The New Rules of Retirement

Strategies for a Secure Future

Second Edition

Robert C. Carlson

WILEY

Published by John Wiley & Sons, Inc., Hoboken, New Jersey.
The First Edition was published by John Wiley & Sons, Inc. in 2004.
Published simultaneously in Canada.

For general information on our other products and services or for technical support, please contact our Customer Care Department within the United States at (800) 762-2974, outside the United States at (317) 572-3993 or fax (317) 572-4002.

Wiley publishes in a variety of print and electronic formats and by print-on-demand. Some material included with standard print versions of this book may not be included in e-books or in print-on-demand. If this book refers to media such as a CD or DVD that is not included in the version you purchased, you may download this material at http://booksupport.wiley.com. For more information about Wiley products, visit www.wiley.com.

Library of Congress Cataloging-in-Publication Data:

Names: Carlson, Robert C., 1957–author.
Title: The new rules of retirement : strategies for a secure future / Robert C. Carlson.
Description: Second edition. | Hoboken, New Jersey : John Wiley & Sons, Inc., [2016] | Includes index.
Identifiers: LCCN 2015050104 (print) | LCCN 2016005041 (ebook) | ISBN 9781119183556 (hardback) | ISBN 9781119183532 (pdf) | ISBN 9781119183495 (epub)
Subjects: LCSH: Retirement–United States—Planning. | BISAC: BUSINESS & ECONOMICS / Personal Finance / Retirement Planning.
Classification: LCC HQ1063.2.U6 C37 2016 (print) | LCC HQ1063.2.U6 (ebook)| DDC 332.024/014—dc23
LC record available at http://lccn.loc.gov/2015050104

Cover Design: Wiley

Printed in the United States of America

10 9 8 7 6 5

To Elaine, my wife and best friend

CONTENTS

Retirement Has Changed ... Again

"**R**etirement and retirement planning are changing ... In the future, there will be more changes to retirement, and the changes will occur much more rapidly."

That was the opening of the first edition of *The New Rules of Retirement*. That opening couldn't have been more accurate, and it still applies today.

Though the first baby boomers hadn't yet reached age 65 when the first edition published (that didn't happen until 2011), they already had an impact on retirement and would continue to transform the post-career years. Other forces and trends joined with the boomers' reaching the silver years to break the old retirement rules. In only 10 years we had to adjust to these and other changes:

- Life expectancy, and therefore the length of retirement, steadily increases.
- Employers and governments continue to reduce benefits to older Americans, leaving retirees more and more on their own.
- Higher-income older Americans are receiving even less support as the government programs become more means-tested.
- Income and estate tax laws changed significantly, requiring updates to plans.
- The nontax factors in estate planning became more prominent and were revised and updated.
- The Affordable Care Act of 2010 introduced many changes to medical insurance and benefit plans, including changes to Medicare.
- Long-term care insurance underwent a couple of revolutions, with both good and bad consequences for retirees.

Of course, few people expected the turmoil in the economy and investment markets and how they would affect retirement plans. The financial crisis of 2008 affected the economy more adversely than any event since the Great Depression of the 1930s. The downturn in the investment markets marked the second decline in the major stock market indexes of more than 50 percent in less than a decade. The Federal Reserve brought interest rates to near 0 percent in response to the crisis, changing the investment plans of many people who were in or near retirement.

The most important lesson from more than a decade of change is: Retirement has changed and will change again.

You need to expect change. Your plans need flexibility, and you need to be ready to adapt and adjust.

Yes, you need a plan for retirement. You also need to realize that it is only a plan. It isn't set in stone, and it isn't a blueprint for the future from which you shouldn't deviate. A plan is based on assumptions about the future. You'll estimate inflation, interest rates, investment markets, the tax law, medical insurance, and more. Reality rarely will match all the assumptions or even come close. Some assumptions will be on target. Others will be a little off the mark, while still others won't even be close.

Plans need to be reviewed and adjusted. When you are in or near retirement, plans need to be reviewed annually. You don't want to review and change plans too frequently, because then you'll be responding to each little change in the investment markets. Regular reviews, however, mean only minor changes in your retirement plan can keep you on track. When too much time passes between plan updates and reviews, then you're likely to need major upheavals to put a plan back on track.

New Help for Retirement

Perhaps the most important change in retirement planning in the last decade is the fresh focus of professionals and academics. When I prepared the first edition of this book, few financial professionals or academics addressed the issues of Americans in or nearing retirement. They were still concerned with helping younger people maximize the accumulation of wealth. They largely neglected the needs of those who were past the accumulation phase of life and were in that post-career spending, or decumulation, stage of life.

Most of those who did offer advice for retirees relied too often on rules of thumb, intuition, and shortcuts to make recommendations. Only a few of us spent the time to create and analyze data to make recommendations. When we did, as readers of the first edition learned, the best actions often were counterintuitive. The rules of thumb and short cuts often led to recommendations that either made sense only in the past or that didn't stand up to analysis.

All that has changed. Now, there is a fairly robust collection of academics and financial professionals vigorously addressing the needs and concerns of older Americans. They use detailed research, data, and analysis to demonstrate the results that would occur from taking different actions under different circumstances. That means retirees and their advisors can spend more time analyzing individual situations and less time constructing models and data. It also means that the problems of retirees benefit from the attention, experience, and intellectual capital of a large number of professionals instead of only a few.

A related change is a new focus on strategies for generating reliable streams of income and cash flow in retirement. Until a few years ago, almost all investment research was geared toward maximizing long-term total returns. With the aging of the baby boomers, there's a realization that a large number of people no longer are interested in total returns. They're interested in making their wealth last, keeping it safe, and generating reliable income to ensure they can pay their expenses for an indefinite period. "Keep my money safe and pay me income" is the new Holy Grail of investing. It is receiving attention from major financial firms, academics, and a range of financial professionals.

In short, those in or near retirement have a lot more intellectual support than they used to, and it will improve retirement advice and outcomes. This intellectual support wasn't available until only a few years ago. Your retirement will be better because of the ideas and research generated.

The Retirement Process

For the first generation or two of American retirees, retirement was an event. A person reached a certain age, usually 65, and then stopped working. Retirement usually was filled with leisure pursuits: travel, recreation, spoiling the grandchildren, and similar activities.

While that model of retirement still exists, more and more Americans are shifting to different retirement models. The old model simply isn't appropriate for many of us.

Extending Careers

One emerging retirement model is to work past the age of 65. There are a number of reasons people do this.

German Chancellor Otto van Bismarck is said to have originated the practice of retiring at age 65 when he created the first old-age social insurance program in 1889. The U.S. Social Security Administration on its website disputes that this was the primary influence on the adoption of 65 as the first full retirement age in Social Security. The SSA points instead to an existing practice of designating age 65 in the U.S. private sector and state retirement systems, as well as actuarial data generated by the government, as the reasons age 65 was adopted.

Whatever the reasons for establishing 65 as the typical retirement age, they don't apply today. People live longer than they did in 1889 or 1935. Age 65 no longer is particularly old and people can live long beyond that, as we discuss later in this book. Many Americans at age 65 are relatively healthy and active. They don't want to stop working.

Research indicates there are many benefits to continuing employment. Mental and physical health often are maintained better with the regular social contact and structure that are part of steady employment. Work also gives a sense of purpose, which is essential at every age.

Of course, many people plan to continue working beyond 65 for financial reasons. The financial crisis of 2008 was a setback to many retirement plans, causing some retirees to seek to return to work while many preretirees began making plans to extend their careers. Since 2008, numerous surveys of Americans ages 40 and over found that many of them plan to continue working longer than they initially planned in order to increase their nest eggs.

Of course, work in retirement doesn't have to be compensated. Volunteer work provides many of the nonfinancial benefits of paid work. Volunteering also can provide psychic income and a sense of purpose because you are contributing to a cause that is important to you.

Keep in mind that retirement age isn't always a matter of choice. About half of retirees report in surveys that they didn't retire when they initially intended. A small percentage of them worked longer than planned, either because they liked what they were doing or needed the money. But most report that they retired earlier than they planned. Only a few retired early voluntarily and because they reached their financial goals. Most retired early involuntarily. Health reasons are a major reason for early retirement. People experience illnesses, injuries, or chronic conditions that make it difficult for them to continue their careers. Others retire early because they lost their jobs and couldn't find satisfactory new positions. After searching for a while, they left the labor force.

Retiring later is a model used by a growing number of people who still are planning and have a choice about when to retire.

Phased Retirement Is Here

A second retirement model growing in popularity is not to retire at all, at least not before health requires it. Leaving a long-time employer and settling down to a few years of travel, relaxation, or just sitting around isn't the game plan for many Americans any more.

Here is a more typical "retirement." A person in his or her late 50s or early sixties will leave an employer after working for that employer for 10 years or more. That employer will be one of four or five during the career. The next six months to one year will consist of relaxing and enjoying life, essentially taking a sabbatical or "career break." The period might include traveling, taking up a long-planned hobby, or spending more time on the activities that used to occupy only weekends and vacations. Then the person will search for a more meaningful way to spend some of his or her time.

The next phase of life has many possibilities. All of them are viable and in use today. It might consist of work in the same occupation the person previously had or in a related field. But it is just as likely to be something in a completely different field or industry. The new work might be full-time. In many cases, however, the work is in a lower-paid position with fewer responsibilities and fewer hours.

Some will keep this new job until it is time for a full-time retirement. Others will keep the job for a few years. Then, the person might shift to another position after deciding the current position is no longer fulfilling. The person might move to a completely unrelated position that involves learning new things. Over time, the hours worked might ratchet down. Even minimum-wage work might be sought at one point just to stay active and earn a little extra money. Eventually, the person might stop working altogether or decide to spend the time on volunteer activities for a charity or the community.

For some this is a planned process. Many others intend to retire and can afford to do so, but in their planning they neglected to consider how they would occupy their time in retirement. They return to the work force because they became bored and realized they had to "reboot" their retirement plans. They need to take some time to decide what would be a meaningful and successful retirement for them. Some people retire two or more times before getting it right.

There are many other scenarios. An executive who loves golfing might "retire" and take a job at his local course or club. Another executive might become a consultant, or take a job with a smaller business that needs an experienced hand, or even take a much lower-paying job to help run a charitable organization. Some hope to work at basically the same jobs for the same companies while working fewer hours, and some employers are trying to restructure positions to accommodate this.

Those who study retirement refer to all these possibilities as *bridge jobs*.

Starting a business in retirement is another course to take. One might start a small, part-time business that is not much more than an attempt to make money at a hobby. Another might have the ambition to build an operation with dozens or hundreds of employees.

These are just a few examples of possible phased retirements. There are likely to be as many retirements as there are retirees.

No longer is there a definite line between work and retirement, and there isn't a standard retirement age. People are more likely to retire in phases or stages, sometimes called *downshifting*.

Retirement Activities to Avoid

This book focuses on actions you can take to make your retirement success-ful and better. For a few minutes, however, let's take a look at retirement advice from a negative perspective. Let's consider the actions you want to avoid if you can, those that have been proven to derail retirement plans.

Sometimes the best way to have good results is to avoid mistakes and losses. We have enough experience with retirement to know which actions and events are most likely to cause retirement to suffer a downward spi-ral. Avoid these and you're well on the way to a successful retirement. Of course, not all these events are within your control. Yet, you can be aware of their potential to upend retirement plans and plan for them by having flexibility in your plans and carrying insurance or other protections when appropriate.

We discuss each of these in more detail in the chapters noted.

Debt

Once it was rare for someone to retire with debt, even a home mortgage. Now, the number of retirement-age Americans with substantial debt is increasing. Some carry debt in retirement as a strategy. They believe lever-aging their assets and income increases their standard of living without incurring much risk. Others are less strategic about their debt. They don't pay down their debt before retirement, and they aren't careful about incur-ring debt in retirement.

It's important to realize that in retirement your finances are less flexible. You have little or no potential for earning more income. Negative finan-cial surprises are likely to occur, especially high medical or long-term care costs. If you're already carrying a fair amount of debt when these expenses arise, you'll have few options for dealing with them. For most people, it's better to eliminate debt before retirement and try to avoid it in retirement, except to deal with emergencies. Details about planning your spending are in Chapter 2.

Spending Too Rapidly

Surveys of retirees and preretirees indicate that many believe they can safely spend 7 percent or more of their assets each year without the risk of running out of money. Financial planners and academics who have stud-ied retirement spending believe the safe spending rate is much lower. This issue is so important we discuss in detail in Chapter 4.

Uncovered Major Medical Expenses

Medicare doesn't cover all your medical expenses, which is something many people don't realize as they enter retirement. Of course, you can't really control when you need medical care. That's why medical expenses and long-term care expenses are the wild cards of retirement planning. We discuss how to plan for these expenses in Chapter 6 and 7.

Helping Others

People want to help their children and grandchildren. Since the financial crisis of 2008 and even before, there's been a trend of *boomerang kids* in the United States. These are adult children fully or partially supported by their parents, either while living on their own or in the parents' homes.

Retirees need to know there's a line of support they can't cross without endangering their own financial security. Too many are in danger of overextending themselves to help their younger loved ones. That's understandable, but it's dangerous. You're likely to spend down your nest egg too fast, and that will leave both you and the younger generation without any financial support.

Help for younger generations must be affordable for you and shouldn't be open-ended or without expectations of results from the youngsters See Chapters 2 and 4 for discussions of how to plan spending and Chapter 11 for ways to help the younger generations.

Flying Solo

Married couples do better financially in retirement than singles. That's partly because divorce is expensive, requiring the same income to support two households. But it's also because too many retirement plans don't include the contingency that one spouse will pass away, costing the household Social Security and other income sources. A solid plan includes financial security for a surviving spouse. See Chapter 3 for some help on providing guaranteed income to the surviving spouse.

Fraud

Financial crooks generally target older Americans. Older Americans usually have enough money to entice the crooks, and they're more vulnerable than younger people. Studies show that people generally are more optimistic and trusting as they age, making them susceptible to fraudulent pitches. Others have reduced cognitive functions, so they don't make decisions as well as they used to. Realize you're more of a target for fraud and establish safeguards (see Chapter 13).

Second Homes

Classic retirement goals often include becoming a "snowbird" or having a vacation home. Too many people, however, don't understand the full financial burdens of these goals. A classic mistake is not to factor in the periodic repairs and maintenance required of the second home. These expenses mount as the home gets older and become significant in retirement when incomes are likely to be lower and finances are less flexible (see Chapter 14).

New Businesses

People with successful careers often consider starting businesses in retirement to stay busy. Before traveling this road, be aware of the high potential for failure and the loss of capital. A retirement business should use only capital that isn't needed to maintain the planned standard of living. Be sure to plan your spending carefully as discussed in Chapter 2 and establish a sustainable spending plan as discussed in Chapter 4.

The New Retirement and You

You can have the retirement you desire. You can have financial independence and security. But you have to plan. Key issues must be carefully analyzed before decisions are made. The earlier you start planning, the better. But it's never too late to plan to improve retirement.

You can opt for the traditional retirement of living off your investments and other sources of income you have while filling your time with leisure or fulfilling activities. Or you can opt for the many other possibilities—or a combination of them. Regardless of the retirement you choose, you won't be alone if you don't participate in the traditional retirement that became common after World War II.

Keep in mind that retirement is a relatively new development. As recently as the turn of the twentieth century, few Americans lived past age 50. Only the very wealthy actually retired. We all are learning new things about retirement every day. Your plan needs to include flexibility, because many things will change. All retirement plans are educated guesswork. Regular adjustments are required as we learn more and facts and circumstances change. Even after you are retired, the plan will have to be modified to keep up with changes, so don't view yourself as being locked in to an inflexible retirement plan.

Now let's get to work. We know that the rules of retirement have changed and will continue to do so. We know every facet of retirement has been affected by change in the last decade or so, and each facet probably will be affected by change again. Let's look in detail at the key parts of retirement finances and the decisions that should be made now in order to enhance the retirement years.

ABOUT THE AUTHOR

Robert C. Carlson is editor of the monthly newsletter *Retirement Watch*. He is also the managing member of Carlson Wealth Advisors, L.L.C. Mr. Carlson is chairman of the board of trustees of the Fairfax County Employees' Retirement System, which has over $3 billion in assets, and was a member of the board of trustees of the Virginia Retirement System from 2000 to 2005, which oversaw $42 billion in assets at the time.

Mr. Carlson was trained as an attorney and accountant, passing the CPA exam. He received his J.D. and an M.S. (Accounting) from the University of Virginia and received his B.S. (Financial Management) from Clemson University. He also is an instrument-rated private pilot. He is listed in several editions of *Who's Who in America* and *Who's Who in the World*.

The New Rules of Retirement

The New Rules of Retirement

Keep my principal secure.
Pay me income.
Protect me from inflation.

These are the goals of more and more Americans age 40 and above. As Americans enter or approach their post-career years, their focus shifts from earning higher income and investment returns to preserving their hard-earned nest eggs. They want to receive steady cash flow from their nest eggs and control their expenses. They want to ensure they'll have enough income and assets to meet their lifetime goals.

Steady, secure income means financial independence. That's why interest in developing a continuing, stable stream of cash is booming.

Unfortunately, your job is becoming harder than ever. Your job is to establish and maintain financial security and independence in those post-career years. Not too many years ago, it was fairly easy to establish and maintain financial independence in retirement. Retirees had assistance and support from former employers and the government. Most of them had pensions. It also was fairly easy to convert a preretirement portfolio into a reliable stream of cash flow that helped replace your working years' income. Things are different now.

Much has changed and continues to change in the economy, the markets, government policies, and employer practices. The Federal Reserve has kept interest rates dirt low since 2008, and it is likely to be years before rates return to historic average levels. The government is cutting programs and increasing fees and taxes. Employers are slashing benefits. Wall Street and the markets aren't helping much. The rules and choices are becoming more complex. All the factors of retirement finance are changed or changing.

Tough, complicated decisions need to be made about IRAs, 401(k)s, medical insurance, investments, taxes, estate planning, and more. Many of the decisions are irreversible. Make a bad decision or two, and the rest of your retirement plan might not matter.

In 1989, only 30 percent of Americans ages 30 and older were on track to be financially unprepared for retirement, according to the Center for Retirement Research. In 2015, 52 percent of Americans over 30 were considered unlikely to be able to maintain their living standards in retirement. About two-thirds of those aged 45 to 60 said in 2015 they will retire later than they had planned, according to the Conference Board. In 2011, that number was only 42 percent. Government data show that after many decades of declining, the average retirement age has been increasing.

Even those who think they're prepared for retirement often aren't. Almost half of all Americans die with financial assets of less than $10,000, according to recent research by James Poterba, an MIT economist. Many Americans enter retirement with what seemed to be substantial and adequate financial assets, but because of mistakes and unforeseen events they spend faster than they anticipated or should have. They end up with few assets.

It doesn't have to be that way for you.

You can be financially secure during your post-career years, free of the worries that will plague many others in the coming years.

But you can't rely on what worked in the past. Following tired "rules of thumb" and traditional cookie-cutter approaches is the road to income insecurity. Don't travel that road. The markets and economy, tax law, estate planning, health insurance, Medicare, Social Security, long-term care, annuities, and all the other financial aspects of your post-career life are being transformed. You need to use strategies and tools that are different from those that worked for previous generations of retirees.

Six Threats to Lifetime Income Security

Most importantly, you need to know how to deal with today's six key threats to lifetime income security. Most of the threats aren't new, but they've been increasing, and so is the danger to your financial security.

Retirement Threat #1: The Foundations Are Crumbling

For decades, Social Security and Medicare provided the secure financial foundation of retirement. They still do. Today, however, those programs are in financial trouble, and they will have to change at some point.

You know about Social Security's problems. If changes aren't made by 2036, a 23 percent cut in benefits will be required to maintain the system, according to its chief actuary. The specifics of its financial condition and potential benefit cuts change annually as estimates are updated, but the general condition doesn't change.

Many people say they don't expect to receive anything from Social Security and aren't including it in their plans. Those are mistakes. Too many people underestimate the importance of Social Security to retirees. Even for many higher-income people who earned at least the maximum Social Security wage base for 35 years, the program replaces 28 percent of pre-retirement income. For low-income beneficiaries, it replaces 90 percent of preretirement income. On average, Social Security benefits are estimated to provide about 40 percent of the average retiree's income. Also, Social Security is the only income most retirees have that is indexed for inflation.

Most current retirees report depending more and more on Social Security as the years pass. They tend to spend down other assets or see the purchasing power of income and assets dwindle because of inflation. That's why it is important that you understand the role of Social Security and maximize your benefits.

If the program goes under or benefits are reduced substantially, many people will have to make major adjustments. I suspect most benefit reductions would be limited to those who aren't already retired or within 10 years of retirement, except for higher income people. Don't give up on Social Security. Instead, realize its importance to your retirement and plan to maximize and protect your benefits.

Medicare is in even worse shape and is closer to insolvency. Without change, Medicare will be bankrupt by 2022, according to the Congressional Budget Office. (Again, the specific estimate changes annually.) In recent years, there have been a few changes in the program, but more are likely. There are likely to be higher premiums, reduced benefits, more means-testing, and a later eligibility age.

Like it or not, Social Security and Medicare are the foundations of the American retirement, and you'll have a tough time replacing them.

In this book you'll learn how to shore up these foundations of your retirement plan. You'll learn to maximize the benefits you receive from these programs and avoid making the mistakes that thousands of retirees make every year. Learn the facts about Social Security and Medicare and they can be valuable assets, effectively adding many thousands of dollars to your nest egg.

Retirement Threat #2: You're on Your Own for Medical Care

Retirement medical and long-term care costs are prime worries of most Americans. About 67 percent of Americans ages 55 to 65 said medical expenses were the top retirement concern, according to a 2012 survey by

Allianz. Many other surveys over the years reported similar results. And rightly so. Medical expenses are the retirement plan wild card.

Medical expenses and health care are among the most misunderstood and underestimated expense for retirees. Consider this:

- Many Americans believe that Medicare or their employer's insurance will cover most retirement medical expenses and long-term care expenses they need. That's not even close to the truth.
- Only 28 percent of employers with more than 200 employees provide retiree medical coverage (compared to 66 percent in 1968). Most of those that still offer retirement medical benefits are reducing benefits and moving retirees to privately run insurance exchanges. Smaller employers often don't provide any retirement medical benefits.
- Medicare pays only 80 percent of *covered* expenses, so you're on the hook for 20 percent of covered expenses with no limit. Plus, there are many medical expenses that aren't covered by Medicare. You need ways to pay for all of those.
- Medicare covers only about half of the average member's annual medical expenses. The average retiree will pay $6,000 to $8,000 out-of-pocket each year for medical care, depending on whose estimate is used. That's the average, so many pay more and some pay considerably more.
- A married couple age 65 today is estimated on average to need more than $270,000 over the next 20 years to pay for their medical expenses that aren't covered by Medicare. Of course, those with above-average needs or who live past age 85 will need more.
- Long-term care expenses generally aren't covered by Medicare. The truth is, Medicare pays for only 25 percent of total nursing home expenses in the United States, and those payments largely are for short-term rehabilitation after an illness or injury. Residents, their families, and Medicaid pay most nursing home expenses.
- Most prescription drugs aren't covered by basic Medicare Parts A and B.
- Medicare now is means-tested. The higher your income is, the higher your Medicare premiums will be for both traditional Medicare Part B and for prescription drug coverage under Part D.
- The Affordable Care Act shifts money away from Medicare, especially the popular Medicare Advantage program, reducing benefits and increasing costs for beneficiaries.

Medical expenses will be one of the three biggest post-career expenses for most people, and they'll only increase as the years go on.

Even many of those who understand they are largely on their own for medical care need to know more than they do. Many pay far too much for Medicare supplement, Part D prescription drug, and long-term care insurance. Recent surveys found that many owners of these policies pay up to twice what they need to.

It doesn't do much good to save and invest for a comfortable retirement and build a legacy for your loved ones only to spend most of your nest egg on medical care and overpriced insurance. You need to stay up to date about Medicare, Part D prescription drug coverage, long-term care, and every other aspect of paying for retirement medical care.

Retirement Threat #3: Avoid the #1 Retirement Planning Mistake

"We didn't realize how much everything would cost, Bob. That's the mistake we made."

Those were the words of a woman who shared, with her husband, a large lakefront house (with an indoor swimming pool) in a secured golf course community in central Virginia. They also owned a condo in Florida to be near one set of grandchildren in winter.

They weren't scrounging for money. But after five years of retirement, the couple were concerned that they had underestimated the cost of retirement. He took some part-time consulting work, and she also found part-time work.

This is not unusual. Ask many retirees what their biggest retirement planning mistake was, and a high percentage will say that they didn't do a good enough job of estimating retirement spending. Ask financial professionals, and they'll also say that most people don't have a good handle on how much retirement costs.

One-third of U.S. adults who haven't retired say they'll need 25 to 50 percent of their preretirement income in retirement, while another third say they'll need 50 to 75 percent, according to a TIAA-CREF survey.

The traditional rule of thumb used by financial advisors is your annual retirement spending will be about 80 percent of your preretirement income. That's far above the estimate many people use, and it still isn't a good way to estimate your retirement spending.

This simple rule of thumb, one of the great myths of retirement planning, gets many people into trouble.

You will spend less (or nothing) in retirement on expenses such as commuting, new work clothes, payroll taxes, 401(k) contributions, and a few other items. It sounds very logical.

But since you aren't working, you have time to fill. That time might be filled by activities that cost money, such as golf, travel, entertaining, eating out more frequently, going to more shows and movies, hobbies, spoiling the grandchildren, or a host of other possibilities. Over time, you also are likely to incur higher medical expenses.

With parents living longer and children needing more financial help, you could end up helping both your parents and your children. That situation has become more and more common.

The truth is that for many people, expenses stay the same or increase in the first years of retirement. The money goes to different expenses. A rule of thumb that actually works is that the higher your income, the less likely your expenses are to decline in the first years of retirement.

If you don't want to wake up in a cold sweat worrying about money a few years into retirement, ignore the general rule. The question is: How much are *you* likely to spend in retirement? Many people learn to their regret that the general rules of thumb don't apply to them. We discuss how to estimate retirement spending in Chapter 2.

Even those who correctly estimate their retirement spending often make a different mistake. They fail to consider how inflation affects the purchasing power of income and assets over time. In fact, the most common retirement planning mistake is failing to consider the effects of inflation in retirement plans. Many people develop a spending plan for the first year or two of retirement that matches their income. But they forget that prices and costs change over time.

Inflation is one of the great enemies of retirees. The average three percent annual inflation of the last few decades cuts your purchasing power in half over 24 years and by close to 20 percent after five years. A more modest 2 percent inflation cuts your standard of living by 20 percent after 10 years. It doesn't happen overnight, but it is painful over time.

And don't use the Consumer Price Index to measure inflation. It measures inflation for a basket of goods purchased by a hypothetical American family. Your household spending is different, and so is its inflation rate. In retirement, for example, you'll probably spend less on housing and more on medical care. There are other differences.

You learn in this book the right way to estimate your retirement expenses, the true effects of inflation, and more.

Retirement Threat #4: Most Retirement Investment Advice Is Wrong and Dangerous

Retirees and those close to retirement traditionally receive the worst investment advice. There've been some improvements in recent years as demand from the Baby Boomers forced changes. Yet, many still receive poor investment advice for the years just before retirement and during retirement.

That's not surprising. Most financial advisors and brokers still concentrate on investors who are going to increase their investment accounts each year. That's a growth business. There's not much growth when clients plan to spend their investment funds and draw down their accounts.

The investment advice for retirees used to be simple. As you age, move most of your portfolio into safe, income-producing investments such as short-term bonds, certificates of deposit, and money market funds. Then, live off the income.

That made sense when retirement lasted about five years, interest rates were higher, and you didn't have to worry about wide changes in the cost of living. Now, this advice could be the most dangerous thing you can do in retirement.

More recently, retirees and preretirees were told to invest like everyone else, using diversified portfolios developed using historic returns and computer programs. They were told to buy-and-hold these portfolios and to count on the long-term trends of ever-rising stock prices to fund their retirements. That's a shame, because the results since 2000 have been awful.

The strategy can work over the very long run. Unfortunately, it often produces poor results in the short run. People in or near retirement can't invest based on 80 years of history. What happens in the next 10 years or so is what matters to them, and the results over the next 10 years often vary greatly from the last 10 years and the historic averages. Investment returns in the five years immediately before and after retirement will make or break your retirement plan.

Another problem with most investment advice is that people are told they have diversified portfolios when they really don't. The truth is that when a portfolio is 60 percent stocks and 40 percent bonds, about 90 percent of your total returns and volatility are tied to the stock indexes. Your retirement security rises and falls with the stock indexes.

When the bulls are running, that's a great thing. But the volatility and poor performance of stocks since 2000 have hurt many retirees and put future retirees in uncomfortable positions.

These days, investing conservatively and for safety isn't rewarding, either, thanks to the Federal Reserve board's zero-interest-rate policy and market manipulation. The Fed is saving the economy by punishing savers and those who simply want a comfortable, safe retirement income. Savers are losing money after inflation and taxes.

You have more choices than the traditional safe, low interest investments and investing for the long term while hoping for the best in the short-term. You don't have to bounce up and down with the stock indexes or sit in cash, losing money to inflation and taxes.

Retirement Threat #5: Retirement Lasts Longer Than Most Think

For the first generation of post-World War II retirees, retirement generally lasted five years or so. Today, many people still believe they have to plan only for 5 to 10 years of retirement. The fact is, a 20-year retirement is common, and 30-year retirements aren't unusual.

People on average still retire before age 65. Though many people now say they plan to work longer and the average retirement age has been increasing, about half of people retire involuntarily and before they expected. The fact is that retirement could last a long time, even if you plan to continue working, because you might not retire when you thought. Even for those who retire at age 65 or later, retirement can last a long time. People simply are living longer than they used to.

Here's a sample of what you need to know about longevity. In a married couple in which each spouse is age 65 today, there's about a 20 percent chance either spouse will live to 95. When both spouses are 55, there's a 43 percent chance at least one will live past 95, according to annuity mortality tables. In about 15 years, the odds will increase by about 50 percent, according to the insurance actuaries.

Many people born in 1946 and later can expect to spend more than 30 years in retirement. Some will spend more time in retirement than they did in their careers.

There's another twist to consider. Life expectancy increases with wealth and education. The wealthier and better educated a person, the greater on average is the life expectancy. Such a person has access to better medical care and is more likely to make smart lifestyle choices. The person's career probably wasn't physically demanding and was unlikely to result in injuries or disability. These factors make an above-average life expectancy more likely, probably about four years longer than the average for his or her age.

Life spans are likely to increase in coming years as science discovers new treatments and cures.

There are many benefits to longevity and longer life spans. But there's one giant negative. The nest egg needed to pay for all those years of retirement can be substantial. You have to save enough money and keep that nest egg growing to pay for all those years of retirement and protect the purchasing power from decades of inflation.

Retirement Threat #6: Your Taxes Won't Go Down in Retirement

It used to be a truism that taxes and tax rates would decline in retirement. That's no longer the case.

These days, someone's taxes and tax rate are less likely to decline after retiring. Even if they do, they're likely to creep up during retirement. In many cases, a person's marginal income tax rate actually increases in retirement, and retirees face some of the highest marginal tax rates in history. Average tax rates are likely to stay the same or increase.

You have to be on constant guard against politicians devising new and creative ways to get their hands on your nest egg. It's only going to get worse as the population ages.

The bottom line is that for most retirees, taxes are one of the three largest items in their budgets. The situation is likely to get worse. Congress and state and local governments are far more likely to increase your taxes than to cut them.

You'll learn effective tax reduction strategies throughout the book, but we focus on ways to plan for lower taxes in Chapter 9.

You Can Create Safe, Secure, Sustainable Lifetime Income

You don't have to stand there meekly and let these risks destroy your nest egg. You can fight and win. You can build a fortress around your assets and generate reliable cash flow.

I believe today is a great opportunity for those who prepare for retirement and adapt to the recent changes and those to come. Be clear that there isn't a magic formula, silver bullet, or single ideal investment. You'll have to look elsewhere for gimmicks and fads. You can create a successful retirement by using a toolbox of strategies and a solid plan. You'll also need to ignore the status quo, conventional rules of thumb, and standard Wall Street advice.

I find that simple solutions often are the best. You need to push past the complexity so beloved by Wall Street and Washington and find strategies that will maximize your cash flow.

Most importantly, remember a retirement plan is a process, not an event. As you've seen, the rules and circumstances keep changing. You can't set-it-and-forget-it. Be sure you're aware of changes, carefully analyze how they affect you, and choose a course of action that will work for you.

We know that retirement in the future will be as different from the retirement of the past as night is from day. Those who planned for retirement only 15 or 20 years ago would be shocked by the task faced by their counterparts today. Many of the issues and questions to be addressed today weren't even on the radar screen not long ago.

The first real generation of American retirees, those who retired in the 1960s and 1970s, developed the image of retirement that many Americans still hold today. For most of the second, third, and fourth retirement generations, things will be different. Sometimes they will be shockingly different.

Many observers paint a gloomy picture of retirement in the coming years. Yet there is no reason for the majority of people to experience a retirement that is less satisfying than was experienced by the first generation of retirees. Most of us should be able to create the retirement we desire.

Retirement is an opportunity. It is an opportunity to do things you never could find the time for. It is a chance to plan how to spend your *next* 50 years. But to take advantage of the retirement opportunity, you have to plan and prepare. Most of all, you need to know the new rules of retirement planning.

In the coming chapters, we'll explore the financial concerns of retirees and preretirees and how they are affected by the trends I've identified. We'll look at how to estimate retirement spending and how much money you should accumulate for retirement. I'll explain the medical expense options and how to pay for long-term care. You'll learn how to invest before and during retirement. I'll show you how to plan an estate, cut taxes, and provide for loved ones. We'll cover these topics and much more. I'm not going to give you the obvious advice, such as start early, invest the maximum in a 401(k) account, and invest for the long term. Think of this book as your instruction manual for the new world of retirement.

You can have the retirement you desire, but you must act now to stay ahead of the dramatic, rapid changes that are taking place. Even those who already are retired are affected and must act. Those who don't learn about and understand the shifting world of retirement will have retirement years filled with worry and anxiety. Those who understand the new rules of retirement will make decisions with confidence and be able to take advantage of all their retirement opportunities.

Start with Spending

T he main goal of a retirement plan is to be sure you have enough income or cash flow to maintain the retirement standard of living you want. To meet that goal, first, you need to estimate how much a year of your retirement standard of living will cost. Second, you need to generate income to pay those expenses.

In this chapter we focus on estimating your retirement spending. In the next chapter we'll begin looking at ways to generate the income needed to fund that spending.

It is difficult to make retirement plans, even something as simple as setting a retirement date, without estimating the cost of your retirement. Every other part of a retirement plan hinges on how much you plan to spend. If that estimate is way off the mark, the rest of your plan will be way off. Some people overestimate how much they'll spend in retirement, and that causes them to reduce their preretirement standard of living so they can save enough for retirement. Others underestimate retirement spending and find they need to make substantial adjustments after retiring.

Even if you already are retired or very close to it, estimating future spending now is important. The steps we discuss in this chapter will give you a good handle on how long your money is likely to last under current practices and let you know if adjustments need to be made. Those who carefully estimated spending before retirement should repeat the exercise every year or so to see how accurate the estimates are and whether the plan needs to be adjusted.

How important is this step?

The greatest fear of most Americans approaching or in retirement is not having enough income and assets to last through retirement.

Survey after survey confirms that. (Some surveys peg medical expenses or the cost of long-term care as the major concerns, but that's another way of saying people are worried about not having enough money to meet these expenses.) Even surveys of wealthy Americans reveal they worry about their standards of living eroding in retirement. I've met multimillionaires who were genuinely concerned that they wouldn't be able to maintain their preferred lifestyles after retiring.

Ask retirees what their biggest retirement planning mistake was, and a high percentage will say that they didn't do a good enough job of estimating retirement spending. Ask financial professionals, and they'll say that most people don't have a good handle on how much the retirement they desire will cost or even how much they are spending today. Another reason to estimate retirement spending is that surveys show that people who estimate their expenses and capital needs, even if they make poor estimates, save more and are better prepared for retirement than those who do not make estimates.

Unfortunately, most of the advice on how much to save for retirement is nothing more than very simple rules of thumb. Longer retirements and greater self-reliance mean that we must dispense with rules of thumb and devise a more accurate estimate of retirement spending and capital needs. Even when a rule of thumb is generally accurate, you shouldn't use it. It might reflect what people do on average, but almost no one is the average. You need to estimate your likely spending.

A number of methods are used to estimate retirement spending. There is no one right way to estimate retirement capital needs or spending, but some ways are better than others. As we've collectively developed more experience with extended retirements, we've learned more about which methods work best.

In this chapter, we'll look at different ways to estimate the amount of money that should be accumulated for retirement. We'll review a couple of widely cited rules of thumb or short cuts. I'll explain why you should avoid those methods. Then I'll point you to some better ways to estimate retirement spending.

The 80 Percent Rule

If you've been exposed to any retirement planning advice, you probably heard the classic and most common formula: Assume that retirement spending will be less than 100 percent of the income of your last pretirement year. The recommended percentage varies. I've heard from 65 percent to 85 percent, but most of the recommendations I've seen are around 80 percent.

The advice is quick, easy, and has a reasonable theory behind it. The theory is that not as much money will be spent in retirement as was spent during the working years. In retirement there won't be Social Security taxes or commuting expenses. There also isn't likely to be the need for as many new suits or other work clothes. Of course, 401(k) contributions won't be made. Perhaps lunches will be eaten at restaurants less often. Other expenses also might decline or disappear.

Some research supports this general rule. Since 1988, every few years Georgia State University, in a project funded by Aon Consulting, has used government data and other sources to determine the percentage of preretirement income that people actually spend in retirement. This percentage is known as the replacement ratio. It is the percentage of your preretirement income that your retirement income and assets have to replace to meet retirement spending needs. The study adjusts preretirement income for postretirement changes such as income taxes, savings, and expenditures related to age and work. The latest study I've seen was done in 2008 and can be found on the Aon website.

One result of the Aon/Georgia State study that often isn't mentioned is that it regularly finds that the replacement ratio depends on income. The lower one's preretirement income, the higher will be the replacement ratio until annual pre-retirement income reaches $60,000. Above that level, the replacement ratio plateaus. But the 2008 study caps preretirement income at $90,000. Some of the earlier studies estimated the replacement ratio for incomes up to $150,000 and found that after the plateau replacement ratios rose steadily as preretirement incomes rose above $90,000.

In the first edition of this book I wrote that on average, a couple with preretirement income of $150,000 would need about 85 percent of that income in retirement. A couple with $50,000 in preretirement income would need only 74 percent of that income in retirement. The replacement ratio, however, rose again for even lower incomes. A couple with $30,000 of preretirement income, for example, needed 78 percent of that income in retirement.

More importantly, the studies over the years have found that the replacement ratio rises steadily over time. For example, in 2001, a preretirement income of $50,000 required a replacement ratio of 74 percent. The replacement ratio rose to 77 percent in 2004 and 81 percent in 2008. At higher incomes, however, the replacement ratio remained fairly steady over time. For a preretirement income of $90,000, the ratio was 76 percent, 78 percent, and 78 percent, respectively.

The Aon-Georgia State studies are interesting and provide useful information for those planning retirement. It would be a mistake, however, to simply take the study results and apply them to your own retirement plan. Using the replacement ratio to help establish a target amount to accumulate is acceptable for someone years away from retirement. As retirement approaches, a more individualized estimate should be made.

While certain expenses will be eliminated after retirement, other expenses might take their place. After retirement, the time that used to be spent working has to be filled. It might be filled with no-cost activities such as watching television, playing cards, walking, visiting nearby friends, or sitting in the park. It also might be filled with hobbies or activities that cost money. These include golf, travel, eating out more often, or going to more movies and shows. The retiree might become a volunteer, which might require employment-type expenses such as commuting, lunches, and clothing. Another popular retirement activity is spoiling the grandchildren.

It's also important to consider some spending wildcards. Medical expenses could rise substantially over time. The amount of medical expenses will depend on personal health, insurance coverage, and where one lives. With parents living longer and children needing more financial help, more retirees end up helping both parents and children at the same time.

The point is that retirement spending is unique for each person or household. Studies and rules of thumb provide averages and estimates. Anecdotal evidence indicates that many retirees find that, contrary to the traditional assumption, their expenses don't decline in retirement, at least not in the first years of retirement. They spend the same and even more after retiring as they did just before retiring. The higher your pre-retirement income, the more likely it is that you'll be in that group. On the other hand, I've known people who said they spend considerably less in retirement than they did before retiring.

The Double Trouble Method

Here is a widely recommended method for estimating retirement financial needs that uses two simple rules of thumb. It's very simple, which explains a lot of its appeal. I sometimes call it the *ballpark method*, because it gives an answer that's "in the ballpark." But the simplicity and the generality of the rules leave a lot of room for error. This method can be helpful to a young person who is looking for some benchmark of how much to save and accumulate for retirement. As one is closer to retirement, the imprecision can make the method dangerous. For some people, the method will greatly overestimate spending, leaving retirees to live far more frugally than they need to. For others, the method underestimates spending and raises the probability of running out of money.

Here's how the method works.

Suppose our friend Max Profits uses the 80 percent rule to estimate his spending in the first year of retirement to be $40,000. He estimates he'll earn a total annual return of 7 percent on his investments. He'll need a $571,429 portfolio in order to draw $40,000 annually to spend ($40,000 divided by .07). That's a simple calculation that produces a retirement savings goal in a few minutes. It gives, however, a very incomplete answer. Someone less than five years away from retirement definitely needs a more accurate estimate. Even people within 10 years of retirement should be focused on a better estimate.

One factor not considered in this estimate is inflation. The cost of living is likely to rise each year, and Max needs to factor this into his plan. Max will need to spend more than $40,000 each year after the first year to maintain that standard of living. That means Max must reinvest a portion of the investment return each year to ensure that the portfolio and its income will maintain their purchasing power. If Max expects 3 percent annual inflation, then he needs to reinvest 3 percentage points of the annual investment return. Max can spend only 4 percent of that 7 percent annual return. That brings the annual spendable income from the portfolio down to only $22,857. To meet his goals, Max needs to either increase the investment return to 10 percent or increase the retirement fund to $1,000,000. If Max's investments will earn less than 7 percent, he will need an even bigger nest egg.

Even after adjusting the method for inflation, there still are key elements missing from the estimate. The method assumes Max receives nothing from Social Security. Although Social Security has its problems and changes are likely to be made, Max is still likely to get $10,000 or more annually from Social Security, perhaps much more, for many years. Factor in Social Security and Max will need to save less than this simple method indicates. Max also should be sure not to overlook any other income sources.

The ballpark method also assumes the investment principal never is touched. Most retirees don't want to dip into their initial capital in the early years of retirement. But there's no reason to assume that the principal won't be touched for life unless the primary goal is to pass the entire principal intact to a spouse, the next generation, or to charity. Otherwise, the method sets the savings goal too high. I think the results should be viewed as a high estimate of the amount that should be saved to meet retirement needs.

There are other simple rules to estimate retirement spending, and they suffer from some or all of those shortcomings.

Your Starting Point

The real question is: How much are *you* likely to spend each year in retirement? I recommend throwing out the general rules. Don't use a rule of thumb about replacement ratios. Don't look at annual retirement spending as a lump sum. Instead, develop a spending estimate that reflects the lifestyle you want.

Retirement planning is about much more than finances. Most people focus on the finances, but successful retirement doesn't start or end with the finances. You need to give some thought about how you want to live in retirement. What will you do with those hours that no longer will be spent working?

Your retirement plan should start with a thoughtful consideration of the lifestyle you anticipate in retirement and then be followed by an estimate of what that would cost today. You'll have daily activities, as well as weekly, monthly, and less frequent activities. You'll have regular necessary expenses for food, shelter, utilities, and medical care. There will be periodic necessary expenses such as replacing cars and things around the house.

Some people refer to this approach as life planning or holistic financial planning. Call it whatever you want. What's important is that the activities you engage in will drive your spending to a large extent. If your lifestyle in retirement isn't much different than your preretirement lifestyle, then your spending estimate will be very similar to your preretirement spending. But if you plan a different lifestyle for at least the first few years of retirement, then your spending might differ greatly from the preretirement years.

Develop a detailed list of possible monthly categories of expenses and decide how much money is likely to be spent on each item in today's dollars. How much do you want to travel? Play golf? Give to the grandchildren? Dine in restaurants? These are all retirement expenses that for more people are higher than before retirement. Don't forget to include taxes—all kinds of taxes.

Medical expenses are the wild card in any retirement budget. The average retiree spends anywhere from $6,000 to $10,000 annually on out-of-pocket medical expenses, depending on whose estimates are used. The estimates include all costs, such as Medicare and insurance premiums, deductibles, copayments, and noncovered expenses. But it is just an average. A particular retiree might spend more or less, depending on health, family history, and insurance coverage. The amount also is likely to increase above the average as the retiree ages. We discuss medical expenses and how to plan for them in detail in Chapter 6. Study the medical expense coverage options carefully before estimating retirement expenditures.

Don't overlook infrequent expenses. These include home maintenance and improvements, appliance replacement, automobiles, travel, and help for family members. For these expenses, divide an estimated annual spending by 12 and put a monthly amount in the spending estimate. This is what accountants call a sinking fund. Suppose you plan to buy a new car every four years at a cost of $40,000. At 3 percent inflation, the cost after the first four years is about $45,000. You could list about $940 per month in the budget to ensure the cost of a new car will be accounted for in your spending plan. A more sophisticated approach is to assume some interest will be earned on the sinking fund. At 3 percent annual interest, the monthly amount to set aside would be about $884.

Once all the amounts are determined, add them to get monthly and annual estimates of the cost of the first year of retirement.

This exercise has several important benefits. Of course, it makes your estimates of retirement spending more accurate. That reduces the probability that you'll run out of money in retirement by spending your nest egg too rapidly. Studies of retirees often show that those who are most satisfied and financially secure are those who engaged in some financial planning before retiring.

The exercise also requires you to spend time thinking about what you will do in retirement. Too many people enter retirement without giving much thought to how they'll spend their time. Through school and their careers, decisions about how to spend most of their time were made by others or by circumstances. In retirement, most of the decisions often are yours. Failure to give careful thought to daily and weekly lifestyles is why a high percentage of people retire more than once. They retire, and then after a while become bored and realize they are wasting a lot of time. They return to work, resolving to retire a few years later and more successfully. The nonfinancial aspects of retirement determine the success of retirement more than the finances. By making this exercise part of your planning, you increase the probability retirement will be a success from both the financial and nonfinancial perspectives.

How Much Will You Really Need?

At this point you have completed the most important step in retirement planning. You've given careful thought to the retirement lifestyle you want and estimated how much that would cost, at least in the first year.

As you go through the rest of the steps in this chapter and this book, don't be alarmed if at first it appears your income and assets don't match well with your spending estimate. That's not a bad thing, since you start a retirement plan by thinking about what you really want to do in retirement and how much that will cost. Your spending plan likely has expenses you could put into several broad categories. There are the essentials or "must haves": food, housing, medical insurance, and the like. Then there are the "nice-to-haves," which could be a range of activities and even upgrades to the essentials, such as a larger home. The final category is aspirational spending, the activities you'd do in an ideal world.

Most people at the first attempt at a retirement plan find that all these expenses are too much for their resources. Then, they go back to their spending plans and make adjustments. Don't be concerned if adjustments need to be made in your first plan after going through the next steps.

After estimating your first year of retirement spending, you need to estimate the length of retirement. Younger people should simply assume an extended period of at least 30 years, though 40 years or more looks like it will be more appropriate as life expectancy increases. For people retiring soon or already retired, we discuss longevity more in Chapter 4.

Next, use the spending and longevity estimates to make a reasonable estimate of how much money you need to fund retirement. That's what the rest of this chapter explains. You'll learn to customize and modify the information to make more reliable estimates of your retirement needs. Keep in mind that there are a lot of tools and technology available today to make calculations much easier. We'll discuss some of the options in this chapter.

The basic next step to determining how much money you'll really need is to adjust the spending estimate for inflation over your working years and retirement. Then, you'll use an assumed investment return to estimate how much money should be accumulated at the start of retirement or for the rest of retirement.

An easy step is to use the many calculators that are available, mostly free, from various financial services firms and websites. Once you've estimated retirement spending, these tools walk you through steps to estimate how much money you'll need for retirement and how much needs to be saved each month. These calculators are available free from most mutual funds, brokers, and other financial services firms. While some still are available in printed format as worksheets, most now are available free through websites. Even many news sites have financial calculators, including retirement planning calculators. Employers that sponsor 401(k) plans also usually have these available on the plan website.

I used to list software packages and websites that I believed were the best to use for retirement planning. Unfortunately, the offerings and their availability change too frequently. Some of the financial services also reserve their better tools to clients instead of making them available to the public. Therefore, I can't offer a list of retirement tools to consider. Instead, I suggest you visit the websites of the major financial services firms, especially mutual funds and discount brokers. You also should find tools on many financial news and strategy websites.

The standalone software available to nonprofessionals has declined significantly. Quicken from Intuit still has a retirement planning function. You also might want to visit the website of Money Tree Software, which has for years offered a software program called Silver Financial Planner. At times, a version of this has been available to consumers, while at other times it was available only in conjunction with financial planners who have the professional version. Of course, a reader also can purchase the professional version, which was less than $500 in 2015.

Obviously some of the calculators try to be more accurate, while others try to keep things simple so that people won't fail to complete the process. The calculators are kept simple by limiting the variables the user can change, such as inflation rates, life expectancy, and some of the details of spending. Some, for example, have you enter an annual lump sum for spending that is constant over time. Others allow more flexibility or detail in the spending estimates. The simplest calculator I'm familiar with is the Ballpark Estimate from the American Savings Education Council. An online version is on its website, www.asec.org, along with links to several other retirement calculators from other organizations. (Like other websites, this one changes over time. This description was accurate when this book was written.)

The basic data used to complete one calculator often can be easily transferred to another calculator. Most people who are planning their retirement would benefit from completing several different calculators and comparing the results. Most of these calculators will estimate how large the investment portfolio should be on the first day of retirement (or today, if you're already retired) to meet the spending goals. For those not already retired, most also will compute how much money should be saved and invested each month to accumulate that sum by the estimated retirement age.

Using multiple calculators is helpful, because you'll see the different results. That tells you how important the different assumptions are and how difficult it is to make an estimate. That should tell you that it is in your interest to revise the estimates regularly and change assumptions as needed.

The web calculators will do all or most of the computations. The best web calculators are those that are more robust, allowing you to change many assumptions. Of course, it takes more time to use these calculators than simpler ones. Members of *Retirement Watch* can download from the members' section of the website a spreadsheet, which allows substantial customization of spending details, especially of the issues discussed next.

Better Planning with Technology

A major reason the simple methods of estimating retirement spending and capital needs were developed was that it was too difficult to make a proper, detailed estimate. A large number of calculations had to be done by hand. Since technology now is widely available and relatively inexpensive, detailed estimates are relatively easy to make. Here are examples of the issues that can be addressed and make estimates more accurate than the simple methods when technology is used to develop a retirement plan.

Customized Inflation.   One of the biggest mistakes in retirement planning is failing to fully factor inflation into the plan. Over 20 or more years of retirement, inflation can make a comfortable income uncomfortably tight or even inadequate. A good retirement planning model, whether it is a simple one or a sophisticated tool using technology, will take inflation into account.

The most common approach is to apply a flat inflation rate to estimated annual spending. Prices of different goods and services, however, do not increase at the same rate. More importantly, your spending probably doesn't match the basket of consumer goods and services that the government uses to compile its inflation numbers. Education expenses have increased faster than overall inflation and are a meaningful portion of the Consumer Price Index, but those expenses don't affect many retirees. On the other hand, medical and long-term expenses also have increased faster than the CPI, and retirees often incur a larger amount of these than is represented in the CPI.

That's why a better approach to estimating inflation is to assign a separate inflation rate to each budget item or at least to groups of similar items. That gives a much better estimate of the inflation the individual is likely to experience during retirement. The recent inflation rates for different items and other information about inflation can be obtained from the Bureau of Labor Statistics of the U.S. Department of Labor website, www.bls.gov/cpi/home.htm.

Some of the web calculators allow different inflation rates to be assigned to each item in the retirement budget or at least general categories of items. Software available to professional financial planners often allows customized estimates of inflation. The difference between this approach and using one inflation rate for the entire annual expenditure won't mean much in the first few years of retirement. After 10 or more years of retirement, however, the compounded difference could be significant.

Irregular Expenses.   Earlier, I explained how to use a sinking fund to factor into the monthly budget expenses that are not incurred each month or even each year. A more precise alternative to the sinking fund is available in some calculators and software. These programs ask for an estimate of the year when these expenses are likely to be incurred. For example, a program might ask how often a car will be purchased and what the cost in today's dollars is likely to be. This information is included in the estimated income and spending for that year. The same can be done for home repairs and replacement of major appliances.

Unlike the simple methods, the more sophisticated software calculates the spending of each year separately instead of assuming uniform spending each year. This can make for a more accurate projection of total retirement spending. It also shows the bumps and fluctuations in spending that are more realistic than the simple models' uniform annual changes in spending.

Mature-Years Spending. Simple retirement models assume the same amount is spent each year all through retirement. The truth is that most people slow down as they age. Sometime between ages 70 and 75 many people choose to travel less, play golf less, and dine out less. In general, they spend less in many areas than when they were younger. Activities and spending might ratchet down again from 75 to 80. We'll discuss this lifetime spending cycle more in Chapter 4.

The simple models don't adjust for this, but some software is written to handle these changes. Without factoring the mature-years spending change into a retirement plan, estimated spending could significantly exceed actual spending. In addition, for married couples, spending usually is reduced after one spouse passes away. Again, failure to adjust for this could lead to an overestimate of retirement capital needs or an underestimate of how much could be spent in the early years of retirement.

Changing Assumptions. Ideally, more than one estimate of retirement spending and capital needs is made. A number of assumptions go into the calculations. Estimates include inflation, investment returns, tax rates, the retirement date, the actual spending on each item, and more. Because of the number of assumptions, it is a good idea to do several projections, changing one or two of the assumptions each time. What happens to the plan if investment returns are less than expected? What happens if inflation is higher? A really good calculator or program allows you to change the investment returns each year. That way you can see what happens if you have poor investment returns the first few years of retirement.

Very small changes in these assumptions can significantly change the results, especially if there still are years to go before retirement and two decades or more to spend in retirement.

Those who don't want to work with the numbers or technology themselves of course should consider working with a financial planner or similar professional. For those readers, this chapter gives you a good idea of what to look for in a plan and the questions to ask.

Uncertainty and Monte Carlo

For years, retirement planning models would assume a steady rate of return is earned on the investments. If a 7 percent investment return is estimated, the method will assume that exactly 7 percent is earned each and every year.

Anyone who has been in or watched the markets for a while knows that isn't the way markets work. Investment returns are likely to be variable. A 15 percent gain one year might be followed by a 5 percent gain the following year, a 12 percent loss the third year, a 20 percent gain the fourth year, and so on. Over time, these variable returns might amount to a 7 percent average annual return. The major stock market indexes, for example, rarely have a year that matches their long-term average annual returns.

Often, the difference between the assumption of steady returns and the reality of variable returns won't make a meaningful difference. That's especially true when a younger person is planning for a retirement several decades in the future. There are times, however, when it can make a big difference. It is most likely to make a meaningful difference when the markets enter a strong bearish phase at the start of retirement. (The periods from 2000 to 2002 and following 2007 were such times. So was 1966 to 1982.) A portfolio's value could fall dramatically during those years. Instead of spending income the first few years, the new retiree would be spending principal. That also leaves less principal to generate gains and income when the markets eventually resume a bullish phase. The result often is that the wealth won't last as long as initially forecast unless spending is reduced.

To deal with this potential problem, the financial community developed a new method to make estimates in retirement plans. The traditional method of assuming a constant rate of return is known as a linear or deterministic model. The alternative is a probabilistic model. The plan produced by a deterministic model shows the specific amount of money projected to be available each year of retirement. The probabilistic method concludes by showing the probability or likelihood that a particular plan of spending, saving, and investing will lead to a successful retirement. Probabilistic models weren't readily available until the late 1990s or early 2000s. The computing power available was too expensive and slow. The declining cost and increased power of technology made this newer approach available to anyone with a newer personal computer or access to a website.

The most common probabilistic model is known as the Monte Carlo simulation. It actually was developed by nuclear scientists at the Los Alamos Laboratory to design atom bombs. Instead of assuming one average annual return, the Monte Carlo simulation calculates the results of a plan under a wide range of possible investment scenarios or outcomes. Some Monte Carlo simulations use many combinations of actual historic returns from the investment markets. Other simulations use random, computer-generated returns (within parameters set by the programmer). The Monte Carlo simulations for financial plans usually calculate 500 or more possible outcomes. That means for a 30-year retirement plan, the program will calculate investment returns over 500 different 30-year periods. The program determines the percentage of times that the investment capital lasts the entire 30-year period or longer, and that is the probability that the plan will be successful. For example, the report might say that there is an 85 percent probability that the nest egg will last through the retirement period under the assumptions used. Most financial advisers recommend changing a plan until there is a 90 percent or greater probability of success.

The Financial Engines website at www.financialengines.com (and available through many 401(k) plans) probably was the first vehicle to make Monte Carlo simulation generally available. Now simulations are on the websites of most financial services firms and financial news and strategy firms.

While the Monte Carlo simulation can be more informative than a simple deterministic model, it has its own drawbacks. A number of assumptions are built into each program. These assumptions include the average annual returns for each investment asset over time and the correlations among the different investments. Correlation is the extent to which the investments rise and fall together. Sometimes these assumptions are explicitly revealed; sometimes the program documentation is not clear about the assumptions. These assumptions could be unrealistic, wrong, or ones with which the user simply disagrees. An incorrect assumption would make the Monte Carlo simulation as unrealistic as the traditional deterministic method.

A large number of iterations is necessary for the simulation to be useful. A program or website that doesn't want to incur the cost of a high number of simulations does a disservice to its users. In a public opinion poll, the number of people questioned determines the probability of error. Likewise, the number of simulations determines the probability of error in the program. Unfortunately, Monte Carlo simulation programs typically don't reveal their probability of error.

Of course, the probabilities are a lot like insurance. Suppose you look at the statistics and decide that there is a low probability of your house burning down this year. So, you don't buy homeowner's insurance. That probability doesn't do you much good if in fact your home does catch fire this year. Likewise, a 98 percent probability of success from a Monte Carlo simulation looks good. But the plan is not a good one if your actual results fall into the 2 percent of outcomes when the plan fails.

More important than the probability of failure is the extent of the failure. If a plan falls short of the goal by a few dollars and a few months, that's not a real problem. Small adjustments in spending can turn the plan into a successful one. But if the plan falls short of success by years and tens of thousands of dollars, that's a different story. Likewise, if a plan is successful and actually will fund the retirement for 60 years, then the plan might be restricting spending too much. The extent of success or failure can matter as much as the probability.

The Monte Carlo simulation also assumes that the retirement plan will be followed. In the real world, however, an investment bear market or some other unexpected and negative event often causes people to change their investment portfolios or other parts of their plans. Reducing stock holdings in a bear market, for example, would reduce a person's ability to participate in a succeeding bull market. But that possible change in behavior is not factored into the probability of success calculated by the simulation program.

Of course, the simulation is only as good as the data on which it is based. That is why the most important part of retirement planning is to develop a realistic estimate of retirement spending, saving, inflation, and other factors. Nothing else matters if those estimates aren't done well.

The Monte Carlo simulation is a useful tool in the retirement planning toolbox. Don't think, however, that because it uses high-level mathematics and computer power that the result is hard science. There are many assumptions and variables in the simulation. Solid judgment and key decisions are at least as important as computer power. You need to realize the limits of the tool.

A Successful Retirement

The key to successful retirement planning is a good estimate of retirement spending. Everything else relies on it. Whichever method is used to estimate retirement finances, keep the following principles in mind.

How to Forecast Spending Successfully

Use Your Own Spending.   Don't use rules of thumb or rely on surveys of other retirees. Decide what you want to do in retirement. Then, estimate how much that lifestyle would cost today. As we discussed earlier, this estimate of annual retirement spending might equal or exceed spending during the working years. It depends on your plans for retirement.

Count on Inflation.   Even low inflation has a strong effect over 10 years or more. A 3 percent annual inflation rate cuts purchasing power in half over 24 years and by close to 20 percent after five years. Even a low 2 percent inflation rate cuts the standard of living by 20 percent after 10 years. For example, after 10 years of only 2 percent inflation, almost $12,200 is needed to buy what $10,000 used to buy (a 22 percent increase). After 15 years, almost $13,500 is needed. If inflation doubles to 4 percent, almost $15,000 is needed after 10 years and $18,000 after 15 years. Here's another way to look at it. A dollar in 1982 had the purchasing power of about 59 cents in 2002. A 1967 dollar equaled about 19 cents in 2002. It won't happen overnight, but it is painful over time. See Table 2.1.

TABLE 2.1 Dollars Needed to Retain Purchasing Power

Years	Inflation Rate		
	3%	4%	5%
1	1.0	1.0	1.1
2	1.1	1.1	1.1
3	1.1	1.1	1.2
4	1.1	1.2	1.2
5	1.2	1.2	1.3
6	1.2	1.3	1.3
7	1.2	1.3	1.4
8	1.3	1.4	1.5
9	1.3	1.4	1.6
10	1.3	1.5	1.6
11	1.4	1.5	1.7
12	1.4	1.6	1.8
13	1.5	1.7	1.9
14	1.5	1.7	2.0
15	1.6	1.8	2.1
16	1.6	1.9	2.2
17	1.7	1.9	2.3
18	1.7	2.0	2.4
19	1.8	2.1	2.5
20	1.8	2.2	2.7
21	1.9	2.3	2.8
22	1.9	2.4	2.9
23	2.0	2.5	3.1
24	2.0	2.6	3.1
25	2.1	2.7	3.4
26	2.2	2.8	3.6
27	2.2	2.9	3.7
28	2.3	3.0	3.9
29	2.4	3.1	4.1
30	2.4	3.2	4.3

A Key Issue Is Which Inflation Rate to Use. People who were planning retirement in the early 1980s would use a 4 percent to 5 percent annual inflation rate. The average annual inflation rate from 1962 to 1982 was 5.9 percent. That turned out to be much too high for the following 20 years, when inflation rose only 3.2 percent annually. Overestimating inflation causes a preretiree to save more money than required and reduces their working years' standard of living. Those planning retirement today might be tempted to use a 1 percent to 2 percent rate, based on recent history, but this would be risky. If inflation rates rise in the future, they won't have saved enough for retirement. For the long term, the inflation rate in the United States has been around 3 percent. Ideally, as we discussed, a separate inflation rate is assigned to each item of proposed retirement spending. The usefulness of that method, however, still depends on being able to estimate future inflation accurately.

Don't Underestimate Longevity. People who retire today have life expectancies that were only dreamed of during their youth. A common retirement planning mistake is to underestimate life expectancy and spend money accordingly. To be safe, most people should count on a retirement of at least 30 years. Married couples should assume at least one spouse will live into his or her 90s, unless there are medical or family reasons that likely limit life expectancy. Many advisors say that the safest advice is to assume that at least one spouse will live at least 15 percent longer than the current life expectancy for his or her age or that at least one spouse will live to 100. That means that many people should plan on 30 or more years of retirement. We'll discuss longevity in more detail in Chapter 4.

Don't Overlook All Possible Income Sources. The tools available from the financial services companies often tend to overstate the amount of investment assets needed. Don't forget other income sources such as Social Security, home equity, a reverse mortgage, and so forth. Inheritances also might be part of the equation. Remember that in the later years, retirees should feel free to spend principal and not rely solely on income and capital gains, unless leaving money to loved ones or charity is the primary goal.

Make More than One Estimate. The primary projection will depend on the best estimates of inflation, investment returns, and other factors. Additional projections also should be made that will show the results if one or more of those assumptions change. Consider making alternate projections with higher and lower inflation and investment returns and some changes in spending. The point is to see how long-term changes in the assumptions change the results. That makes it easier to adjust the plan over the years when it looks as if actual results will differ from the original assumptions.

Stress Testing. Medical expenses and long-term care expenses are the most uncertain spending in most retirement plans. You can make annual estimates of those expenses and assume an inflation increase, but unlike other expenses these expenses have the potential to balloon in one or more years. You might have routine medical treatment and exams for years and then require a major surgery or other treatments in one or more years. You might develop a chronic condition that requires additional expenses every year. Or at some point you might need long-term care.

The best way to deal with such uncertainties is stress testing. Assume that at some point in retirement you are faced with large expenses for medical care or long-term care. How much of those expenses would be covered by insurance or government programs? How would the expenses not covered by insurance or programs affect your retirement plan?

After looking at stress test results, you might modify your plan. You might decide to increase insurance coverage. The trade off is that more insurance increases your annual costs but reduces the uncertainty by covering more of the catastrophic or large expenses. Or you might decide to build more flexibility into your plan. Don't spend as much money annually as your plan seems to allow. That will give you more of a reserve to cover any large medical or long-term care expenses.

Review and Revise Regularly.   No matter your age, remember that the plan is only a plan. It is based on assumptions, and real events are going to differ from at least some of your assumptions. Younger people should review their plans every five years, or more often if significant life changes occur. People in or within five years of retirement should make annual reviews comparing their plans to actual results. Annual reviews enable you to make relatively small adjustments to stay on course. Waiting too long to compare results to the plan might require significant and jarring adjustments to spending or other parts of your plan. Think of a retirement plan as a process that has to be fine-tuned regularly.

How Much Is Enough?

"How much is enough?" is partly a practical question and partly a philosophical one. So far, I've addressed it as a practical question. But let's look at it philosophically for a moment. How much do you really need to reach your goals? If you can't reach all the goals, which goals are the important ones?

Surveys regularly indicate that people could be very happy if they had more money than they actually do have. People at every level of wealth believe they need more money to be happy and to fulfill their goals—it's a natural, very human response. It also is consistent among countries and cultures. As income grows, things that once were luxuries become necessities and are taken for granted. Then we train our sights on what might be available if we had even more money, and shoot for those things. But life is full of choices, and there are precious few of us who can afford everything we would like.

True wealth produces freedom. I've seen too many people who let their things own them, rather than owning their things. A big house or multiple houses, nice cars, club memberships, entertaining, and travel all cost money. They're great as long as the money to support them is available. But not everyone is comfortable with that much overhead or with the investment risks needed to support this kind of spending. In those cases, the people don't own the things, the things own the people. Nice things shouldn't increase one's level of stress. If the pressure of paying for things causes someone to be unhappy or to snap at loved ones, that person probably can't afford those things.

In later chapters, I will demonstrate how to invest to increase returns, reduce taxes and other expenses, and take other steps to make wealth last longer. These steps will enhance retirement. The first step, however, is to make a good estimate of retirement spending and capital needs and develop a plan to accumulate that amount. Spending amounts should be adjusted when it appears that income and assets won't be sufficient to fund the spending.

Not many people begin retirement with all the money they need to pay for their desired retirement. However, that doesn't mean they will outlive their assets or end up living with their children. It just means they have to make some adjustments as they go along. A key to successful retirement is knowing when adjustments need to be made and making adjustments that you can live with. Unsuccessful retirements generally occur when no early planning is done, the retiree lives however he or she desires, and later adjustments are forced by circumstances.

Securing and Maximizing Guaranteed Lifetime Income

The most important financial goal of retirement planning is to establish a secure stream of income or cash flow that will meet your spending needs for the rest of your life. Too often, people lose track of this goal amid all the talk about how much to save, how to invest, and other topics. The ultimate goal is to generate reliable income to pay your expenses for life, what I call establishing your *retirement paycheck*. The more income that can be guaranteed for life, the more financially secure and independent you'll be.

Establishing a lifetime stream of income in retirement was easy for the first post–World War II generation of retirees. Most of them had Social Security and pensions from their employers providing a floor of guaranteed income. With their own savings, they invested in a collection of safe income investments, such as certificates of deposit, treasury bonds, and tax-exempt bonds. They might have taken a little risk with utility stocks, high-dividend yield stocks, and corporate bonds. Such portfolios generated a lot of income, and the principal value didn't fluctuate much. The income and portfolio didn't have to last too long, because most people were retired only 5 to 10 years.

Things are different today. The foremost difference is that yields on most investments have been at or near historic lows for most of the time since 2000. A very valuable portfolio is needed to generate a high income from the investments used by previous generations of retirees. Also, life expectancy has increased to the point that many people should plan on retirement lasting 30 years and perhaps longer. We discuss longevity in more detail in Chapter 5. Inflation is likely to degrade the purchasing power of income over that time. Even modest inflation of 2 percent annually reduces purchasing power by over 30 percent over 20 years. Taxes, all kinds of taxes, are likely to rise steadily and reduce the income available for other expenses. Expenses can be higher, because retirees now pay more of the expenses that in the past were borne primarily by former employers or the government. That trend is likely to continue. There are other obstacles to securing guaranteed lifetime income.

Fortunately, there are many tools available to create your retirement paycheck. There's no silver bullet or single financial product you should use to secure your lifetime income stream. Instead, you need to take full advantage of all the tools available for establishing post-career cash flow, and you need to optimize those tools for your situation.

Today those entering or nearing their post-career years have a number of tools available to them:

- Social Security
- Employer pensions
- Annuities
- Nest egg distribution or spending strategies
- Nest egg investment strategies
- Tax strategies

In Chapter 2, we discussed the importance of estimating lifetime spending reasonably accurately, so you'll know approximately how much income you'll need. In this chapter we discuss how to use Social Security and annuities to establish and maximize a base level of income that's guaranteed for life, no matter how long you live. In Chapter 4, you'll learn how to extend the life of your other investment assets by developing a strategy for spending your nest egg, and in Chapter 5 we review investment strategies that can make your nest egg last longer. In Chapter 10, we discuss issues involving employer retirement plans, so you can maximize the benefits of those plans.

There's a key point to keep in mind regardless of the recommendations you adopt from these chapters. Remember: It's only a plan. Many factors are considered and assumptions are made when developing a financial roadmap for retirement. The real results will differ from the assumptions. You won't forecast everything correctly. Some of the differences will be more favorable than those used in your plan; others will be less favorable.

That's why you can't consider a plan to be set in stone. The plan will have to be revised. Remember to monitor and review your situation, compare it to your plan, and make adjustments when necessary. When circumstances aren't monitored and a plan doesn't have flexibility, a solid lifetime paycheck can shrink or disappear when reality doesn't match the plan. Review the plan at least annually once you're in retirement and even in the five years before retirement. Regular reviews mean you can stay on track with modest changes. Let too much time pass between reviews of and updates to your plan, and you might have to make major, uncomfortable adjustments to get back on track. Regular reviews mean modest changes, and you'll have more confidence.

Retirement income security is a process, not a fixed plan.

Despite the obstacles and challenges put in your path, you can convert accumulated assets and resources into a stream of cash flow that will last the rest of your life and your spouse's. It could even last longer, so you can leave a legacy for your children, grandchildren, and causes that interest you.

Securing Basic Expenses with Guaranteed Income

Before consider strategies to lock in guaranteed lifetime income, you want to prioritize your spending.

In Chapter 2 we discussed how to estimate retirement spending. Within that spending estimate, you'll have several levels of spending. The first level consists of your basic or required expenses. This level includes food, shelter, utilities, insurance, transportation, clothing, and regular medical care. You might have other categories of spending in this level.

The next level of spending is the "nice to have" or preferred spending. These are the expenditures that maintain or somewhat increase your standard of living. This level might include travel, dining out, recreation, entertainment, and a wide range of expenses that are part of your expected retirement lifestyle but that can be reduced or deferred when money is tight.

The third level is what I call aspirational spending. These expenses are for activities and items that you'd like to be part of your retirement, but that you know are "extras." They include "bucket list" types of activities and purchases that you've always wanted but never had the time or money. In retirement, you'll have the time.

The final level is what I call legacy spending. The most common legacy spending is spoiling the grandchildren and providing some financial help to your children. There's also long-term legacy spending. This legacy spending involves conserving part of your estate so it can be left to either family members or charities or both. Your first priority, of course, is to maintain your standard of living in retirement. Many people, however, prefer restricting some of their levels of spending in order to have some legacy spending.

Some spending might be split between two or more levels. For example, you need some clothing, but you probably don't need designer clothes or a large volume of clothes. So, if you're inclined to want a large volume of clothes or expensive clothes that exceed basic need, some clothing expenses will be basic spending and some will be at a higher level. The choice of retirement housing is similar. There's a basic housing cost, and then there is nice-to-have and aspirational housing. Likewise, you might want to play a lot of golf. The cost will vary, however, depending on whether you play on public courses or join a private club. Playing on public courses probably is nice-to-have spending while a private club could be aspirational spending.

After estimating and prioritizing your spending, the next step is to decide how much of the spending you'd like to be supported by guaranteed lifetime income, which includes Social Security, employer pensions, and annuities.

I think it's a good idea for most people to match their basic or required living expenses with guaranteed income. You don't want to worry about being able to pay for food, utilities, and the like. When you don't have guaranteed income paying for those basic expenses, there's a tendency to worry and reevaluate spending and investments each time the investment markets take a tumble. When there are large, sustained market declines, many retirees wonder if their nest eggs will last the rest of their retirement years and often make emotional or panic decisions to change their spending or investments or both.

When basic expenses are covered by guaranteed lifetime income, people are able to take a little more risk with the rest of their nest eggs than they otherwise would. Taking more risk intelligently creates the potential to earn higher investment returns. Higher returns can lead to a higher standard of living in retirement or more legacy spending for family or charities.

The amount of guaranteed income you desire can vary, depending on your financial situation. Someone who hasn't quite saved enough money for a secure retirement might want to increase the amount of guaranteed income. The less financially secure a person is, the lower is the allowable margin of error from low investment returns or other surprises. That's why someone on the edge of a secure retirement might prefer a high level of guaranteed income to ensure the income doesn't fall short for either basic expenses or spending beyond that. Someone who is more financially secure might be comfortable with less guaranteed income. This person's investment portfolio might be large enough that basic expenses and beyond would be covered even after major surprises, such as investment losses and unexpected expenses. A financially secure person might be willing to take more risk in exchange for the potential of earning higher income and having more for the aspirational and legacy spending.

The greatest fear for those in or approaching retirement is running out of money during their lifetimes. Whatever income doesn't come from guaranteed sources must come from working, savings, and investment returns. Those income sources have risk and uncertainty. Maximizing guaranteed income sources reduces risk and uncertainty, and with it, the potential for running out of money.

There are two sources of guaranteed lifetime income for almost everyone: Social Security and annuities. We're going to discuss those in the rest of this chapter. You'll learn how to maximize the benefits of these tools to enhance your financial security.

Secrets to Boosting Social Security Benefits

There's a lot of confusion about Social Security. Of course, there's discussion and uncertainty about the financial condition of Social Security and how long the program will last. More importantly, there's confusion among Americans age 50 and older about the role of Social Security benefits in their retirement plans, the rules of Social Security, and which decisions to make about taking benefits.

The confusion is unfortunate, because decisions need to be made about Social Security benefits. Those decisions generally are irreversible, and the choices can change your lifetime benefits by tens of thousands of dollars, sometimes substantially more than that. The effects of the decisions also can ripple through to your spouse and even to your children. You need to carefully consider Social Security decisions. Ideally, planning for Social Security benefits begins years before you plan to retire. You don't have to begin Social Security benefits when you retire from work. The benefits can begin before or after formal retirement, and the optimum decision for you might be for benefits to commence at a time other than your retirement.

Before retirement, most people don't give Social Security much consideration and think Social Security won't be an important part of their retirement cash flow. Yet, 34 percent of current retirees estimate that Social Security provides 90 percent or more of their retirement income. For most American retirees, Social Security provides a meaningful portion of their retirement income, and it is the only guaranteed lifetime income received by many. It is among the very few available guaranteed and inflation-indexed sources of income. Also, the importance of Social Security to regular cash flow usually increases as one ages. Other assets are spent, and inflation reduces their purchasing power.

Most people have little idea of the level of their retirement benefits. The Social Security Administration (SSA) mailed annual statements of estimated benefits to everyone for years, and then suspended the mailings for a few years. In 2015, SSA reinstated mailing estimated benefit statements to some people, but that policy probably will change again. You don't have to wait for Social Security to mail you a statement of estimated benefits. Estimates are available over the telephone or through the Social Security website any time.

When you receive a benefits estimate, it is likely to be misleading unless you understand how the estimates are developed.

Social Security retirement benefits are based on your highest 35 years of earnings. The younger you are, the more likely the estimate won't be reliable. The estimate assumes earnings will increase at the estimated wage inflation rate from now through retirement age. Your history of promotions, raises, changing jobs for higher salaries, and being laid off is likely to be very different from the steady path assumed in the estimate. If you avoid extended layoffs, you're likely to have several points in your career when your earnings increase significantly because of promotions or job changes. Some people believe the SSA deliberately understates likely benefits in these estimates to encourage people to save more. On the other hand, one or more extended periods of unemployment or stagnant salaries could cause your earnings history to lag the estimates.

As you age, however, the statements generally should be more accurate, but errors at that point are likely to overstate eventual benefits. The estimate assumes you work until the age at which benefits begin and that earnings increase each year at the estimated wage inflation rate. Many people in their 50s and beyond "hit the wall" as far as salary increases go, have periods of unemployment, retire earlier than expected, or take jobs that pay less than their previous positions. In these cases, your 35 highest earnings years could be less than the estimate.

Yet, for some people the estimates still will tend to underestimate benefits. Keep in mind only the 35 highest years of earnings are used. As you work longer, you likely are knocking off low-earnings years from your youth. Even if you suffer a setback and don't earn as much the rest of your career as originally anticipated, you could earn more than in the early years and increase your final benefits.

The online Social Security benefits estimator is more accurate than the mailed estimates. After you register online, the calculator uses your real earnings history. You also have the flexibility online to estimate benefits using different scenarios. The paper statements mailed to people are limited to a fixed set of assumptions and have a higher margin of error.

Another way to look at Social Security retirement benefits is the replacement ratio. This is the amount of your final income that Social Security will replace in the first year of retirement. Social Security benefits are calculated so that the replacement ratio depends on your income level throughout your career. The lower your income, the higher the Social Security replacement ratio is. A low-income worker could have Social Security retirement benefits replace 90 percent of final income. A very-high-income worker could receive closer to 10 percent or less of final income in Social Security benefits.

In 2015, someone who made the minimum wage (about $14,500 annually) would receive Social Security retirement benefits on average of 76.5 percent of final wages. For the median income of $33,120, the replacement ratio declined to 58.4 percent of final income. Someone whose earnings were the maximum wage for Social Security withholding had a replacement ratio of only 28.2 percent, and someone earning $165,150 had retirement benefits of only 18.8 percent of final earnings. The replacement ratio will decline further as income rises, because there is a maximum first-year retirement benefit. No matter how much you earn and pay in Social Security taxes, you won't be paid more in retirement benefits than the year's maximum. (In 2014, the monthly maximum payment for someone at full retirement age was $2,642.) To receive the maximum benefit, a worker would have to earn the maximum Social Security wage base (the maximum salary amount on which Social Security taxes are collected) every year for the 35 highest years of earnings. The maximum payment applies only to someone starting benefits that year. Once benefits begin, they rise with increases (but don't fall with decreases) in the Consumer Price Index each year.

The average U.S. worker receives about 40 percent of final salary income in Social Security retirement benefits.

With the poor performance of the stock market indexes since 2000, low interest rates on bonds, and high volatility in all investments, Social Security is becoming a more important source of income for many Americans, and more are starting to realize how important that guaranteed income and stability is.

Within a wide range of options, you decide when to begin Social Security retirement benefits. Many people don't realize just how much flexibility they have and how much the choices change the amount of benefits. A retiree can substantially increase lifetime cash flow by making the optimum decisions about Social Security.

It is critical for a near-retiree to spend time carefully analyzing the Social Security benefit options. The best choices often are not intuitive or even well-known. Also, the choices that will maximize income have changed over time. Rules of thumb from the past are not ideal for today's retirees.

For married couples, there can be a series of decisions instead of one decision. These decisions have long-term effects on the retiree's income. Just a few of the decisions are: At what age should benefits begin? When should a spouse begin benefits? Should benefits be based on one's own work record or one's spouse's record? Should you change the choice? Contrary to what many people believe, Social Security benefits can be changed under certain circumstances. Beginning Social Security benefits often is referred to as claiming benefits. Choices about when to begin benefits often are called claiming strategies.

Maximizing Social Security benefits can greatly enhance retirement financial security. You could lose opportunities and substantial income by treating Social Security benefits as an afterthought and "bonus income" or by not realizing that you have choices. Social Security is for many people the only part of retirement income that is both guaranteed for life and inflation-protected. These are two qualities many people appreciate only after they've been retired a few years. Social Security benefits also act as a form of life insurance for married couples, since a surviving spouse can receive benefits based on the deceased spouse's earnings history.

There are two other aspects of Social Security benefits that often are misunderstood. For more and more retirees, a portion of the benefits is subject to income taxes. Originally, benefits were tax free. But beginning with the 1986 law, a portion of benefits became taxable. For higher-income beneficiaries, the portion taxed was increased in 1993. There are ways at least some people can reduce the income taxes on their benefits.

The other misunderstood feature of Social Security benefits is how earning income from work after benefits begin affects the benefits paid. The law on that also changed over the years, generating much confusion.

These issues are covered in Chapter 10 on taxes in retirement.

When to Begin Benefits—The Basic Choices

The amount of benefits received depends partly on the age you choose for the benefits to begin. Each person can choose to begin receiving Social Security retirement benefits at age 62 or any time thereafter. (You might be eligible for disability or survivor's benefits at younger ages.) The earlier the benefits start, the lower the initial payment is.

A key concept of Social Security is full retirement age (FRA). If you choose to begin benefits at this age, you receive the full or normal benefits under the program's formulas. Begin benefits earlier, and your monthly checks will be reduced. Begin benefits later, and your monthly checks are increased for each month you wait after FRA to begin benefits until you reach age 70. There's no increase for delaying benefits after 70.

The FRA at the inception of Social Security was 65, but the 1983 reform changed FRA for anyone who was born after 1937, which means for anyone who turns 65 after 2002. The FRA rises roughly two months for each year you were born after 1937, with a break from 1943–1954, until the FRA becomes 67 for those born in 1960 or later. The schedule is in Table 3.1.

TABLE 3.1   Full Retirement Age Schedule

Year of Birth	Full Retirement Age (FRA)	% of FRA Benefits at Age 62	Annual Credit for Delayed Retirement	% of FRA Benefits at Age 70
1936 and before	65	80%	6%	130%
1937	65	80%	6.5%	132.5%
1938	65 & 2 mos.	79⅙%	6.5%	131.42%
1939	65 & 4 mos.	78⅓%	7%	132.66%
1940	65 & 6 mos.	77½%	7%	131.5%
1941	65 & 8 mos.	76⅔%	7.5%	132.5%
1942	65 & 10 mos.	75⅚%	7.5%	131.25%
1943–1954	66	75%	8%	132%
1955	66 & 2 mos.	74⅙%	8%	130.66%
1956	66 & 4 mos.	73⅓%	8%	129.33%
1957	66 & 6 mos.	72½%	8%	128%
1958	66 & 8 mos.	71⅔%	8%	126.66%
1959	66 & 10 mos.	70⅚%	8%	125.33%
1960 and later	67	70%	8%	124%

Other changes made in the 1983 reform were adjustments to the formulas for computing benefits that begin before or after FRA. There is a bigger reduction for taking benefits before FRA than under the previous law, and the bonus for delaying benefits after FRA was increased.

Of course, if you're not working or simply need the income, you might not care about optimizing the lifetime Social Security benefits. You'll need to begin retirement benefits, because you need the income. Also, when there's a personal or family history that indicates living to life expectancy or much beyond is unlikely, waiting to receive benefits might not be the best strategy.

For many other people, however, there is a choice and a reasonable chance of outliving life expectancy. For them, a careful analysis of when to begin Social Security benefits can significantly affect both lifetime income and the benefits available to survivors.

The easiest way to decide when to begin benefits is to compute the simple break-even point. Start with your estimated benefits, which you can find on the Social Security website. Suppose your normal benefit at FRA would be $1,400 per month. Waiting until age 70 would entitle you to $1,820 monthly or 130 percent of the normal benefit, an additional $420 monthly. For this example, we'll say your FRA is 66, which means taking benefits at FRA gives you benefits 48 months earlier than at 70.

To find the break-even point, multiply the normal retirement benefit at age 66 by the number of extra months you'll receive it before age 70. In this example that is $1,400 times 48 for a cumulative early payment of $67,200. Divide that total by the increased monthly benefit for waiting until age 70 ($420). The result is 160. That is the number of months it will take for the total lifetime payments received after waiting until age 70 to catch up with the lifetime payments you would receive by starting benefits at 66. That comes to $13^1/_3$ years. That means after age 79 the decision to delay benefits will pay off. If you die before age 79 and four months, you lost money by waiting to take benefits.

The benefit formula is set up so that the benefit for waiting to receive benefits closely follows the actuarial tables available in 1983. Those who outlive the 1983 life expectancy will come out ahead, and those who do not will lose money by delaying benefits. The system should come out even.

Here's another example. Suppose you turned 62 this year. Your benefits payable at 62 would be 77.5 percent of normal retirement, meaning you'll receive $1,085 monthly at 62 if your FRA benefit were $1,400. FRA for you, however, was 65 and six months. By taking benefits at 62, you will receive the benefits for an extra 42 months. That means total benefits received by FRA would be $45,570. Divide that amount by the $315 additional benefit you would receive by waiting until FRA. You'll find that it will take $144^2/_3$ months for lifetime benefits to make up for waiting until normal retirement age to begin taking benefits instead of starting them at age 62. That means you will have to live until about age 78 to break even for waiting until normal retirement age. Live longer than that, and you benefit by waiting until normal retirement age instead of starting benefits are 62.

As in the other example, the break-even point is designed to be around normal life expectancy as of 1983 for the age group. The system breaks even on average, and those who live beyond life expectancy come out ahead.

This simple break-even calculation does not include all possible factors and can oversimplify the decision.

The monthly increases for delaying benefits aren't steady and equal, points out William Meyer of Social Security Solutions in an article in *The Wall Street Journal*, so the break-even age changes. From age 62 to 63, benefits increase 0.42 percent of the benefit per month of delay. From 63 through 66, they increase at 0.56 percent. From 66 through 70, benefits increase 0.67 percent for each month of delay.

Because of this unevenness, the break-even age changes. There are good times and bad times for singles to begin retirement benefits, and most singles are making the wrong choice.

The worst times for singles to begin benefits, says Meyer, are between 62 years, one month and 63 years, 11 months and from 65 years, five months and 66 years, seven months. Many people take benefits either when they're first eligible or at normal retirement age, and those are among the worst times. He says the break-even age is 78 years when benefits are begun from 62 to 63 but falls to 76 years at ages 63 to 64. The break-even point from then is on a roller coaster through age 70.

There are additional factors to consider before making a decision under the simple break-even analysis.

Once benefits begin, they increase with inflation each year that the Consumer Price Index is greater than 0 percent. That should push the break-even point of waiting a little further into the future. But there's another factor that could act in favor of waiting. When Social Security computes your benefits, it uses your wage history but also increases past wages for general wage inflation. Wage inflation usually is higher than Consumer Price Inflation, so you could benefit more by delaying benefits than is demonstrated by the simple break-even analysis in these examples.

Also, if you're considering delaying benefits, that means you don't need the money at 62 to pay expenses. You have other resources available. You could begin benefits at 62 and invest the money as it is received. Investment returns could increase the advantage of early benefits, and that would push the break-even point of waiting farther into the future. This is the time value of money. Receiving money now is more valuable than receiving the same amount later. Of course, there's risk in this approach. If your investments lose money or earn less than the 8 percent annually that benefits increase by delaying them, you've taken a gamble that didn't pay off. In recent years, earning 8 percent or higher has been a very ambitious goal.

The simple break-even method also doesn't take into account potential changes in inflation, investment returns, and taxes. For example, instead of delaying Social Security benefits you could begin the benefits and draw less money from your investment portfolio. Investment returns could offset the reduction in benefits. When you move beyond the simple break-even method, the calculations become potentially more accurate but also far more complicated. Fortunately, New York Life Insurance Company published a paper in 2015 that did these calculations. The paper concluded that using the additional factors made delaying benefits even more attractive in most cases.

Most Americans begin receiving their Social Security benefits early, though the percentage delaying benefits has increased. About 37.5 percent of men and 42.4 percent of women claimed their retirement benefits at age 62, according to the 2013 Social Security Administration's Annual Statistical Supplement. Even so, more people are delaying benefits than used to, because 10 years ago about 50 percent claimed benefits at 62.

About 31.5 percent of men and 25.2 percent of women now wait until their FRA to claim benefits. Far fewer than 10 percent wait until age 70, when benefits are maximized, and that number's held steady for decades.

For those who retired before the changes started in 2002 and took early benefits, they probably made the right decision. But taking early benefits might not be the right decision for those who come after them.

Don't Leave Money on the Table

The key is that the rules for increasing or decreasing benefits are set so that anyone who lives to life expectancy receives the same lifetime payouts regardless of the age benefits begin. That makes the normal life expectancy the *break-even point*, as discussed in the above examples. Live beyond that point and you will benefit by waiting to receive benefits. Your lifetime benefits will exceed what you would receive by starting at age 62.

But the formulas were set in 1983, the last time Social Security was reformed, using life expectancy tables available at the time. Life expectancies have increased. For example, about half of men currently age 65 will live past age 85. So, more people will benefit from delaying benefits than was the case when the rules were set in 1983.

Another consideration is that the wages in your work history are indexed for increases in overall wages each year. That should increase your wage history and your benefits when you delay receiving benefits, even if you're not working and earning more income. If you actually wait until age 70 to begin benefits, you are likely to receive a higher benefit than the age 70 benefit estimated when you were age 62, because of the annual wage indexing. Also, when you decide to delay retirement and continue generating income from working, your benefits are likely to increase if those wages from those additional years are higher than the wages earlier in your career. Social Security uses only the highest 35 years of wages. If you can replace low early-career wages with higher late-career wages and knock the lower wages out of your top 35 years, that will increase your benefits.

The increase in life expectancy is a reason many should at least consider delaying benefits. If you have no reason to believe your life expectancy will be below average, the delay should make sense. Since half of your age group will live beyond life expectancy, and that life expectancy is higher than what was assumed in 1983, a majority of the age group will receive a higher lifetime benefit by waiting.

Another reason to consider delaying benefits is your spouse. Delayed Social Security benefits are a very low-cost form of life insurance when you were the higher-earning spouse. Your surviving spouse receives the higher of the benefit you were receiving and his or her earned benefit. For the cost of forgoing Social Security benefits a few years, that can be a good deal. We discuss more about spouses and benefits later in this chapter.

There also might be tax benefits when you delay Social Security benefits if that increases your drawdown of IRAs and other qualified retirement accounts. Required minimum distributions from qualified retirement accounts can greatly accelerate as one lives to the late 70s and beyond. In time, these taxable distributions could greatly exceed spending needs. This increases lifetime taxes and reduces the amounts available for heirs to inherit. We discuss that in more detail in Chapter 9. A good strategy can be to spend some money from the qualified retirement plan first, reducing future required minimum distributions and allowing Social Security benefits to increase. The approach might also make it less likely in the future that required minimum distributions from a qualified plan will trigger income taxes on Social Security benefits. Unless you expect to earn higher than an 8 percent after-tax return from your IRA, spending the IRA early to earn higher delayed Social Security benefits can be a good trade-off.

Another reason to delay benefits is that many baby boomers are likely to work past normal retirement age and certainly past age 62. A number of them will try retirement and, for lack of either money or things to do, will return to work. If they begin taking Social Security benefits early, returning to work could cause the benefits to be reduced. Working will increase their benefits later, but it might not be enough to make up for the reduction from taking benefits early.

Introducing Spousal Benefits

So far, we have analyzed when to take Social Security benefits in the context of a single person. Yet, Social Security retirement benefits come with a spousal benefit and several options. It is easy to overlook this when deciding to take benefits, but the age when a person begins his or her retirement benefits affects the level of benefits received by a surviving spouse and in some cases also affects the retirement benefits of a current spouse. Spouses also can increase joint lifetime benefits by coordinating when they take their benefits. Substantial changes were made in the strategies for spouses in the Bipartisan Budget Act of 2015. The law basically eliminated the ability to use several profitable strategies for married couples.

The important rule is that a married person can qualify for Social Security benefits based on either his or her own earnings or the spouse's. More than one quarter of Social Security benefits, in fact, are paid to survivors and family members.

A person who earned wages (or self-employment income) for at least 40 quarters (10 years) qualifies for his or her own Social Security benefits. A married person also is eligible for a retirement benefit that is 50 percent of his or her living spouse's benefit. A surviving spouse is entitled to receive 100 percent of his or her deceased spouse's retirement benefit.

If a person is eligible for more than one retirement benefit, he or she receives only the highest of the available benefits.

Let's look at an example. Suppose Max and Rosie Profits each works until eligible for full retirement benefits. Max is entitled to a monthly benefit of $1,000 based on his earnings history, and Rosie is eligible for $300 based on her earnings history. Because Rosie's earned benefit is lower than 50 percent of Max's earned benefit, she'll receive the $500 spousal benefit based on Max's benefit. Together, they'll receive $1,500 in monthly benefits if they apply for benefits today at FRA.

Suppose Max dies before Rosie. Then, Rosie can change her benefit to the $1,000 per month she is entitled to as Max's widow—100 percent of Max's retirement benefit. She receives only the $1,000 and stops receiving the $500 spousal benefit she was receiving. So, her household income will decline to $1,000. If Rosie dies first, Max continues to receive his $1,000 benefit, because it is higher than 100 percent of Rosie's earned benefit that would be his survivor's benefit. (This example ignores the inflation adjustments that occur while they are receiving benefits.)

Because your spouse's retirement and survivor benefits depend on your benefit, they are something to keep in mind when choosing the starting date for your Social Security benefits.

For example, let's assume a married couple in which the husband earned more than his wife. The husband might decide, considering only his situation that it makes sense for him to begin benefits at age 62. The decision might change, however, if he considers the effect on his wife. As a woman, she is statistically likely to live longer than the husband. If she survives her husband, her survivor's benefit is going to be based on the husband's benefit, unless her earned benefit is higher. Also, during her life she'll receive the higher of her own benefit and 50 percent of her husband's benefit at FRA. For the husband in some situations, delaying Social Security retirement benefits can be a cheap form of life insurance that maximizes his wife's income after he's gone.

More on Spouses and Benefits

Now, we will look in more detail at how spouses' earnings and decisions can affect each other's benefits and how they can coordinate the timing of their benefits to maximize household income. There are options for each spouse that could greatly influence the lifetime Social Security earnings of both spouses. You'll learn that it is beneficial for spouses to coordinate when each begins benefits instead of separately considering their decisions.

Every married person eligible to receive Social Security benefits looks to two work records to determine the amount of benefits received. The person's own work record, of course, is one source. The spouse's earnings record is another. As we discussed earlier, the general rule is that a person receives the higher of the benefits earned under his or her own work record and 50 percent of what the spouse would receive at FRA. Keep in mind, however, that a spousal benefit can't be received until the other spouse actually files to begin receiving benefits. If the higher-earning spouse hasn't filed to receive benefits, the lower-earning spouse can't begin receiving a spousal benefit yet.

Note an important difference between the benefits of a spouse and a surviving spouse. While the higher-earning spouse is alive, the lower-earning spouse's retirement benefit is half of the higher-earning spouse's FRA benefit. But after the higher-earning spouse passes away, the lower-earning spouse's survivor benefit is the retirement benefit the higher-earning spouse actually was receiving if he or she was already receiving benefits. The amount of that benefit will depend on the age when the higher-earning spouse chose to begin benefits. If the higher-earning spouse began receiving benefits before FRA, the surviving spouse will receive less than the full retirement benefit as a survivor benefit.

There is an additional step in the computation of a spouse's benefit. The benefit received is based on a combination of the other spouse's benefit at FRA and the age at which the lower-earning spouse actually begins benefits. There's a reduction in benefits for starting before FRA whether a person's benefit is based on his or her earnings record or the spouse's. If a spousal benefit is begun before FRA, the benefit will be reduced on a sliding scale. If age 62 is selected, the benefit received will be 35 percent less than what he or she would receive at FRA.

Summarizing Spousal Strategies

We will build on the rules already discussed to develop strategies that might further boost the guaranteed retirement income of you and your spouse.

For a spouse to receive retirement benefits based on the other spouse's earned benefits, the other spouse first must be receiving retirement benefits. Let's assume the wife is the lower-earning spouse, and the husband is the higher-earning spouse. If the wife is ready to retire and wants to receive benefits before her husband is ready to, the wife's benefits will not be based on the husband's earned benefits; she can receive only her earned benefits. (The husband can begin receiving retirement benefits while continuing to work, but the earnings limit would further reduce the benefits. This is discussed in more detail later in this chapter.)

The wife can begin receiving benefits based on her own earnings record when the husband is not yet receiving benefits. After the husband begins receiving benefits, the wife can make a shift and receive spousal benefits based on the husband's earnings record. If the wife began receiving benefits before her FRA, the benefits received both times will be reduced by the formula that's used to reduce all benefits received before FRA. Let's look at some examples.

Rosie Profits has reached her FRA and wants to begin receiving benefits. Her husband, Max, hasn't reached his FRA and wants to delay benefits at least until his FRA. Rosie is entitled to $500 monthly at FRA based on her own earnings. When Max reaches FRA, he will be entitled to $1,800 monthly. Rosie can begin receiving $500 now. When Max begins benefits at his FRA, Rosie will receive an additional $400 to bring her total to $900 monthly—half of Max's benefits. (The example also doesn't consider inflation adjustments.)

Suppose Rosie begins receiving her benefits before her FRA. She will receive a reduced benefit based on her earnings history. Let's say her reduced benefit is $400 monthly. When Max retires at FRA, Rosie still will be able to switch to a spousal benefit and receive the additional $400. That will bring her monthly benefit to only $800. By beginning benefits before FRA, she permanently reduced her monthly benefit, even after Max retires at FRA and she begins the spousal benefit.

Now suppose Max begins benefits before reaching his FRA, and Rosie already began receiving $400 monthly before her FRA. Rosie can begin receiving the spousal benefit when Max begins receiving his benefits, but Rosie's benefit will be reduced again. It's reduced once because Rosie began receiving benefits before her FRA, and it's reduced again because Max is taking his benefits before his FRA and receiving less than his full benefit. She should receive less than the $800 monthly in the previous example. The exact reduction will depend on when each of them begins receiving benefits.

As you can see, the rules and scenarios can get complicated. Social Security's website calculators can help explore results under different scenarios. While the best option depends on the specific details, published studies indicate the strategies that are likely to be optimal for many couples. Under these studies, lifetime payouts are maximized when the lower-earning spouse begins taking his or her earned retirement benefits early, say when first eligible at age 62. The higher-earning spouse should wait to at least age 68 before taking benefits and preferably to age 70. Then, the lower-earning spouse can switch to receiving spousal benefits when they are higher than his or her own earned benefits.

Advanced Strategies for Spouses Curtailed by 2015 Law

Until the Bipartisan Budget Act of 2015, Social Security benefit rules allowed some interesting planning strategies for married couples beyond simply deciding when to begin benefits. Congress snuck a major change to Social Security benefits claiming strategies in the law. The change will cost retirees who would have planned carefully tens of thousands of dollars over their lifetimes. The loss is about $50,000 per couple, according to a Bloomberg.com estimate.

The law eliminated or curtailed two claiming strategies that were becoming popular. Apparently, some people in the administration and Congress had been opposed to these strategies and aimed to eliminate them. Instead of the usual process of proposing laws and having them discussed in committees, the provisions were inserted into the budget deal negotiated between the president and congressional leaders. Originally, the strategies were created in a 2000 law, and opponents of the strategies believe they were unintended loopholes or effects of the 2000 changes.

The two strategies are known generally as *restricted application,* or *claim now, claim more later,* and *file and suspend.* Here's a summary of them:

- *Restricted filing.* A married person generally receives retirement benefits of the higher of his or her own earned benefit and 50 percent of the amount his or her spouse would receive at FRA. But a special rule allowed anyone at normal retirement age (age 66 for those retiring in recent years) or older to file an initial claim for spousal benefits only. This allowed the person to receive some Social Security benefits while either continuing to work or simply allowing his or her own Social Security benefits to increase 8 percent annually through age 70. The person was allowed at any time to switch from spousal benefits to earned benefits. One spouse had to have already filed for retirement benefits in order for the other to file a restricted application for spousal benefits only.
- *File and suspend.* Spousal benefits can be received only if the other spouse has filed to claim retirement benefits. The file and suspend strategy allowed the lower-earning spouse to receive the spousal benefit while the higher-earning spouse continued to defer receiving benefits and accrued the 8 percent annual increase from delaying benefits. The higher-earning spouse would file for retirement benefits at FRA or later and then immediately suspend the benefits. Filing for benefits allowed the other spouse to file for the higher of his or her earned benefits and the 50 percent spousal benefit. Suspending the filing didn't affect that. But the suspension reinstated the monthly increase from deferring benefits until the higher-income spouse decided to begin benefit payments.

The strategies are largely eliminated in the 2015 law, but it phased in the changes, so some people still had the opportunity to take advantage. Here are the changes:

- *Restricted filing.* The ability to file a restricted application for spousal benefits at FRA or later is eliminated. The elimination applies to those who turn 62 after 2015 (those born in 1954 or later). Everyone in that age group will be treated as applying for the higher of his or her earned benefits and the spousal benefit whenever applying for benefits.

■ *File and suspend*. This strategy is allowed for six months following enactment of the law, which is April 30, 2016. So, if the higher earning spouse was age 66 or older within the six-month period, the strategy still is available to the couple.

After the six-month grace period, someone who has filed for retirement benefits still can suspend them anytime after reaching FRA. The catch is that benefits also stop to almost anyone else who is receiving benefits based on that person's earnings. That includes spouses and minors and disabled children receiving benefits based on the person's earning history.

So, a higher-earning spouse isn't able to file and suspend in order to allow the lower-earning spouse to receive the higher spousal benefit. Keep in mind that while a spouse is entitled to the higher of his or her earned benefits and 50 percent of the other spouse's FRA benefit, the spousal benefit is payable only after the higher-earning spouse has filed to receive benefits. Now, the higher-earning spouse has to make a choice: file to receive benefits earlier than planned in order for the other spouse to receive the higher spousal benefit, or wait to begin benefits so that the benefit payment will be higher.

A reason the file and suspend strategy made sense was the survivor's benefit. When one spouse dies, the surviving spouse receives the higher of his or her earned benefit and what the other spouse was receiving at the time of death (or was entitled to at FRA if benefits hadn't begun). It made sense for the higher-earning spouse to wait until age 70 to receive benefits if possible, because it ensured that the surviving spouse of the two would receive the highest possible benefit for life. In effect, having the higher-earning spouse delay benefits is a cheap form of life insurance.

The survivor's benefit rule still is in place, and it still makes sense in most cases for the higher-earning spouse to delay benefits until age 70 to ensure the maximum lifetime benefit for each spouse. The lower-earning spouse will have to be content with his or her earned benefits during that time instead of a higher spousal benefit.

Another strategy that isn't affected is for those who have other reasons to suspend benefits after FRA. Suppose Max Profits is younger than 70 and files to begin receiving retirement benefits. Perhaps he was laid off or intended to retire. After some time, Max is back in the workplace and earning enough that he doesn't need the Social Security benefits. He decides it makes more sense to suspend the benefits so that they can earn some delayed retirement credits. When Max eventually resumes the benefits, they will be higher than when they were suspended because of the delayed retirement credits. In that case, he can suspend benefits any time after reaching FRA. But he can't suspend benefits until FRA. So, if he begins benefits as soon as possible at age 62, they can't be suspended until FRA.

The law didn't affect the benefits of divorced spouses. They still can qualify to claim benefits on an ex-spouse's earnings record without regard to whether the other spouse has filed to receive benefits or suspended benefits.

Here's another strategy that's affected. Suppose after filing and suspending benefits, Max decides he not only needs to resume the benefits but he also needs additional cash. Previously, he could have benefits resumed retroactively, receiving a lump sum for up to six months of past benefits plus have his benefit checks resume. Under the new law, the lump sum is no longer available.

Final Words on Spousal Strategies

Though married couples don't have as many options as they did before the 2015 law, there still are options and decisions to be made about when to receive benefits and coordinating them between spouses. Married couples need to take the time to analyze their Social Security strategies.

For example, consider the case of a married couple in which each spouse has a work history that qualifies for Social Security benefits. Let's say the lower earning spouse's benefits will be at least half of those of the higher earner. That means each spouse is likely to receive benefits based on his or her work history.

In this case, it likely is going to make sense for the higher earning spouse to delay receiving benefits until age 70. That ensures he or she receives the maximum possible benefit, and that whichever is the surviving spouse will continue to receive the highest possible benefit of the two. The probability is pretty high, around 60 percent, that at least one of the spouses will live long enough to justify delaying the higher earning spouse's benefits to age 70.

What about the lower-earning spouse? It makes a lot of sense for that spouse to begin receiving benefits early, perhaps as early as when first eligible at age 62. That's because after one spouse dies, the lower-earning spouse's benefit will stop, regardless of which spouse passes first. Also, there's a less than 50 percent probability that both spouses will live past the break-even point when it makes sense for the lower-earning spouse to delay benefits to at least normal retirement age. So, unless there is a family or personal history that raises expectations of both spouses living past their early 80s, it should make sense for the lower-earning spouse to claim early.

The last point is an important one. Family history and expectations of longevity are an important factor. You can't be sure of life expectancy, so you have to develop probabilities. If both spouses have a less than average life expectancy, then claiming early makes sense. If both spouses have longer than average expectancy, then it makes sense for both to delay claiming benefits.

The decision is more difficult when the lower-earning spouse's benefit is much less than half of the higher-earning spouse's benefit. In this case it probably makes the most sense for both spouses to claim benefits when the younger spouse reaches FRA, or when the higher-earning spouse reaches FRA if that occurs second.

The rationale is that the lower-earning spouse's earned benefit is going to be much lower than the spousal benefit of half the higher-earning spouse's benefit. The lower-earning spouse will want to receive the spousal benefit. Claiming any benefit before FRA wouldn't be beneficial, because in addition to being eligible for only a low benefit, the lower-earning spouse's benefit will be reduced further by claiming it early. The lower-earning spouse should wait to FRA so that the benefit won't be reduced.

Also, spousal benefits don't increase after FRA. There is no benefit to waiting any longer to receive a spousal benefit.

A spousal benefit can be received only when the other spouse already is receiving benefits. That means the lower-earning spouse can't receive the spousal benefit until the higher-earning spouse is receiving benefits. The couple has a choice of receiving no benefits at all until the higher-earning spouse is age 70 and has maximized benefits or beginning both benefits at FRA. That's why it probably makes sense for both to begin benefits as soon as the second spouse reaches FRA. It's unlikely that the higher benefits from waiting for the higher-earning spouse to maximize benefits at age 70 will be great enough to justify delaying receiving both the higher-earning spouse's regular benefit and the lower-earning spouse's spousal benefit after FRA.

Various calculators available on the Internet can help make these decisions. Be sure a calculator says it was updated for the 2015 law before using it. Good calculators that charge fees are at www .MaximizeMySocialSecurity.com and www.SocialSecuritySolutions.com. There also are good free calculators at the websites for T. Rowe Price and AARP.

Maximizing Benefits for the Divorced and Widowed

Divorced and widowed taxpayers have other options and rules to consider. We'll first discuss the rules for divorced spouses.

A divorced person can collect retirement benefits based on an ex-spouse's earned benefits when they were married for at least 10 years, have been divorced at least two years, and the ex-spouse seeking to claim on the other ex-spouse's benefits has not remarried. A benefit of the rules for divorced people is that you don't have to coordinate with the ex-spouse. You can make choices without regard to whether the ex-spouse has applied for benefits or is remarried. You don't even have to inform the former spouse.

When the qualifications are met, you are entitled to the higher of your own benefit and one half of your ex-spouse's full retirement benefit if your ex-spouse is qualified for benefits, regardless of whether he or she has applied. Your benefit is reduced if you begin it before you are FRA.

Divorced spouse benefits can be helpful even when you were the higher-earning spouse. One strategy under this rule is for the divorced person to wait until at least age 66. At 66, you can file a claim that is restricted to spousal benefits, meaning collecting 50 percent of the other ex-spouse's earned benefits. Then, at age 70 you can file to claim based on your own earnings record and receive the maximum amount.

Divorced spouses also can receive survivor's benefits. When the other ex-spouse dies, the surviving ex-spouse, if not remarried and at FRA, can collect the higher of his or her own earned benefit and 100 percent of what the other ex-spouse was receiving at the time of passing.

Now, let's look at benefits for widows and widowers, also known as survivor's benefits.

When you are widowed, even if you remarried, take a look at the rules. You might be able to claim higher benefits under a deceased spouse's record even if you remarried.

When the surviving spouse was married to the deceased spouse at the time of death, the surviving spouse receives the higher of his or her earned benefit and 100 percent of the deceased spouse's earned benefit (or what the deceased spouse was receiving at the time of his or her passing). We already discussed that rule.

Survivor's benefits can begin as early as age 60 (age 50 if the survivor is disabled), but benefits will be reduced for taking them before FRA and will be about 71 percent of full benefits by taking them at 60. Full benefits can be received if the survivor waits until his or her FRA to begin the benefits.

Eligibility for survivor's benefits isn't affected when the survivor remarries after age 60, but there are no survivor's benefits when the survivor remarries before age 60. So, if you are widowed and considering remarrying in your late 50s, it might pay to delay the nuptials if your deceased spouse had a higher level of earned Social Security benefits than you or your next spouse.

You can see that the Social Security rules provide a lot of flexibility and choices, especially for married couples. By paying attention to the rules and investigating your benefits under different scenarios, you can maximize this lifetime stream of guaranteed, inflation-indexed income.

Fixing Social Security Claiming Mistakes

Fortunately, the timing of Social Security retirement benefits is not always the one-time decision many believe it is. There might be options for changing your benefits when your circumstances change or you believe you made a mistake the first time.

One strategy for changing your benefits isn't as flexible as it used to be. A complete do-over is possible if you make the decision within the first 12 months of beginning benefits. You file Form 521 with Social Security and repay all benefits received to date. (Interest is not charged on the repayment.) Social Security calls this *withdrawal of benefits*.

Withdrawal gives you a fresh start, as though you never filed a claim to begin benefits. Then, you can wait until FRA, age 70, or whatever starting point you want. You'll receive the higher benefit as though it were your first claim.

Before making a decision, know that the decision to withdraw benefits could affect others who were drawing benefits on your earnings record, such as a spouse or dependent. They might be required to repay benefits or will stop receiving benefits when yours cease.

The second strategy for changing a claiming decision is not as generous but is available to more people. You simply notify Social Security that you want your benefits suspended. The benefits will stop after about a one-month lag.

Two things happen when you suspend benefits. One event is that you stop receiving monthly benefit checks while the suspension is in effect. The other action is that you begin earning delayed retirement credits, increasing your future benefits by about 8 percent annually.

Retirement benefits can be suspended only at FRA or later. If you began receiving benefits before FRA, you can't suspend them until age 66 or whatever your FRA is. After reaching FRA, you can suspend benefits at any time.

Suppose you began receiving retirement benefits at age 62, and then at FRA (66) suspend them until age 70. Your benefits will increase about 32 percent during the delay. You'll never reach the benefit you would have received had you initially waited to age 70 to receive benefits, but the benefits might increase to the level of your initial FRA benefit.

There are a couple of additional points. You can suspend only your own earned retirement benefits, not spousal benefits. So, if you are receiving spousal benefits early, suspending them isn't an option. (You still can switch from a spousal benefit to your own earned benefit.)

Also, Medicare premiums generally are deducted from Social Security benefits. If you're enrolled in Medicare and suspend Social Security benefits, you'll have to begin making separate payments of the monthly Medicare premiums. (This is discussed in Chapter 6.)

Now, let's look at the opposite mistake: Someone who either delayed or suspended retirement benefits and then decided that was a mistake. You can end the suspension of benefits or apply for benefits. Before the Bipartisan Budget Act of 2015, you also could apply for a retroactive lump sum payment of up to six months of benefits. The lump-sum benefit payments no longer are allowed.

In some cases, claiming Social Security benefits is not a one-time decision. There is some flexibility. You can't completely return to your original position in all cases. But if your circumstances changed or you realized you didn't make the optimum decision the first time, there are ways you can improve the situation.

A Caution about Delaying Benefits

There's a tie-in between Social Security and Medicare that you should know before deciding to delay Social Security benefits.

You need to sign up for Medicare Parts B and D at age 65 in most cases. If you don't, you'll pay a penalty of higher premiums for life. See Chapter 6 for details.

When someone is enrolled in Medicare Part B and also receiving Social Security retirement benefits, the Medicare premiums automatically are deducted from the Social Security benefits unless you specifically elect to pay separately the Medicare premiums. Remember also that Social Security benefits receive a cost-of-living adjustment. The COLA is based on the Consumer Price Index for urban wage earners for 12 months ending the third quarter of each year.

There's a "stop-loss" provision in the law. The law says that for people who have Part B premiums deducted from Social Security benefits, higher Medicare premiums can't cause a decrease in the net Social Security benefit. That means if the premiums rise more in dollar terms than the COLA boosts your benefits, you won't be charged the full premium increase.

Usually, this doesn't matter, but there have been three times when Part B premiums increased more than the Social Security COLA, preventing the full Part B premiums from being charged to many Social Security recipients: 2010, 2011, and 2016. In these cases, other Medicare beneficiaries pay the increase in premiums and actually pay more.

The law requires that Medicare premiums cover 25 percent of the estimated cost of the program for the year. When the bulk of Medicare beneficiaries have their premiums paid through Social Security and don't pay their full share of the premium increase, the other beneficiaries make up the difference. Estimates are that about 30 percent of Medicare beneficiaries don't have their premiums paid through Social Security. When the other 70 percent of Medicare beneficiaries don't pay higher premiums, the entire cost increase for the program that year falls on the 30 percent who don't have their premiums deducted from Social Security.

Three groups are likely to bear these higher costs. One group is those enrolling in Part B for the first time that year. They aren't protected by the stop-loss rule. Another group is higher income individuals who are subject to the Medicare premium surtax. The third group is those who are enrolled in Medicare Part B because they are 65 or older but who haven't yet begun Social Security benefits. There's a small fourth group who are enrolled in Part B and receiving Social Security benefits but chose to pay their premiums separately instead of having them deducted from Social Security benefits.

For 2016, the increase in Medicare Part B premiums was going to be substantial. Estimates were that premiums would increase by 50 percent for those without the Social Security stop-loss provision. In the Bipartisan Budget Act of 2015, Congress reduced the proposed increases and borrowed the rest of the money Medicare would need. The beneficiaries who would have owed the substantial premium increases would pay for the debt with $3 monthly premium increases until the debt is paid.

Working Can Reduce Benefits

Your monthly benefits might be reduced if you begin Social Security retirement benefits between ages 62 and your FRA. You aren't supposed to continue earning income from working or being self-employed while receiving benefits during that period. If you earn too much money, the benefits will be reduced. The limit on earned income depends on your age. The limits change each year based on inflation, and you can find the latest limits on the Social Security website.

From age 62 until the year you reach FRA, your benefits will be reduced $1 for every $2 earned over the limit. For 2015, the limit was $15,720.

Suppose Rosie Profits is 62 and commenced her Social Security retirement benefits. Based on her earnings record and the reduction for taking benefits early, she expected to receive $7,200 for the year. But Rosie continued working and expects to earn $35,000. Since she is well over the $15,720 earned income limit, she won't receive any benefits for the year. If she were to earn only $20,000, she would lose $2,140 of benefits. That is determined by subtracting the earned income limit from her earnings of $20,000. She earned $4,280 too much. She will lose $1 for every $2 of excess earnings, so divide $4,280 by two. That gives the lost benefits of $2,140.

The way the limit will be imposed is that Rosie won't receive any benefits from January through April. That would be withholding of $2,400, or $260 too much. She'll receive full benefits from May through December. Then in January the following year she'll be paid the excess that was withheld.

In the year FRA is reached, retirement benefits are reduced $1 for every $3 earned over the limit. The earned income limit for the year of FRA was $41,880 in 2015. This also is indexed for inflation, and the current number can be found on the Social Security website. The limit is applied for each month until you reach FRA. The month you reach FRA, full benefits are paid regardless of how much earned income you earn. The mechanics of computing and withholding the payments are the same as for the year before reaching FRA.

Earned income is any payments of money, property, or services from a job or self-employment. Most sources of income from providing service or selling goods or services count. Not included are sources of investment and passive income such as interest, dividends, capital gains, pensions, and IRA distributions. The Social Security website has details of the types of income that do and don't count toward the earnings limit. When income is from self-employment, only net self-employment income counts. That is gross income minus business-related expenses. For the self-employed, the SSA also looks at the amount of time devoted to self-employment. Someone who works fewer than 15 hours a month on self-employment is considered retired and faces no penalty for excess earnings. Someone who works between 15 and 45 hours a month isn't considered retired if the job requires a lot of skill or the person is managing a sizable business.

Only income earned after the date your benefits begin counts toward the earnings limit. When you begin Social Security retirement benefits during the year, all earned income before the benefits starting date is not counted toward the limit. In those years, the earnings limit is prorated and computed on a monthly basis.

You have to tell the SSA before the start of each year the amount of earned income you anticipate receiving in the following year. The SSA then will compute any penalty and withhold the appropriate amount from your benefits. You are required to tell the SSA if your earned income for the year changes in either direction during the year.

The penalty isn't a complete loss. Once you reach FRA, your benefits will be recomputed. You'll be given credit for both the lost benefits in months when the entire benefit was withheld and also for the earnings you were paid during that period. Continuing to work while receiving benefits might increase benefits over the long term. That's because only your highest 35 years of earnings are used to compute benefits. The years you earn income while receiving benefits could knock out some low-earning years and boost your overall benefit once you reach FRA. The SSA reviews your earnings history each year even after you begin receiving retirement benefits. An earnings year that exceeds one of the previous high 35 years should result in a higher benefit the following year and could result in a lump-sum retroactive benefit increase for the previous year.

A Note about Social Security Solvency

Social Security's long-term solvency has been in question for a long time. Each year the trustees of Social Security and Medicare issue their annual report, and that report updates the precarious financial condition of the programs.

Too many people use Social Security's precarious financial position as a reason to exclude Social Security from their planning. They assume they won't receive anything from the program or should plan as though they won't receive anything. That's a mistake. It can lead to saving too much during your working years and reducing your lifetime standard of living.

While Social Security's long-term financial health is in doubt, it isn't likely to stop paying benefits during your lifetime. The details of the annual trustees' report make clear that the tax revenue coming into the program is likely to be enough to pay 70 percent to 75 percent of all promised benefits for an indefinite period. Changes need to be made to make up the 25 percent to 30 percent of benefits the annual tax flow won't cover, but that is a far cry from saying Social Security will run out of money and fail to pay any benefits.

The gap is likely to be made up in several ways.

Means-testing of the program is likely to continue. Under means-testing, higher-income individuals will receive lower benefits or pay higher taxes or a combination of the two. This might be done directly with straightforward benefit reductions or payroll tax increases. Or Congress will continue its pattern of enacting stealth taxes in which it extracts money for the program indirectly.

Higher payroll taxes also are likely, but these won't affect people who already are retired. They are likely to be targeted at higher-income individuals, such as by raising or removing the ceiling on wages that are subject to payroll taxes. Congress also might do what it has done for Medicare several times and impose a payroll or income tax surtax on higher income individuals that is earmarked for Social Security.

Overall benefits could be cut. I think if that occurs it likely would affect only those under age 50 or 55. Older Americans would be protected because they would be too close to retirement to adjust to the changes. A means-testing approach that reduces the benefits of higher-income individuals is much more likely than an overall benefits reduction.

It's possible that general tax revenue will be used to shore up the program, but I think that's unlikely. It would be more of a last resort.

Higher-income individuals in particular should plan a cushion or flexibility in their retirement plans. They are more likely than others to face changes through benefit reductions and higher taxes.

Guaranteed Income from Annuities

Annuities are another source of guaranteed lifetime income available to almost every American. While Social Security has its share of controversies, annuities sometimes seem to be even more controversial. Only a small percentage of retirement-age Americans own annuities, and many financial advisors generally don't recommend them to clients. The financial media generally issue negative reports about annuities. In fact, I'm sure many people are thinking of skipping this section because they have heard so many negative things about annuities. That would be a mistake.

A properly selected insurance annuity can enhance the financial security of your post-career years. Independent studies show that an annuity can make your portfolio last longer and almost eliminate the risk of outliving your money.

Annuities are controversial for several reasons. There are many different types of annuities. Many different financial products are included under the "annuities" heading. Only a small number of these annuities provide the benefits just mentioned. Too many types of annuities have high fees, limited control, limited liquidity, risk, and terms that few annuity owners fully understand.

In this section we discuss in detail only two types of annuities: immediate annuities and longevity annuities. These are the two types that will generate guaranteed lifetime income at a reasonable cost. They also are easy to understand. We will discuss in less detail a few other types of annuities that often are considered as alternatives to those two types of annuities. Those annuities have their places in some portfolios, but for most people seeking guaranteed lifetime income, immediate annuities and longevity annuities are the best choices.

Most people buy annuities the wrong way. They have contact with a financial professional and are presented with a specific annuity. Then, they try to decide whether or not to put money into it. That's backward. The right approach is the one we've taken so far. Determine your cash flow needs and decide how much of that income you want covered by guaranteed lifetime income. Then, shop for the appropriate vehicle to generate that amount of income. This section is for investors who take the second approach.

Immediate Annuity Basics

An immediate annuity essentially is a private individual pension plan. You transfer a lump sum to an insurer. In return the insurer promises to pay a specific amount to you at regular intervals, and the payments begin within a year after your purchase. Usually the payments are monthly, but they can be quarterly, semiannually, or annually—whichever you select. The payment amounts don't change, except for two variations of the standard annuity, which we'll discuss later.

In the standard, plain vanilla immediate annuity, the payments continue for the rest of your life, no matter how long you live. When you're married, you can elect to have the payments continue for the joint life of you and your spouse, known as a joint life or joint and survivor annuity. The payments continue at the same amount until both of you have passed. There are other options. The payments that continue to your surviving spouse can be reduced from what they were when you both are living. The standard options are for the payments to the surviving spouse to be either 75 percent or 50 percent of the amount paid when both spouses were living.

Another option is for payments to be guaranteed for a minimum period of years, so if you pass away before that period ends the payments will be made to a beneficiary until the minimum payment period ends. Some people select a payment for life with a guaranteed term of years. For example, when you select an annuity for life with 10 years guaranteed that means you'll receive payments for as long as you live. If you pass away before 10 years, your beneficiary will receive payments for the remainder of the 10 years.

The key to remember about all the options is that each option reduces the amount of the payments. An annuity that lasts for your life (a single life annuity) has the highest payout (other than annuity for a fixed period of years that is less than your life expectancy). A joint life annuity generates a lower income payment, because it lasts for two lives. The amount of the reduction will depend on the age of each spouse. An annuity for life with a term certain also will pay less than a single life annuity and probably less than a joint life annuity.

Those are the basics of immediate annuities. They are clean and simple. You deposit money with an insurance company, and it promises to pay you a fixed income for the period of time you select. You are told in advance the amount of the income payments. There are no extra costs or fees. All costs and fees are used to determine the amount of the lifetime payments, so they are embedded in the annuity.

Now, let's look at some details and variations.

Why People Don't Buy Annuities

Economists generally agree that almost everyone should use immediate annuities to secure at least part of their retirement paychecks. More and more financial planners are reaching that same conclusion. Yet, very few people purchase annuities to generate guaranteed income for life. Some economists refer to this as *The Annuity Puzzle*, and there is a growing body of research into the question of why more people don't buy annuities.

People give a lot of reasons for not adding annuities to their financial assets. The most commonly cited reasons for not buying immediate annuities are:

- At the end of the annuity owner's life, there won't be any money available to leave for loved ones or charity.
- When the annuity owner passes away before life expectancy, the annuity owner loses. He or she will have received less in lifetime payouts than the annuity cost. The insurer and its other annuity owners benefit from the unused portion of the nest egg.
- Some people don't want to give up control of their hard-earned nest eggs to an insurer or anyone else.
- Similarly, some people don't like the inflexibility of immediate annuities. Once you make the purchase, the payments are fixed. You can't change the amount of the payment. You also can't take an extra amount when you have unexpected expenses or want to make a major purchase. There are exceptions to this last point; many immediate annuities now will let you take up to 10 percent of the annuity's value in a year.
- Some people think they can earn a higher return with their money, though more people believed that before 2000 than do now.
- Many people find the buying process to be difficult or unpleasant. You have to find and meet with insurance agents or brokers. The prices might not be transparent or easy to compare, and you need to talk to several agents to learn what's available in the market. Once an annuity is selected, it's not as easy to complete the transaction as buying a mutual fund or stock.
- The insurer could become insolvent and stop making payments.
- The fixed amount of the payments will have its purchasing power reduced over time by inflation.

Let's consider these objections and suggest how to view immediate annuities as part of your retirement paycheck solution.

Annuities are a risk management and risk transfer tool. When you are concerned about the potential of outliving your assets and income, you transfer that risk to an insurer by purchasing an annuity. In return, the insurer provides you with income security.

The insurer takes the risks that you'll live a long time or that investment returns will be lower than anticipated. It is cheaper for the insurer to take those risks, because it sells a lot of annuities. Some buyers will live beyond life expectancy, and others won't. For the insurer, those will balance, unless the insurer makes serious errors in its estimates of life expectancies. The insurer also has more tools for dealing with low investment returns and is likely to have estimated lower investment returns than most individuals do. The insurer also essentially plans for an infinite life. It can withstand extended periods of low returns better than you can. It also keeps earning income by selling new policies, and it is likely to be around to reap the benefits when market returns are higher. The insurer also might have a diversified business and profit from selling other types of insurance. Profits in one of the businesses can make up for short-term problems in its annuity business.

Transferring these risks to an insurer isn't free. You have to give up control of the money so the insurer can pool it with the rest of its portfolio and invest for the long term. You might be able to earn a higher return and make the money last longer. But you'll be taking the risk that you won't earn that higher return or that you'll live a long time and deplete the portfolio despite higher returns. Another price you pay for transferring risk to the insurer is that the payments last only for your lifetime. When you live longer than life expectancy, the insurer loses. When you live less than life expectancy, the insurer has a gain. In an annuity transaction, the insurer is taking the risk you'll live a long time, and you're taking the risk you won't.

Insurers are trying to overcome many of the objections people have to immediate annuities by changing contract features. You can buy annuities that guarantee to return some or all of the premiums if you don't live a minimum period, that let you withdraw some of your initial premium even after payments have begun, or that have other features meeting the objections people have to annuities. Keep in mind that each of these features costs money. Each reduces the regular payments you receive from the insurer. My belief is that the annuity features designed to overcome the objections aren't worth their cost. I recommend focusing on standard, plain-vanilla immediate annuities and maximizing your guaranteed lifetime income.

The question you need to ask when considering an annuity is: Which risks are you willing to take, and which do you want to transfer to someone else? When your primary concern is that you might outlive your assets and income, consider purchasing an immediate annuity with part of your nest egg. It doesn't matter if you fear running out of money because of poor investment returns, unexpected spending, or a long life. The immediate annuity covers you in all these cases. Purchasing an immediate annuity transfers a large part of the risk to the insurer. An immediate annuity generates guaranteed lifetime income. When you want guaranteed income for at least part of your retirement cash flow, buy an annuity with part of your assets. When you're comfortable taking all the risks yourself, there's no need to buy immediate annuities.

I think most of the objections to annuities are overcome when you decide to put only a portion of your nest egg into an immediate annuity. Too many people consider annuities as part of an all-or-nothing decision. They consider either putting all their money in annuities or none of it. Very few people should put all or most of their assets into annuities.

People who should consider putting most of their nest eggs in annuities are those with few assets, who aren't comfortable with investing, or have a strong potential for long life expectancy. Most people should consider putting 10 percent to 50 percent of their nest eggs into immediate annuities. That provides them with significant guaranteed income and financial security. It also leaves enough other assets outside the annuity to pay for their spending above the basics, to invest for growth and purchasing power protection, be available for unexpected spending, and to leave to loved ones or charity.

That's why most people should try to have enough guaranteed income to cover essential, fixed, living expenses. Use Social Security, any employer pension, and annuities to generate enough income to cover those expenses. That gives you the income security for your post-career period. The rest of your portfolio can be used to generate additional returns and income to fund nonessential expenses, make up for purchasing power lost to inflation, and establish a legacy fund.

You also don't need to fully fund your annuity allocation at the start of retirement or even all at once. The longer you wait to buy, the higher the income payments will be. The amount of the payments are determined partly by your life expectancy, so the older you are at the purchase date, the higher will be the income you'll receive each month. This is an individual decision, but I suspect most people would do well to purchase immediate annuities around age 70.

Another strategy is not to purchase your annuity allocation at one time. When you purchase an immediate annuity, you lock in current interest rates for the rest of your life. In the post-financial crisis period, you're locking in very low rates. A good strategy is to purchase immediate annuities in annual installments over five years or so, sometimes called an annuity ladder. You can't time interest rate changes to maximize annuity income, but you can avoid locking in all your non–Social Security guaranteed income at one rate by purchasing annuities on a schedule over a period of years. That also gives you some experience with annuities without putting all your planned allocation in them at once. Then, you can suspend or change your purchasing schedule if your experience indicates that's a good idea.

There's one more problem people have with annuities: It's not easy to buy them or to know you're getting a good deal. It's much easier to buy a mutual fund than an annuity. With an annuity, you have to go through a licensed broker or agent. Each broker normally represents only a few insurers; some represent only one insurer. So, to survey the market you need to contact at least several brokers.

Later in this chapter I give steps you can take to reduce these obstacles and inconveniences. I'll show you how to get a good overview of what's available in the market and how to find the best deal for you. You'll also learn how to increase your monthly income for life by as much as 20 percent.

Finding Inflation Protection

Another knock on immediate annuities is that you have no purchasing power protection. Social Security is indexed for inflation, but standard immediate annuities are not. The income payments are fixed. As inflation compounds over time, the purchasing power of your income is reduced.

You might be able to deal with this problem with the rest of your nest egg that is not deposited in the immediate annuities. This portfolio can generate income and returns that will supplement your guaranteed income over time and maintain your purchasing power. Yet, there are no guarantees that the portfolio will generate sufficient returns to maintain your purchasing power and also generate cash to pay for those expenses exceeding the basic living expenses.

Another strategy is an inflation-indexed annuity. This is an immediate annuity that has a cost of living adjustment similar to Social Security's. The income payments are adjusted upward for inflation but not downward for deflation.

When you buy an inflation-adjusted immediate annuity, the payments are increased automatically each year to match increases in the Consumer Price Index or some other selected benchmark. There usually are limits, such as a maximum one-year increase of 10 percent. There's a variation, generically referred to as a growing annuity or growth annuity, that allows you to select a fixed percentage amount the payments increase each year instead of having the payments tied to the CPI. The payments increase by the same amount each year, regardless of what the CPI does. Generally, you can select annual increases of from 2 percent to 5 percent.

The downside to inflation protection through annuities is that there's a cost. With an inflation-indexed annuity, your first-year payment is going to be 20 percent to 30 percent less than that of a fixed immediate annuity. The exact amount will depend on your age, life expectancy estimates of the insurer, and the inflation rates the insurer forecasts. This emphasizes the key point with all annuities and insurance products: You can transfer almost any risk you want to the insurer, but you'll pay something for transferring the risk.

Hint: You don't necessarily want to buy the inflation-indexed annuity that offers the highest first-year payout. The insurer could be assuming future inflation will be very low or that it will earn very high investment returns. You could be hurt down the road if the insurer runs into financial trouble because its assumptions were too optimistic.

A growing annuity should give you a higher first-year payment than a CPI indexed annuity, though that depends on the insurer's inflation estimates and the growth rate you select. Also, you'd know what the income increase would be each year and could factor that into your budgeting and spending, rather than having to wait to see what the year's CPI increase is. Of course, if inflation is higher than the automatic increase rate you selected, at some point you'll need to reduce expenses or supplement the income from another source to maintain your standard of living.

Here's how to compare a fixed annuity to an inflation-adjusted annuity and also compare different inflation-adjusted annuities.

Start with the estimated first-year monthly payment amount of each annuity. Then compare what the payments would be after 10, 15, and 20 years under different inflation scenarios.

For example, assume a 70-year-old could purchase a nonindexed immediate annuity with $500,000 and receive an initial $3,962.93 monthly payment. Assume also that if he selected a 2 percent annual increase, the initial payment would be $3,375.54. If he selected full CPI indexing, the initial payment would be $3,039.18.

Compare how the payments will change over time. After 10 years under the 2 percent option, the payment would be $4,736.07. The payment of the CPI-indexed annuity after 10 years would depend on the inflation rate, and you should assume different inflation scenarios to estimate future payments. It's best to use a computer spreadsheet program to make these calculations.

You need to look at how long it would take for the annual payments of the indexed and growth annuities to catch up with the fixed annuity income. You know that after that period you come out ahead by purchasing the indexed or growth annuity. You want to estimate how long it would take to reach the break-even point under different assumptions.

You also need to consider which risks you want to take. You could accept a lower initial payment and avoid the risk of having high inflation eat away at the purchasing power. But you'll take the risk that inflation will be lower than the insurer is assuming, and you'll end up with lower payments than you would otherwise have received. Or you can select your own annual increase and take the risk inflation will be higher.

Inflation-indexed and growth annuities usually are not sold as separate products. Instead, you shop for an immediate annuity and select an option or rider to have the payments adjusted for inflation or increase automatically at your selected rate.

You also might try to obtain inflation protection with a variable immediate annuity. This is an annuity that begins payments within a year after you purchase it. Your annuity account is invested in investments you select from among those offered by the insurer. After the first year, your payments rise or fall according to how your investment selections perform compared to a return benchmark selected when the annuity was purchased.

I don't recommend this type of annuity for most people. The payments are not fixed, so they don't meet the goal of establishing lifetime guaranteed income. Also, this type of annuity is complicated and has higher expenses. It is better to take your investment risk outside of the annuity where fees are lower and taxes can be managed.

Increasing Annuity Income for Life

After deciding you want a portion of your portfolio in immediate annuities and whether they should be inflation-indexed, it's time to search for the best annuity deal for you. The easiest, surest way to increase your retirement income is to shop for annuities just as you would for anything else. Few retirees or prospective retirees do this, but I've shown over the years that shopping will increase income. Even as the Internet supposedly makes markets more competitive and drives prices down, prices for annuities vary considerably.

Earlier we discussed what's sometimes called *The Annuity Puzzle*. Economists and many financial planners believe most people in retirement should purchase immediate annuities for guaranteed lifetime income. But only a small percentage of retirees do that. I suspect a major reason people don't buy annuities is that the shopping and buying process is less efficient and more unpleasant than the way we buy most other things. Shopping for an annuity still has roadblocks that make it less convenient for consumers than shopping for televisions, books, and even cars. It's more like buying a house. Nevertheless, to obtain retirement security you need to overcome the obstacles and shop for annuities.

Insurers use different assumptions to determine their annuity payouts. They consider estimated investment returns (and recent investment losses), their life expectancy estimates, and their annual expenses and desired profit margin. Each of these assumptions varies between insurers. I suspect some insurers also count on consumers not to shop around.

The financial stability of the insurers also varies and makes a difference in the payouts from annuities. Insurers with better financial positions can pay less because of the increased security they offer. The highest annuity payouts often are offered by insurers with lower financial ratings because they present more risk.

Each insurance broker or agent usually offers products from a small number of insurers. Some deal exclusively with one insurer. To get a good view of what's available in the market through brokers and agents you often have to meet with several brokers and agents.

An easy way to shop is to visit websites, such as www.immediate annuities.com. These essentially are online insurance brokers that deal with a larger number of insurers than the typical agent or broker. You visit the website and type in your age, state of residence, and the amount you want to invest in an annuity. After providing some other personal information, you'll receive a report showing the payouts you'd receive from different insurers. Some websites show the results on the screen. Others mail a package of the proposals to you.

Over the last 20 years or so, every few years I've surveyed the immediate annuity market through websites and brokers. Each time, the survey had the same results. When the survey is limited to insurers that have the top financial safety ratings, there is about a 20 percent difference in the payouts between the highest- and lowest-paying insurers. That's a 20 percent difference in your income every month for the rest of your life. This survey shows that it pays to shop around, despite the inconvenience.

The income can be increased even higher if you want to deal with an insurer that has less than the top safety ratings. Insurers with the lower safety ratings generally pay more on their annuity contracts than the more conservative, higher-rated insurers. You don't have to lower your standards to the lowest-rated insurers to receive higher payouts. Your income can be increased substantially if you're willing to take the risk of using a middle-rated insurer. You don't want to gravitate automatically to the highest-payout annuity. You want to consider the financial stability of the insurer. Be sure you are comfortable over the long term with an insurer's financial stability before buying. An insurer can have a less-than-top financial safety rating and still be a good risk.

One way to increase financial security is to split your annuity purchases among several insurers. The odds of all the insurers you select defaulting should be very low. You balance the payouts of the different insurers with their financial stability and by having diversification of income sources.

Another annuity source to consider if you're still working is your employer-sponsored retirement plan. The 401(k) plans sponsored by many large employers offer an option that lets you purchase the annuity with your 401(k) balance. Compare the payout of this annuity with the private options.

The Advantages of Longevity Annuities

The longevity annuity is a relatively new option, available in the United States only since about 1984. It is a close sibling, however, of the immediate annuity and also is easy to understand.

In a longevity annuity, also known as a deferred income annuity (DIA), you deposit a lump sum with an insurer. Unlike the immediate annuity, you don't receive income payments within a year. Instead, the income payments are delayed anywhere from 2 years to 45 years. You decide on the income starting date when you purchase the annuity. Once income payments begin, they last for life no matter how long you live.

As with the immediate annuity, you can adjust the terms of the longevity annuity and change the risk sharing.

Under the original longevity annuity, the annuity owner took the risk of living a short life. If the owner died before the annuity payments began or before receiving enough income to recover the initial deposit, the insurer benefited. That doesn't have to be the case now. You can have a longevity annuity that ensures at least the initial premium is returned to you as income or paid to a beneficiary.

The standard longevity annuity also doesn't have inflation protection. You know what the annual income will be in the future when you purchase the annuity, but you don't know what its purchasing power will be because of inflation. Now, you can opt for some inflation or purchasing power protection in your annuity.

You also can purchase a longevity annuity that pays income for the joint life of you and a beneficiary, whether a spouse or someone else. That is less expensive than purchasing two separate single life annuities.

As with the immediate annuity, opting for any of these protections or features will reduce the initial income payment. Compare the income you'll receive from a standard longevity annuity to the income from one with inflation protection to decide if the inflation protection is worth the cost.

There are several ways longevity annuities can be used in your retirement plan.

The initial selling point of longevity annuities was as a late-in-life income kicker. The longevity annuity payments would begin at a late age such as 75 or 80. That's when a retiree's financial security is most at risk. At that point, assets and cash flow might be dwindling because of high inflation, low investment returns, or higher-than-expected spending. The longevity annuity income would kick in to restore purchasing power or replace lost income and assets. The initial arguments for using longevity annuities stressed that the annuity could be purchased when the owner was in his 50s or 60s, and the income would begin at a later age.

More recently, longevity annuities have been used differently. Most purchasers buy the annuities when they are in their 50s and 60s and schedule the income payments to begin between ages 65 and 70, when they expect to retire. This can be a good strategy because a longevity annuity usually is cheaper per dollar of income than an immediate annuity. That's because you give the money to the insurance company earlier, and it invests the money for a few years before beginning payments. The additional investment returns are factored into the income you'll receive.

Essentially, you have two strategies to consider for using an annuity to established guaranteed income.

The first strategy is to buy a longevity annuity with part of your nest egg sometime before retirement. The second strategy is to retain the money and invest it until you are ready for the income to begin. Then, you deposit the money with an insurer in an immediate annuity.

Determining which is the better strategy depends on the investment returns you can generate. If you generate higher after-tax, after-expense returns than the insurer company assumes it can, then you probably would buy more lifetime income by retaining and investing the money as long as you can and eventually buying an immediate annuity. Otherwise, a longevity annuity that begins payments in the future would be better. Remember, of course, that the income from the longevity annuity is guaranteed. The investment returns you might earn from investing the money for a few more years aren't guaranteed. They could be either higher or lower than you anticipate. If the returns are lower, then your retirement income will be permanently lower.

Another way longevity annuities are used is to reduce required minimum distributions (RMDs) from IRAs. As we discuss in Chapter 9, the RMDs that must begin after age 70 1/2 can be a problem for IRA owners as they age. The IRS issued regulations in 2014 that allow IRA owners to use a type of longevity annuity, known as a qualified longevity annuity contract (QLAC), to delay some of the RMDs.

Under the 2014 regulations, the amount invested in QLACs isn't used to calculate RMDs, up to a total of $125,000 invested or 25 percent of your IRA balance, whichever is less. The limit is calculated by aggregating all your IRAs. In other words, it is a per taxpayer limit, not a per IRA limit. The limit is determined by comparing the amount invested in QLACs to the IRA balance as of the end of the previous calendar year. Married couples apply the limits per person. Each spouse can invest up to $125,000, or 25 percent of his or her IRA in QLACs. When you own a QLAC in your IRA, the balance in the QLAC isn't used to calculate your RMDs until income begins or age 85, whichever occurs first.

QLACs also can be purchased through participating 401(k) and similar plans and limit RMDs from them. The 25 percent limit applies to each plan, and the $125,000 limit is per person. In 2015, it was difficult to find a 401(k) plan that offered a QLAC as an investment option, but that should change over time.

The $125,000 limit is indexed for inflation, but it will rise only in $10,000 increments. At recent inflation rates, it will take it a while to increase.

Once a QLAC is purchased, limited changes are allowed. Most insurers allow one change to the payout date. You also might be able to add money to the annuity, but a new income payout amount will be calculated for that contribution. That could be a better deal than buying a new, separate annuity with the additional money.

You should know that not all longevity annuities are QLACs. Any annuity issued before the July 2, 2014, date of the IRS regulations doesn't become a QLAC. Your IRA can own a longevity annuity that isn't a QLAC, but it won't help reduce the RMDs. Instead, you have to buy an annuity issued after the regulations. The insurer has to identify it as a QLAC meeting the IRS regulations and not as a standard longevity annuity. Variable annuities, indexed annuities, and other types of annuities also aren't going to meet the QLAC requirements.

You can't own a QLAC in a Roth IRA. You might want to own a regular longevity annuity in a Roth IRA to provide guaranteed income later in life. Only a few insurers issued longevity annuities for years. But the IRS regulations quickly brought change. Major insurers began introducing their versions. In mid-2015, about 10 insurers issued QLACs and 15 offered DIAs.

Another strategy is to use the longevity annuity to protect the purchasing power of your guaranteed lifetime income. You aren't restricted to choosing either an immediate annuity or a longevity annuity. You can purchase both. You can start with an immediate annuity early in retirement to cover your fixed living expenses. You know that inflation is likely to reduce the purchasing power of that income over time. You believe, however, that the income reduction from an inflation-indexing rider on the annuity is too high. Instead, you purchase a longevity annuity at the same time. You have the additional income begin sometime in the future to restore the lost purchasing power of your immediate annuity. You decide when purchasing the longevity annuity when you want the income payments to begin.

Other Annuities You Might Hear About

As mentioned earlier, there are many different types of annuities. They aren't all appropriate for the guaranteed income portion of your retirement plan. None compares to the simplicity, safety, and low cost of an immediate annuity or longevity annuity. Each of the other types of annuities has its own bells and whistles, each of which carries costs. We'll review a few of those in this section.

My bottom line is I think there are times when these types annuities can be useful in the growth stage of a portfolio's life. But insurers are selling them with income riders to make them more attractive to those seeking guaranteed income. I believe this is an expensive way to establish guaranteed lifetime income. Instead, consider these products for a growth portion of your portfolio without the expensive income riders. When you're ready for guaranteed lifetime income, consider immediate annuities or longevity annuities.

Variable annuities with lifetime income riders are available in many versions. They generically are called variable annuities with guaranteed minimum withdrawal benefits or with guaranteed lifetime income benefits.

A variable annuity essentially is a collection of mutual funds in a tax-deferred annuity. You invest with the insurer, and then you choose how your account is invested from among funds offered by the insurer. Your account balance can rise or fall with the performance of your investment selections. Variable annuities often come with a form of life insurance in a guarantee that a beneficiary always will be able to inherit at least your initial premiums, regardless of how the investment account performs.

The guaranteed income rider usually provides that after a period of time passes you can begin taking fixed annual withdrawals from the annuity. It is guaranteed that you can withdraw a certain percentage of the account (usually 3 percent to 6 percent) each year for the rest of your life. The income is guaranteed no matter how long you live and how the investments perform. Even after you've drawn down the account you continue to receive the income for as long as you live. If your investment account performs well, the income can increase over time.

These types of annuities often are very confusing to buyers. I believe most owners of these annuities don't fully understand what they have purchased. Often, for example, the guaranteed income is computed based on a value other than the actual account value on the day the income payments begin. A lesser value is used. The contract has to be read carefully to understand what the income is likely to be under different scenarios.

In addition, significant fees are attached to all these features, and other features are available. The owners who understand the annuities generally are overpaying for the guaranteed income with the hope that the income will increase because the investments will do well. There also are restrictions on the investments and on access to the account value.

If you consider this type of annuity, evaluate it by comparing its potential payoff with alternatives such as investing the money yourself in a portfolio of low-cost investments and to buying an immediate annuity or longevity annuity. To do this type of analysis properly you have to fully account for differences in taxes and fees. The variable annuity does have the advantages of offering benefits to heirs, the potential for the payout to increase, and often more liberal conditions for terminating the annuity or changing your distribution schedule.

Fixed indexed annuities are another option. With these annuities, you make a deposit with an insurer. Your account is credited with interest each year. The amount of the interest is determined by the performance of one or more market indexes or benchmarks. Usually you can select one or more of the indexes from among those offered by the insurer.

These annuities often are very complicated because of the way the interest credited to your account is determined. You don't receive simply the total return of the index for the year minus the insurer's fees. The formulas used to determine the interest are less straightforward. There also are limits on the amount of interest with which you can be credited each year. When the index returns 20 percent in a year, you might have only 5 to 10 percent credited to your account.

I won't go into all the details of these types of annuities, because the details aren't relevant to their potential role in generating lifetime guaranteed income. In recent years, most of the fixed indexed annuities issued were sold with some form of guaranteed income riders similar to those for the variable annuities.

As with the variable annuities, you'll be charged a fee for the income guarantee. The fee usually is charged by reducing the amount of interest credited to your account each year. There's the potential that when earnings for the account are low, the income might not be enough to pay the expenses. Then, the fees could be paid out of principal or previous years' earnings. This is an expensive and uncertain way to generate guaranteed lifetime income.

I believe that fixed indexed annuities and variable annuities can have roles in the accumulation phases of your life. But they are not the best ways to secure guaranteed lifetime income. You're better off focusing on immediate annuities and longevity annuities.

Annuity Safety

When you buy any type of annuity, bear in mind that though the income is guaranteed, it is guaranteed only by the insurance company. You are depending on the solvency of the insurance company to help fund your retirement. Most states have a guarantee fund that covers the annuity obligations of failed insurers, but the coverage varies from state to state. In most states, a maximum of $100,000 is guaranteed. In some cases only the original investment is guaranteed. Earnings aren't covered or are covered at the option of the guarantee agency. Of course, these guarantees are only as good as the solvency of the guarantee fund, and that also varies by state.

That's why you want to examine the financial solvency of the insurer whose annuity you're considering. Examine the ratings issued by the firms that evaluate insurers. These should be readily available from the insurer or broker you're dealing with. Don't be tempted by the highest payout or other attractive features. These terms usually are offered by insurers who are in trouble and need to bring in more money or those that operate with more risk than other insurers. To be especially safe, limit your exposure to any single insurer. Diversify your annuity purchases the same way an investment portfolio is diversified by spreading your annuity purchases among different insurers.

Tapping Your Nest Egg

The missing link in many retirement plans is the withdrawal, distribution, or spending strategy. For a retirement plan to be successful, you need a strategy for drawing down your nest egg. Saving and investing on the way to retirement are important steps. Once you're ready to spend for retirement, you should have a distribution strategy. Your plan must ensure that you spend the nest egg at a rate that is sustainable. You don't want to run out of money. The spending strategy we discuss in this chapter must be coordinated with your estimated spending discussed in Chapter 2. If there's a gap between your spending strategy and the estimated spending, then the estimated spending should be reduced.

Accumulating money for retirement isn't the hardest part, though it's far from easy. Developing a spending strategy is more difficult. Many people enter retirement with what seem to be adequate resources. Yet, recent studies concluded that a high percentage of Americans die owning their home equity and little more. Many retirees end up relying heavily on Social Security to fund their later years' spending.

Some of this shortfall is due to unexpected spending, especially medical and long-term care expenses, and not having insurance or a plan to help with those expenses. Most often, however, the shortfall is due to people entering retirement without a spending plan or with a poorly conceived plan. For example, as we discuss shortly, many financial planners believe that a retiree can safely spend only 4 percent or less of a nest egg per year.

Spend more and you risk running out of money after fewer than 30 years. Yet, surveys of Americans age 50 and over find that most believe they safely can spend safely seven percent or more of their nest eggs each year. Too often, Americans enter retirement with no idea how much they can safely spend each year.

So far in this book, we learned how to estimate how much it will cost to maintain the retirement lifestyle you desire. We also reviewed how to establish guaranteed lifetime income to fund the fixed or basic expenses of retirement. Now, we're going to examine how to determine the amount of the nest egg you safely can spend each year in retirement. By "safely spend," I mean the rate at which you can spend money with a low risk of running out of money during a likely retirement.

A spending strategy can make or break a retirement plan. People who accumulated a reasonable amount of money before retirement found themselves running out of money and having to make changes because they spent money too freely in the early years of retirement. Other people live securely on much smaller nest eggs because they developed reasonable spending plans and kept their lifestyles within those spending plans.

The risk of running out of money is not the only risk of having the wrong spending strategy. Some people are too conservative in their estimates. They live at a much lower standard of living than they could afford. They shortchange themselves during their lifetimes. That's good news for the loved ones and charities who benefit from their frugality, but it means those people deprived themselves of opportunities they could have had during their lives.

The money from this part of your assets is meant to cover those expenses that aren't covered by the guaranteed lifetime income you receive, as we discussed in Chapter 3. When your estimated spending exceeds the sum of your guaranteed annual income and the amount that can be withdrawn under your spending strategy, then you need to make changes in your estimated spending. You need to adjust your planned retirement lifestyle and spending so that they match the sources of cash. Otherwise, your financial security and independence are at risk.

In this chapter, we're going to discuss how you can develop the right spending plan for you. The goal is to determine how much money you can draw from your assets and maintain a low probability of running out of money during a reasonable estimate of your retirement period.

Keep in mind that we're talking in this chapter about spending money other than that used to generate guaranteed lifetime income. We're trying to determine how much we can spend on expenses that aren't covered by Social Security, any employer pension, and any annuities with lifetime guaranteed income.

You can use the strategies in this chapter even if you choose not to have any annuities that pay lifetime income. In fact, when you don't have guaranteed income from annuities or a pension, using these strategies is more important. In that case, your only guaranteed lifetime income is Social Security, so it is more important that you don't spend down your nest egg too quickly.

This was a topic that hardly was discussed only a few years ago. Most retirees simply invested their money in safe investments such as certificates of deposit, short-term and intermediate-term bonds, money market funds, stocks that pay dividends, and the like. They primarily lived off the income from those investments and rarely spent their principal. Because interest rates have been very low since about 1998 and especially since 2008, that strategy isn't viable for most people. You need a lot of money to generate a reasonable income at low interest rates and dividend yields. Retirees and near-retirees have to develop other investment strategies, and they have to spend more than their investment income during retirement.

As I said, this topic hardly was discussed a relatively short time ago. Discussions among professionals began in the 1990s. The discussion in the first edition of this book was one of the few available to a general audience for years. Research and discussions about safe spending formulas became more frequent and numerous over the last 10 years. We're going to review the different strategies, discuss their advantages and disadvantages, and show you the way to develop a spending strategy so that you can tap your nest egg safely.

How Long Should It Last?

A dangerous and frequently made mistake in retirement planning is to underestimate life expectancy. It wasn't necessary for previous generations of retirees to worry about life expectancy. Most only lived about five years after retiring. In recent decades, however, life expectancy for Americans over age 60 has increased. Retirees and preretirees today need to study life expectancy and understand how long they are likely to live. Many will live 20 or 30 years in retirement. It isn't unusual for people to live as long or longer in retirement as they spent in their careers, and that could be more common in the near future. This longevity is why it is vital for a retiree to establish a reasonable distribution policy to reduce the risk of running out of money in retirement.

There are many tools available on the Internet to estimate your life expectancy. One good free calculator I recommend is on the Social Security website. Another simple and useful calculator is the Simple Life Expectancy Calculator on the site of the Society of Actuaries (www.soa .org) that works with Microsoft Excel®.

The SOA's simple calculator lets you estimate the life expectancy of an individual or a couple. In addition to providing average life expectancy, it also provides probabilities for living a certain number of additional years.

For example, a 65-year-old man in 2015 had an average life expectancy of 16.5 years (to age 81.5 years). But he had a 37 percent probability of living another 20 years and a 17 percent probability of living another 25 years. There was a 4 percent probability of living 30 more years. Of course, the numbers were higher for a 65-year-old woman. She had an average life expectancy of 19.2 years and a 50 percent probability of living another 20 years. She also had a 28 percent probability of living another 25 years and a 10 percent likelihood of living another 30 years.

It's important to note that as you age, your life expectancy increases. For example, a 70-year-old man in 2015 has a life expectancy of 13.1 years (age 83.1). That's two years longer than the 65-year-old. The 70-year-old also has a 19 percent probability of living to 90. That's a higher probability than many people realize.

In a married couple, the probability of one spouse living to at least age 90 is fairly high and most couples should plan for that. More and more financial planners say that they prepare financial plans in which at least one spouse lives to 100.

Keep in mind that these are averages. You could live more or fewer years depending on family history, lifestyle, and current health. There are other websites that try to give a more customized life expectancy estimate. You enter personal data and the site prepares an estimate based on the data it has. You can find the ones currently available by entering "life expectancy calculator" in your favorite Internet search engine. In 2015, I found detailed calculators on the websites for the Wharton School at the University of Pennsylvania, bankrate.com, the book *Living to 100*, and insurer Northwestern Mutual.

The 4 Percent Rule

The first published strategy for tapping your nest egg now generally is referred to as the 4 percent rule or the safe spending rate. I was among early critics of using the strategy as anything more than a general guide. It requires modifications for different retirees and situations.

Here are the basics of the strategy. The research assumed that you'd withdraw a percentage of your nest egg the first year. Each year after that, you'd withdraw the same dollar amount that was withdrawn the previous year increased by the inflation rate of the previous year. If your first year's withdrawal was $50,000 and the Consumer Price Index for that year was 4 percent, the second year you would withdraw $52,000. If inflation was 2.5 percent the second year, the third year you would spend $53,300. The original study capped the annual spending increase at 3 percent, even if the CPI increase was higher. Some studies have used a flat annual increase of 3 percent instead of adjusting it for inflation.

Another assumption was that the nest egg would be invested in a traditional portfolio of 60 percent U.S. stocks and 40 percent U.S. bonds. Follow-up studies changed the investment allocation a little but not much, generally assuming a mix of U.S. stocks, U.S. bonds, and cash.

The question the study sought to answer was: What is the maximum percentage of the portfolio that could be withdrawn while maintaining a low risk of running out of money in fewer than 30 years? The answer in the original study and most follow-up studies was greater than 4 percent and less than 5 percent, with the answer usually closer to 4 percent than 5 percent. So, the answer was shortened to the 4 percent rule.

An advantage of the studies is that, unlike most retirement plans developed previously, they didn't assume the portfolio earned a steady average rate of return each year. The researchers realized the danger of what now is called sequence of returns risk. While investments have long-term average annualized rates of return, they don't return the average every year. In fact, U.S. stock indexes rarely have a year in which they return their long-term averages. Instead, the return in a particular year is likely to be much higher or lower than the long-term average.

More importantly, markets, especially stock markets, are likely to have long-term bull and bear markets. In bull markets, returns are likely to be significantly above the long-term average, and in bear markets the returns are likely to be significantly less than the long-term average. These long-term market cycles are likely to persist for years. When someone retires at the start of a long-term bear market, the portfolio is likely to earn significantly less than the long-term average. In the first edition of this book I discussed a study by mutual fund firm T. Rowe Price. The study found that someone who retired in 1968, at the beginning of a significant bear market, would run out of money by 1983 if he spent money at a rate that was sustainable if long-term average return was earned each year. On the other hand, if that person retired in 1982 when the next bull market began and spent at the same rate, his portfolio would last more than 30 years and he would die with a rather substantial net worth. He could have spent far more money during his lifetime.

The research that produced the 4 percent rule factored in this sequence of returns risk. It used different market returns. Some researchers used actual historic market returns. Others had computer programs generate random returns. In either case, the goal was to find a withdrawal rate that would allow a portfolio to last at least 30 years under all or most investment environments. The answer, as I said, is that the safe spending rate is around 4 percent of the portfolio's initial value.

Shortcomings of the 4 Percent Rule

While the rule is a useful starting point, I've been among the critics of the 4 percent rule from the start. Many others have joined over the years.

There are key shortcomings in the rule. In some cases, it is too optimistic. In others, it is too conservative. Here is a summary of the shortcomings:

- The rule doesn't guarantee your money will last at least 30 years. Under the scenarios run in the research, there are high probabilities a nest egg will last 30 years under the assumptions, but the probabilities are less than 100 percent.
- As we discussed earlier, 30 years might not be a long enough test period for many people. Life expectancies are increasing, and there is a reasonable probability that in many married couples at least one spouse will live longer. Saying it is safe to spend at 4 percent for 30 years is not the same as saying it will ensure everyone's nest egg lasts through retirement.
- What really counts is the extent of a shortfall. By how many years or how many dollars does a spending strategy fall short? If the shortfall is by less than a year and a relatively small dollar amount, a few modest adjustments in investing or spending could allow a higher spending rate. But if the strategy runs out of money years before retirement is likely to end, then it is a major problem.
- Different investment portfolios and strategies are going to have different results. A conservative investor who can't bear the volatility of a portfolio that is 60 percent in stocks is likely to earn a lower long-term return than in the studies. For that person, a 4 percent spending rate is too high. On the other hand, a more diversified portfolio than those used in the studies is likely to have better results and substantially reduce the sequence of returns risk. Further, a portfolio that successfully uses tactical asset allocation, changing the portfolio's allocation based on market factors, also is likely to have better results than in the studies. Better investment performance would allow a higher spending rate or cause the portfolio to last longer.
- Where the investment markets are in a long-term bull market or bear market cycle is important. It's often said that the most important years for a retirement plan are the five years before and the five years after retirement begins. When a serious bear market occurs during that period, it will be harder for a retiree to maintain the planned spending level. The portfolio will begin to decline quickly because it will have negative or low investment returns when the retiree begins drawing it down. On the other hand, when there's a strong bull market beginning during this period, the retiree is likely to earn higher returns than anticipated and be able to spend more than initially planned. The 4 percent rule essentially assumes you're starting retirement during a

bad investment period. That's a safe, conservative assumption, but it means people who retire at other times could spend more.

■ It might not be valid to assume historic U.S. investment returns will be repeated. Some researchers argue that the United States was a smaller, faster-growing economy during the periods tested. In the future, for several reasons, they believe the United States is likely to grow at a slower rate. If that's the case, then investment returns are likely to be lower. Historic investment returns probably aren't very relevant to people retiring in the wake of the financial crisis. Several studies indicate that economic growth and investment returns tend to be below average for years following a financial crisis. Some researchers now argue that a safe spending rate taking the current investment environment into account is 2 percent or less.

■ An important flaw in the studies is that no one really spends money in retirement the way the models assume. You'll find very few retirees who total their spending for one year, and then decide they will spend in the next year last year's spending increased by the inflation rate or by a fixed percentage. Spending is more dynamic and changes in a fairly predictable pattern during the retirement years, as we discuss below. Most spending plans also have flexibility. A retiree might be able to spend more in the early years with an understanding that some spending will be reduced or eliminated if investment returns don't meet a minimum level. We'll discuss this in more detail below.

The 4 percent rule is important research, but it should not be followed mechanically in a retirement plan. It is an important benchmark. It should be used as a starting point and modified according to the current investment environment and the individual's situation. In Chapter 2, we demonstrated that the old rule of thumb that people spend in retirement 80 percent of their preretirement income was invalid. Likewise, the 4 percent rule might apply on average but shouldn't be applied by any individual.

There isn't a maximum safe spending rate that will work in all scenarios if you plan to invest for a decent return that subjects you to market risk, interest rate risk, and other risks. Instead of searching for a safe spending rate, you need to either invest for safety and keep your spending within the cash generated or have a flexible spending plan under which your spending increases or decreases with both your goals and market changes.

Understanding Dynamic Spending

The fact is that very few people spend in retirement the way envisioned by the 4 percent rule and many other traditional strategies. Spending changes during retirement. To some extent, the changes are predictable.

The retirement spending cycle has been revealed in the periodic consumption studies done by the Department of Labor. Over decades these studies have revealed a consistent lifetime spending pattern, and spending patterns during retirement also are clear and consistent from the data. The studies were analyzed in a 2014 award-winning article by David Blanchett of Morningstar published in the *Journal of Financial Planning*.

Spending tends to steadily decrease during much of retirement. In fact, lifetime annual spending tends to peak sometime in the average person's 40s or 50s. After age 60, spending tends to decrease on average by a steady 1 percent annually after inflation. That means in current dollar terms the spending might increase because of inflation. But after adjusting for inflation, the real spending tends to decrease by about 1 percent annually. Spending might increase in the later years, due primarily to medical expenses and the need for assistance with daily activities. Blanchett describes this pattern as a "retirement spending smile."

The pattern is logical. When people retire they generally are still fairly young, healthy, and active. They have time to fill that used to be spent working. They also are likely to have a list of activities in which they want to engage that have been deferred because of work or the need to support their children. People also might move or make other significant changes in the early years of retirement that cost money.

As time passes, however, people will have engaged in some of those delayed activities. The novelty of retirement wears off, and they settle into routines. Also, as they age people become less active and could become less healthy.

In addition, the basket of goods and services consumed by a household is not steady during retirement. Most people don't incur the same percentage of their total expenditures on the same categories of expenses over time. It's not surprising that the amounts spent on pensions and insurance decline over time or that medical spending rises as one ages. People also tend to spend less on food as they age, but they give more to charity.

It's important to keep this lifetime spending cycle in mind both when estimating retirement spending and, more importantly, when developing a lifetime policy for drawing down assets.

Keep in mind that these patterns are averages. They differ for different households and for people in different financial situations. For example, Blanchett found households that begin retirement with lower spending than average tend to have lower declines over time than others. Also, households that began retirement with less money than they need to sustain their lifestyles tend to reduce spending at a faster rate than others. Financially secure people might reduce spending at a slower rate than average.

An interesting finding concerns households that are spending less in the first years of retirement than the data indicates they can afford.

These households do increase spending from ages 65 to 75, but the rate of increase declines. These apparently are fiscally conservative households who are concerned about outliving their money. They place a premium on remaining financially secure,' or perhaps their priorities are to leave legacies for their loved ones or charity.

It's possible that this real reduction in retirement spending is due to a recognition of financial constraints that weren't apparent at the start of retirement. It's also possible that it is a choice to spend more in the early years of retirement and to be less active and spend less as they age. The exact reasons for the spending pattern aren't clear from the data, but the pattern is clear and consistent over time.

Blanchett concludes, as I do, that traditional retirement models such as those that use the 4 percent rule overestimate the cost of retirement. Retirement plans should assume that most people will spend more in the early years of retirement when they are more healthy and active and less in the later years.

Another possible conclusion is that retirement assets might not need as much inflation protection as most plans assume. We learned in Chapter 3 that annuities can have inflation adjustments to protect purchasing power over time, but that inflation protection comes at a cost. The studies indicate that full inflation protection might not be necessary. A typical retiree might be better off owning some inflation-adjusted annuities and some that pay the same income for life.

Now, we'll look at retirement withdrawal strategies that assume spending is more dynamic and flexible than the 4 percent rule and traditional retirement models assume.

The Endowment Formula

In *Retirement Watch* newsletter and in the first edition of this book, I introduced the endowment formula as a way of modifying the 4 percent rule. I patterned it after the spending formula used by the Yale University Endowment Fund.

A group of Yale's economics professors and its endowment officials developed the spending rule years ago. Under the rule, spending increases over time only as the markets allow. It also avoids overspending in good years and sharp spending reductions in bad years. In other words, the rule allows market performance to gradually influence spending but keeps market performance from causing sharp changes in year-to-year spending. Yet, it also ensures that the endowment will last as long as the university needs it. Spending adjustments are made automatically, but gradually.

Here's one way to adapt the Yale spending rule for your own retirement fund. First, decide the first year spending percentage of your portfolio. This is where the 4 percent rule studies can serve as a benchmark. You can use 4 percent of the nest egg as your first year spending. Or you can adjust it based on the shortcomings of the 4 percent rule. If you think circumstances when you retire indicate a higher rate will work, consider spending 5 percent or so the first year. If you're more cautious and concerned about future investment returns, select a lower first-year spending rate. Let's say you pick 5 percent. That's the amount you withdraw the first year of retirement.

After the first year, use a formula that divides the annual distribution spending into two portions to arrive at the amount to spend. The first portion is last year's spending plus whatever inflation was last year. Multiply this by 70 percent. The other portion is your target first-year distribution rate from the fund. Multiply this by 30 percent. Add the two numbers, and that is your distribution for the year.

Example: Suppose you have a $500,000 retirement fund. You set a 5 percent spending rule, your first-year spending was $25,000, and inflation was 2 percent. Here's how you do the calculations for the second year.
Last year's spending plus inflation is $25,500. Multiplied by 70 percent, that is $17,850. Five percent of your fund is $25,000. Taking 30 percent of that gives you $7,500. Add the two results, and you will take $25,350 from the fund the second year.

Now, suppose the portfolio declines to $480,000 for the next year, and inflation is 2 percent. One bucket of your spending will be $25,350 (last year's spending) increased by 2 percent, or $25,857. Take 70 percent of that to get $18,100. The other bucket is 5 percent of the fund's new value, or $24,000. Take 30 percent of that, or $7,200. Add the two and your spending is $25,300. You will have a small spending reduction to recognize the reduced value of your portfolio.

For comparison, under a fixed 5 percent plus inflation rule, you would have spent $25,500 the second year and $26,010 the third year.

The endowment spending rule is designed to make your fund last longer than under the strict percentage-plus-inflation rule, as an endowment fund is supposed to last forever. If your portfolio experiences a period of poor investment returns, distributions gradually will be reduced under this method, because 30 percent of the spending is based on the portfolio's value. Under the traditional spending formula, your distributions will increase each year regardless of what happens to your portfolio.

The endowment approach also means you are less likely to be deprived in good times, because if market returns exceed expectations, distributions will rise with the returns.

A benefit of this approach is that about 30 percent of many retirees' budgets tends to be flexible. You can defer purchases of new cars, clothing, and other things. Travel, recreation, and entertainment spending can be reduced. The exact amount of flexibility depends on each retiree's budget and spending patterns.

Because an individual's retirement fund doesn't have to last forever, unlike an endowment, you get additional flexibility. If bad markets cause spending to decline for several years in a row to the point that essential spending is being deferred, you can suspend the spending rule and dip into principal for necessary spending. The next year's spending would incorporate this, because 30 percent of the spending would be based on the fund's value.

Some spending strategies put a limit on the amount that distributions can change in any year and a floor on the amount they can be reduced over time. For example, a strategy might say that the distribution can't rise or decline more than 5 percent in one year or more than 20 percent from the peak. The limits on declines keep really bad markets from severely reducing your spending. But they also mean the nest egg might be spent down faster if poor investment returns persist for years.

A Summary of Other Strategies

There now are a large number of withdrawal strategies to consider for your nest egg. When I wrote the first edition of this book, there were very few. As the first baby boomers reached retirement age, more researchers developed ideas they tested with data. We won't discuss all the strategies in detail. Many were published only in the last few years and haven't been thoroughly tested by other researchers or real life. All try to address the shortcomings of the 4 percent rule while giving retirees spending strategies that deliver high probabilities of never running out of money without forcing a retiree to be overly frugal.

I've selected the ones I think merit your consideration.

Buy Immediate Annuities. In Chapter 3, I mentioned that some people should consider putting all or most of their nest eggs in guaranteed lifetime income products such as immediate annuities and longevity annuities. People who have saved just enough to fund their retirements and who don't think they can handle even short-term reductions in their net worths due to market actions should consider this. Also, people who are going to invest very conservatively anyway might find they have higher incomes if a large portion of their nest eggs is in guaranteed income annuities.

Buy a Ladder of TIPS or Other Bonds. This is a favorite of some economists. TIPS are Treasury Inflation-Protected Securities. These are treasury bonds that pay interest but the value of the bond principal is increased with changes in the Consumer Price Index each year.

Your income doesn't change, but the purchasing power of your principal is protected. Eventually, the bond is redeemed for the amount you invested plus the inflation adjustments.

The belief of the economists is that you don't want to take any risk with the portion of your nest egg that will be used to support your standard of living. So, they recommend buying a ladder of TIPS. A ladder of bonds such as TIPS is when bonds are purchased so that a different group of bonds matures and is redeemed each year. They recommend buying a ladder of TIPS so that enough bonds mature each year to pay your estimated living expenses for the year. They recommend buying 30 years' worth of TIPS, with a different bond or set of bonds maturing each year. There is no interest rate or inflation risk from owning the bonds and holding them to maturity. Unlike buying annuities, this strategy leaves something for loved ones if you pass away before 30 years.

This strategy probably is theoretically correct but isn't practical in the real world. TIPS had extremely low interest rates in late 2015. They were so low that a person would have to have accumulated all his retirement spending before starting retirement and count on almost no investment income to help pay retirement expenses. You also take the risk of running out of money if your retirement lasts longer than 30 years.

Spend No More than a Fixed-Term Annuity Would Pay.   This strategy was published by Laurence Siegel and Barton Waring, and they called it "The Only Spending Rule Article You Will Ever Need." The strategy is simple in principle but can be a little harder to implement.

Basically, they say you should spend no more each year than you would receive from purchasing a term of years annuity that year. A term of years annuity is one that pays a fixed annual amount each year for a certain number of years. After that number of years passes, the payments cease. You can calculate the amount by using a formula that requires you to plug in current interest rates each year. Or you can contact some insurers and determine an average of their payouts.

Let's say you want to assume a 30-year retirement period. (You can adjust this time period up or down.) The first year of retirement you determine what the payout would be from an immediate annuity that was guaranteed to pay the same amount every year for 30 years, assuming you used your entire nest egg to purchase the annuity. You spend no more than that amount the first year. The next year, determine how much income you would receive by purchasing a 29-year annuity with what remains of your nest egg. That's the amount you spend the second year. You go through the same exercise each year.

You're not buying these annuities. You're investing your nest egg as you believe is appropriate. The strategy is used only to determine the maximum amount you'll withdraw from the nest egg each year. Under this approach, your spending adjusts up or down each year based on the value of your nest egg and the latest interest rates. The major downside is that it anticipates depleting your nest egg after 30 years. Of course, you don't have to spend that amount each year. It is a calculation of the maximum amount you should spend. Another potential disadvantage of the strategy is that spending could be volatile from year to year as interest rates and the value of your nest egg fluctuate.

The 20–10 Strategy.   This sounds like another strategy that assumes retirement lasts 30 years. In fact, it covers an infinite period after 20 years. You split the nest egg into two portions. One portion will pay for the first 20 years of retirement. The other portion will pay for whatever period you live after 20 years. Any of the other strategies discussed in this chapter can be used to determine spending for the first 20 years of retirement. The difference is that in this strategy that portion of your nest egg has to last only 20 years, not for an unknown number of years that could be 30 or even well beyond 30 years. A conservative person could buy a ladder of TIPS that mature each year for 20 years. A more aggressive person could invest the nest egg and take withdrawals each year to fund spending. Your goal is for that portion of your nest egg to last for at least 20 years.

The other portion of your nest egg is used to buy longevity annuities that will begin paying income after 20 years. You need to deposit enough in the annuities to generate income that will cover your estimated expenses each year after year 20.

Under this strategy, there won't be anything for your heirs unless the first portion of your nest egg isn't spent during the 20 years or you have some life insurance.

This approach gives peace of mind to some people. They aren't worrying about making their nest eggs last for a lifetime. They know that if they live more than 20 years in retirement, they'll have a steady stream of income for the rest of their lives. Also, by purchasing the annuities 20 years in advance, the annuities are relatively inexpensive.

Follow the IRA Rules.   The tax code requires a minimum amount to be distributed from IRAs after age $70\frac{1}{2}$, as we discuss in detail in Chapter 8. You can use this same formula to decide on the maximum amount to be withdrawn from your nest egg after retiring. As you'll learn in Chapter 8, the required minimum distribution (RMD) formula increases the percentage of the IRA distributed each year, so there's a built-in inflation escalator. The formula also always leaves some amount unspent almost no matter how long a person lives. Some who favor this approach say it produces similar results to the 4 percent rule.

The RMD rules, however, weren't designed for this purpose. They were designed to ensure an IRA is close to empty after a person's lifetime and to limit what can be passed on to the next generation. The distribution pattern doesn't follow most people's spending patterns. In fact, it is the opposite of the retirement spending pattern most people have. A complaint many people have with RMDs is that it increases distributions steadily as they age, forcing them to take distributions they don't want or need. Using the IRA rules is a good way to ensure your nest egg lasts a long time, but it doesn't do a good job of matching the distributions to your likely spending.

Spend a Fixed Percentage of the Portfolio Each Year.   This is a hybrid of the 4 percent rule and the Endowment Strategy. You choose a beginning spending percentage such as 4 percent. You spend up to that percentage of the portfolio each year. The difference is that you don't make any adjustments. Whatever the portfolio's value is at the end of a year, your maximum distribution for the next year is 4 percent of that amount.

A nest egg is likely to last longer under this strategy than under the 4 percent rule, because it doesn't have the regular increases for inflation. Also, the spending changes automatically with fluctuations in the market value of the portfolio. There's an automatic reduction if the portfolio tumbles and automatic increases if markets do well. Also, because there aren't automatic inflation increases, the strategy allows for a higher first-year spending rate than the 4 percent rule.

A potential problem is that the changes in the maximum spending amount are likely to vary greatly from year to year unless the portfolio is invested to remain fairly stable. A traditional portfolio that is 60 percent in stocks and 40 percent in bonds is likely to have wide swings in value from year to year.

Add a Floor and Ceiling.   This is a supplementary strategy that can be added to almost any of those already discussed but was first developed as an improvement to the fixed percentage strategy discussed immediately above. It can reduce the fluctuations in allowable spending and also allow a higher first-year spending rate.

You smooth fluctuations in the maximum spending amount by creating rules that don't allow the spending to vary more than a maximum amount each year. For example, For example, you might say in any year spending can't rise or fall more than 10 percent from the previous year. You could also say spending can't fall more than a fixed percentage below the first year's spending. The wider the floor and ceiling, the less likely you are to run out of money. The tighter the floor and ceiling, the less fluctuations there can be in spending but the greater the risk of spending too much too soon. There are many variations of floor and ceiling strategies, and some researchers developed some detailed formulas for setting the limits.

Other distribution strategies have been proposed in recent years. Some of these have high probabilities of success, but that have fairly detailed rules. Most individuals probably would be unable to follow the strategies, especially as they age, and would need the strategies to be implemented by financial planners who are proficient with the strategies.

Summary

Keep in mind that your investment strategy is a key factor in how successful your withdrawal strategy is. When your investment strategy doesn't come close to meeting your target rate of return, the portfolio is going to diminish faster than anticipated. Also, when the investment strategy causes the portfolio's value to fluctuate greatly from year to year, the maximum distributions are going to fluctuate if you use a flexible formula. A volatile portfolio also means that as you track the success of your strategy, the likelihood of success is going to change a lot from year to year.

No spending formula or plan is perfect. You want to develop a plan that is flexible, recognizes changed circumstances, takes emotions out of the process, and makes gradual changes. I think it is important for a withdrawal or spending rule to make adjustments as the market value of a portfolio changes, but the adjustments should be gradual or smoothed. The endowment formula meets these goals. It also gives you an edge by increasing the likelihood that your fund will outlast the worst markets. Several of the other strategies also provide flexibility with smoothing.

Managing Your Nest Egg

Most investment plans for retirees and preretirees are wrong. They aren't likely to deliver the risk-adjusted returns or income the investor needs to fund spending during the post-career years. Some don't have enough inflation protection or take too much stock market risk for someone in or near retirement.

At this point, you have estimated retirement spending and determined how much income to receive from guaranteed sources of income. You also set a policy for withdrawing money from the part of your nest egg that doesn't generate guaranteed income, your investment portfolio. You're going to review that withdrawal policy regularly and adjust it as necessary to make your nest egg meet your goals.

The next step is to learn how to manage your investment portfolio. You need an investment plan and strategy that will complement the withdrawal strategy. The withdrawal strategy assumes a minimum investment return or income yield. That goal must be met for the nest egg to last long enough to supplement your guaranteed income for life and meet any other goals you have, such as leaving a legacy for loved ones.

The investment needs of retirees and those nearing retirement historically received little attention from either the financial services industry or academics who studied investing. For the first generation or so of retirees that didn't matter. Most of their income came from guaranteed sources, and they didn't live long in retirement. They followed a traditional retirement investment strategy, which we'll discuss shortly, that was safe and generated sufficient income. More recently, that strategy hasn't worked well. Retirees and near-retirees generally had to develop their own strategies or use strategies meant for younger people and hope they worked. Only in the last few years has the unique situation of those in or near retirement been addressed by the industry and academics.

Several useful investment strategies were developed in recent years for retirees and near retirees. First, we'll review some traditional strategies and explain why they aren't suitable or optimum for this group of investors. Then, we'll present an overview of some approaches to investing that are likely to help people meet their goals.

The Classic Advice

The investment advice for retirees used to be simple. As retirement approaches, the portfolio should be shifted from riskier investments—such as stocks—into safer, income-producing investments—such as annuities, bonds, certificates of deposit, money market funds, and some dividend-paying stocks. The theory behind this advice also was simple. A retiree needs regular income to pay expenses. A retiree also does not want the principal of the portfolio to fluctuate as much as stocks do. That's why, according to this advice, a retiree wants a portfolio that pays income and maintains a reasonably stable value.

The strategy made some sense when the average retirement lasted about five years, as it did for those who were in the first generation of retirees. It also made sense when interest rates and dividend yields were much higher than they are now. Also, for those early retirees an investment portfolio was a mere supplement to Social Security and employer pensions.

Things are different now.

The traditional retirement investing strategy is made more difficult by the very low interest rate policy that Federal Reserve has followed most of the time since 2001 and especially since 2008. It's tough to generate sufficient income from an investment portfolio when yields on the safest investments are near historic lows, and yields on investments with much greater risk and volatility aren't much higher.

Other factors also work against the traditional retirement investment strategy.

As we discussed, retirement can last a long time now, 20 years or longer. The key problem over this time is inflation. The purchasing power of income declines steadily over time. Even a low inflation rate will eat away at the purchasing power of income each year. Over 10, 20, or 30 years, the compounding of that inflation will dramatically reduce the income's purchasing power. The purchasing power of the principal also will decline. To maintain purchasing power in the face of inflation, both the income and principal have to increase by at least the inflation rate each year. To maintain the purchasing power of $40,000 when inflation is only 2 percent annually, after 15 years more than $53,000 of income is needed. When inflation is higher, even higher returns are needed to preserve purchasing power.

For a retirement plan to be successful, purchasing power must be maintained over an extended period. Preserving purchasing power requires growth in both the income and the principal, neither of which is likely under the traditional strategy in today's conditions.

The classic investment advice for retirees makes sense now in only a few circumstances. The classic strategy can be used if retirement is expected to last five years or less so that the effects of inflation and changing interest rates would not be severe. The strategy also can work if the income from the portfolio exceeds the amount that must be spent, so that the excess can be reinvested. If inflation is 3 percent annually, an amount equal to 3 percent of the portfolio should be reinvested to maintain the purchasing power of the principal and the income. If the portfolio returns 5 percent when inflation is 3 percent, up to 2 percent can be spent and the rest should be reinvested. The classic strategy also can work when there are other sources of income that will help overcome the loss of purchasing power over time.

Invest Like the Rest

The advice most frequently given to retirees and preretirees the last couple of decades was to invest like everyone else. Don't change the portfolio as retirement approaches to invest for income and safety. Instead, continue to hold a diversified portfolio of assets and invest for total return (income and capital gains) without regard to how much income (interest and dividends) the portfolio generates.

The income produced by the portfolio is spent. When additional cash is needed to pay expenses, some shares of a stock or mutual fund are sold to generate the cash needed. It doesn't matter whether a person is spending income, capital gains, or principal, as long as the total return of the portfolio over time at least meets the target in the retirement plan.

Some versions of this strategy went as far as to say the portfolio should own only stocks. Stocks have the highest long-term return, so they are the assets most likely to make the investor financially secure. Short-term changes in the value of the portfolio don't matter, as long as the long-term return goals are met. Most versions of the strategy recommend that an older person own a lower percentage of stocks than a younger person, but a healthy percentage of the portfolio still is in stocks.

As we discuss in more detail shortly, a modern "diversified" portfolio looks diversified on paper, but the returns and volatility of the portfolio are heavily tied to the stock market indexes. For many portfolios, 90 percent or more of the volatility and returns depend on the action of major stock indexes.

Being tied to the stock market can cause major problems for investors in or near retirement. Stocks can have severe price declines in any year, and they also have extended bear markets in which they lose substantial value and don't recover that value for years. It is difficult for someone who depends on that portfolio to maintain a standard of living for decades to adhere to the investment strategy when it is losing substantial value. Many people who try to follow such a strategy will change their minds and sell all or most of the stocks at an inopportune time.

Another and more significant problem with the strategy applies to those who stick with it. We discussed in Chapter 4 the importance of sequence of returns risk. Suppose a person enters retirement with a traditional portfolio that is highly correlated with the stock market indexes. That person's retirement goals are in jeopardy if a long-term bear market begins near the start of the person's retirement. While the portfolio's value is down, the retiree still has to withdraw money from it to pay expenses. That money is no longer in the portfolio to benefit from the eventual rebound in the investments. That's why a traditional portfolio is more risky for someone in or near retirement than for a younger person.

In Chapter 4 we mentioned the study from mutual fund firm T. Rowe Price that demonstrated a person who retired in 1968 when a bear market was in its early stages would run out of money before the next bull market began in 1982. That's the result of the combination of a decline in a portfolio's value coupled with the portfolio owner's need to withdraw money from the portfolio to fund retirement spending.

Buying-and-holding for the long-term can be a good strategy for a young person who has a career of 30 or more years ahead to be followed by a retirement of 30 or more years. But it is dangerous for someone who already lived most or all of that career and now is looking at leaving the workplace and depending on the portfolio to help finance spending for the rest of his or her life.

Research shows that the most critical investment years for a retirement plan are the 10 years that begin five years before retirement and end five years after retirement. During this period, the nest egg is likely to be at its highest value, and the retirement plans are based on that value. A substantial decline in the portfolio's value during this period is going to reduce its dollar value by a much larger amount than would be the case in the earlier years. The decline also is a more serious setback to the retirement plan, since the plan is based on starting retirement with that higher value. It will take the portfolio a while to recover those losses. In addition, the retirement plan usually assumes the portfolio will continue to earn positive returns and grow to a higher value the next few years. So, the portfolio's value is far behind what was anticipated in the retirement plan and could fall farther behind.

After a person or couple has been retired for more than five years, a portfolio decline has less serious consequences if the portfolio continued to meet its goals during the first five years of retirement. There now is more of a cushion to ride out the losses. The portfolio owner also has become more comfortable living without a steady paycheck, has more confidence in the plan, and is more likely to stay with the overall strategy.

For these reasons, approaching retirement with a portfolio that is strongly correlated with the stock indexes can be dangerous. If stocks have a bear market at that time, the retirement plan might need serious adjustments. At a minimum, the prospective retiree is likely to suffer increased anxiety and reduced confidence.

Two Portfolio Anchors

Before we discuss specific investment strategies for those in or near retirement, there are two other strategies that should supplement any investment strategy. These strategies provide an additional level of protection and safety. They make it easier for an individual to adhere to an investment strategy during periods when it isn't working. They also allow an investor room to take additional risk with the rest of the portfolio and with that additional risk comes the potential for higher returns.

The Safety Fund

The first strategy is to establish a spending or safety fund.

The fund is established by setting aside an amount of cash equal to the anticipated expenses for the next one to five years. The time period is selected by the retiree and depends on how conservative he or she wants to be. A conservative person who wants to be on the safe side would have a spending fund covering up to five years of spending. Someone who isn't as concerned about market fluctuations would establish a one- or two-year fund.

To determine the size of the fund, take your total expected expenses over the period and subtract the amount you expect to be covered by guaranteed lifetime income. Then, you sell enough investments to produce cash equal to the rest of the anticipated expenses for the period. This cash is put in safe, liquid investments. Possibilities are a money market fund or short-term bond fund. You also could put the money in short-term bonds or certificates of deposit if you buy a ladder of the investments so that they mature at different times over the selected time period.

You're not trying to earn a high yield or investment return from the money in this bucket. You want the principal to be safe so that you know you don't worry about having enough money to cover expenses for the time period. You aren't planning to live off the income from this fund; you're going to spend both principal and income. You pay bills with cash from the spending or safety fund.

The advantage of the fund is that you are less likely to worry about short-term fluctuations in the investment portfolio, or even intermediate-term fluctuations. You know there is cash readily available for your expenses over the time period covered by the fund. That should make you less likely to be concerned over a decline in your portfolio or the markets and less likely to overhaul your investment strategy during a bad market period. The fund has the dual effects of allowing you to sleep easier at night and making you less likely to overreact to a change in the markets.

With the spending fund, you also don't have to assess your portfolio each month and decide which assets you're going to sell to raise cash for expenses.

A disadvantage of the strategy is that the money in the spending fund is likely to earn lower returns than the rest of your portfolio. That could lower the long-term return for your investments, which is the usual cost of reducing risk.

After establishing the safety fund, periodically you sell investments from the invested portion of your nest egg to raise cash for the spending fund. There are a number of ways to replenish the fund; you should select the one that works best for you.

You could decide to move cash from the investment portfolio to the spending fund at the same time each month. Some people make the transfer less frequently but still on a calendar schedule: every 3 months, 6 months, or 12 months. Whatever timetable you select, you review the investment portfolio on that schedule and decide which investments should be sold.

Another approach is to let the markets tell you when to make moves. After an investment has had a period of good appreciation, it probably is a higher percentage of your portfolio than planned. You should rebalance the portfolio as part of your regular strategy. You can rebalance the portfolio by selling some of the investment and putting all or some of the cash proceeds in the safety fund. Or after an investment has declined in value and shows a paper loss, consider selling it to take advantage of the tax deduction from the loss and put all or some of the proceeds in the spending fund.

Tax planning probably should have a role whichever approach you take. Income taxes are a major expense for many retirees. You want to plan your asset sales to keep taxes on your investments as low as possible.

As a practical matter, you probably hold investments in different types of accounts: taxable accounts, traditional IRAs, Roth IRAs, and perhaps others. For tax reasons you might not want to have one safety fund.

For example, you might sell some investments in the traditional IRA and move them to a money market fund within the IRA. That way, you aren't taking the amount out of the IRA and into gross income until you plan to spend it. Instead of one safety fund, you might have different safety funds within the different types of accounts you own. The total value of the funds equals what would be in one safety fund.

This strategy often is called the buckets or silo strategy. You have at least two investment buckets or silos. One bucket is for short-term spending and investing. The other bucket is your longer-term positions.

Some financial advisors have elaborate and detailed bucket strategies. They establish multiple investment buckets for different time periods. The buckets for the next few years are invested in safe, conservative assets. Investments for intermediate periods, such as 5 to 10 years away, can take a little more risk but still have a high level of safety. These buckets might be invested in intermediate term bonds and similar investments. The buckets that aren't likely to be spent for 10 years or longer can be invested in riskier assets such as stocks, because the short- and intermediate-term fluctuations shouldn't matter. Those buckets can try to earn higher returns. To pursue one of the more elaborate bucket strategies you probably should use a financial advisor who uses the strategy.

Having Guaranteed Lifetime Income

The other strategy we discussed in Chapter 3. It involves depositing a portion of your nest egg in immediate or longevity annuities to generate guaranteed lifetime income.

In Chapter 3, we discussed the advantages of knowing your fixed expenses will be covered by guaranteed income for life. There are additional benefits to having this guaranteed income. Various studies have demonstrated that having immediate annuities or similar assets as part of a nest egg can make the nest egg last longer. There's never a risk of running out of money, so the guaranteed income can be more effective than bonds or similar investments. In addition, the security of the guaranteed income allows you to take more risk with the rest of the investment portfolio. If this risk-taking is successful, the result can be higher investment returns and more money to either spend during retirement or leave as a legacy to loved ones or charity.

Better Ways to Build Retirement Portfolios

There are many different investment strategies. Of course, they're not all appropriate for investors in or near retirement, and some aren't appropriate for most investors. There are three broad categories of investment strategies that can be used successfully by retirees and those near retirement. The details of implementing these strategies can vary, but the basic elements should be the same as I describe in the following sections.

The High-Yield, Income-Growth Strategy

This strategy was quite common from the early days of the stock market until it began to fade in popularity in the 1960s and 1970s. It still can be effective today, and it might become more popular as investment markets change.

It wasn't too long ago that common stocks had fairly high dividend yields. In fact, stocks of quality companies often had dividend yields that were higher than the yields on their bonds. Retirees and those who wanted to invest for safety would buy common stocks. They weren't too concerned with fluctuations in the prices of the stocks. They simply wanted the dividends. Stocks of high-quality companies would have dividend yields of 5 percent and more.

There's a hidden advantage to investing in dividend-yielding stocks. Companies that pay regular dividends usually increase the dividends and do so on a regular schedule when they can. This is a significant advantage over bonds and other income investments. You need to maintain the purchasing power of your income over time, and a good way to do that is to have the income increase. Regular increases in dividends are an easy, low-risk way to increase your income over time. There are a number of companies that have issued regular dividends for many years and increase those dividends every year or almost every year.

Dividend investing fell out of favor for several reasons:

- *Investors became more interested in the growth of stock prices than in the income stocks could generate.* The post–World War II economic growth was an obvious cause of this. Rapid growth in the economy resulted in rapid growth in stock prices.
- *Changes in corporate and tax policy also were factors.* Corporations can't deduct dividends but can deduct interest payments. It made more sense to many corporate managers to retain their cash and even borrow to fund operations. Let investors benefit from rising stock prices instead of dividends. In recent years, more and more public companies have been borrowing money and using the loan proceeds to buy back their own stock instead of to issue dividends. Buying back stock causes the earnings for each of the remaining shares to increase, and the interest on the loans is deductible. Another factor that diminished the desire for dividends was that for much of the time dividends were taxed the same as ordinary income. Investors were able to keep only a portion of dividend income, so they favored capital gains over dividends. In recent years, dividends were given the same preference

as long-term capital gains, increasing the popularity of dividends among investors.

■ *As investors age, they shift away from stocks.* As the baby boomers enter or approach their retirement years, more investors have been interested in safety and income than capital gains.

You should consider investing a portion of your nest egg in common stocks that pay decent dividends, especially stocks of companies that have long histories of increasing their dividends.

Some investments other than stocks have high yields and income that increases over time. The strategy can be expanded beyond stocks to real estate investment trusts, master limited partnerships, closed-end funds, and some other investments. Many of these vehicles are focused on providing high levels of income to their investors, and having the income increase over time also is a priority.

The strategy is not for trading stocks or even seeking high returns. The goal is to generate income and preferably income that increases over time. To implement this strategy successfully, you have to be unconcerned about the short-term changes in the prices of the investments, whether they are common stocks or other vehicles. Your primary reason for investing is income, and you plan for the income to fund your retirement spending. The prices of the investments will fluctuate. Over time, the prices should increase, but over shorter periods and perhaps longer periods they could decline. You have to understand this and accept it before starting the strategy.

True Diversification

"Buy and hold" has been the mantra of many investment advisors for some time. Most investors were educated to have a buy-and-hold portfolio with all or most of their assets. There are good reasons for buying and holding. Most investors don't make good decisions about when to buy and sell different assets. It's better to endure the ups-and-downs of the markets when you know in advance that you're a long-term investor and will ride the market fluctuations. Simply set up a long-term portfolio that takes a level of risk you can tolerate and is likely to meet your return goals.

Unfortunately, many investors who followed a buy-and-hold strategy since the late 1990s aren't happy. Their portfolios have been more volatile than they expected, and their returns aren't close to meeting their goals.

A buy-and-hold strategy can work. It's a good solution for people who aren't trained in finance and investments or who don't want to spend much time following their portfolios.

The problem isn't with the policy of buying-and-holding a fixed allocation. The problem is that the investment allocations in most buy-and-hold portfolios aren't suitable for long-term holding, especially by someone in or near retirement.

Most portfolios that appear to be balanced or diversified in fact are heavily correlated to the stock market indexes and require strong stock market returns to meet their goals. For example, a portfolio that is 60 percent stocks and 40 percent bonds has about a 98 percent correlation with a 100 percent stock portfolio. Because equities are much more volatile than bonds, the equities drive both the volatility and the total returns of the portfolio. (One study found that a 90 percent stock and 10 percent bond portfolio had returns and risk similar to the 60–40 portfolio.) Such a portfolio is most suitable for a period of strong, positive economic growth and declining interest rates. Or it can be used by someone who is relatively young and can ride out the ups and downs of the stock indexes. If you own one of the traditional buy-and-hold portfolios and in the 10 years before retirement or early in retirement you encounter a long-term bear stock market or even a mediocre equity market, you'll have a problem funding retirement. You won't meet your investment return goals, and that will require adjustments to your spending plans. Certainly in the years since 2000 the traditional buy-and-hold portfolios haven't worked well for many people.

I don't think you want your investment results and quality of your retirement to depend on having the good fortune that the economy and stock markets are in the ideal environment during those important years before and in the early part of retirement. You can avoid that risk by putting together your buy-and-hold portfolio the right way, so that it has what I call *true diversification*.

As I said, the typical buy-and-hold portfolio is heavily dependent on stocks. The portfolio might hold a number of different mutual funds and perhaps other investments, but most of the investments rise or fall with the stock indexes and the entire portfolio will rise or fall with stocks. In investment geek-speak, the investments are highly correlated with stock indexes. More than 90 percent of the returns and volatility of the typical "diversified" buy-and-hold portfolio are tied to the stock market indexes. A long-term stock bear market means an extended period of low or negative returns for such a portfolio. A volatile stock market means a volatile portfolio.

Buy-and-hold investing can work in almost any economic and investment environment when the portfolio has true diversification. The portfolio can't be overweighted to stock market risks and returns. The portfolio should be equally balanced among different risks instead of being dependent on the stock market.

There are different ways to identify the risks you want to balance, but I believe the portfolio should be balanced among investments, strategies, and funds that do well in different economic environments. The major mistake many people make when putting together a buy-and-hold portfolio is they don't consider diversification among different economic environments.

The major influences on investments over periods other than the short term are inflation and economic growth. These factors can either rise or fall. You want investments that do well in each of the possible environments: rising growth, falling growth, rising inflation, and falling inflation. As I said, there are different ways to approach and implement this concept. The idea of balancing risks or drivers of performance is what's important.

Another mistake investors make is to balance investments based on the capital or dollar allocations. That's a mistake because investments have different levels of volatility, or risk. Stocks are the most volatile investments. Bonds aren't very volatile, especially when compared to bonds. A portfolio with true diversification balances the risk or volatility of the investments that do well in each economic environment. You want roughly equal volatility of the portfolio allocated to each investment, not equal amounts of capital. A high volatility investment such as stocks will have less capital allocated to it than a low-volatility asset. You want less capital in the investments with a lot of volatility, such as stocks and commodities, and more capital in low volatility investments. That way, the portfolio should do well in almost any environment and the volatility will be consistent over time.

In addition to having low correlations with the major stock indexes, the investments in a portfolio with true diversification also should have low correlations with each other. This will occur naturally if you consider each economic environment and make sure you have at least one investment that does well in that environment.

The result is that the swings in the portfolio's value are less dramatic and are smoother than for a traditional portfolio. The value of your nest egg won't rise as much in a strong stock market rally, but it won't decline nearly as much in a bearish stock market. You'll recover your losses more quickly than in the traditional portfolio. The portfolio will grow more smoothly and steadily than the traditional portfolio.

The key to higher long-term returns is to avoid large losses. It takes a lot of time and large positive returns to make up major losses. You're better off avoiding the large losses and accepting lower returns in strong stock markets. The result will be long-term returns similar to or higher than those of a traditional portfolio and with less volatility and uncertainty. You'll have higher risk-adjusted returns. That means you earn higher returns for the level of risk you're taking than in a traditional portfolio.

You achieve true diversification and its benefits by adding more types of investments and strategies than are in the traditional portfolio. You want some investments that do well when growth is rising, and some when it is falling. You also want investments that increase when inflation is rising, and some that increase when inflation is falling.

As I said, there are different ways of implementing this strategy. It was pioneered by the hedge fund firm Bridgewater Associates with its All Weather portfolio™. The Bridgewater offering is available only to institutional investors and now is closed to most of them. Others who adapted the strategy usually call it a Risk Parity strategy. Individual investors can build their own versions using mutual funds or exchange-traded funds.

Dynamic Investing for Risk Management

A buy-and-hold portfolio is not for everyone. Some people want to seek higher returns by investing in primarily investments they believe are likely to perform well for a while. Other investors don't want to suffer through significant declines in a portion of their portfolios, even if the declines are temporary. They want to reduce or eliminate investments with the most risk.

Dynamic portfolio management, or tactical asset allocation, can be effective for many investors. You can reduce risk and increase returns through effective management of your portfolio. But there are several caveats to this endorsement. I'm not recommending day trading, market timing, or a strategy with frequent portfolio shifts. I also don't recommend trying to earn the highest returns or locate the next hot investment.

When dynamically managing your portfolio, you're engaged in risk management. Higher long-term returns follow naturally when you manage the portfolio to reduce or eliminate risks you don't want to take, such as owning a lot of stock market positions after stocks have had a strong run and are highly valued. Remember, a key to strong long-term returns is to avoid large losses.

Another caveat is that most people need support and guidance to invest dynamically. One way to obtain this help is to invest in one or more mutual funds that invest dynamically, delegating the decisions to the fund managers. You also could have an investment manager handle your portfolio. Other sources of help with dynamic investing are newsletters and websites. My point is that unless you're involved in the markets regularly, you should obtain help from one or more sources who are experienced with the strategy before using dynamic investment management.

Most people who consider dynamic investing assume it's for investors who are seeking total return or long-term capital gains. But investors seeking primarily income also can benefit from dynamic investing. In fact, I recommend the strategy for income seekers. There is a wide array of income investments to choose from: treasury bonds of different durations, investment grade corporate bonds, high-yield corporate bonds, emerging market bonds (both sovereign and corporate bonds), international bonds, preferred stock, master limited partnerships, floating rate debt, high dividend yield stocks, real estate investment trusts, and closed-end mutual funds that invest in any of the preceding and might use leverage to increase yields.

Income portfolio strategies these days usually fall into two categories. One set of portfolios is filled with the traditional mix of bonds that, when added together, aren't much different from a bond index fund. In recent years, that meant you're earning a low yield, have little or no inflation protection, and watch your principal move up and down in the opposite direction of interest rates. You're at risk of losing a lot of principal when interest rates rise and a lot of purchasing power when inflation rises.

The other category of income portfolios seeks the highest yields. Advertisements will boast of yields of 10 percent, 12 percent, and more, even in today's low interest environment. You don't earn those kinds of yields without taking a lot of risk. You have to invest in securities of financially troubled companies, use leverage, or employ other aggressive strategies. Too often these types of investments suffer losses that exceed the additional yield they paid.

Each of those strategies will work well in a particular market environment and then blow up when the environment changes.

They aren't strategies you can rely on.

A better approach to consider is to invest for high income but also use a dynamic strategy. Since higher-income investments are highly volatile when the economy and markets change, you want to adjust the portfolio periodically.

Just as with other portfolios that use dynamic investing, risk management should be the guiding principle of your dynamic income portfolio. You want to sell or reduce investments that appear to be highly valued or have a high level of risk. You want to add or increase investments that appear to have lower risk and a good potential for appreciation or income. Always seek investments that appear to have a margin of safety. You also should use diversification and balance. No matter how confident you are of a particular market or economic outcome, don't have the portfolio 100 percent dependent on that outcome.

Your dynamic income portfolio won't be restricted to the safest investments. At times, you'll buy investments that are historically risky and you don't want to hold for the long term. You'll buy them when they appear to be low in price and carry less-than-usual risk. In addition, risky investments can be balanced with other investments. A portfolio overall is less risky when you pair investments that separately are risky but aren't correlated with each other. Also, by managing the portfolio dynamically you are able to sell investments when their level of risk is above average and invest the proceeds in less risky investments. You make changes as the valuations and risk of the investments change.

How to Manage Your Portfolio Dynamically. Whether you invest for total return or income, you can use a dynamic investment strategy. Dynamic investing is not market timing. You don't make frequent trades in the portfolio, though you do make periodic changes. The intent is not to try to capture short-term trends in the markets or to respond to the latest headlines and market noise. Instead, the strategy is to sell assets that are overvalued and buy assets that are undervalued or that are likely to benefit from what seems to be the next phase of the valuation cycle. I recommend taking a one-year to three-year outlook when making portfolio adjustments.

The valuation cycle is the most important and most overlooked factor in investment success. Each asset has a long-term cycle during which investors swing from extreme optimism to extreme pessimism and back. Because of that, you can refer to this as the sentiment cycle instead of the valuation cycle. In U.S. stocks, a full cycle can take decades, and there are shorter cycles within the full cycle. For other assets, the cycle might be shorter. The valuation cycle exists for all investments and subsectors of investments. All of us have seen this in action. We know that there will be extreme bull and bear markets for each asset in each generation. We also know that at the same time some investments will be in bull markets while others are in bear markets.

It is important that investors who aren't using a true diversification strategy recognize the valuation cycle and manage their investments with an eye on it. At a minimum, watching the cycle enables an investor to reduce holdings of assets that are in the extremely optimistic phase. That reduces risk and reduces losses when the cycle begins its path toward extreme pessimism.

An investor can't determine the exact top and bottom of a cycle in advance and shouldn't try. What is important is to capture the intermediate trends. An investor who can capture some of the good intermediate trends and avoid some of the bad trends will increase long-term returns with less risk.

As already discussed, in a dynamic strategy you aren't seeking the next hot investment. Instead, the approach should be to reduce risk by limiting exposure to investments that seem overvalued and at risk of tumbling. Eliminating the high-risk assets and seeking those with lower risk automatically avoids the likely big losers. It also positions the portfolio in the assets that are likely to do well over the next few years. The strategy reduces the risk and volatility of the portfolio.

It is not easy to call the turns in a valuation cycle, whether one is trying to call the long-term cycle or the intermediate turns. Identifying turning points isn't any easier for income investments than it is for stocks. You need to use several tools when dynamically managing a portfolio. You need to use more than one factor to determine which investments to buy. Many investors like to identify one valuation factor or other data point to make investment decisions. It's a bad idea. No single piece of data has a strong enough record of accuracy to use it this way. You have to use a number of different factors together and make a decision only when most of them are saying the same thing. Even then, you're likely to make some moves that are on the wrong side of the markets. The best investors carefully track their investment moves and calculate the results. Even the very best find that they are wrong about one third of the time. So, don't expect all your investment moves to be winners.

I recommend using a combination of valuation measures and momentum. Valuation measures show you whether the current price of an investment is high or low relative to historic prices. The better valuation method to use depends on the investment, and no valuation measure is a precise guide to buying and selling. They only indicate whether the value is relatively high or low. An investment can continue at an extreme valuation for some time before turning. That's why I say don't try to pinpoint tops and bottoms. Momentum measures, such as moving averages, indicate whether an investment's popularity is increasing or decreasing. They give you an idea of whether an investment trend is beginning, accelerating, or slowing. Watching momentum helps you avoid buying or selling an investment too soon, which is likely to happen if you use only valuation measures. The risk of momentum measures is that momentum can change very quickly.

Because neither valuation nor momentum signals are precise, it's important to monitor an investment after buying it. Be prepared to conclude that a move was a bad idea and should be reversed.

Also, in dynamic investing, you need diversification and balance to limit the effects of mistakes. The asset you believe has the most potential will be the largest portion of the portfolio, but other investments also should be included.

This has been a brief summary of the key principles of dynamic investing. There are books, newsletters, and websites that describe in detail different approaches to dynamic investing and how to manage investments in different assets.

For those who are willing to do the additional monitoring and trading, dynamic investing can increase income and total returns and reduce risk. My approach to dynamic investing is best described in the lyric of a song that was popular in the 1990s ("The Bug"): "Sometimes you're the windshield; sometimes you're the bug." Dynamic investing can make you the windshield most of the time. Let others risk becoming bugs by seeking the highest returns, following the latest fads, or ignoring the risks in their portfolios.

Your Retirement Investment Strategy

There's no universal right way to manage a portfolio for those in or near retirement. Factors that determine the best strategy for you depend on your interest and knowledge of investments, the amount of time you want to spend on your investments, and your goals and risk tolerance. Some readers of my newsletter, *Retirement Watch*, use each of the main strategies. They have a core portfolio that is managed using a buy-and-hold, true diversification strategy. Some of the portfolio is invested for high income, and another part of the portfolio is invested dynamically. More details about my ideas on investing are in my book *Invest Like a Fox, Not Like a Hedgehog* (Wiley, 2007).

Investing is an area in which many people would be better off seeking help from professionals. One simple, low-cost way to have professionals help you is through mutual funds. There are mutual funds that invest dynamically, buy-and-hold, or use other strategies. You might want to own a portfolio of mutual funds that implement these strategies. You also could have a financial planner help you decide on a strategy and set up the portfolio. The planner might manage the portfolio or offer continuing advice to you. Of course, you also can work with one or more money managers. Interview a number of them to learn their strategies and to determine if you would work well with them. You could give your money to one of them or split your investment assets among several of them. Over time, you might consolidate with one of them or continue to diversify among investment professionals.

Much of the success of a retirement plan depends on achieving the income and total return goals set for your nest egg. It's important that you understand the goals you need to reach. Then, understand the different strategies available to reach those goals and select one or more strategies with which you are comfortable. Finally, implement the plan and don't hesitate to seek the help of financial professionals.

Handling the Medical Expense Wild Card

Medical expenses are among the greatest fears of retirees and preretirees. One survey found that medical expenses and long-term care expenses are more of a worry for retirees than death. Medical insurance and other ways to pay for the expenses are among the least understood (or most misunderstood) parts of retirement finance. It's not surprising.

People are living longer, and aging is associated with higher medical expenses. Also, many people live those longer lives with chronic diseases or conditions. Older Americans often regularly take prescription medications to control diseases or conditions such as high blood pressure, diabetes, high cholesterol, heart disease, and others. There also are treatments and procedures for other conditions that once had no real treatment. These prescription drugs and treatments are doing wonderful things. Yet, someone has to pay for them.

Paying for medical care during retirement used to be simple. Most retirees had medical care covered by their former employers or labor unions. By the 1980s, 70 percent of even *early* retirees still had employer-paid health care coverage. But rapidly rising health care costs—due to longer life spans, more sophisticated medical technology, and greater use of prescription drugs—caused employers and unions to cut back on retiree health coverage. Another important factor was a change in accounting rules. The rules were changed to require companies to recognize on their books today the cost of promised future retirement medical benefits. That helped trigger moves by many companies to reduce or eliminate retiree coverage. The reductions began in the mid-1980s and accelerated through the 1990s and 2000s.

Now, very few employers offer retiree medical coverage. Those that do offer coverage are mostly the largest employers, and even they regularly reduce the coverage. Many of the employer and union plans that offer retiree medical benefits now are integrated with Medicare. Retirees are required to enroll in Medicare, and the employer or union plan covers only some care and expenses that Medicare doesn't.

It's clear that you're largely on your own when it comes to paying for retirement medical expenses. The cost has shifted from former employers to retirees. Even those who have some employer-paid retirement coverage shouldn't rest easy, because most employers can reduce or even eliminate coverage for those already retired. Courts usually uphold their rights to do so.

Yet, many people don't adequately plan for medical expenses in their retirement plans.

While surveys consistently report that Americans are concerned about retirement medical expenses, only about 12 percent take account of medical costs in their retirement planning, according to a 2015 study by Nationwide Financial. More than half admit to knowing very little about Medicare. What's remarkable is that even people who are already retired underestimate their current and future medical expenses. When asked, most underestimated their costs by about 50 percent, according to the Nationwide study. Most respondents guessed at the answer rather than making any calculations or doing research.

Medical expenses are likely to be substantial in retirement and to be a higher portion of your total spending than before retirement. On average, medical expenses rise from 5.64 percent of total spending from ages 45 to 54 to 11.88 percent from 65 to 74 and to 15.08 percent at ages 75 and older, according to the Bureau of Labor Statistics. Medical expenses are a big reason why a recent study found that many Americans when they pass away have only about $10,000 in assets. They often spend their assets on medical expenses and long-term care.

There's also great misunderstanding about Medicare, the government program to help pay medical expenses of those ages 65 and older. Many people believe Medicare will cover all or most of their retirement medical expenses. That's not the case by a large margin, which I'll discuss in more detail shortly.

You're going to have substantial out-of-pocket medical expenses in retirement. The average person covered by Medicare will pay more than $4,300, or $8,600 annually per couple, for out-of-pocket medical expenses, according to the Center for Retirement Research at Boston College. A healthy 65-year-old male will pay cumulative expenses, including premiums, of over $369,000 over the rest of his life. Since women live longer, the average woman will pay 13 percent more, or $417,000. These are only medical expenses; they don't include long-term care costs. Fidelity Investments also develops annual estimates of lifetime retirement medical spending. The Fidelity estimates are somewhat lower than the CRR estimates. Fidelity estimated in 2015 a total of $230,000 lifetime expenses for a 65-year-old couple. Significant differences in the estimates are that Fidelity assumes each spouse lives only to average life expectancy and excludes costs such as over-the-counter medicines and dental care. CRR assumes different life expectancies and has a more comprehensive definition of medical spending.

Remember, in addition to being estimates, these numbers are only the averages. About half the people will spend more, and some will spend substantially more.

Let's look at how you can reduce the uncertainty of your out-of-pocket retirement medical expenses and plan to have them paid. We'll focus on Medicare. Despite its gaps and shortcomings, for U.S. retirees Medicare is the main source of retirement medical insurance.

Some Medicare Basics

More than half of Americans age 40 and older responding to surveys admit to knowing very little about Medicare. That's about the only question about Medicare in the surveys they answer correctly. In fact, many answer even that question wrong, because far more than half of Americans know very little about Medicare. So, those who didn't admit to knowing very little about Medicare were wrong.

Here are some basic facts about Medicare, many of which are surprising to a number of people.

There are several different parts to Medicare.

Part A covers hospital expenses, and most people pay no premiums for it. Part B, also known as traditional Medicare, covers doctors' care and basic medical care, and you pay premiums, which are discussed in more detail later in this chapter. When you are enrolled in traditional Medicare, you also can sign up and pay a premium for a supplemental policy, or Medigap policy. Those policies are issued by private insurers under rules governed by Medicare. The supplemental policies pay some of the deductibles and copayments of Part B and also cover some care that Medicare doesn't. When you're in traditional Medicare, you also can sign up for a Part D plan that will cover some prescription drugs not covered by Parts A and B.

An alternative to Part B traditional Medicare is a Medicare Advantage Plan (Part C). These plans combine elements of Part B and Part D. They often provide a comprehensive care package like an HMO or similar organization, because your basic medical services and prescription drugs are covered by the same package. These have become popular in recent years, enrolling about a third of Medicare beneficiaries. It's not legal to sell you a Medicare supplemental policy or a Part D prescription drug policy when you are enrolled in Medicare Advantage.

Most vision and dental care isn't covered by any part of Medicare, and there are other coverage gaps. You have to pay out-of-pocket for any care that isn't covered by Medicare. For some treatments, such as medical devices, Medicare might not pay for the quality or features you prefer. You have to pay for the difference between the treatment or service Medicare will cover and the one you prefer.

Most of Medicare isn't free. Premiums are required of those who are covered by Part B. Medicare Part B premiums are set each year to cover 25 percent of the estimated costs of the program for the coming year. That means many years they increase faster than the Consumer Price Index, though that isn't always the case. In 2014 and 2015, the premiums held steady but in 2016 they increased substantially.

Most Medicare beneficiaries have the Part B premiums deducted from their Social Security retirement benefits. Medicare premiums are taking a bigger share of Social Security benefits, because Medicare premiums generally increase at a faster rate than Social Security benefits. In 2012, Medicare Part B premiums took 8.2 percent of the average Social Security benefit; in 2000, the premiums took only 5.1 percent of benefits. From 2001 to 2012, average Social Security benefits rose 31 percent while Part B premiums doubled.

There is a protective clause in the law, often known as a *stop-loss provision*. Once you are a Medicare beneficiary and having the premiums deducted from your Social Security benefits, the premiums can't increase by a greater amount than your benefits increase. That means an increase in premiums can't cause your net Social Security benefits to decline. In years when the Social Security COLA is low, the 70 percent or so of Medicare beneficiaries who have their premiums deducted from their Social Security benefits won't share in the full cost increase of Medicare. Instead, the other 30 percent of beneficiaries will have more than a pro rata premium increase to ensure that total premiums pay for 25 percent of Medicare's estimated cost.

Since 2007, higher-income taxpayers have paid a Medicare surtax. This technically isn't a higher Part B premium, though it effectively is. The surtax rises as income rises. Means-testing of this type probably will be a bigger part of the program in coming years. The Medicare surtax was increased for some taxpayers in a 2015 law, with the higher surtax effective in 2017. We'll discuss the surtax in more detail later in this chapter.

In addition to the premiums, you pay deductibles and co-payments for most covered care.

There are many types of care that either aren't covered by Medicare or that have limited coverage.

Changes from the Affordable Care Act of 2010

The Affordable Care Act (ACA) of 2010 (also known as Obamacare) made some changes in Medicare, though the effects aren't fully clear yet.

Insurers were scheduled to be reimbursed less for Medicare Advantage plans than in the past. As a result, members began paying higher premiums, deductibles, and copayments, or receiving fewer benefits, or a combination of both. So far, the lower reimbursements weren't as great as initially forecast, so the effects on beneficiaries haven't been as significant as anticipated. The popularity of the Advantage plans continued to increase.

The ACA attempted to slow the growth in medical care costs by limiting the annual increases in payments to doctors, hospitals, and other providers. But Congress historically didn't let such limits stick, and in 2015 it passed legislation that ended the payment reductions and set a long-term schedule of payment increases.

The Part D prescription drug plans originally had a coverage gap or "doughnut hole." Once a policyholders' annual medical spending exceeded a certain amount, the policyholder had to pay 100 percent of additional prescription drug costs until the total prescription spending for the calendar year exceeded a certain amount. Under the ACA, reductions in the coverage gap are phased in until the gap is eliminated by 2020.

Also, beginning in 2012, Part D members in the doughnut hole pay only 50 percent of the cost for brand-name drugs and 86 percent of generic drug costs. By 2020, they'll pay only 25 percent for both types of drugs after reaching the deductible for their policies.

Most preventive care and screening was included in basic coverage under Medicare beginning in 2011. The usual deductibles and 20 percent coinsurance don't apply to these types of care.

The Limits of Medicare

Traditional Medicare beneficiaries pay on average $4,000 to $9,000 annually out of their own pockets for medical expenses each year, depending on whose estimates are used. The out-of-pocket costs are because of the premiums, deductibles, and coverage limits of Medicare. When Medicare covers a medical expense, in most cases you pay 20 percent of the cost, regardless of how high the cost is. We discuss the limits of traditional Medicare later in this chapter. As mentioned, some people buy a Medigap or Medicare supplement policy to help pay for these limits.

Medicare over the years aggressively reduced its costs by reducing payments to doctors, hospitals, and other providers. As a result, a significant percentage of doctors refuse to take new Medicare patients. The American Academy of Family Physicians reported in 2012 that 19 percent of family doctors are not taking new Medicare patients. Older Americans frequently have complained about difficulty in finding doctors and having to wait longer than other patients for nonemergency care. Those problems are bound to increase, especially for those living in rural areas.

This chapter isn't going to tell you everything about Medicare. You will learn, however, how to incorporate Medicare and other options in your retirement plan, maximize your benefits, and, most importantly, make medical expenses less of a wild card than they are for most people.

You'll learn how to project medical spending in retirement with reasonable accuracy. You'll also know when to sign up for basic Medicare and the other policies. You'll also learn how to evaluate the different choices for Medicare supplement policies and Part D prescription drug coverage. I'll also show you how to deal with some other sticky issues related to retirement medical expenses.

Enrolling in Medicare

Many people unnecessarily increase their retirement medical expenses right from the start. They don't enroll in Medicare or buy the related insurance policies on time, and that results in higher premiums for life. Even if you don't need or want the coverage, there's a time in life when you have to enroll in Medicare or take the risk that when you do enroll you'll pay a premium penalty every year the rest of your life. The rules can be tricky, causing some people to believe they are entitled to a later enrollment deadline when they aren't.

Most people don't have to worry about Part A. You're automatically enrolled when you're eligible, and there are no premiums. If you're among the few who doesn't qualify for premium-free Part A and want to enroll and pay the premiums, your enrollment deadline is the same as for Part B.

The general rule is that you enroll in Medicare Part B within the seven-month period that begins three months before your 65th birthday and ends three months after that birthday. If you're already receiving Social Security retirement benefits before your 65th birthday, you automatically will be enrolled in Medicare Part B or C. When you aren't receiving Social Security before 65, you still are required to enroll in Medicare Part B or C within that initial enrollment period.

If you're interested in Part C (Medicare Advantage), you have to enroll in Part B first. So, the deadline for Medicare Advantage is the same as for Part B.

It doesn't matter whether you are beginning Social Security retirement benefits. In most cases if you don't sign up for Medicare during this time, when you do sign up for it you'll pay a penalty of higher premiums for the rest of your life.

Of course, there are exceptions to the general rule.

There's a no-penalty extension of the Medicare enrollment deadline when you are covered by a qualified medical expense plan during the initial enrollment period. This is an area where people often receive wrong information, so proceed carefully. Qualified coverage means a group plan through your employer (or former employer if you have retirement medical benefits), and the employer has 20 or more employees. That means if you work for (or are retired from) an employer with 19 or fewer employees or are self-employed, any medical insurance doesn't qualify for the extension no matter how good the coverage is. You need to enroll in Medicare during the standard enrollment period to avoid penalties later in life.

Again, you need to be careful with this exception. Some people believe they don't have to sign up for Medicare during the initial enrollment period because they have coverage through the group plan of an employer with 20 or more employees. But many group plans say that once a covered person turns 65, his or her primary insurer is Medicare. The group plan will pay only for care that Medicare doesn't cover. People in this situation probably don't have to enroll in Medicare during the initial enrollment period to avoid the premium penalty. But they could face a higher financial penalty. When they don't enroll in Medicare at 65, they are responsible for all the expenses Medicare would have covered. The employer plan won't cover those expenses. Read your employer plan closely. If it designates Medicare as the primary insurer, you could be responsible for anything Medicare would have covered.

Once you leave an employer or otherwise lose qualified employer coverage after age 65, you have eight months to sign up for Medicare and avoid late enrollment penalties. Here's another trap. When you retire from or otherwise leave an employer, you're entitled to pay for the employer coverage out of your own resources for another 18 months through COBRA. But, while COBRA extends your access to the employer plan, it doesn't extend your special Medicare enrollment period. You no longer are considered to be covered by a qualified employer plan. Instead, you are considered to own an individual policy. You have eight months after leaving the employer to sign up for Medicare and avoid premium penalties, not the 18-month COBRA extension period.

Because of the nuances of the penalty for signing up late for Medicare, verify all the facts before concluding that you have an extension of the Medicare enrollment deadline. Long before your 65th birthday, ask the administrator of an employer group plan in which you are enrolled if the plan is a qualified group plan for purposes of extending the Medicare enrollment deadline. Most plans will send enrollees a letter before their 65th birthday stating whether theirs is a qualified plan for this purpose.

When you miss the initial enrollment period for Medicare, you can sign up only during the general enrollment period from January 1 to March 31 each year. The coverage won't take effect until July 1 of that year.

The penalty for failing to sign up for Medicare on time can be steep. For the rest of your life, the monthly Part B premium is increased 10 percent for each full 12-month period that you could have been enrolled in Part B but weren't.

The enrollment rules for Part D are very similar. The initial enrollment period is the same as for Part B. You also receive a penalty-free extension of the enrollment period if you had "creditable coverage" at the time. Creditable coverage is prescription drug coverage that is on par with a Part D plan. Again, you need to ask your plan administrator if you have creditable coverage. If not, then you don't have an extension of the initial enrollment period. When you had creditable coverage and then lose it, you can enroll in a Part D plan without penalty for two full months after the month in which you lose creditable coverage or were notified of the loss of coverage, whichever is later.

When you miss the initial enrollment period and didn't have creditable coverage, you can sign up for Part D plan during the annual open enrollment period from October 15 to December 7.

The penalty for late enrollment in Part D is more complicated than for Part B and difficult to estimate. The penalty is imposed when after your initial enrollment period there was a period of 63 or more consecutive days when you didn't have Part D or creditable coverage. The penalty is 1 percent of the "national base beneficiary premium" for Part D plans for each full month you delayed enrollment. The national base beneficiary premium changes annually but was $33.13 for 2015.

Suppose Max Profits was without a Part D plan or creditable coverage for 31 months after his initial enrollment period ended and enrolled in Part D in 2015. His penalty is 31 percent of $33.13, or $10.27. This is the penalty Max will pay each month in 2015 as long as he has Part D coverage. The penalty is recalculated each year based on the current national base beneficiary premium and will be imposed on Max each month for the rest of his life as long as he has Part D coverage.

Many people reach age 65 thinking they won't buy a Part D policy because they don't take many prescription drugs yet and don't see a point in paying the premiums. The cost of taking this approach and later needing prescription drug coverage can be steep. A better move is to enroll in Part D when first eligible and purchase the lowest cost policy available to you. Later if you need better coverage, you can switch to a different policy. But keep in mind that you can change policies only during the annual enrollment period, so you'll still go through a period when you believe you need broader coverage but have to wait before purchasing it. You also might have to pay a higher initial premium than you would have if you had enrolled in that plan when you first were eligible, because you're older and the cost of policies in general probably will increase.

Purchasing Medicare supplement or Medigap policies is a bit different from enrolling in Part B and purchasing a Part D policy. The initial enrollment period for Medigap policies is the six months that begin on the first day of the month in which you're both 65 or older and enrolled in Part B. Medigap policies are issued by private insurers under guidelines determined by Medicare. The insurers set their own premiums.

Medicare doesn't impose a financial penalty for purchasing a Medigap policy late. But during the initial enrollment period you're guaranteed to be issued a policy. The insurers who choose to offer Medigap policies can't refuse to issue a policy for health reasons during this period. If you wait to buy a policy after the initial enrollment period, however, the insurer can decline to issue a policy for health or other reasons or can charge you a higher premium. So, you might find that you are unable to buy a policy when you don't take advantage of the initial enrollment period.

Part B Premiums

In Part B, you pay a monthly premium. Remember, if you choose Part C you first have to join Part B. So, you'll still pay the Part B premium, though it might be paid directly to the insurer.

The Part B premiums are calculated so that the total premiums paid during the year are estimated to cover 25 percent of the government's actual costs of Part B. Each fall, the government calculates the premiums to be paid beginning January 1 of the following year. It issues a public notice and also notifies beneficiaries.

Since 2007, Medicare has become more of a means-tested program. Higher-income beneficiaries pay higher premiums than others. The higher premiums are called a surtax and technically aren't premiums or part of the premiums. When first enacted, the premium surtax was set to gradually increase over several years. In 2015, a new law was enacted that increased the surtax for certain income levels. That surtax schedule will take effect in 2019.

The surtax is based on your modified adjusted gross income (MAGI) from two years earlier. Your adjusted gross income is the last line on the front page of Form 1040, Federal Income Tax Return. This becomes MAGI by adding any tax-exempt interest, EE savings bond interest used for education expenses, and excluded foreign earned income for the year. If you're eligible for Part B in 2017, your 2015 MAGI will determine your 2017 surtax.

The surtax begins with MAGI of $85,000 for single taxpayers and $170,000 for married taxpayers filing jointly. The surtax increases as income rises with the individual paying a higher percentage of the

TABLE 6.1   Who Paid Higher Premiums in 2016?

Premium You Pay	% of Cost You Pay	If Your Modified Adjusted Gross Income Is:	
		Single	Married Couples
$121.80	35%	$85,000 or less	$170,000 or less
$170.50	50%	$85,001–$107,000	$170,001–$214,000
$243.60	65%	$107,001–$160,000	$214,001–$320,000
$316.70	75%	$160,001–$214,000	$320,001–$468,000
$389.80	80%	Above $214,000	Above $428,000

estimated costs at higher incomes. Instead of the standard 25 percent of costs, the percentage rises in the different brackets from 35 percent to 50 percent, 65 percent and ultimately 80 percent in the top bracket. The 2015 law changed the tables so that the 65 percent and 80 percent brackets are reached at lower incomes.

Table 6.1 shows the brackets and premiums for 2016.

Beginning in 2019, single beneficiaries with MAGI higher than $133,500 (marrieds filing jointly with MAGI higher than $267,000) will begin paying 65 percent of estimated costs through their premiums. Those earning $160,000 to $214,000 per year ($320,000 to $428,000 for couples) currently pay 65 percent of their costs through premiums but beginning in 2019 will pay 75 percent.

There's a two-year lag between when income is earned and when you pay the premium surtax. The process is that first your return is received by the Internal Revenue Service. Your 2016 income tax return, for example, is received in early 2017. The IRS processes the return and sends the data to the Social Security Administration. The SSA processes that data, calculates your premium, and sends you a letter with the results. For example, the 2016 tax returns will be used to determine 2018 premiums. The SSA will receive the data from the IRS during 2017 and send letters to beneficiaries by mid-November 2017, notifying them of the premiums to be effect January 1, 2018.

Reducing the Premium Surtax

You can reduce the premium surtax by considering it in your tax and financial planning, though you have to plan a couple years in advance. You'd have to be aware of the potential for the surtax to hit you in 2018 when planning your 2016 income.

Since the premium surtax is determined by your MAGI, the best-known traditional income tax deductions won't reduce the surtax. Mortgage interest, charitable contribution deductions, real estate taxes, and other itemized deductions on Schedule A of the income tax return have no effect on the premium surtax. Only the items on the front page of Form 1040 affect MAGI and therefore the surtax.

In addition, some traditional tax planning strategies also won't reduce the surtax, because some forms of income that are excluded under the regular income tax are added when calculating MAGI for the surtax. That means you won't reduce MAGI by turning taxable bond interest into tax-exempt bond interest. You also won't benefit from the foreign earned-income exclusion or from EE savings bond interest that is used for education purposes.

There are other actions that will limit income and also limit MAGI.

You can limit withdrawals from retirement plans and annuities that would be included in gross income. Avoid taking distributions from traditional IRAs, retirement plans, and annuities that exceed your spending needs. Instead, consider taking withdrawals from Roth IRAs or from other accounts.

Another strategy is to manage your capital gains. Avoid selling assets and recognizing capital gains unless there are strong investment reasons to do so or you need the money. Look for assets that have declined in value that can be sold to offset capital gains or other income.

Losses from businesses, partnerships, and the like that pass through to your individual tax return also can be helpful in avoiding the Medicare premium surtax. These will be subtracted from sources of income to determine adjusted gross income.

You don't want the premium surtax to be the main focus of your tax and financial planning. It is one factor to be considered when making decisions about your finances. A strategy that might not seem viable or sensible when considering only federal income taxes might become viable when the premium surtax and other stealth taxes are considered.

When Your Life Changed

Two years elapse between when your MAGI is determined and when the premium surtax is imposed. Events can occur in those two years that change your financial position. The law recognizes this and provides an opportunity for you to appeal the premium surtax. The details of the appeal process should be described with the letter that notifies you what your premium will be.

The SSA will view an appeal favorably when one of the following changes occurred between the time the income was earned and the year the premium surtax is due:

- Divorce
- A spouse's death

- Job loss
- Reduced working hours
- Retirement
- Bankruptcy

When your appeal is granted, you can submit updated financial information and have that used as the basis for determining your premium and any surtax. That means one of these events won't automatically eliminate or reduce the surtax for you. Instead, you have the opportunity to show that one or more events changed your financial situation enough to justify eliminating or reducing the surtax for that year.

Traditional Medicare versus Medicare Advantage

The initial decision is whether to enroll in traditional Medicare, also known as Part B, or Medicare Advantage, also known as Part C. About two-thirds of beneficiaries choose traditional Medicare, though that is down from about 80 percent not too many years ago. Medicare Advantage has been gaining in popularity. This book isn't going to delve into the details of what is and isn't covered in traditional Medicare. That changes almost annually, and you can find the details on the Medicare website or by asking for the free book, *Medicare and You*. With the Medicare Advantage plans, the details of the coverage vary by the plan. I will discuss how to compare the options and decide which is best for you.

Coordinated versus Traditional Care

Medicare Advantage is similar to a health maintenance organization (HMO) and related providers in that all or most of your care is delivered under one umbrella. When you go the traditional Medicare route, you'll select your own primary care physician and any specialists and decide when to make office visits or receive other care. You'll also have to consider buying a Medicare supplement policy and a Part D prescription drug policy. (We discuss details of those policies later in this chapter.)

In a Medicare Advantage plan, all the doctors and specialists are likely to be in the same organization. Care is likely to be coordinated. Many of the plans also are proactive, suggesting when an office visit or other care is needed. Plan employees also might follow up to ensure you are responding as expected or following the doctors' recommendations. An Advantage plan also is likely to have your records together instead of your having to ensure each doctor has access to your complete history.

Also, prescription drug coverage and some of the features of many Medigap policies are part of Medicare Advantage plans. The idea behind Advantage plans is that Medicare reimburses the insurer or plan sponsor more per person than under a fee-for-service plan. The Advantage plan then provides a wider range of services and coordinates care with the expectation of achieving better outcomes than the fee-for-service model. By choosing an Advantage plan, you make one decision instead of three or more (Part B plus Part D and Medigap policies).

Factors in Choosing Between Part B and Part C

When making the choice between Part B and Part C, there are a number of factors to consider. Keep in mind, this is not a lifetime decision. There are opportunities at least annually to switch between Parts B and C or to change from one Part C plan to another. Even if you like your current care and plan, it is a good idea after age 65 to become familiar with the alternatives in your area every year or two. The plans available and their terms change over time and have changed quite a bit in recent years. You might find there is a better alternative even when you like your current arrangement.

Here are some key questions to ask when evaluating your choices.

Do You Have a Choice of Doctors?   Many people are attracted to traditional Medicare because they are allowed to choose their doctors and specialists and when to visit them. The patients aren't given a limited list of professionals from which to choose. They also don't have to go through a gatekeeper or receive permission to see a specialist. Traditional Medicare is fee-for-service. You receive the medical care you want, and Medicare pays for whatever is covered. In an Advantage plan, you have to choose from among the providers selected by the plan if you want the care fully covered. Advance approval from your primary physicians or someone else usually is required to see a specialist or receive treatment if you want the services covered (though there is an appeal process).

Which Doctors Belong to the Plan?   When you're considering an Advantage plan, you can check the list of doctors and specialists in advance. You also might want to check with the offices of any doctors you like so verify if they are covered by the plan. Often, a physician's office will be able to say if the doctor is thinking of adding or dropping participation in some plans.

Which Prescription Drugs Are Covered?   When you look at an Advantage plan, examine the prescription drug coverage in the same way you would for a Part D plan (which we discuss later in this chapter). If you're taking medications regularly, see if they are covered under the plan. Some plans require generic drugs except under certain circumstances. The plan also might limit the choice of drugs when more than one is available for a condition.

What Other Services Are Covered?   Some people want vision, dental, and mental health in one plan. For others, this isn't important. These types of care generally aren't covered under traditional Medicare but might be under an Advantage plan.

What Preventive Care Is Covered?   This is less of an issue since the Affordable Care Act required plans to offer basic preventive tests and services without additional charge and required some consistency between Part B and Medicare Advantage on the issue. Beyond that, however, you might want to see if an Advantage plan limits coverage for other preventive tests. Some plans won't pay for tests unless there are symptoms or a doctor's order. Others cover preventive tests only on a schedule based on age and health history. Ask about any limits on coverage for annual exams and preventive testing and compare that with traditional Medicare if that's important to you.

Is There a Wellness or Disease Management Program?   There usually is with a Medicare Advantage plan. In traditional Medicare, there usually isn't, although it can depend on your choice of doctor. Patients who have or are at risk for chronic diseases might control their conditions better and improve overall health by participating in programs designed to educate them and closely follow their conditions.

What Are the Typical Annual Costs Likely to Be?   Premiums, copayments, deductibles, prescription costs, and other expenses add up. Draw up a schedule of likely medical care during a typical year for you, assuming no new conditions or problems. See how much that would cost under the options being considered.

What Is the Worst-Case Cost?   Select some possible major medical problems and try to estimate what your out-of-pocket cost would be under the different choices.

A Little-Known Medicare Advantage Plan

When you turn 65 or otherwise enroll in Medicare, see if a Medicare Savings Account (MSA) is available in your area. These are similar to Health Savings Accounts, but they are a little different. MSAs are linked to high-deductible Medicare Advantage plans. You would sign up for a high-deductible Medicare Advantage plan and also open the MSA affiliated with the plan. Medicare gives money to the plan each year, and the plan deposits some of that money into your MSA each year. You don't make any deposits in the MSA, and aren't allowed to.

You then can choose to draw money from the MSA to pay for any medical expenses not covered by the Medicare plan or to meet deductibles.

When you use money from the MSA to pay for part of a deductible, it is treated just as if you paid the deductible with your own money. If you don't incur enough deductibles or noncovered expenses to draw down the balance, or choose to pay those costs from other sources, then the MSA balance is rolled over to the next year and you still will receive the next year's deposit. This means you can allow the MSA to compound for years until you really need to draw down the account.

MSAs aren't widely available. There isn't an option in some areas, and in other areas there are only one or a small number of options. The MSA probably isn't a good enough benefit that it should dictate your choice of Medicare plans. But you need to understand what they are so you can decide on the best plan for you.

Shopping for Medicare Supplement Plans

The limits of Medicare coverage are a surprise to many retirees. Some learn the lesson during their preretirement planning. Others don't find out until they incur medical expenses in retirement.

Medicare covers only about half the medical expenses incurred by retirees, according to studies over the years. The specifics vary for each beneficiary, of course. Some people incur far more uncovered expenses than others.

For example, Medicare doesn't cover many types of medical care (dental, vision, most prescription drugs, and some other treatments). It also has limited coverage of some types of care. Most importantly, there's a 20 percent deductible on almost all covered care. So, if you incur a major medical expense, you might have to pay 20 percent of the cost with no limit.

You need a plan to pay the medical care that isn't covered by Medicare. You could plan to pay the uncovered expenses out of pocket and build flexibility to pay those expenses in your saving and spending plans. But that route results in a lot of uncertainty. You can't forecast the amount and timing of the medical expenses you'll incur. You need a big cushion and a lot of flexibility in your retirement plan to choose this route.

Another choice is to join a Part C or Medicare Advantage plan. These plans generally cover more than traditional Medicare. The exact coverage depends on the plan, so check plan documents carefully.

For those who belong to traditional Medicare Parts A and B, the best way to control medical expense uncertainty is to purchase a Medicare Supplement, or Medigap, insurance policy. (You aren't allowed to buy a Medigap policy if you're in Medicare Advantage.) You pay premiums for the policy, which will increase your fixed annual expenses. But the policy will increase coverage and create more certainty about your maximum exposure for medical expense. It's an important protection for those concerned about the uncertainty of retirement expenses or the potential for large, unexpected medical expenses drain their estates.

The first and best time to buy a Medigap policy is your initial open enrollment period, as discussed earlier in this chapter. This is a six-month period that begins the month you turn 65 and are enrolled in Part B. During this period, you can purchase any policy offered in your area and can't be declined or charged a higher premium for health reasons. Once you purchase a policy during this period, the insurer can't cancel your policy as long as you pay the premiums.

After that, you can buy or change a Medigap policy at any time, but the insurer can decline to issue a policy for health reasons or delay coverage of preexisting conditions for up to six months. (Even if the Medigap policy excludes coverage for a preexisting condition, traditional Medicare still will cover its share of the costs of the preexisting condition.) Or you can be charged a higher premium because of your age or health.

Also, as we discussed earlier in this chapter, if you buy a Medigap policy for the first time after your initial open enrollment period, in most cases you'll incur a penalty that results in higher premiums for the rest of your life. The exceptions apply to those who had other types of coverage, such as Medicare Advantage or an appropriate employer plan, during their initial open enrollment periods.

The Medicare Supplement policies are standardized by the federal government. Gone are the days when older people were sold numerous policies with overlapping coverage or few benefits. The types of policies and the benefits that can be offered under each type are standardized. Insurers aren't allowed to sell you duplicative coverage, and that's why Medicare Advantage members aren't allowed to buy Medigap policies. Table 6.2 summarizes the coverage of the different plans that are authorized. Examine the table to determine the plan or plans you want to consider.

Traditionally the advice to maximize your coverage has been to consider Plans F and G. These plans cover most deductibles and copayments under traditional Medicare Parts A and B. They also cover medical care while traveling outside the U.S. and some other costs. The main difference is Plan G doesn't cover the Part B deductible while Plan F does, which means Plan F provides "first dollar" coverage. Another difference is that Plan G isn't guaranteed issue, so the plans don't have to accept less healthy applicants. That allows insurers to make Plan G premiums a little lower and more stable than Plan F as a general rule.

Unfortunately, a law enacted in 2015 requires Plan F to be eliminated by 2020. Congress didn't like the first dollar coverage, believing that it leads to overuse of medical care and higher overall prices. The elimination of Plan F isn't required until 2020, and policies already issued can remain in force beyond 2020. It is likely, however, that the law will cause premiums on those Part F policies to rise substantially over time. That's because

TABLE 6.2   Coverage of Authorized Plans

Coverage Category	Medigap Plan Type									
	A	B	C	D	F*	G	K	L	M	N
Part A coinsurance and hospital costs up to an additional 365 days after Medicare benefits are used up	✓	✓	✓	✓	✓	✓	✓	✓	✓	✓
Part B coinsurance or copayment	✓	✓	✓	✓	✓	✓	50%	75%	✓	✓***
Blood (first 3 pints)	✓	✓	✓	✓	✓	✓	50%	75%	✓	✓
Part A hospice care coinsurance or copayment	✓	✓	✓	✓	✓	✓	50%	75%	✓	✓
Skilled nursing facility care coinsurance			✓	✓	✓	✓	50%	75%	✓	✓
Part A deductible		✓	✓	✓	✓	✓	50%	75%	50%	✓
Part B deductible			✓		✓					
Part B excess charges					✓	✓				
Foreign travel exchange (up to plan limits)			✓	✓	✓	✓			✓	✓
Out-of-pocket limit**							$4,800	$2,400		

*Plan F also offers a high-deductible plan. If you choose this option, this means you must pay for Medicare-covered costs up to the deductible amount of $2,110 (in 2013) before your Medigap plan pays anything.

**After you meet your out-of-pocket yearly limit and your yearly Part B deductible, the Medigap plan pays 100% of covered services for the rest of the calendar year.

***Plan N pays 100% of the Part B coinsurance, except for a copayment of up to $20 for some office visits and up to a $50 copayment for emergency room visits that don't result in inpatient admission.

there won't be a stream of younger and healthier policy holders joining the premium pool. The policies will be held only by older and sicker people, requiring premium increases each year.

Because of the change in the law, Plan G now is the better choice for those who want the broadest Medigap coverage. Existing Plan F owners should consider switching to Plan G if they can to avoid the potential for substantial future premium increases.

The other plans offer less coverage and vary in the coverage they exclude. Less coverage should result in lower premiums than for a Plan F or G policy. As with other types of insurance, you're transferring risk and uncertainty to the insurer in return for higher premiums. Your fixed annual costs from using Plans F or G are higher, but your potential total costs are more fixed and certain, and are much lower if you turn out to need a lot of medical care.

Once you've determined the type of policy you want to consider, take the time to shop around for a policy. Many people are overpaying for Medigap policies by as much as 100 percent because they don't shop around, according to a study by CSG Actuarial. Because the federal government standardizes the policies, the coverage is the same between insurers for each plan type. The differences are in premiums, customer service, and factors such as speed of reimbursements. Some insurers have different expense levels or make different assumptions about the costs they'll incur. Others assume people won't shop around. The important point is that premiums vary considerably for the same type of policy in the same area.

Shopping for Medigap can be fairly easy. You can see summaries and details of all the policies offered in your area on the Medicare website at www.medicare.gov or you can talk through the choices with someone at Medicare by calling 1-800-MEDICARE. Your local Area Office on Aging or other local government agencies or nonprofits might offer assistance, and there are financial planners who also assist in evaluating policies.

Don't buy a policy because it seems to be the best-seller in your area or everyone seems to have it. It might be the best policy, or perhaps the insurer is good at marketing or offers above-average commissions to agents.

Don't automatically select the policy with the lowest initial premium. Some insurers offer low premiums because they are relatively new to the business or are trying to increase market share. Others might simply make poor estimates of their likely revenues and expenses. These types of insurers are likely to increase premiums substantially over time.

You want a financially sound insurer that's issued Medigap policies for a long time. If you really want to do the research and dig into the details, look for an insurer with average-to-low-costs compared to the industry and that pays reasonable but not high commissions to agents.

Another sign that high premium increases are likely down the road is the insurer offers guaranteed-issue policies outside the initial open enrollment period. Guaranteed-issue means a policy will be issued regardless of age or health and everyone the same age is charged the same rate. Such insurers are likely to attract people with health problems.

Another important detail is whether the insurer uses the "attained age" or "issue age" method to determine future premiums. An attained-age insurer bases premiums on the policyholder's age and steadily increases premiums as a person ages. An issue-age insurer bases future increases on the insurer's expenses and overall health costs, not the age of the insured. As a general rule, attained-age policies tend to have lower initial costs but over time are subject to higher increases. Over time with all other things the same, an issue-age policy is likely to cost less and have less volatile premiums.

After purchasing a Medigap policy, even if you shopped carefully when purchasing it and are happy, you should shop around regularly if you're in good enough health to be insurable. Insurers increase premiums by different amounts each year and for different reasons. Your insurer might have incurred more claims than expected or had other expenses increase, to give two examples of events that might cause premiums to rise. A policy that was competitive when you purchased it might not be after a few years. Check the Medicare website to see if there's something better. Don't cancel your existing policy until you've been approved for a new policy and know the premium.

Examining Part D Prescription Drug Plans

Traditional Medicare Part B has very limited coverage of prescription drugs. Generally, only medicine related to a surgery or similar treatment is covered. The prescription medications that many people take on a regular basis aren't covered. Part D was created to provide a prescription drug coverage option for traditional Medicare beneficiaries. The plans have been around only since 2008, but they've been very popular with beneficiaries.

One constant about Part D so far is change. Premiums, other costs (such as deductible and copayments), and coverage all change as insurers gain experience and drug costs and availability change. In some years, average premiums increase substantially, while other years they are fairly stable from year to year. Beneath the averages, there often are plans with major changes in premiums and policy terms from one year to the next.

Part D prescription drug plans are offered by private insurers under guidelines established by the Centers for Medicare and Medicaid Services. The CMS sets the guidelines, reviews proposals from insurers, and decides which plans are approved to be offered. There are several national plans available. Generally, however, an insurer decides in which localities to make a plan available and the premium to charge in each locality. Almost all areas of the country now have low premium, limited coverage plans available. Some populous areas have dozens of plans available, while less populated areas might have only a few plans from which to choose. Details of all the plans are available on the Medicare website or by calling 1-800-MEDICARE and talking with a representative.

Before choosing a Part D plan, consider enrolling in a Medicare Advantage plan. As discussed earlier in this chapter, they combine the hospital care of Part A, doctor's services under part B, and other coverage, such as prescription drugs and dental and vision care. These plans have been rising in popularity, and about one third of those who receive prescription drug coverage under Medicare receive it through Advantage plans.

One goal of many seniors is increasing certainty in their medical expenses. Part D plans increase certainty of prescription drug costs, and Medicare Advantage plans increase certainty of overall medical costs. Consider all your medical coverage together instead of looking only at Part D plans.

Don't ignore Part D policies simply because you aren't taking many prescription drugs around age 65. Remember that there's a penalty if you don't sign up for a policy during the initial enrollment period. You'll pay higher premiums for the rest of your life if you first sign up for a policy after the initial enrollment period, and the longer you delay signing up the higher the penalty is. A better strategy if you don't need much coverage now is to enroll in the lowest-cost policy available to you. Later, if you decide you need more robust coverage you'll have the option of changing policies during the annual open enrollment period. But keep in mind you can switch only during the open enrollment period. So, if your need for broader coverage arises between enrollment periods, you'll bear more of the cost of prescription medicines until you can enroll in a new policy.

Factors to Consider

There are several key factors to consider when reviewing prescription drug plans.

There is an annual deductible, which varies by the plan. The deductible is the amount that you must pay each year for prescription medicine before the Part D policy will pay any costs. Medicare doesn't allow the annual deductible to be more than $360 in 2016, and the amount is adjusted for inflation each year. Some plans don't have a deductible.

Each plan also has copayments or coinsurance. This is the amount you pay on each prescription after you've paid the annual deductible. A copayment is a dollar amount, such as $10 per prescription. Coinsurance is when you pay a percentage of each prescription's cost, such as 25 percent. The copayments and coinsurance usually are based on your receiving only a one-month supply per prescription. Each policy has its own copayments or coinsurance. Some policies will have different amounts for different types of drugs, often known as tiers. The most common tiers are generic drugs and prescription drugs. Often a policy will have a lower copayment or coinsurance for generic drugs than for brand name drugs to encourage policyholders to prefer generic drugs.

You also should study how the policy treats the coverage gap, also known as the doughnut hole. Once you spend a certain amount on prescription drugs for the year, the policy coverage is reduced during the coverage gap. In 2016, the coverage gap begins after you spend

$3,310 on covered drugs. The coverage gap floor changes with inflation each year. In the coverage gap you pay 45 percent of the plan's cost for a brand-name drug, though 95 percent of the price will count as out-of-pocket costs. In the coverage gap you pay only 65 percent of the plan's price for generic drugs, and that will slide down to 25 percent by 2020. But for generic drugs only the amount you actually pay counts as an out-of-pocket cost. You are out of the coverage gap and back to regular policy terms when your total spending for prescription drugs exceeds the upper limit of the coverage gap. The upper limit is $4,850 in 2016.

Once your spending exceeds the upper limit of the coverage gap, you now have catastrophic coverage. Under catastrophic coverage you pay only 5 percent of most prescription drugs for the rest of the calendar year.

Not all Part D plans treat the coverage gap in the same way. Some plans will provide some coverage during the coverage gap.

One way to deal with the gap is to always use your Medicare card when paying for drugs. This likely will get you a lower price than without the card. Another strategy is to use generic drugs or less-expensive brand-name drugs whenever possible. Mail-order pharmacies and low-cost pharmacies also might help control costs. Many pharmaceutical companies offer price breaks for those with lower incomes, and the states also have assistance programs for those with lower incomes. Additional information about the pharmaceutical and state programs is on the website at www.medicare.gov.

Another key feature of a drug plan is the formulary. The formulary is the list of medicines covered by a plan. Don't assume that because you are buying a "prescription drug plan" that it covers all prescription drugs. Each policy has its own formulary, and the differences in formularies can make a big difference in your out-of-pocket costs.

New or experimental drugs often are not covered. Also, coverage might not be available when an approved drug is prescribed for an *off-label* use.

More importantly, a plan might limit the drugs covered for specific treatments. If a generic drug is available, you might be required to at least try it before a brand name is covered. When more than one brand-name drug is available, the plan might cover only one of them. Usually when a specific generic or brand-name drug is required by the plan, you are covered for an alternative only if the preferred drug is not effective for you or you have an adverse reaction. Some medicines come in different forms. For example, a drug might be available as a lotion, cream, or gel. Or it might be available as either a tablet or a capsule. Or a drug might be available in different doses. In all these cases, a plan might not cover all the options.

You can check the formulary for each plan available to you on the Medicare website at www.medicare.gov. If you already are taking drugs, you can see which plans cover them and see the details of the coverage limits. If you are not using drugs, you can review the lists for an idea of how restrictive the plans are. If personal or family history indicates you might need a certain medicine in the future, you can see how the formulary treats it.

The Medicare website lists all the plans available in your area. It also has a tool that searches for plans with certain features and another that compares plans you select. You can enter the prescription drugs you use, and the comparison feature will estimate your out-of-pocket costs for each of the plans, assuming no changes in your use. The comparison feature on the website is an important tool to use when selecting a plan.

There are a few other plan features to consider.

Some plans require authorization from the insurer before a prescription will be covered. That might require some discussion between your doctor and the insurer about the choice of medication.

If you take a prescription regularly, many plans require you to receive it through mail order and from a specific pharmacy. Some plans cover only drugs dispensed through a specific pharmacy or pharmacies.

Choosing a Policy

Once you determine the policy features you want shop around. Insurers count on people not shopping around. Studies have found that premiums for the same coverage can vary as much as 100 percent between different insurers. Use the Medicare website or the staff at 1-800-MEDICARE to compare both coverage and premiums for the policies available to you.

Don't automatically choose a popular plan. A plan might have a large enrollment because it does a lot of marketing or because a lot of low-income members were automatically enrolled in it as the lowest-cost plan. Or an insurer might be trying to increase market share with low premiums for the first year. Instead, look for plan terms that are right for you and an insurer that has experience. Then, look at the premiums.

Once you're enrolled in a plan, be prepared to reevaluate your choice each year during the annual enrollment period. The terms of Part D policies can change a lot from year to year as insurers have more experience or change their business goals. The terms of your policy might change adversely, or better options might join the market.

The Premium Surtax

Higher-income Medicare beneficiaries are subject to a premium surtax on Part D prescription drug policies just as they are on Part B premiums. The surtax officially is known as the Part D income-related monthly adjustment amount (IRMAA). The surtax kicks in at the same income levels for both parts of Medicare. Remember that there is a two-year lag between income and the surtax. Your 2014 modified adjusted gross income determines your 2016 Medicare surtax.

TABLE 6.3   Who Paid Higher Part D Premiums in 2016?

Married Filing Jointly			Singles		
When 2013 MAGI Is		2015	When 2013 MAGI Is		2015
More than	But not over	Part D Premium Addition	More than	But not Over	Part D Premium Addition
$170,000	$214,000	$12.70	$85,000	$107,000	$12.70
$214,000	$320,000	$32.80	$107,000	$160,000	$32.80
$320,000	$428,000	$52.80	$160,000	$214,000	$52.80
$248,000		$72.90	$214,000		$72.90

The amount of the surtax is determined differently for Part D, because the Part D policies are issued by private insurers and have their own premiums. There are hundreds of different Part D policies available each year. You pay your premium plus the monthly addition for your income. The monthly addition can change each year. The monthly addition is transferred to Medicare, though it is collected by your insurer with the regular premium payments.

Table 6.3 shows the additional premiums for 2015.

The Retirement Advantages of HSAs

There's an advantage in the medical insurance changes of the last few years, but few people are maximizing it. The Affordable Care Act of 2010 of course changed insurance for preretirees, whether they buy individual policies or have employer-provided coverage, and you need to know how to use the changes to your advantage in your retirement planning.

The major change is the switch to high-deductible plans in both employer-provided and individual policies. The law and other factors caused premiums to increase significantly for many, and the best way to reduce premiums is to increase deductibles. Insurance with higher deductibles covers fewer routine expenses. The individual pays those expenses out-of-pocket.

A high-deductible policy has advantages and disadvantages, but often carries with it eligibility for a health savings account (HSA). An HSA is a valuable financial tool that isn't exploited by many who are eligible. Your insurer can tell you if the policy makes you eligible for an HSA. If you're married and your spouse has separate medical coverage, check the rules carefully to see if you're eligible to open an HSA and qualify for the full annual contribution.

More than a way to pay for current medical expenses, the HSA can be an important part of your retirement planning. Properly used it often is better than a 401(k) or even a Roth IRA as a planning tool. I believe the advantages of an HSA for retirement planning are so significant that reasonably healthy people who haven't been forced into HSA-eligible coverage during their working years should seriously consider switching to such coverage and maximizing use of the HSA.

The basics of an HSA are simple. Either the account owner or his or her employer makes contributions to the account. (Actually, like a 529 college savings plan, anyone can make deposits into your HSA.) The deposit is deductible from gross income if you make it or excluded from your gross income if the employer makes it. The maximum contribution in 2015 was $3,350 for an individual policy or $6,650 for a family policy. The limit changes each year with inflation. Account owners who are 55 or older add $1,000 to those limits as catch-up contributions. The account can be invested in anything the account administrator allows, and investment earnings of the account compound tax free.

Here's the second big payoff. When distributions are taken from the HSA for qualified medical expenses, the distributions are tax free. So, the money is tax free or deductible going into the HSA, and tax free coming out when used to pay for qualified medical expenses.

Qualified medical expenses are those that are deductible as itemized expenses on your tax return if you had paid for them with after-tax dollars and they weren't reimbursed by insurance. That means an HSA can pay for expenses that aren't covered by many medical insurance plans, such as dental and vision care.

The idea behind an HSA was that you would have the high-deductible policy and use the HSA to pay for deductibles, copayments, and noncovered expenses as they are incurred.

A better strategy is to let the HSA accumulate for your retirement years. Pay current medical expenses from your income, unless some major catastrophic expenses are incurred. Then, use the HSA in retirement to pay for expenses not covered by Medicare, premiums for Medicare supplemental insurance (Medigap) and Part D prescription coverage, and any medical expenses not covered by them.

The HSA also will be available to pay for nonmedical expenses if you need it. When distributions from an HSA are used to pay for other than qualified medical expenses, then the distribution is included in gross income. In that case it works just like a traditional IRA, except there aren't required minimum distributions.

If there is a balance in your HSA when you pass away, the balance is inherited by your estate or a beneficiary you designated with the administrator.

You need to choose an administrator for your HSA, just as you need a custodian for an IRA. There are many available HSA administrators. As with IRAs and other financial accounts, look for low fees, broad investment options, and any other features that are important to you, such as robust online tools or good telephone customer service. Take a look at HSA Bank (www.hsabank.com), which allows accounts above a minimum balance to be invested through TD Ameritrade, and Health Savings Administrators (www.healthsavings.com), which allows investments through Vanguard.

Most HSAs now offer a free debit card that you can use the same as any other payment card to pay for medical services (or anything else if you want to incur the taxes). Most will issue checks that are just like regular bank checks, but for an additional fee. You also can issue payments or transfer funds to one of your other financial accounts either online or over the telephone.

As you reach age 65, there's a tricky interplay between HSAs and Medicare to be aware of.

You're generally required to sign up for Medicare at age 65 unless you meet one of the exceptions. There's also a rule that once you sign up for Medicare, contributions to an HSA no longer are allowed. Neither personal nor employer contributions are allowed.

This means that after age 65 you can't have additional contributions to an HSA unless you meet one of the exceptions for delaying Medicare enrollment past age 65. You can leave money in the HSA and use it as already described after you retire, but new contributions have to stop.

HSA contributions might also have to stop at age 65 if you have filed for Social Security benefits, because you'll automatically be enrolled in Medicare Part A at age 65 if you filed for Social Security benefits, even if you filed for them and then suspended payments.

Filling the Biggest Gap in Retirement Health Care

The biggest gap in your retirement medical insurance probably is one you hardly think about and that gets little attention. Among the many needs not covered by Medicare is dental care. You also won't find dental coverage in Medigap (Medicare supplemental) policies. Unless problems with your teeth and mouth are related to an accident or certain diseases, you won't receive help from these policies and programs.

Apparently, few retirees know about this gap or do anything about it. While 80 percent of children and 54 percent of working adults have some kind of dental coverage, only 30 percent of seniors do. According to one survey, half of Americans ages 65 and older didn't visit a dentist at all in 2014.

There are a number of private options for obtaining dental coverage, but unlike prescription drug, Medigap, and long-term care policies, these options aren't regulated by or associated with Medicare in any way.

You might not think you need help paying for a couple of teeth cleanings a year, and you probably don't. It's the other potential treatments for which you might want some coverage. In many areas, root canals and crowns incur charges of about $1,000 each. Costs can be higher or lower depending on where you live. Dentures, implants, and other treatments that are routine among seniors are more expensive. You might not want to reach into your pocket to pay the retail cost of such treatments when you need one or more of them.

You have two basic options for dental care coverage: dental insurance and dental discount plans.

I suggest you consider a discount plan instead of dental insurance. Most of the time a discount plan controls your out-of-pocket costs better than insurance.

Dental insurance premiums vary around the country, but the premiums typically are around $500 annually. (Age usually isn't a factor in determining premiums.) For this premium you're covered for two cleanings and exams annually and usually for periodic x-rays. In addition, the policies will cover many other dental treatments you might need.

The limits and fine print in the coverage, however, reduce the policies' benefits. There's usually an annual coverage limit of between $1,000 and $1,500. (You can increase the coverage limit a bit by paying a higher premium.) No matter how much dental care you need, the insurance won't pay more than the annual limit. You also will have a copay or coinsurance on most treatments that are covered, usually of 20 percent to 50 percent of the cost.

Also, some important dental treatments might be excluded entirely, especially cosmetic treatments, so check the details before signing up for a policy. In addition, expect a waiting period of 12 months to 18 months for many types of care beyond the routine cleanings to be covered.

The good news in dental insurance is that the insurer negotiates prices with the providers. Your charges for any treatments are likely to be less than the dentist's price to patients who aren't covered, even when the insurer provides little or no assistance for the treatment.

Essentially with dental insurance you're prepaying for two annual cleanings and a few other services plus the negotiated rates.

A better option might be a dental discount plan. These usually have annual premiums of around $100. Again, the cost varies around the country.

The discount plans negotiate with a network of dentists in your area. If you have your dental work done at one of the network dentists, you'll pay substantially less than the dentist's "sticker price." The discounts can be substantial. I reviewed several plans in my area, and the discounts are 40 percent to 50 percent on a range of services, and sometimes are higher. There's rarely a waiting period for a discount plan's benefits.

In addition, usually you can opt for an annual premium of around $200 annually and receive some basic services for no charge, such as one or two annual cleanings and periodic x-rays. So, you'll have coverage similar to that of insurance for a lower premium.

Your regular health insurer or Medigap insurer might offer or be affiliated with one or more dental insurance or discount plans. Plans in your area also can be found at DentalPlans.com or the National Association of Dental Plans website at nadp.org/about/cdorganization.aspx. There also is an insurance plan affiliated with AARP and administered by Delta Dental Insurance Company. Check the AARP website for details.

Health Care Orphans: Covering the Bridge Years

Most Americans retire before age 65, though the average retirement age has crept higher since the financial crisis of 2008–2009. Some retire early involuntarily, because of workforce reductions or personal health problems. Others retire before 65 because they want to. Whatever the reason for leaving the work force, those who retire early need medical insurance. For most people, Medicare eligibility doesn't begin until age 65. Before that, you have to find other sources for coverage of retirement medical expenses.

Some large employers still offer health care coverage to former employees who are under age 65. When large corporations offer buyouts or dismiss large numbers of employees, continuing medical insurance typically is part of the package. Even among large companies, however, the number offering medical coverage is declining. The numbers are even lower outside the universe of large employers.

The Affordable Care Act of 2010 makes finding coverage before age 65 easier than it used to be. People don't have to hunt as hard to determine the policies that are available. Also, insurers no longer can deny coverage because of medical history or unhealthy habits. But the law only made coverage more available than it used to be. The ACA didn't reduce medical insurance premiums, especially for those who are middle-aged or older, and some analysts believe the law increased premiums by requiring more coverage. The premiums for someone age 50 or older can be fairly high and a shock to many people who were used to subsidized employer coverage.

The easiest way to decrease medical insurance premiums is to raise the deductible and copayments. In other words, self-insure for the routine expenses and let insurance cover the higher costs. Changing residences also can change premiums. The cost of medical care and insurance varies around the country based on factors such as the availability of doctors and hospitals. The costs even can vary in areas near to each other, such as by crossing a county line. An individual could reduce premiums by moving to an area where medical care costs are lower.

There also might be other sources of medical insurance. Those considering early retirement should do extensive health insurance research early, several years before deciding to retire. There are many sources to consult to avoid paying too much for a policy with limited coverage. Here are the steps prospective retirees or new retirees need to take:

- Contact your employer. There is at least one option and possibly two options available through the retiree's former employer.

  The Consolidated Omnibus Budget Reconciliation Act of 1985 (COBRA) requires employers with 20 or more employees to offer medical expense coverage to former employees for up to 18 months. The employees have to pay for the coverage, plus they can be charged an administrative cost of up to 2 percent, but this might be a good deal. Coverage is guaranteed. More importantly, an employer policy usually is a group plan, and insurers generally charge less for group premiums than for an older person's individual policy. Under a group policy, younger members subsidize or offset the costs of older members. Using the COBRA provision is a good short-term option, especially for someone who retired unexpectedly or without anticipating the need to secure health insurance. It gives the retiree up to 18 months to find a longer-term solution.

  The COBRA option, however, might turn out to be too expensive. If the employer has what employees consider a good health plan, then it probably has low deductibles and copayments and covers many expenses. The premiums are likely to be high.

  The second option is that the employer might offer some kind of continuing health care coverage to former employees, especially if the employer is large. Again, this kind of coverage is disappearing, but it is worth asking about.
- Check affinity groups, such as professional, trade, alumni, and other associations. Many such associations offer some kind of medical expense insurance plan. These are group plans, so the premiums potentially are lower than for an individual policy. Any retiree or prospective retiree who belongs to an association should check the offerings from such associations. Anyone who belongs to a special interest organization should check available benefits.
- Contact local brokers and agents. There are many health insurance companies in the United States, and each insurance broker and agent works with only a few. Few health insurers work directly with individuals. That is why it is important to comparison shop among several brokers and agents.
- Ask national brokers and agents. A number of websites operate as medical insurance brokers and deal with multiple insurers instead of

only one or two. These can be found through an Internet search engine. A widely used site is ehealthinsurance.com.

- Ask other retirees about their health coverage.
- Get advice from government agencies and the Internet. Local governments generally provide free counseling to older Americans through an Area Office on Aging or similar agency. On the Internet, www .healthfinder.gov offers a lot of free information on health care insurance and buying a policy. It is run by the U.S. Department of Health and Human Services. Of course, for specific policy information you can visit the medical insurance exchanges created under the ACA. If your state set up an exchange, you can visit it. The federal exchange is at www.healthcare.gov.
- Consider short-term health insurance. This is a niche in the insurance industry offering health care coverage for up to 12 consecutive months. The coverage can be much cheaper than most other plans, but there are reasons for the low cost. The policies usually have high deductibles. In addition, preexisting conditions generally are not covered. When the policy expires, longer-term insurance must be obtained. If a chronic disease or lingering injury is incurred while under a short-term policy, then when a longer-term policy is obtained the chronic problem likely won't be covered for the first six months or longer. That's why this insurance generally is sold only to young, unemployed people. Some states prohibit these types of policies.
- Some people return to work either full- or part-time primarily for the health insurance. Or, one spouse remains employed using employer health insurance that covers both spouses until they are both old enough for Medicare.

Planning and Estimating Retirement Medical Expenses

Now that you know about Medicare, you can set up a plan for paying retirement medical expenses and begin to estimate retirement medical expense spending. It is important to incorporate a reasonable estimate of medical expenses in your plan, because being able to pay for medical expenses is a key to a sustainable and successful retirement.

There are several methods to estimate retirement medical expense spending. You could take the estimates for lifetime medical spending we discussed earlier in this chapter from the Center for Retirement Research at Boston College or Fidelity Investments and plug those into your plan. There are potential problems with those methods, which we discussed earlier. These are average expenses, and yours could be considerably higher or lower. Also, those estimates aren't going to reflect your out-of-pocket spending, because they don't account for different types of insurance coverage and different costs around the country.

Another approach would be to consult the Department of Labor's studies of household spending at different age levels. You could assume that you'll spend the same percentage of income on medical expenses at different ages as indicated in those studies. Again, those are averages and might not apply to your situation. It's also difficult to use that approach unless you are fairly certain what your income will be through retirement.

I suggest a more systematic approach to estimate retirement medical expenses. This approach will estimate a baseline for the spending and also can help you develop a plan that will reduce the uncertainty of retirement medical spending.

Most likely, you won't receive much in retirement medical benefits from former employers or unions. Medicare will be your prime retirement medical insurance.

Part A benefits under Medicare are free to most people. So, we start with Part B, also known as traditional Medicare. This will be your main coverage. The standard Part B premium in 2015 was $104.90 per month or $1,258.80 annually. As we discussed earlier, retirees with higher incomes pay a Medicare surtax. That effectively raises premiums, though the surtax technically isn't a premium.

Part B doesn't cover everything. It has deductibles, copayments, and excluded care. Because of that, you should consider a Medicare supplement, or Medigap, policy. You could go without such a policy and save the premiums each year. The policy, however, reduces uncertainty. You have the certainty of paying the premiums each year and know that if you incur any of the expenses covered by the policy, it will pay them. There are a range of Medigap policies, and premiums vary by the type of policy and where you live. You can find current premiums for the different policies available in your area by checking the Medicare website or calling 1-800-MEDICARE. For now, let's take an average cost of $2,000 annually for Medigap policy.

Next, consider prescription drugs. These receive very limited coverage under Parts A and B. Generally, Medicare covers only drugs related to a stay in a hospital, such as those related to a surgery. Yet, prescription drugs are becoming a larger part of medical care and are a significant unplanned expense for many retirees. They usually are listed as the highest portion of retirement medical expenses.

The best way to control prescription drug expenses is by purchasing a Part D prescription drug policy. These policies are issued by private insurers but regulated by Medicare. Policy terms and premiums vary considerably. Some are "barebones" policies that provide limited coverage and have premiums of $40 and less per month. Others have much broader coverage and higher premiums. For projections, you'll want to check prices in your area and use the premiums for a policy you're likely to buy. Check the Medicare website for details or call 1-800-MEDICARE.

For now, we'll use a 2015 national average of about $700 annually in premiums.

As an alternative to this package of policies, you might choose to join a Medicare Advantage plan. These plans combine the coverage of Part B, some Medigap plans, and the Part D and prescription drug policies. Again, the exact coverage and premiums vary by the individual plan. You can see the choices in your area on the Medicare website or by calling 1-800-MEDICARE. Overall, the cost is likely to be similar to the cost for the package of Part B plus Medicare Supplemental and Part D policies.

The premiums for this package of coverage were about $4,000 annually in 2015 using our estimates. Remember, your estimates will vary based on where you live and which policies and terms you choose. You might choose policies with higher premiums and broader coverage to reduce the uncertainty of unexpected expenses. Or you might choose policies with lower premiums and take the risk of large unexpected medical expenses.

You also might assume you're going to incur at least the minimum amount of medical care each year and pay the deductibles. For Part A there's a deductible of $1,260 for each benefit period. (A benefit period generally is a hospital stay.) Under Part A, you also begin paying a daily coinsurance after 60 days in the hospital. The Medigap and Part D policies also will have deductibles and copayments that vary by the policy.

Let's stick with the premiums and say you incur a minimum of $4,000 a year in retirement. That's for one person. If you're married, that likely is doubled. Don't forget the Medicare premium surtax if you're a higher income household.

That is the cost only for one year and is in 2015 dollars. Inflation has to be factored in for future years. Medical expenses generally rise faster than inflation, though Medicare Part B premiums held steady in 2014 and 2015. For example, in Fidelity's annual estimates it used to assume 6 percent annual inflation in medical expenses but beginning in 2010 used lower rates. If premiums are $8,000 for you and your spouse this year, in 30 years of retirement without inflation that's a total of $240,000 in premiums. If annual premium inflation is 3 percent, the one-year premiums in year 30 will be $19,000.

There also is care that isn't covered by any of those policies, most notably dental and vision care. You might choose some separate coverage for those or decide to pay them out-of-pocket.

You can reduce these minimum costs by having less insurance coverage. For example, you could enroll in Part B but not take out a Medigap policy. That would save money at least in the short run, because you won't have the premiums. When you do that, however, you take the risk that you'll be in the half of the population that incurs higher-than-average medical expenses, and you'll have to pay those expenses out of personal funds.

Final Words on Retirement Medical Expenses

Many people approach retirement with misunderstandings about retirement medical expenses. They assume Medicare pays for almost everything or that inflation is low. A 2014 study for Fidelity found that 48 percent of those ages 55 to 64 believed retirement medical expenses are likely to total around $50,000. In this chapter, you were exposed to realistic estimates of retirement medical expenses. You learned the different types of insurance coverage available to U.S. retirees, and in general what is and isn't covered. You also learned how to plan for and reduce the uncertainty of retirement medical spending. I showed you how to develop a reasonable estimate of your retirement medical expenses.

You don't have to live in fear of retirement medical expenses or have them chip away at your financial well-being.

Follow This Plan

Budget for medical expenses. It's not easy to forecast lifetime medical expenses, because your future health is unknown. But don't assume they'll be the same as during your working years. Understand the difference between employer coverage for employees and Medicare. Know the rules about premiums, deductibles, and coinsurance. Also, know which care isn't covered. Then, prepare a separate forecast of medical expenses.

Review the Options

Almost everyone has Medicare Parts A and B. In Part B, you can choose between traditional Medicare and Medicare Advantage. Also, consider whether you should have a Medicare supplement policy to fill the gaps in traditional Medicare. If you opt for traditional Medicare, also consider a Part D prescription drug policy. Finally, consider buying long-term care coverage, which is discussed in Chapter 7.

Don't Miss the Deadlines

You'll face a coverage gap and higher lifetime premiums if you don't sign up for a Medicare part or buy a policy when you're first eligible. For Parts A and B, you'll be enrolled automatically at age 65 if you're receiving Social Security. If you're not, you need to apply for Part B and buy a Part D policy (if you want one) during the period that begins three months before your 65th birthday and ends three months after. But the enrollment dates are extended if you're working for an employer with 20 or more employees or have retiree health coverage from a former employer. Know your deadline and don't miss it.

Consider Extending Your Career

Staying in the workforce longer provides at least two benefits. You keep earning money, and so you can keep adding to your nest egg instead of draining it. Some people work an extra two or more years and earmark all of the additional savings for lifetime medical expenses. Working longer also means you don't retire before age 65 and won't have to seek coverage to fill the gap between your former employer's coverage and when Medicare begins at 65.

Remember Inflation

People often overlook the role of inflation in their retirement planning, as we discussed in Chapter 2. The problem is more acute for medical expenses, because their rate of inflation is higher than for consumer prices.

Shop for Coverage

In Part B, you can choose between traditional Medicare and Medicare Advantage. In most areas, you have a choice of Medicare Advantage plans. There also are a wide range of Medicare supplemental plans (Medigap plans) to consider. In most areas, there also are numerous Part D prescription drug plans.

The terms and costs of these options are very different. The right plan for you depends on how well the coverage suits your medical profile and the cost. Too often, people are paying much more than they need to for medical care because of they don't shop for the right policy. Or they pay too much for a policy, because a similar policy is available for less.

Medicare makes shopping around relatively easy through both its website (www.medicare.gov) and 800 number 1-800-MEDICARE (800–633–4227). Don't hesitate to seek help from Medicare, a seniors' agency, or tax-exempt group in your area, or from a financial planner.

Dealing with the Crisis in Long-Term Care

Long-term care (LTC) is a great American paradox. On the one hand, most people don't want to talk about it. One survey found that 25 percent of adults would rather go to the dentist than discuss LTC. Fewer than 30 percent of adults have had a conversation about long-term care planning with an advisor or loved ones. Yet, paying for LTC and the financial cost of long-term care are the greatest financial concerns of Americans over age 40. They worry that if they need LTC the cost will dissipate all their assets and impose a burden on their loved ones.

LTC generates more confusion and misinterpretation than many other topics. Probably because Americans don't like to discuss LTC, when they do consider or discuss LTC and long-term care insurance (LTCI), the discussions tend to be filled with errors.

One survey of Americans 40 and older revealed the depth of the confusion about and discomfort with LTC and LTCI. About half of people said they understand most people are likely to need long-term care sometime after age 65, but believe they won't be among those who need it. Most people say they expect family to provide needed care, though 60 percent say they haven't discussed this with relatives. They also haven't assessed whether any family members are able to perform the tasks needed for in-home care or would have the time.

The cost of long-term care is significantly *underestimated* by 60 percent of the respondents. Yet, most people significantly *overestimated* the cost of insurance to cover long-term care. They believe the insurance costs far more than it does. Only 20 percent underestimate the cost, and a mere 16 percent stated the correct range. Perhaps that is why only about 5 percent of those 40 and older own LTCI. The mistaken belief of 56 percent of those surveyed is that the annual premium for a healthy 55-year-old couple is $7,000 or more. The actual average cost in 2014 was only $2,700, according to the American Association for Long-Term Care Insurance.

Another mistaken belief is that Medicare or Medicaid will pay for long-term care. Medicare pays only a small percentage of long-term care costs, and those payments primarily are for relatively short-term rehabilitation after an illness or injury. Medicaid does pay a significant portion of the nation's long-term care costs, but coverage isn't automatic. You have to meet the definition of being impoverished before Medicaid will cover you.

About the only question concerning LTC and LTCI answered correctly by a majority of the respondents was when they were asked how familiar they were with the topics: 53 percent said they were not too familiar with the topic, and another 26 percent said they were not at all familiar with it. Another survey found that two-thirds over 40 have done little or no long-term care planning.

Complicating decisions about handling LTC is that the insurance market has been in turmoil since 2009. Insurers began raising premiums substantially on long-term policyholders, some by over 40 percent in one year, even insurers that resisted substantial premium increases in the past. A number of insurers dropped out of the LTCI market. Those insurers that continued to offer LTCI changed their underwriting practices, making it harder for people to obtain LTCI, and for the most part increased premiums. There have been anecdotes and some data indicating that a few insurers increased the number of claims they declined to pay.

Most states imposed rate stabilization laws over 10 years ago to reduce the volatility of premiums. The laws require insurers to justify large premium increases by documenting unusual or unexpected circumstances. Premium increases have to be reviewed and approved by state regulators before they can be imposed. Despite these hurdles, the insurers had the rate increases approved.

Several factors were behind the premium increases and other changes, and they all boil down to actual experience being different from the assumptions made when the policies were written:

- *Interest rates are low.* Rates and investment returns were much higher when the policies were written. Insurers collect premiums and invest them for years before claims are paid. The investment returns are a significant portion of the money insurers use to pay claims and generate profits. Low interest rates led to a significant shortfall of investment income for insurers.

- *People kept their policies.* Premiums were determined assuming a certain percentage of people would pay premiums for a few years, and then let the policies lapse. Fewer people than expected dropped their policies, and over time that leads to the insurers paying more claims than expected when the policies were issued.
- *People are living longer.* LTC is most likely to be needed by those 80 and older. As that age group increases faster than insurers expected, claims on policies are higher than planned.
- *Long-term care costs keep rising.* Again, these increases exceed what insurers planned.
- *Some insurers did a poor job of underwriting.* They issued policies to applicants without thorough medical reviews, underestimating the amount of claims that eventually would be filed by policyholders. That is fairly common in the history of LTCI. In the past, however, the large, experienced LTCI carriers didn't commit that error, but in recent years some of them did.

The result of all these factors is insurance companies lost money on LTCI, or at least earned a lot less than they expected and could earn elsewhere.

In this chapter we're going to discuss LTC. You'll learn the potential of incurring LTC costs and what those costs could be. We'll also discuss the different ways to pay for LTC, including the pros and cons of LTCI. You'll learn how to incorporate LTC in your retirement plan. Along the way I hope to dispel many of the myths and correct the misunderstandings about LTC and how to pay for it.

Will You Need Long-Term Care?

A battle of statistics takes place whenever LTC is discussed.

The U.S. government reported in 2014 that 70 percent of those then aged 65 or older would need some long-term care in their lifetimes. That number is used to make the case that everyone should own long-term care insurance (LTCI). But a close look at the data indicate that only 19 percent of men and 31 percent of women should purchase LTCI, according to a study from the Center for Retirement Research at Boston College.

Both sets of statistics are misleading.

Most people think of LTC as a long-term stay in a nursing home. That's not the case. Despite its name, LTC encompasses a wide range of care, from a few days of rehabilitation after surgery to many years of custodial care in a nursing home. LTC includes home-based care, residence in an assisted living facility, and more.

Within that wide scope, it is no surprise that most of those 65 and older will need some LTC at some point in their lives. Yet, most of that LTC won't be a crushing financial burden. Medicare, for example, pays for nursing home stays of 100 days or less that follow hospital stays of more than three consecutive days. That covers the nursing home stays of 50 percent of men and 40 percent of women, according to the CRR study.

Men on average who enter nursing homes spend a year or less there, while women on average spend about 16 months, according to the CRR study.

The CRR study does much to correct the exaggerations in the government's 70 percent figure, but the CRR study also doesn't tell the whole picture.

Many people believe that LTC is nursing home care, and LTCI is nursing home insurance. Those beliefs are incorrect. A wide range of care counts as LTC.

Most LTC these days occurs outside of a nursing home. A majority of LTC is delivered at home or an assisted living facility. Even most nursing home stays these days are short-term stays for rehabilitation after a surgery, an injury, or major illness. LTC includes part-time or full-time help with two or more of the activities of daily living (ADLs), including dressing, bathing, eating, using the toilet, transferring, and walking. Medical care and treatment often is only a small part of LTC. A home care aid who visits a few hours each day to clean the house and prepare meals is a common form of LTC.

Most people prefer to remain in their homes for as long as possible, and the home care industry has developed to fulfill these wishes. LTCI also has changed over the years so that it covers qualified LTC wherever the care is delivered. Even adult day care now is covered by most LTCI policies.

The information you really are interested in when considering LTC in your plans is the probability of needing any form of LTC for an extended period and how much it will cost. Here's some data that are on point and relevant for your decision.

About 40 percent of people after age 65 will need two or more years of LTC, according to the American Association of Long-Term Care Insurers. Just under half of those over 65 will need some form of LTC for 90 days or more. Women are more likely than men to need LTC for an extended period for two reasons. Women live longer, and the very old are likely to need help with some tasks of daily living, even when they're relatively healthy. Women also have a higher incidence of Alzheimer's disease. This doesn't mean men don't need LTC, but women on average have a greater need.

Most LTC needs are for less than a year. While not the multiyear instances most people fear, they're still significant and expensive. Your plans should determine how you would pay for different potential LTC needs. How will you pay if LTC is needed for 90 days or less? Up to one year? What if you or your spouse needs LTC beyond one year?

I mentioned that most people underestimate the cost of LTC. You can find reasonable estimates of the cost of LTC at the websites of two of the major LTC insurers: Genworth and John Hancock. These insurers publish updated annual estimates of the cost of LTC. In recent years, they began breaking down the costs by locality and type of care (home care, assisted living, and nursing homes). Of course, you can find national figures on the average annual cost of a nursing home or other care, but that doesn't help much in your planning. The cost of care varies considerably around the country.

For example, according to the John Hancock Insurance website, in 2015 in Buffalo, New York, a semi-private nursing home room cost $300 per day today, or $109,500 per year. A home health aide cost $132 for six hours. For a year the cost is $48,180. Adult day care cost $84 per day, or $21,840 for one year of five days a week attendance. A one-bedroom unit at an assisted living facility cost $98 per day, or $35,760 for a year.

Move a little bit up the state to Rochester and the costs were very different. The semi-private nursing home room was $354 per day or $129,210 per year, almost an additional $20,000 per year than in Buffalo. The home health aide was $144 per day, or $52,560 annually. But adult day care cost less in Rochester, $70 per day, or $18,200 annually. Assisted living cost $124 per day, or $45,348 for a year.

Those are examples of the variations in two places in one state. Price variations across the country are more significant. The Genworth and John Hancock surveys also are of median costs in an area. Quality of care and services varies between providers, as does price. A more precise fix on the cost can be obtained by contacting providers in your area and asking about costs and services.

You can see from these examples that even home care is what most people would consider expensive. Keep in mind that these prices are only for the basic services. If someone needs additional services or levels of care, the cost is higher.

These estimated costs are for care in 2015. People generally don't need those services until they are in their late 70s or older. If you are 65 today, you probably won't need the care for another 15 years or longer. In the meantime, the costs are likely to increase at a steady rate. John Hancock's website assumes 3 percent inflation to estimate future costs for all the services. Genworth says the five-year annual growth has varied from 4 percent for nursing homes to 1 percent for a home health aide. Inflation substantially increases the dollar amounts the care would cost in 15 or more years.

LTC is difficult to plan for, because you have a low probability of incurring a very high cost. Many people focus on the low probability portion of the equation, as you can tell from the survey cited earlier. As surveys show, most people also significantly underestimate the potential cost. The result is they put their own independence and financial security at risk as well as the independence and security of their loved ones. If you are among the minority who needs extended LTC, the cost will be extremely high. You own homeowner's and auto insurance for protection from risks that also have low probabilities but high potential costs.

Planning for LTC should be part of every retirement plan. You want to plan for LTC to avoid becoming a burden on your family, to protect the assets of you and your family, and to avoid dependence on others.

LTC planning involves a lot more than buying insurance. This is especially true considering the turmoil in LTCI following the financial crisis and the uncertainty about its future. When planning for potential LTC costs, you need to examine all the options: family, Medicare, Medicaid, LTCI, hybrid, or combination insurance policies (annuities and life insurance with LTC riders), permanent life insurance, and personal assets (self-insurance).

We'll discuss each of these options. For most people, it's best not to rely on only one of the options. Instead, a plan that uses all the tools in the toolbox to some extent is likely to offer a good amount of coverage of potential LTC expenses without costing excessive premiums.

Relying on Family

There's a joke among financial planners and others who discuss LTC with people. The planner is sitting in his office with a married couple who are in their 50s or 60s. The planner says, "Now, let's discuss long-term care insurance." The husband nods toward his wife and says, "You're looking at her."

Many people do consider a spouse or other family members to be their likely source of long-term care. We've all known people who spent a lot of time helping to care for an elderly parent or other relative who no longer could live alone without help. For some people, it works out well. The care isn't needed for an extended period of time, and the parent and adult child might bond in ways that wouldn't have happened otherwise.

No doubt, most of us have adult children or others who are willing to provide help in a pinch. Helping around the house for a period of time, however, is very different from being a primary long-term care provider, especially for an indefinite or extended period of time.

Before considering family as your primary source of LTC, carefully consider all the facets of that decision:

■ *Availability.* For one or more adult children to provide home care, he or she must be available. The person would have to live near you or be able to change his or her life by moving to your home for however long the care is needed. There might be competing obligations to his or her own children or to an employer or both. Even your spouse might not be fully available. If you're elderly and in need of care, it's likely your spouse will have physical limitations that make providing full-time care for someone else difficult.

- *Burden.* Many retired Americans report in surveys that they don't want to be burdens on their children. Providing care for someone is burdensome after a period of time. Even when the caregiver loves the person receiving the care, providing care for an extended period can be stressful and exhausting. The caregiver also is likely to incur expenses to the extent that aren't appreciated, even by the caregiver.
- *Qualifications.* Sometimes caregiving involves doing basic chores around the home: cooking, cleaning, and maintenance. It might even be as simple as directing others who are hired to do the work. That's the case when the person needing care doesn't have any serious physical or mental issues but simply is too old or frail to perform these tasks. Other times the care needed requires a person with some training. These tasks could include monitoring health and administering medication. Even providing assistance with bathing and dressing can require training when certain medical conditions are present. People with dementia and related diseases can be violent or have other types of behavior that are best coped with by someone with training.
- *Fairness.* Often there is one adult child in a family upon whom the burden of caregiving falls. Sometimes only one child is available. Other times only one child is willing to make the effort to provide care. Sometimes after one child begins providing care, the others don't feel a need to help.
- *Family harmony.* When one sibling or other family member provides care to the extent that others don't, discord can be created in several ways. Of course, the person providing the care might feel taken advantage of. The other family members might feel guilty and express that in different ways. Sometimes the caregiver receives compensation, either explicitly or though extra gifts or bequests. The other family members can become jealous of this or believe that the caregiver is overcompensated or used undue influence.
- *Facilities.* Home care is essential when family caregiving is a part of the plan for LTC. While more and more LTC is provided at home, it isn't always possible. Some conditions require residence at a place where professional caregivers or certain facilities are available all or most of the time, such as nursing homes or assisted-living facilities.

In most families, one or more family members are able and willing to provide some care. There are potential pitfalls and disadvantages, however, to planning for family members to be the primary caregivers when LTC is needed. Family caregiving might not be practical or could create long-term problems for one or more family members. In some cases, family caregiving isn't possible because a higher level of care is needed.

What Medicare Offers

In Chapter 6 we discussed some of the myths and misperceptions about Medicare. Perhaps the most widespread and persistent myth about Medicare is that it pays for long-term care, especially nursing home care. Most people believe that, according to surveys. Yet, Medicare won't cover most needs of true LTC.

Medicare was created to cover primarily doctor and hospital expenses. It wasn't and isn't set up to cover custodial care or most other long-term care.

Medicare will cover 100 days or less of LTC following a hospital stay of more than three consecutive days. The coverage is meant for rehabilitation and recovery after a major surgery, injury, or illness. Much of it probably is for short-term nursing home stays but it also can include home care and assisted living care. Earlier we discussed how the study from the Center for Retirement Research at Boston University concluded that this rule covers 50 percent of nursing home stays of men and 40 percent of those of women. But these aren't instances of true LTC. These are short-term stays in nursing homes primarily for physical therapy and to gain the strength before the person can be discharged to home or an assisted living facility.

When we talk about LTC in a retirement plan, we're talking primarily about custodial care. This is needed when a person's age or infirmities make him or her unable to perform at least two of the activities of daily living. LTC also includes instances when dementia or similar conditions mean a person shouldn't live alone or is unable to care for himself or herself. Hospital stays rarely immediately precede these types of LTC, and so Medicare doesn't cover them. These types of LTC aren't covered by Medicare.

Medicaid and Medicaid Trust Strategies

The other government program that pays for LTC is Medicaid. Medicare is the program for those 65 and over, while Medicaid is for all ages but only for those with limited incomes and assets.

Many people assume Medicaid will pay for their LTC, and that is their plan. Medicaid is one of the largest government programs and does pay about 45 percent of the nursing home bills in the United States. Dig a little deeper, however, and you'll see that relying on Medicaid isn't a viable option for many people.

Medicaid doesn't cover any assisted living care, which is a popular and fast-growing type of LTC. Medicaid also pays only limited home care. Home care is the preference of most people and also is a fast-growing type of care.

Medicaid is confusing to many people mainly because it is a joint federal-state program. The federal government provides roughly half the funding and also sets broad rules and guidelines. The level of federal funding varies from state to state. Each state has some flexibility in the details of its program, including who is eligible and which services are covered. There also are pilot or test programs within Medicaid that a state can establish with the approval of the federal government.

To have Medicaid pay for your LTC, you must be a U.S. citizen or have an appropriate visa, be a resident of the state in which you apply, and be 65 or older or permanently disabled or blind. You also must have a Medicaid-authorized professional (often a nurse from a local social services agency) determine that you meet Medicaid's functional limits standards for LTC. Finally, and perhaps most importantly, you must meet the financial tests for Medicaid eligibility.

The financial tests are both an income limit and an asset limit. As I said, each state sets its own rules within federal guidelines. A person might be eligible for Medicaid in one state but not in another. The income limit can be based on either the federal poverty level of Supplemental Security Income (SSI) benefits for the state, sometimes known as welfare. A state can set its income limit as high as 300 percent of the SSI benefit if it wants.

Not all states have formal income limits. The formal income limits generally are around $2,200 per month. Some states simply require a person to spend all or most of his or her income on LTC, perhaps excluding some allowances. The state then will pay any additional LTC costs.

There are allowances that allow you to keep income above the eligibility maximum. A maintenance monthly needs allowance is available when the person needing LTC has a spouse with a limited income. Each state sets its own allowance, and they generally range from $2,000 to $3,000 monthly. A personal needs allowance of $30 or more is available for items not provided by a nursing home, such as personal care items or services, taxi fares, and even movie tickets. Income used to pay for out-of-pocket medical costs can be an allowance.

Income from a trust also might be excluded or treated as an allowance. These trusts are known as qualifying income trusts, supplemental needs trusts, or Miller trusts. A person can have regular sources of income, such as Social Security or annuity distributions, paid into the trust and it won't be counted when determining Medicaid eligibility. To receive that treatment, however, all income and principal of the trust can be spent only on your needs. Also, the state must be remainder beneficiary of the trust so that it receives any assets remaining in the trust after you pass away.

The asset limit usually is tighter than the income limit and the hardest for many people to meet. Generally you total all the assets you own and subtract exempt assets. To be eligible for Medicaid, the remaining amount can be only $2,000, or $3,000 for a married person. That's why this sometimes is known as the impoverishment test. To be eligible for Medicaid, a person must spend or give away assets until he or she essentially is impoverished, except for the exempt assets.

The exempt assets under the federal rules are:

- A home that is the principal residence of the applicant and is in the same state in which he or she is applying for Medicaid. The home can be of any value, but federal rules say the equity can't exceed $500,000 (indexed for inflation), though states can increase that up to $750,000. A state also can require that there be a reasonable likelihood that the applicant will be able to return to the home.
- One automobile of any value if it's used for transportation of the applicant or a household member. An additional automobile may be excluded if it's equipped for use by a handicapped person, if it's needed to go to work or to perform essential daily activities due to distance, climate, or terrain, or if it's used to obtain regular medical treatment.
- Up to $2,000 of personal items and household goods.
- Life insurance with a face value of $1,500 or less per person.
- Burial funds of up to $1,500 each for the applicant and spouse, plus accrued interest.
- Any property essential to self-support, such as property used in a job or business.
- Other resources used to achieve self-support.
- Some types of annuities.

When the applicant is married, all assets owned separately by either spouse or owned jointly are included in the assets of the applicant spouse. Either the applicant or the spouse can ask the state to assess the couple's combined countable assets. This process often increases the exemptions. Exempt assets when the applicant is married are:

- A home of any value if it is the nonapplicant spouse's principal residence.
- The furniture, furnishings, kitchen items, and other household goods in the house without limit.
- The personal effects of the spouse without limit.
- A community spouse resources allowance. This is an additional amount of exempt assets of any type that don't fit in the other categories. The nonapplicant spouse is allowed to keep half of those assets. The federal government says the states can set the allowance from a minimum of $23,844 to a maximum of $119,200 in 2015, with those amounts indexed

for inflation each year. The nonapplicant spouse can keep only half whatever allowance the state sets or the minimum amount of $23,844, whichever is higher. The remaining balance won't affect Medicaid eligibility but must be spent on the applicant spouse's care.

Keep in mind that this is an asset ownership test, not a net asset or net worth test. Any debt owed by the applicant isn't considered. It is possible that a person has a negative net worth, because his debts exceed the value of his assets. Yet, he won't be able to keep all the assets because they exceed the asset limits of the Medicaid eligibility test.

The Asset Shifting Strategies

Many older Americans have seen promotions for seminars and publications on how to shift assets to qualify for Medicaid's nursing home coverage. Here is a brief guide to those strategies and the angles to consider before pursuing them.

As we've seen, Medicaid is the program for those with limited assets and income. Seniors have to be impoverished in order to qualify for Medicaid's nursing home coverage. Medicaid uses both income levels and asset ownership to determine who qualifies for coverage.

The income limits vary a bit from state to state, but can be met by giving as many income-producing assets as possible to a spouse and children. Likewise, the net worth or resource limit can be met by giving away assets that are not on Medicaid's list of exempt property.

The first of the Medicaid strategies is to put wealth into an expensive house. Other assets are sold to buy a house that is bigger than needed and otherwise probably wouldn't be purchased. That way, the wealth is kept in the family but is not counted against Medicaid qualification. Married couples also can load up on an expensive car, personal effects, and household furnishings in many states.

Another strategy is to transfer to individuals or to trusts any other assets that exceed the Medicaid resource limits. These have to be irrevocable transfers under which the original owner is not legally entitled to get the assets back or receive income from them. To discourage these strategies, any assets transferred to a person or trust within 60 months (five years) of applying for Medicaid are considered owned by the applicant when determining Medicaid eligibility.

That means to qualify for Medicaid, either the trust must be funded more than 60 months before entering a nursing home or enough assets must be retained to fund up to the first 60 months of nursing home care. Medicaid then is applied for after 60 months of long-term care.

This 60-month period is known as the look-back period. If you violate the look-back period, then there is a penalty that is an additional waiting period before you are eligible for Medicaid.

Here's how the look-back penalty works. The gifts and transfers you made in the 60 months before applying for Medicaid are divided by the average monthly cost of a nursing home in your area. The result is the number of additional months you must wait to be eligible for Medicaid to cover your LTC.

Suppose someone transferred $300,000 to his children during the 60-month look-back period. He then applies for Medicaid. The average monthly cost of a nursing home in his area is $10,000. Dividing $300,000 by $10,000 results in 30. This means that after the man enters a nursing home and meets Medicaid eligibility requirements, he has to wait an additional 30 months before he is eligible for Medicaid.

Some states allow an applicant to work down the penalty period by paying for nursing home care. In this example, assume that the man entered the nursing home and family members began paying for the care. Each month the man spends in the nursing home is one month off the penalty. Also, each month the man or a family member pays for the nursing home care is another month off the penalty. So, the man is eligible for Medicaid after 15 months instead of 30 months.

The waiting period doesn't begin until the person who made the transfers has moved to a nursing home and has applied for Medicaid coverage and been approved for coverage except for the waiting period.

Suppose a woman transferred $100,000 in assets to her children on November 1, 2015. She moves to a nursing home on November 1, 2016. Her Medicaid application and review were completed by that date. The $100,000 is included in her assets and is deemed to violate the 60-month look-back period. If the waiting period is determined to be 10 months, she won't be eligible for Medicaid until August 1, 2017, 10 months after she moved into the nursing home.

There are other nuances and details to Medicaid eligibility. If you're considering such strategies, don't undertake them without the advice of an attorney who is familiar with Medicaid law in the state where you'll be applying.

Before implementing these strategies, consider the potential drawbacks. The biggest drawback is that Medicaid's reimbursements to nursing homes generally are less than it costs to adequately care for someone. Nursing homes that take primarily Medicaid residents often provide care that is inferior to care in nursing homes that have primarily non-Medicaid residents. Those contemplating these strategies should compare a Medicaid nursing home to one that takes primarily private pay residents. Then those who have resources to pay for non-Medicaid care should decide if they really want to be cared for in a Medicaid facility.

Also, even if the strategies are followed precisely, a state has the option of arguing that transfers made under a Medicaid impoverishment strategy were fraudulent. That has not been seriously tested in the courts, but no one can rule out a state's winning that argument.

The strategies also might generate taxes. Transfers to individuals or trusts are gifts that, after exceeding the annual exemption amount, either are applied against the lifetime estate and gift tax credit or incur gift taxes. These taxes are not a major issue now that the lifetime exemption amount is $5 million, indexed for inflation. But some people will have to consider taxes before undertaking a strategy. The person transferring the property must pay the gift taxes.

The strategies also could increase income or capital gains taxes on the family. The person receiving the gift takes the same tax basis in the property the prior owner had. That means when the donee eventually sells the property, he or she will pay capital gains taxes on all appreciation that occurred during the donor's ownership. If the property were held until death instead and received by inheritance, the basis would be increased to its current market value and capital gains taxes on the past appreciation would be avoided.

Medicaid also has a clawback policy, known formally as estate recovery. States are required to seek repayment of all Medicaid money paid for nursing home care. They are to seek the repayment from the estates of the beneficiaries as well as their families.

It doesn't matter if an asset was exempt from the income or asset limits under Medicaid eligibility rules. The state can seek reimbursement from any asset that's in your estate, including exempt assets. Recovery can be sought from both probate and non-probate estates. The probate estate is assets you owned and that pass through the probate process, such as real estate, financial accounts, and personal possessions. The nonprobate estate includes annuities, life insurance, trusts, jointly owned property, and some other assets. There are some exceptions for a residence. Generally if a house was an exempt asset for Medicaid eligibility, the state won't seek to recover its Medicaid expenses by selling it until your spouse has passed away and any blind or disabled child of yours is at least age 21, if they were living in the house.

Some states are more aggressive than others in seeking recovery from estates and relatives. You should check the situation in your state before deciding that having Medicaid pay your nursing home expenses is part of your plan.

Finally, consider the ethics. Medicaid was set up for poor people, not for people who have the resources to pay for nursing home care but don't want to spend their money that way. Some people think it is unethical to arrange assets so that taxpayers pick up the tab.

Evaluating Long-Term Care Insurance

We discussed earlier in this chapter the turmoil in long-term care insurance since 2009. About half of the major insurers who were in the LTCI market decided to fully or partially leave the market. A number of insurers, though not all, substantially increased premiums on long-term policyhold-ers. It's also become more difficult and more expensive to buy LTCI.

The situation complicates an already difficult decision for many people. A lot of misinformation and confusion typically surrounds LTCI, and the turmoil doesn't help. In this section we're going to look objectively at LTCI and establish guidelines for deciding how to incorporate it in your planning.

Not many people buy LTCI. Insurer industry groups estimate that only about 3 percent to 5 percent of the likely LTCI buyers (mostly those 50 and older) purchased the policies.

The premium increases in recent years scare people away from LTCI, but perhaps they shouldn't. The premium increases were a result of several factors we discussed earlier. In the wake of these factors, insurers have changed practices. They've adjusted to lower investment returns, longer life expectancy, fewer policy lapses, and rising LTC costs. These factors now are incorporated into the process for setting premiums on new policies. The weak insurers and those with little experience in LTC have dropped out of the market. That could mean that for new policy buyers, future surprise premium increases are much less likely.

Many people say they don't purchase the policies because they're expensive. Surveys indicate that could be due to bad information, because a majority of people in surveys estimates the cost of LTCI at about twice what it really costs.

That's not to say that LTCI is cheap. The cost will depend on your age, health history, where you live, and other factors. Where you live is a major factor, because the cost of LTC varies considerably around the country. In 2015, a married couple with each spouse age 55 would pay an annual premium of about $2,350 to cover both spouses. That's a national average premium. If the couple were older or not in excellent health, the premiums would be higher.

We'll learn later in this section that there are a number of provisions in an LTCI policy that can be adjusted to meet the policyholder's needs or preferences. Changes in these provisions can cause the premiums to be higher or lower. Because of that flexibility, a generic premium quote or estimate isn't useful. You can change the policy terms so that you still have coverage but the premiums are more affordable.

Many people say they don't like the use-it-or-lose-it aspect of LTCI. You can pay premiums for decades and pass away without needing much LTCI or filing a claim. In that case, there is no reimbursement to you or your estate. (You can buy policies with a return-of-premium or similar features, but the features increase your premiums.) Of course, most of us do the same each year with homeowner's and automobile insurance. We don't expect to receive much for our premiums and hope we don't have to file a claim.

Instead of focusing on premiums and return of premiums, a better approach to deciding whether or not to purchase LTCI might be to compare the potential benefits of a policy with the potential loss from not having LTCI. An example of how to analyze the issue this way was presented by Joe Tomlinson on AdvisorPerspectives.com in 2015.

In the example, a 55-year-old was paying premiums of $3,400 annually for an LTCI policy that would pay daily benefits of up to $225 for up to five years of care and with inflation protection. The policy would pay benefits only after the first 90 days of LTC. The present value, or cost in today's dollars, of the premiums through age 85 is $60,000.

Looking at data on the need for LTC, Tomlinson estimated that there was a 60 percent probability that no claim would be filed under the policy. That's what keeps many people from buying LTCI. That essentially would mean a $60,000 loss for the man, because no financial benefit would be received from the premiums.

There was 20 percent probability one year of care would be needed. Tomlinson assumed that care would cost $57,000 in current dollars and would rise 3.5 percent annually. Also, the policyholder would pay for the first 90 days of care, and the policy would pick up the tab only after that. The net result is a $12,000 present value loss from purchasing the policy.

There's also a 10 percent probability of needing three years of care. After netting all the factors, that's an $85,000 present value gain from purchasing the insurance.

The probability of needing five years of care was 10 percent. Netting all the factors would result in a $183,000 present value gain from the insurance, according to Tomlinson.

Now, instead of looking only at the insurance, let's add other factors. Assume the man has $250,000 in investment assets at age 55 and invests conservatively. He expects to be able to leave this to his children through his estate. Consider how that goal is satisfied under different scenarios when there is no insurance:

Scenario 1: No need for LTC. That leaves the full $250,000 available for the heirs.
Scenario 2: One year of care is needed. The estate is reduced to $202,000.
Scenario 3: Three years of care are needed. The nest egg is reduced to $105,000.
Scenario 4: Five years of care are needed. The estate is reduced to $7,000.

The different scenarios indicate there is a lot of variability in the amount that will be available to the man's children. It also shows that the financial effects of a low probability event, needing LTC for three to five years, will greatly reduce the estate. That's before considering the scenario that concerns most people, which is a very long need for LTC.

As I said earlier in this chapter, LTC has a low probability but a high potential cost.

The man might decide to essentially self-insure and still try to leave substantial assets for his children by investing more aggressively to earn higher returns. But the investment returns are not guaranteed. The investment strategies could generate low returns or even losses, as well as high returns. That approach introduces another layer of volatility and uncertainty to an already volatile and uncertain situation. Suppose the investment strategies don't work, and the man also needs LTC? Tomlinson estimated that not buying LTCI is more risky than aggressive investing on its own. He estimated that not buying LTCI is six times more risky.

Buying and Designing a Policy

Many of the long-term care insurance policies issued over the years have not paid benefits. There are some estimates that less than 5 percent of policies issued have paid benefits to date. Part of the reason is that the bulk of the people who purchased the policies still are healthy. Another reason is that apparently a large percentage of long-term care policies are allowed to lapse after a few years. The policy owners decide that they cannot afford the premiums or that the premiums are not worth the potential benefits, so they stop paying premiums. Some probably switch to policies they find more attractive. Other policies haven't paid benefits because the policy terms were restrictive. The owners might have needed help with care-related expenses, but their care didn't qualify for reimbursement under their policy terms.

Once a decision is made to buy a long-term care insurance policy, careful consideration must be given to the design of that policy. Always remember that some of the provisions in the policies can be dropped, added, or changed. The terms selected determine the premiums charged and the coverage received. There are five key policy terms that can be adjusted to make the premiums more affordable, while still ensuring that expenses the family cannot afford are likely to be covered.

Customizing a Policy

Following are some key terms and how they can be adjusted to design a custom-made long-term care insurance policy.

Daily Benefit.   Long-term care policies promise to pay a maximum daily benefit for each day of covered care. There usually are separate daily benefit levels for home health care, assisted living, and nursing home. There also might be benefit levels for adult day care and other covered care. The insured picks the daily benefit amounts and counts on personal or family income and assets to make up any difference between the covered amounts and the actual cost.

The national average daily cost of a nursing home is $181 for a semiprivate room. There usually are additional costs. The average daily rate covers room, board, and some basic nursing care. Most residents need additional care, and these generally amount to about 20 percent of the daily cost. The additional costs can be for prescription drugs, physical therapy, personal grooming, and other expenses. Some of these costs might be covered by other insurance. Others won't be. Costs are higher in urban areas and lower in rural areas. The home health care benefit often is set at a percentage of the nursing home benefit, usually 75 percent to 100 percent of the nursing home benefit, though it also can be set as a dollar amount.

Survey nursing home costs before picking a daily benefit, but give careful thought to the area surveyed. The choice of a nursing home or other care facility often is made by a woman in her 40s or 50s. In other words, a daughter or daughter-in-law usually decides where a parent or an in-law resides. When an insured's children live in a different area from the insured, the relevant costs might be those in the area where the children live. The children are likely to move the parent to a nursing home in their area instead of in the parent's area.

Once the cost for an area is determined, decide whether or not the policy should cover the full cost. An individual might not be able to afford $130 or more per day for an indefinite period, but insuring for the full amount might make the policy premium too high. On the other hand, the insured might be able to pay $20 or more per day indefinitely if the need should arise, and reducing the daily benefit by that amount might make the policy affordable. For example, suppose Social Security pays the insured $10,000 annually. If there is not a spouse who would need that income, it is available to pay for long-term care. That means the daily benefit can be reduced by about $27 per day ($10,000 annually).

Keep inflation in mind. Long-term care costs historically rise faster than consumer price inflation. Historically, the average annual increase in LTC is 7 percent. The rate has declined in recent years to the 3 percent to 4 percent range.

Waiting Period. This also is known as the deductible or elimination period. It is the length of time that the insured receives covered care before the policy starts paying benefits. Insurers usually offer waiting periods from 0 to 365 days. Most people choose 90 days. The insured (that's you) pays for all long-term health care during the waiting period. Then, if care still is needed, the insurance company begins paying its obligations under the policy.

Here's a key point that sometimes confuses people. The waiting or elimination period doesn't start to run until you actually begin receiving care that you or someone else is paying for. Some people think that after they've been diagnosed with a need for LTC, they can stay at home and receive help from family and friends for 90 days (or whatever the elimination period is) and then begin LTC that is fully paid by the policy. That's incorrect. You have to begin receiving care that qualifies under the policy and that you pay for to start the elimination period running.

The insured selects the waiting period, and it is a form of self-insurance. Selecting a longer waiting period is similar to selecting a higher deductible on a home or car insurance policy. The longer waiting period reduces the premiums on the policy.

The insured might decide that the policy is only for the worst-case scenario when long-term custodial care is needed for years. In that case, the owner would select a waiting period of 365 days. That turns the policy into a catastrophic long-term care policy and should substantially reduce premiums. The reduction might make the policy affordable or might allow the daily benefit to be raised high enough so that none of the insured's assets are used after the waiting period.

Do a little arithmetic before making a decision. You could have an LTCI policy that pays benefits from the first day you need care, or you could opt for a 90-day elimination period. On average, going for the 90-day elimination period reduces annual premiums by about $750. Also on average, the 90 days of LTC will cost $30,000 or more. You'll have to pay for that. It will take about 40 years of saving $750 to equal $30,000. So, you need to own the policy for a long time for the longer elimination period to be a benefit.

The lesson is that before electing a policy change that reduces premiums, calculate how much responsibility you're taking on and how much it could cost you in the long term. Balance that against the short-term benefit of lower premiums.

Benefit Period.   This is the length of time the policy pays benefits. Many policies call this the maximum lifetime benefit. For example, a three-year benefit period is a maximum lifetime benefit of 365 days times three times the maximum daily benefit. A $150 daily rate would make the lifetime benefit about $165,000.

The maximum lifetime benefit has a great influence on a policy's premium. A maximum of three years of coverage costs about half that of unlimited lifetime coverage. A five-year limit reduces the premium by about 25 percent below the unlimited amount. One of the adjustments insurers made in recent years is not to offer unlimited lifetime benefits. Most policies available now allow the insured to choose a maximum policy benefit of no more than five years.

While most long-term care these days is for a relatively short time, those whose needs extend beyond the short term tend to need care for a considerable length of time. One study reported that long-term home care in general lasted on average 4.5 years, while long-term nursing home care on average lasted for 2.4 years. Remember, these numbers exclude short-term stays and include only people who need LTC for more than 90 days. Only about 9 percent of all nursing home stays are for five or more years, though some studies put that number higher.

The issue for the insured is how much to reduce premiums by taking on the longer-term risk. Those who are using the insurance to protect against the worst case will take the longest benefit period they can afford and use other provisions to reduce premiums. Other policy buyers might be comfortable reducing premiums by assuming they won't exceed the average long-term stay of two and a half to three years.

Inflation Protection. The younger the insured, the more important it is to protect against inflation. Even relatively older insureds, however, should seek inflation protection. The effects of compounded price increases, even at relatively low inflation rates, increase the cost of care substantially over 10 years and longer. Most people should not skimp on inflation protection in a long-term care policy.

The standard inflation protection is a maximum of 5 percent annually. Some policies offer a simple inflation protection option, but the compound inflation protection option offers better protection. After 10 years, the difference is substantial. Compound protection is worth the cost if it does not make the premiums unaffordable. If simple inflation protection is the only option, a better choice might be to drop inflation protection and opt for a substantially higher daily benefit. Usually this offers more protection for the premium dollar.

Inflation protection is expensive, so you might want to consider a higher daily benefit as an alternative to inflation protection. Because of the way insurers determine their premiums, the premiums are likely to be lower when taking this approach. It can make sense to pick a daily benefit that exceeds the current average cost and is close to what the cost is likely to be in 10 or 15 years after inflation. That way the insured is well covered without having to pay for expensive inflation protection.

Covered Care. This used to be a big hole in long-term care policies but now is less of a problem. The policy should cover both skilled and custodial care. The care should be covered whether it is given in a nursing home, assisted living facility, or at home. Many policies now will cover adult day care and some other forms of care. The daily benefit amount will differ, but you want as many types of care covered as possible. Avoid home-care provisions that say only professional licensed home-care services, such as registered or licensed practical nurses, will be covered. Someone who needs home care often needs help with basic chores such as cooking and cleaning. Older policies, in particular, would limit covered care only to those provided by licensed professionals. You should avoid such coverage limits.

Joint Policies.   Many insurers now allow a married couple to purchase one joint policy covering the couple instead of two individual policies. The premiums for a joint policy usually are lower than for two individual policies by about 20 percent. The potential downside of a joint policy is that the first spouse to need LTC exhausts the policy benefits and there is no coverage should the second spouse need care. It's a low probability event but could happen. You need to consider this scenario when deciding on the benefit limits of a joint policy.

The previous six provisions can be used to structure a policy that meets most of an individual's needs and is affordable. The insured must estimate the amount of income and assets that can be devoted to long-term care in the future. Some people will decide they can pay expenses for only a limited time, say 90 days or a year. After that, insurance will have to take over. Others will decide that they can pay a small portion of the expenses indefinitely but that insurance will have to cover most of the cost. Policy provisions can be adjusted to accommodate those two scenarios as well as many others.

Factors Outside the Policy

There are three more factors to consider before buying a policy. These are factors outside the individual policy terms, but they can affect either the cost of your coverage or whether the coverage is available when you need it.

Financial Condition.   Be sure to check on the financial safety ratings of the insurer. The ratings should be available from any insurance agent or broker, as well as from your local library or the Internet. Lower premiums probably are available through the less-sound insurers. However, these policies are designed for long-term protection, so the insured should make relatively certain that the insurer will be around for many years.

Premium Increases.   Premiums will increase. Long-term care policies still are fairly new, and insurers are learning. They made mistakes in the past by grossly underestimating claims. An early indication of probable future increases is how closely the company checks out a prospect before issuing a policy. An insurer that checks out a prospect's health carefully before issuing a policy probably will have a good premium history. An insurer that does little more than require a short questionnaire is likely to be surprised by higher claims than anticipated and to resort to sharp increases in premiums.

The insurance company or broker should provide a history of rate increases for the type of policy being considered. The state insurance department also can provide a premium increase history.

If someone can barely afford a policy now, odds are that after premium increases it won't be affordable in 5 or 10 years and will be dropped—probably just when it is needed most.

These are the key decisions that determine the cost of long-term care insurance and its benefits. What they boil down to is determining the risks the insured is willing to retain and which should be shifted to an insurance company. The specific terms of the policy can mean the difference between making a policy affordable and not being able to purchase one.

The Long-Term Care Partnership.   Over 40 states now participate in the Long-Term Care Partnership Program. The program encourages people to purchase and keep in force private LTCI by relaxing some of the Medicaid LTC rules. When a person has a qualified policy and applies for Medicaid to cover LTC after the policy's benefits have expired, the amount of exempt assets to be eligible for Medicaid is increased by the maximum coverage under the policy, and the beneficiary's estate might be exempt from the requirement that the state seek reimbursement from the estate for any funds spent on LTC.

The Importance of Shopping Around

I mentioned earlier that a high percentage of Americans over age 40 believe LTCI costs substantially more than it really does. That's not surprising, because prices of very similar policies vary considerably. Some insurers apparently count on consumers' not liking to shop for insurance and failing to comparison shop the way they do for other goods and services.

You easily can spend about twice what you should for an LTCI policy. In 2012, premiums on almost-identical policies ranged from $7,129 to $3,815, according to the American Association of Long-Term Care Insurance.

Insurance is an inefficient market. Insurers don't make their premiums readily available to consumers. You generally have to talk with insurance agents, and only a few agents sell policies from more than one company. It can take a lot of work to find a good deal on LTCI, but it is worth the effort.

When Should You Buy LTCI?

Many people who are interested in buying LTCI as part of their protection package are unsure of the age at which they should buy. It's understandable that they don't want to pay decades of premiums before filing claims and receiving benefits. That prospect makes it tempting to wait before buying.

There are some potential benefits to delaying the purchase of LTCI. You won't be paying premiums during the period you don't own the policy. There's a possibility that policy terms could improve, as they have since the policies became mainstream about 30 years ago. The ideal scenario for many people is to purchase an LTCI policy a relatively few years before the benefits are likely to be needed.

The problem is that there can be costs and disadvantages to waiting. While most people don't need LTC until they are in their late 70s or beyond, there are exceptions. There's no way of knowing whether in the next few years you'll have an accident or other event that triggers a need for LTC.

Another reason not to delay is that insurers have a history of changing and upgrading their policies every few years. These changes generally result in premium increases of about 3 percent over the prior version. It might be less expensive in the long term to buy a policy now and lock in current rates, at least to the extent they can be locked in.

The main disadvantage of delay is that you might not be able to buy coverage at any price. The older you are, the more likely it is that you'll have a physical condition that causes an insurer to either deny coverage or offer it only at a very high premium. Table 7.1 estimates the percentage of LTCI applicants in different age groups who were denied coverage in 2014. From the table, it's best to seek coverage in your early 50s. Each year after that your ability to obtain any coverage is reduced.

Compare Group and Individual Coverage

Many larger employers offer group long-term care policies to employees. Employers rarely pay any of the premiums, but use their purchasing power to negotiate favorable terms and premiums for the employees. If a group policy is available, certainly compare it to the individual offerings.

A big advantage of group policies is that an applicant is less likely to be denied coverage for current health problems. Another advantage is that the premiums could be lower than for comparable nongroup

TABLE 7.1   Percentage of LTCI Applicants Denied Coverage

Age	Decline Percentage
55 to 59	37%
60 to 64	39%
65 to 69	46%
70 to 74	50%
75 to 79	63%

policies. Also, the employer has done most of the hard work of the buying process.

Group policies are not without disadvantages. A group policy usually limits the available options. That's one way employers streamline the process and cut costs. There's no disadvantage unless the applicant wants a feature that is not offered or wants to modify a term, such as the elimination period, that is locked in for everyone in the group.

Also, group policies are not always less expensive. Group policies tend to attract people with medical problems who would not qualify for policies or for low premiums on individual policies. A healthy or relatively younger individual might be able to get cheaper rates through a separate policy.

Tax-Qualified or Nonqualifed Policy?

One more factor to consider before choosing a long-term care policy is whether it should be tax qualified. Tax-qualified policies were created in a 1996 law. Their premium payments can be deductible as medical expenses on your income tax return, and any benefits received from these policies are tax free. Before the law, the tax treatment of LTC policies was uncertain, but the premiums were generally believed to be nondeductible. The tax benefits of a tax-qualified policy look tempting, but let's dig a little deeper:

- *The tax deductions are limited.* The first limit is by age. The IRS sets the maximum deduction for each age group annually. In 2015, the maximum premium deductions were: age 40 and under, $370; ages 41 to 51, $700; 51 to 60, $1,400; 61 to 70, $3,720; over 70, $4,660. The amounts are indexed for inflation, and the latest amounts can be found in IRS Publication 502 each year. Another limit is that the deduction is available only to those who itemize expenses on Schedule A.

  A further limit is that the premiums are included with other medical expenses and are deductible only to the extent that when added to other medical expenses, the total exceeds 10 percent of adjusted gross income (7.5 percent of adjusted gross income for those ages 65 and over until 2019). Few people deduct any of their medical expenses because of these limits.

- *Qualified policies have certain required terms and provisions.* One requirement for a qualified policy is that it pays benefits only if the insured cannot perform at least two of the activities of daily living (eating, dressing, bathing, walking, etc.) or is suffering from Alzheimer's disease. In addition, a doctor must certify that care will be needed for more than 90 days. A nonqualified policy, on the other hand, often pays benefits if the insured has a medical necessity, and a minimum need period of 90 days is not required. Thus, nonqualified policies can provide more coverage.

Because the coverage is a bit broader, a nonqualified policy generally costs 5 percent to 20 percent more than a comparable qualified one. Insurers supposedly expect to pay 20 percent to 40 percent fewer claims under the tax-qualified policies, so they charge lower premiums.

■ *While the benefit payments from a tax-qualified policy clearly are* tax free, it is not clear whether benefits from a nonqualified long-term care policy are taxable. The IRS, courts, and Congress have not ruled on the issue. Recipients of benefits under nonqualified long-term care policies usually treat the benefits as tax free, and the IRS has not challenged this treatment to date.

For all these reasons, it is possible that tax breaks under qualified long-term care policies cost more than they are worth. It probably is best to buy the policy you want. After you select a policy, ask about its tax status.

Will LTCI Pay Benefits?

Many people ask: Will a long-term care insurance policy actually pay benefits after I file a claim? Many people apparently are concerned that they will pay premiums for years or decades. Then, when they need care the insurer will decline to pay benefits or find policy loopholes to avoid paying. Media reports, rumors, and data generate uncertainty about the issue.

Reports and anecdotes indicate that in the early days of LTCI, some insurers made their money by collecting premiums and then denying many claims filed by policyholders. In some policies, the conditions under which claims would be paid were vague. Other times, people believed insurers simply denied most claims and made insureds appeal in order to have their claims paid.

Many things have changed since the early days of LTCI, including the process for determining whether a claim should be paid. (Remember, LTCI is fewer than 40 years old.)

The major change was the Health Insurance Portability and Accountability Act of 1996 (HIPAA). The law is best known for its provisions on the privacy of medical records. Another part of HIPAA, however, specified the terms under which benefits would be paid under some LTCI policies. The law defined how disabled a person must be and how the disability is measured to determine when benefits should be paid. While the law applies only to tax-qualified LTCI, most insurers adopted the claims standards as the minimum for all their policies.

There are two possible benefit triggers under LTCI, a physical benefit trigger and a cognitive benefit trigger. A claim should be paid when the insured qualifies under either trigger.

The physical benefit trigger is when the insured is unable to perform at least two of the five or six (depending on the policy) activities of daily living (bathing, dressing, toileting (and in some policies continence), transferring, walking, and eating). The condition is certified by a physician or nurse and must be expected to last at least 90 days. The cognitive benefit trigger is a loss or deterioration in intellectual capacity, such as from Alzheimer's disease or dementia. Some policies provide care is covered if a licensed medical professional certifies that it is needed.

Once a claim is filed, the insurer will evaluate it. The evaluation process varies based on the insurer and the type of claim. The insurer might send one of its employees or contractors to perform an in-person assessment of the insured. Or the insurer might have its staff review medical records or accept a written certification from a licensed healthcare worker. When a policyholder is reported to suffer a severe stroke, for example, the insurer might require only a telephone call or letter from the treating physician. When Alzheimer's or dementia is claimed, the insurer might require a cognitive test by either the patient's doctor or its own staff or contractors.

The fear of some potential LTCI buyers is insurers will use the standards and process to deny most claims. Here's the data I could find. In 2007, nearly 96 percent of LTCI claims received immediate approval. Of the 4 percent that weren't initially approved, about half of those eventually were approved. The other 2 percent were denied because the benefit triggers were not met. This is from a report by the Kaiser Family Foundation published in 2008. The Government Accountability Office reviewed data from five states and found the total number of complaints about LTCI fell from 846 to 721 between 2001 and 2007, but complaints about claims settlement in particular rose from 215 to 315.

The National Association of Insurance Commissioners says the data are hard to interpret, because insurers report data differently. For example, if a claimant is in a nursing home that charges $150 per day but the policy provides for only a $100 daily benefit, some insurers report this as an approved claim while others report it has both an approval of the $100 claim and a denial of the $50 balance. Also, the rise in the number of complaints about claims might be because as the population ages more people are filing claims, so complaints also are likely to rise.

In 2014, a record $7.85 billion in benefits were paid under LTCI policies to 250,000 individual beneficiaries. The total benefit payouts increased five percent from 2013, according to the American Association of Long-Term Care Insurance.

Many fears of nonpayment of LTCI claims were reinforced by a 2007 article in *The New York Times* by Charles Duhigg. The article said *The Times* conducted numerous interviews and reviewed confidential depositions and concluded that "some long-term-care insurers have developed procedures that make it difficult—if not impossible—for policyholders to get paid." It also said that elderly policyholders were faced with "unnecessary delays and overwhelming bureaucracies."

That sounds pretty damning about LTCI and the insurers that offer it. A key qualifying statement, however, comes a little later in the article, where it states that most of the complaints were from policyholders of three companies, two of which were related. These companies experienced a much higher rate of complaints per policyholder than other insurers. At least one of the companies eventually exited the LTCI business and turned its policies over to the state and a trust to administer. The largest long-term-care insurer, on the other hand, received only one complaint for every 12,434 policies. If you want to read the article, go to your favorite web search engine and search for "Charles Duhigg & long-term care."

Almost all insurers will pay promptly claims that qualify for coverage under the policies they issue. But every insurer receives some complaints and denies some claims. It's important that you and others close to you know your policy and understand it. Often claims are filed by someone other the person who bought the policy, or the person who bought it isn't physically or mentally sharp. The elimination period, or deductible, often is a source of conflict between insurers and insureds. Also, the care provider, whether a person or a facility, must have the licenses, certifications, and other standards required by the insurer. Check on that before selecting a provider. Also, be aware of the paperwork and tests the insurer will require to process and pay a claim.

When considering LTCI, don't buy the policy with the lowest premiums. You don't want to trade low premiums today for big problems down the road. You want an insurer with financial stability and that has been in the LTCI business for a while. Check with your state insurance commissioner for histories of both complaints and premium increases regarding each insurer. Be sure you understand the details of the policy before you buy, even if it takes time.

Enhancing LTCI

LTCI is an important and complicated consideration. There are several steps that can generate optimum benefits for you:

- *Shop around*. Despite the number of insurers who left the market after 2009, there still are quite a few insurers offering LTCI. Premiums and policy terms can vary considerably. Take the time to compare similar policies from a range of insurers.
- *Consider innovative policies*. It used to be that you had to determine the maximum benefits you wanted in LTCI and pay premiums for them from the start. There always was an option to reduce benefits when the premiums rose too high, though refunds weren't made for past

premiums paid for the higher benefits. Now, insurers are offering LTCI policies that allow you to increase benefits later without fresh evidence of being insurable. That allows you to lock in a policy at an affordable minimum level of coverage now and increase coverage later if you want.

- *Purchase a joint policy.* Married couples usually can obtain savings of 20 percent or so by purchasing a policy that covers both of them instead of individual policies. Be sure that you understand the coverage limits of the policies you're considering and how they are affected if each of you needs LTC during your lifetimes.

- *Check the claims history.* Most LTCI carriers have been in the business for a long time and promptly pay claims that are due under their policies. There are a few insurers who made a practice of denying claims and forcing the policyholders to appeal in order to receive their benefits. Check the claims history of an insurer with your state insurance department.

- *Don't jump at the lowest premium.* The lowest price isn't necessarily the best deal. The insurer might be inexperienced with LTCI and be making bad assumptions about future claims experience and other factors. Or the insurer might be trying to increase market share by underpricing policies. Too often, the lowest price policies in the first year are the ones that impose sharp premium increases after a few years.

- *Consider long-term partnership policies.* Over 40 states now are in the long-term care partnership. When you have an LTCI policy that qualifies under the partnership, the state is less like to seek reimbursement from your estate if you also need Medicaid to pay for your LTC after the policy benefits are reached.

Exploring the Hybrid or Combination Policies

A minority of people who are in the prime ages for buying LTCI actually buy the traditional stand-alone policies. A major reason for the low ownership rate apparently is the use-it-or-lose-it nature of LTCI. Like auto, homeowner's, and term life insurance, you don't receive benefits from the policy if you don't file a claim. When you don't need LTC in your lifetime, the policy expires with your passing. There isn't a cash value or other amount to be paid to your heirs. If you decide during your lifetime that you no longer want the policy, there also isn't an account to be returned to you. What you received for your premiums is peace of mind that the policy was there if you need LTC.

Because of this issue, insurers developed alternatives. The hybrid, or combination, policies are growing in popularity. In 2014, sales of traditional LTCI declined 24 percent from 2013 for a total of 131,000 policies sold. About 15 years earlier, 750,000 LTCI policies were sold in a year. Meanwhile, hybrid policies (also called linked-benefits policies or combination policies) increased approximately 500 percent in the six years ending 2014, according to the AALTCI.

These are annuities and permanent life insurance policies with LTC riders or benefits attached. You receive the benefits of the annuity or life insurance, but if you need LTC during your lifetime, the policies will pay benefits.

Insurers have different ways of charging for the benefits. With an annuity, you might receive a lower interest rate credited to your account each year than would be the case with a straight annuity. With life insurance, the insurance benefit could be less than if you paid the same premium for a straight permanent life insurance policy, or there could be an additional premium amount for the LTC rider.

Another potential benefit to a hybrid policy is that someone who can't qualify for traditional LTCI for age or health reasons might be able to qualify for a hybrid policy. I'm not saying that anyone can receive LTCI through a hybrid. The insurers do have underwriting standards for these policies. But when the LTC is the secondary benefit under the policy, the insurer might accept some applicants who were denied traditional LTCI. It depends on the insurer and the type of policy.

Some insurance analysts say the coverage under a hybrid policy might not be as robust as stand-alone LTCI. That largely depends on the policy and probably was more true of the early hybrid policies than most of those available now. Some hybrid policies have terms on their LTC riders that are comparable to standard LTCI. Others have differences, such as paying benefits under different conditions, not paying for all the types of care that LTCI covers, and other terms.

When considering a hybrid policy, you need to examine the LTC rider in the same way you would stand-alone LTCI. Consider all the same terms and conditions. Be sure you have the coverage you think you do.

In a hybrid policy, the non-LTCI portion of the policy usually is drawn down before the LTC benefits are used. That means you're spending your and your heirs' money first and the insurance company's money only after your money is exhausted.

Here's an example of one specific annuity/LTC hybrid that first was available in 2013. This is but one example. There are a lot of variations in the details of the hybrid policies, so don't assume every hybrid policy offered to you will have these or similar terms.

The annuity is purchased with a lump sum deposit of from $35,000 to $400,000, or $600,000 for a joint annuity for a married couple. (You also can make a tax-free exchange of an existing annuity.) Your deposit immediately begins accumulating interest. The interest rate in 2013 was 3 percent for deposits over $200,000 and 2.5 percent from lower amounts. The rate changes annually but can't fall below 1 percent.

The LTC benefits were up to three times the annuity's value for those in good health. If you deposited $100,000, you had up to $300,000 of LTC coverage. For those with some health problems but who still qualified for coverage, the LTC benefits were twice the deposit. The cost of the LTC coverage won't increase over time and won't reduce your principal. As interest earnings increase the annuity account value, the LTC coverage also increases. Remember, the cost of the LTC coverage is that your annuity account is credited a lower interest rate than it would receive without the LTC rider.

As with a standard long-term care insurance policy, the LTC benefits are triggered when you can't perform two or more of the six activities of daily living (determined by a licensed medical professional) or are cognitively impaired. Eleven long-term care services are covered, including adult day care, home care, homemaker services, and residence in an assisted living facility or nursing home. There's no waiting period for reimbursements for home health care or respite care, and a 90-day waiting period for other types of care.

Since this is an annuity, your deposit and accumulated interest are available for other uses. You can withdraw up to 10 percent of the contract value each year or schedule regular annuity distributions, such as a single life annuity or a joint life annuity covering the lives of both you and your spouse. Keep in mind that any lifetime distributions reduce your LTC benefit. The account value you don't distribute or use for long-term care can be transferred to your heirs or other beneficiaries.

A withdrawal of the full account within the first nine years faces an early withdrawal fee. The fee is 8 percent of the amount withdrawn the first year and one percentage point less each year until there is no fee for distributions in year 10 and later. This early withdrawal fee, or liquidity fee, doesn't apply to any of the up to 10 percent annual withdrawals.

When LTC reimbursements are triggered, they first reduce your annuity account value. After the account is exhausted, additional LTC reimbursements from the insurer continue until the coverage limit is reached. If you pass away after the account value is exhausted but before using the maximum LTC benefits, your annuity beneficiary receives nothing. Also, if you exit LTC after exhausting the account value, there is no account value left for you to use.

A maximum monthly LTC reimbursement is set by the insurer based on the premiums you deposit. The limit was $4,220 monthly, during the first year, for a 65-year-old male who put in $100,000, which meant there were 72 months of coverage from a $100,000 deposit. Assuming you take the maximum monthly LTC limit, the payments would last 72 months for a single insured and 90 months under a jointly insured annuity. If your monthly reimbursement is less than the maximum, the number of months you'll have coverage is extended. Keep in mind that the maximum monthly payment for LTC is set by the insurer. If you have LTC that costs more per month, you have to make up the difference from other means.

There was no medical exam to qualify for the LTC coverage, only an application and telephone interview.

Married couples can elect Joint LTC Coverage, which can be advantageous. The two spouses share the maximum benefits, which last for 90 months if the maximum monthly reimbursement is taken. This means if the spouses both need LTC but at different times, they have a joint 90 months of care. But if they need care at the same time, the maximum benefit period is shorter because they're using two months of coverage each month they both receive reimbursements.

Of course, the annuity qualifies for the usual tax deferral of interest earnings of the annuity.

Here's an example of how the annuity can work. Max Profits has $100,000 in CDs. He doesn't expect to need the money unless he suffers a financial reversal or has unplanned expenses such as long-term care. He hopes it is available for his children to inherit, but he's keeping it in safe investments partly as an emergency fund for unexpected expenses and partly because he doesn't trust other investments these days.

Max uses the maturing CDs to make a deposit in the annuity. He'll earn 2.5 percent interest for the first year, and it will compound tax-deferred in the annuity. If he needs cash, Max can withdraw up to 10 percent of the annuity's value during a year free from the insurer liquidity charges, and there won't be an early distribution IRS tax penalty as long as he is 59$\frac{1}{2}$ or older. Such distributions would reduce the LTC benefits. After nine years, Max can withdraw the entire amount without penalty if he wants.

Should Max need long-term care while he owns the annuity, he'll have long-term care benefits of more than $300,000 if he qualified for maximum coverage or $200,000 under regular coverage. If Max passes away without taking any distributions or needing LTC, his beneficiaries receive the annuity account value. If he does need LTC, the reimbursements reduce the account value available to his heirs until the account value is spent.

That's one example of an LTC/annuity hybrid policy. There are many variations of the details, and there also are permanent life insurance policies with LTC riders. A common feature of the products is that when you start drawing LTC benefits, these reduce either your annuity account or life insurance benefit first. Only after these are exhausted will the insurer begin paying additional benefits for LTC.

As I said, a major appeal of the hybrid policies is the elimination of the use-it-or-lose-it nature of traditional LTCI policies. If you never need LTC or need only a modest amount, the remaining benefits in the annuity or life insurance are received by your beneficiary. In general you should buy a hybrid policy only when you also have a need or use for either the annuity or permanent life insurance. For example, if you have money you are keeping in safe investments for an emergency or to leave for loved ones, putting some of that money in a hybrid annuity might be a good idea. Also, if you plan to self-insure for at least some of your LTC needs, putting the designated money in a hybrid annuity might be a good way to self-insure.

Using Permanent Life Insurance

Some people plan to use traditional permanent life insurance to fund their long-term care needs. Permanent life insurance comes in several versions. The most common is whole life insurance. You give premiums to an insurer. In return you receive life insurance coverage. You also have a cash value account that earns interest at a rate set by the insurer. You can borrow from the cash value if you need money. Unlike term life insurance, permanent life insurance doesn't expire as long as you pay the premiums. The death benefit always is payable to your named beneficiaries. There are variations with more complications, such as universal life insurance and variable life insurance.

Some people prefer using permanent life insurance because they view it as being cheaper than LTCI and it also will pay benefits eventually, unlike LTCI.

There are a couple of ways permanent life insurance can be used to pay for LTC.

One way would be to borrow against the policy's cash value when LTC is needed. This isn't recommended as a primary way to pay for LTC. The amount you can borrow will be less than your life insurance benefits. Also, the loans will reduce the life insurance benefits eventually paid to your beneficiary. Finally, it is unlikely the cash value will be enough to pay for a significant amount of LTC.

Another way some people use permanent life insurance to fund LTC is to pay for any LTC expenses out of their existing assets and income. This spending will reduce or deplete their estates. After they pass, however, the life insurance policy pays benefits to either their estates or their loved ones. The life insurance ensures that there is a substantial inheritance regardless of how much is spent on LTC.

There are some potential disadvantages to this strategy.

The strategy might not work well when you have a spouse who survives you. The estate could be substantially reduced or even depleted. While the life insurance might be substantial, it might not be enough to sustain your spouse's standard of living for life, including any LTC he or she might need.

Another potential disadvantage is that you need the assets or income to pay for the LTC. Essentially, you need enough liquid assets to pay for the LTC. Otherwise, there's a risk that assets will be sold in a hurry to pay for care or be sold by someone who doesn't know how to maximize their value. If your strategy is to spend down your assets to pay for LTC and then have Medicaid pay for your LTC, be sure to review the rules carefully to ensure you know all the details. For example, the state might seek reimbursement from either your estate or loved ones for the money it spent on LTC.

Forging Your LTC Plan

As we've seen, there are a number of ways to pay for any LTC you or your spouse might need.

A threshold question is who should consider the tools other than paying from personal assets. There are two categories of people who should consider using only personal assets and then Medicaid to pay for LTC.

One group who should consider personally financing LTC is the very wealthy. They can pay for the costs from their own resources. They don't have to be concerned about finding an appropriate policy and paying premiums that might not result in benefit payouts.

There are several factors to consider before deciding you are wealthy enough to self-finance LTC you or your spouse needs.

An important factor is that the cost of LTC varies greatly around the country, as does the definition of very wealthy. Someone who can easily afford LTC in the Midwest might not be able to afford it in New York City. That's why a bright line net worth level of who should consider self-financing LTC can't be developed. It depends on where a person is located or will receive LTC.

The type of assets that comprise your wealth also is important. LTC costs have to be paid in cash. It's not unusual for someone to be wealthy on paper but to have much of that wealth in assets that can't easily and quickly be converted to cash: real estate, small businesses, and other illiquid assets. You probably don't want to have to sell assets, especially at fire-sale prices, to raise cash for LTC. No matter your net worth, if you don't have enough liquid assets to pay for a couple years of LTC plus support your dependents, you probably aren't wealthy enough to self-insure for LTC.

Inflation should be another concern. LTC generally rises faster than the Consumer Price Index, usually at about twice the CPI rate. LTC expenses that seem affordable to you today might not be in 15 or 20 years if LTC costs rise faster than the amount of liquid assets you have.

Keep in mind that others might be depending on your assets. What would happen to the assets available to support them if you need years of LTC? Be sure to consider all the demands on your assets before deciding to self-insure.

The second group of people who should consider self-insuring are those of very modest means. Premiums for LTCI would consume a substantial percentage of their annual incomes, forcing them to dramatically reduce their standards of living. They also probably don't have enough assets to be able to buy one of the hybrid policies to cover LTC. People in this group are those for whom the Medicaid coverage of LTC was created. They should assume that if they need LTC they'll spend down what assets they have until they qualify for Medicaid.

For everyone else, to plan for LTC you need to consider all the tools that are available and use the ones that will work for you. Consider how family can help. Review the benefits you might be able to receive from the government programs, Medicare and Medicaid. Then look at the insurance options. There are individual LTCI policies as well as policies that might be available through employers or other group plans. Take a look at some hybrid policies. You might even want to consider permanent life insurance as a way to restore to your loved ones some of the money you might spend on LTC. Of course, you'll have to self-insure to some extent by paying for LTC from your assets. The government programs and insurance options don't cover LTC costs from day one and also aren't likely to cover all the costs you'll incur.

LTC costs scare many people who are in or approaching retirement. Most people have a low probability of needing the dreaded multiyear residence in a nursing home or at home with full-time assistance. For those who have that need, however, the cost can mount quickly and drain your estate as well as assets of loved ones. That's why you want to develop a plan for covering as much potential LTC expenses as you can and limiting the probability of becoming a financial burden and losing your independence.

Managing IRAs to Last

Individual retirement arrangements (IRAs) are simple at first. You contribute some money each year and select some investments. Congress threw in some complications over the years by changing the contribution amounts and phasing out deductions for contributions as income rises if you participate in an employer retirement plan. Some people need some of their money early and have to deal with the 10 percent early distribution penalty and the ways to avoid it. For most people, however, there's not much more to IRAs than contributing and investing.

All that changes as the late-career years approach.

IRAs are among the most valuable assets people own, especially when they rollover 401(k) accounts to IRAs. It is the main source of retirement financing for many people. People now also can choose between traditional IRAs and Roth IRAs, and they have the option to convert a traditional IRA to a Roth IRA.

Managing your IRA to make it last as long as possible becomes vital. There are many rules to know and traps to avoid.

Taxes and penalties can drain significant cash from IRAs. Traditional IRAs provide tax breaks during the accumulation period. Contributions might be deductible, and income and gains compound in the IRA tax deferred. When money is rolled over from a 401(k), the contributions to the 401(k) weren't taxed, and the income and gains earned on the contributions compounded tax deferred. There's a price to be paid for those tax breaks, and that price is paid when money is distributed from the traditional IRA or 401(k).

Distributions from a traditional IRA are included in gross income and taxed as ordinary income. If the contributions were deductible, those are taxed as ordinary income, as are distributions of income and gains. When contributions weren't deducted, they are tax free when distributed but the compounded income and gains are taxed as ordinary income when distributed.

In effect, you took out a mortgage on your IRA each time you made a contribution. That mortgage comes due in installments when distributions are made. You include the distributions in income (except for distributions of non-deductible contributions), and they are taxed as ordinary income. Another way you pay the mortgage is by having all the taxable distributions treated as ordinary income. Long-term capital gains earned by the IRA, which would receive favorable tax treatment if earned in a taxable account, lose their special tax breaks when earned within an IRA. Those are the costs you pay for the tax breaks of traditional IRAs.

In this chapter, we discuss how to manage IRAs to maximize after-tax wealth and extend the lives of the IRAs. We assume that you are near or in the post-career years. You long ago made decisions about which types of retirement accounts to use and how much to contribute to them. Now, you're approaching the distribution years. You want to know how to manage IRAs and their distributions to maximize how long an IRA will last. In this chapter, we discuss required minimum distributions (RMDs), ways to invest IRAs to last, rolling over 401(k)s to IRAs, converting traditional IRAs to Roth IRAs, and other strategies.

Navigating the Required Minimum Distribution Minefield

Required minimum distributions (RMDs) for those over age 70$^1/_2$ are a key source of lost wealth, and that is only going to get worse. The IRS in recent years concluded that RMD mistakes are a major source of lost tax revenue, so it is cracking down. The IRS receives enough information from IRA custodians to identify people who might have made RMD mistakes. The penalty for not taking the full RMD is 50 percent of the amount you should have distributed but didn't. It's one of the steepest penalties in the tax code.

While it's important to meet the IRS's rules for RMDs, that shouldn't be your only goal. There are planning opportunities for RMDs that can reduce taxes and increase after-tax wealth. You have flexibility and choices, and you need to carefully consider them.

RMDs are required from traditional IRAs after age 70$^1/_2$. The first RMD is required by April 1 of the year after you turn 70$^1/_2$. For example, those who turn 70$\frac{1}{2}$ in 2016 must take the first RMD no later than April 1, 2017, but also can take that first RMD before the end of 2016.

It's often best to take the first RMD in the year you turn 70$\frac{1}{2}$, because you'll have to take the second RMD by Dec. 31 of the following year. That would give you two RMDs in one year if you defer the initial RMD until April 1 of the year following the year you turn 70$\frac{1}{2}$, and then take the second RMD by Dec. 31 of that year. Taking two RMDs could push you into a higher tax bracket, reduce tax breaks, and cause other problems.

In the years after you turn 70$\frac{1}{2}$, you must take an RMD each year by December 31.

You also have to take RMDs from traditional employer plans, but the rules are a bit different. In this chapter, we focus on RMDs from traditional IRAs. There are no required minimum distributions for original owners of Roth IRAs.

To compute your RMD for the year, start with the ending value of the IRA on December 31 of the previous year. When you turn 70$\frac{1}{2}$ in 2016, you use the closing value for 2015, even if you wait until early 2017 to take that first RMD. In years after you turn 70$\frac{1}{2}$, you use the IRA value at the close of the previous year. Those taking regular 2016 RMDs use the IRA values on December 31, 2015.

After determining the correct IRA balance to use, find your life expectancy in the tables furnished by the IRS in Publication 590, available free on the IRS website at www.irs.gov.

There are three life expectancy tables. Table I is for beneficiaries (those who've inherited IRAs). Table II is for married IRA owners whose spouses are both more than 10 years younger than they are and are the sole principal beneficiaries of the IRAs. Every other IRA owner uses Table III, also known as the Uniform Lifetime Table.

After locating the correct table to use, locate your current life expectancy in the table and divide the IRA balance at the end of last year by your life expectancy for this year. If you turn 74 in 2016, your life expectancy under Table III is 23.8. If your IRA balance on December 31, 2015, was $150,000, your RMD for 2016 is $6,303.

When you own multiple IRAs, compute the RMD by aggregating the balances of all your IRAs and dividing the total by your life expectancy. Then, you have flexibility. You can take the RMD from the IRAs in any combination you want. Take it all from one IRA or take different amounts from the IRAs in any ratio you want.

This rule allows you to use the RMD to rebalance your overall portfolio when it's out of balance or simplify your finances by drawing down one IRA at a time.

An RMD doesn't have to be taken in cash. The tax law allows the distribution to be taken in property, and most IRA custodians allow noncash distributions. A property distribution is easy when the custodian is a broker or mutual fund company and the IRA holds conventional assets such as stocks or mutual funds. With most IRA custodians, the form to request the distribution allows you to designate whether you want the distribution to be in cash or in particular assets. To make a property distribution, if you don't already have a taxable account at the custodian, most brokers and mutual fund companies simply set up a new taxable account to receive the distribution. Then, the designated number of shares of the stock or mutual fund is transferred from the IRA to the taxable account.

Consider taking an RMD as a property distribution when you don't need the RMD in cash to pay living expenses and want to continue owning the asset in your portfolio or don't want to incur the costs of selling an asset.

When you take a distribution of property, the fair market value on the date of the distribution is included in your gross income, regardless of what happens to the asset's price the rest of the year. That value also is your tax basis in the asset. If you sell the asset during your lifetime, there will be capital gain on any appreciation or a capital loss if the asset declines in value. The gain or loss is determined by taking the amount realized on the sale and subtracting the basis.

You can take RMDs during the course of the year on any schedule you want, as long as you take distributions totaling at least the minimum amount by December 31. There are different factors to consider when deciding on the timing or you RMDs.

T. Rowe Price did a study some years ago covering the years 1993 to 2003. The study found that an IRA owner who waited as late as possible in the year to take RMDs accumulated a bit more money over time and made the IRA last longer than an owner who took RMDs at the start of the year. The study assumed the IRA owner took distributions in cash. Since investment assets generally were appreciating during that time, it made sense to leave the investments to appreciate in the accounts for as long as possible before selling to generate cash for the distributions.

The result would have been different if the accounts were more conservatively invested or markets weren't booming. In fact, in the Price study, the late-distributing IRA owner was far ahead of the other IRA owner through 1999. After that, the early-distributing IRA owner rapidly caught up because the value of his IRA wasn't declining by as much as the other owner's. Only the stock market rally of 2003 pushed the late-distributing owner back into a clear lead. The timing also wouldn't matter nearly as much if distributions were taken in property instead of cash.

There are other factors to consider before determining the timing of RMDs, and these factors generally favor taking RMDs early in the year.

Early distributions ensure the task is not forgotten or left to a last-minute rush when IRA custodians are busy and likely to make mistakes or perform tasks late. Taking the RMD early in the year also ensures there is no problem in case anything should happen to you during the year. Executors must take RMDs from the IRAs of those over age 70$^1/_2$ who passed away during the year. But many overlook this or take too much time to accumulate enough information to know how much they need to take. The result is a late RMD and a penalty. Taking RMDs early in the year avoids these potential problems.

Don't forget to either factor the RMD in your estimated tax payments for the year or have the custodian withhold an appropriate amount for taxes. You don't want to be hit with an underpayment of estimated tax penalty.

Keep in mind that you always can take more than the RMD from the IRA each year. The RMD is the minimum amount you are required to distribute.

RMDs also are required of beneficiaries who inherit either traditional or Roth IRAs. Those rules are different. The RMDs for beneficiaries should be considered as part of an estate planning strategy, and you should be sure anyone you plan to inherit an IRA from you knows about the rules. We don't discuss them in this chapter.

Strategies to Reduce RMDs

RMDs create tax and financial planning problems for some people. The purpose of RMDs is to force the IRA to be spent down during a person's life expectancy, whether you need the cash or not. When you examine the IRS life expectancy tables and estimate future RMDs under different scenarios, you'll see that the percentage of the IRA that must be distributed each year steadily increases.

The RMD distribution schedule doesn't match the spending patterns or income needs of most retired Americans. They don't steadily increase spending as they age, and many people are more inclined to spend the same or a lesser percentage of their net worth as they age to ensure they don't run out of money. We discussed this in some detail in Chapter 4.

In addition, there are a number of people who have sufficient income and assets outside of their IRAs to sustain their retirement standards of living. They don't need the early RMDs to fund their spending, and they certainly don't need the progressively higher RMDs as the years go by. People in this situation often view their IRAs as emergency spending sources or something they are saving for their heirs to inherit.

You can see how RMDs create tax problems for people in these situations, especially when the IRAs are large because they were funded with rollovers from 401(k) plans.

Remember that IRA distributions are included in gross income and taxed as ordinary income, except for distributions of nondeductible contributions. As RMDs increase over time, they steadily increase gross income and adjusted gross income (AGI). AGI is the last line on the bottom of the front page of Form 1040. AGI is very important, because it determines whether you are subject to what I call the "stealth taxes." These are tax provisions that increase your gross income, reduce tax deductions, or impose additional taxes as income levels rise. We discuss the major stealth taxes in detail in Chapter 9. They include the Medicare premium surtax, tax on Social Security benefits, reductions in personal and dependent exemptions and itemized deductions, the alternative minimum tax, and more.

RMDs put retirees at risk of triggering or increasing the stealth taxes. Many retirees find that as they enter their late 70s and beyond, the RMDs increase to the point that their tax planning is hindered. They are paying substantial income taxes on income they don't need. This reduces their nest eggs and also reduces the legacies they planned to leave to loved ones or charity.

Fortunately, there are strategies for those who don't want that steady increase of distributions during their lifetimes. We discuss them in this chapter. They include:

- *Take money out of the IRA before you are required to, and the earlier the better.* This means draw down the IRA first instead of letting it compound.
- *Convert the traditional IRA to a Roth IRA.* Pay the taxes now, avoid the future RMDs, and have the benefit of tax-free investing and future tax-free distributions from the Roth IRA.
- *Let the RMDs happen, but use the after-tax amount to purchase permanent life insurance.* Your heirs inherit the insurance benefit tax free, and it is likely to be much higher than the after-tax amount of the IRA would be.
- *Use the family bank strategy.* Draw down the IRA early, pay the taxes, and use the after-tax amount to buy a permanent life insurance policy that will serve as a family bank. You can tap the cash value for tax-free loans if you need cash. Otherwise, your heirs inherit the life insurance benefit.

Empty an IRA Early?

The conventional advice is to delay distributions from tax-deferred accounts for as long as possible so that tax-deferred compounding can continue its work. That advice works for most people. Yet it is not the right advice for everyone. As we just discussed, RMDs can increase taxes later in life. Tax deferral can come back to bite the IRA owner instead of providing tax benefits. For people in such a situation, it makes sense to consider taking IRA distributions before being required to. In fact, emptying the IRA early, in effect accelerating taxes, can be more profitable in the long run.

Years ago, when I first addressed the problems of RMDs and owners of "excess IRAs," there were few options. Roth IRAs initially weren't available, and conversions of traditional IRAs to Roth IRAs were allowed only to people with adjusted gross incomes up to $100,000. So, I did the calculations and determined that it can make sense to empty an IRA early instead of maximizing tax deferral. That's still the case today.

For example, Max Profits has a $1 million IRA that earns 9 percent annually, and he is in the top tax bracket. He has to begin RMDs this year, and the first distribution will be $38,168. In five years, the RMD will be $58,250, and at age 82 the distribution will be $102,813. If Max lives to age 90, the RMD is up to $176,238. Max's expenses aren't likely to rise at that rate.

Between federal and state income taxes, Max could be paying close to half these distributions in taxes. If Max hadn't already been in the top tax bracket, the RMDs would push him into it. The RMDs also could increase taxes on Social Security benefits, trigger or increase the Medicare premium surtax, and cause Max to lose other tax benefits because of the phase-out of deductions and exemptions for higher-income taxpayers.

Suppose Max is only age 65, and the rest of the facts are the same. He has to begin RMDs after age 70½, and the first distribution will be $56,154. Five years later, the RMD will be $78,011, and at age 82 the distribution will be $145,308. If Max lives to age 90, the RMD is up to $243,077. At that point, the IRA still is worth more than $2.5 million.

Max and others in similar situations can slash their lifetime tax burden by taking an unconventional step. They can begin taking more from the IRA than the law and their spending needs require.

To make a point, let's take an extreme example and say that Max in the second case lives to 100 and takes only the RMDs. He'll pay just over $2 million in federal income taxes on these distributions at the 35 percent rate. The exact amount of taxes will depend on Max's other income, deductions, and other factors. He still will have over $1.6 million in the IRA at age 100. That amount will be taxed when distributed to him or his heirs.

Suppose instead that, to avoid the higher income taxes down the road, Max decides not to let the IRA grow as much. Max decides to take large enough distributions so that the IRA grows no more than 4 percent from its original balance. Then, the lifetime taxes on the distributions at age 100 are down to just over $1.2 million.

Let's say Max puts into a taxable account the after-tax distributions that exceed the RMDs. That account grows 7 percent annually before taxes, and taxes are paid at a 20 percent rate each year. By age 100, the taxable investment account exceeds $1.75 million. The IRA still is worth over $700,000.

In this scenario, Max's heirs have more after-tax wealth available to them if he limits the growth of the IRA. The IRA still has significant value, and they will be able to spend its after-tax value. All or most of the taxable account is available to them without additional taxes.

Taking the money out early works for a couple of reasons. First, Max no longer is converting long-term capital gains into ordinary income. Once money comes out of the IRA and the after-tax amount is invested in taxable accounts, the appreciation becomes long-term capital gains taxes in 2016 at a maximum rate of 20 percent. Second, Max can control when taxes are incurred. Instead of being forced to take distributions on a schedule whether he needs the money or not, Max can let gains compound in the taxable account and not incur taxes when he doesn't want to. He also can use other strategies to limit the taxes on the taxable account.

The strategy provides an additional benefit to Max's heirs. When an IRA is inherited, the tax basis of the assets is not increased. The beneficiaries who inherit the IRA pay taxes on distributions the same as the original owner would have. In other words, the ordinary income still has to be recognized for the heirs to spend the money. Another way to look at it is that the heirs don't really inherit the full value of the IRA. They really only benefit from the after-tax value.

When assets outside a tax-deferred account are inherited, however, heirs receive a benefit. They are allowed to increase the tax basis of the assets to their current fair market value. That means all the appreciation that occurred during the previous owner's life isn't taxed. The heirs can sell the assets at fair market value and not owe any capital gains taxes. They benefit from the full value of the assets outside the IRA.

Is It Right for You?

The benefits of taking more out of an IRA than the law and spending needs require depend on the individual situation.

The strategy should be considered by those whose IRAs, after considering other sources of income, greatly exceed lifetime spending needs. In effect, the IRA is operating as an emergency savings account, a supplement to other sources of income, or a likely legacy for loved ones. In those cases, benefits can be generated by getting money out of the IRA early instead of letting it compound indefinitely in the IRA.

The earlier one begins the strategy, the better the results will be. (Don't begin before age $59\frac{1}{2}$, to avoid the 10 percent premature distribution penalty.) You will pay income taxes on the early distributions and be able to invest in the taxable account the after-tax amount of the distributions. The taxable account will need time for the investment returns to make up for paying the taxes early.

Also important are the assumptions about rates of investment return, tax rates on and turnover in the taxable account, and longevity. Other factors are whether the RMDs would push the owner into a higher tax bracket, cause the loss of itemized deductions and personal exemptions, or increase taxes on Social Security benefits.

The prime beneficiaries are people like Max: A relatively young retiree whose IRA exceeds by a significant amount likely lifetime spending needs.

Without extra distributions, future RMDs would force large taxable distributions as the owner ages. Lifetime taxes by the owner and his heirs would be much higher than if the IRA were emptied early, the taxes paid, and investment income compounded in a taxable account.

Converting a Regular IRA to a Roth IRA

The Roth IRA is one of the most attractive tax-advantaged vehicles Congress ever created. Congress went a step further and gave many people a chance to convert their traditional IRAs to Roth IRAs. It doesn't matter if the traditional IRA contributions were made because the owner was unaware of the Roth's advantages or was not eligible to make Roth contributions. It also doesn't matter if the traditional IRA was opened before the Roth IRA was created in 1997 or as a result of rolling over a 401(k) or other retirement plan into the IRA. The IRA can be deductible or nondeductible. In any of these cases, the IRA owner might be able to convert the traditional IRA into a Roth IRA. In addition, the IRA owner can choose to convert the entire IRA or any portion of it into a Roth IRA. Once a traditional IRA is converted into a Roth IRA, it is treated the same as an original Roth IRA.

There is a cost to converting a regular IRA into a Roth IRA. Taxes must be paid as though the amount converted were distributed to the taxpayer from the traditional IRA. For example, suppose there is a deductible traditional IRA with a balance of $100,000. If the owner decides to convert the entire amount, then $100,000 must be included in gross income in the year of the conversion. If $50,000 is converted, then $50,000 is included in gross income. If the IRA has nondeductible contributions, then the conversion of the nondeductible contributions is not taxed. (If the IRA owner is younger than age $59\frac{1}{2}$, the 10 percent early distribution penalty does not apply to amounts that are included in income because of the conversion.)

The rules are simple. The trick is determining when it makes sense to incur the cost of converting an ordinary IRA into a Roth IRA. The answer depends on several factors. The IRA owner has to make assumptions about these factors and compare the results of continuing to own the traditional IRA with converting to a Roth IRA. Here are the factors to consider and how they affect the decision:

- *Is money outside the IRA used to pay the conversion taxes?* The more money that is left inside the IRA to benefit from tax-free compounding, the more advantageous it is to convert to a Roth IRA. A conversion is less beneficial if money is taken out of the IRA to pay the taxes—though it still can make sense to convert if the remaining balance is left in the IRA to compound for 10 years or more after the conversion. In addition, if the owner is under age $59\frac{1}{2}$ and uses an IRA distribution to pay conversion taxes, the 10 percent early distribution penalty will be owed on the amount that actually was distributed in addition to income taxes. In that case, it will take longer for the conversion to make sense.

■ *How long will the money be left in the Roth IRA for income and gains to compound before distributions begin?* The longer the money is left in the Roth IRA before beginning withdrawals, the more sense a conversion makes. In most cases for a conversion to pay, the owner should be prepared to leave the Roth IRA alone for at least 7 to 10 years after the conversion, if the average annual total return is at least 8 percent. A lower return will take longer to make the conversion pay off. The payoff period also is affected by whether the money eventually is withdrawn in installments or in a lump sum. The longer the distributions can be delayed or stretched out, the more sense it makes to pay taxes to convert to a Roth IRA.

In fact, one of the best uses of an IRA conversion is when the owner doesn't plan to spend the IRA. The traditional IRA is converted to a Roth IRA, and the owner doesn't take distributions during his or her lifetime. Instead, the Roth IRA is left for younger loved ones to inherit. They receive tax-free income from the Roth IRA. In effect, the original IRA owner has prepaid income taxes for them. A conversion to a Roth IRA can be a great estate-planning tool.

■ *Is there a difference between the tax bracket at conversion and the tax bracket when distributions are made?* The more the tax rate is expected to decline at distribution time, the less sense it makes to pay taxes at today's rate. Keep in mind that the conventional wisdom about tax rates decreasing during retirement frequently might not be true, as will be discussed in Chapter 9.

■ *How much of the IRA will be converted?* Conversion is not an all-or-nothing question. Any percentage of the IRA can be converted to a Roth IRA (depending on the IRA custodian's minimum account requirements). Suppose the owner is using the IRA to pay living expenses now and cannot wait seven years or more after the conversion to begin taking distributions from a Roth IRA. Then the owner might decide to leave enough in the regular IRA to cover expected expenses for seven years or more, and convert the rest into a Roth IRA. Or if the owner doesn't have enough cash to pay taxes for converting the entire IRA, a smaller amount can be converted. The entire IRA can be converted in stages over the years. One strategy is to convert each year only an amount that will keep you from rising into the next tax bracket.

■ *Will Social Security benefits be taxed?* Converting to a Roth IRA also can reduce taxes on Social Security benefits. Distributions from a regular IRA are included in gross income, boosting the amount of Social Security benefits that are taxable. Nontaxable distributions from a Roth IRA are not included in gross income, so they won't make Social Security benefits taxable.

- *How does the state tax the Roth IRA?* Many states automatically conform to federal law, but some states don't grant Roth IRA distributions the same tax-free status they have under federal law. Check your local tax law.
- *Will required minimum distributions from a traditional IRA exceed spending needs?* Minimum annual distributions (discussed earlier in this chapter) are required from a traditional IRA but not from a Roth IRA. The required distributions can dramatically increase income taxes as one ages. If the owner anticipates that required minimum distributions will significantly exceed spending needs, then a Roth IRA should be considered.

How to Decide

Deciding whether to convert a traditional IRA into a Roth IRA obviously involves some projections and number-crunching. There are some general rules that can be used as guidelines. The longer the Roth IRA will be allowed to compound before distributions begin, the more sense a conversion makes. The higher the expected investment rate of return on the Roth IRA, the more sense a conversion makes. A conversion also makes more sense if the taxes are paid with funds that are outside the IRA. A conversion makes less sense if the tax rate will decline after traditional IRA distributions would begin.

Fortunately, there are many convenient ways to do the number-crunching so that general rules don't have to be relied on. A number of websites offer free calculators for projecting the results of a Roth IRA conversion. These calculators allow the user to quickly change the assumptions on the key factors. Most mutual fund firms and brokers have calculators on their websites. The best probably are at vanguard.com, fidelity.com, and troweprice.com. T. Rowe Price also sometimes offers a separate program called IRA Analyzer for a small fee. Many financial publication websites also have calculators.

The mutual fund and brokerage firm calculators often are not full-featured or what the programmers call robust. A more sophisticated Roth IRA calculator can be found at www.rothira.com. A couple of other calculators with no ties to financial products or services are at www.datachimp.com, www.volition.com, www.dinkytown.com, and www.customcalculators.com. I recommend using at least two different online calculators. They almost certainly will get different results, and using different calculators allows you to see which items are variable in the different calculators and which are assumed to be true for all users. Most financial planners also have software calculators that have many features and allow comparisons of many different scenarios. Having a financial planner, estate planner or CPA do the calculations makes sense when the IRA balance is large. For those who don't use computers, many mutual funds and brokers also have worksheets or workbooks that enable the user to make similar calculations on paper.

There is one trick to conversions for those already over age 70$^{1}/_{2}$. Taxpayers who already are subject to the required minimum distributions must take the required distribution for the year of the conversion. A required distribution cannot be avoided by converting a traditional IRA to a Roth IRA.

The best candidate for converting a traditional IRA to a Roth IRA is a wealthy individual who really doesn't need the IRA income, plans to pass the account to the next generation or two, and wants to reduce income and estate taxes. But that is not the only situation when a conversion is appropriate. For example, someone who won't take distributions from the IRA for at least 7 to 10 years and who has enough cash outside the IRA to pay the conversion taxes also could benefit from a conversion. The only way to decide with considerable confidence is to make forecasts using estimates for the factors already outlined.

Tilting Your Finances to Favor a Conversion

You might balk, understandably, at paying the taxes to convert a traditional IRA to a Roth IRA. Or you might run the numbers and find that a conversion doesn't make financial sense for you. In these situations, there are strategies to consider. They can reduce the taxes paid on a conversion and perhaps turn a situation in which a conversion isn't viable to one in which a conversion makes sense.

Look for opportunities to use these strategies:

- *Reduce gross income.* A range of strategies can reduce gross income. You may have enough flexibility to reduce some income received for the year. Reduce optional distributions from IRAs and annuities. Defer salary from employment. Avoid taking capital gains by limiting asset sales during the year of the conversion. Take capital losses to offset gains. Each of these actions reduces gross income.

  Business losses from an S corporation, partnership, LLC, or a proprietorship reduce gross income. There are a number of hurdles in the tax code to taking the deductions. For example, you must materially participate in the activity, and it must be profit seeking and not a hobby. But if you qualify and can time business income and expenses to generate a loss, it will reduce the cost of the IRA conversion.

- *Reduce adjusted gross income.* Gross income minus certain deductions leads to adjusted gross income (AGI). The deductions, listed on Form 1040, include retirement plan contributions, medical insurance premiums for the self-employed, and one half of self-employment taxes. There are other deductions. Study the list to see if you qualify for any of them.

- *Increase charitable contributions.* This is a strategy for people who are inclined to make significant charitable contributions either annually or through their estates. Bunching the contributions in years when an IRA is converted can make a lot of sense. You donate a lot in the year you do the conversion, and the tax deduction from the contributions can reduce the taxes on the conversion. Be sure to do careful tax planning to ensure that the interplay of different tax code provisions doesn't offset some of the benefits of the contributions.

  You don't have to actually give all the money to specific charities the year of the conversion. You can donate to a donor-advised fund, such as those run by Schwab, Fidelity, and many localities. Then, donate the money to specific charities over time.

- *Donate appreciated assets.* You can generate substantial charitable deductions without using cash by donating appreciated assets. When appreciated securities and real estate are donated, you deduct the fair market value on the date of the contribution. You don't owe capital gains taxes accrued during your ownership. This is a way to accelerate charitable contributions without tapping cash or incurring capital gains. Go through your portfolio and consider donating mutual funds, stocks, or real estate that are substantially higher than your purchase price.

- *Take capital losses.* Capital losses offset capital gains for the year dollar for dollar. Additional losses up to $3,000 can be deducted against other income. Any leftover losses can be carried forward to future years and used in the same way.

When you sell assets that have paper losses or you have carryovers of losses from past years, they make it possible to sell appreciated assets and shelter all or most of the capital gains. That generates more cash to pay the taxes for the Roth conversion. You've raised the cash to pay the taxes on the IRA conversion without incurring additional taxes. Or you can consider donating to charity the cash from selling losing assets so the deduction will offset some of your IRA conversion taxes. Run the numbers both ways to see which has the best cash flow.

Changing Your Mind

Once a decision is made on whether or not to convert a regular IRA to a Roth IRA, the IRA owner should continue to monitor the results. Changes in the value of the IRA should trigger a reevaluation of that decision:

- *Suppose a conversion was made.* The law allows this decision to be reversed as late as the date the tax return for the year is due. This is known as a recharacterization. The Roth IRA can be converted back to a traditional IRA and no taxes would be due on the transactions for the year. A recharacterization should be considered when the value of the IRA decreases significantly after the conversion. If the conversion is not reversed, then taxes still are due based on the IRA's value on the conversion date. The owner would be paying taxes on wealth that no longer exists. It makes sense to reverse the conversion. Then, the owner can decide to reconvert into a Roth IRA. A conversion can be done after a recharacterization after a waiting period. The second conversion can't be done until the later of 30 days after recharacterization and the next January 1 has passed.

- *Suppose a traditional IRA was converted into a Roth IRA.* The owner then becomes unemployed or for other reasons suffers a decline in income. The owner determines that the reversal of fortune is likely to continue into the following year and will be severe enough to drop him or her into a lower tax bracket that year. Then it makes sense to recharacterize the Roth IRA as a traditional IRA before the year closes. The conversion can be made the following year when the owner will be in a lower tax bracket and the cost of conversion will be lower.
- *Suppose the owner decided not to make a conversion.* Again, if the value of the IRA drops significantly later in the year, the decision should be reconsidered. If the conversion was not made because the owner did not have enough other assets to pay the taxes, then the lower value of the IRA might make the conversion affordable. In addition, making the conversion when the value is lower means that all appreciation from the new lows will be tax free when eventually distributed from the Roth IRA. Without the conversion, those gains would be taxed as ordinary income.

A recharacterization is simple. A conversion may be reversed any time until the final due date for the tax return for the year, including extensions. That means the decision can be delayed until as late as October 15 of the year following the conversion. The recharacterization is done on Form 8606 filed with the regular tax return, or with Form 1040X (amended tax return) if the regular return already was filed.

When the calculations show that conversion makes sense, the biggest risk is that the government will change the rules. Once many people have accumulated significant wealth in Roth IRAs, Congress might impose some kind of income taxes on future distributions.

Tips for Maximizing IRA Conversion Benefits

There are some strategies that will increase the benefits of an IRA conversion or help you turn a conversion mistake into a benefit.

Convert in Stages.   It can be expensive to convert all of a large IRA in one year. You might not have enough cash to pay the taxes, or the conversion could push you into a higher tax bracket. Instead, convert a portion of your IRAs each year. Convert just enough to keep you from rising to the next tax bracket or triggering stealth taxes.

Convert to Multiple IRAs. Ideally, a diversified traditional IRA shouldn't be converted into one diversified Roth IRA. Instead, each different investment or asset class in the traditional IRA should be put into its own Roth IRA.

You see, the taxes on a conversion are computed on the value of the assets on the date of the conversion. If the converted IRA subsequently declines in value, you still pay taxes on the higher converted value. You could recharacterize the entire IRA, but the overall loss might not be enough to justify all the changes and incurring the waiting period before you can convert again.

When you put each asset in a separate Roth IRA, you have the option to recharacterize (reverse the conversion of) any asset that declined in value and keep the others in their Roth IRAs. You won't be paying taxes on a value that no longer exists, and the rest of your portfolio is safely in tax-free Roth IRAs. You could convert the other asset, probably at a lower value, after the waiting period.

Monitor Converted IRAs. You have the right to reverse a conversion by October 15 of the following tax year. Follow your converted IRA or IRAs and recharacterize those that have declined substantially as you near the recharacterization deadline.

Reconvert. You have another shot at a conversion if you converted assets and then recharacterized them. The reconversion can't occur in the same year as a recharacterization. Also, at least 30 days must pass between the recharacterization and reconversion:

- *Example.* A converted Roth IRA is recharacterized to a traditional IRA on December 15, 2015. The owner can't reconvert until January 15, 2016. He has to wait until the later of the next calendar year and 30 days before reconverting.
- *Example.* A converted Roth IRA is recharacterized to a traditional IRA on July 1, 2015. The IRA can be reconverted on January 1, 2016, because that is the later of 30 days and the next calendar year after the recharacterization.

Roth Accounts Are Not Only for the Young

There are some strategies that will increase the benefits of an IRA conversion or help you turn a conversion mistake into a benefit.

Roth IRAs aren't very old, but they have already spawned some rules of thumb. The most common rule of thumb for Roth IRAs is that they're for relatively younger people. Unfortunately, this rule of thumb is the result of some good research that is distorted and misapplied. It's causing many people to not use Roth IRAs when the vehicles could benefit them people and their heirs.

The rule of thumb began from a sensible base. As we discussed, a Roth IRA needs to compound income and gains for a while to make up for paying taxes early. The tax benefits of the Roth IRA (tax-free distributions, no required minimum distributions on the original owner) are back-end loaded, while the tax benefits of a traditional IRA are front-end loaded. But it doesn't take as long as many people now think for the Roth IRA to pay off, and how long it takes depends on several variables.

Earlier we discussed why it makes sense for most people to let the Roth IRA compound for some years in order for a conversion to make sense. Under likely circumstances, the Roth IRA should compound for 7 to 10 years before taking distributions. Research by others supported this conclusion. The pay-off period depends on investment returns, the difference between tax rates at the time of conversion and the time of distributions, how the taxes on the conversion are paid, and other factors.

Rules of thumb distorted this research. Some advisors routinely say that people older than certain ages shouldn't consider Roth accounts. Yet, a careful look at the facts and the numbers shows converting to a Roth IRA can be a great estate-planning tool, even for older people.

Fortunately, new research specifically addresses the issue of older Americans and Roth IRAs. Before delving into the research, you should know that Roth 401(k)s now are available through many employers, especially large employers. Workers can choose between a traditional 401(k) and a Roth 401(k). This choice is in addition to the choice between a traditional IRA and Roth IRA. You also have the option to convert a traditional IRA or 401(k) to a Roth version.

The new research concludes that many older Americans should consider Roth accounts instead of traditional IRAs and 401(k)s. This applies to both annual contributions to accounts and conversions of traditional accounts to Roth versions, according to a study by Stuart Ritter of mutual fund firm T. Rowe Price.

Let's look at a 50-year-old worker who can choose to contribute to either a Roth or traditional 401(k) plan. He contributes $5,000 annually until age 65, and then begins annual withdrawals. He earns a 7 percent annual return and is in the 28 percent tax bracket the whole time. At first glance, it appears he'd have the same account balance in each scenario, which would be $38,061 after 30 years, according to Ritter's assumptions and calculations.

The Roth balance, however, is tax free. The worker or his heirs will benefit from that full amount. The traditional account, however, will be taxed at the 28 percent rate, leaving the worker or his heirs with only $27,404 to spend. Also, higher distributions have to be taken from the traditional account to have the same after-tax spending money as the Roth version.

The worker could select a traditional 401(k) and invest the income tax savings from his contributions in a brokerage account. But that wouldn't be enough to match the Roth IRA. That's because the brokerage account earnings would be taxed, so it wouldn't compound at 7 percent annually after taxes.

What if the worker is in a lower tax bracket after retirement? Keep in mind that's less likely these days with only a few tax brackets. But Ritter's numbers show that the Roth 401(k) still is a better deal if the worker's income tax rate drops by as much as 10 percentage points in retirement.

What about an older worker? Ritter's work shows that the Roth 401(k) is the better deal for workers into their early 60s.

Of course, these are hypothetical scenarios. They might not apply to you. The Roth option could be even better for you, or it could be a bad deal, depending on the particulars of your situation and what you want to assume about retirement tax rates, investment returns, and other factors. The important point is that you shouldn't let rules of thumb and other people's experiences or views determine your strategy. Take a look at the data.

A strategy we'll discuss more in Chapter 9 involves using a Roth account essentially to help you decide the tax bracket you want to be in during retirement. You'll have other sources of income you can't control, such as Social Security, annuities, distributions from mutual funds or stocks, and required distributions from traditional accounts. When those don't meet your spending needs, you can sell some investments at a long-term capital gains rate of 20 percent and you can tap the Roth account tax free, maintaining your standard of living while controlling your tax bill and rate.

Another advantage of having some money in a Roth account is the flexibility. If you have a large one-time spending need (new car, child's wedding, major home repair), you can take the money from the Roth IRA without pushing yourself into a higher tax bracket or triggering the stealth taxes.

What about conversions of traditional IRAs to Roth IRAs? Are those only for the young or youngish? Not always. In fact, it can make sense for someone to wait until retirement to convert retirement accounts.

Consider that your income might be lower in the first years of retirement than during the working years, so you'll be in a lower tax bracket or at least in a lower portion of the same tax bracket. That makes it less expensive to convert an IRA or 401(k).

Also, a conversion is most likely to pay off (or pay off faster) when the taxes on the conversion are paid from other funds instead of using part of the IRA or 401(k) to pay the taxes. Many people are likely to have lower fixed expenses in retirement, so they're more comfortable tapping other accounts to pay the taxes. You also might have generated some cash from the sale of your home or other preretirement transactions.

You might move to a no-income-tax or lower-income-tax state in retirement. The converted amount is taxed by both the state and federal governments. So, it is less expensive if you've moved to a state with lower taxes.

These factors will make it cheaper or easier to pay for a conversion to a Roth account, and that will reduce the time the Roth account has to compound before the conversion pays off.

We've covered some specific guidance and examples in this discussion. But those shouldn't be your main focus. The main point is that there are variables involved, and what is best for one person on this issue isn't best for another. You need to consider the variables in your case and run the numbers or have a financial advisor run them for you. Rules of thumb aren't the way to make these important decisions. Also, because things change you have to reconsider the decision regularly. Not converting might be the right decision this year, but circumstances could change next year or the year after.

Using RMDs to Buy Life Insurance

Another strategy for reducing or avoiding RMDs will provide a tax-free, guaranteed inheritance to your children and grandchildren and also can provide tax-free lifetime income to your spouse plus funding for charity.

Here's how the strategy works.

First, you change the secondary or contingent beneficiary of your IRA to a charity; your spouse is generally the primary beneficiary. The best bet might be to name a donor-advised fund as the charity. Next, acquire a life insurance policy (ideally a joint and survivor policy issued to both you and your spouse). Then, you use required minimum distributions or regular distributions from the IRA to pay the premiums. It usually is best to have the life insurance benefit be equal to your IRA value and have it owned by an irrevocable trust to ensure it isn't included in your estate for tax purposes. The trust benefits your children, and perhaps the grandchildren. You don't need a trust if you're confident that your estate won't be subject to estate taxes, even after adding in the life insurance benefits.

Here's an example.

Max Profits is 71 and his wife Rosie is 65. Max has a $2 million traditional IRA, and he's going to have to begin RMDs, with the first one being about $73,000. He doesn't need anywhere near that much money from the IRA to fund his expenses, and he certainly doesn't want that much additional taxable income.

Max and Rosie first obtain coverage under a joint and survivor life insurance policy with a benefit of $2 million. Their good health results in a premium of $25,213. They also establish a life insurance trust to be the beneficiary and owner of the policy, with their three children and four grandchildren as future beneficiaries of the trust.

The Profits establish an account at a donor-advised fund and change the beneficiary designation form of Max's IRA to name the fund as the contingent or secondary beneficiary of the IRA. Rosie is the primary beneficiary, so the charity won't receive anything until Rosie passes away.

During Max's lifetime, he takes RMDs from the IRA and contributes a portion of them to the trust to be used to pay the insurance premiums. These should qualify as tax-free gifts to the children under the annual gift tax exclusion if the trust is properly drafted.

After Max passes away, the IRA is available to Rosie for income, and she continues to use a portion of the income to make gifts to the trust to pay insurance policy premiums as needed.

After Rosie passes away, the remaining value of the IRA goes to the donor-advised fund. There are no taxes on this transfer. The children and grandchildren then can serve as directors of the fund and make charitable gifts from the fund over the years in accordance with the bylaws that you had set up years prior.

Also after Rosie's passing, the life insurance policy pays $2 million to the insurance trust, and the trust makes income and principal distributions to the children and grandchildren according to the terms Max and Rosie set when they created the trust. Distributions could be made all at once or over time. The life insurance proceeds avoid all income and estate taxes for both the trust and the beneficiaries.

The result is that the children and grandchildren receive the IRA's full initial value without any depletion by taxes, Max's RMDs, or poor investment returns. Max and Rosie both have access to the IRA during their lifetimes if needed. The remainder of the IRA goes to the charitable fund set up by Max and Rosie, and their children and grandchildren oversee it. Because of the leverage in the insurance policy and the lack of taxes, there is more money available than before, so all these goals can be met.

A number of variations in the details are possible. The Profits can choose from several premium payment schedules for the insurance policy, such as paying the premiums over seven, 10 or 15 years, or paying them annually up to age 100. Instead of naming Rosie as the sole initial beneficiary of the IRA, a charitable remainder trust could be the beneficiary. It would pay Rosie a lifetime income, and any remainder would go to the foundation or other charities. Or after Max's passing the IRA could buy an annuity payable to Rosie for life.

There are many choices for the charitable beneficiary of the IRA. You could name individual charities you like, but naming a donor-advised fund provides more flexibility. You don't know today how much money will be available or which charities will be family favorites. The donor-advised fund allows the decisions to be deferred and allows the charitable contributions to be spread over years. It also provides an opportunity for your offspring to work together selecting charities and to develop the habit of giving.

This strategy was brought to me by David Phillips at Estate Planning Specialists in Phoenix, Arizona (888-892-1102).

The earlier you start on this strategy the better so that you can obtain the lowest cost life insurance. Waiting can only increase the premiums.

Using the Family Bank Strategy

Another strategy to avoid escalating RMDs and a variation of the previous strategy is the Family Bank Strategy.

The IRA is distributed to the owner and the income taxes paid on the distribution. The after-tax amount of the distribution is used to make a single-premium deposit on a permanent life insurance policy. The cash value portion of the policy will have interest earnings each year of about 5 percent to 8 percent that will compound tax free. Eventually, the policy beneficiaries receive the life insurance benefit free of income taxes. During the owner's lifetime, if money is needed, he or she can borrow against the cash value of the policy. The cash value loans are tax free. If they aren't paid back, the loan amount and accumulated interest reduces the death benefit paid to beneficiaries.

This strategy is especially good when you convert only enough of your IRA to bring your taxable income up to the maximum of your tax bracket. For example, a couple earning $150,000 will be in the 28 percent federal income tax bracket until their income reaches about $227,000 (the amount changes each year with inflation). They could transfer another $76,000 annually from the IRA into the Family Bank Strategy before being pushed into the 33 percent bracket.

The really big advantage is that the life insurance benefit is always going to be worth substantially more than the money you transferred into the policy. And, unlike an IRA, market changes aren't going to cause the insurance policy's value to decline. If your loved ones inherit a traditional IRA, they'll really inherit only the after-tax balance, and the balance will change with the markets.

It's possible that even a Roth IRA owner might be better off with the Family Bank Strategy. If the Roth IRA exceeds your likely needs and primarily is for loved ones to inherit, consider turning it into a permanent life insurance policy. That way, your beneficiaries will inherit the tax-free policy benefit, which is likely to be higher than the Roth IRA balance. There's no investment risk with the insurance policy, and you still have tax-free access to the money through loans.

There are four general types of permanent life insurance, and many variations of each. For the Family Bank Strategy, you only want to consider Participating Whole Life or Indexed Universal Life. There's a vigorous debate among insurance professionals who implement the strategy over which type of policy to use. You need to know the arguments on each side and decide which is best for you.

For details about the strategy and how to use it in different situations, read the book by David Phillips, *The Family Bank Strategy*. It's available on Amazon.com or by calling 888-892-1102.

Which Account to Spend First?

Most retirement-age Americans have both taxable and tax-deferred accounts. Many now have tax-exempt accounts, such as Roth IRA or Roth 401(k)s. Each of these types of accounts receives different tax treatment, and sometimes different investments receive different tax treatments in the same type of account. The order in which money is withdrawn from different types of accounts will affect how long the wealth lasts.

In this section, we're going to discuss the best order in which to draw down the different types of accounts to maximize the life of the entire collection of assets. This is one way to determine the sources of your retirement spending over the years. Before making a decision, however, consider the strategy demonstrated in Chapter 9. There we discuss a strategy for remaining in a low tax bracket of 20 percent or so for life. You can take the approach taken in that chapter or in this section.

Now, let's look at the best order in which to draw down accounts.

Fortunately, in most cases, this is an issue for which the traditional thinking is correct. Most people would say intuitively that money in taxable accounts should be spent first and money in tax-advantaged accounts such as IRAs should be spent after that so that the tax-deferred compounding can continue for as long as possible. Money in Roth IRAs should be spent last, since no taxes are incurred.

Most people would be well-served by following that advice. A study published in the *AAII Journal* in May 2002 found that wealth lasted longer when money from taxable accounts was spent first and IRA money was spent only after taxable accounts were exhausted. The higher the rate of return on the investments, the longer wealth lasted by spending taxable accounts first. Also, the higher the individual's tax bracket, the more important it is to allow the tax-deferred compounding of IRAs to continue as long as possible. I've confirmed these results with my own calculations and show in Table 8.1 how long an individual's assets last under different scenarios. The figures assume that the individual's assets are evenly split between taxable and tax-deferred accounts and that each account earns the same rate of return.

TABLE 8.1   Which Account to Spend First?

Rate of Return	Taxable Account First	Tax-Deferred Account First
6%	18+ years	15+ years
8%	25+ years	18+ years
10%	51+ years	24+ years

The second and third columns show how long the owner's accounts will last under the stated distribution order and rate of return.

There is an exception to the general conclusion. The exception is when higher-returning investments are held in the taxable account and the after-tax return is four percentage points or more higher than the return earned by the tax-deferred account. In that case, you want to take distributions from the tax-deferred account first and let the higher after-tax returns compound in the taxable account for as long as possible.

The individual's wealth can be made to last even longer when the taxable accounts are managed and liquidated tax-efficiently. Some basic rules should be followed when managing taxable accounts for maximum longevity.

Investments showing losses should be sold first. A capital loss first offsets any capital gains realized for the year. If the losses exceed the year's gains, then up to $3,000 of net losses can be deducted against other income. If there still are unused capital losses, they are carried forward to future years to be applied in the same way until they are exhausted. Most investors are hesitant to sell losing investments. They don't want to make the loss of capital final. Instead, they want to hold the investments until the values at least recover to their purchase prices. Investors, however, would be better off selling the losing investments, using the tax losses to reduce gains on other income, and spending the sale proceeds or investing them in something else.

After harvesting losses, the next investments to be liquidated from taxable accounts should be those that would incur the lowest taxes as a percentage of their value. Take the taxes that would be incurred from the sale of the asset and divide them by the market value of the asset. The result is the percentage of the asset that would be taxed, in effect the tax rate on that asset. The asset with the lowest tax rate should be sold first.

By following these strategies, a taxable account can, in effect, become a partially tax-deferred account. The longer taxes are deferred, the more after-tax wealth can be accumulated before taxes are paid, and the greater the after-tax wealth will be.

There also might be tax-deferred accounts for which distributions are partially taxed. An example is an IRA with nondeductible contributions. Part of each distribution from such an account will be taxable and part nontaxable. These accounts should be liquidated before the fully taxable IRAs.

Of course, these results were derived from examples using assumptions. Individuals need to determine which assumptions apply to them before adopting a strategy and to consider factors that have not been discussed. For example, state tax laws need to be considered. Some states exempt from state taxes some retirement income, including distributions from IRAs. Retirees in those states might want to take distributions from IRAs up to the exempt amount before selling assets in taxable accounts.

Another factor to be considered is the investor's asset allocation. Taking distributions from any account will change the investor's asset allocation, because the assets sold no longer will be in the portfolio. Changes to the other accounts might have to be made to ensure that the desired ratio between stocks, bonds, and other assets is maintained for the long term. Taxes and other costs could be incurred when rebalancing the portfolio.

Which Investments for Tax-Deferred Accounts?

When you own several different types of accounts, the order in which to withdraw money from the different accounts is not the only issue that determines how long the assets last. Another important decision is how to invest the different accounts. The overall after-tax wealth an individual can accumulate changes depending on which investments are in the tax-advantaged accounts and which are in the taxable accounts. The results surprise many people.

The longstanding conventional wisdom was very simple. It stated that income-producing investments—those that paid regular, taxable interest and dividends such as bonds and stocks with high dividend yields—should be purchased through tax-deferred accounts such as IRAs and 401(k)s. Investments that can earn tax-advantaged capital gains should be purchased through taxable accounts.

The rationale was that in a taxable account, interest and dividends were taxed as ordinary income at the taxpayer's highest tax rate. That didn't leave much income after taxes to compound over the years. Therefore, income investments should be in tax-advantaged accounts where the full income can compound tax-deferred. Stocks and equity mutual funds, if held for more than one year, were subject to a maximum tax rate of 20 percent on their capital gains when held in taxable accounts. If stocks were held in tax-deferred accounts, such as traditional IRAs, the gains would compound tax deferred but the distributions would be taxed as ordinary income. Putting assets with the potential for long-term capital gains (such as stocks) into tax-deferred accounts had the effect of converting tax advantaged long-term capital gains into higher-taxed ordinary income. Tax-wise investors generally want to do the opposite.

While the conventional wisdom was logical, it wasn't always the best advice. The best advice on how to divide investments between IRAs and taxable accounts depends on the individual investor involved.

The conventional advice still works best for investors who buy individual stocks and hold them for a long time. Those investors will be able to take advantage of the lower long-term capital gains rates on investments held for more than one year. The conventional approach also is good for investors who own equity mutual funds and hold them for more than one year, if the mutual funds make no or small taxable distributions each year.

The problem is, many investors do not fall into these two categories. Studies show that whether they own individual stocks or equity mutual funds, individual investors buy and sell too frequently to take advantage of the long-term capital gains rates on most of their equity gains. While that is not the best way to maximize investment returns, it is the way many investors manage their portfolios. Other investors own mutual funds and hold them for more than one year. Many of those funds, however, make taxable distributions each year of a significant portion of their total returns. In these two situations, most of the gains from the stocks and mutual funds would be taxed as ordinary income.

Investors in these situations often can be better off keeping their income-earning investments, such as bonds, in taxable accounts. Their investments with potentially higher returns—such as stocks that are traded after less than one year—that will be taxed as ordinary income should be purchased through tax-advantaged accounts. The tax-deferred accounts protect the annual gains from taxes and allow the gains to compound to a much higher amount than would be possible in a taxable account. Even after paying the taxes when the money is distributed from the tax-deferred account, the investor has more after-tax wealth than would have been accumulated by holding the stocks in a taxable account. The more gains that can be compounded before taxes are incurred, the greater the investor's lifetime after-tax wealth will be.

Another factor to consider is the difference between the investor's ordinary income tax rate and the long-term capital gains rate. An investor who faces the top ordinary income tax rate of 39 percent and a top long-term capital gains rate of 20 percent has a lot at stake in this decision. An investor in a lower tax bracket has a smaller difference between the two rates. He or she still would benefit from getting the allocation right, but the benefit would not be as great.

Perhaps even more important is any difference between the ordinary income tax rate during the accumulation years and during the distribution years. While fewer people see their tax rates decline after retirement, it is possible an investor will be in a much lower tax bracket at retirement. Someone who believes he or she would be in a significantly lower bracket in retirement could come out ahead by putting the highest returning investments in tax-deferred accounts. Taxes would be paid at a much lower rate in the future when the gains are withdrawn.

Owning Nontraditional IRA Investments

More and more IRA owners are considering investments other than traditional stocks, bonds, and mutual funds. It's not surprising. The Federal Reserve's zero interest rate policy boosted returns of stocks and bonds the last few years but probably pulled forward a lot of future returns into those years. For the next 5 or 10 years, returns from traditional investments are likely to be less than historic averages.

The tax law allows your IRA to be invested in a range of vehicles other than publicly traded stocks, bonds, and mutual funds. There are some obstacles you must navigate, but doing so could allow you to invest in unconventional and profitable investments. The most popular unconventional IRA investments probably are real estate and privately traded stock. Other frequent investments are making loans and mortgages and owning some precious metals.

It's the IRA custodians who limit most investments. Your IRA must have an approved custodian or trustee, and most of them are traditional financial institutions that restrict IRA investments to traditional vehicles.

To own nontraditional investments in an IRA, you need a custodian or trustee that allows a true self-directed IRA, one that allows you to invest in any asset permitted by the tax law. (In fact, some let you invest in assets not permitted by the tax law. It's up to you to know the rules and be responsible for any penalties the IRS imposes.) Many traditional IRA custodians and trustees say they offer self-directed IRAs, but they mean only that you can choose from among the traditional investments available on their platforms.

To find a true self-directed IRA custodian or trustee, go to your favorite Internet search engine and search for "self-directed IRA." In addition to articles about traditional self-directed IRAs, you'll find websites for trustees and custodians of true self-directed IRAs.

To use a true self-directed IRA, you should be prepared to pay higher fees across the board. The trustee has to do more work, and there are fewer IRAs of this type so the custodian doesn't have the scale and efficiencies of traditional IRAs. In addition to an annual fee and transaction fees, you might pay to have your IRA's investments valued each year.

A move that might reduce fees is to form a limited liability company and have it wholly owned by the IRA. Then, the LLC makes the investments in its name. But keep in mind the LLC can engage only in transactions allowed for an IRA directly. There will be costs to forming the LLC, and it probably will have to file an annual tax return and pay an annual license fee. So, it doesn't eliminate all the extra costs.

Once you set up the self-directed IRA, either with or without an LLC, the next step is to be sure your investments don't violate IRS rules, especially those against prohibited investments and transactions.

The list of prohibited investments for IRAs is short. It consists of life insurance and collectibles. Collectibles include art, antiques, rugs, stamps, coins, metals, gems, and alcoholic beverages. The IRS can add to the list but hasn't. There are some exceptions. The largest is for U.S.-minted gold coins that are legal tender. An IRA is allowed to own them.

The longer and more significant list is of prohibited transactions. It's easy to make a mistake and stumble into a prohibited transaction and its penalty. You want to avoid prohibited transactions, because the penalty is that the entire IRA will be treated as fully distributed when the prohibited transaction was made. The IRA owner must include the IRA's full value in gross income, regardless of the amount of the prohibited transaction. If the owner has multiple IRAs, only the IRA that engaged in the prohibited transaction is penalized.

Basically, a prohibited transaction is an investment or deal between a related or disqualified person and the IRA. It doesn't matter if the transactions are at fair market value. They are prohibited at any price.

There are six prohibited transactions between IRAs and related parties. The first four are specific, and the last two are general.

The four specific prohibited transactions are:

- A sale, exchange, or lease of property
- A loan of money
- Furnishing goods, services, or facilities
- A transfer or the use of the income or assets of the IRA

The two general prohibitions are: an act in which the related party deals with the IRA income or assets as his or her own; and the receipt of any benefit for the related party's personal account in connection with a transaction involving the IRA's income or assets.

Stated in clear, plain English, the prohibited transactions can be summarized as: No deals are allowed involving the IRA and its owner or a person related to the IRA or its owner. Persons include entities, such as trusts, corporations, LLCs, and others.

A related person for an IRA is the IRA owner; anyone who makes decisions for the IRA; anyone providing services to the IRA; an ancestor, spouse, or descendant of the IRA owner, of the owner's spouse, of a decision maker for the IRA, or of anyone providing services to the IRA; a corporation, trust, partnership, or estate that is 50 percent or more owned by any of the above persons; an officer, director, highly compensated employee, or 10 percent or greater owner of any of the above; and a partner of any of the above.

Though the list of related persons sounds comprehensive, there are some gaps. Not included as related persons are brothers, sisters, step relatives, nieces, and nephews of the IRA owner. Also not included are friends and neighbors of the owner. A "significant other" to whom the IRA owner is not married also is not a related person.

Roth IRAs don't escape these rules. A Roth IRA is subject to the same rules as traditional IRAs and other qualified retirement plans unless specifically exempted. There isn't an exemption to the prohibited investment and transaction rules for Roth IRAs. In addition, the IRS appears to have gone a step further for Roth IRAs. It issued a notice stating that any transaction between a Roth IRA and a "related party" would be considered a tax shelter or an abusive transaction required to be registered with the IRS. For this notice, the IRS considered brothers and sisters as related parties (IRS Notice 2004-8).

Though the list of prohibited transactions is long and comprehensive, the Department of Labor is allowed to grant exemptions and frequently does. It grants exemptions to specific taxpayers for specific transactions and also grants broad class exemptions that apply to anyone who matches the facts in an exemption. Under these exemptions, IRAs and owners have been allowed to engage in transactions involving real estate, stock, loans, and more.

To find details on the exemptions, go the Department of Labor website at www.dol.gov. Look for the "Employee Benefits Security Administration" among the department's agencies. On the home page for the EBSA, look for "Technical Guidance." I'd give a more specific web address, but the Labor Department frequently changes its website. You can look at the class exemptions that have been granted to see if what you want to do qualifies. You also can look at individual exemptions to see if there is something close enough to make it worth your while to apply for one.

With an individual or class exemption, you might be able to use an IRA to buy real estate (including a vacation home), invest in your business, or lend money to a relative. I don't recommend engaging in these transactions on your own. The rules are technical, and you have to comply fully with them. You should consult with an accountant or attorney who is well-versed in the rules for IRAs and retirement plans before engaging in a transaction. The penalty for mistakes is steep and should be avoided.

Beware the Retirement Tax Ambush

T ax rates and taxes will be lower in retirement. That used to be true. Over the last couple of decades it became one of the most dangerous myths in retirement planning, and it is becoming more of a myth each year.

These days, it is rare for a person's tax rate to decline after retiring unless he or she does some careful planning (which we'll discuss in this chapter). For years, without saying so, Congress and the IRS have looked to older Americans to increase government revenues. After all, today's older Americans are the richest generation in history and also a very large generation. That's where the money is. As the Baby Boomers age, those over age 50 will become an even bigger target. Federal income taxes are not the only issue for retirees and preretirees. State and local taxes also generally are rising and likely to continue rising in many states and localities.

Taxes are one of the larger expenses in a retiree's budget—if not the largest.

Retirees face the same tax burdens and rules as other Americans. There also are a number of special tax rules that affect those in and near retirement more than most other Americans.

As a result, retirees today can incur some of the highest marginal tax rates in U.S. history. For example, Social Security benefits were tax free for many decades. Since 1993, when a couple's income is greater than $44,000 ($34,000 for single taxpayers), up to 85 percent of Social Security benefits are included in gross income for each additional dollar earned. Earn an extra dollar of investment income, and not only is that dollar taxed but 85 cents of Social Security benefits also are taxed.

These are the types of rules that can create a marginal tax bracket (the tax rate on the last dollar earned) higher than 70 percent for many seniors. A retiree can face a marginal tax rate of 90 percent or higher if he or she lives in a state with high income tax rates.

More Social Security beneficiaries pay taxes on their benefits each year because the income levels at which the tax takes effect are not indexed for inflation. The percentage of Social Security recipients who pay income taxes on some of their benefits is expected to increase steadily every year.

That is just one example of how the income tax burden increases and the tax code becomes more complicated as retirement nears. There are several areas of the tax code that affect older Americans more than other taxpayers or that are specifically directed at postretirement taxpayers. I call these the *stealth taxes*.

The Stealth Taxes

The tax law is replete with stealth taxes. These are hidden taxes that take money out of people's pockets without increasing tax rates. The taxes are hidden because they can be incurred by actions many taxpayers don't even realize might trigger higher taxes. Often, a taxpayer learns about a stealth tax for the first time only after completing an income tax return and seeing that the tax was triggered. It used to be that only the wealthy worried about stealth taxes, because they are imposed as income increases. In recent years, however, these taxes snared more and more taxpayers, and older taxpayers are among those most likely to pay stealth taxes.

There are six main stealth taxes: the alternative minimum tax (AMT), the Pease tax (the itemized deduction reduction), the PEP (personal exemption phase-out), the tax on Social Security benefits, the Medicare premium surtax, and the 3.8 percent tax on net investment income. There are others scattered throughout the tax code, but they either affect fewer taxpayers or more discrete groups of taxpayers.

The stealth taxes, intentionally or not, are imposed on those in or near retirement more than other groups of taxpayers. Fortunately, taxpayers can avoid or minimize stealth taxes if they know about them ahead of time and take action. We discussed the Medicare premium surtax in Chapter 6. We discuss the others and some other tax issues in this chapter.

To keep income taxes low in retirement and in the years before retirement, you need a dual focus. One focus is to keep adjusted gross income low, which we explain in the next section of this chapter. The other focus is to manage your finances to pay the lowest effective income tax rate. A lower effective tax rate makes your tax bill lower and reduces the amount you need to withdraw from your nest egg to fund your standard of living. We discuss that in a later section.

The Importance of Adjusted Gross Income

There was a time when good tax planning meant reducing taxable income. That's not always the case today.

The stealth taxes aren't based on gross income or taxable income. The focus of these taxes is adjusted gross income (AGI), or modified adjusted gross income (MAGI). They generally are said to be imposed on high-income taxpayers, though that's not always the case because they are based on AGI and MAGI. So, the key to avoiding or reducing the stealth taxes is to reduce AGI or MAGI.

When you look at the standard Form 1040, adjusted gross income is the last number at the bottom of the first page. First, you add all sources of income that are taxable to arrive at gross income. Then, you subtract what are called deductions for adjusted gross income. The remainder is your AGI. Note that itemized expenses such as charitable contributions, medical expenses, and mortgage interest won't help reduce the stealth taxes. Those deductions appear later on the tax return.

MAGI is a special calculation for some of the stealth taxes. It can vary slightly between the stealth taxes, but generally you take AGI and add back a few items that are excluded from gross income when computing the regular income tax. These additional income items usually are tax-exempt bond interest and foreign-earned income.

Reducing AGI and MAGI

Fortunately, there are steps that can reduce the taxes.

There are two broad strategies for reducing AGI. One way is to keep gross income low. The other way is to increase deductions for AGI (except deductions for AGI won't decrease taxes on Social Security benefits.)

The deductions for AGI tend to be for very specific expenses that often don't apply to many people age 55 and over, especially those already retired. But there are some that might be available to you. The deductions include special deductions for teachers, reservists, performing artists, and fee-basis government officials. Also included are health savings account deductions, moving expenses, the deductible part of self-employment taxes, self-employed health insurance premiums, and some self-employed retirement plan contributions. There are a few others that don't have real planning opportunities, such as alimony payments. Some of these deductions periodically are set to expire, but to date Congress has extended them for an additional year or two.

By all means, maximize these deductions to the extent you can. But they don't offer the most planning opportunities for those in or near retirement.

The best opportunities for reducing the stealth taxes are to reduce gross income. Progress here reduces taxes on Social Security benefits as well as the other retiree taxes.

Here are strategies that work best for reducing gross income.

Consider Tax-Exempt Bonds. Here's where things get tricky. Interest from tax-exempt bonds is excluded from gross income for computing the regular income tax. But it is added AGI to create MAGI for most of the stealth taxes. So, it appears there is no benefit from earning tax-exempt bonds instead of taxable bonds.

Because they are tax-exempt, however, the bonds usually pay a lower interest rate than comparable taxable bonds or certificates of deposit. Adding the tax-exempt interest to your other income should result in lower MAGI than if you owned taxable bonds. So, if you own bonds outside an IRA or other tax-favored account, you'll likely owe less in retiree taxes by investing in tax-exempt bonds instead of taxable bonds or CDs.

Defer Income. It might be possible to defer income to future years. Sometimes you have to plan this in advance. Employment income, for example, can be paid in either salary or deferred compensation that will be paid in cash later. If you're still working, you might negotiate to defer and spread out such compensation.

There are other ways to defer income. Don't take distributions from traditional IRAs, annuities, and similar accounts unless you need the money or are required to. Consider the stealth taxes before selling investments, and consider selling assets in installment sales instead of for a one-time payment.

Convert IRAs

When you take distributions from a traditional IRA or 401(k) plan, the distributions are included in gross income and treated as ordinary income, except for nondeductible or after-tax contributions. But Roth IRA distributions aren't included in gross income for purposes of the regular income tax or when computing the retiree taxes. Perhaps even better, with a Roth IRA you aren't required to take distributions after age 70$\frac{1}{2}$. With a regular IRA, those forced distributions trigger higher taxes even when you don't need the income. We discussed the difficulties caused by RMDs in detail in Chapter 8.

The stealth taxes are one reason why converting a traditional retirement account to a Roth IRA can pay off over the long term.

Keep in mind that in the year an IRA is converted, the conversion amount is included in gross income. The converted amount might trigger or increase the Medicare surtax, tax on Social Security benefits, and other stealth taxes. That one-time cost has to be considered in determining whether or not a conversion makes sense.

Manage Your Taxable Investments.   Tax-wise investment strategies are more important when additional gross income might trigger these extra taxes. You don't want taxes to dictate investment strategy, but the potential for higher taxes determines whether a particular investment or strategy is best.

It's a good idea to harvest investment losses. Sell investments that have other-than-modest paper losses to lock in the losses. You can deduct the losses against capital gains and deduct up to $3,000 of additional losses against other income. Any losses remaining after that are carried forward to future years to be used in the same way. If you still like the investment long term, you can buy it back. With stocks, mutual funds, and some other investments you have to wait more than 30 days to repurchase if you want to deduct the loss in the year of the sale.

Be sure your portfolio isn't generating income you don't need. High-dividend stocks and mutual funds that distribute most of their gains each year will increase your gross income and perhaps the stealth taxes. Consider switching to investments that don't increase gross income as much.

Don't trade too much in your portfolio. Keep in mind that each capital gain that isn't offset by deductible losses increases gross income and is a potential trigger for increasing the stealth taxes. Even if you are earning a tax-favored long-term capital gain, it could increase gross income high enough to increase one or more of the retiree taxes.

You also could favor tax-advantaged investments such as master limited partnerships and investment real estate. Again, don't invest only for the tax benefits. But consider how the tax benefits will avoid the retiree taxes and increase your after-tax returns.

Business Losses.   A loss from a business activity can be deducted from other sources of gross income and thereby reduce AGI and MAGI. Business losses might come from ownership of a pass-through entity, such as a partnership, limited liability company, or S corporation. You might be the sole owner or one of several owners. The business losses also could come through a sole proprietorship.

There are some tax rules designed to limit the ability to deduct such losses. The activity must be operated in a business-like manner and with the intention of earning a profit. Also, to deduct the losses on your tax return it can't be considered a passive activity for you. You need to materially participate in the business, which is defined in some detailed IRS regulations.

Some retirees own rental properties that generate tax losses. Others have longtime hobbies, pastimes, or diversions that can be turned into business activities. If you have such an activity, consider participating it in a way that will reduce taxes.

Those are the basics of how to reduce AGI and MAGI. Now, we'll look at another way to manage your retirement finances to minimize all taxes. Following that, we review individual stealth taxes and some additional tax strategies that are important to retirees.

Managing for a Low Tax Bracket

Most retirement tax planning and tax discussions have the wrong focus. They look at marginal tax rates, which is the tax rate on the next dollar of ordinary income earned. If you're married and earning $50,000 annually, for example, your next dollar will be taxed at the 15 percent rate. Or the discussions take your tax bracket as a given and try to reduce taxes a bit by deferring some income or finding ways to increase some deductions.

Those approaches work fine during the working years for most people. While working, most people don't have much influence on their levels of income and therefore can't change their tax brackets. For retired people, some self-employed people, and a few other taxpayers, that's the wrong approach. These groups have more control over both the amount and sources of income they recognize in a year. That's especially true of a retiree who has different types of investment and asset accounts. Different types of income are taxed at different rates, and a retiree can have a lot of flexibility over the types of income recognized each year.

The better approach is to focus on your effective tax rate. This is the percentage of all your sources of income that is paid in income taxes. Many retirees can structure their income so that the effective tax rate is much lower than during their working years and the effective tax rate on someone earning the same amount in salary.

A savvy retiree can keep the tax rate around 20 percent without reducing cash flow by managing investments, retirement plan withdrawals, and other income sources.

Take a look at the important factors. For married couples filing jointly, ordinary income is taxed at the 15 percent rate until taxable income exceeds $75,300 in 2016. (For single taxpayers, the ceiling is $37,650.) Qualified dividends and long-term capital gains are taxed at the maximum 20 percent rate, regardless of their amount. (Long-term capital gains on collectibles, including precious metals, are taxed at a maximum 28 percent rate.) For taxpayers in the 15 percent or lower marginal tax bracket, long-term capital gains and dividends are taxed at 0 percent. In the 25 percent and 35 percent tax brackets, long-term capital gains and qualified dividends face only a 15 percent rate.

Social Security benefits are tax free until adjusted gross income reaches $32,000 for a married couple filing jointly or $25,000 for a single taxpayer. Distributions from Roth IRAs and interest from state and local bonds generally are tax free.

Don't forget those rates are on taxable income. Before getting there, you have exclusions, exemptions, and deductions. You reduce gross income by personal and dependent exemptions. Then, you have either the standard deduction amount or your itemized expense deductions, such as state and local property and income taxes, medical expenses, and charitable contributions. You also might qualify for tax credits, such as the foreign tax credit on foreign investments.

The Benefits of Tax Diversification

To manage your cash flow to stay in a low tax bracket, you first need tax diversification. You need to own different types of investment accounts and have different sources of income. If you follow my recommendations, you'll have some guaranteed lifetime income from Social Security, annuities, and perhaps an employer pension. You'll also have your nest egg in taxable investment accounts, traditional IRAs, Roth IRAs, and perhaps other types of accounts.

Some people try to anticipate what future tax law will be like and tilt their assets toward the types of accounts and investments that would benefit in that regime. They might try to own either all Roth IRAs or all traditional IRAs, for example. That's a difficult strategy to get right. It's better to realize that the tax law will change more than once, and you won't be able to anticipate what it will be at any time in the future. If you try to tilt your holdings toward one type of tax regime and are wrong, you could end up paying much higher lifetime income taxes. Instead, try to have tax diversification. You'll have options in any tax environment and won't be hammered in any particular tax regime. You'll also be better able to manage your cash flow to minimize the effective tax rate.

Determining Your Tax Rate

Retirees often can choose how and when they receive income. By carefully paying attention to the sources of income and the amount of AGI, they have more control over their tax burden. In fact, you can almost determine the tax rate you want to pay. Some planners refer to this as tax bracket management.

Here are the tools you can use to manage your tax bracket and minimize your effective tax rate.

Reduce or Convert Traditional IRAs. One of the greatest obstacles to tax-bracket management is having too much of your nest egg in traditional IRAs or 401(k)s. Most people don't realize this until it is too late.

As we discussed in Chapter 8, traditional IRAs (and other forms of tax deferral) are great during the accumulation years. Yet, they create two problems during the distribution years. One problem is that all distributions are taxed as ordinary income, facing your highest tax rate. The other is that after age $70^1/_2$, minimum distributions are required. As you age, the required distributions increase, and many people in their late 70s and beyond complain that the required distributions far exceed their cash needs and increase taxes.

There are a couple of strategies to consider. One is to take IRA distributions before you need the money. Over time or in a lump sum take money out of the IRA, pay the taxes, and put the rest of the distribution in a taxable account. When you spend the principal in the future it won't be taxed. You'll also be able to invest the money so future income and gains receive favorable tax rates.

The other strategy is to convert all or part of the traditional IRA to a Roth IRA. You pay taxes on the converted amount, but future distributions to you and your heirs are tax free. We discussed this in detail in Chapter 8.

Most people don't want to prepay taxes. It goes against one of the longstanding principles of tax planning. But when taxes will be higher in the future, especially when you'll be faced with an array of stealth taxes, paying taxes now instead of later can make sense. In 2010, favorable tax treatment was offered to those who converted traditional IRAs to Roth IRAs that year. The IRS reported the results and found that conversions increased by nine times over the previous year. Among taxpayers with $1 million or more of income, more than 10 percent did conversions. That means the taxpayers who receive the most sophisticated advice decided paying some taxes early was a good idea when it converted future ordinary income into tax-favored or tax-free income.

An advantage of a Roth IRA is that distributions from it, no matter how large, aren't included in AGI. That is a big help in avoiding the stealth taxes triggered by higher AGI.

More details about these IRA strategies are in Chapter 8.

Time IRA Distributions and Conversions. Consider more than immediate cash needs when deciding how much to distribute from a traditional IRA or 401(k) or how much to convert to a Roth IRA. Consider the rest of your tax picture. Increase distributions or conversions in a year when your tax bracket is lower. Perhaps you have high-deductible medical expenses, a business loss, earned less income, or have other factors that reduce your tax bill. That would be a good year to increase IRA distributions or conversions, because you'll be in a lower tax bracket or have deductions to offset the taxes on the IRA transactions.

Delay Social Security. You need to consider a number of factors before deciding when to take Social Security, as we discussed in Chapter 3. Income taxes are one of the reasons to defer benefits. Social Security benefits are tax free or mostly tax free, unless your AGI is above $44,000. Since delaying benefits increases your retirement benefit, it also increases your potentially tax-advantaged income.

Seek Tax-Advantaged Income. Your taxable accounts should be managed to benefit from tax-exempt income, qualified dividend income, and long-term capital gains. Investments that generate ordinary income, such as interest, should be in other types of accounts or annuities whenever possible. It also is wasteful to take short-term capital gains in taxable accounts without a compelling reason. Hold assets for more than one year to qualify for the long-term capital gains rate.

Use Tax-Wise Investment Strategies. Taxable accounts need to be managed with both taxes and investment returns in mind, resulting in higher after-tax returns. The same strategies we discussed earlier for reducing AGI are good for minimizing taxes on taxable investment accounts.

Manage Your Tax Bracket Annually. When you have tax diversification and the other strategies in place, you are in position to manage your tax bracket, keeping your effective tax rate around 20 percent annually.

You'll have a base of automatic, guaranteed income from Social Security and perhaps some annuities and pensions. After age 70½ you'll also have required minimum distributions from traditional IRAs and 401(k)s. All of that is likely to be taxed as ordinary income. Your taxable accounts might generate qualified dividends, tax-exempt interest, mutual fund distributions, and other income that's outside your control. Much of that should be either tax free (interest on tax-exempt bonds) or tax-advantaged (qualified dividends and long-term capital gains).

When you need cash beyond that to meet your spending needs, you should have flexibility in determining the sources of that cash and how it is taxed. To meet spending needs that exceed the automatic income, carefully choose the sources. You might sell some assets in taxable accounts for long-term capital gains to raise cash. When AGI is nearing the maximum you want, consider Roth IRA distributions to avoid triggering a higher tax bracket or stealth taxes. In a year when AGI is low or you have deductions to offset ordinary income, consider taking extra distributions from traditional IRAs or annuities.

This approach is more work than traditional retirement tax strategies, but the work should pay off by keeping you in a lower tax bracket throughout retirement. With tax diversification and tax bracket management, you can generate substantial cash flow each year while keeping your effective tax rate around 20 percent or even less. Many retirees can maintain their cash flow while avoiding the higher ordinary income tax brackets, the stealth taxes and other burdens Congress aims at you.

The Alternative Minimum Tax

The alternative minimum tax (AMT) is the granddaddy of the stealth taxes. The AMT basically is a separate tax system and is almost a flat tax. A taxpayer computes both the regular tax and the AMT, and then pays the higher of the two. The IRS also computes the AMT for all the returns it processes. If someone didn't compute the AMT who should have, the IRS will send a letter asking for the additional taxes. Many people learn about the AMT for the first time when the IRS or their tax preparers tell them they owe it.

The AMT is computed on Form 6251. The tax starts with regular taxable income. Then a number of adjustments and preferences listed on the form are added back to taxable income. After adding the adjustments and preferences, an exempt amount is subtracted. The AMT is computed on the income remaining after subtracting the exemption. The AMT is close to being a flat tax. The tax rate is 26 percent of AMT income up to $186,300 in 2016. Above that amount a 28 percent rate applies.

Originally, the AMT was designed to ensure that the wealthiest taxpayers did not make generous use of tax breaks to eliminate all income taxes. It was created after IRS data revealed that about 500 taxpayers earned more than $1 million but paid little or no taxes.

Unfortunately, the AMT now traps taxpayers in most income brackets when they have enough tax breaks—even if they have a sizable tax liability under the regular tax. Unexceptional deductions that are added back to taxable income under the AMT include personal and dependent exemptions, state and local taxes, most miscellaneous itemized expenses, and incentive stock option gains.

The reason more and more people became subject to the AMT over the years was that the exemption wasn't adjusted for inflation or income growth. Congress made some partial adjustments in recent years and finally made a permanent "fix" in 2014 that raised the exemption amount and the level at which the 28 percent rate kicks in. But the fix didn't return the exemption to a level equivalent to when the AMT was created. For 2016, the exemption amount is $83,800 for married couples filing jointly and $53,900 for singles taxpayers. The exemption amount is phased out as income rises. For married couples filing jointly, the exemption begins to phase out when income is above $159,700, and for single taxpayers at $119,700.

Under the AMT you're allowed the itemized deductions for charitable contributions and mortgage interest, other than most home equity mortgage interest. You're allowed reduced deductions for some medical and dental expenses. Some business deductions are deferred, such as depreciation and net operating losses.

You're not allowed the itemized deductions for state and local taxes and for miscellaneous expenses. You're also disallowed under the AMT both the standard deduction and personal and dependent exemptions. Tax-exempt bond interest generally is exempt from the AMT, but interest from private-activity bonds is taxed under the AMT.

The full list of tax preferences is in the instructions for Form 6251, available free on the IRS website at www.irs.gov.

There are several ways the AMT can be triggered for retirees and preretirees.

The disallowance of itemized deductions such as state and local taxes and mortgage interest plus the reduction in medical expense deductions can trigger the tax as can the disallowances of the standard deduction for those who don't itemize and personal and dependent exemptions. All these items aren't the exclusive province of the wealthy and can trigger the AMT for others.

Tax items that aren't tax preferences also can interact with the AMT so that they trigger or increase the AMT. Among them are tax-favored items such as long-term capital gains and qualified dividends.

When you have a high amount of capital gains and dividends, you pay a low regular income tax rate. But capital gains and dividends count as income under the AMT, so they can take you above the exemption amount just as quickly as ordinary income does. They also might incur state income taxes, which are deductible under the regular tax but not the AMT. The result of the combination is that you could owe more tax under the AMT than the regular income tax just because you earn a high percentage of your income from capital gains or qualified dividends.

The AMT now applies to eight times as many taxpayers as 20 years ago. Unfortunately, there is no formula that can warn you the AMT might be a problem, because the tax is so complex and has so many moving parts. You have to compute your tax both ways to see if the AMT is a problem.

The AMT can be triggered by taking a large capital gain one year or by having three or more dependents while living in a high tax state. For retirees, required minimum distributions from IRAs can trigger the tax as they increase over the years. Combinations of the different tax preference items or transactions that increase income can unexpectedly make you subject to the AMT. Many people are trapped in a cycle of being subject to the AMT one year but not the next.

Retirees are especially susceptible to a sneak attack from the AMT. A retiree usually receives less taxable income in retirement. Yet, most deductions will remain the same for at least the first few years. Real estate taxes and mortgage interest won't change just because a property owner has retired. Investment advisor fees and other miscellaneous itemized expenses probably will be stable and might even rise. State income taxes will decline a bit with income, but charitable contributions generally stay the same. Even worse, a retiree might have purchased a second home. That increases real estate tax deductions and perhaps mortgage interest expense, and with that comes the risk of paying the AMT.

Most retirees believe that tax-exempt bonds are exempt from all income taxes. They are only partly right. General obligation bonds do not affect the AMT. A number of exempt bonds, however, fund private activities. Interest from these is tax free under the regular tax but is taxed under the AMT. A number of tax-exempt bond mutual funds have about 80 percent of their portfolios in these private activity bonds. A private activity bond is one that is backed not by the general obligation of a government but by an activity that is not considered an essential government function. These activities include airports, stadiums, many commercial properties, and the like.

A retiree also is likely to have more capital gains from the sale of investments than during the working years, and increased capital gains puts the retiree at risk for triggering the AMT. The result for too many retirees is that income declines while tax deductions remain stable and might perhaps increase, which also can trigger the AMT.

Any year you've had changes in any of the items discussed here should cause you to worry about the AMT. Estimate both the AMT and regular income tax both mid-year and close to year-end. If you might be subject to the AMT, there are steps to consider.

When disallowed deductions might trigger the AMT, consider spreading them over two tax years if you can. Otherwise, you receive no tax benefit from the deductions if you're hit by the AMT.

You could defer income. For example, consider spreading a large capital gain over two years instead of one if it is possible. Look for ways to limit distributions from IRAs and annuities. Consider converting a traditional IRA to a Roth. This might make you subject to the AMT in the conversion year but make it less likely in future years. When the law makes the option available, make charitable contributions from a traditional IRA instead of using cash. Or give appreciated stock or other assets to a charity instead of selling the stock and giving cash.

Above all, recognize the potential for the AMT to rear its head when there's a significant new element in your tax picture and estimate your taxes before year-end so you can take action if needed. If you've been preparing your own taxes, a year when the AMT is a possibility is a good time to work with an experienced tax expert.

Taxes on Social Security Benefits

Originally, Social Security benefits were free of income taxes. That went out the door in 1986, when some benefits first were taxed. Taxes were increased on higher income beneficiaries in 1993.

In 1986, taxpayers with adjusted gross incomes above $32,000 began to have up to 50 percent of their benefits included in gross income. In the 1993 tax law, those with an adjusted gross income exceeding $44,000 began to have up to 85 percent of their benefits taxed. Unlike many other provisions of the tax code, these AGI triggers are not indexed for inflation. That means each year more Social Security beneficiaries pay income taxes on some of their benefits simply because inflation increased their nominal incomes.

Suppose Max Profits has adjusted gross income of $31,999. He gets a distribution from a mutual fund that pushes AGI to $32,100. The distribution is taxable. In addition, it triggers taxes on some Social Security benefits that were tax free. Once Max's income exceeds $32,000, each additional dollar of income means more than one dollar is included in gross income—the dollar earned plus up to 50 cents of Social Security benefits. Once Max's adjusted gross income exceeds $44,000, each additional dollar of income could cause up to 85 cents of Social Security benefits to be added to income.

In most states there also are state income taxes on the benefits. That's why those in high-tax states, such as California, who have an AGI above $44,000 can have the marginal tax rate on each additional dollar earned reach 90 percent.

Strategies that Work.   Fortunately, there are steps that can reduce the taxes on Social Security benefits, but first, let's throw out a couple of strategies that won't work. Having the higher-income spouse delay Social Security benefits so that only the lower-earning spouse receives them doesn't work. The lower-earning spouse's benefits still might be taxed. The combined joint income of the two spouses is used to determine the amount of benefits included in income. The tax is not computed separately based on the income of each spouse. Married, filing separately also won't help. In fact, it will make the tax worse, because the benefits will be taxed when adjusted gross income of each spouse is above $0.

If adjusted gross income is significantly above the threshold at which benefits are taxed, there probably is not much that can be done to reduce benefits. Taxpayers who are near the threshold for taxing benefits, however, should consider some strategies that can reduce the amount of Social Security benefits taxed. The strategies are the same as those already discussed to reduce AGI.

Itemized Deduction Reduction

The Pease provision (named after the congressman whose idea it was) affects far more taxpayers than the alternative minimum tax. Pease disallows part of a taxpayer's itemized expense deductions when the taxpayer's adjusted gross income (AGI) is too high. The level at which the itemized deduction reduction kicks in (known as the threshold amount) is indexed for inflation, so it changes each year. In 2016, the provision kicked in when adjusted gross income exceeded $311,300 on returns for married couples filing jointly, and $259,400 for an unmarried taxpayer.

Computing the Pease deduction can get complicated. Itemized deductions are reduced by 3 percent of the difference between the threshold amount and AGI. Up to 80 percent of itemized deductions can be eliminated under the Pease provision.

The Pease provision is particularly hard on taxpayers with volatile incomes or who have one-time income boosts. A large capital gain or retirement plan distribution could make a lot of itemized deductions disappear. Someone who has a high income each year knows he or she will be subject to the itemized deduction reduction and can reliably estimate ahead of time the amount of a deduction that would be lost before writing a check for an itemized expense. But someone with a volatile income or one-time change in income is likely to get trapped by the Pease provision and lose the benefit of a lot of tax deductions. Some of those deductions, such as charitable contributions, could have been delayed until the next year.

Since the provision is based on AGI, the strategies already discussed for reducing AGI will help avoid losing the benefit of itemized expense deductions. When it looks like the loss of itemized deductions can't be avoided in a year, consider deferring any large, discretionary itemized expenses until a future year when the Pease provision might not be triggered.

Saving Personal Exemptions

Personal and dependent exemptions also are phased out as income increases under the personal exemption phaseout (PEP) rules. Each taxpayer gets a personal exemption deduction, one for a spouse, and one for each dependent. The exemption amount is indexed for inflation and was $4,050 in 2016. These deductions are allowed whether expenses are itemized or the standard deduction is taken.

The personal and dependent exemptions are reduced when AGI exceeds a threshold amount. That amount in 2016 was $311,300 on a joint return and $259,400 for a single taxpayer. The formula for reducing the exemptions is complicated. It works out to losing 2.25 cents of each exemption for each dollar income rises above the threshold amount. The formula is that exemptions are reduced 2 percent for each $2,500 or part of $2,500 that AGI is above the threshold. For those who don't use computer software or a tax preparer to do their returns, the IRS offers a worksheet along with the instructions to compute the exemption reduction.

As with the other stealth taxes, the strategies for reducing AGI can prevent the loss of personal and dependent exemptions.

The 3.8 Percent Tax on Net Investment Income

The Affordable Care and Patient Protection Act of 2010 included several new taxes. Among them was the 3.8 percent tax on the "unearned" income of single taxpayers with modified adjusted gross incomes exceeding $200,000 and married couples filing jointly with MAGIs above $250,000. The income thresholds aren't indexed for inflation, so more people will owe them over the years. Though the tax is labeled a Medicare surtax, the proceeds actually will go into general revenues, not the Medicare fund. This tax is separate from all other taxes.

MAGI for this tax is your regular AGI plus any foreign earned income that qualified for the exclusion from gross income.

Unearned income subject to this tax is investment income and includes interest, dividends, capital gains, annuity distributions (taxable distributions only and only when not from a qualified retirement plan), royalties, and passive real estate rental income. Interest income from tax-exempt bonds avoids the tax, though capital gains from sales of the bonds do not.

Taxable distributions from master limited partnerships and real estate investment trusts also count as unearned income. But remember, only taxable distributions are affected. Most distributions from MLPs aren't taxed. On average, MLP distributions are 15 percent taxable income and 85 percent nontaxable returns of capital. But the return of capital portion reduces your basis in the MLP shares, so it increases the capital gain when you eventually sell the shares. On the other hand, you can hold the MLP shares for life. Whoever inherits the shares will be able to increase the basis to current fair market value and avoid taxes on their sale.

Real estate income can be exempt when earned by a real estate professional. To be a professional you must spend a minimum of 750 hours annually managing real estate. That means being involved in the nuts and bolts of managing properties. Those hours also must be more than half of your working hours for the year.

Income and gains earned through pass-through entities such as S corporations, partnerships, and limited liability companies might be exempt. The activity has to qualify as a business for the individual owner. You must pass one of the active involvement tests under the passive activity regulations. The easiest test to pass is to have the activity be your prime source of income, taking 500 hours or more of your time. When none of the tests is passed, the income is passive and subject to the 3.8 percent tax.

Donations of appreciated assets to charity also avoid the tax. That's a reason to consider making charitable donations in appreciated property held in taxable accounts instead of cash.

Business owners need to realize that the surtax will apply to the sale of a business. That's an extra 3.8 percent in addition to the other taxes and the costs of selling.

Unearned income for the tax doesn't include tax-free interest or distributions from qualified retirement plans, such as 401(k)s, traditional IRAs, Roth IRAs, profit-sharing plans, and defined benefit plans. Social Security benefits and life insurance payouts also aren't subject to the tax.

But keep in mind the interplay of tax provisions. Distributions from traditional IRAs are included in AGI. So, large IRA distributions could increase AGI and trigger the 3.8 percent tax on your investment income. This is especially likely as you get older and required minimum distributions increase. But Roth IRA distributions aren't included in gross income. Since they aren't taxable, they don't trigger the investment income tax. It's another factor to consider when deciding whether to convert a traditional IRA to a Roth IRA.

The surtax is imposed on the lesser of net investment income and the amount of MAGI above the threshold. Suppose Max and Rosie Profits have investment income of $30,000 and MAGI of $270,000. Their net investment income is $30,000, and the excess of MAGI and the threshold is $20,000, so they pay the tax on $20,000. Multiplied by 3.8 percent brings a tax of $760. If everything else were the same except their MAGI were $290,000, they would owe tax on the net investment income. That tax would be 3.8 percent of $30,000, or $1,140.

Home Sales and the Surtax.   When the 3.8 percent net investment income tax was first enacted, there was a lot of speculation about how the IRS would rule on its application to sales of homes. Here is how the tax affects home transactions.

When you sell a home at a gain and the home wasn't your principal residence, such as a vacation home, second home, or rental property, all of the gain potentially is subject to the 3.8 percent tax. You'll have a capital gain from the sale of an investment asset, which is investment income.

When you sell your principal residence, however, the investment income tax applies only to the amount that is included in gross income. On the sale of a principal residence, up to $250,000 of gain is exempt for singles and $500,000 for married couples filing jointly.

Remember that only gain is potentially taxed, not the sale proceeds of the home. First, you subtract from the sale price the basis of the home, which includes the original cost plus the cost of any improvements. Second, you subtract selling costs such as broker's commission and closing costs. Only the sale proceeds above that amount are potentially taxed, and only if they exceed the exempt amount.

For most people, the sale of a principal residence isn't likely to be subject to the 3.8 percent investment income tax. Also, none of the sale proceeds are likely to be included in gross income, increasing your AGI so that it is high enough to trigger or increase the 3.8 percent tax on your net investment income.

Avoiding the Surtax.   Of course, as with the stealth taxes, one way to avoid the surtax is to minimize AGI, which we already discussed. There are other strategies unique to the tax:

- *Carefully review major events.* You might think that your income isn't near $250,000, so the tax doesn't affect you. But one-time events could trigger the tax. Suppose you take a large capital gain. That could increase your AGI enough to trigger the tax. Overlooking the potential for the 3.8 percent tax could result in several thousand dollars of additional taxes one year.
- *Know the interplay of tax code sections.* We already discussed several examples of this. Here is another example. When you sell a capital asset at a loss, for the regular income tax the loss is deducted against gains for the year. Any excess loss offsets up to $3,000 of other income, and an additional excess is carried forward to future years. But for the 3.8 percent tax, tax losses offset only gains for the year. Carryforward losses aren't deducted against other investment income to reduce the 3.8 percent tax.
- *Track investment expenses.* The tax is on net investment income. From your gross investment income you are allowed to deduct certain expenses. The deductible expenses include rental and royalty expenses, margin interest to the extent of interest income and short-term gains, investment advice, broker commissions and fees, and state income taxes attributable to investment income.
- *Know what's exempt.* You might be able to restructure things if you're involved in real estate or a small business so that income avoids the 3.8 percent tax. The restructuring would involve your being more actively involved so that the income is business income instead of investment income. Some people will shift from taxable bonds to tax-exempt bonds. Others will carefully plan distributions from annuities.
- *Review trust strategies.* As with other special taxes, the 3.8 percent investment income tax kicks in for trusts at very low levels. For a trust, the 3.8 percent tax kicks in when undistributed investment income exceeds $11,950. Trustees might need to reconsider investment or distribution strategies to reduce or avoid the tax.

Retirees' Special Tax Problem

A special tax problem for many retirees, especially new retirees, is the required quarterly payment of estimated income taxes. After decades of having taxes automatically deducted from their paychecks, many have trouble adapting to a system of paying estimated taxes each quarter. Too often, retirees' payments are late or aren't high enough, resulting in unnecessary penalties. Some retirees prepay too much, providing an interest-free loan to the government.

Those who expect to owe more than $1,000 in federal income taxes that are not prepaid through withholding must make quarterly estimated tax payments. The payment for the first quarter of the year is due by April 15. The other three payments are due June 15, September 15, and January 15. If the deadline falls on a weekend or holiday, the deadline is delayed until the next business day.

The penalty for a late or low payment is interest compounded daily at a rate announced by the IRS each month. The interest rate changes with market treasury rates. Interest is charged from the day the payment was due until the earlier of the date the tax return for the year is due and the date the payment actually is made.

Estimated tax payments must cover all types of taxes due: income, self-employment, tax withholding for household workers, and any others that will be reported on Form 1040. Estimated tax payments are determined by projecting the taxes that will be due for the year, dividing the total by four, and paying that amount each quarter. The IRS assumes that income is earned equally through the year, so estimated payments must be equal. You can't bunch the bulk of your estimated taxes in the fourth payment, unless you qualify for the annualization method, which we discuss shortly.

The first goal is to make payments that are high enough to avoid any penalties. Taxpayers can avoid the penalties by qualifying for at least one of three safe harbors. High-income taxpayers must qualify for the third safe harbor to avoid the penalties. The safe harbors are:

- Pay at least 90 percent of the current year's tax liability through timely estimated tax payments.
- Pay an amount equal to at least 100 percent of last year's tax bill through timely estimated tax payments.
- A high-income taxpayer must pay an amount at least equal to either (1) 90 percent of the current year's tax liability or (2) 110 percent of last year's tax liability. A high-income taxpayer is one whose adjusted gross income on the previous year's tax return was over $150,000 ($75,000 for married individuals filing separately). Those AGI levels are not indexed for inflation.

Another way to avoid an underpayment penalty is through the annualization method. For example, suppose estimated tax payments for the first three quarters of the year were accurate based on the income to date, but income increased substantially during the last quarter of the year. Then, the taxpayer can make a higher estimated tax payment for the fourth quarter and avoid a penalty. This method is for anyone whose income varied during the year and who made payments based on the income as it actually was received. To use this method, Form 2210 with Schedule AI must be filed as part of the income tax return for the year. This form requires a showing of when income was received during the year and that quarterly estimated payments were sufficient for the income received each quarter.

Penalties for failure to pay estimated taxes cannot be avoided by paying the year's taxes with a big check in the last quarterly payment. The IRS expects estimated taxes to be paid equally throughout the year. When payments are not equal, the only way to avoid penalties is to use the annualization method.

Retirees should choose the payment schedule that allows them to retain money as long as possible and keep it working for them, not the government. If income is likely to stay the same or decline this year, prepay 90 percent of this year's tax liability. That way, 10 percent to 20 percent of the final tax liability can be invested until the tax return for the year is filed. The trick with this approach is to make an accurate estimate of the tax bill for the year. If prepayments are too low, the taxpayer will be hit with a penalty. A taxpayer might want to figure the 90 percent amount, then pay a little extra each quarter to ensure there won't be penalties.

If income is likely to increase this year, make payments based on last year's liability. That way, penalties will be avoided and cash will be conserved for as long as possible.

If income will fluctuate and the taxpayer doesn't mind keeping careful track of the cash flows and related tax liabilities, then the annualized method is best. Taxpayers whose income is primarily from capital gains or retirement plan distributions that are discretionary instead of on a schedule might choose this method. It is too much work for most people, but it can save money when income varies throughout the year. The goal should be to estimate income well enough to hold on to the cash as long as possible without incurring any penalties.

When you must pay estimated taxes, you complete Form 2210 with your Form 1040 each year. That will determine if you owe any penalties for late payments or low payments. There are several ways to make payments, and the IRS regularly updates its payment methods. The IRS has electronic payment systems available over either the telephone or the Internet. These can be made with either a direct transfer from your bank account or charges to payment cards. You also can pay by check accompanied by a voucher Form 1040-ES. Details about the estimated tax are in IRS Publication 505, which is available free through the IRS website at www.irs.gov.

There might be an alternative if you don't want to make estimated tax payments or realized that you made a mistake and didn't make high enough payments earlier in the year. When you prepay taxes through withholding, the IRS assumes the payments were made evenly through the year even if they weren't. You can request that income payments to you have income with held.

An option is to have taxes withheld from payments you receive from pensions, annuities, and IRAs. In most cases you can designate the amount you want withheld. Even if it means having a high amount of the payments withheld, you might find it more convenient to have the taxes prepaid through withholding than having to make estimated tax payments.

The withholding option can be especially helpful when in the last quarter of the year you realized that your estimated tax payments were too low to avoid a penalty. You can request that a distribution from your IRA in the fourth quarter have enough withholding to make up the estimated tax shortfall. The IRS will assume that amount was paid evenly during the year, so it might help you avoid a penalty.

Handling Employer Retirement Plans

Employer retirement plans come in two main types. They are very different types of plans and generate different issues and decisions. (I'm talking only about tax-qualified retirement plans in this chapter.)

One type of qualified retirement plan is the defined benefit plan. This is the old-fashioned pension plan that promises the employee a regular payment after retirement. The employee generally has to work for a minimum period to be vested in any defined benefit and for a longer period to qualify for the full or maximum benefit. The retirement benefit usually is a fixed monthly amount payable for life or for the joint life of the employee and his or her spouse. In some plans the payment is indexed for inflation, but not in most private sector plans.

Fewer and fewer private-sector employers offer defined benefit plans. Decades ago, most large employers and many smaller employers offered defined benefit pensions to employees. But a series of tax and accounting changes caused employers to reduce or eliminate defined benefit plans. Now, defined benefit plans are most likely to be offered to government and union employees. A number of large private-sector employers also offer defined benefit pensions, but these pay relatively small amounts to retirees. Retirees are expected to supplement their retirement income with 401(k) plans and other savings. Also, large employers have been steadily scaling back or eliminating their defined benefit plans.

The other type of plan is the defined contribution plan. The well-known 401(k) plan is the primary defined contribution plan. No specific retirement benefit is promised to the employee. Instead, the employee chooses to have a percentage of salary deferred to a 401(k) account. The employer might make a matching contribution of some or all of the employee's contribution. The employee also chooses how the account is invested from among choices offered by the plan. The employee owns whatever amount the account compounds to over time and chooses how to take money out of the account.

The details of each of these types of plans differ greatly among employers. Yet, there are issues common to the each of the plan types. We cover those key issues in this chapter.

Defined Benefit Plan: Take an Annuity or Lump Sum?

When your employer offers a defined benefit retirement plan and it is time to retire, you generally are offered a choice. You can take the lifetime stream of payments offered by the employer, or you can take the entire lifetime benefit in a lump sum. (You also might have this option with a 401(k) plan.)

The decision is critical. You can't change once a decision is made. Once you begin the lifetime payments (often called an annuity or annuitization), that decision can't be reversed. You're locked in to that stream of payments. When you opt for a lump sum instead, you always can choose to use that lump sum to purchase a commercial annuity. But it might not have the same terms as the one you were offered by the pension plan. The annuity offered by the plan no longer will be available to you.

Yet, this decision rarely receives the level of critical analysis it should.

The decision usually boils down to a choice between control and potential returns on the one hand versus security and risk reduction on the other hand.

When you take a lump sum, you have control over the money. You decide how it is invested and how much to spend each year. The control gives you the potential to earn a higher rate of return than was embedded in the annuity payouts. That could give you more spending money over your lifetime and more to leave to your loved ones. Control also means that if in one year you have a large spending need, you can tap into the lump sum for it. Your annual cash flow isn't limited to the annuity payout.

Another advantage of the lump sum is that there is the potential you won't spend it during your lifetime, so some money will be available for your heirs. The annuity payout usually ends on the passing of you or your spouse. There's nothing left for your children or other heirs or for charity.

With the annuity you have security. You'll receive that fixed payment each month for the rest of your life, no matter how long you live.

There won't be anything from the annuity for your heirs, but there probably wouldn't have been anything left of the lump sum if you or your spouse lived to 90 or 100. Plus, the lump sum might have dissipated early through low investment returns or overspending, leaving you to rely on other assets and Social Security to pay your expenses.

Because of the trade-offs, it can be a difficult decision. Yet, it's also a critical decision and one that has to be made.

There are two important steps to take before making a decision.

The first is to determine how good the annuity offer is. The retirement plan should tell you the monthly annuity payment you earned, and it should tell you how much of a lump sum you could receive instead of the annuity. You'd be able to have that lump sum deposited in your retirement account and then roll it over to an IRA. You don't want to take the lump sum as a check or a deposit to a taxable account, because then the entire amount would be taxed in the year you receive it. Once the money is in an IRA, the IRA would be able to buy a commercial annuity.

You want to see the income from a commercial immediate annuity the lump sum would purchase. Follow the instructions for purchasing and comparing immediate annuities in Chapter 3. Contact different insurance agents and brokers to obtain quotes for immediate annuities. This way, you'll learn how much income you can purchase with the lump sum. You'll learn if the annuity is a good deal compared to what is available in the private market or if the lump sum is the better deal. In many cases, the decision is fairly clear at this point. It's obvious that the pension annuity is either a good or bad deal compared to the annuities available elsewhere.

The calculation that pension plans use to determine the lump-sum payment is set by the tax code, and in general it is biased toward a low lump sum. There's a good chance you won't be able to buy a commercial annuity with the lump sum that pays an income comparable to the pension annuity. But don't rely on that general advice. Do the work to determine how much income could be purchased using the lump sum.

There's a second step to take when the lump sum still appears a viable choice. You need to make projections about how long the lump sum would last, or how much you could withdraw from it each year to make it last a long time. You'll have to make estimates about your rate of investment returns, tax bracket, spending rate, and other factors. You need to refer to Chapter 5 for the discussion about tapping your nest egg.

When you believe you'll earn a higher investment return than either an insurance company or than is assumed by the pension plan, you might favor the lump sum. A higher investment return means you're likely to be able to spend more monthly or to have money to leave to loved ones or charity. Or a higher return could mean that you'll earn enough to protect the purchasing power of your income.

To be safe, you should make conservative estimates about your investment returns. Or you should make several projections using different assumptions. That way you'll see what is likely to happen under different scenarios.

The decision really boils down to risk shifting and risk management. By taking the annuity, you transfer to the pension fund the risks that there will be low investment returns or that you'll live beyond life expectancy. You know you won't run out of income during your lifetime, no matter how long you live or how low investment returns are.

You pay for transferring those risks. You have less control over the money and give up the potential of earning a higher return. You also take the risk that you won't live to life expectancy and the pension fund (or its other beneficiaries) will benefit from that. With the annuity, you also might not have any inflation protection. Your other assets will have to provide that.

Choosing Your Annuity

When you decide to choose an annuity over a lump sum from a defined benefit plan, you have another decision to make.

Most pension plans allow you to choose the type of annuity payment you want. Here are the typical annuity payments available:

- *Single life annuity.* The annuity makes payments for the life of the employee. After the employee passes, payments cease.
- *Joint life or joint and survivor annuity.* The annuity makes payments until both the employee and the joint beneficiary pass away. The joint beneficiary usually is a spouse and in most annuities has to be recognized by a state as a spouse. If the employee dies first, the surviving spouse receives payments. Often the amount of the payments to the surviving spouse can be selected before the annuity begins. A 100 percent joint life annuity pays the same amount to the survivor each month after the employee passes away. There usually are options that reduce the payment to the survivor to either 75 percent or 50 percent of what was paid while the employee was alive.
- *Term of years.* The annuity payments are guaranteed to last a stated number of years. If the employee dies before the period expires, payments continue to a named beneficiary or beneficiaries until the term of years ends. If the employee outlives the term of years, the payments end when the number of years ends.
- *Life annuity with guaranteed term of years.* The annuity payments last for the longer of the term of years or the life of the employee. If the guaranteed term is 10 years and the employee lives 5 years, the payments

continue for five more years to a named beneficiary or beneficiaries. If the guaranteed term is 10 years and the employee lives 20 years, the annuity makes payments for 20 years.

The single life annuity usually has the highest monthly payment, though the term of years will be higher if the term is shorter than the life expectancy of the employee. The joint life with 100 percent of the payment continuing to the surviving spouse is likely to have the lowest payment.

The choice often depends on the income and resources that will be available to the surviving spouse. You also need to consider any changes that might be made in a surviving spouse's lifestyle. If the expectation is that the surviving spouse will live in the same house, there might not be a large reduction in the cost of living. There will be a reduction in food, utilities, and some other expenses because there will be only one household member. But many other expenses won't decrease, and there might be increases in other costs, because the deceased spouse won't be available to help with tasks around the house.

If you're married, the tax law says the default payment is a joint and survivor annuity that pays no less than 50 percent of the original amount to the surviving spouse. Your spouse has to agree in writing to any other payment schedule or to a lump sum.

Evaluating Pension Buyout Offers

It's not unusual for corporations to offer a lump sum to employees or retirees in exchange for the employees' relinquishing their pension rights. The number of such offers increased into 2015. Pension buyout offers increased to the point that the IRS issued rules in 2015 that basically prohibit plans from making buyout offers to those already retired and receiving benefits. Offers still can be made to active employees and those who aren't yet receiving their benefits. The offers will continue as long as some plan sponsors believe the offers will benefit the firm financially.

Pension buyout offers generally ask former employees or those nearing retirement if they want to give up the right to receive that monthly check for life in return for one payment that is many times the monthly check.

The law tells pension plans how to compute the lump sums that can be offered. The formula was changed in a 2008 law that phased in the new formula over several years. The new formula in many cases allowed employers to offer lower lump sums than previously were required. Many employers also want to remove the pension obligations from their books. Plus, the quasi-government agency that insures pension benefits raised the premiums it charges employers, making it more expensive to maintain a defined benefit pension plan.

This section discusses the factors to consider when evaluating a pension buyout offer.

Other Benefits

Your pension might have rights and benefits in addition to the monthly annuity. If you're still working, there might be disability benefits or an early retirement subsidy. The pension also might have spousal or survivor benefits. The loss of these benefits often isn't disclosed in the buyout offers, and the lump sum doesn't include money to replace them. It replaces only a single life annuity.

You also should find out if the pension is insured by the Pension Benefit Guaranty Corporation and, if so, the maximum amount of the guarantee. The PBGC guarantees pensions will be paid if the pension fund becomes insolvent, up to a maximum monthly amount that changes each year. If you receive a lump sum, it won't carry a guarantee.

Review any benefit publications or websites available to you, and contact the employee benefits office to see if you are eligible for these and other benefits.

Determining the Value

The lump sum often looks like a good deal compared to the smaller monthly annuity payment. But you need to compare apples to apples by taking a hard look at comparable numbers.

By accepting the lump sum you'd relinquish a guaranteed lifetime income. So, as with the decision of whether to accept an annuity or lump sum at retirement, determine how much it would cost you to replace that guaranteed lifetime income. Most private-sector pensions aren't indexed for inflation. You receive a fixed monthly amount for life. That makes the analysis easy.

Determine the lump sum you would need to buy the same guaranteed lifetime income from a private insurer. We discussed this process earlier in this chapter when discussing whether to take a lump sum or a monthly annuity at retirement and also in Chapter 3 when discussing how to shop for an immediate annuity. The process is the same here. The odds are that to receive the same guaranteed income as your pension, you'll have to pay the insurers more than the lump sum offered.

When you're not already retired or very close to retirement, the inquiry has two parts. Let's say you are 55 and the pension wouldn't begin paying until 65. First, you have to ask the insurers to estimate the lump sum you would need at age 65 to buy an annuity with a monthly payout equivalent to the pension. Second, estimate the rate of return you'd need to earn from investing the lump sum from now to age 65 for it to compound to the amount needed. Another approach is to shop for a longevity annuity. Ask the insurers how much you need to give them today for a monthly payment at age 65 equivalent to what the pension plan would pay.

Another way to evaluate the offer is to calculate how long the lump sum would last. Estimate how much you'd want to withdraw each month for spending. Then, estimate how long the lump sum would last at different investment rates of return at that spending rate. Another approach is to assume you'll spend each month whatever the monthly annuity was going to be. Then, estimate how long the lump sum would last at that spending rate at different investment rates of return.

Conservative investors likely will find that their investment returns won't be enough to allow the account to last for their life expectancies at a spending rate similar to the monthly pension. More aggressive investors might be able to sustain the payouts and even have something left for their heirs, but that assumes the markets cooperate and their actual results match historic returns. Bad markets or investment decisions would leave them worse off than conservative investors.

Taxes

When you receive the monthly pension payments, they likely will be fully taxable as ordinary income. You'll have the after-tax amount to spend. A lump sum can be rolled over into an IRA without incurring immediate taxes. But you'll owe taxes as the money is distributed from the IRA. Or you might convert the IRA to a Roth IRA after the rollover and pay the taxes at that time. In that case, there wouldn't be any taxes on future income and gains earned by the Roth IRA. If you take the lump sum directly instead of having it rollover to an IRA, you'll have to include the entire amount in ordinary income in the year it is received. Those are the most likely tax scenarios. If you have some after-tax contributions in the pension, the results might be a little different for you, because the after-tax contributions won't be taxable when you take them out.

The point is that you need to understand the income taxes that will be owed on whichever option you select. When doing your analysis, be sure you are comparing the after-tax amounts.

Another tax factor is required minimum distributions (RMDs). If you take the lump sum and roll it over to a traditional IRA, after age $70^1/_2$ you'll have to take the RMDs. This could deplete the account faster than you planned and increase your tax burden. You can read more about RMDs in Chapter 8.

Evaluating the Risk Trade-offs

There's a trade-off of risks and costs in the decision. It is the same as we discussed earlier regarding the decision to choose a lump sum or annuity when retiring and in Chapter 3 when discussing whether to use part of your retirement assets to buy an annuity.

With the pension annuity, the pension plan takes the risks of low investment returns or your living a long life. When you keep those risks with the pension plan, you give up control of the money and the potential to earn higher returns with it. By taking the buyout offer, you would be giving up the lifetime guarantee and taking the investment risk yourself.

The buyout offer assumes you'll live to average life expectancy. The lump sum might be more attractive if there are reasons to believe you will be among those with below-average life expectancy. But if you live beyond life expectancy, you'll need higher-than-average investment returns or lower spending for the lump sum to last.

Evaluating a pension buyout offer requires you to consider a range of issues and take several different steps. The most important issue to keep in mind is that accepting the offer means shifting the risks of a longer life and lower investment returns from the pension plan to you. You'd be taking responsibility for achieving adequate investment returns and managing the spending and also taking the risk you might live a very long life.

401(k) Issues and Strategies

There is a lot more to 401(k) and similar accounts than most people realize. There are strategies that could increase your retirement nest egg. There also are mistakes you need to avoid that could reduce the amount available to fund your retirement. We'll look at the key issues and strategies in the rest of this chapter.

Exiting 401(k)s: Facts and Scandals

When you leave an employer, you have a decision to make with your 401(k). It doesn't matter if you are leaving involuntarily, to take another job, or to retire. The choice is the same. Basically, you can choose to leave your 401(k) account with the plan or you can roll it over to an IRA or to a new employer's plan (if the new plan will accept rollovers). You also can take a distribution of the account in cash, but that's usually not a wise choice, since you'd have to include the entire amount in gross income and pay income taxes on it.

The IRA and 401(k) industries were upended in 2013 by a report from the Government Accountability Office. Investigators concluded that the process often is a mess when individuals are leaving an employer and need to decide how to handle their 401(k) accounts.

The 401(k) rollover process is inefficient, and financial services firms that administer 401(k) plans use their positions to heavily market their own IRAs as the preferred option for departing employees, according to the report. The GAO found that consumers leaving an employer sometimes were given misleading or false information about their choices and the fees involved.

One problem is that the process of rolling over an account from the 401(k) plan of the old employer to a new employer's can be difficult. It often requires submitting a lot of paperwork to both plans and long delays. Each employer wants to be sure that no mistakes are being made and that your money isn't going to the wrong account or being siphoned away in an identity theft scheme. So, they double- and triple-check everything. All that takes time.

Another problem is employers don't want to be in the business of giving financial advice to their employees, especially those who are leaving. They leave the advice and information-giving to the plan administrators, who usually are financial services firms eager to have the 401(k) accounts rolled over into IRAs they administer. The report found that 95 percent of money contributed to IRAs in 2008 came from rollovers.

You need to make a decision about what to do with your account when leaving an employer. Do you roll it over or leave it in the 401(k)? The right answer varies from person to person. Your 401(k) and IRAs are among your most valuable assets and your main retirement planning vehicles, if you're like most people. You need to consider carefully this decision and be sure you are receiving complete and unbiased information.

Below I give a framework for making decisions for handling 401(k) accounts when leaving an employer that will enhance your financial security.

A 401(k) Rollover Framework.   Many people automatically roll over their 401(k) accounts in a lump sum when leaving an employer, and the financial services industry certainly encourages that action. It is a good move in many cases, but that might not be the best move for you. Consider all the factors before deciding.

You generally have these options: leave your money in the 401(k) plan (though some employers discourage this), transfer it to the 401(k) plan of a new employer if it allows this, take the distribution in cash, or roll over the account to an IRA.

First, consider any advantages of keeping the money in the current 401(k) plan.

The 401(k) plans maintained by many small and medium-size employers and even some large employers aren't good. They have limited investment options that often aren't among the best funds or asset classes available. The costs can be high. There also might be limits on how often changes can be made in the investments and when money can be taken from the plan.

Some plans, however, especially those at larger employers, can be very good. The employers negotiate low costs and good investment options.

For example, you might be able to invest in institutional class funds that have lower expenses than the retail mutual funds available through IRAs and many 401(k) plans. Large employers also pick up some or all of the account expenses instead of passing them through to employees.

An employer that takes its 401(k) seriously also seeks out the better funds in each asset category, offers a wider range of asset categories instead of just the basic five or so, and works with outside firms to design target date plans or similar asset allocation funds that are better than the off-the-shelf products at most fund families. You'll have more investment choices in an IRA, but a well-run 401(k) narrows your choices down to the better ones you'd find yourself and negotiates lower fees.

A 401(k) plan also is likely to have a stable value fund option, which can be a good place to hide while earning a decent yield when you want to be out of the markets or are mapping out your future. The downside to stable value funds is that they aren't good long-term investments, and there can be a high level of fees embedded in them that result in lower interest being credited to your account than you might earn elsewhere. Stable value funds also usually restrict the number of times you can move your money and require advance notice of changes. If you're considering a stable value fund as a longer-term investment, a better idea might be to roll the account over to an IRA and consider annuities or similar products for the IRA.

A major downside to staying with even a good 401(k) plan is that you can't consolidate your assets in one account. Many people find it easier to manage their investments and reduce procrastination when all or most of their money is consolidated at one broker or mutual fund firm. Consolidation avoids spending a lot of time manually consolidating the accounts and determining what the asset allocation is. Consolidation also might earn you lower fees.

You also need to consider the long term. Some 401(k) plans offer good annuity options when it is time to take retirement distributions or are flexible about setting up distribution schedules or allowing periodic distributions. Others effectively discourage people from maintaining their accounts after retiring by not offering annuity options, limiting distribution options, and making changes cumbersome. Check to see what the plan offers retirees and also what it offers to a beneficiary who inherits the account. Some plans require fast payouts to beneficiaries.

When a 401(k) plan has major drawbacks, your best action is rolling over the 401(k) plan to an IRA or a new employer's plan. If you are joining a new employer that will accept rollovers, consider the same factors in the new plan. You're required to put new deferrals into the new employer's 401(k) plan, but you don't have to roll over your old account to it. Decide whether the better choice is to leave the money in the old plan or roll it over to the new plan.

When the new employer's plan is deficient or you're not going to a new employer, shop around for an IRA. Don't assume the IRA offered by the current 401(k) administrator or custodian is best. Consider investment options, fees, and the different ways you can access the account. Take a look at the list of all fees charged for services. Some IRA custodians offer "no-fee" IRAs, because they don't have an annual custodial fee. Then, they charge a fee every time you want to take money out or make any other transaction.

Doing a Rollover Right.   Once you decide to roll over an employer plan to an IRA or new employer plan, your work isn't finished. There are different ways to do the rollover, and you need to be sure it's done right.

One way to roll over an account is to have the plan issue a check to you. After the check is issued, you have 60 days to deposit the amount in a qualified IRA or employer retirement plan. Fail to make the deposit within 60 days and the distribution is included in your gross income. You'll owe income taxes, and if you're under age $59\frac{1}{2}$ a 10 percent early distribution penalty in addition.

A lot can go wrong in those 60 days. You could be in an accident, get sick, or lose track of things. Also, you could do everything right only to have the new custodian put the money in the wrong account. All these things and more have happened to people. The IRS allows you to ask for a waiver of the 60-day requirement if you think you have a good excuse. But it's expensive to have a proper waiver filed, and the IRS doesn't waive the requirement very often.

Generally, you'll receive a waiver only if the firm receiving the rollover made a mistake, you were free of fault, and you did everything you could to correct the mistake immediately after you learned or should have learned about it. Other than that, a waiver isn't a sure thing. The IRS has even denied waivers when someone died within the 60-day period.

Another reason not to take the check is that the plan has to withhold 20 percent for income taxes. You have to come up with that 20 percent from other sources and deposit it to the new account to make the rollover completely tax free. You'll get a refund of the withholding after filing your income tax return for the year, but you have to find the cash at the time of the rollover to ensure the entire rollover is tax deferred.

My advice: Don't take a check from a retirement plan. You want a trustee-to-trustee transfer. Have the administrator of the plan you're leaving transfer the money directly to the new IRA or employer plan. You'll first have to open the new IRA or other account. With an IRA, you complete a form requesting the IRA custodian to have the funds transferred from the old account. The IRA custodian will contact your 401(k) plan administrator and be sure the account is transferred. There's no 60-day rule with a trustee-to-trustee transfer.

In either case, follow up. Once the account is transferred, be sure it is deposited in an IRA or your new employer's retirement plan. Sometimes firms make a mistake such as depositing transfers into taxable accounts instead of IRAs. You don't want the hassle of correcting this many months after the fact.

A Traditional 401(k) or Roth 401(k)?

Many people know about Roth IRAs, but not many know that Roth 401(k)s have been permitted by the tax law for several years. Employers have been slow to add Roth 401(k) plans, but many larger employers are making them available, and the number of employers offering them is increasing. When an employer offers a Roth 401(k), an employee generally is given a choice between a traditional 401(k) and a Roth 401(k). You also might be able to split contributions between the two. (This doesn't increase your annual contribution limit. You divide the same annual limit between the two accounts.) You also might be permitted to convert a traditional 401(k) to a Roth 401(k), just as is allowed with IRAs.

Like its IRA counterpart, the Roth 401(k) doesn't provide upfront tax benefits. You defer part of your salary into the Roth 401(k), but it still is included in your gross income for tax purposes. The income and gains of the account compound free of income taxes. When you take distributions from the Roth 401(k), they are tax free.

Which type of account is best for you?

The analysis and factors are the same as for an IRA. Generally, the longer the money will compound in the 401(k), the more likely it is that the Roth account will be the better choice. If your tax rate will be the same or higher during retirement as during the working years, the Roth account is likely to be the better choice. See Chapter 8 for more details of the factors to consider and how to make the decision between a traditional and a Roth account.

A general conclusion many make from the factors often is that a Roth 401(k) is the better choice for a younger person. But don't be swayed by a rule of thumb. Middle-aged and older people shouldn't foreclose the idea of electing or switching to a Roth 401(k). The benefits of a Roth 401(k) are so powerful that even older employees should consider the Roth option, according to a study done in 2015 by Stuart Ritter of mutual fund firm T. Rowe Price. This conclusion applies to both annual contributions to accounts and conversions of traditional accounts to Roth versions.

Let's look at a 50-year-old worker who can choose to contribute to either a Roth or traditional 401(k) plan. He contributes $5,000 annually until age 65, and then begins annual withdrawals. He earns a 7 percent annual return and is in the 28 percent tax bracket the whole time. At first glance, it appears he'd have the same account balance in each scenario, which would be \$38,061 after 30 years, according to Ritter's assumptions and calculations.

The Roth balance, however, is tax free. The worker or his heirs will benefit from that full amount. The traditional account, however, will be taxed at the 28 percent rate, leaving the worker or his heirs with only \$27,404 to spend. Also, higher distributions have to be taken from the traditional account to have the same after-tax spending money as the Roth version.

The worker could select a traditional 401(k) and invest the income tax savings from his contributions in a brokerage account. But that wouldn't be enough to match the after-tax value of the Roth 401(k). That's because the brokerage account earnings would be taxed, so it wouldn't compound at 7 percent annually after taxes.

What if the worker is in a lower tax bracket after retirement? Keep in mind that's less likely these days with only a few tax brackets. But Ritter's numbers show that the Roth 401(k) still is a better deal if the worker's income tax rate drops by as much as 10 percentage points in retirement.

What about an older worker? Ritter's work shows that the Roth 401(k) is the better deal for workers into their early 60s.

Of course, these are hypothetical scenarios. They might not apply to you. The Roth option could be even better for you, or it could be a bad deal, depending on the particulars of your situation and what you assume about retirement tax rates, investment returns, and other factors. The important point is that you shouldn't let rules of thumb and other people's experiences or views determine your strategy. Do a thorough analysis, or have a financial planner do it for you, and take a look at the data.

A Roth account has important advantages over a traditional account that could increase their advantage to you, despite your age, which we discussed elsewhere in this book. I'll summarize the key benefits here.

With the Roth account, you aren't required to take RMDs after age 70½. You can let the account compound longer than a traditional retirement account, increasing its benefits, if you have other sources of income to pay for your expenses.

A Roth account also helps you essentially decide the tax bracket you want to be in during retirement. You'll have other sources of income you can't control, such as Social Security, annuities, distributions from mutual funds or stocks, and required distributions from traditional accounts. When those don't meet your spending needs, you can sell some investments at a long-term capital gains rate of 20 percent and you can tap the Roth account tax free, maintaining your standard of living while controlling your tax bill and rate.

Also, distributions from Roth accounts don't help trigger higher Medicare premiums, taxes on Social Security benefits, and other stealth taxes.

Another advantage of having some money in a Roth account is the flexibility. If you have a large one-time spending need (new car, child's wedding, major home repair), you can take the money from the Roth IRA without pushing yourself into a higher tax bracket or triggering the stealth taxes.

The Advantages of After-Tax 401(k) Contributions

Suppose your 401(k) plans doesn't offer a Roth option. Or suppose you're deferring the maximum amount the tax law allows to the 401(k) plan but want to save more.

You can make after-tax contributions to a traditional 401(k) plan. You're aware that pre-tax contributions can be made to a 401(k) up to $18,000 in 2016 (and an additional $6,000 if you're age 50 or older). Most people aren't aware they can make additional deferrals or contributions. The limit on total 401(k) contributions is $53,000 in 2016, or $59,000 for those making catch-up contributions at age 50 or older. That means if you're 50 or older and maximize pretax contributions at $24,000, you can make up to an additional $35,000 of after-tax contributions. The tax law allows these after-tax contributions, and you can make them if your plan also allows them.

Only the first $24,000 of contributions has upfront tax benefits. The additional contributions up to $35,000 will be included in your gross income and subject to taxes. But once in the 401(k), the income and gains on the contributions compound tax deferred. When you take the contributions out of the 401(k), the after-tax contributions aren't taxed. Only the income and gains on the after-tax contributions are taxed.

Plus, the IRS issued regulations in 2014 that provide an added benefit to making after-tax 401(k) contributions.

For years it wasn't clear how to roll over after-tax 401(k) contributions to a Roth IRA. Under the latest regulations, when you're ready to roll over the 401(k) to an IRA, you can separate the after-tax contributions and roll them directly to a Roth IRA. You can do this even if the after-tax contributions weren't in a separate 401(k) account. At the same time, you move the pretax contributions and all the accumulated income and gains to a traditional IRA.

It can be even better if your 401(k) plan allows in-service withdrawals. These are distributions that the tax code allows after age $59\frac{1}{2}$. Even if you continue to work for the employer, you can roll over the account tax free to an IRA. If you have both pretax and after-tax contributions, you can roll the after-tax contributions to a Roth IRA and the pretax contributions and accumulated returns to a traditional IRA. You then have the 401(k) money in IRAs, giving you complete flexibility in managing them. Yet, you can continue to contribute to the 401(k), making both pretax and after-tax contributions if you want.

Some employers restrict how often in-service withdrawals can be taken, but others allow them as often as you want once you are qualified. In these cases, you can make simple online orders to move your after-tax 401(k) money to a Roth IRA on a regular basis, if you want. To keep things simple, if you're going to make frequent in-service withdrawals have the 401(k) invested only in a money market fund so there won't be much income and gains in the 401(k) to complicate things.

Handling Employer Stock in 401(k)s

Many workers own shares of employer stock or other securities through 401(k) or other retirement plans. Few of these workers know the tax break available to substantially reduce the tax burden from selling those shares. By following a few steps, workers can reduce substantially the taxes from selling the employer stock. The tax break has been available for years.

The tax break is known as *net unrealized appreciation,* or NUA. It works like this.

If you sell the employer stock while it is in your 401(k) or other retirement account, you do not get a tax break. The proceeds from that sale eventually will be distributed to you (from either the 401(k) or an IRA rollover) and taxed as ordinary income.

When you retire or otherwise leave the employer and the account still owns the employer stock, however, you have a choice. You can treat the stock the same as other assets, keeping it in the 401(k) or rolling it to an IRA. As distributions of the stock or its sale proceeds are made, they are taxed as ordinary income.

The other option is to follow the NUA procedure. You distribute the stock to a taxable brokerage account and include in gross income in the year of the distribution only the original value or cost basis of the shares. No other taxes are due at that time, no matter how much the shares appreciated since you acquired them.

As you sell the employer shares, long-term capital gains taxes are due on the appreciation that occurred since you acquired the shares. Long-term gain treatment is allowed regardless of how long the shares have been owned either inside or outside of the 401(k).

To receive the NUA treatment, you have to take a lump-sum distribution from the 401(k) plan. This means that all of the assets must be withdrawn from the account in the same calendar year. The rule is firm. The full account must be distributed within the same year. As part of the distribution, have the employer stock deposited in a taxable brokerage account in your name. The rest of the account can be rolled over to an IRA or treated however else you want. The NUA doesn't change the tax treatment of or options for other assets.

The treatment of the employer stock under this procedure is the same whether you purchased the shares through your 401(k) plan or received them as a matching contribution from the employer.

The NUA tax break is available even if the company's stock is not publicly traded. Many private companies regularly determine a value for their stock. These values can be used to determine your basis in the stock. When the stock is distributed to you, the employer should tell you its basis.

The NUA treatment also is available to heirs who inherit a 401(k) account and take a lump sum distribution after the employee's death. It also is available to divorced spouses if they received part of the retirement account under a qualified domestic relations order.

You don't have to use the NUA treatment for all the stock in the plan. For example, shares that have appreciated a lot can be distributed to the brokerage account and taxes paid today on only the basis. Shares that have not appreciated much can be rolled over to an IRA with other account assets; taxes on those shares are deferred until the shares or proceeds from their sale are distributed.

If a person holds the shares until death in a taxable account, the heirs do not increase the tax basis of the shares. The heirs will owe capital gains on the appreciation when they sell the shares, just as the employee would have.

The 10 percent early distribution penalty applies to distributions of employer shares taken as part of an NUA distribution. But if the employee is at least age 55 and takes the distribution after separating from the employer, the 10 percent penalty usually does not apply.

To qualify for the tax break, you also cannot take any withdrawals from the retirement plan before taking a distribution of the stock, even required minimum distributions after age 70$\frac{1}{2}$.

Keep in mind, there might be nontax reasons for selling the stock. If you have doubts about the long-term future for the stock or believe too much of your net worth is in the stock, you might want to sell some or all of it though that means giving up the NUA tax break.

For many people, the traditional strategy still is best. After the top tax rate was increased in 2012, for some other taxpayers at a minimum the strategy isn't as beneficial as before. The top ordinary income tax rate was increased to 39.6 percent from 35 percent. But the top long-term capital gains rate also is increased to 20 percent from 15 percent. In addition, for some people there is the additional 3.8 percent tax on net investment income, which includes sales of employer stock. So, the maximum tax on selling the shares from a brokerage account increased to 23.8 percent from 15 percent.

As I said, for most people NUA treatment still is the best deal. For others, there's less of an advantage of jumping through the hoops for NUA treatment. Still other people will find NUA treatment beneficial but will have to carefully plan future sales of the stock to avoid triggering the 3.8 percent net investment income tax or pushing themselves into the top long-term capital gains tax bracket.

Using a 401(k)'s Brokerage Investment Window

As discussed earlier, the sad fact is that many 401(k) plans aren't very good. They tend to be designed by human resources personnel or business owners, not by investment professionals. They also try to be safe and conventional. The plan might be designed based on what's best for the employer, and that usually means using a single provider for recordkeeping, employee education, and investment options. Or it might be designed primarily for the benefit of the plan administrator.

In short, your choice of investments is limited. You might be limited to investments that aren't particularly good or that charge too much in expenses.

Many 401(k) plans, however, do offer a good alternative. It's known is the business as the brokerage window. Your plan, if it has one, probably uses a different name such as self-directed brokerage account and might even hide the option. But it's a good option for the serious investor with a lot of money in a 401(k) account.

The brokerage window allows plan members to bypass the plan's fund options, open an account through their 401(k) plan at a broker selected by the employer, and invest in most investments that are available in the markets. It's a brokerage account within your 401(k) plan.

Employers generally limit the choices available through the brokerage window, but not nearly as severely as the plan's standard offerings. Most plans allow members in the brokerage window to invest in almost any mutual funds, ETFs, stocks, and bonds available through the broker. Some plans even allow members to invest in options or sell short stocks. The windows usually allow online investing and trading at any time during which other customers of the broker can trade.

Using a brokerage window is not free. There usually is an annual fee of $100 or less. There also are likely to be trading fees on each transaction you make in the portfolio, though there might not be a fee for using no-transaction-fee mutual funds. The funds available through the window also aren't likely to be the institutional share classes available through in-plan funds, so you're likely to pay higher annual expenses in the funds.

Investing your regular contributions also is an issue. Will the plan administrator or broker automatically allocate them in a way you preselect? Or do you have to manually make the investments each month? Are there fees each time you invest the monthly contributions?

Read the 401(k) plan's materials to be sure you know all the fees and restrictions.

Some employers don't want to offer a brokerage window, or they offer one with tight restrictions. They're concerned about legal liability. They don't want employees who make bad investments suing them for making the poor decisions possible. Others are concerned about the government. The Department of Labor in 2012 floated the idea of making employers responsible for any investment selected by 1 percent or more of its plan participants. The proposal was withdrawn but could resurface.

The 401(k) plan brokerage window is not for everyone. If you want a traditional portfolio and your plan offers decent funds, stay within the standard plan. But if you want investments not in the plan offerings or believe the fund choices in the plan are poor, take a look at your plan's brokerage window. When your plan doesn't have a brokerage window, tell the employer you're interested in one.

The Grandkids Need Your Help More than Ever

O ne of the prime financial goals of many older Americans is to help their grandchildren. They believe that the grandchildren's generation will have a more difficult time financially than either their parents or grandparents did. The adult children, meanwhile, either have established themselves or shown that they won't make good use of money that is given or left to them.

The grandchildren aren't expected to inherit much from their parents. The cost of college education and the price of the average home continue to climb to levels unimaginable a few decades ago. Many young people enter their twenties with tens of thousands of dollars of higher education debt. The grandchildren also face the prospect of bailing out the failing Social Security and Medicare systems while dealing with the likelihood that those programs won't be nearly as generous to them as they were to previous generations.

Financial services firms are aware of this interest in helping the grandchildren and offer programs to assist. Unfortunately, not all the programs carry strong benefits or are good in all situations. A strategy that benefits one family could be inappropriate for another. There are heavily promoted strategies aimed at grandparents that are more like gimmicks than smart financial planning. In addition, some strategies that were tried and true only a few years ago are no longer the best choices. It takes more knowledge and deliberation to choose the appropriate method for helping the grandchildren.

Consider the following developments in the quest to help grandparents provide for their grandchildren.

A Small Sum Builds a Large Legacy—The Installment Plan to Building a Legacy

It is remarkably inexpensive and easy to establish a meaningful legacy for a grandchild. Two of the most powerful tools in investing can leverage a small amount into a large sum. Those tools are time and compound returns. You can open a relatively small account today for a grandchild, and when the grandchild really needs the money, the compounded returns over time probably will have greatly increased in value.

Suppose an account is opened with $2,000, and $75 is added to it each month. If the account earns an average return of 8 percent annually, at the end of 20 years it will be worth almost $55,000—though the total contributions were only $20,000. Time and the compounded returns of the investment markets can more than double total wealth. A higher return would, of course, result in more money for the grandchild. That $55,000 should be enough for the down payment on a new home, to start a business, pay off college loans, or pay for other early-adulthood expenses. See Figure 11.1

FIGURE 11.1   How a Small Sum Builds a Legacy

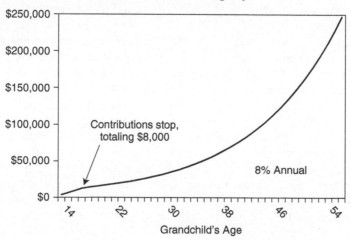

What if the $55,000 is left untouched until the grandchild retires? The grandchild might be disciplined enough not to spend the money, or the account could be created within a trust that limits access to it. If the money compounds at 8 percent annually for another 30 years, the grandchild will have over $500,000—all on the grandparent's $20,000 investment. That's quite a legacy to leave and quite a financial load to take off the grandchild.

Almost any grandparent can use time and compound returns to build a substantial legacy on the installment plan. There is little or no risk that the standard of living of the grandparent will be lowered. This plan also avoids gift taxes, because the annual contributions should qualify for the annual gift tax exemption ($14,000 per recipient in 2016). Estate taxes also can be avoided if the gifts are put in an account that is not in the grandparent's name or legal control. Annual income taxes also should be low. The money can be invested so that there are few taxable capital gains and dividends in most years. Income that is taxable can be taxed at the grandchild's rate.

Table 11.1 shows how the installment plan can work with monthly contributions of $50 and $75. It assumes that the initial investment is $10,000, and the account earns 8 percent annually after taxes. Subsequent monthly investments of $50 and $75 are shown.

A strong impediment to this plan in recent years is that many brokers and mutual funds raised their minimum investment requirements. A little over a decade ago, $100 could open an account in a quality no-load mutual fund. Now, the minimum investment at most financial service firms is $2,500 or more. The few firms that allow low initial investments generally impose higher fees and other expenses. Once the hurdle of the initial deposit is cleared, however, small additional investments can be added on a regular schedule or when money is available.

Brokers and mutual fund companies make it easy to set up these plans using their automatic investment programs (AIP). Under an AIP, once an account is set up, the broker or fund company automatically drafts a set amount from a checking account each month and invests it according to preset instructions (which can be changed). The minimum monthly investment usually is between $50 and $100, though some allow

TABLE 11.1   Monthly Deposit

Years	$50	$75
5	$18,522	$20,334
10	$31,294	$35,842
15	$50,321	$58,947
20	$78,669	$93,370

monthly investments as small as $25 and some require as much as $250. The regular investments can be stopped, usually with 30 days' notice.

Those are the basics of how to make a small investment become a significant legacy. There are, however, details to consider. Different vehicles can be used to establish this legacy, and the final financial results can vary considerably depending on which vehicle is used. Factors that must be considered are income taxes, estate and gift taxes, control over the account, flexibility, and the effect on financial aid for higher education.

We'll look at how all these factors come together. First, we'll examine the best ways to help fund education expenses for a grandchild. Then, we'll look at establishing a legacy that will cover more.

Guide to Helping with a Grandchild's Education

Many grandparents want to help pay for all or some of a grandchild's higher education. So let's look at and compare the different ways available to help fund higher education. A number of these tools also are available to provide wealth in general to a grandchild, so this is a good review even for those who don't want to limit their legacy to higher education. All these strategies, by the way, can be used by parents to help their own children.

The strategies available to help fund college costs—or to provide a legacy in general—have different advantages and disadvantages, which not everyone realizes when choosing a method. Every grandparent needs to carefully consider all the possible effects and choose carefully.

Direct Gifts

The easiest way to help a grandchild is to make a gift of cash or of an investment. The gift later can be used to pay for higher education expenses. Until the expenses are incurred, the gift should be invested to appreciate or compound income.

The benefits of the direct gift are that the money or property is out of the donor's estate, and any income and capital gains earned by the gift are not included on the donor's income tax return and are likely to be taxed at the grandchild's much lower rate. There are no restrictions on the money or how it can be invested or withdrawn.

The disadvantages are that the grandchild has direct control of and unfettered access to the money. It can be invested in whatever strikes the grandchild's fancy. The grandchild may even decide to convert the account to cash and withdraw it.

If the grandchild still is a minor, an account cannot be established solely in the grandchild's name. The assistance of a parent or other adult is required. The easiest approach is for the parent and child to set up a joint account. That arrangement gives either the parent or child the ability to withdraw the money or change how the account is invested. An alternative is to set up a custodial account, such as a UGMA, which is discussed next.

Because of the lack of controls with the direct gift and joint account, they rarely are used to help a grandchild pay for higher education expenses.

The Classic UGMAs

For decades the only vehicle to help fund a minor grandchild's (or child's) education was the Uniform Gift to Minors Act (or Uniform Transfer to Minors Act) accounts, known as UGMA (pronounced ug-ma) or UTMA (pronounced ut-ma). (The name depends on the state in which it is set up.)

These accounts have many advantages. An adult serves as custodian of the account until the child reaches the age of majority. The account is in the minor's name, but the adult controls the investments and withdrawals. Also, a deposit into the account automatically qualifies as present interest under the gift tax law. That means the transfer qualifies for the annual gift tax exclusion, so the transfer is free of gift taxes until all the donor's gifts for the year to that minor exceed the annual limit ($14,000 in 2016). Normally, a gift is not a present interest qualifying for the annual gift tax exclusion unless the recipient has full legal title and control of the property. The tax law carves out a special exception for UGMAs.

Income and capital gains from the account are taxed to the grandchild. That can result in significant income tax savings to the family, because the grandchild is likely to be in a 0 percent or 10 percent income tax bracket, allowing the family to accumulate more after-tax wealth for education.

The disadvantages of UGMAs are less well-known. One disadvantage occurs when the grandchild is ready to attend college and applies for financial aid. Under the formula used to determine financial need at most colleges, a student is expected to spend on college expenses up to 35 percent of assets held in his or her name. The parents are expected to contribute only up to 5.64 percent of their assets each year. (These percentages can vary over time, and different schools can use different percentages.) Grandparents aren't expected to contribute anything.

A UGMA is considered an asset of the grandchild for whom it was established. That means if $20,000 is in the student's name, up to $7,000 must be spent on college during the first year before the student can qualify for financial aid. If the money is in the parents' names, only about $1,000 counts against aid. If the property is in the grandparents' names, none of it is considered during the financial aid qualification process.

If financial aid is a possibility, grandparents and parents should carefully consider whether they want to put assets in the future student's name. Doing so could reduce the amount of financial aid available and require the family to spend more on college expenses than they otherwise would have.

Another disadvantage is that once money or property is placed in a UGMA, the donor cannot get it back. It is important that the donor not contribute money that might at some point be needed to meet emergencies or living expenses. In addition, the UGMA cannot be used to pay expenses that are the legal support obligation of the parents. If the family runs into hard times, the money cannot be used for these legal support items, such as food, clothing, shelter, and medical care.

Also, the youngster gets full legal title to the account immediately upon reaching the age of majority. This is 18 in most states, and 21 in others. There is nothing the parents or grandparents legally can do to keep the youngster from spending the money however he or she wants. Instead of paying for college, the money could be used to purchase a new car, take expensive trips, or on even more alluring items. Because of this feature, many grandparents look for strategies that provide more restrictions on the grandchild's access to and use of the money.

Creating a Trust

The advantages of a UGMA can be obtained without incurring most of the disadvantages by creating an irrevocable trust. A trustee will control and invest the money. Cash will be distributed or used to pay expenses as directed in the trust agreement. Either the trust or the grandchild will be taxed on the income and capital gains, not the parents or grandparents.

Gifts to the trust are present interests and qualify for the annual gift tax exclusion if the trust has a *Crummey* clause. This clause allows the grand-child to take from the trust any new contribution within a certain time after the contribution was received by the trust. Usually 30 days is the time set. If the money is not taken out within that time, it stays in the trust under the terms of the trust agreement. If the child does demand distribution of the money, the grandparent isn't likely to make future contributions.

The trust agreement, which is written by the grandparent, determines when the money is distributed. There are many options available.

Here's one example. The trust agreement might say that money may be spent only for certain purposes—such as education or emergencies—until the child reaches age 21. After 21, the annual income or a percentage of the trust's value is distributed. At age 25, one-third of the principal is distributed. Additional principal is distributed at ages 30 and 35, after which the trust terminates. Those terms are classics for trusts set up to aid youngsters.

Some trusts provide that money is distributed to pay only for educa-tion. Other trusts make distributions as the grandchild achieves certain milestones, such as earning a college degree, holding a job, or reaching a certain age. Trust law is very broad. The standards for distributing and withholding money generally are limited only by your imagination.

Another option is to give the trustee complete discretion over how income and principal will be distributed. The creator of the trust can give the trustee a letter stating the principles to be used, but the trustee is charged with the ultimate decision. That allows the trust to adapt to changing, unplanned circumstances.

An irrevocable trust should contain a clause providing that no distributions will be made when the trustee determines that withholding the money would be in the best interests of the grandchild. This clause protects the money in case the grandchild drifts into substance abuse, gambling, high-risk business ventures, or similar activities. The trustee can resume distributions after determining that doing so again would be in the grandchild's best interest. The trust also should have a clause that allows the trustee to distribute money under special circumstances, such as becoming disabled, needing special medical attention, or wanting extended education.

There are some disadvantages to an irrevocable trust. It costs money to create and maintain the trust. A lawyer must prepare the trust agreement. The trust also has to file separate tax returns and keep separate records. The tax returns can get complicated. In addition, a trustee is needed to manage the trust. To get the maximum tax benefits, an independent trustee is needed. A professional trustee, such as a bank, will do the administrative work, tax returns, and money management for a fee. The administrative and tax work can be split from the investment and distribution management. Whatever the arrangement, creating the trust and having a trustee manage and maintain it will cost money. That's why an irrevocable trust is not a viable option unless a lot of money is involved. Attorney and trustee fees vary around the country, so the advisable minimum size for a trust varies by region.

Another potential disadvantage of a trust is that it reaches the top tax bracket much faster than individuals do. The tax brackets are indexed each year, but a trust paid the top tax rate in 2016 when its taxable income exceeded $12,400. The trustee might be able to manage the investments to avoid the top tax bracket. Otherwise, the family might not get any income tax benefits from setting money aside in a trust for the grandchild.

The trust also might affect the amount of financial aid available. The exact effect will depend on the terms of the trust and whether or not a school chooses to treat the trust as an asset of the grandchild.

Section 529 Savings Plans

A relatively new tool to help fund education expenses is the Section 529 college savings plan. These plans were created by a 1997 amendment to Section 529 of the tax code and have become extremely popular.

The 529 savings plan carries a number of benefits to both the adult who funds it and the future student who is the beneficiary of the account. The plans double as both an education funding tool and an estate planning strategy.

In a 529 plan, a state sets up a college savings trust. An adult opens an account and contributes to it, naming a child or grandchild (or anyone for that matter) as beneficiary. The state invests the money, and the gains earned by the account compound tax-deferred. There are no taxes until money is withdrawn from the account. If distributions are made for qualified education expenses, all compounded income and gains are tax free. If distributions are used for nonqualified purposes, the income and gains are taxed at the beneficiary's tax rate.

Contributions to the trust are considered gifts of present interests, qualifying them for the annual gift tax exclusion. In addition, tax-free gifts can be front-loaded. Up to five years' worth of gift-tax-free contributions can be put into the account in one year and still qualify for the gift tax annual exclusion. When the annual exclusion is $14,000 as in 2016, up to $42,000 per beneficiary can be put into a 529 plan in one year free of gift taxes. A married couple can each put that amount into each account gift tax free in one year.

Front-loading gifts means that the tax-free exclusion for gifts to that beneficiary are exhausted for the five years. In addition, if the donor dies before the five years have ended, a pro rata portion of the gifts will be included in the donor's estate. Otherwise, the money and all its future appreciation are not considered part of the donor's estate.

There are additional benefits to 529 savings plans:

- The donor is considered the account owner and can get the money back when needed under most states' plans. Some states impose an early withdrawal penalty of up to 10 percent of the account's value, some don't.
- The donor can change the beneficiary. If a grandchild decides not to go to college, a new beneficiary can be named.
- The account in one state can be used to pay for education expenses in any state if the state sets up the plan that way.
- Some states give a deduction against state income taxes to their residents who contribute to the 529 plans sponsored by the state.
- There is no preset limit on the earnings under most plans. The money is invested, and most state plans give the donor some ability to choose the investments. If the markets do well, so will the account. On the other hand, there are no guaranteed earnings. An account could lose money, and many have from time to time.
- Some states require that the account be spent by a particular time, usually when the original beneficiary reaches a certain age, such as 30.

Others let the account compound indefinitely, changing the beneficiary several times. This type of strategy can substitute as a trust for part of an estate plan.

■ The U.S. Department of Education stated that for financial aid purposes, the assets will be considered those of the owner. That means the student will not be considered the owner for financial aid calculations. If the grandparents set up the 529 account, the account will not count in financial aid considerations. Individual schools, however, can set their own policy on this issue, and some have taken a different position.

These provisions make the 529 plans more attractive in many ways than other investment-oriented plans such as UGMAs, trusts, and direct gifts of money or investment accounts. The donor gets gift and estate tax benefits, yet can get the money back if needed. The donor still has some control over the account and can change the beneficiary. The grandchild does not get legal title to the account after reaching the age of majority.

However, there are three potential disadvantages to 529 plans. One is that the state usually decides how the account will be invested or at least puts limits on the investment options. In most plans, well-known money management companies such as Fidelity, Vanguard, and TIAA-CREFF invest the money. The donor might have some ability to select the initial investment options and might be able to change them periodically. In a few states the state treasurer invests the accounts, and some states have only one investment plan.

To counter this disadvantage, many states offer additional versions of their 529 plans in conjunction with financial services firms. The account is opened through a firm, usually a broker or mutual fund that has established a relationship with the 529 plan. These accounts generally offer more investment options than the state-managed version of the plan, and investments usually can be changed more frequently. These versions of the plans, however, charge higher fees than the state-managed version.

Another potential disadvantage is that Congress could change the rules. There hasn't been a strong movement in this direction, but it's always possible.

The third potential disadvantage is cost. Each state imposes fees and expenses on the accounts in its plan. The level of these costs varies. Some states set the fees at low levels that cover only their costs. Other states try to make a profit from the 529 plans. In addition, a state can have several plans with different levels of fees for each plan. Many states now have plans that can be sold through brokers and financial planners. These professionals get fees from the plans, and the fees under these versions are higher than for the plans purchased directly from the states.

Most states now offer at least one 529 plan. The terms, costs, and fees of the plans vary, though most have modest fees. Most states also now accept contributions from residents of any state and allow the accounts to finance higher education in any state. That enables you to shop around for the state plan that best suits your needs, investment preferences, and fee levels. The main disadvantage to using an out-of-state plan is the potential loss of a state income tax deduction. States that allow residents deductions for their 529 plan contributions generally allow the deductions only for contributions to their own plans. Also, a few states consider distributions to be tax free only if used to pay for education at a college in their state.

Because most states will open accounts for residents of any state, diversification of plans is possible. Rather than settling on one state plan, a grandparent can split contributions among plans from different states with attractive features. A grandparent might, for example, contribute enough to his own state's plan to get the maximum income tax deduction, and then contribute additional amounts to another state's plan with more attractive features.

The details of the available plans are collected online for comparison at www.collegesavings.org. It is important to review all the terms before settling on a plan. For example, not all plans allow the owner to take the contributions back. Some plans allow the return of contributions but only after a penalty is subtracted. Some plans will transfer an account to another state's plan if desired; others won't.

Prepaying College

Before the Section 529 college savings plan was created, section 529 of the tax code provided only for prepaid college savings plans. These plans still are available. They are not as well-known because financial services firms do not have an incentive to promote them. Yet, they do provide significant benefits to grandparents, parents, and grandchildren. In some ways they are more attractive than the savings plans, especially when investment markets aren't doing well.

Under a prepaid college savings plan, the person opening the account names a beneficiary and tells the state the beneficiary's age. The plan determines how much has to be paid in. The plans generally offer payment options ranging from a lump sum to fixed annual payments. When an account is fully funded, the state guarantees it will pay four years of tuition and mandatory fees at public colleges within the state.

There also is a private college version known as the Independent 529 plan. A list of participating institutions and other details are at www .independent529plan.org. Cash put into the plan earns tuition certificates that can be used to buy tuition at the participating schools. How much education each dollar buys depends on the school the child chooses to attend, because tuition and fees vary among the schools. A disadvantage of the plan arises if the child chooses to attend a public university or a private school that does not participate in the plan. In that case, the plan pays back the original investment plus a 2 percent annual return.

The major advantage of prepaid tuition plans is certainty. If the cost of college grows faster than the plan anticipated, the state or the plan makes up the difference. Likewise, if investment returns lag behind expectations, the state or the plan suffers the loss. On the other hand, if the actual results are better than the projections, the state or the plan benefits.

Certainty can be a major advantage, as many have learned through all the volatility of financial markets since 2000. The cost of higher education also is less certain as states reduced their funding for colleges in the wake of budget problems. Buying into a prepaid plan early locks in the current cost and inflation rate and lets the plan take the risk of higher inflation.

A potential disadvantage is that the guarantee covers only the cost at public colleges within the state sponsoring the plan. Private colleges and those in other states aren't guaranteed. If the grandchild does decide to go to an institution that isn't covered, the state will determine a value for the account and transfer that amount to another institution to be applied to costs there.

A prepaid plan also won't cover all the costs of college. Costs that aren't covered include room and board, textbooks, a computer, and expenses other than tuition and fees.

For financial aid purposes, the prepaid plan is considered the student's asset, and generally will reduce the aid available to the student dollar for dollar.

A prepaid tuition plan has less flexibility than a savings plan. Money generally cannot be withdrawn as it can with a savings plan, other than to transfer it to a college to pay expenses. There also might be limits on the ability to change the beneficiary.

Prepaid savings plans ran into problems during the bear market of 2000–2002. When determining how much a parent needs to pay into the prepaid plan, each state estimates the investment return it will earn on that money. The state also estimates the rate at which tuition and fees will increase. Both sets of estimates turned out to be far too optimistic. Of course, the bear market returns were far less than the estimates. The recession caused states to reduce tuition subsidies, so colleges and universities compensated by substantially increasing their fees.

A number of state plans projected deficits for a few years because of the poor returns. Many significantly raised the amounts that must be paid by new enrollees in the plan. A few states stopped accepting new enrollees until they could resolve the financial issues. It is possible that in some cases the plan might not have enough money to pay all the promised expenses at some point, and the state government will have to decide if it is obligated to fund the deficits.

Coverdell Savings Accounts

Coverdell savings accounts initially were called Education IRAs. The name was changed in the 2001 tax law to honor the late U.S. Senator from Georgia, Paul Coverdell. The 2001 tax law also dramatically increased the benefits of these accounts.

Up to $2,000 per child can be put into a Coverdell account each year. There is no deduction for contributions to the account, income and capital gains are tax deferred, and they are tax free when withdrawn, if used for qualified education expenses. The account must be spent by the time the beneficiary is 30.

Qualified education expenses include tuition, fees, books, supplies, and equipment that are required for enrollment or attendance. Room and board are included if the individual is at least a half-time student. The expenses can be incurred for undergraduate or graduate level courses and also can be used to purchase tuition tax credits under a qualified state tuition program. Since 2002, the accounts also can pay for elementary and secondary school expenses.

An account balance can be transferred or rolled over tax free from the account of one beneficiary to another beneficiary in the same family.

The $2,000 annual contribution limit is phased out when the contributor's adjusted gross income is between $190,000 and $220,000 on a joint return.

The nice thing about Coverdell accounts is that virtually any relative can open an account for the benefit of another relative. If a grandparent's income exceeds the limit, he can give money to a parent to contribute to an account for the grandchild.

A problem with the Coverdell accounts is opening one. Many financial services firms do not offer the accounts. They do not foresee there being enough interest to make the accounts profitable. It was hoped that increasing the contribution limit from $500 to $2,000 would help the situation, but that has not been the case so far. Coverdell accounts also have trouble competing with 529 savings plans and even with taxable accounts when all the features and benefits are compared.

U.S. Savings Bonds

Those saving for college education get a special benefit from U.S. Savings Bonds. Normally, interest on the bonds is tax deferred until the bonds are redeemed. Then the interest is taxable. If the interest is used to pay for college expenses, however, the interest is tax free. The tax-free status of the interest is phased out for bond owners whose adjusted gross income for the year exceeds $116,300 on joint returns and $77,550 for all other returns. The exclusion is completely phased out at modified adjusted gross income of $146,300 on joint returns and $92,550 or more for all other returns.

Savings bonds generally offer safe, solid interest rates. The returns won't be spectacular, and higher interest often can be earned on other types of bonds. The safety of the savings bonds, however, cannot be matched, and the tax-free interest feature can make them a good alternative for a conservative investor.

Just-in-Time Gifts

One widely used strategy avoids all the special vehicles. It uses the gift tax exclusion to avoid gift taxes and also to minimize income and capital gains taxes. Yet, the grandparents retain control of the assets as long as possible.

Under this strategy, the grandparents save and invest in their own names in a taxable account. When it comes time to pay for a year of college, the grandparents make a gift of the investments to the grandchild. The grandchild then sells the investments, pays taxes at his or her rate, and uses the after-tax amount to pay for college. The grandchild is likely to be in a lower capital gains tax bracket than the grandparents and might even be in the 0 percent tax bracket.

A disadvantage of this strategy is the property stays in the estates of the grandparents. That's only a problem if the grandparents might be subject to federal estate taxes. Also, while the grandparents own the investments any income and gains are on their income tax returns. The strategy does, however, avoid the problem of searching for a vehicle that helps the grandkids but doesn't give them too much control, reduce financial aid, or create other problems.

A key advantage of this strategy is that the grandparent retains control of the account. The account also can be set up at any mutual fund or broker the grandparent wants. In addition, the account can be invested in a tax-wise fashion so that the after-tax returns will be competitive with the tax-favored vehicles such as 529 savings plans.

By paying the expenses, the grandchildren also might qualify for tax breaks such as the Hope or Lifetime Learning tax credits for education expenses. Applying those credits to the grandchild's income could make the gains tax free.

An option that builds on this strategy is to have the children pay at least half their living expenses for the year. That makes them independent. They claim their own personal exemptions, the credits for college expenses, and deductions for any loan interest. They aren't likely to hit the income limits at which those tax breaks are phased out. Be sure to keep track of their annual living expenses and be able to show that the children paid at least half their expenses.

The grandchildren's living and college expenses could be paid with gifts received from the grandparents, and the grandchildren still would qualify for the tax breaks. The key is that the gifts must be unrestricted. The grandparents must take the risk that the money will be spent on something else.

Bringing it All Together

You can see that there are many ways grandparents can help pay for a grandchild's education. There is no one right vehicle. A number of factors must be balanced before making a decision. Here are some general rules to consider:

- When money will be invested in the markets to be used years from now, a section 529 savings plan can be the best choice. For a relatively low cost it provides tax advantages and estate planning benefits. The 529 plan also makes it unlikely that the grandchild will spend the money on something more alluring than college. It has minimal impact on eligibility for financial aid and has a great deal of flexibility.
- When the child can be trusted or the grandparent is willing to assume the risk, a good choice is to invest in a taxable account in the grandchild's name. Once the child turns 19, all income and gains are taxed at the grandchild's tax rate unless the grandchild is a full-time student under age 24. The grandparent can invest in his or her own name until sometime after the child turns 19, then give the account to the grandchild. There would have to be a joint account or a custodial account. This approach could severely reduce available financial aid, because the assets are in the student's name.
- If financial aid is a possibility, the grandparents might want to consider investing in their own names. Saving in either the grandchild's name or even in the parents' names could reduce financial aid. Investments could be given directly to the grandchild when college expenses are due. The grandchild could sell the investments, incurring taxes at his or her own rate. A disadvantage is that the grandparents would pay taxes on the investment income at their rates in other years. Another disadvantage is that the property would be included in their estates if they pass away before the money is spent.
- Investing in the grandparent's name keeps many options open. The education expenses can be paid as they are incurred by making gifts of appreciated investments to the grandchild. The taxes on gains are paid at the grandchild's tax rate. In addition, the grandchild might qualify for the Hope and Lifetime Learning tax credits. Saving in the grandparent's name also keeps the grandchild eligible for the maximum financial aid.
- A prepaid tuition plan provides the most certainty. The payment of tuition and fees is guaranteed in return for fixed payments from the parent or grandparent. Additional expenses, such as room and board, can be funded through the other strategies.

Helping Beyond College

Helping to pay for education expenses is not the only way to help grandchildren. Most grandkids can use help beyond education, and many won't even attend college. A grandchild could use assistance to buy the first home, start a business, or even prepare for retirement decades away. Some of the strategies that help save for college also could be used to establish a general legacy for grandchildren. Prepaid college savings plans aren't useful for saving beyond college, and neither are Coverdell Savings Accounts. UGMAs can provide wealth beyond college, though whether or not that happens is completely at the discretion of the grandchild. He or she gets full legal control at the age of majority. Good uses can be made of direct gifts, trusts, and even 529 savings plans. Most of the 529 savings plans don't require the money to be spent until the original beneficiary is age 30; some allow accumulations even longer.

Let's look at how some other ways to help establish a legacy for a grandchild.

Best Way to Help a Grandchild

Perhaps the best tool for providing financial help to a grandchild is a Roth IRA. They were created as retirement accounts, but it is tough to beat the Roth IRA for estate planning and transferring wealth.

The advantages of the Roth IRA are that income and capital gains earned by the account are not taxed. Also, neither the owner nor the subsequent beneficiary pays income taxes on distributions in most cases. These advantages mean investment earnings compound tax free, and then the accumulated amount can be withdrawn without incurring income taxes.

A Roth IRA's advantages are back-end loaded. There is no benefit for creating a Roth IRA, such as a deduction for contributions. There is no age limit on contributions to a Roth and no required minimum distributions (RMDs) for the original owner. With a regular IRA, contributions cannot be made after age $70 1/2$, and required distributions must begin after that age. A beneficiary inheriting a Roth must begin RMDs, but they can be made over the beneficiary's life expectancy. That means for a grandchild, the required annual distributions would be small, usually much smaller than the earnings and the appreciation of the Roth IRA. So the account's value can appreciate for many years until the beneficiary really needs the money.

Those are powerful advantages that cannot be found in any other vehicle. There are several ways the Roth IRA can be used to help loved ones.

Start a new Roth IRA for yourself. A new Roth IRA can be started with annual contributions of up to the annual limit. You might not be eligible to contribute to your own IRA, because the right is phased out as adjusted gross income increases. The limit is indexed for inflation and depends on your filing status.

The owner also must have earned income for the year at least equal to the amount contributed to the Roth IRA. Earned income is salary and wages, not investment income. A contribution also can be made to a Roth IRA for a nonworking spouse as long as the working spouse has earned income at least equal to the total contributions. The earned income requirement keeps a completely retired person from pursuing this strategy.

A grandparent can begin a Roth IRA, name the grandchild as beneficiary, and make regular contributions. After the grandparent passes away, the grandchild becomes the owner. The grandchild must begin taking minimum annual distributions from the Roth and can take additional amounts when desired. Instead of taking additional distributions, the grandchild can let the account continue to compound tax free. If the investment returns exceed the required annual distributions, by the time the grandchild is ready to retire the Roth IRA should provide a meaningful source of tax-free income.

Also, a grandparent who already has a traditional IRA can convert all or part of it into a Roth IRA, naming a grandchild as the beneficiary. This would generate all the Roth IRA benefits for both the grandparent and grandchild. There is a cost to converting a regular IRA to a Roth IRA: The amount converted must be treated as though it were distributed. That means the converted amount must be included in the grandparent's income and taxes paid on it. In Chapter 8 we discussed the circumstances in which it might make sense to convert a traditional IRA to a Roth IRA.

Grandparents also can help set up a grandchild's IRA. There is no minimum age for setting up a Roth IRA. All the taxpayer needs is earned income. It doesn't even have to be enough income to incur taxes. Suppose a grandchild earns a bit of money from babysitting, mowing lawns, or a part-time job. The grandchild naturally wants to spend most of that money. The grandparent can match the earnings with a cash gift that is used to set up a Roth IRA or can make the deposit directly to the IRA. The youngster then lets the income and capital gains compound tax free in the Roth IRA and is still able to spend the money he or she earned.

This can be the best deal for the grandchild. Because the grandchild is setting up the IRA and not inheriting it, there are no required minimum distributions at any time during the grandchild's life. The income and gains can compound for as long as the grandchild lets them. In addition, the money does not have to be left in the IRA until retirement. Distributions from a Roth IRA are tax free if the money has been in the Roth IRA for at least five years and it is withdrawn for one of the following reasons: death, disability, after reaching age 59$^1/_2$, or to pay first-time home buying expenses of up to $10,000. A grandchild can take a tax-free withdrawal to help buy his or her first home. Or the money can compound until after the grandchild reaches age 59$^1/_2$. After that, all distributions are tax free. Money can be withdrawn for other reasons as needed. The gains and income would be taxable, but it would have benefited from tax-deferred compounding over the years.

Don't overlook Roth IRAs just because they don't fit into your retirement plan. Roth IRAs are extremely powerful estate planning tools and can be used by individuals of almost any income level to enhance the future of their loved ones.

No-Tax, Low-Cost Way to Help a Grandchild

A grandparent doesn't need to give away money or property to help a grandchild. Money can be lent to a grandchild.

Here's one plan. Lend $50,000 to a grandchild for five years. The grandchild invests the money and earns 10 percent annually. At the end of five years, the grandchild has accumulated over $80,000 before taxes. The grandchild can repay the $50,000 and still have about $30,000, minus taxes, left as a nest egg. Taxes should be quite low, because the grandchild should be in the lowest tax bracket and the gains should be long-term capital gains. The grandparent's only cost is the earnings from the $50,000 for five years, and the grandchild has accumulated a nice starter fund after only five years.

This is such an attractive deal for taxpayers at any income level that the tax code has imposed a number of hurdles.

A lender is required to charge a minimum interest rate on most loans. If the minimum isn't charged, then it is a below market loan on which a minimum interest rate based on current market rates is imputed. We'll discuss the effects of imputed interest shortly.

There are several key exceptions to the requirement of a minimum interest rate. The first is that a gift loan between individuals, which is what is described here, does not have interest imputed when loans between the individuals do not exceed $10,000, and the loan is not used to purchase or carry income-producing investments.

Another important exception provides no imputed interest on gift loans between individuals when the loans do not exceed $100,000 and the borrower's investment income for the year does not exceed $1,000. If the borrower's net investment income does exceed $1,000, interest will be imputed but only in the amount of the borrower's net investment income for the year.

This obviously is an important exception for loans to grandchildren. A grandparent can lend up to $100,000 to a grandchild interest free, if it is invested primarily for long-term capital gains so that there is little or no taxable annual income. If there is annual investment income, the grandchild should be sure to keep track of investment expenses such as broker's commissions. Those expenses are subtracted from investment income to arrive at net investment income. After five years, the grandchild sells enough of the investments to pay back the loan. There are no tax consequences to anyone, except taxes when the grandchild sells the investment.

Suppose a loan doesn't meet one of the exceptions and has interest imputed. Even then, the results are not bad.

When interest is imputed, the grandparent will be treated as having made a gift to the grandchild equal to the interest that should have been charged but wasn't. Then the grandparent will be treated as having received a payment of that amount of interest income from the grandchild. Because the grandparent can give the grandchild up to $14,000 annually free of gift taxes, gift taxes aren't a problem until the imputed interest is over $14,000.

The grandparent will have interest income equal to the amount of the imputed interest, though it won't be paid in cash. Suppose the imputed interest is $2,000 and the grandparent is in the 40 percent tax bracket. The cost of making the loan will be $800 in taxes on phantom interest income each year.

If a gift loan is made to a grandchild (or any other relative), there must be appropriate paperwork. The IRS doesn't like loans between related parties and tries to treat them as gifts. There must be a real expectation of repayment and the intent to enforce collection. The note should spell out an interest rate and repayment schedule and contain an unconditional promise to repay. The repayment schedule, which can be a balloon payment at the end, must be followed as much as finances permit. There also must be a reasonable expectation that the loan could be repaid. For example, a loan made to a relative with a failing business that is unlikely to recover might be treated as a gift rather than a loan.

One word of caution is that the assets the grandchild purchases might decline in value. I know one wealthy individual who lent money to an adult child and suggested the purchase of a stock he knew well. Unfortunately, the market did not agree with his assessment of the stock. The child soon owned a stock worth half its previous value and still owed the father the full amount of the loan.

Simple, Low-Cost Ways to Help

A grandparent doesn't need to be a multimillionaire to help the grandchildren. The grandparent doesn't even need to be wealthy. There are many simple, low-cost ways to help, and they are tax free. With many of these strategies, the grandparent can see the benefits now instead of imagining how the wealth will be used in the future.

The use of property is a great way to help future generations. For example, a grandparent might have a vacation property or recreational vehicle. The adult children (the grandchildren's parents) might save significant expenses if these assets can be used for family vacations. That savings can be used to help pay for the grandchildren's education or other future needs. Letting others use property costs the grandparents very little, and it usually has no tax consequences.

An increasingly popular strategy is to pay for family vacations. Travel can be fairly expensive, and many families with children have to stretch for or cannot afford a nice trip. A family trip paid by the grandparents can give the family an experience they never would have had or save them thousands of dollars. Grandparents who cannot afford to pay for an entire trip might be able to pay for a portion. Sometimes grandparents will pay for a cruise or a stay at a resort. All the children and grandchildren have to do is get to and from the location and pay for their food.

Technically, paying a share of someone's vacation costs is a gift to them and counts against the annual tax-free gift amount. But the IRS to date has looked only at gifts of money and property. It has not tried to add up holiday gifts, meals, and travel.

Another way grandparents can help loved ones is to have their financial advisors help the grandchildren. Suppose a grandparent gets professional advice on an estate plan, financial plan, or investments. The advice can be tailored to ensure that the needs of the children and grandchildren are considered in the plan. The grandparents also can pass on any advice received.

A further step is for the grandparent to offer to pay the advisors to work with the children or grandchildren. The loved ones would meet with the advisor, and all the information would be confidential between them. But the grandparent will have rendered a valuable benefit, and the advisor can ensure that what the children are doing is consistent with what the grandparent is doing and that the plans are coordinated.

The grandparent also should be able to get a break on fees. Even if the grandparent doesn't pay for everything, the family should get a break by using the same advisor. A family buying as a group probably can negotiate a lower fee than could each individual family member.

Another benefit is that together the younger members of the family learn more about money and sees how finances work. That's a big improvement over leaving your loved ones your assets and expecting them to know how to manage them. Often, being unprepared to handle the family's assets can do more damage than taxes or probate costs.

A grandparent who is in business or is an investor can help family members by letting them benefit from opportunities that come the grandparent's way. When family members are in the same or related businesses, the grandparent can send some potential business or clients to other family members instead of keeping the opportunities for themselves.

Teaching Grandkids Wealth Management

It is nice to give wealth to grandchildren. But an even better gift can be to teach them how to multiply and manage wealth for the rest of their lives.

Young people today are more financially savvy than any prior generation. They own investments, have such high discretionary income that retailers make pitches to them, and even financial services firms are catering to the younger generation. Despite this attention, money, and information, most grandchildren know just enough about money management to be dangerous. That's where grandparents come in. Grandparents can help subsequent generations become better, shrewder financial managers. An additional benefit is that by managing their own funds, the grandchildren will learn to be more responsible people in general.

To help grandchildren on their way, consider these steps:

- Open basic accounts for them. Start with a savings account. It could be an account at a local bank or a money market fund that is easy to access. The grandparent can put in the start-up capital to meet the minimum investment amount, but can tell the grandchild that the startup money is either the grandparent's or is available only for college. Review the account statements with the grandchild from time to time, so that he or she can see how the money grows just by being left alone in the account.
- Use the account to teach the grandchild to save for the long term. For example, the grandparent could say that only up to 20 percent of the balance can be spent, and the rest is being saved for college or some other future need. Also, instead of depositing gifts to the account that the grandchild doesn't know about, give money directly and encourage him or her to save all or most of it. Some people prefer separate accounts—one for spending money, one for long-term expenses such as college, and maybe another for other expenses. Each time the child receives money, a portion is put into each account.
- Give simple lessons to the grandchild. Explain how compound interest and regular savings work, using examples and explanations that the child can understand. Some brokers and mutual funds have education materials to help explain a point. A good book is *The Richest Man in Babylon* by George Clayson, a classic that explains savings and compounding of wealth.
- Encourage the grandchild to save by offering to match new savings with additional gifts to the account.
- Help the grandchild pick stocks for a hypothetical portfolio. It can be a game, but the child will learn and might become interested. Over time, review the selections and how they performed.

- Buy mutual funds in the investment account. Teach the grandchild how to check prices in the newspaper or on the Internet. When the reports from the mutual fund arrive, use these to show the grandchild which companies the fund owns and how they have affected the price.
- Buy a few stocks with the grandchild. This is how a child learns to think like a business owner. When the company reports arrive, the grandchild won't be able to understand most of them. But the grandparent can point out some highlights, such as descriptions of the company's activities and how a few key numbers changed over time.

A grandchild needs to save and invest for a lifetime. Grandparents can get them off to a good start with a few easy steps and some early lessons on how wealth works. With any luck, the grandchild will be able to benefit from a grandparent's wisdom long after the grandparent is gone.

Estate Planning Is More than Taxes

A revolution occurred in estate planning.

Estate planning was in turmoil for more than a decade, but the tax law now is settled. The new rules and strategies are set, and for many people the best strategies are very different from those before the changes began.

The turmoil began with the 2001 tax law that made multiple changes over 10 years and then scheduled a reversion to the 2000 law. A 2010 deal in Washington prevented the reversion and temporarily eliminated the estate tax for most people. The 2010 law, with some modifications, became permanent in 2012. The turmoil in the law is over for at least a while, and with it the major excuse to procrastinate about estate planning.

Less than half of 1 percent of estates of adults who passed away in 2014 incurred the federal estate tax, estimated the Tax Policy Center. That's because each person has a lifetime $5 million lifetime estate and gift tax exemption that increases with inflation each year. The exemption for 2016 was $5.45 million. In addition, the new "portability rules" allow married couples a true doubling of the individual exclusion. A married couple can pass $10 million (indexed for inflation) to future generations free of estate and gift taxes.

Don't conclude from all this, as many have, that because you no longer have to worry about the federal estate tax, you don't have to worry about estate planning. Also, don't conclude that you don't have to consider taxes at all in your estate planning.

You still need a complete, up-to-date estate plan. Everyone does, regardless of the value of your estate. There are many nontax factors that always were an important part of each estate plan but were given less attention in the past because of the importance of estate taxes. Now, those other issues can receive the attention they should. Also, taxes other than the federal estate tax should be an important part of most plans, and you have to look at taxes differently.

A consequence of the 2012 law for most people is that income taxes are a higher burden than federal estate and gift taxes.

Because few estates will face a federal tax burden, now we can focus on the real issues of estate planning. Failure to have a plan or to have a quality, updated plan likely will lead to dissipation of much of your lifetime's wealth by forces other than federal estate taxes. A nonexistent or inadequate plan is an impediment to achieving your plans and goals for the wealth and often leads to family disputes and disharmony.

First, we'll discuss the nontax aspects of estate planning. Then, we'll review the estate tax and basic tax planning strategies to consider as part of your estate plan.

Estate Planning Essentials for Everyone

Tom Carvel and his 800 ice cream stores once were familiar to many Americans, especially those in the northeast region where Carvel's gravelly voice was featured in radio and television ads for the stores. In 1989, ill health forced Carvel to sell the business, and in 1990 he died. Carvel's estimated $200 million estate should have been as simple as a $200,000 estate. He wanted his widow taken care of, then the bulk of the estate donated to charity (they had no children).

Instead, Carvel made almost every possible estate planning mistake. The result was a disaster. Over a dozen lawyers representing many different interests kept the estate tied up in court. The estate dwindled to $60 million or less because of legal fees and other consequences of the litigation. Family members and business associates became estranged and accused each other of various dishonest acts. The whole mess should have ended in 1998 when Carvel's widow, living as a recluse in England, passed away. But her cremation was stopped by an attorney who wanted an autopsy to determine if she was mentally competent at the time of her death, and the disputes continued.

You don't have to be rich to make the mistakes Carvel made. For example, a copy of the will could not be found at the time of his death, and there were reports that the document shredder in Carvel's old office was very busy in the months after his death. The will mysteriously appeared about two years later, after an expensive lost-will court proceeding was concluded.

The problems with Carvel's estate, and thousands of other estates, weren't related to the tax law. There are many essential parts of an estate plan that need to be in place even when taxes aren't a factor. To avoid Carvel-like problems, there are key rules that should be followed in every estate plan.

Best Gift to Leave Your Heirs

When Tom Carvel died, his will was not in the filing cabinet that should have contained it. No one had a copy. In addition, his affairs were a web of corporations and other entities through which property frequently was passed. Paperwork for many of the transactions was incomplete. Carvel apparently kept everything straight in his head, but no one else could figure it out.

The best thing one can do for one's heirs is to organize your estate and leave a clear guide to the estate. The guide has two purposes. One purpose is to make things much easier and less expensive for loved ones. The other purpose is to avoid mistakes, such as overlooked or mismanaged assets.

The ideal way to provide this information is to fill a three-ring notebook with key documents. Yes, even in today's digital word, hard copy documentation is important. The first document would be an instruction letter that gives an overview of the estate and the steps that the executor or heirs should take right away. The alternative is to have survivors spend weeks or months pulling things together, or perhaps paying a lawyer to do so. At a minimum, the letter should identify who should be contacted, give the location of the will and other important documents, and describe funeral preferences.

The letter should be accompanied by copies of key estate and financial documents. Important documents in this package include:

- A list of legal and financial advisors, including the attorney, executor, accountant, insurance agent, bank, broker or financial planner, and financial institutions at which there are accounts.
- An inventory of assets, including a description of what is owned, where it is located, an estimate of its value, approximately when it was acquired, and its tax basis.
- Recommendations for the management or disposition of special property should be stated somewhere in the notebook. Items that warrant this treatment include business interests, real estate, art and collectibles, and any investments about which there is a strong personal attachment.
- Current tax returns plus regularly updated copies of the will, personal financial statements, and details of debts. Estimates of estate taxes and cash flow would be helpful.
- Details of financial accounts including Social Security, insurance, pensions, bank accounts, brokerage accounts, mutual funds, and any other

assets. In most cases, a copy of a recent account statement is sufficient. Another option is to identify where the files for each of the accounts are located.

The notebook should be revised at least annually. The estate executor and at least one other person should be aware of the notebook and where it can be located. Remember that no matter how simple and straightforward things appear to an owner, they often are murky to someone who walks right into the situation and has to begin managing the estate. Make things easier for everyone by getting organized. Most people are surprised by what they learn through this organizing process, and it makes them better at managing their wealth.

Ensuring Your Estate Plan Essentials

Every estate has a host of significant issues other than federal taxes that need to be addressed. To prepare you, here's a roadmap of the key issues for every estate plan. You'll be looking for solutions to each of them that meet your goals, resources, and other factors.

Medical Care

That's right. Medical care is a vital part of a good estate plan. The plan should define how your medical care and needs will be addressed in different circumstances.

First, you'll need documents that provide which decisions will be made and who will make them in case you aren't able to. That means you need a medical power of attorney or medical care directive and perhaps a living will. You also should consider if you want documents such as do-not-resuscitate and do-not-hospitalize orders. You need to focus on both the terms and scope of the documents and, especially with the power of attorney, selecting the person or people to make decisions.

The financial aspect of your medical care also should be covered. Be sure you have adequate insurance or resources to cover most types of medical care. This is discussed in detail in Chapters 6 and 7. Be sure your executor, your spouse, and perhaps others know about your insurance and where to find the details.

Avoiding Disputes

It doesn't matter how much or how little wealth you have. When an estate owner doesn't develop a plan, conflict and chaos often follow. Children, even adult children, can fight over how assets are divided and managed. The presence of a second spouse or other players can make the conflicts worse.

You shouldn't be content with thinking "the kids can work it out." Any estate planner will tell you they often don't. Even when an estate doesn't seem to be worth much, there's a need to clearly state how you want it divided and handled. In most families, there's usually at least one person who'll look for something to fight about with the others if you leave an opening. Almost every estate planner can tell you stories of families spending far more on legal fees than an item or estate was worth.

Consider the possible sources of conflict in your estate. Then, work with your estate planner to develop strategies to minimize or eliminate the conflicts.

Probate

You might not be worried about estate taxes, but the probate process can cost a lot of money and delay settlement of your estate. Probate is the system that ensures your debts are paid, your assets are distributed how you intended, and heirs have clear legal title to assets. Some states have a streamlined and less expensive process, at least for smaller estates, under the Uniform Probate Code. But a number of states still use an older, expensive, cumbersome process. You need to find out which type of state you live in and what would be involved in probating your estate.

When the state has an unattractive probate process, consider avoiding the probate process and how to do it. You can use a living trust, partnerships, limited liability companies, joint title, and other tools. Each has advantages and disadvantages. Discuss them with an estate planner to select the best tools for you.

When you live in or have property in more than one state, the processes of both states must be considered. The bulk of your estate will be governed by the state in which you are resident or domiciled, and any real estate will be controlled by the state where it's located. To avoid probate in two states, you might want out-of-state real estate owned through a trust or limited liability company instead of in your name.

Beneficiary Forms

IRAs, annuities, employer retirement plans, life insurance, and some other assets aren't affected by your will. They are inherited by whoever's named in the beneficiary designation forms. Be sure these forms in both your records and those of the firm sponsoring the asset reflect your current wishes. If you don't do anything else toward estate planning, take this easy step.

Care of Others

You might be helping or anticipate having to help a relative or other person. It might be an elderly parent or other relative. It could be a child or grandchild that has needs. If so, you probably want to develop a plan to ensure he or she has help when it's needed. That might mean buying life insurance or establishing a trust for their benefit.

Asset Management

You're probably managing your investments and other assets well. You're following good advice. You probably also determined who you want to inherit and benefit from the investment portfolio and other assets next. But who will manage the portfolio? Is your surviving spouse or other member of your family capable? Do they have the knowledge and skills to manage your assets and make them last a long time? Have you even discussed this with them?

If not, you need a plan.

One option is to lift the burden from the loved ones, just as you have for years. Plan to have one or more money managers invest the assets.

If that's your plan, find an investment manager now. Don't expect loved ones who don't know how to manage money to be able to select a good money manager.

You can test drive managers by giving one or more managers a portion of your portfolio to manage now. That lets you see not only how they perform but how well they communicate and provide customer service. They'll be in place for you to examine, and over time you can let your spouse or other heirs know that you believe the manager is good and that they should continue to use the firm's services when they inherit the portfolio. If it's the wrong manager, you'll find out soon and be able to make another choice.

Succession

When you own business interests, real estate, or complicated assets such as a collection, succession planning is a must. Look for someone in your family who's able and interested in continuing management of the assets. Then, plan the transition in management and ownership. Don't wait. With businesses and complicated assets, it often takes five years or more of planning for a succession to be successful.

When there's no suitable management successor in the family, you might look for one or more associates who can continue management. They might want to buy the business from the estate or be willing to manage it while family members continue ownership. Or you should develop a plan for how the asset will be sold and the proceeds distributed to your loved ones.

You need to develop a plan of succession or sale now. Too often, when a plan isn't in place the value of the asset isn't maintained during the transition. The estate doesn't receive the full value the business once had. Sometimes the entire value of the asset dissipates.

You might have other issues to address, but these are the most common nontax estate planning issues. Some of these you might be able to resolve on your own. But it's best to meet with an experienced estate planner and discuss the goals and ambitions for your wealth, family, and the rest of your life. Then, you can identify the issues and develop a plan.

Writing a Better Will

A will is not an estate plan, but your estate plan should include a will. Here are some key provisions of wills and the planning process that often are overlooked and can make a big difference in the results of an estate plan.

Estate Liquidity

Estate liquidity is often overlooked but vital. An estate might be valuable, but it also needs cash to pay taxes, debts, and other expenses. If there will be a cash shortage, the owner needs to provide life insurance or a schedule of which assets are to be sold first to raise cash. In some wills, the executor is empowered to take out a mortgage on one or more properties to raise cash.

Specific Bequests

Avoid specific bequests in a will. A specific bequest is when a certain amount of money or particular assets are designated for an individual. Specific bequests can complicate the estate and cause unintended problems. In Tom Carvel's will, 83 people were left relatively small cash gifts. Most of these were former employees who could have been given bonuses after the business was sold. Instead, the gifts increased the size of the will and the cost of administering the estate. They also greatly increased the number of people involved in the will contest and the amount of cash the estate needed.

Specific bequests can create other problems. A specific dollar amount might seem small when the will is written. But the value of other assets might fall in a market decline, or there might be unexpected taxes and other expenses. That cash gift suddenly is a bigger part of the estate than was intended. The gift also might use up scarce cash that is needed for taxes and debts.

A specific property bequest also can have unintended consequences. Suppose a few hundred shares of stock are left to an individual. Over time, however, the market likes the stock and it soars in value. This small gift becomes a meaningful part of the estate, and it is going to someone who was supposed to be a minor beneficiary. Or the stock could drop in value, leaving the beneficiary feeling slighted and with less than intended.

Or the owner might sell the stock after the will is written. Then, the will has to be rewritten or amended, or the executor can be left to figure out what was intended for the beneficiary. Of course, an asset left in a specific bequest might disappear, creating a number of problems.

Small gifts generally should be made during the owner's lifetime. If they are made in a will, there should be some limits. For example, a cash gift can be made through a formula, such as for a specific amount but only up to a certain percentage of the estate's value or its liquid assets. Likewise, a gift of specific property should be limited to a ceiling value or percentage of the estate and only for assets that you're sure you won't sell. But the best bet is to make specific bequests only of unique items, and specify that they be part of the residual estate so they won't come out of the estate first.

Debts and Taxes

Debts and taxes require careful consideration. Without the correct, technical wording, some beneficiaries of an estate might receive their bequests without making any contribution to the estate's taxes and debts. The main beneficiaries shoulder the tax and debt burden through their shares. It is a technical issue, but the owner should be aware of who will bear the burden of the taxes and debts.

Personal Property

Distributing personal property can be the most difficult part of a will. Oddly enough, it is the personal items, even seemingly insignificant ones, which bring out rivalries among the survivors and cause the most disagreements. There should be a plan in the will for dividing the personal property. There are several tried and true methods for doing this with a minimum of distress among heirs.

One option is to have the executor divide the property. A non-family member should be executor for this to work. Or the executor can be directed to sell everything and distribute the cash. Another option is to set up a lottery. The oldest child (or the one who picks the lowest number out of a hat) picks an item first. Then the others pick one item in order. For the next round of picks, the order is reversed. Another method is to have the children pick the items they would like while the parents are alive. The children attach their names to the items. These are just a few ideas.

Changing Circumstances

A final point in estate planning is to expect change. An estate plan is not a one-time event. It needs to be updated whenever there is a change in the personal or family situation. A marriage, divorce, or birth in the family should trigger an appointment with the estate planning lawyer. Significant changes in the estate's property or value also should cause reconsideration of the plan. Even when there are no obvious changes, a lawyer should be contacted for a review every 18 months to three years.

The Estate Tax

The basic outline and computation of the federal estate tax is fairly simple. Your executor compiles a list of all your assets and their values. That is your gross estate. Then a few deductions might be subtracted to arrive at your taxable estate. Your lifetime taxable gifts are added to the taxable estate, because the estate and gift taxes are considered a uniform wealth transfer tax. In other words, you should pay the same tax whether you give property away during your lifetime or after your death. Then the tentative tax on both your final estate and your lifetime gifts is computed. After computing the tentative tax, gift taxes paid during your lifetime are subtracted.

Next, the remaining tax is reduced by the amount of your lifetime estate and gift tax credit. Everyone gets an estate and gift tax credit. The current level of the credit is what exempts most estates from the federal estate tax. Note that since the estate and gift tax are unified, you can use all or part of the credit during your lifetime to make tax-free gifts, and that reduces the amount of credit available to your estate. If you used all or part of the credit to reduce lifetime gift taxes, the amount of the credit that was used is not available to reduce estate taxes.

As I said, in the 2012 law, the lifetime estate tax credit was raised so it shelters an estate worth up to $5 million per person. That amount is indexed for inflation and was set at $5.45 million for 2016. The maximum estate tax rate is 40 percent. There also is generation skipping transfer tax imposed on transfers directly from grandparents to grandchildren or later generations, and it has the same exemption and tax rate as the estate tax.

You can see in the outline of the estate tax in the paragraphs above how the estate and gift taxes are unified. Your lifetime taxable gifts are added to the gross estate to determine the estate tax. Then, the gift taxes you actually paid during your lifetime are subtracted from the tax payable. Finally, the remaining amount of your estate and gift tax credit is used to reduce the tax payable.

This computation should reveal several basic ways to reduce estate taxes. All estate tax reduction planning falls into one or more of these strategies:

- Remove assets from the gross estate or reduce the value placed on assets in the estate.
- Maximize use of the marital deduction and charitable contribution deduction.

- Use the lifetime estate and gift tax credit.
- Don't reduce taxes. Instead, buy life insurance to pay the taxes or provide an inheritance.

Understanding the New Portability

A new feature was introduced in the estate tax in 2010 and remained in the 2012 law. Estate planners call this feature portability or portable credits. It allows married couples to have a joint lifetime exemption equal to two individual lifetime exemptions, because any unused lifetime estate and gift tax credit of the first spouse to pass away can be transferred to the surviving spouse.

Previously, the lifetime estate tax exemption was available only to the individual. It had a use-it-or-lose-it feature. Any exemption amount not used by your estate and your lifetime gifts was lost. To maximize tax savings and avoid losing a credit, it was important for married couples with substantial assets to split title to their assets so that each had an estate of roughly equal value—or at least equal to the lifetime exemption.

Now, a surviving spouse may take the unused exemption amount of the first spouse that passed away and add it to his or her own. It works like this. The estate of the first spouse to pass away is exempt from estate taxes up to $5.45 million in 2016. If that spouse's taxable estate was worth less than $5.45 million, the unused exemption amount transfers to the surviving spouse. When the survivor eventually passes away, he or she can exempt more than $5.45 million of assets by using his or her own exemption plus the unused exemption of the deceased spouse. Together they're sure of exempting up to $10.9 million in 2016.

Consider Max and Rosie Profits with a net worth of $8 million, $6 million in Max's name and $2 million in Rosie's name. Rosie passes away in 2016. Before 2010, her estate would be exempt from taxes, but her unused exempt amount would be lost. Max and Rosie would have been advised to ensure Rosie had legal title to at least the lifetime exempt amount or equal to what Max owned.

Under current law, however, Rosie's estate still is exempt, but that unused estate tax exemption of $3.45 million ($5.45 million [the maximum allowable asset exemption] minus the $2 million that is Rosie's actual net worth) can be transferred to Max. His estate will have both his own exemption of $5.45 million in 2016 plus Rosie's unused $3.45 million exemption, for a total of $8.9 million. Max's exempt amount is increased for inflation each year he lives after 2016, but Rosie's unused amount that carried over to Max is fixed at $3.45 million. It doesn't increase for inflation after Rosie passes away.

To secure the portability of the first spouse's unused exemption, the estate executor must follow IRS rules. In particular, the estate of the first spouse to pass away must file an estate tax return, even if the estate is exempt from filing a return because no tax is due. The return must be filed within nine months of the date of death, though a six-month extension is available. If the executor fails to file a return or misses the deadline, there is no portability and the unused exemption is lost. The executor when filing the return can elect not to allow portability if for some reason you want that or he decides that's best. If an estate tax return is filed but doesn't take a position on the transfer of the unused credit, then it is treated as though the executor elected to transfer the unused credit.

It's important that you name an executor who knows to file an estate tax return, even when one is not required in order for your unused exemption to be portable for your surviving spouse. Filing an estate tax return should be automatic now for someone who was married, regardless of the estate's value. (Some advisors say that couples should consider forgoing the exemption in order to avoid filing an estate tax return. If a return is filed, the IRS might audit it and find some estate or gift taxes are due.)

When the surviving spouse had more than one deceased spouse over his or her lifetime, only the exemption of the last deceased spouse can be used. Here's how that rule works.

Example. Rosie Profits dies, leaving her surviving husband, Max. Rosie had a previous husband who passed away and his estate used only $3 million of his exemption. So, Rosie's estate can exempt $7 million (her $5 million exclusion amount plus the unused $2 million exclusion amount from her first husband). Rosie didn't make any taxable gifts during her lifetime and has a taxable estate of $3 million. Rosie's estate elects to let Max use Rosie's unused exclusion amount, which is $4 million (Rosie's $7 million exemption less her $3 million taxable estate). So, Max's exclusion is increased by $4 million and is $9 million if none of his exclusion was used by taxable gifts. (All these numbers use the basic $5 million exemption without inflation indexing, to keep the example simple.)

A price of portability for the estate of the first spouse to pass away is subject to audit until the audit period for the second spouse to pass away has closed. Also, the carried-over exempt amount from the first spouse to pass away is not indexed for inflation. It's a fixed dollar amount, regardless of how long the surviving spouse lives.

It's a good idea for most estates to take the election, even when the surviving spouse's exemption seems more than sufficient, because the surviving spouse could receive a windfall at some point or could live a long time and have assets appreciate.

The 20-Minute Estate Plan

For most of us, estate planning still should be a key part of our financial planning. We must continue to plan our estates even when there is little risk of owing the federal estate tax.

Estate planning is easier than most people believe. That's because most estate planning experts shroud the topic in complex tax, legal, and insurance jargon. Most people can't get interested in discussions of probate, reversionary interests, split interest trusts, and related topics. Maybe the experts want to add some mystery to the process, or perhaps they don't know how to communicate in plain English. The reasons don't really matter. What matters is that most presentations on estate planning cause people either to avoid planning their estates or to put together hurried, inadequate estate plans.

That's why I've put together this simple guide I call the 20-Minute Estate Plan. It builds on what I already presented and provides straightforward, practical steps that will help an individual put together an estate plan. This isn't a complete self-help guide. Meetings with an estate planner still are essential. The guide makes it easier to work intelligently and economically with an estate planner and to make informed decisions about the various options. That will save time, money, and frustration, and also result in a superior estate plan.

Estate Planning Basics

What is estate planning? It's not simply avoiding taxes or probate. Estate planning is deciding how wealth should be transferred to the next generation (or other recipients of the owner's choice), then determining which legal tools to use to transfer that wealth. Only after establishing how the assets should be distributed does the focus move to considering ways to reduce taxes, avoid probate, and other goals. Lawyers and other professionals like to call the process estate planning, but it really is best to think of it as inheritance planning. That puts the true purpose of the process in the forefront.

To begin the inheritance planning process, take the following steps.

Make a List of All Assets and Liabilities. An effective inheritance plan cannot be prepared without this information. And a professional, no matter how skilled, can't do anything without this starting point. Frequently overlooked assets include pension plans, life insurance policies, trusts of which the estate owner is a beneficiary, and inheritances that are likely to be received. Heirs will inherit only net assets, so a list of all debts needs to be compiled, including whether the debts are secured by certain property.

Decide the Desired Distribution of the Assets in the Future. The traditional goal is for major assets to be inherited first by the spouse if he or she still is alive, then by the children, usually in equal shares. Smaller amounts or specific items might be designated for special friends, other relatives, and charities. Of course, no one has to follow the traditional route. An owner might want to favor one child over others or want the bulk of the estate to go directly to the children instead of his or her spouse. Many people decide to give a portion of their estates to charity. The only major limits are that a spouse cannot be completely disinherited in most states (unless there is a valid prenuptial or postnuptial agreement) and children can be completely disinherited if the intention is made clear in the will. In addition, an inheritance cannot violate law or public policy.

As part of this step, secondary goals also should be considered. For example, should a spouse inherit everything but only in a way that prevents the property from being subsequently inherited by a second spouse or family (or previous family) instead of by your children? Should property be left to children and grandchildren but with strings attached so that they don't waste the property or so they have to reach certain goals before getting the property? There often are ways of accomplishing both main and secondary goals, as long as the goals are clear.

Decide How Much Property Should Be Given Now, and How Much Later.   People often prefer to give some of their wealth while they are alive. There are several potential benefits. If estate taxes are an issue, giving early ensures the assets are out of the gross estate. You also have the benefit of seeing how the wealth is used and benefits the lives of loved ones. Some people use early gifts as a way of testing how their loved ones will handle the wealth. If they believe the wealth is wasted or not used well, they will consider changing either how much they leave someone in the will or give it but with some controls or limits.

Work with One or More Estate Planning Professionals to Develop an Estate Plan.   The plan should achieve the desired goals and also take into account estate taxes, probate, and other concerns. An average middle class individual might need to work only with an estate planning attorney. Wealthier individuals and those with businesses or other complicated assets might need to add an accountant, life insurance agent, business appraiser, trustees, and other professionals.

Implement the Estate Plan after It Is Fully Understood.   That sounds obvious, but apparently it isn't. Many people have great estate plans designed by skilled professionals, but then they fail to fully implement the plans. They don't set up trusts recommended by their planners or fail to transfer assets to the trusts. Maybe life insurance is not purchased as planned, annual gifts to children are not made, or other steps aren't taken. The result is a lot of time and money spent on estate planning but no effective estate plan in place.

Let Heirs Know in General What Is Decided and How Things Are Set Up.   An estate owner also should draft a letter of instructions as described earlier that lists basic information such as where copies of the will are kept, who the financial advisers are, and a summary of assets and liabilities. This document should be updated at least annually and be accompanied by recent tax returns and an outline of your estate plan, at the minimum. The letter should be given to the executor of the estate and to any other key people.

An inheritance plan really involves people more than law, life insurance, trusts, and other legal tools. The focus should be on how to provide for people both now and in the future, and also how one wants to be remembered.

Cutting Off the IRS

I previously listed the four basic strategies for reducing estate taxes: reducing asset from the gross estate, removing future appreciation from the gross estate, increasing deductions, and buying life insurance. Within those four strategies are many options. Not all will be appropriate for you. You decide which are best for you by working with your estate planner.

If your estate plan was in place before 2013, and certainly if it was created before 2010, you need to revise it or at least have an estate planner review it carefully. Here are a few of the more important potential changes:

- *Wills with bypass trusts need to be reconsidered.* Fewer families will need them now, because of the higher estate tax exemption. There still are cases when a bypass trust should be considered as part of an estate plan, but in many cases, the bypass trust could produce results you don't want under the current law.
- *Formulas in wills need to be rewritten when they determine the amount of an estate transferred to a bypass trust or when for any reason they refer to the estate tax exemption amount.* Under traditional formulas, the $5 million exemption will use all or the bulk of most estates. Many surviving spouses will be impoverished under wills in place before the law changed. If your estate plan has a bypass trust or formula clause, you need to visit an estate planner soon.
- *Don't forget state levies.* About 20 states have some form of estate or inheritance tax or both. Often these have much lower exemptions than federal law and will be a more significant burden on your heirs. You might want to revise your will primarily to avoid these taxes. Residents of the states with estate or inheritance taxes might need to do significant estate tax planning even when they will owe no federal estate taxes.
- *Make tax-free gifts.* The wealthy or near-wealthy who have enough assets to pay for retirement should consider removing appreciating

assets from their estates. You want to remove future appreciation from your estate, especially when the assets are appreciating faster than the Consumer Price Index. Otherwise, you take the risk your future estate will be taxable or more of it would be taxable than would be now. You transfer more wealth tax free to heirs when you give property before it appreciates, especially when you can make those transfers free of gift taxes. Even those with modest estates might want to make gifts when they live in states with high estate or inheritance taxes and they have enough to maintain their standard of living.

- *Income shifting is back.* With the higher lifetime exemption, you can transfer a lot of income-generating assets or property with large capital gains free of gift taxes to family members. When they family members are in a lower tax bracket than you, this keeps more after-tax wealth in the family.
- *Use irrevocable trusts.* Property that is transferred during life to an irrevocable trust is excluded from the gross estate. The transferor cannot be a beneficiary of the trust or be able to get the property back. There might be gift taxes owed when the trust is set up, but that should be cheaper than paying estate taxes down the road. If a goal is to avoid gift taxes, just enough property can be put in the trust each year to take advantage of the annual gift tax exemption. An irrevocable trust has the additional benefit of allowing the donor to make the gifts with strings attached. Those strings might protect heirs from themselves and also from being spoiled or otherwise damaged by an inheritance.
- *Buy life insurance to pay taxes or provide an inheritance.* Life insurance is a way to leave an inheritance without altering the ownership of other assets. It is possible that the insurance can provide a larger inheritance than otherwise would be available, especially if a married couple takes out a joint life or survivorship life insurance policy. Life insurance benefits are included in an estate only if the insured had any ownership interests in the policy. Life insurance can be excluded from an estate if the policy is owned either by an irrevocable trust, a limited partnership, or another individual, such as the children.
- *Give to both charity and heirs.* There are various strategies, such as charitable remainder trusts and charitable lead trusts, which allow an estate or a property owner to take advantage of the charitable contribution deduction while providing income or property to heirs for a period of years.
- *Use gift tax discounts.* There are strategies that allow you to give all or part of a property away but also pay gift taxes on only a portion of the value. This is known as a discount gift tax strategy, and discounts of 20 percent and higher are available. Discounts might be possible using family limited partnerships, split interest trusts and a few other strategies for reducing gift taxes.

The Turnabout in Tax Planning

Most of us don't have to worry about federal estate taxes. Yet, taxes still should figure in your estate plan as much as ever. Instead of focusing primarily on federal estate taxes, your tax planning should focus on two other areas. First, you need to focus on reducing federal capital gains and income taxes over the long term. Second, you also need to focus on reducing state taxes on income, capital gains, estates, and inheritances.

Here's the key issue now. When property is included in your estate, most of the time the tax basis of the property is increased to its current fair market value. For example, let's say you purchased mutual fund shares for $10,000 years ago and they now are worth $20,000. If you sell today, you'll pay capital gains taxes on that $10,000 gain. If you give the property to your children to remove it from your estate, which used to be the recommended strategy, they'll take the same $10,000 tax basis you had and eventually have to pay capital gains taxes on that gain and any additional gain when they sell.

Continue to hold the fund shares, however, and they'll be included in your estate. The tax basis will increase to their fair market value at that time. The estate or your heirs who inherit can sell the shares immediately and owe no capital gains taxes. Your loved ones will receive the full value of the shares, not an after-tax value. Or they can continue to hold the shares. Eventually when they sell, they'll owe capital gains taxes only on the appreciation that occurred while they owned the shares.

Bottom line: The longtime rule to remove assets from the estate through direct gifts or transfers to trusts might not be the best advice today. It might be better to hold appreciated and appreciating assets. You'll avoid federal estate taxes unless your estate is very valuable, and you and your heirs will avoid capital gains taxes on the appreciation.

That's why your estate's tax planning strategy should consider all the taxes that might be imposed on an asset. There is the federal capital gains tax, plus any similar tax your state imposes. There also are the stealth and add-on taxes that increase as income rises, including the 3.8 percent net investment income tax and Medicare premium surtax, taxation of Social Security benefits, reductions in itemized deductions and personal exemptions, and the alternative minimum tax. All of these might be avoided by your family when you hold appreciated assets and have them included in your estate. Then, the heirs can sell them at no tax cost.

Even wealthy people who might have part of their estates subject to the federal estate tax should reconsider the extent to which they want to remove assets from their estates. These other taxes cumulatively could total more than the maximum 40 percent federal estate tax, especially if your state doesn't have its own version of the estate tax.

Holding assets in the estate isn't the ideal strategy in every case. If your state is one of the 20 or so plus the District of Columbia (as of 2015) that has some form of estate or inheritance tax or both, you need to compare the tax from holding the asset in your estate to the income tax that would be owed if you transferred the asset now to a loved one. Remember to consider the income tax rate your beneficiary would pay, not that you would pay. For example, if you live in a state with an estate or inheritance tax but your children live in a state without an income or capital gains tax, your family might save money by giving appreciated property to them now instead of holding it in your estate.

You can see that tax planning is more complicated now. Sometimes the right move is intuitive or obvious. Other times, some careful calculations need to be made. You need to evaluate each of the potential taxes that would fall on each asset before deciding whether or not to give property now or hold it.

Here are some general rules:

- Prime candidates to be held in your estate are appreciated investments and your personal residence.
- Depreciated investment properties and business real estate also would avoid income and capital gains taxes by remaining in your estate.
- Appreciated art, gold, and collectibles are likely to be worth holding in the estate because they are subject to a higher maximum capital gains rate—28 percent—than most other assets.
- Any patents, trademarks, and copyrights created by you also are good to hold in the estate, because your tax basis is likely to be zero but a beneficiary of the estate can increase the basis.

On the other hand, there's no tax reason to hold cash. Also, variable annuities and qualified retirement plans (including IRAs and 401(k)s) don't receive an increased basis after the owner's death. All the distributions will be treated as ordinary income whether taken by you or your beneficiary. You might save money by paying those taxes now instead of later.

Avoiding Financial Scams and Abuse

The world is rife with financial scams and abuse, and you're a target. Those are facts we all need to acknowledge. Unfortunately, many people don't know enough about the world of financial scams, to their detriment. Even people who think they know the facts of financial fraud and abuse don't, especially those most likely to be targets. You need to understand financial fraud and abuse and take precautions before it is a problem for you or those you care about.

Most people don't even realize when they've been targeted for or subjected to fraud and abuse, according to a 2015 survey done for FINRA, the Financial Industry Regulatory Authority. The survey asked people if they'd ever been defrauded or targeted for fraud, and most answered in the negative. But the survey also asked people if they'd ever been approached about or participated in certain types of financial transactions, and 84 percent said they had. The financial transactions described in the questions were classic and widespread scams and frauds. That means most people, 84 percent, were targeted for fraud or abuse and didn't realize it.

Several key factors make a person more likely to be a target of fraud and abuse.

Age, of course, makes one a target. That's partly because as people age they tend to become more trusting and optimistic. They're more likely to believe the best results will occur from actions, and that makes them vulnerable to sales pitches.

In addition, cognitive skills diminish as we age. Our "executive think-ing" skills peak as early as age 35 or 40 according to some research. After that, we're less effective at critical thinking and cognitive reasoning, or at least when trying to exercise those tasks quickly. Having diminished cog-nitive skills doesn't mean someone is suffering from dementia or other illnesses. It means they don't analyze and reason as well as they once did, especially when they try to make decisions quickly. Other research shows older people actually make better financial decisions but only when they use wisdom and experience to make good decisions by taking the time to analyze a question in detail.

That's why it is important to take the time to carefully and thoroughly consider important financial and nonfinancial decisions and seek input and opinions from others. You should assume you might be missing one or two things on the first review and "sleep on it." You also should encourage friends and relatives to make decisions more deliberately, so they aren't defrauded.

As you might guess from the FINRA survey, most fraud victims aren't aware of what are known as the *badges of fraud*. These are the factors that indicate a proposal is likely to be a scam or fraud. For example, most people don't know the levels of investment returns that are realistic or that very few investments are guaranteed. Those are just a couple of the badges of fraud most people can't identify.

Other traits are common among fraud victims. They are likely to believe they can tolerate more risk than others (a trait more common among males and higher educated people). They also are less likely to seek advice from friends and family, often because they're afraid asking for input will make them appear unable to make decisions or handle their finances. In fact, seeking advice from people who care about you is a sign of good decision making.

Of course, having some money also makes one a target, but you don't have to be wealthy. Anyone who has a few thousand dollars or more in liquid assets is an attractive target to many crooks.

Comparing Fraud and Abuse

You need to understand financial abuse is different from fraud, and peo-ple are more likely to suffer financial abuse than fraud. Though a some-what nebulous concept, financial abuse is when someone makes improper or illegal use of your property, money, or assets. It can include identity theft, using checks or credit cards without permission, and misusing or stealing property. It also can include inducing someone to sign a docu-ment as well as improperly using a power of attorney, guardianship, or conservatorship.

The key mistake many people make is not realizing perpetrators of financial abuse are highly likely to be people known to and trusted by the victim. When asked about financial abuse, most people say it is likely to be committed by strangers and the greatest threats are from Internet and mail scams or telephone solicitations. In fact, family members or professional advisors are believed to commit about 90 percent of cases of financial abuse.

Financial abuse is most likely to occur when two factors are present. One factor is disability or cognitive decline. The other factor is social isolation. This doesn't mean someone is physically isolated. It means they have significant contact with fewer people and don't spend as much time as they used to with family, neighbors, church members, or whoever else was in their social network for years. It also could mean they never did have much of a social network and have a smaller one now. The abusers tend to isolate people so that others can't learn what is happening to or influence the victims.

Of course, not everyone who is disabled or has cognitive decline is abused. But they are common factors in abuse cases.

Also, an abuser often has some kind of mental or emotional problem. It might be as simple as someone being overwhelmed at being a caregiver or who feels entitled to take advantage of the person. For example, a family member caregiver might conclude that performing the care entitles him or her to make personal use of the victim's car or other possessions without asking or paying for them.

Often, the only help for a victim of abuse is someone else noticing a problem. That's why it is important for all of us to know the factors that can lead to financial fraud or abuse and the signs abuse might be occurring.

You should keep track of friends, family members, and others you know for the warning signs of cognitive decline and social isolation. Social isolation is easy to identify and try to correct. When someone appears to drop out of the social network, try to call or visit the person. If a caregiver or other person acts as a gatekeeper and appears to be isolating the person, there could be a problem.

Also, be alert for changes in spending or investment patterns, erratic or unusual transactions (such as large cash withdrawals), lack of knowledge about personal financial matters or a reluctance to discuss them, and giving a power of attorney to a new person. Unusual fear of or submission to a caregiver also is a warning sign. You can find a checklist of these and other red flags of financial abuse at www.allianzlife.com/sos.

After seeing one or more warning signs, you don't have to investigate or solve the problem. Instead, if you know one or more family members who have been close to the person, you can contact them and express your concerns. Even better, you can report a concern anonymously to local Adult Protective Services, or the long-term care ombudsman if the person is in a nursing home or assisted living. In most states, the report is anonymous by law. The state will look into the details and there won't be consequences to you if it's a false alarm. People are encouraged to report potential abuse if they have only a suspicion. There's no downside to reporting a suspicion, and you could save someone from abuse.

Protecting Yourself from Scams and Abuse

Fortunately, you can take steps to reduce your risk, and many of these steps are very easy to do and cost little or no money.

One easy step is to be alert for key promises and actions that are markers of scams and abuse.

Guaranteed high returns are a definite red flag. It is rare that a legitimate investment offers a guaranteed return. Legitimate guaranteed returns are low. An investment doesn't need to be guaranteed to be suspicious. When the seller says the investment has high potential returns with very low risk, he's likely not being honest. You should be aware of the level of current interest rates on Treasury bonds. All others investment returns spring from the return on these riskless investments. It isn't likely that a legitimate investment can offer substantially higher returns and still be guaranteed or low risk.

Complicated investments or presentations also are warning signs. If you're a sophisticated investor who's using a team to evaluate investments with high minimum investment levels, you might expect to see some complicated deals. Otherwise, complicated strategies, terms, or presentations most likely are used to hide problems with investments. Con artists know that many people, especially as they get older, are embarrassed to admit they don't understand something and are more likely to go along with it.

Someone presenting a legitimate complicated financial offer will know that it is complicated and be prepared to take the time and effort to explain it in detail. When someone presenting a complicated investment isn't willing to answer clearly all your questions and provide the details, that's a red flag.

Urgency is another red flag. There are very few legitimate financial transactions or investments with short deadlines to act. Often, pressure to act quickly is a tool to prevent you from considering all aspects or reviewing it with others.

Don't invest in or buy anything with inadequate disclosure. Anything that meets the legal definition of a security must have a detailed prospectus. Insurance products also are required to provide significant details under state laws. When all you're given are a few brochures and flyers, you should be suspicious. The less information you're given, the more likely it is that the proposal isn't legitimate.

The fastest and easiest way to avoid fraud and abuse is to add more people to your financial team. One simple, effective step is to have more people regularly see your financial statements. There's usually little or no cost to having others mailed copies of your statements or given online access to the statements.

Good candidates for seeing your statements include responsible adult children or siblings, close friends, and professional advisors, such as accountants and estate planners. Their job is to look for unusual transactions, such as large expenditures, new investments, a new pattern of expenses, and similar suspicious activities.

One really good use of a financial team member is as a reviewer and sounding board for making decisions.

For example, an easy, effective way to avoid scams and abuse is to tell anyone who asks for money or proposes an investment to make their case to your advisor or advisors. It might be an accountant, attorney, money manager, or broker. The professional likely will charge an hourly rate for this, but scamsters usually reveal themselves by not following up with your advisor. You even can use a friend or relative who's fairly sophisticated financially and is willing to play the role.

The team approach also is a good way to avoid having one financial advisor take advantage of you through bad deals or excess fees. Make sure all your advisors know who your other advisors are and let each of them know whenever you're contemplating a significant move.

Regular reviews of your finances with each of your advisors or even with a trusted confidante or friend also prevent problems. A team approach also tips you off to someone whose motives are not the best. If someone who's giving you financial advice objects to sharing information or including others in meetings, you should be concerned.

Trusts and powers of attorney also can avoid a lot of problems when the right people are in charge. Likewise, having someone manage or co-manage your money can prevent a lot of problems.

Another way to avoid scams is to minimize what security experts call *pocket litter*, the items you carry around that give valuable information to crooks.

Many people keep significant personal information in their wallets, purses, cell phones, computers, and elsewhere. Experienced criminals who gain access to these items, even if for only a short time, can learn enough to commit identity fraud or set you up for a con.

Take a hard look at what you carry around. At a minimum, use a meaningful password to open electronic devices. Even better is to avoid taking out of your house information that can be useful to criminals such as Social Security numbers, bank and credit card numbers, birthdates, and the like. Carry only what you need.

Making Identity Theft Less Likely

Identity theft isn't making the headlines it did a few years ago. Yet, it's still a major problem. The FTC still estimates that millions of Americans have their identities stolen, and this costs consumers about $5 billion. In 2014, the FTC said fixing credit after a theft took about 175 hours and cost $1,173. In addition, a bad credit report can cause you to be denied a mortgage or auto loan or even a job.

The baby boomers and those who are older are big targets for identity theft. They tend to have money and good credit ratings. Plus, they're vulnerable from a number of sides, such as anyone who helps around the home.

Credit card companies have tightened their protections for customers. Their computers are programmed to identify unusual transactions, and the companies quickly contact the cardholder or freeze an account. But that doesn't stop people from applying for new cards or loans in your name or taking other actions.

If you really want to prevent identity theft, consider these steps.

Check Credit Reports

You're entitled to an annual free copy of your credit report from each credit reporting firm and can obtain it at www.annualcreditreport.com. You should exercise this option annually to see if there are any errors or any activity you didn't initiate. Though you should do it, this is a weak step and only a first step. You would be learning about unauthorized credit applications well after the fact. The real benefit of this step is to correct any mistakes in the report, such as having someone else's history incorrectly applied to your report.

Note that obtaining your credit report is not the same as seeing your credit score. The details of credit scores are considered proprietary, and apparently each lender can determine how the score is computed for them.

Destroy All Debit Cards

Many people like debit cards because, unlike credit cards, they draft the amount directly from your checking or other account. You aren't borrowing money, so interest and finance charges aren't imposed.

The downside is that you don't have all the protections of credit cards. Losses from improper use of your credit card are limited to $50 by law. There's no limit on debit card losses, unless the card issuer voluntarily establishes one. If someone gets your debit card and PIN, they quickly can drain your account.

Debit cards also are less attractive after the Dodd–Frank financial regulation law. The law reduced the fees card processors can charge retailers on each transaction. As a result, the card issuers generally eliminated rewards programs and other bonuses. Because of the identity theft potential and lack of benefits, it might be better to switch from debit cards to credit cards.

Freeze Your Credit Identity

Probably the most effective way to avoid identity theft is to freeze your credit reports. You can contact each of the three major credit reporting firms and direct them to freeze your credit status. Then, they won't be allowed to release your information to anyone. With your credit status frozen, even someone who obtained all the details of your identity won't be able to receive approval for new loans or credit cards.

You periodically might want someone to have access to your credit reports. You might apply for a new job or seek a mortgage or auto loan. In that case, you can ask the services to unlock your account for a set time period. Usually, each time you do this costs $5. Unfortunately, you can't authorize release of your credit report only to certain people or firms. You have to freeze or unfreeze your information to everyone.

When you freeze your credit status, you establish a password or PIN. You need this to unfreeze the account. If you lose the PIN, a process that can take months is needed to verify your identity and unfreeze the credit.

Secure Your Information

Identity usually is stolen through unsophisticated methods. Thieves can enter a home or steal a wallet, cellphone, or personal computer and find all the information they need. In general, someone who has your name, address, birth date, and Social Security number can cause a lot of damage.

People often leave access to this information exposed. They enter key information in their smartphones or computers. They leave sensitive documents accessible in their homes. Even if there are no valuable objects in your home, it pays a thief to break in and grab blank checks, old financial statements, and your passport or birth certificate. You can go on a short vacation and have all this information stolen while you're gone. Documents with this information should be shredded and thrown away or securely locked.

This step is especially important for snowbirds or other second home owners.

Consider Credit Monitoring Services

There are a number of services that track the activity on credit reports by one or more of the credit reporting firms.

Each of the free services generally monitors only one credit reporting firm, usually is owned by the credit reporting firm, and tells you which reports it covers. They also want to upgrade you to a fee-paying service. Usually the free reports are issued at a fixed date, so activity could occur in your account some time before you know about it.

There are other services that will monitor your credit for a fee. These firms say they are proactive and will know as soon as there is new activity in your account. They also look for a wider range of activity, such as requests to change your address and let you know immediately of any changes. This proactive approach can stop someone who's stolen your identity from receiving loans or other credit in your name. Most of these firms also will help you restore your credit record and reclaim your identity if it's stolen.

I'm not convinced these services are worth the cost. Many of the services they offer you can obtain free. For example, you can sign up for a Do Not Mail list at www.dmachoice.org and can opt out of prescreened credit card and insurance offerings at www.optoutprescreen.com. This is in addition to www.annualcreditreport.com. Also, there have been problems at some of the firms. Lifelock, for example, reached a settlement with the Federal Trade Commission in 2010. The FTC alleged that Lifelock used deceptive advertising and that its computer security was lacking. Then, in 2015 the FTC filed a complaint alleging that Lifelock violated terms of the 2010 settlement. You receive more protection at lower cost by freezing your credit reports.

These steps won't completely eliminate vulnerability. There are other ways your Social Security number can be obtained, and a thief can use that to file a false tax return in your name and claim a refund, among other things. But the IRS doesn't hold individuals liable for false refunds (though it isn't as generous with employers who are victims of identity theft). These are the strongest measures you can take and will greatly reduce your risk.

Closing the Door to Your Greatest Fraud Risk

Your greatest risk of being scammed or having your identity stolen might be one you don't suspect. The big headlines are generated when information thieves access the databases of major retailers or other well-known businesses. But the headlines are behind the times.

Information thieves have moved on to medical records.

A medical record often has all the information an identity thief needs in one convenient place: birth date, full name, Social Security number, and often insurance and financial account information. All this information is more convenient and accessible to thieves than ever as medical providers comply with the federal mandate to make medical records digital. Paper records are supposed to disappear or be supplemented by digital versions stored on a hard drive.

An entire medical record often sells for $50 on the black market, according to a 2015 article in *The Wall Street Journal*. A crook can do a lot with a medical record. It can be used in the typical identity theft activities of obtaining loans or credit cards, opening new bank accounts, or filing false income tax returns to claim refunds.

Medical records also can be used to obtain medical care, leaving you stuck with copayments and deductibles on that care. You also might face a canceled plan and errors in your medical history that can take a year or longer to correct.

Digital medical records often are shared quite rapidly among insurers and medical providers, making it hard to correct errors. Unlike credit cards and other financial records, there aren't yet standard procedures in place to correct medical records and reduce the consequences of record theft.

Children and the elderly are the usual targets of medical record theft, a crime that victimized about 1.8 million Americans in 2013 and has increased almost 20 percent annually the last couple of years through 2015.

Medical records are sought by overseas crooks who use their digital expertise to probe the databases of medical providers just as they try to infiltrate major corporations and government agencies. Security from these types of attacks is not high on the priority list of most medical providers. Unlike a lot of other large organizations, a medical provider might not even know its database was breached or probed.

Consumers also are behind in protecting themselves, because medical record theft doesn't receive much publicity. Here are a few steps you can take:

- *Avoid providing Social Security and driver's license numbers to medical providers.* They don't need them, except in rare instances.
- *Ask medical providers to remove these numbers from their existing records.* You have the right to have personal information removed from medical records.
- *Treat old medical documents you possess the same way as financial records.* Shred them instead of throwing them away. Any records you retain should be stored securely. This includes bills, receipts, and diagnosis information.
- *You have the right to review and receive a copy of most of your records from medical providers.* The rights are spelled out in the federal regulations at 45 CFR 164.524. Just as you should with credit reports, it's a good idea to take advantage of this right and review your records for incorrect information, fraudulent charges, treatments you didn't receive, and personal information you want removed.
- *Carefully review the "Explanation of Benefits" you receive periodically from your insurer or Medicare.* These statements often are difficult to decipher, but they can reveal whether someone is using your insurance to obtain treatment under your name or a medical provider is submitting improper charges to the insurer. If you don't understand the treatment code listed, call the provider's billing staff for an explanation.

Choosing the Right Retirement Location

The image of the ideal retirement ingrained in the imaginations of most Americans includes a home in a sun-drenched retirement community.

Reality often doesn't match the ideal. Not every retiree moves to a Sun Belt state. Not every retiree who moves to a Sun Belt state enjoys the experience. Some studies show that 25 percent or more of those who retire to Florida leave the state within five years. I've met retirees who admit to choosing the wrong place to retire. Many people don't realize that despite the publicized exodus of seniors to Florida, Arizona, and other states, most retirees never move from their longtime residences.

Only about 37 percent of retirees have moved in retirement, according to a survey taken in 2015 for Merrill Lynch Bank of America by Age Wave. Another 27 percent say they anticipate moving, but it's not clear they actually will move, when, or where. Many say they anticipate they'll have to move some day for health or medical reasons. A hefty 36 percent say they don't anticipate moving in retirement. So, close to 60 percent of retirees didn't move after retiring, and it wasn't clear they ever will, at least not because they want to.

The biggest reason people give for moving or anticipating a move in retirement is to be closer to family, not to be in a warmer climate or near more golf courses.

Another widespread belief is that when most people move in retirement, they downsize. That is, they move into a smaller, less costly home.

Yet, about half of retirees who move in retirement don't downsize, according to the survey. They move into a home that is the same size or even larger than the one they lived in before retirement. The main reason for not downsizing is so there will be room for family and friends to be comfortable during extended visits. Some even say they want enough room so adult children can live with them if they need to.

The top reasons for downsizing are economic. Most want to lower their monthly housing costs or reduce the burden of maintaining the larger home.

Another stereotype is that most retirees move into an age-restricted community, an enclave restricted to those ages 55 and over. In fact, only 7 percent of retirees say they moved into an age-restricted retirement community.

Even when people move in retirement, most don't move far. About 83 percent of those over age 65 who moved in the year before the survey stayed in the same state. Only about 17 percent of those over age 65 who moved the previous year relocated to a different state. Other surveys over the years found that many in move in retirement stay in the same ZIP code.

One of the most important decisions regarding retirement is where to live. Even someone who gets all the retirement financial decisions right will be unhappy if he or she settles in the wrong place. I know, because I've talked to and counseled retirees. Retirement location questions are among the most common, right after questions about investments and estate planning. Complaints and second thoughts about the chosen retirement location also are very common.

The choice of where to live in retirement also is a very personal one. There are numerous surveys and ratings of various retirement locations. I advise prospective retirees not to take these too seriously. Research can't be very thorough when a survey claims to investigate and rank hundreds of locations each year. I also find it a bit curious that the rankings change drastically from year to year. More importantly, a generic ranking system of locations cannot determine the best location for you. The preferences and priorities of a person or group that's compiling a survey aren't likely to be the same as yours.

There are some real secrets to finding the right retirement location. Unless you want to move a lot, follow my guidelines to finding your happy retirement home. With my recommendations you can use the published retirement location guides, but use them in a different way. It is not important which areas are ranked best by any particular guide. What is important is why a location received a particular rating and the details about the area that are described in the survey. What is most important is what *your* values are and how you rank a location. You very likely will put a different priority on some qualities of a location than the publishers of the various guides.

Start with You

To start, ignore all the guides and descriptions of retirement locations. Start with you. Make a list of your interests, hobbies, favorite things to do, and things you dislike. Then list the things you expect to do in retirement. I think it is best if you start with a general list of activities. Then try to make it more specific by focusing on what you expect the typical day, week, or month to be like, and on what you would like to do at certain times of the year.

This exercise is very similar to the one we conducted in Chapter 2 to develop an estimate of your retirement spending. In fact, ideally you should consider where you want to live when developing your retirement spending estimates.

Next, use these interests to compile a list of qualities that are important for the community in which you would like to live. Do you want to live within a certain distance of a golf course, church, shopping, hiking trails, beaches, fishing, or other activities? Or perhaps you want easy access to libraries, museums, theaters, or racetracks. Most people also have a preference about whether to live in a city, suburb, or rural area.

Consider more than "what." Consider "who." Which people or types of people do you want to be around? If you want to spend a lot of time with the friends you have now or with children and grandchildren, that will greatly influence your decision. Keep in mind that one of the keys to a successful retirement is social contact. People who have a lot of contact with friends and family tend to be happier in retirement than others.

Someone who makes friends easily and who looks forward to socializing might consider the whole country. Also consider your neighbors when looking at individual communities. I find that some retirees don't like living in a community that is full of other retirees. They'd rather be in a community of various age groups. Some prefer to be around people of similar education, profession, or intellectual interests. Others like to be around people of varied backgrounds and interests. Which do you prefer?

There also are other characteristics of the area to consider: Climate, terrain, traffic, crime, taxes, job opportunities, and recreational opportunities. Some people have special interests, such as museums or the opera. Some want to be near first-class medical facilities. Make your list as comprehensive as possible before considering even one location.

Survey the Country

Using your list of interests and preferences, you can start with the big picture and knock out large portions of the country. If you want to golf in the winter, you won't be living in the northern parts of the country. If you like to ski or hike in the mountains, you probably don't want to live in Florida. The list will help even those who plan to split time between two or more retirement homes, because it will help narrow down where those homes should or should not be.

Refine Your Search

After having narrowed it down to a few regions in the country, it is time to turn to the websites, glossy magazines, books, and friends for ideas on places that are worth examining. When considering each possible location, in addition to the list of qualities already described, consider the following factors that I've found often loom large in a retiree's daily life but are too often overlooked.

Look at All the Costs.   Sometimes an inexpensive area is not as inexpensive as it seems, at least not for every lifestyle. Every area seems to have its hidden costs. For example, I met a couple who wanted to reduce their expenses in retirement. So they sold their home in a metropolitan suburban area and used about half the sale price to buy a similar-sized home in a low-cost, less-populated area. They pocketed the rest of the sale price and thought they were on easy street.

However, they found many of their routine activities cost more than they expected. Their new area also did not have the discount superstores or the variety of shopping they were used to, so they would drive for an hour or so to find the shopping they wanted. Basic utilities also cost more in the new location. The list of these little costs and inconveniences went on until they realized the true cost of the location wasn't as low as they expected.

It is important to look at the big costs, such as housing, but it is the little daily costs that often surprise retirees. Health insurance and other health care costs vary significantly around the country. There are no reliable rules of thumb, such as "rural areas are always more expensive than urban areas." You have to verify the cost in each specific location. Once a specific location is under consideration, ask an insurer what the cost would be for you in that location.

Food, utilities, and services also can be eye-openers. I once looked at homes in a community and found that two electric utilities reached the end of their service areas in the middle of the community. One serviced half the community, while the other serviced the other half. Residents said that service and prices differed significantly between the two utilities. The cost of water also varies greatly and shouldn't be taken for granted.

The tighter your budget, the more important all these costs become. Once an area is under serious consideration, take your list of proposed retirement activities and budget and see what each item would cost in the new area. To avoid surprises later, actually take a trip to the grocery store and contact the local utilities to find out what they charge.

Make Sure Low Taxes Are for Real.   There's nothing better for an area's image than to be considered low tax. The label often sticks for decades, even after residents are paying higher taxes. Unfortunately, it often is a false label. For example, many people consider an area to be low tax if it doesn't have an income tax. But the lack of an income tax often is offset by high sales taxes, real estate taxes, personal property taxes, and intangibles tax (which is imposed on investment portfolios). There also can be stuff taxes added by the locality that that greatly increase phone and electric bills.

There also are hidden taxes. Some localities have low property taxes, but they don't provide services that are routinely provided in high tax areas. This fools people who come from areas where, for example, trash collection and other services are included in their property taxes. Only after moving do people find out that in addition to property taxes, they must pay separate fees for these other services.

Another tax trap is that there often are high-tax localities within low-tax states. Localities often set their own rates for property taxes and can impose their own sales taxes. Sometimes a locality can add its own income tax. In these cases, a difference of only a few miles can make a big difference in tax bills.

Contact the local and state tax departments for details about all the local taxes. The Chamber of Commerce might also have good information that summarizes all taxes. Someone who can afford it should meet with a local CPA for details about the taxes and fees. In many areas, real estate agents are required to disclose additional fees imposed on homeowners or they will do so if asked.

Be sure you get information on state and local income taxes, sales taxes, real estate and personal property taxes, and intangibles taxes. Also, take a good look at estate taxes. Sometimes higher inheritance taxes imposed by a retirement relocation can cost your heirs a bundle.

Consider Year-Round Climate and Lifestyle.   Once I was golfing in South Carolina. The starter on the course revealed that he was a retiree from New Jersey who had moved south to avoid snow in the winter. But he found he disliked the South Carolina summers even more than winters in New Jersey. "If I had known about the mosquitoes," he said, "I never would have moved here."

One classic mistake is to retire to an area because of a good vacation or short trip there. Soon after moving, the retiree learns that the daily life in the area is not as enjoyable as a short vacation. Another mistake is to move to a warm area to get a break from dealing with winters. A substantial minority of people who do this eventually change their minds. Sometimes people learn that they really like having four seasons, or at least three. Maybe they don't want to move back to where it is cold six months of the year, but they also don't want year-round summer. Or they find that while winters can be pleasant in a warm climate, the summers can be unbearably hot.

Find Your Community

By now, your choice probably has been narrowed down to a few areas. Now it is time to consider individual communities or subdivisions in these areas. It is possible to pick the perfect area in which to live but to choose a neighborhood or community that causes unhappiness or at least reduces the pleasure of living in the area. Here are a few things to consider when searching for a community.

Demographics.   Florida became a magnet for retirees starting in the 1960s. Now I hear from many near-retirees and new retirees that they don't like Florida and even Arizona retirement communities because the populations are so old. They want to live with a younger, more active group. In addition to age, try to learn about the interests and activities of the community. Some communities have a range of clubs, sports leagues, and social activities. Other communities have more limited activities or have attracted residents who basically stay at home and have a few close friends.

Some people want a leisure-minded retirement community, where the focus is on golf, tennis, and card playing. Others want a learning-oriented atmosphere with a college nearby or with classes, speeches, and lectures. Don't assume every community has all types of activities. Many tend to emphasize some over others.

Security.   Americans of all ages seem more interested in secure communities each year. Do you want a gated community with its own security patrol? Do you want an active neighborhood watch? Some communities also have security measures built into individual living units.

Associations.   In the last few decades, homeowners' and community associations have become another branch of government. State laws usually let an association do pretty much whatever a majority of its members want. That can be good or bad.

An effective association maintains property values and quality of life. But some associations pass detailed, restrictive rules and enforce them to the letter. Rules might encompass the size and design of mailboxes, lawn and patio furniture, and decks. One community association in my area once ordered an entire block of homes to take down their decks because the builder made each one six inches wider than allowed. It is not a bad idea to get a feel for the power and activities of the local association. Some retirement location experts advise you to review association and board meeting minutes for the last year or two to see what the current controversies are and how the group works.

Perhaps more important than the rules and regulations is the financial condition of the community. A homeowners' or community association usually is responsible for the maintenance of common areas and perhaps some other assets. Some HOAs keep dues low by not investing in maintenance or setting aside funds for the inevitable time when assets will need major repair or replacements. Instead, the unfortunate people who are homeowners when those times come must pay special assessments. Check the financial condition of the HOA, especially its level of reserves and how it calculates how much to put in the reserves.

Types of Retirement Housing

Housing for older Americans is a booming industry. There now are many different types of housing available to seniors. There are variations of each type, and some types are common only to some areas of the country. Let's take a brief course in the senior housing options.

Traditional Housing

Of course, a retiree can go into any community and rent or buy an apartment, condo, townhouse, or house just as any adult can. In fact, more seniors probably live in traditional housing rather than any special senior housing.

Planned Communities

Some of these are specifically restricted to seniors, while others use pricing and marketing to ensure that residents primarily will be seniors. These communities tend to differ from regular subdivisions and developments primarily because they have amenities that are especially desirable to active retirees. Golf and other recreation facilities often are prime features. A community center with an active agenda usually is an important element. Housing usually is single family homes or condominiums or both, with design features that are attractive to seniors (examples include one floor level, door handles instead of knobs, and security). The HOA might be responsible for maintenance of all yards and sometimes the outside of all housing units. Usually there is no medical care element to these communities. They are for independent, active people who happen to be retired.

Independent Living

In some places this is called congregate care. These facilities are for seniors who need a little bit of help for activities such as cooking, cleaning, and driving or who anticipate needing some help in the near future. Housing usually is in apartments or condominiums but can be single family homes. Onsite amenities usually include recreation facilities, a convenience store, dining rooms, meeting rooms, a library, social areas, and television rooms. Often there is a shuttle service to local shopping and medical offices, and regular outings are organized. For many, independent living is like being at college.

The buildings usually feature extra-wide hallways and doorways to accommodate walkers, wheelchairs, and motorized scooters, along with other senior-friendly features. Housecleaning and other services usually are available. But, again, onsite medical facilities are limited. Usually the housing unit is purchased or a large deposit is made, and a monthly fee is paid. Additional fees might be paid based on other services used.

Assisted Living Facilities

This often is described as an alternative to nursing homes, but it really is not. Limited medical care is provided at assisted living facilities (which is one reason their basic daily room rate is considerably less than a nursing home rate). Assisted living facilities are for someone who needs help in one or two daily living activities (dressing, bathing, eating, housekeeping, walking, etc.) or perhaps wants help with cooking, cleaning, and similar activities. It is not for someone who needs physical rehabilitation or skilled nursing care. Residents generally live in dormitory-style rooms and have common dining and social areas.

Assisted living facilities generally have to comply with far fewer regulations than nursing homes. Many have a nurse or other licensed medical personnel on site for only part of the day and there are few or no medical facilities on site.

Group homes usually offer assisted living services in townhomes or single-family homes with 15 or fewer residents. These might be subject to less regulation than larger assisted living facilities.

Nursing Homes

These are for individuals who need physical therapy or skilled nursing care on a regular basis. Usually, the care is provided by nurses and other medical professionals under the direction of a physician. Nurses usually are on duty 24 hours a day.

Continuing Care Retirement Communities

The CCRC is a relatively new but fast-growing type of senior housing. CCRCs attempt to put the main types of senior housing in one community:

independent living, assisted living, and a nursing home. Some CCRCs also have townhomes and detached homes in the community.

A resident initially moves to a CCRC when healthy and starts in an independent living apartment, townhome, or detached home. After that, a resident or spouse can move into assisted living and the nursing home as needs require. If a resident never needs either specialized facility, that's fine. But as one ages, there might be the need to move into one of the other facilities. The independent living, assisted living, and nursing home usually are in one building or are connected by walkways so that residents do not need to go outside to visit someone. The community also usually includes the types of amenities found in independent living.

Methods of financing a residence in a CCRC vary. Most often, a large lump sum is paid up front to live in the CCRC. This sum usually is fully or partially refundable to the resident's heirs, though the refund right might disappear after 10 years or so. (In some CCRCs the housing unit is purchased outright. The owner or heirs can sell it.) There also is a monthly fee, which might be the same for everyone or might depend on the services received. In return for these payments, the resident is guaranteed care in the appropriate facility for life.

In recent years, the communities have offered other options. The other options generally require you to pay a lower fee when entering the CCRC, but the fees you pay cover less of the assisted living and nursing home care when you need it. You might have to pay for the services when needed at the market rate.

There are two factors you need to review carefully before deciding on a CCRC. One factor is fee increases. Often there are few or no restrictions on the CCRC's right to increase the monthly fees. Monthly fee increases of 4 percent to 6 percent annually compounded over 10 or more years really add up. Ask about the CCRC's right to raise fees and its history of fee increases. Additional fees are another factor. Ask what services aren't included in the basic fee and what the fees are for those other services. You might find that you're likely to be charged more than the basic fee.

Planned communities generally are suitable for any active retiree. Most senior citizens don't start seeking out the other facilities until their mid-seventies, unless there is a medical problem. So someone younger than 75 who lives in an independent living community or a CCRC might be one of the youngest residents. But some people decide they want to move only once in retirement, so they move to a CCRC or similar community early in retirement.

Someone considering a move into a planned community or CCRC should be aware that the financial strength of the community is very important. You should do all you can to check the financial stability of the firm that will provide the services and lifetime guarantees. In the 1980s, there was some overbuilding in senior housing, and the developers of some communities went bankrupt. It also is important to look at the bylaws, covenants, and other regulations of the community, and know who determines what level of care is needed and when a move into a different level of care can be made.

CCRCs often aren't required to provide the same level of disclosure as HOAs and some other types of communities. They also aren't as subject to as much regulation as some other options. You should gather whatever information you can about the financial condition of the community and any entities related to it before making a decision.

To learn more about CCRCs, consult the websites of AARP and LeadingAge (formerly the American Association of Homes and Services for the Aging). Also check with your local Area Office on Aging and the Long-Term Care Ombudsman for help selecting the right place for you.

Avoiding the Boomerang

The boomerang is when someone retires to a location, decides it was a mistake, and moves back to the original location or somewhere else. It occurs when the original decision was made in haste or without considering all the factors. Here is how to avoid the boomerang:

- *Start the retirement location decision making process about two years before a move might actually happen.* That allows enough time to take all the steps recommended.
- *Don't commit right away.* It is a good idea to rent a place in a new location before buying. Ideally, the rental should be for at least a year in order to get familiar with year-round weather and activities. It also provides time to locate the most convenient and desirable community in the area. An alternative is to rent for a few months at a time each year for a few years before moving. That might provide enough exposure to the area to make a good final decision and also might make for a smoother transition between the old home and the new one.
- *Get involved in the community.* Though renting, act like a permanent member of the community. Get involved in your activities of interest, meet people, and learn about the area. Try to develop the kind of routine that is anticipated for the retirement years.
- *Decide what size home to have after the move.* Be sure to consider factors such as how often family or others will visit, whether an office area is needed, and how many belongings will be in the home.
- *Check financial statements before buying.* Many seniors buy in new communities. It is important to be assured that the community and its amenities will be finished as planned. That means checking out the financial condition of the developer. Also check on the condition of the community association. On the financial statement, see if the fund balance is positive

or negative. Look to see if there is a reserve for future obligations and maintenance; if there isn't, then the current fees probably are too low. Ask about the current level of dues and about past fee increases. Check the current occupancy or sales rates of units. If things are slow, financial trouble could be ahead. Be sure there isn't any outstanding litigation listed in the footnotes to the financial statements. You also might want to review the minutes of board and association meetings for the last year or two to see if maintenance, improvements, or the level of dues have been major issues.

■ *Finally, determine the full cost of a move and be sure it is acceptable.* Moving a household full of goods plus cars and other items can cost tens of thousands of dollars. That expense, plus buying and selling costs, can add up to a stiff price for the relocation.

Most people want to make their retirement location decision only once. To make the right decision, get a head start and be sure to consider all the angles. Finally, consider this option. If there is an area you like for a special reason—say, Florida sunshine for the winter—consider becoming a snowbird. You can rent in that location for a few months during the year and stay in your current home the rest of the year.

New World of Adult Living Choices

Traditional retirement living and housing choices are on the way out. The new generation of retirees is looking for new living experiences. Developers are obliging, giving older Americans more choices than ever. These new choices include building communities outside the traditional retirement havens of Florida and Arizona, but they involve much more than that. The new choices include different types of housing and living arrangements and various types of activities within the communities themselves.

One reason for the new senior living choices is that retirees are relatively young. In many adult communities, about a third of the residents are under age 65. Those under age 55 can amount to 10 percent or more of the residents.

Another reason for the changes is that today's retirements are longer and have more stages than in the past, generally up to three stages. In the first stage of retirement, often at least one spouse continues to work at least part-time. In this stage, the retirees might move to a smaller home but want to stay in the same general area to maintain personal and business relationships and living patterns. In the next stage, retirees might move to a completely different area, perhaps somewhere with warmer weather. In the third stage, retirees move closer to family and friends. Each stage has a range of living choices.

Keys to a Successful Retirement

P eople often tell me that they failed at retirement the first time. And the second. And the third.

These aren't people with serious financial problems. They didn't cut short retirement because they needed the money. Instead, they devoted their retirement planning time and resources to the financial aspects. They neglected the other elements of retirement planning, and those often are the more important parts.

Most retirement planning focuses on the financial side of retirement, which we also can call the hard side of retirement planning. Finances certainly are important to a happy and successful retirement. Yet, they aren't the end of the story or even the most important contributors to retirement success.

The most difficult parts of retirement planning usually are what can be called the soft side of planning. You need to decide how to spend all that time you used to spend working. You need activities that fulfill you and give you a sense of purpose. There's a lot of time to fill, and the amount of time only grows as people live longer and are retired longer. The biggest nonfinancial mistake people make in their retirement planning is neglecting the soft side of planning, and it is the source of many unsuccessful retirements.

The problem is so widespread that in recent years many professional advisors adopted an approach that sometimes is called life planning.

Instead of diving directly into a client's finances, the advisor instead gets to know the client. A proper plan can't be developed until the advisor knows a client's likes and dislikes, hobbies, family, goals, and other interests. In other words, what is important to the person and what does the person enjoy doing? How will that change in retirement? Only after obtaining such knowledge can the financial planning process begin.

That's why we started this journey in Chapter 2 by having you envision the regular activities you want to do in retirement. Only after that could an estimate of your retirement spending be made. Retirement planning begins with deciding how you plan to spend your time. Knowing *you* is the start of retirement planning. It is the essential first step to both the hard side and soft side of planning.

The first step in retirement planning should be to imagine the life you want after your current career. Determine how you'd like to spend your time for at least the first few years and then how that might change in the following years. Where will you live? How do you want to live day to day, month to month, and over the course of a year? Do you know people who already are living that way? Set your life goals first, not your income or asset accumulation goals.

As more than one retiree has told me, retirement can be hard work. The failure of many people to do this work is why people fail at retirement and why some studies indicate that the over-60 age group has higher-than-average rates of depression, substance abuse, and suicide.

The point of saving and investing for retirement is so you can spend time doing things you really want to do. The nest egg sometimes is called *walk away money* or *freedom money*. Being financially secure is helpful to a successful and happy retirement, but it doesn't ensure one. You need more than money.

Many of those who took one or more tries at retirement didn't have a vision of what retirement would be like and how they would be active and fulfilled. They had to try one or more times before they figured out how to be successful at retirement.

The Vacation Retirement

There's a lot of confusion these days about what retirement is or should be.

We all know the stereotypical retirement popularized by those who retired in the 1950s through the 1980s, now known as the vacation retirement. Retired people would spend their time in leisure activities, essentially doing whatever they wanted. It is almost like a second childhood.

When I started advising people about retirement some years ago, it was clear I was helping people reach a point when they would stop working. They looked forward to the vacation retirement. The question I received most often was, "How soon can I retire?" Ceasing work as soon as possible was the goal.

Of course, that was a manufactured image and lifestyle. The surveys indicate only a minority of U.S. retirees pursued that lifestyle. Some believe insurance companies and others in the financial services industry created the image to give people an incentive to save and invest. Others think real estate and travel interests were the creators. I'm not one who believes people can be so easily manipulated by commercial interests. The early generations of retirees probably wanted the vacation retirement after decades of working and the prospect retirement wouldn't last too many years. At this point, it doesn't matter what the origins of the vacation retirement were. While the vacation retirement is what most people associated with the word *retirement*, it certainly wasn't retirement for everyone and probably will apply to fewer people going forward.

It might still be the retirement for you. Now, however, many people say they want to work after age 65. About 70 percent of baby boomers say so, according to AARP surveys. A growing (but still minority) of those over 40 say they won't ever retire.

Though it's a big change, it's not surprising. People are healthier and living longer. Many want to continue contributing and to have meaning in their lives. Others need the money.

Many people need and want the experiences that come with a job and work. Foremost is a sense of purpose and achievement. Many people also benefit from the structure of work. The "every day is Saturday" model of retirement is not for everyone, especially those who still are fairly healthy and active. They don't want to plan each day from a blank slate. They want the structure a job provides for at least part of each week. Being in the workplace also provides regular exposure to new things and people. With the vacation retirement, you wake up one day and all those things are gone. You have to recreate them.

For most of us, the first thing we need to do is drop the assumption of "retirement." We'll be retiring from a particular job or career. But we'll be moving on to other activities, and it's likely those activities will change over the next two or three decades. We might take different jobs, start new careers, or engage in volunteer activities. Many people probably won't actually "retire" until sometime in their 70s or later. Very early in your retirement planning you need to consider the lifestyle you want in retirement. Are you looking forward to the vacation retirement, or are you hoping for something with more structure and purpose?

Two Important, Overlooked Issues

Throughout this book I indicated that many retirement plans overlook key issues. Some don't factor inflation in their spending plans. Others don't pay enough attention to medical expenses and long-term care. Those are two examples of frequent oversights. There are also a couple of soft issues that frequently are neglected in planning.

Where Your Spouse Fits

A few years back, an organization I was associated with had a few high-level tasks that needed to be done. No one at the top executive levels had time to take on the additional work.

The solution was to bring back on a temporary basis a former senior executive.

It worked out well. He had retired recently, so he was current on the issues and had not committed his time elsewhere. He stayed for about six months, completed the projects, and solved the problems. Then, he went back to retirement.

A few months later, he and his wife were invited to the organization's holiday party. During the party, his wife pulled aside the senior executives and asked, "Can't you find him something else to do? He's getting in my way at home."

Common failures of the retirement plans of many married people are they don't realize how retirement will affect the other spouse, and the spouses don't coordinate their plans. Each spouse makes many assumptions about the other during the planning, but they often don't check with each other to be sure the assumptions agree.

One set of problems centers around the daily or weekly routines. Spouses often have trouble harmonizing these activities. One spouse often expected they would spend most of their time together, while the other complains that spouse is in the way or expects to be entertained all day.

This problem largely can be resolved by beginning retirement planning the way I suggest. Imagine your day-to-day retirement life. Each spouse should do this. Give the daily and weekly routines some thought and discuss the ideas with your spouse. If your ideas match up, that's great. Otherwise, it's another part of the retirement plan you'll have to work on.

The day-to-day issues are not the only potential problems between spouses. Big-picture retirement issues also have to be coordinated, which many couples don't do. Fidelity Investments periodically has a survey conducted on the issues. The 2007 version found that 61 percent of spouses disagreed on what the primary source of retirement income would be; 41 percent disagreed on whether at least one spouse would work during "retirement"; and more than 33 percent of couples disagreed about their amount of their life insurance coverage and expected retirement ages. Finances are only part of a retirement plan. Couples need to discuss and decide the other issues.

Caring for Your Mind and Spirit

A very important factor in establishing a successful post-career period is social interaction or human connectivity. Your social relationships are more important to your well-being than money is. More and more research makes this clear.

The relationships could be with family, friends, co-workers, and others in your community. It's not clear why this matters, but regular and close interaction with others is important to maintaining health and a positive outlook. An important point is that the number of relationships or contacts isn't key. What really matters is the depth or closeness of relationships.

You can read some details in two books with similar titles.

The Longevity Project by Howard S. Friedman and Leslie R. Martin analyzed data accumulated from 1,500 individuals over 80 years. The Project periodically interviewed the participants and had them complete questionnaires. Among its findings are that close involvement with friends and communities improves health and longevity and is more important as we age.

The Longevity Prescription by Dr. Robert Butler appears at first to be the latest in a long line of books by doctors in their 80s giving their personal prescriptions for a long life. Butler died in 2010 at age 83. In fact, Butler devoted much of his life to research on aging in the United States and offers much more than his personal experience and reflections.

Reviewing his research and that of others, Butler identified eight keys to a long, healthy life. Two of them are nurturing your relationships and connecting with your community. Butler said social connectivity is so important that, rather than struggling to stay in their homes, most Americans around 80 should seek to move into senior living communities.

Key Retirement Mistakes to Avoid

Most of this book is focused on actions you should take toward a successful retirement. Sometimes, however, the best way to have good results is to avoid mistakes. We have enough experience with retirement to know the major events and actions that are likely to lead to unsuccessful retirements. Avoid these and you're well on the way to a successful retirement. Some of these we discussed earlier in the book, but they bear repeating here.

Debt

Once it was rare for someone to retire with debt, even a home mortgage. Now, the number of retirement-age Americans with substantial debt is increasing. In retirement you have reduced flexibility and substantially less potential to earn a higher income. At the same time, negative financial surprises are more likely, especially high medical or long-term care costs.

The combination of high debt and large surprise expenses can be financially devastating in retirement. You can control your level of debt. Less debt means you have more flexibility and a larger cushion against surprises. For most people, it's better to eliminate debt in retirement.

Spending Too Rapidly

Surveys of retirees and preretirees indicate consistently that many believe they can safely spend 7 percent or more of their assets each year without the risk of running out of money. As we discussed, financial planners and academics who studied retirement spending believe the safe spending rate is much lower. Many say the safe spending rate is around 4 percent of the retirement nest egg. In Chapter 4, we discussed reasons why the safe spending rate might be even lower. Be sure to carefully consider the rate at which you safely can spend your nest egg.

Uncovered Major Medical Expenses

Medicare doesn't cover all your medical expenses, as we discussed in Chapter 6. Realize the potential risk from high medical expenses and use the strategies we discussed to avoid spending too much out of pocket on medical expenses and how to protect yourself from high medical expenses through insurance.

Helping Others

These days, many retirees are overextending themselves to help their younger loved ones. That's understandable, but it's dangerous. You're likely to spend down your nest egg too fast, and ultimately that will leave both you and the younger generation without any financial support. Help for younger generations must be affordable for you and shouldn't be open-ended or without expectations of progress by the younger generation.

Flying Solo

The data are clear that married couples do better financially in retirement than singles. That's partly because too many retirement plans don't include the contingency that one spouse will pass away, costing the household Social Security and other income sources. A solid plan includes financial security for a surviving spouse.

Failing to Adapt

A retirement plan is important. Equally important is to realize it is only a plan. It shouldn't be treated as a one-time exercise that serves as a roadmap to be followed without deviation. A plan is based on a large number of assumptions. It also is based on current laws and circumstances. Actual results are likely to vary quite a bit from the assumptions built into the plan over time. You need to review the plan regularly. Determine where the plan assumptions no longer are valid. Then, revise the plan as needed to stay on course. Don't wait too long to review the plan and consider the changes that need to be made. An annual review means relatively small adjustments each year. Waiting longer to review could mean substantial adjustments will be needed.

Keeping Up with Changes

As just stated, things change. Sometimes circumstances change. Sometimes we learn something new or realize that what we thought we knew wasn't true. That's a theme of this book and the previous version. You can't assume that what you knew or what worked for you years ago still is valid today.

Here are a couple of good examples from the nonfinancial world.

It's widely accepted that people experience cognitive decline as they age. It happens at different rates for different people, but it's been widely accepted that after around age 30, memory and certain mental abilities decline.

Newer research, however, adds to our knowledge and refines that information. The new information calls into question a lot of the conclusions from the early research and shows how we can use our aging minds to our advantage.

It turns out the cognitive tests that are the basis for what most people believe about aging minds were biased in favor of younger people. First, they were biased because of the way the tests were conducted. Younger people were used to taking those types of tests in those types of environments, so they were likely to score somewhat better than older people.

More importantly, the tests were biased because they were carefully structured to minimize the influence of experience on the results. The scientists wanted to measure only raw cognitive ability.

In other words, the tests tested artificial things. In most real-world decision making, experience and knowledge are important. Experience and knowledge become wisdom, and wisdom leads to better decisions.

The bottom line is that older people may process things a bit slower than younger people, but when they take the time to make decisions, older people often make better decisions.

It's important that you know this, because studies also show that people's beliefs about aging influence their behavior. For example, people who have negative stereotypes about aging tend to show greater memory decline than those with positive views of aging.

More importantly, you also can use this new information to improve your cognitive ability and keep your brain young. The best way to do that is to learn new things. Most people believe the way to prevent cognitive decline is to keep the brain working. That's what the first wave of research on brain health indicated. That spawned a wave of older people carrying around crossword puzzle and Sudoku books.

The latest research indicates that learning new things from time to time is better than doing puzzles and games. The brain seems to be more flexible and resilient when it is forced to learn new tasks and information instead of applying or remembering things already known.

Stay abreast of what's new, and your mind will stay fresh.

Another fact everyone knows is that exercise improves health and longevity. The standard advice is to engage in at least a minimum amount of physical activity, but that more is better for most people.

The advice changes and is refined, however, as more data are compiled and analyzed.

Data from the Copenhagen City Heart Study, which has been conducted since 1976, found that male runners lived on average 6.2 years longer than the nonjoggers, and for females the benefit was 5.6 years.

But more exercise apparently is better only to a point. Deeper analysis found those who ran more than four hours a week at 7 miles per hour or faster lost most or all of the benefits of exercise. The greatest health and longevity benefits went to those who ran 1.0 to 2.4 miles per week at a rate of 5 to 7 miles per hour. This group also abstained from vigorous exercise at least two days a week.

This study and others support the notion that too much and too strenuous exercise can damage the heart and other parts of the body. While exercise is better for health and longevity than no exercise, too much exercise can have the same effects as no exercise.

These are two examples of how something many people believe, that seems intuitive, and that becomes a rule of thumb turns out to be not quite true as we learn more and analyze the data in more detail.

Things That Really Matter

We focused most of *The New Rules of Retirement* on your personal finances. We strove to cover all the key financial aspects of retirement and retirement planning.

But the point of this chapter is that there's a heck of a lot more to a successful retirement than money, and a substantial amount of money won't necessarily make your retirement happy or successful. Many people retire once, and then go back to work. A substantial minority of people "retire" several times before it sticks. Lack of satisfaction is what drives them back to work.

Periodically, I review the latest studies of the relationship between money and happiness. By and large, the studies show that once the basic needs of life are met, more money doesn't lead to more happiness. This is true across many different countries, cultures, and demographic groups. Other things lead to happiness and satisfaction, and you have to include these in your retirement plan.

In recent years, the money and happiness studies have tried to dive deeper into the issue.

In 2013, Emily Esfahani Smith wrote a couple of articles in *The Atlantic* discussing the deeper studies. The research indicates that happiness is different from purpose or meaning. People tend to report being happy when their lives are easy and they can have or do what they want. But happiness is fleeting. More lasting satisfaction comes from lives with purpose, even if that makes life difficult for a while. In fact, striving for happiness, wanting to be happy, and planning for happiness don't increase happiness and could contribute to unhappiness.

Most studies of happiness indicate that happy people tend to have a lot of social interaction, are optimistic, and are physically active, among other attributes. Yet, not all people who report being happy are satisfied. Having a purpose makes people more satisfied and, more importantly, makes them feel their lives are meaningful.

That's why many people become somewhat depressed after retiring or losing their jobs. They've lost a lot of their purpose in life, and their lives start to lack meaning.

In your retirement planning, be sure to include one or more things that will give you purpose and a feeling of being meaningful. You don't have to strive to do great things to have a purpose. Volunteering, working part-time, or helping family members or neighbors provide many people enough purpose to give their daily lives meaning.

You still need to plan your finances to be sure you have the time to seek happiness and purpose. But be aware that financial planning isn't the end of retirement planning and won't lead to a successful retirement by itself.

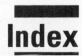

Index

References to figures are given in *italic* type. References to tables are given in **bold** type.

A TIME
FOR TRUMPETS

THE AMERICAN SOLDIER
Staff Sgt. Joseph Arnaldo, New Bedford, Mass.

THE UNTOLD STORY OF THE BATTLE OF THE BULGE

A
Time
for
Trumpets

Charles B. MacDonald

Perennial
An Imprint of HarperCollins*Publishers*

Photographs are courtesy of the United States Army and the individuals pictured (or their relatives) with the exception of the following: German photographs courtesy *Bibliothek für Zeitgeschichte*, Günter von der Weiden, and the Still Picture Branch, National Archives: Strong, Williams, de Guingand, and preparing to execute Skorzeny's men, Imperial War Museum; Vandenberg, Smithsonian Institution; and the ENIGMA machine, National Security Agency.

HarperCollins books may be purchased for educational, business, or sales promotional use. For information please write: Special Markets Department, HarperCollins Publishers Inc., 10 East 53rd Street, New York, NY 10022.

First Quill edition published 1997.

Reprinted in Perennial 2002.

Designed by Bernard Schleifer

Library of Congress Cataloging-in-Publication Data

MacDonald, Charles Brown, 1922-1990.
    A time for trumpets: the untold story of the battle of the bulge/
Charles B. MacDonald.
        Bibliography: p.
        Includes index.
        1. Ardannes, Battle of the, 1944-1945. I. Title.
D756.5.A7M26   1984   940.54'21   84-9043
ISBN 0-688-15157-4

08 09 10 QW 20 19 18 17

For my brother, Rae,
  his wife, Nannie,
  and theirs,
and for the American soldiers and airmen
  who fought in the Ardennes.

Contents

CONTENTS

BOOK IV: THE SHOULDERS

BOOK V: DAMS AGAINST THE TIDE

BOOK VI: THE ROAD BACK

A TIME
FOR TRUMPETS

Prologue

Located in western reaches of the Ardennes region of Belgium, the village of Bande had little distinction. It was just another farming village, lacking the narrow, winding, cobblestoned streets and mountain-like setting of so many villages and towns that help make the Ardennes a picture postcard region.

In early September, 1944, on either side of the main highway through the village—the Grand' Rue—stood a cluster of ten to twelve red brick buildings, mostly dwellings but some with small shops on the ground floor. One was the Café de la Poste. Along a winding side road up a gently sloping hill were other houses belonging mostly to farmers, as might be discerned from their attached barns and from compost heaps almost always located near the front door. At the top of the hill was a small church of drab gray native stone. Much of the nearby land was cultivated, but two or three miles away on every side were forests.

Since less than a thousand people lived in Bande, it was of insufficient importance for the German Army to station occupation troops in the village. The entire region fell under the jurisdiction of the *Kreis-kommandant* in Bastogne, twenty-four miles to the southeast, and there was a detachment of *Feldgendarmerie* eight miles to the northwest in Marche. In a nearby forest, close to a hundred German soldiers lived in wooden barracks, their duty to guard Russian prisoners of war who worked in an ammunition depot.

During the first days of September, 1944, the exhilaration of impending liberation was in the air in Bande. Adding to the excitement, word spread among the villagers that a group of Belgian resistance fighters of the *Armée Secrète* had moved into a nearby wood. Such was the elation of approaching freedom after four long years of omnipresent German soldiers—their hobnailed boots, their imperious commands, their edicts, their requisitions, their unannounced knocks in the night that might mean

9

a loved one seized for deportation—that some of the villagers defiantly
displayed the black, red, and yellow Belgian flag. *A bas les Boches*!

Before daylight on September 5, men of the *Armée Secrète* attacked
the German barracks at the ammunition depot. Three German soldiers
died in the attack. The next day, the Germans surrounded the center of
Bande along the Grand' Rue, ordered the inhabitants from their homes,
and systematically put the torch to every building.

Two days later, on September 8, as troops of the American 9th Infantry Division approached, the last of the German soldiers hurriedly departed. As they left, some of them shook their fists at the obviously
exultant inhabitants. "We'll be back!" they shouted.*

On September 16, 1944, the man who had plunged the world into the
most devastating war in the history of mankind, Adolf Hitler, Chancellor
of Germany and self-styled Führer, summoned a number of senior officers
to his study. It was in a huge, underground steel-reinforced concrete
bunker within the *Wolfschanze* (Wolf's Lair), Hitler's field headquarters in
the swampy pine forest of Gorlitz in East Prussia. Those summoned had
come to constitute a kind of household military staff. Among them was one
of the few wearing the red stripes of the General Staff on their trews whose
advice Hitler still sought and sometimes heeded, the head of the operations
staff of the *Oberkommando der Wehrmacht*, or *OKW* (Armed Forces High
Command), General Alfred Jodl.

The officers were waiting when Hitler entered the study, his shoulders
sagging, his face drained of color, looking considerably older than his
fifty-four years. Although he had recovered from most of the injuries
incurred not quite two months before when conspirators within the army
had tried to assassinate him by setting off a bomb, smuggled into a conference in a briefcase, he still had a ruptured right eardrum and a sometimes uncontrollable twitching of his right arm. He also had spells of
dizziness and a persistent sinus headache. The Führer's voice had become
hoarse (it would later be determined because of a benign growth on his
vocal chords), and he sometimes had such severe stomach spasms that it
was almost impossible for him to keep from crying out, an affliction (it
would also be determined later) attributable to pills prescribed for
flatulence by his personal physician, who was unaware that they contained strychnine and atropine. A steady diet of those pills had turned his
skin yellow, as if he had jaundice, and that very morning, before calling
the officers to his study, Hitler had had what was probably a mild coro-
nary, the third in less than a week.

Taking a seat at his desk, Hitler asked Jodl to sum up the situation on
the Western Front. Jodl first noted the strength of the opposing forces,
which was heavily in favor of the Western Allies—Great Britain, France,

---

*Citations for all direct quotes are part of the bibliography.

and the United States. Of more than a million German casualties incurred over the last three months, said Jodl, almost half had been in the West.

The German troops, he went on, were continuing their withdrawal from southern France, and in northeastern France they were trying to form a new line based upon sturdy old forts dating from the Franco-Prussian War. In the north they were forming new lines along canals and rivers in the Netherlands or falling back from Belgium into the border fortifications, the West Wall. There was one spot of particular concern, added Jodl, referring to a convoluted, heavily forested region encompassing eastern Belgium and much of the Grand Duchy of Luxembourg, where the Americans were attacking and the Germans had almost nothing: the Ardennes.

At the word "Ardennes," Hitler sat erect and ordered Jodl to stop. A long pause followed.

"I have made a momentous decision," the Führer said at last, the firmness of his voice belying his weakened condition, his blue eyes alight with a fervor that nobody had seen since the attempt on his life. "I shall go over to the offensive, that is to say"—he slapped one hand down on a map that lay across his desk— "here, out of the Ardennes, with the objective, Antwerp!"

With those words, Adolf Hitler set in motion preparations for a battle that was to assume epic proportions, the greatest German attack in the West since the campaign of 1940 had brought down the Netherlands, Belgium, Luxembourg, and France in swift and ignominious defeat. It was destined to involve more than a million men and to precipitate an unparalleled crisis for the Allied armies. It was also to involve one of the most egregious failures in the history of American battlefield intelligence. Yet it was also to become the greatest battle ever fought by the United States Army.

It was cold. A damp, penetrating cold, typical for the Grand Duchy of Luxembourg in the second week of December.

Elise Delé and her son Jean plodded through heavy mist along a deserted highway that followed the west bank of the little Our River. To Elise, there was something almost eerie about returning to her village, Bivels, from which every living soul and even the pigs and cows had been evacuated. Yet she badly needed to get to her farmhouse on the steep slope overlooking the village, the house she had long shared with her husband, Mathias, until the Germans in October had taken him away. She had to get warmer clothes for herself and for Jean. Early that morning, December 10, with the approval of the civil authorities in Vianden (not quite two miles from Bivels), she and Jean had set out, Jean pulling a small cart in which to carry back their belongings.

They had passed the first house in the village and were approaching the second when two German soldiers appeared at the door. When they beckoned, Jean dropped the handle of the cart and ran. Elise ran, too, but the soldiers quickly overtook her; it was easier for a thirteen-year-old boy to get away than a woman of forty-one.

At the soldiers' order, Elise went with them across a temporary footbridge over the Our and up a sharp incline beyond to what appeared to be a low-level command post in a concrete bunker of the West Wall. There a young German officer asked what Elise knew about the American soldiers in and around Vianden.

She knew little. The Americans had a post halfway up the steep, cobblestoned main street of Vianden, she said, perhaps eighteen or twenty men. That was all. Those were the only Americans she had seen.

The questioning at an end, the officer appeared to be embarrassed by Elise's presence, as if he was at a loss to know what to do with her; but he refused her every entreaty to be allowed to return to Bivels. At last he put her with some soldiers in a truck heading east.

Elise had no idea where the soldiers were taking her, but when they turned onto a main road, she recognized it as that leading to the town of Bitburg, eighteen miles inside Germany. When they got to Bitburg, the truck stopped at the schoolhouse, and one of the soldiers told Elise to follow him inside. There another German officer questioned her, then sent her to stay in the house of a woman in the town.

The next morning, Elise told the woman she was worried about her son. The soldiers had left no guard, replied the woman. Why not just leave?

Elise was at first too frightened to take her advice. What would the soldiers do if they caught her?

For the better part of two days, Elise stayed in the woman's house. On the 11th, it began to snow, which increased her concern about Jean, and the next afternoon she finally made up her mind to go. As she left the house, she was struck with the change in the town. It was teeming with soldiers and military traffic, and some of the troops wore gray uniforms with black collars, which Elise knew to be the uniform of the SS.

She had traveled about half the distance of her return journey when she came upon two elderly men whom she knew from a village inside Germany opposite Bivels. They invited her to walk with them.

As they continued along the road, Elise began to notice a sharp increase in military traffic. Passing through a wood, she saw great stacks of military equipment piled on both sides of the road just inside the treelines. Not long after that, columns of artillery overtook them, some guns drawn by trucks, others by teams of horses. Each time that happened, she and her companions stepped off the road to get out of the way, but nobody paid them any attention. As they entered another wood, she saw row after row of what looked like small boats.

What was going on? Elise only vaguely remembered when the Germans had come in 1914 and had had little experience with the military other than in 1940, when the Germans had attacked across the Our and driven through Luxembourg and Belgium to the sea, and again just last September, when the Americans had come and made a brief attack across the Our not far from Bivels. On both those occasions, there had been a stream of traffic much like that she was seeing then. Did that mean the Germans were going to attack again? The thought made her all the more anxious to get back to her son.

When Elise and the two German men reached the village where the men lived, she rested in one of their homes; but as darkness fell the next day, December 13, she set out to cover the remaining distance to Bivels. Not far from some concrete pillboxes, she came upon entanglements of barbed wire. As she tried to work her way through, she activated a trip wire, and a mine exploded. Elise was terrified, but because she had been bending forward to negotiate the barbed wire, she was unharmed; and to her immense relief, the noise drew no fire from the pillboxes.

When at last she reached the point where the ground dropped sharply down to the Our, the valley was immersed in a dense fog. She dared not try the descent under those conditions. Lying down in the snow, she tried to sleep, but that was impossible. For what seemed like an eternity, Elise did her best to keep warm by chafing her hands and legs and stamping her feet.

An hour before midnight, the fog lifted. Ignoring the cold, she took off her shoes to cut down on noise and followed a path leading down to the river; but at the river, she saw that the footbridge which she had crossed earlier no longer existed.

Close to weeping from fright and despair, Elise followed the trace of the Our until at last she came to that part of Vianden which lay on the east bank, the only place where the little river diverged as a boundary between Germany and Luxembourg. Although the bridge connecting the two parts of the town had long been destroyed, there was an old man who called across the river to partisans of the Luxembourg underground. Elise knew the partisans helped the Americans to man their post and also occupied the ruins of a tenth-century castle at the top of the town, which in happier times was one of the attractions drawing swarms of tourists to Vianden.

Early in the morning of December 14, two young men from the underground came in a small boat to row Elise across the river. While they crossed, she told them what she had seen behind the German lines. It looked to her, she said, as if the Germans were coming back.

As the three made their way up the main street, the young men insisted on stopping at the Hotel Heintz where the Americans—men of the Intelligence and Reconnaissance (I&R) Platoon of the 28th Division's 109th Infantry—were billeted, to tell them what Elise had seen. Although Elise understood no English, it was obvious that what she had to say excited the Americans. They gave her coffee and something to eat, but like the German officers, the American officer who interrogated her (it was 1st Lt. Stephen Prazenka) refused to release her to look for her son. Instead, the Americans bundled her into a jeep and hurried her back to the town of Diekirch and into the high school, which served as a command post.

There another American officer wearing a red shoulder patch that looked a little like a square-cut bucket questioned Elise at length. Although the officer was calmer than the soldiers in Vianden, there was no doubt that what she had to say highly interested him. So much so, in fact, that he too declined her request to be allowed to find her son. She was soon in the cab of a truck that took her farther west, to the town of Wiltz and another headquarters that appeared to be even bigger and more important than the one in Diekirch.

Elise Delé had no way of knowing it, but a report of what she had to say was quickly on its way up the American chain of command. At headquarters of the VIII Corps in the Belgian town of Bastogne, a clerk jotted down an entry in the G-2 (intelligence) journal:

> From 28th Div to MONARCH 2, Msg # 60, 142320 Dec 44:
> The following is a preliminary interrogation of a Luxembourg woman who has been interrogated by the 28th Inf Div:
> The woman reports that she had been given permission to go to Biewels [sic] where her home is to pick up clothes . . . while there a German reconnaissance patrol took her into custody. . . . [En route to Bitburg] she observed many trucks and horse-drawn vehicles, pontons, small boats, and other river-crossing materiel. In addition, she observed many artillery pieces, some of which were horse-drawn and others truck-drawn. She was again interrogated at Bitburg and while in this town she observed many troops in light gray uniform with black collars (SS troops). . . . She escaped at Bitburg . . . [and] went to Vianden where she was picked up and taken across the river . . . 28th Div considers the informant fairly reliable. . . . Woman's condition is highly nervous, [she] having stepped on a trip wire which detonated a mine. . . . Further check and interrogation is continuing and complete report will be submitted as early as possible.

A short time later, a digest of that message was on its way from Bastogne to the Belgian town of Spa, where at fifteen minutes before midnight on December 14, a corporal entered it into the G-2 journal of the First United States Army. The message said much the same as the one that had gone to the VIII Corps except that it erroneously identified the woman as German.

In Wiltz, in the meantime, the Americans provided Elise Delé with food and comfortable accommodations, but the next morning they refused to allow her to return to Vianden and sent her instead to Bastogne, whence they intended sending her on to Spa. As it turned out, she was destined to spend a long time in Bastogne—most of it taking refuge in a cellar.

BOOK

I

PLANS AND PREPARATIONS

CHAPTER ONE

The Decision, the Setting, and the Plan

By late summer of 1944, few other than a megalomaniac such as Adolf Hitler could have discerned any hope for the beleaguered National Socialist state that Hitler called the Third Reich. Like other German rulers before him, the Führer faced the dilemma of fighting a two-front war, east and west, however much he had tried to avoid it. After conquering France, he had attempted to lure the British into a separate peace; when that failed, he launched what was meant to be a lightning campaign of annihilation against the *Untermenschen* (subhumans) of Russia, whereupon, having "knocked from Britannia's hand the last 'continental sword' at Britain's disposal," he could effectively deal with the British. Yet that strategy too had foundered, on the reef of Russian nationalism and in the sea of Russia's vast expanses.

By late summer of 1944, the Allied armies that had come ashore on June 6 in Normandy and on August 15 in southern France controlled almost all of France, Belgium, and Luxembourg and stood little more than fifty miles from the Ruhr industrial region, whose mines, smelters, and factories were vital to the survival of the German war machine. In Italy, other Allied armies were close to breaking into the Po valley not far from the southern frontier of the Reich; and in the East, during the course of the summer, the Red Army had driven four hundred miles from deep inside White Russia to the Vistula River across from the Polish capital of Warsaw, an advance that conquered half of Poland and put Russian soldiers virtually on the frontier of East Prussia. Red Army troops had been in the Romanian capital of Bucharest for nearly a fortnight and were almost at the gates of the Bulgarian capital of Sofia. Their advances had forced German withdrawal from Greece and had precipitated the kind of defection of Germany's allies that had presaged collapse in World War I. Italy had long since given in and become a battleground; Bulgaria and Romania had defected, with Finland about to follow; and

17

only the presence of German divisions kept Hungary from doing the same.

In five years of war the German armed forces had lost almost three and three-quarters of a million men, the elite of German manpower. Essential raw materials from Russia, the Balkans, Finland, and France were no longer to be had, and neutral Sweden was becoming increasingly reluctant to provide its iron ore to a nation that appeared about to collapse. Thousand-plane raids by Allied bombers on German cities had become commonplace.

Yet Adolf Hitler still saw hope. Or professed that he did.

For all the immense losses in battle, Germany had close to ten million men in uniform, including seven and a half million in the army and another ground combat force, a kind of Praetorian guard of the Nazi Party, the *Waffen-Schutzstaffel*, or SS. There were still others who could be committed to the fight: heretofore-deferred students, men with less than crippling physical defects, nonessential government workers, convalescents from the hospitals, sailors and airmen turned into foot soldiers, new classes made available for the draft simply by extending the age limit at both ends of the induction spectrum (to run from sixteen to sixty).

Nor was there concern, as there had been in 1918, about collapse of the home front. The police state had eliminated the internal Red threat— or at least driven it underground—so that not once during the war years had the ugly noise of street demonstrations reached Hitler's ears. And so ruthlessly had he dealt with the cabal of army officers who tried to kill him—for those most deeply involved, death by hanging on meat hooks, with motion-picture cameras recording the agony—that the chance of a recrudescent opposition was remote. So, too, the air raids and the demand of his enemies for unconditional surrender had cemented the will of the German people.

However damaging the thousand-plane raids, they had failed to prevent German industry from maintaining a remarkably high rate of production. Indeed, not until the late fall of 1944 was German production to reach a wartime peak. Smaller industries had been dispersed to the countryside or moved to the East, where the Russians had few big bombers. A new decree would put workers on a sixty-hour week, impressed foreign workers would be driven ever harder, and production of civilian goods would be drastically cut.

By those methods, German industry during the fall of 1944 was to produce a record million and a quarter tons of ammunition, three-quarters of a million rifles, a hundred thousand machine guns, and nine thousand artillery pieces. Only in tanks was production to decline, and that would be partially offset by record production of self-propelled assault guns from factories previously moved beyond the range of Allied bombers to Czechoslovakia. Hitler also put great store by a new weapon of which some models were already appearing: jet-propelled fighter aircraft three times faster than anything flown by Allied pilots. Once the new jets got into action in substantial numbers, Hitler maintained, they would sweep Allied planes from German skies.

What Hitler needed was time.

For all the crises on the Eastern Front, Hitler was still capable of gaining time there simply by utilizing the age-old process of trading it for space. Although Russian penetration onto the soil of the Reich in East Prussia would be a heavy psychological blow, there was nothing in East Prussia absolutely vital to German survival. (As the master strategist Alfred von Schlieffen had put it: Better an enemy in East Prussia than one on the Rhine.) At the Vistula the Red Army was still three hundred miles from any really critical objective, such as the capital, Berlin, or the coal fields and industry of Silesia. In any case the current Russian offensive had run its course, supply lines too taut to support another great lunge forward until well into the winter.

The Western Front was another matter, for there the Allied armies threatened the vital Ruhr. Yet hope Hitler could see on the Western Front as well. Like the Russians, the Allies had outrun their supply lines, and by ordering diehard holdouts in the French and Belgian ports even as the German armies fell back toward the frontier, he had ensured that for some time to come the Allies would still have to base their supplies on the Normandy beaches or on ports far from the front. There was also the factor of the border fortifications on the western frontier, the combination of concrete antitank obstacles (dragon's teeth), pillboxes, and bunkers known to the German soldier as *Westwall,* and to the Allied soldier as the Siegfried Line. No matter how dated those defenses, Hitler maintained that concrete in any form lent impetus to the defense; and besides, the terrain along the frontier was forbidding.

Space in the East, fortifications and inhospitable terrain in the West thus spelled time, but in the final accounting, time alone was not enough. To stand beleaguered on the defensive while his enemies gradually strangled him was no solution. He had to go over to the offensive, strike a blow that would change everything, prove decisive.

There was no hope for such a decisive blow in the East. The number of new and refitted divisions Hitler could muster for an offensive would simply be swallowed by the great distances and ingested by the Red Army's multitudes. Besides, there was no chance there for a separate peace, for Hitler saw Germany as the last bulwark against the forces of unholy communism, with which he could never traffic. By way of Japan, there had been indications that the Russian dictator, Joseph Stalin, might be willing to parley, but Hitler forbade any dickering with the *Untermenschen.* "Probing the Soviet attitude," he wrote the wife of his foreign minister, Joachim von Ribbentrop, "is like touching a glowing stove to find out if it's hot."

The situation in the West was a different matter. Not only were the distances shorter, the strategic objectives within acceptable range, and the opposing forces far less overwhelming in numbers. Hitler also saw a real possibility of inducing the Allies, for all their proud decrees about unconditional surrender, to accept a separate peace.

Never in history, as he perceived it, had war produced such strange bedfellows as the Western democracies and the Soviet Union. "Ultra-capitalist states on one side," he would tell his generals on the eve of his big offensive, "ultra-Marxist states on the other; on one side a dying empire—Britain; on the other side a colony, the United States, waiting to claim its inheritance." Each of the three, he said, was determined "either to cheat the others out of something or get something out of it." A great victory on the Western Front, Hitler declared, would "bring down this artificial coalition with a crash."

It was absurd for Anglo-American armies to fight a war which, if Germany were defeated, would allow the mucky fingers of communism to grub about in western Europe. Impossible strains among such strange bedfellows would surely develop, and already Hitler thought he detected them, including some in the Anglo-American alliance.

If he could destroy the British and Canadian armies, Britain would be unable to replace its losses, and Canada would hardly be inclined to send another contingent to the slaughter. In which case, would the United States be willing to continue the absurd fight alone? It was obvious that the survival of the United States of America itself was not at stake: And the enemy in the Pacific, Japan—not Germany—had sullied American honor at Pearl Harbor. If a catastrophic blow to the Allied armies should precipitate a separate peace, that would enable Hitler to turn a still powerful army and all Germany's resources to putting an end to the Red menace, thus fulfilling his ambition to destroy communism and the pagan Russian hordes utterly, to level Moscow and Leningrad, blotting their names forever from geography and history alike.

Had not Frederick the Great—who among all the military leaders of history was Hitler's idol, whose maxims were always on the tip of the Führer's tongue to silence the pessimist, invoke new sacrifice, or justify cruel discipline, and whose portrait hung behind the desk in Hitler's study in the Reichschancellery—faced vastly superior forces converging on his kingdom in the Seven Years' War? And had not Frederick, by engaging and defeating his enemies one by one, hung on until the historical accident of the death of the empress Elizabeth of Russia brought to the throne one of Frederick's admirers, Peter III, which split the coalition opposing him? Under intense adversity, would the unholy alliance of capitalism and bolshevism hold up any better? With the British and Canadian armies wiped out, would it not become obvious to the American people that their sons were dying to impose on western Europe the dictatorship of the proletariat?

As early as the last day of July, 1944, when the Allied armies were about to break out of their Normandy beachhead, Hitler, who to that point had adamantly refused to sanction any withdrawal—and replaced his commander-in-chief in the West, Field Marshal Gerd von Rundstedt, for proposing it—admitted to a few intimates that eventual withdrawal to the West Wall might be the only recourse. That would mean, in time, an offensive mounted from behind the protection of the West Wall, a decision which Hitler revealed to a select group on August 19. He planned, he said, to launch an offensive on the Western Front at the beginning of November when heavy fog and rain—poor campaigning weather—traditionally came to northwestern Europe, weather that would seriously interfere with the operations of the Allied air forces.

Not quite a fortnight later, on September 1, Hitler called to the *Wolfschanze* the man he had so recently removed from command, Gerd von Rundstedt, and asked him to return as commander-in-chief in the West. A wizened, venerable old soldier (he was almost seventy), von Rundstedt was to most Germans the paragon of all that was good and right about the German Officer Corps. Hitler disliked him intensely, partly because he was such an obvious exemplar of that elite corps with its plumy elegance, whose officers, Hitler knew, saw him in his role as supreme military commander as an imposter, and partly because Hitler also knew that in private conversations von Rundstedt referred to him mockingly by his rank in the Great War as "the Corporal." On the other hand, after having been relieved in France, von Rundstedt had demonstrated his loyalty by presiding over a Court of Honor to expel those officers associated with the attempt on the Führer's life. Besides, Hitler needed a proud figurehead around which the troops might rally. He needed, too, someone whose presence as commander-in-chief might lull Allied commanders, who would expect that such an experienced and capable old soldier would conduct his campaign according to accepted canons of the military art.

At the meeting in the *Wolfschanze*, Hitler treated von Rundstedt "with unwonted diffidence and respect," while the old soldier "sat there motionless and monosyllabic," but as a loyal German, von Rundstedt agreed to serve. He was to defend for as long as possible in front of the West Wall, then fall back on the fortifications for the decisive battle. Everything depended on that battle, Hitler stressed, for under the conditions existing in the Third Reich, there was insufficient strength to mount an offensive.

Having thus deceived his commander-in-chief, Hitler set about creating the conditions for his offensive. To his minister of propaganda, Josef Goebbels, he gave the assignment of combing the country for enough untapped manpower to create twenty-five new divisions, while others might later be culled from Finland and Norway. To assure von Rundstedt's holding the line, he accorded the Western Front priority on tanks coming off the assembly lines; but to create an armored force to form the steel heart of the offensive, he ordered the four SS panzer divisions then fighting in the West to be pulled from the line and refitted, without telling von Rundstedt why. To control the armor, he created a new headquarters, the Sixth Panzer Army,* commanded by a hard-drinking old crony from the early, street-brawling days of the Nazi Party, SS-Obergruppenführer Josef ("Sepp") Dietrich.

Although von Rundstedt appealed for reinforcements from the new formations, Hitler refused all but minimal help; for as he had anticipated, the Allied armies had outrun their supply lines and would soon grind to a halt. There was a spasmodic climax: an attempt with three airborne divisions to gain bridgeheads over the canals and sprawling rivers of the Netherlands, including the Lower Rhine, and turn the flank of the West Wall; but when that failed, the Supreme Allied Commander, General Dwight D. Eisenhower, had no recourse for a time but to accept a slow, grinding battle of attrition.

As Hitler began more detailed planning for his offensive, one factor remained constant—the goal of destroying the British and Canadian armies, which were located in the far north, mostly in the Netherlands. Although the British had seized the great Belgian port of Antwerp, German troops upon Hitler's specific order still held onto the banks of the Schelde Estuary, which connects the port with the North Sea, and thereby denied Allied ships the use of the harbor. Yet it could be expected that Antwerp would eventually be opened and serve as the principal port for Allied supplies. Since a drive to Antwerp would not only deny the Allies the port but also trap the British and Canadian armies, Antwerp was a strategic objective of the first order.

That objective ruled out launching the offensive against the Allied south wing, for from the Vosges Mountains of Alsace or the hills of Lorraine in northeastern France the route to Antwerp was too long. The shortest distance—no more than sixty miles—was in the north, along the boundary between the American and British armies north of the old Carolingian capital of Aachen, but there the multiple rivers and canals posed serious obstacles to tanks. That left the Ardennes, a region that had long fascinated Hitler, where German armies had attacked with tremendous success in 1914 and again, at Hitler's personal instigation, in 1940.†

At that point, Hitler had no way of knowing how strong the Allied line might be in the Ardennes by the time his offensive was ready. Indeed, even as he reached his decision, there was considerable concern about a drive by a corps of the American First Army through the Ar-

---

*Although Hitler sometimes referred to that headquarters as the Sixth SS Panzer Army, it would officially be accorded the honorific only in the spring of 1945.
†But not also, as is often erroneously remarked, in 1870. That advance was from the Saar-Palatinate through the Wissembourg Gap into Alsace.

dennes and into the contiguous region inside Germany known as the Eifel. There two American infantry divisions had crossed the frontier and penetrated a thinly fortified sector of the West Wall near and astride a high ridgeline, the Schnee Eifel, while a few miles to the south an armored division had crossed Luxembourg, penetrated the West Wall, and headed for the crossroads town of Bitburg. Not until September 17 were hastily assembled troops able to halt the drive at the Schnee Eifel, and even then the Americans retained control of the ridge. Only four days later would German pressure force the armored division to abandon its thrust on Bitburg and retire into Luxembourg.

On the other hand, Hitler might well expect that Allied commanders in 1944 would view the Ardennes much as their predecessors had in 1914 and 1940, as being too compartmented and too heavily forested to accommodate a major offensive. The Supreme Allied Commander in World War I, Marshal Ferdinand Foch, had called the Ardennes "an almost impenetrable massif," and one of his generals, Charles Lanrezac, reputedly said: "If you go into that death-trap of the Ardennes, you will never come out." If Dwight D. Eisenhower in 1944 held a similar view, he too would accord little credibility to the possibility of a German thrust through the Ardennes, so that an attack there could be expected to hit a weak point in the Allied line.

Some days before Hitler made his dramatic announcement at the *Wolfschanze* on September 16, he had directed his plans and operations officer, General Jodl, to study the possibility of an offensive in the Ardennes, and he himself had pored over the results. Opposite the Ardennes, inside Germany, dense forests in the Eifel region provided a ready cloak for the assembly of an attacking force; and however restrictive the terrain, German armies had demonstrated in 1940 that mobile forces could negotiate the Ardennes swiftly.

From the frontier, the route through the Ardennes to the strategic objective of Antwerp was little more than a hundred miles as the Messerschmitt flew, and a drive to Antwerp through the Ardennes would trap not only the British and Canadians but also the American First and Ninth Armies around Aachen—fully half the Allied forces on the Continent—a prize as alluring as that gained in the dash to the sea in 1940. Any coalition that lost half its field strength would surely collapse. At the very least the offensive would eliminate the immediate threat to the Ruhr, thus enabling Hitler to draw on the Western Front for troops to meet the next big lunge by the Red Army.

Although Hitler was aware that he could muster no such power as he had employed in 1940, particularly in the air, he saw methods of overcoming that. It would certainly be November before the new and refitted divisions were ready, and by choosing a period of prolonged bad weather, he would assure that his panzer divisions were well on the way to Antwerp before clearing weather enabled the Allied planes to operate. So, too, he expected to be in Antwerp (it would take a mere week to get there, he said) before Eisenhower could mount a major riposte, for Eisenhower first would have to determine the extent of the offensive, and in responding to such a strategic threat to forces of three nationalities— so Hitler reasoned—the armies of a democratic alliance would require decision at the political level. That too would take time.

At the *Wolfschanze* on September 25, Hitler spelled out in more detail what he had in mind. The artillery preparation was to be massive, followed by infantry assault to achieve a swift penetration and enable a first wave of panzer divisions to begin a rapid drive to seize bridgeheads over the Meuse River, a major military obstacle defining the western and northern reaches of the Ardennes. Quick seizure of bridgeheads over the Meuse was essential for continuing the thrust to Antwerp. At that point, a second wave of panzer divisions was to be committed, while infantry divisions followed and peeled off north and south to protect the flanks of the penetration.

The *Schwerpunkt* (main effort) of the offensive was to be delivered by the four SS panzer divisions of the Sixth Panzer Army, a manifestation of Hitler's faith in the loyalty and ability of the SS units, which even as late as the fall of 1944 were made up in large measure of volunteers. (Naming the SS for the *Schwerpunkt* was also a slap at the army, whose officers had tried to kill him.) The main effort was to be supported by army panzer divisions under another recently created headquarters, the Fifth Panzer Army, commanded by a successful and trusted general brought from the Eastern Front, Hasso von Manteuffel; while infantry divisions under the Seventh Army, commanded by General der Panzertruppen Erich Brandenberger, were to protect the south flank of the penetration. The offensive would require a minimum of thirty divisions, a third of them armored, and Hitler expected the Luftwaffe to support the offensive with more than a thousand planes.

While charging Jodl and his operations staff with devising a detailed plan of operations, the Führer also ordered them to draw up a comprehensive cover and deception plan; for, as Hitler emphasized, secrecy was basic to the plan. Everybody let in on the plan, including clerks and typists, was to sign a pledge of secrecy upon pain of death. Field commanders, including Field Marshal von Rundstedt himself, who was to be the overall commander, were to be brought in only as time, detailed planning, and assembly of forces required.

Hitler may have forgotten that he himself had already been less than discreet about his intentions when, three weeks earlier, on September 4, the Japanese ambassador to Berlin, Baron Hiroshi Oshima, had called at the *Wolfschanze* in company with the German foreign minister, von Ribbentrop, for another of what had come to be periodic conferences. Probably because Japan was Nazi Germany's only ally with muscle, Hitler had long been candid with the Japanese ambassador, yet as the defeats in the field multiplied, he had become uncharacteristically defensive.

When Oshima expressed some concern about the perils facing Germany, Hitler assured him that he still had ample resources for restoring the situation.

> When the current replenishment of the air forces is completed— said Hitler—and the new army of more than a million men, which is now being organized, is ready, I intend to combine the new units with units to be withdrawn from all possible areas and to open a large-scale offensive in the West.

The news astounded Oshima. When? he asked. To which Hitler replied: "After the beginning of November."

A few days later, Baron Oshima reported the conversation to his government in Tokyo where, as in Berlin, nobody was aware that since mid-1941 the United States had been intercepting and decrypting Japanese diplomatic wireless (radio) traffic, a process known by the code-name MAGIC. By means of MAGIC, Oshima's report that Hitler was planning "a large-scale offensive in the West" to start sometime "after the beginning of November" was on the desks of intelligence officers in the Pentagon in Washington almost as soon as it reached the desks of the foreign office in Tokyo.

In Julius Caesar's time, the Ardennes region of what was to become Belgium and Luxembourg constituted the most extensive forest in all Gaul; but over the centuries, as the region passed under the control of one ruler after another, including Charlemagne, much of the land was cleared by agriculture and animal husbandry, so that by the start of the twentieth century only about half of it was still wooded. The most extensive stands that remained were in the east, close to the borders with Germany, almost all of them coniferous, stately firs harvested from time to time for timber, then replanted in orderly rows.

Between the two world wars the Ardennes became a haven for tourists, its countryside dotted with picturesque villages with narrow streets and here and there abbeys and castles, or the ruins of them, a place where tourists partook of the region's renowned venison, wild boar, and marvelously succulent cured ham. A westward extension of the high plateau of the Eifel, so deeply etched through the centuries by serpentine streams that it appears to be less plateau than mountains, the Ardennes presents a rugged face scarred by deep gorges and twisting stream valleys. It has the shape of a big isosceles triangle with an eighty-mile base along the frontiers, extending from an ill-defined point in the north near the Belgian town of Eupen (fourteen miles south of Aachen) to the vicinity of Luxembourg City, the capital of Luxembourg, in the south. Although part of the region protrudes westward beyond the Meuse River, so deep and broad is the cut of the Meuse that for military purposes the region can be said to end there, some sixty miles from the base of the triangle.

As the most extensive stands of forest are close to the German frontier, so too is the most forbidding terrain. For almost the entire length of the frontier, the terrain poses a major obstacle to military movement.

In the north rises the Hautes Fagnes (High Marshes), in effect a ridgeline whose crest marks the highest elevation in the Ardennes (2,777 feet). It is an almost trackless moor covered with forest or peat bogs, the latter providing the source of medicinal waters for the thermal baths of Aachen and of Spa, the Belgian resort whose name long ago passed into English as a synonym for thermal watering places.

Southeast of the Hautes Fagnes, in Belgium's easternmost reaches, dense forests mark the frontier to the vicinity of a road center, St. Vith. Because American troops who attacked there in September held onto the nearby prominent feature just inside Germany, the Schnee Eifel, that ridgeline in the fall of 1944 constituted a part of the obstacles to be faced by any attacker from the east.

The little Our River, which rises in eastern Belgium, becomes a major obstacle as it crosses into Luxembourg, where it marks the frontier and flows through a gorge whose almost clifflike sides are covered with firs. The roads leading west toil upward to a high ridge which American troops, familiar with the Shenandoah Mountains of Virginia, called the "Skyline Drive." Behind that ridge lies another gorge cut by the Clerve and Sûre Rivers. After absorbing the waters of the Clerve, the Sûre drains southeastward to the frontier, where it absorbs the Our and forms the border with Germany (the Germans call it the Sauer) until it joins the Moselle River northeast of Luxembourg City at roughly the southern terminus of the Ardennes.

Along the entire stretch of the Ardennes near the frontier, only one corridor at all conducive to military movement exists, a sector some five miles wide beginning at the northern end of the Schnee Eifel. Taking its name from the village of Losheim, just inside Germany, it is known as the Losheim Gap. The term "gap" is relative, for even though it lacks extensive forest along the frontier, a belt of woodland two miles thick has to be crossed before gaining more open country a few miles deeper into Belgium, and the hills are steep, the valleys deep. Nevertheless, as the Kaiser's armies entered the Ardennes in 1914, a force heavy in horse cavalry pushed through the Losheim Gap in advance of the main body and quickly reached the Meuse. The same thing happened in 1940 when a panzer division under an obscure general, Erwin Rommel, passed through the Losheim Gap to gain the Meuse by nightfall on the third day of attack.

From the high ground along the frontier the terrain slopes gradually downward toward the west, losing some of its convulsive nature except for tortuous meanderings of streams through deep valleys in the extreme north and south. In the center, around Bastogne, the true nature of the region as a plateau is readily discernible, no more of an obstacle to military movement than is always present in a gently rolling landscape. Beyond the little Ourthe River, roughly two-thirds of the distance to the Meuse, the same rolling hills prevail, for the most part, the rest of the way to the Meuse. The Meuse itself follows a south-north course before swinging northeast at the town of Namur. After washing the industrial wastes of one of Belgium's principal cities, Liège, it finally resumes a northward course through the Netherlands to the sea.

The roadnet for such a pastoral region was extensive, although the roads usually twisted and turned in conformity with the stream valleys and in many places passed through thick forests or sharp defiles where they might be readily blocked. As an added obstacle, at every crossroads or road junction stood either a closely knit town or village or at least a collection of stone farm buildings, which almost always constricted the width of the road. Although most of the railroads had been put back into service for military traffic by late 1944, the repairs ended some miles short of the German frontier, and without connections to lines inside Germany, railroads in the Ardennes would have little bearing on the fighting to come.

Not so across the frontier in the Eifel. There, in countryside even more heavily forested than that of the Ardennes, the Germans in preparing for the onset of World War I had constructed a number of rail lines feeding from marshalling yards at Cologne in the north and Koblenz in the south and from other crossings of the Rhine River in between. Since the distance between the Rhine and the western frontier is only about forty-five miles, trains moving along those spur lines have relatively short hauls. The lines lead to towns that are also road centers: Bitburg in the south; Prüm and Gerolstein in the shadow of the Schnee Eifel; and Gemünd and Schleiden in the north. Although the sole arterial line runs along the valley of the Moselle on the southern periphery of the region to the old Roman outpost town of Trier, spur lines lead north from marshalling yards at Trier to Bitburg and the other road centers within the Eifel.

There are no cities in the Eifel and few in the Ardennes. Except for Liège on the northern periphery and Luxembourg City and Arlon to the south, there are only the picturesque villages and an occasional town with a population of two to five thousand. Yet those towns pull together a number of roads and then release them in various directions. So St. Vith near the frontier, Malmédy in the north, and Bastogne and Houffalize in the center would become critical features in any military advance.

The people of Luxembourg reflect a fierce independence befitting a region that has been a separate entity, although not always autonomous, since the tenth century. Of Germanic descent, they speak a dialect, Letzemburgesch, which to the American soldier sounded like German.

The population of the Belgian Ardennes is composed primarily of French-speaking Walloons, but in the northeastern corner most are ethnic Germans, reflecting the fact that before the Treaty of Versailles, the easternmost province, Eupen-et-Malmédy, had long been a part of Germany. In late 1944, in such border towns as Eupen and St. Vith, shop signs were in old German script and almost all the people spoke German. Many—even a majority—might be loyal to Belgium, but the American soldier did not trust them. Almost every home had a photograph of a father or son in German uniform, and few American soldiers bothered to reason that ethnic Germans in regions conquered by the German Army had no choice but to serve the Fatherland.

Situated not far from the North Sea, the Ardennes has a harsh, wet climate, with rainfall averaging 35 to 40 inches a year. Some of the heaviest rains come in November and early December, so saturating the soil that any movement off the roads is difficult; and with them comes the fog or mist that sometimes fails to clear before midday and reappears again in late afternoon. Snow sometimes accumulates up to a foot in depth— deeper in the drifts—and cold, raw winds sweep the heights.

As American intelligence officers would consistently note, the Ardennes presented little attraction for anybody except (they might have added) a tourist. Surely it proffered nothing of strategic importance to German armies forced back on their homeland in desperate straits.

Yet that was reckoning without the fact that by way of the Ardennes it was just over a hundred miles, as the Messerschmitt flew, to Antwerp.

Although Hitler had specifically directed that his offensive be made through the Ardennes, Alfred Jodl and his planning staff studied various alternatives, eventually settling on five, only one of which involved that part of the Ardennes which Hitler had specified, and even that failed to name Antwerp as the objective. As proposed by the planners, that operation would consist of two prongs: a main effort passing through the Ardennes and then turning north, where it would meet a thrust launched from the vicinity of Aachen—a shallow double envelopment which could be expected to trap not the British and Canadians but just the American First and Ninth Armies. Proposing the alternative plans may have been simply a logical procedure for men with General Staff–trained minds; on the other hand, the plan for a shallow envelopment may have been a subtle attempt by Jodl to modify Hitler's grandiose scheme, to reduce it to the dimensions a trained and experienced military planner such as Jodl recognized as within German capabilities.

If such a ploy it was, it failed. The effect was not to lessen Hitler's ambition but to increase it, for he liked the idea of supplementing the

Ardennes thrust with a second prong originating near Aachen; and on Antwerp as an objective, he was immovable.

As finally worked out by Jodl and his staff, the offensive was to be launched along a sixty-mile front from Monschau in the north, some twenty miles southeast of Aachen, whence led the only lateral road across the Hautes Fagnes, to the medieval town of Echternach in the south, downstream from the juncture of the Our and Sûre Rivers. Sepp Dietrich's Sixth Panzer Army, comprising the *Schwerpunkt*, was to attack along a front extending from Monschau to a point within the Losheim Gap, with a panzer division debouching from the gap to follow the path of Erwin Rommel's division in 1940, bypassing opposition, and quickly gaining and crossing the Meuse. (Jodl dug from the archives a copy of the 1940 plan.) Dietrich was to pass south of Liège, cross the Meuse upstream from the city, then head for Antwerp while anchoring his northern flank on the considerable obstacle of the Albert Canal.

On Dietrich's left, General von Manteuffel's Fifth Panzer Army was to attack through and south of St. Vith, cross the Skyline Drive, jump the Meuse upstream from the bend in the river at Namur, and then wheel northwest, bypassing the Belgian capital, Brussels, and protecting the Sixth Panzer Army's southern flank. Erich Brandenberger's Seventh Army, made up primarily of infantry, was to attack on either side of Echternach, and while advancing westward was to peel off divisions to block to the south.

Forty-eight hours after the offensive in the Ardennes began, the Fifteenth Army, composed of infantry reinforced by a panzer and a *Panzergrenadier* (mechanized) division, was to be prepared to attack from the vicinity of Aachen. The basic objective was to pin down American divisions and prevent them from reinforcing in the Ardennes; but if all went well, the attack was to continue southward to reach the Meuse near Liège and trap the Americans around Aachen. Although Hitler spoke grandly of yet another attack in Alsace to tie down American divisions there, plans for that attack, like that by the Fifteenth Army, remained indefinite. So did a suggestion that Army Group H, which defended in the Netherlands, might drive through the Canadians to link with the Sixth Panzer Army at Antwerp, thereby constricting the trap around the Allied armies. Nobody said anything about how the Germans were going to liquidate the more than a million Allied troops who would presumably be trapped.

Accepting the plan, Hitler continued his deception by giving it a code-name, Operation *WACHT AM RHEIN* (Watch on the Rhine), designed to provide a defensive rather than offensive connotation. The next day the head of the *OKW*, Field Marshal Wilhelm Keitel, issued a general order to all commanders on the Western Front asserting that for the mo-

THE GERMAN PLAN

●●●●● ALLIED POSITIONS, DEC 15
━ ━ ━ THE BIG SOLUTION
⇒ ⇐ THE SMALL SOLUTION

Scale:
0   5   10   20   30
MILES

N

AG H
AG B
Rheydt

Rhine

Erft

River

R U H R

Cologne

NETH.
GERM.
WEST
WALL

Roer

Düren

Bonn

Aachen

GERM.

River

FIFTEENTH ARMY

SIXTH PZ ARMY

BEL.

Eupen

HAUTES FAGNES

Spa

Monschau

HÜRTGEN FOREST

ROER DAMS
Gemünd
Schleiden

WEST WALL

SIXTH PZ ARMY

FIFTH PZ ARMY

Gerolstein

Rhine

River

Koblenz

L

E

Malmédy

Losheim

St.
Vith

S
E

SCHNEE
EIFEL
Prüm

F

Moselle

River

Moselle

River

Ouffalize

Clerve River

Our River

LUX.
GERM.

E

I

FIFTH PZ ARMY

SEVENTH ARMY

Wiltz

River

Diekirch

Vianden

WEST WALL

Bitburg

River

AG B

AG G

TIVE

Echternach

Moselle

Trier

Luxembourg
City

ment no German offensive was possible, that the saving of the Fatherland depended upon unyielding defense.

During the afternoon of the same day that Hitler approved Jodl's plan, October 21, he received at the *Wolfschanze* someone he held in special respect, a blond giant of a man who, like Hitler himself, was Austrian: Otto Skorzeny. It was Skorzeny who in 1943 had rescued Hitler's friend and erstwhile ally, Benito Mussolini, from a mountaintop in Italy where he was being held in the wake of Italy's defection; and only a few days before the visit to the *Wolfschanze*, Skorzeny had led a successful raid on the seat of the Hungarian government in the Citadel in Budapest to prevent Hungary's defection. Possibly as an indication of something of the Führer's admiration and trust, Skorzeny may have been the only person briefed in early stages of the planning for *WACHT AM RHEIN* from whom Hitler exacted no written pledge of secrecy.

Wearing the uniform of an SS major, Skorzeny entered Hitler's study and received a warm handshake. "Well done, Skorzeny!" exclaimed the Führer. He had promoted him, he said, to Obersturmbannführer (lieutenant colonel) and awarded him the German Cross in Gold.

After hearing Skorzeny's account of the operation in Budapest, Hitler began a lengthy recitation of *WACHT AM RHEIN*. "One of the most important tasks in this offensive," he said at last, "will be entrusted to you and the units under your command." Skorzeny was to form a special brigade that would precede the attacking armies and seize bridges over the Meuse. The troops were to wear American uniforms, which would enable small detachments to "cause the greatest confusion" by cutting communications and passing false orders. "I know," Hitler concluded, "you will do your best."

A few days later, Skorzeny was dismayed to come upon an order signed by a senior officer of the *OKW*. At the top were the words: "Secret Commando Operations." Units throughout the army, the order read, were to "send in the names of all English-speaking officers and men who are prepared to voluntarily apply for transfer for a special operation" under Skorzeny. All units were also to turn in any captured American vehicles, uniforms, and other equipment.

Skorzeny was livid. Such a widely distributed order was bound to fall into Allied hands. To Skorzeny his operation was compromised from the start, but his superiors would agree to no cancellation lest Hitler himself learn of the gaffe. "It's idiotic," commented Reichsführer-SS Heinrich Himmler, "but it has been done. We cannot hold up your operation now."

Scion of an aristocratic old Prussian family from Mecklenburg, Karl Rudolf Gerd von Rundstedt disdained Nazism and Adolf Hitler. Yet like many another of the senior generals anxious to circumvent the Treaty of

Versailles and restore German military strength, he had pledged himself to the *Fahneneid*, the ancient oath passed down from the Teuton knights requiring every soldier to obey the Emperor unto death, an oath with which Hitler, like the kaisers before him, bound his officers.

Having enlisted in an infantry regiment as an ensign at the age of seventeen, von Rundstedt by the fall of 1944 had been soldiering for more than half a century. Joining the General Staff after the Great War, he had worked hard to dispel the paralysis that the machine gun had engendered, insisting on increased fire support and mobility for the infantryman. Although he believed fervently in the supremacy of the state over the army and despised politics, in 1938 he so disagreed with Hitler's policies—which he considered to be leading to full-scale war at a time when Germany was grossly unprepared for it—that in company with a dozen other top generals he resigned. With the invasion of Poland in 1939, he nevertheless accepted a recall to duty and commanded army groups with distinction in Poland, Belgium, France, and Russia before becoming commander-in-chief on the Western Front.

Von Rundstedt was, to many of his compatriots, the prototype of the Prussian officer, stiff, formal, utterly dedicated to his profession. Some saw him as "excessively modest, too reserved," a man who "led a simple life and was indifferent to money or possessions," one who was "affable to inferiors" and "extravagantly polite to women." He smoked too much and enjoyed an occasional drink. Like most German officers of his time, he had learned the language of the courts; he liked the French and when in France, "chose to speak in French with visiting dignitaries."

By the fall of 1944, von Rundstedt's advanced age was showing. The skin on his face was wrinkled like crepe paper, and even as Hitler recalled him once again to duty, he had been taking the cure at Bad Tölz. Establishing his headquarters in Ziegenberg Castle, in the Taunus Hills east of the Rhine near Bad Nauheim, he made few visits to the troops, a practice far different from the old days. Many of his associates saw the noble old man for what Hitler intended him to be—a figurehead.

Among them was one of his three army group commanders, Field Marshal Walter Model of Army Group B, who was destined to be the tactical commander for Hitler's ambitious offensive. A man of humble origins, in no sense of the nobility, Model had early tied his career to Hitler's. As von Manteuffel put it: "His manner was rough, and his methods were not always acceptable in the higher quarters of the German Army, but they were both to Hitler's liking." He was one of only a few among the thoroughly cowed officer corps who still dared to speak his mind to the Führer and occasionally carried his point. Stockily built, Model found it hard to look the stiff, formal Prussian, but with the aid of a monocle, he managed it.

In Russia, Model had established a reputation as a "lion of defense," and in August, 1944, when Hitler needed a lion of defense on the Western Front, he made him commander of Army Group B and at the same time, briefly, commander-in-chief in the West. To some, Model appeared not only ardent but fanatical. When a commander in Normandy insisted that the remnants of his division be pulled from the line for a rest, Model said: "My dear Bayerlein, in the East our divisions take their rest in the front line. And that's how things are going to be done here in the future." And when Model learned that Field Marshal Friedrich Paulus had surrendered to the Russians at Stalingrad, he was appalled. "A field marshal," said Model, "does not become a prisoner. Such a thing is just not possible." (He would eventually take his own life rather than surrender.)

Sixteen years von Rundstedt's junior, Model treated the old man with due respect, but he ran his army group with little reference to Ziegenberg Castle. Von Rundstedt, for his part, conscious of the peculiar position in which Hitler had placed him (about the only authority left to him, he was to note, was "to change the guards in front of my own headquarters"), accepted Model's deference as his due but made no effort to interfere with Model's trading on his prerogative as bearer of a marshal's baton to deal directly with Hitler. Relations between the two were "correct but not cordial."

As October passed its midpoint, von Rundstedt at Ziegenberg Castle and Model at his headquarters in a former sanitarium for alcoholics near Krefeld, northeast of Aachen, received summonses to send their chiefs of staff to the *Wolfschanze*. Neither knew why, but both assumed for a taste of Hitler's choler, for the Americans had finally captured Aachen, the first German city of appreciable size to fall. Von Rundstedt nevertheless instructed his chief of staff, General der Kavellerie Siegfried Westphal, to seize the occasion to press his repeated unanswered pleas for reinforcements to prevent a breakthrough beyond Aachen to the Rhine.

Arriving at the *Wolfschanze* on the morning of October 22, General Westphal and Model's chief of staff, General der Infanterie Hans Krebs, first had to sign the pledge required of those let in on Hitler's secret: To guard it or be shot. Following the Führer's daily situation conference, all but fifteen of the participants were asked to leave, whereupon Hitler himself took the floor. To the surprise of Westphal and Krebs, he said not a word about the fall of Aachen. Instead, he unfolded an astounding plan: *WACHT AM RHEIN*.

As Westphal and Krebs listened in stunned silence, Hitler outlined the forces that were to be employed. There were to be thirty divisions: eighteen infantry and twelve panzer or *Panzergrenadier* divisions. To Westphal and Krebs, such largesse was heady news, but their enthusiasm cooled when Hitler told them that von Rundstedt's command would have to provide nine of the divisions, including six panzer divisions. Those would have to be pulled from the line in sufficient time to be refitted with replacements in men and equipment before the offensive. For general fire support, there were to be five motorized antiaircraft regiments, twelve artillery corps, and ten rocket projector brigades. There would also be additional general support troops, such as engineer and signal battalions, and the Luftwaffe was to provide at least 1,500 planes, including 100 of the new jets.

Although Hitler said that he wanted to attack early in November, it would be impossible to assemble all the troops by that time, so that the offensive was to begin on November 25, a date, his meteorologists had promised him, that assured inclement weather with poor visibility to conceal the buildup. In the meantime, he intoned, there was to be no let-up in the defensive battle, yet not one of the formations intended for *WACHT AM RHEIN* was to be committed to bolster the defense. With that, Hitler dismissed his generals, ordering them to return to their headquarters and draw up detailed operational plans.

When Westphal reported back to his chief, von Rundstedt was appalled. While admitting that Hitler's choice of the Ardennes for the offensive represented "a stroke of genius," he saw the plan as far too ambitious. As he was to put it later, "all, absolutely all conditions for the possible success of such an offensive were lacking." Even to hold on along the frontier while the men and supplies for the offensive were readied would be problem enough, for there were clear indications that the Americans were preparing new drives in both north and south, the First and Ninth Armies in the Aachen sector and the Third Army in Lorraine. If the German armies should reach and cross the Meuse, which von Rundstedt seriously doubted they could do, both flanks would be highly vulnerable; and to expect to advance all the way to Antwerp without encountering a major counterblow was crediting the Allied commanders with a languor and a dearth of resources they had yet to exhibit. About all Hitler's plan could be expected to achieve, in von Rundstedt's view, was a salient or bulge in the line, costly and indecisive, like those Ludendorff had forged during the Great War.

It was with considerable relief that von Rundstedt learned that Hitler's fair-haired boy, Walter Model, shared his misgivings. "This plan," Model said, when General Krebs presented it to him, "hasn't got a damned leg to stand on."

Without consulting each other, both commanders adopted the same method of trying to whittle down the grandiose scope of their Führer's plan by devising an alternative more in keeping with the reality of German resources. To both, Antwerp as an objective was out of the question. Von Rundstedt proposed a drive through the Ardennes to cross the Meuse between Liège and the bend at Namur for a juncture with a simultaneous attack launched from the north, thereby trapping the Americans around Aachen in a double encirclement. Model proposed instead a single encirclement with all the forces committed through the Ardennes, then driving north.

On October 27, von Rundstedt went to Model's headquarters to discuss Hitler's proposal and his and Model's suggested alternatives. The three army commanders who were to be involved—Sepp Dietrich, Hasso von Manteuffel, and Erich Brandenberger—also participated in what was their first initiation into the secret brotherhood in which they were to serve as potentates. After several hours of discussion, von Rundstedt directed Model to resolve the differences between their two plans. Conscious that the two commanders needed to present a united front if they were to have any power of persuasion with Hitler, Model prepared a final plan almost identical to von Rundstedt's.

As the commander of the Fifth Panzer Army, General von Manteuffel, put it, it was a matter of the "grand slam"—Hitler's plan—versus the "little slam"—von Rundstedt and Model's. (Von Manteuffel was an avid fan of contract bridge.) In time, the generals came to refer to them as the "Big Solution" and the "Small Solution." Since the Small Solution was virtually the same as that proposed earlier by General Jodl, its chances of getting past the Führer were predictably thin.

That failed to deter the old soldier and the ardent young Nazi commander from joining forces to do battle. In the first place, they sensed an ally in Alfred Jodl. In the second, although well aware that Hitler as supreme dictator had debased, broken, and even executed many of their compatriots while they and most of the others in the officer corps had looked on benignly, they were also aware that there were few field marshals of their stature and proven loyalty left to do the Führer's bidding. They were in a position to risk the Führer's fury.

They sensed Jodl's thinking when on November 2 a courier brought a written copy of Hitler's plan with a covering note from Jodl. In the note, Jodl wrote that Antwerp as the objective was "unalterable," but he added, "although from a strictly technical standpoint, it appears to be disproportionate to our available forces." He continued: "In our present situation, however, we must not shrink from staking everything on one card."

The next day, when Jodl followed up the written instructions by visiting Model's headquarters, he faced the combined protests of von Rundstedt, Model, and von Manteuffel—whom von Rundstedt had personally invited to be present. Von Manteuffel—as von Rundstedt intended—carried the weight of the argument, a fresh voice in the controversy. "General," he said to Jodl, "I think under your plan that we can reach the Meuse—but only if certain conditions are met." Every man, every tank, every plane, every gallon of gasoline, every round of ammunition as promised by Hitler would have to be on hand when the movement began, and the attack by the Seventh Army to protect the south flank would have to be materially strengthened. As von Manteuffel's statement inferred, he saw no possibility of an advance beyond the Meuse on Antwerp.

Jodl had thus heard another advocate of the Small Solution, but he had his orders. The Führer's plan, he replied, was "irrevocable." A week later, on November 10, the issue appeared to be closed when Hitler signed a formal operational directive specifying an offensive exactly as he himself had originally envisaged it.

Yet the man with over a half century of honorable service in the uniform of his country continued to protest, striving to spare the troops whose trust he bore the sure debacle he envisaged if Hitler persisted in his plan. Along with Model, von Rundstedt proposed yet another Small Solution: an attack from the north with some of the divisions scheduled for *WACHT AM RHEIN* into the northern flank of the American Ninth Army, which on November 16, along with the First Army, had begun a major offensive in the Aachen sector but had failed to achieve a breakthrough. That posed a chance to destroy some fourteen American divisions, which would have been weakened by their offensive, thereby setting up conditions conducive to a big German offensive to be mounted later on the order of the one Hitler had in mind.

Hitler saw through the gambit. "Preparations for an improvisation," Jodl replied in Hitler's name, "will not be made." Yet when it became apparent that the target date of November 25 was unrealistic and Hitler agreed to delay until December 10, von Rundstedt vowed to continue to try to effect a change. He saw a chance when Hitler called him and Model to a conference at the Reichschancellery in Berlin on December 2. Pleading preoccupation at the front, he sent his chief of staff, Westphal, to represent him, a form of protest not to be lost on Hitler; but he also sent two whom he hoped still might persuade Hitler to reconsider: von Manteuffel, who obviously stood high in the Führer's regard or he would not have brought him as a relatively junior general from the Eastern Front for such a major assignment in the offensive; and Hitler's old crony, Sepp Dietrich.

Nobody, including von Rundstedt, thought highly of Dietrich, but he was a favorite of Hitler's, and to his military colleagues he had already made clear the derision he felt for the job assigned him and the Sixth Panzer Army:

> All Hitler wants me to do is to cross a river, capture Brussels, and then go on and take Antwerp! And all this in the worst time of the year through the Ardennes where the snow is waist deep and there isn't room to deploy four tanks abreast let alone armored divisions! Where it doesn't get light until eight and it's dark again at four and with re-formed divisions made up chiefly of kids and sick old men—and at Christmas!

Von Manteuffel and Dietrich constituted von Rundstedt's big artillery, his fortress guns detailed to fire a final, decisive salvo. Yet the rounds fell short. Dietrich failed to speak at all, and von Manteuffel achieved only some minor changes, mostly of a tactical nature. Hitler nevertheless threw a sop to his faithful Nazi, Walter Model, by changing the codename to that used by Model in his plan for a Small Solution: *HERBSTNEBEL* (Autumn Mist). That was all.

What the field commanders failed to recognize—or to accept—was the desperation that lay behind Hitler's plan, a desperation reinforced by the Führer's megalomania and his distrust of his generals, whose ineptitude and disloyalty, he was convinced, were responsible for bringing Nazi Germany to the brink of destruction. From the day his generals tried to kill him, he had been convinced that he and he alone could save Germany, that some divine providence had spared him for that role, and that the way to do it was to exploit the dissensions he deemed inherent in the misalliance of his adversaries and to "continue this battle until, as Frederick the Great said, one of our damned enemies gets too tired to fight any more."

Destroying ten or fourteen or twenty American divisions around Aachen would not do it. He had to create conditions in which one nation could blame the other for the debacle that engulfed its troops, to sow mutual distrust, to deal such a blow that the people of Britain, Canada, and America would demand that their leaders bring their boys home. Surely, at some point—at that point—the Western democracies would realize that it was Adolf Hitler who had long been fighting their battle for them, the battle to keep the pagan Communist hordes out of civilized Europe.

Hardly had Hitler dismissed the four commanders on December 2 than he ordered preparations to begin for a move from the *Wolfschanze* to underground concrete chambers amid the wooded Taunus Hills little more than a mile and a half up a winding road from Ziegenberg Castle. From there—the *Adlerhorst* (Eagle's Aerie)—he personally would direct his grand offensive, as he had done from the same place for his triumph in 1940, under a design little altered from the one he had had in mind that day in September when he had slapped the map on his desk and first announced his decision: "Here, out of the Ardennes, with the objective, Antwerp!"

CHAPTER TWO

The Deception and the Intelligence Apparatus

Adolf Hitler and his intelligence chiefs considered that they had the most secure enciphering system for wireless communications in the world. It was impossible, they were convinced, to break its codes.

It consisted of a machine that looked like a bulky portable typewriter in a varnished wooden case measuring 7 by 11 by 13 inches. The letters on the keyboard were arranged like those on a typewriter, but there the similarity ended. There were no numbers or punctuation marks, and on a deck behind the keyboard, the twenty-six letters of the alphabet appeared in alphabetical order in three rows. When an operator punched a letter on the keyboard, one of the letters on the deck lit up but never the letter the operator punched; and if the operator punched the same letter another time, yet another different letter lit up.

As the operator worked, an assistant wrote down the letters as they appeared on the deck, and what he put down looked to be merely a jumbled collection of meaningless letters. The assistant then transmitted the jumble of letters in Morse code by wireless. Equipped with the same type of machine, the operator for whom the message was intended typed the jumbled letters onto his keyboard, whereupon they appeared on the deck in the same order in which the original operator had typed them and spelled out a meaningful message.

Like almost any transmission by wireless, the jumbled message could be intercepted. Yet it could be decoded, in theory, only by someone equipped with the same type of machine, and even then the decoder would have to know what particular setting the sender had used on his machine that day, for there were literally millions of possible settings. By late 1944, the Germans were changing the settings at least once a day, and there were different settings each day for each of the services that used the machine: the army, the navy, Luftwaffe, SS, Gestapo, and such civilian services as the *Reichsbahn* (German State Railroads).

The machine was known as the Enigma, named after the *Enigma Variations* in which the British composer Sir Edward Elgar described his friends in musical cipher. A Dutchman invented and patented it in 1919, but when he was unable to build a marketable machine, he sold the patents to a German engineer and inventor, Artur Scherbius. As successfully designed and developed by Scherbius, the machine was intended for commercial use to protect business secrets. By the time Hitler came to power in the early 1930s, the Enigma had been vastly improved. The reforming and expanding Wehrmacht adopted the machine as its basic enciphering device and continued to increase its capabilities and complexity while retaining its compactness and portability, which made it ideal for use in the field.

As Hitler began his preparations for *WACHT AM RHEIN*, it was apparent that somehow the Western Allies were obtaining German secrets, but so convinced was Hitler of the security of the Enigma—and as a dictator, so obsessed about traitors—that he attributed the leaks to some spy within his inner circle of advisers. Yet for something so vital as *WACHT AM RHEIN*, he could take no chances. He forbade transmission by telephone, telegraph, or wireless of any information that could in any way be connected with the offensive, including the supposedly deceptive codename he himself had coined. Anything dealing specifically and identifiably with the offensive had to be transmitted by officer courier, the Gestapo on his tail; and all else had to be justified by another codename, *ABWEHRSCHLACHT IM WESTEN* (Defensive Battle in the West), which was already in use for the fighting around Aachen.

To justify to foe and uninitiated friend alike the massing of men and supplies, the German command pointed to the imminent American offensive to be launched from positions near Aachen toward the Rhine and the industrial region of the Ruhr. The first paragraph of almost every movement order contained the words "in preparation for the anticipated enemy offensive." When the Sixth Panzer Army, for example, had completed its organization and its SS panzer divisions were refitted and prepared to move west of the Rhine, an entry in the War Diary of von Rundstedt's headquarters (known as *Oberbefehlshaber WEST*, or *OB WEST*) read: ". . . there can be no doubt that the enemy will commit maximum strength and maximum matériel to force the breakthrough to the Rhine. Our own defensive measures must be attuned to this. . . . Hence the Commander-in-Chief WEST will order the transfer of Sixth Panzer Army to the OB WEST theater on 7 November. . . ."

Then the Sixth Panzer Army moved, not into the Eifel whence it was to launch its attack, but onto the open plain near Cologne at which the Americans were to aim their November offensive; and there the Germans intentionally bungled their security, parading their preparations before the eager eyes of Allied intelligence. Not until three days before the offensive was to begin would the Sixth Panzer Army make the move of some thirty-five miles into the Eifel, and then only at night.

For the Fifth Panzer Army, which had seen its first commitment in control of a few panzer brigades in a futile counterattack in September against the Third U.S. Army's south flank in Lorraine, there was the problem of disengaging from the front in Lorraine and moving north for some apparent purpose not associated with the offensive. Since such a move could hardly escape Allied notice, von Manteuffel's headquarters appeared in late October in the line near Aachen, where it assumed command of two corps already committed. The Americans were obviously going to employ armor in their coming offensive; it was wholly logical for the Germans to oppose them with a headquarters schooled in the use of armor.

The shift of the Fifth Panzer Army served an added purpose in that it halved the sector then held by General Brandenberger's Seventh Army, which to that point had been responsible for both the Aachen sector and the Eifel. Von Manteuffel's entry into the line left Brandenberger responsible only for the Eifel, a reality to which Allied intelligence was long accustomed. Who might suspect that the Seventh Army had a new mission?

As the target date for the German offensive approached, it became essential to pull von Manteuffel and his headquarters back from the line in preparation. To mislead the enemy, the headquarters of the Fifteenth Army, which had been responsible for the sector opposite the British in the Netherlands, secretly relieved the headquarters of the Fifth Panzer Army and assumed an alias, *Gruppe von Manteuffel*, in the process getting into a proper position for mounting an attack in support of *WACHT AM RHEIN*. In the Netherlands, the headquarters of the Twenty-fifth Army, which took over from the Fifteenth Army, called itself the Fifteenth Army, while a bogus headquarters calling itself the Twenty-fifth Army pretended through false wireless traffic to be assembling west of the Rhine near the assembly area of the Sixth Panzer Army. When pulled from the line, von Manteuffel and his headquarters hid behind the innocuous name of *Feldjägerkommando z.b.V.* (Military Police Command for Special Assignment).

There was less complexity in relieving Field Marshal Model and his Army Group B of some of their responsibilities, for any intelligence officer would recognize that in commanding a front extending from the North Sea across the Netherlands into Germany and thence south almost to the Moselle River—more than 150 airline miles—Army Group B was overextended. Without unusual provisions for secrecy, a new headquarters, Army Group H, assumed control of the front in the Netherlands, leaving Model responsible only for the Aachen sector and—most importantly—the Ardennes-Eifel.

* * *

As those shifts took place, Field Marshal von Rundstedt's problem was to halt the American attacks, or at least to contain them sufficiently so that they would not jeopardize the German offensive. There was some space to be traded for time in the south, where on November 8 the Third U.S. Army began to attack from the vicinity of Metz aimed at gaining the German frontier and penetrating the West Wall in the Saar-Palatinate, that corner of Germany lying in the angle between the Moselle and the Rhine. Nor was there particular concern about the First French and Seventh U.S. Armies that had driven up from southern France, for even should those armies get through the forbidding Vosges Mountains, the broad moat of the Rhine would bar the way. The critical sector was in the north.

There von Rundstedt gained some respite in that once the Allied attempt to jump the canals and rivers of the Netherlands with airborne troops failed, the British commander, Field Marshal Sir Bernard L. Montgomery, had to turn his attention to clearing the seaward approaches to Antwerp. Failing to clear the sixty-mile approach to Antwerp from the sea when the port fell without a fight in early September had been one of the more serious tactical lapses of the campaign, and Hitler's order to build a strong defense along the banks of the Schelde Estuary a most prescient reaction.

As the Allied attack began in mid-October, the Germans opened dikes that industrious Dutchmen through the years had erected to keep out an antagonistic North Sea, and it took the Allied soldiers—mostly Canadians—almost a month to battle through mud, muck, and flood before the last German soldier fell back from the banks of the Schelde. Even then minesweepers required three weeks to cleanse the channel, so that not until November 28—three months after the British took Antwerp—was the first supply ship to drop anchor in the port.

Around Aachen, von Rundstedt had neither leeway nor respite. As the First and Ninth U.S. Armies began their offensive there on November 16, the jump-off line was in some places no more than six miles from the little Roer River, the only obstacle remaining before the open plain comprising the last twenty-five miles to Cologne and the Rhine.

To be sure, the American command had aided von Rundstedt during October and early November by attacking with inadequate strength to clear a vast stretch of woodland south and southeast of Aachen, an extension of the forests of the Ardennes and the Eifel known as the Hürtgen Forest. As the Americans attacked, they ignored the fact that on the upper reaches of the Roer River the forest concealed two big dams, the Schwammenauel and the Urftalsperre. Should the Germans blow the dams, they could produce a single destructive flood wave in downstream lowlands where the Roer marks the start of the Cologne Plain, or by calculatedly releasing the waters slowly, a flood that might last for two weeks or more to prevent crossings of the Roer or trap any force that had jumped the river.

Those dams thus were of critical importance to von Rundstedt, for even should his defense falter in front of the Roer, he could still gain at least two weeks on behalf of Hitler's offensive by manipulating the waters of the river. Conversely—and unknown to von Rundstedt—the American command was belatedly to become aware of the importance of the dams. Just three days before the German offensive began, the First Army was to mount an attack to seize them, an event that was to have an effect on Hitler's offensive far out of proportion to the number of American troops involved.

In the end, the German defense held. It was a remarkable achievement, accomplished as part of a resurgence that some Germans, in remembrance of World War I's Miracle of the Marne, referred to as the "Miracle of the West." Lashed by Hitler's ambition and regimented by the rigorous discipline of the police state, Nazi Germany and its army during the fall of 1944 demonstrated a resilience not unlike that of the giant Antaeus in Greek mythology, who regained his strength whenever he touched Mother Earth.

During the last half of 1944, the German Army refitted the skeletons of thirty-five divisions that had been stripped of flesh on either the Eastern or Western Front and built fifteen new divisions. With a salaam to the German people (*das Volk*), Hitler traded on national pride by calling them *Volksgrenadier* (people's infantry) divisions, an honorific previously reserved for infantry divisions that had performed with extraordinary ability and valor.

In selecting that name, Hitler drew an unanticipated intelligence bonus. Only recently he had issued a public decree calling for a levy of the rank and file of the German people to flock to the defense of the Fatherland. He called that force the *Volksturm*, and both the Supreme Allied Commander, General Eisenhower, and the commander of the 12th Army Group, Lt. Gen. Omar N. Bradley, who was responsible for the Ardennes, confused the two, seriously underestimating the capabilities of what they termed the new *Volksturm* divisions.

Some of the new and refitted divisions had to be returned to the Eastern Front and some helped hold the line in the West, but others joined the four SS panzer divisions as part of the Führer's strategic reserve. Without Hitler's knowledge, von Rundstedt used a few of the divisions to relieve others temporarily so that they might be pulled from the line for quick rehabilitation before the offensive, but few of them stayed in the line for long. With Hitler's approval, some of the newly formed general support artillery and rocket units were employed at some length, in the process eating into ammunition reserves stockpiled for the Ardennes but at the same time gaining battle experience. So, too, ten to twenty thousand men who might have helped fill the strategic reserve had to fight as individual replacements in the defensive battles. Yet in the end, of twenty-eight divisions specifically designated for the offensive, only an SS panzer division, a *Volksgrenadier* division, and two panzer divisions were never able to get out of the line for the refitting necessary for participating in the offensive. The process of getting the others ready, plus two reinforced brigades, nevertheless pushed forward Hitler's target date another five days, to December 15.

That the soldiers making up the new and refitted divisions bore little resemblance to the well-trained, thoroughly indoctrinated, splendidly equipped troops that had swept out of the Ardennes in 1940 was obvious to all. It was only with moderate hyperbole that General Dietrich, who had a reputation for grousing, complained of divisions filled mainly with "kids and sick old men"; but even though under the new decrees sixteen- and seventeen-year-olds were liable for service, few below the age of seventeen were actually assigned to army combat units, although there were many under that age and even younger who served as volunteers or quasi-volunteers in the SS divisions. So, too, even though men through age sixty were theoretically liable for service, few of anywhere near that age were actually called, and seldom did a man over forty-five find himself in a combat unit. The principal weakness of the troops was a lack of training for those men only recently called up and for the thousands upon thousands hastily transferred from the navy, the Luftwaffe, and rear echelon assignments. Yet the numbers at least—a total of more than 250,000 for the first wave—were impressive, and there was still a residue of considerable size of combat veterans and hard-nosed noncommissioned officers to infuse flint into the new and refitted formations.

In equipment, the most serious shortage was motor transport. Even the best-equipped divisions had no more than 80 percent of the vehicles called for under their tables of equipment, and one *Panzergrenadier* division had sixty different types of motor vehicle. Providing spare parts for such a fleet would have been a nightmare, but there were few spare parts for vehicles in any case. Another panzer division, the *Panzer Lehr* (so named because it had originally been a training demonstration division), had only enough half-tracks to transport one of its *Panzergrenadier* battalions; the others had to use trucks or bicycles.

On the other hand, the amount of artillery the army managed to amass was impressive. There were nine of the new artillery units, known as *Volksartillerie* corps, each equipped with fifty to a hundred pieces, and seven of the new rocket, or *Volkswerfer*, brigades, each with more than a hundred rocket projectors; and both types of units were fully motorized. The difficulty with those and other corps and army artillery units was that the guns were of varying caliber and even manufacture—there were, for example, more than a smattering of French and Russian pieces. That complicated ammunition supply. The total of all general support artillery and rockets was 1,900 pieces, a powerful array, and that was in addition to artillery organic to the divisions. Much of the divisional artillery was horse-drawn, but the German soldier had long been accustomed to that.

While the Eastern Front and other parts of the Western Front starved through the fall for want of armored vehicles, Hitler allotted to Army Group B and the strategic reserve 2,168 tanks and assault guns (German statistics always lumped the two together). Most of the assault guns were a lightly armored, self-propelled, high-velocity 75mm. piece, which was an effective antitank weapon as well as a superb weapon for supporting infantry in the attack.

Since some 700 tanks and assault guns had to be held, at least for a time, with the Fifteenth Army for the projected attack in support of *WACHT AM RHEIN*, that left approximately 970 for the opening wave of the offensive and around 450 for the follow-up force. Hitler's beloved SS panzer divisions had priority on those. The total numbers available fell short of the 2,500 that had participated in the Blitzkrieg through the Ardennes in 1940, but it was a powerful force nevertheless.

As expected, it was in tactical aircraft that the Germans were weakest. Despite Hitler's early prediction of at least 1,500 fighter-bombers, the commander of the Luftwaffe, Reichsmarshal Hermann Goering, could promise only a thousand and was actually able to deliver only a few more than that, and those in driblets except on one spectacular occasion. That figure bore no comparison with the two thousand available in 1940.

Those forces were all that Hitler could muster for an offensive in the sixth winter of the war. Given the condition of the Third Reich by that time and the vast superiority in men, weapons, and equipment of its enemies, to assemble even that much while still fighting on two fronts was an exceptional achievement. That the numbers were no fewer was attributable in large measure to the defensive stand of a presumably defeated German soldier who had regained his strength upon touching Mother Earth, and to the performance of his leaders, the old soldier Gerd von Rundstedt and the lion of defense Walter Model.

Transporting the attack divisions to their assembly areas and accumulating and transporting the ammunition, rations, and fuel that they would need in the opening days of the offensive was another remarkable achievement. By Hitler's order, the assignment went to General Jodl's chief, the head of the *OKW*, Field Marshal Keitel. Under a head of state less unorthodox than Adolf Hitler, an officer in Keitel's post would have been in the forefront of the strategic and tactical planning for the offensive; but Hitler himself had all but usurped that role, and Keitel was not a man to press his prerogatives with his Führer. (Some made a pun on his name, calling him *Lakaitel*, meaning "Little Lackey.") Yet the head of the *OKW* was an efficient administrator, and he brought to the logistical assembly for the Ardennes that not unworthy talent.

The workhorse of the buildup was the *Reichsbahn*. By 1944 the state
railroad system was so thoroughly tied in with the Wehrmacht that it was
in essence an adjunct of the military. Ever since the swift and massive
concentration for the Franco-Prussian War in 1870, which had astounded
the world, the German General Staff had looked to the railroads as the
basic instrument for strategic concentration, which explained the creation
of spur lines into the Eifel before the Great War. In preparation for the
Ardennes offensive, engineers reinforced the pillars and supports of all
the rail bridges over the Rhine lest some lucky hit by an Allied bomb
should send an entire bridge crashing into the water.

A lucky hit it probably would have been, for Allied airmen considered
bridges of any kind to be one of the most difficult of targets. Ringed with
multiple batteries of flak guns, the bridges over the Rhine were doubly
inaccessible, and throughout the fall of 1944, as official priority focused
on other targets, Allied airmen made no concentrated effort to take out
the Rhine bridges.

For the trains themselves and the marshalling yards there was no such
immunity. Yet darkness and rain or a sky heavily overcast were all elements basic to Hitler's entire plan. Each train carried its own antiaircraft
guns, which tended to keep the *jabos*, as the Germans called Allied
fighter-bombers, at high and usually ineffective altitudes; and the cabs of
locomotives had long been plated with armor to cut down on casualties
from strafing among engine crews. For the final run across the Rhine into
the Eifel, engineers timed their movement for an overnight trip, and if
anything untoward intervened, there were a number of tunnels in which
to hide until bad weather or nightfall came again. Laborers were so organized for quick repairs at the marshalling yards that seldom, even after a
heavy air attack, did bomb damage interfere with operations for longer
than forty-eight hours. The fact that through much of the fall Allied airmen made German oil production rather than transportation their
number one target also helped the railroads.

The campaign against oil had its effect, although not nearly to the
extent that Allied analysts perceived. By stringent rationing, by drawing
on stockpiles, and by taking extraordinary measures to bring oil from
Hungary (except for synthetic oil plants, the only source remaining), Keitel managed to meet the anticipated requirement of not quite five million
gallons, but about half of that would still be on the east bank of the
Rhine as the offensive began. There was no intent to rely on captured
Allied stocks of gasoline—any such stocks would be a bonus—for sufficient supplies were on hand. Yet that was not to say that there would be
no problems in getting fuel forward to the troops who needed it.

In trying to keep the offensive secret, moving the German fighter aircraft westward, however few in numbers, posed a special problem. Any
careful observer of the air scene during the early weeks of autumn could
have discerned that the Luftwaffe had virtually abandoned close air sup-

port for the Western Front in order to concentrate its available aircraft for defense of the industrial centers. Since Allied air attacks against the homeland continued without let-up, any move of fighter aircraft back to the West would appear to be odd. In the event, Reichsmarshal Goering failed in his attempt at secrecy, but how the Allied command reacted to the failure was another matter.

Toward the end of the first week of December, corps commanders who were to be involved in the offensive were at last let in on Hitler's secret, and on the 10th, the division commanders. Late the next afternoon, von Rundstedt, Model, von Manteuffel, and approximately half the corps and division commanders (the others were to be called in the next day) gathered at von Rundstedt's headquarters in Ziegenberg Castle. Ordered to divest themselves of their side arms and briefcases, they boarded a bus, which began a circuitous tour in darkness and rain through the countryside lasting half an hour and ending finally at the *Adlerhorst*, actually a three-minute ride from Ziegenberg Castle.

Dismounting, the generals passed between a double row of armed SS guards, standing rigidly to attention, and descended into a deep underground conference room. As they sat down around a large square table, an SS guard assumed a position behind each chair, glowering with a ferocity that made at least one of the generals, Fritz Bayerlein, fear even to reach for his handkerchief.

Entering with Keitel and Jodl, Hitler took a seat at a long narrow table at one end of the room. He was, von Manteuffel noted, "a broken man, with an unhealthy color, a caved-in appearance." His hands trembled, and to von Manteuffel, who had seen him less than a fortnight earlier, he appeared to have aged even in that short time: "His body seemed still more decrepit, and he was a man grown old, completely overworked and tired."

Yet when Hitler began to speak, his appearance changed. A kind of fire came into his eyes, and as his speech gathered momentum, he grew ever more forceful. For more than two hours he harangued his audience, speaking extemporaneously of German history, German destiny, the glories of Frederick the Great, the absolute necessity for *Lebensraum* for the great German people, the virtues of what he called the preventive war he had begun in 1939, the necessity for a nation to display not only toughness, stubbornness, and endurance but also daring, "to make it clear to the enemy that whatever he would do he will never be able to count on a capitulation, never, never, never!" People had doubted him over Austria, over Czechoslovakia, over France, but he had triumphed, and he would triumph again. It was then that he began his tirade about the strange bedfellows the war had aligned against Germany—"Ultra-capitalist states on one side; ultra-Marxist states on the other." A great victory would "bring down this artificial coalition with a crash."

The next day, as Hitler briefed his second set of generals, he granted his commanders a minor concession: a twenty-four-hour postponement for last-minute preparations at the front. *Null-Tag* (literally, Zero Day), the jump-off date, was set for Saturday, December 16. There was to be no further postponement.

The naming of a final target date set in motion a plan previously worked out in meticulous detail for a three-day movement to forward assembly areas, a plan based in large measure on the secrecy achieved in preparation for a number of German offensives in World War I and for the concentration in 1940. Although the troops were to be told nothing of what they were about to do until the night before the jump-off, the *Volksdeutsch* (ethnic Germans from Alsace and other border regions) had already been combed from the combat units lest they go over to the enemy with some small but revealing knowledge of what was to come. Troops marched only by night, taking cover by day in forests and cooking only with charcoal fires. Special security detachments prowled in search of anybody who violated camouflage discipline. Patrolling on the existing front line was restricted to the most trusted soldiers lest somebody who had observed more than he should might desert. There was to be no increase in artillery fires above the norm.

Those troops not already in the line—a few of the *Volksgrenadier* divisions had already relieved units not scheduled for the offensive—were allowed to advance at first no closer than twelve miles toward the front, then to move progressively forward over the last two nights, first to a line six miles from the front, then two. In concern for the noise created by tanks and in recognition of their mobility, the restraining line for panzer units was farther to the rear. On the last two nights, as tanks and artillery pressed closer to the front, troops covered the roads with straw to muffle the sound, and planes flew low over American positions in hope of concealing or at least disguising the noise.

To eighteen-year-old Pvt. Helmut Stiegeler, the snow and the cold reminded him that Christmas was only a short time away. "Our thoughts wandered to our folks back home, no one talked to the other, and silently we marched along, unaware of what was ahead of us." The next night, the night before the jump-off, Stiegeler and other men of the 12th Volksgrenadier Division's engineer battalion at last learned what they were to do. After an evening meal of sweet rice with plums, "each group was given a bottle of booze, and off we went."

Meanwhile, for all the efforts at secrecy, there had been yet another lapse in security at the governmental level when on November 15 the Japanese ambassador, Baron Oshima, was invited to confer with Foreign Minister von Ribbentrop at Sonnenberg, sixty miles east of Berlin. During the conversation, Oshima asked about the offensive in the West that

Hitler had told him would be launched sometime "after the beginning of November." Had there been any change in that intention?

Although von Ribbentrop was evasive about details and timing, he confirmed that Hitler still intended to take the offensive in the West. Then, again, it might be the East.

There were some, suggested Baron Oshima, who believed that the big German offensive in 1918 had hastened Germany's defeat, that without it the war might have ended differently. Would it not be "a wise plan for Germany to fight a war of attrition?"

"Absolutely not!" rejoined von Ribbentrop. "The Chancellor believes that we cannot win this war by defense alone and has reiterated his intention of taking the offensive right to the bitter end."

In reporting that conversation to Tokyo, Baron Oshima sneered at the possibility of a German offensive. It was, he said, "one of the instances in which truth from the mouth of a liar reaches the highest pinnacle of deceptiveness"; but a few days later he changed his view. Thinking back to his earlier conversation with Hitler, he notified Tokyo that he believed "we may take at face value" the intent of the German leadership to mount an offensive, for "a Germany whose battle lines have contracted virtually to the old territory of Germany . . . will have no choice but to open a road of blood in one direction or another." And probably, he added, in the West.

As always, those two messages from Oshima to his government were soon on the desks of intelligence officers in the Pentagon.

"He who defends everything," Frederick the Great used to admonish his generals, "defends nothing." During the fall of 1944 the Supreme Allied Commander, General Eisenhower, had sixty-five infantry, airborne, and armored divisions with which to cover a front extending from the North Sea to Switzerland, a distance, not counting local twistings and turnings, of over five hundred miles. Had he divided the front equally among his divisions, each would have been responsible for just over seven miles, which would have constituted a fairly cohesive linear defense. Yet what if the enemy should penetrate the line; where was the reserve to eliminate the penetration? Besides, nobody won wars by defense alone. The problem was how to gain sufficient strength for an attack.

Eisenhower's solution was to concentrate his forces within two sectors where the terrain was most conducive to advance: one concentration south of the Ardennes pointed toward the Saar industrial region; the second, and larger, north of the Ardennes pointed toward the Ruhr. To make those concentrations possible, he employed only minimal forces to defend the other sectors, particularly in Alsace and the Ardennes. Even so, Eisenhower was unable to hold out a reserve.

As the alignment developed, the British 21st Army Group with the

First Canadian and Second British Armies under Field Marshal Montgomery was in the far north, mainly in the Netherlands. To the far south, the 6th Army Group, commanded by Lt. Gen. Jacob L. Devers, had the Seventh U.S. and First French Armies, mainly in Alsace. The American 12th Army Group, under General Bradley, was in the center: the Ninth Army north of Aachen, the First Army around and south of Aachen, and the Third Army in Lorraine.

While the First Army's greatest concentration was in the vicinity of Aachen, its commander, Lt. Gen. Courtney H. Hodges, was also responsible for the Ardennes. The assignment fell in turn primarily to the VIII Corps, which had to cover a front extending from the Losheim Gap in the north to a point southeast of Luxembourg City in the south, a distance of about sixty miles. Since the VIII Corps had only three infantry divisions, that meant a defensive frontage for each division of about twenty miles, more than double the length of front normally assigned a division to defend. In the northern reaches of the Ardennes, from the Losheim Gap to the vicinity of Monschau, the southernmost division of the V Corps held a front of similar length, so that only four divisions were responsible for the entire eighty-mile front through the Ardennes.

The Allied deployment reflected what became known as Eisenhower's "broad front strategy," which was actually nothing more than a version of an age-old, time-tested practice of advancing in parallel columns. Yet to Eisenhower's chief British subordinate, Field Marshal Montgomery, it was anathema. In late summer and through the autumn, Montgomery insisted that the Allied command possessed neither the strength nor the logistical resources to support two major drives into Germany. He wanted the entire front to go on the defensive except in the sector north of the Ardennes, where he wanted to concentrate sufficient strength and sufficient logistical support to launch and sustain a juggernaut all the way to Berlin.

It was a proposal not without reason or merit, but Montgomery—who was inclined to argue his proposals in imperious tones—weakened it by insisting that the entire attacking force, to be composed of British, Canadians, and Americans, be under his command; indeed, that he be designated as overall ground commander for the entire Western Front. To American generals, the proposal appeared to reek of personal ambition, an attempt to usurp a portion of Eisenhower's prerogative as Supreme Commander, a position that had gone to an American for the basic reason that the United States would be furnishing the preponderance of forces. ("Monty's suggestion is simple," Eisenhower confided at one point; "give him everything, which is crazy.")

Yet there were other reasons why Eisenhower turned Montgomery down. There was no way, his logistical planners told him after detailed study, that the existing resources could be reallocated to make it possible to sustain an offensive all the way to Berlin. The basic problem was the lack of ports close to the front, a problem to which Montgomery himself had contributed by failing to clear the banks of the Schelde Estuary once Antwerp fell with its port facilities intact. There was also a possibility that the German armies were less nearly finished than seemed apparent from the overwhelming defeat inflicted on them in France, that they might muster reserves to deal telling blows to any thrust whose flanks would be exposed for several hundred miles. Eisenhower himself had seen, at a place in North Africa called Kasserine Pass, the damage supposedly defeated German forces could wreak.

It was a serious difference of opinion, one replete with rancor. German agents may well have passed some word of it to Berlin, thereby contributing to Hitler's belief that a grand offensive in the West stood a chance of splitting the Anglo-American alliance. Yet for all the rancor, the fact was that it was nothing more than a difference of opinion between a commander and a subordinate, albeit the two senior field commanders of the two principal powers in the Allied coalition; but those were two powers that had achieved a degree of cooperation and coordination never before known in coalition warfare. Although serious differences of opinion and such human failings as national chauvinism and personal antagonism well might recur under the impact of severe adversity at the front, would even the spectacle of the two senior commanders coming to blows be sufficient to wreck such a close-knit coalition?

The exchanges between Eisenhower and Montgomery over strategy and command occurred at a time of heady optimism, an optimism reflected in intelligence reports at every level. In late August, for example, the G-2 at Eisenhower's Supreme Headquarters, Allied Expeditionary Force (SHAEF), Maj. Gen. Kenneth W. D. Strong, had written: "Two and a half months of bitter fighting, culminating for the Germans in a blood-bath big enough even for their extravagant tastes, have brought the end of the war in Europe within sight, almost within reach." It was a view the Supreme Commander himself fully shared. "The defeat of the German armies is complete," he noted a few days later in the course of dictating an office memorandum, "and the only thing now needed . . . is speed."

At headquarters of the First U.S. Army, the G-2, Col. Benjamin A. Dickson, saw political upheaval within Germany or insurrection within the Wehrmacht as likely to hasten the end of the war. The commander of the First Army, General Hodges, had sent General Bradley a bronze bust of Hitler taken from a house in the Belgian border town of Eupen and told the commander of the 12th Army Group that, given ample ammunition and an additional division, the First Army would "deliver the original in thirty days." However much Hodges jested, the incident reflected the prevailing state of mind.

Only one among the G-2s in the senior commands sounded a note of caution. At headquarters of the Third U.S. Army, Col. Oscar W. Koch (pronounced Kotch) remarked that for all the debacle that had befallen the enemy, "his withdrawal, though continuing, has not been a rout or mass collapse." All indications pointed to the fact that the Germans were determined "to wage a last-ditch struggle in the field at all costs." The enemy, he noted, was "playing for time," and weather and terrain would soon be on his side.

Yet Koch's was a lone voice, and despite the stiffening of resistance in the lowlands of the Netherlands, at Aachen, in the Hürtgen Forest, and in the rolling hills of Lorraine, the optimism was slow to dissipate. Meeting in Washington in October, the Allied body charged with directing the conduct of the war, the Combined Chiefs of Staff—made up of the service chiefs of both Britain and the United States—still saw hope of an early victory. They wanted Eisenhower to institute extraordinary measures to assure victory before the year 1944 came to an end: shift the strategic air offensive from all but the most immediately remunerative targets; employ all troops and stockpiles of supplies without regard for withholding reserves; and make use of a heretofore super-secret proximity fuse (VT or POZIT) that exploded an artillery shell by radio impulse in the air just short of the target, thereby sharply increasing the lethal fragmentation effect of the burst.

Eisenhower himself at that point urged caution. The approaches to Antwerp still had to be cleared, he told the U.S. Army's chief of staff, General George C. Marshall, and the port facilities of Antwerp were essential to the final battle. Eisenhower nevertheless saw the possibility of taking the Ruhr before the end of the year or at least of gaining a bridgehead over the Rhine.

Those were the goals of the American offensive that opened near Aachen on November 16, but after almost a month of fighting and a cost to two American armies of 125,000 casualties (killed, wounded, missing, and so-called nonbattle casualties), the American troops were gazing not at the fabled Rhine but at an obscure, flood-threatened Roer only six miles beyond the line from which they had started. Furthermore, they were powerless to cross the little river until somebody got around to doing something about the dams upstream.

The fact that German troops who in September had appeared thoroughly beaten had fought back with such determination and relative success, the Allied commanders attributed to German stubbornness, to blind faith in the Führer, to devotion to the home soil, and, most of all, to the solid generalship of Gerd von Rundstedt. There were other contributing factors: abominable weather, constricted terrain, the West Wall, some few continuing logistical problems on the Allied side. Yet nobody saw in the stalwart German stand any grand design that might threaten the survival of the Allied armies.

Indeed, Allied intelligence officers perceived the heavy fighting as contributing to the possibility of a sudden German collapse. Even before the November offensive began, Eisenhower's G-2, General Strong, noted that the Germans were losing the equivalent of a division every few days and were being forced to shift meager reserves hither and yon as one threat subsided and another arose. "The dwindling fire brigade," wrote Strong, "is switched with increasing rapidity and increasing wear and tear from one fire to another." When the Germans failed to react with a strong counterattack against the American offensive that opened near Aachen on November 16, the First Army's G-2, Colonel Dickson, considered that they had lost any opportunity for a decisive blow and saw the possibility of large-scale surrenders leading to the collapse of the German state.

As late as December 12, only four days before the Germans were destined to emerge from the mists and snows of the Eifel into the Ardennes, the report of the 12th Army Group's G-2, Brig. Gen. Edwin L. Sibert, noted: "It is now certain that attrition is steadily sapping the strength of German forces on the western front and that the crust of defenses is thinner, more brittle and more vulnerable than it appears on G-2 maps or to troops in the line." At about the same time, Field Marshal Montgomery's G-2, a don from Oxford University, Brig. E. T. Williams, was declaring: "The enemy is in a bad way . . . his situation is such that he cannot stage a major offensive operation."

"Gentlemen," Secretary of State Henry L. Stimson reputedly stated in 1929 when abolishing a small State Department–funded cryptanalysis branch known as the Black Chamber, "do not read one another's mail." Yet the remark failed to deter the Signal Intelligence Section of the army's Signal Corps and the navy's Office of Naval Intelligence from trying to read the mail of potential enemies, particularly that of the Japanese, which led to the remarkable achievement of MAGIC. On the other hand, that attention to one aspect of the dirty work of spying failed to carry over into the field of battlefield intelligence.

In the United States Army, seldom did an officer consciously pursue a career in battlefield intelligence. The 12th Army Group's G-2, General Sibert, for example, got into intelligence simply because somebody flagged his file after he served a tour of duty as military attaché in Brazil; and the First Army's G-2, Colonel Dickson, was a reserve officer who when called to active duty in 1940 drew an assignment in intelligence only because he was proficient in French and German. Seldom did G-2s move on to high command; those gems went to chiefs of staff and to plans and operations officers, the G-3s. The G-2 and his counterpart at regimental and battalion level (S-2) held one rank below that of the G-3 or S-3, and before war came, they often drew lowly extra duties such as club officer or command historian.

In the British Army, by contrast, intelligence was a prestigious field.

Eisenhower's G-2, General Strong, for example, planned a role in intelligence from his days as a cadet at the Royal Military Academy at Sandhurst, where he became fluent in French, German, and Italian. Following a prewar tour as an assistant military attaché in Berlin, he headed the German Section of the War Office, then served successively as chief of intelligence of the Home Forces and of Allied Force Headquarters in the Mediterranean.

That was not to say that American intelligence officers were incapable. As with any group of staff officers, their abilities varied; but almost to a man they encountered the antipathy of other members of their staffs arising from the long-established low estate of the intelligence officer. (General Sibert said he often heard the remark: "I wonder what is wrong with him that he is in G-2.") For Colonel Dickson at the First Army's headquarters, the situation was compounded by a personality conflict with a strong-willed chief of staff, Maj. Gen. William B. Kean—who, many said, virtually ran the First Army (the staff called him Captain Bligh)—as well as between himself and the G-3 section.

Benjamin Abbot ("Monk") Dickson got his nickname from childhood playmates in Washington, D.C., who dubbed him "Monkey"; his older brother shortened it to "Monk," calling him that when the two were at West Point, and it stuck. He was a handsome man, over 6 feet, 3 inches tall, angular, mustached; and at thirty-seven years of age he maintained the same weight (190 pounds) at which he had played on the football team at the Military Academy. In the classroom Dickson displayed a photographic memory, a talent that was to serve him well in the profession he eventually entered. He graduated from West Point in one of the accelerated classes during World War I and served in the American Expeditionary Force in Siberia; but after assessing the chances of promotion in the postwar army as poor, he resigned, earned a degree in mechanical engineering from the Massachusetts Institute of Technology, and went into the warehouse business in Philadelphia.

Having maintained a reserve commission, he returned to active duty as a captain in 1940 and soon rose to become a corps G-3 in North Africa, where he gained a reputation as a pessimist, which stuck with him even though events at Kasserine Pass proved his point. He also gained the confidence of his commander, General Bradley, who took him along to England when forming the staff of the First Army; but when Bradley, after the invasion of Normandy, moved up to command the 12th Army Group, a readymade staff was waiting, so that Dickson, Kean, and the others were left behind.

Going beyond the usual resentment of one headquarters for the next senior headquarters, the First Army's staff officers saw their counterparts at the 12th Army Group as Johnny-come-latelys, lacking their own battlefield experience, and some on occasion played on their past association with General Bradley to bypass his staff and deal directly with the general. None resentéd his counterpart at the 12th Army Group more than did Dickson, for Edwin Sibert was a career artilleryman who had never served in intelligence until to his surprise he was plucked from an artillery command with an infantry division in the United States to become G-2 at headquarters of the European Theater, which was essentially an administrative and logistical headquarters. On the basis of experience in North Africa and Normandy, Dickson viewed Sibert's job—and his rank—as rightfully his. Although Dickson later denied that he held any animosity for Sibert, his contemporaries saw it otherwise; one remarked that he "hated Sibert and the latter reciprocated."

Whether for that reason or for some other, coordination between the G-2 sections of the First Army and the 12th Army Group was minimal. Except when specifically asked, Dickson never visited headquarters of the 12th Army Group, and when he wanted to consult a G-2 at a higher level, he went to Brigadier Williams at headquarters of the 21st Army Group. Under the American staff system, there was no chain of command among intelligence staffs: Dickson served his commander, Sibert his; and even though Dickson served at a subordinate level, Sibert had neither command nor technical jurisdiction over him.

To Monk Dickson's associates in intelligence at higher levels, he was a volatile man, a pessimist, an alarmist. It was sufficient, for example, whenever Dickson learned that the Russians had lost contact with a division on the Eastern Front, for him to list it in the enemy's order of battle in the West. At times he might have several divisions listed in the West that other intelligence officers knew to be elsewhere. They called them "Monk's shrubbery." Although the practice caused no real harm, it contributed to the view of Dickson as an alarmist, a man who sometimes had to be sat on.

At an operational level—army group and below—prisoners of war constituted a basic source of intelligence. American intelligence officers considered themselves particularly adept at gleaning information from German prisoners, for they might employ as interrogators refugee German Jews whose appearance belied their race but whose knowledge of Germany enabled them to gain a prisoner's confidence and ask penetrating questions. Thus the intelligence officers saw no reason to question what they learned from prisoners during much of the fall of 1944, and since most of those who surrendered were dregs, their morale low, the interrogations tended to reinforce the view that Germany would be unable for long to continue the fight. So, too, did the capture of prisoners from such special units as so-called stomach battalions, composed of men with digestive problems who required a special diet. Did not the very existence of those units indicate that the Third Reich was running out of manpower?

In France and Belgium, civilians had also been a basic source of intelligence, but with the crossing of the German border, information from civilians had virtually ceased to exist. It was much the same story with special agents from the Washington-based Office of Strategic Services (OSS), who had found it relatively easy to penetrate the lines in France but who had little success inside Germany.

Furthermore, relations between the First Army's headquarters and the OSS were strained. In Normandy, Colonel Dickson had found the OSS agents to be individualistic, their demands on the army's communications too heavy; and he had convinced General Hodges to kick them out, with the exception of a small section under Capt. Stuyvesant Wainwright that engaged in counterespionage and antisubversion. ("I don't want a man from OSS," Dickson reputedly declared, "nor a dwarf, nor a pygmy, nor a Goddamned soul.") In the office of the OSS detachment at headquarters of the 12th Army Group, some wag placed under a picture of Hitler the caption: "He fools some of the people some of the time but he fools Dickson all of the time."

The strain increased when somebody at the First Army's headquarters wrote a parody of a prisoner-of-war report, allegedly representing an interrogation of Hitler's latrine orderly. Finding it amusing, Captain Wainwright sent it to his OSS superiors at the 12th Army Group, where everybody missed the point and took the parody seriously. An order was soon on the way to the First Army to fly the prisoner back to SHAEF for further questioning, much to the subsequent embarrassment of the OSS.

In the long run, it probably made little difference that the First Army had only one small section of OSS operatives, for those located at headquarters of the 12th Army Group had every license to operate in the First Army's sector and beyond it into enemy territory. Yet not a single OSS agent penetrated the line and entered the Eifel before the enemy's offensive began.

Another basic source of battlefield intelligence was aerial reconnaissance, including that conducted by artillery observation aircraft. Despite many days of inclement weather in the month preceding the German offensive, seldom were all reconnaissance aircraft grounded. During that month of November, the 67th Tactical Reconnaissance Group of the IX Tactical Air Command, which supported the First Army, flew 361 missions, of which two-thirds were considered successful. Yet seldom were missions flown over the region that was to prove critical, the Eifel, for the basic concern was the sector in the north between the Roer River and the Rhine. Although there were many requests for reconnaissance over the Eifel, air officers assigned them low priority, and when weather was marginal, pilots usually elected to fly over the presumably more important region to the north. In the critical last five days before the German attack, pilots of the 67th Tactical Reconnaissance Group flew only three missions over the Eifel, all three on December 14 over Trier.

Partly because a portion of the Eifel lay in the projected zone of advance of the Third Army and partly because airfields of the reconnaissance group of the XIX Tactical Air Command, which supported the Third Army, were better situated than those of the IX Tactical Air Command's reconnaissance group for missions over the Eifel, the commander of the Third Army, Lt. Gen. George S. Patton, Jr., gained approval for pilots of the 10th Tactical Reconnaissance Group to include the Eifel in their coverage. The reports of that group were thus added to the accumulated knowledge of what was going on in the Eifel, as were the reports of the pilots of fighter-bombers flying attack missions and those of two available night fighter squadrons, although neither of those squadrons had more than ten P-61 night fighters, so that their contribution was limited.

At corps and army headquarters, there were Signal Radio Intelligence Companies that constantly monitored the enemy's voice radio communications, usually at division level and below. By that monitoring or by radio directional finding, the companies often picked up the shift of German divisions. Yet German radio security was in general excellent, and those companies discerned "absolutely no indication" of what was about to happen in the Ardennes.

Yet another source of operational intelligence was the front line itself, where outposts day after day looked across at the enemy and where patrols almost every night probed the line. Many an American soldier who gazed out on the Eifel in those days would later recall reports he had submitted that, in his opinion, should have told his superiors that something was afoot; but in most cases he was unaware of the various sieves the information he provided had to pass through. Before ever reaching the First Army, the word he passed back went through S-2s at battalion and regiment and G-2s at division and corps. Each in his turn evaluated the message, reflecting in the process his own preconceptions, his own appreciation of the enemy situation, so that in the end many a front-line soldier's report failed to go much beyond the regimental level, and when it did, it might be deflated by an S-2's or a G-2's observation about it. When on December 12, for example, a front-line regiment reported hearing tanks, the division G-2 noted: "No confirmation, may have been tracked vehicles."

At the optimum, operational intelligence worked in two ways: up and down. Subordinate units passed up such information as they gleaned and deemed important, while G-2s at higher commands passed information back down, in the process taking advantage of their broader knowledge as evaluated and correlated from more diverse sources. One of those sources was strategic intelligence, and in that field the Allied command had a special capability.

"A sonnet written by a machine," wrote a brilliant young British mathemetician, Alan Mathison Turing, "will be better appreciated by another machine." Turing was a person with "the unpredictable way-wardness of genius"—he once changed all his money into silver, melted it down into ingots, buried them, and never could recall where he had left them. As war came to Europe in 1939, young Turing (described as having "long hair, rumpled and dirty clothes"), a graduate of Cambridge University and of the Institute of Advanced Studies at Princeton University, was a member of a team made up primarily of Cambridge dons assembled for the specific purpose of attacking the German enciphering machine, the Enigma. The dons proceeded on a variation of Turing's theory of the sonnet: A riddle created by a machine can best be solved by another machine.

Turing and his colleagues worked under the cover of a technically nonexistent Government Code and Cipher School. It was based in a modest though architecturally flamboyant pseudo-Tudor–Gothic mansion known as Bletchley Park, located in Buckinghamshire outside the grimy railway-junction town of Bletchley some fifty miles northwest of London. Most of the work took place in Hut 6, one of several temporary wooden buildings erected on the grounds of the estate.

The work at Hut 6 received strong assistance from Polish crypt-analysts, who in the years before the war had enjoyed a modest success in breaking some of the ciphers of the early Enigma machines by means of a machine they called the "Bombe," a combination of six Enigmas joined together. As war neared, the Poles turned over both to the British and to the French a Polish-constructed copy of the Enigma along with plans and drawings of the Bombe.

By the spring of 1940, Turing and his colleagues had built the first of what was destined to be a series of ever more complex machines designed to attack the Enigma. It was "a large copper-coloured cupboard" about 6 feet tall, "which on first glance looked like an oriental goddess." They called it the Mark I Heath Robinson, after a satirical British cartoonist who drew weird, fanciful machines supposedly capable of extraordinary feats; but they usually referred to it by the original Polish name, the Bombe.

It was a forerunner of the computer yet not a true computer, for it worked on electromechanical rather than electronic principles and had no memory. Once wireless interceptors picked up an enemy signal, it was copied onto a tape and fed into the Bombe, which proceeded at a speed far beyond that of the human mind to determine which of the more than a million keys or variations of them had been used to encipher the message.

For all the miraculous ability of the Bombe, it had to have extensive human help. That was where the cryptanalysts came in, for through long months of working with Enigma intercepts and creating a vast databank of intercepted signals, they had discerned certain patterns in the transmissions. They had early learned, for example, that the letter punched by the operator never showed up in the encoded message as the same letter; thus X or Y or whatever could represent only one of twenty-five letters, not one of twenty-six. They had also learned to capitalize on the laxity of the German operators, many of whom after setting the machine and closing it, selected as the day's key the three letters that were visible in windows on the lid, and the operators dutifully repeated the key at the start of every message they transmitted. Constant repetition of the key could in time mean something in regard to the overall code.

Over a long period of time the cryptanalysts became familiar with the various headquarters making the transmissions, thereby ascertaining the call sign of the sender and usually the call sign of the recipient, for the traffic between the various headquarters was fairly constant. By directional radio finding, they could also determine the geographical location of both sender and recipient. Even though call signs changed daily, the German operator had only so many for his own headquarters and for those with which he communicated, so that in time the cryptanalysts could develop a catalogue of call signs and geographical locations for various headquarters.

So, too, the cryptanalysts could capitalize on the fact that military units were usually required to transmit situation reports at much the same time each day, and those usually contained standard opening phrases, such as "Morning report from Seventh Army," or "Evening report from Fliegerkorps II." From the hour of transmission and from the standard phrases, the cryptanalysts might determine the code letters used that day for the hour and the standard phrase.

By feeding all those clues and more into the Bombe, the cryptanalysts usually provided enough information for the amazing machine to turn the clues swiftly into a break of the day's code. From that point it was simple for the Bombe to decipher all intercepted signals enciphered in that particular code.

Wireless intercept stations in various parts of Britain fed one signal after another to Bletchley Park, literally thousands every day. They went to Hut 6, where the Bombe deciphered them. Then messengers passed them to one of two other huts—if army or air force messages, to Hut 3; if naval intercepts, to Hut 5. The material that emerged from those two huts as translated and interpreted messages was known by the codename ULTRA.

A staff of more than a hundred manned each hut, working in shifts around the clock, filling in missing letters or words (for seldom was an intercept perfectly received), translating the messages, and from a vast collection of data recorded on index cards providing interpretation of the message, which to differentiate the interpretation from the message was always carefully labeled "comment." Many of the people who did the work were in uniform, but most who filled in the letters and words and did the translating were civilian dons highly proficient in German and accustomed to the painstakingly slow functioning of the pedagogue. Beginning in 1942, Americans joined the staff, most of them lawyers in uniform.

By late 1944, deciphered, reconstructed, and translated messages, reinciphered in Allied codes and known as flimsies, were going in abundance from Hut 3 directly over special communications links to more than fifty Allied air and ground headquarters, including Eisenhower's SHAEF, all three army groups under Eisenhower's command, all army headquarters, and all major air commands, down to and including tactical air commands. There the information was received by small sections known as Special Liaison Units, or SLUs, which in British practice usually consisted of an officer and two or three men, but which in American practice were usually slightly larger.

The number of people within the headquarters privy to the ULTRA material—indeed, to the very fact that there was such a thing as ULTRA—was sharply limited, usually to the commanding general, his chief of staff, and his G-2. Information provided by ULTRA was not to be reported in G-2 summaries, periodic reports, or intelligence estimates unless it could be truthfully ascribed to some other source.

A specially designated officer in Hut 3 determined which headquarters got which flimsy, but that was usually a decision involving only major commands, such as SHAEF or the Allied command in Italy. Which headquarters got what appeared in code letters at the top of the flimsy: for the 12th Army Group, for example, WM; for the First Army, YK; and the list of code letters was usually long, for if it was considered to be of interest to Eisenhower's headquarters, it was considered to be of interest to all commands under Eisenhower.

The volume of flimsies reaching an SLU was large but seldom overwhelming, and Bletchley Park provided an indication of a flimsy's importance by assigning it a number of Zs from one to five. Although the identification or location of enemy units as obtained through ULTRA might be posted on a special situation map maintained by the SLU, a flimsy had to be destroyed within twenty-four hours of receipt. Heads of the SLUs were nevertheless permitted to make notes so long as they bore no identifiable relation to the original source material. That provided at least a modicum of institutional memory, as did the comments often provided with a message by Bletchley Park.

Since all commanders receiving ULTRA information knew that the data came from the enemy's own messages, none was inclined to discount it. ULTRA had, after all, given fairly explicit warning of the enemy's counterattack in Normandy designed to cut off Allied spearheads that had broken out of the beachhead.

In most headquarters, procedures for passing ULTRA information to the commander were much the same. Each morning the head of the SLU or his representative briefed the commander and senior members of his staff along with the comparable air commander (the commander of the

Ninth Air Force, for example, with General Bradley; the commander of the IX Tactical Air Command with General Hodges). Commanders and all of the few other officers cleared for ULTRA were free to visit the ULTRA room at any time, and whenever a message came in labeled with five Zs, the head of the SLU had to take it personally to the commander, no matter what time of day or night.

The only exception to those procedures was at headquarters of the First Army, where the G-2, Colonel Dickson, insisted on presenting the ULTRA briefing himself, a briefing from which he excluded the head of his SLU, Lt. Col. Adolph G. Rosengarten, Jr. For a time Dickson merely employed the raw messages, but in the weeks before the start of the German offensive, he began to use a briefing paper prepared by Rosengarten. Although Dickson resisted having the ULTRA officer from the IX Tactical Air Command, Lt. Col. James D. Fellers, attend, he had to bow to pressure from the commander of the IX Tactical Air Command, Maj. Gen. Elwood R. ("Pete") Quesada.

As the German Army fell back on the frontier in early fall, the volume of wireless traffic decreased, for there the telephone took over many of the chores of communication. Yet Hitler's order forbidding transmission by wireless of any information that might be connected with the impending offensive had little additional effect on the number of intercepted messages pouring into Bletchley Park, certainly not enough of a reduction to indicate that anything untoward was afoot; for if day-to-day functions and operations were to continue, the German Army, and particularly the Luftwaffe and the *Reichsbahn*, had to use wireless. So, too, wireless was a basic means of conveying the disinformation that the Germans wanted the Allies to hear.

Thus all that was really missing was any reference to an offensive in the Ardennes, and interceptors and cryptanalysts continued to handle around fifty messages a day dealing with the Western Front. What those messages had to tell Allied intelligence chiefs and their commanders in the weeks immediately preceding the German offensive was considerable.

CHAPTER THREE

What Did the Allies Know?

On September 27, 1944, Bletchley Park deciphered a message from Operational Headquarters of the *Waffen-SS* dated September 18, directing that all SS units on the Western Front be pulled from the line for rest and refitting, beginning with the 1st, 2d, 9th, and 12th SS Panzer Divisions, the 17th SS Panzergrenadier Division, three separate heavy (Tiger) tank battalions, and headquarters troops of the 1st SS Panzer Corps. All were to be assigned to "the staff of Sixth Panzer Army, the setting up of which has been ordered under Oberstgruppenführer Sepp Dietrich."

That there was a nine-day delay between the sending of the German message and Bletchley Park's deciphering it was probably attributable to cryptographic difficulties, for a delay of that length was unusual. The deciphered message went out in late afternoon of the 27th to General Eisenhower's headquarters and all subordinate commands down to and including armies and tactical air commands. Four days later, on October 1, the SHAEF G-2, General Strong, noted in his weekly intelligence summary that the Germans were withdrawing armor from the line in an apparent effort to provide a panzer reserve north of the Ardennes. Strong made no mention of specific divisions nor of the Sixth Panzer Army.

Throughout October, ULTRA provided further details about the withdrawals. In mid-October, for example, a message from Field Marshal Keitel revealed that the Sixth Panzer Army was to be the *OKW* reserve, which meant that neither Field Marshal Model nor Field Marshal von Rundstedt had control over it; it was a *strategic* reserve for the *Führerhauptquartier*, Hitler's headquarters.

Other messages located assembly areas for the divisions, mostly east of the Rhine in Westphalia, just north of the Ruhr, or dealt with the training areas where the divisions were to refit. Still others told of difficulties in releasing certain units from the line, noted altered withdrawal schedules, and revealed that the SS panzer divisions were to be brought to full strength. A further message revealed that Hitler himself had ordered the withdrawals and the creation of the Sixth Panzer Army. Yet another revealed a certain urgency: headquarters of the 1st SS Panzer Corps was to join the Sixth Panzer Army by October 20 "at latest. Longer delays by corps could not be permitted."

Throughout the month, neither General Strong nor any other Allied intelligence officer in intelligence summaries, periodic reports, or estimates of enemy intentions made mention of the Sixth Panzer Army. Strong first named it at the end of the first week in November, citing a German deserter as the source of the information; and at the same time Strong remarked that the Fifth Panzer Army had disappeared from the line in Lorraine, which, unknown to Strong at the moment, was the first step in the move of General von Manteuffel's headquarters to the Aachen sector.

What preoccupied Strong, Sibert, Dickson, and the other intelligence chiefs was what the Germans intended to do with the SS panzer divisions. Was it counterattack, or spoiling attack?

General Sibert at the 12th Army Group expressed the generally held view that it would be counterattack, to be launched once the First and Third U.S. Armies achieved a breakthrough toward the Rhine and the Ruhr. General Strong believed that whatever action the Germans took, it would occur in November, which was what the MAGIC intercept of Baron Oshima's report of his conversation with Hitler had indicated: an offensive in the West sometime "after the beginning of November." Nobody mentioned that the SS panzer divisions constituted—as ULTRA had reported—not a reserve for Model or von Rundstedt but for *OKW*, for Hitler.

In early November, ULTRA began to provide evidence of a hurried move of German fighter aircraft to the West. Beginning on the 8th, the Luftwaffe command in the Netherlands sent the first of a series of messages dealing with the expected arrival of fighter groups at airfields in its sector. The messages displayed an air of haste and secrecy in regard to "the special contingency known to you."

On November 16, in a message from a higher Luftwaffe command ordering daily reports on the serviceability of all aircraft, the sender used the term "*Jägeraufmarsch*," which the officials in Hut 3 considered to be worth a comment. In a military context, the comment read, *Aufmarsch* "denoted the assembly of forces for a planned operation," a term which the Germans had used in that sense when describing "the Allied dispositions on the eve of D-Day." Other messages meanwhile told of a buildup of fighter aircraft at fields inside Germany close to the front, and by November 23 it was clear that the hurried *Jägeraufmarsch*—whatever it was for—was complete.

Neither at Bletchley Park nor at any Allied air or ground headquarters on the Continent did anybody divine the purpose behind the *Jägeraufmarsch*. Years later it would be clear that the haste reflected

Hitler's original intention of launching his offensive before the end of November, but nobody on the Allied side could discern that at the time nor even why the Germans moved the planes at all.

In the new locations, the aircraft still might intercept Allied bombers raiding German cities or they might support a German counterattack when the American armies broke through toward the Rhine. When the transfers produced no increase in the paltry amount of air support the German ground troops were receiving, support of the expected German counterattack appeared to be the answer.

Nor did the fact that the bulk of the transfers ended on November 23 provide any clue, and nobody saw any particular significance in a revelation by ULTRA early in December of the creation of a new headquarters, *Jagdführer Mittelrhein* (Officer Commanding Fighters, Central Rhineland), although it was soon obvious from strength reports to that headquarters that it controlled the newly transferred aircraft. Any Allied attempt to determine the meaning of the shifts was all the more difficult because in most cases, in keeping with Hitler's stringent security plan, the German commanders and operators who sent the messages Bletchley Park deciphered knew little or nothing of the purpose themselves.

Starting in early November, troops of the Sixth Panzer Army began to transfer to the west bank of the Rhine. Duly noting the moves, Allied intelligence officers began a guessing game as to the exact location of the assembly areas. The game was essentially meaningless, for all deduced that the assembly areas were in the vicinity of Cologne, a location from which the SS divisions might readily counterattack a thrust toward the Ruhr.

Noting that the enemy had apparently created or rebuilt at least five SS panzer or panzer divisions and five parachute divisions during September and October, a "truly colossal effort," General Strong at SHAEF concluded that the Germans intended "a final showdown before the winter," and deemed it logical that they would use their newly created reserve against an Allied drive in the north. General Sibert at the 12th Army Group continued to think much the same, while Colonel Dickson at the First Army saw the possibility of a spoiling attack from positions northwest of Aachen to drive down both banks of the Meuse River, a maneuver not unlike the Small Solution proposed to Hitler by von Rundstedt and Model, although Dickson presupposed no accompanying drive through the Ardennes.

By November 20, almost all were of one mind: The Sixth Panzer Army's mission was to counterattack once the American armies crossed the Roer River, probably with the help of the Fifth Panzer Army, whose arrival in the Aachen sector they had quickly spotted, for three divisions of that army were behind the Roer River in a position to assist the Sixth Panzer Army. It was a few days later before they picked up the bogus headquarters, *Gruppe von Manteuffel*, but when they did so they saw through a part of the German deception by identifying the arrival of headquarters of the Fifteenth Army. At that point they concluded that von Manteuffel controlled two armies, the Fifth Panzer and the Fifteenth, and ULTRA, at least, learned that the Fifth Panzer Army had moved out of the line. The German attempt through false wireless traffic to conceal the Fifteenth Army's relief in the Netherlands by the Twenty-fifth Army failed utterly.

Meanwhile, ULTRA was continuing to feed the intelligence officers a steady diet of intercepted messages, mainly dealing with troop movements by rail and related requests for air protection. In a message sent with high priority, Model's Army Group B in early November asked the Luftwaffe for fighter protection for the unloading of troop trains in the vicinity of Cologne. That was the first of more than thirty similar intercepted and decoded messages over the weeks remaining before the German attack, always originating with Army Group B. Although many requests were for protection in the north near Cologne, most (sometimes communicated with "almost shrill urgency") were for the Rhine crossings between Bonn, just beyond the northern reaches of the Eifel, and for Koblenz, at the confluence of the Moselle River with the Rhine, whence the main rail line along the southern periphery of the Eifel ran along the Moselle to Trier. From any of those rail crossings of the Rhine, trains might use the spur lines into the Eifel; and in the last days before Hitler's deadline, most requests were for protection in the vicinity of Koblenz, well away from the sector in the north where Allied eyes were focused. At the same time, the Luftwaffe was ordering subordinate commands to fly counter-reconnaissance screens to keep allied aircraft away from the marshaling yards at Koblenz and Trier.

Of greater interest, many of the requests were for aerial protection of railheads inside the Eifel. On December 2, for example, Army Group B wanted fighter cover not only for Trier but for Wittlich, Gerolstein, and Bitburg, all deep inside the Eifel. In a request for protection on December 3, Army Group B named the ground units involved in the movements: the 326th Volksgrenadier Division at Gerolstein, in the shadow of the Schnee Eifel (and not far from Monschau, where the division subsequently attacked); the 62d Volksgrenadier Division at Wittlich, due east of Bitburg (and a relatively short march from St. Vith, where that division attacked); and the *Führer Begleit Brigade*, an armored brigade built around Hitler's inner palace guard and never before employed at the front, at Cochem on the main rail line along the Moselle. On December 7, Army Group B wanted fighter cover for virtually the entire Eifel. And all the while, none of the planes providing cover either for the rail movements or the railheads came from those airfields so recently reinforced with additional fighter aircraft.

With some exultancy, the cryptanalysts with the help of their ingenious Turing engine began early in November to break the codes of the

Reichsbahn. Of some eight hundred trains used to move the German attack force into position, ULTRA picked up signals on almost half, clearly indicating a massive movement toward the Western Front.

On occasion, the messages revealed intense urgency: on November 10, about a week after the movements began, the Director-General of Transport insisted that the Sixth Panzer Army order all units "to ensure punctual transport," for it would be "impossible to make up any delays once they had occurred" because "all formations already [were] being moved at highest possible tempo." The day before, he noted with some agitation, the 2d SS Panzer Division had fallen thirty-six hours behind schedule, the *Panzer Lehr Division*, twenty-four, and the 12th SS Panzer Division, twelve. Maintaining the tight schedules was clearly of major importance: Even a twelve-hour delay was reason for concern.

Even as ULTRA was reporting rail movements and requests for their aerial protection, reconnaissance and fighter pilots of the IX and XIX Tactical Air Commands were picking up many of the movements. Despite the bad weather that Hitler counted on—and got—and despite the tendency of the pilots to concentrate on regions to the north where ground intelligence officers expected the enemy to strike, there was many an indication of buildup in the Eifel.

In fairly clear weather on November 18 and 19, for example, pilots reported heavy rail movements at various points in the Eifel: at Gemünd, near the Roer River dams; at Gerolstein; and at Bitburg. Marshaling yards at Koblenz and Trier were aswarm with activity. Pilots reported trains loaded with tanks, ambulances, and other vehicles, hospital trains, troop trains. Sometimes there were truck convoys marked with white square panels in an apparent effort to simulate American convoys. A few pilots reported what looked to be piles of equipment alongside the roads just inside the treelines.

In the first two weeks of December the weather proved even more restrictive, but there was continued evidence of buildup nevertheless. Many sightings were again in or near the Eifel: at Koblenz, Prüm, Gemünd, Münstereifel (a few miles east of Gemünd), Gerolstein, Trier. Despite having only a few Black Widow planes each, the two American night reconnaissance squadrons also turned in considerable evidence of buildup: columns of what looked to be vehicles with dim-out lights, which would indicate truck convoys, on many of the roads west of the Rhine, and in some places irregular patches of shielded lights away from the roads, which might indicate troop assembly areas. One pilot reported a battery of searchlights turned on briefly near Kaiserslautern, which was well south of the Moselle River in front of the Third Army, but—it might have been noted—only a few miles by rail from the Eifel.

On November 24, ULTRA began to decipher what became a series of requests from Army Group B—some betraying "an increasingly urgent note"—for aerial reconnaissance missions that when viewed in the context of a German counterattack in the north near Cologne made little sense. The first asked for reconnaissance of the region around Eupen and Malmédy, which was the most direct route from the Eifel to the American supply center of Liège and for American reinforcements moving south into the Ardennes; and also of roads along the Prüm-Houffalize axis, which was one of the most direct routes, via St. Vith, into and through the Ardennes. On December 3, Army Group B again asked for reconnaissance of the area around Eupen and Malmédy: "Are forces being brought up in Monschau area and what forces? Where are troop movements and concentrations and tank assemblies?"

Beginning on November 29 there were odder requests still: for aerial reconnaissance of crossings of the Meuse River from Liège past the bend in the river at Namur and upstream for fifty-five miles past Dinant to Givet. A few days later the Luftwaffe gave that assignment to a special detachment of jet aircraft, and night reconnaissance also began. Reconnaissance was "to be forced through at lower level if weather prevents high level flight." On December 3, a message said that reconnaissance of the bridges over the Meuse was "of the greatest urgency." And five days later, on the 8th: "A good photo of Mass [Meuse] crossings from Maastricht to Givet still with priority over other tasks." As late as December 14, demands for those photos and for others of the road center of Ciney a few miles short of the Meuse were still coming in. What could crossings of the Meuse River in the Ardennes, far from the German concentration near Cologne, have to do with a German counterattack near Cologne?

ULTRA revealed all those things; and more too. For every request for reconnaissance of the region around Eupen and Malmédy, there were at least three more for reconnaissance around Aachen and repeated requests for aerial protection for trains unloading in the vicinity of Cologne. Reconnaissance pilots reporting rail movements and possible truck convoys in the Eifel were also reporting movements farther north that well might be deduced to feed a buildup near Cologne, and railheads and marshaling yards other than those in or close to the Eifel were also busy.

So, too, on December 11, Bletchley Park deciphered a message from Field Marshal von Rundstedt:

> Large scale attack against Western Germany might begin in very near future. Allies would probably try to seize Rhine crossings by air landings on large scale. Most important therefore that defense at Rhine bridges should be in constant state of readiness. . . . *Wehrkreis* [county] commanders to report by 18th whether all preparations for defense of Rhine crossings made.

In response to concerns about the thinness of the front in the Ardennes as expressed by the commander of the VIII Corps, Maj. Gen. Troy H. Middleton, General Eisenhower and General Bradley visited Middleton on November 8, lunched with him at his headquarters in a Belgian Army caserne in Bastogne, then toured lower headquarters near the front. They left at the end of the day well aware of widely spaced positions; but since the Germans, like the Americans, appeared to be using the sector to give depleted divisions a rest and new ones a taste of combat experience, they entertained no real concern for what Bradley would later call a "calculated risk." Besides, Bradley had already sent a newly arrived 9th Armored Division to the Ardennes in October to serve Middleton as a reserve.

One of Bradley's subordinates, the commander of the Third Army, General Patton, was less sanguine. On November 24 he wrote in his diary that "the First Army is making a terrible mistake in leaving the VIII Corps static, as it is highly probable that the Germans are building up east of them."

That entry no doubt reflected a growing concern on the part of Patton's G-2, Colonel Koch, he who had never been so optimistic about the condition of the German forces as were his intelligence colleagues in other commands. Since the southern portion of the Eifel was an extension of the Third Army's projected zone of advance, Koch paid it special attention; it was at his suggestion that Patton had obtained approval for reconnaissance aircraft supporting the Third Army to reconnoiter over the Eifel. Koch was particularly concerned about the threat that would accrue to the Third Army's north flank should the Germans emerge from the Eifel into the Ardennes. By December 9, he was sufficiently worried to invite his commander to a special intelligence briefing.

As Koch put it to Patton, the enemy had at least thirteen divisions out of the line, including six panzer or SS panzer divisions and at least four parachute divisions. Koch had also learned—presumably from ULTRA—that three divisions had left Scandinavia for the Western Front. Although most of the armor was in the north near Cologne, the 2d Panzer and 12th SS Panzer Divisions had recently been reported moving south. By Koch's reckoning, the enemy had four *Volksgrenadier* divisions in the line opposite the First Army's VIII Corps, two panzer divisions with a total of 105 tanks in immediate reserve, and three *Volksgrenadier* divisions nearby. Considering what the VIII Corps had in the line, the German concentration was greater, comparatively, than it was opposite the rest of the First Army or the Third Army. Koch concluded that the Germans intended either to shift the reserve forces in the Eifel north or south to meet American threats, to use them to try to lure American divisions away from the main attack, or "to launch a spoiling or diversionary offensive."

A short silence followed Koch's presentation, then discussion began. Nothing was to be allowed to interfere with the Third Army's plan for a renewed offensive on December 19, Patton declared at the end, but the staff was to begin "limited outline planning" to meet any threat that might emerge from enemy action in the Ardennes. "We'll be in a position," said Patton, "to meet whatever happens."

The next day, December 10, Colonel Koch put his concern in writing. Strongly impressed by the withdrawal of German divisions from the line, particularly panzer divisions, at a time when the enemy's defensive need was so great, he predicted that the Germans probably intended "to mount a spoiling offensive in an effort to unhinge the Allied assault on *Festung* [Fortress] *Deutschland*." Yet three days later he weakened his earlier warning about the Ardennes by falling into line with the view prevailing among his intelligence associates: that the enemy was planning a counterattack with the Sixth Panzer Army in the north.

At headquarters of the First Army, Colonel Dickson was also becoming concerned. One event that set him worrying was the capture in late November by troops of the Ninth Army of an order issued on October 30 by the 86th Corps, which called on all units of the corps to screen for men who had "a knowledge of the English language and also the American dialect," and who might volunteer for "a special unit" the Führer had ordered "for employment on reconnaissance and special tasks on the western front." The order also directed that "captured U.S. clothing, equipment, weapons and vehicles" were to be collected as "equipment of the above troops." Otto Skorzeny's fear that the Allies would obtain a copy of that order had come to pass.

In several informal discussions with Dickson, the head of the First Army's SLU (ULTRA), Colonel Rosengarten, recalled the German offensive through the Ardennes in 1940 and noted that "desperate men are likely to take desperate measures." Possibly as a result of those discussions, Dickson prevailed on his commander, General Hodges, to ask General Bradley for two divisions to back up the line in the Ardennes. No, said Bradley, he had none to spare.

On December 8, Monk Dickson presented to Hodges a map labeled "Study of Enemy Armored Reserves" on which the head of his G-2 target section, Lt. Col. Clarence M. Mendenhall, had tabulated German troop and armor concentrations, as well as stockpiles of ammunition and bridging equipment based on information gathered from all intelligence sources. Mendenhall had labeled each location priority "Red Bomb" (one), "Blue Bomb" (two), or "Brown Bomb" (three). Those labeled Red and Blue Bombs were troop concentrations close to railheads or rail junctions through which troops and supplies were known to pass. Of a total of fifty-three targets, twenty-nine were in the sector north of the Eifel, twenty-six of which were labeled Red Bomb; in the Eifel, some as far back as the Rhine, there were twenty-four, ten of them labeled Red Bomb. Priority clearly was in the north.

Convinced that Allied bombing of the enemy's railroads had been at random and never sufficiently concentrated to knock out all lines in a given area at once, Dickson wanted all the targets hit in a concentrated offensive by medium and heavy bombers. When General Hodges approved, as did the commander of his supporting tactical air command, General Quesada, the request went forward to the commander of the United States Strategic Air Forces in Europe, General Carl Spaatz, who controlled the heavy bombers. It came back disapproved: "Targets unremunerative."

By December 10, Dickson had become convinced that the Germans were going to make a move somewhere soon. He was scheduled to go on a long-delayed four-day leave to Paris the next day (although still subject to the return from leave of the G-3, Brig. Gen. Truman C. Thorson), and even though he had no concern about leaving his intelligence duties to the "deft, sure hand" of his deputy, Col. William Silvey, he considered the German buildup so threatening that before departing, he wanted to convey "a solemn warning." On the 10th, he issued G-2 Estimate No. 37, on which he had worked at considerable length—a document he and others would later claim should have been sufficient to alert the Allied command to the offensive in the Ardennes.

In the estimate, Dickson used the terms "all-out counterattack" and "all-out counteroffensive" interchangeably, although technically they are two different things. "An extremely intelligent PW," he noted, "stated that every means possible is being gathered for the coming all-out counteroffensive." Morale among recently captured prisoners of war had "achieved a new high," as "expressed by attempts to escape and avowed eagerness . . . to rejoin the battle for Germany." With a jibe at Adolf Hitler, who often boasted of success in military operations based on his intuition, Dickson wrote that "von Rundstedt, who obviously is conducting military operations without the benefit of intuition, has skillfully defended and husbanded his forces and is preparing for his part in the all-out application of every weapon at the focal point and the correct time to achieve defense of the Reich west of the Rhine by inflicting as great a defeat on the Allies as possible."

Among enemy capabilities, Dickson mentioned as "current" continuing to defend along the line of the Roer River with particular attention to the Roer River dams, which the enemy recognized as "a tactical ace." When American troops crossed the Roer, a second capability would be likely: "a concentrated counterattack with air, armor, infantry, and secret weapons at a selected focal point at a time of his own choosing." It was "plain" that the enemy's strategy was "based on the exhaustion of our offensive to be followed by an all-out counterattack with armor, between the Roer and the Erft [a small stream midway between the Roer and the Rhine]." The "continual building up of forces to the west of the Rhine" pointed "consistently to his staking all on [that] counteroffensive."

The focal point, wrote Dickson, was "between Roermond and Schleiden." Roermond, which lay within the sector of the 21st Army Group, is twenty-two miles north of Aachen; Schleiden is within the northern reaches of the Eifel near the Roer River dams, almost due east of Monschau. That placed the focal point well north of the Ardennes.

To deduce from that prediction that Dickson anticipated an offensive out of the Eifel into the Ardennes would be to strain credulity. Although he noted that the enemy's armored reserve appeared "to be quartered in houses and barns along the railroads generally in a semi-circle from Düsseldorf to Koblenz [thereby placing some of it in the Eifel] with Cologne as a center point," his only specific reference to the Ardennes was to remark "a definite pattern for the seasoning of newly-formed divisions in the comparatively quiet sector opposite VIII Corps prior to their dispatch to more active fronts." He did note the presence in back-up positions in the Eifel of the 2d and 116th Panzer Divisions but believed they were being readied to counterattack to deny the First Army capture of the Roer River dams, which may have been the reason he extended the likely sector for enemy action as far south as Schleiden.

At General Bradley's headquarters in a drab brownstone office building belonging to the Luxembourg State Railways, across a cobblestoned Place de Metz from the Luxembourg City railroad station, Edwin Sibert was also beginning to have some concern about the Ardennes. In late November, as he and General Bradley had driven through the region en route to visit Field Marshal Montgomery's headquarters in northern Belgium, they had both remarked the absence of troops and installations behind the lines. When they discussed the possibility of a German thrust through the Ardennes, Bradley said that "when anyone attacks, he does it for one of two reasons. Either he is out to destroy the hostile forces or he's going after a terrain objective." Neither, said Bradley, could be attained in the Ardennes. Yet even should the Germans attack there, it was hardly likely that they could make "decisive progress" through such "broken, relatively roadless country"; and if they tried, "we could chew them up."

Hardly had Bradley and Sibert returned to Luxembourg City when a disturbing ULTRA intercept reached Sibert's desk. It was the first order to the Luftwaffe to reconnoiter crossings of the Meuse River from Liège to Givet, with reconnaissance "to be forced through at lower level if weather prevents high level flight." So concerned was Sibert that he sent his deputy, Col. William H. Jackson, to SHAEF and thence to London to visit the top British intelligence agencies to see if he could get any additional information. Jackson departed on December 1 but soon cabled that he could find out nothing more.

On December 10, the terrain expert in Sibert's G-2 section, Maj. Ralph Ingersoll—in civilian life, a prominent newspaperman—asked Sibert to come to his office, where on a wall map he pointed out detraining areas in the vicinity of Bitburg. Instead of just moving inexperienced or recuperating divisions in and out of the Eifel, said Ingersoll, the Germans might be building up there by a stratagem of moving three divisions in and two out while hiding the extra one.

The theory impressed Sibert enough for him to relate it to General Bradley, who promptly asked the Supreme Commander, General Eisenhower, for a newly arriving armored division as an additional reserve for the Ardennes; but Eisenhower said no. He needed the new division for reinforcing the Seventh Army to help it support renewal of the Third Army's offensive. Furthermore, there was some concern that if the Germans struck other than in the north, it might be in Alsace, where Allied lines were also thin and such French cities as Metz and Nancy were within easy reach.

For all the rising interest in the Ardennes, Sibert believed any threat there to be minimal compared to the buildup of German armor in the north near Cologne. Even on that score, Sibert thought that Monk Dickson in his G-2 Estimate No. 37 was exaggerating. Indeed, he found Dickson's latest assessment so pessimistic that when General Strong telephoned from SHAEF to complain and to urge that Sibert "get Dickson straightened out," Sibert agreed something should be done. Strong was also concerned about "Monk's shrubbery," for Dickson had bolstered his pessimistic case by naming some German units identifiable only through ULTRA (that was a no-no) and known in fact to be located on other fronts.

Lacking either technical or command supervision over Dickson, Sibert chose to counter Dickson's alarm by issuing a more sober report himself. That he failed to telephone Dickson or to ask for a conference appeared to say something about the state of relations between the two.

By chance, that was the point at which the G-2 section, in response to criticism that its intelligence summaries were dull and therefore seldom read, chose to call in the newspaperman Ralph Ingersoll to dress them up. Ingersoll's first rewrite was of G-2 Summary No. 18, which Sibert issued on December 12, the summary in which Sibert remarked that attrition was eating heavily into German strength and that the front was more brittle and vulnerable "than it appeared on G-2 maps or to troops in the line." The "deathly weakness" of the infantry divisions, "plus the inevitability" that the enemy had fewer and fewer replacements, the report continued, made it "certain that before long he will utterly fail in his current attempt to withdraw and arrest his tactical reserve so that he will be forced to commit at least part of his panzer army to the line." The report concluded: "With continuing Allied pressure in the south and in the north, the breaking point may develop suddenly and without warning."

The ideas, the opinions were Sibert's, based on his own beliefs and on Kenneth Strong's recent report stressing heavy German losses; but it was unfortunate, Sibert was to remark years later, that that was the first report to be dressed up by Ingersoll. He "stressed the optimistic picture, so it looked a lot better than it should." Whatever the case, G-2 Summary No. 18 was to haunt Edwin Sibert for the rest of his life.

In the offices of SHAEF's G-2 section in the Trianon Palace Hotel at Versailles, General Strong was still optimistic because of the continuing high level of German attrition, yet he mentioned that until the Sixth Panzer Army was committed, "We cannot feel really satisfied." Noting continuing troop movements in the Eifel, he remarked that "the procession is NOT yet ended."

Although Strong saw the troop movements in the Eifel as just that—a procession, troops passing through—he nevertheless joined those who were directing increased attention toward the Eifel and the Ardennes. For "at least a fortnight" before the German attack began, he called attention at morning briefings conducted by the chief of staff, Lt. Gen. Walter Bedell Smith, to three possible uses of the reserve panzer divisions. They could go to Russia; counterattack an Allied penetration; or "stage a relieving attack through the Ardennes." As was the custom, he presumably listed the possibilities in descending order of probability, and as General Smith was to recall, Strong also suggested that the relieving attack might be made in Alsace.

It may have been Strong's growing concern that prompted General Eisenhower, as he motored through the Ardennes on December 7 on the way to a conference with Montgomery, to remark that the Allied command might be in for "a nasty little Kasserine." It was definitely Strong's concern that prompted Bedell (pronounced Beedle) Smith to urge Strong to go to Luxembourg City and alert General Bradley.

Strong made the visit during the first week of December at the time when General Sibert was also beginning to look with some anxiety at German activity in the Eifel. Strong talked first with Sibert, then spent more than half an hour with Bradley, who told him that he was "aware of the danger" but that he had "earmarked certain divisions to move into the Ardennes area should the enemy attack there." If so, he told nobody else about it and issued no directive. In any event, those at Bradley's headquarters in Luxembourg City looked on Kenneth Strong as a worrywart.

Bradley had by that time already spoken again about the possibility of a German strike in the Ardennes with the commander on the ground, a reserve infantry officer and former dean of Louisiana State University,

Troy Middleton. Bradley saw an attack in the Ardennes as "only a remote possibility," at most a spoiling attack involving four to six divisions.
If it should happen, Middleton was "to make a fighting withdrawal, all
the way back to the Meuse River if necessary." (Middleton never told his
division commanders that.) He was to locate no major gasoline or supply
depots within the area to be given up. (Bradley never told Courtney
Hodges that.) As Middleton withdrew, Bradley was to order armored
divisions to hit the enemy's flanks. (Bradley never alerted any division to
that role.)

If Middleton continued to harbor any particular concern, it could
hardly have been as a result of any warning from his intelligence officer,
Col. Andrew R. Reeves. In a report on December 9, Reeves estimated
the enemy opposite the VIII Corps to consist of four infantry divisions
with a total strength of 24,000 men. That, if correct, meant that the enemy's line was almost half as thin as that of the widely stretched VIII
Corps. "The enemy's present practice," wrote Reeves, "of bringing new
divisions . . . to receive front line experience and then relieving them out
for commitment elsewhere indicates his desire to have this sector of the
front remain quiet and inactive."

Both Reeves and Middleton could, of course, read the intelligence
reports sent down from higher echelons, and they must have remarked
the difference in tone between that from Dickson of the First Army on
December 10 and that from Sibert of the 12th Army Group on the 12th.
In any event, it was obvious that higher command expected nothing to
happen on the front of the VIII Corps, for Middleton received an order,
as a corollary of the attack by the First Army to seize the Roer River
dams, to stage a feint near his southern boundary in Luxembourg in hope
of drawing enemy strength from the north.

The assignment went to the 23d Special Troops, a deception unit
equipped with such devices as sonic gear to simulate heavy motor traffic
and inflatable rubber tanks. Assuming the guise of the 75th Infantry Division, which was actually en route from England to the Continent, the
men of the detachment wore the division's shoulder patch and marked
their vehicles as if they belonged to the 75th Division. Radio traffic sim-
ulating a division headquarters and supporting units went out intentionally in an easily broken code. Proceeding for five days, the so-called
rubber duck operation showed up on German situation maps for a while
as a question mark; but by December 15, von Rundstedt's headquarters
had decided that no new division existed, and the question mark disappeared. The only ones genuinely fooled were the Americans, for at headquarters of the VIII Corps, they read reports from the front of increased
enemy radio and vehicular traffic as a response to the deception operation, and some troops of the 4th Infantry Division in the line in Luxembourg were later to wonder why the 75th Division never came forward to
help them.

Middleton nevertheless still nursed a considerable concern. To the commander of the Ninth Army, Lt. Gen. William H. Simpson, who stopped by Bastogne on December 5 after a conference with General Bradley in Luxembourg City, he confided "in strong terms" that he was convinced the Germans had altered their practice on his front. "Whereas previously the Germans had been unloading troops in the rear area, bringing some up to the front line and then moving them to other sectors," he thought at that point that they were pretending to do the same thing but "were actually building up a large force in the rear area."

To subordinates, at least, Middleton displayed no such concern, as exemplified on December 10 when he heard from the commander of the 2d Infantry Division, Maj. Gen. Walter M. Robertson, who at the time was responsible for that part of the front which included the Schnee Eifel. On the 8th and the 9th, the 2d Division's outposts had reported intense enemy activity, including heavy motor traffic. By the 10th, the activity had slackened, leading Robertson's G-2, Lt. Col. Donald P. Christensen, to conclude that one unit had replaced another in the line and that "the relief is now complete."

Yet Robertson was still worried, not necessarily about any broad German plan but about his own front, for the troops on the Schnee Eifel might be trapped by German drives around both ends of the ridge. That night as he talked in his office in St. Vith with his chief of staff, he telephoned Middleton, who declined a request for aerial reconnaissance the next day. "Go back to sleep, Robbie," he said. "You've been having a bad dream."

The corps commander whose responsibility included the northern portion of the Ardennes, Maj. Gen. Leonard T. ("Gee") Gerow of the V Corps, was preoccupied throughout much of November with an attack in the Hürtgen Forest, and later—as the date for the enemy's offensive approached—with the attack to take the Roer River dams. Gerow's G-2, Col. Thomas J. Ford, noted that prisoners were reporting the presence of SS troops "in towns close to the front," but he presumed they were "possibly surveying the new Roer River defense line."

The 2d Division's G-2, Colonel Christensen, whose division was to be relieved in the Schnee Eifel sector to carry the main weight of the attack for the dams, was more concerned. He expected the Germans to react to the American attack with local counterattacks, but also envisaged the possibility of "a major counterattack" just south of the dams. Christensen had in mind a counterattack with two panzer divisions, for it seemed "probable" that two were located several miles east of the dams.

Considering Gerow's own strength in that sector—three infantry divisions, a combat command of armor, and a cavalry reconnaissance squadron—the possibility of a counterattack by two panzer divisions was hardly to be taken lightly. Such a counterattack, Gerow believed, posed the greatest threat to his south wing, where one of his divisions (like those of the VIII Corps) was spread thin along a twenty-mile front southeastward from Monschau to the Losheim Gap, and where the attacking 2d Division would be depending for support of its attack upon a single road running through a dense forest close behind the front. That prompted Gerow to designate a fall-back position in that sector should it be required. He chose a stretch of high ground that would come to be known as the Elsenborn Ridge.

In the mineral resort town of Spa, at the First Army's headquarters in the Grand Hôtel Britannique—which twenty-six years before had served the same purpose for von Hindenburg and Ludendorff—Monk Dickson—his trip to Paris again delayed by General Thorson's failure to return because of bad flying weather—was becoming not only concerned but agitated. He learned on the 14th that "many PWs" were saying an offensive was soon to begin, probably "between the 17th and 25th of December," while others spoke of "the recapture of Aachen as a Christmas present for the Führer." There were further reports of heavy reinforcements pouring toward the front in the general area between Düren and Trier, which encompassed the entire Eifel.

That night, during a staff meeting held in General Hodges's office—it had once been von Hindenburg's—Dickson suddenly slapped the situation map in the area between Monschau and Echternach. "It's the Ardennes!" he exclaimed.

Yet Courtney Hodges and Dickson's compatriots on the First Army's staff knew Monk Dickson as an impetuous man. (In September, he had burst into Hodges's sleeping van with a monitored radio report saying von Rundstedt had ordered army troops to disarm the SS and appealed to the German people to join him in obtaining an honorable peace, which when checked turned out to be an American "black propaganda" broadcast designed to confuse the German people.) Indeed, a basic reason for the conflict within the staff was the G-3 section's failure except on rare occasions to listen to Dickson. On the night of December 14, nobody paid much attention to his outburst.

As evidenced by Dickson's next G-2 periodic report, issued the following morning, he himself saw no reason to put his impetuosity on record. The enemy, he assumed, "was resorting to his attack propaganda to bolster morale of the troops," although, he cautioned, it was possible that "a limited scale offensive will be launched for the purpose of achieving a Christmas morale 'victory' for civilian consumption." As for the Ardennes, he remarked only that the VIII Corps had reported that "an abrupt change of routine of enemy personnel opposite 9th Armored Division strongly suggests that new troops may have arrived in that area," to which he—or a subordinate—commented: "Very likely a recently arrived

Volksgrenadier Division coming in to relieve 212 Volksgrenadier Division."

With that, Dickson finally set off for his four-day leave in Paris. Before he went, he may have seen the message that arrived in the headquarters from the VIII Corps shortly before midnight on the 14th: It told of "a German woman" who had come through the lines and spoken of seeing "many horse-drawn vehicles, pontoons, small boats, and other river-crossing equipment," as well as "many artillery pieces, both horse-drawn and carried on trucks," in the vicinity of Bitburg.

The observations were not those of a German woman but of Elise Delé. Reproducing the report for transmission to subordinate commands, somebody added the comment: "A very interesting report. Build-up of troops has been confirmed by Tac/R [aerial reconnaissance] and PW statements. However, presence of large numbers of engineers with bridging equipment suggests preparation for offensive rather than defensive action."

Word went out to the 28th Division to investigate with ground patrols, but that was all.

As Monk Dickson left for Paris, all the other senior intelligence officers were at their posts. None expressed any new concern for the Ardennes, although one whose remarks had gone unnoticed by the others—Lt. Col. Anthony Tasker, a British officer serving as G-2 of the First Allied Airborne Army—had for two weeks been pointing toward the Ardennes as a likely spot for the anticipated German strike. Making his predictions at daily headquarters briefings, he pointed particularly to the thinly held sector on and near the Schnee Eifel. Yet headquarters of the First Allied Airborne Army was out of the line in England and, not being engaged in operations, was publishing no intelligence estimates; and since Tasker had no intelligence input that the other commands lacked, who would have paid any attention anyway?

There was clearly no concern at headquarters of the 21st Army Group. Field Marshal Montgomery's chief of staff, Maj. Gen. Francis ("Freddie") de Guingand, was on leave in England, and Montgomery himself had written General Eisenhower for permission to spend Christmas in London with his son. In Luxembourg City, General Bradley was getting ready to depart on the morning of the 16th for Versailles, where he was to participate in a conference at SHAEF's main headquarters on a critical shortage of American infantry replacements. In Spa, the First Army's commander, General Hodges, during the afternoon had received a "visiting galaxy" of professional baseball players (including Frankie Frisch, Bucky Walters, Dutch Leonard, and Mel Ott) and had then conferred for an hour with the commander of the VIII Corps, General Middleton. Since he had a bad head cold, he retired early in his requisitioned villa, Le Bocqueteau, atop a ridge two miles outside Spa in a community of expensive villas known as Balmoral. After returning from Spa to Bastogne, General Middleton also went off early to his sleeping van.

At Versailles on the 15th, an Allied air commanders' conference heard Eisenhower's G-3, Maj. Gen. Harold R. ("Pinky") Bull, report that the First Army's attack on the Roer River dams had failed to provoke a reaction from the enemy's panzer reserve and that on the VIII Corps front there was "nothing to report." Eisenhower's air intelligence officer, Air Commodore C. M. Grierson, then rose to relate that the Luftwaffe had continued to move fighter aircraft westward but that the shifts were "defensive" only.

At Bletchley Park, somebody put into the file a flimsy deciphered and sent to headquarters on the Continent on December 12: "Jadg Corps II aware 11 hours [December] 10th that all SS units were observing wireless silence."

Colonel Dickson at headquarters of the First Army had come closer than anybody to predicting what was about to happen in the Ardennes. Yet despite his brief impetuous outburst—"It's the Ardennes!"—Dickson, too, represented part of a general intelligence failure. Yet ULTRA and many another intelligence source had provided a lot of information that, properly interpreted and mixed with other material, should have told Eisenhower, Bradley, Hodges, Middleton, and Gerow what was about to hit them.

What ULTRA had failed to do was to be specific, to say exactly why Hitler was shifting fighter aircraft westward and building a large reserve with panzer and SS panzer divisions as its core. Allied commanders had come to expect ULTRA to be specific, to tell them not only what but when and where. When neither ULTRA nor their other intelligence sources told them those things, they failed to penetrate Hitler's masterful deception scheme to parade the assembly of the Sixth Panzer Army in the north while preparing secretly to attack in the Ardennes.

Only toward the end had Strong, Sibert, and Dickson, with some help from Koch of the Third Army, begun to pay attention to the Ardennes, to become aware of the move of enemy units into the Eifel. Yet even then they expressed no conviction—with the exception of Dickson's outburst—that the Germans intended a major blow in the Ardennes. It would represent, as Walter Bedell Smith was to remark later, "a dying gasp. No Goddamned fool would do it." In no way did the intelligence officers alert their commanders to a threat in the Ardennes serious enough or imminent enough to warrant any change in Eisenhower's offensive plans north and south of the region. To skitter and react with nervous defensive moves to every possibility open to the enemy is tantamount to surrendering all initiative.

The fact was that throughout the autumn and up to the last, almost all the intelligence specialists were assessing German intentions with three propositions in mind:

- First, that von Rundstedt, a capable old soldier, was in full charge on the Western Front. Had not the sturdy German defense all through the fall reflected the steady hand of an experienced commander acting according to time-tested and long-accepted tactics and principles? That gave verisimilitude to the theory, which even a doubting Oscar Koch finally accepted, that the German armor would be used sanely and rationally to counterattack the impending Allied drive toward the Rhine and the Ruhr.
- Second, so hardpressed was von Rundstedt both north and south of the Ardennes, partly as a result of having pulled divisions from the line to form a reserve, that he was finally having to shift divisions in either direction to counter upcoming American offensives. That accounted for the rail and motor traffic in the Eifel.
- Third, as General Sibert reported on December 12, German losses had been so great that the front was more brittle and more vulnerable than it appeared to be, and the enemy—as Brigadier Williams so forcibly noted—was in no condition to mount a major offensive. A general belief that the Germans were desperately short of fuel for tanks and planes fed that assumption. One intercepted message after another told of crippling fuel shortages. Who could have guessed that those messages told in fact of a desperate effort to accumulate enough fuel to launch a major offensive?

The enemy could still do something—the feeling was—but not much.

The basic failure was to have neglected to look beyond Gerd von Rundstedt to Adolf Hitler and to have recognized the desperation that motivated the Führer. The great German military theorist Carl von Clausewitz, in his famous treatise *On War*, written while he headed the *Kriegsakademie* early in the nineteenth century, had spelled it out:

> When the disproportion of power is so great that no limitation of our own object can ensure us safety from a catastrophe, or where the probable duration of the danger is such that the greatest economy of forces can no longer bring us to our object, then the . . . forces will, or should, be concentrated in one desperate blow. . . . He who is hard pressed . . . will regard the greatest daring as the greatest wisdom—at most, perhaps, employing the assistance of subtle stratagem.

Allied intelligence officers had committed the most grievous sin of which a G-2 is capable. They "had looked in a mirror for the enemy and seen there only the reflection of their own intentions."

CHAPTER FOUR

The Last Few Hours

The heavy drain of the long war had forced the German Army early in 1944 to reduce the strength of its infantry division from just over seventeen thousand men to just under thirteen thousand and to cut one of the battalions from each of three infantry regiments, although a so-called Fusilier battalion under division control was normally employed like a seventh infantry battalion. At slightly over fourteen thousand men, the American division had a thousand more men and nine infantry battalions. To make up, in part, for the cuts, the Germans vastly increased individual automatic weapons, especially a machine pistol known as the *Schmeisser*, whose high cyclic rate of fire made a kind of emetic or *b-r-r-r-r-r-p* sound so that the American soldier called it a "burp gun."

In most other aspects of armament, the two divisions were roughly similar. The individual American rifle, the M-1, was semi-automatic; that of the German, a bolt-action piece. Light air-cooled machine guns were comparable, except that the German piece had a much higher cyclic rate of fire, which produced such rapid fire that the German soldier called it the "*Hitler-Säge* (Hitler's Saw)." The Americans had a heavy water-cooled machine gun dating from World War I, which the Germans had abandoned. The Americans also had another weapon dating from the Great War, the Browning Automatic Rifle, called the BAR (pronounced as if spelling it). Basic mortars were similar: the American, a 60mm. and an 81mm.; but on the American side there were limited numbers of a much more powerful weapon, the 4.2-inch chemical mortar, designed for firing chemical shells but effective with high explosive and white phosphorus. Both sides had individual antitank rockets employing a shaped charge: the Germans a one-shot *Panzerfaust* and the Americans a bazooka, named for a makeshift musical instrument played by a hillbilly radio comedian, Bob Burns.

The crew-served American antitank weapon, a towed 57mm. piece, was little better than a pea-shooter against German tanks, while the German division had eighteen self-propelled 75mm. assault guns, normally used as close support for attacking infantry but effective against tanks. As a kind of assault gun, each American infantry regiment had six towed short-barreled 105mm. howitzers in a Cannon Company. Both divisions had three medium (105mm.) artillery battalions and one heavy battalion (150mm. for the Germans, 155mm. for the Americans) for a total of forty-eight howitzers.

To provide increased direct fire support for the infantry and better antitank defense, it had become standard practice by the fall of 1944 to attach to each American infantry division a tank battalion and a tank destroyer battalion. The tank battalion had a company (thirteen) of lights and three companies (fifty-three) of mediums; and some recently arrived battalions had an assault gun platoon with six tanks equipped with a 105mm. howitzer. The tank destroyer battalion had either a towed 3-inch gun (so-designated because it was a copy of a naval weapon) or a 76mm. (same as a 3-inch) or 90mm. self-propelled gun.

Those attachments made the American infantry division considerably stronger in men and firepower than the German *Volksgrenadier* division and at least the equal of the German *Panzergrenadier* division, which had organic medium tank and tank destroyer battalions and a contingent of half-tracks for transporting its grenadiers. Since the American division had a wealth of motor vehicles, plus the attached tanks and tank destroyers, it was as mobile as the *Panzergrenadier* division.

Neither the *Panzergrenadier* nor the parachute division had had to take the sharp reductions imposed on the *Volksgrenadiers*, so that both types of divisions still had nine battalions of infantry. The parachute divisions were considered to be elite, and in months long past they had been made up almost entirely of volunteers; but after heavy losses in an airborne assault on Crete in 1941, Hitler had become disenchanted with airborne troops. Airborne training virtually ceased, and among the parachute infantry in the Ardennes, few had any parachute training. The name parachute division had become nothing more than an honorific.

The German panzer and SS panzer division had a panzer regiment with two tank battalions and a self-propelled tank destroyer battalion. Most of the divisions in the Ardennes had around 130 tanks and tank destroyers combined. The *Panzergrenadiers* of both types of divisions— four battalions in the army division, six in the SS division—were supposed to ride in half-tracks. Only one of three artillery battalions in the army division and one of four in the SS division was self-propelled. The army division had thirteen thousand men, the SS division, twenty thousand. And all the SS divisions were beefed up with an attached tank or tank destroyer battalion, a *Nebelwerfer* (rocket) battalion, and a heavy 170mm. artillery battery.

Most American armored divisions had three tank battalions equipped with a total of 177 medium tanks, a self-propelled tank destroyer battalion, three medium artillery battalions (all self-propelled), and three battalions of armored infantry (one of the war's great misnomers, for when battle was joined, the armored infantryman fought outside his half-track with no more protection than any other foot soldier). Two divisions—the 2d and 3d Armored—were different, having been organized under an earlier table of organization with more tanks but fewer infantry than the other armored divisions.

Both sides had general support artillery, plus such specialized units as signal, quartermaster, ordnance, engineers, and the like; but in those specialized units, the Germans were at a dual disadvantage in numbers and quality. Such a basic item as tank recovery vehicles, for example, was in critically short supply, and several engineer battalions had never erected a bridge before. The American units, on the other hand, were at full strength, thoroughly trained and experienced in the field. American engineer battalions, trained in addition to their engineer duties to fight as infantry, were to prove to be a hidden reserve.

The one major German advantage was the quality of German tanks vis-à-vis those of the Americans. The Americans still had seventy-seven light tanks in their armored divisions and still used the light tank as a basic weapon in cavalry reconnaissance units, but its armor was absurdly thin and its 37mm. piece of no value except for firing canister against enemy infantry. The standard American tank was the 33-ton Sherman, most still equipped with a short-barreled 75mm. gun, although some had an improved long-barreled 76mm. high-velocity piece. By December 1944, the Sherman would have to be considered almost obsolescent, its only advantage over German tanks being a greater rapidity of fire (as a result of a gyrostabilizer and power traverse) and somewhat greater mobility. Like German tanks, it used regular gasoline rather than Diesel and was thus readily put to the torch: Some crewmen called it, after a popular cigarette lighter, the "Ronson." No American heavy tank had yet reached the battlefield.

The workhorses of the battlefield for the panzer and SS panzer divisions were medium tanks: the 27-ton Mark IV, a mainstay for the entire war, which mounted a long-barreled 75mm. gun; and the 47-ton Mark V Panther, which also mounted a 75mm. gun but had much thicker armor than either the Mark IV or the Sherman. Although the Sherman fought on equal terms with the Mark IV, it could knock out a Panther only with a shot to the side or rear.

The Germans also had behemoths, a 63-ton Mark VI Tiger and a 68-ton Royal or King Tiger, both of which were heavily armored and mounted a deadly high-velocity 88mm. gun. Although reports from American soldiers would indicate that the Tiger was omnipresent, only about 150 of them were to fight in the Ardennes, employed in separate battalions usually attached to a panzer or SS panzer division. The only American weapon that could consistently be counted upon to knock out a

Tiger was the tank destroyer equipped with a 90mm. gun, which had been developed originally as an antiaircraft weapon. A Tiger advancing with machine guns blazing or 88 blasting was a near-paralyzing sight.

The Ardennes was at once the nursery and the old folks' home of the American command. New divisions came there for a battlefield shakedown, old ones to rest after heavy fighting and absorb replacements for their losses.

In the north, covering Monschau, was the 102d Cavalry Group, a light force equipped with armored cars, light tanks, and a few self-propelled 75mm. assault guns. From Monschau southeast to the Losheim Gap and the boundary with the VIII Corps, the 99th Infantry Division, which had been in the line for five weeks but had yet to mount an attack, held a front approximately twenty miles long. Like almost all American divisions arriving in Europe in the fall of 1944, the 99th had been raided for replacements and shortly before shipping overseas, filled its ranks with men transferred from ground units of the Army Air Forces, from antiaircraft units, and from the Army Specialized Training Program (ASTP), the last an ill-starred experiment to provide technical training in colleges and universities for men with high IQs. (The program was sharply cut back as battlefield losses mounted.)

For long, only a cavalry reconnaissance squadron had held the five-mile width of the Losheim Gap. After repeated requests for reinforcement from the commander of the 2d Division, General Robertson, to whom the cavalry was attached, headquarters of the 14th Cavalry Group had arrived on December 11 to assume control of that squadron and brought with it a second squadron. That such a small force was entrusted with defending the critical Losheim Gap demonstrated the complacency with which American commanders viewed the possibility of a German offensive in the Ardennes. Yet other commanders on the ground were concerned. The 99th Division protected its right flank next to the gap with its only reserve infantry battalion, and the 2d Division placed one of its two reserve infantry battalions on its left flank close to the gap. The only other deference to the gap as a historic *débouché* was provided by the commander of the VIII Corps, General Middleton, who placed eight of his thirteen corps artillery battalions in positions from which they could fire either into the Losheim Gap and or in the sector around the Schnee Eifel.

Since early October, the 2d Division had held an eighteen-mile front that included the Schnee Eifel and extended southwest beyond the ridge almost to the Luxembourg border. To free the 2d Division for the First Army's attack on the Roer River dams, the 106th Infantry Division, fresh off the boats and flush with new men, mostly from the ASTP, began taking over on December 10.

In late November, the veteran 28th Infantry Division, having lost five thousand men in bloody fighting in the Hürtgen Forest, replaced another division that had been resting in the Ardennes, taking over a twenty-five-mile front along the Our River all the way south to the juncture of the Our and the Sûre. In effect, the 28th held nothing more than an outpost line.

With the arrival of the 9th Armored Division in late October as a reserve for the VIII Corps, General Middleton in order to provide the men with some battle experience, used the armored infantry battalion from one of the three combat commands to hold just over two miles of the 28th Division's front, intending to rotate the battalion with others. The tanks of that battalion's combat command were kept in reserve a few miles to the rear. Although the 9th Armored Division's other two combat commands were in reserve farther to the rear, one began to move on December 13 to provide an armored reserve for the attack to take the Roer River dams.

On December 7, the veteran 4th Infantry Division, having incurred almost as many casualties in the Hürtgen Forest as the 28th Division, took over the rest of the line—some twenty miles from the vicinity of Echternach to the boundary with the Third Army southeast of Luxembourg City. Since the southern boundary of the German offensive was to be a few miles south of Echternach, only a portion of the 4th Division was destined to become involved in the fighting.

In addition to the thirteen general support artillery battalions of the VIII Corps, General Gerow of the V Corps had just over six battalions concentrated near his southern boundary to support the attack on the Roer River dams. Thus there were 228 artillery pieces in addition to the 276 organic to divisions that would be capable of firing at some point within the Ardennes. It was an impressive assembly, yet far fewer than those available to the attacker. Middleton also was to have the support of an engineer combat group of four battalions and another of three battalions operating in rear areas of the VIII Corps under control of headquarters of the First Army. In the entire VIII Corps, there were 182 self-propelled tank destroyers and 242 medium tanks; they would be considerably outnumbered.

The men who manned the foxholes in the Ardennes knew that in comparison to attacking, they had it good. When not in their holes, they had warm, dry places to sleep in: houses, cellars, or bunker-type squad huts made from logs of the big fir trees, covered with sandbags. Some had heating from stoves mostly taken from nearby villages. Except in the most exposed positions, the troops almost always had hot food, and they could attend religious services back at battalion or regimental headquarters. From time to time, a man got to go on a forty-eight-hour pass to regimental or divisional rest camps well to the rear, where he could take a shower, sleep on a cot, buy a watered beer, have coffee and doughnuts dispensed by smiling American girls in Red Cross uniforms, see a movie, or, on rare occasions, a USO show, and, even more rarely, find a whorehouse where you had to stand in line, but what the hell?

There was, nevertheless, a war on. The Germans shelled with mortars and artillery, got nervous when a new division moved in and sent combat patrols to find out what was going on. The battalion S-2 was forever demanding that companies send out patrols to nab a prisoner, to determine what the enemy was up to; and to cover the great gaps in the line (sometimes up to a mile or more between units), contact patrols had to operate on a fairly regular basis. So porous was the line that German soldiers whose homes were in the eastern corner of Belgium sometimes slipped through to spend a night with their wives or girlfriends in St. Vith or nearby villages, and German agents mingled with the GI patrons of bars and cafés in the bigger towns. On occasion a German patrol might hit an installation in the rear of the line, a battalion headquarters or a supply point, lay mines on roads, or sometimes string a strand of heavy wire across a road within American lines so that the driver of a fast-moving jeep with windshield down might be decapitated.

On one occasion a German patrol ambushed three medical officers—a lieutenant colonel and two majors—killed them, and stripped them of their uniforms. A few days later, in the reserve positions of the 9th Armored Division's Combat Command B, as three officers were going to their mess hall, they passed three medics, a lieutenant-colonel and two majors, who were escorting three women wearing nylons and heavily veiled. The two parties exchanged salutes, but as the armored officers sat down to their meal, almost as one they did a double take. What was it about those medical officers? They had red crosses on their helmets and on the brassards on their arms, but something was wrong. No American medic ever carried a weapon, yet all three had .45-caliber pistols strapped to their waists. And nylons? What woman in wartime Luxembourg had nylons?

The three officers dashed outside, their weapons at the ready, but they were too late. Nobody was to be seen.

As *Null-Tag* finally approached, senior German commanders had no more faith in the Führer's grand design than when they had first heard of it. Individually, without consulting one another, neither von Rundstedt, Model, nor von Manteuffel made any plans for operations beyond the Meuse. Although von Manteuffel, at least, hoped to gain bridgeheads over the river just in case Hitler "had more forces hidden up his sleeve," he was convinced that that was the only way the offensive might continue toward Antwerp, for if by some strange good fortune the German armies should reach the Meuse without encountering "strong enemy forces," those forces would surely be lying in wait on the other side of the river.

Nor did Sepp Dietrich display any greater optimism. In conjunction with his chief of staff, Brigadeführer der Waffen-SS Fritz Kraemer, a General Staff–trained officer for whom von Rundstedt and Model had arranged appointment in order to afford the Sixth Panzer Army professional tactical and strategic direction, Dietrich had drawn up a plan, with the tacit consent of von Rundstedt and Model but without the knowledge either of General Jodl or Hitler, to alter the Führer's dictate. Instead of passing south of Liège and crossing the Meuse west of the city, the Sixth Panzer Army was to cross on both sides of the city. That would put Dietrich in position to implement the Small Solution. Should it come to that.

Hitler for some reason became suspicious, for on the eve of the offensive, after nightfall on December 15, he telephoned Model. "There will be no deviation by the panzer units east of the Meuse toward the north," he admonished. "The Sixth Panzer Army must keep clear of the covering front to be built up between Monschau and Liège. Do not let Dietrich become involved in the fighting along his northern flank." To which Model replied, *Jawohl, mein Führer*, and shortly telephoned back to say he had given the instructions to Dietrich. "All the efforts of Army Group B," said Model, "will be directed toward the thrust to Antwerp."

As for the other army commander, General Brandenberger, whose Seventh Army was to secure the southern flank of the penetration, there was no way he could be optimistic. To attack and then to defend more than eighty miles of up-and-down Ardennes countryside from Echternach to the Meuse River at Givet, he would have only four infantry divisions, no tanks, and a mere handful of tank destroyers and assault guns. An earlier hope of taking Luxembourg City had to be abandoned, but even with that modification, Brandenberger's appeared to be an impossible assignment.

Despite the presence to the south of the Third U.S. Army and its commander, George Patton, for whom German generals had immense respect, Hitler showed less concern about the south flank than about the north. Enlarging on an idea originally suggested by Model, Hitler on December 8 suddenly developed a new interest in parachute troops. He wanted a battalion of just over a thousand paratroopers to drop behind Monschau astride the only north–south road leading across the moors of the Hautes Fagnes, there to block American reinforcements from the north until Dietrich's troops could arrive to erect a solid defensive shoulder. Making the link-up was to be the assignment of a special task force equipped with twenty-one experimental *Jägdtigers* (tank destroyers), 82-ton monsters mounting an awesome 128mm. gun, the mainstay of German antiaircraft defenses, on a Tiger chassis.

The airborne attack fell to a veteran paratrooper who had fought on Crete, a man of the old Catholic aristocracy, Col. Graf (Count) Friedrich August von der Heydte. To assemble the troops, Hitler ordered commanders of all parachute regiments to send a hundred of their best soldiers, which predictably set in motion the game long practiced in every army of getting rid of misfits and incompetents. Yet when men of von der Heydte's old unit, the 6th Parachute Regiment, learned of the mission, some 250 of them took off and reported to their former commander, who somehow managed to convince his superiors to allow him to hold onto them.

At that point, von der Heydte had only a few days left in which to prepare his rag-tag force, few of whom had ever made even a practice parachute jump; and the man to whom von der Heydte was to be responsible, Sepp Dietrich, was less than cooperative. When von der Heydte reported at his headquarters near Münstereifel, Dietrich had been drinking heavily. Since a parachute drop would alert the enemy, declared Dietrich, it would have to be made only a few hours before the ground attack started, which would mean a night drop.

Von der Heydte pointed out that to jump at night into a region of forests and moors with such inexperienced troops as he possessed would be suicidal, but Dietrich refused to budge. Don't worry, Dietrich assured him. The paratroopers would have to hold for only a few hours before the big *Jägdtigers* reached them.

The commander of another special force, Otto Skorzeny, already concerned that the order requesting volunteers for his mission had surely fallen into Allied hands, had encountered little to encourage him in his assignment of penetrating the American line with German soldiers masquerading as Americans. From the first he was concerned that soldiers wearing the enemy's uniform would be violating International Laws of War and subject, if captured, to execution; but legal counsel assured him that the laws permitted wearing enemy uniforms as a *ruse de guerre*, forbidding only fighting while wearing them. His men could wear their German uniforms underneath and take off the American ones before opening fire. (That, Skorzeny knew, was claptrap.)

Skorzeny also recognized that it would be impossible to create a cohesive brigade, which was the size unit he considered necessary, out of random volunteers in the short time available. Only with difficulty did he persuade Jodl to give him two infantry battalions and a company of tanks. Those were to be the core of the 150th Panzer Brigade of 3,300 men.

The response to the call for volunteers who spoke American "dialect" left Skorzeny in dismay. Only ten, mostly former merchant seamen, spoke perfect English with some knowledge of American slang. Another 125 had a fair command of English, and about 200 others had learned a little English in school. A few could say yes and no. That was all.

The quest for American uniforms and equipment was at least as discouraging. Although Skorzeny asked for twenty American tanks, he got two, one of which quickly broke down with transmission trouble. Skorzeny had to make do with twelve Panthers camouflaged to look like Shermans, sufficient only, Skorzeny ruefully observed, to "deceive very young American troops seeing them at night from very far away." Of ten armored cars received, six were British, but in any case they soon broke down. There were about fifteen American trucks and thirty jeeps.

The first consignment of uniforms turned out to be British. When a consignment of American field jackets arrived, they had a big triangle—indicating prisoner of war—painted on the back. There were a few American mortars and antitank guns but no rounds for them and possibly enough M-1 rifles to arm half the brigade but with limited amounts of ammunition. It was soon obvious that Skorzeny would be able to disguise only those men in a commando company who were to spread confusion in the American rear, and even those would lack much of the paraphernalia that American soldiers usually wore and carried.

Skorzeny also had another security scare. Although his troops were sealed in their training area at Grafenwöhr, near Nuremberg, so wild were the rumors circulating among them as to their mission that Skorzeny was sure some word would leak to Allied intelligence. Yet how to stop the rumors? Skorzeny decided at last to let them fly, the wilder the better.

A few days later, when Skorzeny was visiting at Grafenwöhr, a lieutenant assigned to the commando company asked to speak with him privately. "Sir," said the young officer, "I believe I know the real objective of the brigade." Skorzeny bristled. Had somebody talked? But the lieutenant quickly continued: "The brigade is to go straight to Paris and capture Allied headquarters!" He himself wanted to help; he had lived in Paris and spoke French fluently. Although he recognized that Skorzeny had probably already drawn up a plan, he had some ideas he hoped Skorzeny would consider. After slipping through the lines in American uniforms, the men would rendezvous at the Café de la Paix on the Place de l'Opéra, and from there proceed to capture or assassinate General Eisenhower and his staff.

As far as Skorzeny could make out, the lieutenant had based his reckoning on the codename Skorzeny had chosen for the operation: *GREIF.* It meant a mythical bird, but in another sense the word could mean "Grasp." "Well," said Skorzeny, "go and think it all over very carefully and work out the details. We'll have a further talk—but mind you, keep as silent as the grave."

By the time night fell, Skorzeny reckoned, almost every man in the camp believed he knew what the mission was: Kill Eisenhower.

Aside from spreading confusion in the American rear, Skorzeny's mission was to seize three bridges over the Meuse in the zone of the Sixth Panzer Army between Liège and the bend in the river at Namur. Once *Volksgrenadier* divisions had broken the American line, which Skorzeny assumed would be accomplished before the end of the first day, he was to send three task forces (two of which would have twelve tanks each) through the darkness, bypassing opposition, and seize the bridges before the Americans could blow them. Jeeps carrying drivers and riders disguised as Americans were to lead the way.

One of Skorzeny's three task forces was to accompany another special group, a beefed-up *Kampfgruppe* (battle group) of the 1st SS Panzer Division known as the *Liebstandärte Adolf Hitler* (Hitler's Own), a division which traced its origins to Hitler's first bodyguard, initially organized by Sepp Dietrich. The commander of the *Kampfgruppe* was SS-Lt. Col. Joachim Peiper, who at age nineteen had become an officer candidate in the SS, and except for a brief stint on the staff of Reichsführer-SS Himmler had spent the next ten years with the *Liebstandärte Adolf Hitler* and stood high in Hitler's personal favor. (Possibly reflecting the SS distaste for names of biblical origin, Peiper had come to prefer to spell his first name "Jochen.")

The moment the *Volksgrenadiers* achieved a breakthrough, *Kampfgruppe Peiper* was to drive through the northern reaches of the Losheim Gap toward the bridge over the Meuse at Huy, midway between Liège and Namur. Over a route specially chosen because it had fewer bridges than the others—at some points, Peiper was later to complain with considerable justification, a route "more fit for bicycles" than for tanks—Peiper was to dash for Huy without regard for his flanks, avoiding likely opposition, and where possible bypassing it if encountered. In the interest of speed, the armored spearhead of Peiper's column could hardly be expected to burden itself with large numbers of prisoners of war, but whether they were to be cared for by troops following later in the column or just what was to be done with them would in time become a matter of major importance and tragedy.

As each German soldier marched to his jump-off position in the Eifel and on the evening of December 15 learned for the first time what he was to do, reactions varied widely. Some received the news stoically, much like Private First Class Stiegeler whose group "was given a bottle of booze, and off we went." Others doubted that anything substantial could be accomplished: Had they not lived on promises ever since the retreat from Normandy? Where were the miracle weapons the official communiqués promised? Many of those transferred from rear echelon posts and from the navy and the Luftwaffe were depressed. At a time when the war was practically over, why should they have to fight and probably die for a lost cause?

Thousands received the news with resignation. In the 2d SS Panzer Division, for example, 1st Lt. Erich Heller and his young officer friends, all of whom had fought in Normandy, "agreed that the war was virtually lost," but even so, they "had no idea of not doing their duty." The people at home were taking terrible punishment from the bombers, yet they were holding firm, doing what was expected of them. As soldiers at the front, could they do less?

For some, it was, in any case, a battle for survival, for if Germany lost the war, the people would be, at best, enslaved. If not, why the demand for unconditional surrender? Why the Morgenthau Plan to abolish German industry and turn the country into a pastoral, agricultural land?

Still others saw the possibility of achieving something that might alleviate postwar Germany's fate. A sergeant in *Kampfgruppe Peiper,* Karl Wortmann, thought they would succeed, "not necessarily a great victory but gaining as much territory as possible to embarrass the Americans and demonstrate success to the German people." A regimental commander in the 12th Volksgrenadier Division, Col. Wilhelm Osterhold, intended to lead his troops as capably as possible, "perhaps in the process achieving something that might lessen the harsh treatment that was in store for Germany."

Thousands more received the news with enthusiasm. As one German officer wrote in his diary: "There is a general feeling of elation; everybody is cheerful." Pvt. Klaus Ritter and his young friends in the 18th Volksgrenadier Division were "euphoric . . . in four weeks they would actually be in Paris!"

For many, faith in the Führer's ability to set matters right remained, and since all news came through a controlled press, they had no real knowledge of how grim was Germany's plight. Countless numbers among them welcomed the chance at battlefield booty: to feast on American rations, to smoke cigarettes with real tobacco in them ("A choice between Camels and Chesterfields!"), to get a pair of the good leather boots the *Ami* wore. Others welcomed retribution: a chance to pay back the *Ami* for the destruction of German cities, for the bombing of civilians, to chase him forever from German soil.

In the SS panzer divisions, morale was highest of all. Noted one SS trooper to his sister:

> I write during one of the great hours before we attack . . . full of expectation for what the next days will bring. Everyone who has been here the last two days and nights (especially nights), who has witnessed hour after hour the assembly of our crack divisions, who has heard the constant rattling of Panzers, knows that something is up . . . we attack and will throw the enemy from our homeland. That is a holy task!

On the back of the envelope, he scribbled: "Ruth! Ruth! Ruth! WE MARCH!"

A member of an old Virginia family, Walter Melville Robertson had received a commission in the infantry from West Point in 1912. Seeing no overseas duty during World War I, he served the usual between-wars assignments, mostly with infantry regiments at isolated U.S. posts in the West and Southwest, but he also served as an instructor at the Command

and General Staff College and at the Army War College. Early in 1940, he went to Fort Sam Houston, just outside San Antonio, Texas, to join one of the U.S. Army's more renowned regular units, the 2d Infantry Division, with which Robertson's destiny was long to be linked. Possibly because he and his wife had no children, the 2d Division became a kind of family to him. Mild-mannered and soft-spoken, he had the reddish hair and florid complexion of an Irishman and also "a temper when tested too far." No drinker, something of a loner, he seldom mingled socially with his officers, but they had deep respect for his ability as a commander.

Robertson first commanded a battalion in the 9th Infantry, then the regiment itself, then the 23d Infantry, whereupon he became assistant division commander and finally assumed command of the division. Under his command, the 2d Division came ashore on OMAHA Beach the day after D-Day. At fifty-six, Robertson was a few years older than most division commanders.

When at the end of the first week of December Robertson went to headquarters of the V Corps in Eupen to receive the order for the attack on the Roer River dams, one aspect of the plan of attack troubled him deeply. Approaching the dams from the south, he would have at first only one road over which the entire division would have to advance and also depend upon for supply. It ran from the town of Büllingen north through Krinkelt and Rocherath, two villages so close together that they appeared to be one (American troops called them the "twin villages"), thence for six miles through a dense fir forest to the first objective, a road junction known as Wahlerscheid and marked by a customshouse, a farmhouse, concrete dragon's teeth, and a thick cluster of pillboxes of the West Wall. The enemy strongpoint sat astride one of the wide gaps in the defensive line of the 99th Division. *(See map, Chapter Eight, p. 164.)*

For almost the entire distance, the road ran behind and almost parallel with the 99th Division's positions along the German frontier, from one to three miles away. If the Germans should penetrate the 99th Division's extended line and cut the road at any point along the nine miles from Büllingen to Wahlerscheid, whatever portion of Robertson's troops had passed over the road would be trapped. There would be no way out except on foot, for there was not even a trail leading westward except for a dirt track from Krinkelt-Rocherath through the village of Wirtzfeld, thence over a meandering course to the town of Elsenborn, and for more than half a mile the track ran along a stream bottom with soil of such consistency that not even a jeep could negotiate it.

Once troops of the 106th Division began to take over on the Schnee Eifel, Robertson's engineer officer, Lt. Col. Robert W. Warren, put his 2d Engineer Battalion to work to improve that track to make it passable at least for one-way traffic. Yet that would merely alleviate Robertson's problem, not solve it, for the track through Wirtzfeld was near the start of what would be the division's lone supply route, so that a cut along the wooded six-mile stretch north of Krinkelt-Rocherath might still trap the division. So, too, would an enemy thrust into Krinkelt-Rocherath, and there were two fairly good roads leading into the twin villages through frontier forests from German positions.

A heavy snowstorm was pelting the northern reaches of the Ardennes and the Eifel when Robertson's troops began to move from the Schnee Eifel region to assembly areas in and near a Belgian Army caserne close behind the 99th Division's front, Camp Elsenborn. In an effort to achieve surprise, there was no patrolling to pinpoint the enemy's defenses before the troops of the leading 9th Infantry began to march north from Krinkelt-Rocherath into the fir forest soon after daylight on December 13.

There was at first no enemy, but the going was slow. Although the storm had passed, warming weather made the snow heavy, and because the road was known to be mined and at intervals blocked by felled trees, the men had to plow through the forest on either side, sometimes grappling through growths of wet young firs, at other times subjected to falling snow from towering branches of the bigger ones. By the time the column neared the enemy-held road junction around noon, everybody was drenched.

The hope for surprise quickly vanished. A hundred yards in front of the pillboxes the forest cover ran out, and the first men to emerge from the woodsline drew a blast of fire from rifles and automatic weapons, while mortar and artillery shells exploded in the treetops and threw a lethal shower of fragments onto the forest floor. In some places rows of barbed-wire entanglements six to ten deep barred the way to the pillboxes, and the snow hid a veritable quilt of deadly antipersonnel mines.

That first day, the men of the 9th Infantry made not a dent in the German position, and night brought with it a numbing cold that froze the men's wet uniforms almost stiff. Through the night patrols probed without success to try to find a weak spot in the defenses, while most of the men tried to keep warm by painfully etching some kind of cover from the frozen earth. It was a miserable pattern that would be long repeated, and all the while medical jeeps formed a steady procession back down the forest road, laboriously swept of mines by the engineers.

Meanwhile, a few hundred yards to the southeast of Wahlerscheid, three of the 99th Division's battalions attacked down into deep ravines and up precipitous wooded hillsides in an effort to pin down other enemy troops and prevent them from reinforcing at Wahlerscheid or pushing through the forest to cut the lone supply route. In almost every case on the first day, German fire stopped those men, too, and the cold night was just as painful for them as for the men of the 2d Division. Over the next two days those men nevertheless wrenched gains of a few hundred yards from the stubborn defenders and the hostile forest.

Several miles to the north, beyond Monschau, an untried infantry division, the 78th, attacked southeastward in support of the 2d Division's attack over rolling, open ground dotted with villages and pillboxes, the northern prong of what the corps commander, General Gerow, hoped would become a double envelopment converging on the dams. Gains were painfully slow, but one battalion managed on the first day to advance a mile and a half to seize two villages, and on the next, a company slipped past defended pillboxes to take a third.

Then the Germans began to counterattack. By late afternoon of the third day, the company in the forward village still held, but its position was precarious; and after nightfall a prisoner provided the disturbing news that a previously unidentified 326th Volksgrenadier Division was assembled nearby.

Back at Wahlerscheid, as dusk approached on the second day, December 14, ten men slithered unnoticed by the Germans under one barbed-wire entanglement after another until all the rows were behind them, and in their wake other men cut a four-foot gap through the wire. Yet the men had no communications with their company headquarters, where some confusion existed because the company commander had just been wounded and evacuated. The men of the patrol had long since retired before word of what they had accomplished reached the battalion commander, Lt. Col. Walter M. Higgins, Jr.

When the next night came—December 15—and the 9th Infantry was as far as ever from cracking the defenses at Wahlerscheid, Higgins decided to try to exploit the little gap in the wire. Soon after dark, an eleven-man patrol, guided by one of the men who had helped forge the gap the night before and equipped with a sound-powered telephone, moved through the gap. Around 9:30 P.M., the patrol leader whispered into the telephone. The patrol had surrounded a pillbox and the Germans seemed unaware that anything was going on.

That was all Higgins needed. Within minutes, first one company then another was plodding single file, following a band of white tape through the gap in the wire. When another battalion quickly followed, the assault began. The men moved swiftly, blowing the doors of pillboxes with explosive charges, killing or capturing the occupants, prodding sleepy Germans from their foxholes, and capturing seventy-seven in one sweep at the customshouse. With Wahlerscheid at last in hand, a second regiment, the 38th Infantry, was soon moving forward to help exploit the breach.

Elsewhere on the Ardennes front, in the final hours before the Germans were to doff their cloak of deception, all remained relatively quiet, but there were a few last-minute indications that something untoward might be stirring. Late on the 15th, the 4th and 106th Divisions each took two prisoners, all of whom stated that they had been told a big attack was coming. Yet two were deserters who said they put little store by what they were told, for they had been promised big things before and nothing happened. Another impressed his interrogators, but he was so heavily sedated because of wounds that detailed questioning had to be delayed. The fourth, an ethnic Pole, was eager to talk. Interrogated at a regimental headquarters, he said the Germans would attack sometime between December 16 and Christmas "in a large-scale offensive, employing searchlights against the clouds to simulate moonlight." But the 106th Division's G-2, Lt. Col. Robert P. Stout, delayed reporting that information to the VIII Corps until he could talk personally with the prisoner.

For several nights, outposts of the 106th Division had been reporting the noise of tracked vehicles, and on the 15th, Colonel Stout noted that the night before there had been the "sound of vehicles all along the front after dark—vehicles, barking dogs, motors." A prisoner, Stout added, had said that "soldiers who come under the category of '*Volkliste III*' [one of the categories of *Volksdeutsch*]" had been withdrawn from the front, but Stout made no effort to read significance into the information.

A few miles to the south, outposts of the 28th Infantry Division reported that there appeared to be new and more disciplined troops opposing the division. The soldiers had fresh uniforms, including overcoats, and outside the pillboxes there was "much saluting and double-timing of guards."

A few more miles to the south, the G-2 of the 4th Infantry Division, Lt. Col. Harry F. Hansen, told his commander, Maj. Gen. Raymond O. Barton, that there were "large enemy formations in Bitburg." Although Barton had no thought of a big enemy offensive, he did assume that the Germans might stage a large raid, possibly to seize General Bradley's headquarters in Luxembourg City. With that in mind, he sent Hansen to talk with General Sibert, but Sibert discounted the idea. Barton nevertheless ordered all men who were in rest centers farther back than regimental headquarters to return to their units, and on the 15th he assembled his regimental commanders to discuss counterattack plans.

On both the 14th and 15th, worried civilians from villages and towns near the Our River began to turn up in the town of Diekirch, several miles back. The Germans were up to something, said the civilians, though they knew not what. "Don't worry," Americans from a Counter-Intelligence Corps detachment in Diekirch told them; "Jerry will never come back." Unconvinced, the civilians either continued to make their way farther from the front or looked up friends and relatives with whom to stay in Diekirch.

Around midnight on the 14th, in response to the information imparted by Elise Delé, a patrol from the 28th Division's 109th Infantry crossed the Our River at Vianden and crept warily up the high ground beyond. The men investigated one pillbox after another, all of which the Germans had long occupied, but they found not a man in any of them. What did that mean?

On the 28th Division's north wing that night, Pfc. John B. Allard, a nineteen-year-old member of Company F, 112th Infantry, volunteered for a patrol also mustered in response to the information from Elise Delé. Having recently learned that his twin brother in another regiment of the division was missing and presumed dead, Allard had made a point of becoming "a more active participant in combat patrol activities." Led by 1st Lt. Donald Nikkel, the twelve-man patrol slipped past German outposts across the Our from the village of Ouren, surrounded a pillbox, and seized it without a fight. While two men escorted twenty prisoners to the rear, the others stayed in the pillbox all the next day while watching with concern as one German formation after another arrived and settled down in nearby woods.

When night came on the 15th, Allard and other members of the patrol started back; but in every direction they came upon German troops, back-tracked, then tried again. In the end, they decided to brave it and in the darkness walked straight through a bivouac where Germans were sleeping in two-man tents. In some of the tents, candles were glowing. After wading the icy Our, Allard and the others reported what they had seen to their company commanders, but as they headed for their cellars, dawn of December 16 was only a few hours off.

In late afternoon of December 15, a farmer named Nikolaus Manderfeld left the village of Afst in the Losheim Gap to walk a little over half a mile along a snow-covered trail leading to the settlement of Allmuthen. One of only ten farmers whom the Americans had allowed to stay in Afst to care for the *bêtes*, as the locals called their pigs and cattle, Manderfeld's home was in Allmuthen, but neither Americans nor Germans occupied that little settlement. Manderfeld wanted to check his house to see if all was well.

Manderfeld was almost there when three German soldiers emerged from behind it, their machine pistols at the ready. One with binoculars around his neck demanded to know what Manderfeld was doing there. Accepting his explanation, they asked what he knew about the American positions. There were a few Americans in Afst, he said, and maybe about forty in the next village of Krewinkel.

"Tomorrow," said the soldier with the binoculars, "the heavies'll start firing again. We'll begin the final offensive. By the day after tomorrow, we'll be in Liège. In four days Antwerp will be ours!"

That night, after Manderfeld returned to Afst and was sitting by the stove in the house where he and all the other men were staying, he told his friends what had happened, but nobody believed him. Klaus Manderfeld always was a great one for tall stories.

Had Nikolaus Manderfeld spoken to the American soldiers in Afst, he might have found a more receptive audience, for the Americans were indeed concerned. The night before, the pattern of enemy behavior had abruptly changed. For long weeks the enemy had appeared to be nervous at night, firing flares and occasionally letting go with a burst from a machine gun or a burp gun; but the night before, there had been not a single flare and the darkness was eerily silent. So, too, an accustomed parade of putt-putting V-1 buzz bombs passing overhead en route toward Liège and Antwerp came to an end.

It was the same on the night of the 15th as 2d Lt. Max L. Crawford led an eight-man patrol from Troop C, 18th Cavalry Reconnaissance Squadron, to set up an ambush in Allmuthen and try to grab a prisoner. At first the men circled the cluster of farmhouses, attached barns, and manure piles at a distance, then, hearing nothing suspicious, they moved to a trail junction across from one of the houses. While three men took up positions across the trail from the house at an open shed filled with hay, others deployed closer to the trail junction, and Lieutenant Crawford and Cpl. John Banister took cover alongside the attached barn. From inside the house, the two heard low voices and a muffled cough.

The patrol had been in position only a short time when a group of about thirty Germans, some pulling a sled loaded with something and all talking unconcernedly, approached the trail junction. According to Crawford's instructions, the men were not to fire if badly outnumbered, but when several of the Germans began to walk toward the hay shed, Pvt. Richard King, armed with a Thompson submachine gun, considered that he had no choice. The Germans were almost on top of him as he fired.

Considering that the little patrol "didn't have the chance of a snowflake in hell," Crawford's second-in-command, Sgt. David Herzog, yelled to take off. Most of the men made it, scrambling back to a rendezvous point previously agreed upon, but the Germans captured one man and were so close to Crawford and Banister that they dared not move. For more than two hours they flattened themselves against the side of the barn while soldiers passed in and out of the house, sometimes so near it seemed to Crawford and Banister they could have reached out and touched them. It was close to midnight before they dared try to escape, and however carefully they set their feet down in the snow, it seemed as if they were moving like elephants and that the loud crunching noises would surely give them away.

At long last, they were far enough from the house to make a run for it. Getting back to Afst close to one o'clock in the morning, Lieutenant Crawford reported to the squadron's S-2 what had happened. No patrol, said Crawford, had ever run into that much enemy activity in Allmuthen.

That same night of December 15, at the southern terminus of the Skyline Drive in Diekirch, a glamorous German-born film star, Marlene Dietrich, heading a USO troupe, performed to the raucous applause of hundreds of GIs. She went to bed as soon as possible after the performance, for she had to get up early the next morning to travel north to the sector of the 99th Infantry Division, where she was to make informal appearances at several regimental rest camps close behind the front.

Within the Eifel on December 15, German intelligence officers took a last look at the American side of the line. The only possible trouble spot appeared to be in the extreme north near Monschau, where on the 13th an apparently small-scale American attack had begun. That might pose problems for the northernmost unit in the offensive, the 272d Volksgrenadier Division, which had been hit by the northern prong of the American attack. The other division that was to attack at Monschau, the 326th Volksgrenadier Division, had just arrived in an assembly area for the jump-off and was thus unaffected by the American attack.

Otherwise, the American front appeared much the same as it had for some days: the 4th, 28th, and 99th Divisions and the recently arrived 106th Division, which German intelligence had quickly identified. The 2d Division presumably had moved to a reserve position and thus would probably have to be reckoned with at some point during the offensive but not right away. Possibly because the 2d Division had removed all unit markings from its vehicles and all of its distinctive big Indianhead shoulder patches before beginning its attack, and possibly too because three battalions of the 99th Division had also been involved in the attack, the Germans had failed to discern the presence of the 2d Division at Wahlerscheid. They still expected to encounter in that sector only the thinly spread 99th Division.

At most, the Germans believed the Americans had about 370 tanks in the entire Ardennes, and they felt fairly sure that the 12th Army Group had no major reserves. Yet from agents they had learned that the 82d and 101st Airborne Divisions had assembled in northern France, where they were presumably resting after a long stay in defensive positions in the Netherlands following participation in the Allied airborne operation in September. The bars in Rheims and surrounding towns were filled at night with rowdy paratroopers.

In assembly areas close behind the front that night, commanders read out a message from Field Marshal von Rundstedt and endorsements from Field Marshal Model and the appropriate army commander to their men. Von Rundstedt's message said:

> Soldiers of the West Front!! Your great hour has arrived. Large attacking armies have started against the Anglo-Americans. I do not have to tell you anything more than that. You feel it yourself. WE GAMBLE EVERYTHING! You carry with you the holy obligation to give everything to achieve things beyond human possibilities for our Fatherland and our Führer!

At von Rundstedt's headquarters in Ziegenberg Castle, the keeper of the *OB WEST* War Diary made a final entry for the day at midnight: "Tomorrow brings the beginning of a new chapter in the Campaign in the West."

BOOK

II

THE FIRST DAY

CHAPTER FIVE

In Front of St. Vith

Scion of one of the oldest of the hereditary nobilities of Prussia, Hasso Eccard von Manteuffel was, at forty-seven, young for an army command and at 5 feet, 2 inches, and 120 pounds, hardly of the physique to inspire awe in subordinates. When he was a cadet-officer candidate at the age of fourteen at the Berlin-Lichterfelde Academy, they had to remove a portion of his rifle barrel to enable him to manipulate it in drill. At last old enough for military service in 1916, he served on the Western Front as a lieutenant of infantry, where he was wounded slightly by shrapnel.

Long an avid and expert horseman, von Manteuffel transferred after the war to the cavalry and became enthused over the possibilities of armor as espoused by a young major, Heinz Guderian. He joined the Inspectorate General of Armored Forces soon after Guderian in 1934 became its chief of staff. Then, as later, von Manteuffel (like Gerd von Rundstedt) was apolitical, "in the true Prussian tradition."

Although von Manteuffel saw Hitler's attack on Russia as a mistake, he volunteered for front-line service, commanded a *Panzergrenadier* battalion, and soon replaced the fallen commander of his regiment. During the unsuccessful drive on Moscow, he performed with such distinction that he gained promotion to colonel and received the Knight's Cross to the Iron Cross.

As the German retreat began in heavy snows and below-zero cold, von Manteuffel ran afoul of his army commander, Colonel-General Walter Model. Model ordered von Manteuffel to make an attack, but hardly had it begun before von Manteuffel called it off: the snow was so deep his men could barely move. Outraged, Model went to von Manteuffel's headquarters and threatened court-martial, but the division commander defused the issue by sending von Manteuffel with the advance party for the division's impending transfer to France. By the time von Manteuffel saw Model again, the diminutive soldier—his friends called him "*Kleiner*" ("Little")—had commanded a division in North Africa and had returned

101

to the Eastern Front to lead an elite panzer division, *Grossdeutschland*. He so impressed Adolf Hitler in the process that the Führer summoned him to the *Wolfschanze* to jump him past corps command to the rank of General der Panzertruppen and command of the Fifth Panzer Army on the Western Front.

In October, 1944, as the Fifth Panzer Army shifted to the command of Army Group B, von Manteuffel with some trepidation reported to Field Marshal Model's headquarters near Krefeld. Entering Model's office, he saluted and noted with relief that Model returned the salute. "You remember our conversation in 1941?" asked Model. "Now we two have the same task; we are good friends."

More than anybody other than Hitler himself, von Manteuffel put his imprint on the way the big offensive was to begin. As part of the unsuccessful effort to talk Hitler out of the Big Solution, he found an opportunity, when he saw Hitler at the Reischschancellery on December 2, to convince the Führer to make changes. Rather than a two- to three-hour artillery preparation, he argued that a short, concentrated preparation would accomplish much the same effect while lessening the enemy's alert. Rather than attack at 10 A.M., which would leave little more than six hours of daylight for the first day's operation, he wanted the artillery preparation to begin well before daylight at 5:30 A.M., followed a half hour later by a ground assault assisted by artificial moonlight to be created by bouncing the light of giant searchlights off the clouds. ("How do you know you will have clouds?" asked Hitler. Responded von Manteuffel: "You have already decided there will be bad weather.")

Having donned the uniform of a colonel of infantry and spent a night in a pillbox overlooking the Our River, von Manteuffel had personally determined that outposts of the American 28th Division's 110th Infantry pulled back from the river at night. He thus proposed no artillery fire along the river, so that the assault troops could begin crossing while the artillery was hitting American positions a mile or so beyond on the Skyline Drive. Since he also discerned that the positions of the 28th Division's 112th Infantry, which were on the German side of the Our, were widely spaced, he asked authority to forego an artillery preparation there so that troops might infiltrate between and in rear of the American positions before the hour of attack.

To all those proposals, Hitler agreed.

Split seconds before 5:30 A.M. on Saturday, December 16, an American soldier from Company K, 110th Infantry, manning an observation post atop a concrete water tower along the Skyline Drive in the village of Hosingen, telephoned his company commander. In the distance on the German side of the Our, he could see a strange phenomenon: countless flickering pinpoints of light. Moments later both he and his company commander had the explanation. They were the flashes of German guns, for at Hosingen, along the rest of the Skyline Drive, and at many another point along what had been the quiet front in the Ardennes, the morning darkness suddenly came alive with a maelstrom of bursting shells.

No experienced mechanized cavalry commander—least of all a stickler for spit-and-polish and soldiering by the rules such as Col. Mark A. Devine, Jr.—would have viewed the positions of the 18th Cavalry Reconnaissance Squadron with anything less than dismay. Devine and headquarters of the 14th Cavalry Group had assumed responsibility for the cavalry squadron on December 11. To defend the Losheim Gap, the roughly eight hundred men had had to sacrifice the one genuine asset of lightly armed mechanized cavalry: mobility. They instead occupied little fixed islands of defense, mainly in widely separated farm villages, most of them built in depressions—"sugar bowls," the troops called them—

providing some relief from the raw winds that swept the heights but affording little advantage for military defense.

To compound Devine's problems, one of his three troops (at 145 men, a troop was about 40 men smaller than a rifle company) had been detached to strengthen defenses at the other end of the Schnee Eifel. On the other hand, Devine had the assistance of twelve towed 3-inch guns and two reconnaissance platoons of the 820th Tank Destroyer Battalion, as well as the self-propelled 105mm. howitzers of the 275th Armored Field Artillery Battalion, attached to the 106th Division but detailed to support of the 14th Cavalry Group.

In large measure, the positions occupied by the cavalrymen reflected those prepared originally by units of the 2d Division, which upon first arriving in October had had no cavalry attachment. Thus the stronger positions—if any could be called strong—were in the south close to the Schnee Eifel, blocking roads leading from the Losheim Gap into the rear of the Schnee Eifel, for holding those roads was critical to maintaining the positions on the high ridge. All the roads led by one route or another to the upper valley of the Our River, and thence down the valley to the village of Schoenberg, where a road coming around the south end of the Schnee Eifel joined up. From Schoenberg, St. Vith is only six miles to the west.

Unknown to the cavalrymen, the boundary between the Sixth Panzer Army to the north and the Fifth Panzer Army ran through the southern portion of the Losheim Gap. That was designed to provide running room for *Kampfgruppe Peiper* and the rest of the 1st SS Panzer Division in the bid for a swift drive to the Meuse, while at the same time affording General von Manteuffel just enough space for swinging a pincer around the north end of the Schnee Eifel.

The southernmost unit of the Sixth Panzer Army, the 3d Parachute Division, intent on opening up routes for the tanks, thus hit, for the most part, the north portion of the 14th Cavalry Group's positions, where the little islands of defense consisted of only two to four towed tank destroyers and a few riflemen and machine gunners from one of the reconnaissance platoons of the attached tank destroyer company. Most of the other cavalry positions were in the path of two regiments of the 18th Volksgrenadier Division, supported by the bulk of the division's artillery and reinforced by a battalion of forty 75mm. assault guns and as many self-propelled tank destroyers, equipped with long-barreled 75s. The *Volksgrenadiers* were seeking access to the valley of the Our and the road to Schoenberg, there to link with their division's third regiment coming around the other end of the Schnee Eifel.

Just before 5:30 A.M. on December 16, men on outpost duty in the villages in the Losheim Gap saw the same kind of spectacular flickers of light on the horizon as had the soldier on the water tower atop the Skyline Drive. Moments later followed a bombardment from artillery, rockets, and mortars such as no one in the 18th Cavalry Reconnaissance Squadron had experienced before. Amid the thunder the troops could make out the distinctive screeching sound of rockets (the Americans called them "Screaming Meemies") from the *Nebelwerfer*, a multiple-barreled, electrically fired rocket launcher.

Yet little of the shelling hit the villages in the southernmost reaches of the Losheim Gap, the villages of Weckerath, Roth, and Kobscheid. That reflected the fact that German patrols had found an undefended area of more than a mile between Weckerath and Roth, and at the last minute General von Manteuffel decided to eschew an artillery preparation there while sending a column through the gap to gain a leg on the march to the valley of the Our. A battalion of *Volksgrenadiers* was soon pushing unhindered in the darkness toward the village of Auw, whence the road continued to the Our. There was also another road from Auw leading south atop the first ridgeline behind the Schnee Eifel, a road which troops of the 2d Division had named "Skyline Boulevard."

Hardly had the artillery fire lifted elsewhere and passed on to targets farther to the American rear than German searchlights flicked on, providing a kind of eerie moonlight made the more effective by reflection off the snow. It was a new and in some ways disturbing experience for the men in the Losheim Gap, but they soon realized that the illumination helped them at least as much as it did the attackers.

At Kobscheid, as at all the cavalry posts, the defenses had been heavily reinforced with .50-caliber machine guns taken from the squadron's armored cars. Those and other weapons manned by two platoons of cavalry opened fire just as the Germans reached barbed wire encircling the village. Throughout the day the fight at Kobscheid eddied back and forth, but for the most part the cavalrymen held their own.

Not so at Roth, which sat astride the most direct route to the Our. The Germans needed Roth to move reinforcements and supporting guns for the foot column that had already bypassed the village, so that from the start the *Volksgrenadiers* attacking Roth had strong support from assault guns. Consisting of a lone platoon of cavalry, the few men of Troop A's headquarters under Capt. Stanley E. Porché, and two of the virtually immobile towed 3-inch tank destroyers, the defenders of Roth were hardpressed from the start. Although Colonel Devine tried to send a platoon of light tanks to help, the tankers found the road blocked by those *Volksgrenadiers* who had slipped past Roth. By late morning, hope for Captain Porché and his men was fading.

At Weckerath, only a few men from headquarters of Troop C were in the village, but a troop of light tanks quickly arrived to help. From the village, the crews of the light tanks could see what looked to be about fifteen tanks—they were either assault guns or tank destroyers—accompanied by a battalion of infantry marching through the gap between Weckerath and Roth. Although the tanks opened fire, as did 75mm. assault guns on a ridgeline farther back, the Germans plodded on. The pincer around the northern end of the Schnee Eifel was moving methodically into place, and there was little the cavalrymen could do about it.

At Krewinkel, the next village to the north, where a platoon of cavalry and a platoon of attached reconnaissance troops had been jolted by the opening artillery barrage, the men watched incredulously through the eerie half-light created by the searchlights as a column of men from the 3d Parachute Division marched down the road, talking, whistling, singing as if they were on a hike. The commander of the little garrison, 1st Lt. Kenneth Ferrens, waited until the Germans were almost atop the outer coils of wire before he gave his men the signal to fire.

The first fusillade wreaked terrible damage on the German column, but those men who survived quickly dispersed and pressed the attack. About fifty got inside the village, where fighting raged at close quarters; but the Americans, firing from dug-in positions and from a sturdy stone church and schoolhouse, had the advantage. "Surrender, Americans," yelled some of the Germans. "You are surrounded!"

Full light of day was still to come when the Germans began to withdraw. One man among the last to leave shouted toward Lieutenant Ferrens's command post: "Take a ten-minute break, soldier. We'll be back." To which Ferrens responded: "And we'll be waiting for you—you son of a bitch!"

In the meantime, Troop C's executive officer, 1st Lt. Aubrey L. Mills, had made it through a hail of small-arms fire into Krewinkel with a half-track loaded with ammunition. As Lieutenant Ferrens had promised, the defenders were thus ready and waiting when German paratroopers wearing white camouflage suits made a second assault. Some got into the lower, eastern fringe of the village, but that was all. At least one hundred and fifty Germans died in the two assaults; miraculously, only two Americans were wounded and one killed, Lieutenant Mills. Having continued past Krewinkel a few hundred yards to the next village of Afst, Mills had just started back when he took a bullet between the eyes.

At Afst, which was the only other village occupied by the cavalrymen, the glow from the enemy's searchlights also provided a first view of attacking Germans for Lieutenant Crawford and the men of his platoon. Like Ferrens, Crawford waited until the white-suited Germans were close to the outer wire before signaling his men to fire. Not one German got inside the wire before the leaders whistled withdrawal, leaving behind thirty dead.

At the drab settlement of Lanzerath, near the northern extremity of the Losheim Gap on the forward slope of a high ridgeline, Susanne ("Sanny") Schür lived with her parents in a house on the eastern edge of the village, overlooking a wide valley toward the pillboxes of the West Wall and the German village of Losheim. When twelve American soldiers came to stay in the Schür household, digging an emplacement for a machine gun in the garden, Sanny slept at night between her mother and father, concerned that the soldiers might molest her. An attractive young woman of twenty-five, she found it baffling that nobody ever made a pass at her. The soldiers were always polite and would never let her carry heavy loads. She warmed their rations for them, and they gave some to her and her parents. (Sanny particularly liked the K-ration cheese, which had little slivers of bacon in it.)

When the German shelling began before daylight on December 16, Sanny and her parents retreated to the cellar. Most of the Americans joined them, then as the shelling continued, the men who had been manning the machine gun in the garden also came to the cellar. The shelling had stopped and some time had passed when the door at the top of the cellar stairs opened and another American appeared. He said something to the other soldiers (Sanny understood no English), and they hurried upstairs.

When Sanny went to get her father a cup of coffee, she found all the soldiers gone. They had obviously left in a hurry, for they had abandoned much of their equipment, including their radio.

Sanny had just returned to the cellar when she heard heavy footsteps overhead. Mounting the stairs, she opened the door warily to find an irate SS-trooper. Why had she allowed the Americans to fire a machine gun from her garden? Noticing the American radio, he grabbed it and smashed it against the wall. When he stormed out of the house without searching it, Sanny hastily gathered all the American equipment and hid it under the potatoes in the cellar. In the process, she came upon a note addressed to her by one of the soldiers:

> This is just a present for being so nice to us during our stay here. I am sorry we couldn't have stayed longer. I will remember your kindness and good luck to you, also to your mother and father.

[signed] Russell.

> PS: If I ever come back through here, I will stop to see you.

Sanny Schür had witnessed the departure of part of Lanzerath's tiny garrison, a squad of reconnaissance troops and the crews of two 3-inch guns of the 820th Tank Destroyer Battalion. Others who witnessed the swift withdrawal were men of the Intelligence and Reconnaissance (I&R) Platoon of the 99th Division's 394th Infantry, who just a few days earlier had occupied log-covered foxholes in a copse of fir trees atop a hill just north of Lanzerath only a few hundred yards up the slope from the Schürs' house.

"If they can't sign off on the phone," said Pfc. William J. Tsakanikas, to his platoon leader, 1st Lt. Lyle J. Bouck, Jr., as the half-tracks towing

the guns disappeared, "they might at least wave goodbye as they leave."
To Tsakanikas and Bouck, the departure from Lanzerath looked like a
bug-out, yet even if it was, Bouck, at least, was inclined to afford the
crews some compassion, for so vulnerable were towed antitank guns (no
matter the caliber) that their first shot was often their last.

It was, indeed, a bug-out; but at 9:30 A.M. the cavalry commander,
Colonel Devine, made it legal by ordering all the towed 3-inch guns to be
pulled back to the vicinity of his headquarters in Manderfeld, for at two
other villages near Lanzerath, the crews of six of the towed tank destroyers were under siege from overwhelming numbers of paratroopers. Although most of the men got away, they managed to save only two of the
guns.

The crisis in the Losheim Gap was all the more alarming for Mark
Devine because he was frustratingly aware that he had been able to
achieve no defensive coordination with the 106th Division. When he first
arrived on December 11 to assume responsibility for the sector, he had
learned from the commander of the 18th Cavalry Reconnaissance Squadron, Lt. Col. William F. Damon, Jr., that the 2d Division had prepared a
plan, in case the Germans came around the north end of the Schnee Eifel
through the Losheim Gap, to counterattack with a reserve infantry battalion supported by attached tanks. Although Devine had gone promptly
to the 106th Division's command post in St. Vith to try to affirm the
continued existence of that plan, the division commander, Maj. Gen.
Alan W. Jones, and his staff were too preoccupied with the myriad details of getting their division into the line to be bothered with a counterattack plan. It was, after all, a quiet sector, and nothing was likely to
happen. Once the problems of relieving the 2d Division had been dealt
with, there would be time enough to coordinate with the attached cavalry.

Thus frustrated, Devine put his staff to work on a plan of his own to
be executed should something happen before he could coordinate with
the 106th Division. He decided on a fighting withdrawal from the original
positions in the villages to a ridgeline marked by his headquarters village
of Manderfeld, and from there, if required, to a second ridgeline two
miles behind Manderfeld. He intended bringing forward the 32d Cavalry
Reconnaissance Squadron, which had only recently arrived and was then
well to the rear in the town of Vielsalm, repairing its light tanks and other
vehicles. As the 32d Cavalry counterattacked, he would pull the 18th
Cavalry back. The commander of the 32d Cavalry, Lt. Col. Paul Ridge,
and his staff reconnoitered possible routes for the proposed counterattack, while Devine's staff worked to get the plan ready for distribution on
the morning of December 16.

Because the opening artillery barrage knocked out all wire communications to the forward posts and German jamming made radio communi-

cations difficult, Devine at first had little information about what was happening, and he was not one to go forward under fire to find out for himself. He nevertheless assumed the peril sufficient to order Colonel Ridge to bring his 32d Cavalry forward.

After ordering the tank destroyers in northern reaches of the Losheim Gap to fall back, Devine alerted the cavalrymen in the villages in front of Manderfeld to be ready to withdraw at 11 A.M., by which time he hoped the 32d Cavalry would have arrived. The response from Kobscheid and Roth was less than encouraging. From Kobscheid came word that it would be impossible to withdraw during daylight, but the troops probably could hold and escape after dark. From Captain Porché in Roth there was even less hope. A last radio message soon emerged: enemy self-propelled guns were "seventy-five yards from CP, firing direct fire. Out." Of a garrison of ninety men at Roth, three were killed and eighty-seven surrendered.

When Colonel Devine asked General Jones by telephone for help, Jones replied that he culd provide nothing "at this time." In which case, said Devine, he had no choice but to fall back to the Manderfeld Ridge, whereupon he hoped to counterattack with the 32d Cavalry Reconnaissance Squadron. The fact that Devine might be able to counterattack eased concern for the Losheim Gap at headquarters of the 106th Division. At any rate, in St. Vith, they had troubles enough of their own.

When the withdrawal from Weckerath, Krewinkel, and Afst began, so close was the enemy that it was a shoot-out in the tradition of stagecoaches beset by Indians in the Wild West. The cavalrymen clambered aboard any vehicle that could move: jeeps, half-tracks, armored cars, light tanks, holding on with one hand so they could shoot with the other. Because of the cold and lack of any opportunity to warm transmissions and engines in advance, the vehicles could make only about ten miles an hour. At that agonizingly slow pace, they had to run a gauntlet of Germans on both sides of the road.

Two light tanks led the way, machine guns blazing, while men clinging to the lurching vehicles fired their individual weapons. Although most of the Germans took cover, they fired repeatedly, while some stood erect waving their arms and shouting for the Americans to surrender. The last man to leave Afst, Lieutenant Crawford, fired a bazooka to prevent a self-propelled gun from charging the rear of the column. Despite the German fire, not a man was killed and only one wounded.

At Kobscheid, the two platoons held throughout the afternoon. Soon after nightfall, the remaining sixty-one men sabotaged their vehicles, broke into three groups, and slipped out of the village to a rendezvous point in a wood lot a few hundred yards away. Over the next three days, bumping into and shying away from German columns and shaking German patrols that followed their tracks in the snow, they made their way to St. Vith.

As the main body of the cavalry began to dig in on the Manderfeld Ridge, it was obvious from patrol reports that the Germans were pushing around both flanks. To cover the southern flank, Devine sent a troop of the 32d Cavalry to Andler, a village affording entry to the valley of the Our. To seal the northern flank and reestablish contact with the 99th Division, he sent another troop of the 32d Cavalry with the assault guns of the 18th Cavalry, formed as a task force under Maj. James L. Mayes, driving up the road along the crest of the Manderfeld Ridge toward Lanzerath. The task force reached a road junction half the distance to Lanzerath but there ran into a battalion of the 3d Parachute Division supported by self-propelled guns and some of the towed 3-inch guns captured earlier from the Americans. There was no getting past them.

With the Germans moving unchecked around the north flank, Devine saw no hope of holding the Manderfeld Ridge. Around 4 P.M. he asked the 106th Division for permission to withdraw to the next ridgeline two miles behind Manderfeld while continuing to anchor his south flank at Andler, which would still deny the Germans access to the road down the valley of the Our in rear of the Schnee Eifel. General Jones approved.

To Devine, it seemed inexplicable that the Germans made no effort to interfere with the withdrawal. The reality was that except at Andler, the 14th Cavalry Group had ceased for the moment to be of concern either to the 18th Volksgrenadier Division or to the 3d Parachute Division. The *Volksgrenadiers* had yet to reach Andler, and when they got there, they were to turn away from the cavalrymen to push down the valley road to Schoenberg. Meanwhile the paratroopers, however belatedly, were busy accomplishing their mission of opening routes for the 1st SS Panzer Division.

That night, as the cavalrymen dug in on their new position without contact with the enemy, their commander, Colonel Devine, went to St. Vith to talk with General Jones and try to get help. Jones said he was too busy at present to speak with him but told him to stick around the command post until he found the time. Devine was still waiting when daylight came. That he stayed without raising any kind of a fuss was out of character, for to at least one who knew Devine well, he seemed like "a volcano about to erupt"; and to wait all night in St. Vith displayed an odd complacency for a colonel with long years of service who had to be aware that his command was in serious peril.

Operating essentially with a single cavalry reconnaissance squadron, the 14th Cavalry Group had done about all that could have been expected from such a light force. The cavalrymen had sounded the alarm and delayed the enemy, which were the roles of cavalry on defense. They had done their job, moreover, with minimal casualties and in a sector where the attacker outnumbered the defender far more heavily than anywhere else on the first day of the offensive. Nevertheless, at the end of the day the failure to hold the original positions posed a critical peril for the 106th Division.

The most immediate peril came from the battalion of *Volksgrenadiers* that had infiltrated the gap between Weckerath and Roth and headed for Auw, where only a company of the 81st Engineer Combat Battalion, the 106th Division's organic engineers, barred the way. Since the village was at the end of the enemy's infiltration route, it drew a heavy bombardment in the German artillery preparation. Tumbling from sleeping bags, the engineers hurried to the cellars, there to find the local inhabitants—the village was inside Germany—already dressed and taking cover, which prompted some of the men to recall having seen a young woman the night before going from house to house. When the shelling ended and nothing else happened, the company commander, Capt. Harold M. Harmon, turned out his road work details as usual; but only one platoon had departed beyond recall when in mid-morning German small-arms fire erupted.

Some of the engineers dashed for previously prepared defensive positions, others for the houses. They were making a good fight of it until German assault guns appeared and began a brutal and systematic fire. Just before German grenadiers closed in, one American platoon and men of the company headquarters made a run for it, some in jeeps, some on foot, heading for the next village of Andler.

For the remaining platoon, the escape route led across an open field, so there was little hope of getting out unless somebody somehow could distract the enemy's attention. Cpl. Edward S. Withee made that job his. "I'll stay," he said. "Get going." Armed with a Thompson submachine gun, Withee began a steady fire while the rest of the men raced across the open ground to safety. When all had escaped, Withee somehow managed to surrender.

Although the Germans had yet to gain Andler and access to the valley of the Our, they already possessed at Kobscheid and Auw entrée to two roads leading in behind the Schnee Eifel. From Kobscheid a farm track led to the village of Schlausenbach and headquarters of one of the 106th Division's regiments; and from Auw a road ran along the top of the ridgeline immediately behind the Schnee Eifel: Skyline Boulevard.

There was obviously nothing the 14th Cavalry Group could do at that point to help the 106th Division block its north flank except to try to hold at Andler. That Troop B, 32d Cavalry Reconnaissance Squadron, was preparing to do; but on the ridgeline extending to the northwest, which constituted the 14th Cavalry Group's third delaying position, there was less resolve.

Lacking direction from Colonel Devine, who was still in St. Vith, some commanders were looking for excuses to continue to retire. One of those was the commander of the 32d Cavalry's Troop A, 1st Lt. Robert B. Reppa, who was concerned that his little force stood all alone on the north end of the new defensive line and that he had no contact with anybody. Although he asked for authority to move north to join the troops of the 99th Division in the village of Honsfeld, he had yet to receive it when he decided to act on his own. He and his men reached Honsfeld shortly after 9 P.M., there to find a captain from the 99th Division organizing a defense of the village with men from a regimental rest center and anybody else who happened into the village. Reppa might have done better to have stayed where he was.

To break past the Schnee Eifel and take the road center of St. Vith, General von Manteuffel had two *Volksgrenadier* divisions under the 66th Corps. To ensure close coordination for the pincers carrying out the dual envelopment of the Schnee Eifel, he insisted that the corps commander, General der Artillerie Walter Lucht, make one division responsible for both prongs.

General Lucht chose to give the assignment to the 18th Volksgrenadier Division, primarily because that division had been holding the line there since late October and thus had some familiarity with the terrain. He also directed the 62d Volksgrenadier Division, newly rebuilt from remnants of a division destroyed on the Eastern Front, to attack alongside the 18th Volksgrenadier Division's southern flank, take a bridge over the Our River at the customs post of Steinebrück, five miles southeast of St. Vith, and support the 18th Volksgrenadier Division's drive on St. Vith. Except for the assault guns and tank destroyers that were mostly with the pincer moving around the north end of the Schnee Eifel and a battalion of assault guns with the 62d Volksgrenadier Division, neither division had any armor. All the Fifth Panzer Army's tanks were either farther south making the main effort against the Skyline Drive or in reserve with restrictions on their use imposed by Field Marshal Model. Because von Manteuffel needed the roads funneling through St. Vith to broaden the base of his drive to the west, he nevertheless insisted that the town be taken on the first day of the offensive.

When a military force first attacks, then stops the attack and shifts to the defensive, the positions it assumes usually reflect the positions reached as the attack came to an end. As those defenses are already prepared, a relieving force arriving later finds it easier, especially if the enemy is close, simply to occupy the old positions and make only minor adjustments. That is particularly true if the positions embrace some terrain feature that higher command insists must be retained in the same strength with which it had been held before—such as the Schnee Eifel.

When the 2d Division took over in the vicinity of St. Vith in early October, it assumed responsibility from the two divisions it relieved of two salients into the West Wall, one atop the densely forested, often fogenshrouded Schnee Eifel, the other some seven miles to the southwest

Steinebrück

423D INF
424TH INF

Bleialf

Buchet

Ihren Cr.

Grosslangenfeld

18TH
VG DIV

Winterspelt

Eigelscheid

Burg Reuland

BELGIUM
GERMANY

WEST

WALL

62D
VG DIV

Heckuscheid

Our River

106TH DIV
28TH DIV

Grosskampenberg

WEST

WALL

Lützkampen

116TH
PZ DIV

WEST WALL

N

IN FRONT OF ST. VITH
FIRST DAY — DEC 16

Scale:
0   1   2   3
MILES

near the village of Grosskampenberg. The salient near Grosskampenberg was on open ground, dominated by pillboxes on higher ground still held by the Germans, so exposed that movement to or within the positions by daylight was impossible; and even in a sector where both sides were inclined to live and let live, the Germans were nervous lest the Americans exploit that partial penetration of the West Wall. They threw in frequent mortar and artillery concentrations and probed the positions with strong patrols.

After tolerating the situation for almost a month, the division commander, General Robertson, convinced his corps commander, General Middleton, to allow him to blow up the captured pillboxes and retire to positions prepared in advance a few miles to the rear. Having accomplished that at the start of November, the division's southernmost regiment from that point held a well-prepared although elongated line in the vicinity of Grosskampenberg and a village a little to the north, Heckhuscheid.

Yet despite those adjustments, the regiment's line still reflected something of the original dispositions. The new positions covered two relatively minor roads leading west, while on the regiment's north wing, a major road leading to the crossing of the Our River at Steinebrück and on to St. Vith was the responsibility of what could only be described as an outpost. Astride that road at the hamlet of Eigelscheid stood 130 men of the regiment's cannon company, operating not in their normal role as infantry fire support with towed short-nosed 105mm. howitzers, but as infantrymen.

The outpost at Eigelscheid was all the more vulnerable because to the north, the main positions of the next regiment, atop the Schnee Eifel, were almost four miles away. In between were to be found only the division's reconnaissance troop (50 men) and an attached troop of the 18th Cavalry Reconnaissance Squadron (145 men). In addition, at the village of Bleialf, guarding the south flank of the positions on the Schnee Eifel, was a provisional (meaning makeshift) battalion composed of an antitank company, a platoon of a cannon company operating as infantry, a rifle platoon, and an I&R platoon. The grand total came to about 350 men.

The principal points of entry into what was to become the 106th Division's sector, all of which funneled into St. Vith, were thus barred in less strength than any other part of the overextended line: the cavalry in the Losheim Gap defending the route around the north of the Schnee Eifel; the makeshift battalion at Bleialf astride the principal route around the south end of the high ridge; and a cannon company fighting as infantry astride the road leading to the Our at Steinebrück.

In rear of the two regiments on the Schnee Eifel, the roadnet afforded an enemy coming around either or both ends of the ridgeline an opportunity for not one but two envelopments. From the village of Auw in the Losheim Gap, there was the road running south along a relatively high ridgeline to Bleialf—Skyline Boulevard—thus affording a route for a shallow envelopment. From Andler in the Losheim Gap there was the road following the trace of the Our River to link with a road from Bleialf at Schoenberg, thus affording a route for a deeper envelopment. The only major road leading to St. Vith ran through Schoenberg, and the entire division, including all of its artillery battalions, had a river at its back.

Atop the Schnee Eifel, the defensive positions were well prepared, the product of two months' work by the men of the 2d Division. Almost all foxholes had log cover, and the troops had dry sleeping quarters either in pillboxes or in squad huts constructed from logs. Yet that was about all that could be said for the positions except that they were on dominating ground. Even that advantage was largely negated by a dense coniferous forest covering the entire ridge, which sharply limited both observation and fields of fire.

As with the salient in the West Wall near Grosskampenberg, the commander of the 2d Division, General Robertson, was unhappy with the salient on the Schnee Eifel, and early in November he had asked permission to withdraw the two regiments to the open ridgeline carrying the Auw–Bleialf road, Skyline Boulevard. His corps commander, General Middleton, agreed, but neither General Hodges nor General Bradley would approve on the grounds that the positions on the Schnee Eifel represented a penetration of the West Wall that might later be exploited in any general advance toward the Rhine. Neither of those commanders nor any of their senior staff officers chose to have a first-hand look at the ground.

Despite their denial, Robertson made up his mind that should the two regiments on the Schnee Eifel be threatened with envelopment, he would pull them back to Skyline Boulevard. Yet the fact that Robertson was planning to move to Skyline Boulevard, which would still be subject to envelopment, rather than behind the Our River, was an indication that he was not thinking in terms of any major enemy offensive, and he made no effort to construct alternate positions, nor did the 2d Division prepare a plan of withdrawal.

The division did prepare a counterattack plan based on the possibility of a limited enemy thrust around one end or the other of the Schnee Eifel. In that event, Robertson intended to employ an infantry battalion that he held in reserve well to the rear at the village of Born, just north of St. Vith, and possibly a second infantry battalion held in reserve near Steinebrück, plus an attached medium tank battalion, the division engineer battalion, and attached antiaircraft half-tracks. That force appeared to be adequate for any contingency, for as the letter of instructions outlining the plan put it, "a major offensive in this sector is not probable."

That there was nevertheless concern about the whole area, including the Losheim Gap, was reflected in General Middleton's placing the bulk of his corps artillery in positions from which to fire into some part of the sector. Seven of those battalions were brigaded under headquarters of three artillery groups, while the eighth, the 275th Armored Field Artillery Battalion, was attached to the 106th Division for support of the 14th Cavalry Group. Forward observers from all the battalions maintained observation posts in the line and all charted prearranged concentrations on points of likely trouble; the 275th Armored Field Artillery Battalion, for example, registered two hundred concentrations that might be called for by number within the Losheim Gap.

The eight battalions represented a powerful reinforcement. On the other hand, the firing positions of three of them were east of the Our River behind the Schnee Eifel and thus shared one of the weaknesses inherent in the 106th Division's positions—a river at their back. If the enemy should achieve a major penetration, support from the corps artillery battalions would be short-lived, for few commanders would risk the loss of big corps guns, not only 105mm. howitzers but also 155mm. and 8-inch guns and howitzers.

Despite the support inherent in the presence of the corps artillery, the defensive positions inherited by the 106th Division—and particularly the positions of the two regiments on the Schnee Eifel—were an invitation to disaster, the only possible rationalization being that nothing ever happened in the Ardennes. Small wonder that General Jones and his regimental commanders were upset. Yet there was little they could do about it, for in order to conceal and facilitate the 2d Division's relief and movement to the attack on the Roer River dams, the relief had to be accomplished man for man, gun for gun, with the 2d Division leaving its heavier weapons in place in exchange for those of the 106th Division.

Like many divisions that had failed to get overseas before American battlefield casualties began to mount, the 106th had undergone several levies on its trained troops. During the year of 1944, the division had to relinquish more than seven thousand men, representing 60 percent of enlisted strength. In their place, arriving only a short time before the division embarked for shipment overseas, were 1,200 men from the ASTP, 1,100 from training as air cadets, 1,500 from other divisions not yet scheduled for overseas, and 2,500 from various disbanded small units, mostly service troops. That the 106th Division was not the only division to go through that debilitating process afforded scant comfort.

Like most veteran divisions in Europe, the 2d Division by that time had accumulated weapons well in excess of normal issue, particularly machine guns, and when men of the 106th Division had no machine gun to exchange, the men of the 2d Division took their extra weapons with them. Although the 2d Division left its extensive telephone lines intact—a line ran to almost every squad—those were of little use to incoming troops who lacked the large numbers of sound-powered telephones that over the months the 2d Division had seized from the Germans. Unlike the 2d Division, the 106th Division had no attached tank battalion, and its attached tank destroyers were not self-propelled but towed. The lack of tanks, in particular, was a serious, even crippling, disadvantage.

Division headquarters was set up in a former hospital, St. Joseph's Kloster, run by a Catholic order in St. Vith. The Germans had used it as a hospital, but the 2d Division later put a tarpaulin over the large Red Cross on the roof. There General Robertson and his staff briefed General Jones and his. At Robertson's order, an officer was to remain behind at each battalion and regimental headquarters, and a senior noncommissioned officer with each company to spend the first night with the new units. For a division that was to jump off in the attack the morning after its last regiment was relieved from its defensive positions, that was about all that men and commanders of the 2d Division could be expected to do for the newcomers.

Except to tell the men for God's sake take off those neckties, and in at least one case, to assure a worried soldier: No, you don't stand guard at right shoulder arms. And to tell each and all how lucky they were. It was a quiet sector, a little mortar and artillery fire, an occasional patrol, but that was all. A piece of cake.

For men thus assured, the artillery barrage that began at 5:30 A.M. on December 16 was a jolting experience, even though the artillery available to the German 66th Corps was considerably less than elsewhere along the front. Atop the Schnee Eifel, the shells ripped into the big fir trees, sending branches crashing to the forest floor, but since the positions were sturdy and covered with logs, few casualties resulted. At the same time, heavy shelling hit the villages behind the ridgeline, particularly Schlausenbach and Buchet, sites of the command posts of the two regiments on the Schnee Eifel. Shelling was also heavy on the two villages barring major roads, Bleialf and Eigelscheid. It was heavy, too, on road junctions in the rear, including Schoenberg and St. Vith, which took a pounding from big railway guns. Telephone lines at the front went out early, including those to supporting artillery battalions, and the units of the 106th Division had had little experience using radios.

As in the Losheim Gap, nowhere along the entire extended line of the 106th Division did the Germans take advantage of the artillery preparation to close quickly with the defenders. On the Schnee Eifel, that was by design. All that the 18th Volksgrenadier Division planned there were a few thrusts during the course of the day by strong patrols to conceal the fact that in order to free troops for the pincer movements north and south, nothing more than the division's field replacement battalion of two hundred men had been left to face the Schnee Eifel. Although General von Manteuffel had considered that the Americans might respond to his attack by driving down the eastern slopes of the Schnee Eifel to cut off his spearheads, he concluded in the end that an inexperienced division would hardly react that way.

Men of the 422d and 423d Regiments on the Schnee Eifel handily repulsed such patrols as tried to climb the steep slope, and when the day came to an end, they considered that they had done their job well. The 2d Division troops had warned them that when a new division entered the line, the Germans would react with strong patrols, and that was what they thought had happened.

At Bleialf, there was no such misplaced confidence, for a half hour after the artillery fire lifted, a battalion of *Volksgrenadiers* struck the village. The impetus of that thrust threw back the bulk of the provisional battalion, while other Germans advancing up a railway cut at the southern edge of the village severed contact with the attached troop of the 18th Cavalry.

Telephoning General Jones in St. Vith, the commander of the 423d Infantry, Col. Charles C. Cavender, asked for return of his 2d Battalion, which had been held at Born as the mainstay of the division reserve. Jones refused. It was too early in the fight to part with half his little reserve. Left with no other choice, Cavender assembled a makeshift counterattacking force built around his Service Company (the regimental supply troops), a company of the 81st Engineer Battalion, every man who could be spared from Headquarters Company, and the remainder of Cannon Company, all fighting as infantry. With help from supporting artillery and a brace of towed 3-inch guns from the 820th Tank Destroyer Battalion emplaced on a hill overlooking Bleialf, that conglomerate force penetrated the village and in house-to-house fighting retook all the houses except for a few on lower ground near the railroad.

A few hundred yards to the south, against the men of Troop B, 18th Cavalry Reconnaissance Squadron, the German attack began in earnest just as it was getting light. By mid-morning, with the help of supporting artillery, the cavalrymen had the situation in hand but were running low on ammunition. Four men in an armored car commanded by Sgt. Wade H. Bankston managed to work forward from troop headquarters in Winterscheid, a thousand yards to the rear, and distribute a resupply of ammunition just before the Germans struck again; but when ammunition began to run low a second time, German fire made it impossible to get forward with more. By radio, the troop commander, Capt. Robert G. Fossland, reported his situation to Colonel Cavender, to whose regiment the cavalrymen were attached. In a rare display of concern for an impossible situation, Cavender responded: "If you can't hold, you may withdraw."

Under covering fire from three armored cars, all three cavalry platoons fell back, bringing their wounded and their equipment with them. Reaching Winterscheid, they began preparing an all-around defense of the village, out of contact with men of the 424th Infantry in Bleialf and those of the division's reconnaissance troop to the southeast in the village of Grosslangenfeld. As troopers began to drift into Winterscheid, the cavalrymen soon learned that the 106th Reconnaissance Troop—little larger than a platoon—had gone to pieces under the first impact of the enemy attack.

In the sector of the 424th Infantry to the southwest, the 62d Volksgrenadier Division attacked with two regiments abreast with the main effort directed at Eigelscheid and the road to Steinebrück while a supporting attack not quite two miles to the south aimed at high ground marked astride its crest by the village of Heckhuscheid. It was at

Heckhuscheid that the first Germans appeared, just as a misty dawn was beginning to break.

The positions of the 3d Battalion at Heckhuscheid had the shape of an inverted L (⅂), with Company L holding a cluster of houses on a hillock at the angle (a road junction) and other positions on a reverse slope extending to the north, while Company K extended the line from the cluster of houses into Heckhuscheid. The Germans quickly seized the cluster of houses, from which they were able to provide supporting fire for an assault against the rest of Company L's position. The assault forced the men of Company L back to the next ridgeline, where they held until the battalion's reserve company counterattacked and restored the position. Among some two hundred German prisoners were a battalion commander and his reconnaissance officer.

Subjected to heavy fire from *Nebelwerfers*, Company K in Heckhuscheid nevertheless repulsed several attacks and in the process captured a wounded German officer. On his person the company commander, Capt. Richard J. Comer, found a map case containing a document that looked to be of considerable importance. It was an order from the G-3 of the 46th Corps, "Subject: Undertaking GREIF," and it told of Germans operating in American uniforms, explaining how they were to identify themselves to other Germans. Comer rushed it to the rear. By early afternoon it was in the hands of the division G-2, Colonel Stout.

A few hundred yards south of Heckhuscheid, near Grosskampenberg, a misty day had fully dawned when the first Germans struck the 424th Infantry's other forward battalion. Those Germans were from the 116th Panzer Division, spilling over from that division's thrust against a neighboring regiment of the 28th Division. The Germans passed diagonally across the front of the battalion's flank, which enabled the men on that flank to exact a heavy toll. Because the German objectives appeared to be a road leading from Lützkampen, in the 28th Division's sector, into the rear of the 424th Infantry, and a bridge over the Our at the village of Burg Reuland, the battalion commander, Lt. Col. Leonard Umanoff, covered his open flank by positioning his reserve company astride the road.

Hardly had that company moved into position when five Mark IV tanks appeared. Small-arms fire forced the tank commanders to close their turrets, a 57mm. antitank gun knocked out one, and Pvt. Gilbert E. Thomas stopped another with a bazooka. When the other three fell back, that ended the threat to the 424th Infantry's right flank.

Meanwhile, the critical spot for the 424th Infantry was at Eigelscheid on the road to Steinebrück, where the commander of the 62d Volksgrenadier Division, Col. Frederick Kittel, was hoping for a swift penetration, whereupon he intended to commit a battalion on bicycles to seize St. Vith in a *coup de main* and there, he hoped, capture trains loaded with gasoline. As Kittel soon learned, it was a plan far too ambitious for the inexperienced troops involved. Even had it succeeded, they would have found no gasoline stocks in St. Vith, for the closest American railhead to the town was ten miles away.

Soon after daylight, the little band of defenders in Eigelscheid saw a mass of Germans in a long skirmish line on the skyline at a road junction a few hundred yards to the front. To the American soldiers, the inexperience of the German troops seemed apparent, for they stood erect, advanced in bunches, and fired their weapons wildly without regard for specific targets. They also appeared to be either drunk or doped, and the men of Cannon Company could hear their leaders swearing and shouting: "*Marschiert schnell! Schnell!*" ("Move quickly! Quickly!").

The commander of Cannon Company, Capt. Joseph Freesland, called for round after round of artillery fire from the supporting 591st Field Artillery Battalion. With each concentration, the German line would waver, but amid shouting and blowing of whistles, the men re-formed and continued forward. One man with a bugle exhorted the troops with bugle calls until American fire cut him down. Fire from four heavy .30-caliber and three .50-caliber machine guns the men had borrowed from the regiment's reserve battalion strongly augmented the fire of the company's carbines and M-1s.

Early in the fighting, Captain Freesland raced by jeep to the regimental headquarters in a village to the rear to ask for help from the reserve battalion located near Steinebrück only to learn that since General Jones had designated that battalion as part of the division reserve, the commander of the 424th Infantry, Col. Alexander D. Reid, could release it only with Jones's approval. As with Colonel Cavender of the 423d Infantry, the answer was no. By the time Freesland got back to his company, the situation had markedly deteriorated. With the collapse of the 106th Reconnaissance Troop at Grosslangenfeld, just over a mile to the north, another German force was advancing on Eigelscheid from that direction, and along the main road appeared four self-propelled 75mm. assault guns.

Again Freesland rushed back to the regimental headquarters. That time Colonel Reid told him that the assistant division commander, Brig. Gen. Herbert T. Perrin, had arrived at Winterspelt, the first village behind Eigelscheid. Perhaps Perrin could prevail upon General Jones to release the reserve battalion.

When Perrin heard Freesland's story, he took it on his own to call forward a rifle company from the reserve, Company C, which despite German shelling was soon on the march to join Cannon Company in Eigelscheid. Not long before noon, Perrin gained Jones's approval to move up the rest of the battalion; but by the time those companies got to Winterspelt, the defenses of Eigelscheid were about to collapse and Winterspelt itself was under attack from German troops moving up a dirt track from Grosslangenfeld.

At Eigelscheid, the commander of a detachment of 57mm. antitank guns, Staff Sgt. Rocco P. DeFelice, although wounded, brought the fire of one of his guns to bear on the four German assault guns. He knocked out two before fire from one of the others demolished his frail piece.

By that time, the *Volksgrenadiers*, by sheer weight of numbers, were beginning to break into the houses. When Captain Freesland ordered one of his platoons on the southern fringe of the village to fall back, the platoon leader, 2d Lt. Crawford Wheeler, told his men to obey, but he himself refused to budge. "Somebody's got to stay here and do the job," he shouted. The last anybody saw of Wheeler, one of the assault guns was firing point-blank into his position.

In the end, there was no holding Eigelscheid. Early that afternoon, in a sudden snow squall, the survivors of Cannon Company (eleven men were wounded and twenty-six were missing) made a fighting withdrawal along with the men of Company C back to Winterspelt to join the rest of the 1st Battalion, augmented by a company of the 81st Engineer Battalion. There the men prepared to stand, just two miles by way of a winding, rapidly descending road in front of the important bridge over the Our River at Steinebrück.

Except at Eigelscheid, the 424th Infantry's defenses were intact and the enemy's ambitious plan for a swift thrust to St. Vith thwarted, but the augury for the morrow was less than good. The 591st Field Artillery Battalion had fired over 2,600 rounds, which was about all the artillerymen had on hand, and soon after nightfall, astride the road to Steinebrück, troops of the 62d Volksgrenadier Division renewed their attack, striking hard at Winterspelt.

A crisis was thus developing close to the south flank of the 106th Division. Yet it had nowhere near such perilous connotations for the survival of the division as the crisis that had evolved on the north flank with the withdrawal of the 14th Cavalry Group. There the command post of the 424th Infantry at Schlausenbach, the regiment's direct support field artillery battalion, and the division's general support 155mm. howitzer battalion all were in immediate peril. And unless the northern pincer of the 18th Volksgrenadier Division could be blunted, both regiments on the Schnee Eifel soon might be trapped.

Only recently promoted to the rank of colonel at age thirty-two, George L. Descheneaux, Jr., was one of the youngest regimental commanders in the United States Army. With the start of the enemy's artillery preparation early on December 16, Descheneaux awoke in the house where he was billeted and hurried next door to his command post in the village's tiny *gasthaus* beside a little stream running through the valley.

So, thought Descheneaux, that ethnic Pole the men of Company E had captured the day before had not been nuts. He had said the Germans were going to attack before Christmas, and from the weight of shells falling on Schlausenbach, he knew what he was talking about.

By 8:30 A.M. there were reports of Germans infiltrating up a wooded draw between Kobscheid and Auw in the direction of Schlausenbach, then another report of fifty Germans in white camouflage suits on high ground between Schlausenbach and Auw. Patrols dispatched from the regimental reserve, Company L, soon returned with two defiant prisoners.

In addition to the command post, Descheneaux was concerned about his supporting artillery, for both his own direct support battalion, the 589th, and the general support howitzers of the 592d were emplaced a mile or so from Schlausenbach along either side of Skyline Boulevard near the hamlet of Laudesfeld. They thus were vulnerable to any German push down the road from Auw. When the company of the 81st Engineer Battalion at Auw folded in mid-morning, it was obvious that those artillery battalions would soon be under attack unless Descheneaux could do something about it. Employing his reserve, Company L, as a nucleus, Descheneaux added portions of his Antitank and Cannon Companies, fighting as infantry but supported by Cannon Company's howitzers, and ordered the force to retake Auw and block access to Skyline Boulevard.

Even as the men were assembling, three German assault guns (the Americans took them to be tanks) began to push south from Auw along the little road inappropriately christened a boulevard. From a previously prepared outpost along the road, a bazooka team hit the first gun, and a howitzer from Battery A, 589th Field Artillery Battalion, also hit it with a round of direct fire, setting the gun on fire. The other two assault guns fell back along the road to a point where the lay of the land hid them from view.

The action produced momentary relief for the men and howitzers of the 589th Field Artillery Battalion, but there was ample evidence that German patrols were operating in woods near the firing positions, and an enemy force blocked the only exit—little better than a logging road—for Battery C's pieces. As nightfall approached, the howitzers were in obvious peril, and the general support 155mm. pieces soon might be no better off.

Colonel Descheneaux's little counterattack, which began around 2 P.M., even as the artillerymen first engaged the assault guns, was making some progress when Descheneaux had to call it off. Because Germans were pressing up the wooded draw leading to Schlausenbach, he was forced to establish a defensive line to protect his headquarters. That left nobody to block for the artillery.

Early on the morning of December 16, General Jones ordered half his division reserve, the 2d Battalion, 423d Infantry, commanded by Lt. Col. Joseph P. Puett (the battalion that was located at Born and whose services Jones had denied the commander of the 423d Infantry), to move by truck to St. Vith and await instructions. As Puett waited in the division headquarters, Jones and his staff were discussing, sometimes heatedly, whether to pull the two regiments off the Schnee Eifel and back to Skyline Boulevard. At one point, Jones telephoned the corps commander to raise the issue. (General Middleton was to say later that he was concerned that if the two inexperienced regiments began to withdraw, they "might go half-way to Paris.") Jones decided finally to leave the regiments in place.

Shortly after midday, General Jones told Colonel Puett to proceed to Schoenberg and sent a radio truck with him so that Puett could report what he found when he got there. At the village, Puett saw vehicles from the 14th Cavalry Group streaming through, but the word was that a troop of cavalry was still at Andler, thus blocking the road that led down the valley of the Our to Schoenberg. Reporting all that to Jones, Puett told him also that he had heard from the 589th Field Artillery Battalion, which needed help.

Well after nightfall, around 7:30 P.M., Jones radioed Puett to go to Skyline Boulevard and help the 589th and 592d Field Artillery Battalions to displace. Having by that time released his other reserve infantry battalion for commitment at Winterspelt, Jones wanted to maintain some flexibility with Puett's battalion and told Puett "not to get heavily engaged." Yet by denying Puett mobility, Jones virtually ensured that that would happen; once Puett reached the artillery battalions, he was to release his trucks for return to the rear.

As commander of a reserve battalion, Colonel Puett had made a point of reconnoitering as many roads as possible in the division's sector and in the process had discovered the existence of a corduroy (log) road leading up a steep incline through a fir forest. Known as the Engineer Cut-Off, it had been constructed by engineers of the 2d Division to bypass the junction of Skyline Boulevard with the Schoenberg-Bleialf road, which was under enemy observation and frequently shelled (the troops named it "88 Corner"). Calling in a platoon leader, 2d Lt. Oliver B. Patton, Puett told him to go by jeep by way of the Engineer Cut-Off to Skyline Boulevard, locate the artillery battalions, and return to guide Puett's battalion forward.

With a driver and two other men, Patton reached the Engineer Cut-Off, but as the jeep bounced over the logs in the darkness Patton heard what sounded like tanks approaching and shouts in German. Patton ordered his driver to turn the jeep off the road as if it were wrecked, and everybody hid in the woods while what appeared to be several tanks (they would have been either assault guns or tank destroyers) drove by with German infantry accompanying them.

Once the Germans had passed, the men pulled the jeep from the ditch, pushed it to get it started again, and continued on their way. Locating the positions of the 589th Field Artillery Battalion, they picked up a guide to ensure that they would find their way back again and returned without difficulty to Schoenberg. (The German vehicles and soldiers Patton and his men encountered on the Engineer Cut-Off apparently constituted a patrol and may have subsequently established a roadblock at 88 Corner.) By midnight, Puett's battalion had reached the artillery positions, where Puett found that Jones's order not to get heavily engaged was like telling a man to take a swim but not get very wet.

Early in the evening, from his command post at the *gasthaus* in Schlausenbach, George Descheneaux asked General Jones for authority to pull back his northernmost battalion from the Schnee Eifel to form a new line blocking to the north between the Schnee Eifel and Schlausenbach. Not until a little after 11 P.M. did Jones grant that authority, so that it was midnight before the battalion began to move. By that time, Colonel Puett's battalion had arrived. Soon a line was forming, consisting of two battalions and Company L and extending from the Schnee Eifel past Schlausenbach and across Skyline Boulevard.

That line, thin as it was, conceivably might block envelopment of the Schnee Eifel from the north along the road from Kobscheid to Schlausenbach or along Skyline Boulevard—the shallow envelopment—but along the principal approach to Schoenberg from the north—the road following the trace of the Our and the possible route for a deeper envelopment—the only defenders were the hundred or so men of Troop B, 32d Cavalry Reconnaissance Squadron, at Andler. If that little force collapsed, or if the conglomerate force that had retaken Bleialf at the other end of the Schnee Eifel should fold, the way to Schoenberg and its critical bridge over the Our River would be open. And once the Germans got to Schoenberg, anybody and anything still on the east bank of the Our River would be trapped.

While attending the University of Washington, Alan Walter Jones earned a commission as a second lieutenant of infantry through the ROTC and entered the army in 1917; he elected to stay on after the Great War and between wars went through all the appropriate service schools. He had commanded the 106th Infantry Division (nicknamed the "Golden Lions" from a shoulder patch depicting a yellow lion's head) since the division's formation in the spring of 1943.

A stockily built man with full, rounded face, jet-black hair, heavy eyebrows, and a thin mustache, Jones had just turned fifty when he brought his Golden Lions into the line. Outwardly calm, he was a person who seldom revealed his emotions. Yet because he was sharply conscious that he had never been responsible before for men's lives in combat, the ill-chosen, overextended positions he had inherited troubled him far more than they had apparently disturbed General Robertson. Jones also had an intense personal concern. His only son, 1st Lt. Alan W. Jones, Jr., was on the staff of one of Colonel Cavender's battalions, and Alan's wife, Lynn, back in Washington, D.C., was pregnant with her first child.

Almost from the start of the German artillery preparation on December 16, General Jones was convinced that what was hitting his division was something big. What else could explain the reports from the 28th Division to the south and the 99th Division to the north of similar heavy barrages?

Yet for a long time Jones did little in reaction to the crisis. Having denied one of his two reserve infantry battalions to Colonel Cavender for use at Bleialf, it was almost noon before he authorized the battalion near Steinebrück to move to Eigelscheid and Winterspelt and after midday before he sent Colonel Puett's battalion to Schoenberg. The last two decisions may both have been made easier by the fact that at 11:20 A.M. the corps commander, General Middleton, attached to the 106th Division a battalion of corps engineers, the 168th, a part of which was soon in St. Vith, so that even after committing two infantry battalions, Jones still had a small reserve. In the meantime, Jones had denied Colonel Devine's plea for help in the Losheim Gap, for what had he to send?

Around midday, the commander of the First Army, General Hodges, at Middleton's request, released to the VIII Corps the 9th Armored Division's Combat Command B, which had only recently left the corps to serve as a reserve in the attack on the Roer River dams. Since the combat command was in an assembly area twelve miles north of St. Vith near the village of Faymonville, and was already on one-hour alert for possible commitment in support of the attack on the dams, its men and armored vehicles could have been in St. Vith in less than two hours; but General Middleton wanted to learn more of the enemy situation before committing what constituted one of only two armored combat commands available to him as reserves. Although he attached the 9th Armored Division's CCB to the 106th Division, it was to remain in its assembly area and be committed only with Middleton's approval.

Darkness was approaching when the combat command's liaison officer, 1st Lt. Raymond L. Lewis, arrived back from a mission to the 2d Division to find the headquarters in a schoolhouse on the edge of Faymonville astir with the news of the attachment. He left promptly to travel the few miles to the village of Ligneuville, where his commander, Brig. Gen. William H. Hoge, was enjoying an early dinner with a friend, Brig. Gen. Edward W. Timberlake, commander of the 49th Antiaircraft Artillery Brigade, in one of the more charming old inns in the Ardennes, the Hôtel du Moulin, long renowned for its cuisine.

Grimy from a day on the road, young Lewis reluctantly interrupted the dinner to tell General Hoge that General Middleton wanted him to telephone. As Hoge left to make the call, General Timberlake invited Lewis to sit down and eat. As far as Lewis was concerned, the hotel was still renowned for its cuisine, for the chef had done things with U.S. Army ground beef that Lewis had never known a mess sergeant to do.

After putting CCB on a ten-minute alert, General Hoge left at 6 P.M. for St. Vith, arriving at General Jones's headquarters in the St. Joseph's Kloster a half hour later. On the ground floor it was pandemonium—noncommissioned officers and clerks running about, junior officers arguing in loud voices. Going upstairs, he found Jones in his office, remarkably composed.

Jones wanted Hoge to move his combat command into the Losheim Gap at Manderfeld, arriving there at dawn the next day to counterattack and erase the enemy penetration threatening the positions on the Schnee Eifel. In the meantime, Jones wanted a platoon of self-propelled tank destroyers at St. Vith immediately to protect his headquarters.

Hardly had Hoge left the headquarters than Jones received a telephone call from General Middleton. He was sending more help, said Middleton. A combat command of the 7th Armored Division was to arrive at St. Vith at 7 A.M. the next morning, December 17, and the entire division was to follow.

With Jones when he received that news was the assistant G-2 of the VIII Corps, Lt. Col. William H. Slayden, whom Middleton had sent to the 106th Division as an adviser until the division could become acclimated. Slayden knew that the 7th Armored Division was at least sixty miles away in the Netherlands. Whereas the head of the ponderous column might conceivably reach St. Vith by seven o'clock the next morning, it would be long hours before an entire combat command could arrive, and longer than that before the combat command would be ready to attack. Yet Slayden kept his views to himself. Both Middleton and Jones had attended more service schools and studied far more logistical tables than he had. Who was he, a lieutenant colonel, to say that his corps commander, a major general, was, at best, abysmally misinformed?

When Jones heard the news that he was soon to get a second combat command of armor—and, in time, an entire armored division—he felt as if somebody had removed a sack of lead from his back. Although he recognized that the principal crisis he faced involved the two regiments on the Schnee Eifel, he was also seriously concerned about the Germans at Winterspelt, who were apparently bearing down on the crossing of the Our River at Steinebrück. Yet at that point, he had the means to deal with both. It would be better, he decided, to use the 9th Armored Division's CCB at Winterspelt, thereby freeing the narrow streets of St. Vith of that combat command's host of tanks and other vehicles. That in turn would allow unfettered passage of the combat command of the 7th Armored Division through St. Vith and out on the road to Schoenberg to the relief of the troops on the Schnee Eifel.

At the schoolhouse in Faymonville, General Hoge was about to end his briefing of his commanders for the move to the Losheim Gap and Manderfeld when a call came through from St. Vith informing him of Jones's change of plan. The greater distance involved, Hoge decided, dictated that his command get on the road immediately. His subordinate commanders hastened back to their units to pass the word along.

As the evening wore on in the St. Joseph's Kloster, Alan Jones, for all his relief over the morrow's promised help, began to question his decision to leave the two regiments up on the Schnee Eifel. At some time late in the evening, he decided to propose withdrawal. He soon had the corps commander on the telephone for a conversation that was destined to have a major impact on the outcome of the battle in front of St. Vith.

Ralph G. Hill, Jr., was a captain in command of a detachment of three other officers and five enlisted men detailed to serve, once the U.S. Army entered Germany, as a military government for a *Wehrkreis*. Hill and his detachment had arrived in eastern Belgium in September at a time when it appeared that American troops were about to penetrate well beyond the German frontier. When the drive ended atop the Schnee Eifel, he and his detachment assumed responsibility for handling relations with Belgian civilians in and just north of the Losheim Gap. On the order of the commander of the first division to occupy defensive positions north of the gap, Hill evacuated some ten thousand civilians from the region, leaving behind only some four hundred inmates and attendants of an asylum for geriatric patients in the division headquarters town of Bütgenbach, and around two hundred farmers, who were to care for the *bêtes*.

When the 99th Division assumed responsibility for the area in November, the division commander, Maj. Gen. Walter E. Lauer, found the lowing of the cattle upsetting (two hundred men were unable to keep them all milked on schedule) and ordered Hill to get rid of them. Since driving the animals westward would tie up military traffic for days, the only solution appeared to be slaughter.

Hill had the Belgian farmers set up twelve butchering stations, and when American supply trucks had delivered their loads in Bütgenbach, the Belgians reloaded the empty trucks with meat, which the drivers delivered to towns and cities to the rear. There the civilian authorities, if notified in advance, would be happy to provide men to unload it. Yet in order to notify the civilian authorities, Hill needed a reliable communications system.

Carrying a flashlight and a field telephone, he went across the street from the house where he was billeted in the town of Büllingen and descended the stairs into the cellar of the post office. There he found an underground telephone cable and a long row of terminal points. Connecting his field telephone to each in turn, he finally got a response:

"*Bonn hier.*" He had reached a female operator in the German city of Bonn alongside the Rhine.

When the woman learned she was talking to an American soldier in Büllingen, she thought it hilarious. Where did her switchboard indicate his call was originating from, Hill asked. When she said Spa, Hill disconnected her and as soon as possible sent a man to Spa. Once the man located the terminus of the cable and convinced civilian authorities to run a line to headquarters of the First Army in the Hôtel Britannique, Hill had the communications network he needed. To make it more comprehensive, he arranged for lines to be run to headquarters of the 99th Division in Bütgenbach and to headquarters of the 2d Division (later the 106th) in St. Vith.

On December 16, Ralph Hill faced another day of supervising the butchering of cattle and arranging for receiving and shipping the meat. When he tried to place a telephone call to Eupen through the 99th Division's switchboard, the operator told him the line was out, cut by "paratroopers." Talking to the signal officer, he learned that the line had gone out before daylight, that the officer had sent out a trouble-shooting crew that failed to return, and that a second crew had found the men of the first dead in a ditch. When the signal officer learned that Hill had a line to Spa and thence to Eupen (headquarters of the V Corps), he was elated and quickly put such a load on Hill's little switchboard that Hill had to ask him for operators to help.

If the 99th Division was having communications problems, thought Hill, perhaps the 106th Division was too. When that proved to be the case, Hill immediately handled a call from General Jones to General Middleton. As it turned out, lines from the two divisions to their respective corps headquarters were in and out throughout the day, but by seven o'clock that evening both were in again and Hill let the 99th Division's operators go.

It was late in the evening when the 106th Division's line to the VIII Corps at Bastogne went out once more, and a call came through Hill's switchboard for MONARCH 6 (codename for Middleton). Hill connected it and listened in. It was General Jones, talking in riddles in case the Germans were tapping the line, about his regiments on the Schnee Eifel. He thought it would be wise to withdraw his "two keys [regiments] from where they are because they are very lonely." He knew, Jones continued, that he would have "two big friends [combat commands] to rescue them in the morning," but he thought it would "be wise to prevent a scissors working on them."

Middleton responded that Jones was the commander on the ground. "You know how things are up there better than I do," he said.

At that moment, a call came into the switchboard from the 99th Division. Since the departing operators had taken their telephones with them, leaving Hill with only one, he disconnected Jones and Middleton momentarily to tell the caller he would get back to him when the line was free; but he quickly reconnected Jones and Middleton. That brief period—only seconds—may have been the time when Middleton added, "but I agree it would be wise to withdraw them."

When Jones put down the telephone, he was convinced either that Middleton wanted him to leave his regiments in place or that he was putting the onus of the decision entirely on him. "Well, that's it," he said to one of his staff. "Middleton says we should leave them in." A short while later that decision appeared to be confirmed when Jones saw an order from Middleton—issued earlier in the day but just arrived—directing no withdrawals unless positions became totally untenable and designating a line not far behind the existing front that was to be held "at all costs." Jones apparently failed to note that that line in his sector was the west bank of the Our River, well behind the Schnee Eifel.

Meanwhile at Bastogne, when General Middleton put down his phone, he turned to a member of his staff. "I just talked to Jones," he said. "I told him to pull his regiments off the Schnee Eifel."

That night the 106th Division's G-2, Colonel Stout, noted in his periodic report: "The enemy is capable of pinching off the Schnee Eifel area . . . at any time."

CHAPTER SIX

The Skyline Drive

For the Fifth Panzer Army's main effort, General von Manteuffel planned for two panzer corps to attack abreast. The 58th Panzer Corps, commanded by Generaloberst Walter Krüger, was to attack on either side of the border village of Ouren, on the Our River ten miles south of St. Vith. It would then cross the northern reaches of the ridgeline the Americans knew as the Skyline Drive and jump the Meuse River just downstream from the bend at Namur. The 47th Panzer Corps, commanded by General der Panzertruppen Heinrich Freiherr (Baron) von Lüttwitz, was to cross the Our a few miles farther south, jump the Skyline Drive, take the road center of Bastogne nineteen airline miles beyond the German frontier, and seize crossings of the Meuse upstream from Namur.

Each of the panzer corps had only two divisions, one panzer, one *Volksgrenadier;* but General von Manteuffel had two panzer units in reserve, the *Führer Begleit Brigade*, which had the strength of a little better than half a panzer division, and the *Panzer Lehr Division*. Von Manteuffel could commit the *Führer Begleit Brigade* only with the approval of his superior, Field Marshal Model; but as soon as General von Lüttwitz's 47th Panzer Corps put in a bridge behind its *Volksgrenadier* division, he intended to use the *Panzer Lehr* with that corps.

Originally a part of the Pennsylvania National Guard, the 28th Infantry Division, which had been fighting since Normandy and had incurred such losses in the Hürtgen Forest that people had begun calling its red bucket-shaped keystone shoulder patch the "Bloody Bucket," held such an elongated defensive front that each of the panzer corps was destined to strike little more than a regiment. In the north, Krüger's 58th Panzer Corps faced only some three thousand or so men of the division's 112th Infantry, while von Lüttwitz's 47th Panzer Corps faced the 110th Infantry. (The division's third regiment, the 109th Infantry, was to become involved with the supporting attack by the Seventh Army.) Thus the ratio of attacker to defender was roughly ten to one.

The Germans that Private First Class Allard and other members of the patrol from Company F, 112th Infantry, came upon on the night of December 15 while making their way back across the Our River near Ouren were from the 560th Volksgrenadier Division. Created from occupation troops in Denmark and Norway, the division had seen no combat and had had only limited training, and one of its three regiments had yet to arrive from Denmark. Its running mate, on the other hand, the 116th Panzer Division, known as the *Windhund* (Greyhound) Division, had a long, distinguished record on the battlefield, having fought in Normandy and having previously dealt the 112th Infantry a crippling blow in the Hürtgen Forest. The division was nearly at full strength in men and had close to a hundred tanks—mostly Panthers—and assault guns.

The positions held by the 112th Infantry constituted an extension of the line of the 106th Division and had the same basic weakness: a river at the back. Yet nothing ever happened in the Ardennes, so why relinquish ground within the pillbox belt of the West Wall dearly bought with American blood? Only two of the regiment's battalions were in the line—one in and around the village of Lützkampen, close to the flank of the 106th Division's 424th Infantry; the other a little to the southwest near the village of Sevenig. The third battalion occupied back-up defensive positions on the west bank of the Our but was, in essence, a reserve. Although the regiment had lost almost two thousand men in the Hürtgen Forest, the commander, Col. Gustin M. Nelson, considered the replacements to be well trained and highly motivated.

The 112th Infantry was defending the sector where General von Manteuffel had decreed that there should be no artillery preparation so that eighty-man shock companies might infiltrate up wooded draws between the widely spaced American positions, attack from flanks and rear, and strike swiftly for bridges over the Our (two at Ouren and two farther north). When the searchlights flicked on in the early morning darkness of December 16 and German artillery opened fire to north and south but not on the positions of the 112th Infantry, the men in the foxholes were left to wonder—however reverentially—why not them too?

In the darkness a small German force attacked mortar positions behind the 3d Battalion near Sevenig, but the mortarmen had well-prepared foxholes near their pieces and fought off the assault. Another force caught a platoon of Company L at breakfast, captured the kitchen, killed the platoon leader, and put the men to flight.

The first indication that Germans were moving in behind the 1st Battalion near Lützkampen came with word of the ambush of a kitchen truck returning from the front, but there was little other evidence of the enemy presence until approaching daylight revealed German troops marching in the open. When one of the shock companies came under devastating flanking fire from the 424th Infantry to the north, that part of the attack collapsed. As twenty-five Germans emerged from a wood to move past an exposed crossroads, small-arms fire killed four and the rest surren-

SKYLINE DRIVE
FIRST DAY - DEC 16

Scale:
0 ½ 1 2 3 4
MILES

N

Burg Reuland

Our River

BELGIUM
GERMANY

West Wall

106TH DIV

28TH DIV

Lützkampen

Weiswampach

Ouren

Harspelt

Sevenig

116TH PZ DIV

BELGIUM
LUXEMBOURG

Trois Vierges

112TH INF

110TH INF

560TH VG DIV

Heinerscheid

Clerve River

Urspelt

N12

Fishbach

Antoniushof RJ

Reuler

Clervaux

Marnach

Dasburg

2D PZ DIV

Munshausen

SKYLINE

Drauffelt

Our

Hosingen

26TH VG DIV

Bockholz

Wilwerwiltz

Café Schinker

Gemünd

Holzthum

Walhausen

FIFTH PZ ARMY

SEVENTH ARMY

Wiltz

Consthum

DRIVE

Clerve River

Wiltz River

Weiler

Kautenbach

110TH INF

109TH INF

Hoscheid

dered. The battalion commander himself, Lt. Col. William H. Allen, manned a .50-caliber machine gun protecting an antitank gun near his headquarters. When he had exhausted his ammunition, a score of Germans lay dead and forty surrendered.

Meanwhile, a group of forty Germans had moved through the darkness toward the southernmost of the two bridges at Ouren. At close to 9:30 A.M., men of the 3d Battalion's Headquarters and Cannon Companies, having rushed to foxholes previously prepared for a close-in defense of Ouren, spotted them. "Get them when they cross the bridge!" yelled the personnel officer, Capt. William B. Cowan. The men thought at first that the Germans were prisoners on their way to the rear, but when it became obvious that they were armed, everybody heeded Cowan's order to fire. Some of the Germans fell on the bridge, others made it across a little farther, and only a few managed to get away. Somebody on the German side nevertheless reported overeagerly that the 560th Volksgrenadier Division had seized a bridge across the Our.

With the coming of daylight, German artillery and *Nebelwerfers* at last opened fire, but since the German troops were in and behind the American line, the artillerymen had to direct most of their fire well to the rear against American artillery positions and villages beyond the Our. American mortars and artillery at the same time caught Germans in the open or in the draws and exacted a heavy toll.

Shortly before noon, the commander of the 112th Infantry, Colonel Nelson, ordered his 2d Battalion to move from the west bank of the Our through Ouren and counterattack to clear the enemy from between the village and the 3d Battalion's positions. By nightfall, that sweep was complete and the positions abandoned by the platoon of Company L restored.

Also shortly before noon, the commander of the 116th Panzer Division, Generalmajor Siegfried von Waldenburg, decided to commit tanks to try to get his *Panzergrenadiers* moving. The first attempt ended in failure when fire from the adjacent 424th Infantry knocked out two tanks and three others fell back. Soon after that, the commander of the 58th Panzer Corps, General Krüger, informed that the *Volksgrenadiers* had taken one of the two bridges at Ouren, ordered von Waldenburg to end his try for the two bridges farther north and join in the fight to take Ouren itself. That was what halted the threat to the 424th Infantry's flank.

The dragon's teeth of the West Wall in front of the 3d Battalion's positions sharply restricted the routes available to the German tanks and made them ready prey for American guns. A second German attempt to get tanks forward failed when Pfc. Paul C. Rosenthal, the gunner in the crew of a towed 3-inch tank destroyer supporting the 424th Infantry, expending only eighteen rounds, knocked out five. A third try failed when the lead tank of a group of five set off a mine and the others turned back under fire from 57mm. antitank guns. A fourth and fifth attempt failed when towed guns of a company of the 630th Tank Destroyer Battalion, attached to the 112th Infantry but firing from dug-in positions on a ridge behind the Our, knocked out six. A final foray, by three German tanks equipped with flamethrowers, ended with another assist by towed tank destroyers supporting the 424th Infantry.

Since the report of a captured bridge at Ouren proved to be false, the only real success to which the 58th Panzer Corps might point at the end of the first day was a small bridgehead established by the *Volksgrenadiers* over the Our in an undefended sector downstream from Ouren. There the bridge had long been destroyed, its debris blocked the site, and felled trees and mines denied egress along the exit road on the far bank, so that there was little hope that German engineers could bridge the river swiftly. That meant that the two bridges at Ouren, although denied by American defenses against which the Germans had made few inroads, still constituted the most likely way for the 58th Panzer Corps to get past its first obstacle in the drive for the Meuse.

It had clearly been a less than rewarding day for Krüger's 58th Panzer Corps. Although the losses of the 116th Panzer Division were moderate, they included thirteen tanks and at least eighty men captured, and one of the leading shock companies had been wiped out by flanking fire from men of the 424th Infantry. The inexperienced *Volksgrenadiers* had lost close to a thousand men. Of greater importance, the 112th Infantry had delayed one of von Manteuffel's two main columns for twenty-four hours.

On the other hand, as night fell on December 16, the men of the 112th Infantry knew that their foe was still there and hardly likely to desist after only one day of attack. "Nobody able to sleep and no hot meals today," one man wrote in his diary. "This place is not healthy anymore."

Hurley Edward Fuller was known as a curmudgeon. A Texan, he had enlisted in the United States Army in 1916, the next year attended officer candidate school and obtained a commission as a second lieutenant of infantry, and went to France, where he fought in the bitter campaign in the Argonne Forest. Fuller was for long disenchanted by that experience, but he stayed in the army, where he established a reputation as a capable but irascible commander, a man with a cantankerous disposition. After commanding the 2d Division's 23d Infantry for a year and a half, he brought the regiment ashore in Normandy on D-Day plus 1 but lasted in combat only ten days before the soft-spoken but firm Walter Robertson relieved him of his command. Something about having maneuvered his regiment into an untenable position.

Still determined to fight, Fuller had gone to an old friend, Troy Middleton of the VIII Corps, also a veteran of the American Expeditionary Force, and asked for help. Although Middleton recommended to General

Bradley, then commanding the First Army, that Fuller be given another chance, Bradley was moved up to command the 12th Army Group and nothing came of Middleton's recommendation until November, when a vacancy developed in the command of the 110th Infantry. As the 28th Division had just been transferred to the VIII Corps, Middleton suggested to the division commander that Fuller fill the slot.

Assuming command of the 110th Infantry in late November, only a few days before turning fifty, Colonel Fuller moved the regimental command post from a farm village to the more comfortable locale of Clervaux. A charming old town set astride a bend in the Clerve River in a deep, narrow basin formed by the merging of four precipitous wooded gorges, the narrow streets, framed by houses and shops with sharply pitched roofs, were dominated by a château. Dating from the twelfth century and situated on a promontory near the eastern edge of town, the château, although small, had most of the usual attributes of a castle except a moat: two turreted towers, a massive stone entranceway with heavy wooden doors built to withstand siege, a cobblestoned interior courtyard, and dungeon-like cellars. Long a magnet for tourists, Clervaux had the hotels to go with it, thus making the town an ideal rest center for troops of the 110th Infantry and for other units of the 28th Division. Colonel Fuller established his headquarters in the Hôtel Claravallis in the western part of town near the railroad station.

Hurley Fuller made few changes in the dispositions of his troops from those of his predecessor, for what choice had he? The deep gorge of the Our River in front of his regiment was so forbidding that his division commander, Maj. Gen. Norman D. Cota, had elected to achieve such concentration as was possible on a twenty-five-mile front at either end of the line: in the north, where the 112th Infantry held a bridgehead beyond the Our River, and in the south, where the 109th Infantry constituted, in effect, a part of the defenses of Luxembourg City. That left the 110th Infantry responsible for fifteen miles of front in the center. And to add to the regiment's difficulty, Fuller had to furnish the division's sole infantry reserve, a battalion positioned a few miles behind the Clerve River near a principal highway leading to Bastogne.

Since manning a fifteen-mile line close alongside the Our with two battalions was an obvious impossibility, the regiment stationed squad-sized outposts near the river during the daytime and patrolled a mile or so of open slopes and steep-walled draws between the river and the Skyline Drive at night. So, too, with the available troops, a solid defensive line along the Skyline Drive was impossible. Instead, the regiment blocked each of five roads leading up from the valley of the Our and on to the west with a rifle company, garrisoning either a village astride the ridge road or a village just in front of or behind it. The two points of greatest concern were at Marnach, through which ran a principal road leading through Clervaux and on to Bastogne; and at Hosingen, roughly in the center of the regimental sector, through which another road led fairly directly to Bastogne.

Each of the two battalions ostensibly held out a reserve company, but both of those were also responsible for defending a village just behind the Skyline Drive through which other roads to the west also passed. In other villages there were only makeshift forces, consisting of the regimental antitank company deployed as infantry and such as was left of the two weapons companies once their heavy machine guns and 81mm. mortars had been parceled out to the rifle companies.

The wide frontage also forced the supporting 109th Field Artillery Battalion into the unusual tactic of widely separating its three firing batteries to enable at least one battery to reach a portion of the front. Even so, to ensure coverage for the entire front an attached battery from a corps artillery unit had to help out. Because of the distance between the infantry positions on the Skyline Drive and the enemy beyond the Our, the firing positions had to be established close behind the crest of the Skyline Drive in unusual proximity to the infantry.

Like the other regiments of the 28th Division, the 110th Infantry had received approximately two thousand replacements for the men lost in the Hürtgen Forest, mostly riflemen and machine gunners, the soldiers with whom combat always deals most harshly. On the assumption that the Ardennes front would remain quiet, Colonel Fuller intended rotating the reserve battalion from time to time with the forward battalions.

On the German side, during the three nights preceding the assault, one of the German Army's more experienced units, the 2d Panzer Division, which had taken heavy losses in Normandy but had retained a solid cadre of experienced noncommissioned officers and officers, made its move forward by the prescribed stages. Rebuilding of the division had started fairly early in the fall, so that the replacements were of better caliber than those reaching other divisions at the last minute. The division had eighty-six tanks, two-thirds of them the latest model Panthers, and twenty assault guns; but the chronic shortage of motor transport afflicted the division much as it did other units. The commander was a newcomer, Col. Meinrad von Lauchert, a seasoned campaigner of the Eastern Front whom General von Manteuffel had requested to replace a commander who lacked experience with armor.

Veteran of many a fight on the Eastern Front, the 26th Volksgrenadier Division—one of the infantry divisions that had earned its honorific in battle—had moved into the Eifel in October and had held a front almost as wide as that of the 28th Division. Defending in such a quiet sector had enabled the division commander, Col. Heinz Kokott, a dignified, soft-spoken man of scholarly mien, to re-equip and build up his division with little interference. By December, Kokott had some seventeen thousand men, considerably more than the recently formed *Volksgrenadier* divisions, but, like everybody else, short on motor transport.

The experienced *Panzer Lehr Division* was one of only a few divisions that even though earmarked for the Ardennes offensive, had been committed to help hold the line in advance of the offensive. In a counterattack role against the Third Army, the division had incurred heavy losses in both men and tanks. On the night of December 15, the division had only fifty-seven Mark IV and Panther tanks, although it had received some relief in the attachment of an assault gun brigade and two battalions of self-propelled tank destroyers. The division commander, Generalleutnant Fritz Bayerlein, a short, stocky man of forty-nine who reminded some people of an aggressive terrier, created a task force—an advance guard—composed of reconnaissance troops, two companies of *Panzergrenadiers*, and a company of Panthers, which he intended to commit early to exploit the gains of the 26th Volksgrenadier Division.

As dictated by General von Manteuffel, the troops were to make direct attacks on American positions at only two places, Marnach and Hosingen, in order to open the two principal roads leading west. Units not designated for those attacks were to practice what had become known in World War I as "Hutier tactics" (after a German general, Oscar von Hutier), whereby the troops advanced in small units avoiding prepared enemy positions, leaving them to be mopped up by other units coming later.

Since the 26th Volksgrenadier Division had become accustomed to putting outposts across the Our after dark and had learned that American troops withdrew their outposts at nightfall, supporting engineers started building a bridge at the village of Gemünd even before the artillery preparation began. Further north at Dasburg, in the sector of the 2d Panzer Division, that could not be done, for access to the site of the demolished bridge—the only site in the vicinity where a bridge might be built—was blocked by an electrically operated iron gate anchored in stalwart concrete stanchions, a part of the West Wall defenses, and the commander of the 600th Army Engineer Battalion which was to construct the bridge, Maj. Georg Loos, was unable to locate the key needed to operate the electrical mechanism. The only alternative was to demolish the gate with explosives, and lest the noise should give away what was happening, that could be done only after the artillery preparation began.

Meanwhile, two German soldiers carrying a radio had slipped past the American positions and made their way down a steep forested slope into the northern fringe of Clervaux. They sneaked past the château and holed up in a room in the rear of the Pharmacie Molitor, across from the Hôtel Central in the heart of town. From the pharmacy, they would have a good vantage point, once daylight came, for directing artillery fire on targets within Clervaux.

The pinpoints of light that the American observer atop the water tower in Hosingen reported at 5:30 A.M. on December 16 were the belch-

ings of 554 organic or attached artillery pieces and *Nebelwerfers* of the
67th Panzer Corps. As German patrols had long ago established the location of the American positions, the fire was markedly accurate on the
forward villages, while *Nebelwerfer* rockets cascaded into the narrow
streets of Clervaux, awakening the men quartered there on leave and
sending civilians scurrying for their cellars or for those of the old château.

The shelling also awakened the regimental commander, Colonel Fuller, and his executive officer, Lt. Col. Daniel B. Strickler, on the second
floor of the Hôtel Claravaliis. Strickler hurried into Fuller's room, No.
10. "What do you make of it?" asked Fuller. "All this big stuff," Strickler
responded, "is a sure sign we're in for a fight." Dressing hurriedly, both
officers rushed down to the operations room off the lobby of the hotel.
Every telephone line to the front-line units, they discovered, was out. So
was the line to division headquarters seven miles to the southwest in the
town of Wiltz.

Late on December 15, the commander of the 3d Battalion, 110th Infantry, Maj. Harold Milton, had directed a training mission to be conducted early the next morning for a section of 81mm. mortarmen.
Protected by a squad of riflemen from Company L, the mortarmen were
to move forward from the Skyline Drive and fire on a village just beyond
the Our River. The squad of riflemen had already moved out when the
German artillery preparation began. As it lifted, Major Milton canceled
the mission, and Company L's commander, 1st Lt. Bert Saymon, sent
two men in a jeep to tell the riflemen to return.

Reaching a crossroads atop the Skyline Drive marked by a lone building, the Café Schincker, the two men in the jeep told riflemen of one of
Company L's platoons defending the crossroads where they were going
and that they and the squad of riflemen would soon be returning. In
darkness and thick fog, the jeep continued to the east. A minute or so
later, the men at the crossroads heard a squeal of brakes and a burst of
small-arms fire. When they later saw shadowy forms moving past the
crossroads, they were unable to make out whether they were Germans or
their fellow riflemen on the way back. Lest they shoot their own men,
they held their fire.

At the Café Schincker crossroads and almost everywhere else, a heavy
ground fog early on December 16 helped the troops of the 26th Volksgrenadier Division get past the defensive positions atop the Skyline
Drive. Men of Company K in Hosingen could hear troops crossing the
highway to the north, but they could see nothing. South of Hosingen, the
Germans were almost on top of one of Company K's platoons before
the Americans spotted them; nobody from that platoon got away. Other
Germans surprised Battery C, 109th Field Artillery Battalion, in firing
positions behind Hosingen. Although the artillerymen lowered the muzzles of their howitzers and opened fire with fuses set for one or two sec-

onds, the Germans continued to attack, so that for a long time that battery would be fighting for its life and unable to provide any fire support for the infantry.

Also having crossed the Skyline Drive unimpeded, company-sized enemy forces got almost atop the villages of Holzthum and Consthum, on the reverse slope of the ridge below the Café Schincker crossroads, and were trying to slip past undetected when men of the 3d Battalion's reserve in Holzthum, Company L, and of the battalion headquarters in Consthum took them under fire. As heavy fighting erupted for both villages, it alerted men of a battery of the attached 687th Field Artillery Battalion just outside Consthum and enabled the artillerymen to set up a close-in defense bolstered by two half-tracks of an antiaircraft battalion, each with quadruple-mounted .50-caliber machine guns.

In at least one case, the fog worked against the Germans. Making out a large body of men approaching, the crew of another U.S. half-track with quad-50 machine guns was unable to determine at first whether they were Germans or Americans. When the approaching troops halted at the sight of the half-track, the crewmen assumed the worst. As they waved the men forward "in friendly fashion," the Germans decided that their own side had captured the half-track and advanced. They were within a hundred yards when the gunner pressed the button that fired the four machine guns in tandem. Close to a hundred Germans fell.

At the only positions of the 110th Infantry on the forward slope of the Skyline Drive, which the first German units were supposed to bypass, the Germans in fact stumbled onto the positions. There a detached platoon of Company I, protecting a battalion observation post behind the village of Wahlhausen, and the rest of Company I, at the village of Weiler, spotted the Germans in time to bring mortar and artillery fire to bear. Those Germans were destined to be pinned down for the rest of the day.

In the meantime, atop the Skyline Drive at Hosingen, which the Germans needed both as a principal route westward and as egress along the best road leading uphill from the bridge at Gemünd, somebody failed to press the attack in keeping with the importance of the objective. After overrunning the platoon of Company K south of the village, the Germans made only a feeble stab at the village itself. It was a lack of aggressiveness that as the day passed could hardly be ignored by the division commander, Colonel Kokott.

To the north, in the zone of the 2d Panzer Division, the leading battalion of *Panzergrenadiers* stumbled into an American minefield soon after crossing the Our River, which so delayed the advance that it was full daylight and the fog had thinned when the men drew up to the village of Marnach astride the Skyline Drive. Since Marnach with its entry to the road to Clervaux was not to be bypassed, the *Panzergrenadiers* began immediately to attack. Yet Company B and a platoon of towed guns of the 630th Tank Destroyer Battalion were on full alert and the attack failed. The defenders in the village nonetheless were soon uncomfortably aware that other Germans were bypassing Marnach on either side, heading down a steep slope toward Clervaux and the positions of their supporting artillery, Battery B, 109th Field Artillery Battalion.

In the Hôtel Claravallis, Colonel Fuller soon had radio contact with headquarters of his 1st Battalion and his supporting artillery, but so far away was headquarters of the 3d Battalion in Consthum that he was unable to get through, nor could he raise the division headquarters in Wiltz. Turning to his executive officer, Colonel Strickler, he told him to go to Wiltz and inform the division commander, General Cota, that his regiment was under heavy attack, then proceed to Consthum and stay there to oversee the defense of the regiment's south wing.

By 9 A.M. the telephone line to division headquarters was back in again, and through the division switchboard, Fuller was able to talk with Major Milton in Consthum. At about the same time, he received a radio call from Battery C, 109th Field Artillery, under siege in its firing positions behind Hosingen. The Germans had captured one of the battery's twelve howitzers, and even though the artillerymen were still fighting for the others, they needed help desperately.

Telephoning Cota in Wiltz, Fuller demanded (he was not the type of man to ask) release of his 2d Battalion from the division reserve. A big, blustery New Englander known as Dutch, who could be as strong-willed as anybody, Cota refused. It was too early, the situation not developed fully enough, for him to part with his lone infantry reserve. On the other hand, since reports reaching Cota from his other two regiments indicated that the 110th Infantry's situation was the most serious, he afforded Fuller two companies of medium tanks of the 707th Tank Battalion, long an attached fighting colleague of the 28th Division. (The third company was with the 109th Infantry; the company of lights with the 112th.)

Since the tanks were in a village alongside the Clerve River only two miles from Battery C's positions, a platoon was soon on the way. Reaching the nearby village of Bockholz without difficulty, the five tanks enabled the artillerymen to drive off their foe, retake their captured piece, and resume firing.

Two companies of tanks—thirty-four Shermans—was a considerable force, but in view of the multiple and widely spaced crises confronting the 110th Infantry, it could hardly be employed in the most advantageous fashion as a single unit. Faced with calls for help from almost every direction and under orders to give no ground anywhere, Colonel Fuller parceled out his newly obtained support piecemeal, a platoon here, half a platoon there. He kept one platoon in reserve in Clervaux and ordered two platoons to what he considered to be the most critical spot of all, Marnach, astride the German route to Clervaux.

The 1st Battalion commander, Lt. Col. Donald Paul, had already tried to help hardpressed Company B in Marnach by sending a strong patrol south from Company A, which was on the regiment's north flank in the village of Heinerscheid and had yet to come under attack. The patrol got only halfway to Marnach before running into Germans who were bypassing the village. Pinned to the ground for a while by small-arms fire, the men of the patrol finally managed to fall back just in time to help their company repel a first attack on Heinerscheid.

Colonel Paul then ordered his reserve, Company C, located with Cannon Company two miles southwest of Marnach on the reverse slope of the Skyline Drive at the village of Munshausen, to move to Marnach and clear Germans from the southern fringe of the village. The company, under Capt. Carrol Copeland, had already begun to march when Colonel Paul learned that Colonel Fuller had two platoons of medium tanks earmarked for Marnach. At Paul's request, those ten tanks headed for Munshausen to overtake and join Company C. The men of Company C had meanwhile come under heavy small-arms fire in which Captain Copeland was wounded; they pulled off the road and were trying to advance cross-country. The tankers failed to spot them but nevertheless succeeded in reaching Marnach.

Once the southern edge of Marnach was clear of Germans, Colonel Paul had intended sending infantry and tanks together southward to sweep the enemy from the Skyline Drive and move into Hosingen, which he mistakenly believed had fallen. When Company C failed to reach Marnach, Paul ordered one of the tank platoons to retrace its steps, pick up the men of Company C, and help the infantry defend Munshausen. The other platoon of tanks, commanded by 1st Lt. Robert A. Payne, was to drive alone on Hosingen.

In the confusion nobody appeared to notice that those instructions left Company B in the critical village of Marnach without tank support. Indeed, Colonel Fuller, who sanctioned the drive on Hosingen, thought the other platoon had stayed in Marnach. When that platoon turned up in Munshausen, hc was convinced that the platoon leader had bugged out.

Machine guns blazing, Lieutenant Payne and his tanks swept the two-and-a-half-mile stretch of the Skyline Drive between Marnach and Hosingen free of Germans—at least for a time—and found, with relief, that Company K still held Hosingen. Indeed, Company K and a company of the division's organic 103d Engineer Battalion, which was also in Hosingen, had stood virtually ignored while Germans eddied around them to north and south.

A mile south of Hosingen at the crossroads marked by the Café Schincker, in the meantime, men of the platoon of Company L defending the crossroads saw a jeep approaching at mid-morning from the east. Since that was the road taken before daylight by the jeep sent to recall the squad of riflemen scheduled to participate in the training exercise, the men waved to the occupants. In response, they drew a burst of fire from burp guns. Screeching around the corner onto the main road atop the Skyline Drive, the jeep raced up the road toward Hosingen, leaving the men at the crossroads agape; but they had time to note that the jeep bore Company L's markings on the bumpers.

Down at the Our River, German engineers were working hard to put in bridges, but it was a slow process. Because the bridges had to be stout enough to support big Panther tanks, the girders were heavy, and the terrain around the bridge sites was so confined by the deep river gorge that no heavy equipment could get forward to help. All had to be done by hand; furthermore, the Our, normally a placid stream, was swollen from rains and melting snow. During the morning the commander of the Fifth Panzer Army, General von Manteuffel, visited both sites. While lamenting the slow progress, he considered that the engineers were doing the best they could under the circumstances.

Shortly after 1 P.M., Major Loos's engineers finally completed the bridge for the 2d Panzer Division at Dasburg, whence ran the road to Marnach and Clervaux. The Mark IV and Panther tanks were nevertheless slow to cross, for a narrow, precipitous approach road on the east bank had a succession of hairpin turns that was hard for the ponderous tanks to negotiate. Only ten had crossed the span when the next tank in column took the last turn too short, crashed into one side of the bridge, and plunged into the water. Except for the driver, the crew escaped; but repairing the bridge consumed another two hours, so that it was late afternoon before tanks could begin crossing again. At about the same time, around 4 P.M., engineers of the *Panzer Lehr Division* completed a bridge downstream at Gemünd.

Throughout the afternoon, German pressure was intense almost everywhere except at Hosingen, and almost everywhere the American troops were running low on ammunition. As darkness approached, each little garrison was virtually surrounded, yet nowhere had they given in, although Company L in Holzthum held at that point only a few houses and a barn. On the other hand, the complexion of the battle was about to change, for with two bridges across the Our River, the Germans would soon have the added strength of tanks and other armored vehicles.

Additional firepower was first apparent on the forward slope of the Skyline Drive near Wahlhausen, where the lone platoon of Company I was holding at the former battalion observation post. Soon after it was fully dark, flak wagons with quadruple-mounted 20mm. guns joined the attack. Almost out of ammunition, the platoon leader, 1st Lt. Jack Fisher, radioed for artillery fire on top of his position. He got it, but that failed to stop the Germans. Only one of Fisher's men got away. Fisher himself, although captured, soon eluded his guards in the darkness and eventually made his way back to the battalion headquarters in Consthum.

The rest of Company I in the nearby village of Weiler was in little better shape than the detached platoon. Surrounded and virtually out of ammunition, the company commander, Capt. Floyd K. McCutchan, determined to break out after nightfall. He himself took charge of one group of fifty men while 1st Lt. Edward Jenkins led a second group of similar size.

Although the two groups were supposed to rendezvous at a designated point along the Skyline Drive, Jenkins and his men got diverted by an encounter with a German patrol, never reached the rendezvous point, and ended up the next day at a village still in American hands along the Clerve River. McCutchan and his group, meanwhile, waited in vain all night for Jenkins's arrival. The next day, they fought their way past one German force after another until at last they reached the road behind Consthum, where an ambulance driver told McCutchan that troops of the 3d Battalion still held the village. Turning over the wounded to the driver, Captain McCutchan and the thirty-five men still left to him plodded wearily up the road toward Consthum and back into the fight.

Meanwhile in Clervaux, Colonel Fuller early on the afternoon of the 16th rounded up sixty men of the 110th Infantry who had been on leave in the town and sent them to Reuler, a village just north of the Marnach road, there to protect the firing positions of Battery B, 109th Field Artillery. They arrived just in time to help half-tracks of the division's attached antiaircraft artillery keep the Germans from overrunning the battery. Yet it was obvious to all that the howitzers would soon have to displace or fall into German hands. Near nightfall they managed to get out and took up new firing positions alongside the Clerve River in the shadow of the château in Clervaux.

In late afternoon, Fuller again appealed to General Cota for release of his 2d Battalion from the division reserve, but again Cota refused. What about some two hundred men from other units of the division who, like the sixty of the 110th Infantry, had been on leave in Clervaux? Those, said Cota, Fuller could use.

Organized into a provisional company, those men and the few officers among them, armed only with rifles and carbines, began to dig in to block hairpin curves in the road from Marnach as it descended into Clervaux. The crews of two heavy .30-caliber machine guns soon joined them and after nightfall a platoon of 57mm. antitank guns. The little force was obviously makeshift and thin, but except for the platoon of Shermans in reserve, it was all Fuller had for defense of his headquarters town. For a last-ditch defense within the town itself, he ordered cooks, clerks, MPs, anybody who could be spared from his duties in the headquarters, to organize the old château as a strongpoint.

Defense it would be, for there could be no question of withdrawal. Early in the day, General Cota had passed on the order from the corps commander, General Middleton, directing all units to hold until their positions became "completely untenable." Even then, they were not to withdraw beyond a specified line, which in the 110th Infantry's sector included Marnach and thus Clervaux. Cota himself later in the day reinforced Middleton's order by admonishing everybody to hold at all costs.

Orders or no, the sorely pressed men of Company B in Marnach were close to going under. Their commander had been wounded early in the fighting and evacuated, so that the 1st Battalion's executive officer, Capt. James H. Burns, had assumed command.

An hour after nightfall, Burns reported by radio that the Germans were attacking again supported by half-tracks firing machine guns. That was the last word to come from the men who had so stoutly defended Marnach, but a continuing noise of firing from the village gave Colonel Fuller hope that some of them were still holding out. If only he could get his hands on his 2d Battalion, he might restore the position at Marnach and save Clervaux.

Around 9 P.M., General Cota telephoned Fuller. He was considering releasing the 2d Battalion, said Cota; if he did, what would Fuller do with it? He would attack, Fuller replied without hesitation, to relieve Marnach. And if that proved successful, he would continue south to Hosingen, where early that evening the Germans had at last launched a heavy attack against Company K.

OK, said Cota. He could have the battalion minus one rifle company, which Cota retained to protect the division headquarters.

As Fuller drew up his plans for an attack before daylight the next morning, he learned that Cota had ordered the 707th Tank Battalion's light tank company, which had spent the first day uncommitted by the 112th Infantry, to attack at daylight down the Skyline Drive to Marnach. That prompted Fuller to delay the 2d Battalion's attack an hour to coincide with the drive by the light tanks. At the same time, the medium tank platoon at Munshausen, along with a platoon of Company C's riflemen, was also to drive on Marnach.

As December 16 neared an end, the commander of the 47th Panzer Corps, General von Lüttwitz, had to accept that he had fallen well short of his first day's objective, crossings over the Clerve River. That was attributable in part to the delay in getting bridges installed across the Our; but even when the bridges were in, the *Panzer Lehr Division* was in for more delay when vehicles mired on the unpaved roads leading from Gemünd and blocked them. The failure was also attributable in part to the unsuccessful application of the Hutier tactics by units of the 26th Volksgrenadier Division, for except at Hosingen and at the Café Schincker crossroads, the *Volksgrenadiers* had been unable to avoid a fight. They were like a man who tries to sneak past a hornet's nest, only to find the hornets swarming at him so ferociously that he has to stop and try to destroy the nest. Nor had the Hutier tactics worked much better for the two *Panzergrenadier* regiments of the 2d Panzer Division.

The Germans had taken only three defended positions: Marnach, Weiler, and the position held by a single platoon of Company I near Wahlhausen. With the arrival of the 26th Volksgrenadier Division's reserve regiment, they finally mounted an attack at Hosingen, but there Company K and its engineer support were still strong. Only at Holzthum was another American force near caving in, so near, in fact, that the commander of Company L, Lieutenant Saymon, ordered his platoon at the Café Schincker crossroads to fall back to Holzthum to help, but the platoon was unable to break into the village and had to go instead to join the defenders at Consthum.

The fact that the Germans had failed to achieve their objective was also attributable to the intrepidity of the American soldier. With only two battalions supported for part of the day by two companies of medium tanks, the 110th Infantry had held off four German regiments and had nowhere been routed. That was around two thousand men versus at least ten thousand. And the men of the 110th Infantry had done it at times without normal artillery support, so hardpressed were two of the four supporting batteries. Considering the odds, nowhere on the first day of the German offensive was there a more remarkable achievement by the American soldier.

Yet how much more punishment could those men take? Hundreds dead, hundreds wounded, possibly more than a hundred captured, and the survivors all short of ammunition. There were hopes for the morrow, of course, when two-thirds of the reserve infantry battalion—about six hundred men—was to join the fight. What the American commanders could not know was that just before midnight, Mark IV tanks of the 2d Panzer Division—all resistance finally eliminated at Marnach—were beginning to assemble in the village, to be ready with the start of a new day to head downhill toward the little town of Clervaux and its two bridges over the Clerve River.

CHAPTER SEVEN

The Southern Shoulder

Erich Brandenberger and his Seventh Army were like poor relations from whom the patriarch of the family expects big things but to whom he provides little material assistance. Adolf Hitler expected the Seventh Army to protect the southern flank of his offensive all the way from the German frontier to the Meuse River, a distance of about eighty miles, and to do it with a parachute and three *Volksgrenadier* divisions dependent almost entirely on horse-drawn transport. Assuming the Seventh Army reached the Meuse and aligned its four divisions to hold equal portions of the south flank, that would mean a defensive sector for each division of twenty miles, which could hardly be considered much of a barrier to a counterattack from General Patton's Third Army to the south. Yet Hitler was paying scant heed to the south flank, for he was counting on surprise and speed to get the Fifth and Sixth Panzer armies across the Meuse before the Americans could counterattack, so that he expected the first American riposte only after his troops got beyond the Meuse. At that time, he figured, Eisenhower would be too concerned about stopping the forward thrust of the offensive to pay much attention to its flanks.

Hitler's senior field commanders saw it differently. They all were well aware of the tactical dictum that had emerged from the Great War and long been taught at the *Kriegsakademie,* a dictum with which American commanders were also familiar, for it had been taught too through the interwar years at the U.S. Army's Command and General Staff College at Fort Leavenworth, Kansas: The way to deal with an enemy penetration is to hold tight at the shoulders to deny any widening of the penetration and thus limit the force the enemy can project in his forward thrust. Once the lines are stabilized, cut off the penetration at its base.

Both Field Marshals von Rundstedt and Model urged Hitler to strengthen the Seventh Army, and General von Manteuffel made a last effort at the Reichschancellery on December 2 to get at least a *Panzergrenadier* division for Brandenberger, whose advance was crucial for the

146

protection of his own south flank. But Hitler refused. Any additional unit given the Seventh Army would be either one less unit available to propel the two panzer armies swiftly over the Meuse or one less unit for the second wave he was counting upon to exploit the crossings of the Meuse all the way to Antwerp.

That left General Brandenberger—at fifty, a bald, bespectacled, paunchy man who was a conservative but experienced commander—with 2 corps headquarters, 4 divisions, 30 assault guns, 427 artillery pieces and rocket projectors, and no tanks, more a reinforced corps than a field army. In Brandenberger's view, the best he could hope to accomplish was to make a penetration with one corps on his south wing in the vicinity of the border town of Echternach and erect a defensive barrier about eight miles short of Luxembourg City. With the other corps he would penetrate close along the flank of the Fifth Panzer Army, gaining as much impetus as possible from that army's advance, and drive—if fortune smiled—as far as the region south of Bastogne, there to assume defensive positions facing south toward Arlon. Getting to the Meuse, Brandenberger reasoned, was chimerical.

On the other hand, as elsewhere in the Ardennes, the forces available to the Seventh Army, however limited, dwarfed the defensive strength immediately available to the opposing American units. Each of the two divisions of the 85th Corps next to the Fifth Panzer Army faced a single battalion (eight hundred men) of the 28th Division's 109th Infantry on the west bank of the Our River—seven battalions against one—while one of the two divisions of the 80th Corps faced an armored infantry battalion of the 9th Armored Division and the other a regiment of the 4th Division, the 12th Infantry, both of which held positions on the west bank of the Sûre River below the juncture of the Our and the Sûre.

Yet in that sector, as in few other places, there were some American reserves. With the arrival of the 60th Armored Infantry Battalion to gain battle experience, the 109th Infantry had been able to pull a battalion into reserve, and the 28th Division's commander, General Cota, had afforded the regiment a medium tank company of the 707th Tank Battalion and a company of towed tank destroyers. As a component of the 9th Armored Division's Combat Command A, the armored infantry battalion had the back-up of the combat command's medium tank battalion and a company of self-propelled tank destroyers. Although the commander of the 4th Division, General Barton, had two more regiments, both were holding elongated fronts farther south; and since Barton had no way of knowing German intentions, he would be reluctant to draw on those regiments until he determined the extent of the German attack. Barton also had a self-propelled tank destroyer battalion and a medium tank battalion, but in the wake of the hard fighting in the Hürtgen Forest, both were far under strength and even those vehicles that survived the forest fighting needed repairs and overhauls.

THE SOUTHERN SHOULDER
FIRST DAY · DEC 16

Scale: 0   1   2   3   4
MILES

In artillery, the defenders were to have at first less than a fourth of the strength available to the Germans. The 109th Infantry had its usual light 105mm. howitzer battalion plus the 28th Division's general support 155mm. battalion, which Cota had allotted the regiment because of the possibility of a German move against Luxembourg City. The 60th Armored Infantry Battalion had an armored field artillery battalion with self-propelled 105mm. howitzers in support, and the 12th Infantry its usual 105mm. howitzer battalion. General Barton also had his organic 155mm. howitzers and two corps field artillery battalions, but those were positioned farther south, where the infantry's lines were even thinner than in the 12th Infantry's sector.

Of the two divisions of the 85th Corps commanded by General der Infanterie Baptist Kniess, the more ambitious assignment went to the 5th Parachute Division on the north wing. Hoping to benefit from the rapid advance expected of the *Panzer Lehr Division* just to the north, the paratroopers—in reality, mostly recently converted Luftwaffe ground troops—were to cross the Wiltz River, in effect, a southward extension of the Clerve, a goal expected to be reached by the end of the first day. They would then continue west, bypassing the 28th Division's headquarters town of Wiltz, and finally form blocking positions south of Bastogne.

The 352d Volksgrenadier Division was to cross the Our a little farther south, seize dominating ground in the angle formed by juncture of the Our and the Sûre, and push on toward the westward reaches of the Sûre and the towns of Diekirch and Ettelbruck. Having crossed the Sûre, the troops were to build defensive positions on the heights beyond. One of the newly formed 13,000-man *Volksgrenadier* divisions, made up mainly of converted airmen but with a sprinkling of shore-based sailors, the 352d had been holding the line in the Eifel for several weeks but had pulled back during the night of December 12 to prepare for the attack. (Which explained why nobody fired when Elise Delé set off a mine and why the patrol of the 109th Infantry that crossed the Our before daylight on the 15th at Vianden found nobody in the pillboxes.) Most of the Seventh Army's skimpy allotment of assault guns was with those two divisions.

Reflecting the greater ambition of the objectives assigned the 85th Corps over those assigned the Seventh Army's other corps, two-thirds of the artillery pieces and rocket projectors fired their preparation in the 109th Infantry's sector. Most of the fire hit headquarters towns and artillery positions in the rear, little of it against the forward infantry. So accurate was the shelling in Diekirch, where the regiment's reserve battalion was billeted, that men of the battalion's intelligence section went looking for an observer in their midst. As the story reached the troops—possibly apocryphal—they found a radio antenna erected over a cobbler's shop and inside, operating a radio set, "a good-looking blond." (Are all female spies blond and good-looking?) The word passed among the troops that "she was summarily shot."

Little of the snow that was present in northern reaches of the Ardennes was to be found that morning in central Luxembourg, for what had been snow farther north had fallen as rain and sleet there; but the same kind of heavy fog that obscured German movement elsewhere hugged the ground. (Although the Seventh Army had a few of the big searchlights used farther north, few American troops remarked on any effects.) In the fog and darkness, the Americans saw nothing of the Germans crossing the Our in assault boats; and at Vianden, engineers of the 5th Parachute Division were on top of the roadblock maintained outside the Hôtel Heintz before men of Lieutenant Prazenka's I&R Platoon awoke to their presence. Everybody in the little platoon was either killed or captured.

The German advance against the extreme northern wing of the 109th Infantry reflected orders to the paratroopers to sidestep opposition wherever possible. One column bypassed Company F, which was dug in on a ridge commanding a meandering road leading from Vianden, and toiled slowly toward the southern reaches of the Skyline Drive. Another force entered the undefended village of Walsdorf, a little over a mile behind Vianden, which prompted the 2d Battalion commander to commit a company to dig in facing the village. When the paratroopers began to emerge from Walsdorf in late afternoon, heading toward the 2d Battalion's headquarters village of Brandenburg, the commander of the 109th Infantry, Lt. Col. James E. Rudder, who had only recently taken over the regiment after having led a Ranger battalion ashore on D-Day in Normandy and later in the Hürtgen Forest, sent a company from the regimental reserve to help the headquarters troops hold Brandenburg.

The other of the 2d Battalion's forward units, Company E in Fouhren—almost due south of Vianden astride the principal highway leading down to the valley of the Sûre and thence to Diekirch—had more difficulty. Both the 5th Parachute Division and the adjacent 352d Volksgrenadier Division needed either that highway or a secondary road that also passed through the village. Paratroopers passing to the north, *Volksgrenadiers* to the south, soon isolated Fouhren, and Company E's radio failed. Paratroopers and *Volksgrenadiers* alike poked at the village through the day, but possibly because it lay on the interdivisional boundary, they made no coordinated assault. At the end of the day, Company E was still in place.

Volksgrenadiers passing south of Fouhren nevertheless posed a considerable threat, for they soon held two nearby undefended villages, one on the main highway leading down to the Sûre valley, the other on a side road also providing access to the valley. Should they reach the valley road, they would cut the supply route to the 3d Battalion's positions in the angle formed by confluence of the Our and the Sûre. Having taken advantage of the fog, German patrols had already begun to fire on one of the batteries of the 108th Field Artillery Battalion alongside the valley road. Shortly after midday, Colonel Rudder committed a company from his reserve battalion, supported by a platoon of medium tanks, to drive the Germans from the two villages and later reinforced those with the final company of his reserve.

Among the last to be committed was Company B's Second Platoon, accompanied by two Sherman tanks. The platoon leader, 1st Lt. James V. Christy, had seen action before, but as was the case in all the rifle companies of the 109th Infantry, many of his men had only recently reached the front as replacements. One of those was Tech. Sgt. Stanislaus Wieszcyk, one of hundreds of noncommissioned officers combed from support units, given a few days of refresher training, and put into the infantry. Over Wieszcyk's protest ("Listen, Lieutenant, I got these stripes for running a consolidated mess hall at Camp Fannin, Texas!"), Christy had made him his platoon sergeant, second in command; either he did the job his stripes at that point called for or he would lose them.

By nightfall, the platoon and its two supporting tanks had advanced well along the road from the Sûre valley toward Fouhren. In the darkness, it was eerie moving forward with flashes of artillery fire lighting the night sky in seemingly every direction. The men were tired, hungry, and upset over the losses they had taken during the day. Lieutenant Christy "could sense the uneasiness of the soldiers."

The lead tank suddenly came to a halt. Going forward, Christy found the tank commander determined to proceed not another inch without riflemen in front of him to guard against antitank rockets from *Panzerfausts*. Turning to Sergeant Wieszcyk, Christy told him to get a squad out front. "The guys have had more than enough today," responded Wieszcyk. "They won't go."

The young lieutenant gulped, but he quickly turned to the commander of the tank. "How many men do you want in front of this tank to move it?" The tank commander said one good soldier would do. "You've got him!" said Christy. "Follow me."

With pounding heart, Lieutenant Christy stepped out in front of the Sherman and started walking into the darkness. He had gone only a short way and the tank had scarcely begun to rumble forward behind him when Christy made out a figure on his left. It was Wieszcyk. "OK, Lieutenant," said Wieszcyk, "you made your point." Close behind him was the entire First Squad.

Before digging in for the night, the two reserve companies made it to the fringes of the two villages, thereby blocking both roads leading to the valley of the Sûre but without dislodging the Germans from the villages. Company E remained isolated in Fouhren, and Colonel Rudder had committed the last of his infantry reserve.

Meanwhile, against the high ground in the angle formed by the confluence of the Our and the Sûre, German infantry, having crossed the Our unobserved in the fog and darkness, had attacked positions of the 3d Battalion early in the morning. As defensive positions went in the Ardennes, those were fairly compact: two rifle companies dug in on steep bluffs overlooking the Our and the third in reserve, while the battalion's right flank drew protection from the deep cut of the Sûre. To the waiting Americans, the attacking Germans appeared to be "fanatically hopped up"; many of them charged "wildly, screaming and firing their weapons until killed or wounded." Whether courage drunk from bottles or some other kind, it was undeniably courage and drew grudging admiration from the defenders, but it went for nought. In what General Brandenberger was later to call "very bloody fighting," the Germans made no dent in the 3d Battalion's line, while artillery fire observed from the forward positions pummeled them throughout the day along the banks of the Our, seriously interfering with attempts to put in a bridge just downstream from Vianden.

As the first day of the attack against the 109th Infantry came to an end, Colonel Rudder saw "no cause for alarm." While there was no doubt that the attack was in considerable strength, Rudder considered his regiment to be "in a good position" with "a distinct advantage of terrain." The Germans had yet to employ any tanks or assault guns, and Rudder still had the bulk of a company of medium tanks on hand. Although Company E remained isolated in Fouhren, isolation on the battlefield held few concerns for an officer with Rudder's background in the Rangers, and a renewal of the counterattack by his reserve battalion should remedy Company E's situation with the coming of a new day.

Men of the 9th Armored Division's 60th Armored Infantry Battalion held on a high plateau between the Sûre River in the north and a little stream known as the Ernz Noire (Black Ernz) in the south. With an eye to tourism, Luxembourg officials called the terrain to the south "*La Petite Suisse* (Little Switzerland)." The name denotes no great heights but instead spectacular sandstone rock formations in the deep gorge of the little Ernz Noire, formations carved by the elements over the centuries, sometimes isolated and looking like misshapen chimneys, elsewhere clustered like the ruins of some grotesque fortress. Except for the verdant forest cloaking the gorge, the officials might also have called it "*le Wild West*," for to many an American soldier familiar with the rock formations on the buttes and mesas of southwestern states, it looked like a setting for cowboys and Indians. The gorge lies some three to five hundred feet below the surrounding tableland, and in some places its walls are sheer cliffs.

Unlike the deep cut of the Sûre River, which afforded flank protection for the 109th Infantry's 3d Battalion, the gorge of the Ernz Noire did nothing to strengthen the armored infantrymen's positions, for three roads cut perpendicularly across it. One of them led directly into the rear of the American positions at Beaufort, where the battalion commander, Lt. Col. Kenneth W. Collins, had his headquarters in a castle dating from the twelfth century, that Victor Hugo, who spent time in the region as an exile, called "a vision." Farther up the gorge, the other two roads led toward firing positions of the 3d Armored Field Artillery Battalion. Furthermore, responsibility for the Ernz Noire belonged to the neighboring unit, the 4th Division's 12th Infantry, and as Colonel Collins knew, the 12th Infantry was so overextended that only a small outpost was in a position to block German movement up the gorge.

Collins also was considerably concerned about his north flank, for more than a mile separated his men from the closest positions of the 109th Infantry. To cover that gap—or at least to give the alarm—he had only a squad positioned in the settlement of Hogenberg, looking down on the German village of Wallendorf and the juncture of the Our and the Sûre, the spot where American armor in September had crossed and headed for Bitburg. Yet Collins's main positions were compact and located atop steep bluffs with good fields of fire into the valley of the Sûre.

Like both forward battalions of the 109th Infantry, the 60th Armored Infantry Battalion faced seven enemy battalions, an entire division, the 276th Volksgrenadier, recently arrived from Poland, where it had been rehabilitated after disastrous losses in Normandy. Most of the new men were young conscripts who had received adequate basic training, but they had neither tanks nor assault guns.

The division's objective was somewhat indefinite—merely to cross the Sûre, annihilate the Americans who stood in the way, and gain high ground to the southwest from which to constitute part of a blocking position to be formed by the 80th Corps facing in the direction of Luxembourg City. Just where that line was to be established depended upon how much ground the two divisions of the 80th Corps were able to gain, but they hoped to reach a point eight miles from Luxembourg City. Contrary to what the Americans were to perceive, the capital of Luxembourg was not an objective. Neither were the transmitters of Radio Luxembourg, one of Europe's most powerful stations, located just over halfway between the frontier and Luxembourg City at Junglinster, although to the American commanders both seemed likely targets.

Since the bulk of the Seventh Army's artillery supported the north wing of the attack, the preparation in the sector of the 60th Armored Infantry Battalion was less than awesome, about a thousand rounds, most of which fell on the battalion headquarters village of Beaufort and on the artillery positions farther back. Yet that was sufficient to knock out all telephone lines within the battalion.

The first Germans the armored infantrymen spotted early on December 16 appeared to constitute nothing more than patrols; but by late morning, that first impression had proven to be deceptive. When the fog lifted, the men could see swarms of Germans crossing the Sûre near Wallendorf and downstream near the village of Dillengen, just down the bluff from the foxholes of Company A. Supporting artillery took both sites under heavy fire, but still the Germans continued to cross.

The little outpost at Hogenberg was quickly overwhelmed, and the men of both forward companies were soon aware that the wooded draws leading to their positions were thick with Germans. Shortly before midday, an attack launched from the houses of Dillingen forced back a platoon of Company A, but the battalion's reserve company moved forward quickly from Beaufort to restore the line. As night fell, except for the outpost at Hogenberg, the 60th Armored Infantry's positions were intact. The battalion commander, Colonel Collins, nevertheless continued to worry about the possibility of the Germans moving up the roads from the Ernz Noire and isolating his companies and their supporting howitzers.

The commander of the Seventh Army, General Brandenberger, considered the 212th Volksgrenadier Division the most capable of his four divisions, which was why he assigned the division the task of anchoring the army's south flank and why he withheld one regiment as an army reserve. Burned out in fighting on the Eastern Front, the division had begun rebuilding in September around a cadre of experienced junior officers and noncommissioned officers and with conscripts judged to be better than average, including a considerable number of seventeen-year-olds. Yet the division had only four assault guns and the usual handicap posed by horse-drawn artillery.

As for the American 4th Infantry Division, having arrived in Luxembourg only at the end of the first week in December, it had had little time in which to reorganize and absorb replacements for the five thousand casualties incurred in the Hürtgen Forest. All rifle companies were still short by at least forty men, the size of a platoon, and they would have been even more understrength had not General Barton, concerned about a possible enemy raid on Luxembourg City, recalled the men who had been in rest centers to the rear.

The German artillery barrage that began at 5:30 A.M. on the 16th struck only the division's northernmost regiment, the 12th Infantry, and most of the shells fell on company and battalion command posts and artillery positions. While heavy and surprising for what was supposed to be a quiet sector, the preparation was hardly enough to create much alarm in old hands who had experienced German shelling since the early days in Normandy. It was nevertheless sufficient to knock out most telephone lines forward of the battalion headquarters (or else, as most men believed, German patrols deliberately cut them).

Concealed by the fog and darkness, the *Volksgrenadiers* crossed the Sûre on both sides of Echternach, a medieval town of some five thousand people (all previously evacuated) on the west bank of the Sûre almost at the center of the 12th Infantry's positions. Having defended the West Wall opposite the sector for several weeks, the *Volksgrenadiers* had plotted the American positions accurately and moved swiftly to encircle the outposts.

Southwest of Echternach, the Germans overran a squad-sized outpost each of Companies I and L, but the men in other companies managed to fall back on the main positions in the villages of Osweiler and Dickweiler, located in rolling, high farm country about a mile back from the Sûre. In Echternach itself, all three of Company E's rifle platoons in widely separated positions came under fire from Germans who had infiltrated nearby buildings, as did the company headquarters in a hat factory on the southern edge of town. At the village of Lauterborn, just over a mile behind Echternach, where Company G provided a back-up position along the main highway to Luxembourg City, all three of the company's squad-sized outposts were cut off, but to a man they were eventually to make their way to safety, some after wandering behind German lines for up to four days.

The effect of the German infiltration was far more damaging against the outposts of Company F. Three were located northwest of Echternach near the village of Berdorf, on a lip of high ground overlooking the Sûre, or just back from it in farm buildings, all held in platoon strength. The fourth, manned by an under-strength squad, was in the gorge of the Ernz Noire near the point where the first of the perpendicular roads crossing the gorge led to Beaufort. All four outposts fell, everybody either killed or captured except for two men from the outpost along the Ernz Noire and thirteen who had gone on a routine contact patrol. Four of those men were also captured later in the day, but the nine others eventually made their way out, some after playing cowboys and Indians with the Germans among the big rock formations in the valley of the Ernz Noire.

By late morning, the Germans had surrounded all five of the forward companies: Company I in Dickweiler, Company L in Osweiler, Company G in Lauterborn (which had the effect of cutting off Company E in Echternach), and what was left of Company F in a resort hotel a hundred yards outside Berdorf. Yet their presence still posed considerable difficulties for the Germans, for the American positions controlled every road leading into the 12th Infantry's sector except that up the valley of the Ernz Noire.

Shortly before noon, General Barton granted the regimental commander, Col. Robert H. Chance, authority to commit his reserve battalion and released to him a platoon of medium tanks of the attached 70th Tank Battalion and two platoons of the battalion's light tanks, rushed forward from assignment guarding Radio Luxembourg. Chance sent one company with some of the tanks marching on Berdorf to relieve the men of Company F in the nearby hotel and another with the rest of the tanks toward Lauterborn to relieve Company G.

The force advancing on Berdorf failed to make it, encountering strong resistance near the village and precipitating a fight that was destined to continue well into the night. The force moving on Lauterborn did better. Overcoming resistance on a hill just outside the village, it continued forward, and as night began to fall, reached a mill on the edge of Lauterborn. There the force rescued a small group of Americans who through the afternoon had undergone what had been, at best, an unnerving experience.

As the Germans advanced on Lauterborn, about forty of them captured fifteen Americans manning an outpost built around a 57mm. antitank gun. Continuing to advance, the Germans marched the Americans up the road in front of them, heading toward the millhouse that was occupied (although the Germans had no way of knowing it) by Company G's command group. Alongside the road outside the millhouse stood a low stone wall; as the prisoners passed behind the wall, they had cover, but the Germans were still in the open. The men of the command group opened fire. Armed only with rifles and a single BAR, the command group nevertheless managed to keep the Germans pinned to the ground until the relief force arrived.

At Osweiler and Dickweiler, the two forward companies of the 3d Battalion held their own. At Osweiler, the Germans fell back after making an assault that cost them fifty men, and even though twenty Germans managed later to get into a few of the houses, they pulled out after dark. At Dickweiler, the Germans made only a halfhearted effort against the village until late afternoon, by which time the battalion commander, Maj. Herman R. Rice, had sent fifteen men from his reserve company riding three medium tanks to the village. As two German companies attacked, everybody held his fire until the Germans were so close that the tank commanders feared their tanks might be hit by *Panzerfausts*. When at last the infantry company commander signaled fire, the effect was devastating. A German company commander and fifty of his men were killed; another company commander and thirty-five men surrendered; and the other survivors fell back in disorder.

A hundred yards east of Berdorf, the commander of Company F, 1st Lt. John L. Leake, had established his headquarters in the Parc Hôtel, built in the early 1930s when tourism was beginning to develop into a major industry in Luxembourg. As the hotel's brochures proclaimed, the Parc Hôtel occupied a *site isolé*—a high, open plateau only a few hundred yards from one of the more spectacular rock formations in the gorge of the Ernz Noire known as the *Ile du Diable* (Devil's Island)—and featured both *confort moderne* and *cuisine distinguée*. Since Leake and the members of his command group had to make do with U.S. Army victuals prepared by their own less than accomplished chefs, they could provide no testimony to the distinguished cuisine, but they could attest to the modern comforts of the beds and the plumbing, and the isolated site afforded excellent fields of fire.

Since all communication had failed, Lieutenant Leake had no early knowledge of the tragic fate of his outposts, located a mile from the hotel, but in the wake of the early morning shelling, he was markedly concerned about a lack of communications with his battalion headquarters and the artillery. Since his executive officer, 1st Lt. Richard McConnell, was planning to go to the rear to dispose of cash left over from paying the men, he urged McConnell to hurry back with the company's radio, an SCR*-300, which had been left for repair. McConnell was about ready to leave by jeep but was waiting for the first sergeant to complete the morning report when a soldier came running up. It was a man from the crew of a nearby 57mm. antitank gun. Did anybody know anything about a column of troops marching up the hill from the direction of the Hamm Farm?

*Signal Corps Radio

Almost simultaneously men manning an observation post on top of the hotel called down that they could see a column of troops approaching. Rushing to the roof, Lieutenant Leake saw Germans advancing, one file on either side of the road. At Leake's urging, Lieutenant McConnell and his driver took off in their jeep immediately, wheels spinning, under orders to report to battalion the approach of "a possible enemy patrol" and to hurry back with the SCR-300.

As Lieutenant Leake was soon aware, what he had seen was no German patrol but the vanguard of an entire battalion. The bulk of the battalion bypassed the Parc Hôtel and entered the unoccupied village of Berdorf, while the group seen from the observation post moved into a cluster of houses just short of the hotel and opened fire.

Inside, Leake, three other officers, and fifty-five men took refuge. Other than their rifles, they had only a few BARs, one .50-caliber machine gun, and little reserve ammunition. Such extra ammunition as the company had on hand was in a small shed in the garden, which was impossible to reach in the face of fire from the German-held houses. Two men who had been working in the shed were trapped there.

As the Americans took up firing positions at the hotel's windows, the Germans were unable to advance. Meanwhile, those in the village of Berdorf moved about freely until Company F's first sergeant, Gerveis Willis, placed a BAR in a window near the entrance to the hotel and opened fire on a crossroads at the edge of the village. Willis reckoned that he killed eight men before the Germans began to respect his marksmanship and avoid the crossroads.

Lieutenant McConnell had in the meantime reached battalion headquarters in a village a few miles back and found the company's radio fully repaired. Conscious of Lieutenant Leake's urgent need for the radio, he dismissed his other mission of getting rid of the excess money and with his driver, Cpl. John Mandichak, headed back for the Parc Hôtel. As they reached the crossroads in Berdorf, Germans at close range opened a hail of fire. Mandichak dived out his side of the jeep and ran into a barn, where he hid under a pile of hay until nightfall and then slipped away, the beginning of a seven-day odyssey that was eventually to bring him to safety in American lines. Diving out the other side of the jeep, McConnell ran into a house, but the Germans spotted him and he had to surrender.

A German sergeant took McConnell's bag of money, examined the contents, then handed it back with a smile. Having sold newspapers as a youth in Miami, McConnell had picked up some Yiddish and found that he could converse, after a fashion, with the sergeant. His company commander was with a German group that had just taken the Parc Hôtel, said the sergeant; he was sending the lieutenant there. At the point of a rifle, McConnell started up a straight, exposed road leading directly to the hotel's entrance.

When McConnell and his guard got within twenty-five yards of it, McConnell realized that the German sergeant was wrong. Those were American soldiers at the windows. "Don't shoot," McConnell shouted; "they'll shoot me." Since it was obvious to the German soldier, too, that Americans, not Germans, held the hotel, he used his prisoner as a shield and backed down the road to Berdorf.

At that point, the German sergeant saw a chance to use his prisoner to engineer surrender of the Americans in the hotel. Summoning his squad and with McConnell in the lead at the point of a gun, he headed up the road. As the group got close to the hotel, one of the soldiers yelled from a window: "Are all those your prisoners?" McConnell shouted back: "Hell, no. I'm the prisoner!"

Lieutenant Leake was momentarily at a loss to know what to do, but he made up his mind quickly and shouted his order to his men loud enough for McConnell to hear: "Pick your targets. It's just like shooting ducks in a gallery. Squeeze 'em off and don't waste ammo!"

McConnell understood, but for the benefit of the Germans, he shouted back: "Don't shoot!" Then he added: "And don't miss!"

At one of the windows, Cpl. Robert Hancock drew a bead on the German closest to McConnell. He "could see the lieutenant's shoulder and the Jerry's left pocket"—he held on the pocket.

At Lieutenant Leake's signal, everybody fired at once. The first volley dropped all but two of the Germans. Along with McConnell, those two—one of them the sergeant—ran behind a nearby building that shielded them from the hotel but exposed them to the two men from Company F who had been trapped in the supply shed. Each choosing a target, the two men fired, killing one German but only wounding the sergeant. (The man firing at the sergeant was new to the front and reluctant to kill anybody. He had consciously aimed at the sergeant's buttocks.)

"Now," said McConnell to the sergeant, "you had better give up." To which the sergeant responded: "I give up."

McConnell cradled the German in his arms, an act that presumably kept the Germans in nearby houses from opening fire, and took him into the hotel. There he and the others were careful to treat their prisoner with consideration, for they were all too conscious that before long, their roles might be reversed.

As the afternoon wore on, that appeared to be ever more likely, for even though the Germans in the nearby houses attempted no assault, German artillery pummeled the hotel, caving in the attic and part of the third floor, and there was no sign of a relief force coming to the rescue. Just after nightfall there was the sound of heavy firing on the far side of Berdorf, which indicated that somebody was trying to get through, but it eventually died away.

By early evening of December 16, the 12th Infantry continued to hold all its positions except those outposts overrun in the first German surge during the early morning fog and darkness, but it was clear that the Germans were continuing to build their strength. So intense was the pressure against Companies I and L at Osweiler and Dickweiler that the regimental commander, Colonel Chance, sent the last company of his reserve battalion to the 3d Battalion's command post to be ready to move to the two villages early the next day. The companies had no choice but to hold, for in mid-afternoon the 4th Division commander, "Tubby" Barton—as West Point classmates had long ago nicknamed him—had ordered that there was to be "no retrograde movement" in the 12th Infantry's sector.

However hardpressed the 12th Infantry, Barton was still hesitant to call on his other two regiments for help, for there was no guarantee that the German attack was not to expand. He nevertheless took the gamble of ordering his southernmost regiment to release its reserve battalion to move north early the next morning. He also directed much of the artillery supporting other parts of his front to shift to positions from which to fire in support of the 12th Infantry; and from the commander of the 9th Armored Division, he got the promise of a company of medium tanks to arrive the next morning from that division's CCA and augment his own badly depleted tank battalion. He also alerted the 4th Engineer Battalion and the 4th Reconnaissance Troop to be ready for commitment at an hour's notice.

On the German side, the commander of the Seventh Army, General Brandenberger, viewed the day's developments with some equanimity. Although he lamented the fact that American artillery fire had prevented installing even one bridge to enable his few assault guns to enter the fight (a mile to the north, the *Panzer Lehr Division* refused the use of its bridge, pronounced "too busy"), there were positive points as well. While it was true that the 5th Parachute Division had fallen far short of crossings over the Wiltz River, it was also true that each of the army's four divisions had penetrated the American front at one point or another, and Brandenberger perceived the failure to advance farther as attributable to his enemy's local reserves, all of which he assumed had been committed by the end of the day. At that point it was "a matter of making the breakthrough a thorough one before the enemy had a chance to bring up stronger reserves."

What Brandenberger could not know was that he was destined to meet a stronger reserve sooner than he anticipated. A few minutes before midnight, the commander of the VIII Corps, General Middleton, telephoned General Barton. At daybreak the next morning, said Middleton, a combat command of the 10th Armored Division was to leave an assembly area in the Third Army's sector only thirty-five miles from the 12th Infantry's positions. Barton was to have the use of that combat command.

CHAPTER EIGHT

The Northern Shoulder

When he spoke, it was as if he strained his words through gravel. The illegitimate son of a Bavarian servant girl, he was short and burly and looked like a man who depended for his livelihood on slaughtering pigs on a farm, which he did as a youth, or cutting meat at the butcher's, which he did after his discharge from the army at the end of the Great War until he joined the SS in 1928 and became Adolf Hitler's chauffeur and bodyguard. Five years later he organized and commanded the Führer's household troops, the *SS-Leibstandärte Adolf Hitler*, and in the summer of 1934 acted as chief executioner in Hitler's notorious purge of Nazi ranks, which became known as the Night of the Long Knives.

He commanded the *SS-Leibstandärte Adolf Hitler* as a regiment in France in 1940, then headed it as a brigade in Greece and finally in Russia as a division, renamed the 1st SS Panzer Division (*Leibstandärte Adolf Hitler*). He was commanding an SS panzer corps in Normandy in the summer of 1944 when the cabal of army officers tried to kill the Führer. Hitler promptly made him head of a newly formed panzer army, but that command disintegrated in the defeat in Normandy and the retreat to the West Wall. Whereupon Hitler designated him to rebuild the SS panzer divisions, command the Sixth Panzer Army, and make the main effort in the offensive through the Ardennes.

While admitting the man's personal bravery, the German Army's generals despised him. His World War I rank of sergeant "attached to him perpetually in the minds of the aristocratic members of the German General staff." He was, said von Rundstedt, "decent, but stupid." To senior army commanders, he had at most the ability to command a division, which was why Model and von Rundstedt arranged to have the experienced and capable Fritz Kraemer assigned as his chief of staff. He was also sinister and ruthless: In Russia, when he learned that the Russians had murdered six of his troopers, he ordered all Russians captured over the next three days to be shot, and more than four thousand died.

By late 1944 he was drinking too much, seldom actually drunk but often close to it. By that time, also, he had come to decry his Führer's rash and clumsy interference with battlefield command, which explained his conniving to alter Hitler's plan for the Sixth Panzer Army's crossings of the Meuse so that if the offensive failed, his army would be in a position to implement the Small Solution.

Yet the man was careful to conceal his discontent from the Führer, and to Hitler none of his shortcomings mattered. He had been loyal since that night long ago in 1923 when Hitler had attempted to seize power in the *Feldherrnhalle* in Munich and failed. Hitler knew that the troops adored the man, that they would die for him; and Hitler was convinced that he, above all others, could be trusted.

That was why Hitler chose Sepp Dietrich as the one to lead the beloved SS panzer divisions to victory and save the Third Reich.

As befitted the force making the main effort, the Sixth Panzer Army was by far the strongest of the three armies attacking in the Ardennes. Dietrich had three corps headquarters, five parachute and *Volksgrenadier* divisions, four SS panzer divisions (counting attached separate tank and assault gun battalions, eight hundred tanks and assault guns), and more artillery and *Nebelwerfers* than the Fifth Panzer and Seventh Armies combined, an awesome one thousand pieces.

With two *Volksgrenadier* divisions, the 67th Corps was to attack on both sides of Monschau to get onto the Hautes Fagnes, the high moors just beyond the frontier, there to join von der Heydte's parachutists and the big *Jägdtigers* with 128mm. guns in blocking American reinforcements. South of Monschau, after a parachute and two *Volksgrenadier* divisions achieved penetrations, two SS panzer divisions of the 1st SS Panzer Corps were to make the main thrust in the vicinity of the twin villages of Krinkelt-Rocherath and through the northern reaches of the Losheim Gap. Two more SS panzer divisions under another SS panzer corps were to constitute a second wave, and most of Skorzeny's brigade was to operate in support of Dietrich's army.

Roads were, of course, vital to swift advance by the German armor. None of the roads in the sector to be traversed by the SS panzer divisions was ideal, but the planners designated five as adequate. Two emerged from the Losheim Gap, while the other three in the vicinity of Krinkelt-Rocherath crossed a broad expanse of high ground that the Americans called the Elsenborn Ridge. Since the network of through roads was so limited, it was vital that the SS panzer commanders adhere strictly to the routes assigned them, so vital that Hitler invoked his pet tactic of demanding compliance upon pain of death. To fail to obtain use of any of the five roads would impose a severe strain on the execution of the plan; to fail to gain as many as three could well be disastrous.

Not that anybody expected any difficulty, for all knew that their ad-

PLANNED ROUTES OF ADVANCE
I SS PANZER CORPS

ROUTES
A,B,C — 12th SS Pz Div
D — KG Peiper, 1st SS Pz Div
E — 1st SS Pz Div (-)

versary was inexperienced and vastly overextended. At either end of the Sixth Panzer Army's jump-off line, there was only a cavalry reconnaissance squadron and, in between, holding a twenty-mile front, the 99th Infantry Division. Even as the German troops crept through the snow and darkness on the night of December 15 to their attack positions, they and their commanders were still unaware that close behind the 99th Division was the 2d Infantry Division.

What Dietrich did soon learn was that two elements of his plan had already gone awry. One of the *Volksgrenadier* divisions that was supposed to attack at Monschau had been unable to break free from defensive positions farther north, so that the 67th Corps would have only a single division. Nor was there to be any help from von der Heydte's parachutists, at least not, as intended, before the attack started. Some of the trucks carrying the parachutists to the airfields from which their planes were to take off ran out of gasoline before they got there. By 10 P.M., when the planes were scheduled to take off, only 400 out of 1,200 parachutists had arrived. There would be no airborne attack that night.

Nowhere along the Ardennes front was the German artillery preparation more intense, more spectacular than in the sector of the Sixth Panzer

Army. To Cpl. Rudi Frübeiser of the 3d Parachute Division, it was "an earth-shaking inferno." To Tech. Sgt. Ben Nawrocki of the 99th Division's 393d Infantry, it seemed that "all hell broke loose . . . The ground shook." The operations officer of the 394th Infantry, Maj. William B. Kempton, called it "thunderous." For Pfc. Thor Ronningen of the 395th Infantry, who was asleep in a foxhole in Höfen, close to Monschau, it was "a terrifying experience to wake up to the crash of the artillery and the ear-splitting scream of the rockets. The ground shook like a bowl of Jell-O." And Maj. Günther Holz, commander of the 12th Volksgrenadier Division's tank destroyer battalion, said that "the earth seemed to break open. A hurricane of iron and fire went down on the enemy positions with a deafening noise. We old soldiers had seen many a heavy barrage, but never before anything like this."

In Höfen, the shelling crumbled many of the buildings, filling the streets with debris, and set some of the houses on fire, illuminating the foggy night with a lurid glow. Along the rest of the 99th Division's line, where most of the defensive positions were within or on the edge of fir forests, shells exploded in the treetops, knocking off big limbs and spraying the forest with jagged metal. Yet even though the overall effect was awesome, the damage to the defenders was minimal. Wire communications went out almost everywhere, but so widely spaced were the positions that many of the shells fell on undefended sectors, and elsewhere the men were well dug in, their foxholes roofed with logs.

At the road junction of Wahlerscheid, where the 2d Division was attacking, there was no shelling, for the Germans planned no attack in that sector. Nor was there any artillery fire on the town of Monschau. One of the most picturesque towns in all Germany, Monschau was in peacetime a favorite of honeymooners and—so the word went—of Adolf Hitler himself. Set in a deep gorge astride the upper reaches of the Roer River (at that point more like a mountain stream gurgling over a rock-strewn bottom), the town consisted of charming medieval buildings, their upper stories of white stucco and exposed wood framing ranged along cobblestoned streets little wider than sidewalks. Somebody—some said it was Model, others Hitler himself—had ordered that there was to be no shelling of Monschau.

The artillery was still firing when the big searchlights lit the sky with a milky glow. If the light helped the Germans in their attack, it also helped the Americans in their defense, particularly at three places where the attackers closely followed the artillery preparation. There were only three places where that happened along the entire front: against the 38th Cavalry Reconnaissance Squadron at Monschau; against a lone battalion of the 395th Infantry at Höfen; and against two battalions of the 393d Infantry dug in where two woods trails emerged from the forest almost due east of Krinkelt-Rocherath to join a highway following the trace of the

THE
NORTHERN SHOULDER
FIRST DAY · DEC 16
Scale:
0   1   2   3   4
MILES

Belgian-German frontier, a road the Americans called the "International Highway."

To Pfc. Bernie Macay, whose Company B, 393d Infantry, faced that highway, it seemed there were thousands of Germans. He and the men with him "could see them against the skyline as they came over the hill. It seemed like they were coming right at us and for some reason ignoring everybody else." At Höfen, the Germans approached "in swarms," moving forward at a slow, methodical walk; and at Monschau, men of the 38th Cavalry Reconnaissance Squadron saw shadowy forms plodding toward them. With a round in the chamber of every rifle and machine gun, and with 37mm. guns on the light tanks loaded with canister, the men waited for the Germans to reach the barbed wire in front of their positions.

As elsewhere in the Ardennes, the defensive line around Monschau was thin. The cavalry's strongest positions, including a line of fifty machine guns culled from jeeps and armored cars, were northwest of the town behind a railroad track. They had been emplaced there to deny access to the town of Mützenich, on high ground behind Monschau; for Mützenich more than Monschau was the key to access to the highway leading onto the Hautes Fagnes. Immediately north of Monschau, the defensive line swung to the other side of the railroad in order to deny entry to Monschau, while at the southern edge of the town, where a road cut across the deep gorge of the Roer, the cavalrymen had a roadblock backed up by light tanks. The squadron had direct support from the 62d Armored Field Artillery Battalion, and the pieces of two corps artillery battalions were within easy firing range.

At Höfen, the commander of the 3d Battalion, 395th Infantry, Lt. Col. McClernand Butler, had managed to hold only a single rifle platoon as a reserve. Even so, his line was thin, but having defended the town since early November, the men were well dug in and their fields of fire across ground rising steeply toward the positions were excellent.

Butler had the support of a battalion of the 99th Division's artillery; and two nights earlier, a company of towed guns of the 612th Tank Destroyer Battalion, attached to the 2d Division, had arrived in Höfen in order to be ready to provide support when the men of the 2d Division broke through at Wahlerscheid and fanned out to other objectives in front of Höfen. The crews dug in their twelve 3-inch guns and camouflaged them with bed sheets.

Despite the small size of the defending force, the Germans had no such numerical superiority as they had elsewhere in the Ardennes, primarily because of the failure of one of the two *Volksgrenadier* divisions to arrive but also because the other, the 326th Volksgrenadier Division, was depleted. One battalion had yet to arrive; another had been siphoned off the day before to help repel the attack by the 78th Division, a part of the attempt to take the Roer River dams; and yet a third, having briefly held the pillboxes at Wahlerscheid, had been relieved there the night before by the division's replacement battalion (less than an hour before the 2d Division's 9th Infantry carried the position) and would be unable to reach the line of departure for an attack before daylight on the 16th. Instead of two divisions with fourteen infantry battalions, there was thus a single division with only four battalions immediately available.

The Germans struck the cavalry on either side of the gorge of the Roer River in front and just to the north of Monschau. As a German set off a trip flare, the waiting defenders opened fire as one. When the cavalry commander, Lt. Col. Robert E. O'Brien, called on the commander of the 405th Field Artillery Group, Col. Oscar A. Axelson, for help, Axelson decided, even though the super-secret proximity fuse had yet to be released officially, that he would use it. The shells bursting in the air above the approaching Germans were terrifying and devastating. As

60mm. mortars fired illumination rounds, the cavalrymen could see the Germans falling back in "headlong retreat."

Exulting in that success, Colonel O'Brien was nevertheless conscious of the meager strength of a cavalry reconnaissance squadron and early asked for reinforcements. In response, the commander of the V Corps, General Gerow, sent the 146th Engineer Combat Battalion, whose men arrived soon after nightfall and began to dig in before Mützenich, the gateway to the road to the Hautes Fagnes and to Eupen, where Gerow had his headquarters.

At Höfen, meanwhile, the defenders waited as the men of two German battalions trudged up the steep hill toward their positions through the murky illumination of the artificial moonlight. They were less than two hundred yards from the American foxholes when "every weapon the battalion possessed opened fire" and "practically swept" most of the Germans away. Yet so persistent was the assault that in at least three cases, dying men pitched forward into the foxholes.

Only in the center of the elongated town at the seam between Companies I and K was there any German success. There some thirty or so got into the houses, but as the others fell back, harassed at every step by the towed tank destroyers firing high-explosive rounds, the infiltrators held on for less than an hour. When it was over, at least a hundred Germans were dead, possibly more, and nineteen captured. The contrast in American casualties was striking: four killed, four missing, seven wounded. If the Sixth Panzer Army was to break through at Monschau-Höfen and secure its northern flank on the high moors beyond, General Dietrich obviously would have to come up with greater strength for the 67th Corps.

Yet success or failure for the Sixth Panzer Army rested ultimately not with the 67th Corps but with the 1st SS Panzer Corps, a few miles to the south along the approaches to Krinkelt-Rocherath and a cluster of other frontier villages, and in the Losheim Gap. And there the Germans had the same great numerical superiority they possessed at most other places. Striking to gain access to two woods trails leading to Krinkelt-Rocherath, the entire 277th Volksgrenadier Division (built around remnants of an infantry division that had been virtually destroyed in Normandy) was destined to hit only three American battalions, while a little farther south the entire 12th Volksgrenadier Division was to hit but two battalions.

Once past the frontier forests and villages, in the process opening up routes for the SS panzer divisions, the two *Volksgrenadier* divisions were to cross the Elsenborn Ridge and swing northwest to block in the direction of the Hautes Fagnes. The task of opening other routes for the panzers farther south in the Losheim Gap fell to the 3d Parachute Division, which was then to follow *Kampfgruppe Peiper* closely but peel troops off to face north and protect Peiper's supply route.

On the American side, the commander of the 393d Infantry, Lt. Col. Jean D. Scott, who had been ordered to demonstrate by fire in support of the attack by the 2d Division and the 395th Infantry, seized the opportunity to better his positions. He decided to attack with a portion of his 3d Battalion to take a dominating forested hill, the Rath Berg (American troops called it "Rat Hill"), just off the battalion's north flank. The 3d Battalion had accomplished that handily; but the added defensive responsibility had absorbed all but a platoon of the reserve company.

Thus there was scant back-up for a line of foxholes extending more than two miles, all of the line inside dense fir forest except for a short stretch where the holes were on the fringe of the forest looking out over the International Highway. The foxholes constituted more a series of platoon strongpoints than a solid line, and the critical point was that at which the woods trail leading four miles back to Krinkelt-Rocherath joined the highway. Beyond the International Highway, the Germans still held the pillboxes of the West Wall, and open draws led up to the highway from German villages behind the pillboxes.

The critical junction of the woods trail and the highway was the responsibility of Company K under Capt. Stephen K. Plume. Yet the main thrust against Plume's company hit not there but along the woodsline a little to the south. There two battalions of Germans were almost on top of Company K's foxholes just as the artillery preparation lifted, and the outcome dramatically illustrated the advantage the Germans forfeited at most other places by failing to follow their artillery fire closely. Except for the platoon astride the woods road, the first rush overwhelmed all of Company K. If the men of the remaining platoon were to survive, they had to fall back, and Captain Plume ordered them to withdraw immediately to the company command post.

Because communications were out, it was close to 8 A.M. before the battalion commander, Lt. Col. Jack G. Allen, learned of Company K's fate. Since the collapse jeopardized Company L on the other side of the woods trail, Allen told that company to fall back to defend the battalion command post and soon directed Company I, a mile away atop Rat Hill, to do the same. The men of Company I had to fight to get there, but by noon a defensive position encompassing the battalion command post was forming, based in part on old positions dug when the battalion had a reserve company.

On the German side, the commander of the 1st SS Panzer Corps, Generalleutnant der Waffen-SS Hermann Priess, was markedly upset by the failure of the *Volksgrenadiers* to achieve a quick penetration so that the 12th SS Panzer Division (*Hitlerjugend*) could get going on the drive to the Meuse. Around noon, he ordered a battalion of *SS-Panzergrenadiers* to help, but that failed to carry the 3d Battalion's position. The *SS-Panzergrenadiers* did push down the woods trail as far as the deep cut of a creek called the Jans Bach, thereby succeeding in blocking the 3d Battalion's only road to the rear.

There was no question but that Colonel Allen and his men were fighting for their lives. The regimental commander, Colonel Scott, could send no help, for what had been his reserve battalion had moved on December 13 to help in the 395th Infantry's attack in support of the 2d Division; but early in the afternoon, the commander of the 99th Division, Maj. Gen. Walter E. Lauer, released a company from his only reserve, a battalion of the 394th Infantry, to go to Allen's assistance. Allen sent guides to the rear to lead the company forward over firebreaks, thereby avoiding the Germans on the road.

As night fell, the German pressure decreased, for German commanders had to reorganize their units in the face of heavy, even crippling losses. Before the attack, regiments of the 277th Volksgrenadier Division had been critically short of officers and noncommissioned officers—hardly a single front-line company had more than a single officer—and as those leaders tried to inspire their inexperienced troops by example, they had been among the first to fall. The Germans probably lost as many as three hundred men, for when a thaw came at last to the Ardennes in the spring, local inhabitants found the draws leading up to the International Highway thick with German bodies. American losses were also heavy, some three hundred either killed, wounded, or captured, three-fourths of them from Company K, including the commander, Captain Plume, who was captured.

Just to the south, Maj. Matthew L. Legler's 1st Battalion, 393d Infantry, underwent the same kind of numerically overwhelming assault as did the 3d Battalion. Yet most of Legler's positions were at the edge of the forest, overlooking the International Highway and generally open ground, so that the men of the 1st Battalion had an advantage not shared by their neighbors. With machine guns, mortars, and artillery, they exploited excellent fields of fire to exact a heavy toll. Not one German got inside the American positions, and within an hour the assault was at a halt.

Under strong pressure to obtain a quick penetration for the waiting tanks of the 12th SS Panzer Division the commander of the 277th Volksgrenadier Division, Col. Wilhelm Viebig, committed his reserve regiment. At 8 A.M., that regiment and the survivors of the other attacked behind a heavy concentration of artillery fire and rockets. Again many a German fell, particularly noncommissioned officers and the few junior officers who were herding the troops forward, but the sheer weight of numbers soon began to tell.

The first breakthrough came on the right where the International Highway entered the woods, and where, in order to cover the second woods trail leading back to Krinkelt-Rocherath, most of Company C's positions had to be within the forest with limited fields of fire. A half hour after the renewed assault began, two of Company C's platoons fell back, but the Germans failed to pursue their advantage, seemingly content merely to occupy the foxholes and loot them. An hour later, two of Company B's platoons also caved in.

At that point, Major Legler committed his reserve company to restore Company B's positions. Employing marching fire, the men retook most of the foxholes.

Yet Legler needed help to reoccupy Company C's positions. When he appealed to the regimental commander, Colonel Scott, all Scott could provide was the Mine Platoon from the Antitank Company, composed of a lieutenant and twenty-five men. When they reached the battalion command post, the operations officer, Capt. Lawrence H. Duffin, was waiting with thirteen men from the Headquarters Company. Taking command of the little force—less than a full-strength rifle platoon—Duffin led the men up the trail, soon to find Company C's command post under attack. Fixing bayonets, the men charged. They killed twenty-eight Germans, and the rest fell back to the foxholes they had captured earlier. With Company C's survivors, Captain Duffin formed a new line based on the command post.

By midday, the 1st Battalion, 393d Infantry, still maintained a fairly cohesive defense, but the battalion had lost four hundred men, more than half its foxhole strength. The Germans were nevertheless slow to continue the attack, a reflection of their own heavy losses.

With the coming of darkness, the Germans took advantage of the gaps they had forged on the flanks of both the 1st and 3d Battalions to send strong patrols—some composed of more than fifty men—to probe deep into the forest. Sometimes the Germans called out in English in an effort to trap the unwary. Sometimes they fired their burp guns wildly, seemingly on the offchance that they might hit somebody.

For men of both American battalions, it was a cold, miserable night. Anybody who slept did so only fitfully, and if anybody ate, he had only frozen C- or K-rations, for there could be no fires. Medical officers and aid men in both battalions tried to make the wounded as comfortable as possible, but both aid stations were overflowing. Through much of the day medics of the 1st Battalion had been able to take out most of their wounded by jeep, but nobody dared make the run after nightfall. Evacuation of the wounded from the 3d Battalion ended early when the Germans cut the woods trail at the Jans Bach.

Just to the south of Major Legler's battalion, the northernmost unit of the 394th Infantry, the 2d Battalion, had also become embroiled with the 277th Volksgrenadier Division but against nothing like the heavy odds faced by the two battalions of the 393d Infantry. All that the German division commander, Colonel Viebig, had left to throw against that battalion, located mostly within the woods alongside the International Highway, was the division's Fusilier Battalion.

The men of that battalion were slow to follow up the artillery preparation and paid the inevitable consequences. Mortar and artillery concentrations zeroed in earlier rained down on them, while machine gunners and BAR-men unleashed a torrent of small-arms fire. In less than half an hour, the Germans were falling back.

They tried again in mid-morning with the help of three assault guns, but a heavy concentration of fire from the 155mm. guns of the 99th Division's general support artillery battalion erupted around the vehicles and sent them scurrying to the rear. Some of the Fusiliers nevertheless worked their way within hand grenade distance of one of the platoons of Company E; but since all men of the platoon had overhead cover on their holes, the platoon leader, Tech. Sgt. Fred Wallace, called for artillery fire on top of the positions. Most of the Germans were killed, and such few as survived were quickly rounded up.

Except for occasional shelling, that was all that happened on December 16 to the 394th Infantry's 2d Battalion. The men were proud of their stand. All their positions were intact and the casualties few. Yet most were aware that something serious—they knew not what—was happening to their neighbors off either flank, and at the command post deep in the forest, the battalion staff had to cope with a special problem. Their commander had gone to pieces, cowering in a corner of one of the log huts, his head between his knees.

To anyone with a map, it would be obvious why the Germans made no major thrust against the 394th Infantry's 2d Battalion, for in rear of the battalion, the only passage through the forest was over firebreaks and muddy logging trails. But just a few miles farther south two paved roads and a railroad led into the 99th Division's positions, and there waited *Kampfgruppe Peiper*, the tank-heavy task force of the 1st SS Panzer Division, ready to begin the thrust on which Adolf Hitler's principal hope rode for quick seizure of crossings over the Meuse River. There, too, the entire 12th Volksgrenadier Division was to make the penetration and was to have some help from adjacent troops of the 3d Parachute Division. To defend against that formidable force, there were only two U.S. battalions of the 394th Infantry (one of them designated as the division reserve and short a company) and the regiment's I&R Platoon.

For the Germans, the two roads were crucial. The main road led up a gently rising incline from Losheim to an intersection with the International Highway at Losheimergraben, a crossroads settlement consisting of a customshouse and a few other buildings. It then passed through dense forest to open country and a cluster of villages and towns—Hünningen, Mürringen, Büllingen, and Bütgenbach—continuing westward to Malmédy and beyond. The other road, just south of the railroad, also had a connection from Losheim and ran through the Belgian frontier village of Lanzerath. From there it passed a cluster of buildings known as Buchholz Farm and a nearby railroad station, which American troops called Buchholz Station (actually, Losheimergraben Station), and on to the west by way of the village of Honsfeld. The main road through Losheimergraben was to be used by a column of the 12th SS Panzer Division; the other by *Kampfgruppe Peiper*.

Wilhelm Osterhold was a slight, wiry man with a black mustache, known among the troops of the 12th Volksgrenadier Division's 48th Regiment as one who believed that a regimental commander led his troops from the forward ranks. A career soldier, Osterhold had entered the army not to accommodate any military bent but in search of refuge from National Socialism. When Hitler and the Nazis came to power in the 1930s, Osterhold's father, a staunchly anti-Nazi representative in the Reichstag, had been arrested for distributing anti-National Socialist literature and sent to a concentration camp. That left a black mark against every member of the family, and the only way young Osterhold could see of evading it was to submerge himself in the army. It had proven to be a good choice, for Osterhold knew that on at least one occasion, Nazi authorities had raised questions about him, but by that time he had become an officer with a record, and his superiors covered for him.

Colonel Osterhold's 48th Regiment was to make the 12th Volksgrenadier Division's main effort, its first goal to seize the crossroads at Losheimergraben and open a path for a column of the 12th SS Panzer Division. Like other units of the division, Osterhold's regiment had lost heavily in late September after arriving hurriedly from the Eastern Front to halt the American drive near Aachen and in the process earning the honorific *Volksgrenadier* in the days when the name had some meaning. The replacements who had only recently joined the regiment were young and inexperienced, but hospital returnees who had fought in Russia had joined the ranks of veteran noncommissioned officers and junior officers.

For the assault, Osterhold had the support not only of all his division's artillery but also of two *Volksartillerie* corps. He also had fifteen 75mm. assault guns, while another regiment of his division was to make a supporting attack up the line of the railroad close by on the south.

To Colonel Osterhold, as to the other soldiers at the front that morning, the artillery preparation seemed awesome, but as he and his men soon discovered, it did little damage. To Osterhold, the fire plan appeared to have been drawn up far away in Berlin.

In a fan-shaped defense of the crossroads, the Americans of the 1st Battalion, 394th Infantry, got their first indication of the enemy's approach soon after the artillery fire lifted with the appearance in the diffused glare from the enemy's searchlights of a U.S. jeep on the road from Losheim. The jeep approached a concealed outpost containing a

57mm. antitank gun, but the crew of the antitank gun was so stunned to see an American vehicle that nobody fired. Turning around, the jeep raced back to Losheim, then reappeared a short time later preceding a 75mm. assault gun.

The crew of the antitank gun let the jeep pass but opened fire on the assault gun. A first round knocked off a track, a second penetrated the hull, and a third set the assault gun on fire. Only the commander, a lieutenant, got out, and he was badly wounded. Men in positions a little farther up the road killed the occupants of the jeep with small-arms fire.

Because the going was slow up steep wooded draws which the Germans had to use to reach other portions of the 1st Battalion's positions, it was well into the morning before the defenders saw any of the enemy; but when the Germans came, they came in strength. Two battalions of the 48th Regiment hit the seam between two American companies in the thick forest northeast of Losheimergraben; then one of the battalions swung down the line of Company B's foxholes in the direction of the crossroads, taking the positions in flank. With the attacking Germans was Osterhold himself, frustrated because he was unable to establish radio contact with his supporting artillery, and when he finally did get through to call for fire, the artillery fell short on his other battalion, disrupting that part of the attack.

The assault against Company B nevertheless continued, so that by early afternoon the company had lost sixty men, including the leader of an attached heavy machine-gun platoon, Tech. Sgt. Edward Dolenc, last seen firing his machine gun with twenty or more Germans piled in front of it. Because the other half of the German thrust had been disrupted by the misdirected artillery fire, the men of Company C were free to try to reestablish their neighboring company's positions, but with little success. Night was falling when Colonel Osterhold and one of his battalions reached the edge of the woods overlooking Losheimergraben. Osterhold was reluctant to continue further without assured fire support from either artillery or assault guns.

In the woods on the other side of Losheimergraben, what appeared to be two platoons of Germans bounced off positions of Company A astride the International Highway and worked their way toward the crossroads. Only the men of Company D's 81mm. mortar platoon, their mortars dug in around a farmhouse a hundred yards short of the crossroads, stood in the way. The Germans were almost on top of one of the mortar positions before the crew spotted them across a firebreak no more than fifteen yards away.

Looking out from the mortar position, Pfc. Robert Newbrough saw a German soldier holding a potato masher hand grenade, the first German soldier Newbrough had ever seen close up. The German was "just as startled" to see him, Newbrough decided, as he was to see the German. Newbrough was debating what to do when his sergeant called by telephone for the other mortars to fire almost on top of his position. Elevating the tubes to almost ninety degrees, the mortarmen in the other positions opened fire. Once the shells began to burst, the surviving Germans fled. Newbrough, as he put it, "didn't know where and didn't care."

As night came, the 1st Battalion still held most of its original positions, except for the penetration that had split Company B. Yet the commander, Lt. Col. Robert H. Douglas, doubted how much longer he could hold on. Along the main road leading from Losheim to Losheimergraben, he was disturbingly aware, he had only about fifty men left, a heterogeneous group from various units that had coalesced around a platoon leader, 1st Lt. Dewey Plankers. If the Germans launched a strong thrust up the highway, that little group would be hardpressed to stop it.

With the authority of the commander of the 394th Infantry, Col. Don Riley, Douglas early that evening called on four platoons from the 3d Battalion, ostensibly the division reserve, to dig back-up positions astride the highway behind Losheimergraben. Yet by usurping those platoons, Douglas raised the possibility of the men of the 12th Volksgrenadier Division taking him in the rear, for even before the *Volksgrenadiers* had hit his battalion, they had struck the supposedly reserve positions of the 3d Battalion off his flank; and even though the Germans had absorbed considerable losses, they were still there.

Constituting the 99th Division's only reserve, the 3d Battalion, 394th Infantry, commanded by Maj. Norman A. Moore, was located in and around the little rural railroad depot that the Americans called Buchholz Station. Because one of the rifle companies had been sent as a reserve for the 395th Infantry's attack (and was to be committed later on the 16th to help Colonel Allen's battalion of the 393d Infantry), Moore had only two rifle companies, one of which he established at Buchholz Station; for even though the battalion was supposed to be in reserve, nobody else was defending the line of the railroad, which ran through a deep cut in the forested hills along the frontier and was an obvious route of advance should the Germans attack.

Not that Moore or anybody else in the 3d Battalion was expecting an attack any more than anybody else in the 99th Division or elsewhere in the Ardennes. Indeed, on the morning of the 16th, once the unusual phenomenon of German shelling had passed and nothing else had happened other than the appearance of a strange luminous glow on the horizon, the men of Company L began to prepare for breakfast. Their company kitchen having arrived at the position only the night before, they were anticipating their first full hot meal in several days.

The chow line had yet to form when somebody noticed a group of just over fifty men walking through the fog along either side of the railroad track. Somebody shouted, Who were those guys? One man thought they might be men of the company's Weapons Platoon coming for breakfast, but he yelled at them anyway to halt. When someone in the approaching group began shouting orders in German, 1st Sgt. Elmer Klug fired with his carbine.

For the other men of Company L, that was all the signal they needed. Everybody within sight of the German column opened fire. The Germans scattered, some into the woods on either side of the railroad, others to the protection of a freight car on the tracks. Cpl. George F. Bodnar managed to fire four bazooka rockets into the freight car but was unable to get close enough to assess the results.

Constituting the advance guard of the leading battalion of the 12th Volksgrenadier Division's 27th Regiment, the Germans had obviously been surprised, but their commander quickly fed in reinforcements. For the rest of the morning, fighting around the station and in the adjacent woods raged at close quarters, while Major Moore brought up his remaining rifle company to help. Some of the Germans reached the round-house close to the station, whereupon Tech. Sgt. Savino Travalini, leader of the battalion's Antitank Platoon, fired enough rockets from a bazooka to flush them, then cut them down with fire from his rifle when they tried to escape.

As German pressure eased around noon, Company L's cooks prepared to serve the long-delayed breakfast, but shells from German mortars and artillery rained down in such numbers that the meal was soon forgotten. The men of the 3d Battalion, 394th Infantry, were to get nothing to eat that day.

When the early night of the Ardennes winter closed in around the little railroad station, American troops still held the station and positions on either side, thus blocking the nearby road leading from Lanzerath to Honsfeld and a woods trail leading from the station into the rear of the 1st Battalion's positions at Losheimergraben. Yet the defenses were flimsy at best, made the more so after the regimental commander authorized sending the four platoons—more than half the 3d Battalion's remaining riflemen—to back up the positions at Losheimergraben. That prompted Major Moore to abandon the railroad station in order to put greater strength on the Honsfeld road (meaning only two platoons) and the trail.

In the day's fighting, the Germans had lost at least fifty killed and thirty captured, about equal to American losses. Yet to the little cluster of Americans who remained, it was obvious that the Germans would be back. As far as they knew, unless a small band of men of the 394th Infantry's I&R Platoon was still holding out nearby on a wooded hillock overlooking the village of Lanzerath, they were all that stood in the way to prevent the Germans from turning the south flank of the 99th Division.

Lyle Joseph Bouck, Jr., was anticipating nothing special for his birthday, which was December 17, but he had taken note that it was an important one, his twenty-first. Only two others among the seventeen men in the I&R Platoon, which Bouck commanded, were younger. Yet Bouck already had six years of military service behind him. In his home town of St. Louis, he had enlisted in the National Guard at the age of fourteen, and at eighteen he had completed Officer Candidate School at Fort Benning and been commissioned a second lieutenant. After assignment to the 99th Division, he had attracted the attention of the 394th Infantry's intelligence officer, Maj. Robert L. Kris, who picked him to command the regimental I&R Platoon. Its combat mission was just what the letters I and R stood for: intelligence and reconnaissance, which meant, mainly, patrolling.

Six days earlier the regimental commander, Colonel Riley, had ordered Lieutenant Bouck to go with his platoon to the vicinity of Lanzerath and pick a defensive position to serve as an outpost for the 99th Division's south flank. There was nothing on that flank, Riley knew, but the 14th Cavalry Group with a single cavalry reconnaissance squadron in the line, and the sector, Riley also knew, was the historic Losheim Gap. Any force penetrating into the gap might turn north to trap not only the 394th Infantry but the entire 99th Division. A single I&R Platoon could hardly be expected to stop a strong thrust, but it could give the alarm.

What Bouck and his men found was a readymade outpost. Some two months earlier, before the 4th Division (which had made the attack that captured the nearby Schnee Eifel) had left for another assignment, a battalion of that division's 12th Infantry had dug the foxholes to protect a flank abutting on the Losheim Gap. To Lieutenant Bouck, it seemed an excellent position. The foxholes were covered with logs and looked out from the edge of a fir forest onto a field sloping down to the highway that passed through Lanzerath, an extension of the International Highway. Not only were there good fields of fire onto the highway but also onto a road junction a few hundred yards outside Lanzerath where a road branched off and led past Buchholz Farm to Honsfeld. When the weather was clear, you could look over the tops of the houses in Lanzerath into a wide valley beyond, where lay the village of Losheim and the dragon's teeth and pillboxes of the Siegfried Line.

So ideal was the position as an outpost that Colonel Riley ignored the fact that it lay just outside the 99th Division's southern boundary and told Bouck to occupy it. As Bouck and his men moved in, they established contact with the crews of the four towed guns of the 820th Tank Destroyer Battalion and their supporting reconnaissance troops, who constituted the 14th Cavalry Group's little strongpoint in Lanzerath. Although Bouck was aware that such a small force as his could hardly be expected to hold at length, he was pleased with the commanding nature of his position, and he congratulated himself that he and his men had managed to accumulate more weapons than normally allotted an I&R Platoon: To augment their M-1 rifles, they had scrounged several BARs, two .30-caliber machine guns, and a .50-caliber machine gun mounted on a jeep.

The night of December 15, Lyle Bouck was wary. Every night since moving into the position, there had been strange noises rising from the valley beyond as if heavy vehicles were moving about. Did that portend what the intelligence officer, Major Kris, had warned him about, that there might be a German reaction to the attack under way to seize the Roer River dams? Taking no chances, he ordered every man to stay alert throughout the night.

Bouck and all his men were thus awake when at 5:30 A.M. the valley behind Losheim came alive with pinpricks of light on the horizon that soon turned into flickers. There followed the thunder of what seemed to be hundreds of guns, then the crash of shells on Lanzerath, and then right on top of the I&R Platoon's positions. Despite their foxhole cover, the men breathed with relief only after the barrage passed on beyond them in the direction of Buchholz Farm. Not long after that the sky lit up with a strange glow, made all the more eerie by a heavy fog.

A first cousin of Sanny Schür—in whose house some of the reconnaissance troops supporting the tank destroyers in Lanzerath lodged—Adolf Schür lived with his parents and an older brother at the northern edge of the village, just down the hill from the woodsline where six days earlier a small group of Americans had moved in. At sixteen years of age, Adolf was enjoying his friendship with the Americans in Lanzerath. They gave him and his family good-tasting canned food, sugar, and real coffee, and they taught him some English words. He was sure they were swear words and vulgarities, for the soldiers laughed when he repeated them, but Adolf liked the attention that afforded him.

Early in the morning of December 16, when the shelling began, Adolf took refuge with his family in the cellar; but when it had stopped, he hurried upstairs eager to see what might happen. Not long after daylight, he saw his American friends hitching their big guns to their half-tracks and heading north out of the village. That must mean the Germans were coming, but Adolf found it odd that the Americans would leave without firing a shot.

There was no time to determine whether the little group of Americans a hundred yards away at the woodsline on the hill was still there before German soldiers came marching up the road through the village. There was a line of men in the mottled uniforms of paratroopers on either side of the road, their rifles slung from their shoulders, not at all as if they expected trouble. A few dropped out of the column and entered the Schürs' house, ostensibly looking for a drink of water, but when they spotted the sugar and American rations that Adolf's mother was saving for Christmas, they took them, then rejoined the column outside.

Up on the hill, after recovering from the jolt of seeing the crews of the tank destroyers fleeing, Lieutenant Bouck puzzled over why no German attack had followed the heavy artillery barrage. With three of his men, he went into Lanzerath and from the second story of a house, looked out over the valley toward Losheim. Despite the fog, he could make out streams of German troops marching up the road from Losheim in his direction.

Hurrying back to the hilltop position, Bouck radioed his regimental headquarters what he had seen and begged for artillery fire on the approaching Germans, but the officer with whom he spoke obviously thought Bouck was out of his mind. No artillery fire followed.

Turning to his men, Bouck told them to get ready to fight. In view of the apparent size of the German force, most of the men wanted to withdraw, but Bouck ordered them to hold. From their commanding position, Bouck believed, they could do heavy damage to the German column.

The men were in their foxholes, their weapons trained across a snow-covered field onto the road below, when the first Germans emerged from the concealment of the barn attached to Adolf's house. Bouck told the men to hold their fire. The first Germans, he reasoned, were probably an advance guard; he wanted to wait until the main body was in his men's sights.

A hundred had passed when there was a break in the column, then a group of three men alone. That, thought Bouck, would be the command group. His runner, Private Tsakanikas (one of the few men in the platoon who was younger than Bouck) drew a bead on the three, and Bouck was about to give the order to shoot when a blond-haired girl of about thirteen emerged from a house beyond the road. Running to the three figures, she pointed uphill toward the I&R Platoon's positions.

Lest the child be killed, Bouck hesitated. In that split second, one of the Germans yelled something, and the column of paratroopers dived for the ditches on either side of the road.

From the barn of his father's house, Adolf Schür was watching. "Goddamn!" he muttered. "Mother fucker! Son of a bitch!"

The predictable attack—by what turned out to be a battalion of the 3d Parachute Division's 9th Regiment—soon followed. To Bouck and his men, it seemed stupid. The paratroopers had no fire support except for some men firing from the ditches along the road, no mortars, no artillery; but still they tried to rush the hundred yards uphill across an open, snow-covered field to get at the American position. To many in the I&R Platoon it was a painful assignment to fire at them. They could see their faces, and they were only kids. The fire caught some of them trying to cross a barbed-wire fence bisecting the field and left them hanging on the wire.

All the while Lieutenant Bouck was appealing by radio to headquarters of the 394th Infantry for artillery support. An officer finally told him there would be no artillery; all the guns were preoccupied on other missions.

"What shall we do then?" asked Bouck.

"Hold," the answer came back, "at all costs!"

Bouck pondered what that meant. Hold until every man was dead?

Around noon a white flag appeared; the Germans wanted to evacuate their wounded. At Bouck's order, the men held their fire, but no sooner was the task completed than the Germans returned to the assault just as before, frontal assault up the steep hill, by that time littered with German corpses. From beyond the road light mortars coughed some support, but because of the overhead cover on the foxholes, the fire did little damage.

In the barn next to the Schürs' house, Adolf's brother, Eric, and his father, Christolf, came up from the cellar to join Adolf. Christolf had been a drummer in the Great War. "Now," he told his sons, "you can see what war is really like."

Atop the hill, Lieutenant Bouck was again on the radio to his regiment. He was reiterating the vain requests for artillery support when what sounded like an explosion in his ear knocked him to the ground. A burst of automatic fire had struck his radio, destroying it. Only stunned, Bouck recovered quickly.

Conscious that ammunition was running low, Bouck told Tsakanikas to take whoever wanted to withdraw and get out, but Tsakanikas refused to go without Bouck. "No," said Bouck, "I have orders to hold at all costs. I'm staying."

Bouck was nevertheless beginning to have his doubts, for his men had accomplished about all they could. For the better part of a day they had occupied what appeared to be a German battalion and had frustrated any advance in the direction of Honsfeld into the division's exposed flank. Given the growing shortage of ammunition, he could hold little longer in any case. He called for two men to go to the regimental headquarters and return either with ammunition and reinforcements or with authority to withdraw; but neither man made it.

Down the hill in Lanzerath, a German sergeant, Vince Kühlbach, protested against continuing to attack the Americans across the open field, and in gathering dusk fifty Germans assembled behind the Schür house and began advancing against the flank of the position. As the darkness thickened, the paratroopers were soon in among the foxholes, pulling the occupants out at gunpoint, clearing one foxhole after another. A burst from a burp gun into the foxhole that Bouck shared with Tsakanikas caught Tsakanikas in the right side of his face, blowing out his right eyeball and leaving it "hanging limply in the cavern where his cheek had been." Bouck himself was hit in the leg.

Downhill, Adolf Schür was struck by the sudden silence. Soon he saw Americans coming down past his house, their helmets gone, their hands above their heads. Then came the wounded, not many, only five or six. A German soldier and an American lieutenant were supporting one man whose face looked as if it had been blown away. Adolf watched in morbid fascination and followed the procession until the wounded and their guards went into the Café Scholzen.

Inside the little tavern, Bouck and Tsakanikas lay on the floor beneath a cuckoo clock hanging on the wall. They had been there for what seemed to Bouck a long time when the clock signaled midnight. It was December 17. He was twenty-one years old, thought Bouck; he had become a man.

Because American commanders had anticipated that the Germans would make some kind of riposte in response to the attack on the Roer River dams, their first reaction early on the morning of December 16 was that that was what was happening. At 8:30 A.M., the former commander of the 1st Infantry Division, Maj. Gen. C. Ralph Huebner, who was acting as deputy commander of the V Corps in anticipation of assuming command when General Gerow moved up to take command of a new army headquarters, visited General Lauer at headquarters of the 99th Division in the town of Bütgenbach, and the two agreed that that was the case. From a forward headquarters in the village of Wirtzfeld behind the twin villages of Krinkelt-Rocherath, the commander of the 2d Division, General Robertson, was at first unaware that anything untoward was happening other than the unusually heavy German artillery fire just before dawn; yet that, too, could have been a predictable reaction to the attack by Robertson's troops at Wahlerscheid.

The first indication Robertson had that the 99th Division might be in trouble came later in the morning in a roundabout way via a telephone call to Robertson's artillery commander, Brig. Gen. John H. Hinds. The caller identified himself as a captain on the 99th Division's staff and asked for loan of the battalion of towed tank destroyers that was attached to the 2d Division. Hinds thought it so strange that a junior officer should make the request and to him, the artillery commander, rather than to Robertson, that he reported the call immediately to Robertson. Concerned as he had been since the start of his division's attack lest the Germans cut the lone road leading to his attacking regiments, Robertson hurried with Hinds to the 99th Division's headquarters in an imposing villa in Bütgenbach.

What they found appalled them. The living room of the house was in tumult, crowded with enlisted men and officers, everybody seemingly trying to talk at once, and at one side of the room the division commander himself, General Lauer, playing a piano—as was his wont in times of crisis.

"Can't we go to your CP where we can talk?" Robertson asked above the din.

"This *is* my CP," replied Lauer.

As Robertson discerned the situation from Lauer, the Germans had attacked the 99th Division at several points, but Lauer insisted he had matters in hand. On the basis of the confusion at the command post, Robertson was inclined to think otherwise.

Robertson and General Hinds headed back for Wirtzfeld more concerned than ever about the 2d Division's lone supply route, and the thought struck Robertson that he had better begin considering withdrawal from the attack at Wahlerscheid. Yet his mission still was to exploit the capture of the pillboxes, and barring a change in orders, that had to have priority. To increase his forces for the exploitation, he directed the commander of his reserve regiment, the 23d Infantry, to begin moving his regiment forward. A battalion was soon on the way to a bivouac alongside the forest road a mile or so beyond the twin villages.

Before noon, Robertson learned that he was to lose the combat command of the 9th Armored Division that had been attached to his division to help in the drive for the Roer River dams. That, Robertson assumed, was a result of the German attack against the 106th Division in the 2d Division's old defensive positions near St. Vith, word of which reached Robertson through the corps commander, General Gerow.

Gerow, like Robertson, was worried. Early in the afternoon he asked the commander of the First Army, General Hodges, for authority to call off the 2d Division's attack and move the division back to the positions he had charted earlier on the Elsenborn Ridge. Obviously less concerned than Gerow about what might be developing, Hodges refused.

In mid-afternoon, Gerow telephoned Robertson, ordering him—apparently at General Lauer's request—to release the two remaining battalions of his reserve, the 23d Infantry, for attachment to the 99th Division. One battalion was to go to the village of Hünningen, a short distance behind the Losheimergraben crossroads and the positions of the 394th Infantry, there to occupy defensive positions that Lauer, in concern for the fragile nature of his division's south flank, had ordered dug long before. The other battalion was to move into the forest east of Krinkelt-Rocherath and at dawn on the 17th attack to restore the positions of Colonel Allen's 3d Battalion, 393d Infantry.

That General Lauer would ask the help of those two battalions told Robertson something of how serious Lauer's situation had become. He had almost decided to take it on himself to halt his division's attack and withdraw when he had a visit from Gerow's deputy, Ralph Huebner. Both were convinced that the 2d Division should withdraw. As Huebner departed, he told Robertson: "Go slow and watch your step; the overall situation is not good."

No division commander as experienced as Robertson was could have been unaware of the precarious position of his command. All three battalions of the 9th Infantry and two of the 38th were fighting at

Wahlerscheid—those of the 9th Infantry seriously depleted by the heavy fighting for the road junction—and the remaining battalion of the 38th Infantry was well forward in reserve. A battalion of the 23d Infantry was also forward, as were two battalions of the 2d Division's artillery, even more dependent than the infantry, should it come to withdrawal, on the single road leading back through the dense forest to Krinkelt-Rocherath. The 99th Division's 395th Infantry also depended upon that road for survival.

Hardly had Huebner left Robertson's command post than Robertson, without notifying General Gerow, telephoned the commanders of his two attacking regiments and told them to halt their attacks and hold where they were. Although he added an order to renew the attacks the next morning, he left the hour open, and the attacks were to be launched only on his specific command.

That done, Robertson went forward up the critical road to ensure that both regimental commanders fully understood what they were to do and that they alerted their battalions to begin planning for withdrawal. Then back in his headquarters in a farmhouse on the edge of Wirtzfeld, he and his chief of staff, Col. Ralph W. Zwicker, sat up well past midnight refining the withdrawal plan.

At the 99th Division's headquarters a few miles away in Bütgenbach, General Lauer exhibited far less concern. Lauer was exceedingly proud of the way his inexperienced troops had fought that day, and nowhere had there been a penetration in depth. At midnight, he reported personally by telephone to General Gerow that he had heard from all his units, and his "entire front was practically established on its original line—that the situation was in hand and all quiet." Yet his south flank, he added, did have him "considerably worried."

Lauer's report was far more optimistic than the actual situation justified and was particularly strange in that Lauer knew that men of the 394th Infantry's Company A had captured a copy of Field Marshal von Rundstedt's order telling his troops that their "great hour" had arrived: "WE GAMBLE EVERYTHING!" Lauer hardly could have continued to believe that his division was encountering a mere local reaction to the attack for the Roer River dams.

Admittedly, Lauer did have the added strength of the battalion of the 23d Infantry in the woods east of Krinkelt-Rocherath and of the other battalion moving into prepared positions at Hünningen. The battalion at Hünningen would help strengthen the division's southern flank, about which Lauer was so concerned. Although he knew nothing of the fate of the 394th Infantry's I&R Platoon outside Lanzerath, he knew he still had some troops near Buchholz Station, and not far away at Honsfeld the commander of the 394th Infantry's rest center was forming a provisional company from men who had been at the center to defend the village.

Thus there was at least a shield—albeit thin—covering the division's southern flank.

On the German side of the International Highway, the commanders were markedly disappointed with the results of the first day's fight. Most had expected that as early as 7 A.M.—and surely well before nightfall—columns of the 1st and 12th SS Panzer Divisions would have been well past the forward American positions on their way to the Meuse. Yet nowhere had there been a penetration sufficient for the panzers to exploit.

One man who was particularly concerned was Otto Skorzeny, whose special brigade was to follow the panzer divisions. Trying to go forward to Losheim to find out what was happening, he encountered roads so jammed with vehicles and horse-drawn artillery that he had to walk almost six miles to get there. Since it was obvious the day's objectives were out of reach, and since the success of Operation *GREIF* depended upon surprise and speed, he was tempted to call off the operation. Yet if the panzer divisions got through that night or early the next morning, he decided finally, there still might be a chance of reaching the Meuse, in which case his men's seizing the bridges "could be decisive."

For his part, the commander of the 1st SS Panzer Corps, General Priess, was fuming. Having already ordered a battalion of *SS-Panzergrenadiers* to try to achieve a breakthrough in the direction of Krinkelt-Rocherath, he told the commander of the 12th SS Panzer Division, Brigade-fuhrer der Waffen-SS Hugo Kraas, to commit two more battalions of *SS-Panzergrenadiers* supported by two companies of Mark IV tanks and two companies of Panthers. When Kraas protested the attachment of his tanks to the 277th Volksgrenadier Division, Priess relented and put Kraas himself in charge. From that point, the assignment of breaking through the forest to Krinkelt-Rocherath fell to the 12th SS Panzer Division with such help as the badly depleted 277th Volksgrenadiers might provide.

In front of Losheimergraben, the commander of the 12th Volksgrenadier Division, Generalmajor Gerhard Engel, exhorted the commander of his tank destroyer battalion, Major Holz, to bring his assault guns into play at the crossroads. At the same time an even more determined commander, Joachim Peiper, arrived on the scene a few miles to the south at Lanzerath.

Shortly before midnight, Peiper pushed his way into the Café Scholzen. On the dingy floor wounded Germans and Americans were sprawled against the walls. Under a cuckoo clock mounted on one wall slumped an American lieutenant holding a soldier who had lost part of his face and was bleeding profusely over the lieutenant's uniform. Other Germans seemed simply to have chosen the tavern as a place to sleep. What was the matter? Had everybody simply "gone to bed instead of waging war?"

Peiper was already in a foul mood. All day he had waited, his tanks and half-tracks using up precious gasoline in traffic jams, and still no penetration to spring his column loose. In the end he had simply plowed his way forward, ordering his tank commanders, if they had to, to run down the horse-drawn artillery that was clogging the roads. Then to arrive at the Café Scholzen and find that everybody appeared to have called off the war for the night.

Locating the commander of the 9th Parachute Regiment, Col. Helmüt von Hofmann, Peiper learned that he was delaying his attack until morning because the woods between Lanzerath and Honsfeld were heavily fortified, defended by at least a battalion, and the road was mined. Had he personally reconnoitered the American positions? demanded Peiper, uncaring that as a lieutenant colonel he was grilling a senior officer. Well, no, replied von Hofmann, but . . .

In disgust, Peiper demanded that the colonel reinforce him with one of his parachute infantry battalions. He was going through.

CHAPTER NINE

Reaction at the Top

At fifty-one years of age, Omar Nelson Bradley still had a touch of rural Missouri about him. He spoke with a high-pitched voice in a flat Midwestern accent. His hair was thinning and his ears protruded. To many, he had the air of a schoolteacher, as well he might, for his father had been one in Missouri and he himself had spent thirteen of his first twenty-three years of commissioned service teaching either in the ROTC, at West Point, or at The Infantry School.

It was at The Infantry School at Fort Benning that Bradley had first come into contact with a man who was destined to become the U.S. Army's chief of staff and to make an indelible imprint on the conduct of the war: George Catlett Marshall. Bradley's class of 1915 at West Point would be known as "The Class the Stars Fell On"—fifty-nine of them became general officers—and a number who received their stars, including Dwight D. Eisenhower and Omar Bradley, could attribute their accession in large measure to the fact that George Marshall recognized their talents.

On the morning of December 16, Omar Bradley awoke in his room in the Hôtel Alfa, looking out over the Place de Metz in Luxembourg City, to confront a dismal day: cold, damp, foggy. It came as little surprise when at breakfast in the hotel's plain ground-floor restaurant his aide, Lt. Col. Chester B. Hansen, told him that it would be impossible to fly to a scheduled appointment with General Eisenhower at SHAEF's main headquarters in Versailles. Yet Bradley considered the business to be discussed so significant that he determined to proceed by car. Indeed, in order to stress its importance, he planned to accompany his personnel officer, Brig. Gen. Joseph J. ("Red") O'Hare, on the first leg of a trip to Washington, where O'Hare was to press the War Department for more infantry replacements for the European Theater.

To get an early start on the four-hour drive, Bradley decided to forgo the usual nine fifteen situation briefing at his headquarters, but as it turned out, he missed nothing of significance. As his olive drab Cadillac sedan threaded through the fog-enshrouded streets of Luxembourg City and out onto an icy highway leading to Verdun and Paris, a briefing officer from the operations section was noting that there had been little change along any part of the front. That included the sectors of the First Army's V and VIII Corps. When a briefing officer from the intelligence section had his say, he noted that the 326th Volksgrenadier Division had been identified moving north through the Eifel, which, he added, "might be the answer to the numerous vehicular movements in the northern VIII Corps sector." Nobody yet knew anything of the portentous events already taking place in the Ardennes—searchlights, heavy artillery fire, ground attacks—which at one point were occurring little more than twenty miles away.

After a stop for lunch in a transient officers' mess at the Ritz in Paris, Bradley and his party went on to Versailles, reaching Eisenhower's headquarters in the Trianon Palace Hotel early in the afternoon. They found the Supreme Commander in a pleasant mood: He had learned earlier in the day of his promotion to the rank of General of the Army, which carried with it five stars, the equivalent of field marshal in other armies. He had also just had an enjoyable diversion, the wedding of his orderly, Mickey McKeough, to a soldier from the headquarters, Pearlie Hargreaves.

It was late afternoon—almost dusk—when a colonel from SHAEF's G-2 section tiptoed into the room where Eisenhower, Bradley, O'Hare, and several members of Eisenhower's staff were talking. He handed a note to Eisenhower's G-2, General Strong. Glancing at it, Strong interrupted the conference to say that the Germans had attacked at five points along the front of the VIII Corps. Although the attacks had begun early in the morning, there was as yet no word as to their size or extent.

As Strong moved over toward a situation map to indicate the points of enemy attack, Bradley found it impossible to believe that the enemy could be launching more than a spoiling attack with perhaps four to six divisions, designed to upset the First Army's attack for the Roer River dams and the Third Army's impending attack against the Saar industrial region south of the Ardennes. After all, only a few days earlier Bradley's G-2, General Sibert, had remarked on the "critical dilemma" faced by the German command, and even General Strong, who had warned of possible enemy action in the Ardennes, had spoken only of "a relieving attack."

A short while later a message arrived indicating that eight German divisions not previously identified on the Ardennes front were involved in the attacks. Recalling how Bradley on a number of occasions had wished for the Germans to come out of their pillboxes and fight in the open, Eisenhower's chief of staff, Bedell Smith, put a hand on Bradley's shoulder. "Well, Brad," he said, "you've been wishing for a counterattack. Now it looks as though you've got it."

"A counterattack, yes," replied Bradley, "but I'll be damned if I wanted one this big."

Yet Bradley was still unconvinced that the Germans were launching anything more than a spoiling attack. No, said Eisenhower, it was no spoiling attack. (Eisenhower, apparently through the MAGIC intercepts of Baron Oshima's messages, knew something Bradley did not know.) Calling for a situation map that showed two American armored divisions out of the line, the 7th Armored Division with the Ninth Army in the north and the 10th Armored Division with the Third Army in the south, Eisenhower said he thought Bradley should "send Middleton some help. These two armored divisions."

Still Bradley caviled. While agreeing that it would be prudent to shift the two divisions, to remove a division from the Third Army just as General Patton was preparing to launch a big offensive was bound to upset Patton. "Tell him," Eisenhower came back, "that Ike is running this damn war."

When Bradley got Patton on the telephone, Patton was indeed irate. It was nothing more than a spoiling attack, Patton insisted, and Troy Middleton could handle that himself. "I hate like hell to do it, George," Bradley responded, "but I've got to have that division. Even if it's only a spoiling attack as you say, Middleton must have help." That done, Bradley telephoned his staff in Luxembourg City with instructions to tell General Simpson of the Ninth Army to put the 7th Armored Division on the road. He also directed both Patton and Simpson to alert any other divisions that were out of the line for a possible move to the Ardennes.

Bradley and Eisenhower had dinner that night in Eisenhower's imposing requisitioned stone villa in nearby St. Germain-en-Laye, a villa earlier occupied by Field Marshal von Rundstedt. Afterwards, they "cracked a bottle of champagne" to celebrate Eisenhower's promotion and played five rubbers of bridge.

Shortly before eleven, as the two were at the point of retiring, they learned of a message just received in SHAEF's ULTRA room in an attic above the palace stables. Bletchley Park had intercepted and decrypted a signal ordering the German air command in the Netherlands, Jägdkorps II, to be prepared the next morning, the 17th, to "support the attack of 5 and 6 Armies." Eisenhower and Bradley could hardly have been unaware that that meant the Fifth and Sixth Panzer Armies.

After Bradley finally got to bed around midnight, he found it difficult to fall asleep, and when he did, he slept fitfully.

In an age of virtually instantaneous communications by telephone, telegraph, and radio, it was taking a surprisingly long time for information about the German offensive to reach Eisenhower's headquarters.

Except for the late night flash from Bletchley Park, there was, even more than eighteen hours after the start of the German artillery preparation, little to go on.

The artillery preparation itself was in large measure responsible. Almost everywhere the shelling knocked out telephone lines leading from front-line units, and even in experienced regiments, rear headquarters were often slow in the wee hours to realize that lines were out and switch on their radios. Add to that the time it took an officer to pass a message to a corporal or a sergeant for transmission to the message center, then the time it took the message to move up the chain of command: from battalion to regiment to division to corps to army to army group to SHAEF. So, too, as with intelligence reports, there was a process of selection: What was important enough to pass up the line? Although there was no problem with telephone lines at corps level and above, the two corps headquarters were slow to get solid information to pass along. And for some reason, neither Eisenhower nor Bradley deigned to pick up the telephone and talk directly with the senior commander most intimately concerned, Courtney Hodges of the First Army.

In early afternoon, the text of von Rundstedt's hortatory field order to the German troops, captured by the 99th Division's 394th Infantry, reached headquarters of the First Army, whence it passed quickly to headquarters of the 12th Army Group. It stopped there. Not until early the next morning were Eisenhower and Bradley in Versailles to learn of it, and then it was by means of an ULTRA intercept sent from Bletchley Park:

> Rundstedt on sixteenth informed soldiers of West Front that hour of destiny had struck. Mighty offensive armies faced Allies. Everything at stake. More than mortal deeds for Fatherland and Führer. A quote holy duty unquote.

No American commander on the Western Front had more concern for the men serving under him than did Courtney Hicks Hodges, commander of the First Army. He personally saw to it that towns behind the line were set aside as rest centers for the exclusive use of combat troops, where, by his direction, the men were to eat, drink, loaf, and "do whatever they wish within the limits of propriety." On at least one occasion, he told his jeep driver to halt while he got out to stand by the road as trucks sloshed past carrying bearded, grimy, bone-tired infantrymen of the 4th Division from the fighting in the Hürtgen Forest. As he watched, tears came to his eyes. "I wish," he said, "everybody could see them."

Hodges's concern may have stemmed from the fact that only he among all the senior U.S. commanders in Europe had seen war at the level where men do the dying. In charge of a machine-gun company in the grim Meuse–Argonne campaign of World War I, he had received the nation's second highest award for valor, the Distinguished Service Cross. So, too, only he among the senior commanders had served as an enlisted man. Having failed geometry in his plebe year at West Point, Hodges had joined the army as a private but had earned a commission only a year behind his former classmates at the Military Academy.

With gray hair and mustache (he was six years older than Bradley), Hodges looked more businessman than soldier. Georgia born, he was soft-spoken. He was also taciturn. Lacking personal eccentricities, he seemed essentially colorless, but both Bradley and Eisenhower thought highly of him. His only fault, it seemed to Eisenhower, was that "God gave him a face that always looked pessimistic." Bradley had "implicit faith in his judgment, skill, and restraint."

Hodges and Bradley had served together at the Army War College and on the faculty of The Infantry School (where Hodges, too, impressed George Marshall and where Bradley later succeeded Hodges as commandant). When Bradley commanded the First Army in the invasion of Normandy, Hodges was his deputy, serving with the sure knowledge that after Bradley moved up to command an army group, Hodges was to get the First Army. Inheriting Bradley's staff (with the exception of the G-1, Red O'Hare, whom Bradley took with him), Hodges made no changes, for he himself had helped select most of the officers.

Shortly before 7 A.M. on December 16, as Hodges—still bothered by a head cold—was preparing to sit down to breakfast in his requisitioned villa outside Spa, he received first word of enemy action in the Ardennes: German attacks against the cavalry in the Losheim Gap and "the heaviest artillery fire ever received in the 28th Division area." Hodges went quickly to his office in the Hôtel Britannique, where news of other attacks all along the line as far south as Echternach soon came in, some "in large patrol strength and others in battalion strength."

On the basis of the early reports, Hodges perceived the greatest threat to be against the 106th Division and in the Losheim Gap. Just before ten thirty, he directed General Gerow of the V Corps to release Combat Command B of the 9th Armored Division from attachment to the 2d Division and turn it over to Troy Middleton of the VIII Corps to be used to help the 106th Division. At noon, Hodges ordered the commander of the VII Corps in the vicinity of Aachen, Maj. Gen. J. Lawton Collins, to place a regiment of the 1st Infantry Division, which had recently come out of the line after fighting in the Hürtgen Forest, on six-hour alert for possible movement to the Ardennes. An hour later he told Collins to put the entire 1st Division on six-hour alert along with a combat command of the 3d Armored Division. Even so, when Gee Gerow telephoned to ask authority to call off the 2d Division's attack for the Roer River dams, Hodges said no. If the Germans were trying to divert that attack, why give them what they were after?

The news in early afternoon of the capture of von Rundstedt's order would seem to have made it clear that more than a spoiling attack was under way, even more so because the order bore an endorsement from the commander of the 12th Volksgrenadier Division, General Engel: "This call to arms to be made known to all soldiers without exception at once before beginning of attack." Yet that fact occasioned no particular alarm.

Hodges's junior liaison officers, whom he always maintained at the divisions to keep his headquarters informed, were reporting that even though some companies and battalions had given ground and some were isolated, there had been no major German penetration and nobody saw the situation as critical. (As late as 4:15 P.M., the 28th Division, which all along its extended front was under heavy attack, reported that "the situation for the division is well in hand.") Furthermore, in late afternoon Hodges received word from the 12th Army Group that he was to get the 7th and 10th Armored Divisions. Hodges was "neither optimistic nor pessimistic," but on the evidence he had received to that point, he believed not only that he could "handle" the attack but that it afforded an opportunity to inflict heavy losses on the enemy.

Nevertheless, before retiring for the evening, he ordered the 1st Division to send one of its regiments immediately to help the 99th Division, and by midnight the 26th Infantry was on the way. He had still to retire when a German plane strafed the road in front of his villa and dropped two bombs nearby.

Shortly after Hodges finally went to bed that night of December 16, word came through a radio intercept from the XXIX Tactical Air Command, which supported the Ninth Army, that planes were preparing to take off from airfields east of the Rhine near Paderborn to drop parachutists behind the First Army's lines. Somebody on Hodges's staff alerted the guard at the gatehouse in front of the villa to watch for parachutists and doubled the guard.

At two other headquarters buildings within Belgium, there was no such ambiguity. The V Corps was based in the Belgian Army's physical training institute on Bellmerin Strasse, Eupen; the VIII Corps had its headquarters in a red-tiled caserne in Bastogne that belonged to the Belgian Army. At both headquarters, the capture of von Rundstedt's order removed any doubt about what the Germans were up to. For the VIII Corps there was an additional indication with the 106th Division's capture of the order providing details of Skorzeny's Operation *GREIF*, and on the body of a fallen officer of the 116th Panzer Division someone found not only a copy of von Rundstedt's order but similar orders issued by Field Marshal Model and General von Manteuffel.

Model: We will not disappoint the Führer and the Fatherland, who created the sword of retribution. Forward in the spirit of Leuthen!

> *Von Manteuffel:* Forward, march, march! In remembrance of our dead comrades, and therefore on their order, and in remembrance of the tradition of our proud Wehrmacht!

In passing along those orders and von Rundstedt's, the VIII Corps G-2, Colonel Reeves, noted: "These documents indicate the scope of the German offensive, and its importance becomes apparent from the impressive list of high-ranking German generals whose signatures appear thereon. The GRIEF operation appears to be a part of a large-scale offensive."

Gerow and Middleton also discounted the optimistic reports from some of their units, such as that from the 28th Division that all was "well in hand." Middleton was all the while getting full and candid reports from the inexperienced Jones of the 106th Division (who had yet to learn the old dodge that one's own command looks better if the enemy's successes appear to be less), and it was clearly obvious that something serious was happening in the Losheim Gap. Gerow, too, received cheerful reports, the 99th Division telephoning that "by 1130 hours we had practically restored our line to its former positions," but that failed to deter him from asking Hodges's permission to call off the 2d Division's attack and pull the division back to the Elsenborn Ridge.

At the headquarters of the 12th Army Group across from the railroad station in Luxembourg City, there was no such view of what the Germans were trying to accomplish. "The sudden attacks and seemingly overpowering array of six enemy divisions . . . should not be misinterpreted," wrote General Sibert. "The quality of divisions involved, the piecemeal efforts to launch small-scale attacks and the apparent lack of long range objectives would seem to limit the enemy threat." Sibert in fact saw the enemy's attack much as did his boss, General Bradley, back in Versailles, as "a diversionary attack" to disrupt the American attacks north and south of the Ardennes. "Until the magnitude of the enemy's attack increases in more cohesive action or until one or more elements of the Sixth SS [*sic*] Panzer Army are committed. . . ." Sibert concluded, "the day's events cannot be regarded as a major long term threat."

The key phrase was "piecemeal efforts." That looked to Sibert to be the case partly because of erratic reports from the front and partly because the inexperienced German troops were generally slow to follow up their artillery fire, so that there was no impression of one grand assault. Yet those attacks still occurred over an extended front, all the way from Monschau in the north to Echternach in the south. Should not that fact in itself have conveyed some meaning?

Whether the ex-journalist, Ralph Ingersoll, massaged that report or not, what it had to say was clear. The intelligence section at headquarters of the 12th Army Group was as yet unprepared to go back on its earlier miscalculation of what the enemy was capable of doing. General Sibert nevertheless put somebody to work trying to contact the First Army's G-2, Monk Dickson, on leave in Paris. The word finally got through to Dickson: Sibert suggested that he make his way as quickly as possible to Luxembourg City.

Among the German army commanders, there was disappointment that in the first day of the grand offensive they had gained considerably less than they had intended. Yet there was no despair. He who had expected the least, General Brandenberger, was the most optimistic: He considered that his Seventh Army was close to a breakthrough. For General von Manteuffel, the Fifth Panzer Army's gains "did not come up to expectations," but he hoped to make up for lost time by continuing to attack through the night. There was more concern in the Sixth Panzer Army, if not with the commander, General Dietrich, then with his more pragmatic chief of staff, General Kraemer. He thought the unexpectedly strong resistance from Monschau to Losheimergraben was predicated upon his enemy's expectation of rapid reinforcement from the north, and because the 326th Volksgrenadier Division had failed to break through at Monschau and von der Heydte's parachutists had failed to jump, there was nothing to keep those reinforcements from arriving.

In late afternoon, Kraemer himself telephoned von der Heydte, telling him it was vital for his parachutists to jump that night and block the highway leading south across the Hautes Fagnes. "Hold on as long as possible," Kraemer told him, "two days as a minimum, and do as much damage as you can to the reinforcements."

From the first, Friedrich von der Heydte had been concerned about the inexperience of his young parachutists and when he learned the background of the Luftwaffe crews that were to fly him to the drop zone, he was appalled. Although the crews belonged to the renowned "Stalingrad Squadron," which had flown supplies to Field Marshal Paulus's besieged troops at Stalingrad, the only man remaining who had actually flown those missions was the squadron commander. None of the others had ever dropped parachutists in a combat operation; none had ever flown a combat mission of any kind; and none had ever flown his Junkers 52 aircraft at night. Von der Heydte could see nothing ahead but disaster.

When most of the parachutists failed to reach the airfields on the night of December 15, von der Heydte hoped with some degree of fervor that the operation might be canceled. Headquarters of the Sixth Panzer Army quickly sent an investigating officer to conduct a formal inquiry into von der Heydte's failure to take off, and von der Heydte was clearly under suspicion of sabotaging the operation. (Was he not a cousin of the officer who had planted the bomb back in July in the plot to kill the Führer?) Yet General Kraemer's order to jump on the night of the 16th ended both the investigation and von der Heydte's fervent hopes of a cancellation.

Just before midnight, 112 Junkers 52s began to taxi to take-off positions on two airfields near Paderborn. By tradition, von der Heydte as commander was in the leading pathfinder plane and would jump first. He would be jumping with his right arm in a splint, hurt a few weeks before in an airplane accident in Italy.

As the planes took off and searchlights lit up one by one to guide them to and over the Rhine, von der Heydte began to have some hope that the inexperienced pilots and navigators might yet deliver his troops to the correct drop zone. In time, he could make out the trace of the front, distinguishable by the flash of artillery pieces and the light of smoldering buildings. As the planes flew over, there was no mistaking it, for to help maintain formation, the pilots were flying with their navigation lights on, and heavy antiaircraft fire erupted. When they were over the drop zone, the pathfinder planes dropped incendiary bombs to mark it, and von der Heydte—his right arm strapped to his side—dove into the night.

As he neared the ground a strong wind seized his parachute, and when he landed, the impact knocked him unconscious. When at last he came to his senses, he found himself alone. Taking a compass bearing, he began to walk toward the designated rendezvous, a road junction known as Belle Croix astride the north-south highway leading across the moors.

There he found 20 of his men—20 out of 1,200. Others were to turn up in time, but for the most part the planes had scattered the parachutists all the way from the Rhine to the Hautes Fagnes and some far to the north in the sector of the Ninth U.S. Army beyond Aachen.

In the *Adlerhorst* amid the forested hills of the Taunus, Field Marshal von Rundstedt made no effort to spare his Führer his own pessimistic evaluation of the first day's events. There was no question, he said, that the offensive had achieved total surprise, yet the main effort by the Sixth Panzer Army had failed to achieve a penetration. That meant a loss of at least a day, making it questionable whether the army could reach the Meuse.

The report infuriated Hitler. The weight of the Sixth Panzer Army's SS panzer divisions had yet to be felt, he said. Once they got going, they would "crush everything before them."

When the briefing was over, well after midnight—late nights were commonplace with the Führer—Hitler got on the telephone to the commander of Army Group G, General der Panzertruppen Hermann Balck, who was responsible for the front south of the Ardennes. Balck thought at first he was in for yet another diatribe admonishing him to hold fast, yield not a foot of ground, but he soon found that the Führer had something different to say.

Good old dependable Dietrich, said Hitler, had punched a hole in the Losheim Gap, and *Kampfgruppe Peiper* was poised for the march to the Meuse. Von Manteuffel was encircling the Schnee Eifel, already had tanks on the heights overlooking Clervaux, and would be on the way to Bastogne and the Meuse as soon as it was daylight. And the weather! The forecast was for more of the same—fog, drizzle, perhaps some light snow, but in any case, weather to keep Allied planes on the ground.

Despite himself, Balck, a hardened old soldier, became caught up in his Führer's enthusiasm.

"Balck! Balck!" Hitler exulted. "Everything has changed in the West! Success—complete success—is now in our grasp!"

The reality of what actually happened on that first day lay somewhere in between Hitler's elation and the incomprehension of Omar Bradley and Edwin Sibert of the 12th Army Group. Bradley and Sibert were finding it difficult to accept that the German blow in the Ardennes was a major offensive ("No Goddamned fool would do it!"), and Hitler was reading more into his armies' successes than was actually there.

In the far south, all four divisions of Erich Brandenberger's Seventh Army had crossed the Our and Sûre Rivers, which in view of the thin American positions was hardly to have been prevented; but unknown to Brandenberger, he was soon to be facing American reserves. At Marnach, von Manteuffel's tanks were indeed "on the heights overlooking Clervaux"; but everywhere else the 28th Division's 110th Infantry was still making a fight of it, and how soon von Manteuffel's two panzer corps could get across the Clerve River and on with the drive for Bastogne and the Meuse remained to be seen. So, too, the 28th Division's 112th Infantry was still holding firm.

From the American viewpoint, the most critical sector as night fell on December 16 was the Losheim Gap and the threatened encirclement of two regiments of the 106th Division on the Schnee Eifel. Yet there, too, it remained to be seen how long it would take von Manteuffel's *Volksgrenadier* divisions to gain St. Vith and open the roadnet in the vicinity, a roadnet critical for sustaining a broad-based advance to the Meuse. Since the cavalry at Monschau and the 99th Division at Höfen and along the International Highway had stopped the Sixth Panzer Army's *Volksgrenadier* divisions, the critical sector for the Germans, too, was the Losheim Gap; for in northern reaches of the gap, Joachim Peiper, as Hitler said, was genuinely "poised for the march to the Meuse."

Despite the fight put up by the men of the 99th Division, which, as von Rundstedt noted, had produced a delay of at least a day in the quest for the Meuse, chances for a breakthrough along the International Highway were good, particularly east of Krinkelt-Rocherath where the 12th SS Panzer Division was getting ready to take over the assignment. If the added weight of tanks could produce a quick breakthrough there, the

Germans would score a success they had no inkling of, for they would trap the 2d Division. The 12th SS Panzer Division would also be past the first big hurdle in a drive for the Meuse close along the flank of *Kampfgruppe Peiper* and the 1st SS Panzer Division.

Nevertheless, except in gaining total surprise, nowhere on December 16 had the Germans achieved any of their first day's goals. The soldiers whom Hitler saw as "the Italians" of the Allied side—how could a nation as heterogeneous as the United States of America, with its mixture of ethnic and racial types, field a capable fighting force?—had nowhere turned and run. When men in foxholes refuse to admit overwhelming odds, advance through or past them may be inevitable, but it is seldom either easy or swift.

III

THE PENETRATIONS

CHAPTER TEN

Kampfgruppe Peiper

Handsome, "well bred . . . dashing and resourceful," Joachim Peiper at a youthful twenty-nine brought to the Ardennes long months of combat experience in Russia, where he had risen from command of one of the 1st SS Panzer Division's *Panzergrenadier* battalions to command of the division's panzer regiment. He had been awarded Nazi Germany's highest award for valor, the Knight's Cross of the Iron Cross, and had earned the admiration of his troops for bravery, sangfroid, and ruthlessness. He personally led a night attack on the village of Pekartschina with flamethrowers mounted on his half-tracks and burned the village to the ground—other units of the division called Peiper's *SS-Panzergrenadiers* the "Blowtorch Battalion." In one drive, the panzer regiment under Peiper's command claimed 2,500 Russians killed and only 3 captured, which was testimony to the brutality, fanaticism, and mounting desperation that characterized the ideological, racist war in the East, at least as Peiper practiced it. Many of the men who came with Peiper to the Ardennes had also experienced that savagery.

Peiper received his orders for what his superiors called "the decisive role in the offensive" three days before the start of the attack from the commander of the 1st SS Panzer Corps, General Priess. In the course of the briefing, Priess passed along an order of the day from the Sixth Panzer Army's commander, General Dietrich, which reflected Hitler's exhortation to his senior commanders at the *Adlerhorst*. The offensive represented "the decisive hour of the German people" and thus was to be conducted with "a wave of terror and fright" and without "humane inhibitions."

As Peiper himself later recalled the order, the German soldiers were to be reminded of "the innumerable German victims of the bombing terror." He was also "nearly certain" that "it was expressly stated that prisoners of war must be shot where the local conditions of combat should so require it." Although that proviso was incorporated into the

Kampfgruppe's order for the attack, Peiper himself made no mention of it in his oral briefing to his commanders, for they "were all experienced officers to whom this was obvious."

The word to kill prisoners nevertheless reached almost all subordinate units. One company commander enjoined his men to "fight in the old SS spirit," and added: "I am not giving you orders to shoot prisoners of war, but you are all well-trained SS soldiers. You know what you should do with prisoners without me telling you that." A private recalled that not only were they to take no prisoners but "civilians who show themselves on the streets or at the windows will be shot without mercy." One non-commissioned officer urged his men to think of the thousands of German women and children buried in the rubble of German cities; then they would know "what you as SS men have to do in case you capture American soldiers." The offensive was aimed at "the murderers of our mothers, fathers, and children."

Serious questions were to arise later as to the methods through which those testimonials, including Peiper's, were elicited. On the other hand, it would be hard to maintain that all that was about to happen in abject violation of the basic rules of international warfare was the result of nothing more than spontaneous reaction to the pressures of the battlefield.

Kampfgruppe Peiper was a powerful force of approximately four thousand men. Peiper had seventy-two medium tanks, almost equally divided between Mark IVs and Mark Vs (Panthers), roughly the equivalent of one and a half American tank battalions. He also had five flak tanks; a light flak battalion with self-propelled multiple 20mm. guns; about twenty-five assault guns and self-propelled tank destroyers; an artillery battalion with towed 105mm. howitzers; a battalion of *SS-Panzergrenadiers*; around eighty half-tracks; a few reconnaissance troops; and two companies of engineers, although the column was supposed to move so rapidly that the engineers carried no bridge construction equipment. Attached to Peiper were one of Skorzeny's four-man teams disguised as Americans; one of Skorzeny's task forces with seven hundred men and twelve Panthers disguised to look like Shermans; and thirty 68-ton Mark VI (King Tiger) tanks of the 501st SS Heavy Panzer Battalion. Because the Tigers were slow and cumbersome, Peiper put them at the rear of his column, to be called forward once the advance reached more open country close to the Meuse.

The rest of the 1st SS Panzer Division was to proceed in three columns. Composed of the division's reconnaissance battalion, one was to follow Peiper in order to deal with any threat to resupply. Two others were to proceed through the lower portion of the Losheim Gap: one composed of the 2d SS Panzergrenadier Regiment (minus a battalion with Peiper), reinforced by the division's twenty remaining tanks and most of its twenty-two self-propelled tank destroyers; the other composed of the

1st SS Panzergrenadier Regiment with a few of the tank destroyers. The division commander, Col. Wilhelm Mohnke, his headquarters and support troops, and the bulk of the division's artillery were to bring up the rear. Should Peiper's column be held up, one of the other columns was to assume the mission of seizing the bridges over the Meuse.

As Peiper calculated it, his column would be about fifteen miles long and in the sharply compartmented terrain of the Ardennes, mostly road-bound. If he was to accomplish his mission of driving swiftly to the Meuse without regard for his flanks, he needed the heavy firepower of the Mark IVs and Panthers to the fore, intermixed with *SS-Panzergrenadiers* riding in half-tracks, who would be called upon as required to help the tanks. Peiper established his command group midway in the column, but he himself would usually be well forward in one of the leading half-tracks.

In Lanzerath in the early hours of December 17, it took the commander of the parachute battalion that Peiper had commandeered considerable time to roust his men from the houses where they had settled down for the night. Thus it was close to four in the morning before the leading vehicles of *Kampfgruppe Peiper*—two Panthers and three half-tracks—began the advance on the first objective of Honsfeld. Four Mark IV flak tanks, each equipped with a 37mm. cannon, and two flak wagons, with quadruple 20mm. pieces, were next in line, followed by more half-tracks transporting *SS-Panzergrenadiers* and tanks with paratroopers clinging to the decks. A company of paratroopers advanced on foot to provide flank protection as the column moved through woods between Buchholz Farm and Honsfeld.

Where were the mines and well-manned American defenses that Colonel von Hofmann had predicted? Peiper's leading vehicles encountered nothing, and only those vehicles well back in the column came under any fire from the two platoons of Company K, 394th Infantry, at the farm and in the nearby woods. The platoons quickly disintegrated under fire from the quad-20s on the flak wagons. One American remained: a radio operator hiding in the cellar of the farmhouse. He counted the German vehicles as they passed and reported the number by radio to his regimental headquarters; he got up to twenty-eight half-tracks and thirty tanks before the Germans rooted him out.

Just over a mile short of Honsfeld, a road from within the Losheim Gap joined the Lanzerath-Honsfeld road. As Peiper's lead tank reached the road junction, the driver came upon American vehicles heading into Honsfeld. He fell in behind one of them and followed.

In Honsfeld, the captain commanding the 394th Infantry's rest center had had a busy day. He first had to welcome Marlene Dietrich, who was supposed to entertain the troops, then hurriedly send her back. As the

KAMPFGRUPPE PEIPER
DEC 17

Scale:
MILES
0 1 2 3 4

←N

WEST WALL

Losheimergraben
Losheim
Buchholz
Sta.
Lanzerath
Manderfeld
Auw
Andler

Krinkelt
Mürringen
Hünningen
Honsfeld
2D SS PZ GR REGT
Wallerode

Rocherath
Wirtzfeld
Büllingen
KG PEIPER
Schoppen
Möderscheid
Amblève
Born

Elsenborn
Bütgenbach
Dom. Bütgenbach
Faymonville
Ondenval
Thirimont
Amblève R.

Camp Elsenborn

Waimes
Baugnez
MASSACRE SITE
Ligneuville
Amblève R.
Recht
Poteau

Malmédy
Stavelot
FUEL DEPOT
Wanne

situation everywhere along the front worsened, he used the men from the rest center, augmented by stragglers, to form a provisional company and placed them in positions behind a creek a few hundred yards to the east and south of the town. Two platoons of towed guns of the 801st Tank Destroyer Battalion backed up that line from the edge of the village. When two platoons of towed guns of the 612th Tank Destroyer Battalion arrived around three o'clock in the morning, borrowed from the 2d Division, the commander of the 801st's guns told the leaders of those two platoons to bed down for the rest of the night; he would direct them into firing positions at daylight.

Earlier, when Lieutenant Reppa and his troop of cavalry arrived from the Losheim Gap, Reppa checked in with the captain from the 99th Division, who asked him to be prepared to send out patrols the next morning but suggested his men bed down for the night in the village. Reppa did as he was told, but he sent an armored car commanded by Sgt. George Creel to take up a position just beyond the last house in Honsfeld along the road entering the village from the south (the direction of Lanzerath) and give the alarm should the Germans approach.

In the armored car close by the road, Creel and his crew through much of the pitch-black night saw nothing to disturb them. Now and then American vehicles approached, sometimes several traveling together, all fleeing from the Losheim Gap and continuing into Honsfeld and beyond. Most had their "cat's-eye" blackout lights on, but sometimes a soldier walked ahead of a vehicle with a flashlight to guide the way.

It was close to 5 A.M. and another American vehicle had just passed when Creel blinked in disbelief. Coming up the road was a lone soldier carrying a white handkerchief and guiding the "biggest damn tank" Creel had ever seen. The tank passed so close to the armored car—within three or four feet—that despite the darkness, Creel could make out a small black swastika on it. As the tank passed, Creel tried to fire, but a trailer attached to his armored car blocked his field of fire.

From farther down the road there was a sudden flurry of small-arms fire from the American infantrymen. It lasted less than a minute before the infantrymen broke for the rear, and crews of the tank destroyers joined them. Everybody was soon engaged "in a wild scramble, trying to separate themselves from an enemy that seemed to be all around them, yet was not visible." Creel and his crew took off on foot to try to warn Lieutenant Reppa but were unable to get into the center of the village.

The two leading Panthers of *Kampfgruppe Peiper* were soon past the first scattered houses of Honsfeld. As they entered the heart of the village, they came to an S-bend in the road—at that point more a street than a road—and a building on either side narrowly restricted passage. It took considerable backing and filling before the big tanks were able to get past. Three half-tracks—Peiper himself riding in one of them—followed closely.

Once past the S-bend, the German crews could make out jeeps, armored cars, light tanks, and towed tank destroyers parked beside almost every house. At the order of the commander of the advance guard, 1st Lt. Georg Preuss, machine gunners in the tanks and on the half-tracks opened fire, spraying the buildings and all the while continuing to advance. They reached the far edge of the little village with not a shot fired back at them.

Karl Wortmann was a big, strapping man, well over 6 feet tall and solidly built. He had enlisted in the *Waffen-SS* as a youth and was proud of his service. A noncommissioned officer, Wortmann was the aiming gunner for the 37mm. cannon on the third of four flak tanks closely following Peiper's lead tanks into Honsfeld. Early traces of a foggy daylight were bringing increased visibility when the first flak tank edged around the S-bend and past the buildings closely flanking it.

A U.S. antitank gun opened fire. The first round hit the flak tank, but it kept moving. A second round hit the second vehicle, immobilizing it. Bypassing the immobilized tank, the driver of Wortmann's flak tank continued to advance. Although the antitank gun fired a third time, it missed Wortmann's vehicle. Wortmann could see that the gun was firing from a barn concealed by a hedge. Taking aim with his 37mm. piece, he knocked it out with one round.

As small-arms fire erupted from the upper stories of houses into the open turrets of the flak tanks, gunners on flak wagons equipped with quad-20s returned the fire. It took some twenty minutes before the last of the Americans either fled or surrendered. Wortmann and his crew found the men who had manned the antitank gun hiding in the cellar next to the barn from which they had fired.

By that time, more half-tracks carrying *SS-Panzergrenadiers* and tanks with paratroopers on them were pouring into the village. Dismounting, the foot troops fanned out to clear any resistance that remained.

In one of the houses, Lieutenant Reppa was dozing in a chair. At the sound of the first German tanks passing, he snapped fully awake. "Those don't sound like ours," he said to his first sergeant, William Lovelock. The two rushed to a window just as a shell exploded and illuminated a German half-track passing outside.

Reppa's initial shock quickly turned to dismay that Sergeant Creel had failed to give any warning. Then Reppa determined to make a run for it, but first he had to send messengers to the houses where his other men had bedded down and tell them to do the same. He was briefing the messengers when a tank loaded with paratroopers stopped just outside the house. Jumping to the ground, the paratroopers headed for the door, their rifles and burp guns at the ready.

"*Heraus!*" a German commanded.

"We can't make it," Reppa muttered, half to himself. "We can't do a damn thing."

Going to the door, he opened it, threw up his hands, and shouted: "*Kamerad!*"

Variations of that scene were taking place all over Honsfeld. At the first fire from the German tanks and half-tracks, many men fled, some even managing to escape with their jeeps and other vehicles; but others, rudely awakened, saw their best chance of survival in surrender.

Just when the murder started and how widespread it was, nobody could say. But it happened.

Three houses from the center of the village on the road to Büllingen, an SS officer prodded eight sleepy Americans, barefoot and in their underwear, at gunpoint from the house, lined them up beside it, and mowed them down with a burp gun. From another house, five American soldiers emerged under a white flag. A group of German soldiers opened fire with rifles and burp guns, killing four and wounding the fifth, and as the wounded soldier cried for help, a tank ran over him and crushed him. From yet another house, four men carrying a large white flag tried to surrender, but a machine gunner in a German tank opened fire, killing all four.

Elsewhere, seventeen men from the 612th Tank Destroyer Battalion and an officer, 1st Lt. Laurens B. Grandy, kept up a steady fire for a time but eventually concluded that their situation was hopeless. When Grandy and one of the men emerged with half a tablecloth as a flag of surrender, a German soldier told them to have everybody leave his weapon and file out with hands overhead. All eighteen were standing in a row, hands raised, when a German noncommissioned officer jumped from a half-track, raised his burp gun, and killed the two men at the end of the row. One of the Americans took that as a signal to run: Staff Sgt. Billy F. Wilson fled to the back of the house, then dodged from one building to another to reach a field and the concealment of a hedgerow. Some four hours later he made his way to safety.

Pfc. William T. Hawkins was with a group of approximately a hundred men whom the Germans herded together after they had surrendered, many of them also from the 612th Tank Destroyer Battalion. They were standing in a closely packed group with hands overhead when German machine gunners opened fire, killing—it appeared to Hawkins—some twenty to thirty men. Then for some unexplained reason the firing abruptly stopped, and the survivors were soon marching down the road toward Lanzerath.

As about 250 prisoners plodded down one side of the narrow road, more of *Kampfgruppe Peiper's* tanks and half-tracks were moving forward. Some of the drivers of the vehicles veered toward the prisoners as if to run them down. Soldiers on the tanks swung at the prisoners with the butts of their rifles, knocking some men down. Still others took pot-shots with their rifles. If an American fell, the guards would let nobody help him. A machine gunner in one tank fired a few rounds into the air, then lowered his gun and killed two prisoners. An SS officer fired his pistol into the forehead of one of the men.

As those things happened, the Americans would dive for the ditches or jump behind trees, but their guards quickly prodded them out. In only one case did a guard intervene. He looked to be no more than eighteen; when an SS officer ordered him out of the way so he could take a shot at the prisoners, the young German refused, standing instead with his arms outstretched to protect the prisoners behind him. Frustrated, the officer went on his way.

By the time the column of prisoners reached Lanzerath, somebody had added two Belgian civilian men to the tail. As the last of the column was passing the Café Palm, just across the road from Adolf Schür's house, a soldier jumped from a passing tank, grabbed the two civilians, and forced them into a barn next to the Café Palm. Several shots sounded. An hour later, one of the men dragged himself across the road and into the Schür's barn, where Adolf found him.

Adolf helped the man into the kitchen, where Frau Schür bathed his wounds—he had been shot twice in the nape of the neck. The other man, he said, was dead. Although there were several German paratroopers in the kitchen, they made no objection to helping the civilian. An SS trooper came in later, seemingly intent on finishing the man off, but Christolf Schür protested vehemently, and the presence of the other sol-diers appeared to intimidate the SS trooper. After a time, he left.

One more terrible deed remained to be done in nearby Honsfeld. Two nights later, after seventeen-year-old André Schroeder and the few other civilians still living in Honsfeld had repaired for the night to the staunchest cellar in the village, as was their custom, five SS troopers called down from the top of the stairs. They wanted somebody, they said, to show them the way to Büllingen. Although Schroeder volunteered to do it, the Germans spotted sixteen-year-old Erna Collas, whom every-body in Honsfeld considered to be the prettiest girl in the village. They insisted that she show them the way.

Erna went with the soldiers but never returned. In the spring, after the snows melted, they found her body in a shallow grave alongside the road to Büllingen, shot seven times in the back. There was no way of telling whether she had been raped.

After reaching the far edge of Honsfeld, Colonel Peiper sent a half-track to reconnoiter his assigned road leading west. The weather was turning warmer; most of the snow, except in the woods, was melting; and Peiper was concerned that the road, which showed on his map to be little more than a cart track, would not support his heavy vehicles. The reconnaissance confirmed his fears.

The alternative was to proceed northwest, to the town of Büllingen, which was on the route assigned to the 12th SS Panzer Division. Hearing the noise of battle from the direction of Losheimergraben, Peiper deduced that the tanks of that division had yet to get past the crossroads. He decided to take the chance of going to Büllingen, then turn back onto his assigned route before the other German column reached Büllingen. Not only was it a better road; Peiper had heard that there was American gasoline in Büllingen, and after all the delays and peregrinations of the day before, his vehicles were badly in need of fuel. That Hitler had decreed death to any commander impinging on the route of another held little concern for Peiper.

While waiting at the edge of Honsfeld for the column to close up, Peiper started a company of the paratroopers that he had appropriated in Lanzerath on the march to Büllingen in half-tracks accompanied by a single tank. He told the battalion commander to return with the rest of the paratroopers to his own regiment.

There would be little to prevent *Kampfgruppe Peiper* from taking Büllingen. A town with a normal population of two thousand people, it lay four miles behind the 99th Division's line at Losheimergraben and served as a center for troops supporting the division. Within recent days, it had also served those supporting the 2d Division, for Büllingen sat astride the main supply route for the troops who were attacking at Wahlerscheid. The service batteries of two of the 99th Division's artillery battalions were there. So was Capt. Ralph Hill's little Civil Affairs detachment with Hill's telephone connection in the basement of the post office, so helpful the day before to commanders of the 99th and 106th Divisions. Then there was the 2d Division's Quartermaster Company and a company of the division's organic 2d Engineer Battalion; and several hundred yards outside the town on either side of the road to Honsfeld, artillery observation pilots of both the 2d and 99th Divisions had turned the fields into airstrips for their frail little L-5 aircraft.

At the instigation of the commander of the V Corps, General Gerow, the First Army at midnight on December 16 released a battalion of combat engineers, the 254th, for attachment to the 99th Division, which sent the battalion to Büllingen to defend the town to the east (the direction of Losheimergraben) and to the south (the direction of Honsfeld). The first company arrived at 4 A.M.—the same time at which Peiper was starting his move from Lanzerath—and went into position just east of the town. Company B followed an hour later. As the men marched along the road toward Honsfeld, they came upon the airstrips and nearby the 924th Field Artillery Battalion's Service Battery, which was occupying a few isolated houses along the road. Rather than set up a defense close to those installations, the company kept going all the way to the far edge of a growth of scrub brush little more than a thousand yards short of Honsfeld. There the Americans began to dig in.

The third company arrived only at daybreak and stopped short of Büllingen to assume a reserve position on the road leading back to Bütgenbach—site of the 99th Division's headquarters—at a road junction marked by a manor house and several outbuildings that the Americans knew as Dom. Bütgenbach (dom. is a map abbreviation for *domaine*, meaning estate). A platoon of towed guns of the 612th Tank Destroyer Battalion was already in position there, a reserve for the two platoons that had gone on to Honsfeld.

As the engineers of Company B marched along the road toward Honsfeld, one man dropped out of the column to pound on the door of a house which served as a billet for the pilots of the 99th Division's L-5 planes. "The Germans are coming!" he shouted. Nobody questioned how he knew. While the pilots went to their planes and warmed up the motors, the crewmen loaded the detachment's gear onto trucks.

At the edge of the patch of scrub brush on a hill overlooking Honsfeld, the men of Company B, 254th Engineers, had had scant time to dig in when around 6 A.M. they heard tracked vehicles and German voices. They opened fire. In the darkness, the men could make out German soldiers piling off a tank and six half-tracks; they were the paratroopers that Peiper had sent ahead of his main column. The engineers repulsed a first assault and what appeared to be two more; but shortly after 7 A.M., as it was beginning to get light, twelve German tanks joined the attack. Lacking any defense against the tanks, the engineers broke. Some fell back toward Büllingen, others toward Dom. Bütgenbach.

While the main body of Peiper's force was still coming forward, Peiper dispatched two patrols along dirt tracks roughly paralleling the main road to Büllingen. Five tanks and several half-tracks went beyond the railroad connecting Honsfeld and Büllingen to come at Büllingen from the east. There they shot up the company of engineers that was defending near the railroad and continued into town.

The other patrol, consisting of a tank and several half-tracks, took a route to the left of the main road and approached the 99th Division's airfield just as the pilots were getting ready to take off. As the tank's machine guns opened fire, each pilot in turn took off in the direction of the tank, as if dive-bombing it (although they had no weapons), and so intimidated the gunner that all but one plane got away, that one left behind in the mud. Only then did the pilots of the 2d Division's planes realize that something was wrong and race for their airstrip. A sole pilot escaped in his plane.

When the commander of the 924th Field Artillery Battalion's Service Battery, Capt. James Cobb, learned what was happening, he was at his battalion's headquarters in Krinkelt. He raced back in his jeep to his

command post along the road to Honsfeld and ordered twelve men under
1st Lt. Jack Varner to form a roadblock between the two airstrips. They
had just gotten into position with two .50-caliber machine guns and two
bazookas when a column of German vehicles with two tanks in the lead
appeared along the main road from Honsfeld.

Sgt. Grant Yager hit the second tank with a rocket from a bazooka,
and as the crew piled out, the machine gunners and other men with carbines opened fire, but the return German fire was deadly. At least two
men were killed, and both the two-man machine-gun crews were
wounded. Except for one of the machine gunners, Pfc. Deloise Rapp,
who was wounded twice in one foot and played dead, and Lieutenant
Varner, who was out of sight behind a hedgerow, the men surrendered.
(Rapp eventually crawled to a basement, coming upon Lieutenant Varner
in the process. Although Rapp was certain Varner could have escaped
after nightfall, Varner refused to go without Rapp, who was unable to
walk. Both were captured.)

As tanks and half-tracks plowed onto the 2d Division's airstrip, shooting up the remaining planes, the Germans permitted Sergeant Yager and
two other men to administer first aid to one of the wounded, Pvt. Bernard Pappel, who had been hit in a leg and an arm. As they treated him,
a German officer in a light-colored leather jacket began berating Yager in
German, but when Yager was unable to understand, he turned away. It
was so unusual for an SS officer to wear a light-colored jacket—SS jackets were always black—that numerous witnesses to Peiper's march were
later to remark on it. The man was the commander of Peiper's *SS-Panzergrenadier* battalion, Maj. Josef Diefenthal.

When the column was ready to continue into Büllingen, the Germans
ordered Yager and the two men with him onto the hood of a half-track.
As it moved forward, the men heard a single pistol shot. "My God!"
yelled one of the men with Yager. "They shot Pappel in the head."

Inside Büllingen, there was no fight.

Shortly after 7 A.M., the company of the 2d Division's engineers in
the town received orders to mine the roads leading into Büllingen and to
prepare all bridges for demolition, but they were still loading mines into
their trucks when German tanks and half-tracks appeared—the German
patrol that had come into the town from the east. Some of the engineers
managed to get out of town, mostly along the road to Losheimergraben.
There they joined men of the 254th Engineers who had escaped the fight
just east of Büllingen and augmented the defenses of the battalion of the
23d Infantry that had moved the day before into Hünningen. Others hid
in cellars, but over the next three days the Germans routed them from
their hiding places.

The men of the 2d Division's Quartermaster Company in Büllingen
were lining up for breakfast when those same five German tanks and

accompanying half-tracks appeared. The Americans dived for basements, from which they could see an elderly man emerge from his house. Wearing a Nazi armband and carrying a burp gun, he gave every passing tank a Nazi salute, then directed them to the railroad station where there were large stocks of supplies.

At the station, the tanks shot up parked trucks and trapped some men of the 2d Division's Signal Company in the basement. To escape detection, the men had to strangle their little dog mascot, Queenie. Those men as well as almost all those of the Quartermaster Company and seven of the pilots and ground crewmen of the 2d Division's artillery aircraft managed to hide through the rest of the day and get out of town after nightfall.

Because the other artillery service battery in Büllingen was along the road to Bütgenbach, those troops escaped with most of their vehicles and equipment. So did Captain Hill and his Civil Affairs detachment; but most of the men of Captain Cobb's battery, including the commander himself, were either captured immediately or ferreted from cellars the next day. Of sixty-nine officers and men in the battery, only eleven got away.

At a big, treeless square in Büllingen that served in normal times as the cattle market, Peiper's tanks and half-tracks found the gasoline they were hoping for in a small depot only recently established by the 2d Division's Quartermaster Company. The Germans used captured Americans to help fuel their vehicles. When each vehicle was filled up, Peiper hurried it out of town to the southwest along the road leading back onto his assigned line of march.

A flank patrol of five Mark IVs took the road toward Bütgenbach, but at Dom. Bütgenbach the guns of the 612th Tank Destroyer Battalion opened fire, knocking out three of the German tanks. The others quickly turned back, and the American gunners, along with the company of engineers in position there, were left to wonder (albeit with considerable relief) why the foe had turned away from them.

So long was Peiper's column that even as the first vehicles left Büllingen, others were still far to the rear on the road from Honsfeld and even farther back in and beyond Lanzerath. They proved to be ready targets when in mid-morning the skies cleared enough to permit two squadrons of the 366th Fighter Group, assigned for the day to support the 99th Division, to attack. Pilots of the 389th Squadron bombed and strafed Peiper's column, sending vehicles scurrying for concealment. They subsequently claimed thirty German tanks and other vehicles destroyed; but like infantrymen making their estimates of enemy losses, seldom were the claims of pilots in the air justified by the reality on the ground. When the second squadron, the 390th, moved in to attack, a squadron of ME-109s appeared. Although the American pilots shot down seven German planes, they had to jettison most of their bombs while doing it.

*   *   *

Inside Büllingen, Karl Wortmann and the crew of his flak tank delighted in the booty. When the radio operator handed Wortmann a small rectangular wax-coated cardboard box, Wortmann was at a loss to know what was in it. Breakfast, said the radio operator. Wortmann found that hard to believe, but he watched the others and quickly learned how to get at the food. Cigarettes, too. Although Wortmann had never smoked, he was unable to resist taking along several cartons. Like the crews of many other vehicles, Wortmann and his men stashed every empty space in their flak tank with whatever they found: food, cigarettes, field jackets, gloves, boots.

There were to be reports later that in Büllingen, Peiper's men killed fifty American prisoners who had helped them fill their vehicles with gasoline. The reports were false. *Kampfgruppe Peiper* took about two hundred prisoners in and around Büllingen, and somebody murdered Private Pappel; but there was no repetition of the mass atrocities committed in Honsfeld. Since others were destined to happen later, who could say why?

In capturing Büllingen, *Kampfgruppe Peiper* had seemingly trapped the bulk of the 2d and 99th Infantry Divisions. Most of the men, most of the artillery pieces, and most of the supporting tanks and tank destroyers of the two divisions were located somewhere along or near the road leading northeast from Büllingen through the twin villages of Krinkelt-Rocherath and the forests near the road junction of Wahlerscheid. At that point there were only two ways out of the trap. Infantrymen might make it on foot through the forest over firebreaks and muddy logging trails; vehicles and artillery pieces just might make it over the farm track leading from Wirtzfeld, behind Krinkelt-Rocherath, to the little town of Elsenborn and nearby Camp Elsenborn. Yet for all the efforts of the 2d Division's engineers to improve that muddy lane, no one knew how long it would stand up under heavy traffic. What was more, if the Germans who had taken Büllingen continued on to Wirtzfeld and Krinkelt-Rocherath, they could roll up the two divisions from the flank. Or should they continue to Bütgenbach and then swing north up the road to Elsenborn, they could come in behind everybody, even men trying to get out of the forest on foot: two divisions and their attachments, possibly as many as thirty thousand men.

That was what Walter Lauer thought was about to happen. "The enemy," Lauer noted later, before Peiper's objectives had become clear, "had the key to success within his hands but did not know it."

Walter Robertson thought the same. Just a few minutes before 7 A.M. on December 17, from the 2d Division's forward headquarters in a house on the edge of Wirtzfeld, Robertson telephoned the commandant of the division's Special Troops, Lt. Col. Matt F. C. Konop. German tanks had broken through and were on their way to Büllingen, said Robertson. He wanted Konop to get every man and every gun he could put his hands on to form "a last ditch defense of the CP." Such unaccustomed agitation was there in Robertson's voice that for a brief moment Konop failed to recognize who was talking.

The minute Robertson hung up, Konop was on the phone to the various headquarters units, telling them to get cooks, clerks, jeep drivers, MPs, whoever, out to form a line on the southern fringe of Wirtzfeld in front of the command post. He tried to warn the Quartermaster Company in Büllingen, but the telephone line was out.

It was a fairly impressive little defensive force that Konop assembled. Aside from the heterogeneous collection of men from the division headquarters, there were others from the division artillery's command post, also located in Wirtzfeld. The presence of the division artillery commander, General Hinds, facilitated repositioning a battery of 105mm. howitzers and another of 155mm. howitzers so that they could fire on the approaches to Wirtzfeld from Büllingen. There were a few 57mm. antitank guns and four half-tracks equipped with quad-50 machine guns. Even so, the little force would have been no match for a determined armored thrust from Büllingen, which was what Robertson and everybody else thought was coming.

Not long after 8 A.M., the worst appeared about to happen. Five German tanks and several half-tracks—the force that had entered Büllingen from the east and driven to the railroad station—appeared out of the mist on the Büllingen road, where it crossed a ridgeline eight hundred yards outside Wirtzfeld. Just at that moment Konop's defense received a strong boost with the arrival of five self-propelled tank destroyers of the attached 644th Tank Destroyer Battalion. The destroyers quickly knocked out four of the tanks and a half-track and sent the other vehicles hurrying back into Büllingen.

After leaving Büllingen, Colonel Peiper halted his leading vehicles at a crossroads so that the column could close up. During the pause, a half-track reconnoitered a dirt track that led more directly than the main road to the next point on Peiper's route, the village of Möderscheid. Since the road appeared to be serviceable, Peiper took it and from Möderscheid proceeded northwest toward the village of Schoppen. On the way, the Germans captured the two-man crews of two ambulances, plus Staff Sgt. Henry R. Zach, two junior officers (1st Lt. Thomas E. McDermott and 2d Lt. Lloyd A. Iames), and six other Americans in a four-jeep convoy. They loaded some of the prisoners on their vehicles but made the four jeeps join the column.

About midway between Schoppen and the village of Faymonville at a little chapel, St. Hubert, Peiper found another side road that appeared promising and would enable him to avoid Faymonville and the adjacent fair-sized town of Waimes, where he might well run into opposition. It was little more than a country lane, but Peiper risked it, and his vehicles made it.

The lead tank was approaching the village of Ondenval when an American 6×6 truck appeared. The machine gunner in the tank fired, hitting the truck and sending it careening into a ditch, where it turned over on one side. As the tank passed by, the German gunner gave the truck another burst of fire, as did the gunners in several other tanks that followed.

Inside the cab of the truck, two American engineers huddled. Miraculously, the German fire hit neither man. When the noise of the German vehicles had passed, the two scrambled out, raced to a nearby railroad embankment, clambered to the other side, and began to run back south in the direction from which they had come.

That little episode marked the beginning of what was to prove a series of fateful encounters between *Kampfgruppe Peiper* and Americans of the 1111th Engineer Combat Group.

Just up the road from Ondenval in the schoolhouse in the center of Waimes was a forward hospital run by a platoon of the 47th Field Hospital. By early morning of December 17, the surgeons, nurses, administrative officers, technicians, and orderlies were aware that something unusual was happening at the front, for the rumble of artillery fire was almost constant and during the night the number of incoming patients markedly increased. In mid-morning, a sudden spate of patients hurriedly evacuated from a hospital run by another platoon of the 47th Field in Bütgenbach appeared, and close behind them the medical personnel of that platoon.

Orders soon arrived to transfer all patients to a hospital in Malmédy; then came orders for the platoon that had been in Bütgenbach to follow, but the hospital in Waimes was to continue to function. Throughout the rest of the morning, ambulances continued to arrive from the direction of Bütgenbach. Although busy with patients, at least one of the nurses, 2d Lt. Mabel Jessop, felt a gnawing anxiety. Were the Germans coming? Were she and the others in the platoon considered expendable? When it came time for lunch, she had trouble swallowing "the usual cold, tasteless mixture of canned hamburger and dehydrated potatoes."

As Peiper's column proceeded from Ondenval around midday over a winding back road to the village of Thirimont, Peiper rode in a half-track with the commander of the *SS-Panzergrenadiers*, Major Diefenthal. The leading tanks tried to go all the way through Thirimont along a dirt road that led directly to a principal north-south highway, N-23, which connected Malmédy with the little resort town of Ligneuville and thence with St. Vith. Peiper wanted to get to N-23 by the shortest route, for he needed to reach Ligneuville in order to pick up another road leading west. It was a back road, but by taking it he might avoid likely American strength on the highway that passed through Malmédy; and, in any case, that highway was assigned to the 12th SS Panzer Division.

Just beyond Thirimont, Peiper's luck with country lanes ran out: The lead tank bogged down at a ford where the little road crossed a small stream. The column thus had to swing northwest at Thirimont to pick up N-23 at a road junction known as Baugnez, then turn south to Ligneuville. Peiper himself had abandoned the lead vehicles at that point, having climbed down from Major Diefenthal's half-track to question an American soldier (Peiper spoke excellent English) who had been captured, along with his jeep, while he was trouble-shooting telephone lines.

Kampfgruppe Peiper was about to have its second brush with men of the 1111th Engineer Combat Group. They were two men—a sergeant and a private—sent out scouting in a jeep by their company commander from the 291st Engineer Combat Battalion in Malmédy, who had learned of a German breakthrough in the vicinity of Bütgenbach. The two had turned left at the Baugnez road junction in the direction of Waimes and Bütgenbach when something caught their eye down the hill to the south in the direction of Thirimont, from which a secondary road led up to the highway they were on.

Moving down the secondary road, they hid in the edge of a wood bordering the road to watch wide-eyed the scene below them. Tanks, tanks, half-tracks, and more tanks. Wary that at any moment they might be discovered, they waited long enough to count sixty-eight German vehicles, thirty of them tanks, then avoiding the highway by which they had come, took a winding back road toward Malmédy.

At one o'clock, the word finally came to the schoolhouse in Waimes: Evacuate immediately! Patients and surgical teams went first and within ten minutes were on their way toward the road junction at Baugnez, where their trucks and ambulances turned right onto Highway N-23 and proceeded down a steep hill into Malmédy.

The nurses were next, ten of them crowded into a single ambulance. The vehicle was nearing a point where a woods ran out and open fields led to the road junction of Baugnez when shells began to explode in the road ahead. As the driver pulled the ambulance to the side of the road, the nurses clambered out and into the ditch. Only then did they notice that there were six trucks also stopped, men taking cover in the ditch beside them.

More shells, so close that Lieutenant Jessop thought the gunners must surely know exactly where they were and expected "to be blown up with the next blast." As some of the men from the trucks began to crawl down the ditch toward Waimes, the nurses turned to follow, and as they turned

they could see big German tanks entering the road below them and making for the junction at Baugnez.

The nurses were soon filthy with mud, drenched by the slush and
snow. When two American trucks came along the road from the direction
of Waimes, they waved them down frantically, told the drivers what had
happened, climbed aboard, and headed back to the schoolhouse in
Waimes.

Only scant minutes earlier, a long column of tanks, half-tracks, and
trucks of the 7th Armored Division's Combat Command R (CCR) had
passed through Malmédy, one of two march columns by which the 7th
Armored Division was moving south at General Bradley's order to help
the 106th Infantry Division near St. Vith. The last of CCR's vehicles had
climbed the road out of Malmédy and past the Baugnez road junction
when a small convoy of three serials transporting 140 men entered the
other side of Malmédy. The convoy belonged to Battery B, 285th Field
Artillery Observation Battalion.

The 285th Field Artillery Observation Battalion was one of those
technical units that, however small, make important contributions to a
modern army in the field. The men did mapping and surveying, but for
the most part theirs was a sound-and-flash unit, whose mission was to
detect the location of enemy mortars and artillery and pass that information to howitzer and gun battalions. The battalion had only a Headquarters Battery and two operational batteries, A and B. Seldom did the
battalion function as a unit: Its two batteries were usually parceled out
individually where needed.

Commanded by Capt. Leon T. Scarborough, Battery B had recently
been operating near Aachen, and when the 7th Armored Division received the order to move south, so did Battery B. Even though the battery was not attached to the armored division, Captain Scarborough
arranged for a slot in one of the division's two march columns and then
left with a small billeting detail to precede the convoy and prepare for the
battery's arrival at its new location.

Battery B's route led through Eupen, across the Hautes Fagnes to
Malmédy, and on to the south. There were thirty-three vehicles in the
convoy: jeeps, three-quarter-ton trucks, 6×6 trucks, and a command car.
The vehicles were numbered B-1 to B-33.

Cpl. Ernest W. Bechtel was one of the men assigned to a 6×6,
Number B-26, one of only a few that had no tarpaulin over the bed. As
the men were loading, Bechtel spied his best friend, who was also a
neighbor back in his home town in Pennsylvania, Cpl. Luke B. Swartz.
He was standing with his head bowed just behind the next truck, B-25.
"Hey," called Bechtel, "why don't you ride with me on B-26?"

"No," replied Swartz, "it's beginning to sleet. I'll ride on one of the trucks with a tarp." Besides, he went on, it was his last day anyway. "Ernie," he said, "I'll not be going home. Something terrible is going to happen to most of us today, but you'll be going back. Tell the folks back home I love them."

"What the hell are you talking about?" demanded Bechtel.

Without further word, Swartz climbed aboard B-25 just as the convoy got under way. Bechtel boarded B-26.

It was a cold, miserable ride through the murky early morning of December 17. On the way the column paused briefly for the men to search for German paratroopers, and shortly after midday, as the vehicles entered Malmédy, it was apparent to almost everybody that something unusual was happening. The narrow, winding streets of the town were jammed with military vehicles, most of them going in the opposite direction from that of Battery B's convoy and their drivers obviously in a hurry to get out of town. As the trucks neared the center of town, civilians began to run alongside, shouting *Boches! Boches!* and pointing in the direction Battery B was going.

When the lead vehicle of the convoy reached one of the last houses on the edge of Malmédy before N-23 began its ascent to Baugnez, the commander of the 291st Engineer Combat Battalion, Lt. Col. David E. Pergrin, came out of the house, flagged down the convoy, and talked to the 285th Field Artillery Observation Battalion's executive officer, Capt. Roger L. Mills, who was in command. There had been a German breakthrough near Bütgenbach, said Pergrin; it might be wise for the convoy to swing to the west along the 7th Armored Division's other march route.

Mills pondered the advice briefly. No, he decided; if he lost his position in the march column, it might be difficult to get back in. He would continue on N-23.

Seemingly inexorably, fate was drawing *Kampfgruppe Peiper* and that small American unit to a rendezvous at the road junction known as Baugnez. Had there been no boggy ford on the road leading west from Thirimont, *Kampfgruppe Peiper* would never have gone to Baugnez. Had Captain Mills heeded Colonel Pergrin's advice, there would probably have been only one American—a military policeman—at the road junction when *Kampfgruppe Peiper* got there.

At 12:45 P.M., two military policemen at the Baugnez road junction directed the last vehicle of the 7th Armored Division's CCR down N-23 and watched it disappear in the direction of Ligneuville. They had about an hour to wait before the next scheduled convoy appeared, that of the division's artillery. (They knew nothing about Battery B.) Since a single man could handle anything that passed in the meantime, one climbed into a jeep and headed down the road to Malmédy. The man left behind was Pfc. Homer D. Ford.

Most of Battery B's vehicles had begun the ascent toward Baugnez when the man in charge of the truck known as B-26, Sgt. James Barrington, became ill. As the driver brought the truck to a halt, Barrington staggered from the cab, vomiting. While two other trucks, B-27 and B-28, waited, the driver of B-26 searched for an aid station. It took ten minutes to find one and leave Sergeant Barrington there. (He was suffering from food poisoning.)

As the three trucks headed out of Malmédy, they came upon a group of men from the 291st Engineer Combat Battalion placing explosive charges against stately ash trees that lined either side of the road. "We're going to blow this row of trees," the engineers warned. "Once you're through, you can't return." Determined to catch up with the convoy, the men in charge of the three trucks told their drivers to keep moving.

As the trucks continued up the steep hill, the noise of heavy firing broke out: the *crump-crump* of big shells, the din of machine-gun fire. The lead driver slowed down. What was going on?

Only moments later, a jeep came roaring down the hill apparently out of control, but it came screeching to a halt just before colliding with B-26. An officer in the front passenger seat was bleeding profusely from a wound in the neck, and the driver was almost incoherent. All the men in B-26 could make out was the word "Krauts!"

By that time, shells had begun to burst alongside the highway nearby, and the noise of firing up ahead had become thunderous. It would be suicide to drive on. Somehow the drivers of all three trucks managed to turn around in the narrow road and head back toward Malmédy. The engineers, they noted with considerable relief, had yet to blow the trees across the road.

Back on the fringe of Malmédy, where Colonel Pergrin had the command post for his 291st Engineer Combat Battalion, the two men who had been scouting in the direction of Thirimont brought their jeep to an abrupt halt in front of the house. Pergrin found it hard to believe the story they told.

"There's a big Kraut column coming, Colonel! They've got tanks and half-tracks and armored cars, everything, and there's a hell of a lot of 'em. It looks like the whole German Army!"

Pergrin had barely gotten all the details of what the two men had to say when the noise of heavy shelling and machine-gun fire drifted down the hill south of Malmédy. "That little FAOB outfit," Pergrin said, half to himself, "has run smack into that Kraut column."

A small advance party, consisting of two vehicles and fifteen men (mostly route markers, who were to be dropped off at intersections to guide the way), had already disappeared down the road in the direction of Ligneuville when a round from a German tank fell just in front of the first vehicle of the main column, a command car in which Captain Mills

MASSACRE OF
BTRY B, 285TH FA OBS BN
AT BAUGNEZ
DEC 17
1 - Café Bodarwé
2 - Site of Massacre
3 - Lejoly House

was riding with Battery B's executive officer, 1st Lt. Virgil T. Lary, Jr. The driver braked to a precipitous stop, and the truck behind swerved as its driver applied the brakes.

At that moment, a jeep arrived from the direction of Ligneuville, an officer in the passenger seat. It swerved to a halt beside the first truck, but Staff Sgt. William H. Merriken and others in the truck shouted to the driver to keep moving. Go to Malmédy and get help! Gunning the motor, the driver careened down the road, dodging in and out of the vehicles of the convoy and through a hail of German fire at an incredible speed.

Round after round came from the German tanks, raking up and down the American column. Machine guns. Mortars. Several of the trucks exploded. Many crashed into the ditches on either side of the highway. The kitchen truck caught fire.

Battery B, 285th Field Artillery Observation Battalion, had met *Kampfgruppe Peiper*. Having spotted the American column while moving up the secondary road from Thirimont, the German tanks and half-tracks had veered off and charged across open fields toward N-23 and Baugnez, firing as they advanced.

Most of the men dived for cover in the ditches or behind vehicles, and many opened a futile fire with M-1s and carbines. A few ran for a nearby wood, but German fire cut them down. Cpl. Warren Schmitt ran to a little stream a few yards from the road, flopped down in the edge of the icy water, and pretended he was dead. Captain Mills and Lieutenant Lary both vaulted into a ditch. Everywhere there was firing and the heavy, raucous noise of churning tank treads.

Men in the vehicles near the tail of the column were unable to see what was happening. One thought the column had come upon German paratroopers; because a V-1 buzz bomb was passing overhead, several thought everybody was firing at that. But as the German tanks and half-tracks reached the highway, the rear vehicles, too, were caught up in the maelstrom. One of those vehicles was an ambulance with two medics from the 1st Division's 26th Infantry, Pvts. Roy Anderson and Samuel Dobyns, who had missed their unit's convoy as it moved to join the 99th Division and had tacked onto the tail of Battery B's column. A round from a German tank set the ambulance on fire.

At the road junction, as the Germans struck, Private Ford was still directing vehicles past. When three or four men from one of the trucks ran in Ford's direction, he motioned them to come with him and dashed behind one of the few buildings close by, a café run by Mme. Adèle Bodarwé. From there, Ford spotted a small shed and swiftly hid in it with the other men.

Inside the café, Madame Bodarwé watched the carnage in horror. Even though her son had been forced to serve in the German Army, she was a loyal Belgian. With her that morning was a farmer neighbor, Henri Lejoly, who was not necessarily pro-German but thought it well to side with whoever appeared to be in charge. He went to the door of the café and waved warmly to the Germans.

Firing was still rampant when an American jeep arrived driven by a German officer. It was Peiper. While questioning his American prisoner, he had heard the sound of firing up the hill and hurried forward. When he saw what was happening, he was annoyed, both because of the delay and because of the needless expenditure of ammunition against a helpless target—"those beautiful trucks, which we needed so badly, all shot up."

Only with difficulty did Peiper manage to stop the firing, and as it ceased, American soldiers emerged from the ditches, their hands in the air. The Germans herded them together roughly in small groups, many of them relieving the prisoners of rings, watches, cigarettes, and gloves. Almost every German soldier appeared intent on getting a pair of gloves.

Germans guarding one group wanted three men to drive the American trucks. Several said they could not drive; three others, Master Sgt.

Eugene L. Lacy and Cpls. Thomas J. Bacon and Ralph A. Logan, said they could. The Germans ordered them to move three undamaged trucks to the head of the column but there told them to dismount and join a group of several other men standing in a line along the road. A German with a pistol went down the line of men, putting the barrel first to one man's forehead, then another's. He was going to shoot them all, he said, because American planes were bombing his people. Standing nearby, slightly wounded, Captain Mills intervened. The men, he insisted, were to be treated honorably as prisoners of war. The German put away his pistol.

By that time, Colonel Peiper had established control over his men, and tanks and half-tracks began moving again down the hill in the direction of Ligneuville. One half-track stopped to pick up the ten men whom the German had threatened to shoot. (They were subsequently left under guard in Ligneuville and later marched into Germany.) Peiper left the scene in Major Diefenthal's half-track.

Homer Ford, the military policeman, and the men who had hidden with him in the shed, soon joined the ranks of prisoners. Henri Lejoly pointed out their hiding place to the Germans.

In time, the Germans herded all the prisoners into a field to the west of N-23, a hundred yards south of the road junction and the Café Bodarwé. All told there were approximately 130: Of the 140 men making up Battery B, a total of 64 (those who had left early with the battery commander, the route markers, the men in trucks B-26, B-27, and B-28, and the 10 who, however inexplicably, the Germans had sent on to Ligneuville) were safe; but the number of prisoners was augmented by men from other units. Some had been taken earlier, such as the medics from the two ambulances captured near Möderscheid, several MPs, and Sergeant Zach, Lieutenants McDermott and Iames, and others from the four-jeep convoy. Others again, such as the two medics from the 26th Infantry, Anderson and Dobyns, had simply happened on the scene. And the MP who had been on duty at the road junction, Private Ford.

The Germans herded the men tightly together only sixty feet from the highway, roughly in eight rows, hands above their heads. Some men jostled briefly for position, for they disliked being in the front row. The weather was damp and raw, the ground soggy underfoot with here and there a patch of old snow. The men's hands grew numb from holding them up and from the cold, for hardly anybody still had gloves.

Some of the men were uneasy, but the majority were complacent. Although most recognized that their captors were SS troops, hardly anybody expected treatment different from what might be expected of regular troops. Quite obviously the Germans were merely waiting for trucks with which to transport them to the rear, where they were destined to pass the Christmas of 1944 as prisoners of war.

A German officer—later identified as Maj. Werner Poetschke, commander of the 1st SS Panzer Battalion (perhaps conveniently so identified, for by that time he had been killed on another battlefield)—stopped two Mark IV tanks and directed them into position covering the prisoners. Once they were in place, he ordered one of the commanders, Sgt. Hans Siptrott, to open fire. Siptrott in turn ordered his assistant gunner, Pvt. Georg Fleps, a twenty-one-year-old SS volunteer from Romania who already had his pistol at the ready, to shoot.

Fleps fired. Standing beside Lieutenant Lary, Lary's driver collapsed backward from the impact of the bullet, toppling men behind him in an accordion action, so tightly were they all grouped. With the shot, the prisoners began shouting and jostling, and at least two in the front rank, Pfc. James P. Mattera and one of the medics, Dobyns, bulldozed their way toward the rear. Some of the officers yelled for the men to stand fast lest they provoke more shooting.

No provocation was needed. Private Kleps fired a second shot with his pistol, killing a medical officer, 1st Lt. Carl R. Guenther; then somebody shouted: "*Machen alle kaputt!* (Kill them all!)," and machine guns on both tanks opened fire.

Those who survived the first deadly fusillade flung themselves to the ground, burying their faces in the mud and trying to burrow under the bodies around them. The firing continued, the machine guns raking back and forth across the prostrate forms. There were screams, groans, cries of agony "almost like a lowing."

To the men who still lived, it seemed that the firing went on for an eternity. It actually lasted about fifteen minutes. Yet for a full two hours afterward, men on passing German vehicles amused themselves by firing a few bursts into the clump of bodies.

At long last, the cries and moans of the wounded died out and the noise of German vehicles on the road faded away. To the survivors, the silence was eerie. A few dared a glance to see whether any Germans were left, but most kept their heads glued to the ground. The silence at last ended with the sound of German voices and approaching footsteps. Engineers of the 3d SS Pioneer Company were moving into the field to finish off anybody who might have survived.

Upon first reaching the field, the Germans stood "for a few minutes to observe the Americans who were still moving or otherwise showing signs of life." Then they fanned out to finish them off. One of the engineers shot "four or five" with his pistol, making sure he put the muzzle only a few inches from the man's heart. As he remarked later, "I was sure I killed each man at whom I fired." Other Germans asked men to speak up, promising medical treatment, and a few made the mistake of responding. One German allowed an aid man to minister to one of the wounded, then killed them both. The medic, Dobyns, made a run for it, which so surprised the Germans that he succeeded in covering twenty-five to thirty yards before fire from a machine gun cut him down. Although wounded four times, Dobyns was still alive, but the Germans presumed him dead and left him alone.

By that time, nobody still living could be unaware of what was going on. Each man tried desperately to control his breathing, not only to keep his body still but to prevent vapor from showing in the cold as he exhaled. To many a survivor it seemed that the pounding of his heart would surely give him away, and for some, no attempt to appear dead would suffice, for as the Germans systematically kicked them in the head or the groin, it was almost impossible to keep from reacting.

Shot in the calf and the foot, Lieutenant Lary recalled that a German came his way,

> shooting here and there. A bullet went through the head of the man next to me. I lay tensely still, expecting the end. Could he see me breathing? Could I take a kick in the groin without wincing? . . . He was standing at my head. What was he doing? Time seemed to stand still. And then I heard him reloading his pistol in a deliberate manner . . . laughing and talking. A few odd steps before the reloading was finished and he was no longer so close to my head, then another shot a little farther away, and he had passed me up.

Almost miraculously, others than Lary still lived. In the front row, Sgt. Kenneth Ahrens had been shot in the back, his uniform so soaked with blood that the Germans apparently had no doubt that he was dead. Sergeant Merriken, with two machine-gun bullets in his back and a pistol bullet in one knee, found himself amazed at how calm he was, but praying "that someone would survive and tell what the Germans had done." Then there was Cpl. Michael T. Sciranko, shot in an upper thigh; Cpl. Albert M. Valenzi, hit in both legs; the MP, Homer Ford, hit in an arm; the medic, Dobyns, shot four times; his buddy, Anderson, unwounded; Cpls. Theodore J. Paluch and Charles F. Apperman, also unwounded. Sergeant Zach was hit in the leg and the hip, and Pvt. John H. Cobbler, hit six times, somehow still survived.

As the executioners left the field and silence again descended, men began to venture a whisper, a soft, agonizing query to try to determine if they were alone or if somebody else was alive. Here and there somebody answered, and one human being gained courage from the proximity of another.

"They'll be back," said one man; "we've got to make a run for it." "No, no," urged another; "wait until dark." Lary was among those who wanted to wait until dark. Mattera was one of those who wanted to go, so traumatized by the cold, the shock, and the presence of death that he was convinced he would never escape detection a second time.

"Let's go!" shouted Mattera and rose to his feet "in slow motion, resembling a drunken man." However much Lary disagreed, he was one of those who took the cue, rose, and began to run.

Some twenty men tried it, most heading for the Café Bodarwé. "No," yelled Mattera, "head for the woods!" But few heeded him. Twelve men took refuge in the café. Lieutenant Lary headed there at first but at the last minute went for the shed behind it and covered himself with straw. Three other men fell to the ground some distance behind the café and played dead again. All the while Germans were firing machine guns, and Lary saw one man fall. When the Germans saw men enter the café, they set it on fire and as the Americans emerged to escape the flames, shot them down.

On the edge of Malmédy, the commander of the 291st Engineers, Colonel Pergrin, had decided at last to risk a look in the direction of Baugnez and headed there with his jeep and his communications sergeant, William Crickenberger, armed with a Thompson submachine gun. As they came within sight of the burning Café Bodarwé, they left the jeep and began walking. Off to the right, three men emerged from the woods: Sergeant Ahrens and Corporals Sciranko and Valenzi. All three were wounded and babbling incoherently. Helping the men to the jeep, Pergrin and Crickenberger hurried back to Malmédy, where so intense was the men's shock that it took Pergrin an hour and a half to get the story of what had happened. Once he had it, he rushed a message to General Hodges in Spa, telling both of the massacre and something of the size of the German force.

Up on the hill near the road junction, darkness turned out in the end to be the only salvation for those few who still survived and for those who had run but had yet to reach safety. A few still hiding among the dead crawled away, mostly to the woods, whence they somehow made their way down the hill into Malmédy. Four men, among them Sergeant Zach, hid in the smoldering ruins of the café, where they were rescued the next morning by an artillery officer passing in a command car.

Three men tried to take cover in a house along a dirt road behind the café, but the people inside bolted their doors and refused to let them in; the men hid behind the house until darkness came. After seeing that, Sergeant Merriken, his wounds almost incapacitating, crawled into a woodshed near the house. He had either dozed off or lost consciousness when he revived to see a figure crawling toward the shed. Arming himself with a piece of wood, he prepared for the worst; but it turned out to be Pfc. Charles E. Reding, who had braved the flames inside the café until the Germans left, then crawled away, the only survivor from the café.

Blood from Merriken's back wounds had dried, gluing his shirt to his back, and he had to drag his right leg like "a chunk of lead." But with the help of Reding, who was unhurt, the two crawled across fields and Highway N-23, and as daylight came, hid in a thicket. Late in the day an elderly farmer approached, spotted them, and signaled with his head and his eyes for the men to come to his house. There the man and his wife hid them through the night, at one time turning away a German patrol that knocked at the door. The next day the woman walked into Malmédy and returned with an ambulance and American aid men.

Others who made it were the medics Anderson and Dobyns; Corporal Paluch, who played dead behind the Café Bodarwé; and Homer Ford. So did Corporal Schmitt, so numb from hours of immersion in icy water that he could only crawl. And the man who had been wounded six times, John Cobbler, but he died later while being evacuated by ambulance from Malmédy.

Mattera eventually reached an outpost of the 291st Engineers on the edge of Malmédy. "Forget the password!" he shouted. "I'm from Lancaster County, Pennsylvania . . . outfit wiped out . . . the Germans are coming!"

To four sisters—Bertha, Ida, Marie, and Martha Martin—who lived in a farm house with their aging father, the appearance of a young American, "wild-eyed, blood-spattered," on the doorstep was a terrifying experience. He said his name was Lieutenant Lary. They sat him on a chair beside the kitchen stove and washed and bound his bloody foot. They thought he was going to die, but when he rallied in the warmth, Marie and a neighbor, Martha Marx, fashioned a crutch for him and practically carried him down the precipitous hill into Malmédy. They reached Colonel Pergrin's command post at three o'clock in the morning. When Pergrin heard Lary's story, the testimony of the sole surviving officer, he sent his assistant operations officer, 1st Lt. Thomas Stack, to Spa to describe the massacre personally to General Hodges.

Hodges immediately ordered his inspector general to begin an investigation. And his aide, Maj. William C. Sylvan, noted in his diary: "There is absolutely no question as to its proof—immediate publicity is being given to the story. General Quesada [commander of the IX Tactical Air Command supporting the First Army] has told every one of his pilots about it during their briefing."

At the Baugnez road junction, the Germans threatened to kill Henri Lejoly, despite his protestations that he was German, for Lejoly had seen what had happened; but they eventually let him go. What happened to Madame Bodarwé would never be determined. She simply disappeared, and her son, back from the wars, was never able to find her or her body.

Five nights after what came to be known as the Malmédy Massacre, a heavy snow fell, mercifully blanketing the bodies of the eighty-six dead (seventy-two in the field where the main massacre occurred) and temporarily concealing the evidence of the most heinous crime inflicted on American troops during the course of the war in Europe. The forty-three men who escaped that dreadful field that Sabbath afternoon would always wonder why they had been spared. So would those men of Battery B who missed the tragic rendezvous, such as Sergeant Barrington, Corporal Bechtel, and the others in vehicles B-26, B-27, and B-28. And Bechtel would long reflect on the premonition of his friend, Luke Swartz. For as Swartz had predicted, he had died in the "something terrible" that he had somehow discerned was about to happen to Battery B, 285th Field Artillery Observation Battalion.

CHAPTER ELEVEN

"The Damned Engineers"

As daylight waned on December 16, Otto Skorzeny sent three of his teams disguised as American soldiers to try their luck at penetrating the front. Four men rode in each jeep, which to Skorzeny was logical, for there were seats for four. Skorzeny failed to note that the Americans had so much transport that seldom did four ride in one jeep, and when it became known that Skorzeny's four-man teams were abroad, any jeep with four men in it aroused suspicions. At least one man who spoke English well, usually a former merchant seaman, rode with each German team, and if forced to communicate with the Americans, he tried to do all the talking.

Of Skorzeny's three large task forces, only one got started on the original mission of seizing bridges over the Meuse. Attached to *Kampfgruppe Peiper*, the force took position well back in the column, and to Peiper's disgust, displayed no inclination to do what it was supposed to do: move out in advance and make a quick dash for the bridge at Huy. Since Peiper had no command authority over the task force, there was nothing he could do about it. Because the other two task forces were to accompany the 12th SS Panzer Division, what they did depended on the progress of that division.

On December 17, Skorzeny sent another of his disguised teams with Peiper and six others to penetrate the line on their own. All probably got through, but how much they accomplished was another matter.

One of the few to cause any confusion—and that minimal—reached a road junction atop the Hautes Fagnes known as Mont Rigi. By the time a convoy of the 1st Division's 16th Infantry arrived during the afternoon of December 17, the Germans had changed the road signs, so that the convoy took not the most direct route to its destination at the town of Waimes but a roundabout route through Malmédy. As American MPs arrived at Mont Rigi, the Germans jumped into their jeep and raced away. The misdirection added about an hour to the convoy's driving time.

Although there was considerable cutting of telephone lines, no serious disruption of telephone service developed. The difficulties experienced by the 99th and 106th Divisions happened before any of Skorzeny's men went into action, probably the work of patrols from the attacking divisions or of civilians.

The first team to be captured was that which accompanied *Kampfgruppe Peiper*. Only half an hour after the team moved ahead to operate on its own, a military policeman stopped the jeep. When the men were unable to give the password, the MP detained them, and discrepancies in their uniforms and what they had in their pockets gave them away. They wore neither leggings nor combat boots, and only one had a regulation U.S. Army belt. Whereas American soldiers used specially printed invasion currency, the men had dollars and pounds, and all carried the German soldier's personal document, the *Soldbuch*. The night before they were to be shot as spies, American authorities permitted captured German nurses in a nearby cell to sing Christmas carols for them.

Just before dark on December 18, engineers manning a roadblock on the highway leading into Malmédy from the Baugnez road junction saw a jeep approaching. In it were what appeared to be four American soldiers and two more on the hood. As the jeep neared the roadblock, one of the soldiers on the hood jumped off and ran toward the roadblock. "They're Krauts!" he yelled. "The men in that jeep are Krauts!" When those inside the jeep opened fire, the other man on the hood jumped off. As the driver of the jeep tried desperately to turn around in the road, the engineers returned the fire. They killed one man who tried to run, and the other three surrendered. They had been bringing two prisoners to what they thought to be German-held Malmédy.

Two teams claiming to have reached the Meuse returned to German lines after only twenty-four hours, having accomplished nothing more than a look around; and a third team was to come near the river on Christmas Eve but would not live to tell about it. Yet another team reached the Meuse at a bridge midway between Huy and Namur. When the driver of the jeep failed to produce a valid trip ticket, an MP at a checkpoint before the bridge arrested the four occupants. They turned out to be wearing Nazi armbands beneath their field jackets and there were German weapons and explosives in the jeep.

The leader, Lt. Günther Schulz, talked freely. He gave the objective of the offensive in considerable detail and catalogued the role of Skorzeny's brigade. A principal goal, he said, was to penetrate SHAEF headquarters to assassinate General Eisenhower and other senior officers. Skorzeny himself, and some fifty men, were to rendezvous in Paris at the Café de la Paix on the Place de l'Opéra and proceed from there to

Versailles. (Was Schulz the lieutenant who had advanced that scheme to Peiper?)

To Americans in the Counter-Intelligence Corps, Skorzeny's reputation lent credence to what Schulz had to say. Early the next morning, December 18, a disturbed colonel on the SHAEF staff brought the information to General Eisenhower. Although Eisenhower scoffed, he soon discerned that the less he cooperated with security arrangements, the more men the Counter-Intelligence Corps detailed for his protection. He finally agreed to move from his villa in St. Germain-en-Laye to a house close to the headquarters in Versailles and gradually accepted the heavy guards, constant changing of routes to and from the headquarters, and other minor inconveniences. An officer who bore a remarkable resemblance to Eisenhower, Lt. Col. Baldwin B. Smith, moved into the villa in St. Germain and took the Supreme Commander's usual route to and from the headquarters each day. In Paris, a detail staked out the Café de la Paix without results.

General Bradley, too, had to endure the concern of his staff for his safety. His personal plane moved from a nearby civilian airfield to a secure military base across the frontier in France, and no longer could he travel in a sedan. Instead he rode in a jeep without general's stars on the bumper and with escort jeeps equipped with machine guns ahead and behind. His staff also insisted on obscuring the stars on his helmet. At the urging of the security officers, he used the rear entrance of the Hôtel Alfa and finally consented to move from his room at the front of the hotel to one at the back.

That there were Germans roaming about in American uniforms led to increased security checks everywhere. Many a soldier, including senior officers, found it insufficient to know the day's password: He also had to answer queries on such Americana as state capitals, who was the current husband of film star Betty Grable (it was band leader Harry James), who were "dem Bums" (the Brooklyn Dodgers baseball team), and what was the name of President Roosevelt's dog (Fala). As Skorzeny himself was later to note, his men set off "a real spy mania in the American back areas," but it resulted in nothing more than minor inconveniences and had little or no effect on operations.

Skorzeny's concern that his men might be treated as spies turned out to be real, for the American command paid no heed to the nicety, as presumed by Skorzeny's legal advisers, that it was acceptable to wear the enemy's uniform as a *ruse de guerre* so long as you did not actually fight in it. Eighteen of Skorzeny's men were captured; eighteen were shot.

A last gasp by one of Skorzeny's teams occurred on Christmas Eve, when four men in a jeep crashed through a checkpoint established on the road leading to a bridge over the Meuse at Dinant by men of the British 3d Royal Tank Regiment. A short distance beyond the checkpoint, the jeep hit a necklace of mines the British had emplaced to be pulled across the road should a vehicle refuse to stop. For a moment there was immense concern, for all four occupants were blown to pieces and all wore American helmets and overcoats. Relief prevailed when the guards found the four were wearing German uniforms underneath.

Combat Command B, 9th Armored Division, William Hoge commanding, began leaving its assembly area near Faymonville for St. Vith to help the 106th Division at 2 A.M. on December 17, two hours before Joachim Peiper started his thrust from Lanzerath. Had the orders that Hoge originally received held—to move into the Losheim Gap—the combat command would have left Faymonville at daybreak and at some point would have bumped into *Kampfgruppe Peiper.*

Even as it was, a small portion of Hoge's command was destined to have a brush with Peiper, for at the town of Ligneuville, down a steep slope from the Baugnez road junction, there was an ad hoc force made up of the company kitchens and supply trucks and also Service Company of CCB's 14th Tank Battalion. The combat command had been engaged in a crash program to install grousers on the tracks of its armored vehicles to widen the tracks and improve footing on muddy ground. The work had been completed except for two Shermans and a 105mm. assault gun, which were unable to accompany the combat command because their tracks had been removed in preparation for installing the grousers. Also in Ligneuville was General Timberlake's headquarters of the 49th Antiaircraft Artillery Brigade, situated in the Hôtel du Moulin, at a curve in the road near the northern edge of town.

Because General Timberlake was in touch by radio with one of his big 90mm. firing batteries near Bütgenbach, he learned fairly early in the morning of a breakthrough in the 99th Division's sector. He ordered his men to pack and be ready to leave Ligneuville at short notice and subsequently ordered departure right after the noonday meal.

When the noise of cannon and machine guns erupted somewhere to the north of Ligneuville, the commander of the ad hoc force, Capt. Seymour Green, set off in his jeep toward the Hôtel du Moulin in hope of getting a better fix on the location of the firing. He was parked beside the road when a tankdozer (a Sherman equipped with a bulldozer blade) came down the hill at breakneck speed. "German tanks!" shouted the driver. "Captain, I was shot at by German tanks!"

The tankdozer had been on loan to the 2d Division, was returning to the 14th Tank Battalion in Ligneuville, and had just passed the Baugnez road junction when Peiper's advance guard began shooting up Battery B's convoy. That sent the operator dashing for Ligneuville.

Passing word to the kitchen and supply trucks to get out of town, Captain Green and his driver headed uphill toward the sound of the firing, while General Timberlake and his staff rushed from the Hôtel du Moulin to make their getaway. At a sharp curve in the highway above

Ligneuville, Green told his driver to stop while he proceeded on foot. "If anything happens," he said, "go back."

As Green rounded the curve, he found himself practically face to face with a German tank. The sight so stunned him that he stood rooted to the spot. As the tank approached, Green threw away his carbine and raised his hands in surrender.

Continuing down the hill, the German column was in full sight of men of the 14th Tank Battalion's Service Company, who were working on the two Shermans and the assault gun on a hill overlooking the highway. The tankdozer joined them there, and when the first German tank appeared—a Panther commanded by Peiper's adjutant, 1st Lt. Arndt Fischer—a round from the 76mm. gun on the tankdozer sent it up in flames. As the driver of Peiper's half-track drove to cover behind a house, Peiper jumped down and helped bandage Lieutenant Fischer, who was badly burned.

Angered at the loss of an officer whom he considered a personal friend, Peiper grabbed a *Panzerfaust* and set out to destroy the American tank, but a round from a German tank knocked the tankdozer out before Peiper got to it. The German tanks also knocked out the immobile Shermans and the assault gun, but the encounter prompted Peiper to delay while he sent *SS-Panzergrenadiers* to clear the town. Peiper himself entered the Hôtel du Moulin, where he spent a half hour helping himself to food left behind by General Timberlake and his staff.

Peiper's goal at that point was to get onto a road just beyond Ligneuville that led west to the town of Stavelot. Although that would represent another encroachment on the 12th SS Panzer Division's assigned route, the road, however poor, was better than one assigned him farther south, and even though Peiper had lost radio contact with headquarters of his division, he assumed from the lack of noise of battle in Malmédy that the other division was still far behind. After Stavelot, he would return to his assigned route at Trois Ponts, so named from three bridges in and near the town at the juncture of the Amblève and Salm Rivers. From there he would proceed to Werbomont on the north-south Bastogne-Liège highway, which would put him past the worst of the Ardennes terrain and provide fairly easy going to the Meuse at Huy, only twenty-five miles beyond Werbomont.

Peiper himself had gone on his way when a Belgian farmer's wife, Mme. Marie Lochem, who was in her barn tending her cows, looked out to see just over twenty American soldiers marching up the street. A German sergeant, Paul Ochmann, culled eight of them to dig graves for three dead Germans. Once they had finished, Ochmann lined them up in a row. As Madame Lochem watched in horror, the sergeant shot one of the prisoners in the head, then another, and another, until all eight lay prone on the ground.

Seven of the men were dead, but the eighth, Cpl. Joseph P. Mass, received only a grazing wound. Throughout the rest of the afternoon he pretended to be dead. As it got dark, he crawled to a clump of trees, where in time a Belgian man brought him food and pointed the direction to St. Vith; but in trying to get there, Mass lost his way and was captured again.

From a window in the Hôtel du Moulin, the proprietor, sixty-nine-year-old Peter Rupp, a German by birth but a Belgian by loyalty, witnessed the executions and feared for the lives of fourteen other Americans held in the hotel, among them Captain Green. As Ochmann entered the hotel, Rupp confronted him. "Murderer!" he shouted. "You killed eight of them! I saw you put the pistol in their mouths!" The German sergeant hit Rupp in the jaw with his fist, knocking out two of his teeth.

A watching SS officer told Ochmann to kill all the prisoners and the old Belgian as well, and Ochmann was on the point of herding the prisoners out of the hotel when another officer countermanded the order. Immensely relieved, Rupp was nevertheless concerned that somebody else might do the prisoners in. Going down to the cellar, he came back with bottles of wine and cognac, which he passed to the German soldiers. In a short while, the prisoners were all but forgotten.

David Edward Pergrin studied civil engineering at Pennsylvania State College and at the same time earned a U.S. Army commission through the ROTC. Not quite six feet tall, he was broad-shouldered, solidly built (he played football at Penn State), and wore glasses. As a lieutenant colonel at the age of twenty-five, he took the 291st Engineer Combat Battalion overseas, where in England it became part of the 1111th Engineer Combat Group, commanded by a veteran of World War I, Col. H. Wallis Anderson, then led it on a variety of engineering tasks through the Normandy hedgerows and on into the Ardennes. Casualties had been remarkably light; one man lost both legs to a mine, but nobody had been killed.

As winter approached, the group commander, Colonel Anderson, assigned one of his three battalions the task of operating sawmills to provide timber for squad huts and other amenities at the front. Another drew the job of building and maintaining roads close behind the front just north of the Losheim Gap, while the third, Pergrin's 291st, served as security for Anderson's headquarters but at the same time operated some sawmills and did road maintenance as required. It was not without intention that the battalions of the 1111th Engineer Combat Group were deployed so as to provide a screening force for the First Army's headquarters town of Spa.

As befitted the role of security for group headquarters, Pergrin's battalion was closest to Anderson's command post in Trois Ponts. Pergrin's own headquarters was just up the hill to the west in the village of Haute-Bodeux. One company was farther west, at Werbomont. A second was billeted in one of the more imposing buildings in the Ardennes, the Château de Froid-Cour (built early in the twentieth century but in the style of a medieval castle), just outside the village of La Gleize, overlooking the scenic valley of the meandering Amblève River. The third was in Malmédy. The three companies of the 291st Engineers were thus either astride or near the central leg of the route that Peiper wanted to take in his quest to reach the Meuse River.

That line-up was destined to remain much the same despite the fact that on December 16, Company A, under Capt. James H. Gamble, began to move from Werbomont closer to the front, assigned to follow the advance of the 9th Armored Division's CCB to remove any demolitions the Germans might have implanted in the Roer River dams. One platoon was already forward, operating sawmills in the villages of Montenau and

Born, midway between Malmédy and St. Vith. Although Captain Gamble hoped to billet the rest of his company in Born, the place was so bulging with support troops of the 106th Division that he continued a few miles on to the village of Amblève, near the headwaters of the little river behind the Losheim Gap. There he found space for his command post in the schoolhouse and billets for his men in houses and barns close by.

Gamble and his men had passed from the French-speaking part of Belgium into the German-speaking part, and they disliked it. "The people of the village watched them unload in a silence as chill and gray as the stone houses." The atmosphere seemed heavy with a sense of foreboding, and there were rumors of a German breakthrough somewhere along the front.

The feeling of uneasiness spread that night through many of the men of the 291st Engineer Combat Battalion. Indeed, the day had begun with an unusual occurrence, four shells from big German railroad guns falling in Malmédy. Then, during the night, the telephone line between the battalion headquarters and the group headquarters went out, which was highly unusual that far behind the front; and when troubleshooters found the break, it was obvious that somebody had cut the line. A short while later, group headquarters passed along an alert disseminated by headquarters of the First Army to watch for German paratroopers. Through much of the night at Amblève, the guard on duty outside Captain Gamble's command post heard heavy traffic on the main road through the town. Had he left his post to check, he would have found vehicles of the 14th Cavalry Group pulling back from the Losheim Gap.

The coming of daylight brought considerably more concern. A platoon of Company B, leaving Malmédy to work on the road leading from the Baugnez junction east toward Bütgenbach, found a steady stream of American vehicles heading west, jeeps and trucks from rear echelon supply units, but also some artillery pieces and big antiaircraft guns. When the platoon leader, 1st Lt. Frank W. Rhea, Jr., arrived in his jeep to check on the platoon's work, the heavy traffic so disturbed him that he drove on in the direction of Bütgenbach to determine what was happening.

Rhea got as far as a road junction just short of Bütgenbach. From there he could hear the sound of small-arms and artillery fire and could see American fighter-bombers attacking some target out of sight beyond the hills. "What's going on here?" Rhea asked an MP on duty at the intersection. All hell had erupted before daylight, said the MP, and the Germans had broken through the 99th Division's lines.

Rhea hurried back to alert his company commander. On the way, he told his men to drop their roadwork and return to Malmédy. As the men passed the road junction at Baugnez, the town in the valley below them looked "like a giant anthill somebody had stirred with a stick." Vehicles were pouring in on two sides and out the other two.

*   *   *

In Amblève that morning, the man on radio duty in Company A's command post, Cpl. Albert C. Schommer, pulled back the blackout curtains and looked outside. Military vehicles of virtually every description were streaming through the village, and not far to the north Schommer could see American planes attacking. He called for 1st Sgt. William H. Smith to take a look.

Smith was so concerned that he jumped into a weapons carrier and drove off to see what he could find out. He returned around ten thirty to report to his company commander, Captain Gamble: "A whole column of German tanks [is] up there, headed in this direction. If we don't get out of here fast, we're not going to get out at all!" (Smith had seen *Kampfgruppe Peiper* on its way to Möderscheid, only a mile and a half from Amblève, and had no way of knowing that at Möderscheid, Peiper was to swing west away from Amblève.)

Although Gamble had no authority to pull back, the choice appeared to be between pulling back and being overrun. He made his decision, telling Sergeant Smith to have the men siphon gasoline from the equipment vehicles so there would be enough for those carrying troops, but he was relieved when a message arrived from Colonel Pergrin: Pull back to Werbomont.

The men were having some difficulty taking down a radio antenna installed on the roof of the schoolhouse when one of them raised a pair of binoculars. He let out a yell. At a road junction not over a mile to the southeast, there were several half-tracks, German soldiers milling about, and what looked to be three German tanks. The man had spotted not *Kampfgruppe Peiper* but one of the 1st SS Panzer Division's other columns. Whoever it was, it speeded Company A's withdrawal.

As the column stopped in Montenau to pick up the platoon operating a sawmill there, Captain Gamble learned that the platoon was desperate for gasoline. The platoon leader, 1st Lt. Archibald L. Taylor, had sent two men in a 6×6 to Malmédy to get more, but they had come back on foot telling of having been shot up by German tanks and their truck overturned alongside a railroad embankment near the village of Ondenval.

Company A, 291st Engineers, made it out, but barely. As Lieutenant Taylor's platoon, bringing up the rear, left Montenau, Germans of the 1st SS Panzer Division were coming in the other side; and as Company A tried to turn west, the little convoy ran into one of the most stifling traffic jams to beset the U.S. Army during the course of the war in Europe. Men of the 7th Armored Division with their tanks, half-tracks, trucks, and artillery were trying to get into St. Vith, and a lot of other people in their vehicles and some with their big guns were trying to get out. Only by using forest trails and logging roads was Company A able to bypass the traffic jam and make its way (albeit slowly) toward the west and in late evening of December 17 reoccupy its old billets in Werbomont.

* * *

When Lieutenant Rhea of Company B, 291st Engineers, returned to Malmédy from his reconnaissance toward Bütgenbach, he reported to his company commander, Capt. John T. Conlin, what he had learned. Conlin promptly telephoned Colonel Pergrin at his headquarters in Haute-Bodeux. Pergrin told him to begin setting up blocks on the roads leading into Malmédy, and he and his staff headed for the town. Although Malmédy was only thirteen miles away, it took forty-five minutes for Pergrin to get there, for almost all the way he was bucking the traffic of the march column of the 7th Armored Division that was heading for St. Vith by way of Trois Ponts.

When Pergrin did reach Malmédy, it was what Lieutenant Rhea had learned of the breakthrough near Bütgenbach that prompted him to warn Battery B, 285th Field Artillery Observation Battalion. Less than an hour after his unheeded warning, another convoy entered Malmédy: that of the 7th Armored Division's artillery. Convinced that the Germans were aiming for Malmédy, since as a road center it was an obvious military objective, Pergrin tried to talk the commander of the artillery's convoy into staying to provide support for the defense of the town; but the officer in charge insisted that his orders were to go to St. Vith, and he was not about to disobey orders.

The vehicles of one of the artillery battalions managed to inch through the congested streets to get onto the road to Stavelot and Trois Ponts, but it proved such a mammoth task that the convoy commander turned the rest of the vehicles around to go back to Eupen and from there get onto the march route. The delay thus imposed was destined to come close the next morning to bringing the 7th Armored Division's artillery into direct confrontation with *Kampfgruppe Peiper.*

As the artillery convoy pulled back from Malmédy, something akin to pandemonium was enveloping the town. An evacuation hospital, a replacement depot, quartermaster units, ordnance units, all began to pull out. Their vehicles added to the congestion already brought about by vehicles of withdrawing units passing through the town. Civilians joined the exodus with bicycles, pushcarts, wheelbarrows, children's wagons, anything in which to transport a few pitiful belongings.

If Colonel Pergrin was to have any hope of keeping the Germans out of Malmédy—indeed, of even delaying them appreciably—he had to have more than the 180 men of Company B and his headquarters, and the only sure way to get help was to call on the rest of his battalion. At that point he had no way of knowing where Captain Gamble's Company A was located in the course of withdrawing from Amblève, but he still had Company C in the Château de Froide-Cour at La Gleize. He promptly ordered that company to Malmédy, stressing that in the process the company was to drop off a squad to establish a roadblock at Trois Ponts and another at Stavelot. If the Germans took either town, they would cut off Malmédy from the west; and if they gained Stavelot, they would be only a short distance from the First Army's headquarters at Spa and even closer to a mammoth gasoline depot along a secondary road leading north from Stavelot to Spa.

That order dispatched, Pergrin made his reconnaissance toward the Baugnez road junction, in the course of which he picked up Ahrens, Sciranko, and Valenzi, and learned of the massacre at the road junction and something of the size of the German column. Unknown at first to Pergrin, the message he sent the First Army's headquarters telling of the massacre and the German column started a limited number of reinforcements heading for Malmédy. For again, if Malmédy should fall, the Germans would have access to roads over which to probe deep into the First Army's rear, not only to Spa but to Liège with its big supply installations.

The only troops at General Hodges's immediate disposal for reinforcing Malmédy quickly had been serving as a kind of palace guard for the First Army's headquarters. They consisted of two separate (nondivisional) infantry units—the 526th Armored Infantry Battalion and the 99th Infantry Battalion, the latter made up of Norwegian Americans and Norwegian citizens (escapees from occupied Norway, merchant seamen stranded in the United States after their vessels were lost) all of whom had volunteered to serve in the U.S. Army. He also had at hand a company of towed 3-inch guns of the 825th Tank Destroyer Battalion. Those three units were soon on their way to Malmédy, and upon arrival all were to come under the commander of the 99th Infantry Battalion, himself a Norwegian American, Lt. Col. Harold D. Hansen.

Early on the afternoon of December 17, a Belgian customs officer, twenty-six-year-old Nicolas Schugens, left by bicycle from the village of Wanne, just south of Stavelot, where he had been living temporarily, to go to a new customs assignment at the border point of Steinebrück. As he left Wanne, the local youths were getting ready for a football match with men of the Royal Air Force who manned a nearby radar post. Cycling through that part of Stavelot on the south bank of the Amblève River, he could see beyond a stone bridge over the stream into the main part of town, where American soldiers were strolling, some with Belgian girls in their Sunday best on their arms.

Near the bridge, Schugens turned south and began to pedal up a steep hill along a narrow, twisting road leading to Ligneuville. He had gone about two miles when he came upon an old man, who shouted that German tanks were coming. "Go to the devil," responded Schugens; "you're crazy." Not long afterwards, he came upon a *garde-champêtre* (rural policeman), who in considerable excitement told him the same thing. Again Schugens said he was crazy and continued on his way, but not without some wariness.

A short while later, Schugens stopped to listen. Was that the rumble of tanks? It seemed incredible. But then came the unmistakable sound of machine guns firing.

That was enough for Schugens. Turning his bicycle around, he took a short cut over a forest trail to Wanne. Because Schugens was in the customs service, he had avoided being drafted into the German Army when the Germans came in 1940, but he was not about to risk it again. Hurrying to his house, he gathered a few possessions and took off again on his bicycle, headed west, he knew not where.

As he left, he told the young men playing football that German tanks were coming. They said he was crazy and went on with their match.

Sgt. Charles Hensel commanded the twelve-man squad (plus a truck driver) from Company C, 291st Engineer Combat Battalion, that the company commander had designated to establish a roadblock at Stavelot. It was completely dark—around 6:30 P.M.—when Hensel and his men got there. Surprised to find great numbers of trucks, their headlights blazing, milling around the town (supply troops billeted there were pulling out), Hensel and his men crossed the bridge over the Amblève and began the steep ascent beyond, where Nicolas Schugens had passed on his bicycle just a few hours earlier. For a short distance there was a line of houses on the left of the road, but they ran out where the ground dropped off sharply toward the deep valley of the Amblève below.

Hensel stopped the truck at a sharp bend in the road, such a sharp bend that any vehicle would have had to slow down to negotiate it. A rocky escarpment bordered one side, and on the other, the drop to the valley of the Amblève was precipitous. Hensel put his men to work installing mines: They had no concern for American vehicles, for the word they had was that anything that came down the road would be German. Hensel placed a bazooka team just down the road from the mines, while one man, Pvt. Bernard Goldstein, went beyond the bend in the road to a small stone shed to serve as a lookout.

Goldstein had been there only a few minutes when he heard tracked vehicles approaching, obviously tanks inching their way slowly along in the darkness, and he could hear men speaking German. The tanks were only a few yards away when Goldstein stepped out into the road, his M-1 rifle at the ready. "Halt!" he commanded.

On the way up to Goldstein's position to guide a companion for Goldstein, Sergeant Hensel heard the incredible command. As paratroopers jumped off the tank and opened fire with rifles and burp guns, Hensel and the man with him dropped to the ground and fired a few rounds from their rifles; but when the tank opened up with its machine gun, they scurried back around the bend in the road. Goldstein clambered up the rocky hill to the west, while the bazooka team fired a rocket that by sheer luck damaged the German tank.

Hensel and his men waited at the roadblock for twenty minutes, but the Germans made no effort to continue. Although several men tried to get forward to look for Goldstein, German fire turned them back. When Hensel heard the tanks backing up the hill, he told everybody to mount the truck, and to prevent the Germans from realizing that he and his men were leaving, the truck coasted down the road to the bridge over the Amblève. Hensel intended making his stand there.

Incredibly, there was to be no need for a fight at the bridge right away. Bone-weary, the venturesome Joachim Peiper had ceased to be his usual volatile self. Had there been no delay in Ligneuville, Peiper would have reached the heights overlooking Stavelot before it got too dark for him to discern that the vehicles in the town were not moving in but pulling out. So, too, there would have been no roadblock manned by a handful of engineers at the canalized stretch of road above the town to add to the impression that Stavelot would be staunchly defended. As it was, Peiper assumed he was in for a fight, and before it started, he needed to give his men some rest. They had been on the road three days and nights almost without pause.

The delay afforded American commanders a few hours to do something about defending Stavelot. It also enabled the 7th Armored Division's artillery convoy to thread its way through the town and on to Trois Ponts and St. Vith.

When Sergeant Hensel and his men reached the bridge at Stavelot, a platoon of engineers was preparing it for demolition. It was probably a platoon of a company of the 202d Engineer Combat Battalion, which had recently arrived from the Third Army and, while resting, was attached temporarily to the 1111th Engineer Combat Group. With that platoon on hand and apparently in charge, Hensel decided to rejoin his own platoon in Trois Ponts.

The intrepid Private Goldstein found his way to the bridge around midnight, but the lieutenant in charge of the engineers sent him with another man as an outpost. The two ran into Germans in the last houses of the town. The other man was mortally wounded, and Goldstein took three bullets in his right hip and leg but eventually crawled back to the bridge.

Soon after midnight, the engineers attempted to blow the bridge, but the charges failed to go off. What they did not know was that among their midst were two of Skorzeny's men disguised as Americans who had done something to sabotage the attempt. (A patrol from a company of the 5th Belgian Fusilier Battalion, which was responsible for guarding the gasoline depot north of Stavelot, had become suspicious of those two men earlier in the evening; but since the Americans appeared to accept them without any concern, the Belgians said nothing.)

In the meantime, when the commander of the Norwegian battalion, Colonel Hansen, reached Malmédy, he agreed with Colonel Pergrin that even though Malmédy appeared to be the German objective, reinforcements should be sent to help the squad of engineers in Stavelot. They got a message to the 526th Armored Infantry Battalion to drop off a company there along with a platoon of towed tank destroyers; and around three o'clock on the morning of December 18, that little force, commanded by the 526th's executive officer, Maj. Paul J. Solis, moved into Stavelot.

Major Solis delayed another attempt to blow the bridge, for he intended putting a roadblock on the other side of the river. Two squads of infantry, a 57mm. antitank gun, and two towed tank destroyers were making their way up the steep hill beyond the Amblève when, shortly before daybreak, *Kampfgruppe Peiper*'s mortars and assault guns opened a preparation fire for the delayed attack on Stavelot. That fire prompted the men to fall back; but as the trucks towing the antitank pieces tried to turn around, direct fire from German tanks farther up the hill knocked out the towed tank destroyers and the trucks. The men who survived hurried back across the bridge.

As German paratroopers headed down the road for the bridge, three of Major Solis's 57mm. antitank guns sprayed the bridge and the approach with canister. The paratroopers took cover in houses near the bridge to await arrival of German tanks.

By that time the light was sufficient for the gunners of two remaining towed tank destroyers, commanded respectively by Sgts. Martin Hauser and Louis Calentano, and emplaced atop a knoll along the road from Malmédy, to make out German tanks descending the steep hill on the other side of the river. Each of the tank destroyers knocked out two German tanks, but other tanks made it to the bridge, where the 57mm. antitank guns were no match for them. Paratroopers and *SS-Panzergrenadiers* soon followed the tanks across the bridge.

At that point, the last vehicles of the 7th Armored Division's artillery convoy were passing through the town—antiaircraft half-tracks with quad-50 machine guns. They paused to give the American infantry a hand but soon pulled out to continue their march by way of Trois Ponts for St. Vith. So, too, the company of the 202d Engineers that had been resting in the town did a yeoman job of fighting for a while, but like the half-tracks, had no real commitment to defending the town and soon pulled out.

So overwhelming were the odds against Solis's lone armored infantry company that at 8 A.M., Solis ordered withdrawal. Most men and the two tank destroyers fell back along the road to Malmédy, but Solis himself, in a half-track, withdrew along the road to Spa. After a delay of more than twelve hours, much of it self-imposed, Peiper had his passage through Stavelot.

Equipped with British uniforms and weapons, the 5th Fusilier Battalion was the first unit of the Belgian Army to be formed after the country's liberation, drawn in large measure from men who had fought in the underground resistance. In early December, the battalion was attached to the First Army to be used primarily for guarding supply installations. One of the tasks assigned the 3d Company under Capt. Jean Burniat was to guard the American gasoline depot, which contained almost a million gallons, on the Stavelot-Spa road. The gasoline was in 5-gallon Jerricans stacked alongside the road, mostly just inside a forest, but some of it on open ground between the forest and the first houses of Stavelot.

As Solis approached the first stacks of Jerricans in his half-track, Lieutenant Detroz of the Belgian Army beckoned him. He and his platoon were the guards—and only defenders—of the depot, and Detroz was convinced that the Germans would soon go for the gasoline. Since the ground on one side of the road rose sharply and on the other dropped off sharply, Detroz suggested piling Jerricans across the road and setting the gasoline on fire. The Belgians and the men with Solis were soon secure behind a great wall of flame.

Although Colonel Peiper had no knowledge of that gasoline depot, a German flank patrol consisting of a few tanks and half-tracks, possibly attracted by the great clouds of smoke, climbed the road from Stavelot. The tanks tried to maneuver past the roadblock, but the sharply sloping ground, as Lieutenant Detroz had figured, prevented it. The patrol turned back.

Peiper's delay in front of Stavelot had afforded time for Colonel Anderson of the 1111th Engineer Combat Group to prepare a defense of what looked to be the next town on the route of the German armored column—his own headquarters town of Trois Ponts. As Anderson pulled his headquarters back, he left defense of Trois Ponts in the hands of his executive officer, Maj. Robert B. Yates. Around midnight on the 17th, Company C, 51st Engineer Combat Battalion, arrived and began preparing the two bridges in the town for demolition while a platoon of the 291st Engineers did the same at a bridge farther south. The engineers were aided by a 57mm. antitank gun of the 526th Armored Infantry Battalion and its crew when a half-track towing the gun threw a tread and had to fall out of the battalion's convoy.

Just before the highway from Stavelot reached Trois Ponts, it curved to the right to run through two railroad underpasses. At the exit of the second, the road came to a dead end before the Amblève River: There one either turned left to enter Trois Ponts over two of the three bridges that gave the town its name or right to follow the trace of the Amblève. Peiper wanted to turn left to pass through Trois Ponts and continue beyond to Werbomont.

By the time the leading tanks of *Kampfgruppe Peiper* moved out of Stavelot, the engineers at Trois Ponts had prepared their bridges for demolition, the two over the Amblève and Salm Rivers in Trois Ponts and the

third over the Salm River a mile south of the town as well, for by an
unlikely but possible roundabout route, the third bridge might also provide access to the town. There was no time to prepare the two railroad
underpasses for demolition; instead, a four-man crew—Buchanan, Higgins, Hollenbeck, and McCollum—positioned the 57mm. antitank gun on
the road between the second underpass and the first bridge. When the
leading German vehicle poked its nose beyond the second underpass, the
crew was to fire, thereby providing time for the engineers to blow the two
bridges. The men were aware that theirs was virtually a suicide mission.
When somebody remarked that they had only seven rounds of ammunition, they said that if they failed to accomplish their mission with those
seven rounds, they would have no need for any more.

It was just after eleven o'clock on December 18 when the lead vehicle
of *Kampfgruppe Peiper*, a Panther, emerged cautiously from the second

underpass. The four-man crew of the 57mm. antitank gun fired. So close was the range that there was little likelihood of their missing, but so puny was their weapon that there was also little likelihood of their knocking out a Panther. That first round nevertheless damaged a track on the tank—but not its 75mm. gun. With one round the tank knocked out the 57mm. piece and killed all four of the crew, but behind those intrepid men the first bridge went up in a great blast of dust, debris, and sound, and the second went up soon after.

There was at that point no way Joachim Peiper and his tanks could get into Trois Ponts from that direction, and for the first time since Peiper started out on his remarkable trek, despair engulfed him. No one understood more clearly than he how badly he needed to get into Trois Ponts. Could he have done so, Peiper was convinced he would have reached the Meuse that night.

Yet at that point a little rock-strewn river defied him. No major obstacle for infantry, the Amblève has such steep banks that it is an insurmountable barrier for tanks and other vehicles. If Peiper was to have any hope of reaching the Meuse, he somehow had to find another way of getting across the river or else face a serpentine, circuitous route along the trace of the river through terrain where passage might be blocked at any number of points.

Consulting a map, Peiper saw that along that road following the trace of the Amblève there was another bridge across the river, downhill from the village of La Gleize near the hamlet of Cheneux; and from there a secondary road led to the road connecting Trois Ponts and Werbomont. If he could seize that bridge—and if it was sturdy enough to support his tanks—he still might make it to the Meuse.

Although Peiper paid scant attention to the possibility, there was one more route by which he might have gained Trois Ponts: the bridge over the Salm south of the town. The job of destroying that bridge belonged to a platoon of Company A, 291st Engineers.

When Peiper began the attack early that morning, the 18th, he had been obsessed with the thought that he faced a major fight to get through Stavelot. In search of an alternate route, he sent a company of Mark IVs along a dirt road leading down the left bank of the Amblève to the village of Wanne (site of the football match the previous afternoon between locals and men of the RAF) and thence to Trois Ponts by way of the railroad station on high ground overlooking the town. Should Peiper be delayed further at Stavelot, those tanks still might secure passage at Trois Ponts.

As it turned out, the hope was vain, for by the time the Mark IVs reached the railroad station, Peiper's main column was approaching and the two bridges in Trois Ponts were already down. On the other hand, if the tanks gained the bridge over the Salm south of Trois Ponts, vehicles might follow a road from Wanne to that bridge and so enter Trois Ponts through the back door.

From a hiding place near the bridge, the noncommissioned officer in charge of the company of 291st Engineers, Sgt. Jean B. Miller, watched as the Mark IVs reached the railroad station. Since Miller had heard the blasts of the two bridges going up in Trois Ponts, he felt sure the Germans would make a try for his bridge. He had not long to wait.

Miller and his men watched from concealed positions as paratroopers who had ridden the tanks moved cross-country downhill toward the bridge. The Germans approached warily, while Miller waited with one hand on the key to the detonator. Some of the Germans began removing the mines that the engineers had implanted in the road in front of the bridge, while others examined the bridge for demolitions.

Still Miller waited. Some of his men, watching breathlessly from their hiding places, wondered what was wrong with their sergeant. It was only when several of the Germans were on the bridge and walking across that Miller finally turned the key. The bridge went up with a thunderous roar, taking several of the paratroopers with it. At that point there was no way for Peiper to get into Trois Ponts.

It was with considerable relief that Peiper learned soon after midday that his advance guard had found the bridge across the Amblève at Cheneux intact and strong enough to support his tanks. That would enable him to get out of the tortuous valley of the Amblève and back en route for the Meuse by way of Werbomont.

Yet he was reckoning once again without the seemingly ubiquitous American engineers.

When news that the German armored column had passed through Stavelot reached headquarters of the First Army, the commander of the IX Tactical Air Command, General Quesada, whose headquarters was in nearby Verviers, telephoned the commander of the 67th Tactical Reconnaissance Group, Col. George W. Peck. He wanted volunteers, said Quesada, to try to break through the low cloud cover and locate the German column. Two pilots, Capt. Richard Cassady and 2d Lt. Abraham Jaffe, were soon in the air in F-6 reconnaissance aircraft.

Since the Germans were obviously moving in or near the valley of the Amblève, Cassady and Jaffe concentrated their search there. To get under the cloud cover, they sometimes had to fly less than a hundred feet off the ground. Then suddenly both pilots spotted what they were after: a column of tanks and other vehicles stretching from La Gleize seemingly all the way back to and beyond Stavelot. To pin down the exact location, they made three runs over the column, and only during the last did the Germans recover enough from their surprise to fire at the planes.

Cassady and Jaffe promptly radioed the IX Tactical Air Command of their find, and Quesada ordered fighter-bombers of the 365th and 368th Fighter Groups to attack. In four-plane flights, sixteen P-47 Thunderbolts roared in, first making a bomb run with 500-pound bombs, then returning to strafe. Some planes worked the column as far back as Stavelot, there shooting up ten German tanks that appeared to be attacking the town.

For most of the German troops, it was an unaccustomed, terrifying experience, since even those with long service on the Russian front had seldom been exposed to attack from the air. Yet losses were few: only some of the smaller vehicles knocked out, a few men killed, a few wounded.

The attack seemingly at an end, the vehicles pulled out of their hiding places and resumed the march. The head of the column was across the bridge over the Amblève and entering Cheneux when sixteen more Thunderbolts broke through the low cover. Near the bridge two half-tracks went up in flames, many of the men in them killed or wounded, and a 500-pound bomb hit the front of a farmhouse, disabling a Panther that was passing on the road. The explosion also blew up a command car and the officers in it.

Peiper's flak tanks with their 37mm. guns and flak wagons with 20mm. pieces fought back, scoring hits on three planes and sending one careening out of control. The gunners could see it disappear over the wooded hills to the north, leaving behind a thick trail of smoke.

The American pilots, as usual, overestimated the damage they did, claiming thirty-two armored vehicles destroyed, which was a vast exaggeration. Peiper actually lost only a few half-tracks and lesser vehicles and the lone Panther at Cheneux. What was of greater importance to both sides was the delay imposed by the attack. The American planes were at it for the better part of two hours, and even after they went away, it took time to get the disabled Panther off the road at Cheneux so that the column could get moving again.

The American pilots had bought almost two and a half hours for men of Captain Gamble's Company A, 291st Engineers. It was time that the engineers needed badly.

Many years before, Wally Anderson as a lieutenant had pondered the moves of Pancho Villa along the Mexican border. As commander of the 1111th Engineer Combat Group, Colonel Anderson pondered the moves of Joachim Peiper. Like Peiper, he consulted a map. Where was the German column headed? Since the Germans had tried to get into Trois Ponts, they obviously intended to move westward along the road to Werbomont. Relegated at that point to the serpentine valley of the Amblève, the Germans, Anderson deduced, would seize the first opportunity to get out of the valley and back onto the Werbomont road.

Aware that the bridge over the Amblève near Cheneux could accommodate tanks, Anderson reasoned that the Germans would use it to gain

egress from the valley, but it was too late to hope to destroy that bridge.
Yet if the Germans used the bridge at Cheneux to get back onto the road
to Werbomont, they would also have to cross another bridge on the way
to Werbomont over the Lienne Creek near the hamlet of Habiémont.
Although the Lienne is smaller even than the Amblève, it too is deeply
incised and forms an effective barrier for vehicles, including tanks.

Colonel Anderson promptly radioed headquarters of Company A,
291st Engineer Combat Battalion, in Werbomont. Captain Gamble was
to send a detail immediately to prepare the bridge over the Lienne for
destruction.

Other than the men of the company headquarters, there were only
about fifteen of Company A's engineers left in Werbomont; the rest were
either at Trois Ponts or Malmédy or out hunting German paratroopers. A
platoon sergeant, Staff Sgt. Edwin Pigg, assembled those men left and
the necessary wire and TNT and loaded all onto the only available truck,
one that had burned out its valves on the hurried trip back from Amblève
the day before and could go no faster than ten miles an hour.

Because the truck moved so slowly, Sergeant Pigg and his detail did
not reach Habiémont and the bridge over the Lienne until 3 P.M. An
hour later they were busy wiring the bridge when a small convoy approached carrying Colonel Anderson and men of the group headquarters
and those whom Colonel Pergrin had left behind in his headquarters in
Haute-Bodeux. The First Army's engineer officer had ordered Anderson
to fall back.

All the way from Trois Ponts the vehicles of that convoy had passed
civilian refugees trudging along with little bundles of possessions. At one
point, as the convoy was forced to slow down, someone knocked on the
side of a command car in which Tech. Sgt. John L. Scanlan and another
soldier were riding. It was an old man and an old woman. "Please, Mon-
sieur," the man pleaded, "take us with you. We are Jewish. We lived
through the Nazi occupation but we cannot stand any more." The two
men shifted to one side of the seat and helped the old couple in.

Had it not been for the bombing by American planes, neither the old
couple nor anyone else in that convoy would have escaped. The last vehicle passed the point where the road from Cheneux joined the Trois
Ponts–Werbomont road no more than a half hour before Peiper's leading
tank got there.

At just about the same time, the little band of Company A's engineers
completed wiring the bridge near Habiémont. By that time they had a
new commander, one of the company's officers, 1st Lt. Alvin Edelstein,
who had arrived with Colonel Anderson's convoy. Although it was
rapidly growing dark, the man charged with turning the detonator key,
Cpl. Fred Chapin, could make out the first German tank as it rounded a
curve not more than two hundred yards away. Others were close behind.

Seeing the Americans near the bridge, the gunner of the first tank opened fire. Although the round did no damage, it prompted Chapin to duck, and when he looked up, he was unable to spot Lieutenant Edelstein, who was to give the signal to blow the bridge.

When he finally saw him, the lieutenant was waving wildly as if to say Blow it! Blow it! Chapin turned the key and saw a "streak of blue lights, the heaving blast of dust and debris, and knew he had a good blow."

Joachim Peiper reputedly pounded one knee with his fist in sheer frustration and muttered: "The damned engineers! The damned engineers!"

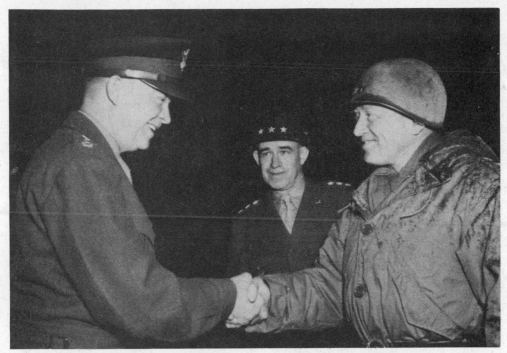

Dwight D. Eisenhower, Omar N. Bradley, George S. Patton, Jr., in Bastogne

Bernard L. Montgomery

Courtney H. Hodges

The Enigma machine

Kenneth Strong

Edwin L. Sibert

E. T. Williams

**THE
INTELLIGENCE
CHIEFS**

Benjamin A. Dickson

Oscar Koch

William H. Simpson

Troy H. Middleton

Leonard T. Gerow

J. Lawton Collins

Hoyt S. Vandenberg

Pete Quesada

Panther tank (Mark V)

Sherman tank (M-4)

Walter M. Robertson

Walter E. Lauer

Alan W. Jones

Norman D. Cota

Raymond O. Barton

Robert W. Hasbrouck

Adolf Hitler

Alfred Jodl

Gerd von Rundstedt

Walter Model

Joseph Sepp Dietrich

Hasso von Manteuffel

Nebelwerfer

Antiaircraft half-track

Captured Tiger tank (Mark VI)

Erich Brandenberger

Hermann Priess

Walter Krüger

Heinrich von Lüttwitz

Friedrich von der Heydte

Otto Skorzeny

Joachim Peiper

Henri Lejoly

Victims at Baugnez

Lyle Bouck, Jr.

Long H. Goffigon

William D. McKinley

Derrill M. Daniel

David E. Pergrin

Marlene Dietrich

Bruce C. Clarke

Hurley E. Fuller

Elise Delé

Renée Lemaire

Wilhelm Osterhold

Karl Wortmann

Preparing to execute prisoners of Skorzeny's Brigade

Gasoline depot near Stavelot

Matthew B. Ridgway

James M. Gavin

Anthony C. McAuliffe

Leland S. Hobbs

Maurice Rose

Samuel M. Hogan

Walter Bedell Smith

Francis de Guingand

Manton S. Eddy

Ernst Barkmann

Daniel B. Strickler

Léon Praile

Ernest Harmon

Creighton Abrams

William R. Desobry

Hal D. McCown

Gerhard Tebbe

Fritz Bayerlein

CHAPTER TWELVE

The Race for Bastogne: The First Phase

Behind blackout curtains, lights burned through the night of December 16 in almost every office in the Grand Hôtel Britannique in Spa alongside once well-kept lawns where guests come to take the cure of the mineral waters used to stroll down to a little rock-strewn river, the Vesdre, and the bandstand alongside it. Well before daylight, the commander of the First Army, General Hodges, was in his war room in what had once been an elegant suite.

Although immensely concerned, Hodges was still disinclined to accept that the enemy's attack was anything more than an attempt to thwart his drive on the Roer River dams, and when General Gerow telephoned just after 7 A.M. to ask again for permission to halt the 2d Division's attack on the dams and pull the division back, Hodges resorted to the device of the uncertain commander: Leave the decision to the man on the ground. Still unhappy about calling off the attack, he told Gerow to handle the situation as he saw fit.

Otherwise, Hodges could feel a certain comfort in that reserves were on the way: the 9th Armored Division's CCB and the entire 7th Armored Division to St. Vith; a battalion of combat engineers and a regiment of the 1st Division to help the 99th Division (the rest of the 1st Division would also be arriving soon); and the bulk of the 10th Armored Division to help north of Luxembourg City. Yet his relative peace of mind was short-lived, for first reports were soon in of *Kampfgruppe Peiper*'s break-through at Honsfeld. Hodges was quickly on the telephone to his colleague in the Great War and longtime friend, the commander of the Ninth Army, "Big Bill" Simpson. The 30th Infantry Division, Hodges knew, was out of the line just north of Aachen, and he needed it. Badly.

Shortly before noon on the 17th, the 30th Division's commander, Maj. Gen. Leland S. Hobbs, received a call telling him to get his division on the road. "I don't know any details," said the chief of staff of the XIX Corps, "but you are going south. I think it is only temporary." To Hodges, it appeared that *Kampfgruppe Peiper* intended either to take Malmédy and swing northwest on Liège or to continue to the Bastogne-Liège highway and then turn north on Liège. In either event, he intended using the 30th Division to block a move on Liège.

General Hodges also telephoned headquarters of the 12th Army Group in an effort to reach General Bradley to ask for two airborne divisions—the 82d and 101st—which constituted the Supreme Commander's only reserve; but Bradley was out of touch, on the way back to Luxembourg City from his meeting with Eisenhower in Versailles. He was not expected back until late afternoon.

In the Trianon Palace Hotel in Versailles, Eisenhower's staff was also thinking about the two airborne divisions. While General Bradley was still en route back to his headquarters, the chief of the SHAEF planning staff, a British officer, Maj. Gen. John F. M. ("Jock") Whiteley, telephoned Bradley's chief of staff, Maj. Gen. Leven C. Allen, to remind him that the two divisions were available. "I'll put it up to Ike, if you wish," said Whiteley.

Although Allen was quick to say yes, there had been no word on General Eisenhower's decision when Bradley got back to his headquarters. He went immediately to the war room for a look at the situation map, which showed that the Germans had committed fourteen divisions. "Pardon my French," said Bradley, "but where in hell has this son of a bitch gotten all this strength?"

Yet even though Bradley referred to the offensive as "Rundstedt's all-out attack," he still looked on it with parochial vision. He still believed that it was deliberately designed to disrupt the First Army's attack for the Roer River dams and the impending offensive by the Third Army, and that if von Rundstedt could force the American command "to pull our strength" away from the Third Army's sector, "he will achieve his primary purpose." He saw the enemy's geographical objective to be Liège in an attempt to disrupt American supply and noted that the Ninth Army should be alert to the possibility of an attack to link with the main thrust on Liège (the Small Solution). To a suggestion that he move his headquarters back from Luxembourg City, Bradley responded: "I will never move backwards with a headquarters. There is too much prestige at stake."

Soon after Bradley's return, General Hodges called asking for the two airborne divisions. Bradley immediately put in a call to Eisenhower, but it was 7 P.M. before Eisenhower, reluctant to part with his last reserve, gave his permission. Everybody in Luxembourg City and Versailles agreed that the divisions should move to Bastogne, not with an eye to turning Bastogne into a bastion but in recognition that the road network there would afford multiple options. When Bradley told Hodges he was to get the divisions, Hodges already wanted to exercise an option: He needed only one division at Bastogne; the other he wanted to block Peiper at Werbomont.

In a venerable French Army barracks at Sissons, thirty miles southeast of Rheims, Maj. Gen. James M. ("Slim Jim") Gavin, at thirty-seven years of age the youngest commander of an American division, the 82d Airborne, had just returned from a performance for his troops by the Ballet Russe de Monte Carlo. He was sitting down to dinner at his headquarters when he received a telephone call from an old friend, the chief of staff of the XVIII Airborne Corps, Col. Ralph D. Eaton. Eisenhower's headquarters, said Eaton, "considered the situation on the Ardennes front critical," and the 82d and 101st Airborne Divisions were to move immediately to the Ardennes.

At General Hodges's request, the divisions were to be committed under the command of the XVIII Airborne Corps. Since the corps commander, Maj. Gen. Matthew B. Ridgway, was away in England (conducting a postmortem on the lengthy battle the two divisions had concluded not quite three weeks before in the Netherlands), as was the senior division commander, Maj. Gen. Maxwell D. Taylor, commander of the 101st Airborne Division (in Washington at Ridgway's behest to prod the War Department into increasing the strength of the airborne division), Gavin was to serve as acting corps commander.

Although some men from both divisions were on pass to Paris, they would be sent forward later. Since the 82d Airborne Division had had longer out of the line to recover from the fighting in the Netherlands, the division was to move first, shortly before dawn the next morning, December 18, and go to Bastogne. The 101st was to follow as soon as possible. In keeping with General Hodges's wish, it was to make for Werbomont.

The necessary orders issued, Gavin departed shortly before midnight to consult with Hodges in Spa. Aware that he might run into Germans, he and two members of his staff set out in darkness, fog, and light rain in an open jeep "prepared for any eventuality."

With the news that an airborne division was coming to Bastogne, the commander of the VIII Corps, Troy Middleton, could relax a little. As he was disturbingly aware early in the evening of December 17, the center of his front was falling to pieces, leaving him to wonder whether he or the Germans would be in Bastogne to welcome the airborne troops when they got there.

It was thus with additional relief that Middleton later in the evening saw the commander of the 10th Armored Division, Maj. Gen. William H. H. Morris, Jr., enter his headquarters in the Heintz barracks (named for a lieutenant from Bastogne who was killed in World War I). On the way north from the Third Army, the 10th Armored Division had already passed to Middleton's command under orders to counterattack the flank of the enemy's penetration north of Luxembourg City. Middleton changed that order. While the bulk of the division was to pursue its original mission, Morris's leading combat command, then bivouacked near Luxembourg City, forty miles from Bastogne, was to move as rapidly as possible the next day to Bastogne. To Middleton's immense concern, a race for Bastogne had developed, and he had precious little left to throw off the sled to the wolves.

Just how long it would be before General von Lüttwitz and his 47th Panzer Corps could get across the little Clerve River and begin traversing the fifteen remaining miles to Bastogne depended primarily upon the 28th Division's 110th Infantry, sorely pressed but still holding at the end of the first day's fighting along the Skyline Drive. It also depended, to a lesser degree, upon what happened to the division's other two regiments, the 109th Infantry to the south and the 112th Infantry to the north; for if the Germans could overrun or even bend back those regiments in the manner of the sweep of a windshield wiper, the 110th Infantry would be left to fight alone.

Whether the 109th Infantry could provide any help to the central regiment depended in turn upon the advance of the German 5th Parachute Division, the northernmost unit of the Seventh Army. For once past the first tier of villages behind the Our River, the paratroopers were to aim for Wiltz, where the 28th Division's commander, Dutch Cota, had his headquarters, only twelve miles from Bastogne. That advance would take place along the seam between the two American regiments, and at the seam, in the village of Hoscheid atop the Skyline Drive, there was only a small American force: a portion of the 110th Infantry's Antitank Company with three Shermans and the 707th Tank Battalion's assault gun platoon, six Shermans mounting 105mm. howitzers.

At two thirty on the morning of December 17, General Cota telephoned the commander of the 109th Infantry, Colonel Rudder, at his headquarters in the Hôtel Lieffrig in Ettelbruck. Earlier in the night, several German assault guns had crossed the Our on a weir near Vianden and with a parachute battalion had moved up a winding road toward the Skyline Drive and Hoscheid. That looked to Cota as if the Germans intended taking Hoscheid, then driving down the Skyline Drive to cut off Rudder's regiment. Cota ordered Rudder to send a platoon each of infantry and tanks to reinforce Hoscheid.

The tanks and the soldiers riding on them failed to make it, for the paratroopers had already cut the Skyline Drive south of Hoscheid. Stopped a half mile short of the village, the relief force could provide no help; Rudder eventually had to call it back to help a besieged battery of field artillery.

The tanks, assault guns, and men of the Antitank Company fighting as infantry nevertheless held throughout the day but at nightfall, almost out of ammunition, the foot troops climbed aboard the vehicles to make a run for it back to positions of the 687th Field Artillery Battalion and then to fall back with that battalion to Wiltz. The stand at Hoscheid had delayed the parachute division for a day, but at that point the paratroopers had split the two American regiments. From then on, the 109th Infantry would be totally involved in trying to prevent the Germans from expanding the southern shoulder of their penetration.

At the other end of the Skyline Drive, where the 112th Infantry's positions were on the German side of the Our River and where the Germans had failed on the first day to get a bridge over the river at Ouren, the Americans through the night could hear the noise of German tanks. A battalion of the 116th Panzer Division was moving into the village of Lutzkampen for renewed attack before daylight on the 17th. Through much of the night searchlights played against the clouds, keeping the American line in a kind of twilight and helping *Volksgrenadiers* and *Panzergrenadiers* to move into attack positions.

An hour before dawn, the searchlights went out, and German artillery and *Nebelwerfers* opened fire all along the two-battalion line. As the shelling lifted, eighteen tanks advanced from Lutzkampen. Although men of the 1st Battalion managed to stop most of the accompanying *Panzergrenadiers*, the tanks fired methodically into the foxholes with machine guns and cannon, broke through, and turned down the road toward Ouren, in the process cutting in behind the 1st Battalion's headquarters village of Harspelt.

Just before the artillery preparation began, in response to repeated pleas for help from the regimental commander, Colonel Nelson, a platoon of self-propelled tank destroyers from the 9th Armored Division's CCR had reached Harspelt. Those destroyers opened up on the German tanks at short range, knocking out four but in the process losing all but one gun.

As the surviving tanks continued toward Ouren, observers for the 112th Infantry's Cannon Company, whose 105mm. howitzers were just across the Our, spotted them only eight hundred yards away. The gunners depressed their pieces, bore-sighted them, and fired. With the second round, the first tank went up in flames. The German tanks quickly returned the fire, knocking out one of the howitzers; but the others continued to fire, eventually knocking out three more of the tanks and damaging two.

While the remaining tanks pulled back behind a rise in the ground,

American fighter-bombers appeared, also as a result of repeated calls for help from Colonel Nelson. That sent the German tanks scurrying for concealment in nearby woods. Although the time of the fighter-bombers over a cloud-shrouded battlefield was brief, the German tankers had become wary.

Again Nelson appealed to his division commander, General Cota, for help. The parent unit of the tank destroyers that had helped at Harspelt, the 9th Armored Division's CCR, was in reserve, Nelson knew, at Trois Vierges, only eight miles from Ouren. Although Cota passed along the request for the armor to the corps commander, General Middleton, that was the only reserve left to Middleton, other than three engineer battalions, to block the roads to Bastogne. Middleton said no.

Back on the heights beyond the Our, four more German tanks emerged from Lutzkampen and with help from *Panzergrenadiers* pushed much of the 1st Battalion back into woods near the positions of the 229th Field Artillery Battalion. In mid-morning, the tanks fired on the artillery pieces, but the American gunners used direct fire to turn them back. When infiltrating *Panzergrenadiers* took the gunners under fire later in the day, Colonel Nelson ordered the battalion commander, Lt. Col. John C. Fairchild, to move his howitzers to the other side of the Our.

The inexperienced *Volksgrenadiers* of the 560th Volksgrenadier Division, often advancing as they had done the first day in column or closely bunched, attacked the 3d Battalion in the village of Sevenig and nearby pillboxes. They captured a few of the pillboxes, but in a repeat of the first day's counterattack, the 2d Battalion crossed the Our from its reserve position and retook them.

As the day wore on, Colonel Nelson could take comfort in that most positions were still intact, but he was disturbingly aware that hundreds of Germans had infiltrated into the rear of his men, some of them firing with burp guns and rifles on his own command post in Ouren. The infiltrators had virtually surrounded his 1st Battalion; and although he had no reason to believe that the battalion had folded, he had lost radio contact with the commander, Colonel Allen, in Harspelt.

In mid-afternoon, Nelson sent his executive officer, Lt. Col. William F. Train, on a roundabout route to Wiltz, avoiding the embattled positions of the 110th Infantry, to report personally to General Cota on the regiment's condition. Nelson wanted Cota's authority to pull everybody back behind the Our. As it turned out, Cota was thinking the same thing, and even before Train arrived, he had gained General Middleton's approval. The only limiting proviso was that the two bridges over the river at Ouren be destroyed.

By the time the 3d Battalion began to withdraw early in the evening, the German infiltrators had occupied that part of Ouren lying on the east bank of the Our and had seized the bridge south of the village over which the 3d Battalion was supposed to withdraw. Suspicious, the battalion commander, Maj. Walden F. Woodward, sent a patrol to the bridge and learned that the Germans were there. Having earlier sent all his vehicles to the rear, Woodward led the infantry to a ford farther south and crossed, feet wet but safe.

On the west bank at Ouren, Colonel Nelson and the men of his headquarters departed under sporadic small-arms fire. Although a rear guard kept the Germans away from the bridge joining the two sections of the village until most of the troops had left, the Germans were too close for the Americans to think of preparing the bridge for demolition.

When Nelson reached Weiswampach, at the northern extremity of the Skyline Drive, he learned that a patrol had failed to contact the 1st Battalion to inform Colonel Allen of the withdrawal. Nelson was worried, for he knew that without orders, Allen would never fall back.

It was near midnight when a communications sergeant finally established intermittent radio contact with Allen's command post. Getting Allen on the radio, Nelson asked if he recognized his voice. When Allen said yes, Nelson told him: "Get all your boys together and visit Blue [3d Battalion] and then White [2d Battalion]." Considering the location of those two battalions, that could mean only one thing: Withdraw by way of Ouren. Allen said he understood.

The Germans had already forced one of Allen's companies back onto the adjacent 424th Infantry of the 106th Division, but Allen set out with the rest of the battalion. As the column neared the bridge linking the two sections of Ouren, Allen, like Woodward, sent a patrol to see if the Germans held the bridge. They did, reported the patrol, but with only half a squad.

Allen determined to bluff his way through, and even if he failed, he considered he could overwhelm six Germans. Ordering his men into a column of twos, he put an officer who spoke German in the lead. In the darkness just before dawn, with the officer shouting commands in German, the men marched in closed ranks across the bridge. Nobody challenged them, and nobody fired a shot.

For two days men of the 116th Panzer and 560th Volksgrenadier Divisions had fought to take the two bridges over the Our at Ouren, but once they held them, they discovered that neither bridge could handle even a tank the size of a Mark IV. Rather than delay the advance while reinforcing the bridges, the corps commander, General Krüger, arranged for his tanks and half-tracks to cross on the bridge of the neighboring 47th Panzer Corps at nearby Dasburg. The delay was of paramount concern to General von Manteuffel, who had been convinced that the 116th Panzer Division's route was the fastest way to the Meuse River.

During the night of the 17th and all through the 18th, as Krüger's divisions plodded across the Our, they gave the 112th Infantry a respite and an opportunity to dig in on a new position covering Weiswampach, roughly a thousand yards behind the Our. Throughout the day of December 18, men at the southern end of the position could see German tanks, half-tracks, and troops filing past. Howitzers of Cannon Company and the 299th Field Artillery Battalion harassed them but were unable to stop the procession.

When the infantry commanders found time to count noses, they learned that despite two days of heavy fighting, the 112th Infantry had emerged in relatively good shape. After having dealt the foe considerable losses, including a probable twenty-one tanks, the regiment still was an effective fighting force.

In mid-afternoon of December 18, Colonel Nelson received an order from General Cota by radio to withdraw through Trois Vierges, on the main St. Vith–Bastogne road, Highway N-12, and fight a delaying action back toward Bastogne. By that time, Nelson knew that the 9th Armored Division's CCR had left Trois Vierges and suspected that the Germans filing past his southern flank had moved in. He saw only two ways of getting to Highway N-12 on the Bastogne side of Trois Vierges. He could cut across the German route of advance between the Skyline Drive and Trois Vierges, which he saw as impossible without tanks or self-propelled tank destroyers; or he could circle well around Trois Vierges.

Notifying Cota that he intended bypassing Trois Vierges, Nelson led his regiment before daylight on December 19 to a point north of the town and was getting ready to swing around it when he received a radio message from the 28th Division's headquarters telling him to occupy a new line, essentially the old position he had just left near Weiswampach. Believing the staff at Wiltz to be out of touch with the situation and convinced at that point that he could accomplish neither mission, Nelson got into a jeep and rode a few miles to the north to the town of Vielsalm, where the commander of the 106th Division, General Jones, had shifted his headquarters from St. Vith.

Once Nelson explained the situation, Jones welcomed him with fervor, for Jones needed every man he could get, and as if by miracle, a commander had appeared who had at his disposal a complete regimental combat team—a company of engineers, a battalion of artillery, a few towed tank destroyers, and an entire regiment of infantry. "From now on," said Jones, "you are attached to the 106th Division, and I will take full responsibility."

Like the 109th Infantry, forced by the Germans back to the south, the 112th Infantry had been forced back to the north, no longer to be involved even peripherally in the struggle to keep the Germans away from Bastogne. From the start that job had belonged, in any case, almost entirely to Hurley Fuller and the 110th Infantry Regiment.

Between the hours of midnight, December 16, and daylight, December 17, much happened that was to have a telling effect on how well and how long the 110th Infantry could continue to do its job. (*See map, Chapter Seventeen, p. 355.*) Having finally gained control of two-thirds of the 2d Battalion from the division reserve, Colonel Fuller had ordered the battalion to counterattack at daylight, retake Marnach atop the Skyline Drive, and block the principal road into his headquarters town of Clervaux. Yet things were happening that were going to make that difficult.

The action began in Clervaux, the picturesque town astride a bend in the Clerve River whose bridges the 2d Panzer Division needed in order to get through the town onto a high plateau beyond and thence to Highway N-12, leading to Bastogne. Soon after midnight, assisted by the two Germans equipped with a radio who had slipped into the Pharmacie Molitor, German artillery and *Nebelwerfers* began to bombard the town. The shelling proved to be covering fire for German patrols, which entered the town in the darkness and began to harass the 110th Infantry's headquarters installations, including the men of Headquarters Company who were holed up in the old château. In reaction to the shelling and the patrols, Battery B, 109th Field Artillery Battalion—which had already displaced from its original firing positions to others near the château in Clervaux—had to displace farther to the rear. That put its howitzers out of range for supporting the counterattack.

Other German actions were to deny the counterattacking 2d Battalion all artillery support. Bypassing Company A's strongpoint on the Skyline Drive at Heinerscheid, a company of *Panzergrenadiers* attacked Battery A's firing positions behind the Skyline Drive, knocked out or captured three half-tracks of the 447th Antiaircraft Artillery Battalion, and overran the guns. The artillerymen saved not a single gun, nor was there any opportunity to spike them. By 4 A.M. Battery A had ceased to exist except for a few men who made their way out on foot.

The overrunning of Battery A and the displacing of Battery B left only Battery C, south of Clervaux at Bockholz, and Cannon Company, nearby at Munshausen, in position to deliver any fire in support of the 2d Battalion's counterattack. Yet both those units were preoccupied with providing support for the hardpressed strongpoints on and behind the central and southern portions of the Skyline Drive, and both were soon to come under strong German ground attack.

As men of the 2d Battalion (less one company) moved onto the ridge north of Clervaux before daylight, planning to get past Reuler and into Marnach, German tanks and half-tracks were already emerging from Marnach, aiming both for Clervaux and for the same high ground that the 2d Battalion occupied. So canalized was the road from Marnach to Clervaux that the commander of the 2d Panzer Division, Colonel Lauchert, decided to opt for a second route that led from the ridge north of the town, through a succession of hairpin turns, into the western end of the town near the railroad station and Colonel Fuller's headquarters in the Hôtel Claravallis. To get into Clervaux by the back door.

Hardly had the American infantry begun to advance than Company F on the left bumped head-on into German troops emerging in a skirmish line from a woods. It took the company the better part of two hours to drive those Germans back. At the same time, Company E ran into Germans in a draw close to Reuler. A stiff fight was going on there when Colonel Fuller radioed the battalion commander, Lt. Col. James R. Hughes, to send a platoon to block the Marnach-Clervaux highway. A platoon of Company E tried, but a single rifle platoon had no chance of stopping the tanks and half-tracks that were by that time clanking down the road toward Clervaux.

Part of the armored assistance Fuller was counting on in the counterattack on Marnach—a drive by the eighteen light tanks of the 707th Tank Battalion down the Skyline Drive from Heinerscheid—quickly ran afoul of German self-propelled guns. As the tanks neared the hamlet of Fishbach, not quite midway between Heinerscheid and Marnach, the guns knocked out eight of them, and *Panzerfausts* accounted for three more. Five other tanks escaped to the west, while the other two, although damaged, limped back to Heinerscheid and the perimeter defense of the 110th Infantry's Company A.

A second drive in support of the counterattack had slightly more success—that by a platoon of medium tanks commanded by 1st Lt. Raymond E. Fleig with a platoon of Company C's infantry riding on the decks. Repeating a maneuver executed the day before, the force moved from Munshausen northeastward on Marnach. The tanks and infantry reached the edge of Marnach and held a few houses against a swift riposte by German tanks and *Panzergrenadiers*, but since the little force clearly would be unable to retake the village without help, Colonel Fuller in mid-morning ordered it back.

Faint hope stirred for Colonel Fuller that same morning with the unexpected arrival of more tank support. Earlier, the corps commander, General Middleton, had ordered the 9th Armored Division's CCR at Trois Vierges to move to a reserve position closer to Bastogne and attached the combat command in place to the 28th Division; but it was not to be used without Middleton's approval. Yet the 28th Division's commander, General Cota, was so desperate for help that he exceeded his authority and sent a staff officer to commandeer a company of tanks from CCR's column: Company B, 2d Tank Battalion.

With seventeen Shermans, the commander, Capt. Robert L. Lybarger, reported to Fuller in Clervaux around 10:30 A.M. on the 17th. Fuller promptly sent a platoon to Heinerscheid to support Company A, another to Reuler to help Colonel Hughes's 2d Battalion, and the third to clear Germans from the eastern end of Clervaux. As on the first day of the offensive, Fuller was expending his armor in little increments, but under orders to hold at all costs everywhere, he saw no alternative.

Those platoons moving to Heinerscheid and Reuler were in for rude receptions. The platoon going to Reuler was entering the killing zone of the bulk of the 2d Panzer Division and soon paid the consequences: three out of five tanks knocked out in what was for the crewmen their first combat experience. The platoon going to Heinerscheid arrived just as an attack by the 116th Panzer Division's reconnaissance battalion, having crossed the Our at Dasburg, was nearing a climax. As Company A's defense collapsed, the platoon lost two tanks, but the other three managed to make their way to join the platoon at Reuler.

It was the lot of the men in those tanks to arrive just as the tanks and *Panzergrenadiers* of the 2d Panzer Division were mounting a climactic attack to clear the heights above Clervaux and get into town by the back door. As night was falling, the Germans drove the five surviving tanks and about two hundred infantrymen out of Reuler. At the same time, other German tanks in the nearby village of Urspelt were knocking out four of the five light tanks that had survived the early morning shootout on the Skyline Drive at Fishbach. Before fleeing with men of the 1st Battalion's headquarters, the crew of the fifth tank put a thermite grenade down the muzzle of its cannon.

The collapse at Urspelt left the Germans free to come in behind the men of Colonel Hughes's 2d Battalion, who were trying to make a stand on an open ridge between the two villages, and the infantrymen and their five tanks were soon surrounded. Convinced that the situation was hopeless, Colonel Hughes ordered the tanks to form a rear guard while the infantry tried to escape in the darkness in small groups. After allowing the infantry a reasonable time, the tankers were to blast their way out of the encirclement.

In the pre-dawn darkness of December 18, only about sixty of the infantrymen made it. The withdrawal was even more disastrous for the tanks. Moving cross-country, four either threw a track or bogged in the mud and had to be abandoned. The fifth, with men of the other crews clinging to the decks, made it to the Clerve, but in attempting to ford the river, mired in the soft bottom. It, too, had to be abandoned.

The back door to Clervaux was open.

South of Clervaux, at Munshausen, Bockholz, Holzthum, and Consthum behind the Skyline Drive, and at Hosingen and Hoscheid astride the high ridge, every American strongpoint was under heavy attack. Assisted by assault guns that had at last toiled up the muddy roads from the deep valley of the Our River, not only were troops of the 26th Volksgrenadier Division attacking the strongpoints but others were bypassing them and edging down back roads through thick forests to get at the bridges over the Clerve.

The first of the positions to be abandoned was that of Battery C, 109th Field Artillery Battalion, just outside Bockholz, where four assault guns joined the *Volksgrenadiers* that had given the battery such a difficult time the day before. Rather than suffer annihilation, the battery commander in mid-morning ordered withdrawal. Despite German fire, the artillerymen hitched their howitzers to their trucks and made a getaway, losing but two howitzers in the process and eventually occupying new firing positions on the other side of the Clerve.

At nearby Munshausen, Company C and Cannon Company were under attack all through the 17th with the Germans so close that the gunners had difficulty depressing their howitzers low enough to hit them. The companies were without the tank support they had had on the first day, for soon after Lieutenant Fleig's tank platoon withdrew from Marnach, Colonel Fuller ordered Fleig and the platoon of infantry that accompanied him to help out in Clervaux.

Learning in early afternoon of the heavy pressure at Munshausen, Fuller withheld the infantry platoon for the defense of his command post but sent Fleig and his tanks back to Munshausen. As the tanks moved up from the river valley toward the village, a *Panzerfaust* knocked out one, and when the others reached the fringe of the village, so many of the buildings were in flames that the tankers assumed no Americans remained. Two rounds from a bazooka, which the tank crewmen took to be from a *Panzerfaust*, convinced them.

In reality, the man firing the bazooka thought the tanks were German, and Company C and Cannon Company were in full control of Munshausen. They had been under attack by the 2d Panzer Division's reconnaissance battalion, which was providing flank protection for Colonel Lauchert's main drive, and late in the afternoon Lauchert afforded a company of Panthers to help. With that added strength, the reconnaissance battalion reached the center of the village, but as the company commander rode erect in the turret of the first Panther, an American rifleman shot him in the head. That took the spirit out of the attack, and the Germans fell back to the fringe of the village.

By that time, Cannon Company had lost two of its six howitzers, and near midnight the two company commanders agreed that unless they withdrew, everybody would be lost. Because the Germans were too close to hope to get the howitzers out, the men spiked them and broke into small groups to try to escape. Although there were still more than two hundred men, so thick were the Germans in the river valley that few made it.

When men of the 2d Panzer Division's reconnaissance battalion swarmed over Munshausen the next morning, they were impressed by the number of their comrades who had been shot through the head. There was no anger at that, merely admiration for those whom they were for long to speak of as "the sharpshooters of Munshausen." What did anger them was finding the body of one of their company commanders, Capt. Heinz Nowak. Something of a maverick, Nowak had endeared himself to his men. The night before, he had marched off alone into Munshausen "swinging a souvenir American bayonet like a baton." When his men found him, he was dead on a path near the church, the bayonet protruding from his throat.

Incensed, the men wanted to kill their American prisoners, but a sergeant intervened. The war would soon be over, he said, and "measures would be taken against those who mistreated prisoners of war."

At Hoscheid, the few men of Antitank Company with their tank and assault gun support, under attack all day on the 17th from paratroopers of the 5th Parachute Division, made their escape after nightfall. At nearby Holzthum in mid-afternoon, the few survivors of Company L— the company commander, Lieutenant Saymon, and forty men—slipped away to join the defenders of the adjacent village of Consthum.

Atop the Skyline Drive at Hosingen, Company K, Lieutenant Payne's platoon of Shermans, and Company B of the 103d Engineers were under heavy attack following the late arrival west of the Our of the 26th Volksgrenadier Division's reserve regiment. The continued American possession of Hosingen was so irksome to the commander of the 47th Panzer Corps, General von Lüttwitz, that he early sent the *Panzer Lehr Division*'s advance guard to help. He had to have unfettered passage through the village if the advance guard was to cross the Clerve downhill from Hosingen and exploit the gains of the 26th Volksgrenadier Division. So badly did he want the village that he told Colonel Lauchert to loan a few of his Panthers and Mark IVs of the 2d Panzer Division to assist the attack from the north.

Faced by such an overwhelming force, the defenders of Hosingen were doomed. By noon the village was surrounded, the men fighting desperately from the houses, Lieutenant Payne's five tanks dashing here and there in response to one threat from German tanks and assault guns after another. Although Company K's commander, Capt. Frederick Feiker, pleaded for artillery support, not a single battery was still within range. By nightfall the engineers were isolated in one part of the village, the infantry and three remaining tanks in a perimeter defense of Company K's command post in another; and ammunition was perilously low.

When Captain Feiker radioed his situation to his battalion commander, Major Milton, in Consthum, Milton told him to break into small groups and infiltrate out to join the remainder of the 3d Battalion in Consthum. So close were the encircling Germans, said Feiker, that that would be impossible. Not long after daylight on the 18th, all ammunition exhausted except for a few hand grenades and a few smoke rounds for nonexistent 60mm. mortars, Feiker asked Milton what he was to do. The decision, said Milton, was his.

Not long after that, a radio operator reported: "We've blown up everything there is to blow except the radio, and it goes next." The men in Hosingen, who had stymied superior forces for two days and into a third, at last surrendered. That they numbered little more than three hundred came as a surprise to their captors. That only seven had died in the prolonged fight came as almost as much of a surprise to the defenders themselves.

At Consthum, where the remnants of the 3d Battalion blocked two roads leading to the 28th Division's headquarters town of Wiltz, the defenders held under heavy pressure all through the 17th. During the morning of the 18th, the regimental executive officer, Colonel Strickler, who had been at Consthum almost from the start, obtained General Cota's approval to withdraw. While the battalion commander, Major Milton, got the men and three surviving tanks ready to pull out, Strickler left by jeep in a hail of bullets to determine whether a bridge over the Clerve at the village of Kaustenbach was still in American hands. It was not, but no Germans were there either, and the survivors of the fight at Consthum eventually made their way back to help defend Wiltz.

By that time, almost all the other bridges over the Clerve south of Clervaux belonged to the Germans. Soon after nightfall on December 17, men of the 26th Volksgrenadier Division seized intact a bridge at Drauffelt, downhill from Hosingen, another a mile downstream between Drauffelt and Wilwerwiltz, and a third at Wilwerwiltz. A day late, the *Volksgrenadiers* with the help of the *Panzer Lehr Division* could at last begin their role in the race for Bastogne.

In Clervaux on December 17, the first crisis arose around nine-thirty in the morning when Mark IVs and half-tracks approached along a steeply descending road from Marnach. Colonel Fuller promptly sent the platoon of five Shermans from the 707th Tank Battalion that he had held in reserve in the town climbing around three steep hairpin curves in the road at the edge of Clervaux to meet them. At a bend high above the rooftops of the town, the two forces met in a blaze of fire. The Americans lost three tanks, the Germans four, and the remaining tanks on both sides fell back.

Rather than returning to Clervaux, the two surviving American tanks turned left at the third of the hairpin curves along a road following the trace of the Clerve to the south, ostensibly to get more ammunition at the headquarters of their company. Whatever the reason, Colonel Fuller was to get no more help from them. Nor did he get much support from the platoon of tanks of the 9th Armored Division's CCR that he sent to help the infantry clear the Germans from the eastern end of Clervaux. There the platoon lost two tanks to German fire—one to a long-range shot from a German tank high above the town, the other to a *Panzerfaust*—and the remaining three withdrew without telling Fuller to their parent unit well beyond the Clerve. Those were the only tanks of Company B, 2d Tank Battalion, to survive the company's baptism of fire.

The departure of those tanks was what prompted Fuller to order Lieutenant Fleig's tank platoon from Munshausen to Clervaux. To get there, Fleig had to take a roundabout route down to the valley of the Clerve and thence up the little road following the trace of the river to the lower of the steep hairpin curves above the town. As Fleig's lead tank reached the road junction, a Mark IV high up the road above Clervaux near an overlook, where in happier times hikers and tourists paused to look down on the picturesque rooftops of the town, opened fire. The infantrymen aboard the tanks dove for whatever cover they could find while the gunners of the two tanks slugged it out. The Sherman won, and the wreckage of the Mark IV formed a perfect roadblock for preventing any German vehicle from getting into Clervaux along the road from Marnach.

Because of that roadblock, German tanks made no new effort to enter Clervaux from that direction. Instead, several tanks assumed firing positions on high ground uphill from the destroyed Mark IV and from time to time threw direct fire into the town.

While Lieutenant Fleig and his tanks waited at the edge of town, the commander of the infantry platoon, 1st Lt. Jack D. Haisley, made his way to the Hôtel Claravallis and reported to Colonel Fuller. Although Fuller wanted Haisley and his men to help defend his command post, he wanted Fleig's tanks to go back to Munshausen, for by that time Company C and Cannon Company were hardpressed and Fuller had just received armored assistance for Clervaux from another source.

In early afternoon, in response to Fuller's continuing pleas for help, General Cota sent another small contingent from the 9th Armored Division's CCR, a platoon of self-propelled tank destroyers. When the destroyers reached the Hôtel Claravallis, Fuller directed them up the road toward Marnach to engage the German tanks that were firing into the town. A short while later, all five came racing back in such precipitate haste that at the first hairpin curve above the town one of them overturned. Picking up the crew, the others continued through the town and beyond the Clerve. Nobody in Clervaux saw them again.

By that time, most men of the provisional company formed earlier from men on leave in Clervaux and sent out along the Marnach road had gradually drifted back into the town, a kind of disintegration not uncommon among hastily formed provisional units where the individual soldier has no unit loyalty. Those men became caught up in the fight against steadily growing numbers of *Panzergrenadiers* infiltrating the town from various directions, and a few of them joined the defenders in the château. At one point, some of the Germans got within two hundred yards of Fuller's command post before Lieutenant Haisley's infantry platoon, a single 57mm. antitank gun, and several stragglers and MPs turned them back.

Throughout the afternoon, Fuller appealed time after time to General Cota for permission to withdraw any of his men and guns that could still get away to a new position behind the Clerve and so block the road leading to the St. Vith–Bastogne highway. Yet each time either Cota or his chief of staff, Col. Jesse L. Gibney, refused. Newly come to the 28th Division, Fuller was not yet a trusted member of the family, and who was to say whether his dolorous assessment of the situation was accurate?

Dutch Cota was nevertheless torn, for it was possible that he might be presiding over the demise of one of his proud regiments. On the other hand, he knew there was a race on for Bastogne, and his corps commander still insisted that he hold at all costs. Cota finally did agree to send Fuller Company G, which he had withheld when releasing the 2d Battalion from division reserve.

Not long after dark, around 6:30 P.M., Colonel Hughes radioed Fuller from his encircled position on the ridge north of Clervaux that six German tanks had bypassed him and were heading for Clervaux along the road leading into town from the rear. Again Fuller got Colonel Gibney on the telephone, but again Gibney refused permission to withdraw. Even as the two were talking, a staff officer ran into the room to tell Fuller that six German tanks were approaching the hotel. Fuller told that to Gibney. He would obey the order to hold, said Fuller, but as a Texan, he wanted Gibney to know that he was assigning him the same fate as befell the defenders of the Alamo.

At that moment three shells from German tanks exploded one after the other inside the ground floor of the hotel beneath the room from which Fuller was talking. What was that? asked Gibney. Fuller told him. When Gibney began to say something more, Fuller interrupted; he had "no more time to talk," he said brusquely, and rang off.

Fuller had just turned from the telephone when a blast of machine-gun fire tore into the ceiling of the room he was in, and tank fire continued to blast the ground floor. All lights went out. Going into the corridor, Fuller felt his way to his own room, No. 10, to get his carbine and overcoat. He was determined to get out some way and reconstitute as much of his regiment as he could put together on the other side of the Clerve.

As Fuller entered No. 10, he found ten men taking refuge there. Just at that moment a rocket from a *Panzerfaust* exploded into the room, wounding five of the men, including one who was blinded. By the light of German flares outside, Fuller hurriedly bandaged the man's eyes.

As Fuller was working, an MP entered. He had found a way out of the building, he said, if anybody wanted to take the chance. Fuller and the others, including the blinded man, all said yes. With the blinded man holding Fuller by the hand, the MP guided them across the hall to No. 12 and over to the only window in the room.

Someone had thrown a narrow iron ladder from the window across a twelve-foot space between the rear of the hotel and the landing of a fire escape built onto the side of a sheer cliff. (Had the men but known, in a short corridor off the main hall stood a large armoire hiding a door that led directly onto the fire escape.) With the blinded man still holding on, Fuller walked across the ladder to the landing, then up a few metal steps which soon gave way to steps carved out of the side of the cliff. The military policeman and eleven others followed.

At the top, Fuller, winded, paused briefly to catch his breath, then led the little group westward toward the village of Esselborn. There, he knew, one of the 2d Battalion's companies had once been billeted so that there still might be a telephone with which to contact Cota. He also hoped he might find Company G there, but in both cases his hopes were vain.

After rebandaging the blinded soldier's eyes, Fuller left him and another man whose wounds made it difficult for him to walk in the care of an unarmed soldier. With the rest, he set off again in the hope of finding some part of the 2d Battalion that had been fighting north of Clervaux.

Back at the Hôtel Claravallis, not long after Colonel Fuller made his escape, a switchboard operator put in a call to headquarters of the 28th Division. Germans were all over the command post, said the operator, and a tank had stuck its cannon inside the lobby of the hotel. Just as taught in communications training, the operator in a solemn voice said formally: "This switchboard is now closed."

By midnight of December 17, the fight by the center regiment of the division whose officers and men wore the bloody bucket shoulder patch was nearing an end. Yet some who somehow managed to get across the Clerve River were to fight again along Highway N-12—the St. Vith–Bastogne highway—and only the next day, December 18, was resistance to end in Hosingen and Consthum. So, too, there was still to be a fight by men of the 110th Infantry's Headquarters Company, holed up in the old château in Clervaux.

The order received by the commander of Headquarters Company, Capt. Claude B. Mackey, was to hold at all costs. For a little band of about eighty officers and men, armed only with carbines and M-1s plus a single .50-caliber machine gun, that was absurd. Yet it was the order Mackey had received and that was what he intended to do.

It was, Mackey might note, a romantic setting for a last stand: the ancient twelfth-century fortress with its thick stone walls, its turrets, and its firing apertures (designed for the crossbow but easily adaptable for a rifle or a carbine), perched atop a promontory commanding not only the entire town of Clervaux but also the two bridges over the winding Clerve River, the highway leading in from Marnach, and to some degree the open ridge to the north. The château's one weakness as a bastion was the lack of a moat; and whereas the massive wooden doors between the entrance towers may well have been a genuine obstacle to a medieval battering ram, they would pose no real obstacle to a twentieth-century tank.

Even before dawn on December 17, the Americans had to close the big doors leading into the inner courtyard and take to the apertures, for infiltrating *Panzergrenadiers* were making their presence felt with determined fire from rifles, burp guns, and machine guns. Sometimes the men opened the doors slightly to let in some American soldier seeking refuge, so that in time their numbers grew to 102, which included the regimental communications officer, Capt. John Aiken, Jr.

Since the château housed the regiment's message center, there was a half-track in the inner courtyard with a radio, an SCR-193, by means of which the men could maintain contact with the division command post in Wiltz. In the dungeon beneath, there were eighteen German prisoners of war and some seventy-five civilians, mostly elderly men, women, and children. Because the château housed Headquarters Company's kitchen, food and water were ample for all.

Sixteen-year-old Jean Servais, who had taken refuge in the château with his parents, found the siege a lark. Much of the time he roamed around watching the soldiers with fascination. During the height of the shelling, he came upon one soldier calmly playing a popular American

tune on a piano and paying no heed to the shells bursting nearby. At one of the apertures, he watched another soldier, cigarette dangling from his lips, his rifle equipped with a sniper-scope, calmly and deliberately squeeze off his rounds; before Jean turned away for some other diversion, the man hit four Germans, one of whom rolled like a heavy stone down the steep wooded slope just across the Clerve from the château.

Before daylight on December 18, a Sherman—from where and what unit, nobody inside the château knew—took up position in the outer courtyard. After daylight, as German tanks shoved aside the destroyed Mark IV on the road above the town and began descending the hill, the Sherman opened fire. From the road, the Sherman was difficult to spot, but somebody eventually picked it up. A first round merely scratched the armor plate, but a second entered between the turret and the hull, blowing off the gun. The Sherman's crew somehow survived and eventually reached safety beyond the Clerve.

The firing from inside the château still indicated clearly that only armored vehicles could make it through Clervaux with impunity. That no doubt contributed to the German decision to get rid of the troublesome hold-out. Fire from tanks and assault guns soon set a portion of the château to burning, and smoke billowed in the little courtyard. Considering the end to be near, Captain Aiken ordered the half-track and its radio destroyed with thermite grenades.

Around noon on the 18th, a German tank rammed the big doors blocking the entrance, poised there, and fired a round from its cannon. To Mackey and Aiken, there appeared to be no point in resisting any longer. They brought out a white flag.

As the Americans, the civilians, and the German prisoners all filed out, Jean Servais supported an American who had lost considerable blood from a wound in his cheek. Because of that, the Germans herded him together with the Americans. For Jean, the events had ceased to be fun. At the first opportunity, he slipped away.

CHAPTER THIRTEEN

The Race for Bastogne: The Second Phase

For the commander of the Fifth Panzer Army, Hasso von Manteuffel, the commander of the 47th Panzer Corps, General von Lüttwitz, and the German division commanders, the race for Bastogne took on added urgency during the evening of December 17 with news through an intercepted radio message that the Allied command had ordered two American airborne divisions to Bastogne. The way the German commanders figured it, the airborne troops would reach Bastogne during the night of the 18th or early on the 19th. That made the continued slow progress on the second day of the offensive all the more upsetting. Not only getting Bastogne but also reaching and crossing the Meuse River appeared to von Manteuffel "already imperiled."

Since the Fifth Panzer Army's primary goal was to cross the Meuse, the 2d Panzer Division in pursuit of that goal was to bypass Bastogne to the north. Yet if Bastogne could not be taken swiftly, it would tie down German forces needed elsewhere while at the same time affording the Americans a base from which to launch a counterattack that, as von Manteuffel put it, "could seriously endanger the German attack." Thus it was critical that the *Panzer Lehr Division*, with help from the 26th Volksgrenadier Division, beat the American reinforcements to Bastogne and thereby free the *Panzer Lehr* to join the 2d Panzer Division in the drive for the Meuse.

The commander of the *Panzer Lehr Division*, the feisty General Bayerlein, believed that General von Lüttwitz during December 17 had seriously jeopardized his chances of a *coup de main* at Bastogne. Von Lüttwitz had committed one of Bayerlein's *Panzergrenadier* regiments against the unyielding American defenders of Consthum. And he had also appropriated Bayerlein's advance guard, the special task force he had created for quickly exploiting the early gains—an armored reconnais-

sance company, two companies of *Panzergrenadiers*, and a company of Panthers—against the strongpoint at Hosingen. By late afternoon of the 17th both forces had incurred heavy casualties.

Once von Lüttwitz early in the evening of December 17 learned that the 26th Volksgrenadier Division had a bridge over the Clerve River at Drauffelt, he nevertheless moved swiftly to get the *Panzer Lehr* marching toward Bastogne. He ordered Bayerlein's advance guard pulled back from Hosingen and shifted immediately to the bridge at Drauffelt, to be followed by the division's previously uncommitted *Panzergrenadier* regiment. As the advance guard moved forward, Bayerlein reinforced it with fifteen Mark IV tanks, a company of engineers, and a battery of self-propelled artillery that had toiled through the traffic jams endemic on the muddy roads leading up to the Skyline Drive from the valley of the Our.

Von Lüttwitz was taking a chance that the forces of the *Panzer Lehr* and 26th Volksgrenadier Divisions could jointly use the bridge at Drauffelt and a steep, winding road leading from the river valley toward the St. Vith–Bastogne road, Highway N-12. As soon became evident early on December 18, to expect men moving basically on foot but with a mix of motor vehicles and horse-drawn transport to share a single narrow, muddy road with armored vehicles was to presume the millennium. Even the breakdown of a single vehicle meant a traffic jam of immense proportions until the vehicle could be shoved off the road. Bayerlein's armor was soon "flowing to the west not in a quiet, even stream but . . . irregularly from traffic congestion to traffic congestion, slowly and clumsily." The German commanders and the troops could only be thankful that for yet another day low clouds and a misty rain concealed them from Allied fighter-bombers. It was mid-afternoon before the armor could at last break free of the congestion.

To the north, at Clervaux, the 2d Panzer Division encountered no such difficulties, for the road through Clervaux belonged exclusively to the division. That was not to say there were no delays, for the hairpin curves on the approach to Clervaux and the narrow streets were tricky for the big tanks to negotiate, and until well into the day small-arms fire from the château made it difficult for anything other than tanks and assault guns to get through. Yet there was another route around the town to the north, and even before daylight on the 18th, advance elements of the 2d Panzer Division were on their way westward across the river, headed for Highway N-12.

On the American side, the commander of the VIII Corps, General Middleton, was running distressingly low on troops with which to slow the German advance. Late on the 17th, he at last agreed for General Cota to withdraw the 110th Infantry behind the Clerve with the idea of forming a new delaying line west of the river, but that approval came too late for Hurley Fuller and almost all the regiment except Colonel Strickler and the remnants of the 3d Battalion in Consthum. Those remnants, plus previously uncommitted Company G, were about all the 110th Infantry could still contribute as an organized force to further delay in front of Bastogne. Other than what remained of that embattled regiment, all that Middleton had left to throw into the fight were three engineer combat battalions, a separate (nondivisional) armored field artillery battalion, and the 9th Armored Division's Combat Command R.

It was precious little with which to delay three German divisions, including two panzer divisions, long enough to allow the 10th Armored Division's CCB and the airborne division to get to Bastogne. At best, Middleton knew, not until late afternoon of the 18th could the combat command reach the town, and it might be well into the night before the first airborne troops arrived, which meant that only the next day, the 19th, could he hope to get any of the airborne troops into the line.

Middleton sent one of the engineer combat battalions (the 44th) to help Cota at Wiltz, and the other two (the 35th and 158th) to form a screen of outposts in villages just beyond the eastern periphery of Bastogne. Earlier assigned to general support of the 28th Division, the armored field artillery battalion (the 58th) was to support all units in front of Bastogne. Having also earlier ordered the 9th Armored Division's CCR from Trois Vierges to an assembly area closer to Bastogne, Middleton toward evening on the 17th told the commander, Col. Joseph H. Gilbreth, to establish two roadblocks in an effort to stay the German advance.

As yet untested in battle, the 9th Armored Division's CCR had the usual components of a combat command: a battalion each of armored infantry, medium tanks, and armored field artillery, and a company each of self-propelled tank destroyers, armored engineers, and antiaircraft artillery (half-tracks mounting quad-50s). Yet the fighting had already drawn off a portion of Colonel Gilbreth's command: a platoon of tank destroyers to help the 112th Infantry near Ouren; another to help the 110th Infantry at Clervaux (although four of the five guns had come back); and a company of medium tanks appropriated by General Cota to help the 110th Infantry, of which only three survived.

At Middleton's order, Gilbreth was to establish one roadblock at a road junction known as Antoniushof, the meeting of the road from Clervaux with Highway N-12, and another at a junction known as Fe'itsch, where a secondary road from the valley of the Clerve at Drauffelt joined N-12 only eight miles from Bastogne. The terrain in the vicinity of the two junctions is unusual for the Ardennes—high and rolling, devoid of the deep ravines and heavy woods cover to be found in most other places, and it afforded ample fields of fire for armored vehicles. In a fairly straight line, the highway followed the crest of the high ground. Unfortunately for armor on the defensive, there were only two or three buildings at each road junction and thus little cover or concealment for tanks and tank destroyers.

Task Force Rose at Antoniushof—named for the commander of Company A, 2d Tank Battalion, Capt. Lawrence K. Rose—consisted of Rose's company of Shermans, a company of the 52d Armored Infantry Battalion, and a platoon of armored engineers, while a battery of the 73d Armored Field Artillery Battalion was close enough to provide support. Unknown to Rose, another American unit was nearby: Company G, 110th Infantry, which General Cota had withheld when releasing the 2d Battalion from the division but had at last released early in the evening on the 17th to go to Clervaux.

Arriving after midnight in the village of Donnange (the 2d Battalion's former reserve position on a side road just off the main highway from Antoniushof to Clervaux), the men of Company G spotted the silhouettes of what looked to be German tanks on high ground just beyond the village. Because the company had no radio and thus no way of knowing what was happening in Clervaux, the commander, Capt. George N. Prestridge, decided to hole up for the night. To put some distance between his company and the possible German tanks, he pulled his men from Donnange to dig in behind the village.

At the other road junction, Fe'itsch, not quite four miles down N-12 in the direction of Bastogne, there would also be limited help from men of the 110th Infantry. A former commander of the regiment, Col. Theodore A. Seely, had arrived at the road junction. Having been slightly wounded in the Hürtgen Forest, Seely had refused evacuation but until his wound healed had remained at the division headquarters as an extra regimental commander while Colonel Fuller took over his regiment. When Cota lost contact with Fuller and his command post in Clervaux, he ordered Seely to "go find your regiment and take command of it."

At the Fe'itsch road junction, Seely found several junior officers from the regimental headquarters who had escaped from Clervaux and with them began to reconstitute a headquarters in a farmhouse a half mile behind the junction. When the armored task force that was to establish a roadblock at Fe'itsch arrived, Seely had ten officers and a hundred men, who took position on a flank of the task force.

Named after the commander of the 2d Tank Battalion, Lt. Col. Ralph S. Harper, the task force at Fe'itsch had Harper's remaining company of Shermans and a company of armored infantry. Except for a battery with Task Force Rose, the 73d Armored Field Artillery Battalion was in position to provide support.

Not quite three miles behind the road junction the commander of CCR, Colonel Gilbreth, established his headquarters in the village of Longvilly. To provide a screen for it, for his artillery battalion, and for a nearby 58th Armored Field Artillery Battalion, Gilbreth formed a small task force to occupy high ground north of the main highway between Fe'itsch and Longvilly. Commanded by the head of the 52d Armored Infantry Battalion, Lt. Col. Robert M. Booth, the task force had Booth's remaining line company, a platoon of light tanks, and a platoon of self-propelled tank destroyers.

As daylight came on December 18, that was the alignment facing the armor of the 2d Panzer Division coming up from the valley of the Clerve at Clervaux and the *Panzer Lehr Division* along with the bulk of the 26th Volksgrenadier Division toiling up from the valley at Drauffelt. With those defenders, plus a thin screen of engineers in the villages behind them, rested the chances of keeping the Germans out of Bastogne long enough for reinforcements to get there.

Just outside Donnange at daybreak on December 18, a man from the 109th Field Artillery Battalion, Sgt. Charles T. Johnson, who had been detailed along with a second lieutenant and a radio operator as a forward observer team for Company G, 110th Infantry, volunteered to go into the village and find an observation post to determine if the silhouettes the men had seen on the skyline the night before were indeed German tanks. With the team's jeep and radio operator, Johnson entered the village, then climbed the church steeple and peered through the mist with his binoculars. On the high ground not two hundred yards from where the men of Company G had dug in were four tanks. The U.S. Army, Johnson knew, had no tanks that big.

Sending the radio operator back to alert Company G, Johnson established radio contact with the fire direction center of his battalion and was getting ready to call for a fire mission when he looked back toward Company G's positions. Having learned of German tanks so near, Captain Prestridge was marching his men back to the protection of the houses in the next village of Lullange. Quick to spot the movement, the German tanks began firing, and the infantrymen broke into a run to gain the cover of the houses.

Climbing down from the steeple, Johnson found his radio operator waiting with the jeep behind a stone wall. They, too, raced back to Lullange.

The German tanks failed to follow the withdrawal, for their goal was the road junction at Antoniushof, but an hour later a company of *Panzergrenadiers* supported by mortars attacked Lullange. From an observation post in a house, Johnson was able to bring down effective artillery fire, and the attack collapsed.

During the action, Johnson was appalled at the conduct of his lieutenant. Lips trembling, his head in his hands, the officer cringed in a corner of the room.

With the support of assault guns, the Germans in late afternoon attacked again. Although Johnson moved immediately into his observation post, try as he might he was unable to raise the 109th Field Artillery Battalion on the radio. The instrument appeared to be dead.

They might as well fall back, said the lieutenant. A forward observer was no good without a radio.

It gradually dawned on Johnson that the terrified lieutenant had sabotaged the radio in order to have an excuse to fall back. Johnson refused to go, but the lieutenant drew his pistol and ordered him to join him. The officer was shaking, tears in his eyes. "My God," thought Johnson, "this is the kind of thing that happens in the movies!" Having no radio and facing a desperate man, Johnson decided to go along. If they made it out, he would turn him over to the MPs.

Dodging mortar shells, the two took off across an open field and after nightfall found Colonel Seely's command post near the Fe'itsch road junction. While Johnson waited, the lieutenant went inside, but when he failed to return, Johnson asked the sentry at the door what had happened. The colonel, said the soldier, had put the lieutenant under arrest.

*   *   *

Through the night of December 17, Hurley Fuller had gotten nowhere in his efforts to return to the east bank of the Clerve River and find his 2d Battalion. At every turn, he and the few men still with him ran into Germans or German tanks. By daylight, Fuller had become separated from everybody except a lieutenant, David Wright, but soon came upon fifty men of the 630th Tank Destroyer Battalion. They were trying to turn their jeeps and trucks around on a narrow woods trail in order to head south, for they too had run into Germans going the other way.

Fuller and Wright joined them, but hardly had they begun to move when the little column came under fire from German tanks. There was no way past, and Fuller detected German infantry trying to encircle them. He ordered the vehicles set on fire and led the little force—the size of a platoon—to a nearby hillock, where the men dug in. They held there through the afternoon, losing fifteen men to German fire. When night came, ammunition was so low that Fuller told the troops to break into small groups and try to escape.

Fuller himself, with Lieutenant Wright and three men, had gone about a mile when they stumbled upon a German assembly area in a wood. Although the Americans hid, one of them suddenly jumped up and began shouting, "*Kamerad!*" (He told Fuller later that a German was pointing a rifle at him.) Fuller and the others tried to run but without success, and in the melee somebody hit Fuller on the back of the head, knocking him unconscious.

Fuller came to to find he had a flesh wound from a bayonet in his stomach. Kicking him, his captors forced him to his feet, and along with Lieutenant Wright and the three men herded him to a battalion head-quarters. Once an interrogator had discerned his captive's rank, Fuller was soon on his way by truck to headquarters of the 2d Panzer Division on the other side of the Clerve in Bockholtz.

During the morning of the 18th, the 2d Panzer Division's reconnais-sance battalion felt out the positions of Task Force Rose at Antoniushof, and in early afternoon *Panzergrenadiers* and Mark IVs and Panthers at-tacked. Under direct fire from the big guns, Rose's armored infantrymen broke and fled in some confusion down Highway N-12 toward the Fe'itsch road junction. Fire from the tanks also forced the battery of field artillery to withdraw. That left only Captain Rose's Shermans and his assault gun platoon, and seven of the tanks (over a third of Rose's strength) were soon knocked out. Although Colonel Gilbreth asked per-mission to pull the remnants of Task Force Rose back to reinforce Task Force Harper at Fe'itsch, General Middleton refused.

Whether Rose could have made his way to Fe'itsch in any case was problematical. By the time night fell, he had had to relinquish the road junction itself, which afforded German tanks free passage in the darkness along N-12 to Fe'itsch. With or without orders, Rose finally decided to break out in another direction, toward the northwest and Houffalize, ten miles north of Bastogne. Five of the tanks and the assault guns made it; but near Houffalize, they ran into the 116th Panzer Division's reconnaissance battalion, which was moving forward after bypassing the 112th Infantry's positions near the frontier. Only a few of Rose's men escaped, eventually to make their way to Bastogne.

The end came even more quickly for Task Force Harper. In early darkness, *Panzergrenadiers* began to attack, reinforced a few hours later by Mark IVs and Panthers, which were equipped with new infrared night-sighting devices. It was no contest. Only three of the American tanks—or so it seemed to the Germans—offered any appreciable resistance, and when Colonel Harper was killed, the defense fell apart. The company of armored infantrymen broke first, but the surviving tanks soon followed, scurrying down the highway to Longvilly, where Colonel Gilbreth rallied them for defense of his headquarters.

Despite the collapse of Task Force Harper, Fe'itsch was not yet fully in German hands, for most of the stragglers from the 110th Infantry were still there. Shortly before dark, Colonel Seely had gained reinforcements, men from Captain Prestridge's Company G, who had been driven from Lullange. Even so, Seely had little hope of holding for long, and inside his command post in the farmhouse near the road junction, he had already told some forty officers and men to divide themselves into groups of three and four to be ready if necessary to pull out.

It would not be long before that time came. When a sentry came in to tell Seely that he could hear a tank approaching, Seely went outside. He could see nothing, for it was dark and a heavy fog had descended, but he could hear the tank. To Seely's accustomed ear, it was a Sherman, yet advancing so tentatively that Seely was convinced the driver was unfamiliar with it. Hurrying back inside the house, he yelled for attention. "There's a tank coming down the road," he shouted; "it's very close. It's an American tank but it's not an American driver. Go! Go! Go! Fast!"

Everybody dashed for the rear of the house. Most made it out windows and a back door, but not Seely himself. He, his operations sergeant, James M. Hanna, and the commander of the 109th Field Artillery Battalion, Lt. Col. Robert E. Ewing, were at the back of the group scrambling for the exits. They were opposite the door to the cellar when they heard the tank stop in front of the house. Seely yelled to the others to get into the cellar, and the three tumbled downstairs. For a moment, Seely congratulated himself on his foresight, for he and his companions had hardly started down the stairs when the tank put a round from its 75mm. gun through the center of the first floor.

On the other hand, Seely realized quickly that his decision had only short-term benefits. The single outside door of the cellar was open, and it faced the front of the house and the German-operated American tank. Seely still figured that in the foggy darkness he and the others might escape during a break in the German column; but that break never developed, for in the fog and darkness, the German vehicles were bumper to bumper.

In time, a half-track stopped directly in front of the house. Jumping down, a German soldier approached the door to the cellar, stuck his head in, and turned on a flashlight six inches from Colonel Seely's face. There was no possibility of escape.

Splitting up the three prisoners, the Germans put Seely on the hood of a half-track. As the column inched toward Longvilly, Seely took advantage of a pause, jumped off, and headed for a wood. Although bursts of fire followed him, he escaped without injury, but his freedom was to be short-lived. Groping through the dense fog, he bumped into the side of another German half-track.

Recaptured, Seely was to stay with that half-track for three days until a German company commander recollected that he had captured a senior officer and sent him to the rear. At headquarters of the 2d Panzer Division, his presence confused his interrogators. They had already captured one colonel, whom they had identified as the commander of the 110th Infantry, and they knew that two other regiments of the 28th Division, the 109th and 112th, were still intact. Thus they deduced, not without some logic, that Seely commanded the 111th Infantry, which, indeed, had been a part of the division before the U.S. Army adopted a triangular structure for its divisions. Seely said nothing to correct their error.

Colonel Gilbreth and the remnants of Task Force Harper in Longvilly were left in the meantime to wonder why the German tanks that had dealt such a blow at Fe'itsch failed to follow up their advantage, for through the night the Germans made no assault on Longvilly. The answer was that the 2d Panzer Division was not headed for Bastogne but for the Meuse. At a road junction a half mile outside Longvilly, the troops and vehicles of Colonel Lauchert's division turned off the main highway onto a road bypassing Bastogne to the north.

Whereas that turn spared the stragglers and headquarters troops in Longvilly, it trapped Task Force Booth, the small force that Gilbreth had established on high ground to screen Longvilly and his supporting artillery. Having lost radio contact with Gilbreth's headquarters, Colonel Booth during the night decided to try to save his little force by moving cross-country in hope of gaining American lines someplace, he knew not where. At seemingly every turn, the men and light tanks bumped into Germans. Although they managed to back off from those encounters, not quite three miles from the starting point at the village of Hardigny, a strong force of tanks and *Panzergrenadiers* cut the little task force to pieces. Eventually, in some cases after up to six days of wandering, some 225 men made their way into Bastogne.

In mid-afternoon of December 18, when the advance guard of General Bayerlein's *Panzer Lehr Division* and one of the *Panzergrenadier* regiments at last broke free of the traffic jam along the road leading up from the valley of the Clerve, Bayerlein, who was forward, split the column at the village of Eschweiler. He planned to take advantage of two roads leading toward Bastogne. Bayerlein sent the advance guard up the road on the left, while he himself moved with the *Panzergrenadier* regiment and fifteen Mark IV tanks on the right.

The road that Bayerlein was traveling led to the Fe'itsch road junction, but about a mile short of it Bayerlein took a back road leading directly toward Bastogne. As he made the turn, he could hear the sounds of fighting at Fe'itsch, and fiery tracer bullets gave the night "a fantastic aspect." Not long after 6 P.M., Bayerlein and his force drew up at the hamlet of Neiderwampach, less than six miles from Bastogne.

On the verge of victory in the race for Bastogne, Bayerlein pondered how to proceed from there. There were two choices. He could turn south to get onto a principal hard-surfaced highway leading from Ettelbruck and the valley of the Sûre River into Bastogne; or he could continue to the west along a side road to get onto the road from Fe'itsch and Longvilly to Bastogne at the village of Mageret, three miles from Bastogne. Because the side road was the more direct, because Bayerlein knew that American reinforcements would soon be arriving in Bastogne, and because he considered it unlikely that such a minor road would be defended, he chose the side route. Besides, civilians assured him the road was excellent. Nevertheless, concerned about its condition, he employed at first only a platoon of tanks and a company of *Panzergrenadiers*.

For a time, Bayerlein worried that he might have made a mistake, for the little road grew progressively worse until finally it was nothing but a muddy farm track. Yet for the most part his vehicles managed to traverse it, and at Mageret he found only a small detachment of the 158th Engineer Combat Battalion. Soon in control of the village, Bayerlein was preparing to head down the highway toward the goal of Bastogne when he received disturbing news. According to a Belgian man, a large American force with at least forty tanks and other vehicles, including artillery, had only a short time before passed through Mageret going in the direction of Longvilly.

If Bayerlein turned at Mageret to move into Bastogne, the American force would be in his rear. He had at that point only his *Panzergrenadiers*, a battery of artillery, and fifteen tanks, and much of that force still had to inch forward over the muddy track from Niederwampach. Did he dare turn his back on such a strong American force?

*   *   *

Preceding the main body of the 10th Armored Division's CCB, the commander, Colonel Roberts, reported into General Middleton's headquarters in Bastogne just before 4 P.M. on December 18. The Heintz Barracks was less bustling than usual, for at the direction of the commander of the 12th Army Group, General Bradley—with whom Middleton at that point had much better communications than with his immediate superior, General Hodges—Middleton had already started most of his headquarters troops moving to the rear, retaining only key staff officers and their assistants. He himself was determined to remain, despite admonitions from Bradley to the contrary, until he could brief Roberts and the commander of the airborne division.

Like most experienced armored commanders, Colonel Roberts, who had taught armored doctrine at the Command and General Staff College, was always wary of the way doughboy generals might employ armor. They had a tendency to use it in the fashion that helped bring the downfall of the French Army in 1940, not as a powerful massed force but in increments, often as infantry support. And Middleton—Roberts was aware—was a doughboy general.

Middleton's first question fulfilled all Bill Roberts's concerns: "How many teams can you make up?"

Reluctantly, Roberts responded: "Three."

Once Roberts had formed the three teams, said Middleton, he was to send one north of Bastogne on the Liège highway to the village of Noville; a second to the southeast to block the highway leading from Ettelbruck; and a third (in fact, the first to be formed) to what looked to be at the moment the most threatened point, Longvilly. However much Roberts disagreed with the splitting of his command, he conceded mentally that the corps commander knew more about the situation than he did.

Having had experience with wholesale retreat at Château-Thierry in May, 1918, Roberts wanted to know what he should do about stragglers. "Sir," he said, "I want authority to use those men." Middleton promptly agreed and the next morning issued an order specifically authorizing Roberts "to take over all or any part" of the 9th Armored Division's CCR "in case they show the slightest inclination to retire."

The force that Colonel Roberts sent to Longvilly was Team Cherry, named for Lt. Col. Henry T. Cherry, commander of the 3d Tank Battalion. Cherry had one of his own medium tank companies, two light tank platoons, a company of the 20th Armored Infantry Battalion, and a few reconnaissance troops, engineers, and medics.

It was Team Cherry that passed through Mageret on the way to Longvilly not long before General Bayerlein reached Mageret. Team Cherry had, in fact, not forty tanks—as the Belgian had told Bayerlein—but only seventeen mediums, ten lights, and no artillery. Whether the Belgian simply overestimated the American strength or deliberately misinformed Bayerlein was never determined, for the man was never identified. What mattered, in any case, was that the word of the American force made Bayerlein cautious and delayed even a probe toward Bastogne for six hours and a genuine attack considerably longer than that.

Roberts had yet to leave Middleton's headquarters in Bastogne when Middleton had another visitor, the commander of the 101st Airborne Division's artillery and, in General Taylor's absence, the acting division commander, Brig. Gen. Anthony C. McAuliffe. When McAuliffe left Camp Mourmelon, near Rheims, his orders were to go, not to Bastogne but, in accord with the wishes of General Hodges, to Werbomont. He had come by Middleton's headquarters only because he was some distance ahead of the trucks transporting his troops, had some time to spare, and welcomed a chance to find out the situation from Middleton.

What McAuliffe could not know was that when the commander of the 82d Airborne Division and acting commander of the XVIII Airborne Corps, General Gavin, reached the First Army's headquarters in Spa, he had found Hodges increasingly concerned about the threat posed by *Kampfgruppe Peiper*. Since Gavin's division was ahead of McAuliffe's, Hodges told Gavin to move to Werbomont to stop Peiper while the 101st Airborne Division went to Bastogne. Gavin got that word to his convoy, but it failed to reach McAuliffe's.

It did reach General Middleton, and he told McAuliffe. While it was still light, McAuliffe and his G-3, Lt. Col. Harry W. O. Kinnard, picked out an assembly area just west of Bastogne and sent a military policeman to a road junction to divert the march units of the 101st Airborne Division's convoy to Bastogne. Yet some of the march units had already passed the junction.

Acting commander of the division artillery because of General McAuliffe's change in roles, Col. Thomas L. Sherburne, at the head of the 101st Airborne Division's convoy, was becoming irritated by the accordion-like action of the 82d Airborne Division's convoy ahead of him. Fed up with the constant stop-and-go, stop-and-go, Sherburne paused at a crossroads northwest of Bastogne, wondering whether he might not gain time by detouring on a roundabout route to Werbomont by way of Bastogne. When a sergeant of military police told him that some hours earlier General McAuliffe and his party had turned toward Bastogne, Sherburne told the MP on duty at the crossroads to divert all march units of the 101st Airborne Division to Bastogne. By that chance development, the division was soon on its way to where the American command wanted and vitally needed it.

That was not to say that movement to the assembly area just outside Bastogne was swift. The trucks carrying men of the airborne division had to buck heavy traffic generated by service units withdrawing from Bastogne, and officers of those units, under orders to fall back, insisted on priority on the road. In the congestion, once a group of vehicles came to a halt, many a driver dozed off, so that in the end it took MPs moving up and down the column to awaken drivers and keep the traffic flowing in both directions.

First units of the 101st Airborne Division nevertheless began arriving in the assembly area near Bastogne around midnight on December 18. The men were cold and wet, having ridden in big cattle trucks through rain with no overhead cover and having left Camp Mourmelon so hurriedly that many lacked helmets, ammunition, some even weapons; and hardly anybody had overcoats or overshoes. They were to have little sleep and little time to prepare for the battle ahead of them, but what mattered was that they were there.

The advance guard of CCB's Team Cherry, commanded by 1st Lt. Edward P. Hyduke and composed mainly of light tanks and armored cars, reached the edge of Longvilly around 7 P.M. on the 18th. As far as Hyduke could make out, the village was jammed with men and vehicles of the 9th Armored Division's CCR. Rather than risk getting his vehicles intermingled with those of CCR, Hyduke halted his column and radioed Colonel Cherry, who came forward and went into Longvilly to talk with CCR's commander, Colonel Gilbreth.

Gilbreth was elated to learn of Team Cherry's arrival, for at that hour Task Force Harper was still holding at the Fe'itsch road junction and Gilbreth assumed Team Cherry would help. Colonel Cherry quickly squashed the idea; his orders, he said, were to go no farther than Longvilly.

Learning that Gilbreth had no plans other than to carry out his orders to hold at all costs, Cherry headed back to Bastogne to explain the situation to Colonel Roberts and get a decision as to where to position his command. He told Lieutenant Hyduke, in the meantime, to deploy the advance guard in fighting positions on the Bastogne side of Longvilly, thereby avoiding confusion with CCR. Hyduke chose positions on high ground along the highway near a roadside religious shrine, the grotto of St. Michael.

As Colonel Cherry passed back through Mageret, General Bayerlein and his tanks and *Panzergrenadiers* had just arrived. Although Cherry's jeep drew some small-arms fire, Cherry thought it was from trigger-happy American stragglers, picked up speed, and proceeded on his way. In Bastogne—where Colonel Roberts had yet to receive Middleton's order telling him to prevent CCR from retiring—Roberts told Cherry that should CCR withdraw, Cherry was to cover the withdrawal; but no matter what, Team Cherry was to hold.

When Cherry started back, he got no farther than the hamlet of Neffe, a half mile short of Mageret, where he had earlier established his headquarters in a nearby château. There he learned that at least a strong

German patrol was in Mageret. By radio, he ordered the commander of the armored infantry company with Team Cherry, Capt. William F. Ryerson, to send a patrol to open the road through Mageret.

Ryerson sent two squads of armored infantry in a half-track. Short of the first houses, the men dismounted and made their way on foot to a crossroads in the center of the village. There they determined that in fact at least three German tanks and a company of infantry were in the village, too much for two squads to think of tackling.

Just as the men were getting ready to pull out, they heard the noise of a tracked vehicle approaching from the rear. Were they to be trapped? After a breathless wait, they found it to be a self-propelled tank destroyer, which CCR's commander, Colonel Gilbreth, had sent to clear Mageret. Along with the tank destroyer, the two squads withdrew.

When Captain Ryerson radioed word on the enemy's strength to Colonel Cherry, Cherry ordered him to leave Lieutenant Hyduke's force as a rear guard and turn the medium tanks and armored infantry to clear the Germans from Mageret. That Ryerson prepared to do, but it was to be a difficult assignment, partly because an ugly situation was about to develop in Longvilly.

In late evening of December 18, Colonel Gilbreth faced a crisis. He had lost Task Force Rose and much of Task Force Harper, he had no contact with Task Force Booth and no way of knowing whether it still existed, his own field artillery battalion and the separate 58th Armored Field Artillery Battalion were under intermittent shelling from German tanks and assault guns and direct pressure from German patrols, and he himself and his headquarters were in what amounted to the front line, no place from which to direct a battle. Shortly before midnight, Gilbreth told his staff and headquarters troops to prepare to withdraw to Bastogne, while the combat troops (mainly the men, half-tracks, and tanks that had fallen back from the Fe'itsch road junction) were to stay behind to hold Longvilly and screen the artillery.

Word for the headquarters troops to withdraw went out in a grim setting. Pitch darkness, a clinging fog, German searchlights in the distance, fiery arcs of tracer bullets, eerie flickers of flares. There was shelling, the occasional chatter of burp guns from German patrols, and everywhere untold confusion. To many a man it looked like Armageddon, and somewhere just over a hill or two, maybe three, there was a place where he could escape it: Bastogne.

There was no way to confine word of the withdrawal to the few who were supposed to execute it, and for men who had just experienced the enemy's deadly power at the Fe'itsch road junction, it was easy to convince themselves that the order to fall back applied to them too. At the appointed hour for men of the headquarters to depart, seemingly every man, every vehicle, every gun in Longvilly converged on the western exit from the village. Soon there was panic, an ugly panic.

Somehow Colonel Gilbreth and his staff managed to stop it. Gilbreth "cut the column in the middle" and ordered that not another vehicle, not another man, including the headquarters troops, was to leave Longvilly until daylight. Yet in the meantime, those vehicles that had succeeded in getting out of the village added to the congestion already created on the narrow highway leading to Mageret by the presence of Team Cherry's half-tracks and tanks.

On the German side that night, the commander of the 47th Panzer Corps, General von Lüttwitz, unaware that American reinforcements had reached Bastogne but expecting them at any time, ordered an all-out attack to take the town at daylight the next morning, December 19. In keeping with General von Manteuffel's original plan, the 2d Panzer Division was to continue along its route, bypassing Bastogne, and because the 5th Parachute Division was lagging far behind and thus exposing the south flank of the panzer corps, a regiment of the 26th Volksgrenadier Division was to screen that flank. Every other force available to the corps was to drive for Bastogne. From Mageret and along the next road to the south, the *Panzer Lehr Division* was to make a two-pronged thrust against the town, while two regiments of the 26th Volksgrenadier Division marched north through Longvilly to gain the village of Bizory and pivot against Bastogne from the northeast and north.

Neither von Lüttwitz nor the commander of the *Volksgrenadiers*, Colonel Kokott, knew of the presence of Team Cherry along the Mageret-Longvilly road, and they thought the Germans held Longvilly. That was not the case, but neither did the Americans, for with the first traces of daylight, all that was left of the 9th Armored Division's CCR began a disorderly exodus onto the road to Mageret. Once on the road, the vehicles had no place to go, for on one side the ground dropped off sharply into a marsh and on the other it rose steeply. The only exit from the road, a steep, muddy farm track leading north to the hamlet of Arloncourt, was blocked by vehicles that had tried to get out that way during the night; and at Mageret, the Germans still held the village.

At daylight, the commander of Team Cherry's armored infantry company, Captain Ryerson, tried to execute his assignment of driving the Germans from Mageret. Because of the obstacles on either side of the highway, Ryerson had trouble getting tanks and half-tracks turned around to make the attack. Their job was made the more difficult by the crush of CCR's vehicles, which in some places jammed the highway by moving abreast of Ryerson's vehicles in the other lane of the two-lane road. Not until mid-morning was Ryerson able to get a small force headed for Mageret with a medium tank in the lead.

Some three hundred yards outside Mageret, the highway passed through a cut and at the far end of it swung left. As the leading tank reached that point, a German antitank gun knocked it out. The tank burst into flames, partially blocking the road.

Dismounting from the half-tracks, infantrymen tried to get past the burning tank, but small-arms fire from Mageret turned them back. Shells from two 105mm. assault guns slowed the firing for a while, but each time the infantry tried to advance, it increased again.

The infantry was still trying to make it when two half-tracks of the 482d Antiaircraft Artillery Battalion, attached to CCR, raced forward, their drivers obviously determined to get out no matter what. Team Cherry's infantrymen shouted for the half-tracks to stop, but the drivers paid no heed. Just as they reached the bend in the road, they spotted the burning tank. Seeing that they were about to crash, drivers and the other men on the half-tracks jumped clear. With the half-tracks wrecked against the remains of the tank, no vehicle was going to get through.

For much of the morning, the blocked American column escaped major interference from the Germans, for General von Lüttwitz's order to attack at daylight was unrealistic. During the night advance, troops had crossed and recrossed unit boundaries, and some order had to be established. So, too, the division commanders felt compelled to delay in order to bring up food and ammunition and to afford their men at least a few hours' rest.

It was late morning before Colonel Kokott got his two *Volksgrenadier* regiments on the move, one to cross the Mageret-Longvilly highway, the other to pass through Longvilly. Hardly had they begun to advance when they came under fire from Lieutenant Hyduke's force from Team Cherry on the high ground near the grotto of St. Michael, the only American force along the highway occupying a viable fighting position. It took three hours for Kokott to get an attack organized against Hyduke's force, but when it started he had help from a portion of the *Panzer Lehr Division,* for General Bayerlein was determined to deal with the armored force in his rear before committing himself to an all-out attack against Bastogne.

For all Bayerlein's concern about that armored force, he himself was at that point directing less than full attention to conduct of the battle. In a wood outside Mageret, his troops had found a platoon from an American field hospital, and among the staff, a "young, blonde, and beautiful" American nurse attracted Bayerlein's attention. Through much of December 19, he "dallied" with the nurse, who "held him spellbound."

When German artillery, *Nebelwerfers*, and tanks at last opened fire, they pummeled not only Lieutenant Hyduke's positions but the trapped convoy of American tanks, half-tracks, self-propelled artillery, armored cars, trucks, jeeps, and ambulances along the road between Longvilly and Mageret. Here and there vehicles were soon burning, sending up great clouds of black smoke. Crews of the tanks and self-propelled artillery tried to fight back, firing at German tanks at long range—and occasionally scoring a hit—but for the most part, the men and machines along the highway were helpless. Only along some short stretches of the road were there woods providing concealment, and only where the road passed through the cut near Mageret was there any protection from the enemy fire.

Lieutenant Hyduke, his men, armored cars, light tanks, and tank destroyers (he appropriated the lone surviving platoon of CCR's 811th Tank Destroyer Battalion) held near the grotto of St. Michael for a little more than an hour, in the process knocking out eight German tanks, but time finally ran out. Ordered by Colonel Cherry to fall back on the main body of Team Cherry, Hyduke had to order his remaining vehicles destroyed, for there was no way they could get past the double bank of vehicles along the constricted highway behind them.

As darkness fell, somebody managed to push aside the vehicles blocking the steep track leading north from the highway to Arloncourt, and most of the self-propelled artillery and a few other vehicles inched out along that route. Many men headed cross-country on foot (among them the forward observer from the 109th Field Artillery, Sergeant Johnson). The coming of darkness also enabled Ryerson's armored infantrymen at last to gain enough of a foothold at the edge of Mageret to afford access to a dirt road leading west in the general direction of Bastogne. Once tanks had shoved aside the wreckage that blocked the highway at the cut in the road, Ryerson was able to get most of the surviving tanks and other vehicles out by that route. He got most of the wounded out the same way.

Team Cherry and the 9th Armored Division's CCR paid dearly along the Mageret-Longvilly road. The effect when combined with earlier losses at Antoniushof and Fe'itsch was that CCR had virtually ceased to exist. Its armored field artillery battalion got none of its howitzers out, although the corps battalion, the 58th, lost only four pieces. Team Cherry lost 175 officers and men—a fourth of the command—7 light and 10 medium tanks and 17 half-tracks. Under the circumstances, it was incredible that any men or vehicles escaped.

To those casualties in the race for Bastogne would have to be added those incurred by the 28th Division's 110th Infantry and its attached and supporting units. And their losses were horrendous. The 110th Infantry lost 2,750 officers and men wounded, captured, and killed—virtually the entire regiment—and almost all its vehicles and the six howitzers of its Cannon Company. Company B of the 103d Engineers was wiped out. The 109th Field Artillery lost a hundred men, all the howitzers of one battery, and two of another. Except for nine medium tanks, most of them crippled, and five assault guns, the 707th Tank Battalion lost two entire companies of medium tanks, a company of lights, and most of the crews. So, too, the 630th Tank Destroyer Battalion lost most of its men and all but six of its towed guns, and a company of the 447th Antiaircraft Artillery Battalion was also virtually erased. CCR's Company B, 2d Tank Battalion, lost fourteen out of seventeen medium tanks and most of the crews.

It was impossible to ascertain with accuracy what the fight cost the Germans, but losses of forces on the attack almost always exceed those of forces on the defense. What mattered, in any case, was not the losses in men, machines, and guns but the loss in precious hours.

Had the 2d Panzer Division and the 26th Volksgrenadier Division crossed the Clerve River on the first day, December 16, the Germans would have captured Bastogne, and the *Panzer Lehr Division* would have been free to join the 2d Panzer Division in a drive to the Meuse with almost nothing in the way. Muddy roads, traffic jams, and difficulty in installing bridges across the Our River were partly responsible for the delay, but in the main the men of the 110th Infantry were responsible, both on the first day and the second. All of that accomplished by easily the most overextended regiment on the American front, a regiment that only a few weeks before had had its guts ripped out in the Hürtgen Forest.

Those delays, combined with that imposed by the 9th Armored Division's CCR, enabled American reinforcements to win the race for Bastogne. Yet even after the 10th Armored Division's CCB arrived, the Germans still might have seized the town had it not been for Team Cherry, which for all the "mischance and confusion" along the road between Longvilly and Mageret, had posed such a threat (real or imagined) that General Bayerlein had delayed the final thrust on Bastogne by his *Panzer Lehr Division*. Perhaps a minor accolade might be accorded the unidentified American nurse who diverted Bayerlein from focusing on his appointed task at a critical hour.

Even after the arrival of troops of the 101st Airborne Division in their assembly area just outside Bastogne around midnight of the 18th, the town was still in dire peril, for only a combat command of armor, a lightly armed airborne division, a few artillery battalions, and a few other small units were available for Bastogne's defense. In winning the race for Bastogne, the Americans had nevertheless forced General von Manteuffel to face a critical decision: Bastogne, the Meuse, or both? Much would hinge on that decision, and it was not von Manteuffel's alone to make.

CHAPTER FOURTEEN

The Defense of Wiltz

When General Cota late on December 17 obtained authority to pull the 110th Infantry behind the Clerve River, so little was left of the regiment that all Cota could hope to do was delay for a time at his headquarters town of Wiltz. But why Wiltz? What would a delay at Wiltz accomplish?

Holding Wiltz would block three minor roads that converged on the town: one climbing up from the valley of the Clerve at Wilwerwiltz; another meandering along a wooded, clifflike hillside high above the scenic trace of the little Wiltz River from the confluence of the Wiltz and the Clerve at Kautenbach; and a third entering the town from the south off the Ettelbruck-Bastogne highway. Since the Germans had roads north of Wiltz leading to Bastogne—of which Cota was surely aware by daylight of December 18—and since delaying at Wiltz would leave nobody for blocking the principal Ettelbruck-Bastogne highway, who needed those roads through Wiltz? Holding the town however long would do nothing to keep the Germans out of Bastogne.

It looked to be one of those decisions taken at any number of places in the early days of the German offensive that rested on nothing more logical than that American troops were there; ergo, American troops should stay until the Germans kicked them out. Why not let Wiltz go and instead defend the Ettelbruck-Bastogne highway? For anybody holding Wiltz, leaving that highway unprotected was, in any case, asking for disaster.

With a population of four thousand, Wiltz was, in essence, two towns: the first a picturesque quarter, set high on a ridgeline and dominated by a château dating from the thirteenth century that overlooked the deep-cut valley of the Wiltz; and the second a more prosaic quarter on low ground to the west, close along the river. The roads from Kautenbach and the Ettelbruck-Bastogne highway entered upper Wiltz; that from Wilwerwiltz, lower Wiltz.

Having released the 110th Infantry's Company G from the mission of defending the division's command post, Cota had left only a provisional battalion formed from headquarters and postal clerks, bandsmen, telephone linemen, drivers, MPs, whatever. Men of that battalion were digging in outside Wiltz during the morning of the 18th when the corps commander, General Middleton, sent help: the six hundred-man 44th Engineer Combat Battalion, commanded by Lt. Col. Clarion J. Kjeldseth. When Cota learned that the 10th Armored Division's CCB was moving up from the Third Army, he sent a liaison officer to the commander, Colonel Roberts, asking his help, in particular to block the Ettelbruck-Bastogne highway. Roberts replied, sorry; he had his orders to go to Bastogne.

From Wiltz, Cota sent two companies of the engineers beyond the little Wiltz River to block roads in the villages of Eschweiler and Erpeldange leading up from the valley of the Clerve, while the third company and the provisional battalion constituted a reserve. The other two roads were of no particular concern at the moment, for Colonel Strickler and what was left of the 110th Infantry's 3d Battalion were soon to withdraw from Consthum to help defend upper Wiltz.

Fire support was limited: six crippled Shermans and five assault guns of the 707th Tank Battalion, six towed guns of the 630th Tank Destroyer Battalion, a few half-tracks of the 447th Antiaircraft Artillery Battalion, and a few armored cars of the 28th Reconnaissance Troop. On the southeastern fringe of upper Wiltz were the 105mm. howitzers of the 687th Field Artillery Battalion, which had fallen back in stages from their original firing positions near the southern end of the Skyline Drive.

General Cota was actually preparing a party to which no German commander wanted to come. General von Lüttwitz of the 47th Panzer Corps had no interest in Wiltz other than to assure that nobody made a foray from the town into his flank, which was why he told the commander of the 26th Volksgrenadier Division, Colonel Kokott, to withhold a regiment to keep an eye on it. So, too, even though Wiltz lay in the zone of the Seventh Army's 5th Parachute Division, the commander of that division, Col. Ludwig Heilmann, had no designs on Wiltz. He wanted to move as fast as possible to blocking positions south of Bastogne, and that could best be achieved by bypassing Wiltz.

Around midday on December 18, it nevertheless appeared to the Americans that a battle for Wiltz was beginning with German attacks at Eschweiler and Erpeldange; but those attacks, which overran two of the towed tank destroyers, were actually a part of the *Panzer Lehr Division's* efforts to get out of the valley of the Clerve and gain Bastogne. The attacks still forced American troops back to the Wiltz River, only a few hundred yards from the first buildings of lower Wiltz. Lest the sole remaining tanks and assault guns of the 707th Tank Battalion be lost, Cota

DEFENSE OF WILTZ

DEC 18 -19

Scale:

0   1   2   3   4

MILES

N

Munshausen

Drauffelt

PZ LEHR DIV

Eschweiler

Wilwerwiltz

Erpeldange

26TH   VG   DIV

Weidingen

Wiltz

River

WILTZ

Consthum

TO
BASTOGNE

Clerve

Kautenbach

CAFÉ
SCHUMANN

River

5TH   PCHT   DIV

Sûre   River

TO ETTELBRUCK

ordered withdrawal behind the Wiltz and the bridge destroyed; but for some reason, the bridge remained intact.

To the surprise of the defenders, the Germans failed to follow. As *Panzer Lehr*'s columns moved on, the regiment of the 26th Volksgrenadier Division assigned to guard the flank arrived. Yet, that regiment had no intention of attacking Wiltz and exerted so little pressure that early the next day, December 19, Cota ordered the engineers to push out again to Erpeldange, there to block the road from Wilwerwiltz with a little greater margin of safety than at the crossing of the Wiltz River on the very fringe of Wiltz. Seeing that move as a possible threat, the *Volksgrenadiers* attacked and drove the Americans a second time across the Wiltz River. That time the engineers blew the bridge.

*   *   *

Before daylight that morning, the 19th, General Cota sent his headquarters out of Wiltz to relocate ten miles to the rear in Sibret, southwest of Bastogne. A platoon of the 42d Field Hospital, which had been operating in the old château in upper Wiltz, also departed, taking most of the patients, but twenty-six were in such serious condition that the surgeons ruled they would have to be left behind. Several surgeons and technicians volunteered to remain with them. The provisional battalion also remained in Wiltz, and Cota himself departed only in late afternoon after Colonel Strickler and the remnants of the 110th Infantry's 3d Battalion had arrived from Consthum. Cota left Strickler in command at Wiltz.

By that time, a genuine attack against Wiltz was in the making. Not that the commander of the German parachute division, Colonel Heilmann, wanted it any more than before but because he was having trouble maintaining control of his regiments, whose commanders were as inexperienced in battle as were most of the troops. Rather than following orders to bypass defended villages, the paratroopers fought for them: They wanted loot and a warm place to pass the night. That was the basic reason why the parachute division was trailing its neighbors to the north; and partly by chance, the same thing happened at Wiltz.

Trying to get past the town, the parachute division's advance guard lost its way and in mid-afternoon of the 19th blundered into the firing positions of the 687th Field Artillery Battalion on the fringe of upper Wiltz. The artillerymen used direct fire from their howitzers to knock out assault guns accompanying the paratroopers, but in the process, they expended all their artillery rounds.

As night fell, the American battalion commander, Lt. Col. Max E. Billingsley, ordered withdrawal to a rendezvous point at a crossroads on the Ettelbruck-Bastogne highway four miles outside Wiltz, known from an inn located there as the Café Schumann crossroads. After assembling there, Billingsley intended displacing farther to the rear, for since he had no ammunition, there was no point in risking loss of his howitzers.

When the commander of the 110th Infantry's 3d Battalion, Major Milton, saw the howitzers leaving, he assumed that a prepared withdrawal plan was in effect. Unable to contact Colonel Strickler by radio to verify it, Milton told his force of about two hundred men to follow the artillery. They had reached a three-pronged road junction, where two roads from Wiltz join the Ettelbruck-Bastogne highway less than a mile from the Café Schumann crossroads, when a messenger from Strickler overtook them in a jeep. There had been no order to withdraw, the word was, and if Milton continued, he would jeopardize the rest of the garrison in Wiltz.

Milton sent word with the messenger that he would await instructions at the road junction. Having no further word after waiting more than an hour, he borrowed the only jeep remaining to the battalion, that of the artillery liaison officer, and went back to Wiltz and Strickler's headquarters.

There he learned that the defense of the town was collapsing. Ammunition was nearly exhausted, and on the heights east of upper Wiltz, a regiment of the 5th Parachute Division had made several dents in the line. Almost all the U.S. tanks and assault guns were either destroyed or immobilized, the crews of those few still functioning so exhausted that at every pause, they fell asleep. There had been no contact for hours with the 28th Division's headquarters at Sibret; and advance parties sent to assembly areas west of Wiltz to which the units in the town were to withdraw returned with word that German paratroopers held them. It began to look as if Wiltz was surrounded.

With that news, Strickler saw no hope of any orderly withdrawal. Instead, he told all commanders to try to pull back with their units intact. Should that prove impossible, they were to break into small groups and try to work their way westward. Move out, said Strickler, as soon as ready.

With two other officers of the 3d Battalion whom Major Milton had encountered at Strickler's headquarters, Milton began to make his way on foot back to his battalion at the road junction. On Strickler's orders, the battalion was to block the Ettelbruck-Bastogne highway until the units leaving Wiltz could get past. Executing that order presupposed the continued existence of the residue of his battalion.

Not long after Major Milton first left for Wiltz, the men of his battalion, having begun to dig in on either side of the Ettelbruck-Bastogne highway at the road junction, heard the sound of marching feet. Because Milton had said that the men were to fire only if attacked, the officers passed the word to hold fire. A platoon of German paratroopers, each man pushing a bicycle, paraded past.

When the Germans disappeared, the officers assembled the men on the highway with the idea of continuing to withdraw when heavy firing broke out in the direction of the Café Schumann crossroads. The men scurried for cover. When it became apparent that the firing was some distance away, they began to return to the road; but not all of them. At least half the men had decided to take off, to try to make their way out individually or in small groups.

As the officers were preparing to march the remaining men toward the Café Schumann crossroads, headlights blazed behind them along one of the roads from Wiltz, and a burst of machine-gun fire erupted. The firing came from an American armored car, which was leading a convoy of various types of American vehicles, all with headlights on. The men in the convoy were trying to brazen their way out. Having spotted three figures on the road, the machine gunners on the armored car had fired.

Moments later, the headlights picked up the clump of men from the

3d Battalion. Recognizing them as Americans, the driver stopped. After a hurried conference, the two groups joined forces, and the men of the 3d Battalion clambered aboard the vehicles. One who clung to the side of the armored car in the lead was the erstwhile commander of Company L, Lieutenant Saymon.

The three figures at which the armored car's machine gunner fired had in the meantime pulled themselves from the ditches: Major Milton and the two officers accompanying him. Arriving at the spot where Milton had left his men, they found nobody, and from the direction of the Café Schumann, they heard heavy firing. All that was left to do, the officers agreed, was to head west as best they could. Several days later, having picked up a few stragglers along the way, they arrived in Sibret.

The artillerymen of the 687th Field Artillery Battalion reached the Café Schumann crossroads not long after full darkness descended. After placing outposts on all four points of entry to the crossroads, the battery commanders were getting ready to feed their men, then continue the withdrawal.

At the outpost southeast of the crossroads on the Ettelbruck-Bastogne highway, small-arms fire erupted. The platoon of German paratroopers that had just marched past Major Milton's men had reached the crossroads. The paratroopers quickly deployed and attacked. Spread out in fields and woods around the crossroads with the vehicles and artillery pieces, few of the artillerymen got involved in the fight, for the attack centered on the crossroads itself, where the only Americans were the officers and men of the battalion headquarters inside the café.

As the firing began, the commander of Battery A, Capt. Norris D. McGinnis, whose howitzers were beyond the crossroads in the direction of Bastogne, told his men to pull out. At that point the battery had only three guns, which were destined to get out and eventually join the defenders of Bastogne. That was about all that was to be left of the 687th Field Artillery Battalion.

The fight for the crossroads was in full swing when up the road, in rear of the paratroopers, appeared the convoy of vehicles with headlights on. Stunned, the Germans at first held their fire, but when about half the vehicles had passed, they opened a blaze of fire. A *Panzerfaust* knocked out a half-track close behind two leading armored cars, blocking the road. Another knocked out a tank farther back in the column. Fire from burp guns and machine guns swept men from the vehicles "like autumn leaves before a strong wind." Most who survived the first fusillade dived for the ditches, but the ditches already belonged to the Germans.

Small-arms fire swept off most of the men clinging to the sides of the two leading armored cars, but as the machine gunners worked their weapons relentlessly, a few continued to hold on, including Lieutenant Saymon. After what seemed an eternity, the two armored cars finally broke free and were soon on their way toward Bastogne. Although hit in the left leg, Saymon was still holding on.

At the crossroads, the screams and moans of the wounded mingled with the sound of continued firing. Inside the café, officers of the battalion headquarters considered their situation hopeless, and if anything was to be done for the wounded, they would have to surrender. The operations officer, Maj. Edgar P. German, who spoke German, called for a cease-fire. The Germans complied.

As the officers had hoped, the Germans helped move the wounded into the café, but for a time there was a question whether the able-bodied would survive. Overhearing German conversations, Major German detected that the paratroopers were under orders to speed their attack, and handling a large body of prisoners would delay them. A sergeant was adamant that the prisoners should be shot, but before he could act, a captain arrived. There would be no killing of prisoners, he decreed.

In the melee, the 687th Field Artillery lost almost all its vehicles and all howitzers but the three of Battery A. As for the men, many melted into the darkness even as the surrender was taking place, and a few eventually made their way to safety. The Germans marched those who surrendered away from the crossroads and held them temporarily in a wood. From there, the men could hear renewed firing at the crossroads.

That was German fire directed at another column of vehicles trying to escape from Wiltz, made up primarily of men of the provisional battalion who had climbed aboard anything with wheels or tracks that could still function. As the men in that convoy soon learned, the Germans had by that time installed mines across the main highway at the three-pronged road junction and backed up the roadblock with paratroopers and machine guns.

When the leading half-track hit a mine, it blew up. The driver of the next vehicle, a half-track of the 447th Antiaircraft Artillery Battalion, its quad-50s blazing, drove deliberately into the minefield; that half-track, too, went up in a deafening explosion, but it got rid of the mines. As the paratroopers fled, the sacrifice made by the men in the half-track provided a safe path for the vehicles that followed.

The encouragement the rest of the men gained from that experience was short-lived, for just down the road was the Café Schumann crossroads. There the paratroopers had erected another roadblock amid the wreckage of American vehicles and the bodies of American and German dead. As the convoy approached, a *Panzerfaust* hit the first armored car at point-blank range. Turning over from the impact, the vehicle burst into flames, lighting the scene for German machine gunners so well that it was difficult for them to miss their concentrated target.

Yet the Germans were dealing with near-desperate men, and amid the pandemonium three dozen of them rushed forward from the rear of the

American column, firing and hurling grenades. The Germans fell back. Once a half-track cleared a passage through the wrecked vehicles, the convoy continued toward Bastogne.

Again the men's encouragement was to be short-lived. Only a few hundred yards beyond the crossroads, they came upon another road-block. Vehicles burned; men fell left and right. The few survivors threw themselves into the ditches, then took advantage of the darkness to crawl away, eventually to get far enough from the scene of the carnage to dare to rise and run. Many were destined to blunder into German positions or to come across German patrols; but some—nobody would ever know just how many—eventually made their way out.

The experiences of the men in those two convoys were much like those of all others who tried to get away from Wiltz that terrible night, for there was no denying the inevitable consequences of an ill-advised decision to fight a delaying action with no provision for keeping escape routes open. The last organized unit to attempt to leave, the 44th Engineer Combat Battalion, lost more than 160 men in the withdrawal; added to the casualties incurred inside Wiltz, that meant that the battalion had lost more than half its strength.

Every man who got out had his own personal odyssey: kindness from Belgian civilians whenever he dared enter a village, but mostly bitter cold, hunger, fear, lack of sleep, water-logged feet often leading to trench foot. Those few who turned south into the heavily wooded country along the Sûre River had the greater fortune, for the Germans had yet to push far to the south. Yet few men knew that, and since many had heard the names of only two places to their rear—Bastogne and Sibret—those drew them like lodestones, particularly Bastogne. For any number of men, heading for those places was their undoing, since those were the two towns for which the Germans were heading. It was only with fortitude, perseverance, guile, and a triple helping of luck that anybody got through.

One who did get through was the commander in Wiltz at the end, Dan Strickler. Before ripping a map off the wall in the command post and burning it, Strickler tore out the section depicting the region around Bastogne and thrust it inside his shirt. He also made sure he had a compass.

An hour before midnight, Strickler, the 28th Division's assistant G-3, Maj. Carl W. Plitt, and Strickler's driver, Cpl. Robert Martin, took off in Strickler's jeep. They had gone only a short distance in the direction of the Café Schumann crossroads when German mortars and machine guns opened fire. In trying to evade the fire, Martin drove the jeep into a ditch, and it was impossible to get it out. At that point, they had no alternative but to proceed on foot, moving north to get around the Café

Schumann crossroads, then to cross the Ettelbruck-Bastogne highway farther along, and head west for Sibret.

The trek that began with that decision turned out to be grueling and nervewracking. A crackling noise in the woods. Was it Germans? In one case, it turned out to be an American corporal, the division chaplain's assistant. Later other American soldiers emerged in ones or twos, mainly MPs, among the last to leave Wiltz, so that in little more than an hour Strickler's group increased from three to ten.

Reaching the Ettelbruck-Bastogne highway, the group paused for a long time to observe the pattern of German traffic before seizing a quiet moment to dash across. Avoiding roads and villages, the men plodded on through "mud, fields, streams, forests, underbrush, and over barbed-wire fences and stone walls." Whenever they paused to rest, most dropped off to sleep, then awoke trembling from the cold. They drank from streams, but there was nothing to eat.

As daylight neared, Strickler halted the men in a patch of woods overlooking a village. If daylight revealed no Germans, he intended sending someone into the village to find food. He was about ready to venture it when a man and a boy ran up from the village into the woods. The man explained that he was fleeing lest the Germans deport him as a laborer. The name of his village, he said, was Tarchamps.

Strickler, checking the map inside his shirt, realized that he and his group had covered over half the distance to Sibret. Considering that they had moved cross-country and in the dark, they were making remarkable progress.

While Strickler was questioning the civilian man, a German column roared by on the road below, assault guns with soldiers riding on the decks interspersed with captured American jeeps and trucks. Pulling deeper into the woods, Strickler insisted that the man and his son come along; he could trust nobody.

The little group sat out the daylight hours of December 20 in the woods. Although two other small groups of fleeing American soldiers stumbled upon the hideout, all agreed that their chances of escape were better in small groups than together.

Strickler's goal that night was to get across the major Arlon-Bastogne highway; but as he and his men reached the highway, German traffic was almost constant and every three hundred yards or so there was a listening post. In time they finally reached a point where the highway passed through a wood, and a slow, careful search revealed no listening post. Even so, Strickler decided to wait to cross until around 3 A.M. when the Germans might be less alert. Then all went well, except that there turned out to be a barbed-wire fence on the far side of the road and in the darkness, several men drew blood as they tugged frantically at their clothing to free themselves, expecting a German vehicle to appear at any moment.

Beyond the highway, at the first village, German armored vehicles were entering, and dogs emerged, barking furiously. At the next, which Strickler identified as Hollange, it appeared so quiet that he decided to risk an attempt to get food. While the others hid behind a haystack at the edge of the village, Strickler and his driver, Corporal Martin, approached a house.

As they neared, a farmer appeared at the door with a lantern. Asking in halting French for food, Strickler also asked if there were many German soldiers. As he raised the lantern for Strickler to have a look, Strickler saw the hallway full of sleeping Germans and in an adjoining room an officer sprawled across a bed.

"*Merci beaucoup*," said Strickler, and pretending nonchalance, he and Martin walked away. The farmer must have thought that they, too, were Germans, and at that point Strickler had no wish to alter the impression.

To get away from Hollange, the men had to wade a stream that turned out to be waist deep. So wet and cold that it was hard to keep moving, they reached another wood from which they could look down on Hollange. At daylight the village came alive with German soldiers, who mounted bicycles and rode away.

To Strickler, there was no question but that they had to do something to get dry. Drawing back deep into the woods, he took the chance, over the objection of several of the men, of lighting a small fire, and the men took turns drying their clothing.

During the break, one man pulled a K-ration packet from his jacket. He agreed to share it (he had little choice) and the ten divided it carefully. Each had five sips of bouillon, a nibble from a cracker, and a single bite of the egg-and-ham mixture that came with a breakfast meal.

Setting out again as the night of December 21 approached, they ran almost immediately into dense, briar-laced undergrowth that tore at their uniforms and their skin. Famished, exhausted, disgruntled, and frightened, some of the men were close to delirium, but Strickler pressed them on. When they finally emerged from the undergrowth, they were so fatigued that they took their chances in the open and marched down a dirt road until they came to a hamlet. They knocked on several houses before a man finally opened his door.

Strickler said his men had to have food, and the Belgian invited them in. Two days before, he told them, American troops had blown a bridge just beyond the hamlet, and he was expecting the Germans at any moment. He nevertheless produced ersatz coffee, milk, bread, butter, and jam.

An hour later, food in their stomachs and the warmth of the Belgian's fire a pleasant memory, they set out again. Some three miles away, American sentries challenged them. They had reached Vaux-les-Rosières astride a principal highway leading southwest out of Bastogne to the town of Neufchâteau. Having had to relinquish Sibret, General Cota and what was left of the 28th Division's headquarters had paused there for the night.

By daylight on December 20, men of the 5th Parachute Division controlled Wiltz. When they found an occasional American straggler, they sent him to the old château in upper Wiltz to help with the wounded. There the surgeons and technicians left behind by the 42d Field Hospital cared both for the seriously wounded Americans left behind and for German casualties. Shouting that one of the surgeons, Capt. Harry Fisher, was Jewish, the Germans took him away, leaving his colleagues to assume grimly that the Germans shot him. In reality, the Germans used him to work at a front-line aid station just outside Bastogne at the village of Marvie and employed him at other forward aid stations until the end of the war.

There were two other Americans in Wiltz of whom the Germans had no knowledge. One was Sgt. George Carroll, found, painfully wounded in the shoulder, by an elderly couple in lower Wiltz, M. and Mme. Jean-Pierre Balthasar. Reluctantly—for it was a terrible risk—the couple hid him in their attic. The second was Pvt. Ralph Ellis, one of a few to escape from the positions of the 110th Infantry's Company C and Cannon Company on the other side of the Clerve River.

Hiding by day and traveling by night, fording both the Clerve and Wiltz Rivers, Ellis reached the fringe of lower Wiltz just at daylight on the 20th. Exhausted, starving, half-frozen, his feet so numb that he had to look down at them to make sure he was walking, he made his way to a deserted house on the edge of town, found a half-empty container of oatmeal, ate it raw, and climbed into a bed.

Madame Balthasar was deeply concerned about the wounded soldier in the attic, and when German soldiers arrived to be billeted in the house, she became even more worried. She decided to climb the hill to upper Wiltz and the Clinique St. Joseph. There she found a sympathetic volunteer nurse—she gave her name only as Mademoiselle Anna—who agreed to bring some medicine and help Madame Balthasar's *invité* (her guest).

Just over a week later, the number of Americans hiding in Wiltz increased by one more. As the Germans were evacuating the hospital in the château, Sgt. Lester Koritz, a member of the 28th Division's G-2 Section whom the Germans used as an interpreter in the hospital, hid in the basement until everybody left. After dark he made his way to a tobacco shop run by two spinster sisters, Mariechen and Elise Goebel, whose acquaintance he had made earlier. They took him in.

Ralph Ellis by that time had begun to forage at night for food, but he was becoming almost delirious, his feet dark, swollen, and pus-filled. Unless he could find help, he decided, he was going to die. One night he made his way to another deserted house deeper inside lower Wiltz and the next morning inadvertently showed himself at a window. A man saw him: Louis Steinmetz, who worked with the Red Cross and was also a member of the underground resistance. Steinmetz and his sister-in-law took Ellis in, and when Steinmetz went to the Clinique St. Joseph for ointment, Mademoiselle Anna deduced that he too was hiding an *invité* and offered to help.

In time, the civilians brought all three Americans to a common hiding place. They were still hiding and caring for them—Ellis's feet in critical condition—when in early January American liberators came for a second time to Wiltz.

CHAPTER FIFTEEN

Developing Crisis at St. Vith

The commander of the 106th Infantry Division, Alan W. Jones, was expecting to have at his disposal soon after daylight on December 17 a combat command of the 7th Armored Division. His corps commander, Troy Middleton, had told him so.

On the basis of that information, Jones had changed his orders to the 9th Armored Division's CCB, which had been preparing to attack into the Losheim Gap to block the open north flank of the two regiments of the 106th Division on the Schnee Eifel (regiments which Jones, on the basis of a misunderstood telephone conversation with Middleton, deemed he had no authority to withdraw). The assignment to help those two regiments was to pass instead to the 7th Armored Division, while the 9th Armored Division's CCB helped the 106th Division's third regiment, the 424th Infantry, farther south. Although the 424th Infantry was in no immediate danger of encirclement, its left wing appeared to be about to give way, which would open to the Germans a direct route to St. Vith, a route even shorter than that leading from the Schnee Eifel.

Although the contemporary U.S. Army field manual on the armored division specified no accepted rate of march, experience had shown that armor moving in convoy under semitactical conditions rarely exceeded ten miles per hour. When the commander of the 7th Armored Division, Brig. Gen. Robert W. Hasbrouck, received the order to move to St. Vith, his division was in the southern tip of the Netherlands, sixty miles and a minimum of six hours away from St. Vith; and not until close to 5 A.M. the next morning, December 17, were the first of Hasbrouck's vehicles to obtain road clearance and begin to march. Under the best of road conditions, that meant that not until well into the day of December 17 could any substantial part of the division reach St. Vith, and even then planning and deploying for an attack would consume additional time. Jones and Middleton should have had some appreciation of all that.

*   *   *

310

However far away the 7th Armored Division, General Jones already had one of the "big friends" that Middleton was sending to help him: General Hoge's CCB, 9th Armored Division. The leading vehicles of Hoge's convoy entered St. Vith just as day was breaking and halted close to Jones's command post in the St. Joseph's Kloster. Hoge and his staff were inside talking with Jones when small-arms fire rained down on the column of vehicles. It was coming from the second floor of a house. As machine gunners on half-tracks returned the fire, infantrymen broke down the door on the ground floor and raced upstairs. There they found spent cartridges littering the floor and three men in civilian clothes firing German rifles. The soldiers took no prisoners.

Inside the command post, General Hoge learned that before daylight, the Germans had mounted a heavy attack at Winterspelt against men of the 424th Infantry: Cannon Company, forced back the day before from nearby Eigelscheid, and the 1st Battalion, committed late the day before to help hold Winterspelt. Hoge was to use his armored infantry to seize high ground strengthening the position at Winterspelt, while his tanks remained behind the Our River for use as the situation developed.

On the way from St. Vith to the Our crossing at Steinebrück, Hoge got the impression that the situation at Winterspelt was worse than General Jones knew, for CCB's column came upon more than a hundred stragglers from the 424th Infantry retreating in disarray toward St. Vith. Hoge stopped to talk with the men, and at his urging, junior officers among them agreed to form a provisional company and reinforce CCB's 27th Armored Infantry Battalion.

As Hoge soon learned, the defenders of Winterspelt had broken, most of them falling back onto other positions of the regiment, although a platoon leader, 1st Lt. Jarrett M. Huddleston, Jr., had rallied a few men in front of the important bridge across the Our at Steinebrück. The Germans nevertheless held the high ground looking down on the bridge.

By noon, CCB's armored infantry, with the help of a platoon of the 14th Tank Battalion, had retaken that first stretch of high ground, and in mid-afternoon General Hoge decided to commit the rest of his tanks to retake Winterspelt. The tanks were ready to move when Hoge received a message from General Jones. Hoge was to attack if he wished, said Jones, but after nightfall he would have to withdraw. Having authorized the adjacent 112th Infantry of the 28th Division to retire behind the Our River, the corps commander, General Middleton, had told the 424th Infantry to do the same.

Rather than spill blood to take meaningless ground, Hoge called off the attack.

As daybreak approached on December 17, all that stood in the way of the 18th Volksgrenadier Division clamping a pincers around the two regi-

ST. Vith
DEC 17-19

GERMAN ATTACKS
U.S. POSITIONS

Scale:
0 1 2 3
MILES

N

SCHNEE EIFEL

Losheim
Manderfeld
Lanzerath
Weckerath
Roth
Kobscheid
18TH VG DIV
Auw
19
422D INF
576
Oberlascheid
423D INF
Radscheid
Buchet
Engineer Cut-off
Bleialf
Laudesfeld
18-19
504
Grosslangenfeld
Eigelscheid
Grosskampenberg
Andler
Schoenberg
17
18TH VG DIV
Ihren
62D VG DIV
Winterspelt
Lützkampen
Heuem
River
Our
Steinebrück
Elcherath
Heckhuscheid
Herresbach
Setz
17
THE PRÜMBERG
17
Braunlauf Cr.
Our River
Burg Reuland
Our
2D PZ GR REGT
Wareth
Amblève
SIXTH PZ ARMY
FIFTH PZ ARMY
Meyerode
FB BRIG
Wallrode
17
19
19
Amblève
Born
Hünningen
St. Vith
106TH INF DIV
7TH ARMD DIV
Grufflange
No23
17
Rodt
Crombach
Beho
19
Recht
Poteau
Salm River
Salm
116TH PZ DIV
Petit Their
Salmchâteau
Gouvy
19
Salm River
Vielsalm
Bovigny
Ourthe
WEST WALL
River Our

ments of the 106th Division on the Schnee Eifel were two small forces. At Bleialf, at the southern end of the Schnee Eifel, waited the little conglomerate that the commander of the 423d Infantry, Colonel Cavender, had mustered the first day to retake the village; and at Andler, behind the northern part of the Schnee Eifel at a point of entry into the valley of the Our River, was a lone troop of the 32d Cavalry Reconnaissance Squadron with nothing more powerful in its arsenal than machine guns and 37mm. cannon mounted on thin-skinned armored cars. If either or both of those small forces collapsed, the Germans would soon be in Schoenberg, where the roads from Andler and Bleialf joined. That in turn would trap the 422d and 423d Regiments and their supporting artillery on the far side of the Our and open a direct route to St. Vith.

During the night of December 16, two of the U.S. artillery battalions were in immediate danger: the 589th, supporting the 422d Infantry, and the 592d, the division's general support 155mm. howitzers. The firing positions of both were just off the Auw-Bleialf road (the so-called Skyline Boulevard) down which the Germans had attacked southward from the direction of Auw. Although the arrival at midnight of Colonel Puett's infantry battalion from the division reserve provided some protection, the two battalions were still virtually in the front line. The division artillery commander, Brig. Gen. Leo T. McMahon, ordered both to displace, to be followed by the third battalion, the 590th, which supported the 423d Infantry.

The 155mm. howitzers of the 592d made it out except for one left stuck in the mud and another that missed the Engineer Cut-Off and was destroyed by German fire at 88 Corner, possibly from the assault guns Lieutenant Patton had encountered earlier. Before daylight the remaining howitzers assumed new firing positions near St. Vith.

The 105mm. howitzers of the 589th Field Artillery Battalion tried to displace to the vicinity of the battalion's Service Battery along the Bleialf-Schoenberg road just over a mile short of Schoenberg, which would still leave the pieces with a river behind them. Because the Germans blocked the only road leading out of Battery C's positions, none of that battery's howitzers was able to get out. Except for one piece whose prime mover ran off the Engineer Cut-Off, the other two batteries made it to the new positions. Yet there the crews soon discovered that they had merely exchanged one hot spot for another.

That was because at Bleialf—one of the two critical spots that had to be held lest the Germans gain Schoenberg—the German regiment comprising the southern arm of the 18th Volksgrenadier Division's pincer movement struck just before dawn on the 17th with the help of a few assault guns. The little provisional force in Bleialf folded, and as the first vestiges of a fog-shrouded daylight appeared, the Bleialf-Schoenberg road was open to German advance.

Not long after, so was the Andler-Schoenberg road, for there the 32d Cavalry Reconnaissance Squadron's Troop B had no chance of holding the village. For the first time in the offensive King Tiger tanks entered the fighting, the leading tanks of the 506th Heavy Panzer Battalion, big, slow, and cumbersome but also powerful and terrifying. A separate unit attached to the Sixth Panzer Army, the battalion had gone outside the army boundary in search of a road capable of handling the big tanks and merely stumbled into the fight for Andler.

Lest the entire troop be lost, the commander, Capt. Franklin P. Lindsey, Jr., asked permission to fall back and establish a roadblock on the road to Schoenberg, but that authority was still to come when fire from the tanks drove part of the troop to the west. Facing collapse, Lindsey ordered the rest to head for Schoenberg. Learning there that Bleialf had also fallen, Lindsey kept moving through Schoenberg to the village of Heum, two miles behind Schoenberg along the road to St. Vith.

The *Volksgrenadiers*—but not the big tanks—followed closely and at 8:45 A.M. stormed across the bridge over the Our River at Schoenberg, a critical bridge that nobody on the American side had made any plans to demolish. At that point the American troops to the east—two regiments and attached units, two divisional artillery battalions, and parts of three corps artillery battalions—had no way of getting out unless somebody came to their rescue, unless they could find some other escape route, or unless they could fight their way out. If their predicament needed any further confirmation, the experiences of the artillery battalions soon provided it.

Although the corps commander, General Middleton, had expected that in the event of trouble in the Losheim Gap or around the Schnee Eifel, he would get a lot of help from those powerful corps artillery pieces, that was not to be. Partly because there was little central coordination of fires by the newly arrived 106th Division, but primarily because the guns had a river at their backs.

The two surviving firing batteries of the 589th Field Artillery Battalion with their seven remaining howitzers reached their new positions along the Bleialf-Schoenberg road not long before full daylight. They had yet to begin firing when a truck tore down the road from the direction of Bleialf, the driver shouting that the Germans were right behind him. It was a truck from the battalion's Service Battery, located only a short distance up the road. In the absence of the battalion commander, Lt. Col. Thomas P. Kelly, Jr., who was still trying to save Battery C's howitzers, the executive officer, Maj. Arthur C. Parker III, ordered withdrawal behind the Our.

In the scramble to get onto the highway, the three remaining guns of Battery B bogged in mud and were unable to make it. So did one of Battery A's four howitzers. The other three raced downhill into Schoenberg, across the bridge over the Our, and through the village only minutes ahead of the *Volksgrenadiers* coming from Andler.

Close behind those pieces, a few trucks carrying men of Battery B also got through Schoenberg, but not the last one. In that truck was the battery commander, Capt. Arthur C. Brown, who delayed leaving the battery's position until he could check for stragglers. As the truck in which Brown was riding headed down the steep hill into Schoenberg, a group of black American soldiers shouted and waved frantically; moments later Brown was to understand that those men were trying to warn him that the Germans were inside Schoenberg, but Brown's instantaneous reaction was to step on it. So he told his driver.

A short distance beyond the bridge, Brown spotted a German assault gun (he saw it as a tank) between two buildings. Brown emptied his pistol at the observation slots, which provided just enough time for the truck to get past before the assault gun fired. So close was the round that "the canvas on the truck bellied in from the blast."

As Brown's truck passed the last houses and cleared a rise in the road, another German assault gun sat full astride the narrow road. There were dead and wounded Americans in the ditches, and others stood with arms stretched overhead in surrender. Brown's driver brought the truck to a screeching halt and all aboard dived for the ditches. Most were captured, but Brown and a few others made it to a nearby wood. After a harrowing seven days, they eventually reached American lines.

The black soldiers Brown had encountered near the bridge were men of the 333d Field Artillery Battalion, a part of the 333d Field Artillery Group, whose firing positions had been beyond the river. Their group commander, Lt. Col. John P. Brewster, had begun the day before to extricate his three battalions, all of which were east of the Our; but as was evident from the presence of those soldiers in Schoenberg, not everybody made it out.

Shortly after the offensive opened, in mid-morning of the 16th, Colonel Brewster felt compelled to shift a battery of the 740th Field Artillery Battalion from positions near Auw lest it be overrun. The battery joined the battalion's other two firing batteries south of Schoenberg near the village of Amelscheid. By mid-afternoon, Brewster was convinced that he should displace all his batteries behind the Our; but at the request of the 106th Division's artillery commander, General McMahon, who assured Brewster that his division was going to hold, Brewster agreed to leave a firing battery of each battalion in place.

At daylight on the 17th, Brewster realized that was a mistake, for he learned of the penetrations at Bleialf and Andler. He promptly ordered the three remaining batteries to displace. That of the 740th Field Artillery Battalion got through Schoenberg ahead of the *Volksgrenadiers*. Not so the other two.

Battery C, 333d Field Artillery Battalion, was still in firing positions north of Schoenberg when at 8:15 A.M. *Volksgrenadiers* attacked. Seeing the situation as hopeless, the battalion commander, Lt. Col. Harmon S. Kelsey, who had stayed behind with the battery, ordered the howitzers abandoned. He and his troops headed for Schoenberg in three trucks, but once they debouched onto the Andler-Schoenberg road, they ran into Germans headed for Schoenberg. Kelsey ordered the trucks abandoned, every man for himself. He and most of the others were captured, but about a dozen men escaped, and later in the day a few others got away when an American fighter-bomber strafed as the Germans were marching them to the rear. Men of the 333d's Service Battery had much the same experience; only twenty-seven of them eventually made their way to St. Vith.

From positions just south of Schoenberg near Amelscheid, Battery B, 771st Field Artillery Battalion, was about ready to depart by way of Schoenberg when a truck that had already left came racing back with word that the Germans held Schoenberg. Having occupied the positions for several weeks, the battalion commander, Lt. Col. Mark S. Bacon, was more familiar with the terrain than were commanders in the 106th Division, and he knew a way out. He led Battery B along a woods trail to a narrow bridge across the Our downstream from Schoenberg at the hamlet of Setz. From there, having bypassed Schoenberg, the men and their guns got onto the road leading to St. Vith.

The last of the three organic battalions of the 106th Division, the 590th Field Artillery Battalion, waited through the night for word from General McMahon to begin its exodus; but communications with the division's command post were out, and not until daylight did the word finally come. Men of the battalion's survey section in the lead ran into a German roadblock on the Bleialf-Schoenberg road not far from the lower end of the Engineer Cut-Off, and the first howitzers to displace came under punishing German shelling just as they turned onto the cut-off. Those two events convinced the battalion commander, Lt. Col. Vaden C. Lackey, that he and his men stood a better chance by staying where they were until relief came. As he ordered all howitzers back to their original positions, the fate of the 590th Field Artillery Battalion was from that point tied inexorably to that of the infantry the artillerymen supported.

One more small group of the 598th Field Artillery Battalion had still to make an effort to get through Schoenberg. The group consisted of twenty-five officers and men, including the executive officer of Battery A, 1st Lt. Eric F. Wood, Jr., who had stayed behind to try to get his mired howitzer onto the road. At last they despaired and piled aboard three jeeps.

As the jeeps headed down the hill into Schoenberg, the men saw "men in greenish uniforms running back and forth in the main street." A burp gun fired. Bullets "zipped around" the men's ears, and they "dove off the jeeps into the ditch." Determining that the closest concealment was a wooded hill just north of the road (it was to figure prominently in later action as Hill 504), the men climbed laboriously to the top. As a heavy barrage of mortar rounds fell, they scattered, every man for himself.

It remained for Troop B, 18th Cavalry Reconnaissance Squadron, attached to the 423d Infantry, whose commander, Captain Fossland, had pulled back the day before into Winterscheid just outside Bleialf, to make the final try that day to get through Schoenberg. The 106th Reconnaissance Troop having collapsed at Grosslangenfeld and Bleialf having fallen, Troop B had no neighbors. When Fossland radioed his plight to the commander of the 423d Infantry, Colonel Cavender authorized him to try to withdraw through Schoenberg but warned him that the Germans might be in the village.

Along with thirty officers and men of the 106th Reconnaissance Troop, Troop B in mid-afternoon headed for Schoenberg. With no difficulty, the column reached the Bleialf-Schoenberg road near where the 589th Field Artillery Battalion had tried to establish new firing positions. Part of the column had turned onto the highway heading for Schoenberg when a jeep coming from the direction of Bleialf pressed into the column—a jeep filled with Germans. One of Troop B's armored cars fired its 37mm. gun, and the jeep crashed into a ditch, a mass of wreckage and tangled bodies.

Wary of what lay ahead in Schoenberg, Captain Fossland halted the column short of the first houses and sent a platoon under 1st Lt. Elmo J. Johnston to reconnoiter. With Johnston riding in the first of three armored cars, the men started out just at dusk, crossed the bridge over the Our without interference, and turned left along the road to St. Vith. Up ahead, Johnston could make out a long line of American 6×6 trucks filled with Germans. His first reaction was that they were prisoners headed for the rear, but if so, why were they carrying rifles and burp guns?

Shouting a warning over the radio to the vehicles following, Johnston told his driver to step on the gas, and the drivers of the other two armored cars did the same. As they raced past the column of trucks, the gunners on all three vehicles fired canister from their 37mm. pieces, and German soldiers tumbled from the trucks to find cover. Johnston's armored car got all the way past the German column before German fire knocked it out. Fire from an assault gun caught the other two armored cars, and of six jeeps with Johnston, only the last one got away.

When that jeep returned to Captain Fossland, he saw no alternative but to destroy his remaining vehicles and split his men into small groups to make their way out as best they could. (He knew nothing of the nearby bridge across the Our at Setz, used earlier by Colonel Bacon and his artillerymen.) A few of them, including Fossland himself, eventually succeeded.

The experience of Fossland's column along the last segment of the Bleialf-Schoenberg highway and of Johnston's men in the village demonstrated that the Germans had yet to establish a hold on that part of the highway or to prepare to defend the village against breakout attempts. The problem lay with the regiment of the 18th Volksgrenadier Division that was supposed to move from Bleialf to Schoenberg. The men of that regiment were slow to push through little groups of Americans they encountered along the road, so that not until nightfall did the German pincers actually close at Schoenberg. Yet that had little effect on the fate of those Americans trapped east of the Our, for even if only one arm of the pincers was in Schoenberg, the principal way out was blocked.

Yet as Colonel Bacon had demonstrated, that was not the only way out. Between Schoenberg and embattled Steinebrück, downstream from Schoenberg, there were four small yet nonetheless negotiable bridges over the Our. The one used by Bacon at Setz led onto the Schoenberg–St. Vith highway, which by late in the day was thick with German traffic; the other three led to woods trails that eventually joined the Steinebrück–St. Vith highway, which was under the control of the 9th Armored Division's CCB. Whoever tried to use those bridges would first have to get across the Bleialf-Schoenberg highway, but that would be a far easier assignment than trying to fight through Schoenberg.

Like most commanders of the trapped units, few of the men who tried individually or in small groups to infiltrate back to St. Vith were familiar with the general terrain or the roads. They had been there only a few days, and few knew any route other than that from St. Vith to Schoenberg by which they had arrived. Hardly anybody among the fleeing soldiers had a map and very few had a compass. Yet somehow over the next few days and nights, some managed to elude the Germans and make their way to safety. How many would never be known: perhaps two hundred or so on the 17th and 18th, probably another two hundred or so after that. Then again, many another failed, blundering into German positions or rounded up by German patrols.

One who reached the west bank of the Our but still failed to gain American lines was the executive officer of Battery A, 589th Field Artillery Battalion, Lieutenant Wood. When American troops swept back through the area in late January, they found Wood's body in the forest behind Schoenberg not far from St. Vith near the village of Meyerode. Wood was officially listed as killed in action on December 17, the same day that he and others from his battalion had come under mortar fire near Schoenberg and scattered. When his body was found in the forest near Meyerode, seven dead Germans lay close by.

To Wood's father, a brigadier general on General Eisenhower's staff, that was an indication that his son had died not on the 17th but weeks later after having conducted a heroic guerrilla struggle in the German rear. In support of that theory, Wood's father accumulated affidavits from civilians in the village of Meyerode.

While moving through the woods near Meyerode late in the afternoon on December 17, Peter Maraite came upon two American soldiers, one a young officer. After convincing them he was to be trusted, he invited them to his house in Meyerode, where he and his wife fed them and they spent the night. When the two departed the next morning, they said they intended to reach St. Vith, only three miles away, but failing that, they meant to collect American stragglers in the woods and harass the Germans.

Over the days and weeks that followed, civilians in Meyerode heard occasional small-arms fire in the nearby woods. Sometimes wounded German soldiers stumbled from the woods into the village, and from time to time civilians heard German soldiers complaining and swearing about resistance in the forest. Word spread in Meyerode that a small group of Americans was roaming the woods, ambushing German work parties and preying on supply columns, and that the leader was a young officer, "very big and powerful of body and brave of spirit."

Residents of Meyerode later found the body of a young American officer in the woods—a big man "with single silver bars upon his shoulders," and close around him the bodies of seven German soldiers. That officer, Wood's father maintained, was his son, and for his valor in the forest, he should be awarded posthumously the Medal of Honor.

If, indeed, Lieutenant Wood fought a small-scale guerrilla war in the thick forest between Schoenberg and St. Vith, he was a man of incredible intrepidity. Almost every U.S. soldier trapped behind German lines had but one goal, to reach American lines, and whoever those two men who spent the night in Peter Maraite's house were, they were only a relatively short distance from American lines. What kind of charisma enabled Wood to persuade other Americans to abandon that goal (so close at hand) and join him in a long-running, virtually hopeless vendetta in the frozen woods? Where was the food to be found to sustain themselves over days and weeks? And what about ammunition?

For the Belgian civilians, at any rate, there were no doubts. Whether Lieutenant Wood died on December 17 while trying to reach St. Vith or whether he did, indeed, fight on with a small band of men, the Belgians erected a monument to him in the forest where, they say, he for long continued the fight. Set at the edge of a patch of fir trees along an almost eerily silent gravel trail, it is a touching memorial.

After the 106th Division's field artillery battalions displaced before daylight on December 17, General Jones ordered Colonel Puett to withdraw his 2d Battalion and reconstitute a reserve at Schoenberg. Yet hardly had Jones issued that order than he learned of German success at Bleialf, and before Puett could make any headway in moving to Schoenberg, word came of the German breakthrough at Andler. A short while later the division's signal officer, Lt. Col. Earle Williams, tapped a telephone wire along the Schoenberg–St. Vith road to tell Jones that the Germans had taken Schoenberg. All Colonel Puett could do at that point was to join his parent regiment, the 423d Infantry, to become part of an all-around defense.

At 9:45 A.M., General Jones gave the two trapped regiments their first authority to pull back. "Withdraw from present positions," the message read, "if they become untenable." Yet the message reflected a continuing belief on the part of Jones that with the arrival of the 7th Armored Division, matters would be set right. The division expected to clear out the area "west of you," the message went on, during the afternoon.

Meanwhile, word from Captain Lindsey's Troop B, 32d Cavalry Reconnaissance Squadron, was that the troopers were trying to delay along the Schoenberg–St. Vith road at Heuem, but that little force was all that stood between the 18th Volksgrenadier Division and St. Vith. In midmorning, Jones told the commander of his 81st Engineer Combat Battalion, Lt. Col. Thomas J. Riggs, to throw together some kind of force to block the road as far to the east as possible.

Riggs had few of his own men available. Two of the line companies were still attached to forward regiments, and of the third, which the Germans had overrun the day before at Auw, there were only sixty-four men, making a total from the 81st Engineers and the division headquarters defense platoon of just over a hundred. Although corps headquarters had released the 168th Engineer Combat Battalion to General Jones, only the headquarters and a single company were immediately available, perhaps 175 men. There was also a platoon of the 820th Tank Destroyer Battalion, which had lost its towed guns while fighting with the 424th Infantry, but three replacement pieces arrived from an ordnance depot to the rear. The one bright spot for Riggs was the presence of ten of the original twelve 155mm. howitzers of the 592d Field Artillery Battalion, which had escaped the entrapment beyond the Our.

Riggs's instructions were to move down the road toward Schoenberg as far as Heuem to join Captain Lindsey's cavalry; but when the 168th Engineer Combat Battalion's reconnaissance officer, 2d Lt. Harry Balch, reached Heuem, he found Lindsey and his men withdrawing. They had orders, said Lindsey, to join a line the 14th Cavalry Group was trying to form north and northeast of St. Vith against Germans moving through the Losheim Gap, and nothing Balch could say would stop them. The Germans, said the cavalrymen, were just around the next bend in the road.

It took Balch little time to verify that. When he passed the information to his own commander, Lt. Col. William L. Nungesser, and to Colonel Riggs, the two agreed that it would be folly to try to hold Heuem. If the engineers were to have any time to dig in before the Germans were upon them, they would have to choose the last possible defensive position short of St. Vith itself. That was high ground, mostly wooded, a mile outside the town, known as the Prümerberg. From the Prümerberg, the ground dips down sharply—almost a bluff—to the town in the valley below. Choosing that position might afford the engineers precious minutes to get ready, but should their line fold, German guns would have a commanding position from which to fire directly into St. Vith.

The 592d Field Artillery Battalion provided the engineers a little time when around noon 1st Lt. George Stafford as pilot and 2d Lt. Alonzo A. Neese as observer took off in an observation plane from the 106th Division's airstrip. Flying low because of poor visibility, the plane picked up a German column along the highway about two miles beyond where the engineers were digging in. A first volley of 155mm. shells hit an assault gun in the lead, sending it up in flames, and accompanying infantry scattered.

Not quite an hour later, three German assault guns emerged cautiously around a bend in the road only a few hundred yards from where the engineers were digging in. Moving off the road into a field, one of the assault guns bogged down; and as the crew dismounted, the commander of Company B, 168th Engineers, 1st Lt. William E. Holland, killed everybody with a .50-caliber machine gun. A bazooka team knocked out a second assault gun, and the third withdrew. Moments later three P-47 fighter-bombers appeared and made several strafing runs along the road leading through the woods from Schoenberg.

The fact that the German probes along the main highway from Schoenberg to St. Vith were tentative reflected General von Manteuffel's plan for taking St. Vith. Since woods along the main highway sharply canalized an advance, he intended the final assault to come from the village of Wallerode, just over a mile and a half northeast of St. Vith, where more open ground would make it possible to bring more strength to bear. Consisting of a company each of assault guns and engineers and *Volksgrenadiers* mounted in half-tracks, the 18th Volksgrenadier Division's Mobile Battalion was to make the assault. Reaching Schoenberg at noon, the battalion had to toil along a woods trail leading to Wallerode, so that not until after nightfall did the battalion arrive.

The regiment of *Volksgrenadiers* that had taken Schoenberg nevertheless continued to probe up the main highway toward St. Vith. As patrols sought to determine the location of the American line, the little band of some three hundred American engineers on the Prümerberg kept glancing backward hoping to see reinforcements in the form of the men and tanks of the 7th Armored Division.

*   *   *

Bruce Cooper Clarke, forty-three years old, was a big man, well over 6 feet tall, with a heavy frame, broad shoulders, and a barrel-like chest. Raised on a farm in New York State, he enlisted as a youth in the National Guard, then received an appointment to the Military Academy at West Point. After spending most of his early military career with the engineers, he transferred to armor as the U.S. Army was forming its first mechanized units. He entered combat in Normandy as commander of the 4th Armored Division's CCA, but on October 30, he faced an unwelcome transfer. When General Bradley relieved the commander of the 7th Armored Division, he elevated the commander of the division's CCB, General Hasbrouck, to command the division and needed a strong replacement for Hasbrouck. That was to be Clarke.

On December 16, Bruce Clarke was dining with General Hasbrouck, who suggested that he should take a three-day leave in Paris. Clarke had been looking for a break so that he might have an operation for gallstones, an illness he was controlling only with constant medication, and three days was insufficient for that; but he welcomed the break anyway. He had had no rest since coming ashore in Normandy.

Back at his billet, Clarke pulled out his Eisenhower jacket and replaced the colonel's eagles on the shoulders with the single stars of a brigadier general. That was the only pair of stars he possessed, for he had received his promotion just nine days before.

He was about ready to leave for Paris when the telephone rang. It was Hasbrouck. The 7th Armored Division, he said, had received orders to move immediately to Bastogne. Why, he did not know. In any event, Clarke's CCB was to lead the march, and Hasbrouck wanted Clarke himself to head immediately for Bastogne: "Find out what you can from General Middleton. Take a radio jeep so you can let me know what's happening."

So much for the Eisenhower jacket and Paris. Within the hour Clarke was on his way to Bastogne, where he arrived at 4 A.M. on the 17th. Middleton, who had trouble sleeping because of bursitis, was awake in his sleeping van. Giving Clarke a quick rundown on the German attack, he said he intended using the 7th Armored Division to help the 106th Division at St. Vith; but first, said Middleton, he wanted Clarke to catch a few hours' sleep.

That Clarke did, and when he awoke, he radioed General Hasbrouck that the 7th Armored Division was to go not to Bastogne but to St. Vith. He suggested that the division assemble at the town of Vielsalm on the Salm River eleven miles behind St. Vith. During the conversation, he learned that because of difficulty in obtaining road clearance, the division had begun to march only at 5 A.M. It would be late in the day before even Clarke's CCB in the lead would be available for commitment at St. Vith.

After a quick breakfast, Clarke left for St. Vith, where he arrived at

General Jones's command post at ten thirty. By that time the German trap had closed on the two regiments beyond the Our River, and so effective was German jamming of radio frequencies that Jones received only an occasional message from them. Jones wanted Clarke to counterattack immediately with his combat command "and break that ring that these people have closed around the Schnee Eifel."

It pained Clarke to have to tell Jones that only he, his operations officer, his aide, and his driver had reached St. Vith. He had no idea when his combat command would arrive.

As *Kampfgruppe Peiper* prepared to start its drive for the Meuse before daylight on December 17, the other two columns of the 1st SS Panzer Division also prepared to begin their advance through the Losheim Gap. Except for Major Diefenthal's battalion of *SS-Panzergrenadiers* with Peiper, the columns included the division's two *SS-Panzergrenadier* regiments supported by twenty-two self-propelled tank destroyers and twenty Mark IVs and Panthers.

The roadnet assigned those columns was skimpy at best. Only three roads for the two columns, and all converging either at Manderfeld or on the ridge behind the village. From there the roads were even poorer—mainly woods trails—through a belt of forest two to three miles wide. Only beyond the forest did the roadnet open up.

Whoever drew the inter-army boundary paid scant attention to the route assigned to the southern column of the 1st SS Panzer Division, for from Manderfeld that route led through Andler and Herresbach, both within the Fifth Panzer Army's zone of advance, thence to Vielsalm, behind St. Vith even deeper within the Fifth Panzer Army's zone, and on to the Meuse at Huy. As soon as the skimpy roadnet within the Sixth Panzer Army's zone jammed with traffic, commanders of units in the southern column predictably said to hell with the boundary and moved through Andler. That produced traffic congestion of monumental proportions, which soon brought officers from both panzer armies fuming and swearing onto the scene, including the commander of the 66th Corps, General Lucht. Yet for all the fuming and swearing, nobody went very far very fast.

That difficulty with traffic was why few units of the 14th Cavalry Group—other than Captain Lindsey's Troop B, 32d Cavalry, at Andler—experienced any enemy pressure through much of the day of December 17. Yet the 14th Cavalry Group continued to retire nevertheless.

While Colonel Devine was waiting on the night of the 16th to see General Jones in St. Vith, the corps commander, General Middleton, telephoned with a complaint from the 99th Division that the cavalry had lost contact with the division's right flank. Promising to rectify it, Devine telephoned the commander of the 18th Cavalry Reconnaissance Squadron, Colonel Damon, to move what was left of his command back

through the thick belt of forest stretching the width of the Losheim Gap
to the village of Wareth, and from there establish contact with the 99th
Division.

The departure of Damon and his command was what had left Lieutenant Reppa and his troop of the 32d Cavalry alone in the northern reaches
of the gap and prompted Reppa to abandon his position and go to
Honsfeld. Which put him the next morning right in the path of
Kampfgruppe Peiper.

Those departures left only two components of the 14th Cavalry Group
still forward in the Losheim Gap: Lindsey's troop at Andler and headquarters and Troop B, 32d Cavalry, two miles to the northwest at Herresbach, just in front of the wide belt of forest. There the commander of
the squadron, Colonel Ridge, visibly shaken by all that was happening,
had found an excuse to go back to Vielsalm, virtually abdicating his command in favor of his executive officer, Maj. John L. Kracke. Early in the
evening, a passing artillery officer told Kracke that the unimproved trails
leading west through the forest were impassable, and Kracke began to
worry that he and the command might be trapped.

Around midnight, Kracke sent an officer to reconnoiter the only
improved road through the forest, that leading northwest to Wareth.
Somebody had blocked the route, the officer reported, by felling trees
across it.

That left only the woods trails. Reconnoitering one of those, the
squadron's motor officer, Capt. Samuel E. Woods, concluded that it was
in good enough shape to warrant a try. At eight thirty on the morning of
the 17th, with Colonel Devine's approval, withdrawal began. By that
time a disparate array of vehicles had accumulated—at least two hundred—not only those belonging to the cavalry but others from tank destroyer, antiaircraft, and medical units.

It was fortunate for the men in that column that the Germans exerted
no pressure, for even without it, the trek through the forest was a nightmare. Vehicles bogged down; others with chains on their wheels pulled
them out. Then the same thing happened over and over again. At a sharp
curve on the side of a steep hill, a shoulder of the road gave way, and
Captain Woods had to form a work party to fell trees and keep it passable. Not until early afternoon was the last vehicle past that chokepoint.

At last returned from the fruitless wait in St. Vith, Colonel Devine
had approved Kracke's withdrawal because it fitted with a new plan he
had devised. All units of the 14th Cavalry Group—including Captain
Lindsey's, by that time fighting a delaying action on the Schoenberg–St.
Vith road—were to form a new line north of St. Vith extending from
Wallerode northeast to the village of Born. To General Jones, Devine
reported that he was withdrawing to "a final delaying position" and sent a
map overlay depicting it. Jones approved, at least tacitly, for he had dire

need of some kind of block north of St. Vith if the 7th Armored Division was to be able to get into the town.

In setting up the new line, Devine came into conflict with the commander of his artillery support, Lt. Col. Roy U. Clay. Clay was already piqued because Devine, unsure of the location of isolated American troops, refused to allow Clay's self-propelled 105mm. howitzers to fire on Schoenberg and villages in the Losheim Gap. When Devine told Clay to place his pieces in the new line in positions from which to employ direct fire, Clay refused.

Detailed to support the 14th Cavalry Group but not under Devine's command, Clay hurried to the command post of the 106th Division's Artillery, to which his battalion was attached. He was "mad as hell," he told the artillery commander, General McMahon, because there were "Germans all over the place" and Devine refused to allow him to shoot. Before McMahon could respond, a captain spoke up: As liaison officer from headquarters of the VIII Corps Artillery, he was attaching Clay's battalion to the 7th Armored Division. Clay could fire "anytime and any place" he wished.

When Clay returned to his howitzers, he found Colonel Devine abandoning the final delaying position so recently established from Wallerode to Born. He had learned that to the north, Germans were already farther west than Born and thus might cut in on the rear of the new line. He ordered everybody back to the vicinity of Recht, a crossroads village several miles behind Born. Having had no contact with the enemy except for Captain Lindsey's harsh encounter just before daybreak at Andler, the 14th Cavalry Group had nevertheless retired during the day a distance of more than ten miles.

The operations officer of the 38th Armored Infantry Battalion, Maj. Donald P. Boyer, moved with his jeep and driver about an hour in advance of his battalion, which was a part of the 7th Armored Division's CCR. Driving along the division's eastern march route through Malmédy and the road junction at Baugnez, Boyer was on his way to Vielsalm to pick out an assembly area for his battalion. Shortly after midday on December 17, he reached the hamlet of Poteau marking a road junction where the Ligneuville-Vielsalm road joined the principal highway connecting Vielsalm and St. Vith. Boyer found it hard to believe what he saw: "a constant stream of traffic hurtling to the rear (to the west) and nothing going to the front (to the east). We realized that this was not a convoy moving to the rear; it was a case of 'every dog for himself'; it was a retreat, a rout."

What Boyer saw was undeniably ugly. Here a 6×6 with only a driver, there another "with several men in it (most of them bareheaded and in various stages of undress), next perhaps an engineer crane truck, then several artillery prime movers," some of them towing howitzers, "command cars with officers in them," jeeps, "anything which would run and which would get the driver and a few others away from the front." He was "seeing American soldiers running away."

What Boyer failed to appreciate was that most of the people in those vehicles were moving away from the front under legitimate orders. Some of the vehicles were from the squadrons of the 14th Cavalry Group that mistakenly got onto the road to Poteau rather than to Recht. Others were from the 771st Field Artillery Battalion that had withdrawn from the vicinity of Schoenberg to Wallerode but had to displace again; still others were from the 740th Field Artillery Battalion, which was trying to move its 8-inch howitzers from positions near Schoenberg; and both battalions were following orders from the artillery officer of the VIII Corps, Brig. Gen. John E. McMahon, Jr., who had directed all of the corps artillery battalions in the vicinity of St. Vith, with the exception of Clay's 275th Armored Field Artillery Battalion, to fall back.

Do you leave precious general support howitzers and guns without infantry protection in positions so close to the front that they are likely to be overrun? Do you leave heavy engineer equipment in the same predicament? Do you leave ordnance, quartermaster, signal, and medical installations to be annihilated or captured?

The bulk of the traffic moving westward on the St. Vith–Vielsalm road late on December 17 constituted a legitimate exodus. That it had gotten out of control was another matter. At the order of the corps artillery officer, five of the retiring corps artillery battalions had avoided the St. Vith–Vielsalm road, taking other roads to the south, but the other two—the 740th and the 771st—had no choice. Anticipating problems, the 106th Division's Military Police Platoon had early moved into position to control the traffic, but the sheer volume overwhelmed the few MPs who were available.

When congestion inevitably developed, individual drivers, sometimes at the behest of their officers, broke out of the column and tried to push ahead in the eastbound lane. Since the road was twisting and narrow, little more than a hard surface poured onto an existing dirt road without first eliminating the bumps, rises, and sharp bends, the eastbound lane was soon as jammed as the westbound lane. And when the first vehicles of the 7th Armored Division arrived and tried to get through the road junction at Poteau, a traffic jam of epic proportions quickly developed. It took the commander of the 7th Armored Division, General Hasbrouck, five hours to negotiate the eleven miles from Vielsalm to St. Vith.

The American commanders might have taken some consolation from the fact that the same thing—only worse—was happening on their enemy's side of the front, and two of the senior German commanders got caught up in it. The commander of the Fifth Panzer Army, General von Manteuffel, was trying to get to Schoenberg, where he intended to pass the night at headquarters of the 18th Volksgrenadier Division in an effort to put some spark into that division's attack on St. Vith; but the roads were so blocked that he eventually got out of his command car and began to walk. The same thing happened to the commander of Army Group B, Field Marshal Model, and each used his rank, with little success, to try to get the traffic moving.

The two came upon one another in the night.

"And how is your situation, Baron?" asked Model.

"Mostly good."

"So? I got the impression you were lagging, especially in the St. Vith sector."

"Yes," said von Manteuffel, "but we'll take it tomorrow."

"I expect you to," responded Model. "And so that you'll take it quicker, tomorrow I'm letting you use the *Führer Begleit Brigade.*"

Inside the 106th Division's command post in St. Vith that afternoon, staff activity could be considered hectic, but General Jones himself was calm. At one point, on the telephone to General Middleton, he told the corps commander not to worry. "We'll be in good shape. Clarke's troops will be here soon."

Around 1:30 P.M., the door to Jones's office burst open and the cavalry commander, Colonel Devine, almost fell in. "General," he gasped, "we've got to run. I was practically chased into this building by a Tiger tank, and we all have to get out of here."

To General Clarke, Devine looked like a man who had been through too much. "I suggest we send Colonel Devine back to Bastogne," said Clarke. "Maybe he could give General Middleton a first-hand account of the conditions up here." Devine saluted and left.

An hour later, the sound of small-arms fire emerged from the east. Going to the third floor of the St. Joseph's Kloster, Jones and Clarke could see a small group of Germans at the edge of the woods on the bluff overlooking the town. "General Clarke," said Jones, "I've thrown in my last chips. I haven't got much, but your combat command is the one that will defend this position. You take over command of St. Vith right now."

Clarke accepted, the first step in what was to become a confused command arrangement destined to persist through much of the remainder of the fight in and around St. Vith. Clarke was junior to three other brigadier generals on the scene: Jones's assistant division commander and his artillery commander and the commander of the 9th Armored Division's CCB, General Hoge. Furthermore, Clarke's division commander, General Hasbrouck, had one less star than did General Jones, and he, too, was junior to Hoge. It remained to be seen how that confusion of stars would work out.

In mid-afternoon, hoping that CCB would soon be arriving, Clarke sent his operations officer, Maj. Owen E. Woodruff, to the first crossroads outside St. Vith at the village of Rodt to guide the vehicles in and make sure the road was clear of westbound traffic. With little to occupy him at Jones's headquarters, Clarke soon joined Woodruff. He found the major looking dejected and part of a field artillery battalion without howitzers monopolizing the road. The artillery commander, said Woodruff, insisted on using the road and was threatening to shoot him if he interfered.

Clarke soon had the lieutenant colonel in front of him at attention. "You get your trucks off this road so my tanks can get up here," the imposing Clarke thundered. "If there's any shooting done around here, I'll start it."

Shortly before four o'clock the first vehicles of the 7th Armored Division's CCB arrived, those of Troop B, 87th Cavalry Reconnaissance Squadron. "Keep going down this road," said Clarke to the troop commander. "You'll run into a great big lieutenant-colonel named Riggs. Tell him that you're attached to him, and he'll tell you what to do."

Troop B was soon going into position with its armored cars, light tanks, and assault guns on the left of the thin engineer line on the Prümerberg, covering some of the open ground between the Prümerberg and Wallerode to the north. The Germans may well have heard the cheer that arose from the engineers when the reinforcements appeared.

General Hasbrouck reached St. Vith close behind Troop B. As he conferred with Jones and Clarke in the St. Joseph's Kloster, night was falling, and the main body of CCB was still toiling forward along the congested road from Vielsalm. Quite obviously, there could be no attack that night to relieve the men—including Alan Jones's son—who were trapped beyond the Our River on and in the shadow of the Schnee Eifel. Hope remained nevertheless for an attack by CCB early the next morning.

As other units of CCB filtered into St. Vith, so imperative was the need to reinforce the thin line on the Prümerberg that Clarke felt impelled to commit them piecemeal as they arrived without regard to their parent battalions. The first to follow the cavalry troop into the line were a company of the 23d Armored Infantry Battalion and a company of mediums of the 31st Tank Battalion.

The 38th Armored Infantry Battalion arrived soon after. Normally a component of CCR, that battalion had reached Recht, where CCR began to establish a headquarters, when Hasbrouck ordered it forward for attachment to CCB. General Clarke put the commander, Lt. Col. William H. G. Fuller, in charge of the critical defenses in front of St. Vith, which Fuller reinforced with two of his line companies (the third had been diverted by mistake to Vielsalm). The line on the Prümerberg received additional reinforcement with the arrival of another company of the 168th Engineer Combat Battalion.

By midnight of December 17, a fairly cohesive defense had been established in front of St. Vith with three companies of armored infantry, a company of medium tanks, and a troop of cavalry; and Fuller pulled the engineers who had first established the position into reserve for a time so that they might reorganize. The line extended from the vicinity of Wallerode in the north across the Prümerberg, there blocking both the main highway from Schoenberg and a secondary road leading less directly from Schoenberg. A few hundred yards south of that road, the line ended. Although the Germans probed the developing line several times during the night with strong patrols, they made no attack. They were planning to take St. Vith the next morning with a strike by the 18th Volksgrenadier Division's Mobile Battalion from Wallerode.

Hasbrouck also sent the rest of the 87th Cavalry Reconnaissance Squadron, which was normally a part of other combat commands, to St. Vith, and Clarke put the two remaining troops of the squadron to the north and northeast of the town to block two principal roads that had been exposed by withdrawal of the 14th Cavalry Group. That enabled Clarke to hold the remainder of CCB as a reserve behind St. Vith: three-fourths of the 23d Armored Infantry Battalion, all but a company of the 31st Tank Battalion, and a company of the 33d Engineers.

South of St. Vith, General Hoge's CCB, 9th Armored Division, and Colonel Reid's 424th Infantry, 106th Division, conformed to General Jones's retirement order and during the night of the 17th pulled back across the Our River. The combat command kept most of its strength in reserve along the road from Steinebrück to St. Vith, with outposts along the river and light tanks patrolling woods trails to the east. Hardpressed during the day only on the flanks at Winterspelt and near Grosskampenberg, the 424th Infantry got its supporting 591st Field Artillery Battalion out first, then leapfrogged its infantry battalions to the west bank of the Our. The regiment had to leave behind considerable equipment and supplies.

Arriving in late afternoon, the 7th Armored Division's Combat Command A moved into an assembly area southeast of Vielsalm, there to be in a position to block any enemy move from the south while at the same time serving as a division reserve. In view of the uncertainty of the situation everywhere around St. Vith, General Hasbrouck kept CCA on thirty-minute alert.

Headquarters of the 7th Armored Division third combat command, CCR, divested of its armored infantry but still in charge of the Shermans of the 17th Tank Battalion, was at Recht on the Ligneuville-Vielsalm road with the tanks in an assembly area nearby. Although Recht was to have been the center of the 14th Cavalry Group's latest defensive position, only three reconnaissance teams, made up mainly of armored cars, arrived there; the rest of the cavalry became entangled with the morass of vehicles on the St. Vith–Vielsalm road in and near Poteau. Colonel Devine had established his headquarters in Poteau, but when the cavalry's vehicles finally broke through the traffic jam, they continued to the next village of Petit Thier.

Artillery available at first in what was fast shaping up as a horseshoe defense of St. Vith was limited. The 424th Infantry still had its direct support battalion, but the other pieces that had made it back from beyond the Our (the three 105mm. howitzers of the 589th Field Artillery Battalion and the ten 155mm. howitzers of the 592d) had displaced from the vicinity of Wallerode and had yet to occupy new firing positions. The 9th Armored Division's CCB also had its usual support, the 16th Armored Field Artillery Battalion; but because of the necessity of a detour to avoid the road junction at Baugnez, only one of the 7th Armored Division's three battalions arrived during the night. Not until midday on the 18th were the other two to be ready to fire, and none of the three was close enough to St. Vith to provide support for the critical defensive line on the Prümerberg.

There were also a few batteries of corps guns still on hand south of Vielsalm, and close behind St. Vith was the 275th Armored Field Artillery Battalion, so recently attached to the 7th Armored Division. The commander, Colonel Clay, found General Clarke on the road near St. Vith and told him he was sick of retreating. "I want to shoot," said Clay.

When General Jones learned in mid-afternoon of the 14th Cavalry Group's withdrawal from the Wallerode-Born line, he ordered Colonel Devine to his headquarters in St. Vith. Dusk was approaching, around four o'clock, when Devine set out from his new command post in Poteau with three jeeps escorted by an armored car. Among the party were Devine's executive officer, Lt. Col. Augustine D. Dugan, and his operations officer, Maj. Lawrence J. Smith.

Because the main road to St. Vith was still hopelessly jammed, Devine and his party moved by way of Recht to a wooded crossroads known as the Kaiserbaracke, there to gain access to N-23, the Ligneuville–St. Vith highway. In St. Vith, Devine saw either General Jones or his operations officer, for he received orders to return his squadrons to the Wallerode-Born line.

On the way back to Poteau via the Kaiserbaracke, Devine and his party became aware as they neared the crossroads of what looked in the darkness to be German tanks a few hundred yards off the road. Just as the armored car in the lead reached the crossroads, a German sentry close beside it yelled, "*Halt!*" An officer riding erect in the commander's position in the armored car put the muzzle of his .45-caliber pistol full in the man's face and fired. As the gunner on the .50-caliber machine gun opened up, tracer bullets illuminated some fifteen lightly armored German vehicles just off the road.

The armored car backed up, forcing the jeep in which Devine and his operations officer, Major Smith, were riding into a ditch. Devine's driver quickly sensed trouble and climbed aboard the armored car. The other two jeeps also escaped, but Devine and Smith were left behind, eventually to crawl away until they gained a railroad right of way that Smith knew led to Poteau.

They reached Devine's command post in Poteau shortly before midnight. There Devine immediately summoned the commander of the 18th Cavalry Reconnaissance Squadron, Colonel Damon, told him to "take over," and "left the room and went to bed." Before daylight, his staff arranged his evacuation through medical channels.

Hardly had Colonel Damon assumed command when word came from General Jones reiterating the order for the cavalry to return to its former positions. Somebody managed to intercept the last troop of the 32d Cavalry Reconnaissance Squadron as it was passing through Poteau and get it turned around and facing back in the direction of Born. Yet in the darkness and amid all the confusion of heavy traffic through Poteau, all that accomplished was to bring the traffic through the road junction to a dead halt.

A short time later, a message arrived from headquarters of the 106th Division repeating an order from headquarters of the VIII Corps for "the commander of the 14th Cavalry Group" to report to Bastogne. That was the outcome of Jones's and Clarke's unhappy encounter with Colonel Devine that afternoon and was meant to bring Devine (not the current commander, Colonel Damon) to Bastogne. Yet Damon had no way of knowing that. Handing over the group to the commander of the 32d Cavalry Reconnaissance Squadron, Colonel Ridge, Damon left for Bastogne.

Within half an hour, Devine's executive officer, Colonel Dugan, returned following his escape by jeep from the encounter at the Kaiserbaracke. Senior to Ridge, he assumed command of the group, and Ridge promptly repaired to his accustomed post in Vielsalm. Like Devine, Ridge was evacuated through medical channels as a nonbattle casualty.

During the afternoon of December 17 at Recht, the acting commander of the 7th Armored Division's CCR, Lt. Col. Fred M. Warren (the regular commander was on leave in Paris), learned from a passing jeep driver that the Germans had captured Ligneuville, only three miles to the north. Warren and his operations officer, Maj. Fred Sweat, drove up the road and just south of Ligneuville came upon some of the men of the trains (supply trucks and troops) of the 9th Armored Division's CCB who had escaped from the town.

Assured that the Germans were, indeed, in Ligneuville, Warren and Sweat hurried to St. Vith and the 106th Division's command post to give the alarm. There they came upon their division commander, General Hasbrouck, who told them to return to Recht and hold the village as long as possible.

Having given up CCR's armored infantry battalion to the defense east of St. Vith, Warren was reluctant to use his tanks to defend the village without infantry protection. Although he appealed to the division headquarters for at least a company of armored infantry, word came back that none was available. The headquarters was as yet unaware that a company of CCR's own armored infantry battalion had been mistakenly diverted to Vielsalm.

In early evening, the driver for the 7th Armored Division's chief of staff, Col. Church M. Matthews, arrived on foot in Recht with the news that during the afternoon he and Matthews had happened upon a German armored column outside Ligneuville. The Germans had shot up the jeep and killed Matthews.

The Germans that Matthews and his driver had encountered were part of the tail of *Kampfgruppe Peiper*, which had no intention of turning south toward Recht, but Warren could not know that. Should the Germans take Recht, they might move on to Poteau and soon be in Vielsalm, only seven miles away, in the process cutting off all the American troops who were trying to build a defense of St. Vith. Overcoming his qualms about committing tanks without infantry protection, Warren called in a company of the 17th Tank Battalion.

Whatever the intent of *Kampfgruppe Peiper*, Colonel Warren was well advised to prepare to defend Recht, for the southernmost column of the 1st SS Panzer Division had at last gotten some troops and vehicles through the traffic jams to the rear and onto the assigned route through Recht and Vielsalm. Those were men of the 1st SS Panzergrenadier Regiment under Col. Max Hansen.

The defenders of St. Vith were about to face the first of what would turn out to be multiple crises. Unlikely heroes of that first crisis were to be the men of the 14th Cavalry Group.

CHAPTER SIXTEEN

Shaping the Defense of St. Vith

At Recht (*see map, Chapter Fifteen, p. 312*) the attack that CCR's head-quarters troops, the three reconnaissance teams of the 14th Cavalry Group, and the company of mediums of the 17th Tank Battalion were expecting came at 2 A.M. on December 18. Dismounted *SS-Pan-zergrenadiers*, strong on automatic weapons and *Panzerfausts*, penetrated the village and by the light of flares searched for the American tanks. After forty-five minutes of heavy fighting, CCR's acting commander, Colonel Warren, came to the conclusion that he was in danger of losing an entire company of medium tanks and ordered withdrawal.

The headquarters troops and the few armored cars belonging to the 14th Cavalry Group fell back on Poteau, while the tanks moved southeast toward the battalion's assembly area near the hamlet of Feckelsborn. From there, the tankers commanded an abandoned railroad underpass between the hamlet and Recht, and when daylight came, they drove back every German attempt to get through the underpass.

At Poteau, Colonel Warren and his staff found the highway through the hamlet blocked. They spent most of the remaining hours of darkness trying to get traffic rolling but eventually despaired and moved on foot down the Vielsalm road to Petit Thier. Had the Germans who captured Recht marched immediately on Poteau, they could have wreaked havoc on the stalled column.

The new commander of the 14th Cavalry Group, Colonel Dugan, found meanwhile that there was still fight left in the remnants of his group; it was a matter of exerting leadership to bring it out. The stub of an unlit cigar clenched between his teeth, Dugan was here, there, and everywhere, trying to get the clogged traffic under way and at the same time reorganize his command sufficiently to comply with General Jones's order to reoccupy the Wallerode-Born line. Damon the night before and Dugan in the early morning told headquarters of the 106th Division that any task force from the 14th Cavalry Group trying to reoccupy the Wallerode-Born line was doomed. Since it was obvious by that time that the Germans were already in Wallerode, Jones modified the order to require reoccupying only Born; but he was adamant on that.

Since the bulk of the 32d Cavalry Reconnaissance Squadron had already retreated all the way to Vielsalm, Dugan ordered the squadron to return, but the traffic jam precluded it. With the help of Major Mayes of the 18th Cavalry Reconnaissance Squadron, Dugan created a small task force from the remnants of that squadron reinforced by the 32d Cavalry's assault guns. Because the traffic jam blocked one of only two roads to Born, Task Force Mayes headed out the road to Recht. Although Dugan expected the task force to encounter Germans before reaching Born, he was unaware that *SS-Panzergrenadiers* had captured Recht. No matter what, he had to comply with his order from Jones.

In darkness and fog at 7 A.M. on the 18th, Task Force Mayes had gone only 250 yards beyond the last houses of Poteau when a rocket from a *Panzerfaust* struck the second vehicle, a 75mm. assault gun, setting it on fire, and German small-arms fire erupted. The task force had run head-on into an attack by troops of the 1st SS Panzergrenadier Regiment on Poteau. Fighting a delaying action, Task Forces Mayes's armored cars, half-tracks, and assault guns fell back on the road junction.

For the rest of the morning, those cavalrymen held the road junction at Poteau against a determined infantry attack supported by self-propelled tank destroyers. Typifying the élan the men brought to the fight, Staff Sgt. Woodrow Reeves clung to the outside of his light tank, the better to direct the fire of his gunner, and when an officer ordered him to get inside, Reeves replied: "Can't, Lieutenant; too busy shooting Germans." When a group of Germans set up a machine gun on a wooded hillock overlooking the road junction, a patrol of cavalrymen swarmed from Poteau to knock it out. Somebody got on the radio frequency of a battalion of the 7th Armored Division's artillery and brought in fire support. Through it all, Colonel Dugan, cigar still held between his teeth, circulated among the soldiers, grinning, encouraging, exhorting.

The fighting built a fire under the drivers of the vehicles clogged along the highway through the hamlet. Somehow the column at last began to move, but in some cases there was panic. The crews of eight 8-inch howitzers of the 740th Field Artillery Battalion abandoned their pieces (although the 7th Armored Division eventually recovered them). Some vehicles still on the St. Vith side of the road junction turned back to try to find another way out.

The cavalrymen, for all their valor, were nevertheless engaging in a markedly uneven fight. The Germans were closing in when Colonel Dugan soon after midday ordered withdrawal down the road toward Vielsalm. Reaching Petit Thier, Capt. William G. North, Jr., and Staff Sgt. Walter Gregory climbed into the steeple of the church, smashed a hole in the roof to afford observation, and adjusted artillery fire on Poteau. Probably as a result of that fire, the cavalrymen were able to continue their withdrawal under no pressure from the enemy.

From that point, all that was left of the 14th Cavalry Group was attached as a task force to the 7th Armored Division. Finally afforded an opportunity to fight rather than withdraw, and provided with firm leadership, the cavalrymen had performed at Poteau as they had on the first day of the German offensive. Unfortunately, the performance came too late to save the commander who rallied them, Colonel Dugan. In a general house-cleaning of senior commanders in the group, General Middleton summarily relieved Colonel Dugan of his command.

Because 1st Lt. Joseph V. Whiteman had worked his way through college selling Indian blankets, his colleagues called him "Navajo." A member of the 23d Armored Infantry Battalion, Whiteman acted as the battalion's motor officer during the trip south but fell behind the convoy when his truck developed engine trouble.

Arriving in Vielsalm late in the afternoon of December 17, Whiteman joined the crews of several half-tracks that for one reason or another had also fallen behind and headed for St. Vith to rejoin his unit. Because of the traffic jam, the half-tracks were able to get no farther that night than Petit Thier. Just as Whiteman and the others were preparing before daylight the next morning to continue, they heard "all hell break loose up the valley toward Poteau."

When the surviving vehicles of the 14th Cavalry Group fell back through Petit Thier, Lieutenant Whiteman made up his mind to defend the village, else the Germans might overrun the 7th Armored Division's artillery and move into Vielsalm. With the half-tracks, Whiteman established a roadblock in front of the first buildings in Petit Thier and began to corral reinforcements. He soon had two assault guns, two tanks, and two tankdozers that had become separated from the 31st Tank Battalion, as well as eighty-four men of the 106th Division's 424th Infantry, whose lieutenant said he was "out of ammunition, out of chow, and out of orders." Whiteman said he could provide all three. Before the day was done, Task Force Navajo had forward observers from all three of the division's artillery battalions, a platoon of self-propelled tank destroyers, and a company of engineers, to whose commander, senior to Whiteman, command of the task force passed.

Early on December 18, the commander of the 9th Armored Division's CCB, General Hoge, sent his liaison officer, Lieutenant Lewis, to St. Vith to learn the dispositions of the 7th Armored Division's CCB. As Lewis approached the St. Joseph's Kloster, one of General Clarke's staff officers stopped him in considerable agitation. German tanks were approaching St. Vith along the road from the north, he said, and all that stood in the way was a reconnaissance troop. Could General Hoge send somebody to help?

Climbing into Lewis's jeep, the two "drove like mad" to Hoge's command post in a beerhall along the road to Steinebrück. Hoge decided to go to St. Vith himself, but before departing he told Lewis to direct the commander of the 14th Tank Battalion, Lt. Col. Leonard E. Engeman, to get a strong task force ready to move out. Minutes later Hoge telephoned from St. Vith, telling Engeman to get under way.

Composed of two medium tank companies, a company of self-propelled guns of the 811th Tank Destroyer Battalion, a reconnaissance platoon, and a few antiaircraft half-tracks, Engeman's task force reached St. Vith shortly before noon to find not one but two German attacks moving against the town. The 18th Volksgrenadier Division's Mobile Battalion had debouched from Wallerode onto the highway leading from Amblève into St. Vith, while contingents of the 1st SS Panzergrenadier Regiment had reached a hamlet on N-23 not quite a mile outside St. Vith. Holding one of the tank companies in reserve on the fringe of St. Vith, Colonel Engeman sent the other up the Amblève road and the tank destroyers up N-23.

As the men in the tank destroyers soon learned, General Clarke had already sent a company of his own tanks and a company of armored infantry marching on the hamlet on N-23, while another company of tanks provided fire support. In less than an hour the *SS-Panzergrenadiers* were fleeing the hamlet, and the results were much the same along the road from Amblève. The 9th Armored Division's tanks knocked out four assault guns and drove the Mobile Battalion back on Wallerode. As General Clarke placed one of his tank companies in a position from which to cover the north flank, the 9th Armored Division's men and vehicles returned to their own command.

Early on December 18, the commander of the 7th Armored Division's Combat Command A, Col. Dwight A. Rosebaum, went to St. Vith in search of his division commander, General Hasbrouck, only to learn that Hasbrouck was in Vielsalm. En route there, Rosebaum laboriously threaded his way through the coagulated traffic at Poteau only minutes before the Germans attacked the road junction. At the division headquarters in the Middle School on the Rue de l'Hôtel de Ville in Vielsalm, he told Hasbrouck that in his view, there appeared to be no immediate threat to the division's south flank, certainly nothing comparable to the threat developing on the north. He recommended that Hasbrouck shift his combat command to Poteau.

With Hasbrouck's agreement, Rosebaum left his company of light tanks, a company of engineers, and some antiaircraft half-tracks to screen the division's south flank while he headed with the rest of his command for Poteau by way of St. Vith. Because the remnants of the 14th Cavalry Group had to abandon the road junction before anybody from CCA got there, the 48th Armored Infantry Battalion had to fight to gain a foothold

among the houses. That was achieved by nightfall, and the armored infantrymen with tank support cleared the last *SS-Panzergrenadiers* from
Poteau the next day.

The alleviation of the threat to Vielsalm was not attributable solely to
the arrival of CCA at Poteau. It came about also because *Kampfgruppe
Peiper* had run into trouble at Stoumont and La Gleize, and American
countermeasures were threatening Peiper's line of supply. The commander of the 1st SS Panzer Division, Colonel Mohnke, had lost interest
in propelling his own southernmost column toward the Meuse by way of
Vielsalm. He instead turned everything available to him due west in an
attempt to reach Peiper and with him continue the drive to the Meuse.

South of St. Vith, yet another threat loomed on December 18, though
of less serious proportions. There, even as General Hoge was responding
to the cry for help against German thrusts from the north, men of the 62d
Volksgrenadier Division were trying to get across the Our River at
Steinebrück and have at St. Vith from that direction.

At Steinebrück, the bridge over the fast-flowing little Our was still
intact, intentionally left so after the withdrawal the night before in the
outside hope that some of the troops trapped in the vicinity of the Schnee
Eifel might fight their way to Steinebrück. By noon on the 18th, it was
obvious that Germans infiltrating across the river were converging on the
bridge in such numbers that General Hoge had to give the word to blow
the bridge or risk the Germans seizing it. While a platoon of light tanks
laid down suppressive fire, a platoon of armored engineers succeeded in
blowing half the span.

Since the Our had ceased to be a barrier anywhere else, there was
little point in the 9th Armored Division's CCB continuing to overextend
itself to hold the low ground along the river. Better to fall back to the
first range of hills and establish contact with the 7th Armored Division's
CCB on the left and the 106th Division's 424th Infantry on the right.

Having first conferred with General Jones in St. Vith, General Hoge
withdrew after nightfall on the 18th. He chose an area of high ground
generally behind and commanding the Steinebrück–St. Vith highway,
and at a point close to St. Vith barred the road. The new position also
blocked access to the little valley of the Braunlauf Creek, which formed
an avenue of approach into the rear of the defenders of St. Vith.

Although troops of the 62d Volksgrenadier Division were quick to
build up beyond the Our, they made no immediate move against the new
American line, for the regimental commander at Steinebrück, Col.
Arthur Jüttner, wanted first to rebuild the bridge in order to get his assault guns across the river. For that, Jüttner had a company of impressed
Russians who traveled with the regiment to perform such onerous tasks
as peeling potatoes, digging entrenchments, and building bridges over icy
streams.

Also on the south flank but well to the west, where the 7th Armored Division's CCA departed its assembly area to move to Poteau, the light forces left behind began patrolling in search of enemy buildup. On the way to check the village of Gouvy, half-tracks of the 440th Antiaircraft Artillery Battalion, along with a platoon of light tanks, came upon three Mark IVs serving as a flank patrol of the 116th Panzer Division, which was advancing on nearby roads toward Houffalize. The half-tracks and light tanks might have been in serious trouble had not the first round from one of the Mark IVs knocked out an air-compressor truck; its carcass blocked the road and kept the German tanks from getting at the American column. After firing a few rounds at long range, the Mark IVs withdrew.

Scouting about, the antiaircraft troops at a railroad depot a short distance from Gouvy found an American railhead containing, among other stores, great quantities of C- and K-rations. Thinking the Germans were closing in, the guards had set the depot on fire, but it was soon extinguished. The food was to prove a godsend for the men defending St. Vith.

At the railhead were also 350 German prisoners of war awaiting transportation to the rear. Since a highway westward from Vielsalm was still open, that was soon accomplished.

Among the myriad monumental problems facing the commanders and troops of the 422d and 423d Infantry Regiments and their attached units east of the Our River was that of communications with their division headquarters in St. Vith. Mainly because of German jamming, communications were at best erratic. From time to time messages got through to the 423d Infantry, and occasionally through the artillery net to the 590th Field Artillery Battalion, but almost every message had to be repeated over and over until finally received, usually several hours after the original transmission.

That was the case with the message that General Jones sent in mid-morning of December 17 telling the two regiments to withdraw if their positions became untenable but explaining that the division intended to clear out the area to the west of them that afternoon. Colonel Cavender of the 423d Infantry received the message around 3 P.M. and finally got a copy of it to Colonel Descheneaux of the 422d Infantry just after midnight. By that time, the message was obviously out of date, for there was no indication that anybody had cleared out anything to the west.

Both commanders were nevertheless content to hold where they were. They had strong, well-prepared positions on the Schnee Eifel, and through the day of the 17th, their men had been adjusting them for all-around defense. If promised resupplies by air arrived, they were confident they could hold out long enough for a relief column to break through.

It was thus with something less than enthusiasm that the two commanders received a message sent by General Jones at 2:15 A.M. on December 18 directing the regiments to fight their way out and in the process destroy the enemy along the Schoenberg–St. Vith road. (Colonel Descheneaux bowed his head and almost sobbed: "My poor men—they'll be cut to pieces.")

The message was ambiguous: The two regiments were "to destroy [the enemy] by fire from dug-in positions S[outh] of Schoenberg–St. Vith R[oa]d." Cavender and Descheneaux took that to mean that they were to drive southwest across the Bleialf-Schoenberg road, draw up to the Our River downstream from Schoenberg in the vicinity of Setz, and there dig in to provide fire on that portion of the Schoenberg–St. Vith road running alongside the river, thereby to support a relieving attack by the 7th Armored Division. Then the two regiments might cross the Our to safety. Avoiding Schoenberg made sense, for the Germans would surely be strongest there, the obvious spot for the Americans to attempt a breakout; and although neither commander was aware of it, almost everybody who had escaped since the Germans closed the trap at Schoenberg had done so by crossing the Our downstream from Schoenberg.

Although General Jones designated no overall commander for the breakout attempt and Colonel Cavender made no attempt to assert his seniority to assume command, the two officers made every effort to coordinate their plans. That in itself was difficult, for they had no communication with each other except by patrols. They nevertheless made plans to attack the next morning with Cavender's 423d Infantry, which was closest to the Bleialf-Schoenberg road, in the lead in a column of battalions. At that point there was still hope of bringing out the regimental vehicles in the wake of the infantry, and even though the 590th Field Artillery Battalion was running short of ammunition, it would be possible to provide some artillery support for the 423d Infantry's attack.

At 10 A.M. on the 18th, Colonel Puett's 2d Battalion—the former division reserve—set off in the lead, heading west toward the hamlet of Radscheid along the Auw-Bleialf highway (Skyline Boulevard) to gain the entrance to the Engineer Cut-Off leading to the Bleialf-Schoenberg road. Puett's men made good progress, and the lead scouts were soon at the juncture of the Engineer Cut-Off with the Bleialf-Schoenberg road. But Puett was worried. Germans were pressing down Skyline Boulevard from the direction of 88 Corner into his left flank and rear. By radio, he asked Colonel Cavender to commit another battalion to block that threat.

Puett's message reached Cavender only minutes after Cavender received another from General Jones: There was to be no counterattack by the 7th Armored Division from St. Vith to Schoenberg, said the message. Cavender and Descheneaux were to shift the direction of their attack to take Schoenberg, then drive on to St. Vith on their own.

The message came as a jolt. The two regiments had left the cover of their prepared positions to meet and assist a relieving force, and now that they were in the open and exposed, they learned that there was to be no relieving force. Furthermore, they were to attack Schoenberg, a bridge and a road junction that the Germans obviously saw as critical. Yet because of the difficulty with communications, there was no way to debate the issue with General Jones, no recourse but to obey the order.

By that time, German fire had so increased that most of the men of Puett's battalion were pinned to the ground, unable to move in any direction. Sending a messenger to inform Colonel Descheneaux of the new order, Cavender ordered his 3d Battalion under Lt. Col. Earl F. Klinck to bypass Puett's battalion and proceed along a farm track that became a woods trail leading from Radscheid in the direction of Schoenberg. Klinck was to cut the Bleialf-Schoenberg road at the foot of a wooded height overlooking Schoenberg—Hill 504—and continue less than a mile into the village.

Klinck and his men crossed Skyline Boulevard near Radscheid without difficulty and had moved unimpeded into the wood a third of the way toward their objective when at the Ihren Creek they ran into small-arms fire. They nevertheless continued to advance until Company L on the left was within a few hundred yards of the Bleialf-Schoenberg highway. With that company halted, Klinck committed Company K to help, and the two companies plodded forward until Company L's left platoon cut the highway near the base of Hill 504. There Klinck consolidated his battalion for the night.

In response to continued pressure against Colonel Puett's battalion from Germans pushing down Skyline Boulevard from 88 Corner, Colonel Cavender at dusk committed his 1st Battalion; but as darkness fell, confusion set in, and the battalion made little progress. Late in the evening Cavender pulled the battalion back to Oberlascheid, just downhill from Radscheid, to prepare to join the drive on Schoenberg the next morning; but Company A, unable to disengage, had to stay behind.

Cavender at that point knew nothing about the success of Colonel Klinck's 3d Battalion in reaching the Bleiaif-Schoenberg road close to Schoenberg. Radio communications with the battalion had failed soon after the jump-off, and messengers sent back by Klinck never reached Cavender. At long last, a patrol from Cavender's headquarters located the battalion, and Cavender himself was preparing to go forward when another message got through from headquarters of the 106th Division:

> Attack Schoenberg; do maximum damage to enemy there; then attack toward St. Vith. This mission is of gravest importance to the nation. Good luck.

Cavender and his staff found the appeal to patriotism degrading; they were already trying to do what the order said in any case. Once Cavender had returned from talking with Colonel Klinck, he ordered his other two battalions to close up on the 3d Battalion and renew the attack on Schoenberg early the next morning. As far as he knew, he would be doing the job alone, for a messenger sent to notify Descheneaux of the change in plan had failed to return, and every effort to locate the 422d Infantry during the afternoon had failed.

Colonel Descheneaux and his regiment were actually close by. In keeping with the plan for the 422d Infantry to follow the 423d across the Bleialf-Schoenberg road, Descheneaux had attempted no attack but instead had assembled his units a mile north of Oberlascheid and just short of Skyline Boulevard. It was a slow, laborious march to the assembly area from the heights of the Schnee Eifel three miles away, but the men were nevertheless in fairly good spirits. Some grumbled about having to give up their prepared positions, and all were aware that before leaving their positions, they had drawn the last C- and K-rations available to the regiment. Yet on the morrow the 422d Infantry was going on the offensive, at last to do something about the predicament in which it found itself. The word was, too, that an armored division was on the way to help, and there would also be—so the word had it—resupply by air.

Having, in fact, learned of the new order to attack Schoenberg, Descheneaux that night called his battalion commanders together. The regiment was to attack the next morning with two battalions forward. The first objective was the wooded high ground overlooking Schoenberg known as Hill 504. Although there could be no artillery support, the regiment still had some ammunition for its 60mm. and 81mm. mortars. Descheneaux had no specific word as to the plans of the 423d Infantry, but he assumed that the regiment would be moving forward on his regiment's left.

By daylight on December 19, Colonel Cavender had all three of his battalions forward. Deep in the forest, he had just completed giving the attack order and told his battalion commanders to synchronize their watches. Said Cavender: "It is now exactly 9 o'clock."

As if his words were a signal, the woods erupted with bursting artillery shells. "It sounded like every tree in the forest had been simultaneously blasted from its roots." Everybody scattered, but for some it was too late, among them the commander of the 1st Battalion, Lt. Col. William H. Craig, who was mortally wounded. At about the same time, German infantry overran the firing positions of the 590th Field Artillery Battalion, whose guns had moved across Skyline Boulevard to support the attack.

Despite that disastrous prelude, the attack began as scheduled at 10 A.M. Farthest forward and on the left flank, Company L, commanded by Capt. John B. Huett, moved with two platoons abreast astride the road to Schoenberg; but the men had gone only a short distance when fire from assault guns and from flak guns mounted on half-tracks rained down. Hope stirred when a Sherman tank nosed around a bend in the road: Was that the start of the promised counterattack by American armor? Hardly. Not after the tank opened fire with its machine guns and the men could see German helmets protruding from the turret.

At the rear of the company came a deluge of small-arms fire from *Volksgrenadiers* moving down the road from Bleialf. What was left of Company L was in a vise. Although Captain Huett managed to pull the survivors onto the wooded lower slopes of Hill 504, in early afternoon, as ammunition was running out, *Volksgrenadiers* charged the position. Thirty-two men managed to surrender.

To Company L's right, the rest of the 3d Battalion, moving through the forest, gained a position on Hill 504 from which the men could look down on Schoenberg, but that was as far as they could go. Again deadly fire from assault guns and from flak guns mounted on half-tracks. Colonel Klinck pulled his men back slightly to gain some defilade and told them to dig a perimeter defense.

As for the 1st Battalion, Company C was the regimental reserve, and although Company A had finally managed to disengage and fall back on Radscheid, it happened too late for the company to participate in the attack. That left only Company B. That company got across Hill 504 and gained a clearing only five hundred yards short of the highway leading north out of Schoenberg to Andler. But there the omnipresent assault and flak guns cut the company to pieces.

Colonel Puett's 2d Battalion, advancing on the regiment's right flank, also gained a position on Hill 504 from which to look down on Schoenberg. Unable to contact Colonel Cavender by radio, Puett decided to drop down into the valley of the Linne Creek leading to the Schoenberg-Andler road and get into Schoenberg from that direction. In early afternoon, the men started to move, but hardly had they entered the valley when a blaze of small-arms fire struck them from the other side. Men of the 422d Infantry had taken them to be Germans.

Although the firing was soon stopped, the battalion, already reduced to 450 men, was badly disorganized. Out of contact with the regimental commander, Puett saw no alternative but to cast his lot with the 422d Infantry.

That regiment began its attack almost as inauspiciously as did the 423d Infantry.

The 1st Battalion on the right got virtually nowhere. As the men of Company C crossed Skyline Boulevard, they came under fire from assault guns and machine guns, and even though some of the men gained a bare knob beyond the road, continued fire broke up that group. As other men of the battalion were emerging from the assembly area up a draw leading to Skyline Boulevard, German assault guns were waiting. Almost all of the men of the two companies were either killed or captured.

Farther away from the German guns, men of the 2d Battalion on the left had considerably more success. They got across Skyline Boulevard with little difficulty and continued beyond the Ihren Creek to high ground occupied by the only surviving platoon of Company C.

Joined by Colonel Descheneaux, those men continued to advance and in early afternoon came out onto the forward slope of open ground leading down to the Schoenberg-Andler road. Below them vehicles lined the road bumper to bumper. Word spread that the vehicles were American, not to fire; but that was wishful thinking. Hardly had the men stood up and started down the slope when fire from machine guns and assault guns in the stalled column swept the hillside.

That was about the same time that Colonel Puett's battalion came under small-arms fire in the valley of the Linne Creek. The firing was from the 422d Infantry's 3d Battalion, which had come up in the woods to the left of the 2d Battalion. That mistake straightened out, Puett sent patrols up the creek valley in search of a covered route into Schoenberg, while he himself sought out Colonel Descheneaux, who was pulling his 2d Battalion back from the open slope into nearby woods.

To Puett it was obvious that Descheneaux saw no hope of continuing the attack, but he himself was determined to make one more try. He left to rejoin his battalion.

As for Descheneaux, it had become a question not of continuing the attack but of surrendering. What triggered his decision was the appearance of tanks behind him on Skyline Boulevard. For a brief moment there was hope that the 7th Armored Division had at last arrived, but when the tanks opened fire, that thin hope vanished. The tanks were from the *Führer Begleit Brigade*, on their way to participate in the attack on St. Vith but traveling by way of Skyline Boulevard to Andler in an effort to avoid the bottleneck of Schoenberg.

Descheneaux could move neither forward nor backward. Almost in despair, he called together his battalion commanders, including the commander of the 598th Field Artillery Battalion, Colonel Kelly, who had joined the regiment after failing to get out of the pocket with his battalion. All knew that little food remained, drinking water only from streams, virtually no medical supplies, only a few rounds of mortar ammunition, and small amounts of ammunition for the rifles and machine guns. The promises of relief by the 7th Armored Division and resupply by air had been empty.

"We're sitting like fish in a pond," said Descheneaux to the assembled commanders. Just at that moment men bearing a stretcher passed. On it was the young commander of Company M, Capt. James Perkins, one leg missing, blood pouring from the stump. As the litter bearers deposited

Perkins at the makeshift aid station nearby, Descheneaux could hear the moans of other wounded.

"My God," he said, "we're being slaughtered!" Asserting that he himself had no wish to die simply for glory, Descheneaux asked his commanders what they thought. All were reluctant to surrender but saw no choice.

The commander of the 589th Field Artillery Battalion, Colonel Kelly, protested. In little more than an hour, he pointed out, it would be dark and they could try then to get away.

Descheneaux rejected the suggestion. "As far as I'm concerned," he said, "I'm going to save the lives of as many men as I can, and I don't care if I'm court-martialled."

As men began to smash their weapons against the tree trunks, George Descheneaux broke down. Sitting with his feet in a slit trench, he "cried like a baby." Looking up, he saw several young officers staring at him. Their eyes looked cold. Was it pity, Descheneaux asked himself, or hate?

When Descheneaux requested a volunteer to go under a white flag to arrange surrender, it seemed to the executive officer of Puett's 2d Battalion, 423d Infantry—Maj. William J. Cody Garlow, a grandson of "Buffalo Bill" Cody—that Descheneaux was looking directly at him. "OK, Colonel," said Garlow, "I'll go." Borrowing two white handkerchiefs, he tied them together and set off alone, not thinking to take with him someone who spoke German.

Coming at last to a German position, Garlow waved the handkerchiefs frantically. German soldiers beckoned him in but then scrambled from their foxholes to strip him of his watch, a few bars of candy, and a pint of whiskey. Knowing no German, Garlow was unable to communicate that he had come not to surrender himself but to arrange his unit's surrender.

At last a young lieutenant with crew-cut hair arrived. When he spoke in English, Garlow explained his mission and demanded that the soldiers return his property. The lieutenant barked a command, and the men complied. Accompanied by a squad, the two officers were soon on their way toward the woods where Descheneaux and his troops, some of them in tears, were waiting.

There Colonel Puett had returned from his reconnaissance to learn of Descheneaux's decision. Puett found it unbelievable and told Descheneaux he intended getting his battalion out. No, said Descheneaux, he had already sent out a white flag. If Puett and his men tried to escape, it would go hard on everybody else. He specifically ordered Puett himself not to try it.

Going back to his battalion, Puett told his men what was happening. Anybody who wanted to try to make it out alone or in small groups could take off. About seventy-five men faded into the woods.

A few hundred yards away in the woods atop Hill 504, the commander of the 423d Infantry, Colonel Cavender, was arriving independently of Colonel Descheneaux at the same decision: that it would be best to surrender. Calling his battalion commanders together, he surveyed the condition of their units. The 1st Battalion had virtually ceased to exist; Colonel Klinck's 3d Battalion had lost well over half its strength, including all of Company L; and Colonel Puett's 2d Battalion had disappeared.

There was no ammunition left, said Cavender, except for the few rounds each man still had on his person. Nobody had eaten all day. The supporting artillery had already been overrun.

The officers detected what was coming. "I know it's no use fighting," said one of them, "but I still don't want to surrender."

"I was a GI in the First World War," said Cavender, "and I want to see things from the soldier's standpoint." He was silent for a moment. "Gentlemen," he said at last, "we're surrendering at 1600 [4 P.M.]."

One of those whom Cavender surrendered was the son of his division commander, Alan W. Jones, Jr.

The 422d and 423d Infantry Regiments, along with their attached and supporting units—the 589th, 590th, and 592d Field Artillery Battalions; Companies A and B, 81st Engineer Combat Battalion; Battery D, 634th Antiaircraft Artillery Battalion; Company C, 820th Tank Destroyer Battalion; Companies A and B, 331st Medical Battalion; the 106th Reconnaissance Troop; and Troop B, 18th Cavalry Reconnaissance Squadron —lost more than eight thousand men in the fighting atop and in the shadow of the Schnee Eifel.

Many men got out before the surrender, including almost all the 592d Field Artillery Battalion, part of the 589th, and some of Troop B, 18th Cavalry, along with a few men of the 106th Reconnaissance Troop; and still others had been wounded, captured, or killed before the mass surrender. Some made it out individually or in small groups after the surrender, notably forty men and two lieutenants, Harold A. McKinley of Company A, 423d Infantry, and Ivan H. Long of the I&R Platoon, 422d Infantry. Like most of those who escaped, men in that group hid in the woods by day and traveled by night, often guiding on the path of V-1 buzz bombs.

How many men surrendered en masse in late afternoon of December 19 would never be known exactly. The 106th Division lost 6,879 men captured, to which would have to be added those captured from attached units for a total slightly above 7,000. Assuming an average strength of the infantry battalions at the time Cavender and Descheneaux surrendered their regiments to be five hundred men—possibly an overestimate—approximately three thousand Americans surrendered in the two mass capitulations. Thus the oft-suggested spectacle of some eight to nine thousand Americans plodding into Germany with hands overhead was false.

There were men from both regiments who continued to fight even after the regimental commanders surrendered. For some the fight was brief, for a cruel rumor spread that the 9th Armored Division had recaptured Bleialf, and many men, including those left in charge of the 422d Infantry's vehicles, headed for Bleialf. The rumor being baseless, the men paid dearly for their desperate gullibility.

Meanwhile, fragments of the 422d Infantry began to coalesce on high ground a few hundred yards outside the village of Laudesfeld, Hill 576, not far from the old firing positions of the 592d Field Artillery Battalion. There half-tracks of the 634th Antiaircraft Artillery Battalion, originally emplaced to protect the artillery, had held their ground while the fighting surged around them. By midnight of December 19, some five hundred men had assembled on the hill, and under the overall command of the 2d Battalion's executive officer, Maj. Albert A. Ouellette, they organized for defense.

Almost every man had arrived with some ammunition, and on the antiaircraft half-tracks and a few other vehicles were some twenty .50-caliber machine guns. At least as important, there were enough rations for each man to have two meager meals for two days. The men with the antiaircraft half-tracks thought they still had radio communication with their battalion headquarters in St. Vith and reported that they were holding out. Even though they received no acknowledgment of the message, the fact that they had sent it provided hope that a relief column might eventually break through.

The next day, December 20, artillery fire began to pummel the position. German troops ringed it closely, as any attempt to move about the open hill in daylight quickly affirmed; but the Germans made no assault. The Americans, in time, obviously would have to surrender.

Late that day, a German reconnaissance car flying a white flag and carrying a German medical officer approached. He wanted to arrange a truce, said the officer, to assure safe evacuation of both German and American wounded in the vicinity; but while he was about it, he suggested that the Americans surrender.

At the invitation of the German, Major Ouellette sent with him a lieutenant who returned a few hours later with word that the Germans had artillery pieces trained on Hill 576 and infantry poised to follow an artillery preparation to sweep the hill. The lieutenant knew it to be fact, for the Germans had paraded their preparations before his eyes.

Although some of the junior officers still wanted to hold out, Major Ouellette saw no reason for further loss of life. On the promise of a cease-fire through the night, he agreed to surrender early the next morning. So closely ringed was the position that probably none of those who tried to sneak away during the night succeeded.

At 8 A.M. on December 21, the last organized resistance east of the Our River ended. It marked the conclusion of the most costly defeat for American arms during the course of the war in Europe.

Even as the men beyond the Our River surrendered, General Jones and his staff were still trying to get them resupplied by air. It was a task that had proven utterly frustrating.

Colonel Cavender had first asked for an airdrop early on December 17 and specified the most needed items. Somebody on Jones's staff contacted the air officer at headquarters of the VIII Corps, Lt. Col. Josiah T. Towne, and word went back to Cavender to expect a drop that night.

It never came. Towne relayed the request through the IX Fighter Command to the IX Tactical Air Command, which, in turn, had to refer it to headquarters of the First Army for approval. Not until early the next morning, December 18, did the request reach England and headquarters of the IX Troop Carrier Command, whose C-47 transport planes would have to fly the mission. Ground crews loaded forty planes of the 425th Troop Carrier Group with ammunition and medical supplies; but the weather was closing in, and only twenty-three took off.

Those planes arrived during the afternoon of the 18th over a base at Florennes, in Belgium, where they were supposed to land, but the controller waved them off. The base was too busy to accommodate them. Most of the planes eventually landed at a base in France. The commander himself did land at Florennes, only to learn that nobody knew anything about the mission and that no fighter escort was available.

During the early afternoon of December 19, somebody at the 106th Division's headquarters asked headquarters of the VIII Corps if supplies had been dropped. It was late in the evening—and men of the 422d and 423d Regiments were already trudging deep into Germany—before a reply came back: "Supplies have not been dropped. Will be dropped tomorrow weather permitting."

It never took place. As senior commanders had accepted awkward defensive positions on the Schnee Eifel in the belief that nothing ever happened in the Ardennes, so they had failed to provide adequate machinery for responding to a sudden need for resupply by air. For except in pre-planned airborne operations, nobody ever got surrounded.

Along the horseshoe-shaped defense protecting St. Vith, the Germans during December 19 made only reconnaissance probes. That was not what General von Manteuffel intended. He was counting on the arrival of the *Führer Begleit Brigade* and a strong thrust to take St. Vith on the 19th, but traffic conditions in the German rear were still appalling. Von Manteuffel himself went again to Schoenberg, where he found the traffic stacked up three abreast on the Schoenberg-Andler road. The 18th Volksgrenadier Division was still using two of its three regiments and all

but one of its artillery battalions against the trapped Americans east of
the Our and would be able to turn its full strength against St. Vith only
after eliminating them.

During the day von Manteuffel met near Wallerode with the commander of Army Group B, Field Marshal Model, and the commander of
the 66th Corps, General Lucht. There was little the three officers could
do other than vow to get the attack moving early on the 20th. By that
time the 62d Volksgrenadier Division should have the bridge at
Steinebrück rebuilt, at least two of the 18th Volksgrenadier Division's
regiments should be forward, and the *Führer Begleit Brigade* should be
ready to make the principal thrust down the Amblève highway into St.
Vith. Then again, that depended upon untangling the traffic jams on the
roads in the rear.

During the afternoon of December 19, the commander of the 9th Armored Division's CCB, Bill Hoge, strode into a schoolhouse in the village
of Crombach, two miles outside St. Vith, where Bruce Clarke had moved
his command post. "Who do I work for?" demanded Hoge. "I was sent
down here by First Army to be attached to Jones and the 106th Infantry
Division. Where is Jones? Now I don't know what the situation is. Maybe
I had better go back to Bastogne and find out."

Clarke tried to placate him. There was no need to deal with Jones; the
two of them could work things out together.

On a map, Clarke noted that the positions occupied by Hoge's CCB
the night before were for the most part forward of a railroad track built
on a high embankment. He knew, said Clarke, that the Germans were
going to hit him hard and that sooner or later he was going to have to
give up the town of St. Vith, which would eliminate the only route of
withdrawal for those of Hoge's troops forward of the embankment. When
Clarke suggested that Hoge withdraw that night behind the embankment,
Hoge agreed.

It was on that same day, December 19, that Colonel Nelson of the
28th Division's 112th Infantry reported to General Jones to announce the
availability of his regiment and its supporting artillery battalion. Attaching the regiment to the 106th Division, Jones notified General Middleton,
who subsequently approved. Jones told Nelson to tie his regiment's defenses to the right flank of the 424th Infantry and block the main highway
leading to Vielsalm from the south, a road that was, in effect, an extension of the Skyline Drive.

By midnight of December 19, a horseshoe-shaped defense of St. Vith
had taken form. No reinforcements were to be expected. The next move
was up to General Lucht and his 66th Corps.

CHAPTER SEVENTEEN

In Front of
Luxembourg City

On the southern shoulder of the German offensive, amid the frontier villages, woods, and steeply rolling hills between the southern reaches of the Skyline Drive and the Our River, and below the confluence of the Our and the Sûre on either side of the Ernz Noire ("Little Switzerland"), the American troops at the start of the second day were having their difficulties. Yet they were considerably better off than many of their colleagues elsewhere, primarily because they were facing no German armor but only a parachute and three *Volksgrenadier* divisions of General Brandenberger's Seventh Army. Those German divisions were in fact having problems throwing bridges across the Our and the Sûre in order to bring forward such fire support as they did possess: horse-drawn divisional artillery and the equivalent of an under-strength battalion of self-propelled assault guns.

There, too, even though Brandenberger had assumed at the end of the first day that his adversary had committed all his local reserves, there were actually reserves still to make their presence felt. Although the 109th Infantry's Colonel Rudder had committed his reserve infantry battalion, primarily in an effort to rescue Company E, surrounded in Fouhren, he still had a company of medium tanks of the 707th Tank Battalion to add weight to a renewal of that effort. During the night, the 60th Armored Infantry Battalion, in the line to gain battlefield experience, had reverted to control of its parent command, the 9th Armored Division's CCA, and the bulk of that combat command's tanks and self-propelled tank destroyers were still to enter the fight.

On the high plateau east of the Ernz Noire, generally astride the highway linking Echternach and Luxembourg City, the 12th Infantry's Colonel Chance had committed the last of his reserve battalion; but the commander of the 4th Division, Tubby Barton, had arranged to borrow a company of medium tanks from the 9th Armored Division's CCA. Taking a chance that the German offensive would not expand to the south,

Barton was bringing forward the reserve battalion of his southernmost regiment, the 22d Infantry. He also still had in reserve his organic reconnaissance troop and engineer combat battalion.

More important still was another reserve whose early commitment Brandenberger could in no way have anticipated. That was the 10th Armored Division's CCA, which at daybreak on December 17 began moving to Luxembourg from the sector of the Third Army in northeastern France. The combat command was to be available at the start of the third day, December 18.

American commanders intended on the second day, December 17, to use their local reserves to rescue surrounded units, strengthen threatened units, and block exits from the gorge of the Ernz Noire leading into the rear of the units on either side. Rudder of the 109th Infantry was to rescue Company E in Fouhren; Collins of the 60th Armored Infantry Battalion was to block roads leading into his rear from the Ernz Noire and maintain contact with his line companies on the wooded heights overlooking the Sûre River; and Chance of the 12th Infantry was to rescue the men of Company F in the Parc Hôtel outside Berdorf and the men of

Company E in Echternach and to reinforce the hardpressed men of the 3d Battalion southeast of Echternach in Osweiler and Dickweiler.

In the northern part of the 109th Infantry's sector, where the commander of the 85th Corps, General Kniess, was trying to break the 5th Parachute Division loose in order to lean on the advance of the adjacent *Panzer Lehr Division*, the Germans were content to bypass most isolated defensive positions in favor of pushing on to the Skyline Drive. Yet if they were to open a road for their drive to the west, they had to have Hoscheid on the Skyline Drive. That was what had led to the day-long fight for the village, ending after nightfall with American withdrawal. A road westward at last available, the 5th Parachute Division from that point became, in effect, an adjunct of the Fifth Panzer Army's drive for Bastogne.

The situation of the 5th Parachute Division at Hoscheid was similar to that of the 352d Volksgrenadier Division at Fouhren. The *Volksgrenadiers* needed the village in order to gain access to the valley of the Sûre River at Diekirch and their assigned road leading west; but without support from assault guns, it was difficult to force the 109th Infantry's Company E from Fouhren. Because of American artillery fire, it was late in the night of December 17 before a bridge was in place to allow assault guns to cross the Our. Yet even though two American companies trying to gain Fouhren had help from a platoon of medium tanks, the *Volksgrenadiers* managed to prevent them from breaking through to the village.

When Company E radioed in some desperation for food and ammunition, Colonel Rudder ordered a patrol to try to get through after nightfall, but again Fouhren remained out of reach. The last word from Company E came by radio an hour after midnight. When a patrol from the I&R Platoon, accompanied by a tank, got within two hundred yards of the village at daylight, the men could see that the house that had served as the company command post had burned to the ground. Company E, 109th Infantry, had ceased to exist.

The collapse at Fouhren meant increased pressure on the 109th Infantry's 3d Battalion close by in the angle formed by confluence of the Our and the Sûre, for it left that battalion's northern flank exposed. Eliminating that battalion was critical to the German advance, for it was forward observers with the battalion who were directing the shelling of the 352d Volksgrenadier Division's bridge site. At dawn on December 18, a German regiment hit the 3d Battalion's north flank and surrounded and captured a platoon of Company K, but the battalion held.

Despite that stand, the positions of the 109th Infantry were fast becoming untenable, for there was no way to halt German movement between the widely spaced American positions. By midday of December 18, German forces the size of companies and even battalions were moving almost with impunity behind the American-held villages. Here and there they overwhelmed little outposts trying to fill the gaps between villages: a brace of 57mm. antitank guns, a few men from Cannon Company fighting as infantry, a squad of engineers defending a roadblock.

As early as the pre-dawn hours of December 17, a battery of 105mm. howitzers of the 107th Field Artillery Battalion just behind the southern reaches of the Skyline Drive came under small-arms fire from German patrols; and in the early afternoon on the 18th, an entire battalion of *Volksgrenadiers* attacked that battery and a nearby battery of 155mm. howitzers of the 108th Field Artillery Battalion. While neighboring batteries took the Germans under fire, two half-tracks from the 447th Antiaircraft Artillery Battalion raced up the Skyline Drive, their quad-50s blazing, and chased the Germans off the road. From the north, the platoon of tanks sent to try to break through to Hoscheid returned and helped drive the Germans away. The artillery pieces were for the moment safe, but it was obvious that all the artillery in support of the 109th Infantry would have to displace.

By that time, Companies F and G had fallen back on the 2d Battalion's headquarters village of Bastendorf, and remnants of Companies A and B, having failed to reach Fouhren, fell back under fire to a road junction less than half a mile from the road following the trace of the Sûre River into Diekirch. If the men of the 3d Battalion were to withdraw from their positions in the angle formed by confluence of the Our and Sûre, they would need that road.

Early that same afternoon, December 18, two assault guns supporting a battalion of *Volksgrenadiers* hit the road junction. With the first rounds, the German guns knocked out six 57mm. antitank guns and one of three medium tanks still fighting with Company A. For a moment it looked like a breakthrough; but with the help of the two surviving tanks, the infantry rallied and held.

To Colonel Rudder, the near disaster at the road junction underscored the need to pull his regiment back and consolidate along a new line. Although he had in mind eventual withdrawal behind the Sûre River, he asked authority at first merely to consolidate on high ground near Diekirch. The men were well dug in on the high ground by the next afternoon, the 19th, when German artillery, having at last crossed the Our, opened heavy preparation fire. Yet the attack by *Volksgrenadiers* was weak. In more than three days of fighting, the 352d Volksgrenadier Division had lost heavily, and in the attack that afternoon, the division commander, Colonel Erich Schmidt, was seriously wounded.

That night Colonel Rudder asked General Cota for permission to withdraw behind the Sûre. Cota suggested instead that Rudder fall back along the Ettelbruck-Bastogne highway, thereby rejoining the 28th Divi-

SKYLINE DRIVE
SECOND DAY - DEC 17
Scale:
0 ½ 1 2 3 4
MILES
N

Burg Reuland

Our River

BELGIUM
GERMANY

West Wall

106TH INF DIV
28TH INF DIV

Lützkampen
116TH PZ DIV

Ouren
Harspelt

Sevenig

BELGIUM
LUXEMBOURG

Weiswampach

Trois Vierges

112TH INF
110TH INF

GERMANY

River LUXEMBOURG

560TH VG DIV

Heinerscheid

Clerve River

N12

Urspelt

Fishbach

Antoniushof RJ

Reuler
Clervaux
Marnach

2D PZ DIV

Dasburg

Munshausen

SKYLINE

Our

Drauffelt

Clerve River

Hosingen

Bockholz

26TH VG DIV

Wilwerwiltz

Café Schinker

Holzthum

DRIVE

Walhausen

Gemünd

FIFTH PZ ARMY

SEVENTH ARMY

Consthum

5TH PCHT DIV

Wiltz

Wiltz River

Weiler

Kautenbach

110TH INF
109TH INF

Hoscheid

sion; but because of the 5th Parachute Division's advance, Rudder believed that would be less a withdrawal than an attack. "Use your own judgment," said Cota finally. "You are on the ground."

Under protective artillery fires, most of the troops left Diekirch before midnight along the road to Ettelbruck and before daylight the following morning were digging in on high ground south and west of Ettelbruck. From those positions they could cover both the Ettelbruck-Bastogne highway and the principal highway leading south from Ettelbruck to Luxembourg City. An attached company of the 28th Division's organic engineers blew bridges both at Diekirch and at Ettelbruck.

In Diekirch, at the first rumor that the Americans were going to abandon the town, the civilians erupted from their cellars into the streets. They had started to flee early on December 16, but in order to keep the roads open for military movement, local officials at the behest of officers of the 109th Infantry had halted the exodus. Over the next few days, the local *gendarmerie* had helped the Americans by housing German prisoners of war in the town jail. Fearing reprisals, the civilians were determined to leave, and with Colonel Rudder's approval, they followed the Americans out of town. More than three thousand men, women, and children set out in freezing cold and darkness along the roads leading south.

For the 60th Armored Infantry Battalion between the Sûre River and the gorge of the Ernz Noire, the basic concern was likely German movement up the undefended gorge and egress along one of the three roads leading into the rear of the American positions. There was also the possibility of envelopment from the north, where on the first day the Germans had eliminated a small outpost which the armored infantry battalion commander, Colonel Collins, had positioned there to give the alarm.

During the night of December 16, the commander of the battalion's parent unit, Col. Thomas L. Harrold of the 9th Armored Division's CCA, took a few steps toward blocking those possibilities. He sent the 19th Tank Battalion's company of light tanks to screen the northern flank; he attached a troop of the 89th Cavalry Reconnaissance Squadron to Collins to patrol the road from the Ernz Noire into Collins's headquarters town of Beaufort; and he sent another troop plus the 76mm. self-propelled guns of Company B, 811th Tank Destroyer Battalion, to block the other two roads leading up from the gorge.

Those were timely steps, but they were insufficient to prevent German infiltration. During the night of the 16th, troops of the 276th Volksgrenadier Division worked southward through some woods in the rear of Collins's companies, and others occupied a ridgeline between Beaufort and the forward companies. Although a counterattack by the attached cavalry cleared the ridgeline, the Germans in the woods remained, which meant that the line companies of the 60th Armored Infantry Battalion were cut off.

At the same time, a regiment of *Volksgrenadiers* moved unopposed up the gorge of the Ernz Noire to the settlement of Müllerthal, where the road along the bottom of the gorge met another bisecting the gorge, an intersection that soon became known to American troops as "the T." From Müllerthal, the Germans threatened the village of Waldbillig, not far behind firing positions of the 3d Armored Field Artillery Battalion.

Early that afternoon, a troop of cavalry reinforced by four self-propelled tank destroyers tried to drive the *Volksgrenadiers* from Müllerthal, but on a narrow, winding road leading down into the gorge, a German with a *Panzerfaust* knocked out the leading tank destroyer, blocking the road. Dismounted cavalry got nowhere, and as daylight waned, the American force withdrew to the top of the gorge.

As night came on the 17th, *Volksgrenadiers* at the other end of the gorge poured into Beaufort. Colonel Collins ordered his headquarters troops to withdraw while the attached troop of cavalry under Capt. Victor C. Leiker fought a rear guard action. Leiker's troop managed to hold for about two hours, just long enough for self-propelled pieces of the 3d Armored Field Artillery Battalion near the next village to displace.

During the night, the only radio still affording communication with the trapped companies of the 60th Armored Infantry Battalion, one belonging to an artillery forward observer, ceased to function. Yet that was of little concern for the moment in view of the fact that the commander of CCA, Colonel Harrold, was assembling a force to attack early the next morning to relieve the armored infantrymen and "drive the enemy into the river." And it was an impressive force: two companies of mediums of the 19th Tank Battalion, a company of the 9th Armored Engineer Battalion mounted in half-tracks to fight as infantry, a troop of the 89th Cavalry Reconnaissance Squadron, and the 60th Armored Infantry Battalion's I&R Platoon. The attack was to begin from what was fast becoming CCA's new defensive line, extending from Waldbillig northward along a ridgeline through the village of Savelborn and on to screening positions of the light tanks in Ermsdorf.

On the German side, the commander of the 276th Volksgrenadier Division, Generalleutnant Kurt Möhring, was at the same time preparing to attack the center of that line at Savelborn, from which Harrold's attack was to debouch. Möhring had a battalion of *Volksgrenadiers* and an antitank company with fifty-four *Panzerfausts*.

Unknown to General Möhring, his failure to build a bridge quickly across the Sûre, which had resulted in a slow buildup beyond the river, had prompted his superior, General Brandenberger, to call upon Field Marshal Model at Army Group B to send a replacement for Möhring. As it turned out, Möhring was riding in his command car that evening near Beaufort when fire from an American machine gun killed him.

The next morning, the steps Möhring had taken to assemble a force near Savelborn served the 276th Volksgrenadier Division well. Before daylight, as the Germans were preparing to attack Savelborn, the 60th Armored Infantry Battalion's I&R Platoon, in the vanguard of the attacking American force, entered the woods outside the village. German fire killed the platoon leader at the outset and in the end virtually wiped out the platoon.

After daylight, the main body of CCA's attacking force followed along the same road through the woods, and to men in the half-tracks and tanks, there appeared to be a *Panzerfaust* behind every tree. In what seemed to be only minutes, the *Panzerfausts* knocked out a light tank and six Shermans. The commander of the leading medium tank company, Capt. Arthur J. Banford, Jr., his own tank shot from under him, ordered withdrawal. Pleading insufficient foot troops to protect the tanks, the entire column fell back on Savelborn, an inauspicious first offensive action for those troops of CCA, and it left the men of the 60th Armored Infantry Battalion to fend for themselves.

In the beleaguered positions of that battalion, the artillery forward observer late in the afternoon of December 18 finally managed to repair his radio. By order of Colonel Harrold, the men were to make their way out by infiltration. That night and over the next two nights 400 men made their way to safety; but in the three-day fight, the 60th Armored Infantry Battalion lost close to 350 men, most of them during the withdrawal.

The new line to be held by the 9th Armored Division's CCA extended for more than seven miles, from Waldbillig alongside the Ernz Noire through Savelborn and Ermsdorf and beyond. Yet despite the length of that line, a gap between the combat command and the 109th Infantry of four miles still existed. That regiment's depleted 2d Battalion soon moved into the gap, a stopgap measure, at best, but as it turned out, all that was needed.

A new commander for the 276th Volksgrenadier Division, Col. Hugo Dempwolff, made it his first priority to reorganize his command, for casualties had been heavy. Still lacking a bridge over the Sûre, he arranged during the night of December 18 to pass his artillery and supplies over bridges belonging to the two adjacent divisions; and when his engineers at last completed a bridge late on the 19th, he was able to move forward three assault guns that the commander of the Seventh Army, General Brandenberger, had scrounged from some place. Only with the arrival of those guns was Colonel Dempwolff prepared for the 276th Volksgrenadier Division to return to the offensive, and by that time higher command had arrived at other plans.

By daylight on December 17, the slight superiority in numbers possessed by the commander of the 212th Volksgrenadier Division, Generalmajor Franz Sensfuss, over the 12th Infantry's Colonel Chance—five infantry battalions (one regiment served as the Seventh Army's reserve) against three—had disappeared. For the commander of the 4th Division, General Barton, had ordered the reserve battalion of his southernmost regiment to the threatened sector and his organic engineer battalion into the line as infantry. That made it five against five, and Barton had a decided edge in artillery, tanks, and tank destroyers, for Sensfuss had only four assault guns and as yet no way to get them or his horse-drawn artillery across the Sûre River.

Although Sensfuss's engineers had thrown a bridge across the Sûre on the first day of the offensive, American artillery fire knocked it out before the first vehicle could cross. That night the German engineers brought down searchlights close to the river opposite Echternach. They planned to build a bridge based on the stone piers of an earlier bridge that had served the town since the Middle Ages; but American shelling again interfered. Falling back, the engineers had to wait for daylight before building a bridge at another site downstream, and not until late afternoon of December 18 did that bridge begin to serve the division.

The first move General Barton made early on December 17 to meet the continuing German threat was to send the 4th Reconnaissance Troop and the 4th Engineer Combat Battalion, before daylight, to an obvious point of danger: the high ground above the gorge of the Ernz Noire not far from Müllerthal and the road intersection known as the T. When in the early morning *Volksgrenadiers* reached Müllerthal, Barton decided to reinforce by creating Task Force Luckett, headed by a former commander of the 12th Infantry, Col. James S. Luckett, then carried as an excess officer with the division headquarters. In addition to the reconnaissance troop and the engineers, Luckett was to have eight Shermans which Company B, 70th Tank Battalion, had by that time managed to put into some kind of operating order, the tank battalion's mortar platoon, and the reserve battalion of the adjacent 8th Infantry. Calling on that battalion was a risk, for the German offensive still might expand southward; but knowledge that the 10th Armored Division's CCA was on the way made Barton's decision easier.

When the eight Shermans arrived in mid-afternoon of the 17th, Colonel Luckett sent them to block the gorge of the Ernz Noire a half-mile upstream from Müllerthal, and when the 8th Infantry's reserve battalion reached the scene, the 2d under Lt. Col. George L. Mabry, he added the infantry to that block. Yet, ironically, General Barton had created a block against a German force that threatened not his 12th Infantry but rather the 9th Armored Division's CCA; for the Germans in the gorge were from the 276th Volksgrenadier Division, whose zone of advance lay on CCA's side of the gorge. Barton and Luckett would be left to wonder why the Germans made no effort to emerge from the gorge into the rear of the 12th Infantry.

Elsewhere the 12th Infantry spent the second day of the German offensive trying to rescue surrounded units and reinforce others.

The regimental commander, Colonel Chance, again sent Company B, reinforced by a platoon of light tanks and four mediums, to clear the village of Berdorf and rescue the men of Lieutenant Leake's Company F. That was no easy assignment, for Berdorf was an elongated village extending for more than half a mile along a spine formed by the highway leading from the 2d Battalion's headquarters village of Consdorf. Accompanied by the light tanks, half of the infantrymen worked house by house up the spine, while the rest of the men and the four medium tanks bypassed the village over open ground between the village and the Ernz Noire. That route led to Lieutenant Leake's little force in the Parc Hôtel.

As the four tanks neared the hotel, it looked to Lieutenant Leake as if they were maneuvering to get into position to fire on it. As indeed they were; for since Lieutenant McConnell had lost Company F's SCR-300 during his fracas with the Germans in Berdorf, Leake had had no way to report his position. How to reveal to the tanks that Americans held the hotel? Leake had no identification panels, no flares, nothing.

One man suddenly remembered that in rummaging through the drawers of a dresser in one of the rooms, he had come across an American flag. He rushed to find it, and a volunteer climbed to the shattered roof of the hotel and waved it frantically.

As the tanks and their accompanying infantry reached the hotel, the rest of Company B was pushing the Germans past the road junction a hundred yards away in Berdorf, but that was as far as the attack carried before nightfall brought a halt. Leake and his men continued to hold the hotel, for that provided good flank protection for the men in Berdorf.

In the center of the 12th Infantry's sector on December 17, Colonel Chance sent Company A to reinforce Company G in Lauterborn, astride the last high ground before the highway dropped down into Echternach, whereupon the two companies were to drive to the relief of Company E inside Echternach. Because the Germans held high ground on either side of the highway leading into Lauterborn, it took Company A the better part of the day to get into the village, and by that time it was too late to continue the attack. The men of Company E remained isolated in Echternach.

On the right of the 12th Infantry's sector, in Osweiler and Dickweiler, the third line company of Chance's reserve 1st Battalion, Company C, reinforced the defending companies of the 3d Battalion; and in midmorning, the reserve battalion from the 22d Infantry, the 2d under Lt. Col. Thomas A. Kenan, detrucked behind the two villages. The men of one company climbed immediately onto the decks of a company of tanks borrowed from the 9th Armored Division's CCA and headed for Osweiler. On the way they flushed and routed a company of Germans in some woods alongside the road and in the process freed sixteen men of Company C, captured during the company's move to Osweiler.

In mid-afternoon, the rest of Colonel Kenan's battalion headed for Osweiler on foot. The column was nearing the crest of a ridge a mile short of the village when a column of Germans appeared. Taken by surprise, the men of both columns dropped to the ground and opened fire. The fight was a stand-off until darkness came, when the Germans disengaged, and the next morning Kenan's men resumed their march to Osweiler.

The Germans had been on their way to Scheidgen, close by Consdorf and headquarters of the 12th Infantry's 2d Battalion. There the Germans gained their only success of the day when a platoon of self-propelled tank destroyers abandoned the village without a fight. With only a few men from the headquarters available to defend Consdorf, the battalion commander, Maj. John W. Dorn, spent an anxious night, but the Germans made no effort to push beyond Scheidgen.

At the end of the second day of the German offensive, the trace of a new defensive line was beginning to take shape in the 12th Infantry's sector. Osweiler and Dickweiler on the right were firmly held (a fact soon recognized by the German commander, General Sensfuss, who made no further attempt to take those villages). So, too, on the left, Task Force Luckett had firmly anchored the line along the upper reaches of the Ernz Noire. The weakness was in the center, where there was a gap between Osweiler and Consdorf along the principal highway through the sector—the road from Luxembourg City to Echternach (which General Sensfuss also recognized and intended to try, with his limited means, to exploit).

Out in front were two projections. Company B and Lieutenant Leake's little band at Berdorf constituted one; Companies A and G in Lauterborn and Company E in Echternach constituted the other. Except for the danger to the men in those projections, the 12th Infantry at nightfall on December 17 was in fairly good shape, and reinforcements were arriving. They consisted of a corps engineer battalion, the 159th, which General Barton put in reserve near his left flank lest the enemy break through the adjacent sector, and the 10th Armored Division's CCA.

After conferring with General Middleton in Bastogne, the commander of the 10th Armored Division, General Morris, met with Barton in Luxembourg City and agreed on how to use CCA. Since the entire 10th Armored Division, except for CCB at Bastogne, was to be committed in Luxembourg, CCA was not attached to the 4th Division. The two commanders nevertheless agreed that the armor would attack the next day, the 18th, through the positions of the 12th Infantry, to drive the Germans back across the Sûre.

In early afternoon, Barton worked out the details of that commitment with CCA's commander, Brig. Gen. Edwin W. Piburn. One task force was to clear the gorge of the Ernz Noire; a second to push through Berdorf and thence into Echternach; and a third to retake Scheidgen, link with the infantry in Lauterborn, and continue into Echternach. Since Barton was most concerned about the possibility of the Germans debouching in strength from the Ernz Noire, the first of Piburn's task forces to arrive was to be committed there. It was unfortunate that the first task force contained the bulk of the combat command's medium tanks, for the gorge of the Ernz Noire was no place for tanks.

As the three task forces began to advance early on December 18, the Germans made their move to exploit the gap between Osweiler and Scheidgen. Two German battalions drove south along secondary roads close by the main highway leading to Luxembourg City, in effect cutting into the rear of the American troops at Osweiler and Dickweiler and, if the advance continued, into the rear of the neighboring 8th Infantry.

Fortunate it was for the Americans that those two German battalions had lost heavily in the first two days of fighting, for in the sector where they struck, the 12th Infantry had no prepared defensive positions. In both cases, the Germans bumped into forces that had to turn from other duties to fight back—in one hamlet, the 12th Infantry's Cannon Company, caught as the cannoneers were moving into new firing positions; in another, the rear command post of the 2d Battalion, 22d Infantry, whose headquarters troops had the support of only a platoon of towed tank destroyers. Yet in both cases the Americans held off the Germans long enough for a few medium tanks to get forward and enable them to withdraw.

The German commander, General Sensfuss, may not have realized it, but he had at last achieved a breakthrough, for in the hamlets ahead hardly anybody stood in the way. Yet both German battalions, already under strength, had taken heavy losses during the day and were in no condition to exploit their gains. Once General Sensfuss had learned of the arrival of American armor, he convinced General Brandenberger to release his third regiment from the Seventh Army's reserve, but it would be another twenty-four hours, at best, before that regiment got across the Sûre River.

Meanwhile, the attacks by the three task forces of the 10th Armored Division's CCA achieved little, particularly the attack aimed at clearing the enemy from the gorge of the Ernz Noire. Tanks of the 11th Tank Battalion entered the gorge upstream from German-held Müllerthal, but because the road at the bottom of the gorge was narrow and closely confined on both sides by woods, the width of the attacking front was the width of one medium tank. When a round from an antitank gun damaged the leading tank, it took considerable time to work the rest of the column around. It was late afternoon before the head of the task force reached Müllerthal, there to confront a strong German position.

CCA's second task force, composed of the 61st Armored Infantry Battalion and a company of Shermans, moved to Berdorf and there joined the 12th Infantry's Company B in clearing the rest of the village. Progress was slow. When night came, the Germans still held a few houses in Berdorf and the task force had made no progress on its second assignment of pushing beyond Berdorf into Echternach.

The third and smallest task force (composed of a company each of medium tanks and armored infantry) found only an enemy rear guard in Scheidgen and with the help of two companies of the 159th Engineer Combat Battalion soon took a commanding height overlooking Lauterborn. Once inside the village, the two companies of the 12th Infantry delayed their planned push into Echternach to await arrival of the tanks.

Yet when the tanks got there, the task force commander, Lt. Col. John R. Riley, considered it too late in the day to continue into Echternach. While the task force holed up for the night at the mill alongside the road to Echternach, where Company G had its command post, Riley sent two tanks accompanied by two squads of infantry into Echternach to ascertain how the 12th Infantry's Company E was faring.

Fairly well, as it turned out. The company commander, 1st Lt. Morton A. Macdiarmid, had established his headquarters near the edge of town in a hat factory along the road to Lauterborn, the Rue de Luxembourg, and his kitchen in the garage of the adjacent Hôtel de Luxembourg. The headquarters was under no particular enemy pressure, and Macdiarmid had withdrawn such men of the rifle platoons as could make it back to the command post; but others in outposts elsewhere in the town, including an entire platoon, were cut off.

What Macdiarmid wanted was not relief from the assignment of defending Echternach but tanks to help extricate the men who were cut off. Although the commanders of the two tanks were unwilling to risk the peril of *Panzerfausts* in narrow streets after nightfall, they promised to return along with additional tanks the next morning.

On December 19, the commander of the 10th Armored Division's CCA, General Piburn, changed his mind about employing tanks in the gorge of the Ernz Noire. To General Barton, Piburn proposed that the road forming the top of the T at Müllerthal could be neutralized by holding high ground on either side of the gorge, thereby freeing Piburn's tanks to constitute a reserve that would be readily at hand should the Germans try to emerge from the gorge. Barton agreed, an all-too-rare example of reconsideration of an ill-considered original commitment.

For a second day CCA's central task force continued to clear Germans from Berdorf, but slowly. The Germans made a bastion of every house, and from time to time the task force had to send tanks to the rear to clear German patrols from the supply route leading back to Consdorf.

All the while, Lieutenant Leake and his sixty men continued to hold the Parc Hôtel just outside the village. German artillery fire still ripped into the roof and rockets from *Panzerfausts* tore big holes in the east side. Maintaining a constant vigil at doors and windows, the American soldiers amused themselves by trying to pick off Germans who carelessly showed themselves in nearby houses. Not an American was killed and only one wounded, hit in the leg by a random enemy machine-gun bullet.

On the night of December 19, a dense fog descended. Under its concealment *Volksgrenadiers* inched close to the hotel, in some places no more than twenty yards away, and dug in so quietly that none of the sentries in the hotel detected them.

Before daylight the next morning, a crushing blast tore a great hole in the east side of the hotel, and the *Volksgrenadiers* attacked. Since it was too foggy and dark to make out the advancing Germans except when they fired their weapons, the defenders of the hotel relied for the most part on hand grenades. For half an hour "it was a desperate fight." Then almost as suddenly as the German firing had begun, it ceased.

With the coming of daylight, the Americans could see that during the night the Germans had also dug in on the west side of the hotel—the side facing Berdorf—apparently hoping the Americans would abandon the hotel and withdraw in that direction. The coming of daylight also revealed that the demolition preceding the German attack had blown open a sealed door in the basement leading to a room containing hundreds of bottles of liquor, liqueurs, and a barrel of beer, but Lieutenant Leake allowed nobody to touch it.

As it turned out, there would be little time for imbibing in any case, for Leake and his men soon had to abandon their sanctuary. Leaving behind their lone prisoner, the German sergeant who had been shot in the buttocks, they joined Company B and the armored task force in Berdorf just after nightfall for withdrawal to Consdorf. As on the German side, higher command had come up with a new plan for that part of the front.

On December 19, General Patton was beginning to turn more of the troops of his Third Army northward toward the southern shoulder of the German penetration. Command of the VIII Corps having passed to Patton, he created a provisional corps headquarters to control those troops of the VIII Corps still in Luxembourg and others coming in. Under the commander of the 10th Armored Division, General Morris, the headquarters controlled Morris's division (except for CCB at Bastogne), headquarters and CCA of the 9th Armored Division, the 109th Infantry, and the 4th Infantry Division.

Retaking the ground the Germans had seized in the first four days of the offensive no longer had a high priority. What mattered was holding a firm line to allow time for additional troops from the Third Army to arrive. With that in mind, General Barton was to form a line extending from Osweiler and Dickweiler through Scheidgen and Consdorf to the positions held by Task Force Luckett overlooking the Ernz Noire at Müllerthal, while the 10th Armored Division's CCA pulled back in reserve. Which meant withdrawal from Berdorf, from Lauterborn, and from Echternach.

On the German side on December 19, the commander of the 80th Corps, General der Infanterie Franz Beyer, was also ordering his troops to shift to the defensive. Although the 212th and 276th Volksgrenadier Divisions had failed to push the shoulder of the penetration as far south as plans called for, the two divisions, in Beyer's opinion, had gone as far as they were capable of going. The time for a major American reaction to the offensive, Beyer reasoned, was drawing near, and he needed to get his men dug in and ready for it when it came. That was tacit admission that the forces at the base of the southern shoulder—blessed from the start with more ambition than resources—had ground to a halt.

Two small offensive tasks remained. Beyer wanted the 276th Volksgrenadier Division to take the village of Waldbillig so as to afford those troops in the gorge of the Ernz Noire at Müllerthal a route of egress from the gorge. The Germans accomplished the takeover against cavalry of the 9th Armored Division's CCA during the afternoon of the 20th. The other task was to eliminate the Americans who were still holding in Echternach.

To that task the commander of the 212th Volksgrenadier Division, General Sensfuss, turned his personal attention, for to Sensfuss, that little band of Americans represented the height of impudence. They obviously could be eliminated at will and their presence had little effect on German operations, yet they persisted in sticking it out in the town. To wipe them out, Sensfuss called on his division's Fusilier Battalion and his four attached assault guns.

Arriving in Echternach from the dreadful carnage in the Hürtgen Forest, men of the 12th Infantry's Company E were delighted with their new assignment. The front was quiet, and they were in sole charge of a town where five thousand people normally lived and all had been evacuated, leaving the men free to plunder for whatever goodies the American troops who had preceded them had missed or left behind. That included ample stocks of wine, champagne, brandies, canned foods, apples, and potatoes. "Really, it was swell; the boys were getting rested up and they were showing signs of being able to smile again." Few were aware—and probably could have cared less—that they occupied a town that in peacetime was one of Luxembourg's premier tourist attractions, whose population swelled every spring for a folk festival honoring St. Willibrord, the town's patron saint, and featuring a "dancing procession," in which young men and women, linked by white scarves, did a kind of jumping jig through the streets and into the cobblestoned Place du Marché.

Although the men were widely scattered in outposts in various parts of town, reinforced in some cases by heavy machine gunners and 81mm. mortarmen of the 2d Battalion's weapons company, all were in buildings, warm, dry, relatively secure. Carrying details brought three hot meals a day from the company kitchen in the garage of the Hôtel de Luxembourg. If any Germans were inside the town during daytime, they never showed themselves; and at night no American stirred from his post or his billet, so that anything that moved in the dark streets was considered to be German and worthy of a few hand grenades.

Back at the 2d Battalion's headquarters in Consdorf, the operations officer, Capt. Paul H. Dupuis, learned that there was a 1937 Plymouth sedan in Echternach with low mileage but lacking a battery and with a hole in the gasoline tank. The battalion commander, Major Dorn, told Dupuis that if he got the automobile running, he could take it on a week's leave to Paris, and Dorn himself would go next. Late on December 15, Captain Dupuis went to Echternach to spend the night at Company E's headquarters and see what he could do the next morning to get the Plymouth running. That was why Dupuis was in Echternach when the enemy's artillery preparation began, and he elected to stay to provide such assistance as he could to Macdiarmid.

Germans were soon crossing the river at various points in rubber assault boats, sometimes driven back by the fire of Company E's outposts but at other sites unseen and undeterred by the defenders. By mid-afternoon, *Volksgrenadiers* were roaming parts of the town almost at will, taking the scattered outposts under fire, and in some cases surrounding them. Lest the outposts be picked off one by one, Lieutenant Macdiarmid ordered everybody to fall back on the hat factory and the Hôtel de Luxembourg. Yet some men were unable to break away, including the entire First Platoon.

At dusk on the first day, December 16, a small group of Germans tried to storm the company headquarters, but cooks with the help of fire from a .50-caliber machine gun mounted on a jeep in the doorway of the garage drove them off. For long after that, the Germans ignored the men in the hat factory and the Hôtel de Luxembourg, concentrating instead on knocking off the few outposts that had been unable to withdraw. The men of the First Platoon nevertheless held fast.

When the two tanks from Task Force Riley entered Echternach in late afternoon of December 18, hope rose for the First Platoon's rescue. It quickly fell again with the refusal of the tank commanders to move about the town after dark. True to their word, both tank commanders nevertheless returned the next morning, the 19th, with the rest of their platoon. Accompanied by riflemen from Company E, the tanks quickly broke through to the First Platoon and brought the men back to the hotel.

The commander of the 4th Division, General Barton, expected at that point that Company E would withdraw, for he had directed that a message authorizing withdrawal should go forward with the tanks. Yet no such message reached either Dupuis or Macdiarmid. As far as they knew, Barton's early order that there was to be "no retrograde movement" by any unit of the 12th Infantry was still in effect. Not that it bothered Dupuis, at least; he had been surrounded as a company commander in the Hürtgen Forest, and a relief force had broken through. As evidenced by two visits from American tanks, relief could be accomplished in Echternach at any time. Radio communications to the rear were sometimes in, sometimes out, but nobody ordered withdrawal, nor did Dupuis or Macdiarmid ask authority to withdraw.

It was during the afternoon of December 19, not long after the rescue of the First Platoon, that the German commander, General Sensfuss, turned his personal attention to erasing the American position in Echternach. In mid-afternoon, men of his Fusilier Battalion slipped into buildings facing those held by Company E and opened fire with burp guns, machine guns, and *Panzerfausts*. From a position alongside a building not three hundred yards away, an assault gun opened a systematic and destructive fire. If that kind of direct shelling continued, Company E would be unable to hold out much longer.

Just before dusk, Captain Dupuis told one of Company E's platoon leaders, 1st Lt. Richard L. Cook, to take a volunteer and one of the company's jeeps from the garage, make a dash up the hill to Lauterborn, and "for God's sake get the tanks." Accompanied by Staff Sgt. Michael J. Siscock, Lieutenant Cook left just before dark, pulling swiftly out of the garage, swinging into the Rue de Luxembourg on two wheels, and racing up the road toward Lauterborn. The German assault gun fired, but the shot was wild.

At Lauterborn, Cook encountered frustration. The commander of the armored task force, Colonel Riley, refused to venture his tanks in the streets of the town after dark, particularly under the foggy conditions prevailing that night, and the commander of CCA, General Piburn, upheld him. They understood, in any case, that Company E was to withdraw during the night to Lauterborn, and throughout the night the armored troops waited in vain for the infantrymen to appear.

Early that same evening, December 19, Company E did receive an order by radio to withdraw during the night, but unknown to Task Force Riley, Captain Dupuis had replied that it would be impossible to conform. In the darkness, he said, platoon leaders would be unable to make sure that every man received the order to pull back, and neither he nor Lieutenant Macdiarmid wanted to risk leaving somebody behind. They would have to wait for daylight.

When daylight came on December 20, nobody outside Echternach knew what was going on with Company E, and what was more, hardly anybody appeared to give a damn. Task Force Riley was getting ready to withdraw in conformity with the plan for the 10th Armored Division's CCA to constitute a reserve behind a new defensive line, and shortly before noon the bulk of the task force began to move. At the request of the commander of the 12th Infantry, Colonel Chance, a platoon each of medium tanks and armored infantry stayed behind to join the 12th Infantry's Company G in an effort to break into Echternach and rescue Company E; but there was no getting through. As darkness came, everybody fell back through Lauterborn all the way to the new defensive line.

For the men of Company E, it made no difference at that point in any case. Beginning at two o'clock that afternoon, four German assault guns opened a devastating fire on the buildings held by those men and by the machine gunners and mortarmen of Company H, and there was nothing they could do to stop the deadly fire. General Sensfuss himself led his fusiliers in the attack and was slightly wounded.

Among the defenders, Sgts. Daniel B. Stresow and John Redovian in the Hôtel de Luxembourg ran back and forth between floors in an effort to avoid the German shells. At long last, having ripped great holes in the front of the hotel, the German gunners turned their fire on the garage next door. From an upper story window, Stresow and Redovian could see the entrance to the garage and German shells bursting around it. They "heard groaning and an officer appeared, yelling to cease fire."

"Gee," said Stresow to Redovian, "the company commander is surrendering the company." Then the two sergeants "saw the kitchen crew and a few others line up outside with their hands in the air." Stresow had "an awful feeling" deep inside his stomach.

Twenty men of Company H and 110 of Company E surrendered, victims of a debacle that never should have happened. Captain Dupuis and Lieutenant Macdiarmid never asked if there had been a change in General Barton's order for no retrograde movement, which they clearly should have done before their situation grew critical. Even in the absence of such a request, commanders at battalion and regiment with broader knowledge of the overall situation should have ordered Company E out. By the time that finally happened, after dark on the fourth day, December 19, the reluctance of Task Force Riley to employ its tanks in Echternach in the dark left Company E to the mercy of the enemy.

The timidity of Task Force Riley reflected a similar timidity in all the 10th Armored Division's CCA and also in the 9th Armored Division's CCA. Neither combat command made any determined effort to exploit its marked superiority in armor, mobility, and firepower. With rare exceptions, the two combat commands had encountered nothing more formidable than *Volksgrenadiers* sometimes armed with *Panzerfausts*, and in almost every case they had recoiled in a kind of paranoid dread of what else might be out there.

Not until December 19 was anything else out there with the 212th Volksgrenadier Division, and then it was only four assault guns; and not until the next day was anything else out there with the 276th Volksgrenadier Division except three assault guns. Crews of American Shermans had legitimate concerns when they faced the superior armor of the Panther and even more so when they faced the superior armor and armament of the Tiger—but seven 75mm. assault guns against 102 Shermans?

In three days of fighting, the 9th Armored Division's CCA lost one light and six medium tanks—all to *Panzerfausts*—and in two days of fighting, the 10th Armored Division's CCA lost not a single tank. Did those statistics reflect clever deployment and maneuver or reluctance to close with the enemy? The crews of the Shermans of those two combat commands treated their tanks with the deference and protectiveness that an old-time cavalryman might have lavished on his horse.

Rightly or wrongly, foot soldiers, who seldom had anything between them and their enemy except the muzzles of their rifles, sometimes had a hard time understanding the concerns of men who rode behind several inches of armor plate.

CHAPTER EIGHTEEN

In Defense of the Twin Villages

At the designated rendezvous point for the German paratroopers near the Belle Croix road junction atop the Hautes Fagnes, Colonel von der Heydte eventually gathered not quite three hundred of his men, less than a fourth of those who jumped before daylight on December 17. The men had only their individual arms and the ammunition they brought with them, for the supply panniers were as widely scattered as the parachutists themselves. Although somebody found von der Heydte's radio, the drop had smashed it, which left no way to communicate with the Sixth Panzer Army.

When von der Heydte and his men saw the convoys carrying troops of the 1st Infantry and 7th Armored Divisions southward across the Hautes Fagnes, they dared not attack nor even harass them, so few were their numbers. Before daylight on the 18th, while a group of paratroopers was resting in the ditches near a crossroads, an American convoy was upon them before they had a chance to hide. As soldiers on the trucks waved sleepily—the German paratrooper's helmet resembled that of the American soldier—the Germans with immense relief waved back.

By noon on the 18th, von der Heydte had established a kind of base camp deep within a forest, from which small patrols moved to attack single American vehicles and to scrounge for food. Concerned about two men who had each broken an arm in the parachute jump, von der Heydte detailed six American prisoners to escort the men to the main highway and arrange to get them to a hospital. He gave the prisoners a note addressed to the commander of the 101st Airborne Division, General Taylor, against whom von der Heydte had fought in Normandy, asking that he "please treat my jump casualties as well as my regiment has treated casualties of your division."

By nightfall of December 20, von der Heydte was convinced that nobody was going to break through to him. (Because of American bombing, the big *Jägdtigers* with their 128mm. guns that were supposed to relieve von der Heydte never got past a railhead in the northern reaches of the Eifel.) Although von der Heydte had no way of knowing how the offensive was going, it seemed clear from the failure of the Sixth Panzer Army to reach the Hautes Fagnes and from a continuing stream of American convoys moving south that the battle hardly could be going as planned. On the assumption that the Germans had captured Monschau, von der Heydte released thirty other American prisoners and headed there with his men.

Reaching a creek not far from the Eupen-Monschau highway, the paratroopers came upon an American outpost line designed to keep them cooped up in the forest. After a brief skirmish, the Germans withdrew; but when patrols could find no way out of the forest past the American blocks, some of them supported by tanks, von der Heydte despaired of getting through with his entire force moving together. He himself was growing desperate: His splinted arm was hurting, he feared his feet were frostbitten, and he had eaten not a morsel since before the jump early on the 17th. There would be a better chance of getting through, he decided, if the men broke into groups of three. In the end, only about one-third— a hundred men—succeeded in reaching German lines.

Traveling with his executive officer and his orderly, von der Heydte himself came upon a farmhouse, where he stopped to rest and learned that the Americans still held Monschau. Convinced that his condition was delaying his companions, he insisted that they go on without him.

That night, the 21st, von der Heydte finally reached Monschau. He had to knock at the doors of several houses before someone answered. When the owner let him in, von der Heydte asked for pen and paper, wrote a note in English, and asked the man's fourteen-year-old son to take it to the Americans. He was turning himself in.

On maps of Belgium, no Elsenborn Ridge appears. The commanders and staffs of the American units that fought against the northern prong of the German offensive arrived at that name to designate a high ridgeline on the German side of the town of Elsenborn and nearby Camp Elsenborn. It is shaped like a boomerang, with the highest point, at just over two thousand feet between Elsenborn and the village of Wirtzfeld, forming the southern prong of the boomerang and its slopes dropping off sharply to a reservoir, the Lac de Bütgenbach. To the northeast of the highest point, two other crests form the other prong of the boomerang. The ridge constitutes the watershed for the area, and while broad and sprawling rather than sharply defined, it is clearly the dominant high ground for miles around.

Shortly before seven o'clock on the morning of December 17, as Walter Robertson learned that German tanks were headed for Büllingen, it began to look as if the commander of the First Army, General Hodges, had waited too long to approve calling off the 2d Division's attack and withdrawing the division to the Elsenborn Ridge. As headquarters troops scurried to form a last-ditch defense of the division's forward headquarters in Wirtzfeld, Robertson finally received the word he had been so anxiously awaiting: Call off the attack and withdraw.

Yet with German tanks in Büllingen, the only way left for his troops and most of those of the 99th Division to get out was through Wirtzfeld over the back road to Elsenborn that his engineers had been working hard to make passable. Lose Wirtzfeld and that escape hatch would be closed. So too it would be barred if the Germans took the twin villages of Krinkelt-Rocherath just to the east of Wirtzfeld. If the 2d and 99th Divisions were to survive, they had to keep the Germans out of the twin villages and Wirtzfeld long enough for everybody to funnel through. Robertson saw the job of directing that fight to be his.

The most serious threat at that point appeared to be from the German tanks in Büllingen, which might drive north on Wirtzfeld or northeast on Krinkelt. Aside from ordering a last-ditch defense of Wirtzfeld, Robertson directed the only reserve still at his immediate disposal, a battalion of the 23d Infantry, to drop off a company at the southern edge of Krinkelt and the rest of the battalion to occupy high ground between Wirtzfeld and Büllingen.

There were two other routes by which the Germans might get into the twin villages: one led from the crossroads at Losheimergraben northwest through Mürringen, the other over the two trails through the forest from the International Highway due east of the twin villages. Because Robertson had lost communications with headquarters of the 99th Division, he had no way of knowing how well the troops of that division were blocking those approaches; but he could take some comfort in the knowledge that a battalion of his own 23d Infantry, attached to the 99th Division, was in a back-up position along each of the approaches.

Robertson could only hope that the defenses along the two approaches would hold long enough for him to get at least some of his battalions back from Wahlerscheid to hold Krinkelt-Rocherath and Wirtzfeld. Then when everybody had reached the twin villages, he would pull all his men back to the Elsenborn Ridge.

The withdrawal would be facilitated by the fact that Robertson had anticipated it and the night before had alerted the commanders of the six battalions at Wahlerscheid to plan for it. Under Robertson's plan, the 38th Infantry was to defend the twin villages, while the 9th Infantry, which had incurred the greater losses at Wahlerscheid, joined the battalion of the 23d Infantry that was defending Wirtzfeld. Once those defenders were in place, the 99th Division's 395th Infantry, which with two of its battalions and an attached battalion of the 393d Infantry had attacked in support of the 2d Division at Wahlerscheid, was also to pull back and cover the north flank of the defenders of the twin villages. Rob-

DEFENSE OF THE TWIN VILLAGES
DEC 17

Scale:
0 1 2 3 4
MILES

N

Wahlerscheid

WEST

Olef Creek

WALL

Jans Bach

Camp Elsenborn

Elsenborn

ELSENBORN RIDGE

ROCHERATHER
BARACKEN

1

2

277TH
VG

12TH SS
PZ DIV

LAC DE
BÜTGENBACH

Rocherath

Krinkelt

Wirtzfeld

Bütgenbach

Büllingen

Dom. Bütgenbach

Mürringen

International Highway

12TH
VG
DIV

PEIPER

Air
Strips

Hünningen

B-254 E

KG

Honsfeld

Buchholz
Sta.

Losheimergraben

Losheim

1 - 3D BN, 23D INF
2 - McKINLEY'S BN

Lanzerath

ertson personally went to the command post of the regiment to inform the commander, Col. Alexander J. Mackenzie, and to tell him that on his own authority he was attaching Mackenzie's regiment to the 2d Division.

The first unit to withdraw was to be the 38th Infantry's reserve battalion, not yet committed, which was to defend the southern periphery of Krinkelt, at that point seemingly under the gravest threat. Two of the division's artillery battalions that were forward along the Wahlerscheid road were to follow, then the three battalions of the 9th Infantry and, finally, the two remaining battalions of the 38th Infantry. Three companies of mediums of the attached 741st Tank Battalion and two companies of self-propelled guns of the 644th Tank Destroyer Battalion were to find places in the withdrawing column. (The 741st's light tanks and the third company of tank destroyers were committed elsewhere.)

Having issued those instructions, Robertson left his forward command post and moved up the road leading to Wahlerscheid. Through much of the rest of the critical day to come he would be driving up and down that road, watching the men of his division execute one of the most difficult of all military maneuvers: withdrawal in broad daylight in close contact with the enemy and in the face of violent enemy attacks from another direction. The extinction or survival of the 2d Division and much of the 99th Division hinged in large measure on Robertson's actions along that road.

At the crossroads settlement of Losheimergraben, where Colonel Osterhold's 48th Regiment of the 12th Volksgrenadier Division was trying to open a path for the 12th SS Panzer Division, Osterhold had trouble again on the second day of the offensive getting fire support for his *Volksgrenadiers*. When an assault gun tried to move forward to help, an antitank gun concealed among the houses immobilized it, and not until midday did Osterhold finally establish radio contact with his supporting artillery. Only then could the *Volksgrenadiers* get up close to the first house.

In English, Osterhold called out for the Americans in the house to surrender, but he received no answer. "I want to talk with your commander," Osterhold yelled. "I warn you not to fire at me. May I come out?" When an American voice answered, telling him to advance, Osterhold and several of his men walked forward. He found thirty men and a lieutenant in the cellar, many of the men holding hand grenades from which they had already pulled the safety pins. They stood not a chance, Osterhold told the young officer; better they should give up. When the lieutenant assented, the Germans helped find the safety pins for the grenades.

The final conquest of the crossroads at Losheimergraben was strongly reinforced by another regiment, which exploited the American decision the night before to pull half the rifle strength from Buchholz Station to prepare a back-up position behind Losheimergraben. Early on the 17th, the men of that regiment passed quickly through the station and continued north into the rear of the defenders of Losheimergraben. Since that move jeopardized all three battalions of the 394th Infantry, the commander, Colonel Riley, in early afternoon ordered everybody to fall back on the prepared positions at Hünningen and Mürringen, where the attached battalion of the 2d Division's 23d Infantry was already in position at Hünningen.

The 394th Infantry had incurred heavy losses at Buchholz Station and at Losheimergraben, and the maneuver to pull back was not to prove easy. Yet what really mattered at the moment was that no Germans had gotten past Losheimergraben in time to interfere with the 2d Division's withdrawal from Wahlerscheid.

To twenty-two-year-old 1st Lt. Long Haley Goffigon, who grew up on a truck farm on Virginia's pastoral eastern shore and got his military training in ROTC at Virginia Polytechnic Institute, it seemed there was an occupational hazard in commanding a company's First Platoon. When it came to making assignments, it was easiest for the company commander to say: First, Second, Third, which meant that the First Platoon as often as not got more than its share of hairy tasks. That was what happened just before nightfall on December 16, when Goffigon's First Platoon of Company I and the rest of the 23d Infantry's 3d Battalion arrived at a road junction on the fringe of a dense fir forest due east of the twin villages of Krinkelt-Rocherath. As everybody tumbled from the trucks, sure enough, the company commander called out: First, Second, Third.

As it turned out, Goffigon and his First Platoon assumed a defensive position astride a road leading east through the forest. At first glance, it appeared to have its rewards, for there Goffigon found foxholes already dug, some with overhead cover—a back-up position prepared earlier by some supporting unit of the 99th Division. Although there were not enough holes for the entire platoon and the crews of two heavy machine guns that arrived later, the rest of Company I, extending the line in the woods to Goffigon's right, had no holes at all, and digging them in snow-covered frozen earth with small individual entrenching tools was difficult.

On the other hand, as Goffigon soon discerned, his position had major drawbacks. He was on the extreme left flank of the 3d Battalion with nobody on his left to prevent the Germans from pressing through the woods and getting in behind him. He was also astride the only road through that part of the forest, a road along which to the east, his company commander told him, a battalion of the 99th Division's 393d Infantry was fighting for its existence. If the Germans broke through that battalion and continued through the forest, that road would be the main axis of advance, and only he, the thirty-five men of his platoon, and his attached machine gunners stood directly in the way.

When Goffigon and Company I first arrived, defense was not the issue. The battalion commander, Lt. Col. Paul V. Tuttle, Jr., was under orders to attack to help the 3d Battalion, 393d Infantry, reestablish its positions along the International Highway; but during the night that changed. Since the commander of the embattled battalion, Colonel Allen, thought he could do that on his own, Tuttle's battalion was to form a back-up defensive position.

It was close to two thirty in the morning when that word came, so that nobody made any effort to readjust the battalion's positions to provide more strength along the road. The battalion was responsible in any case for another road that entered the right flank of its position, the road leading from the 393d Infantry's 1st Battalion. The Germans might come along either road or both. Thus Tuttle's battalion remained in a linear defense covering more than half a mile of thick forest with both flanks in the air.

Even aside from the poor position, the 3d Battalion, 23d Infantry, was ill prepared to defend for any length of time; for in keeping with orders, the battalion had left its former positions near St. Vith with only a basic load of ammunition, which meant just a few bandoleers per man. Since the battalion was attached to the 393d Infantry, supplying the battalion was that regiment's responsibility, but every appeal to that hardpressed regiment for more ammunition brought no result. During the night, the battalion's supply officer went to the rear to do the job himself, but before he could get back, *Kampfgruppe Peiper* cut the supply route at Büllingen.

The battalion was also notably weak in antitank defense. There were no antitank mines and only a few bazookas and rockets. As the battalion entered the woods, there were two 57mm. antitank guns from the 393d Infantry at what became Lieutenant Goffigon's position, but sometime during the night the crews of those guns hitched up and slipped away. The only hope Goffigon would have for stopping German tanks lay with two Shermans from the 741st Tank Battalion, commanded by 1st Lt. Victor L. Miller, which arrived just before daybreak on the 17th and took up positions in rear of Goffigon's platoon.

Deeper in the woods, early on December 17, the commander of the 393d Infantry's 3d Battalion, Colonel Allen, ordered his men and the company of the 394th Infantry that had joined the battalion late the day before to attack to regain the battalion's original positions. Hardly had that effort begun when the situation on the German side markedly changed. A second battalion of *SS-Panzergrenadiers* joined the fight and with it a platoon of what was eventually to be four companies of the 12th SS Panzer Division's tanks.

In the dense forest, bazooka teams were able to keep the tanks at some distance, but Allen's position soon became critical nevertheless. Almost everybody was running out of ammunition, and the wounded were piling up in the aid station with no way to evacuate them. Talking by radio with the commander of the 393d Infantry, Colonel Scott, Allen asked authority to withdraw, to which Scott—with General Lauer's approval—in mid-morning agreed. The battalion was to pull back through the 23d Infantry's 3d Battalion, reorganize behind those positions, and return to the line on the left of the attached battalion. At the same time, Scott ordered his 1st Battalion to withdraw down the other woods trail and extend the other flank of the 23d Infantry's 3d Battalion.

As Allen's men prepared to withdraw, they found places on vehicles for all but fifteen of the more seriously wounded. The battalion surgeon, Capt. Frederick J. McIntyre, and a few of his aid men volunteered to stay behind with those men.

Around eleven o'clock, while one company acted as a rear guard, the 393d's 3d Battalion began pulling out, machine guns on jeeps blazing away into the forest on either side of the road through the woods. As the men passed through Lieutenant Goffigon's platoon, Goffigon and his men begged them for their ammunition, and many donated what they had left. Two men dropped out of the bedraggled column to fight with Goffigon's platoon.

To everybody in the 23d Infantry's 3d Battalion, it was obvious that the Germans would be close behind the withdrawing column. How long the battalion could hold; how long its ammunition would last; and how well two Shermans might deal with accompanying German tanks—on all those factors might well depend the fate of those other men of the 2d Division who were beginning to withdraw through the forest from Wahlerscheid to the twin villages and Wirtzfeld. Indeed, the fate of everybody in the 2d and 99th Divisions who had yet to gain the twin villages or Wirtzfeld might well depend upon how long the 23d Infantry's 3d Battalion could hold—and when it got right down to it, upon how long Lieutenant Goffigon and the men of the First Platoon, Company I, could hang on.

For troops in close contact with the enemy in daylight, there could be no quick response to the word that they were to pull back, abandoning the positions they had won over four days at high cost. (They were later to call Wahlerscheid "Heartbreak Crossroads.") Withdrawal was easy enough for the 38th Infantry's uncommitted reserve battalion, which headed down the forest road to the twin villages around nine o'clock on the 17th and was soon digging in on the southern and southeastern fringes of Krinkelt. Not until over two hours later, at 11:20 A.M., was the first of the committed battalions of the 9th Infantry able to start back; and not until 1 P.M. would the last of the 9th Infantry's three battalions pull out.

That was the 1st Battalion under Lt. Col. William D. McKinley, which had made the first attack at Wahlerscheid. Around 3 P.M. the battalion finished reorganizing in the woods and began the long foot march down the road toward the twin villages. The men were cold, wet, exhausted from the four days in the line, their ranks reduced by shot, shell, and winter weather to four hundred officers and men, little more than the normal strength of two rifle companies.

As the men began to march, neither McKinley nor the commanders of the two battalions of the 38th Infantry that still had to begin their withdrawal were aware of what was happening in the woods east of Krinkelt-Rocherath, not far from the road into the twin villages that everybody had to use. Neither was General Robertson, who was still moving up and down the forest road, here lending a word of encouragement, there resolving a dispute over priority on the road; for when the 23d Infantry's 3d Battalion had become attached to the 99th Division's 393d Infantry, the battalion had passed out of the 2d Division's communications net.

Hardly had the last men from the 393d Infantry passed through the 23d Infantry's 3d Battalion when Lieutenant Goffigon spotted troops forming up in a wooded draw down the hill from his positions. For a short time, there was some doubt whether they were yet more withdrawing Americans or Germans; but as they headed up the road, unaware that the Americans stood in their way, Goffigon could make out their duck-billed caps and their *feldgrau* greatcoats. Goffigon, his men, and the attached machine gunners of Company M greeted them with a hail of fire. Company M's 81mm. mortars and Company I's little 60mm. mortars also fired, and Goffigon's company commander, Capt. Charles B. Mac-Donald, called for artillery fire. The result was depressing: only three rounds. As the afternoon wore on, that proved to be the only response to every request for fire, for the supporting battalion of the 99th Division's artillery was critically short of ammunition.

Those rounds and the fire from the rifles, mortars, and machine guns nevertheless drove the Germans back, but as they regrouped in the draw, Goffigon spotted something potentially more disturbing. Where the road crossed the forward slope of a ridge beyond the draw, he saw a cluster of tanks. One of the three-round salvos from the artillery dispersed them, but as the German foot troops began another assault, the presence of the tanks weighed heavily on Goffigon's mind. Particularly when he discovered that the two Shermans had withdrawn a considerable distance down the road behind his position, which the tank commander, Lieutenant Miller, said was to achieve better firing positions.

As the Germans returned to the attack, the assault lapped over against the rest of Company I and the left wing of Company K. To the defenders, the assaulting Germans seemed to be oblivious of casualties, fanatically so, as well they may have been, for they constituted two battalions of *SS-Panzergrenadiers* of the 12th SS Panzer Division, their ranks filled mainly with seventeen- and eighteen-year-old volunteers from the Hitler Youth.

The second assault nevertheless faltered, and again the Germans fell back to reorganize in the draw. Then once again came the shrill commands, the blowing of whistles, and a third assault.

Except for Goffigon's platoon, the defenders had little protection other than the trunks of the big trees. They nevertheless took few casualties, for no mortar or artillery fire accompanied the assaults; but squad and platoon commanders were soon reporting almost desperately that they were running out of ammunition.

By that time the assault had spilled over against the battalion's third unit, Company L, and MacDonald and the other company commanders were pleading with their battalion headquarters for more ammunition. They got only a reply that became maddening in repetition: "We're doing all we can!" Without more ammunition, MacDonald told the battalion's operations officer, Company I would be unable to hold much longer. The orders, the reply came back, were to hold at all costs.

The dwindling supply of ammunition soon became subordinate to another threat: German tanks. There were five of them, big Panthers. From his foxhole close alongside the road, Lieutenant Goffigon could see them waddling forward, their treads clanking noisily on the frozen surface of the road, infantry close behind them. Artillery fire dispersed the infantry, but the tanks kept coming.

Captain MacDonald sent a runner to tell the two Shermans to move forward, but as the runner discovered, Lieutenant Miller's tanks had fallen even farther back, all the way to the road junction at the edge of the forest. Although MacDonald appealed to his battalion commander, Colonel Tuttle, to order the tanks to return, Tuttle said no. The Shermans stood no chance against Panthers in a frontal engagement, and there was no place to maneuver off the road within the forest.

To MacDonald, that signaled the end. How could men in foxholes with nothing but their rifles stand up to tanks?

"For God's sake, Captain," Goffigon yelled over his sound-powered telephone, "get those tanks down here. These bastards are sitting seventy-five yards away and pumping shells into our foxholes like we were sitting ducks!"

Over the SCR-300 to battalion, MacDonald told Colonel Tuttle that without the two Shermans, he would be unable to hold. Tuttle said again that the orders were to hold at all costs, and if he ordered the Shermans forward, he was convinced the tank commanders would defy him.

MacDonald's light machine gunners, their ammunition exhausted, were filing rearward past the slit trenches of the company's command post. As MacDonald tried to stop them, Goffigon reported over the telephone that his position was collapsing. When he and his platoon runner, Pfc. John Welch, climbed from their hole, they realized for the first time that except for dead men in some of the holes, they were the only ones left of the First Platoon. In a hail of machine-gun fire from the German tanks, Goffigon and Welch took off through the woods alongside the road.

At that point MacDonald saw no chance for his company other than to try to form a new line along a firebreak a few yards to the rear of his command post. Unable to contact Goffigon, he told the other platoon leaders to fall back to the firebreak. There the men of the company headquarters and a machine gunner held briefly; but once the rifle platoons began withdrawing, they went to pieces under the German fire.

Company I's collapse left Company K's left flank exposed, and before the company commander, 1st Lt. Lee Smith, could get word to his left platoon to withdraw, the Germans overran one of the squads. As the riflemen scrambled through the woods, the German tanks passed undisturbed along the road until they neared the road junction at the edge of the forest. There the two Shermans of the 741st Tank Battalion gave battle. They knocked out two Panthers but in turn succumbed to return fire. Most of the crewmen died in the fight, including Lieutenant Miller.

As Company L also fell back, an American line in front of the twin villages ceased to exist. Although Company I had parried the *SS-Panzergrenadiers* for close to three hours, the German tanks decided the issue in less than thirty minutes. As the opposing tanks fought their duel at the edge of the forest, the time was 4 P.M., an early winter dusk was gathering, and along the road from Wahlerscheid to the twin villages, three of the 2d Division's withdrawing battalions had yet to pass.

Close to 4 P.M., Walter Robertson happened to stop by the command post of Colonel Mackenzie's 395th Infantry in the woods off the Wahlerscheid road. There he learned for the first time that Colonel Allen's battalion of the 393d Infantry had withdrawn from the forest and that "the Germans had broken through" his 3d Battalion, 23d Infantry.

With jeep and driver, Robertson hurried back to the Wahlerscheid road and at a crossroads a short distance north of Rocherath (the Rocherather Baracken) overtook the last company of the 9th Infantry's 3d Battalion, Company K, which had fallen behind during its battalion's withdrawal. Jumping from his jeep, Robertson found the company commander, Capt. Jack J. Garvey. Swiftly he ordered Garvey to move his company into a defensive position astride a complex of roads and farm trails near an isolated farmhouse, just over halfway between the woodsline to the east and Rocherath. Robertson also commandeered a platoon of heavy machine guns and the battalion's Ammunition and Pioneer Platoon and sent them with Company K.

Returning to his jeep, Robertson headed back up the road toward Wahlerscheid until he came upon the front of the column of the depleted 1st Battalion, 9th Infantry, Colonel McKinley's battalion. Appropriating ten 6 × 6 trucks belonging to the 395th Infantry, Robertson told McKinley to load as many men as possible onto them while the rest followed on foot, whereupon Robertson in his jeep led the way to the Rocherather Baracken, then turned southeast toward the complex of roads and trails and the farmhouse where he had sent Company K. McKinley was to hold the road network, said Robertson, "until ordered otherwise."

William Dawes McKinley, twenty-eight years of age, a grand-nephew of President William McKinley, grew up on U.S. Army posts and never considered any career other than that of an army officer. After graduation from West Point, he had long service with the 2d Division's 9th Infantry; and as the regimental executive officer in Normandy, he was personally leading a platoon in an attack when he took two machine-gun bullets in the stomach. He returned to the regiment in September. Friendly, cheerful, seemingly fearless under fire, McKinley was utterly devoted to his troops.

In fading light amid patches of unmelted snow, the men of McKinley's 1st Battalion, 9th Infantry, began wearily to dig in, bitter after four days and nights of hard fighting to be thrown back into the line to make up for some unit that had failed to do its job against (they believed) a local counterattack. McKinley put two of his depleted companies forward, tied in with Company K at the farmhouse, and held his third, which was down to just over fifty men, in reserve on what he thought was an exposed north flank. (Colonel Allen's battalion of the 393d Infantry was actually in position there but some distance away.)

Coming upon the commander of a detachment of three self-propelled guns of the 644th Tank Destroyer Battalion at the Rocherather Baracken, McKinley got from him a number of antitank mines, which McKinley's men stockpiled for use once they could be sure all American tanks and other vehicles had made their way out of the woods to the east. The commander of the tank destroyers also provided fifteen bazookas and ample rockets to go with them.

By 6 P.M. in murky darkness, "absolutely black," McKinley's battalion and Company K (totaling perhaps as many as six hundred men) had prepared a defensive position of sorts. It consisted mainly of hastily dug foxholes along thin low hedges marking the perimeters of fields, but since an artillery battalion had earlier occupied the area, there were a few log-covered dugouts, one of which McKinley used as a command post. For a time, "communication with the world outside of the battalion was non-existent." It was around six thirty when the artillery liaison officer, 1st Lt. John C. Granville, finally got his SCR-610 to work and established contact with the 9th Infantry's usual artillery support, the 15th Field Artillery Battalion.

Only minutes after Granville established that contact, Company B reported three tanks approaching. On the possibility that they might be American tanks escaping from the forest, McKinley told Company B to hold its fire; and by the time the men discovered that the tanks were German, to have revealed their positions by opening fire would have been suicidal. The tanks passed through the line and turned toward Rocherath along a road that ran behind the foxholes of Company A and in front of the farmhouse occupied by Company K's command group.

Hearing tanks approaching, two men from Company A, Sgt. William Floyd and Pfc. Herbert P. Hunt, left their foxholes to make sure they were American. The two men were standing alongside the road as the tanks and accompanying infantry neared. To Hunt, what followed was incredible: The German infantrymen (they were *SS-Panzergrenadiers*) passed by, some laughing and joking, scarcely looking in his and Floyd's direction. Then came the tanks, "splashing Billy and me with mud and slush. One of the tank commanders, standing in the open hatch of his tank, gave us the vulgar middle finger gesture as he passed."

As Hunt and Floyd hurried back to their company commander to ask for artillery fire, the tanks pulled off the road and cut their engines. Since the company's radio had failed, the two, accompanied by their platoon sergeant, Tech. Sgt. Charles Reamer, headed for headquarters of the battalion's weapons company, Company D, to use that company's radio; but as they were passing by, machine guns on the tanks fired. The first burst killed Reamer and Floyd. Hunt escaped and made his way to Company D's command post. Shells from the company's 81mm. mortars and artillery were soon exploding all about the tanks, and one went up in flames.

By the light of the burning tank, the men of Company A opened fire on the foot troops, but that fire revealed to the Germans for the first time that they were behind an American line. The two surviving tanks turned against Company A's foxholes, methodically showering them with machine-gun fire and grinding them with their heavy treads. To Hunt, it looked like the end of his company, but in the darkness the tanks failed to find many of the positions.

Aware at that point that anything that came down the road would be German, men of Company B hastily laid mines on three trails leading into their position. Hardly had they finished when four tanks accompanied by *SS-Panzergrenadiers* approached. The mines immobilized two of them, and as the other two turned off the road, bazooka teams stalked them and knocked them out. Their tanks eliminated, the *SS-Panzergrenadiers* went to ground.

Half an hour later, more tanks with *SS-Panzergrenadiers* approached in a column that looked in the darkness as if it stretched all the way back to the forest. Lieutenant Granville called for artillery fire close to Company B's foxholes, then called for the gunners to walk it back to the forest. As the German tanks dispersed, the men could hear the screams of German wounded.

At about the same time, seven German tanks passed along a road just outside Company A's positions. Artillery fire knocked out four of them, but three continued in the direction of Rocherath.

Although the Germans were taking heavy losses, that failed to stop them. The commanders of all three American companies were soon aware that individual German tanks were slipping past foxholes where the defenders were dead or wounded or had no way of coping with tanks. Bazooka teams from all three companies went in search of them. The commander of Company B, 1st Lt. John Melesnich, himself accounted for one tank with a bazooka; a man from Company K, Pfc. William A. Soderman, got three before machine-gun fire wounded him severely; and a machine-gun section leader from Company D, Sgt. Charles Roberts, and a squad leader from Company B, Sgt. Otis Bone, took a can of gasoline from an abandoned American half-track, poured the gasoline on the rear deck of an immobilized German tank, and set it on fire with a thermite grenade.

Not quite an hour went by before the Germans struck in strength again with three columns of tanks and infantry coming up all three trails leading from the forest. Lieutenant Granville screamed into his radio for fire on all three routes. "If you don't get it out right now," he shouted, "it'll be too goddamn late." Receiving no acknowledgment of his message, Granville "reached out for God to take him by the hand." Three minutes later the artillery responded with a deep-throated rumble. Nobody could survive such a shelling as that.

As Granville was later to learn, so vital did General Robertson consider Colonel McKinley's position that he afforded the battalion priority on all artillery under his control not engaged in some other essential mission. That included all four of the 2d Division's battalions and three corps battalions of 155mm. howitzers.

When the Germans fell back around midnight, a silence—"almost frightening"—descended over the American positions. In the hiatus, Colonel McKinley sent a message to the 38th Infantry, to which his battalion was attached: "We have been strenuously engaged, but everything is under control at present."

Even as General Robertson turned McKinley's battalion to the cluster of roads northeast of Rocherath, two battalions of the 38th Infantry were still marching down the forest road from Wahlerscheid, so that the defense of the twin villages had not fully formed. The 38th Infantry's reserve battalion, the 3d, was on the southern and southeastern fringes of Krinkelt; the regiment's Antitank Company had placed its nine 57mm. antitank guns at various points along the fringes of the villages; and the regiment's Service Company fighting as infantry held on the northeastern edge of Rocherath, where two of the roads leading from McKinley's position joined before entering the village. The regimental commander, Col. Francis H. Boos, established his command post in Rocherath at an X-shaped crossroads near the center of the village.

By that time all supporting units of the 99th Division had left the twin villages, but stragglers continued to pour in, including many men of the 23d Infantry's 3d Battalion, knocked from the woods to the east. Those men in most cases either attached themselves to units of the 38th Infantry or in small groups holed up in houses without knowledge of who else was near.

One of the units of that battalion, Company L, made it out of the woods almost intact except for one platoon caught by German shelling. The company commander, 1st Lt. Walter E. Eisler, Jr., still had 120 officers and men; and as he entered Krinkelt, he came upon the seemingly ubiquitous division commander, General Robertson, who attached the company to the 38th Infantry. Eisler and his men extended the north flank of the regiment's 3d Battalion along the eastern edge of Krinkelt. To their delight they found a house in their sector containing a ration of liquor intended for the officers of the 393d Infantry.

On the way to the twin villages, the 38th Infantry's 1st Battalion ran into a thunderous barrage from German artillery and *Nebelwerfers* at the crossroads north of Rocherath, the Rocherather Baracken. One rifle company had already passed, but the other two lost twenty-two men to the shelling, cutting sharply into ranks already depleted at Wahlerscheid. The concussion from one shell knocked the battalion commander, Lt. Col. Frank. T. Mildren, to the ground, but he arose unhurt. He hurried into Rocherath to put his lead company into position, but it was some time before the other two could reorganize and continue into the village.

Last to arrive from Wahlerscheid, the 38th Infantry's 2d Battalion also took some casualties from shelling at the Rocherather Baracken. The commander, Lt. Col. Jack K. Norris, left Company F to defend the crossroads; put Company E between the crossroads and Service Company's position at the road junction on the northeastern edge of Rocherath; and at the order of his regimental commander, sent Company G to defend the regimental command post.

The twin villages and the countryside between them and the forest were at that point "a scene of wild confusion." Artillery fire from both sides was pummeling the ground; German machine guns were firing at long range from the edge of the forest, their bursts liberally laced with tracer bullets that created arcs of what looked like dotted lines of neon; and a radar set abandoned by an antiaircraft unit near the edge of the woods was smoldering, a fiery concave skeleton. Men in the twin villages could see the burning German tank inside Colonel McKinley's position. Houses in both villages were on fire. Flares flickered eerily, burned out, and fell to the ground. As one officer saw it, "the night was ablaze with more noise and flame" than he had "thought possible for men to create." Into that cauldron the men made their way, cold, tired, miserable, stumbling, cursing the night, the misty rain, the unknown, their fate.

Toward the twin villages churned the three German tanks that had slipped past Colonel McKinley's Company A. With them was the tank battalion commander, SS-Lt. Col. Helmüt Zeiner, and forty *SS-Panzergrenadiers*. They bumped into the men of Service Company at the road junction on the northeastern edge of Rocherath but in the face of heavy fire, sideslipped around Service Company's flank into Rocherath.

By that time, the two companies of Colonel Mildren's 1st Battalion, hit by the shelling at the Rocherather Baracken, had worked their way into Rocherath and then to Krinkelt. They fanned out to houses and thin hedgerows east of a church that in normal times served parishioners of both villages and roughly marked an otherwise indiscernible boundary between the two. Most of the men dug in or took up firing positions inside the houses, but the company commanders pushed a few men farther to the east as outposts to give the alarm should the Germans approach.

Among those men was Pfc. John T. Fisher. He and the other men of two under-strength squads occupied two farmhouses on either side of a road on the fringe of Krinkelt, whereupon the sergeants posted several men, including Fisher, in ditches at a juncture of trails not far from the houses to serve as listening posts close to a 57mm. antitank gun. The men had been there only a short time when they heard the noise of tanks "just creeping along." As the tanks drew nearer, somebody threw a hand grenade and "all hell broke loose." The Germans fired a flare, a first round from a tank's cannon knocked out the antitank gun, and Fisher and the others ran back to the farmhouses.

In one of the houses, Fisher found himself with most of the men of his squad. German troops were soon milling around the building, and one man suggested that he drop a grenade from a window and open fire with his BAR, whereupon everybody was to take off. He had dropped the grenade and was about to fire when a round from a German tank exploded inside the house. The blast wounded Pvt. Donald Foulke in both legs, and before anybody could escape, the Germans rushed in, seized the men, and at gunpoint forced them outside, six of them, including Fisher.

Were they the only ones who had been in the house? Assuming the Germans would provide help for the wounded Foulke, the others told them about him. One of the Germans entered the house, fired a burst from his burp gun, and came back out.

Terrified, one American dropped to his knees, pleading obsequiously with the Germans to spare him and proffering cigarettes. A German knocked him down with his rifle butt. As the man began to weep uncontrollably, the Germans escorted him and two others to the far side of the house. Several bursts from burp guns, a scream, then silence.

When the Germans returned, they ordered Fisher and the other two remaining Americans to line up against a wall of the farmhouse. Three of the Germans raised their rifles, another a burp gun. Just as they fired, Fisher and one of the others dropped precipitately to the ground while the third fell to his knees, pleading in agonized tones: "Lord, have mercy!" A burst of fire from the burp gun knocked him to the ground.

As all three men feigned death, the Germans went away. After waiting what seemed like hours but was only a matter of minutes, Fisher asked if the other two were alive. Both said yes, but both were severely wounded, and the man who had dropped to his knees soon died.

When Fisher dared raise his head to look around, the other man had slipped away. Waiting a few more minutes to make sure no Germans were around, Fisher himself ran off into the night.

Less than half an hour after that encounter, the three German tanks, with some *SS-Panzergrenadiers* riding on the decks and others on foot, struck the men of the 38th Infantry's 1st Battalion. Having had time to dig in, Company A held fast, but the men of the other two companies went to pieces under fire from machine guns and cannon. Company B's commander, Capt. William S. MacArtor, his command group, and many of his men simply disappeared into the night. (They were captured.) The survivors of Company C joined men of the Antitank Company holding houses near the regimental command post.

As the tanks continued, they gained one of two main streets running through the villages, a street with the church on one side and on the other, a few yards up the road, a house occupied by Colonel Mildren and the 1st Battalion's headquarters group. With the approach of the tanks, officers and men alike rushed to the windows and opened fire with any weapon at hand.

Seizing a machine gun that had no tripod, Pvt. Grover C. Farrell stepped into the street in the path of the first tank. Firing from the hip, he marched straight for the tank. Possibly in concern for the *SS-Panzergrenadiers* on the deck, the tank commander pulled his vehicle back.

Colonel Zeiner's three tanks and what amounted to a platoon of *SS-Panzergrenadiers* were giving an impression of a German attack out of all proportion to the numbers involved. That was partly because of the heavy drumbeat of German artillery fire that pounded the twin villages, setting buildings on fire, and partly because the German force had bounced off opposition when encountered: Service Company first, then the 38th Infantry's 1st Battalion. The turn of the 38th Infantry's Company K came next.

As the tanks pulled back from Colonel Mildren's command post, they bumped into the positions of Company K, where the men were under orders from their battalion commander, Lt. Col. Olinto M. Barsanti (who was concerned for withdrawing troops of the 99th Division), to fire only if men or vehicles could be positively identified as enemy. That was why the men let the tanks through. When they at last opened fire, two of the tanks turned on glaring spotlights, blinding the defenders, and wailing sirens added to the confusion.

As that first spate of fighting for the twin villages began, many of the tanks and self-propelled tank destroyers available for the defense were scattered. Four platoons of the 741st Tank Battalion's Shermans were either in Wirtzfeld or in the extreme southern end of Krinkelt looking toward likely German advance from Büllingen, and two tanks under Lieutenant Miller had already been knocked out at the edge of the woods east of the twin villages. The battalion commander, Lt. Col. Robert N.

Skaggs, held his remaining tanks near his command post, ready to move to threatened sectors. He sent a platoon when Service Company came under attack, but when the German tanks bounced off the position, no direct encounter occurred. When word came later that Company K was under attack, Skaggs sent three tanks to help. Zeiner's tanks knocked out all three. Close to the church, the three tanks burned through much of the rest of the night.

By midnight, Colonel Zeiner had come to the conclusion that he faced vastly superior American strength in the twin villages. He, his tanks, and the little band of young *SS-Panzergrenadiers* went into hiding and before daylight sneaked out of town with eighty prisoners they had captured. They had given the troops of the 2d Division, most of them coming into the villages after nightfall under heavy shelling, quite a scare. It was with considerable relief that Colonel Boos reported to General Robertson around 2 A.M. on the 18th: "Action quieting; believe we can hold."

During the afternoon of December 17, in conformity with the decision by the commander of the 394th Infantry, Colonel Riley, and General Lauer's approval, the regiment had begun to withdraw to the vicinity of Mürringen and Hünningen. For two of the battalions, the 1st and 3d, which had fought at Buchholz Station and at Losheimergraben, it was far from easy. They fell back under fire from *Volksgrenadiers* dogging their footsteps. It was well after dark before remnants of the 1st Battalion —roughly 250 men—were sufficiently organized to occupy previously prepared reserve positions on high ground outside Mürringen. The commander of the 3d Battalion, Major Moore, had even fewer men (all of Company K was missing) and both battalions lost many of their vehicles.

In the woods north of Losheimergraben, the 2d Battalion was less severely pressed but continued to be handicapped by the presence of a battalion commander reduced to "a quivering hulk." Leaving a small covering force in place, the companies withdrew in orderly columns, carrying their mortars and machine guns by hand as they trudged uphill and down along snow-covered trails through the thick forest. In keeping with the plan, the covering force fell back just before dark but when unable to find the battalion's assembly area, continued into Mürringen.

The main body of the battalion was having problems because the command group lost contact—and communications—with the companies. Chancing upon Company C of the adjacent 1st Battalion, 393d Infantry, which had decided with the coming of darkness to wait until daylight to continue the withdrawal, the command group over a failing SCR-300 regained radio contact with the companies and talked them to Company C's position. By that time, daylight on December 18 was fast approaching. Unable to contact the regimental headquarters by radio, the command group decided to push on after daylight to Mürringen in hope that the rest of the regiment would be found there.

It would prove to be a false hope.

Under heavy attack in the reserve positions at nearby Hünningen soon after nightfall on the 17th, the commander of the attached 1st Battalion, 23d Infantry, Lt. Col. John M. Hightower—a great hulk of a man—asked Colonel Riley for authority to withdraw. Hightower's battalion—and Riley's regiment to only a slightly lesser degree—was stuck out beyond any other American force in a salient with but a single road out, that through Krinkelt. Only support from a battalion of the 2d Division's artillery and a battalion of corps guns was enabling Hightower's men to hold. Riley's supporting artillery battalion of the 99th Division was out of ammunition.

Yet Riley said no. He had so little knowledge of the location of his own troops—including his 2d Battalion still somewhere out there in the woods—and thus so little control over them, that he dared not risk withdrawal, and to permit Hightower to pull back would bare his southern flank.

A short while later, around ten o'clock, Hightower received a message relayed through his artillery liaison officer's SCR-610 telling him that his battalion was no longer attached to the 394th Infantry but instead to the 2d Division's 9th Infantry in Wirtzfeld. An hour later, a message from the commander of the 9th Infantry, Col. Chester J. Hirschfelder, told him: "Pull back to new positions or you will be cut off."

By that time, Hightower's men were so closely engaged with the enemy that Hightower considered an attempt to withdraw might prove disastrous. By means of the artillery liaison officer's radio, he told Hirschfelder so, but another message quickly followed: "Withdraw immediately. Hirschfelder."

When Hightower informed Colonel Riley of that order, Riley was still reluctant to see the battalion depart. Yet when he queried his division headquarters, General Lauer verified Hightower's attachment to the 9th Infantry and told Riley that he, too, was authorized to withdraw if he considered his position to be untenable. Still knowing nothing of his 2d Battalion in the woods, Riley remained hesitant. In view of the critical shortage of ammunition and no artillery support, he nevertheless came to the conclusion that he had no real choice. The two commanders agreed to coordinate their withdrawals to begin two hours after midnight.

Having heard that a fight was raging in Krinkelt, Colonel Hightower thought at first that he would have to abandon his vehicles, but he was yet to give that order when an ambulance driver appeared. He had just come through Krinkelt, he said, and he could guide the vehicles out. As worked out with Riley, the ambulance driver was to lead the way, followed by vehicles of the 394th Infantry, then by Hightower's vehicles. Men of the 394th Infantry were to move on foot along the east side of the road to Krinkelt, thereby affording some protection for the vehicles.

Hightower elected to bypass Krinkelt with his foot column and move cross-country to Wirtzfeld.

As Hightower had anticipated, withdrawing from Hünningen proved to be difficult. Two companies managed to break contact with little problem, but for the third, Company B, which had borne the brunt of the fighting, it was different. Because the company's little walkie-talkie radios had ceased to function, the company commander, Capt. Kay B. Cowan, had to get word to his platoons by runner, and two sent by different routes to the First Platoon never made it. Nobody heard anything more from that platoon, and of 175 men who had entered the fight in Company B, only 47 made their way out. Of 65 men in attached antitank and heavy machine-gun platoons with the company, only 19 escaped.

The withdrawal of the bulk of what was left of the 394th Infantry and of Hightower's battalion of the 23d Infantry began soon after 2 A.M. on the 18th. It was a black night, and the Germans, alerted to withdrawal by the departure of Hightower's troops, pounded Mürringen and the road to Krinkelt with interdictory shelling. As the men began the dismal march, nobody was really sure who held Krinkelt or even Wirtzfeld.

In deciding to commit the 12th SS Panzer Division against the twin villages, the commander of the 1st SS Panzer Corps, General Priess, missed his chance for a quick run around the flank of the 2d and 99th Divisions through Büllingen and Bütgenbach. Throughout much of the fateful day of December 17, only small detachments of towed tank destroyers, light tanks, and stragglers barred that route, mainly at Dom. Bütgenbach, the manor house and outbuildings astride the highway roughly midway between Büllingen and Bütgenbach. But then American reinforcements had arrived.

The reinforcements were from the 1st Infantry Division's 26th Infantry, which at the order of the First Army's General Hodges late on the 16th, had started south from an assembly area near Eupen where the entire division was recuperating from the terrible fight in the Hürtgen Forest. Although the 26th Infantry had been absorbing replacements and hospital returnees, few of the companies had more than a hundred men, many of them newcomers. In the 2d Battalion, the officers and men of two companies were almost all replacements, for those two companies had been cut off during the fighting in the forest and everybody in the forward positions either killed or captured.

In early morning of the 17th, the 26th Infantry reached Elsenborn, where the executive officer, Lt. Col. Edwin V. Van Sutherland (the regimental commander, Col. John F. R. Seitz, was on leave but would soon return), learned that his regiment was attached temporarily to the 99th Division. At the division's interim command post in a café in Elsenborn, Sutherland found the staff in "a state of shock," with little knowledge of the situation of either American or German forces. Yet it was obvious

that somebody needed to block the principal highway leading from Büllingen to Bütgenbach. To do that, General Lauer sent the 26th Infantry to
defend Bütgenbach.

At Bütgenbach, Colonel Sutherland held one battalion in reserve,
sent another to high ground overlooking Büllingen about three-quarters
of the way between the two towns, and sent his remaining battalion
marching down the main highway to Dom. Bütgenbach. As the battalions
moved out early on the afternoon of the 17th, the 26th Infantry's normal
artillery support, the 33d Field Artillery Battalion, arrived.

The battalion that went to Dom. Bütgenbach was the 2d, commanded
by Lt. Col. Derrill M. Daniel. During the night of the 17th, Daniel's men
dug in on a reverse slope between Büllingen and Dom. Bütgenbach and
put outposts on the crest. No longer was the way open for the Germans
to exploit their early capture of Büllingen.

As darkness was falling, Daniel called his company commanders to his
command post in the manor house. Many of the men, said Daniel, had
heard tales of American troops surrendering or running away. That was
not going to happen in the 2d Battalion, 26th Infantry, and he wanted
every man in the battalion to know that he as their commander had
adopted a motto for the battalion: "We fight and die here."

CHAPTER NINETEEN

To Gain the Elsenborn Ridge

Moving cross-country from Hünningen, the foot column of Colonel Hightower's battalion of the 23d Infantry encountered few problems. Before daylight on December 18, the battalion was occupying a reserve position behind the twin villages.

It was not so easy for the vehicular column. As the vehicles neared Krinkelt, so many houses were burning and so heavy was the shelling that the commander of the 394th Infantry, Colonel Riley, assumed the Germans held the village and ordered the vehicles abandoned. As the drivers and others on the vehicles started moving cross-country toward Wirtzfeld, they were soon joined by most of the men of the 394th Infantry who were making the exodus on foot.

Not so the commander of Company M, Capt. Joseph Shank, who as commander of a weapons company had a number of vehicles in the column. Why abandon the vehicles without at least some effort to get through Krinkelt?

With a few men, Shank proceeded into Krinkelt, where he found an American tank. From the crew he learned that the Americans did, indeed, hold most of Krinkelt and that the vehicles should have no difficulty passing through the southern edge of the village to gain the road to Wirtzfeld. Returning to the vehicles, Shank found enough men to drive them all (the drivers from the 23d Infantry had stayed with theirs), and the column got under way. Passing through Wirtzfeld before daylight, the vehicles continued to Camp Elsenborn, where General Lauer was in the process of assembling and reorganizing his division.

As daylight came on December 18, there were still considerable numbers of men from both the 393d and 394th Regiments in the woods, stragglers and men in organized units alike.

One of the units was the 394th Infantry's Company K, which had become separated from the rest of the 3d Battalion during the withdrawal and had never reached Mürringen. With the coming of daylight, the men saw a few German vehicles between the woods and Mürringen, and the company commander, Capt. Wesley J. Simmons, decided not to risk trying to enter the village. He led the company along a wooded draw leading toward Krinkelt; but because of the noise of battle there, he avoided the village and passed instead along a draw leading to Wirtzfeld. Except for seventy men lost in the first two days of the offensive, Simmons brought his company out intact.

Company K had long since moved on when shortly after noon on the 18th, the 394th Infantry's 2d Battalion, its distraught commander still more a hindrance than a help, reached the woodsline overlooking Mürringen. With that battalion was all that remained of the 393d Infantry's 1st Battalion, which except for Company C was not much.

Since all appeared to be quiet in Mürringen, two companies advanced on the village, but as they neared the first houses, they met "a withering hail of enemy small arms fire." Still in radio contact with a corps artillery battalion, an artillery liaison officer with the 393d's 1st Battalion called for fire, which enabled the infantrymen to fall back to the woods.

By the time those two companies could reorganize and the withdrawal resume, it was growing late and a rapidly developing mist helped conceal the column. Much like the men of Company K, the remnants of the two battalions entered the draw short of Krinkelt and headed for Wirtzfeld. Somebody in the gathering dusk took them to be Germans and brought down heavy shelling. That split the column, some men heading for Krinkelt, others for Wirtzfeld. When at last there was time to count heads, it turned out that the 394th Infantry's 2d Battalion had emerged with almost six hundred officers and men, but the 393d Infantry's 1st Battalion had fewer than three hundred.

One more of the 99th Division's regiments was still in the forest: Colonel Mackenzie's 395th Infantry, minus the battalion that was at Höfen but with an attached battalion of the 393d Infantry. At the order of General Robertson, to whose division the regiment was attached, all three battalions had pulled back several hundred yards on the 17th to positions from which to protect the Wahlerscheid road as the units of the 2d Division withdrew. Then on the 18th, they withdrew farther to positions a thousand yards short of the Rocherather Baracken, there to provide flank protection for the defenders of the twin villages.

Late in the afternoon of the 18th, Colonel Mackenzie received a coded radio message from the 99th Division's headquarters ordering the regiment to fall back to the Elsenborn Ridge. To Mackenzie, that seemed odd, for he had received no order negating his attachment to the 2d Division, and he knew that the 2d Division was still holding Krinkelt and Rocherath. While conforming to the order by directing his battalions to withdraw, Mackenzie went ahead of them to the division headquarters in Camp Elsenborn.

When Mackenzie arrived, an hour before midnight, General Lauer was shocked to see him. He had sent no such message, and the regiment was still attached to the 2d Division. Mackenzie had no choice but to turn his men around and go back.

The origin of the withdrawal order could never be determined. It could have been that the Germans had captured a copy of the American code and sent the message; yet that would appear unlikely, for if equipped with such a valuable tool, why would they use it only once? Nor did the Germans make any effort to occupy the 395th Infantry's positions. It could have been that somebody on Lauer's staff, aware that the 99th Division's other two regiments had withdrawn but unaware of the 395th Infantry's attachment to the 2d Division, sent the message. Whatever the case, the weary men had to retrace their steps in the darkness (when one battalion commander refused to order his men back, Mackenzie relieved him of his command), and before daylight on December 19, the regiment was once again in position.

Early in the evening of December 17, after having spent much of the day on the Wahlerscheid road, General Robertson finally joined his headquarters, which on his order had withdrawn from Wirtzfeld to Camp Elsenborn. From the new command post, Robertson talked by telephone with the commander of the V Corps, General Gerow. Robertson explained that he intended to hold the twin villages and Wirtzfeld until all troops forward of the villages had retired, then fall back to the Elsenborn Ridge.

Around midnight, Robertson conferred with General Lauer. The two agreed that while the 2d Division should continue to hold Krinkelt-Rocherath, all other troops of both divisions were to start preparing a new line on the Elsenborn Ridge.

Robertson also conferred that night with the operations officer of the 1st Division, Lt. Col. Clarence E. Beck, and learned with considerable relief that the entire 1st Division was on its way south. Other units of the division were to extend the 26th Infantry's line westward from Bütgenbach in the direction of Malmédy.

That development sharply diminished Robertson's concern for his south flank, but he was still worried about the other. Between the 395th Infantry and the detached battalion at Höfen, there was a gap of ten miles. Although the entire gap was densely wooded, the Germans could move infantry with light support weapons over logging trails to reach the Elsenborn-Monschau highway and get in behind the Elsenborn Ridge from that direction. All Robertson had at hand to bar the way were the 2d Reconnaissance Troop and the 15th Field Artillery Battalion, whose firing positions were astride the road. That open flank continued to perturb Robertson for two more days until units of the 9th Infantry Division began to arrive; but to his immense relief, the Germans made no effort to exploit the gap. Had the Germans been able to break through at Höfen or Monschau, thus opening the road leading south to Elsenborn to tanks, the situation would have been graver still.

Having failed on the first day of the offensive to penetrate either the American cavalry at Monschau or the 395th Infantry's 3d Battalion at Höfen, the 326th Volksgrenadier Division on the 17th concentrated an entire regiment with a company of assault guns against Höfen, but to no avail. In a pre-dawn assault, some Germans got into the village but were soon wiped out in confused fighting or ejected. After daylight, some of the *Volksgrenadiers* broke through, so threatening the battalion command post that the commander, Colonel Butler, called for artillery fire on it; but when the towed guns of the 612th Tank Destroyer Battalion held off the German assault guns, the *Volksgrenadiers* were unable to sustain their penetration.

That turned out to be the last German effort to break through in the north. Why the 326th Volksgrenadier Division desisted was evident from a quick look around the battlefield at Höfen. There on December 17, fifty Germans surrendered and more than five hundred died. As on the day before, the contrast with American losses—five killed, seven wounded—was striking.

Just before daylight on December 18, as Colonel Zeiner pulled out of Krinkelt with the three tanks that had created such a tumult in the twin villages through much of the night, he saw a formidable German force poised at the woodsline ready for a major assault to take the twin villages. While sending his three tanks to the rear for refueling, Zeiner himself joined the attacking force.

That force consisted of most of the surviving tanks of Zeiner's battalion—probably around eighty—and a dozen *Jädgpanthers* (tank destroyers) each equipped with an 88mm. cannon on a Tiger chassis, which probably accounted for numerous reports by American soldiers of Tiger tanks in the twin villages. In addition to two battalions of *SS-Panzergrenadiers* that were to accompany the tanks, an attached regiment of the 277th Volksgrenadiers was to cover the open northern flank. The commander of the 12th SS Panzer Division, Brigadier Krass, exhorted his subordinate commanders in no uncertain terms to make quick work of the twin villages and get on beyond the Elsenborn Ridge. Sharp messages to that effect from Model and von Rundstedt had been pouring into headquarters of General Dietrich's Sixth Panzer Army with increasing frequency, and Dietrich was quick to pass the vitriol down the chain of command.

During the night of December 17, Bill McKinley and his little band from the 1st Battalion and Company K, 9th Infantry, had done what their division commander asked of them: They had held at the cluster of roads and trails northeast of Rocherath long enough for the two battalions of the 38th Infantry that were still withdrawing from Wahlerscheid to reach the twin villages. By their stand, they had prevented the Germans from cutting the road into Rocherath at the Rocherather Baracken and had sharply restricted routes remaining to German tanks to get into the twin villages. Yet they still had a job to do. They were to continue to hold until the 38th Infantry's 2d Battalion could get firmly entrenched behind them.

Once the action died down at midnight, communications men laid a telephone line to that battalion, and squad, platoon, and company commanders took inventory of their ranks. Somehow the battalion's supply officer got a resupply of small-arms ammunition and bazooka rockets as far forward as McKinley's command post in a dugout a hundred yards behind the line of foxholes. Through the night, supporting artillery delivered interdictory fires on the open ground between McKinley's positions and the forest and on the two trails leading through the forest, the only avenues of approach for German tanks and half-tracks. (Such a morass had those trails become that only tracked vehicles could negotiate them.)

Shortly before 7 A.M. on the 18th, the battle erupted again. Tanks and tank destroyers poured machine-gun and cannon fire into the foxholes of McKinley's men, and *SS-Panzergrenadiers* were close behind. At Lieutenant Granville's call, American artillery quickly responded. Around the farmhouse and along the roads, trails, and spare little hedgerows, there was fire, noise, and confusion—a reprise of the melee of the night before.

Back and forth the fighting ebbed. Incredible the courage of men on both sides: Germans constantly pursuing the fight, climbing over their own dead, ignoring their losses; Americans holding fast in their holes, refusing to panic, resolved not to give in. In only one case did any defender break. Having run out of rockets for their bazooka, seven men from Company B's left platoon made a dash for the rear, but Colonel McKinley himself, stepping from his dugout, stopped them and ordered them back. The men turned and retraced their steps.

At close to nine o'clock the commander of Company A, 1st Lt. Stephen E. Truppner, radioed that tanks and infantry were all over his position and called for artillery fire on his own foxholes, the only chance, he said, for any of his men to survive. As Truppner requested, Granville put the fire of a full battalion of guns on the company's positions for half an hour, no doubt killing many Germans who were caught in the open; but when it ended, no further word came from Lieutenant Truppner.

Hard on that success, the Germans overran the positions of Company K in the vicinity of the farmhouse. From the basement of the house, the company commander, Captain Garvey, could see Germans prodding those few of his men who were still alive from their foxholes, while a German tank approached the house and halted with its cannon only a few feet from the front door. Aware that it would be a matter of seconds before the tank blasted the house to pieces, Garvey told a man who spoke German to call out that his company commander would surrender to a German officer. When a German lieutenant arrived, Garvey and his command group filed out with their hands above their heads.

Around 11 A.M., Colonel McKinley at last received the word he was anxiously awaiting: Beginning at noon, he and his men were to withdraw behind the 38th Infantry's 2d Battalion. Yet so closely were his men locked in combat that McKinley saw little possibility of extricating anybody without close fire support from tanks or self-propelled tank destroyers.

Almost as if by a miracle, the leader of the battalion's antitank platoon, 1st Lt. Eugene Hinski, spotted four Shermans of Company A, 741st Tank Battalion, that were patrolling near the Rocherather Baracken. Running to them, Hinski asked the platoon leader, 2d Lt. Gaetano Barcellona, if he wanted to fight. "Hell, yes!" Barcellona responded.

When Barcellona reported to McKinley, he learned that the greatest difficulty involved four German tanks located between the farmhouse and Rocherath that would be able to fire on the route of withdrawal. Barcellona was to split his platoon, two tanks maintaining concealed positions while the other two moved into the open to lure the German tanks from their hiding places.

The maneuver worked. Barcellona's tank destroyed one of the German tanks with a single shot and another with three. As the two others turned toward Rocherath, another of the Shermans disabled one with a shot in the rear, while the other escaped into the village.

With supporting artillery fire landing close to the American foxholes, two of the Shermans moved toward the left flank of McKinley's position and two toward the right, their machine guns blazing. Under cover of that fire, the infantrymen began to withdraw with, under the circumstances, "unbelievable control." As the men left their holes, the *SS-Panzergrenadiers* tried to close, but the machine-gun fire sent them to ground. Colonel McKinley and his operations officer, Capt. James Harvey, were the last to leave. As they headed down the road toward the Rocherather Baracken, they heard Germans shouting for them to surrender.

Counting Company K and other attachments, Colonel McKinley had gone into position with something like 600 men; he got out with 217. Among the survivors were only five men from Company A and twelve from Company K.

McKinley and the men of the 1st Battalion and Company K, 9th Infantry, had performed an incredible feat. By their stand, they had enabled two battalions of the 38th Infantry to reach the twin villages for a defense that otherwise probably could not have been mounted. ("You have saved my regiment," Colonel Boos told McKinley.) They had left the ground around the cluster of roads and trails and the farmhouse littered with German dead and the carcasses of seventeen tanks and tank destroyers.

For all the pertinacity and valor displayed by a number of other battalions of the 2d Division during the fight for the twin villages, none performed with more fortitude and sacrifice than the men of McKinley's battalion and Company K. And for all the heroic defenses of many another American unit during the German offensive, probably none exceeded and few equaled McKinley's battalion and Company K in valor and sacrifice.

Even as that terrible fight developed northeast of Rocherath, the main body of the attacking German force crept through the early morning darkness to the very edge of Krinkelt and Rocherath, and behind a heavy barrage of artillery and *Nebelwerfers* struck the twin villages. All day the battle raged and all that night.

To many an American soldier fighting for his life in what was fast becoming the rubble of the two farming villages, the big German tanks appeared terrifying and seemingly invincible; but that was far from the reality. Indeed, what happened to the German armor in the twin villages well demonstrated why armored commanders were reluctant to risk their big battle wagons among the houses and streets of villages and towns; for there they were particularly vulnerable to stalking bazooka teams and to tanks and tank destroyers lying in wait in concealed positions.

The German tanks became even more vulnerable under the pounding of the 2d Division's four artillery battalions reinforced by three corps battalions, for even when that fire failed to knock out a tank, it might break a track or a sprocket wheel, leaving the tank sitting "like a crippled goose in front of the hunter." So, too, once concern for the withdrawing vehicles of the 99th Division had eased, antitank mines on roads and trails might immobilize a tank and leave it immobile prey to intrepid men with bazookas. Even nightfall failed to end the searches, for the light from burning tanks and buildings enabled them to continue; and once the American infantrymen had gotten over the first shock of blinding searchlights on some of the German tanks, they used the lights to guide them to the tank's sides and rear.

As everywhere during the German offensive, the 75mm. guns on the American Shermans and the 76mm. cannon on both the towed and self-propelled tank destroyers were usually ineffective against the frontal armor of Panthers; but the experienced American crews knew they could deal a death blow with a shot in side or rear. Lying in ambush, with the darkness and fog helping them to avoid detection, they could wait for the advantageous shot at close range. Even crippled tanks still might be effective under those circumstances: two immobilized Shermans concealed in a lane in Rocherath accounted for five German tanks that incautiously passed in front of them.

Holed up in the houses, American infantrymen were in favorable positions to get in a shot from a bazooka from an upper story into an open turret or onto a rear deck. (From a house on the eastern edge of the village, Lieutenant Goffigon and his runner, Private Welch, had holed up with two other men from the 23d Infantry's 3d Battalion; when a German tank appeared in the street just outside the house, a single rocket knocked it out, blocking the street and any further movement there by

German tanks.) Seldom were the German crews able to escape a destroyed tank, for even if the vehicle failed to burn, Americans in the buildings picked them off as they emerged from their turret or the escape hatch.

In the center of the twin villages, where Rocherath and Krinkelt imperceptibly joined, no front line existed. Americans held some houses, Germans others.

When the tank of a platoon leader of the Third Company, SS-Sgt. Willi Fischer, reached the center of the villages near the church, the scene looked to be a "tank grave." Just ahead of Fischer, Beutelhauser's tank was knocked out; close beside it, Brödel's tank was burning, Brödel hanging lifeless in the turret. Still others were knocked out, some still aflame. To Sergeant Fischer, it was "a cruel sight."

As another platoon leader, SS-Sgt. Gerhard Engel, arrived at a house near the church where Colonel Zeiner had established his command post, the commander's face reflected "depression and resignation." Even as Engel reported to Zeiner, a Panther approaching the command post not a hundred yards away turned into "a flaming torch," knocked out by an immobilized Sherman whose crew still fought from the tank.

In the first surge into the twin villages, a force of *SS-Panzergrenadiers* seized a house alongside the main road through the villages just north of the church. All through the day and night those men held on, the deepest German penetration, and had not American troops continued to hold the houses across the road, the Germans would have cut the villages in half.

Just to the north of Rocherath, once McKinley and his men had withdrawn, the Germans moved in strength against the 38th Infantry's 2d Battalion in the vicinity of the Rocherather Baracken. Those were men of the attached regiment of the 277th Volksgrenadiers protecting the 12th SS Panzer Division's flank. Small-arms and artillery fire broke up two German assaults against the crossroads, but tanks approaching from the direction of McKinley's former position got in among the northern buildings of Rocherath. Five were within a hundred yards of the 38th Infantry's command post before tanks and tank destroyers knocked out four and the fifth withdrew.

Another tank approached the command post of Colonel Mildren's 1st Battalion close to the church. As it neared an intersection, two American soldiers in a jeep roared out of a side street. Coming to a precipitous halt, they dived for cover. The tank flattened the vehicle, but in the process its turret jammed and was unable to traverse. The driver headed for a concrete utility pole, banging it with his cannon in an effort to loosen the traversing mechanism, but the pole snapped. He hit a second pole; it too snapped but not before the turret broke free.

As the tank continued toward Mildren's command post, the battalion's communications officer, 1st Lt. Jesse Morrow, fired a bazooka into its rear. The tank brushed against a house and veered into a ditch, immobilized; but the crewmen still had fight in them. As Morrow prepared to fire a second rocket, the tank's cannon spat fire. Morrow collapsed, wounded only slightly in the neck but knocked unconscious by concussion. The tank might have finished him off had not another soldier thrown a thermite grenade into the turret.

In early afternoon, the Germans struck again at the Rocherather Baracken, swept across the Wahlerscheid road, and got in behind the crossroads, cutting a farm track leading to Wirtzfeld. Colonel Boos promptly committed the two companies of the 23d Infantry's 1st Battalion that constituted a reserve behind the twin villages. Those two companies—their strength still pretty much intact despite their earlier fight at Hünningen—drove the Germans back and dug in to extend the flank of the position at the Rocherather Baracken.

In a house on the eastern edge of Krinkelt, two men from the command group of Captain MacDonald's Company I, 23d Infantry (who with the rest of their company had fallen back from the woods to the east) had taken refuge the night before—Pfc. Hugh Berger, an eighteen-year-old who took comfort in reading his Bible every night, and Pfc. Willie Hagan, an older career soldier. Soon after the German attack began on the 18th, a tank came up beside the house. Finding a bazooka without a sight, Berger fired but missed. Hagan quickly shoved another rocket into the bazooka, and Berger fired again. "You got him," yelled Hagan; "you knocked hell out of the sonofabitch!"

As the hatch opened, only one German emerged, a hand blown off, his face "like fresh ground meat." The two men carried him into the house and put him on a bed; but as the German began to revive, he shouted loudly and seemingly irrationally. With all that noise, said Hagan, he was bound to give their position away.

"If I stop that noise," said Hagan, "you won't ever tell, will you, Berger?"

"No, Willie," said Berger, "I'll never tell."

Early in the day's battle, the commander of Antitank Company, Capt. James W. Love, came upon two men, both badly wounded, each supporting the other, who told Love that they had been captured, lined up against a wall, shot, and left for dead. Private Fischer and his companion in tragedy also told their story, and there were reports that in the forest east of the twin villages a squad of Company K, 23d Infantry, had been summarily executed. Others told of SS troops bayonetting American wounded.

Word of those incidents spread as only word can spread among men fighting for their lives. Men of the 2d Division had faced SS troops before, back in Normandy. As the fighting for Krinkelt and Rocherath continued, they gave no quarter.

To many an American and German alike, the battle for the twin villages was as close as they would ever come to Armageddon. Yet through it all the American supply routes leading back through Wirtzfeld remained open, so that lack of ammunition never became a general problem, and the wounded, when the fight in their immediate vicinity permitted, could be evacuated. Although losses among artillery forward observers were high, communications with the seven supporting artillery battalions remained constant, and the German artillery fire never came close to matching the American fire in volume or intensity. By late afternoon, senior American commanders in the twin villages were convinced that they could hold indefinitely, and Colonel Boos released the two hundred tired and battered survivors of Colonel McKinley's battalion to go back for rest at Camp Elsenborn.

Yet for all the confidence, withdrawal was in the offing. During the afternoon, General Robertson met with Gereral Lauer and the commander of the 1st Division, Brig. Gen. Clift Andrus, and worked out a plan for retiring to the Elsenborn Ridge to positions to be tied in with those of the 1st Division. The men of the 2d Division had done the job Robertson had asked of them, and there was no point in staying longer in the twin villages; for the villages constituted a salient forward of positions the 1st Division had begun to occupy and which the 9th Division was soon to move into farther north. Furthermore, the high ground of the Elsenborn Ridge was far more advantageous for a defense. To facilitate occupation of the new positions, the corps commander, General Gerow, early in the evening attached the 99th Division to the 2d, with Lauer acting as Robertson's deputy.

On the German side, commanders had to accept the fact that in quest of a quick route across the Elsenborn Ridge, they had stumbled into a deadly cul-de-sac. Although it was still vital to gain the Elsenborn Ridge, for the ridge controlled all three roads assigned the 1st SS Panzer Corps for the drive to the Meuse, the critical problem at the moment was the necessity to open the southernmost of those routes—that through Bütgenbach. The corps commander needed that road in order to get supplies and reinforcements through to *Kampfgruppe Peiper*, and it needed the high ground in the vicinity of Bütgenbach to cloud the eyes of American artillery, which was making a shambles of all efforts to succor Peiper along the lesser road Peiper himself had taken.

In passing through Bütgenbach, the 12th SS Panzer Division would pose a threat to the Elsenborn Ridge. That would assist a new thrust against the ridge to be mounted by a unit released from the Sixth Panzer Army's reserve, the 3d Panzergrenadier Division, with the help of the 12th and 277th Volksgrenadier Divisions.

Before daylight on December 19, those tanks of the SS panzer division that got the word and could still maneuver began withdrawing from Krinkelt and Rocherath. The American defenders were soon aware that the ratio of their strength versus that of the enemy had markedly changed. *SS-Panzergrenadiers* nevertheless made some attacks to cover the German withdrawal, but small arms and artillery fire took care of those with little difficulty. In early afternoon, the Americans began systematically destroying all American and German vehicles, weapons, and equipment that could not be extricated. General Robertson had decided that the time had come not to withdraw but, as his order put it, "to move to new positions" on the Elsenborn Ridge.

Once Robertson gave that order in mid-afternoon on December 19, all vehicles not essential for continuing defense began infiltrating in ones and twos to the rear; and at the hour designated for the withdrawal to begin—just after nightfall at 5:30 P.M.—the little road from Wirtzfeld that meandered back to Elsenborn, the road on which the 2d Division's engineers had worked so prodigiously, became one-way for traffic pulling out. While the 395th Infantry conducted its own withdrawal over logging trails and cross-country to an assigned sector on the Elsenborn Ridge, the 38th Infantry's units began to peel off a battalion at a time from north to south. Tanks of the 741st Tank Battalion and self-propelled guns of the 644th Tank Destroyer Battalion, plus the I&R Platoon and a contingent of engineers, formed a rear guard. Once all units of the 38th Infantry had passed through Wirtzfeld, the rear guard retired to that village while the 9th Infantry and the 23d Infantry's 2d Battalion withdrew.

Because the Germans were in close contact, there was no concealing the fact that a withdrawal was under way, and German artillery and *Nebelwerfers* soon took the twin villages and Wirtzfeld under fire. Under strict orders to walk, not run, most of the withdrawing troops obeyed the order despite the shelling, and medics were able to load men wounded by the shellfire onto departing vehicles. Some vehicles bogged on muddy sections of the withdrawal route, but there were enough men on foot nearby to get them moving again.

At 2 A.M. on December 20, the withdrawal was complete except for six men of the 38th Infantry's Headquarters Company, who had taken refuge from the shelling in Wirtzfeld in a cellar. There they fell into a sleep of exhaustion. When they awoke after daylight, all they could see from the cellar window were German boots. They waited until heavy concentrations of American artillery fell on the village and sent the Germans fleeing for cover, then ran for it.

Close behind the 1st Division's 26th Infantry, which reached Bütgenbach late on December 17, came another of the division's regiments, the 16th Infantry. While the division's third regiment hunted paratroopers near Eupen, the 16th Infantry began to extend the defensive line along the highway leading from Bütgenbach to Waimes, three and a half miles to the west in the direction of Malmédy. The first troops of that regiment arrived early on December 18.

It was none too soon for 2d Lt. Mabel Jessop, nine other nurses, a few medical and medical administrative officers, and the technicians of the platoon of the 47th Field Hospital in the schoolhouse in Waimes. Following the near collision with *Kampfgruppe Peiper*, the nurses had returned to Waimes and with the other medical personnel reopened the hospital, however limited the facilities. Although worried that the Germans might come, they were at a loss to know how to get to safety.

By the morning of December 18, the hospital not only had new patients but close to fifty able-bodied stragglers who still had their weapons. That disturbed the medics, for under terms of the Geneva Convention, no arms were allowed in a medical facility. They made the men deposit them in a remote part of the building.

In mid-morning, Lieutenant Jessop paused in her work to go into a corridor for a cigarette. As she looked out a window, she saw two soldiers enter the courtyard, weapons at the ready. One was a German captain; the other wore an American uniform with a sergeant's stripes and a shoulder patch denoting the 5th Armored Division. "Your hospital is under arrest," shouted the man in American uniform. "Everybody line up in the yard!"

As everybody conformed—the medical administrative officer in charge would allow none of the stragglers to go for their weapons—the German in American uniform announced that patients and all medical personnel were to load into American vehicles and head for German lines. The able-bodied soldiers were to walk.

As loading began, the soldier in American uniform embraced a middle-aged woman in the street. Word spread (rightly or wrongly) that the man was a native of Waimes and that the woman was his aunt.

Amid the confusion of loading, one of the ambulance drivers slipped away. On the fringe of the town, he found three half-tracks with quad-50 machine guns. In a matter of minutes, they were racing for the schoolhouse, and the German captain and his companion were on the run. Bullets chased them down the street, but they got away.

Less than an hour later, Lt. Col. Charles Horner arrived, wearing the shoulder patch of the 1st Infantry Division. A battalion of the 16th Infantry was on the way, said Horner, and the patients, nurses, and medics were to prepare for evacuation.

Derrill McCollough Daniel had commanded one or another of the 26th Infantry's battalions since the 1st Division's assault landing in North Africa in 1942 and the 2d Battalion since the landing in Sicily in 1943. At thirty-nine, he was one of the senior battalion commanders in a division that had long taken pride in a nickname derived from its shoulder patch, the "Big Red One." Born in South Carolina, Daniel obtained his commission through ROTC at Clemson, the state's agricultural and mechanical college, and then pursued advanced degrees, including a Ph.D. in entomology. By the time he entered the army as a reserve officer in 1940, he was a recognized authority on the biological control of insect pests.

As the men of Daniel's 2d Battalion dug in during the night of December 17 between Büllingen and Bütgenbach at Dom. Bütgenbach, the battalion had the support of four self-propelled guns of the 634th Tank Destroyer Battalion and five Shermans of the 745th Tank Battalion. Under strength by some two hundred men, Daniel nevertheless withheld a rifle platoon to serve as a counterattacking force with the tanks.

Daniel put the tanks behind a rise in the ground near Dom. Bütgenbach and concealed the tank destroyers among the hedges and buildings of the settlement from which they could cover both the main road from Büllingen and another road leading up from the south that joined the main one just short of Dom. Bütgenbach. He placed six 57mm. antitank guns within the line of forward foxholes. His regiment's 3d Battalion covered his left flank from high ground between Bütgenbach and Büllingen. Although his right (or western) flank was open, the regimental executive officer, Colonel Sutherland, had withheld the regiment's third battalion in Bütgenbach as a reserve.

All through December 18, while *SS-Panzergrenadiers* and tanks of the 12th SS Panzer Division tried to wrest the twin villages from men of the 2d Division, Daniel's men had time to dig deep, cover their foxholes with logs, and reinforce them with sandbags. Patrols probed toward Büllingen, determining that the Germans still held the town. Late that afternoon, when an armored car emerged from Büllingen and approached the line of foxholes, a 57mm. piece knocked it out, killing three of the crew and wounding a fourth. The men turned out to be from the 12th SS Panzer Division.

Despite heavy, almost continual American artillery fire on Büllingen (a civilian in the town noted 3,500 rounds in one day alone, and the town was virtually leveled), some two hundred *SS-Panzergrenadiers* and a dozen tanks assembled there and before daylight on December 19 headed up the road toward Dom. Bütgenbach. Fire from the 33d Field Artillery Battalion drove back all but three tanks. Those got past the line of foxholes and headed for the buildings of Dom. Bütgenbach, firing their machine guns as they went; but by that time the 1st Division's 5th Field Artillery Battalion had arrived, and a few salvos from its big 155mm. howitzers convinced the German crews to turn back. Once they had withdrawn beyond the line of foxholes, either the self-propelled tank destroyers or the 57mm. guns knocked out two of them. (For the only time during the German offensive, the 57mm. was an effective weapon against German tanks; somewhere the 26th Infantry had scrounged a few rounds of British Sabot ammunition, which had a high muzzle velocity, making the rounds capable of penetrating heavy armor.)

Two hours later the Germans were back, probing for a soft spot with a company of *SS-Panzergrenadiers* and two tanks, but again American artillery broke up the attack. The shelling sent the *SS-Panzergrenadiers* reeling back in disorder and knocked out one of the tanks.

Through the rest of the day, only occasional shelling hit the American positions; but during that time, Colonel Zeiner, the surviving tanks from Krinkelt-Rocherath, and the rest of the 12th SS Panzer Division's tanks reached Büllingen. Shortly after midnight, accompanied by *SS-Panzergrenadiers* and an attached regiment of the 3d Parachute Division, ten of Zeiner's tanks moved out along the road toward Dom. Bütgenbach. As one of the Germans later noted, "exceedingly heavy artillery and mortar fire" erupted. (By that time, all four of the 1st Division's artillery battalions were in place, along with a battery of 90mm. antiaircraft artillery, a corps artillery battalion with 155mm. howitzers, another with 4.5-inch guns, a battery of 8-inch guns, and a battalion of 4.2-inch chemical mortars.) The Germans "suffered most serious losses." Although a few tanks got past the line of foxholes, tank destroyers knocked out two of them, and the rest fell back.

A few hours later, shortly before daylight on the 20th, the Germans tried again, with eight Panthers in the lead. A shell from some source knocked out the company commander's Panther, setting it on fire, and three more fell victim to artillery fire.

Several tanks nevertheless broke into Company E's position. By the light of flares fired by 81mm. mortars, the crew of a 57mm. antitank gun put four rounds into one of them, sending it up in flames. The light from the flames enabled the gunner, Cpl. Henry F. Warner, to put four more rounds into a second tank, knocking it out; but after the fourth round, the breech block on the gun failed to open. As a third tank appeared, heading directly for the gun, all the crew but Warner dived for foxholes.

Staying with his piece, Warner tried desperately to free the breech block. When the tank was but a few feet away, the turret opened, and the head and shoulders of the German tank commander appeared. Firing his .45-caliber pistol, Warner dove into a foxhole. Still the tank advanced on an apparent collision course with the 57mm. piece and the foxholes of the crew; but just as it reached the first hole, it stopped and went into reverse. Stealing a quick glance, Warner could see the commander slumped over the rim of the turret.

In the fights for the twin villages and for Dom. Bütgenbach, Colonel Zeiner had lost so many tanks that he had to consolidate those that survived into a single company.

Inside Büllingen before daylight the next day, December 21, twenty young SS troopers of the 12th SS Panzer Division, quartered in a house belonging to a farmer, Albert Kohnenmerger, were sleeping in the cellar. Most were boys, fifteen to seventeen years old, and they had already participated in the attacks on Dom. Bütgenbach and experienced the dreadful wrath of the American artillery. Kohnenmerger was with them

in the cellar when noncommissioned officers arrived to order them back
to the attack. The Belgian farmer watched in silent pity as the boys began
to weep. As they gathered their gear to move out into the cold night,
tears streaked down their faces.

Those young Hitler Youth were on their way to participate in the
strongest thrust yet to be launched against Colonel Daniel and his men.
By that time, in the wake of repeated demands from the SS panzer division commander, Brigadier Kraas, the artillery and *Nebelwerfers* that had
been ranged against Krinkelt-Rocherath had been relocated to fire on
Dom. Bütgenbach, so that for the first time the attackers had powerful
fire support.

The artillery and *Nebelwerfers* began firing three hours before dawn
on the 21st and despite heavy counter-battery fire from American guns,
continued until the first hint of light appeared in the sky. The shelling set
three of the outbuildings at Dom. Bütgenbach on fire, including a barn
used as an aid station, and tore great gaps in the line of foxholes.

As Colonel Daniel's men waited for the inevitable ground attack to
follow, their position was slightly stronger than before because engineers
had laid antitank mines on both roads leading into Dom. Bütgenbach.
Daniel also had ten more 57mm. antitank guns and a company of infantry
from the regiment's reserve battalion. He used a platoon from that company to reinforce his Company G, which had lost so heavily that he had
had to use his lone reserve platoon to fill gaps in its line. On the other
hand, the enemy's prolonged shelling negated much of that additional
strength, for despite overhead cover on the foxholes, casualties were
heavy.

As two battalions of *SS-Panzergrenadiers* approached under covering
fire from at least thirty tanks and tank destroyers, each battalion taking
one of the two roads leading into Dom. Bütgenbach, Daniel called on his
supporting artillery to place "a ring of steel" in front of his position. A
total of twelve battalions responded: all battalions of the 1st and 2d Divisions; a battalion of the 99th Division (the only battalion of that division
within range); and three corps battalions, plus a battalion of 4.2-inch
chemical mortars. Through the entire morning, German soldiers, displaying incredible courage (the Americans saw it as fanatical), tried to break
through that ring of steel, but not a man made it. They died in droves.

The German tanks eventually found a weak spot: the battalion's open
right (western) flank. There Colonel Daniel had placed three of his newly
arrived 57mm. antitank guns. One of them scored a hit on the drive
sprocket of a Panther, and as the tank backed up, exposing its thinner
side armor, the gun knocked it out, setting it on fire. When a Mark IV
appeared out of the fog, the same gun knocked it out, but a round from a
Panzerfaust destroyed the American gun. A round from a Mark IV destroyed a second of the 57mm. guns, and machine-gun fire from another
wiped out the crew of the third; but not far away was the gun for which

Corporal Warner was the gunner. Warner got in a shot against the rear of a Mark IV, sending smoke billowing from it. Then a burst of machine-gun fire from the dying tank mortally wounded Warner.

The German tanks were at that point free to roam up and down the foxhole line, shooting up the holes, crushing the occupants with their treads. As more tanks appeared, a U.S. self-propelled tank destroyer knocked out seven in rapid succession, but five others continued toward the buildings of Dom Bütgenbach. Two Shermans knocked out two of the German tanks before they themselves succumbed to the firing. Taking cover behind the one remaining barn, the three surviving German tanks began to blast Daniel's command post in the manor house.

Inside the house, Colonel Daniel appealed to his regimental commander, Colonel Seitz, for a fresh company of infantry armed with extra bazookas. Borrowing a company from the neighboring 18th Infantry, Seitz sent it forward; but that company could not arrive until mid-afternoon, and Daniel's need was immediate.

Daniel nevertheless got the help he needed: a platoon of self-propelled guns of the 613th Tank Destroyer Battalion had just reached Bütgenbach, and those were the new 90mm. pieces. Concealed by a smoke screen, the four guns of that platoon raced down the road from Bütgenbach. When the platoon leader reported, Daniel told him to place his guns in protected positions from which they could fire through the barn at the German tanks behind it.

Fire from the 90mm. guns soon prompted two of the German tanks to make a run for it, but as they came out of hiding, the big pieces knocked them out. The third tank remained in place until late afternoon, when rounds from the battalion's 81mm. mortars at last forced it to try to escape. An early evening mist enabled the crew to make it.

It was close to nightfall when the Germans finally abandoned their day-long attempt to ram through the defenders of Dom. Bütgenbach. It was a costly effort. American patrols later reported enemy dead beyond the main line of resistance "as common as grass." One patrol actually counted 300 bodies in one sector alone, and men of a Graves Registration unit in an early count found 782 dead. In addition, the Germans left behind the hulks of forty-seven tanks and tank destroyers. The defenders lost 5 57mm. antitank guns, 3 Shermans, a tank destroyer, and close to 250 men.

Impressed by the weight of the attack, Colonel Daniel briefly contemplated falling back to high ground closer to Bütgenbach, for his position constituted a distinct right-angle corner in the line, joining the positions of his regiment's 3d Battalion and those of the 2d and 99th Divisions, facing east, with those of the rest of the 1st Division, facing south. Yet when the reserve company from the 18th Infantry arrived, Daniel reconsidered. It was he who had coined the motto, "We stand and die here," and his men had fought by it, many of them dying in the process. There was to be no falling back.

As it turned out, the attack on December 21 represented the highwater mark of the German attempts to break through to Bütgenbach, outflank the Elsenborn Ridge, and succor *Kampfgruppe Peiper*. Not that the German command desisted. The next day, the 22d, the Germans attacked again, but as before they were unable to penetrate the deadly curtain of American artillery fire.

Again a few tanks broke through, not into the 2d Battalion's positions but into those of the 1st Battalion, which Colonel Seitz had committed to extend Daniel's line south to Bütgenbach. Those tanks got into Bütgenbach itself, but without infantry support, they were reduced to playing a deadly game of hide-and-seek with tank destroyers and bazooka teams. Some briefly took cover within the walls of the hospital for geriatric patients, whose inmates were still there, but the bazooka teams eventually knocked all the tanks out.

Like Bill McKinley of the 9th Infantry, Derrill Daniel attributed the success of his battalion to the big guns that backed him up. "The artillery did a great job," he noted later. "I don't know where they got the ammo or when they took time out to flush the guns, but we wouldn't be here now if it wasn't for them."

On that critical day of December 21, American artillery in support of the 2d Battalion, 26th Infantry, fired more than ten thousand rounds in an awesome display of firepower. It was no wonder that not a single *SS-Panzergrenadier* or paratrooper got past the line of foxholes. Yet the artillery would have been of little consequence had not intrepid infantrymen and antitank crewmen held their ground with incredible courage and pertinacity. Like McKinley's men, Daniel's had made one of the truly epic stands against the big German offensive.

By December 21, American troops opposing the northern prong of the German offensive had "knocked a part of Hitler's personal operations plan into a cocked hat." The division commanders, the corps commanders, Dietrich, Model, von Rundstedt, and eventually Adolf Hitler himself all had to face the fact that the Sixth Panzer Army and Hitler's beloved SS troops had failed to do the job Hitler asked of them.

At that point, the Sixth Panzer Army faced a formidable American line. In the north, the veteran 9th Infantry Division moved in to back up the cavalry at Monschau and the infantry at Höfen, and to extend the line southward to link with the 2d and 99th Divisions on the Elsenborn Ridge. Each of those battered but still viable divisions held only a regimental front, with a second regiment of each division manning a second line of defense, and the third regiment of each division in reserve. Separated from the positions of the 2d Division only by the Lac de Bütgenbach, the

1st Division extended the line to the west from Bütgenbach all the way to Waimes and a juncture point near Malmédy with another veteran division that had hurried south to oppose *Kampfgruppe Peiper*. Those four divisions, which included three of the most experienced in the United States Army, formed a solid shoulder against any expansion of the German offensive on its northern wing.

Not that the Germans would not try. Hardly had the men of the 2d and 99th Divisions entrenched on the Elsenborn Ridge than fresh troops of the 3d Panzergrenadier Division tried to penetrate the 99th Division's line. The attack came through the forest well north of the twin villages up the valley of the Schwalm Creek; but it got nowhere. When the spring thaw came in 1945, local civilians found German bodies stacked in the valley of the Schwalm three and four deep.

There the infantry could again pay tribute to its sister arm, the artillery, for in few places during the course of the war in Europe did the American command amass such a concentration of firepower. Word passed among the infantry on the Elsenborn Ridge that the artillery massed behind them was hub to hub, which was almost literally the case. There were sixteen battalions of divisional artillery, which included four 155mm. howitzer battalions, plus seven battalions of corps artillery: 155mm. howitzers, 155mm. guns, 4.5-inch and 8-inch guns. There were in addition the 105mm. howitzers of the Cannon Companies of twelve regiments. The total number of guns capable of firing in front of all or portions of the four divisions was 348, plus tanks and tank destroyers and a battalion of 4.2-inch chemical mortars. To control that tremendous collection of firepower, the corps commander, General Gerow, deputized the 2d Division's artillery commander, General Hinds, who was free to call upon any battalion other than divisional battalions that might be engaged in a priority mission for their own troops.

Once more, on December 26, the Germans would test the defenses of the Elsenborn Ridge with an attack against the 99th Division by a newly arrived 246th Volksgrenadier Division, but hardly had the attack begun before a deadly rain of shells broke it up. Nobody was going to get through the ring of steel those artillery pieces were capable of laying down.

Between December 13 and 19, the 2d Division had penetrated a heavily fortified section of the West Wall, then executed an eight-mile daylight withdrawal while in close contact with the enemy and assumed defensive positions at the twin villages facing in another direction. There they came immediately under heavy attack, held the villages for two days and nights while troops of the 99th Division streamed through, and then broke contact and withdrew to new positions on the Elsenborn Ridge. It was, as the division commander, General Robertson, noted, "a pretty good day's work for any division. Leavenworth [Command and General

Staff College] would say it couldn't be done, and I don't want to have to do it again." He was not alone in that assessment, for the commander of the First Army, General Hodges, told Robertson: "What the 2d Division has done . . . will live forever in the history of the United States Army."

What the 2d Division had done was to block an attack by Sepp Dietrich's Sixth Panzer Army constituting the main effort—the *Schwerpunkt*—of Hitler's offensive. With the exception of the push by *Kampfgruppe Peiper* and the 1st SS Panzer Division, that main effort had failed to get more than three to four miles beyond the German frontier and had failed to open three of the five routes assigned to the 1st SS Panzer Corps for the drive to the Meuse. And the fourth route, that taken by *Kampfgruppe Peiper*, was subject to a powerful array of American artillery; while a fifth, that through Vielsalm, was still blocked by other American troops.

Credit for sealing the third route belonged to Colonel Daniel's 2d Battalion, 26th Infantry, 1st Division. But for the heroic stand of that battalion, the 12th SS Panzer Division, foiled at the twin villages, might have broken through at Bütgenbach, outflanked the Elsenborn Ridge, and undone everything the 2d Division had previously accomplished.

So, too, part of the credit for stopping the drive belonged to the inexperienced soldiers of the 99th Division. From greatly overextended defensive positions, they had kept the Germans at arm's length for the first day and almost all of the second, which turned out to be—by a hair's breadth—the time needed to enable the men of the 2d Division to reach the twin villages. The Germans had expected to penetrate the 99th Division's line and commit their armor soon after daylight on the first day. Despite some disarray in command at the division level, the fighting men of the 99th Division had denied that expectation by many hours.

German losses were never determined with any degree of accuracy, but they were obviously tremendous. It was because of heavy losses that the 326th Volksgrenadier Division abandoned its attacks at Monschau and Höfen, and after only one day of attack, the 277th Volksgrenadier Division could contribute little to the continuing drive against the twin villages. After the fight at Losheimergraben and some assistance in the attacks at Dom. Bütgenbach, the commander of the 12th Volksgrenadier Division, General Engel, told his superiors that, without reinforcements, his division was incapable of attacking.

In the fight for the twin villages, the 12th SS Panzer Division started out with 105 tanks and self-propelled tank destroyers, plus a dozen *Jädgpanthers* of the 560th Army Tank Destroyer Battalion. Allowing for some duplication in counting, Brigadier Kraas lost sixty-seven tanks and tank destroyers in the rural streets and lanes of the twin villages and the surrounding landscape and at Dom. Bütgenbach, forty-seven more. The 12th SS Panzer Division had ceased to be a viable force.

On the American side, the stand at the twin villages amply demonstrated the importance to the infantrymen of tanks and tank destroyers. Without the three companies of Shermans of the 741st Tank Battalion and the two companies of self-propelled pieces of the 644th Tank Destroyer Battalion, the infantrymen, however determined, probably would have been unable to hold. A company of towed guns of the 612th Tank Destroyer Battalion and three guns of the 801st Tank Destroyer Battalion were much less effective. Lacking the Sabot ammunition employed by the 57mm. pieces at Dom. Bütgenbach, the 2d Division's antitank guns were virtually worthless; but bazookas were effective, and the artillery turned out to be the most effective antitank weapon of all.

When the 2d and 99th Divisions counted their losses, the totals were less than might have been expected. For the 2d Division, just over a thousand men killed and missing, and since the division had few men captured, most of those could be presumed dead. The 99th Division lost not quite one thousand four hundred men killed and missing, but a considerable number of those—perhaps five hundred—were captured. The total loss for the two divisions, including wounded, was close to five thousand men.

Stymied on the northern shoulder, the Germans had to swing their remaining weight southward to roads already overcrowded. Whether, despite the failure of their *Schwerpunkt*, they could still accomplish their goal—or at least reach the Meuse River—remained to be seen.

DAMS AGAINST THE TIDE

CHAPTER TWENTY

Command Decisions

Bernard Law Montgomery was an ascetic. One of nine children in an Anglo-Irish family of modest means, he decided early that life was an unending struggle to be conquered only by hard work, integrity, and moral courage. After finishing the military academy at Sandhurst, he served a tour with the British Army in India, where he found the atmosphere conducive to furthering his asceticism: no late nights, no tobacco, no alcohol, little consort with women. Happily married to his profession, he nevertheless took a wife in 1927 and had a son, David, to whom he was devoted; but when his wife died ten years later, he once again dedicated himself almost exclusively to the military and his role in it. As he rose steadily in command and rank to become one of Britain's ablest soldiers, he made conscious, determined efforts to be seen and identified by his troops, who for the most part adored him. Yet at the same time he developed attributes of arrogance and imperiousness that irritated many of his colleagues and, when the time came, American commanders in particular.

Like his superior, the Chief of the Imperial General Staff, Field Marshal Sir Alan Brooke, Montgomery deeply resented the fact that British troops had to serve under American command, and he exploited every possible opportunity to broaden his own role. While acting as overall ground commander under Eisenhower in the invasion and the campaign in Normandy, he had been content; but when Eisenhower, according to plan, assumed personal command in the field on September 1, 1944, Montgomery launched his campaign to alter Eisenhower's strategy and send the bulk of the Allied forces under his command in a single grand offensive north of the Ardennes, which would well serve his ambition to become once again the overall ground commander. It was a campaign still going on in one form or another when the Germans launched their offensive.

Montgomery may well have seen the offensive as a heaven-sent opportunity to gain his goal. Within hours after learning of it, he sent teams of picked junior officers, known by the codename PHANTOM, who acted as his eyes and ears on the battlefields, hurrying to the Ardennes. Either they misinformed him of the extent of the American problem or he chose for his own ends to paint the picture in colors gloomier than actually warranted.

In a telegram to Field Marshal Brooke on December 19, Montgomery spoke of "great confusion and all signs of a full-scale withdrawal . . . a definite lack of grip and control . . . an atmosphere of great pessimism. . . ." "The command setup," he continued, "has always been very faulty and now is quite futile, with Bradley at Luxembourg [City] and the front cut in two." He had told Eisenhower's deputy chief of operations, the British officer Jock Whiteley, that Eisenhower should put him in command of all troops north of the German penetration. Somebody, Montgomery added, meaning either the Combined Chiefs of Staff, of which Brooke was a member, or the British prime minister, Winston Churchill, should give Eisenhower "a direct order . . . to do so."

By December 19, the broad shape of the German offensive and the altered form that American defense might impose on it had begun to become apparent, particularly on the shoulders of the penetration. In front of Luxembourg City, which some on the American side still saw as a possible German objective, the American troops had given little ground; and by the 19th, they were forming a line anchored near the German frontier and the Sûre River at Osweiler and Dickweiler and extending northwest toward high ground overlooking Ettelbruck, and that part of Erich Brandenberger's Seventh Army facing the line was going over to the defensive. On the north shoulder, by the 19th, Monschau, Höfen, and the twin villages had held; the 1st Division had arrived to extend the shoulder from Bütgenbach westward toward Malmédy; and the 9th Division was arriving to strengthen the line north of the Elsenborn Ridge. As events over the next few days were to demonstrate, nobody was going to get past the Elsenborn Ridge.

The center, on the other hand, was in a state of flux. Although American troops were coming in to try to bottle up *Kampfgruppe Peiper*, Joachim Peiper and his tanks deep behind American lines at La Gleize and Stoumont still posed a serious threat. It was late on the 19th that the trapped men of the 106th Division in front of St. Vith surrendered; but a surviving regiment of that division, a regiment of the 28th Division, CCB of the 9th Armored Division, and the entire 7th Armored Division, had formed a defensive peninsula, a kind of horseshoe, based on St. Vith, thereby forcing the German columns onto overcrowded roads on either side. So, too, a combat command of the 10th Armored Division and the 101st Airborne Division had won, by the slimmest of margins, a race for the road center of Bastogne.

Yet between St. Vith and Bastogne there was a gap measuring on the diagonal twenty miles. Through that gap had surged two panzer divisions, the 2d and the 116th; and by late on the 19th, they had reached the north-south highway connecting Bastogne through Houffalize to Liège. There the gap was somewhat narrower, about fifteen miles across, partly because the defenders of Bastogne had pushed their line out several miles north of the town and partly because the 82d Airborne Division was arriving a few miles north of Houffalize in the vicinity of Werbomont.

Between Houffalize and Werbomont were two highways leading to the east that American supply trucks were still using. Both led to the Salm River: one to Trois Ponts, where the little band of engineers that had blown the bridges there in front of Peiper was still holding, and the other to the rear of the horseshoe at St. Vith. Yet there was nobody to defend those roads other than a few outposts dropped off by the 7th Armored Division's supply trains.

Nor were there other than scattered units to oppose a continued advance by the 2d and 116th Panzer Divisions toward the Meuse. The commander of the VIII Corps, General Middleton, had managed to find a few engineer battalions and a Canadian forestry company to demolish bridges and cover crossing sites over the Ourthe River, which meandered across the gap; but that was all.

By the 19th, only four days after the start of the offensive, American strength in the Ardennes had grown to close to 180,000 men, double the numbers there when the offensive began. Instead of an armored and five infantry divisions, there were three armored and ten infantry (including two airborne) divisions, and another armored division, the 3d, was arriving. It was a display of mobility that German commanders would find difficult to believe. Although Eisenhower had no more reserves per se, he could, by shuffling the lines north and south of the penetration, produce three more divisions from the vicinity of Aachen and more than that from the Third Army.

The Germans at that point had committed four panzer and thirteen parachute and *Volksgrenadier* divisions, and the *Führer Begleit Brigade* was soon to appear at St. Vith. Sepp Dietrich still had two uncommitted SS panzer divisions, and Field Marshal Model at Army Group B had a reserve of a panzer, a *Panzergrenadier*, and a *Volksgrenadier* division. There were presumably other divisions in a so-called Führer Reserve; but apart from two divisions, the 9th Panzer and the 15th Panzergrenadier, the field commanders could never be sure that such a reserve actually existed. Those two divisions were for the moment earmarked for possible use in the projected supporting attack by the Fifteenth Army around Aachen.

What the Germans called Hitler weather—mist, fog, low-lying clouds, drizzle—was still holding, which meant that the heavy Allied advantage in airpower was yet to be brought to bear. While mounting a maximum effort by fighter-bombers against the attacking ground forces, the Allied air commanders wanted to turn their medium bombers against communications centers and railheads in the Eifel in order to shove German unloading and supply points all the way back to the Rhine; yet that would be impossible so long as the Hitler weather held. Tactical aircraft managed only a few sorties during the first four days with just one notable achievement—the dramatic intervention against *Kampfgruppe Peiper* during the afternoon of December 18—and mediums flew only one mission, a blind bombing attack through the clouds that probably did little damage.

While shielding the ground columns, the Hitler weather also worked against the Luftwaffe. German fighters made only a few appearances: over the northern shoulder as *Kampfgruppe Peiper* was breaking free early on the 17th; over Krinkelt-Rocherath that afternoon; and in the skies over St. Vith the same day. Most operations by the Luftwaffe were night bombing missions against American supply installations in the vicinity of Liège, but like the tactical missions, they did little damage. Nor was it likely that the Luftwaffe could maintain even that much effort for long, for on December 17 alone, American antiaircraft guns knocked down 54 German planes while Allied fighters destroyed 114.

As late as December 18, senior American commanders still saw the German offensive as a spoiling attack designed to disrupt American offensives north and south of the Ardennes and still thought the drive was aimed at the supply installations around Liège. Late on the 18th, for example, although General Bradley saw the situation as "worse than it was at noon," he still looked on the offensive as an opportunity for Patton "to rush the Siegfried Line and hurry our way to the Rhine." General Eisenhower was thinking much the same way: to take advantage of what appeared to be an imprudent move out of the West Wall fortifications by containing the Germans with minimum forces while simultaneously launching offensives all along the rest of the front other than the Ardennes to converge along the Rhine River. (That was paying no attention to the fact that the Germans north of the Ardennes still held the Roer River dams.)

Plans for moving troops of Patton's Third Army northward against the German penetration nevertheless proceeded. Meeting with Bradley in Luxembourg City early in the afternoon of the 18th, Patton said he could intervene "very shortly" with three divisions, including the 4th Armored Division. A combat command of that division and a corps headquarters began moving north that night, to be followed early on December 19 by the rest of the armored division and an infantry division and during the night of the 19th by a second infantry division. It appeared fairly certain, Bradley told Patton, that Patton was to assume command of Middleton's VIII Corps.

Having pretty well completed building a wall against expansion of the penetration at the northern corner—or "door post," as the Germans called it—Patton's counterpart in the north, Hodges of the First Army, was primarily concerned at that point with the big gap between the northern wall and the defenders of Bastogne. The 82d Airborne Division could fill a portion of the gap, as could the incoming 3d Armored Division; but Hodges felt compelled to withhold most of the armored division as a reserve. An infantry division, the 84th, was also soon to arrive, sent south from the Ninth Army.

Faced with German troops only a few miles short of the headquarters town of Spa, Hodges during the 18th moved his headquarters to the rear to another watering place, Chaudfontaine, just outside Liège, the site of his rear headquarters. There were lingering reports that headquarters of the First Army panicked, but those appeared more a misinterpretation of soldiers hurriedly packing and getting out of town than a reality. Hodges himself, for example, and the principal members of his staff waited around the Hôtel Britannique into the evening expecting a visit by the commander of the 82d Airborne Division, General Gavin. When Gavin failed to arrive, they left around 10 P.M. That hardly looked like panic.

In Chaudfontaine, Hodges moved into a room on the second floor of the Palace Hotel with an office across the street in the Hôtel des Bains. That street was a principal highway leading into Liège, and the noise of traffic on it plus the passage of buzz bombs overhead at all hours later prompted Hodges to move again, to Tongres, some fifteen miles on the other side of Liège.

By the morning of December 19, General Eisenhower had a better fix on his enemy than he had on the 18th, partly because of material provided by ULTRA. He had learned, for example, that the Germans were getting ready to commit two SS panzer divisions under the 2nd SS Panzer Corps, and there had been more calls for aerial reconnaissance of the bridges over the Meuse. By that time, Eisenhower also knew the identities of most of the seventeen German divisions thus far committed. The increasing German strength gave added meaning to the earlier intercept of von Rundstedt's hortatory order to the troops, which pointed to considerably more than a spoiling attack.

Eisenhower's thinking about how to meet the offensive thus had undergone considerable change when, at his summons, his senior commanders joined him and key members of his staff at 11 A.M. on December 19 at the 12th Army Group's rear headquarters in Verdun. The meeting took place on the second floor of a stolidly ugly French Army barracks in a room heated only by a pot-bellied stove. The commanders—Bradley, Devers, and Patton, along with a few members of their staffs, and Eisenhower's deputy supreme commander, Air Chief Marshal Arthur W.

Tedder—had assembled when Eisenhower's G-2, General Strong, and G-3, General Bull, at last arrived. "Well," said Eisenhower with a touch of irritation, "I knew my staff would get here; it was only a question of when."

As the generals took their places at a long table, Eisenhower admonished them. "The present situation," he said, "is to be regarded as one of opportunity for us and not of disaster. There will be only cheerful faces at this conference table." To which Patton responded: "Hell, let's have the guts to let the sons of bitches go all the way to Paris. Then we'll really cut 'em up and chew 'em up."

A new infantry division, Eisenhower revealed, had just arrived in France and would be moved forward swiftly. Three infantry divisions then in Britain were to accelerate their shipping schedules, and he was asking that divisions in the United States alerted for early movement ship their infantry regiments in advance. He was also asking authority to use artillery shells equipped with the super-secret radio-controlled proximity fuse. (He was unaware that Colonel Axelson of the 406th Field Artillery Group had already put the fuse to work with good results at Monschau.)

All offensive action, declared Eisenhower, was to cease. Although commanders were to be prepared to give ground, if necessary, to shorten lines and free reserves, there was to be no withdrawal beyond the Meuse River. General Devers was to shift the boundary of his 6th Army Group northward to free some of Patton's troops for a drive into the enemy's south flank, while Simpson's Ninth Army was to do the same to free divisions of the First Army. Because Hodges was too preoccupied at the moment with containing the German thrusts, there could be no counterattack immediately from the north, but Patton was to mount an attack to reach Bastogne and from there eventually drive northward to link with a later attack by the First Army. (The belief that Hodges was in no position for an early attack and the desire to link with the American troops in endangered Bastogne thus served to obviate the obvious possibility of cutting the Germans off at their base with simultaneous attacks by Hodges southeastward on St. Vith and Patton northward up the Skyline Drive; but unknown to Eisenhower, Hodges was even then contemplating an early drive on St. Vith.)

Turning to Patton, Eisenhower asked: "When can you start?"

Patton responded: "As soon as you're through with me."

Eisenhower wanted him to be more specific.

"The morning of December 21st," said Patton. "With three divisions."

That was only a little more than thirty-six hours away. "Don't be fatuous, George," said Eisenhower. "If you try to go that early, you won't have all three divisions ready and you'll go piecemeal. You will start on the twenty-second and I want your initial blow to be a strong one! I'd even settle for the twenty-third if it takes that long to get three full divisions."

The man who only a few hours earlier had argued vehemently with General Bradley over releasing any of his troops was at that point exultant. Having already drawn up three proposals with his staff, he had but to go to a telephone and give a codeword to put the plan to move on Bastogne into action.

Patton would have liked to have seen the Germans drive westward some forty or fifty miles, then chop them off and destroy them, but he recognized that he would never muster support for that kind of daring. As he set about directing a ninety-degree turn by one of his corps and shifting the troops more than 150 miles to the north for an attack to begin two and a half days later—a maneuver that would make Stonewall Jackson's peregrinations in the valley campaign in Virginia and Gallieni's shift of troops in taxicabs to save Paris from the Kaiser look pale by comparison—he remained supremely confident. To his wife, Beatrice, Patton wrote: "Remember how a tarpon makes one big flop just before he dies."

It was well into the evening when General Eisenhower and his party returned to Versailles. As the Supreme Commander went to his office in the Trianon Palace Hotel, his intelligence officer, General Strong, retired to his billets, which he shared with the deputy chief of operations, Jock Whiteley. Strong soon learned that Whiteley had been pondering the telephone call he had received early in the day from Field Marshal Montgomery suggesting that Eisenhower place Montgomery in command of all troops north of the German penetration.

Although Whiteley was no partisan of Montgomery's, the more he thought about the proposal, the more sense it made. Since General Bradley was determined to remain in Luxembourg City, how could he give the northern part of the front the attention it deserved? He was sure that Bradley's communications with the First Army's new headquarters in Chaudfontaine must be poor, for communications from Versailles to Chaudfontaine were poor.

When Strong agreed that the move was warranted, Whiteley telephoned Eisenhower's chief of staff, General Smith, and asked for an audience. Going with Strong to Smith's office, he made his proposal and in return got a taste of Bedell Smith's well-known hair-trigger temper. He had always counted on Whiteley, snapped Smith, to maintain "a completely Allied outlook," yet there he was "talking like a damned British staff officer."

Whiteley nevertheless stuck by his proposal. It was based, he said, strictly on military considerations. Smith could fire him, but he stuck by it.

Picking up the telephone, Smith got Eisenhower on the line and told him of Whiteley's proposal and Strong's concurrence. By that time, his flare-up of temper had passed, and when he put down the telephone, he told the two British officers: "General Eisenhower says we can decide this matter after our staff meeting tomorrow morning."

Although it was then close to eleven o'clock in the evening, Eisenhower was still in his office, a cavernous room normally used for meetings and banquets. Rising from his desk, he walked over to a big situation map that covered part of one of the walls.

As Eisenhower pondered the map, he noted to himself that Whiteley's proposal made sense. The critical battle might well be joined on the northern shoulder of the penetration, and Bradley was too far away to exercise close personal control. Before the German offensive was over, it might well be that all Allied troops north of the penetration would become involved. He needed a single commander to coordinate the four armies located there. Besides, Montgomery's 21st Army Group had the only considerable reserve then available on the Continent, the 30th British Corps, which had been out of the line getting ready to renew the offensive. Although Eisenhower as Supreme Commander had full authority to call on that corps, and if Montgomery objected to its use, he had no question but that the Combined Chiefs of Staff would back the Supreme Commander, it would be better, should British troops be required, that Montgomery himself commit them.

On the other hand, Eisenhower mused, some of the senior American commanders (particularly Bradley and Patton) would resent the move, primarily because it involved the imperious, abrasive Montgomery. However temporary the change in command, some would see it as a surrender to Montgomery's persistent arguments that he be made overall Allied ground commander, and some hotheads might even see it as a loss of confidence in Bradley.

Yet as Eisenhower continued to study the map, it became ever clearer that he had to do it. With a grease pencil, he drew a line across the map from Givet on the Meuse River eastward through the Ardennes and across the German frontier to Prüm. All forces north of that line—the First and Ninth Armies, the First Canadian Army, and the Second British Army—were to be temporarily under Montgomery; those south of the line—the VIII Corps and the Third Army—under Bradley.

Going to the telephone, Eisenhower told Bedell Smith to notify Bradley of his decision. As might have been expected, the news jolted Bradley. Indeed, he was "completely dumbfounded—and shocked." When he had left Eisenhower only a few hours earlier, the Supreme Commander had given no inkling of a change in command. Although there had been, in fact, some problems with telephonic communications to Hodges, his communications people were laying new lines, including one west of the Meuse. He thought the staff at Versailles was beginning to panic when in fact there was nothing to justify undue alarm. Although he failed to say so to Smith, he also believed it would be a loss of face for him and the entire American command; and it particularly rankled that he would have to relinquish his beloved former command, the First Army, which he had earlier tried to safeguard from Montgomery's clutches by inserting Simpson's Ninth Army into the line between the First Army and the British.

Bradley nevertheless felt compelled to admit that if it were anybody but Montgomery, even another British commander, and certainly if it were an American commander, the proposal made sense, was "the logical thing to do." Furthermore, should the Germans get across the Meuse, Montgomery's 21st Army Group would be in jeopardy. Against that possibility, Montgomery would want to hold onto the 30th Corps; but if he were in command of the northern front, he might be disposed to use his reserve to keep the Germans from getting across the Meuse. "There's no doubt in my mind," said Bradley finally, "that if we play it the way you suggest, we'll get more help from the British in the way of reserves."

Assured by Smith that the change was to be temporary, Bradley gave his consent, an act, he was to note near the end of a long life, that was "one of my biggest mistakes of the war." As Eisenhower personally notified Bradley the next morning, the change was to take effect at noon that day, December 20.

Unaware that a change was in the offing, Field Marshal Brooke had in the meantime responded to Montgomery's demand that he be placed in command in the north by going, not to the Combined Chiefs of Staff (there was no time for that) but to the prime minister, Winston Churchill. Late in the night of the 19th, Churchill telephoned Eisenhower. Whether Churchill intended to push Montgomery's candidacy would never be known, for early in the conversation, Eisenhower volunteered that he intended giving Montgomery temporary command in the north. In typical Churchillian fashion, Churchill assured him "that British troops will always deem it an honor to enter the same battle as their American friends."

As Eisenhower had anticipated, Patton, like Bradley, resented the decision. Patton thought Eisenhower did it either "through the machinations of the Prime Minister" or in the hope of getting help from British divisions. In any event, he saw Eisenhower as "unwilling or unable to command Montgomery."

Conscious of the pain caused to Bradley and the possibility of misinterpretation of the move as a loss of confidence in Bradley, Eisenhower suggested to the U.S. Army's chief of staff, General Marshall, that it "would be a most opportune time to promote Bradley." Although Marshall agreed, he noted that because the Congress had adjourned for Christmas, that was for the moment unfeasible.

As presented to Bradley, the basic reason for the change was the difficulty of Bradley's communicating with Hodges. Without question, face-to-face discussions between the two commanders would have been difficult. One or the other would have had to circle by road or by air far around to the west of the Meuse, and if the Germans crossed the Meuse, that might prove to be impossible. Although communication by telephone would be no real substitute for direct contact, Bradley was correct in that some telephonic communications—whether sufficient to the demand would remain problematical—still existed, but by circuitous and not always reliable routes. As early as December 22, the Germans forced men manning a repeater radio station at Jemelle, near Marche, to abandon their post; and the next day they cut the main telephone line, a buried cable, and two days later another, an open-wire circuit.

In the final analysis, Bradley himself was the author of his own discontent. It was he who located—or approved—a forward headquarters in Luxembourg City, only fourteen miles behind the front, considerably closer than any of his three subordinate army headquarters and most of the corps headquarters. Nor could it be argued that that location was central to his three army commands, for it was considerably closer to the headquarters of the Third Army than to those of the First and Ninth Armies. (Was that to keep close tabs on the impetuous George Patton?)

It looked like an affinity on the part of somebody for the creature comforts of a big town, that plus the general belief that the Germans were already beaten. Even so, Bradley's dogmatic refusal to relocate his headquarters reflected an undue concern for the reaction of the civilians of the Luxembourg capital. There were already thousands of refugees all over the Ardennes, and the withdrawal of Hodges's headquarters from Spa had generated others; furthermore, however miserable the plight of refugees, Europeans over the centuries had grown to live with the comings and goings of conquerors.

At headquarters of the First Army in the Hôtel des Bains in Chaudfontaine, the news of the change in command "created undercurrents of unhappiness." As Bradley looked on his former command with affection, so did the members of the First Army's staff on their former commander, and Montgomery with his "cocky mannerisms" would do little to ease the pain of separation. When Montgomery arrived at the headquarters around noon on the 20th with his chief of staff, General de Guingand, he had already received reports on the situation at the front from his PHANTOM couriers, and rather than consult the First Army's operations map, he referred to a small one of his own. To one of the members of his entourage, he seemed to stride into the headquarters "like Christ come to cleanse the temple."

The Americans had rebuffed Montgomery in happier times, but now, in their hour of trial, they deigned to call on him. In Montgomery's view, had they but listened to him, followed the strategy he advocated, made him the overall ground commander, no hour of trial would have arrived.

When it came time for lunch, Montgomery declined General Hodges's invitation, turning instead to eat alone from a lunchbox and Thermos. No matter that that was his usual practice when dining away from his headquarters, the Americans saw it as an affront.

Having been told by Eisenhower that he approved giving up ground if necessary in order to gain reserves, Montgomery proposed withdrawing from St. Vith and softening the angle of the northern corner by pulling back from the Elsenborn Ridge. Hodges and his staff saw that as a typical Montgomery maneuver, a step to "tidy the battlefield." In their view, what American blood had bought, American soldiers held onto. When Montgomery saw that they reacted as if he intended to strip them of their birthrights, he demurred temporarily, but the matter of withdrawal from St. Vith was to arise again.

While considering, as did Hodges, that Liège was a basic German objective, Montgomery believed that German ambition went beyond Liège. It looked to him as if the Germans intended swinging northwest and crossing the river between Liège and the bend at Namur, in which case Hodges needed to extend his retaining wall southwestward as far as Marche and assemble a strong reserve behind the Ourthe River between Marche and the Meuse to counterattack whenever the Germans had outrun their resources. To command that reserve, Montgomery insisted upon having the commander of the VII Corps, Maj. Gen. J. Lawton ("Lightning Joe")* Collins, whom he considered to be one of the more capable American corps commanders.

Courtney Hodges also thought highly of Collins; indeed, there were those who said that Joe Collins was Hodges's fair-haired boy. Hodges was already considering pulling headquarters of the VII Corps from the line east of Aachen and assembling enough troops to counterattack southeast from Malmédy on St. Vith in hope of linking with a drive by Patton up the Skyline Drive—a move advocated both by Gerow of the V Corps and Middleton of the VIII Corps.

To flesh out the VII Corps, Collins was to have the 84th Infantry Division, already under orders to move from the Ninth Army to the Ardennes, and the division that Eisenhower had remarked at Verdun as having just reached France, the 75th Infantry Division. At the suggestion of Montgomery's operations officer, Brig. David Belchem, Montgomery ordered the Ninth Army's reserve, the 2d Armored Division, to the Ardennes to provide Collins with a third division. The corps was to be employed not, according to Hodges's plan, to drive on St. Vith, but according to Montgomery's, as a reserve between the Ourthe and the

---

*Although Collins was an audacious commander, the nickname derived not from swift battlefield maneuver but from his having earlier commanded the 25th ("Tropic Lightning") Infantry Division in the Pacific.

Meuse. Whether the Germans would allow the Allied command the luxury of withholding a reserve remained to be seen.

Even before assuming command in the north, Montgomery ordered his 30th Corps with four divisions (a fifth was to follow later) to move to a deep reserve position some thirty miles north of the Meuse. That put the corps in position not only to counter a crossing of the Meuse but also to counter any German attempt to take advantage of the thinning of the American line around Aachen. Montgomery also sent detachments to secure bridges over the river between Namur and Liège.

As Montgomery left Hodges's headquarters, he was concerned about Hodges's health. To Montgomery, Hodges appeared to be exhausted, a candidate for a heart attack, and he thought he should be relieved of command. At the first opportunity, Montgomery telephoned Bedell Smith, telling him that as a British officer, he himself was unwilling to relieve an American general but he thought Eisenhower should relieve Hodges.

When Eisenhower learned of it, he thought he knew immediately what was wrong; Montgomery had failed to realize that God had given Hodges a face that always looked drawn and pessimistic. He promptly sent off a note to Montgomery advising him that Hodges was "the quiet reticent type and does not appear as aggressive as he really is. Unless he becomes exhausted he will always wage a good fight."

As early as December 18, the commander of the Fifth Panzer Army, Hasso von Manteuffel, had concluded that the German offensive had failed, that there was no hope of reaching Antwerp (which he had never anticipated in any case), and that even the Meuse River appeared to be out of reach. The only army commander who was enjoying any real success, he passed his pessimistic opinion on to the commander of *OB WEST*, von Rundstedt, and to the chief of the armed forces operations staff, General Jodl, both of whom had already come to much the same conclusion.

As von Rundstedt saw it, the way to salvage something from the offensive was to mount the projected attack by the Fifteenth Army to drive in behind the American forces in the vicinity of Aachen, thereby forestalling the shift of any more American divisions to the Ardennes. He ordered the Fifteenth Army to attack early the next morning, December 19.

Hitler promptly overrode him. Were his defeatist field commanders trying to set up conditions for shifting to their Small Solution? There was to be no attack by the Fifteenth Army. And to ensure it, he ordered the two divisions of the Führer Reserve that were earmarked for use with the Fifteenth Army—the 9th Panzer and 15th Panzergrenadier Divisions—to move to assembly areas in northern reaches of the Eifel. That put them beyond reach for unauthorized commitment with the Fifteenth Army, and Hitler reiterated that neither division was to be employed without his specific approval. With everything else remaining, von Rundstedt was to exploit the penetrations already achieved in the Ardennes.

Since the Sixth Panzer Army had failed to get past the Elsenborn Ridge, the commander of Army Group B, Field Marshal Model, with von Rundstedt's endorsement, ordered the main effort to shift on December 20 to the Fifth Panzer Army. At Hitler's order, General Dietrich nevertheless had to continue to hammer away for four more days in what turned out to be a continuing futile effort to get past the Elsenborn Ridge; but the Sixth Panzer Army's role was inexorably changing from getting across the Meuse to protecting the Fifth Panzer Army's north flank.

As a first step in that shift, one of the uncommitted SS panzer divisions, the 2d *(Das Reich)*, was to swing around to the south of St. Vith, follow the path of the 116th Panzer Division, and turn north against the line the Americans were building up along the north flank of the German penetration. Meanwhile the other SS panzer division, the 9th *(Hohenstaufen)*, was to move through the Losheim Gap, cross the Salm River upstream from the route taken by *Kampfgruppe Peiper*, and swing north against the developing American line close alongside the 2d SS Panzer Division. Vital to the new role of the Sixth Panzer Army was the necessity for the main body of the 1st SS Panzer Division to make contact with *Kampfgruppe Peiper*, and the new alignment could never be fully developed without the road network in and around St. Vith to take the place of the network denied by the American stand on the Elsenborn Ridge.

Although nobody told Adolf Hitler, the German field commanders were no longer thinking in terms of reaching Antwerp—if, indeed, they had ever thought seriously in those terms. Their long-range goal was to use the Sixth Panzer Army to pin the American forces along the northern flank while the Fifth Panzer Army crossed the Meuse in the vicinity of Namur, then swung northwest toward Aachen to trap those American forces facing the Sixth Panzer Army south of Liège and at the corner at the Elsenborn Ridge.

A variation on the Small Solution.

As was the case at Eisenhower's headquarters, realization of the portent of what was happening in the Ardennes was slow to come to the people in Allied capitals. That was basically because of a system of strict censorship imposed on all news by the headquarters, not only on news transmitted to Britain and the United States but also on what was aired or printed in Belgium and France.

Before the invasion, the exiled government of Belgium had agreed to voluntary censorship, while France had agreed to subject its press and radio to the same restrictions as SHAEF imposed on British and American correspondents. Although an occasional newsman violated the restrictions, retribution in the form of withdrawn credentials inevitably followed, and that might mean being sent home.

The official radios in Belgium, Britain, and France began transmitting some reports of what was happening on the second day, December 17, but most of the first newspaper accounts came only on the third. No Washington newspaper, for example, had any mention on the second day, although *The New York Times* carried a story on page 19 under a one-column headline: GERMAN ASSAULT ON FIRST ARMY FIERCE. The correspondent noted: "It was a new and violent move in the enemy's campaign to delay and harass us and make every yard of our advance as costly as possible." The banner headlines across front pages came only on the third day, December 18.

There was at first no particular concern among the people of Brussels and Paris. Neither the official radio nor the newspapers engaged in sensationalism, and only a few months earlier the people had seen with their own eyes a thoroughly defeated German Army limp back to the homeland. To most people it was unbelievable that such a crippled force could mount a really viable threat to Allied armies, whose power was plain for all to see. Most housewives were concerned less with what was happening at the front than with finding something special for Christmas dinner among the rationed stocks in the shops.

As the days passed and it was obvious that the weather was preventing Allied planes from operating, some concern began to arise. There were tales from refugees, reports by telephone from friends or relatives close to the front, and word that the British Army had established road blocks on the approaches to Brussels. Some even saw the possibility of a second occupation with inevitable reprisals, but for most the concern never developed into more than a gnawing worry. The Germans obviously were advancing with no such speed as they had displayed in 1940. Nobody in either Brussels or Paris took to the roads.

Seeing supporting units hastily falling back in the first days, newsmen at the front were shocked and dismayed by what they took to be panic. Many fled to Maastricht in the Netherlands, where they tried to send dispatches reporting wholesale flight, but the censor saw what they wrote as "sheer hysteria" and squelched it. At least one of the newsmen, Wes Gallagher of the Associated Press, was later grateful. "What could have been an unholy mess," he noted, "was saved by the good sense of front line field censors."

American newsmen in particular were nevertheless outraged at the little information SHAEF's press office provided and at the little the censor would pass. An "angry session" erupted at Versailles on December 19 with reporters demanding the release of more details. "May I say," shouted George Lyon of the Office of War Information, "that SHAEF's policy . . . is stupid?" Another said that "everybody across hell and forty acres" knew what was going on, and the American people were entitled to know.

Nothing remotely critical of the Allied command or the troops appeared in print in the early days. What had befallen "our troops" and "our men" was obviously a result of the fortunes of war, and even though Christmas would be "tinged by sorrow, anxiety, and a graveness of spirit," all was sure to be set right in time. President Roosevelt and the White House made no public comment, and a spokesman for the War Department urged that "the situation should not be viewed with panic." The American public would "do well to reserve its judgments and fears until enough time has passed for a clarification of the situation." The Germans, he said, were incapable of a decisive victory.

The military editor of *The New York Times*, Hanson Baldwin, made one of the first criticisms. Writing on Christmas Eve, he noted that the Allied command appeared to have been surprised threefold: with regard to time, place, and size of the German forces. American intelligence officers appeared "to have made the same mistake they made before and during the hedgerow fighting in Normandy," which was to underestimate "the capacity and will of the enemy to fight."

Two days later *The Washington Post* noted editorially that "our command was caught napping." The blame clearly belonged to "the intelligence service," and the government should remember that and create a strong intelligence arm in the postwar era. Yet except for British newspapers, which saw in the events an opportunity to push for a larger command role for their countryman, Field Marshal Montgomery, that was about as sharp as the criticism ever became.

CHAPTER TWENTY-ONE

The War Against *Kampfgruppe Peiper*

As Joachim Peiper and his armored column descended into the deep valley of the Amblève River at Stavelot early on December 18, distance and terrain disrupted radio communications with headquarters of the 1st SS Panzer Division. Throughout the day, while American engineers at Trois Ponts and near Habiémont were frustrating Peiper, he knew nothing of what was happening behind him—whether the 3d Parachute Division was moving forward to hold his lifeline at Stavelot, whether the 12th SS Panzer Division had broken through to drive along his northern flank, whether the rest of the 1st SS Panzer Division was advancing to link with his rear. Nor did he have any information as to what steps the American command was taking to counter his drive. What he did know from the actions of the American engineers and from the attack during the afternoon by American fighter-bombers was that he had lost his principal ally: surprise.

Only near midnight, when a liaison officer managed to get forward with an ultra high-frequency radio, was he able to reestablish contact with his division headquarters. To his concern, he learned that two American divisions, the 7th Armored and the 30th Infantry, were moving into the Ardennes from the vicinity of Aachen. Although both those divisions had been in reserve and out of contact with German units, American radio security was so poor that German intelligence had quickly picked up their movements.

Having seen the bridge over the Lienne Creek near Habiémont blown in his face just at nightfall, Peiper had sent reconnaissance detachments with half-tracks and assault guns upstream and down in an effort to find another bridge. Although both detachments located bridges, they were in each case too fragile to carry his tanks. One of the detachments nevertheless crossed to the west bank of the Lienne, but there in the darkness ran into a company of American infantry supported by two self-propelled tank destroyers. Only one of the German vehicles escaped, an armored car in which the detachment commander, Lieutenant Preuss, was riding.

As darkness deepened, Peiper saw no choice but to pull back to the north bank of the Amblève by way of the bridge he had taken intact near Cheneux. Leaving a strong force to defend Cheneux in the event he needed the bridge later, he assembled his command in and around the village of La Gleize. Up to that point, his losses had been relatively light, a total of thirteen tanks—three at Dom. Bütgenbach, four in front of Wirtzfeld, one at Ligneuville, four at Stavelot, and one at Cheneux—plus two flak tanks and a few half-tracks and smaller vehicles. During the night, seven of his attached Tiger tanks and the division's reconnaissance battalion joined him.

Peiper at that point considered that there were two ways he could continue the thrust to the Meuse. Beyond La Gleize and the next town of Stoumont, the road followed the valley of the meandering Amblève close alongside the river, with steep, clifflike wooded hills on the other side, so that a few men with antitank mines might block it at any number of places; only ten winding miles later did the road enter more open country at the Bastogne-Liège highway. Yet there was supposed to be a bridge not far beyond Stoumont, between the hamlet of Targnon and a railroad stop, known as Stoumont Station, that afforded passage across the Amblève and a return to the road he was trying to reach that led to Werbomont. Given the confined nature of the road beyond Stoumont Station, getting that bridge appeared to be Peiper's only real hope, and even that was dependent upon the great imponderable of gasoline.

What Peiper did not know was that he was practically within spitting distance of enough gasoline to take him not only to the Meuse River but to the North Sea and back several times. In the woods along a secondary road only a few miles north of La Gleize was the second and larger of the First Army's big depots with more than 2 million gallons of gasoline, guarded as night fell on the 18th by only about a hundred men of a rear echelon headquarters with five half-tracks and three assault guns reinforced by a few men of the Belgian Fusiliers. Although two 90mm. antiaircraft guns and four more half-tracks with quad-50s arrived after nightfall, it was still a defensive force in no way capable of dealing with the strength Peiper might throw against it. Yet not until the next morning did any Germans move toward the depot; and then it was only a flank reconnaissance patrol of a few armored vehicles, under orders to fall back if encountering resistance, which it did.

Thus Peiper in his ignorance worried and fretted in La Gleize about the growing shortage of fuel. As his exhausted troops bedded down for the night, it was Peiper's second self-imposed delay, and it was to have consequences even exceeding those that followed the delay before Stavelot. For his patrols determined during the night that the road to Stoumont Station was not to be Peiper's for the asking.

*   *   *

Long weeks earlier, in Normandy, a battalion of the 30th Division's 120th Infantry had held onto a hill, although surrounded, for six days and helped frustrate a Hitler-ordered offensive aimed at cutting off American spearheads that had broken out of the beachhead. After that, a turncoat American radio propagandist for the Nazis known as "Axis Sally" referred to the 30th Division as "Roosevelt's SS," a name in which the men of the division took a certain pride. The division's true nickname was "Old Hickory," after President Andrew Jackson, which reflected the division's origin in the Carolinas-Tennessee National Guard.

Night had fallen on December 17 by the time most of the vehicles carrying troops of the 30th Division to the Ardennes got on the road. A few German planes flew over the column, dropping flares and an occasional ineffective bomb and making a few futile strafing passes, and there were reports of German paratroopers but no real difficulties. As the column started out, the plan was that the division would back up the defenders of the twin villages and Bütgenbach, but with news of *Kampfgruppe Peiper's* breakthrough, the massacre at Baugnez, and later Peiper's attack on Stavelot, all that changed. In the end, the 117th Infantry went to Stavelot, the 120th Infantry to Malmédy, and the 119th Infantry to Spa, there to be prepared to defend the First Army's headquarters town but also to be ready for commitment elsewhere, depending on which direction *Kampfgruppe Peiper* took from Stavelot.

Those assignments made, General Hodges asked the division commander, Maj. Gen. Leland S. Hobbs, to come to Spa.

As Hodges made that request, he already had a visitor, the temporary commander of the XVIII Airborne Corps, James Gavin, who had just made an all-night trip by jeep from his 82d Airborne Division's encampment in northern France. Gavin went immediately to the War Room, where he talked with Hodges, as well as the chief of staff, Bill Kean, and the operations officer, Tubby Thorson.

It was at that conference that Hodges, in concern for the threat posed by *Kampfgruppe Peiper*, decided to order the 82d Airborne Division to bypass Bastogne and move to Werbomont to stop Peiper, leaving the 101st Airborne Division to go to Bastogne. From the Hôtel Britannique Gavin drove to Werbomont, where at the bridge over the Lienne Creek near Habiémont, he talked with the engineer officer assigned to destroy the bridge, Lieutenant Edelstein. Then continuing on to Bastogne, Gavin made sure the acting commander of the 101st Airborne Division, General McAuliffe, understood the change in orders. He returned in the evening to Werbomont by way of Houffalize. (Only later was Gavin to learn that advance contingents of the 116th Panzer Division had already driven past Houffalize.) As Gavin reached Werbomont around 8 P.M., first troops of the 82d Airborne Division were arriving.

The regular commander of the XVIII Airborne Corps, General Ridgway, had in the meantime hurried back with his staff by air from England. He spent the night of the 18th at Middleton's headquarters in Bastogne and drove after daylight to Werbomont, there to establish his corps headquarters in a farmhouse across the road from General Gavin's, which at that point became the headquarters of the 82d Airborne Division. That done, Ridgway drove to Hodges's relocated headquarters in Chaudfontaine. There he learned that he was to have control of the 30th Division's 119th Infantry, a portion of the 3d Armored Division, which was on the way to the Ardennes from the Ninth Army, and the 82d Airborne Division. It was a small force indeed with which to stop Peiper and at the same time fill a gap between Werbomont and the Ourthe River, a gap of some fifteen miles toward which other German armored columns were driving. Yet that was Ridgway's assignment.

As Leland Hobbs entered the Hôtel Britannique around noon on December 18, many of the First Army's headquarters units were packing, getting ready for the shift to Chaudfontaine. General Hodges had just received word from pilots of cub planes flying from the First Army's airstrip just outside Spa that the big German armored column had turned away from Trois Ponts and was heading up the valley of the Amblève toward La Gleize and Stoumont. That obviously presented the enemy commander with three choices. He could continue to follow the valley of the Amblève; cross the bridge at Cheneux and head for Werbomont; or turn north at one of several points on Liège.

In any case, the German column had to be stopped. When Hobbs left the headquarters and found the commander of the 119th Infantry, Col. Edward M. Sutherland, he had orders to send one of Sutherland's battalions to hold along the Lienne Creek in front of Werbomont until troops of the 82d Airborne Division could assume that task. The rest of the regiment was to block the German column in the valley of the Amblève. As part of the battalion that moved to the Lienne Creek, it was Company F that devastated one of Peiper's reconnaissance detachments along the creek that night.

Early the next morning, the commander of Company F, 1st Lt. Edward C. Arn, was astounded to see a jeep pull up outside his headquarters and a two-star general in the uniform of a paratrooper jump out. "I'm Jim Gavin of the 82d Airborne Division," said the general. His men, he explained, were soon to relieve Arn's, and if Arn had no objection, he would "go on up ahead and have a look around." A few minutes later one of Arn's platoon leaders, 2d Lt. Kenneth Austin, called over his walkie-talkie radio. "I wish to suggest that you have me relieved," said Austin; "I'm going nuts. There's a two-star general in a jeep . . ."

Meanwhile, the rest of the 119th Infantry had headed in late afternoon of the 18th for the valley of the Amblève River. Traveling behind a reconnaissance screen that found the road clear of Germans at least as far as Stoumont, the leading 3d Battalion detrucked in that town.

Since it was well after dark, the commander, Lt. Col. Roy C. Fitzgerald, Jr., told his men to dig defensive positions for the night. The wisdom of that decision was soon revealed when patrols, sent probing in the direction of La Gleize, returned with word that they had seen Germans openly talking and smoking less than a thousand yards away along the highway near the imposing Château de Froide-Cour. As best the men could discern in the darkness, there were some thirty-five to forty tanks.

At about the same time, Peiper's patrols discovered that the Americans were near. Ordering an attack before dawn to seize Stoumont and push on to the bridge across the Amblève just short of Stoumont Station, Peiper spent much of the night moving among his troops, joking with them, bantering, encouraging them. He was concerned that fatigue and the day's frustrations were taking a toll of his men's enthusiasm and esprit.

Around mid-morning of the 18th, the 117th Infantry's 1st Battalion reached the gasoline depot in the woods above Stavelot. There just forward of the woodsline, Belgian Fusiliers were still maintaining a roadblock by burning gasoline in the road. Since the fire denied any use of the road, the battalion commander, Lt. Col. Robert E. Frankland, ordered a halt to the burning; but since it might be some time before vehicles could pass, he told his men to detruck and proceed on foot. His fire support—three assault guns and a platoon of towed tank destroyers—would have to wait until the fire died down. Nor would Frankland have artillery support, for his regiment's supporting artillery battalion had yet to arrive.

Having anticipated early reinforcement by troops of the 3d Parachute Division to hold Stavelot and the vital bridge over the Amblève, Peiper had left only a small security detachment in the town. As Frankland's infantrymen approached, men of that detachment opened fire. The Americans nevertheless gained the first houses and gradually worked their way farther into town. The towed guns of a platoon of the 823d Tank Destroyer Battalion finally bypassed the roadblock at the gasoline depot and assumed firing positions overlooking the houses.

Early that afternoon ten Mark IVs suddenly appeared, racing into Stavelot along the road from Trois Ponts. Those tanks might have done terrible damage had not the fighter-bombers that were attacking Peiper's column near Cheneux roared to the attack. They knocked out no tanks, but they drove them to cover.

By nightfall, the men of the 117th Infantry's 1st Battalion held half of Stavelot, the towed tank destroyers had entered the town, as had three Shermans of the 743d Tank Battalion, and the 118th Field Artillery Battalion was ready to fire. All that was fortunate, for the fight for Stavelot was only just beginning.

Soon after midnight, a Tiger, one of a number of the 501st Heavy Panzer Battalion following in Peiper's wake, approached the town square along the street leading up from the bridge over the Amblève. Men of a platoon of Company A under 1st Lt. Robert O. Murray, Jr., knocked it out with a bazooka fired at close range, and the great carcass blocked the narrow street. As two following Tigers tried to turn into even narrower side streets, they had to back and fill to make the turns, leaving them vulnerable to Murray's bazookamen. Well-placed rockets knocked them out.

By midday of December 19, Frankland's infantry had cleared all of Stavelot except for a few houses on the western edge along the road to Trois Ponts. Although the men had gained the buildings facing the river near the bridge, the bridge itself was still intact. Just across the river was a force of the 2d SS-Panzergrenadier Regiment, a contingent of one of the other columns of the 1st SS Panzer Division under orders from the division commander, Colonel Mohnke, to open a route to Peiper. With the *SS-Panzergrenadiers* were four Panthers. From an observation post on the high ground behind Stavelot, Colonel Frankland's artillery liaison officer called for such heavy fire beyond the river that the *SS-Panzergrenadiers* ran for cover, but the tanks continued to roll toward the bridge.

At first they had cover from a row of houses, but forty yards short of the bridge, the cover ran out. The crew of a towed 3-inch gun covering the bridge—Sgt. Clyde Gentry was the commander, Cpl. Buel Sheridan the gunner—could see the tanks pass behind the buildings and waited nervously for the first one to appear at the other end. It was a Panther.

Before the tank could turn toward the bridge, presenting the protection of its heavy frontal armor, Sheridan got in two shots. The first missed, but the second ripped the turret off. A second Panther made it to the center of the little stone span under a hail of rounds both from Sheridan and from the crews of other towed guns before a round so damaged the turret and the gun that neither could traverse.

When two more Panthers emerged, Sheridan hit one in a track; as the driver tried to back up, he ran into a ditch and there foundered helplessly. The other came to a halt behind the last house, the muzzle brake on its cannon visible, but it made no further effort to advance.

That ended the attack from the south bank of the Amblève. Yet even as that fight was going on, another developed at the western end of town, the work of the 1st SS Panzer Division's reconnaissance battalion. Commanded by Maj. Gustav Knittel, that battalion had passed through Stavelot the night before to reach Peiper at La Gleize. Once Peiper learned of the American capture of Stavelot, he summoned Knittel to his command post in a farmhouse near the Château de Froid-Cour and told him to retake the town.

That was Knittel's first chance to talk with Peiper since his arrival. As he got ready to depart, he paused. "They've killed a good few at the crossroads," he said.

"The crossroads?" asked Peiper.

Yes, Knittel responded. The one where the road turned toward Ligneuville. "There're a lot of *Amis* dead there."

That was the first indication Joachim Peiper received that anything untoward had happened at the road junction at Baugnez. At about the same time, his superior, the commander of the Sixth Panzer Army, Sepp Dietrich, was also receiving his first information on the massacre. His chief of staff, General Kraemer, handed him a piece of paper containing a report of a radio broadcast from *Soldatensender Calais*, a British propaganda station over which German prisoners of war beamed reports aimed at the German soldier. According to the broadcast, some sixty Americans had been "shot by the enemy as they were surrendering or had already surrendered."

A message went out almost immediately from headquarters of the Sixth Panzer Army to subordinate units to conduct "an immediate enquiry whether anyone knew anything about the shooting of some American prisoners of war." Otto Skorzeny was one who received the message, and he reported in the negative. To Skorzeny, "such a crime was quite unthinkable in the German Army." The commander of the 1st SS Panzer Division, Colonel Mohnke, also submitted a negative report.

For the attack against the western side of Stavelot, Major Knittel obtained three Mark IVs to strengthen his own force of light tanks, armored cars, and half-tracks. Dividing his force, Knittel sent the main body directly up the road from Trois Ponts and the other part up a back road through the hamlets of Parfondruy, Ster, and Renardmont, on high ground overlooking Stavelot. Knittel hoped to pass beyond those hamlets and get in behind the Americans at Stavelot.

Knittel's means in no way matched his ambition, nor did he take into account the gunners of the 118th Field Artillery Battalion. Against the two German attacks at Stavelot that afternoon, the cannoneers fired three thousand shells. So rapidly did they work their pieces that they had to cool the tubes with water. As night came on December 19, Colonel Frankland's battalion of the 117th Infantry still had a firm grip on Stavelot, and during the night the infantrymen all but sealed their hold when a contingent of the 30th Division's 105th Engineer Combat Battalion, working behind a smoke screen under the noses of Germans on the other bank of the Amblève, at long last blew the stone bridge over the river.

The engineers who blew the bridge made a major contribution to continued defense of Stavelot, but their accomplishment failed to put an end to German efforts to force a way through the town, for unlike Peiper, the follow-up force of the 1st SS Panzer Division, commanded by Lt. Col.

Rudolf Sandig, had bridging equipment. Before daylight the next morning, December 20, a hundred men of the 2d SS Panzergrenadier Regiment, covered by heavy fire from tanks and self-propelled tank destroyers, began wading the icy, swift-flowing little river. Theirs was an incredibly difficult assignment, for at that spot both banks of the river were steep concrete revetments.

By the light of flares, American soldiers in the buildings facing the river had little difficulty picking off the men struggling through the water. Some concentrated their fire on those carrying makeshift ladders and on anybody who looked to be an officer, while supporting tanks fired white phosphorus shells in an attempt to light the scene by setting fire to houses on the other bank. When that failed, Sgt. William Pierce swam the river with a can of gasoline, emptied it against the side of a house, and set it afire.

A few of the Germans nevertheless managed to get into the first row of houses near the bridge, but their presence masked the fire of their supporting tanks and tank destroyers. Lieutenant Murray's platoon of Company A had little difficulty retaking the houses, and the German attack collapsed.

The killing of Belgian civilians by soldiers of *Kampfgruppe Peiper* began early on December 18 as the first Germans passed through Stavelot. Along a street leading to the road to Trois Ponts, a machine gunner on a half-track fired into the kitchen of the house of M. Gengoux, killing his fourteen-year-old son José. Nearby, Joseph Albert and his daughter, Denise, hiding in their cellar, heard a noise upstairs, and when M. Albert went to investigate, a German soldier shot him dead. On the fringe of Trois Ponts, two soldiers engaged M. Warnier and his wife briefly in conversation, then killed them both.

The next day, also among the few houses of Trois Ponts standing on the north bank of the Amblève, five German soldiers entered the house of M. Georgin, where Georgin, his wife, and three young neighbors were in the kitchen. "They are hiding terrorists here!" shouted one of the soldiers. Another ordered young Louis Nicolay to follow him, and as soon as they got outside killed him. Yet another ordered M. Georgin to accompany him, but when they were out of the house, Georgin made a run for it. As the German fired his burp gun, Georgin pretended to be hit and fell to the ground. "*Kaput,*" said the German to his companions, but he made no effort to investigate. Inch by inch, Georgin crept toward the bank of the Amblève, then leapt to his feet and threw himself into the swirling waters. As he reached the far bank, the Germans fired, almost severing one of Georgin's arms, but he got away. Nobody else in M. Georgin's house survived.

That night, the 19th, on the fringe of Stavelot, Mme. Régine Grégoire was taking refuge in a neighbor's cellar with her two children (aged four and nine) and twenty-three other people, all women and children except for two elderly men. A hand grenade rolled down the steps and exploded, harming nobody, but a second one wounded Madame Grégoire slightly in the leg. Shouts came from the top of the stairs: *"Heraus! Heraus!"*

Since Madame Grégoire spoke German (she was a native of Manderfeld in the Losheim Gap), she called out that there were only civilians in the cellar. When the Germans insisted that she come out, she went upstairs with her children in tow, there to find a dozen German soldiers whom she recognized by their uniforms as SS. Although she insisted there were only women and children in the cellar, and the two elderly men, the Germans demanded that everybody come into the garden.

There the soldiers pushed Madame Grégoire and her children to one side but forced the others to stand or kneel alongside a hedge. One soldier with a pistol, another with a rifle, then executed them methodically. They ranged in age from four to sixty-eight. Only Madame Grégoire and her children were spared.

Those were but a few incidents in what became an orgy of killing in Stavelot, Trois Ponts, and the hamlets of Parfondruy, Ster, and Renardmont. Here an old man and his wife; there a farmer in his barn; elsewhere twelve people collected in ones and twos and brought together in a house, executed, the house burned; one woman lying in her bed.

Of a population of just under a hundred people in Parfondruy, twenty-six were murdered. As best the Belgian authorities could determine, 138 people died in brutal, senseless executions.

For defending Stoumont, the men of the 3d Battalion, 119th Infantry, had the support of eight towed pieces of the 823d Tank Destroyer Battalion, which took up firing positions on the forward edge of town covering the highway from La Gleize and open fields on either side of the road. Although the 119th Infantry's normal artillery support had yet to arrive, the regimental commander, Colonel Sutherland, had the promise of support from the 400th Armored Field Artillery Battalion, newly attached to the 30th Division, although whether the self-propelled 105mm. howitzers would arrive in time remained to be seen. As soon as Sutherland learned that the Germans were close, he obtained from General Hobbs a promise of a company of mediums from the 743d Tank Battalion, the 30th Division's usual tank support, to arrive at dawn. Sutherland held his 1st Battalion in reserve near his headquarters three miles up the valley of the Amblève.

Also present at Stoumont were two weapons seldom employed in a ground role: powerful 90mm. antiaircraft guns. Under the command of 1st Lt. Donald McGuire, the two guns belonged to Battery C, 143d Antiaircraft Artillery Gun Battalion, which only a few days earlier had arrived from the United States. Such was the concern at headquarters of the First

Army about Peiper that even before anybody knew troops of the 119th Infantry were going to Stoumont, the First Army's antiaircraft officer, Col. Charles G. Patterson, ordered Battery C to go there and block Peiper.

Around 7 A.M. on December 19, with the first indications of daylight but with a dense fog blanketing the valley, Peiper threw his *SS-Panzergrenadiers* and his company of paratroopers against Stoumont. As those troops, supported by tanks and assault guns, began to advance, Lieutenant McGuire's two big antiaircraft guns were moving into position near a farmhouse along the La Gleize highway where a platoon of the 119th Infantry's Company I had established a roadblock. The crewmen were so nervous about their first combat that in trying to maneuver one of the guns into position, they got the prime mover entangled with the gun, and both mired in a ditch. The crew of the remaining gun dug it in near the farmhouse.

As the Germans approached, the fog and darkness were such that the crews of attacking tanks and defending antitank pieces alike could discern few targets. Lieutenant McGuire had yet to see his first tank when an infantry lieutenant ran up asking for two men "to take care of a tank." Although neither Pfc. Roland Seamon nor Pvt. Albert Darage had ever fired a bazooka, they volunteered, and the lieutenant, giving them a quick lesson with the weapon, told them to aim for the rear of the tank. As the two crept warily through the fog, each with a loaded bazooka, they found not one German tank but four, two of them Tigers, two Panthers. Each man fired into the rear of one of the tanks. "Biggest Goddamned noise I ever heard," said Seamon later. As both tanks began to burn, machine guns on the other two raked the roadside, and Seamon and Darage fell back to the farmhouse.

A short while later, one of the other tanks—a Tiger—came into the vision of McGuire's remaining 90mm. gun. A first round hit near the tank's left front sprocket, while a second sheered off most of the barrel of the tank's cannon. "The escape hatch flew open, and the crew boiled out."

By that time, German foot troops were closing in on the farmhouse, and a half-track bringing ammunition to McGuire's gun went up in flames. Since the exploding ammunition was threatening the gun crew, the sergeant in charge ordered his men out and put a rifle grenade down the barrel. Moments later ammunition stacked close to the gun exploded.

Although the outpost at the farmhouse was fast collapsing, the men of the 119th Infantry at other places were turning Peiper's *SS-Panzergrenadiers* and paratroopers back, and Peiper was soon aware that the concern he had felt the night before was real: fatigue and frustration had taken something out of his men. As he himself rallied the foot troops, he saw the incredible spectacle of many of his tanks backing up. At Peiper's order, the tank commander, Major Poetschke, moved personally to get the vehicles moving forward again. Seizing a *Panzerfaust*, he went from tank to tank, threatening "every commander to shoot him down if he went back one more meter."

Just as the German attack picked up momentum, part of the promised defensive tank support—two platoons of Company C, 743d Tank Battalion, under 1st Lt. Walter D. Macht—arrived in Stoumont. Those ten tanks hurried to the fringe of the town, but they arrived scant minutes too late, for Company I astride the road to La Gleize was falling apart. As the infantry broke, a round from a German tank knocked out one of the towed tank destroyers, small-arms fire killed the entire crew of another, and most of the other crews, unable to manhandle their ponderous pieces, joined the flight.

Inside Stoumont, near Colonel Fitzgerald's command post in the schoolhouse, Company I's leaders managed to stem the hegira. There the tanks and a bazooka accounted for six German tanks, either destroyed or disabled, but *SS-Panzergrenadiers* continued to pour into town. After two hours of fighting, little of Company I remained (the company later counted twenty-four survivors). Since the advance into the center of Stoumont threatened the other two rifle companies to the southeast and northeast of the town, Fitzgerald ordered them to withdraw. The men of Company L had a covered route of retreat; those of Company K, on the other hand, had to join the survivors of Company I and Fitzgerald himself in flight down the main road toward Targnon and Stoumont Station while fire from German tanks and assault guns exploded all around them.

Fairly early in the fighting, word of the crisis in Stoumont reached the regimental commander, Colonel Sutherland, who promptly sent Company C of his reserve battalion forward in trucks. As the trucks reached Targnon, the men of Companies I and K passed them fleeing the other way. Five hundred yards beyond the hamlet, the company commander, Capt. Donald R. Fell, ordered his men to dismount and continue on foot.

As Fell drew closer to Stoumont, he came upon the commander of the American tanks, Lieutenant Macht, whose mediums were falling back by bounds, one group providing covering fire while the other withdrew, then repeating the process. Incredibly, Macht had lost not a tank, but all were rapidly running out of ammunition. Together, he and Fell agreed to conduct a fighting withdrawal until additional reinforcements arrived. That was already beginning to happen, for a battery of the 400th Armored Field Artillery Battalion had reached firing positions, but by that time there was little that artillery support could do to resolve the crisis.

With German foot troops and tanks close behind, Fell's infantry and Macht's tanks fell back through Targnon and thence down the hill toward Stoumont Station at the bottom of the valley. At a sharp bend in the road just short of the station, they gained some help from a 90mm. antiaircraft gun that the commander of Battery C, 1st Lt. Jack Kent, had been trying to move into Stoumont but, despairing of that, had put into position near the station. The big piece knocked out a half-track and two Panthers before pressure from the approaching *SS-Panzergrenadiers* prompted Kent to order his gun destroyed.

At Colonel Sutherland's command post, the commander of the 30th Division, General Hobbs, had arrived. He was swiftly in touch with headquarters of the First Army, asking for additional tank support. Without it, it appeared that Peiper would soon force his way out of the valley of the Amblève and—as the American commanders believed—turn on Liège. From one of Sutherland's staff officers, Hobbs had learned that the 740th Tank Battalion, newly arrived in Europe, was waiting to draw tanks and equipment from an ordnance depot at Sprimont, only a few miles from Sutherland's command post. When Hobbs asked for that battalion, General Hodges approved.

As it turned out, there were precious few tanks and little equipment at that ordnance depot. The battalion commander, Lt. Col. George K. Rubel, and most of his men had arrived at the depot the day before on the theory that they soon would be committed somewhere; but they had found that it was a repair depot with only about fifteen tanks that could be made operable. The crewmen worked through the night, robbing parts from other tanks to get those operating and in the end appropriating anything that would run and had some firepower—self-propelled 105mm. howitzers, self-propelled tank destroyers, nine light tanks, towed 75mm. pack howitzers, armored cars, whatever. Few of the vehicles had radios, so that the men in them would have to communicate by visual signals.

By the time word came for the 740th Tank Battalion to move to help the 119th Infantry, Company C, commanded by Capt. James D. Berry, had fourteen Shermans, five duplex-drive (amphibious) Shermans, and an M-36 (a self-propelled tank destroyer with a 90mm. piece). As Berry moved past Sutherland's command post, he told one of the staff officers: "They're bastard tanks but we're shooting fools."

When Berry and his bastard tanks neared Stoumont Station, Lieutenant Macht's tanks, down to only a few rounds of ammunition among them, and the 119th Infantry's reserve 1st Battalion, commanded by Lt. Col. Robert Herlong, had blocked the valley road a thousand yards behind the station at a point where the railroad and the river on one side and a steeply rising wooded cliff on the other sharply restricted passage. By that time, the 119th Infantry's normal artillery support, the 197th Field Artillery Battalion, was ready to fire, and any of Peiper's tanks coming past Stoumont Station would do so at their peril.

While Macht's tanks withdrew, Berry's took their place. At the order of Colonel Sutherland, Colonel Herlong and his infantry, with Berry's support, were to drive back up the road and gain a good line of departure for retaking Stoumont the next morning.

It was around four o'clock, with the evening closing in and fog swelling up from the river. A Sherman commanded by 2d Lt. Charles D.

Powers led the way. In the gathering fog and darkness, Powers knew that all might depend on his getting in the first shot. Hugging the cliff side of the road, he rounded a curve just short of Stoumont Station. Ahead of him, barely discernible in the haze, he made out the form of a Panther. When he fired, his shot ricocheted off the gun mantlet and penetrated downward into the driver's compartment, setting the tank on fire.

Continuing to advance cautiously, Powers made out another Mark V. Again he got off the first shot, but it ricocheted off the heavy front slope plate, and Powers's gun jammed. Standing in the turret, he signaled for help from Staff Sgt. Charles W. Loopey, who was close behind in the M-36 tank destroyer. The first round from Loopey's 90mm. gun set the German tank on fire. With Powers's gun at last cleared, the lieutenant continued forward. Finding a third Panther, he knocked off the muzzle brake from its cannon with his first round and with two more set the tank on fire.

With darkness descending and the three destroyed Panthers forming an effective roadblock, Berry's Company C, 740th Tank Battalion, in its first taste of combat, and Herlong's 1st Battalion, 119th Infantry, holed up for the night, blocking the road and the valley of the Amblève at Stoumont Station. As the commander of the 119th Infantry, Colonel Sutherland, knew, he was to get his 2d Battalion back that night from its assignment in front of Werbomont protecting the assembly of the 82d Airborne Division, so that on the morrow he would have two full battalions for retaking Stoumont. In response to persistent demands from headquarters of the First Army, Sutherland sent what was left of Fitzgerald's 3d Battalion to block a secondary road leading through woods north of Stoumont to Chaudfontaine and Liège.

What Berry, Herlong, Sutherland, Hobbs, Gerow, Hodges, and everybody else on the American side could not know was that Joachim Peiper had no intention either of driving on Liège or of continuing up the valley of the Amblève. What he wanted to do was get out of the valley by way of the bridge between Targnon and Stoumont Station. Although a patrol had discovered that that was only a footbridge, the original bridge having been destroyed as the Germans retreated in September, there was a ford nearby with firm footing.

Nevertheless, as night came on December 19, Peiper recognized that taking even that route was beyond his means. The day's fighting had left his gasoline tanks almost dry. (Peiper was still unaware that salvation in the form of 2 million gallons of American gasoline was to be found not far away in the woods just north of La Gleize.)

By radio, he asked permission to use his small amount of remaining fuel to turn around and fight his way back to the rest of the 1st SS Panzer Division, but the division commander, Colonel Mohnke, said no. Peiper was to hold where he was until the rest of the division broke through to him, perhaps in two to three days, whereupon the entire division was to resume the drive to the Meuse.

During the night of the 19th, some help did reach *Kampfgruppe Peiper:* a battalion of the 2d SS Panzergrenadier Regiment, moving mostly on foot by way of a wooden span over the Amblève at the hamlet of Petit-Spai, just upstream from Trois Ponts and the railroad underpasses through which the road from Stavelot led to Trois Ponts. German engineers had been working on that little bridge since the previous night, and it was finally capable of carrying light vehicles. When the *SS-Panzergrenadiers* crossed, they were able to take a small amount of gasoline with them.

Yet even that makeshift supply route might soon be denied Peiper, for the net around him was tightening on both banks of the Amblève.

Early on the morning of December 19, the commander of the 82d

Airborne Division, General Gavin, knew little of the situation—friendly or enemy—in front of his assembling troops at Werbomont. His orders were to push out to the east and southeast in hope of establishing contact with the 7th Armored Division and the other defenders of St. Vith.

It turned out for the most part to be an uncontested march, for there were no Germans short of the Salm River except for the defenders that Colonel Peiper had left to hold Cheneux and the nearby bridge over the Amblève. By nightfall, one of Gavin's regiments was in Rahier, close to Cheneux, where civilians told the men that the Germans held Cheneux. Men of another regiment penetrated the next day, December 20, all the way to Trois Ponts. There, much to their surprise, they found the men of Company C, 51st Engineer Combat Battalion, who on the 18th had thwarted *Kampfgruppe Peiper* by demolishing the three bridges in and around Trois Ponts. (Said the engineer commander, Major Yates, to the paratroopers, "I'll bet you guys are glad we are here.") Patrols from that regiment, the 505th Parachute Infantry, were soon pushing up the valley of the Salm, where they established contact with patrols from the 7th Armored Division.

On the other side of the Amblève, early on December 20, a powerful force was joining the 30th Division for the fight against *Kampfgruppe Peiper:* the 3d Armored Division's Combat Command B. The 3d Armored Division was one of those two American armored divisions in the European Theater (the other was the 2d Armored) organized under a Table of Organization and Equipment, subsequently superseded, which called not for three separate tank and armored infantry battalions, as with later divisions, but for two tank regiments (four medium and two light battalions) and an armored infantry regiment (three battalions). Each of the two divisions had not quite 4,000 more men than the later armored divisions and 55 more medium tanks (232 as opposed to 177). Although there was no separate headquarters for a Combat Command Reserve, the division commanders usually held out portions of their commands as a reserve under the control of one of the regimental headquarters.

As the 3d Armored Division's CCB reached the scene, the combat command had two full medium tank battalions, a battalion of armored infantry, a company of armored engineers, and a battalion of self-propelled 105mm. howitzers. Ordered to clear the north bank of the Amblève between Stavelot and La Gleize, and in conjunction with Sutherland's 119th Infantry to clamp a vise on *Kampfgruppe Peiper*, Brig. Gen. Truman E. Boudinot divided his combat command into three task forces, all three to drive along woods roads leading into the valley of the Amblève from the vicinity of Spa.

The largest of the three, named for its commander, Lt. Col. William B. Lovelady, consisted of a battalion of tanks and a company of armored infantry. The task force passed without incident through the woods to gain the valley highway near the village of Coo, in happier times a center for tourists visiting a nearby waterfall. As Lovelady's tanks turned down the road toward Trois Ponts, a small German column appeared around a bend in the road. Consisting of a few self-propelled guns, some infantry, and a few trucks carrying gasoline, the column had crossed the Amblève over the wooden bridge at Petit-Spai. Lovelady's tanks quickly ripped it to pieces, and the presence of those tanks ended the little trickle of supplies reaching Peiper by way of Petit-Spai and split Major Knittel's reconnaissance troops at Stavelot from *Kampfgruppe Peiper*.

The central task force, commanded by Maj. Kenneth T. McGeorge and consisting of a company each of medium tanks and armored infantry, headed for La Gleize by way of the woods road leading past the big gasoline depot near the hamlet of Cour. And the third task force, commanded by Capt. John W. Jordan, which had a company of light tanks, a few mediums, and a company of armored infantry, moved toward Stoumont along the woods road blocked earlier by the 119th Infantry's 3d Battalion to prevent Peiper from turning north toward Liège. Since both of those task forces ran head-on into Peiper's strength, neither was able to get past the woodsline overlooking La Gleize and Stoumont.

Less than a quarter of a mile outside Stoumont, on a steep hillside overlooking the road to Targnon, stood the St. Edouard Sanitorium, a large four-storied brick building maintained by a Catholic order for convalescent children and young girls and the elderly. As the two priests and the sisters staffing the sanitorium learned of the German advance, they had no choice but to remain, for there was no way to evacuate their frail charges. They were immensely relieved when after nightfall on December 18, American troops arrived in Stoumont, and twenty of them established an outpost in the sanitorium.

Their relief was short-lived. In mid-morning of the 19th, as the sisters herded everybody into the basement—250 civilians all told—the Germans attacked, and the little band of Americans surrendered. "You have nothing to fear from us," a German noncommissioned officer assured the priests and the sisters, "if you do nothing. But we had to shoot some people in Stavelot who fired on our troops from the windows of the houses." It was the old rationale, noted the sisters, the shibboleth of *francs-tireurs* that the Germans had used as long ago as the Great War to justify the killing of Belgian civilians.

To the commander of the 119th Infantry's 1st Battalion, Colonel Herlong, it was obvious that if he was to pass along the highway below the windows of the sanitorium and retake Stoumont, he would have to seize the big building. With artillery support at last available and a company of the bastard tanks of the 740th Tank Battalion, some of them fitted overnight with radios, Herlong began his attack early on December 20 through fog swirling up from the river bottom.

Almost at the moment the attack began, a Panther covering the road opened fire, but the leading American tank, commanded by 1st Lt. John E. Callaway, knocked it out with a round that "opened its muzzle up like a rose." A few hundred yards farther along the road, Callaway knocked out two half-tracks, but it was soon evident that those vehicles were only outposts. The Germans had pulled back from Targnon, and beyond the hamlet they had liberally strewn antitank mines, covered by fire from infantry dug in on the steeply rising slope above the road. It took all day for Herlong's infantry and the supporting tanks to eliminate those Germans and get past the minefields.

As night was approaching and fog was again rising from the river bottom, Herlong's force had come within the length of a few football fields of Stoumont when a round from a German gun damaged the leading tank, commanded by 2d Lt. David Oglansky. Although Oglansky's gun was disabled, his motor still functioned. In view of the approaching darkness, the commander of the tank company, Captain Berry, with Herlong's approval, ordered the attack halted for the night and Oglansky's tank placed sideways as a roadblock. While one of the rifle companies dug in around the tank, the other two started up the hill to take the St. Edouard Sanitorium.

On the downhill side of the sanitorium was a stone retaining wall, a kind of glacis, some five feet high, sufficient to prevent a vehicle (even a tank) from climbing it but no real obstacle for men on foot. After a short artillery preparation, men of the two companies clambered over the embankment and under concealment of the fog and gathering darkness stormed the building.

As Father Hanlet, one of the two priests in the basement of the sanitorium, described it:

> Fighting raged around us and over our heads . . . and in the halls and the rooms. . . . Suddenly, a door to the basement opened and shots echoed on the stairway, evoking heart-rending cries: "Civilians! Civilians!" Some American soldiers descended: we were saved! What joy, what relief! The Sister Superior recited a dozen rosaries for the eternal rest of the soldiers killed in the battle . . . while the Americans set up their guns on the first floor and, in the kitchen, made hot water for tea, coffee, and chocolate. Our liberators were as happy as we were.

Although the Americans promised that they would evacuate everybody at daylight, that was not to be, for the strategic location of the St. Edouard Sanitorium was no less apparent to Joachim Peiper than it was to Robert Herlong. Supported by tanks firing from a road above the sanitorium, a hundred *SS-Panzergrenadiers* shouting "*Heil, Hitler!*" charged the building. The fight raged from room to room, and the German tanks moved in close enough to fire into the windows.

Down on the road below, Captain Berry's tanks tried to come to the rescue, but they were unable to get beyond the steep embankment. A *Panzerfaust* set one afire, and when German flares lit the landscape, German tanks from their positions higher up the slope knocked out two more.

Most of the Americans in the sanitorium eventually got out to form a line along a hedge only fifty yards from the building. Thirty-three surrendered, but in an annex to the building, Sgt. William J. Widener and eleven other men held out. Well into the night, Widener called out sensings to an artillery observer in the defensive line on the grounds.

Meanwhile, down in the basement Father Hanlet moved to help an American who was badly wounded in the arm and losing blood rapidly. Although Father Hanlet applied a tourniquet, he was so concerned the man still might die that he administered the last rites of the church. "Thank you," the man whispered. "I understand what you have said and done. My wife is very Catholic; should I die, she will be pleased. Thank you."

The Germans soon brought in another American, wounded in the knee, and two wounded Germans. The sole German medic was so busy that Father Hanlet, recalling that one of the American prisoners appeared to be a medic, suggested that the Germans enlist his help. Soon the two medics were working side by side.

Taking pity on the American whom the priest thought was dying, a German noncommissioned officer lit a cigarette and placed it between the man's lips. The man took a few puffs and seemed to revive. Fumbling in his pockets, he came up with a piece of chocolate and handed it to the German. The sergeant thanked him, but turning away, he whispered to the priest: "I can't eat it; it's covered with blood."

Outside, two hours before daylight, the Germans tried to expand their success at the sanitorium by a foray out of Stoumont along the highway to Targnon. When a round from a self-propelled gun knocked out Lieutenant Oglansky's tank, set in place as a roadblock, Oglansky told his crew to head for the rear while he took command of a nearby tank. He was hardly aboard when a *Panzerfaust* knocked it out, setting the tank on fire. Other *Panzerfausts* knocked out two more tanks, which also began to burn. Together with Oglansky's immobile tank, the three burning vehicles effectively blocked the road. The heat from the flames was so intense that nobody could get near, nor could the *SS-Panzergrenadiers* get past.

When combined with heavy shelling from supporting artillery, that put an end to the sortie from Stoumont; but Herlong's infantry and Berry's tanks were in no shape to renew their attacks on the sanitorium and Stoumont right away. The wild night had cost both forces dearly, including the loss of almost half the two rifle companies that fought at the sanitorium.

* * *

Only a few miles away on the other side of the Amblève River, the 82d Airborne Division's 504th Parachute Infantry during the afternoon of December 20 sent a patrol probing toward Cheneux. The regimental commander, Col. Reuben H. Tucker, was anxious to take the village, both because it was on higher ground than Rahier, where his troops were located, and because Cheneux and the nearby bridge in German hands posed a threat to the entire airborne division. As the patrol soon discovered, the Germans were in Cheneux in force: most of Peiper's light flak battalion with its self-propelled 20mm. flak guns and a company of the newly arrived battalion of the 2d SS Panzergrenadier Regiment that had crossed the wooden bridge at Petit-Spai the night before.

In mid-afternoon, with a heavy mist limiting visibility to two hundred yards, Tucker sent two companies in an approach march formation across open fields toward Cheneux. The mist made it impossible to bring down accurate artillery fire, so that the only real fire support the companies had was from a 77mm. assault howitzer mounted on a half-track that the Germans had left behind when they withdrew before the destroyed bridge near Habiémont. Men of both companies soon went to ground, punished by fire from machine guns and flak guns in Cheneux. As night fell, the company commanders pulled their men back to the edge of a small wood.

When Colonel Tucker learned of the withdrawal, he insisted that the companies resume the attack. Concealed by the darkness, the paratroopers made good progress at first, despite barbed-wire fences that tore at their uniforms and their flesh. They were within two hundred yards of a roadblock on the edge of the village before German gunners opened a withering fire. Again the men went to ground, but as the firing continued, Staff Sgt. George Walsh of Company B jumped to his feet and shouted: "Let's get the sons of bitches!" That got the attack moving again. Men fell left and right, wounded or dead, some left hanging on the barbed-wire fences, but the survivors plodded on.

Walsh and a few other men were soon atop the roadblock. Walsh himself tossed a hand grenade into a flak wagon, knocking out the crew. A second man jumped aboard another flak wagon and slashed the gunner's throat with his knife. Hand-to-hand fighting was still going on when two self-propelled tank destroyers, which Colonel Tucker had been trying to locate for hours, at last moved forward. With the help of those pieces, the survivors of the two companies soon had a toehold in the village, but so few men were left that they were unable to clear the rest of the buildings. Although the battalion commander, Lt. Col. Willard E. Harrison, came forward, he could provide no help, for his remaining company was on a separate mission elsewhere.

Colonel Tucker, meanwhile, decided on a wide encirclement of the village to get in behind the Germans at the bridge over the Amblève and soon had his 3d Battalion on the march. It was late afternoon of the next day, December 21, before that battalion gained high ground overlooking the bridge; but at that point the Germans in Cheneux were cut off, and Company G, sent to reinforce, attacked to clear the village. In gathering darkness, some of the Germans escaped to make their way across the Amblève. They left behind fourteen flak wagons, a battery of self-propelled 105mm. assault guns, six half-tracks, a few trucks and other vehicles, and mounds of dead *SS-Panzergrenadiers.*

In the attack on Cheneux, the two companies of Harrison's battalion lost 23 men killed and 202 wounded, including all the officers of Company B. That brought Company B down to eighteen men, and Company C to thirty-eight men and three officers.

The story of the attack of those two companies was another of those incredibly heroic actions. But however courageous, the unsupported infantry attack across open fields laced with barbed-wire fences was as ill-conceived and senseless as many of the herdlike German assaults, such as those against Lieutenant Bouck's I&R Platoon outside Lanzerath. Afforded time to mount an attack with accurate artillery support—or even with the support of just the two tank destroyers—those companies could have taken Cheneux at far less cost and with no great forfeiture of time.

CHAPTER TWENTY-TWO

The Last Days of *Kampfgruppe Peiper*

The stands by American troops in front of the Elsenborn Ridge and at Dom. Bütgenbach were having a marked effect on the fortunes of *Kampfgruppe Peiper*. First, they denied Peiper help from the 12th SS Panzer Division along his north flank. Second, because they made it necessary for the 3d Parachute Division to hold an elongated defensive front extending all the way from Bütgenbach to Waimes, they denied him help from the paratroopers in keeping his supply route open at Stavelot.

Meanwhile, in the Losheim Gap, the fitful but nevertheless time-consuming fight by men of the 14th Cavalry Group had delayed the advance of the rest of the 1st SS Panzer Division, trying to get through to Peiper and bring him gasoline. The massive traffic tie-ups in the gap had further delayed the follow-up force, as did brushes with the defenders of the developing horseshoe defense of St. Vith at Poteau.

By the time engineers supporting Colonel Frankland's battalion of the 117th Infantry had destroyed the bridge over the Amblève in Stavelot, only seven Tiger tanks plus Major Knittel's reconnaissance battalion of the follow-up force had come through, and Frankland's troops had repulsed two attempts by tanks and a battalion of the 2d SS Panzergrenadier Regiment to get across the river, once before the bridge was blown, once after. The remaining battalion of that regiment (one had been with Peiper from the start) had nevertheless crossed during the night of the 19th over the wooden bridge at Petit-Spai. Throughout December 20, a few men and light vehicles continued to cross that span; but early on the morning of December 21, when a self-propelled tank destroyer tried to cross, the bridge collapsed.

To the commander of the 1st SS Panzer Corps, General Priess, to try to continue to gain any advantage from *Kampfgruppe Peiper*'s breakthrough seemed sheer folly. It was time, in Priess's view, to cut the losses, to tell Peiper to fight his way out. Yet Priess's superior, Sepp Dietrich, disagreed completely, for Dietrich was determined to wring

450

every possible advantage from the one success his Sixth Panzer Army had achieved.

At Dietrich's order, Colonel Mohnke on December 21 was to employ every available resource to break through to Peiper. He was also to employ an additional resource, Otto Skorzeny's 150th Panzer Brigade, in order to take Malmédy and open up roads that might be employed to get through to Peiper, and also to get in behind the stalwart American opposition on the Elsenborn Ridge.

On the American side, senior commanders were sensing the kill, and as soon as *Kampfgruppe Peiper* could be eliminated, General Hodges intended driving through to relieve the troops at St. Vith and close the gap between Malmédy and St. Vith. To facilitate control of that attack, he placed the entire 30th Division and the 3d Armored Division's CCB under General Ridgway and the XVIII Airborne Corps.

Using the 150th Panzer Brigade as a regular ground combat force was the idea of Skorzeny himself, who had become convinced as early as the evening of the second day of the offensive, December 17, that his brigade would be unable to accomplish its mission of seizing bridges over the Meuse. When he made the suggestion at Dietrich's headquarters around midnight, Dietrich told him to report to Mohnke, who had established his headquarters in the Hôtel du Moulin in Ligneuville. The fact that the journey would involve Skorzeny's going beyond the German frontier, which Hitler had expressly forbidden, was of no concern to Skorzeny.

Part of the rationale in attacking Malmédy was that early in the offensive one of Skorzeny's operatives had reported entering the town and finding it lightly held. Unknown to Skorzeny, that had markedly changed. Although Colonel Pergrin's little band of 291st Engineers was still there, the engineers had been strengthened early by Colonel Hansen's Norweigians and by part of the 526th Armored Infantry Battalion, then by all of the 30th Division's 120th Infantry. Amid the hills and valleys behind the town there were six artillery battalions, and December 21 was the date on which American artillery was to be free—as authorized by the War Department at General Eisenhower's request—to use the VT or POZIT fuse on its shells.

Skorzeny's was "a motley crew." A few men had full American uniforms, including dog tags; others had American trousers and boots but German tunics; still others had American field jackets but German trousers; and some were in full German uniform. There were a few captured American jeeps and armored cars, but the ten tanks available to Skorzeny were either Mark IVs or Panthers, most of which had been fitted with sheet metal to create sloping sides in an attempt to make them look like American tanks, and painted with the Allied marking, a white star in a white circle. Along with a few assault guns and mortars, those would provide the only heavy fire support, for Skorzeny had no artillery at his disposal.

Three hours before daylight on December 21, as a dense fog blanketed the valley of the little Warche River, which runs through Malmédy, one of two German columns struck down Highway N-23 past the Baugnez road junction along the principal road into the town from the south (*see map, Chapter Twenty-one, p. 443*). Almost all of the 120 men involved wore all or some part of American uniforms, but they got nowhere. Late the previous day, the Americans had captured one of Skorzeny's men, who revealed that the Germans would attack at three thirty the next morning, and the defenders were on full alert. The leading half-track set off a mine and exploded, throwing vehicle parts, equipment, and human flesh high into the big ash trees lining the road, the same trees Pergrin's engineers had been planning to blow five days earlier but which still stood.

Men of the 120th Infantry's 1st Battalion stopped that thrust, and the artillery, making plentiful use of the new fuse that produced deadly air bursts, finished the Germans off. By the time daylight came, none other than dead Germans was to be found along the road from Baugnez.

Skorzeny's main force, which included all ten tanks, attacked by way of a dirt road leading along a winding route from Ligneuville to the Malmédy-Stavelot highway a mile southwest of Malmédy, then over a temporary but sturdy wooden bridge carrying the highway across the Warche River just before the little stream wends southward to join the Amblève. Since the highway and most of Malmédy itself were on the south bank of the Warche, the Germans had no need of the bridge in order to take the town, but they would need it to turn toward Stavelot or to use the road to Spa. Although the 291st Engineers had prepared the bridge for demolition, they had yet to connect the detonator, and as two American engineers arrived to do that, they were too late. Skorzeny's attack was already under way, signaled by a blaze of light as the Germans crossed a field and tripped wires the defenders had installed to set off flares.

Part of the infantry, accompanied by a single Panther, swung toward Malmédy, where the Norwegians of the 99th Infantry Battalion were dug in atop a railroad embankment. In the fog and darkness some of the Germans, shouting in English "Surrender or die!," made it to the foot of the embankment, but machine-gun fire and hand grenades rolled down from above finished them off. When the Panther tried to break through a roadblock where the Malmédy-Stavelot highway passed under a trestle, a round from a towed piece of the 825th Tank Destroyer Battalion damaged it and prompted the commander to pull back, and American artillery again took command of the field. Under the devastating fire of shells equipped with the VT fuse, some of the Germans panicked, running not away from the air bursts but full into them, all the while shouting *"Kamerad!"*

The going was rougher near the bridge, for there were to be found the other nine German tanks. One early set off an antitank mine and began to burn, but the others were soon shooting up the landscape. The tanks forced back a platoon of the 120th Infantry's Company K that was manning a roadblock in front of the bridge, partly because the crews of two towed tank destroyers were away from their pieces as the Germans struck. When one tank crossed the bridge and headed toward Stavelot, a forward observer for 81mm. mortars, 2d Lt. Arnold L. Snyder, knocked it out from the rear with a bazooka. Pfcs. Francis S. Currey and Adam Lucero hit the turret of another with a rocket from a bazooka, so damaging the tank that it was unable to fire, and the crew abandoned it.

From a steep bluff along the road to Spa, three towed tank destroyers drove several of the remaining tanks to cover behind a masonry wall beside a house. Two self-propelled tank destroyers then drove forward from a roadblock along the road to Stavelot, crumpled the wall with fire from their 76mm. pieces, and knocked out two of the tanks.

With the German tanks reduced to four, much of the sting passed from the attack, but fighting continued into the early afternoon, mostly around a paper mill and houses near the bridge where some of the Germans holed up. From a hill overlooking the battlefield, Otto Skorzeny could see the turn the fight was taking and ordered everybody to fall back, but none of the tanks succeeded.

That evening, as Skorzeny was driving to Colonel Mohnke's command post in the Hôtel du Moulin in Ligneuville, he came under artillery fire, and a fragment ripped the flesh over his right eye. Although he reported to an aid station, where medical officers removed the fragment and sutured the wound, he refused evacuation.

Except for minor defensive assignments, the attack on Malmédy marked the end of Skorzeny's participation in the offensive and that of the 150th Panzer Brigade. Neither of Hitler's two special units—von der Heydte's and Skorzeny's—had accomplished much of anything.

As part of the renewed effort to break through to Peiper, the battalion of the 2d SS Panzergrenadier Regiment that had twice tried to cross the Amblève at Stavelot tried again on the morning of the 21st. Again the *SS-Panzergrenadiers* attempted to wade the stream, their weapons held high above their heads; but they displayed considerably less spirit than on the day before, and they had no tank support. The attack quickly collapsed. Although a few men of the battalion were later to get across the river along an undefended sector between Stavelot and Trois Ponts, the presence of Task Force Lovelady prevented them from reaching Peiper. All they could do was augment Knittel's reconnaissance troops in the hamlets overlooking Stavelot, eventually to be mopped up along with Knittel's men by troops of the 117th Infantry supported by Lovelady's tanks.

The 1st SS Panzergrenadier Regiment, which had seen little fighting except for a brief encounter against the forming American line behind St.

Vith, made Mohnke's main effort, supported by self-propelled tank destroyers and tanks transferred from support of the other *SS-Panzergrenadier* regiment. The troops were to get across the Salm River at Trois Ponts and farther upstream.

By that time, a company of the 82d Airborne Division's 505th Parachute Infantry had established a small bridgehead beyond the Salm on the heights around the railroad station across from Trois Ponts, and the rest of the regiment had dug in at likely crossing sites upstream. At the hamlets of La Neuville and Grand Halleux, the paratroopers wired two bridges across the Salm for demolition but delayed blowing them in anticipation of the projected drive on St. Vith.

Trying to cover a front of close to eight thousand yards—more than four miles—the paratroopers were nowhere strong. Such a distance would have been a severe test for an infantry regiment, and parachute regiments were considerably smaller than infantry regiments. Their three battalions had only three companies as opposed to four in infantry battalions, and the companies even at full strength had only 140 men.

The main German thrust hit Company E around the railroad station on the high ground across the river from Trois Ponts. Commanded by 1st Lt. William J. Muddagh, the 110 men of the company fought back with determination, using one platoon as a counterattacking force whenever a penetration seemed about to develop, and making good use of the fires of the 456th Parachute Field Artillery Battalion. Yet it was a fight against markedly uneven odds. Although the battalion commander, Lt. Col. Benjamin V. Vandervoort, wanted to withdraw the company, his regimental commander, Col. William E. Ekman, had ordered the bridgehead established, and Vandervoort was out of communication both with Ekman and the division headquarters. Unwilling to order withdrawal without higher authority, Vandervoort sent first a platoon then all of Company F across the debris of the destroyed bridge in the heart of Trois Ponts to join the fight on the far bank.

Those two companies were holding their own, partly because the ground was so soggy that the German tanks and tank destroyers were unable to close, when in early afternoon the assistant division commander, Col. Ira P. Swift, arrived at Vandervoort's headquarters. Maintaining the little bridgehead, said Swift, was costing more than it was worth. Although conscious of the difficulty of withdrawing in daylight while engaged at close quarters, he saw that as preferable to having the two companies cut to pieces.

As the paratroopers began to pull back, a few men at a time, the Germans quickly sensed what was happening and launched a final charge. For the paratroopers, it became a case of *sauve qui peut*. Men raced down the steep hill, stumbling, falling; some jumped from the cliff into the river; others scrambled frantically over the debris of the bridge. Almost all the men of Company F made it to safety, but Muddagh's Company E left half its strength on the far bank.

Although the SS troops had eliminated the little bridgehead, they were still unable to cross the river. Major Yates's engineers covering the remains of the bridge with fire saw to that. And when the German attempts ceased, the engineers subjected what was left of the bridge to a second demolition, then withdrew to be committed elsewhere with the main body of their battalion.

Late in the day, upstream at La Neuville and Grand Halleux, the Germans mounted lesser attacks; but in both cases, as German vehicles drew near, the paratroopers blew the bridges. Through the night and into the next day, the 1st SS Panzergrenadier Regiment continued to try to cross the Salm, and in several places small groups made it, for there was no solid defensive line; but each time the paratroopers either killed the Germans or drove them back. Nobody was getting through to help *Kampfgruppe Peiper*.

Early on December 19, the commander of the 30th Division, General Hobbs, sent his assistant division commander, Brig. Gen. William K. Harrison, to command all the forces around Stoumont—Colonel Sutherland's 119th Infantry and Task Forces McGeorge and Jordan of the 3d Armored Division's CCB—in order to take Stoumont and capture La Gleize. He was under some pressure to get the job over with, for not only was the presence of *Kampfgruppe Peiper* holding up a drive to close the gap between Malmédy and St. Vith; it was also delaying a transfer of the 3d Armored Division's CCB elsewhere to oppose rampaging German tanks.

However unsuccessful the German sortie from Stoumont down the highway toward Targnon before daylight on December 21, it nevertheless delayed the start of what Harrison intended as a three-pronged attack on Stoumont; for Harrison had to afford the commander of the 119th Infantry's 1st Battalion, Colonel Herlong, time to get his troops into some kind of order following that foray and the costly fighting for the St. Edouard Sanitorium. In the interim, the 119th Infantry's Cannon Company joined the 197th Field Artillery Battalion in heavy shelling of the sanitorium and the town, while the 119th Infantry's 2d Battalion under Maj. Hal D. Mc-Cown began a long foot march through the woods above Stoumont to push downhill from the woods, cut the La Gleize-Stoumont highway, and have at Stoumont from the rear.

When Herlong's infantry soon after midday at last renewed the attack against the sanitorium—still a prerequisite for the drive on Stoumont—a few men managed to get inside the building; but when a German tank moved in close and began firing through the windows, those men fell back under the concealment of a smoke screen fired by mortars. Nor did an attempt by Task Force Jordan to drive into Stoumont from the woods north of the town fare any better, for again fire from German tanks denied exit along the narrow road leading out of the forest.

Only Major McCown's 2d Battalion achieved any success. Encountering no opposition during the long march through the woods, the battalion in early afternoon debouched into the open and quickly cut the highway between Stoumont and La Gleize. As soon as the Germans discovered the battalion's presence, tanks and assault guns began firing from both Stoumont and La Gleize, and Peiper started preparing a counterattack; for the cutting of the highway left only a meandering dirt road alongside the river linking his two forces.

Because Task Force Jordan's tanks were supposed to join McCown's battalion but failed to show, McCown set out with his orderly and radio operator to find them. The three were climbing a steep, wooded slope when a German soldier jumped from behind a bush. Although McCown killed him with fire from his grease gun, other Germans opened fire. As McCown and the other two dropped to the ground, a voice called from behind them: *"Kommen sie hier!"* Turning, McCown saw a line of Germans covering them, weapons at the ready. All three surrendered.

Although General Harrison was yet to learn of McCown's capture, he came to the conclusion in late afternoon that there was no point in subjecting McCown's battalion to enemy riposte along the La Gleize–Stoumont highway when the attack to take the sanitorium and Stoumont had gained nothing. He told the battalion to retrace its steps through the woods.

When General Hobbs telephoned Harrison for "the real picture down there," Harrison made no effort to mask his concern. Two of the 119th Infantry's battalions had been badly battered, even demoralized, and American tanks were no match for the big German tanks firing from dug-in positions. "That place [Stoumont]," said Harrison, "is very strong. I don't think those troops we have now, without some improvement, can take the thing. That is my honest opinion." The trouble was, Harrison went on, that he could "only get light artillery fire on the town, and the Germans can shoot at us with tank guns and we can't get tanks to shoot back unless they come out and get hit."

It was a rare display of candor that would have endeared Harrison to his troops had they but known of it. Since Hobbs had long worked with his assistant division commander and trusted his judgment, he agreed to delay further attack until he could explore alternatives.

One who was seeking some way to help break the impasse was the commander of the 740th Tank Battalion, Colonel Rubel. Having found a spot in Targnon from which direct fire could be poured into Stoumont, he sent a member of his staff foraging for a 155mm. self-propelled artillery piece. Shortly before dark, the officer returned with it—where he got it from was never recorded; it was just one of those incidents that happened often in the Ardennes when a tank, a gun, a small group of men came briefly upon the scene, did a job, then passed on without record. Before darkness forced a halt, the artillery piece fired some fifty of its big, ear-splitting shells into Stoumont.

Another member of Rubel's tank battalion, Captain Berry, was also seeking a way out of the impasse. Soon after nightfall, he reconnoitered around the fringes of the sanitorium in search of some way to get his tanks over or around the stone retaining wall below the building. Finding a spot where he thought he could construct a short corduroy road to enable his tanks to get past, he called for volunteers among the infantry to help. Using felled trees and empty shell casings, the men toiled relentlessly. Shortly before midnight, a road was in place.

As snow was beginning to fall, four tanks, including one in which Berry himself rode, headed for the sanitorium. Successfully navigating the corduroy road, the tanks—like the German tanks before them—drew up close to the building and fired point-blank through the windows. The Germans found that as punishing as had the Americans and soon took off.

To Father Hanlet and the other civilians in the basement, the silence that followed was eerie, almost as terrifying as the incessant explosion of shells they had so long endured. One shell had even penetrated a wall of the basement and lodged among one of the supporting arches, but amid a loud chorus of rosaries, it had failed to explode.

Father Hanlet rushed upstairs. The Germans had gone! He was confident the Americans would soon arrive, and *merci Dieu*, not one of his charges, for all the harrowing ordeal, had been hurt. Furthermore, the seriously wounded American to whom the priest had administered the last rites was still alive and appeared to be holding his own. Stepping across the stiff bodies of fallen Americans and Germans, Father Hanlet paused to say a prayer for the dead.

It was close to mid-morning of December 22 when General Harrison, noting an apparent absence of German activity at the sanitorium, sent a patrol to investigate. With the sanitorium at last in hand, Harrison changed his mind about renewing the attack on Stoumont and prepared again to move up the highway and down from the woods to the north.

Unknown to Harrison, the Germans in the sanitorium represented a rear guard designed to conceal as long as possible the fact that Peiper had fallen back from Stoumont to concentrate his entire force in and around La Gleize. At noon on the 21st, Peiper had called his commanders to his headquarters in the farmhouse near the Château de Froid-Cour and told them his plan. Since the Americans had already demonstrated that they could cut the highway connecting La Gleize and Stoumont, and the American paratroopers on the other side of the Amblève might well cut the dirt road linking the two places, he intended to avoid the risk of having his force split by falling back on La Gleize. There he would await reinforcement by the rest of the 1st SS Panzer Division, or, if that failed, attempt to return to German lines.

In preparation for the withdrawal, Peiper ordered all American prisoners and German walking wounded to move from the Château de Froide-Cour to cellars in La Gleize. Seriously wounded Americans and Germans in the château were left in the care of a German medical sergeant and two American aid men. Also left behind on a whitewashed wall of one of the rooms in the basement was a charcoal drawing of Christ, thorns on his head, tears on his cheeks—whether drawn by a German or an American nobody would ever know.

Unfortunately for Peiper and his men, they had completed their withdrawal and the Americans had occupied Stoumont and pushed on beyond the Château de Froide-Cour when, during the night of the 22d, twenty transport planes of the Luftwaffe finally responded to strident demands from General Dietrich to drop supplies to Peiper, and almost all dropped their containers in and close around Stoumont. When daylight came, American fire stymied virtually every German effort to recover the containers. Among those few that were recovered were containers filled with such nonessential (however welcome) items as cigarettes and Schnapps, and one held nothing but Luger pistols.

Peiper got enough gasoline from the containers to move a few tanks to better defensive positions and to recharge the batteries of some of his vehicles so that the crews could operate their radios, but that was all. Nor was an effort to float gasoline cans down the Amblève River any more successful.

Hal Dale McCown, twenty-eight years of age, a native of Arkansas and an honor ROTC graduate of Louisiana State University, was one of Peiper's prisoners of war, captured during the course of the first offensive action conducted by the 119th Infantry's 2d Battalion since he had assumed command of the battalion a few weeks earlier. His captors took him to a farmhouse, where a German lieutenant colonel questioned him (McCown was unaware at the time that the officer was Peiper). McCown duly gave only his name, rank, and serial number.

Losing interest, Peiper told the guards to take McCown away. They conducted him to a cellar in La Gleize lit by a single unshaded electric bulb. A young officer seated him so that the light was full in his face and a noncommissioned officer toyed menacingly with a Luger. So obviously staged was it that McCown found it difficult to suppress a smile. He replied the same way to every question: name, rank, serial number.

Eventually tiring of the charade, the officer sent him to a cellar in a house adjoining the village schoolhouse and left him there with four lieutenants from his own regiment and four guards. In a bookcase, McCown found a book by a British novelist of the 1920s, E. Phillips Oppenheim,

The Great Impersonation, and began to read to pass the time, but darkness soon put an end to the diversion.

Late in the evening of December 21, a guard took McCown to Peiper's new command post in the cellar of a farmhouse on the fringe of La Gleize. When the two were alone, it became obvious that Peiper wanted to talk. His English, McCown found, was almost perfect, and the man appeared to be amiable and cultured. He also appeared to be supremely confident that Germany would yet win the war. A new reserve army that Himmler was raising . . . secret weapons.

Think of the good Hitler was accomplishing, said Peiper. "We're eliminating the Communist menace, fighting your fight." So, too, Europe united under the Führer would bring a new, productive era to the old Continent. "We will keep what is best in Europe and eliminate the bad." Yet it was soon clear to McCown that Peiper was engaging in bravado, that he was too intelligent not to recognize not only the immediate plight of his command but the inevitable fate awaiting Nazi Germany.

Aware that Peiper was holding more than a hundred Americans as prisoners of war, McCown's immediate concern was for their safety. Like almost everybody else on the American side by that time, McCown had heard of the massacre of American prisoners near Malmédy, and he felt fairly certain he was talking to the man whose troops had done the deed. As Peiper's senior prisoner, said McCown, he felt a responsibility for the well-being of the others whom Peiper held. Would Peiper give him his personal assurance that the prisoners would be treated according to the Geneva Convention?

"I give you my word," said Peiper.

La Gleize had already taken heavy shelling from American artillery, but with the 119th Infantry's occupation of Stoumont and the Château de Froid-Cour, forward observers had an unobstructed view of the village. By midday on the 22nd the village was under almost constant shellfire, but except for an occasional direct hit, Peiper's tanks were virtually impervious to it.

Soon after midday, the commander of the 740th Tank Battalion, Colonel Rubel, set up his borrowed 155mm. self-propelled artillery piece alongside the Château de Froid-Cour, and close by the 105mm. pieces he had found at the ordnance depot at Sprimont. With a clear view of La Gleize, the gunners wreaked havoc on the buildings in the village, and one of the rounds from the 155 chopped the top off the spire of the village church. From farther away, the 155mm. howitzers of the 30th Division's 113th Field Artillery Battalion added the fury of their fire, much of it shells armed with the VT fuse. Little would be left of La Gleize but rubble, and those German soldiers who survived the carnage would ever after have a name for the village: *Der Kessel* (The Cauldron).

In the little cellar alongside the schoolhouse, McCown's guards took cover beside their prisoners, McCown and the four lieutenants. In early afternoon, a shell hit a wall of the cellar, tearing a gaping hole in it and sending rubble cascading inside. Moments later, another shell burst near the hole in the wall, spraying the cellar with rubble and shell fragments, killing one of the American lieutenants, and wounding three Germans, one of them mortally.

On the eastern fringe of La Gleize, in the cellar of the farmhouse that served as Peiper's headquarters, Peiper was sharply conscious of the terrible pounding his men—and his wounded—were taking in the village. He was particularly concerned with what appeared to be a big artillery piece employing direct fire from (so he thought) a window of the Château de Froid-Cour, but he considered he could not spare the ammunition to try to knock it out. Like gasoline, food, and medical supplies, ammunition was virtually exhausted.

Despite an ultra high-frequency radio brought to him earlier, communication with his division headquarters was erratic. The day before he had radioed that all supplies were exhausted and asked permission to break out, but only on the afternoon of the 22d did a reply come, and it was infuriating: "If *Kampfgruppe Peiper* does not punctually report its supply situation, it cannot reckon on a running supply of fuel and ammunition." There were six Tiger tanks that belonged with Peiper located near Stavelot, the radio voice continued. What did Peiper want done with them? Send them, Peiper replied sarcastically, by air to La Gleize.

Composing himself, Peiper asked again for authority to break out. He could do it, he said, only on foot, without vehicles and without wounded.

As the operator signed off, apparently to consult with Colonel Mohnke, Peiper felt sure authority to fall back would come. Possibly because of what had happened at the Baugnez road junction, he was concerned about leaving his wounded and called for Major McCown to be brought to the command post. He wanted to make a deal, Peiper told McCown; he wanted McCown's assurance that the American commander who occupied La Gleize would return the wounded to German lines. In exchange, he would leave all the American prisoners behind except McCown himself, whom he would release once the German wounded were repatriated.

"Colonel," McCown responded, "that proposal is a farce. For one thing, I have no power to bind the American command regarding German PWs. All I can do is sign a statement that I heard you make the offer. I can do nothing more."

Peiper settled for that. McCown wrote the statement, and he and another captured officer, Capt. Bruce Crissinger, commander of Company A, 832d Tank Destroyer Battalion, signed it. Since Crissinger was to stay behind with the other prisoners, he retained the statement.

Returning to the radio, Peiper asked if approval had come to break out. "May we break out?" his radio operator asked. "I repeat, may we break out?"

The answer was yes, but only if vehicles and wounded were brought along.

Blow up the radio, Peiper told the operator. Without vehicles, without wounded, he was getting out.

Through much of the day of December 23, from a sandpit just outside La Gleize, big Karl Wortmann watched the shelling of the village. Having started out with *Kampfgruppe Peiper* as a gunner on a flak tank, he had become, in the wake of casualties, a section leader, but one of his two flak tanks had been knocked out near the sanitorium in Stoumont. He and the men of his surviving tank watched the shelling in dismay: white phosphorus shells, shells that burst in the air, shells that plowed the ground and ripped open the buildings. As Wortmann was wont to do late each day, he left the position and headed into the village for the *Kampfgruppe*'s command post to check on developments. Don't forget, his men called after him, as they did each day, "by all means bring back something really good to eat." At least, thought Wortmann, his men still retained their gallows humor.

Wortmann was unable to get to the command post, for the shelling was too intense. The men he encountered were dazed, numbed by it. He hastened back to his own men and his flak tank.

The night was bitterly cold, the ground covered with a deep snow. Wortmann had no idea of the time, but he knew it was well past midnight and he feared he had dozed off and was dreaming. Or was that a real voice calling out, "Merry Christmas, Merry Christmas"?

Jumping from the tank, Wortmann ran toward the sound. It was a messenger from Peiper's command post. Why, demanded Wortmann, was he saying Merry Christmas when Christmas was still a day away? It was the codeword, said the messenger; it meant "immediate escape— blow up your tanks and follow!"

By the time Wortmann and his men had implanted delayed demolition mines in their tank and made their way into La Gleize, the village appeared to be deserted. Wortmann had no idea of the route for the breakout. He was beginning to despair when one of his men found a trail of footprints in the snow, a track left by hundreds. Following it, he and his men soon came upon the tail of the withdrawing column.

Behind a small advance guard, Peiper himself led the column of some eight hundred men with Major McCown by his side and two men from the headquarters detailed to guard McCown. At a farmhouse, Peiper ordered two Belgians, Laurent Gason and Yvan Hakin, to join him as guides. They led the Germans to a small wooden bridge spanning the

Amblève underneath the remains of a demolished railroad bridge. As the men crossed, they could hear the first of the explosions of the demolitions placed in their vehicles, either with delayed fuses or by a small engineer detail left behind with the assignment. When the head of the column reached the crest of a wooded hill beyond the river, the men could see fires burning in La Gleize.

With the coming of daylight, Peiper released the two Belgians and ordered his men to conceal themselves in the woods. All through the day, Peiper, McCown, and McCown's guards trooped about the forest trying to determine the best route to take when night came again. Having had only four pieces of dried biscuit and two swallows of cognac, McCown was desperately hungry, but there were no rations for anybody. Late in the day an officer gave him a small piece of hard candy from a K-ration. That helped.

Shortly before nightfall—it was Christmas Eve—the column began moving again behind a strong advance guard. With such discipline did the eight hundred men move that McCown was convinced they could have passed within two hundred yards of an outpost without being detected. Over and over McCown heard the word that any man who fell behind the column was to be shot. Later in the night he saw some men crawling in an effort to keep up.

Karl Wortmann was a part of the advance guard when around 11 P.M. a patrol of American paratroopers tried to seize the leading men. Firing broke out, "fierce, wild shooting." There were casualties and cries for medics, and Peiper himself was grazed by a bullet.

As the Germans around Major McCown scattered for cover, McCown lay still, awaiting some order from his guards. When it failed to come, he arose cautiously and began to walk slowly at right angles from the direction of the firing, all the while glancing back to see if anybody was covering him or following. Sure at last that he was alone, he turned and headed directly toward where the firing had come from.

He was walking slowly and whistling "Yankee Doodle" as loudly as he could when a voice shouted: "Halt, Goddamn it!" McCown permitted himself half a smile. He had made it.

The German column meanwhile continued to withdraw, got across the highway paralleling the Salm River south of Trois Ponts, and took refuge in a gully long enough to give such first aid as was possible to the wounded. Although patrols searched for a bridge, none was to be found. There was nothing to do but wade or swim.

Some of the taller men, including Wortmann, formed a chain spanning the forty-foot width of the river, arms locked, every other man facing in the opposite direction. The others began to cross upstream from the chain, but despite that precaution, the swift current carried some men downstream to their deaths. No one could stand the icy waters for long, so that men forming the chain had to be constantly relieved and replaced.

It was well after daylight when the last man crossed, and as the column headed for the village of Wanne, where long days before Peiper's passing had interrupted a football match, American artillery opened fire. More men wounded, some killed, blood on the snow. When the survivors finally gained the barns and houses of the village, their uniforms were so frozen that it was a major task to get them off.

Of some 4,000 men who had started the attack with *Kampfgruppe Peiper*, plus about 1,800 men of Major Knittel's reconnaissance battalion and the additional battalion of the 2d SS Panzergrenadier Regiment that had later joined Peiper, only those 800 made their way out of the entrapment. A few wounded also made it, for while the wooden span over the Amblève at Petit-Spai still stood and while Peiper still had access to it, he had evacuated many of his wounded. He nevertheless had to leave behind 80 wounded in the Château de Froid-Cour and just over 300 in La Gleize. Unknown to Peiper, he also left behind fifty *SS-Panzergrenadiers* in the woods above La Gleize who never received the code word, "Merry Christmas," and subsequently fought to the death. Out of a force totaling 5,800 men, Peiper lost close to 5,000.

Just how many tanks and other vehicles *Kampfgruppe Peiper* left behind at Cheneux, La Gleize, Stoumont, and Stoumont Station was difficult to determine, for U.S. Army counts and later counts by civilians in the area differed. Based in large measure on tanks and other vehicles known to have started out with the column, the figures were probably sixty tanks, including seven Tigers; three flak tanks; seventy half-tracks; at least fourteen 20mm. flak wagons; twenty-five 75mm. assault guns and 105mm. and 150mm. self-propelled howitzers; plus trucks and smaller vehicles. To that total would have to be added others lost along the way: thirteen tanks, two flak tanks, and here and there a half-track, plus six mediums and three Tigers at Stavelot. The total number of tanks was eighty-seven, including five flak tanks and ten Tigers.

Although Peiper confessed to Major McCown that his men killed 7 American prisoners at La Gleize, when, according to Peiper, they tried to escape, the conduct of the SS troops toward 170 other American captives was satisfactory. So, too, apparently, toward Belgian civilians, for even though twenty-three civilians died at Cheneux, La Gleize, and Stoumont, in only one case, when an older couple died as a result of rounds fired from an automatic weapon through the window of their home, was there any indication of deliberate killing.

Peiper had fallen far short of his goal of reaching the Meuse, yet he had accomplished more than he probably realized at the time and certainly much more than Skorzeny's disguised infiltration teams or von der

Heydte's parachutists. Peiper had provoked genuine concern in the American command, and by his continued presence, he had so delayed an American drive to close the gap between Malmédy and St. Vith that by the time he withdrew, conditions were no longer conducive to making it. He had also kept a powerful American combat command tied up for almost five days when it was critically needed elsewhere.

A tragic and in some ways incredible postscript to the war against *Kampfgruppe Peiper* remained to be enacted.

Skies had yet to clear fully over the Ardennes on December 23 when twenty-eight medium bombers, B-26 Marauders of the Ninth Air Force's IX Bombardment Division, headed for the German town of Zulpich, site of a railhead for the German Army some thirty-three miles northeast of Malmédy. The pilots of most of the planes soon realized they were off course and either aborted their mission or bombed alternate targets; but six others, also thinking they were bombing an alternate target, dropped eighty-six 250-pound general purpose bombs on Malmédy. All six pilots reported "excellent results."

So they were. Someone at the 30th Division's headquarters telephoned frantically to headquarters of the First Army: "Planes are bombing Malmedy. We haven't a line left to anybody in town. Get them off." But by that time the damage was done. The bombs hit squarely in the center of town, destroying buildings, blocking streets with rubble, burying civilians and soldiers alike.

Adding to the destruction, fires erupted and for a time raged out of control, for the little town's fire-fighting equipment was never intended to cope with such a holocaust. Here and there men of the 291st Engineers dynamited buildings to create firebreaks, but it was well into the night before the fires were under control. By that time the school's playground was carpeted with dead civilians. Dazed survivors with tears streaking down dust-stained faces asked incredulously of the soldiers: "American planes?"

Twice before, in Normandy in July, American bombs on two successive days had fallen short on men of the 30th Division as they waited to participate in the big attack to break out of the beachhead. The division lost 138 men killed, hundreds more wounded, and for long afterward old-timers in the division spoke sardonically of the Ninth Air Force as the American Luftwaffe; and whenever American planes attacked in support of the 30th Division, General Hobbs always insisted on a wide margin of safety between the bomb line and his troops. Yet again American aircraft had attacked men of the 30th Division. And not once but twice.

In the early afternoon of December 24, Christmas Eve, Colonel Pergrin and men of his 291st Engineers were still digging survivors from the rubble created by the bombing the day before when a flight of eighteen heavy bombers, B-24 Liberators, droned overhead, and "what the medium bombers did the day before was nothing compared to what the eighteen B-24s did." They leveled the entire central core of the town. A desperate telephone call from the 120th Infantry went through to head-quarters of the 30th Division: "These planes are on us again; they are about to ruin us. Can you call them off?" Yet again the damage had already been done.

Just as the bombers approached, men of the 291st Engineers had fi-nally tunneled into a cellar to rescue a few men of the 120th Infantry trapped there, and Colonel Pergrin had squeezed through the opening. Then the bombs exploded, and a nearby freestanding wall collapsed, seal-ing the cellar again. It took the engineers an hour to dig Pergrin and the others out.

Fires again broke out. Entire streets were burning, and as night fell, "it looked as if the whole town could go up in flames." Dead civilians were once more laid out in rows in the schoolyard.

The struggle to dig out from the two bombings was still under way on Christmas Day when around 2:30 P.M. another flight of B-26 Marauders approached the town. Thirty-six planes were on their way to bomb St. Vith, which was by that time in German hands. Most of the planes found their targets, but four mistook Malmédy for St. Vith and dropped sixty-four 250-pound general purpose bombs.

In a town crammed with refugees, authorities in Malmédy never were able to determine exactly how many civilians died over those three terri-ble days, but the figure was probably at least 125. American losses were 37 killed and close to 100 wounded, and the center of the pretty little town was a ruin.

Many an American soldier long attributed the bombings to a map appearing in the soldier newspaper *Stars & Stripes*, which erroneously showed Malmédy to be in German hands. Yet that theory took no ac-count of the fact that big identification panels were prominently displayed on rooftops of the town. Through the years, surviving inhabitants tried to arrive at some explanation: Were the Americans expecting to lose the town and wanted to turn it into a chokepoint, as they did at such places as St. Vith, Houffalize, and La Roche? Yet why would they do that when their own troops were still there?

None of those theories explained the tragic bombings. It was, in fact, the human equation: pilot error. Nothing more, nothing less.

CHAPTER TWENTY-THREE

The Defense of St. Vith

Armor is an offensive weapon, created essentially to exploit a breakthrough achieved by infantry or armor or a combination of both. Few commanders of armored combat commands and divisions would endorse the use of their tanks, self-propelled tank destroyers, half-track–mounted infantry, and self-propelled artillery in a defensive role. Leave that to the separate tank and tank destroyer battalions whose basic assignment is support of the infantry.

Yet there are obviously times when a commander has no choice but to use his armor defensively. When that happens, no armored commander wants to be bound by the dictum (so often propounded by infantry commanders) to hold a static defensive line at all costs. Impose maximum delay but give ground rather than be overwhelmed, then counterattack, not necessarily to regain and hold the ground relinquished but to impose further delay. The object: to take full advantage of armor's mobility.

As the commander of the 7th Armored Division's CCB, Bruce Clarke, put it during the course of the fight for St. Vith: "This terrain is not worth a nickel an acre to me." Before an enemy in far superior strength, he could afford to give ground grudgingly, Clarke believed, because a few hundred or a thousand yards here and there was of no real value to his opponent. If his opponent was to succeed, he had to make great strides and make them swiftly, and only by outmaneuvering or by overwhelming and annihilating the defenders could he do so. As was demonstrated when Clarke urged his colleague, Bill Hoge of the 9th Armored Division's CCB, to pull back behind the railroad line southeast of St. Vith because Hoge's only route of withdrawal was through St. Vith, and Clarke felt sure he would in time lose the town.

Clarke's division commander, Bob Hasbrouck, thought the same way. When on December 17, for example, the acting commander of CCR, Colonel Warren, told Hasbrouck of a developing threat to the village of

466

DEFENSE OF BASTOGNE
DEC 19-22

U.S. PSNS. MORN. 19 DEC
U.S. PSNS. 22 DEC

Scale 0 1000 2000
YARDS

Recht, near Poteau, Hasbrouck told him to defend the village, not to the death, but as long as possible.

While the new commander of Allied forces opposing the northern portion of the German penetration, Field Marshal Montgomery, was making his first visit to headquarters of the First Army in the Hôtel des Bains in Chaudfontaine around noon on December 20, the 7th Armored Division's chemical warfare officer, Lt. Col. Frederick Schroeder, walked into the hotel. He had been on the road since early morning, driving from the division's headquarters in Vielsalm on a roundabout route to avoid *Kampfgruppe Peiper*. He brought with him a letter from his division commander, General Hasbrouck, for an old friend of Hasbrouck's, the First Army's chief of staff, Bill Kean.

With that letter, Hasbrouck provided the first solid information the First Army's headquarters had received about the situation at St. Vith. The 7th Armored Division, wrote Hasbrouck, was defending a line from Poteau southeastward to include St. Vith; the 9th Armored Division's CCB was extending the line southwest of St. Vith; and the 106th Division's 424th Infantry and the 28th Division's 112th Infantry curved the line around to the west. The infantry regiments were "in bad shape." Only a few reconnaissance troops, tank destroyers, light tanks, and stragglers were available to extend the southern flank beyond the positions of the 112th Infantry; and off that flank, Hasbrouck reported, the 560th Volksgrenadier and 116th Panzer Divisions were moving in the direction of Houffalize. Unless he got help, those divisions would soon cut him off from the rear.

Colonel Schroeder arrived with that message even as Field Marshal Montgomery was proposing that the First Army pull back from St. Vith, in the process canceling the drive General Hodges had ordered by the 82d Airborne Division to push up to the Salm River and establish contact with the rear of the defenders of St. Vith. Since Hodges wanted to hang on to St. Vith in order eventually to close the gap between Malmédy and St. Vith, he used the threat to Hasbrouck's rear to justify continuing the 82d Airborne Division's advance to the Salm.

Montgomery still wanted to withdraw from St. Vith. As he saw it, the real crisis appeared to be developing well to the rear, with a possible German sweep beyond the Ourthe River to cross the Meuse between Liège and Namur. A salient at St. Vith, sticking out far beyond other positions, merely absorbed troops needed elsewhere and endangered their existence. On the other hand, he agreed that continued advance by the airborne division might prevent the Germans from trapping the troops at St. Vith and facilitate their withdrawal later.

Although Hodges pursued the point no further, he continued, in his own counsels, to plan to close the gap between Malmédy and St. Vith, which carried the obvious intent of leaving the defenders of St. Vith in place. Furthermore, once the 82d Airborne Division gained contact with Hasbrouck's rear, the forces around St. Vith were to pass to the command of the XVIII Airborne Corps. The commander of that corps, Matthew B. Ridgway, was an airborne soldier not given to worrying about being surrounded and not accustomed to giving ground.

For the German command, December 20 was a day of disappointment around St. Vith. Model, von Manteuffel, and Lucht had been planning an all-out attack to take the town starting at daylight, a three-pronged envelopment with the 62d Volksgrenadier Division attacking from the southeast along the road from Steinebrück; the 18th Volksgrenadier Division attacking along the two roads from Schoenberg, which converged just behind the American defensive line on the Prümerberg, just short of St. Vith; and the *Führer Begleit Brigade* attacking from the north.

In releasing the *Führer Begleit Brigade* to General von Manteuffel—in effect, directing him to use it—Field Marshal Model thought he would gain quick access to the roadnet at St. Vith, whereupon he intended sending the brigade driving swiftly for the Meuse or cutting in behind the opposition on the Elsenborn Ridge that was stymieing the Sixth Panzer Army. Yet the monumental traffic jams in the Losheim Gap and at Schoenberg continued to delay both the 18th Volksgrenadier Division and the *Führer Begleit Brigade*, and not until after daylight on the 20th would a bridge be ready at Steinebrück for the 62d Volksgrenadier Division. Those factors dictated at least another twenty-four-hour delay before a major assault on St. Vith could begin.

Commanded by Col. Otto Remer, the *Führer Begleit* (Escort) *Brigade* had been built around the nucleus of a battalion which Remer had commanded with the mission of protecting Hitler at his headquarters on the Eastern Front in the Gorlitz Forest. A prompt reaction to the attempt on Hitler's life in July had brought Remer to the Führer's personal attention, propelling him into that small fraternity of relatively junior officers, such as Skorzeny and Peiper, whom the Führer especially favored. In the wake of the big Allied airborne attack in the Netherlands in September, Hitler had become so concerned lest parachutists drop on his headquarters and attempt to capture him that he summoned Remer to the *Wolfschanze* and told him to enlarge the *Führer Begleit* from a battalion to a brigade.

Remer was occupied with doing that when in late November Hitler revealed that he was moving his headquarters to Berlin and wanted Remer to reorganize his brigade as a combat force to be employed on the Western Front. (He failed to bring Remer in on his grandiose plan for an offensive.) As finally formed, the brigade was a powerful force, something like a strongly reinforced American combat command. Remer had three mobile grenadier battalions, an artillery battalion of 105mm. pieces, a flak regiment with twenty-four 88mm. guns (the regiment had provided antiaircraft protection for the *Wolfschanze*), and contingents of antitank troops and engineers and a panzer battalion with forty-five Mark IVs and thirty-five assault guns. Because the panzer battalion and some of the grenadiers came from the renowned *Grossdeutschland Panzer Division*, which was on the Eastern Front, prisoner identifications were later to cause considerable concern and bafflement to American intelligence officers.

So anxious was General von Manteuffel to get the drive going on St. Vith that even though he had lost all hope of mounting a major attack on December 20, he told Remer to use whatever he had on hand to get something moving quickly. Before daylight on the 20th, a company each of infantry and tanks tried to move from Wallerode on St. Vith, but by that time the overall commander on the Prümerberg, Colonel Fuller, had extended his line to cover that approach to St. Vith, and much of the 7th Armored Division's artillery had moved forward to positions close enough to augment the fires of the 275th Armored Field Artillery Battalion. The probe got nowhere.

An ambitious man, Otto Remer was actually less interested in helping to take St. Vith than in beginning a drive for the Meuse, for which he needed crossings of the Salm River at Vielsalm and a short distance upstream at Salmchâteau. Displaying some of the same independence as Skorzeny and Peiper, Remer decided, without consulting von Manteuffel, to shift the thrust of his effort away from St. Vith to the roads behind the town that led to those crossing sites. At midday on the 20th, he sent a battalion each of tanks and infantry to take the village of Rodt, where he intended to get on the highway leading to Poteau and thence to Vielsalm; but as the four leading tanks crossed the brow of a hill, 90mm. guns of the 814th Tank Destroyer Battalion knocked out all four with an expenditure of only seven rounds. Remer decided to call everything off until his full brigade arrived.

By that time, the commander of the defenses in front of St. Vith, Colonel Fuller, had assembled a fairly sizable force in an arc stretching from the main highway into St. Vith from the north across the heights of the Prümerberg to a draw southeast of the town near where the railroad and the road from Steinebrück entered St. Vith. Fuller had two companies of his own 38th Armored Infantry Battalion (the third company— armored infantry battalions had only three line companies—was with CCA at Poteau), two of the 23d Armored Infantry Battalion (the third was a part of CCB's reserve), a composite force of about four hundred men of the 81st and 168th Engineers, a troop of the 87th Armored Cavalry Reconnaissance Squadron, and a platoon of the 423d Infantry that had been the 106th Division's headquarters guard.

In support were a company each of the 31st Tank and 814th Tank Destroyer Battalions. Most of the tank destroyers were in reserve in St. Vith, but in recognition that the road from Steinebrück was a likely ave-

DEFENSE OF ST. VITH
DEC 21 - 23

Scale:
0   1   2   3   4
MILES

nue of attack and because there was a six hundred-yard gap between Fuller's line and positions of the 9th Armored Division's CCB, four guns were in position on that flank with the 23d Armored Infantry Battalion's Company B. The eleven available medium tanks were positioned to cover open ground near Wallerode, the second and lesser highway leading from Schoenberg, and the main highway crossing the Prümerberg.

Fuller's position had three obvious disadvantages: a lack of unit integrity, for the troops had been committed piecemeal; the gap on the southern flank; and a lack of depth. The lack of depth was particularly serious for the men on the Prümerberg, since close at their backs the ground dropped off sharply—almost a bluff—which was much like having a river behind you.

On specific order from General von Manteuffel, the *Führer Begleit*

Brigade on December 21 was supposed to hit St. Vith from the north; but the commander, Otto Remer, nevertheless persisted in his aim of getting onto the highway leading to Vielsalm. That left the attack on the town to the 18th Volksgrenadier Division and a regiment of the 62d Volksgrenadier Division.

Because the 18th Volksgrenadiers still had problems reaching their jump-off positions, it was 3 P.M. before German artillery began a preliminary bombardment, but when it came, it was punishing. Some of the veteran armored infantrymen swore they had never undergone anything like it. Screaming rockets from *Nebelwerfers* added terror to the fire and tore gaps in the line, and on the Prümerberg, where most of the foxholes were inside the woods, tree bursts were deadly. The shelling wounded the commander of the tank company, Capt. Robert Foster, and one of his tank commanders, and sent a platoon leader into shock; but the executive officer, 1st Lt. John J. Dunn, made his way forward to take over.

At four o'clock, as dusk was approaching, the shelling lifted to command posts in the rear and to St. Vith, and *Volksgrenadiers* all along the line swarmed to the attack. Artillery of the 7th Armored Division and of the 275th Armored Field Artillery Battalion responded with alacrity. Germans fell left and right, yet others, constantly exhorted by their noncommissioned officers, continued to push forward. By the time night fell, small groups of Germans were behind the line, roaming in the rear, killing messengers, bringing command posts under fire.

On the southern flank, the 23d Armored Infantry Battalion's Company B was quickly in trouble. Although the four tank destroyers with their 90mm. pieces provided yeoman support, they were soon out of high-explosive shell and reduced to firing armor-piercing rounds, which had little effect on the *Volksgrenadiers*. Quickly discerning the gap between Company B and the 9th Armored Division's CCB, the Germans pressed into it.

When the company commander, Capt. Dudley J. Britton, called for tanks, the commander of the 31st Tank Battalion, Lt. Col. Robert C. Erlenbusch, told Lieutenant Dunn to send four that were in a concealed position behind the Prümerberg. The tanks started out, but one quickly broke down, and the commander of the 168th Engineers, Colonel Nungesser, who was roaming up and down the line watching for trouble spots, saw the peril where the main highway crossed the Prümerberg as too great and ordered the tanks back. When Dunn learned of the shift, he ordered his own command tank to join him; sent two tanks that were covering the open ground facing Wallerode to the southern flank; and ordered the other three to the highway on the Prümerberg. Thus five tanks were soon in position there.

On the southern flank, Company B was fast going to pieces. As infiltrating Germans approached Britton's command post in a house, they yelled in English: "Come on out!" To which Britton yelled back: "Fuck you, come on in!"

Although Britton's headquarters troops drove those Germans off, so thickly were the *Volksgrenadiers* surging through the gap on the company's flank that Britton saw no alternative but to withdraw. With his tank destroyers, he hoped to hold a few hundred yards back where the highway from Steinebrück passed beneath the railroad. Yet by that time two of Britton's platoons were surrounded and were unable to break away, and when Britton and his remaining platoon reached the railroad, events happening elsewhere made it impossible to form a new line.

On the Prümerberg, it was almost full dark, around 5 P.M., when six Tigers of the 506th Heavy Panzer Battalion, which had earlier appeared with devastating results at Andler, approached along the highway from Schoenberg. Lieutenant Dunn radioed his five tanks on the hill to get into positions from which they could cover a rise in the road, and when the Tigers crossed the rise, to open fire simultaneously.

The tankers were ready, but as the Tigers crossed the rise, they fired high-velocity flares which burst behind the American tanks with a brilliant light. That blinded the American gunners and silhouetted their tanks. In a matter of seconds, the German gunners had knocked out or disabled all five tanks, killing or wounding most of the crews. Having demolished the American tank support in one powerful blow, the German gunners began knocking out machine-gun crews as fast as they could be replaced. Nobody could long stand such a pounding, and the survivors along the highway broke for the rear.

Stunned by those events, the overall commander of the forces in front of St. Vith, Colonel Fuller, told the commander of the 81st Engineers, Colonel Riggs, to take over. He himself was heading for General Clarke's headquarters "to plan alternate positions." When he got there, he told Clarke he couldn't take it any more. Preoccupied with other events, Clarke told him to report to the medics, who subsequently evacuated him through medical channels. (Soft-hearted medical officers appeared predisposed to soft-hearted treatment of field grade officers.)

Back on the Prümerberg, despite the breakthroughs along the southern flank and the main road from Steinebrück, there was still an American line in front of St. Vith. In between those two roads, the infantrymen, cavalrymen, and engineers were still holding, along with two tanks guarding the other road from Schoenberg; and on the open ground facing Wallerode, both Company A, 38th Armored Infantry, and Company A, 23d Armored Infantry, although hardpressed, were still intact. The company of the 23d Armored Infantry had just been reinforced by sixty men of the 106th Division, consisting mostly of the men who had made their way out of the entrapment beyond the Our River with Lieutenants McKinley and

Long. Before returning to the fight, they had had a twenty-four-hour rest in the schoolhouse at St. Vith.

Inside St. Vith, on the other hand, confusion was rampant. The big Tigers, *Volksgrenadiers* clinging all over them, were soon lumbering down the steep hill along the highway, and even though an occasional group of Americans and a tank destroyer or two tried to make a stand, nobody could hold for long. In the darkness, vehicles of all types began streaming out of town toward the west, American soldiers clambering aboard on any available space.

Around 9:30 P.M., General Clarke got word to Colonel Riggs to withdraw to a new line to be formed on the first high ground behind the town. Riggs was able to get that order to few of the men, and with the Germans in St. Vith, it was impossible to withdraw in any case. A few got out individually or in small groups, but many, including Riggs, were captured.

It was close to midnight when the commander of the 38th Armored Infantry's Company A, Capt. Walter H. Austey, on the open ground facing Wallerode, finally established radio contact with his battalion's executive officer and learned of the order. With some seventy men, he began to withdraw in a heavy snowstorm, but many men lost contact in the snow and darkness, and only Austey and thirty-three others escaped.

Men of the 23d Armored Infantry's Company A got the word even later. Finally succeeding in making a field artillery radio function, Cpl. Harold Kemp contacted the 275th Armored Field Artillery Battalion. "What are our orders?" asked Kemp. After a brief delay, the word came back: "Go west! Go west!"

Well over a hundred men lined up in single file to begin the withdrawal, but in the darkness and blinding snow, the column soon broke apart and most of the men lost their way. Only twenty-one finally reached General Clarke's command post, among them none of the men from the 106th Division who had struggled to make their way back across the Our River to St. Vith.

The 7th Armored Division's CCB lost heavily in the defense of St. Vith: at least nine hundred soldiers who had stood in front of the town. Of eleven tanks, four survived (one of them commanded by 1st Lt. Will Rogers, Jr., son of the American humorist), along with most of the tank destroyers. The debacle left Clarke with only one full company of armored infantrymen.

As Clarke made the decision to withdraw from in front of St. Vith, he notified the commander of the 9th Armored Division's CCB, General Hoge, who would have to pull back his north flank to conform with the new line Clarke hoped to form a thousand yards behind St. Vith. Although Hoge's troops had sustained some pressure during the day from the 62d Volksgrenadier Division, they had handled it with little difficulty.

By midnight, Clarke's new line was forming. Officers stationed on roads and trails halted stragglers and directed them to the new positions, which in view of the shortage of infantry, would be porous at best. Clarke had his usual 31st Tank Battalion, a company of the 814th Tank Destroyer Battalion, and the bulk of the 17th Tank Battalion, which normally fought with CCR but which had become available after CCA took charge in the vicinity of Poteau.

Fortunately for Clarke and his men, the Germans were in no position to pursue their success in capturing St. Vith immediately. Most roads leading into the town converged along narrow streets at a traffic circle near the southern edge of the town, not far from the St. Joseph's Kloster, which quickly became a bottleneck with effects as stultifying as those already experienced at Schoenberg and in the Losheim Gap. Men of all three regiments of the 18th Volksgrenadier Division and one regiment of the 62d Volksgrenadier Division poured into the town, eager to get at the booty and the warmth of the houses, and units were soon almost hopelessly intermingled. Support troops raced down from the Prümerberg to join what rapidly became "a kind of scavenger hunt," and officers and men in captured American vehicles added to the confusion. Still searching for a way around the stalled traffic in the Losheim Gap, some contingents of the Sixth Panzer Army also entered the town; and as usual, SS officers among them were truculent and imperious, refusing to obey the orders of other officers or military policemen. Once again the commander of Army Group B, Field Marshal Model, had to get out of his command car and walk.

On December 22, after all of the *Führer Begleit Brigade* had at last arrived, Colonel Remer intended to get on with his self-appointed task of capturing Rodt and gaining the main highway to Vielsalm—a first step toward the glory of a drive to the Meuse. A strong infantry patrol had found a way around Rodt the day before. Remer sent an infantry battalion to follow that route and reach the highway, while his other two infantry battalions attacked the village itself. At the same time, twenty-five tanks were to bypass the village and attack it from the rear.

The juncture point for the defenses of Combat Commands A and B, Rodt was weakly garrisoned by Service Company of the 48th Armored Infantry Battalion. With strong support from the 275th Armored Field Artillery Battalion, the Americans of that company nevertheless turned back one German battalion and allowed only a few men from the other to get into the fringe of the village. The battalion that was following the route taken earlier by the patrol bumped into the 48th Armored Infantry's vehicle park, where drivers and mechanics manned the .50-caliber machine guns on the half-tracks to turn the Germans back. Remer's tanks nevertheless got behind the village. When they attacked, the few men of Service Company had no way to stop them.

In capturing Rodt, Remer drove a wedge between Combat Commands A and B, and with Germans in both Rodt and St. Vith, two troops of the 87th Armored Cavalry Reconnaissance Squadron between the two villages had to pull back to General Clarke's new line. At about the same time, men of CCA around Poteau captured prisoners whose identity told the American commander, Colonel Rosebaum, that he faced a strong new force: the 9th SS Panzer Division.

That division had finally threaded its leading units through the coagulated traffic in the Losheim Gap under orders from General Dietrich to cross the Salm River and drive westward and, if possible, rescue *Kampfgruppe Peiper* in the process. The division had no interest in Vielsalm other than to guard against interference by the American armor known to be in the vicinity and merely left a task force to guard the division's flank in front of Poteau.

That Colonel Rosebaum could not know. Confronted with possible attack by an entire SS panzer division that might cut off all American troops east of the Salm River by a drive through Poteau on Vielsalm, Rosebaum abandoned any further contest with the *Führer Begleit Brigade* and pulled back to form a close-knit semicircular defense of the vital road junction at Poteau.

That action further widened the rift between CCA and CCB, which in turn prompted General Clarke to fall back to a new line based on the village of Hinderhausen, southwest of Rodt, and his old headquarters village of Crombach. While Clarke's headquarters moved to the village of Commanster, deep in a vast expanse of forest (the Grand Bois) which screened the approaches to Vielsalm, the withdrawal proceeded with little difficulty. Except for the *Führer Begleit Brigade*, still consolidating at Rodt, most of the Germans facing Clarke were still involved in the disorganization and confusion that was St. Vith.

Unhindered by the bottleneck at St. Vith, two regiments of the 62d Volksgrenadier Division meanwhile continued to attack the 9th Armored Division's CCB, their goal being to gain the Salm River at Salmchâteau. In mid-morning of December 22, a company of *Volksgrenadiers* broke through the line of the 27th Armored Infantry Battalion, plodded through deep snow up the constricted valley of the Braunlauf Creek, and opened fire on the battalion's headquarters in a large farmhouse in the settlement of Neubrück. The commander, Lt. Col. S. Fred Cummings, Jr., his staff officers, and headquarters troops, firing from the windows, drove off a first assault; but with a second, a few Germans got into the basement, which at the rear of the house was on ground level. Since the defenders were almost out of ammunition, Cummings agreed to surrender.

Wounded in the attack, the German commander, a captain, insisted on medical treatment for himself, one of his lieutenants, and several of his men. Since the Germans had also overrun the battalion aid station in a nearby farmhouse, they brought the battalion surgeon, Capt. Paul J. Russomano, and several of his medics to treat their wounded. Pleading a shortage of medical supplies, Captain Russomano convinced the German officer to allow him to send an ambulance for more.

When the ambulance departed, the Germans ordered their prisoners to march toward German lines. They had gone only a short distance when they came under a crossfire from the machine guns of two platoons of American tanks. When the guards ordered everybody back to the farmhouse, the battalion's intelligence officer, Capt. Glen L. Strange, ducked under an abandoned half-track and eventually worked his way to one of the tank platoons.

At the farmhouse, in the meantime, the German captain insisted that he and the other German wounded be evacuated to German lines under a flag of truce. The ambulance having returned—but not before the driver had alerted General Hoge's headquarters to what was happening—the wounded Germans—and at the captain's insistence, Captain Russomano—departed in it.

By that time, a platoon of tanks under 1st Lt. David P. Duck, with twenty infantrymen rounded up by Captain Strange riding on the decks, was heading for the farmhouse. Duck's tank fired two quick rounds of high explosive, one into each floor of the house, then thrust its 76mm. piece through the front door. The Germans boiled from the windows, hands overhead. Colonel Cummings, his staff officers, and his headquarters troops followed, none of them injured. Although the Germans held onto Captain Russomano, two months later they sent him under a white flag into American lines.

The issue of who was in overall command of the conglomerate of American forces in the vicinity of St. Vith remained for long unsettled. In response to General Hasbrouck's message carried by his chemical warfare officer to the First Army's headquarters, General Hodges noted that Hasbrouck was to "retain" under his command the 112th Infantry; the 9th Armored Division's CCB; and the 106th Division. That disturbed Hasbrouck, first, because none of those units had been under his command and second, because he was a one-star general and the commander of the 106th Division, General Jones, was a two-star. Furthermore, Hasbrouck was also junior to the commander of the 9th Armored Division's CCB, General Hoge.

Hasbrouck promptly sent another message to the First Army's headquarters. He also sent a copy to Jones for his information and another to General Ridgway, for by that time, late on December 20, patrols of the 82d Airborne Division on the other side of the Salm River had established contact with patrols of the 7th Armored Division, and with that contact all forces in the vicinity of St. Vith passed to the command of

Ridgway and the XVIII Airborne Corps. Hasbrouck pointed out the differences in ranks and noted that Jones was still in command of the 106th Division and that Hoge's combat command and the 112th Infantry were attached to that division. The next day, Ridgway responded by "discontinuing" attachment of the 106th Division to Hasbrouck but directing Jones "to cooperate with 7th Armored Division to carry out corps orders."

Cooperation had been the order of the day in any case. What bothered Hasbrouck far more than who was in charge was the survival of his division, a question that came up shortly before midnight of December 21 after the defenses in front of St. Vith collapsed. Aware that Ridgway wanted to hold the St. Vith salient and attack to close the gap between Malmédy and St. Vith, Hasbrouck's old friend, Bill Kean, told Ridgway—even though he knew that his superior, General Hodges, also wanted to attack—that Hasbrouck was "not expected to sacrifice his command out there." Whether to continue to hold or to withdraw, said Kean, was a decision that should be Hasbrouck's alone.

Despite the loss of St. Vith, Ridgway still believed the troops beyond the Salm could hold; for the 82d Airborne Division was beginning to build a fairly firm line that should prevent the Germans from cutting off the salient from the rear, and he hoped that the 3d Armored Division soon might attack to remove all threat of encirclement. Not long after midnight, he ordered the forces in the salient to shorten their lines by withdrawing to an oval-shaped defensive position in front of and encompassing Vielsalm—a position that came to be known as the "fortified goose egg"—there to await relief by the 3d Armored Division. To resolve the command problem, he attached the 7th Armored Division to the 106th Division, which meant that General Jones was in overall command.

Hasbrouck, Hoge, Clarke, and Rosebaum were all decidedly unhappy with Ridgway's defensive plan. Although the shortening of lines would help, the goose egg would still have an extensive perimeter and would embrace the vast forest in front of Vielsalm, the Grand Bois. When viewed on a map, the roads looked extensive; in fact, all were dirt trails except for a gravel highway that cut diagonally across the forest. How could tanks—or even mounted infantry for that matter—be shifted to meet developing threats? What, too, if the airborne troops failed to keep the rear of the goose egg accessible? It was one thing to supply lightly armed airborne troops by air; but armor? Clarke called the plan "Custer's Last Stand."

Before daylight came on December 22, all commands were nevertheless beginning to comply with the order to form the fortified goose egg; but soon after dawn, Hasbrouck wrote out a long recital ~f the situation in the salient for transmission to Ridgway. First, he called attention to the dearth of roads and to the fact that all supplies would have to come over a single bridge at Vielsalm. Then he pointed out that even that bridge might be denied should the 2d SS Panzer Division, identified south of the salient, drive the airborne troops back even as much as three thousand yards. Hasbrouck also noted that Clarke's CCB had lost heavily in front of St. Vith, fully half the command. "I don't think," concluded Hasbrouck, "we can prevent a complete breakthrough if another all-out attack comes against CCB tonight."

Hasbrouck quite clearly wanted to withdraw. Just as he finished writing, word arrived of the *Führer Begleit Brigade*'s attack on Rodt and of the attack against the headquarters of the 9th Armored Division's 27th Armored Infantry Battalion. In a postscript, Hasbrouck told of those attacks; and lest any doubt of the seriousness of the situation still remained, he added: "In my opinion if we don't get out of here and up north of the 82d before night, we will not have a 7th Armored Division left."

Meanwhile, a British captain had arrived at Hasbrouck's command post in the Middle School in Vielsalm. He was a PHANTOM, one of Field Marshal Montgomery's junior liaison officers. Ushered in to see Hasbrouck, the captain asked what Hasbrouck thought should be done with the 7th Armored Division. If holding beyond the Salm was considered to be vital, said Hasbrouck, he would assuredly continue to hold, but he personally recommended withdrawal.

When that word reached Montgomery, he went to Chaudfontaine to confer with General Hodges. The time had come, said Montgomery, to withdraw. Reluctantly, Hodges agreed, and the order went out to the XVIII Airborne Corps.

Matthew Bunker Ridgway, forty-nine years old, was born into an army family, and the U.S. Army had been his life. He was a man of great personal courage (he wore a harness with a hand grenade attached to each of the front straps, not, he maintained, because he wanted to create a distinctive image but because he might need them). His airborne troops from as far back as the days when he had commanded the 82d Airborne Division admired his toughness and called him "The Eagle." He drove himself relentlessly and saw no reason not to drive others the same way. You won wars, in Ridgway's view, not by giving ground but by taking it and holding it.

In early afternoon of December 22, General Ridgway arrived at the Middle School in Vielsalm. Although he knew of Field Marshal Montgomery's order to withdraw and the fact that there was probably no way of circumventing it, he was reluctant to acquiesce until he had a feel himself for the situation on the ground.

In Hasbrouck's headquarters, Ridgway talked with Hasbrouck and with Jones, whose headquarters was also in Vielsalm, in a Belgian Army barracks built originally for the *Chasseurs Ardennais* close by the Salm River. In one hand, Ridgway held Hasbrouck's recent message urging withdrawal and fearing for survival of the 7th Armored Division. Holding aloft the message, Ridgway demanded in a scathing tone: "Did you read this before you signed it?"

Replied Hasbrouck: "Yes, sir, I most assuredly did."

With that reply, Ridgway's attitude changed. What, he asked, were the prospects for holding the fortified goose egg until a relief force arrived? In response, Hasbrouck cited all the things wrong with the position: the woods, the dearth of roads, the fatigue of the troops, the reduced strength. Jones, on the other hand, he who had remained rosily optimistic in the St. Joseph's Kloster at St. Vith even as two-thirds of his command was about to be lost, said he thought it could be done.

Although that was what Ridgway apparently wanted to hear, it obviously irritated him. Beckoning to Hasbrouck, he told him to come along; he was going forward to have a look for himself.

At General Clarke's command post in Commanster, the two met with Clarke and with the commander of the 424th Infantry, Colonel Reid, much of whose regiment was to form the reserve within the goose egg. What, Ridgway asked each commander, was the combat efficiency of his command? About 50 percent, said Reid; 40 percent, said Clarke.

There was one more commander Ridgway wanted to talk to, one who had been on the football team at West Point when Ridgway had been the manager, a man whom Ridgway knew from long acquaintance to be "calm, courageous, imperturbable" and in whom he had "absolute, implicit confidence." If Bill Hoge told him things were bad, he would know without doubt that things were bad.

Although Hoge was on the road, Ridgway contacted him by radio and arranged to meet at a farmhouse. There Ridgway tried a ploy.

"Bill," he said, "we've made contact with you now. This position is too exposed to try to hold it any longer." He had no intention he said, of leaving Hoge's combat command in place "to be chopped to pieces, little by little." Watching closely for Hoge's reaction, he said he intended to begin withdrawal that night. "We're going to get you out of here."

Hoge: "How can you?"

That terse response told Ridgway all he needed to know. "Bill," he said, no longer employing artifice, "we can and we will."

Back in Vielsalm after dark, Ridgway summoned General Jones to Hasbrouck's command post. He found Jones's attitude "strange." How could he be so optimistic when he seldom left his command post and knew so little about what was happening? He seemed to Ridgway to be "casual, almost indifferent, little interested in the fact that that night we were going to bring his people out of the trap."

In Hasbrouck's presence, Ridgway relieved Jones of his command and put all the troops in the salient under Hasbrouck. Apparently unaware that Hoge was senior to Hasbrouck (or ignoring the fact in view of the difference in the size of the forces the two commanded), he assigned

Hoge as Hasbrouck's deputy, although Hoge was too busy with his own combat command ever to assume the post. To soften the blow of relief for Jones, Ridgway made him deputy commander of the XVIII Airborne Corps.

The sudden relief added to the strain created by all that had happened to the fledgling 106th Division—which Alan W. Jones had so expectantly brought into the line not quite a fortnight before for an introduction to combat in a quiet sector—was too much for Jones, one of the more tragic figures in the events that occurred in the Ardennes. Shortly after midnight, he suffered a serious heart attack. Medics evacuated him to a hospital in Liège.

There were something like twenty thousand American troops in the salient beyond the Salm River, more than a hundred medium tanks, around seventy self-propelled tank destroyers, scores of half-tracks, trucks, and other vehicles, and the howitzers of nine field artillery battalions. There were only two ways out: either through Vielsalm or not quite two miles up the river to the south, through Salmchâteau.

Three principal roads led to the exits: the main St. Vith–Vielsalm highway passing through Poteau and entering Vielsalm from the north; the gravel road cutting diagonally through the Grand Bois and Commanster into Vielsalm from the southeast; and the highway following the valley of the Salm into Salmchâteau from the south. Because that highway was on the west bank of the river and accessible at points to the south, the bridge at Salmchâteau was not vital, but the town, which was also on the west bank, was, and the town was outside the defensive line established west of the river by troops of the 82d Airborne Division.

Getting onto any one of those three routes was the big problem, particularly for the heavy vehicles of the artillery and the armored units, for in many cases they would first have to feed their vehicles over narrow woods trails and farm tracks. Despite nearly a foot of snow, the ground underneath was still soft and with the passage of only a few heavy vehicles was soon churned into a morass. "The mud makes it pretty difficult," General Clarke told General Hasbrouck late in the night of the 22d. "I don't know how we're going to do it."

There was also an enemy to be reckoned with. Since early in the evening an intense combat had been raging for control of Crombach, and there was considerable doubt whether the Shermans of Colonel Wemple's 17th Tank Battalion could break away without incurring heavy losses. Soon after midnight, men of the 62d Volksgrenadier Division advanced up the valley of the Braunlauf Creek and again broke into the settlement of Neubrück, that time in numbers not to be denied. A few miles to the south *Volksgrenadiers* got into a village and overran a platoon of medium tanks.

In late evening of the 22d and on into the early hours of the 23d, the artillery battalions began a phased withdrawal along with a part of Colonel Reid's 424th Infantry that had moved into reserve near Commanster, but neither General Clarke nor General Hoge thought it possible to begin his withdrawal. It was close to five o'clock in the morning of December 23 when General Hasbrouck sent a message to both of them. Just beyond the river along the highway leading west from Salmchâteau, the 2d SS Panzer Division's reconnaissance battalion was attacking positions of the 82d Airborne Division; unless the withdrawal began soon, "the opportunity will be over." It would be necessary "to disengage whether circumstances are favorable or not," otherwise it would be impossible to execute "any kind of withdrawal with equipment."

During the night, a cold wind had begun to blow out of the east, bringing what weathermen call a "Russian high." Although both Clarke and Hoge noted it, they saw little hope that the ground might freeze in time to aid their withdrawals; but after receiving Hasbrouck's message, Clarke stepped outside his command post in a beerhall in Commanster and tested the ground. He could hardly believe it. Checking first with Hoge, then reporting to Hasbrouck, he was exultant. "That cold snap has frozen the road," he said. "I think we can make it now."

So did Hoge. First in the march table, his troops were unable to get under way until close to 7 A.M., and even before the first vehicles reached Vielsalm, full daylight had come. The last battalion of the 424th Infantry, which served as a covering force for Hoge's withdrawal, nevertheless soon followed but got out only under sustained small-arms fire. Provided covering fire by a platoon of 105mm. assault guns, Colonel Wemple's tanks in Crombach also managed to break contact and—thanks to the freeze—move cross-country, eventually to get on the route of withdrawal through Commanster. The crush of traffic was soon so great where the road narrowed to pass through the village that General Clarke himself took a hand in keeping it moving.

A short distance northwest of Crombach, at Hinderhausen, Colonel Erlenbush's 31st Tank Battalion and the two remaining troops of the 87th Armored Cavalry Reconnaissance Squadron faced Otto Remer's *Führer Begleit Brigade* less than a mile away across open fields in Rodt. Having churned the roads and trails around Rodt into a morass, Remer's vehicles had been unable to attack, but that too changed with the coming of the freeze. Putting a few tanks in the lead, Remer sent a battalion of infantry moving on Hinderhausen.

By that time, Remer had changed his objective. At the order of General von Manteuffel, he was to turn south and get on a road to Salmchâteau, there to join General Krüger's 58th Panzer Corps, which with the 2d SS Panzer and 116th Panzer Divisions was fast becoming the new *Schwerpunkt* of the German offensive.

The only route of withdrawal for the men and vehicles at Hinderhausen was a woods trail eventually leading to Commanster, a rutted track that General Clarke himself the day before had found almost impossible to negotiate even in a jeep. The tanks and a company of tank destroyers, infantrymen clutching for dear life to any handhold on the sides and decks, were forming for the withdrawal when the German column came into sight. While the cavalrymen deployed their vehicles as a rear guard, two of the tank destroyers knocked out the leading tanks with their 90mm. guns. The withdrawal began.

God bless the Russian high! The ruts were far from solidly frozen, but the footing was good enough for tracked vehicles. Although one tank threw a track, the driver managed to get it off the trail into a grove of seedling firs. The covering force soon followed with little attempt by the Germans to pursue, for Otto Remer had at last found an order to his liking: To turn the *Führer Begleit Brigade* south to Salmchâteau and join the 58th Panzer Corps in the drive for glory to the Meuse.

The next force to withdraw was Colonel Rosebaum's CCA in and around Poteau. At mid-morning the troops of the 9th SS Panzer Division that had been left to block toward Vielsalm attacked, but Rosebaum's tanks had little difficulty stopping them; and soon after midday, out of a sky that was at last beginning to brighten, a flight of P-38 Lightnings of the 370th Fighter Group appeared. Unable to establish radio contact with the unit they were supposed to support, the pilots chose a target of opportunity, the Germans in front of Poteau.

When word came shortly before 2 P.M. for CCA to withdraw, the Germans failed to react. Nor did they follow the withdrawal closely, which enabled the few men of CCR who were defending the village of Petit Thier to climb aboard their half-tracks and other vehicles and depart without a round fired at them.

The last troops scheduled to come out were those on the southern flank: the 112th Infantry and the task force that Hasbrouck had created to screen the open portion of that flank, named for its commander, Lt. Col. Robert B. Jones, commander of the 7th Armored Division's 814th Tank Destroyer Battalion. Jones had two companies of his self-propelled tank destroyers, his reconnaissance company, a company of light tanks, and the remnants of the 14th Cavalry Group.

Before daylight on the 23d, General Hasbrouck ordered the commander of the 112th Infantry, Colonel Nelson, to send one of his battalions to a village due east of Vielsalm, there to block trails leading through the Grand Bois to Vielsalm; that battalion thus eventually withdrew through Vielsalm. He ordered another battalion to provide close-in defense of the bridge at Vielsalm and with a company defend the bridge at Salmchâteau until the withdrawal was completed, then demolish it. That left Colonel Nelson with only one battalion, headquarters troops, and attached engineers and towed tank destroyers.

With that force, Nelson was to screen south of the village of Beho, where the route of withdrawal for Hoge's combat command joined the road to Commanster. Once the armor passed, the infantry was to fall back on the village of Rogery, there to block a secondary road (it fed into the Salm valley highway by means of a bridge over upper reaches of the river) and await General Hasbrouck's order to withdraw. That was supposed to come as soon as all but Nelson's men and Task Force Jones had departed, for Task Force Jones was supposed to be the last out.

Using a radio belonging to a liaison officer from Hasbrouck's headquarters, Nelson reported at 1 P.M. that everybody was out except his force and Task Force Jones, but no order to withdraw followed. A few minutes later, seven German tanks preceding truck-mounted infantry appeared in front of Rogery, an advance guard of the *Führer Begleit Brigade* on the way to Salmchâteau.

A towed gun of the 630th Tank Destroyer Battalion knocked out one tank, and one of two 90mm. guns loaned to Nelson by the 814th Tank Destroyer Battalion knocked out another. (The 112th Infantry's executive officer, Colonel Train, found himself caught between the tank destroyers and the German tanks; the shells passed over his head "like subway trains.") The other German tanks fell back, but the infantry dismounted and attacked.

Seeing no point in a last-ditch fight when withdrawal was in the offing—indeed, should have been under way had the order but come from Hasbrouck—Colonel Nelson in mid-afternoon decided the time had come to get out. Under cover of fire from the tank destroyers, he sent his vehicles across the nearby bridge over the Salm to gain the valley highway and his infantry cross-country to cross the stream on a railroad bridge.

It was well after dark by the time Nelson's troops reached the valley highway. To their amazement and dismay, they found the road blocked by vehicles two and three abreast—the vehicles of Task Force Jones, which were supposed to have followed their own withdrawal. Inching forward in a jeep on a shoulder of the road, Nelson learned that as the light tanks heading Jones's column had approached Salmchâteau, German tanks had opened fire, knocking out several of the light tanks and blocking the road. The *Führer Begleit Brigade*'s advance guard had hit Nelson's position at Rogery, then continued toward Salmchâteau along a farm track.

There were at that point no American troops in Salmchâteau. Just before dusk, the company of the 112th Infantry stationed at the bridge asked paratroopers of the 82d Airborne Division, who occupied high ground to the west of the town, to blow the bridge. That done, the infantrymen joined the paratroopers in their defensive line. Destruction of the bridge would have no effect on the withdrawal of Colonel Nelson and Task Force Jones, for they were already across the Salm; but the departure of the infantry company left the town open to German occupation, and the Germans soon moved in.

With most of the 2d SS Panzer Division immobilized while awaiting gasoline, the commander of the division's reconnaissance battalion, Maj. Ernst Krag, had set out on December 22 to prepare the way for his division's advance northwestward alongside the 116th Panzer Division by getting onto the main highway leading west from Salmchâteau. Having no success penetrating positions of the 82d Airborne Division along the highway (it was those thrusts that had prompted Hasbrouck's concerned message to Clarke and Hoge at 5 A.M. on the 23d), Krag sent a portion of his command to Salmchâteau. There he might at least establish contact with other Germans forces he knew to be advancing from the direction of St. Vith.

Although Colonel Nelson sent his I&R Platoon, a platoon of engineers, and a platoon of infantry to get into Salmchâteau, they had no success, and by that time the stalled column along the valley highway was feeling the wrath of an enemy sensing a kill. Tanks and infantry of the *Führer Begleit Brigade* followed up the American withdrawal from Rogery and continued toward the Salm and the bridge leading to the valley highway over which Colonel Nelson's vehicles had passed. A platoon of the 814th Tank Destroyer Battalion under 1st Lt. Hugh T. Bertruch, Jr., stood in the way.

A brilliant moon had risen. Lieutenant Bertruch's tank destroyers opened fire, using their machine guns to discourage the infantry and their 90mm. pieces to stop the German tanks. In a blazing firefight, the tank destroyers knocked out seven German tanks but lost all their own guns. As the survivors among the crews fell back down the hill into the valley, they found engineers ready to blow the bridge leading to the valley highway. The demolition stopped the *Führer Begleit Brigade* from driving full into the flank of the immobilized column along the road.

Only the bright moonlight prevented utter confusion from developing among that column. The men and vehicles of Task Force Jones and of the 112th Infantry were hopelessly intermingled; and a detachment of engineers from the 82d Airborne Division, under orders to blow a culvert near the end of the column to block the road, seemed determined to do their task and get back to their command. The 112th Infantry's executive officer, Colonel Train, stopped them; but once he turned away to other tasks, they did the job they were ordered to do and to hell with the consequences. That trapped a few light tanks and an ambulance, and the guns of the *Führer Begleit Brigade* dealt with them swiftly.

Somebody at last discovered a secondary road leading off the valley highway to the west. There was no choice but to take it, try to bypass Salmchâteau, and come into the 82d Airborne Division's lines along the highway behind the town. It took much of the rest of the night to do that, men and vehicles often moving cross-country (once again, prayers of thanks went up for the Russian high). Some of the first men to gain the airborne division's line found the paratroopers getting ready to bring down artillery fire on what they took to be an approaching German column.

Before daylight came on December 24, most of the men and vehicles of Task Force Jones and the 112th Infantry had escaped. Colonel Nelson estimated that he lost only eighteen out of more than a hundred vehicles. To his chagrin, at ten o'clock in the morning he at last received a copy of the order from General Hasbrouck for him to withdraw—an order sent at 1 P.M. the day before.

In Vielsalm on the night of December 23, a small detachment of airborne engineers, covered by a platoon of the 508th Parachute Infantry's Company A under 1st Lt. George D. Lamm, prepared to demolish rail and road bridges spanning the little Salm River. Early that evening, word came from the 7th Armored Division that everybody scheduled to withdraw through Vielsalm had passed; but unless pressed by the Germans, the engineers intended to delay until midnight to allow for stragglers. While the bulk of Lamm's platoon covered the bridges from the west bank, Lamm led an eight-man patrol to the far bank to discourage any Germans trying to reach the bridges.

A little after 10:30 P.M., Lieutenant Lamm and his men spotted a platoon of Germans coming along the street leading to the highway bridge. Lamm told his men to open fire, then to fall back while he covered their withdrawal. He then moved back over the railroad bridge, pulling the fuse to the demolitions there, while one of the other men did the same at the highway bridge.

To the dismay of all, neither charge went off.

While the airborne engineers rewired the charges, setting them for a thirty-second delay, Lamm led the patrol back to the west bank. Once the engineers pulled the fuses, the patrol rushed back. The railroad bridge went up with a roar; but again, at the highway bridge nothing happened.

Despite fire from a German tank on high ground inside Vielsalm, Lamm once more led the patrol forward, again engineers set the fuse, and again the patrol fell back across the bridge. Yet again, nothing happened.

For a fourth try, Lamm attacked across the bridge to drive Germans back from nearby houses. As the patrol withdrew, the engineers fired a bazooka into the demolitions to make sure they went off. They did, but they blew only the flooring from the bridge, leaving supporting joists intact.

From the west bank, Lamm and his platoon kept up a steady fire while engineers went back for more explosives. For close to an hour, the paratroopers held the Germans away from the remains of the bridge until at last new explosives were in place.

He had so much TNT under the joists, shouted the engineer officer, that Hitler was bound to hear the explosion in Berlin. Waiting nearby around a bend in the road, one of General Hoge's liaison officers, Lieutenant Lewis, allowed as how the lieutenant knew what he was talking about: "The earth shook and fragments went high in the sky."

Hasso von Manteuffel had intended taking St. Vith and its important network of roads by the end of the first day of the offensive, December 16. He got the town only at the end of the sixth day, December 21. Even then it was a bottleneck, and the roads beyond were still denied until the end of the eighth day, December 23. It was a critical, crushing delay, second in importance in disruption of German plans only to the stand of American troops on the northern shoulder in front of and along the Elsenborn Ridge.

It had not come easy nor without heavy cost. Because most of the troops involved immediately after the withdrawal went into action farther west, the losses east of the Salm were difficult to pin down. Probably as many as five thousand men killed, wounded, or captured. The 7th Armored Division alone lost fifty-nine medium tanks. Losses in the two infantry regiments, which on the south flank of the salient had been out of the mainstream of the action, were severe but less than might have been expected. Including the fighting in the first few days of the offensive, for example, the 112th Infantry lost seven hundred men.

For much of the late afternoon of December 23 and into the evening, Bob Hasbrouck was at the western end of the highway bridge in Vielsalm to welcome his men to a new lease on life. The Supreme Commander, General Eisenhower, promptly sent a letter of commendation to all the units. And the man then in charge of the troops along the northern edge of the German penetration, Field Marshal Montgomery, even as he ordered the withdrawal, sent a message saying: "They can come back with all honor. They come back to more secure positions. They put up a wonderful show."

It remained for the 30th British Corps, which by that time had assembled in watchful waiting behind the Meuse River, to forward the most terse and yet most moving tribute. All the message said was *"A bas les Boches!"*

For the rest of their lives, Robert Hasbrouck, Bruce Clarke, William Hoge, Dwight Rosebaum, Alexander Reid, Gustin Nelson, and many another commander who had fought in the salient beyond the Salm River would be grateful to Field Marshal Montgomery for getting them out of what they saw as a deathtrap for their commands. Yet to the credit of Matthew B. Ridgway, he had gone to the scene himself and for all his preconceptions to the contrary, had determined that withdrawal was imperative.

CHAPTER TWENTY-FOUR

The Defense of Bastogne

A market town with a population in 1944 of slightly over four thousand, Bastogne stands on a plateau at 1,600 feet elevation. The plateau lacks the vast expanses of forest and the turbulent terrain of most of the Ardennes; much of it is open pastureland amid rolling hills with occasional wood lots of coniferous trees. The town has no natural defense features other than the surrounding hills, but concentric circles of farm villages with sturdy brick and stone buildings provide solid anchors for defensive positions.

Until the late seventeenth century, when Louis XIV's troops demolished the town's fortifications, Bastogne had been a bastion of considerable military importance, primarily—as again in the winter of 1944—because of its central position astride the high plateau and its nexus of roads. In December 1944, five major and three secondary highways converged on a shop-lined square near the southern edge of town. It was those roads that made Bastogne important to Americans and Germans alike.

Early on December 19, the presence of what was left of the 9th Armored Division's CCR at Longvilly and of the 10th Armored Division's Team Cherry on the road between Longvilly and Mageret seriously interfered with efforts of the 47th Panzer Corps to get an attack under way against Bastogne. Throughout the day, their presence prevented the 26th Volksgrenadier Division from getting into position to attack the town from the northeast through the village of Bizory. The commander of the Panzer Lehr Division, General Bayerlein, was so intimidated that he made only tentative probes against the town from the east. (General von Manteuffel was furious with Bayerlein for getting off onto side roads and becoming involved at Mageret. If he was unable to read a map, why didn't he ask one of his staff officers to do it for him?) Even the commander of the 2d Panzer Division, Colonel von Lauchert, whose tanks were bypassing the town on the north en route to the Meuse, felt compelled to leave a few of his artillery pieces behind to counter the American tanks and artillery near Longvilly.

The delays thus imposed—plus the presence near Bastogne of the other two teams of the 10th Armored Division's CCB—would go a long way toward enabling the Americans to consolidate their hairbreadth victory in the race for Bastogne. One of the other two teams, commanded by Lt. Col. James O'Hara, was blocking the principal highway to the southeast in the direction of the Café Schumann crossroads and Ettelbruck; and since the Germans were trying to get into Bastogne along other roads, O'Hara and his men had only brushes with the enemy on the first day. Not so the team commanded by Maj. William R. Desobry.

William Robertson Desobry, twenty-six years old, grew up on army posts but considered himself a Texan. When it came time for college, he chose not West Point but Georgetown University in Washington, D.C., and entered the army through the ROTC. With the commander of the 10th Armored Division's CCB, Colonel Roberts, the veteran of the Great War, young Desobry had established almost a father-son relationship.

As Desobry came into Bastogne on the night of December 18, Roberts pointed on a map to the village of Noville, four miles northeast of Bastogne on the principal highway to Houffalize and Liège, Highway N-15, and told Desobry to go there. He had no way of knowing, said Roberts, who was there: Americans, Germans, or nobody. General Middleton nevertheless had designated the village as an outpost for Bastogne at the limit of artillery support positioned close to the town.

"You are young," said Roberts, "and by tomorrow morning you will probably be nervous. By midmorning the idea will probably come to you that it would be better to withdraw from Noville. When you begin thinking that, remember that I told you it would be best not to withdraw until I order you to do so."

Desobry's was a small force of around four hundred men, including a company of Shermans of the 3d Tank Battalion, a company of the 20th Armored Infantry Battalion, and a few engineers, medics, and reconnaissance troops. When Desobry and his men reached Noville, about all they could discern of the village without a map (hardly anybody had a map in the early days at Bastogne) and in darkness and fog, was that it was a collection of houses, barns, a beerhall, a church, and a schoolhouse. Most of the buildings lined the Bastogne-Houffalize highway. And the whole place stood on windswept ground, for only at a little cemetery in a depression off the highway were there any trees.

Establishing a defense to the east, north, and northwest, Desobry sent outposts onto three roads leading into the village. Anticipating stragglers from other units, he told his men to hang onto any engineers and infantry who appeared to be willing to fight (*see map, p. 467*).

It was close to four o'clock in the morning when the men on the road leading from the east and the village of Bourcy heard half-tracks approaching. Not certain whether they were American or German, a sentry yelled: "Halt!" As the leading half-track braked abruptly, someone shouted something in German. From an embankment above the road, the men in the outpost hurled hand grenades into the half-track, and a duel with more hand grenades ensued. To get away from the rain of potato mashers, the man in charge, Staff. Sgt. Leon D. Gantt, ordered the men to fall back a short distance toward Noville. As the Americans disengaged, the half-tracks turned and headed back toward Bourcy.

Silence was settling in again when the men in Noville heard a strange rumble in the distance that as it drew closer became a dull roar. German tanks and other tracked vehicles were moving west along a road bypassing Noville to the north. In the fog and darkness, it was an eerie sound.

Shortly after 6 A.M., the men in the outpost along the Houffalize road heard tanks approaching. Because American stragglers had been feeding through the outpost for some time, they held their fire. Then, as two German tanks came into view, their gunners opened fire, knocking out two Shermans in the outpost. At Desobry's order, that outpost and the other two fell back.

Daylight was slow to develop through the thick fog. Visibility was still meager when two more German tanks approached down the Houffalize road accompanied by *Panzergrenadiers*. Tanks, machine guns, bazookas, rifles—every American weapon within range opened up. The *Panzergrenadiers* scattered and disappeared in the fog, while the two German tanks went up in flames. From that time the two hulks served as a partial roadblock along the Houffalize road.

It was mid-morning, around ten thirty, when the fog suddenly lifted "as if it were a [theater] curtain" to reveal an awesome spectacle. For the first time the defenders could see that they were on relatively low ground dominated by ridgelines to the north and northeast. On the high ground to the north were fourteen German tanks arrayed in a skirmish line, and on the other ridge and at various other points around the landscape there were more, altogether possibly as many as fifty or sixty. Quite obviously, Team Desobry was facing the might of an entire panzer division.

Partly because Colonel von Lauchert had difficulty getting his *Panzergrenadiers* to accompany the tanks over the open ground, the fight quickly became a duel between armored vehicles, mostly at long range and often influenced by the vagaries of the fog, which swirled and eddied, sometimes rising, sometimes descending. Just as the duel opened, a platoon of self-propelled guns of the 609th Tank Destroyer Battalion raced into the village. Those guns and the Shermans drew some advantage in that the buildings of the village afforded a degree of concealment and protection.

In quick succession, the American pieces hit nine of the fourteen tanks on the ridge to the north, setting three on fire, and as another German tank headed down a farm track leading to Noville, a round from somebody's gun set it ablaze. With a 37mm. gun, an armored car scored a hit at some vulnerable point on a Panther and knocked it out; the gunner himself found it hard to believe.

In the flaming encounter, the 2d Panzer Division lost seventeen tanks, plus the two destroyed earlier on the Houffalize road. Team Desobry lost a single tank destroyer, four smaller vehicles, and thirteen men wounded.

However one-sided the victory, it left Major Desobry acutely conscious of the size of the enemy force he faced and of the vulnerability of his position. As was soon demonstrated, German tanks and assault guns could sit in defiladed positions on the high ground above the village and pour their fire almost with impunity on Desobry's defenses, gradually destroying the protection of the buildings in the process.

Desobry was thinking, just as Colonel Roberts had predicted, that it would be better to withdraw from Noville. He also remembered that Roberts had said he was not to withdraw without permission. Radioing Roberts, he requested that permission.

Shortly before midnight on December 18, Col. Julian J. Ewell led his regiment, the 501st Parachute Infantry, into an assembly area three miles west of Bastogne. His was the first contingent of the 101st Airborne Division to arrive from Camp Mourmelon. A few hours later he received a summons to report to what was left of headquarters of the VIII Corps in the Heintz Barracks on the northern fringe of Bastogne.

There Colonel Ewell—a wiry, blunt-spoken man, something of an iconoclast, little given to formalities and speaking with a mountaineer's twang—found the situation map so covered with red markings indicating German units that "it looked as if it had the measels." The members of the corps staff appeared to be punch drunk from fatigue, but General Middleton and the interim commander of the 101st Airborne Division, General McAuliffe, were alert and calm. Having little knowledge of what was going on east of Bastogne with Team Cherry and the 9th Armored Division's CCR, the two had agreed to husband the bulk of the airborne troops for defense of the town but to send a regiment to the east to develop the situation.

That job was to be Ewell's. Pointing to the highway leading through the hamlet of Neffe and then through Mageret and Longvilly—the road along which Team Cherry and CCR were soon to be fighting for their lives—McAuliffe told Ewell to move out along it, "make contact, attack, and clear up the situation."

It was still dark and foggy when at 6 A.M. Ewell's leading 1st Battalion, commanded by Maj. Raymond V. Bottomly, Jr., passed on foot through the Place St. Pierre at the northeastern edge of Bastogne and out onto the road leading to Neffe and Mageret. As the troops approached

Neffe, daylight had come, but a heavy fog still limited visibility to a few hundred yards.

The paratroopers had just passed the last curve in the road before it descended straight into Neffe when a German machine gun opened fire. Shells from German tanks soon followed. The only weapons available to Bottomly capable of dealing in any way with tanks were seven 57mm. antitank guns, and because of the straightness of the road, it was impossible under German fire to get those into firing positions. Until a battery of short-tubed 105mm. howitzers of the 907th Glider Field Artillery Battalion could arrive, there was little Bottomly could do to get his men into Neffe.

Just outside Neffe the commander of Team Cherry, cut off from his command by the presence of General Bayerlein's tanks and *Panzergrenadiers* in Mageret, had established his command post in a château; and in Neffe he had created a roadblock with the 3d Tank Battalion's Reconnaissance Platoon, equipped with armored cars and light tanks. Around six o'clock that morning, two of Bayerlein's tanks with two platoons of infantry had probed through Neffe in the direction of Bastogne.

That probe was nothing more than a tentative thrust conditioned by Bayerlein's concern for the armor to his rear, but it was strong enough to eliminate the Reconnaissance Platoon's roadblock, and with *Panzergrenadiers*, Bayerlein turned against Cherry's command post in the château. All through the morning, Cherry's headquarters troops ran from window to window, firing a few rounds from each to give an impression of strength. They gained some respite with the approach of Major Bottomly's paratroopers, for the Germans had to turn some troops in that direction; and in early afternoon a platoon of paratroopers worked around to the south to reach the château. Despite that reinforcement, Colonel Cherry decided, once the château caught fire from German shelling, to retrace the route of the paratroopers and get out. He was not driven out, reported Cherry, he was "burned out"; and he was not withdrawing, he was "moving."

In the meantime, the second of Colonel Ewell's parachute infantry battalions arrived. Since Bottomly was unable to advance on Neffe, Ewell decided that he might get at the hamlet by occupying Bizory, which stood atop high ground a few hundred yards north of Neffe. He sent his 2d Battalion to Bizory, which the paratroopers found was still being held by a few men of the 158th Engineers.

Hoping to eliminate the German opposition in Neffe by a drive from Bizory into Mageret, behind Neffe, Colonel Ewell ordered the battalion commander, Maj. Sammie N. Homan, to take Mageret. That effort ended near a woodlot on the crest of high ground between the two villages where Homan's men ran into the 26th Volksgrenadier Division's reconnaissance battalion, the only contingent of the division that had at last gotten past Longvilly to drive on Bizory. "For the time being,"

Homan reported laconically to Ewell, "I cannot think of taking Mageret."

The 501st Parachute Infantry's 3d Battalion was, in the meantime, having trouble getting forward because of the exodus from Bastogne of headquarters and logistical units of the VIII Corps. In the process, some of the men managed to cadge helmets, rifles, and ammunition from those troops, and as they passed through the main square in Bastogne, from headquarters troops of the 10th Armored Division's CCB.

When the battalion finally broke free of the congestion in early afternoon, Ewell told the commander, Lt. Col. George M. Griswold, to bring the bulk of his battalion to the hamlet of Mont, on the Bastogne-Neffe road, from which he intended coming upon Neffe from the south by way of the château that had been Colonel Cherry's command post. To protect the flank of that maneuver, he told Griswold to send a company farther south into the village of Wardin, where, so Ewell believed, the company would find a part of Team O'Hara, one of the three teams of the 10th Armored Division's CCB.

Team O'Hara was actually a thousand yards beyond Wardin astride the Bastogne-Ettelbruck highway, but since Wardin was close on the team's north flank, Colonel O'Hara had recently dispatched his S-2, Capt. Edward A. Carrigo, and one of his infantry company commanders, 1st Lt. John Drew Devereaux, to check out the village. As the two officers entered in a jeep, Devereaux driving, civilians rushed from their houses, obviously distressed.

Devereaux stopped his jeep and jumped on the hood. An actor who not many months before had been appearing on Broadway and a member of the august theatrical family, the Barrymores, Devereaux appeared to relish his role. "Don't be afraid," he called out in French. "We Americans are here to stay. Keep to your cellars, and don't be afraid."

Continuing through the village, Devereaux and Carrigo had just passed the last house when a projectile of some kind hit the bumper of their jeep. It failed to explode, but through the fog the two officers made out a German armored car and a half-track. Turning around quickly, they hurried back into Wardin. Slowing the jeep, Devereaux announced to the civilians: "The Germans are coming. Get back to your cellars."

As the two officers raced out of Wardin, the paratroopers of Company I, 501st Parachute Infantry, commanded by Capt. Claude D. Wallace, Jr., were plodding on foot toward the village. They got into Wardin just as the Germans were coming in the other side in strength, the second prong of the attack on Bastogne planned by General Bayerlein for his *Panzer Lehr Division:* a battalion of *Panzergrenadiers* supported by seven tanks.

The 130 or so men of Company I were no match for such a force. They fought bravely—one man knelt with a bazooka in the middle of the little dirt road that passed for a main street and knocked out the leading

German tank before return fire cut him down, and other men with bazookas accounted for three more—but there were still other German tanks and too many *Panzergrenadiers*.

When Colonel Ewell learned that Company I was in trouble, he ordered Captain Wallace to pull back, but it was too late for many of the paratroopers. The company lost all of its officers and forty-five men, most of them killed or so badly wounded that they had to be left behind. Captain Wallace was among those who died. For all Lieutenant Devereaux's high promises to the inhabitants of Wardin, their village at that point belonged to the Germans.

The pattern of all that happened that day, December 19—repulse at Neffe, occupation of Bizory but repulse in the thrust on Mageret, and repulse at Wardin—convinced Julian Ewell that the offensive phase of his commitment was over. Going to McAuliffe's headquarters, Ewell asked permission to occupy a defensive line along high ground extending southward from Bizory. Although Ewell discerned that some people on McAuliffe's staff thought him timid, McAuliffe approved; and Colonel O'Hara soon received authority to fall back to a position astride the Bastogne-Ettelbruck highway just north of the village of Marvie, there to tie in with Ewell's line.

At the same time, General McAuliffe afforded Ewell a battalion of the 327th Glider Infantry to serve as a reserve behind that flank. The new line was only just over a mile outside Bastogne, which would limit maneuver; but as doubters on McAuliffe's staff would soon learn, what they had taken to be Julian Ewell's timidity was, in reality, the better part of valor.

When Colonel Roberts in his command post in the Hôtel Lebrun on the Rue de Marche just off the main square of the town received Major Desobry's request for permission to withdraw from Noville, he was torn. Desobry's position was obviously dominated by German-held high ground, and there was a better defensive position atop a ridgeline a few miles behind Noville at the settlement of Foy. Under the conditions of the commitment of his combat command at Bastogne, Roberts considered that he had authority to approve the withdrawal of any part of his command. On the other hand, they were not going to hold Bastogne without steadfast defense everywhere. Before granting the authority, Roberts left to have a talk with General McAuliffe in the Heintz barracks.

On the way, Roberts bumped into the airborne division's assistant commander, Brig. Gen. Gerald J. Higgins. As he was explaining the situation at Noville to Higgins, Lt. Col. James L. LaPrade and the men of his 1st Battalion, 506th Parachute Infantry, appeared and with them their regimental commander, Col. Robert F. Sink. Higgins promptly ordered Sink to send a battalion of his paratroopers to reinforce Desobry, and

Colonel LaPrade and his men simply kept on walking in the direction of Noville.

Returning to the Hôtel Lebrun, Colonel Roberts radioed Desobry: "You can use your own judgment about withdrawing, but I'm sending a battalion of paratroopers to reinforce you." That settled the issue for Desobry. As soon as the paratroopers arrived, he intended to attack to take the high ground from which German guns were doling out such misery, and with the high ground in hand, he hoped to be able to hold on at Noville.

Like the other battalions of the 101st Airborne Division, LaPrade's was short of helmets, weapons, overshoes, coats, and ammunition. Learning of that, Desobry told his Service Company in Bastogne to try to do something for the men. Loading several vehicles with supplies, 2d Lt. George C. Rice drove through LaPrade's marching paratroopers and deposited them at the head of the column so the men could pick from them as they passed. He did that three times before the paratroopers got all the way to Noville.

As the paratroopers entered the village, German shelling was continuing. Desobry and LaPrade nevertheless mounted their attack against the high ground in early afternoon, but nowhere did it gain more than five hundred yards. The fire from German tanks on the ridges was devastating, and the attack coincided with a German thrust on Noville that Colonel von Lauchert had been trying to get under way ever since his tanks had absorbed such heavy losses that morning. Again the *Panzergrenadiers* deserted their tanks on the open ground, and again the 2d Panzer Division lost heavily in tanks; but the American attack came nowhere near gaining the high ground overlooking Noville.

Shortly before nightfall, McAuliffe's deputy, General Higgins, went to Noville for a first-hand look at the situation. As he was conferring with Desobry and LaPrade on the ground floor of a house that served as their joint headquarters, German shells exploded outside, prompting LaPrade to pull a big armoire in front of the most exposed window, which faced the highway just outside the house. Hardly had Higgins gone when the commander of the 506th Parachute Infantry, Colonel Sink, also arrived for a first-hand look.

Shortly after Colonel Sink left, the battalion maintenance officer parked his tank recovery vehicle just outside the house and came inside to report that he had completed his work and was returning to Bastogne. In the gathering darkness, gunners on German tanks made out the outline of the vehicle and began shooting at it. They missed the vehicle, but several rounds hit the house.

One tore through the armoire. Colonel LaPrade fell to the floor dead. Major Desobry also fell, unconscious, with one eye virtually torn from its socket and a serious wound in the back of his head.

Medics rushed Desobry by jeep to the 506th Parachute Infantry's aid station, then by ambulance to the airborne division's collecting station, set up in tents at a crossroads near the division's original assembly area west of Bastogne. There surgeons saved his eye and while he was still under anesthetic, put him in an ambulance ready for evacuation. But when the anesthetic wore off, Desobry was to find himself on the way into Germany, a prisoner of war.

Late that night, six armored vehicles—a mixture of tanks and half-tracks—approached the crossroads and opened fire on the collecting station. Just as the firing began, a twelve-truck convoy on the way to the rear for supplies arrived; although the drivers fought back with the .50-caliber machine guns mounted above the cabs of their trucks, their cause was hopeless. German fire soon knocked out all the trucks, setting some of them alight, which clearly illuminated the big red crosses on the nearby tents. Everybody in a truckload of wounded waiting to be moved into the collecting station was killed.

After fifteen minutes of firing, a German officer entered the main tent and ordered the senior officer, the division surgeon, Lt. Col. David Gold, to surrender. All medics and all patients were to load on American vehicles.

Three medical officers and a few men managed to slip away into the night and tell their story in Bastogne. Most of the attackers, they said, wore civilian clothes, and when a patrol reached the site, the men found no American dead or wounded, only dead men of military age in civilian clothes.

There was some speculation later whether the raid on the collecting station might have been the work of Belgian Nazis who accompanied German units in the offensive. (They included the Belgian quisling, Léon DeGrelle, whom the Germans intended to head a new government in Belgium.) Although the Germans may have staged the raid to look like the work of civilians, there was no question that the officer who demanded Colonel Gold's surrender was a German, and the dead in civilian clothes wore the identification discs of German soldiers.

Back from Noville, General Higgins told General McAuliffe that the men in Noville were "way out on a limb" and in his judgment "had better get out." While the two were still talking, Colonel Sink arrived. He wanted his battalion of paratroopers out.

Although McAuliffe reckoned he had the authority to pull back his own troops, it was the corps commander, General Middleton, who had ordered that Noville be held; and at that stage, McAuliffe had no command authority over troops of the 10th Armored Division's CCB. (Nobody apparently thought to consult with Colonel Roberts, who considered he had authority to pull his troops back.) Instead, McAuliffe telephoned Middleton at his new corps headquarters seventeen miles away in

Neufchâteau. "No," said Middleton. "If we are to hold on to Bastogne, you cannot keep falling back."

That night in Noville, December 19, in the same dense fog that blanketed every corner of the Ardennes, the paratroopers, the armored infantrymen, the crews of the armored cars, medium tanks, and tank destroyers stood to their posts. Early in the evening, McAuliffe sent forward five self-propelled guns of the 705th Tank Destroyer Battalion, long-barreled 76mm. pieces—less powerful than the 90mm. but considerably more powerful than the regular 76mm.—which had just arrived in Bastogne with the rest of the battalion following a run from the Ninth Army. Also early that evening, another battalion of the 506th Parachute Infantry moved into Foy, just over a mile down the highway toward Bastogne.

All through the foggy night, small groups of *Panzergrenadiers*, sometimes accompanied by a tank or two, probed the perimeter, leaving the defenders praying for the coming of daylight. When it came, they wished for the night again, for the German shelling increased and two German tanks raced at full speed along the shoulders of the Houffalize road, fire from their machine guns keeping American troops pinned deep in their foxholes.

As the tanks drew up alongside the first building in Noville, the crews failed to note in the fog that they were within ten yards of an American bazooka team. The first rocket from the bazooka set one of the tanks on fire.

A short distance up the highway, Staff Sgt. Michael Lesniak dismounted from his tank, had a look, returned to his tank, and moved into the center of the road. Before the Germans knew what was happening, Lesniak's gunner fired and with his first round knocked out the other German tank. Yet a third tank that had stayed some distance behind the others threw a few shells into the village before falling back. One of those hit Lesniak's tank, damaging the traversing mechanism on the turret.

That was but the start. For the next two hours, groups of *Panzergrenadiers* supported by a few tanks probed at various points. Here and there a fight would flare and as defending tanks or tank destroyers lent a hand, would diminish, only to spring up again at another spot. Fog and smoke from burning buildings obscured the scene.

Again a German tank, a Panther, got through along the Houffalize road and came to a halt in front of a house serving as the command post for the company of the 20th Armored Infantry Battalion. As the tank swung its cannon toward the front door, the company commander, Capt. Omar Billet, said a silent prayer. He got a quick answer: only twenty yards away, Sergeant Lesniak was able to traverse the damaged turret on his tank just far enough to enable his gunner to get a bead on the Panther.

The gunner fired three quick rounds from his 75, which did no apparent damage, yet that was enough for the German crew. The driver put the tank in reverse, only to run over a jeep, crushing it and fouling one of the tracks on the tank. Dragging the jeep with it, the tank continued to back up but next collided with a half-track. The collision tipped the tank precariously far over to one side; the crew bailed out and raced from the village under concealment of the fog.

As on the day before, the fog in mid-morning suddenly lifted. In a reserve position near the rear of the village, the crews of the guns of the 705th Tank Destroyer Battalion could see on the high ground to the east a skirmish line of fifteen German tanks. With the first salvo, the gunners knocked out four and, as the crews tried to flee, took them under fire with .50-caliber machine guns. The other tanks turned back beyond the crest of the hill.

As the fog lifted, the two officers who had succeeded LaPrade and Desobry—Maj. Robert F. Harwick of the paratroopers, Maj. Charles L. Hustead of the armor—verified something they had long suspected: The Germans had moved in on their rear and cut the road to Bastogne. The situation was actually worse than they knew, for the Germans had also driven back the battalion of paratroopers that had occupied the settlement of Foy, forcing them to retire to high ground just to the south.

Again unknown to Harwick and Hustead, for all communications had failed, General McAuliffe was trying to send help. He ordered a battalion of the 502d Parachute Infantry, which had assembled as the division reserve around the village of Longchamps, not quite three miles southwest of Noville, to push through. The battalion got as far as a village about a mile from the Foy-Noville stretch of the main highway, but there ran into some of the Germans who had cut in behind Noville.

By that time, McAuliffe had decided that it was no longer a matter of reinforcing the defenders of Noville but of getting them out. That time he made no reference to General Middleton, for in mid-morning Middleton had attached Colonel Roberts's CCB to McAuliffe's division, which afforded McAuliffe command authority over the troops of CCB, and he had come to the conclusion that if he tried to continue to hold at Noville, every man there would perish. McAuliffe planned at first an attack by two parachute infantry battalions to open a way out, but the commander of the 506th Parachute Infantry, Colonel Sink, argued that there was no time for that.

When at last, around 1 P.M., radio contact was reestablished through the artillery net, the order went out to the two majors in Noville to fight their way out. The battalion of paratroopers on the high ground behind Foy was to help by retaking Foy; when the men in Noville heard the noise of that attack, they were to take off.

To Majors Harwick and Hustead, the chances of a successful withdrawal looked bleak. The road from Noville to Foy ran straight as a ruler, open fields on either side, not a single tree, the only cover or concealment a lone farmhouse on the left of the road some five hundred yards short of Foy. Since the lifting of the fog in mid-morning, the atmosphere had become almost clear so that for the German gunners visibility was close to perfect.

The two officers nevertheless prepared to depart. A company of paratroopers on foot, supported by three tanks, was to lead, followed by four half-tracks and five tanks providing an armored escort for vehicles carrying more than fifty wounded. Most of the rest of the men were to follow in vehicles of some kind, while another company of paratroopers on foot, supported by four tank destroyers, formed the rear guard.

As if acting as a signal for the withdrawal to begin, the curtain of fog descended again. The foot troops in the lead made the march with few problems, and all might have gone well for everybody except for a freak incident. As the first half-track preceding the vehicles carrying the wounded came abreast of the farmhouse outside Foy, the armored shutter over the slit through which the driver looked out to drive fell shut. When the driver raised his arm to lift the shutter, an officer thought the man had been wounded and pulled the hand brake. As the vehicle came to an abrupt stop, the half-track behind it rammed into the rear. In accordion fashion, every vehicle along the entire column came to a halt.

At that moment, small-arms fire struck the head of the column, some coming from the ditches on either side of the road, some from the farmhouse. As machine guns on the leading half-tracks blazed, men all along the column took to the ditches.

In time, the drivers of the half-tracks got their vehicles moving again and with machine guns still blazing, were soon inside Foy; but wary of what lay ahead in the fog, the driver of the first of the five U.S. tanks preceding the vehicles with the wounded was reluctant to push forward. He stalled until the armored commander, Major Hustead, arrived and ordered him to take the farmhouse under fire and get going.

The house was soon ablaze, and all five tanks began to move, only to be caught broadside by fire from three German tanks firing from somewhere beyond the farmhouse. Rounds hit the two leading tanks, setting the first on fire and disabling the second, in the process seriously wounding the driver.

Amid the confusion, the tank company commander, Capt. William G. Schultz, who had been riding in the fifth tank, walked up to the third tank and climbed aboard. On the theory that if he advanced, the rest of the column would follow, Schultz started off and got all the way through Foy before a round from a German tank knocked his tank out. Schultz and the crew nevertheless made it on foot into Bastogne.

Back near the farmhouse, nobody had followed Captain Schultz's example; for as the fourth tank started forward, a round from a German tank set it on fire and knocked the turret off into the road, blocking it. Only one tank was left, that in which Captain Schultz had been riding. Its driver, having learned that the driver of the second tank had been wounded but not that the tank was disabled, had gone forward to drive that tank. Major Hustead tried to find him, but without success, so he looked around for another driver from among the crews. Nobody professed to be able to drive a tank. That may well have been true, for there were specialists other than drivers in the crew of a tank; but nearby paratroopers and armored infantrymen refused to believe them. They swore at them and called them yellow bastards.

Far back in the column, everybody was growing restive. Swinging off the road to the west, a large group of paratroopers moved through the fields and gained Foy with no difficulty. The four tank destroyers with the rear guard followed and like the paratroopers, reached Foy without incident.

As the tank destroyers moved beyond Foy, an officer with the paratroopers who had retaken the settlement stopped one of them and told the driver, Pfc. Thomas E. Gallagher, to come with him. He had spotted the three German tanks that were firing at the withdrawing column. When Gallagher said he was short of crew and had no gunner, two other paratroopers climbed aboard. With a paratrooper doing the firing at a range of two hundred yards, Gallagher's tank destroyer knocked out one of the tanks, and the others turned away.

Delivered from the damaging fire of the German tanks, the remaining men and vehicles—including those carrying the wounded—worked their way off to the west of the road. The vehicles included the fifth tank, manned and driven by paratroopers, who climbed aboard swearing that somehow they would learn how to drive "the son of a bitch."

Darkness was near when the last of the survivors from Noville pulled into Bastogne. Team Desobry had gone to Noville with fifteen medium tanks; only four came back. The team also lost five tank destroyers and approximately half its 400 officers and men, while the 506th Parachute Infantry's 1st Battalion lost 212 killed, wounded, and missing.

Team Desobry had nevertheless imposed telling losses on the 2d Panzer Division, at least thirty tanks and perhaps as many as six hundred to eight hundred men. Ironically, while fighting in defense of Bastogne, Team Desobry had made its greatest contribution in delaying the panzer division's drive for the Meuse River by at least forty-eight hours—two days that were to have a telling effect.

For the attack on Bastogne on December 20, each of the attacking German divisions was short a regiment. Only with American withdrawal from Wiltz during the night of the 19th was Colonel Kokott's third regiment freed of the task of screening the corps flank before Wiltz, too late for the regiment to join the attack the next morning. So, too, one of the *Panzergrenadier* regiments of the Panzer Lehr Division had been delayed by the steadfast defense of men of the 110th Infantry on the other side of the Clerve River at Consthum, and as daylight came on December 20, that regiment was still toiling over roads turned by churning vehicles into a morass of mud.

The obstacle posed by Team Cherry and the 9th Armored Division's CCR at last eliminated by a combination of German guns and American withdrawal, Colonel Kokott was finally free to drive with one regiment on Bizory, the other on the Houffalize highway to get into the town from the north. But by that time both those routes were blocked: the one through Bizory by Major Homan's battalion of Ewell's 501st Parachute Infantry; the Houffalize highway by a battalion of Sink's 506th Parachute Infantry; the 3d under Lt. Col. Lloyd E. Patch. That battalion was preoccupied through much of the day with the drive to retake Foy and facilitate withdrawal of the troops in Noville. Partly for that reason, a problem developed along a railroad that served as a boundary between the two regiments.

Down the line of that railroad late on the 20th, a battalion of *Volksgrenadiers* supported by seven assault guns headed toward Bastogne, the way barred only by a patrol from Homan's battalion. That patrol nevertheless delayed the German advance long enough for both Colonel Ewell and Colonel Sink each to send a company to plug the gap.

The *Panzer Lehr Division* had no more success against the line that Colonel Ewell had formed on the eastern approaches to Bastogne. As two battalions of *Panzergrenadiers* supported by tanks attacked after nightfall from Neffe, fire from every artillery piece engaged in the defense of Bastogne converged on the hamlet. The Germans lost three tanks, and the attack got nowhere, while fire from the machine guns of five of the 705th Tank Destroyer Battalion's self-propelled pieces helped stop a second thrust. Only with the coming of daylight did the gunners learn why their fire was so effective: The Germans had been trying to advance in the darkness across a field laced with barbed-wire fences forming feeder pens for cattle. Bodies lined the base of every fence, and many hung on the wire.

Late on the night of December 20, the commander of the 47th Panzer Corps, General von Lüttwitz, could point to only two successes in the fight for Bastogne. The Americans had withdrawn from Noville, and well after nightfall, a task force built around the 26th Volksgrenadier Division's reconnaissance battalion and commanded by Maj. Rolf Kunkel skirted the town on the south and without opposition reached the Bastogne-Neufchâteau highway at the town of Sibret. There *Kampfgruppe Kunkel* found that a company of the Seventh Army's 5th Parachute Division had arrived first and was trying to drive headquarters of the 28th Division out of the town. When Kunkel's men joined the fight, General Cota again had to displace his headquarters; and the highway to Neufchâteau, the main supply route for the troops in Bastogne, was at that point severed.

Yet there was little joy that night in the headquarters of any German commander involved in the fight for Bastogne. To try to break the impasse, von Lüttwitz begged General von Manteuffel to allow the 2d Panzer Division to continue from Noville into Bastogne, but mindful of Hitler's insistence on getting to and over the Meuse, the commander of the Fifth Panzer Army said no. ("Forget Bastogne and head for the Meuse!") Made fully aware of his superiors' priorities, von Lüttwitz during the night ordered General Bayerlein to leave a *Panzergrenadier* regiment to help Kokott at Bastogne and send the rest of the *Panzer Lehr Division* skirting the town on the south and heading for the Meuse.

By December 20, virtually all the forces that were to participate in the defense of Bastogne had assembled, and as General Middleton had notified both General McAuliffe and Colonel Roberts during the morning, McAuliffe was in overall command. The principal component of the defensive force, the 101st Airborne Division, had left some men behind for housekeeping chores at Camp Mourmelon, but most of those who had been on leave when the division hurriedly moved out had come forward. At that point the division had just over ten thousand men in three parachute infantry regiments, a glider infantry regiment, an engineer battalion, four artillery battalions, and the usual technical support units. Because casualties in the Netherlands had been heavy, there were many replacements, but the division as a whole was a veteran outfit with high esprit.

By the 20th, Colonel Roberts's CCB, 10th Armored Division, had already lost heavily, Team Cherry having been almost annihilated and Team Desobry at Noville having taken severe losses in men and tanks. Yet Team O'Hara still had a full company of medium tanks, and Colonel Roberts found eight new tanks in Bastogne with their ordance crews, who had been on their way to deliver the tanks at the front. Thus CCB still had about thirty tanks, and the 420th Armored Field Artillery Battalion was intact.

Since Colonel Roberts had come under McAuliffe's command and thus no longer had full control of his armor, his basic concern was to see that the airborne commanders made proper use of it, that once tanks and tank destroyers did a job, they were not held as forts among the foxholes but returned to Bastogne, there to be ready for quick commitment at some other spot as trouble developed. With that in mind, Roberts virtually abandoned his command post in the Hôtel Lebrun to spend most of his time at McAuliffe's side.

The 9th Armored Division's CCR was no longer a viable fighting force. Only its supporting 73d Armored Field Artillery Battalion had emerged from the fighting at Longvilly in any way intact; the battalion still had eight howitzers. Nine tanks that had escaped the disaster attached themselves to Major Homan's battalion of the 501st Parachute

Infantry at Bizory, and some enterprising officer, finding fourteen of the combat command's mediums far to the rear at Neufchâteau, led them back. Under a tank company commander, Capt. Howard Pyle, those tanks, supported by sixty armored infantrymen, were to fight as Team Pyle. Other men of CCR—armored infantrymen, tankers without vehicles, whomever—became part of a makeshift force, Team SNAFU, acronym for a popular soldier expression of the time, "Situation Normal, All Fucked Up."

Conscious that there would be many stragglers in any big battle, Colonel Roberts early prepared a net to catch them; a junior officer among the stragglers suggested the name; and an officer from the 110th Infantry, Capt. Charles Brown, commanded the team. Roberts set up a detail in the town square to assign the men—many of whom were hollow-eyed, semi-coherent—a place to sleep and to feed them a hot meal. Within twenty-four hours, most were sufficiently recovered to join Team SNAFU.

The stragglers were mainly from CCR and the 28th Division. During the morning of December 20, that division's assistant commander, Brig. Gen. George A. Davis, with General Middleton's permission, took three hundred of the men who wore the red keystone shoulder patch to rejoin the division. Team SNAFU nevertheless numbered about six hundred men, used to man close-in roadblocks on the edges of Bastogne, to form small task forces, and to serve as individual replacements.

Given the losses sustained by the two armored combat commands, the arrival of the 705th Tank Destroyer Battalion was a godsend. On the way from the Ninth Army, the commander, Lt. Col. Clifford Templeton, had dropped off eight guns to hold a crossing of the Ourthe River at the village of Ourtheuville on the Marche highway until his supply vehicles got past, and he lost a gun at Noville; but he still had thirty-six with their powerful long-barreled 76mm. pieces.

The defenders were strong in artillery. Like the howitzers of an infantry regiment's Cannon Company, the pieces of the 101st Airborne Division's 105mm. howitzer battalion had short barrels, which limited their range but not their power. The division's other three battalions had 75mm. pack howitzers. There were also CCB's and CCR's support battalions. Most of the 28th Division's 109th Field Artillery Battalion reached Bastogne too, and there were four battalions of corps guns with 155mm. pieces. (A fifth, the 58th Armored Field Artillery Battalion, with only four guns following the fight at Longvilly, passed through the town before anybody thought to stop it.) There were stragglers among the artillery pieces as well, such as three guns of the 687th Field Artillery Battalion that had escaped the fate of the rest of the battalion at the Café Schumann crossroads. That made eleven battalions of artillery—about 130 pieces.

* * *

Both General Middleton and General McAuliffe were anticipating that the defense of Bastogne would soon be augmented by the Third Army's 4th Armored Division. During the night of December 18, Middleton had learned that the division was on the way northward, one of the early shifts of troops of the Third Army even before General Eisenhower's conference with his senior commanders at Verdun on the 19th. The 4th Armored Division, Middleton understood, was to be attached to his VIII Corps.

Around midnight on the 19th, the 4th Armored Division's Combat Command B under Brig. Gen. Holmes E. Dager arrived at the village of Vaux-les-Rosières, astride the Neufchâteau-Bastogne highway approximately halfway between the two towns, there to become a part of the VIII Corps. Yet that day at Verdun, General Patton had promised Eisenhower to mount a major offensive on December 22 to push through to Bastogne; and Patton had sent headquarters of the III Corps under Maj. Gen. John Millikin to prepare for the offensive at Arlon, well south of Bastogne on the principal highway leading into the town from the south, many miles from Vaux-les-Rosières. Millikin understood that the entire 4th Armored Division was to be his for the attack on the 22d.

Before daylight on the 20th, somebody on General Middleton's staff ordered General Dager to send a task force from CCB into Bastogne along the highway from Vaux-les-Rosières, the Neufchâteau-Bastogne highway—a company each of tanks and armored infantry and a battery of self-propelled artillery. Although Dager resented having his command whittled away like that, the force set out at ten thirty that morning under Capt. Bert Ezell of the 8th Tank Battalion with orders "to aid CCB of the 10th Armored Division."

In Bastogne, Captain Ezell talked with General McAuliffe, then reported, at McAuliffe's order, to Colonel Roberts in the Hôtel Lebrun. Roberts sent Ezell to a reserve position not far from the town of Sibret on the Bastogne-Neufchâteau highway, there to await, as both Roberts and McAuliffe thought, the arrival of the rest of the 4th Armored Division.

In the meantime, General Dager established radio contact with headquarters of the division and protested the diminution of his command. After having been Patton's chief of staff, Maj. Gen. Hugh J. Gaffey had only recently assumed command of the 4th Armored Division and was incensed that somebody appeared to be making off with a third of his new command. With Patton's approval, he ordered Dager to recall Ezell's little force and bring all of CCB back to the vicinity of Arlon to join the rest of the 4th Armored Division for the attack on the 22d.

By such quirks are battles and sometimes even campaigns decided. Had Middleton been allowed to hold onto the 4th Armored Division's CCB and with it keep open the Neufchâteau-Bastogne highway, Bastogne probably never would have been surrounded. Even if the Germans had cut the Neufchâteau-Bastogne highway, the 4th Armored Division might have capitalized on the location of CCB and attacked from Vaux-les-Rosières instead of from Arlon. Which would have spared many officers and men of the 4th Armored Division a great deal of misery and, in some cases, death.

The arrival of many of the paratroopers without their personal gear foretold that there would long be supply shortages in Bastogne. Nor did an airborne division travel with the big supply trains to be found with infantry and armored divisions. Yet Colonel Roberts had arrived with his trains full and would be able to share, and most of the artillery units (other than those of the airborne division) had fairly ample supplies of rations and ammunition.

Scrounging supply officers soon found that many of the units attached to the VIII Corps had left behind large stocks of supplies, including a Red Cross depot with great amounts of flour for doughnuts, so that pancakes appeared on everybody's breakfast menu. So, too, the town of Bastogne had some reserves of food, and the poultry, pig, and cattle population in the surrounding farm villages was a resource not to be ignored.

Nevertheless, should the town be surrounded and subjected to siege, there was bound to be hardship and concern, in particular, for ammunition and gasoline. A further problem quickly developed when the 101st Airborne Division lost its collecting station, along with most of the surgeons and other medics, creating a severe shortage of surgeons and medical supplies.

During the afternoon of December 20, General McAuliffe left Bastogne for a talk with General Middleton at his new headquarters in municipal offices in Neufchâteau. How long could he hold Bastogne? asked Middleton. For at least forty-eight hours, replied McAuliffe, possibly longer. Middleton said he was determined to hold the town, but he was none too sure it could be done. In any event it was critical to keep the Neufchâteau-Bastogne highway open. As McAuliffe departed, Middleton admonished him with a smile: "Now don't get yourself surrounded."

Climbing into his command car, McAuliffe told his driver to gun it. He was none too sure that Bastogne was not already surrounded. A half hour after he got back there, the Germans cut the Neufchâteau-Bastogne highway at Sibret.

For the civilian population of Bastogne, the first day of the German offensive, December 16, was calm. Since it was a Saturday, the shops along the Grand' Rue were doing a bustling business. Not until the next morning, as the congregation in the Church of the Franciscan Fathers spilled out after mass into the Place St. Pierre, was there anything other than rumor to indicate that something unusual might be happening. A long column of refugees from Luxembourg, among them the fathers from the Benedictine abbey on the heights behind Clervaux, was trudging through the square.

Around noon on the 17th, electricity all over town went off, but everybody assumed it was simply a malfunction and temporary. There was still no indication that the fighting was approaching the town, but at 5 P.M. an American staff officer passed to the acting mayor, Leon Jacqmin, an order for a curfew. Yet as always happens when civilians get caught up in battle, nobody told them much of anything. They were expected simply to take to their cellars and stay out of the way.

By the morning of the third day, December 18th, there was no mistaking the sound of artillery fire, and American stragglers began to enter town. By midday, some of the people were leaving, pushing carts, pulling children's wagons piled high with possessions; but some three thousand people remained.

One who departed was Abbé Jean-Baptiste Musty, head of the Bastogne Seminary on the Place St. Pierre. He was anxious to get his fifty boys to safety. Early on the 20th he accompanied them on foot out onto the highway leading northwest across the Ourthe River toward the village of Bande and the town of Marche.

As the fighting closed in at Bastogne, some people stayed in their own cellars, while others joined neighbors whose cellars were sturdier. More than six hundred—including a hundred students—crowded into the underground corridors of the Boarding School of the Sisters of Notre Dame, others nearby in a shelter beneath the choir in the Franciscan church, and others again under the thick vaults of ancient cellars in another monastery, the Récollets. One who lived in a cellar among strangers was the woman from Bivels, Luxembourg, whom American intelligence officers had brought to Bastogne to tell her story of a German buildup beyond the Our River: Elise Delé.

Facing the possibility that the town might be surrounded, M. Jacqmin called for volunteers to take stock of available resources. There was considerable coal, they found, at the railroad station. Somebody discovered stocks of German drugs and dressings in Father Musty's seminary. More than 7 tons of flour and 2 tons of tinned biscuits turned up. There was a central abattoir for butchering pigs and cattle from nearby villages, and the boarding school had bakery facilities. There were also two doctors.

The people of Bastogne were facing a long, tedious, uncomfortable, hazardous underground existence, which some of the elderly would not survive, but nobody was to lack for essentials. They would live "in a sort of dream," having little way of knowing how serious their plight, how went the battle, whether the Germans would finally take the town, and if they did, what would be their fate. Yet their plight was easier than that of the people in surrounding villages, for those people sometimes got caught up in the actual fighting and felt the terrible blows of the powerful American artillery. (Within the town and the defensive perimeter, 115 civilians were killed.)

Renée Lemaire, thirty years old, was a beautiful young woman with strikingly blue eyes and a thick cascade of brown hair. She had studied and trained for four years at the Brugmann Hospital in Brussels to become a visiting nurse and then worked under the auspices of the Ixelles Hospital in Brussels.

Close to Christmas, 1943, Renée met Joseph, the son of an elderly widower for whom she was providing nursing care. They discovered mutual interests—both adored playing the piano, and Renée loved to sing while Joseph played—and soon they were in love and planning marriage.

Near the end of February, 1944, Renée was on night duty at the hospital for a week, and when it ended, she went to Joseph's house. The doors and windows were locked. From neighbors she learned that the Gestapo had taken Joseph and his father away. They were Jews.

Devastated, Renée nevertheless continued her work. But after the liberation, in late fall of 1944, she obtained permission to spend a month with her family in Bastogne, where her father, Gustave, had a hardware store in the Grand' Rue. Her mother, an older sister, Gisèle, and a younger sister, Maggy, were also there.

Like others in Bastogne, the Lemaires welcomed American soldiers to their home, and Renée was swiftly caught up in the glories of the liberation, the laughter of the Americans, the delights of their K-rations, their coffee and chewing gum, their kindness "made in U.S.A." Soon Renée was laughing again, her eyes sparkling. She played the piano in the living room while the soldiers sang, and she learned their songs: "Mexicali Rose," "I'll Walk Alone," "Paper Doll." One of the soldiers, Jimmy, tall and handsome, started coming often to the house, and the two went for long walks together.

On December 17, Jimmy came once more. His unit had sudden orders to leave. "Don't forget, Renée," he said. "I'll be back. I promise you."

As the fighting drew close, the Lemaires retreated to their cellar, which they shared with neighbors and from time to time with American soldiers. One was a medic, Frank, with the 10th Armored Division's CCB. When Frank learned that Renée was a nurse, he asked if she would help at his aid station in a large store near the railroad station, the "Sarma."

Beginning the next day, Renée worked long hours at the aid station together with another young woman, an immigrant from the Belgian Congo, Augusta Chiwy, and each night they returned to their cellars exhausted. But their presence, noted the surgeon, Maj. John T. Prior, was "a morale factor of the highest order."

*　　　*　　　*

Word that the Germans had cut the highway leading from Bastogne to Neufchâteau during the night of December 20 was quick to pass among the troops around Bastogne. Most men assumed that at that point, they were surrounded.

Among the American commanders, the news of the cutting of the highway stiffened their resolve to hold Bastogne, for at that point what was the alternative? They might not have to hold for long, in any case, for the attack General Patton had promised General Eisenhower at Verdun was to begin early on December 22, and the expectation was that Patton would have little difficulty in breaking through swiftly to Bastogne.

Strictly speaking, Bastogne was not yet surrounded. At last free to pass through Noville, columns of the 2d Panzer Division were soon swinging around the town to get onto the Bastogne-Marche highway, in the process cutting all roads to the northwest; but it took longer for the *Panzer Lehr Division*, swinging around Bastogne to the south and heading for the Meuse by way of St. Hubert, sixteen miles due west of Bastogne, to cut all roads leading west.

Both those divisions were, in any case, en route away from Bastogne, so that any buildup west of the town was the responsibility of the 26th Volksgrenadier Division. Having despaired of getting into the town from east or north, that was what the division commander, Colonel Kokott, intended doing. While the attached regiment of *Panzergrenadiers* of the *Panzer Lehr Division* struck from the south, Kokott's third regiment, which had just arrived, was to attack along with *Kampfgruppe Kunkel* from the southwest and west. Yet it would take some time to get the regiment into position, so that the job of cutting the roads and completing the encirclement of Bastogne fell to Major Kunkel.

On December 21, as Kokott accompanied his third regiment along the path taken earlier by *Kampfgruppe Kunkel* south of Bastogne, he became optimistic that the town would soon fall. In the villages along the route, he found no defenses, and here and there he saw small groups of Americans fleeing. Those were the last escapees from Wiltz or somewhere else to the east, but Kokott took their presence to mean that the defenses of Bastogne were falling apart.

Field Marshal von Rundstedt also thought Bastogne would soon fall. Through Field Marshal Model at Army Group B, he directed General von Manteuffel to proceed immediately to reduce the town, but still under the mandate of doing nothing to interfere with the drive of the panzer divisions for the Meuse. At headquarters of the 47th Panzer Corps that night, von Manteuffel found General von Lüttwitz optimistic, primarily because the leading force of the Seventh Army, the 5th Parachute Division, had at last begun arriving on the south flank of his corps. With the parachute division blocking the highways from Arlon and Neufchâteau, von Lüttwitz would no longer have to keep looking over his shoulder for fear an American relief force might be advancing on Bastogne from the south.

Colonel Kokott found no defenses in the villages south of Bastogne because there were none, for General McAuliffe had first concentrated on the obvious threats from east and north. Only the 326th Airborne Engineer Battalion stood south of Bastogne, manning roadblocks on the Arlon highway, astride a secondary road facing the village of Assenois, and on the Neufchâteau highway, and Kokott had passed south of those roadblocks. German movement there nevertheless prompted McAuliffe to send two battalions of the 327th Glider Infantry to augment the engineers and build a line facing south.

It was the attempt by *Kampfgruppe Kunkel* to get in behind Bastogne that produced the heaviest fighting on both the 21st and 22d. There most of the heavy American artillery battalions were to be found, with nothing more than little clumps of infantry to protect them, and only the fourteen tanks of Team Pyle to serve as a mobile defensive force.

As a first step in completing the encirclement, *Kampfgruppe Kunkel* early on December 21 set out from Sibret on the Bastogne-Neufchâteau highway for the village of Villeroux, a mile beyond the highway. Unknown to the Germans, in the vicinity were three of the American 155mm. artillery battalions. The Germans quickly came upon the 771st, and the gunners abandoned their pieces and fled; but before the German column could continue, the tanks of Team Pyle appeared. Although the Germans forced the tanks back on the village of Senonchamps, the brief engagement afforded time for the gunners of the other two corps artillery battalions, the 755th and the 969th, to pull their pieces back to Senonchamps.

At the edge of Senonchamps, Team Pyle made a stand. Helped by the quad-50s of a battery of the 796th Antiaircraft Artillery Battalion, the tanks inflicted such losses that Major Kunkel called off the attack for the night.

Senonchamps was of considerable importance to the defense of Bastogne, for from it ran two secondary roads leading to the Bastogne-Marche highway, one of them joining the highway only a mile from the first buildings of Bastogne. In and around the village, in addition to Team Pyle, was the 10th Armored Division's 420th Armored Field Artillery Battalion, whose commander, Lt. Col. Barry D. Browne, had collected a few light tanks, three mediums, and thirty infantry stragglers to create a force that became known in time as Team Browne.

As elsewhere in the Ardennes before daylight on December 22, snow began to fall in and around Bastogne. In mid-morning, *Kampfgruppe Kunkel* renewed its attack, but fire from the American tanks quickly broke it up. Three more times during the afternoon the Germans tried to break into Senonchamps while infantry worked through nearby woods to get at the American howitzers; but nowhere did they succeed. As night began to fall, General McAuliffe sent a company of the 327th Glider Infantry and a hundred men from Team SNAFU to help protect the artillery pieces.

The remnants of yet another corps artillery battalion were farther west near the village of Tillet, the 58th Armored Field Artillery Battalion with four guns salvaged from the fight near Longvilly. As the battalion fell back from Bastogne, the artillerymen encountered men of the 101st Airborne Division's Reconnaissance Platoon, who had been trying to find a road open to St. Hubert. They reported that the Germans were in Tillet in strength.

As the two forces linked to try to find a way around the village, trucks attempting to transport unneeded impedimenta of the 501st Parachute Infantry away from Bastogne joined them. The column soon encountered a roadblock, which the Reconnaissance Platoon attacked and eliminated, but behind it was a far stronger German force. Forming a perimeter defense, the commander of the artillery battalion, Lt. Col. Walter J. Paton, radioed Bastogne for help. General McAuliffe could send none, and as Paton tried to turn back to Bastogne, he found that the Germans had moved in behind him.

Soon after daylight the next morning, the 22d, a contingent of the *Panzer Lehr Division*'s reconnaissance battalion attacked. By noon, assault guns had disabled all but one of the four howitzers, and Paton saw no alternative but to try to break out on foot. With fire from the last howitzer, the men destroyed the 501st Parachute Infantry's trucks and the other vehicles. Screened by falling snow, they set out. Not quite seven hours later, they trudged into Neufchâteau, having lost not a man.

By nightfall on December 22, the rough outline of a perimeter defense of Bastogne—characterized by Colonel Kinnard, the 101st Airborne Division's G-3, as "the hole in the doughnut"—was beginning to emerge. The defensive line was closest to the town on the east and the south, just over a mile off. And in the still unsettled portion of the perimeter west of town, a finger-like projection held by a battalion of the 327th Glider Infantry extended for almost six miles along the Bastogne-Marche highway. That projection obviously would have to be withdrawn.

Except at Villeroux and Senonchamps, the enemy's jockeying for position had provided a welcome respite. That cheered McAuliffe and his staff, but another development dampened the cheer: the matter of supplies. There had been some hope on the 22d for resupply by air, but the snowstorm had squashed that. Supplies of small-arms ammunition were running low. Most critical of all, they were short of shells for the artillery pieces, without which the defenders would have little hope for survival.

All the gunners had dug pits that enabled them to switch their pieces to fire in any direction, which was essential, but it quickly ate deeply into the stocks of ammunition. By nightfall on the 21st, it was obvious that the gunners would have to conserve their shells for crises; and German trucks, half-tracks, and tanks bypassing the town to north and south moved almost with impunity, while infantry commanders and artillery forward observers swore in frustration.

By noon of December 22, all four of the artillery battalions of the 101st Airborne Division were down to two hundred shells each, and General McAuliffe was contemplating imposing a ration of ten rounds per gun per day. The man who had succeeded McAuliffe as the division's artillery commander, Colonel Sherburne, lied through his teeth whenever men and officers asked him how the ammunition was holding out, but to McAuliffe he told the grim truth.

Within the town, all aid stations had become makeshift hospitals, and since nobody could be evacuated, the wounded piled up. The few exhausted surgeons shook their heads sadly as men died who with proper medicines and operating facilities might have lived. In the Sarma, where Renée Lemaire and Augusta Chiwy were helping as nurses, Major Prior had close to a hundred patients, thirty of them seriously wounded. There were no beds; the men lay on blankets on the floor, and even blankets were scarce.

In a church near the center of town, patients in the 501st Parachute Infantry's aid station lay in rows on the floor with scarcely enough room between them for the medics to walk. In front of an altar in an alcove, two surgeons worked steadily, hour after hour. So crowded did the church become that the regiment had to open another aid station in a garage, where the men lay on their blankets on top of sawdust. Against a back wall the surgeons placed those men who under the existing conditions had no chance of surviving.

Yet all that misery might soon come to an end, for at mid-morning on the 22d, McAuliffe's headquarters received a brief but encouraging message: "Hugh [General Gaffey of the 4th Armored Division] is coming."

Around noon on December 22, near a farm belonging to Jean Kessler, not far from the Arlon highway, men of a platoon of Company F, 327th Glider Infantry, watched in astonishment as four Germans, one of them carrying a large white flag, appeared in front of the foxhole line. Two sergeants left the platoon's command post in the farmhouse to see what was afoot, Oswald Y. Butler and Carl E. Dickinson, accompanied by a medical aid man, Pfc. Ernest D. Permetz, who spoke German.

Amid falling snow stood two German enlisted men and two officers: a major and 1st Lt. Hellmuth Henke, of the *Panzer Lehr Division*'s operations section, who spoke English. "We are parliamentaries," said Lieutenant Henke, "and we want to talk to your officers." At a few words in German from the major, Henke corrected himself: "We want to talk to your commanding general."

Butler and Dickinson conducted the four to the farmhouse. Leaving the enlisted men under guard, the platoon leader, 2d Lt. Leslie E. Smith, blindfolded the officers and led them a few hundred yards to the rear to the company command post. There the Germans handed the company commander, Capt. James F. Adams, a typed message, one page in German, the second in English, apparently done on an American or English typewriter, for the diacritical marks over some of the vowels in the German had been inserted in ink.

It was an ultimatum from "The German Commander" addressed "to the U.S.A. Commander of the encircled town of Bastogne." There was "only one possibility," read the message, "to save the encircled U.S.A. troops from total annihilation: that is the honorable surrender of the encircled town." The American commander was to have two hours in which to consider the ultimatum, whereupon, if he rejected it, German artillery was prepared "to annihilate the U.S.A. troops in and near Bastogne." Serious civilian losses from that fire, the message concluded, "would not correspond with the wellknown American humanity."

Captain Adams promptly contacted headquarters of the 327th Glider Infantry. The commander, Col. Joseph H. Harper, was away; but the operations officer, Maj. Alvin Jones, alerting General McAuliffe's command post to what was happening, drove to Company F's command post. Leaving the German officers, still blindfolded, with Captain Adams, Jones hurried with the message to the Heintz Barracks, while along the line of foxholes, men took advantage of the unaccustomed quiet to get out of their holes, stretch, build fires, shave, go to the latrine.

At the barracks, where in response to German shelling, McAuliffe had moved his command post into a cellar beneath the main building, Major Jones asked to see McAuliffe personally. Saluting, he said he had a message from the German commander, an ultimatum, and passed the papers to McAuliffe's chief of staff, Lt. Col. Ned D. Moore.

"What does it say, Ned?" asked McAuliffe.

"They want you to surrender," said Moore.

"Aw, nuts!" said McAuliffe.

When McAuliffe got around to composing a reply to the ultimatum, he was at a loss as to what to say.

"That first crack you made," said his G-3, Harry Kinnard, "would be hard to beat."

"What was that?" asked McAuliffe.

"You said 'Nuts!'"

With a pen, McAuliffe wrote: "To the German commander: Nuts! From the American Commander."

By that time, the commander of the 327th Glider Infantry, Colonel Harper, had arrived at the headquarters and insisted on taking the reply back himself. When he reached Company F's command post, he ordered the German officers to be put in a jeep and driven, still blindfolded, to

Lieutenant Smith's platoon headquarters at the Kessler farm. To the immense relief of the Germans, their blindfolds were at last removed.

Lieutenant Henke told Harper that he and his companion were authorized to negotiate details. Would he be so kind as to give them the answer from the American commander?

"The answer," said Harper, "is 'Nuts!'"

Although Henke had spent years in the import business and spoke excellent English, the reply perplexed him. He translated literally for the major, but neither of them understood. Was the reply, asked Henke, negative or affirmative?

"The reply," answered Harper, "is decidedly not affirmative, and if you continue this foolish attack, your losses will be tremendous.

"If you don't understand what 'Nuts!' means," Harper continued, "in plain English it is the same as 'Go to hell!' And I will tell you something else; if you continue to attack, we will kill every goddamn German that tries to break into this city."

The German officers came to attention and saluted. "We will kill many Americans," said Henke. "This is war."

"On your way, Bud," said Harper, then to his everlasting regret added: "And good luck to you."

The surrender demand was the work of the commander of the 47th Panzer Corps, von Lüttwitz, who sent it without consulting his superior. When General von Manteuffel learned of it, he was furious, for quite clearly he lacked sufficient artillery to make good on the threat. Lest the lack of retaliation should make the German command appear ridiculous, von Manteuffel put in a call to the Luftwaffe to bomb Bastogne.

CHAPTER TWENTY-FIVE

To Relieve Bastogne

By late 1944, George Smith Patton, Jr., at fifty-nine years of age, was already something of a legend in the United States Army and a darling of the American press. It had not always been so. After word had leaked out that in Sicily Patton slapped two American soldiers whom he suspected of malingering, newsmen had gone for his jugular. An impolitic remark before a ladies' club in England before the invasion had set the jackals to howling again, but General Eisenhower had stuck by Patton, confident of his ability on the battlefield.

His dash across France from the Normandy beachhead in late summer appeared to justify Eisenhower's loyalty; and a fickle press, suddenly adoring his posturing, his profanity, his flashy uniforms, glistening helmet, pistols on each hip, nicknamed him "Old Blood and Guts" and turned him into an idol of the American public. Soldiers who had hated him in Sicily came to love him. All they needed to say was that they were in "Patton's army"; everybody knew which army that was.

A man of independent means, married to a woman of even greater wealth, George Patton had no economic need to devote his life to the United States Army. He did so because he loved it, lived and breathed it, and in it he could fulfill a deep emotional need to excel, to star. An avid student of military history, he "wrote knowingly on the phalanxes of Greece, the legions of Rome, the columns of Napoleon, and the mass armies of World War I. He could compare the tank to the heavy cavalry of Belisarius." Nobody loved the profession of arms more than did George Patton.

He was a man given to extreme ups and downs. Thus he could kick and scream like a child deprived of a toy when on December 16 General Bradley ordered him to relinquish an armored division to the First Army in the Ardennes, then three days later enthusiastically embrace the sending of a major portion of his army into the Ardennes. The difference was that in the second case, he, George Patton, was to be the star.

514

*   *   *

On December 20, Patton summoned General Middleton to meet him in Arlon. "Troy," Patton greeted him, "of all the goddamn crazy things I ever heard of, leaving the 101st Airborne to be surrounded in Bastogne is the worst!" Well accustomed to Patton's outbursts, Middleton merely pointed out patiently the importance of the network of roads at Bastogne.

"All right, Troy," said Patton, "if you were in my position, where would you launch the attack? From Arlon or from Neufchâteau?"

Middleton replied that he would make the main attack along the Arlon highway and east of it, "to cut off the Krauts instead of pushing them straight ahead." On the other hand, to get to Bastogne as quickly as possible, he would send the 4th Armored Division up the highway from Neufchâteau, which was seven miles closer to Bastogne than Arlon. He might have added that from where the American line had stabilized along the two roads, it was twelve miles to Bastogne on the Arlon highway, nine miles on the highway from Neufchâteau.

No, said Patton, he wanted to keep his divisions concentrated. He would send the 4th Armored Division up the highway from Arlon, the infantry divisions through the countryside east of that road.

Patton's decision may have been based on nothing more than the fact that he had earlier approved General Gaffey's recalling General Dager's CCB from the Neufchâteau-Bastogne highway to Arlon. On the other hand, to Patton, relieving Bastogne was as irritating as a burr under the saddle to a horse, for Patton was not after Bastogne but St. Vith, thereby hoping to cut off the German forces that had penetrated far to the west and destroy them. Yet he had his orders to relieve Bastogne.

It hardly appeared to be a momentous decision in any event, for as an officer in the 4th Armored Division summed up the view held in the division's command circles: "The general impression was that we could just cut our way through." It would turn out to be an unfortunate decision, nevertheless, for as might have been anticipated, there were far fewer Germans along the Neufchâteau highway than there were along the highway from Arlon.

George Patton made good on his promise to attack on December 22, not only in the direction of Bastogne but also farther to the east, to remove any lingering threat to Luxembourg City. As early as December 19, the commander of the Seventh Army's 80th Corps, General Beyer, had recognized that an American reaction would soon be coming and had ordered the bulk of his troops to dig in and hold what they had gained. Yet the American attack there involved at first only one regiment, for not until late on December 23 did the commander of the Third Army's XII Corps, Maj. Gen. Manton S. Eddy, get his supporting artillery in place and all the veteran 5th Infantry Division forward. Thus it was not until the morning of the 24th that an attack began in earnest to drive the Germans back across the Sûre River.

The 5th Division advanced northward on both sides of the Ernz Noire, while the 10th Armored Division's CCA and a task force from the 9th Armored Division's CCA extended the attack to the west. The advance moved across ground and through villages recently relinquished by men of the 4th Division's 12th Infantry and the 9th Armored Division's 60th Armored Infantry Battalion: Müllerthal, Lauterborn, Berdorf, the Parc Hôtel, Waldbillig, Beaufort.

By nightfall of the first day, the armor reached that part of the Sûre River that flows from west to east and forms the angle at the juncture with the Our where men of the 109th Infantry had defended at the start of the German offensive. The infantry in the meantime had slower going but on Christmas Day reached high ground at various points overlooking that part of the Sûre that forms the boundary between Luxembourg and Germany. Late that day and all the next, artillery forward observers called down heavy concentrations, many of them aerial bursts with the POZIT fuse, on hapless Germans trying to get to the other side of the river, whether across a lone remaining vehicular bridge or the few footbridges, in rubber boats or by swimming. By that time the two defending German units, the 212th and 276th Voldsgrenadier Divisions, were shattered, infantry companies down to twenty-five or thirty men, a few reduced to no more than ten.

In Echternach, the first patrols of the 5th Division's 10th Infantry to enter the town searched in vain for any trace of Captain Dupuis, Lieutenant Macdiarmid, and the men of the 12th Infantry's Company E. The relief force that Dupuis had counted on with such trust had at last arrived—as Dupuis had said it would—but six days too late.

In addition to the 4th Armored Division, charged specifically with breaking through to Bastogne, Patton's main attack employed two infantry divisions, the 26th and 80th, both experienced and both fairly well rested after brief periods out of the line. All operated under headquarters of the III Corps, commanded by General Millikin, but the commander and his staff were engaging in their first operation. The zone of attack encompassed twenty-four miles, from the Alzette River inside Luxembourg (Ettelbruck is near the juncture of the Alzette and the Sûre) to the Neufchâteau-Bastogne highway.

The task assigned to the infantry divisions was essentially to clear territory between the Alzette River and the Arlon-Bastogne highway, thereby protecting the right flank of the 4th Armored Division and advancing the line so that when relief came to Bastogne, there would be no narrow corridor leading into the town but a broad expanse of American-controlled territory extending eastward. That also conformed with Patton's ambition to proceed beyond the relief of Bastogne with a general movement of the entire southern flank in a drive on St. Vith.

In the vernacular of the foot soldier, whoever picked the terrain over which the 26th and 80th Divisions advanced had a taste for shit. It was like a roller-coaster; it had deep hollows and ravines; it was heavily wooded; and it had a roadnet that Charlemagne's knights would have complained about. The obvious first phase line for the advance was the deep, meandering, generally wooded gorge carved by western reaches of the Sûre River.

Fortunately for the men of the two divisions, the Germans were not only ill-prepared but totally unprepared to meet an attack. Except in front of the American armor, where the 5th Parachute Division had arrived, nobody was manning the ramparts. The commander of the Seventh Army's 85th Corps, General Kniess, was still trying to get his other division, the 352d Volksgrenadier Division, forward from Ettelbruck over a road that turned off the Ettelbruck-Bastogne highway a few miles outside Ettelbruck and meandered westward through little farm villages for an eventual connection with the Arlon-Bastogne highway. As the American infantrymen began plodding through the snow before daylight on December 22, the 352d Volksgrenadiers were not in defensive positions but on the march.

Observers for the American artillery battalions and the crews of tanks and tank destroyers could hardly believe their eyes: Germans in vehicles or on foot were passing in column before them, unaware that their foe was anywhere near. The 26th Division caught the head of the column while the 80th Division hit the middle and the tail. Although the German regiment bringing up the rear quickly deployed in defense of Ettelbruck, a regiment of the 80th Division broke through farther west and continued under a bright moon to take the village of Heinerscheid and cut the important Ettelbruck-Bastogne highway. Before nightfall the next day, the 23d, a company pushed ahead to seize a bridge over the Sûre River.

The leading German regiment, hit by the 26th Division, reacted quickly, making a fight for it at the village of Grosbous, in the process driving out a company of the 28th Division's 109th Infantry that had been holding there. Yet it was farther to the west that the more significant development occurred, for there first units of a fresh German force appeared.

Those were advance elements of the *Führer Grenadier Brigade*, which like the *Führer Begleit Brigade* had been created around a nucleus of troops that had once protected the *Wolfschanze*, albeit on the outer rather than the inner protective rim. Consisting of six thousand men, many of whom had fought with the *Grossdeutschland Division* on the Eastern Front, the brigade had two battalions of infantry mounted on half-tracks and trucks, an assault gun battalion, and a battalion of forty Mark IV and Panther tanks.

The going through the rugged country between the Alzette River and the Arlon-Bastogne highway was no longer to be easy. To add to the newly acquired strength of the *Führer Grenadier Brigade*, the commander of the Seventh Army, General Brandenberger, received from the Führer Reserve the 79th Volksgrenadier Division. With those forces, Brandenberger—who had established his headquarters in nearby Wiltz—intended to counterattack south of the Sûre River to drive the Americans back and regain control of the Ettelbruck-Bastogne highway.

From that point, both the 26th and 80th Divisions had a brutal slugging match on their hands. As it opened, the commander of the 80th Division, Maj. Gen. Horace L. McBride, had to relinquish at his corps commander's order two of his infantry battalions to help the 4th Armored Division. And in view of the presence of the *Führer Grenadier Brigade*, General Millikin told the commander of the 26th Division, Maj. Gen. Willard S. Paul, to advance with caution.

That brigade turned out to be less of a threat than it might have been, for the American advance forced piecemeal commitment, and the German commander, Col. Hans-Joachim Kahler, was seriously wounded by artillery fire while on reconnaissance the night of December 22. So, too, the venom of American fighter-bombers, at last released by the clear weather on the 23d, seriously interfered with the arrival of all units of the brigade and of the 79th Volksgrenadier Division, for the planes made a bottleneck of the bridges to the rear over the Our River.

It was a grim fight, as bitter in the brutal cold as any that occurred anywhere during the battle in the Ardennes. Men died by the score on both sides, but by the day after Christmas the two American infantry divisions had carried the field. Except at a few points, they controlled all the rugged countryside south of the Sûre River, held two small bridge-heads over the river, and had regained Ettelbruck. There the attack came to a halt to await General Patton's pleasure in continuing the drive north-ward to erase the bulge the Germans had created in American lines.

During the drive across France the 4th Armored Division had estab-lished a reputation as a slashing, freewheeling outfit, and it was George Patton's favorite; but as the division prepared to drive on Bastogne, there were problems. The division was short of tanks, and many of those that remained had clocked so much mileage that breakdowns were frequent. The division had also recently lost its veteran commander, sent home for medical reasons; and for the new commander, General Gaffey, it was to be a first fight with a division command. There were also many replace-ments among the tank crews and the armored infantrymen.

The armor began its advance in two columns, one combat command up the Arlon-Bastogne highway, another up secondary roads just west of the highway. Demolitions executed earlier by engineers as a precaution against German advance delayed both columns.

It was mid-afternoon of the 22d before CCA on the main highway approached the town of Martelange and the deep gorge of the Sûre River, not quite half the distance from Arlon to Bastogne. There a com-pany of the 5th Parachute Division denied access to the sites of two de-molished bridges, and not until well after midnight did a company of armored infantry succeed in getting to the far bank. Engineers then dis-covered that the banks were too steep for either pontoon or treadway bridges. They would have to take the time to erect a Bailey Bridge, which would not be ready until mid-afternoon of the second day, December 23. Patton had charged the 4th Armored Division to "drive like hell," but it wasn't working out that way.

Progress was better with CCB on the secondary roads west of the highway. Only after coming abreast of Martelange did that column en-counter enemy fire, and then only small-arms fire from outposts that quickly fell back. By nightfall on the 22d, CCB had reached the village of Burnon, just seven miles from Bastogne; but that column, too, had to pause to replace a demolished bridge.

Before daylight on the second day, CCB resumed its advance, only to find the next village of Chaumont defended by a company of the 5th

RELIEF OF BASTOGNE
DEC 22 - 26

- U.S. POSITIONS, 26 DEC
- ARMORED ATTACKS

Scale:
0 1 2 3 4
MILES

Noville

Champs

Foy

Longvilly

Hemrolle

Bizory

Bastogne

Mageret

Neffe

Senonchamps

Wardin

Moircy

Marvie

Sibret

Assenois

Lutrebois

Clochimont

Hompré

Harlange

Remichampagne

Chaumont

Vaux-les-Rosières

Remoiville

Burnon

Sûre

River

CCR, 25 - 26 DEC

Warnach

Arsdorf

Neufchâteau

CCB, 22 - 26 DEC

CCA, 22 - 26 DEC

CCR, 23 - 24 DEC

4TH

Martelange

ARMORED

DIVISION

Habay-La-Neuve

Arlon

Parachute Division. In a combined tank-infantry assault in the afternoon, CCB's tanks bogged down on slopes turned soft by the sun, but the armored infantrymen rooted the paratroopers out alone. Yet hardly had the infantrymen reported their success when ten German assault guns and what the Americans took to be five Tiger tanks with paratroopers clinging to them opened a deadly fire.

That morning at headquarters of the 26th Volksgrenadier Division near Bastogne, five *Ferdinand* tank destroyers, which had long-barreled 88mm. guns mounted on a Tiger chassis, had arrived. They were part of the 653d Heavy *Panzerjäger* Battalion, which had recently come from Italy and was scheduled for commitment in Alsace; but somehow those five *Ferdinands* had been diverted to the Ardennes. The division commander, Colonel Kokott, cared not where they came from nor how they got there, for they seemed heaven sent to prevent the American drive from the south from cutting into the rear of his division at Bastogne.

Kokott promptly sent the tank destroyers southward along with ten of his assault guns. They arrived just in time to enable the paratroopers to retake Chaumont, and the German guns exacted a heavy toll of the American tanks mired on the hillside outside the village.

That night General McAuliffe sent an obviously concerned message from Bastogne to the 4th Armored Division: "Sorry I did not get to shake hands today. I was disappointed." A short while later, somebody on his staff sent another: "There is only one more shopping day before Christmas!"

During the afternoon briefing of December 22 at headquarters of the Ninth Air Force in a big office building in Luxembourg City across the Place de Metz from headquarters of the 12th Army Group, Maj. Gen. Hoyt S. Vandenberg listened in gloom to the prediction of his chief meteorologist, Maj. Stuart J. Fuller. A low front, said Fuller, had settled in the general vicinity of the Rhine River, and he could see no break in the clouds for at least four more days. After the briefing was over, the two talked in Vandenberg's office. There were high pressure areas both to the west and to the east, Fuller noted, but he saw no possibility of either arriving quickly.

At breakfast the next morning in the nearby Hôtel Kons, Fuller was happy to acknowledge that he had been wrong. The cold winds of the Russian high had at last driven the clouds away. All morning officers and airmen lined the windows of the big headquarters building, gaping at the sky, and by noon the streets of Luxembourg City were full of people craning to see the show: One parade after another of medium B-26 Marauders, and seemingly everywhere, the fighter-bombers, P-47 Thunderbolts and P-38 Lightnings "like shoals of silver minnows in the bright winter sun." By nightfall, the Ninth Air Force had flown almost 1,300 sorties.

* * *

Nobody was more jubilant over the break in the weather than the men in and around Bastogne. At nine thirty that morning, teams of pathfinders landed to mark a drop zone between Senonchamps and the town. Shortly before noon came the unmistakable hum of vast numbers of motors, then the big C-47 transport planes lumbered into view, looking for all the world like pregnant geese against the sky, and the hum became a thunder. As the big planes slowly plowed through the air at little more than a thousand feet above the ground, out of their bellies plunged parapacks with parachutes of red, yellow, orange, blue, and white.

Men watched in awe from their foxholes, others from windows and the streets of the town, and crowds of civilians emerged from their catacombs for what seemed to be a miracle, "resupply coming from the sky." They "applauded, shouted with joy, cried"; they were saved, "lost hope rekindled." To at least one paratrooper, Capt. Laurence Critchell of the 501st Parachute Infantry, it was difficult "not to feel a sentimental pride of country."

As the planes followed their low course, German antiaircraft gunners, ignoring the presence of hordes of fighter-bombers flying cover, opened fire. A few planes came in trailing smoke, but not a single pilot veered from his course.

One of the planes had dropped its load and was gaining altitude when antiaircraft fire knocked out its controls. Having often flown in the cabin of a C-47, Captain Critchell was able to imagine the scene inside: "the two American youngsters struggling with the controls, the cockpit windows showing nothing but uprushing earth, the instinctive start backwards toward the cabin, and then—."

Before it was over, 241 planes had dropped 144 tons of supplies in close to 1,500 packets. A few fell inside German lines, but not many, and some fell in the town itself. (The next day, Christmas Eve, one of the soldiers gave a white silk parachute to the nurse, Renée Lemaire, who planned to take it home that night and eventually make it into a wedding dress.)

The resupply failed to meet all needs, particularly for medical supplies and ammunition for the 75mm. pack howitzers of the parachute artillery battalions; but that might be remedied on other days. What mattered was that even as a supply crisis was beginning to grip the defenders, the skies had cleared and relief had come. Informed that the troops had recovered 95 percent of the packets, McAuliffe's G-3, Colonel Kinnard, allowed as how that was "close enough for government work."

That day and over the next four days, with a hiatus on Christmas Day because of unfavorable weather over air bases in England, 962 C-47s dropped 850 tons of supplies. On December 26, there were in addition eleven gliders, some of which brought in surgeons. During the five days, the Germans shot down nineteen planes and badly damaged fifty more.

None the less welcome were attacks by fighter-bombers, directed to their targets by Capt. James E. Parker of the Ninth Air Force, who had come into Bastogne on December 19 and scrounged a high-frequency radio from Colonel Roberts's CCB. Parker directed the first planes, which were on the scene by 10 A.M. on the 23d, to the northwest and west, in front of the positions of the 502d Parachute Infantry and a battalion of the 327th Glider Infantry. The Germans had been building up heavily there, and because of the ammunition shortage, the artillery had been unable to do anything about it.

The snow helped the pilots tremendously, for German vehicles left telltale tracks leading to assembly areas in the forests. Against those the fighter-bombers used Napalm, setting the forests on fire. Before the day ended, there were fires all around the circle of American positions so that the smoke made it seem "almost as if the fog was closing in again." Either with explosive bombs or with Napalm, the fighter-bombers hit every village within a mile or two of the perimeter, some of them numbers of times. They flew more than 250 sorties each day.

The clearing weather enabled the commander of the Ninth Air Force, General Vandenberg, to put in motion a plan of aerial reaction he had devised soon after the start of the German offensive. The first priority was to blunt the enemy's armored spearheads and the motor transport supporting them by every available means while at the same time knocking out his railheads and communications centers in the Eifel—Prüm, Nideggen, Bitburg—and the bridges he was using to bring supplies and reinforcements across the Rhine.

The two objectives were in a way contradictory, for in order to provide the necessary fighter escort for the mediums that hit the targets inside Germany, many fighter-bombers had to be withdrawn from the primary goal of blunting the spearheads. Vandenberg solved it by calling on the Eighth Air Force in England to send two groups of P- 51 Mustangs to the Continent to provide escort.

Partly as a result of the shift of American forces north of the German penetration to Field Marshal Montgomery's command, British fighter-bombers became readily available in accord with needs discerned by American air commanders. With the shift, the IX and XXIX Tactical Air Commands passed to operational control of the British Second Tactical Air Force; but on the theory that the IX Tactical Air Command's General Quesada had a better feel for the support needed, the commander of the Second Tactical Air Force, Air Marshal Sir Arthur Coningham, sent a liaison officer to Quesada's headquarters and put British planes at Quesada's disposal. At Quesada's request, most British fighter-bombers flew escort, attacked German airfields, or flew armed reconnaissance along the Rhine. Yet whenever Quesada needed British planes for close support of the ground troops, the liaison officer called them in.

On December 23, Colonel Kokott struck again at Bastogne, using the fresh regiment of the 26th Volksgrenadier Division along the Marche highway northwest of the town and the attached *Panzergrenadier* regiment between the Ettelbruck and Arlon highways to the southeast. In conjunction with the attack from the northwest, the *Volksgrenadier* division's *Kampfgruppe Kunkel* renewed its thrust against Team Browne at Senonchamps.

They were strong attacks, but Team Browne stopped *Kampfgruppe Kunkel* a third time. Then, rather than risk being cut off in the projection along the Marche highway, the commander of the 327th Glider Infantry's 3d Battalion, Lt. Col. Ray C. Allen, withdrew by phases to an arc-shaped line conforming to the shape of the defensive perimeter on either flank. To the southeast, the *Panzergrenadiers* in a night attack wrested half the village of Marvie (just off the Ettelbruck highway) from Team O'Hara, but they seriously depleted their ranks in the process.

At that point neither von Manteuffel, von Lüttwitz, nor Kokott held out much hope of taking Bastogne without considerable reinforcement. When Hitler on the 23d released two divisions from the Führer Reserve—the 9th Panzer and the 15th Panzergrenadier Divisions—von Manteuffel hoped to get both. Instead, Field Marshal Model sent all but one regiment of the *Panzergrenadier* division to bolster the drive for the Meuse. While awaiting the arrival of that regiment, which had artillery and tank support, Colonel Kokott on the 24th held fast at Bastogne.

Early that day, General von Manteuffel attempted to force the issue of Bastogne. In a message that—as he intended—soon reached General Jodl and Hitler himself, he asked what he should do: Turn all resources to capture Bastogne, or continue to emphasize the drive for the Meuse? Having insisted in advance of the offensive on the utmost importance of Bastogne, Hitler at that point appeared to have lost interest in it. The answer came back: Use all available forces to gain the Meuse.

Hitler nevertheless remained ambivalent about Bastogne, for he found it galling that what was apparently a small American force could hold onto the town. That night he ordered an aide, Maj. Johann Mayer, who was at the front, to go to headquarters of the 47th Panzer Corps to find out what was wrong. By the time Mayer left the headquarters, General von Lüttwitz had convinced him of the stiffness of the American resistance, which Mayer promised to pass on to the Führer; but, said Mayer, Hitler insisted that Bastogne must be taken the next day, Christmas Day.

That conformed in any case with what General von Manteuffel was planning. For an experienced military man, continuing enemy holdout astride the nexus of almost all roads in the area was unacceptable. Since the regiment of the 15th Panzergrenadier Division was arriving that night, he ordered an all-out attack for the following morning. Attacking on Christmas Day might take the Americans by surprise, and in the wake of the bombing of Bastogne, which was scheduled that night, provide the Germans with a psychological advantage.

That Christmas Eve along the perimeter of foxholes surrounding Bastogne, men grew pensive and quiet. Some for the first time "felt fearful," as if "the end was at hand." They shook hands, wished each other a Merry Christmas.

In command posts and in cellars, wherever there was light, men could read a Christmas message from their commander, General McAuliffe. "What's merry about all this, you ask? We're fighting—it's cold—we aren't home." Yet, wrote McAuliffe, every man in the Bastogne perimeter could take comfort from the fact that the defenders of Bastogne had "stopped cold" everything thrown at them from every direction. They were writing a page in "world history" and in the process "giving our country and our loved ones at home a worthy Christmas present." The 101st Airborne Division's G-2 Periodic Report that night depicted a circle of enemy positions and activity around Bastogne in red ink and in the center (the hole in the doughnut), in green ink, the words "Merry Christmas."

Early in the evening, as McAuliffe was walking past the police station, he heard German prisoners inside singing carols. He paused to listen: *"Stille Nacht,"* *"O Tannenbaum."* On an impulse, McAuliffe went inside. "We'll be in Antwerp in a few weeks," shouted one of the prisoners in English. "We'll soon be freed," shouted another, "and it is you who'll be the prisoner." And still another: "You'll like it there, General; it is most comfortable and cozy."

McAuliffe waited for them to quiet down. He had come by, he said at last, to wish them all a Merry Christmas.

Earlier in the day, McAuliffe had received a message from General Patton: "Xmas Eve present coming up. Hold on." Yet there was to be no Christmas Eve present. When McAuliffe returned to his command post that night, he spoke by radio with Middleton in Neufchâteau. "The finest Christmas present the hundred and first could get," said McAuliffe, "would be relief tomorrow."

As Middleton was aware, there was little chance of that. Indeed, in view of all the problems the 4th Armored Division was encountering, General Patton was ill-advised to send his message, for it raised false hopes. It had taken CCA until midday on December 24 to clear the first village beyond the Sûre River on the Arlon-Bastogne highway, the village of Warnach, still nine miles from Bastogne. Although CCB on the secondary roads west of the highway was less than five miles from Bastogne, that combat command was still battling the assault guns and *Ferdinands* that had appeared the day before with such effect at Chaumont. And the threat posed east of the highway by an arriving *Führer Grenadier Brigade* had prompted General Gaffey to commit CCR there to protect the division's flank. Hopes of a quick, bold thrust to Bastogne had faded.

The basic problem was the stubbornness of the German paratroopers. Whenever the tanks gained ground or a village, the paratroopers would counterattack or infiltrate back, and it took time to clear them out. That was what had prompted General Millikin to call for two battalions of the 80th Division's infantry to help; they were to join the fight on Christmas Day. At midnight he also shifted the boundary of the 26th Division to the west, to give that division full responsibility for the *Führer Grenadier Brigade*, and ordered CCR back to Neufchâteau to make a supporting attack along the Neufchâteau-Bastogne highway.

Inside Bastogne, around eight thirty on Christmas Eve, men heard the approaching drone of a swarm of big planes, their motors throbbing in a manner uncharacteristic of American planes. For almost all the Americans in the town, the bombing that followed was a new and terrifying experience. First came magnesium flares that made the night seem brighter than day and anybody caught in the open feel naked; then the bombs.

The first fell near a railroad overpass close to the Heintz Barracks. Inside the cellar of the camp's main building, it seemed to the only newspaperman in Bastogne, Fred MacKenzie of the Buffalo *Evening News*, that "an all but imperceptible movement swept along the passage"; it was men "drawing their physical parts into tight knots to resist shock." Then a "thin, shrieking whistle and a thunderous roar beat down their senses."

In a building next door to the department store, the Sarma, which served the 10th Armored Division's CCB as an aid station, the medical officer, Major Prior, was preparing to go to the aid station to write a letter for a young lieutenant who was dying of a chest wound. As he started to step out the door, one of his men reminded him that it was Christmas Eve and suggested they open a bottle of champagne. The two had just begun to drink when they detected "the screeching sound" of the first bomb either of them had ever heard. It sounded as if it was heading straight for them. They threw themselves to the floor.

In the aid station, along with a number of the medics, Renée Lemaire was in the kitchen. At the screech of the bomb, she either dashed into the cellar or somebody pushed her there for safety. As the bomb hit, it seemed to those who survived as if it came straight down the chimney. The blast blew those in the kitchen out through a large plate glass window. It buried those in the cellar.

What remained of the building was soon in flames. As Major Prior and others gathered in the street, they pulled anyone they could from the ruins, their work hampered by two strafing runs from a German plane. Several men volunteered to be lowered through a window at sidewalk level into the cellar and succeeded in rescuing three wounded men before the entire building collapsed.

Twenty of the wounded in the aid station died in the bombing. Also Renée Lemaire. Many days later men dug the bodies from the debris, and Prior himself carried Renée Lemaire's remains to her parents, encased in the silk folds of a white parachute, like the one she so treasured for her wedding dress.

In two runs over Bastogne, German bombers—most of them Junkers 88s—dropped approximately 2 tons of bombs, low in terms of what American bombers usually delivered (seldom less than 20 tons), but enough to do heavy damage to a town the size of Bastogne. One bomb hit the command post of CCB's Team Cherry, killing four junior officers, among them Captain Ryerson and Lieutenant Hyduke who had figured so prominently in the fighting along the Longvilly-Mageret road. The chief damage was to buildings around the main square, and when the fires had burned themselves out, most were charred skeletons. A town that had hardly been touched earlier in the war at that point "wore that ghastly air of desolation" that had come to so many other places in Europe.

For the all-out attack on Bastogne on Christmas Day, Colonel Kokott had been counting on the entire 15th Panzergrenadier Division. He got instead a *Panzergrenadier* regiment with only two of its three battalions forward, plus two battalions of self-propelled artillery and eighteen Mark IV and Panther tanks. Although the commander, Col. Wolfgang Maucke, protested the lack of time for reconnaissance and proper preparation, his was a powerful force, and to it would be added one of Kokott's *Volksgrenadier* regiments and the bulk of his divisional artillery.

Wearing white camouflage capes to match the snow, their supporting tanks painted white, the *Volksgrenadiers* and *Panzergrenadiers* moved forward shortly after three o'clock on Christmas morning, seeking to puncture the American line west of Bastogne in two places: that of the 502d Parachute Infantry at the village of Champs, a little over two miles north of the Marche highway; and that of Colonel Allen's battalion of the 327th Glider Infantry between Champs and the highway. In the darkness, *Volksgrenadiers* quickly got inside Champs. Such intense fighting at close quarters developed that the battalion commander, Maj. John D. Hanlon, was reluctant to send reinforcements until daylight would enable them to tell friend from foe. He nevertheless sent two companies marching toward high ground close by, to which the company inside Champs might retire if forced from the village.

At the same time, a battalion of *Panzergrenadiers* on foot and another riding the eighteen available tanks struck Allen's glider infantrymen. Midway between Champs and the Marche highway, the tanks broke through and headed for the village of Hemroulle, between Champs and Bastogne. In the darkness, several of the tanks passed through the firing positions of the 755th Field Artillery Battalion. As soon as the artillerymen made out the distinctive muzzle breaks on the cannon, they opened fire with machine guns, but the tanks were too close for the 155mm. howitzers to be brought to bear.

Just outside Hemroulle, seven of the tanks, *Panzergrenadiers* still aboard, swung west in an attempt to cut into the rear of the American lines. They were soon approaching the command post of the commander of the glider infantry, Colonel Allen. The commander of Company C, Capt. Preston E. Towns, telephoned Allen to warn that the tanks were approaching.

"Where?" Allen asked.

"If you look out your window now," said Towns, "you'll be looking right down the muzzle of an eighty-eight." So he was. Allen and his staff took off, fire from the tanks following them closely in growing daylight.

The same tanks were soon nearing the command post of the 502d Parachute Infantry in the Château Rolle, a thousand yards behind Champs, where at midnight a Belgian priest had celebrated mass for American soldiers and for civilians who had taken refuge in the château. The headquarters troops, soon joined by walking wounded from the regimental aid station in the stables, rushed to man a position where a tree-lined road leading to the château joined the Champs-Bastogne road. Inside the château the regimental commander, Lt. Col. Steve A. Chappius, his executive officer, and his radio operator, the only three left, could see the German tanks approaching.

German tanks were also heading toward the two companies of the 502d Parachute Infantry that at Major Hanlon's order were marching toward beleaguered Champs. Two self-propelled guns of the 705th Tank Destroyer Battalion fired on them, but German gunners quickly knocked those out. Retiring to a nearby woodlot, the paratroopers fired on the *Panzergrenadiers* riding the tanks, prompting them to seek such cover as they could find in ditches and folds in the ground.

Two other guns of the 705th Tank Destroyer Battalion fired, knocking out three of the tanks; the paratroopers accounted for another with a bazooka; and the scratch force from the 502d's headquarters got another, also with a bazooka. One continued toward Champs, but there the paratroopers, still in command of the village, knocked it out. The seventh turned back toward Hemroulle, but there the crew surrendered, for at Hemroulle the other German tanks had encountered a maelstrom of American fire.

The commander of the German tanks had early radioed Colonel Kokott's headquarters that he had reached the western edge of Bastogne. Although Kokott for long believed the report and thought he was at last about to achieve the success that had so long eluded him, the tank commander had confused Hemroulle with Bastogne. The eleven tanks that entered the village quickly ran into an intense fire from a variety of sources: four of the 705th's tank destroyers, tanks supporting Team Browne, the 463d Parachute Field Artillery Battalion, and bazookas manned by foot troops from whatever formation. Each tank sustained such a variety of hits that it later proved impossible to determine just what kind of fire had delivered the *coup de grâce*.

At Hemroulle, the Germans had again come within just over a mile of Bastogne, as they had in the opening engagements on the other side of the town outside Neffe, at Wardin, and along the railroad between Bizory and Foy; but once again they had failed to get through. Under pressure from Generals von Manteuffel and von Lüttwitz, a dispirited Colonel Kokott launched, as he himself termed it, a last "desperate effort," before daylight the next morning, but to no avail. For all that the all-out attack on Christmas Day accomplished, Kokott, von Lüttwitz, and von Manteuffel might as well have formed a trio and stood in the snow singing *"Tannenbaum! O Tannenbaum!"*

The knowledge that American armor was driving up from the south to relieve Bastogne had long plagued Heinz Kokott. That was why he earlier had dispatched assault guns and the heaven-sent *Ferdinands* to retake the village of Chaumont, and as early as December 23 he had turned some of the attached *Panzergrenadiers* of the *Panzer Lehr Division* and some of his own *Volksgrenadiers* to face south along the highway to Arlon. That and the highway from Neufchâteau were his principal concerns. But late on Christmas Day, when he learned that an American armored column had entered the village of Hompré, less than four miles from Bastogne, a secondary road leading north from Hompré through the village of Assenois became of intense concern. That night he hurried a depleted battalion of his *Volksgrenadiers* to Assenois.

Unlike most American armored divisions, the 4th Armored Division seldom employed its CCR as an integral tactical unit but instead shuffled tank and armored infantry battalions in and out as CCA or CCB needed them and used the headquarters to control battalions requiring rest and replacements. The basic components of the reserve combat command on Christmas Day—the 37th Tank Battalion under Lt. Col. Creighton W. Abrams and the 53d Armored Infantry Battalion under Lt. Col. George L. Jaques (pronounced Jakes)—had nevertheless worked together frequently, but both were under strength. The armored infantry battalion was short 230 men, and Abrams had only 20 medium tanks. Also available to CCR were a platoon of self-propelled tank destroyers, the self-propelled 94th Armored Field Artillery Battalion, and an attached battery of 155mm. howitzers of the 177th Field Artillery Battalion.

Ordered to Neufchâteau at midnight on Christmas Eve, CCR began to advance along the highway leading to Bastogne shortly before noon on Christmas Day. The first objective was Vaux-les-Rosières, from which the 28th Division's headquarters had recently been rudely ejected. At that point only a replacement engineer battalion was holding the village as an outpost for the town of Sibret farther along the highway. As CCR's tanks raced into Vaux-les-Rosières, their machine guns crackling, the German engineers dived for cover and at the first opportunity surrendered.

Rather than come at what were apparently strong German defenses at Sibret frontally, CCR's commander, Col. Wendell Blanchard, turned the column off the main highway at Vaux-les-Rosières onto a secondary road that he trusted might be less strongly defended and from which he could later turn to drive on the defenses of Sibret from the flank. A demolished bridge delayed the column for an hour until a bulldozer arrived to push the debris of a stone wall into the stream, and at the village of Remoiville, the column paused to allow four battalions of artillery to pummel the buildings. That proved to be a prudent decision, for when tanks and armored infantry rushed into the village, they routed an entire battalion of the 5th Parachute Division from the cellars.

By that time it was dusk, and a crater in the road barred further advance until it could be filled. That was to be done during the night. The next day Colonel Blanchard intended to continue along the secondary road until he had come abreast of CCB at Hompré, then swing back against Sibret for what obviously would be a major engagement.

With help from sixteen P-47s of the 362d Fighter Group, CCR during the morning of December 26 took the next village of Remichampagne and cleared nearby woods. Around 3 P.M., the leading tanks reached a road junction just short of the village of Clochimont where, according to Colonel Blanchard's plan, the column was to swing northwest on Sibret.

The tank battalion commander, Colonel Abrams, was at that point becoming wary, for he knew that there were strong German forces in Sibret, and by turning in that direction he might be exposing a flank to other German forces beyond Clochimont in the vicinity of Assenois. Before moving out, he sent tanks scouting in both directions.

As Abrams and the infantry commander, Colonel Jaques, were standing at the road junction discussing their next move, they saw C-47 aircraft dropping supplies at Bastogne. That so vividly underscored the plight of the men at Bastogne that Abrams took an ever-present cigar from his lips and proposed that they say to hell with Sibret and barrel-ass through to Bastogne by the shortest route, a secondary road from Clochimont through Assenois. Jaques agreed, but as the two officers made their decision, they neglected to tell their commander, Colonel Blanchard.

Abrams radioed his operations officer, Capt. William A. Dwight, to come forward with what was known as the C Team: Company C of the 37th Tank Battalion and Company C of the 53d Armored Infantry Battalion. He also radioed for assistance from three battalions of artillery in support of CCB. When Captain Dwight arrived, Abrams told him his objective and the plan and put him in charge. Said Abrams: "This is it."

It was 4:20 P.M. and dusk was fast approaching when six Shermans under 1st Lt. Charles P. Boggess moved out in the lead, followed by the armored infantrymen in their half-tracks. At 4:35, Boggess radioed that he was nearing Assenois and asked for artillery fire. Abrams himself radioed the artillery: "Concentration Number Nine; play it soft and sweet."

Four artillery battalions and the separate battery of 155s opened fire. The 155s and three of the light battalions fired ten volleys each on the center of the village, while one battery of the 94th Field Artillery Battalion hit the forward edge in hope of knocking out antitank guns, and the other two fired on woods flanking each side of the road just beyond the village. It was an intense bombardment, a total of 420 rounds, "soft and sweet."

At a dip in the road just before the village, Lieutenant Boggess called for the artillery to lift. Not waiting to make sure Abrams had received the message, he gunned his tank and was soon beside the first buildings. "Smoke from burning buildings and dust caused by the artillery . . . made the center of Assenois almost as dark as night," but not a German was to be seen. Two tanks took a wrong turn into a side street, and an infantry half-track strayed into the tank column behind the third tank.

As planned, one battery of artillery was still firing into the center of the village to keep the Germans under cover. Those shells were no real problem for the thick-skinned tanks, but they were for the Americans in the open-topped half-tracks. A round knocked out one of the half-tracks, killing four men, and the armored infantrymen in the others jumped down to find whatever cover they could.

At that moment at least a hundred Germans, a mixture of paratroopers and *Volksgrenadiers,* surged up from the cellars. While most of the American tanks and the lone half-track continued past the last houses of the village and up a hill beyond, the fight for control of Assenois raged between the foot troops, fierce, close-in combat.

The advancing column consisted at that point of three medium tanks in the lead, the stray half-track, and two more Shermans bringing up the rear. As Lieutenant Boggess in the leading tank neared the woods beyond the town, where the trees were close to the road on both sides, his machine gunners maintained a steady fire to keep any Germans pinned to their holes. So fast were the tanks moving that the half-track and the other tanks following it soon fell behind. That afforded time for Germans in the woods to put a few antitank mines on the road. The half-track hit one and exploded.

Riding with one of the tanks, Captain Dwight directed them onto the shoulders of the road, and while they pinned down the Germans in the woods with fire from their machine guns, surviving armored infantrymen removed the mines. Then with the infantrymen hanging on, the tanks raced ahead to catch up with the others.

Meanwhile, as Lieutenant Boggess emerged from the woods, just over a hundred yards ahead of him, at a point where a farm track crossed the road, he saw a small pillbox (an old Belgian fortification) and American troops nearby, seemingly getting ready to assault it. With a quick round from the tank's 75, Boggess's gunner knocked out the pillbox and sent the American troops diving for cover. Standing in his open turret, Boggess shouted: "Come here! This is the 4th Armored!"

As the men emerged, their commander, 2d Lt. Duane J. Webster of the 326th Airborne Engineer Battalion, came forward, and Boggess leaned down from his perch to shake his hand.

At 4:50 P.M. on December 26, Boggess and his men lifted the siege of Bastogne.

At first sight of the three tanks, someone in the 326th Airborne Engineer Battalion reported—with some error—to General McAuliffe's headquarters the approach of "three light tanks believed friendly." That brought McAuliffe hurrying to an observation post nearby. There Captain Dwight found him and saluted.

"How are you, General?" asked Dwight.

"Gee," said McAuliffe, "I'm mighty glad to see you."

Meanwhile, as Colonel Abrams prepared to go forward, he received a radio message from the commander of CCR, Colonel Blanchard. What did Abrams think of the possibility, asked Blanchard, of breaking through to Bastogne that night?

Not until an hour after midnight did the 53d Armored Infantry Battalion clear all Germans from Assenois and from the woods behind the village, thereby ensuring at least a minimally secure route into Bastogne. In the process, the armored infantrymen took 428 prisoners.

Yet even before the route was minimally secure, 260 of the most seriously wounded men in Bastogne departed in 22 ambulances and 10 trucks. The others were soon to follow, and the next day, December 27, the first supply convoy entered the town with tanks of the 4th Armored Division providing escort. Having arrived in Paris from the United States on the 26th, the commander of the 101st Airborne Division, General Taylor, declined an offer from General Gaffey to send him into Bastogne in a tank and with his driver made the trip in a jeep.

The siege of Bastogne was over. It had cost the 101st Airborne Division 1,641 casualties; the 10th Armored Division's CCB, 503; the 9th Armored Division's CCR considerably more; others among the artillery and Team SNAFU; and from the 4th Armored Division, 1,400.

As the men in and around Bastogne soon learned, the end of the siege spelled no end to the fighting. Bastogne was no longer a hole in a doughnut but a balloon on the end of a string, and the string was vulnerable. In the days ahead, the defenders of Bastogne were destined to face their most severe test; for the failure to capture Bastogne and events taking place elsewhere in the Ardennes had at last convinced Adolf Hitler that he had to alter the objective of his offensive. Under a new plan, taking Bastogne was more important than ever.

CHAPTER TWENTY-SIX

In Front of the Ourthe River

The Ourthe River has two sources. An east branch rises in the high ground near St. Vith and flows westward past Houffalize, while a west branch rises in the high plateau near Bastogne and joins the other branch five miles west of Houffalize, whence the river cuts a wriggly swath through the center of the Ardennes and eventually flows into the Meuse at Liège. Although the river is small and in many places shallow, the banks are often steep. The west branch and the main course form the last military obstacle of appreciable importance in front of the Meuse; for beyond them is a high plateau, the Condroz, with rolling farm and pastureland and, in comparison with the rest of the Ardennes, relatively little forest cover.

After the 7th Armored Division reached Vielsalm and St. Vith on December 17, the division commander, General Hasbrouck, had seen no point in risking his supply stocks and trucks that far forward. Instead, he ordered the commander of his trains, Col. Andrew J. Adams, to displace nineteen miles to the rear to the town of La Roche astride the Ourthe River. A good direct highway, bisecting the Bastogne-Liège highway (N-15) several miles north of Houffalize at a crossroads called Baraque de Fraiture, connected La Roche with Salmchâteau and thus with the division headquarters at Vielsalm.

As the units of General Krüger's 58th Panzer Corps—the 116th Panzer and 560th Volksgrenadier Divisions—finally broke through the 28th Division's 112th Infantry, they faced a gap created when the 110th Infantry fell back toward Bastogne and the 112th Infantry moved northward into the developing St. Vith horseshoe. The only Americans in that gap were men of the 7th Armored Division's Trains, the 9th Canadian Forestry Company, and the 51st and 299th Engineer Combat Battalions. At the order of the corps commander, General Middleton, those forces were preparing bridges for demolition along the west branch of the Ourthe and

IN FRONT OF THE OURTHE
DEC 21 - 26

- U.S. PSNS, DEC 21
- AXIS OF GERMAN ATKS, DEC 21 - 26
- U.S. PSNS, DEC 26

Scale:
0 1 2 3 4
MILES

along the main course of the river at La Roche and farther downstream, with particular attention to a major crossing site ten miles from La Roche at the village of Hotton.

By early morning of December 19, General von Waldenburg had sufficiently reorganized his 116th Panzer Division to send his reconnaissance battalion scouting to the west. Since the word was that Houffalize was stoutly held (in reality, it was only an outpost established by the 7th Armored Division's Trains), the reconnaissance troops bypassed the town to the south and early that afternoon drew up to the west branch of the Ourthe, only to find the bridge demolished. When patrols reported a Bailey Bridge a few miles upstream at the hamlet of Ourtheuville, von Waldenburg told the reconnaissance troops to seize it.

The corps commander, General Krüger, countermanded the order. A cautious commander—which was why General von Manteuffel afforded two of his three panzer divisions to von Lüttwitz instead of to Krüger—

Krüger reasoned that the Americans were bound to blow the bridge, and besides, the reconnaissance troops were trespassing in the zone of advance of von Lüttwitz's 47th Panzer Corps. He told von Waldenburg to backtrack to Houffalize, where patrols had discovered only a small American outpost in the town, and resume the advance on the other side of the main course of the Ourthe. Because of that decision, it was not until noon the next day, December 20, that the 116th Panzer Division got moving again toward the goal of the Meuse River.

The delay afforded time that the commander of the XVIII Airborne Corps, General Ridgway, sorely needed. Having ordered the 82d Airborne Division to move up to the Salm River in the rear of the troops at St. Vith, he was anxiously awaiting arrival of the 3d Armored Division to fill the gap between the airborne division and the Ourthe River.

Nobody at that point knew much of anything about the whereabouts of the enemy in that gap; but there had been reports from truck drivers of a German column near Houffalize, and before the day was out, small German patrols were probing roadblocks established by the 7th Armored Division's Trains at La Roche. In view of the uncertain enemy situation, the 3d Armored Division was to assemble some distance back in the vicinity of Hotton. After traveling through the night, the troops arrived early on December 20.

It was only part of a division, for the First Army's General Hodges had detached CCA to remain in the vicinity of Eupen as a backstop in case the Germans got across the Elsenborn Ridge (and, at the same time, to hunt for parachutists) and had sent CCB to help the 30th Division get rid of *Kampfgruppe Peiper*. That left the division commander, Maj. Gen. Maurice Rose, with only a battalion each of armored infantry, light tanks, medium tanks, and armored field artillery, plus a company of engineers and the 83d Armored Reconnaissance Battalion—not quite a third of Rose's usual strength.

With that small force, Rose was to occupy a thirteen-mile segment of the Bastogne-Liège highway extending north from Houffalize as far as the village of Manhay, where the highway from Trois Ponts to Hotton cut across. If the Germans intended moving north on Liège, that highway— N-15—was vital for them. If they intended moving west, it was still vital, for from it roads led west from the crossroads at both Baraque de Fraiture and Manhay. General Rose's broader mission was to provide a screen for the assembly of General Collins's VII Corps as a counterattacking force on the plateau beyond the Ourthe, the Condroz.

In view of the dearth of information on the enemy, the width of the zone of advance, and the paucity of forces, General Rose tried to maintain flexibility by creating three task forces and a fairly sizable reserve. Consisting of four hundred men, each task force had a company of medium tanks, a battery of self-propelled artillery, light tanks, and reconnaissance troops. The reserve included a company of medium tanks and a battalion of armored infantry.

The advance toward the Bastogne-Liège highway began in early afternoon of December 20. That was only a short time after the leading troops of the 116th Panzer Division, their countermarch at last completed, set out along their new line of march, designed to take them over the Ourthe both at La Roche and downstream at Hotton, the same sector through which two of the 3d Armored Division's task forces were headed.

On the left, outside that sector, a task force under Lt. Col. Matthew W. Kane encountered no enemy and soon reached the crossroads at Manhay. On the right, it was much the same at first for a task force under Lt. Col. Samuel M. Hogan, heading for La Roche, in normal times one of Belgium's more popular tourist attractions. Entering the town's picturesquely narrow streets nestled deep in the valley of the Ourthe beneath the ruins of an eleventh-century castle, Hogan found with considerable relief that men of the 7th Armored Division's Trains and assorted stragglers held the town. Because it had appeared earlier that the Germans were approaching La Roche from the south, where most of the supply stocks were located, the trains commander, Colonel Adams, had shifted the bulk of them to the village of Samrée, a few miles up the Salmchâteau road.

Continuing along the river road beyond La Roche, Hogan's reconnaissance platoon ran into a roadblock. German fire knocked out the leading armored car, setting it on fire and blocking the road. When Hogan reported that development to the rear, word came back to hold fast for the night; Hogan himself was to return the next morning for a possible change of orders. As the men settled down in La Roche, they loaded their vehicles with rations and cigarettes from the 7th Armored Division's stocks.

The center task force under Lt. Col. William R. Orr had in the meantime headed down the valley of the little Aisne River, a tributary of the Ourthe, to gain the La Roche–Salmchâteau highway at Samrée, then continue to the crossroads on Highway N-15 at Baraque de Fraiture. In early afternoon, as the head of the column reached the village of Dochamps two miles short of Samrée, the 7th Armored Division's quartermaster, Lt. Col. Andrew A. Miller, raced into the village in a jeep. He needed help, said Miller, to protect his supplies at Samrée.

German patrols preceding the main body of the 116th Panzer Division had entered Samrée, but since Miller gathered that a task force of the 3d Armored Division was coming, he believed he could hold them off until the armor arrived. As supply troops continued to load trucks with rations, ammunition, and gasoline, Miller went to look for the U.S. tanks.

Hardly had Miller returned with the promise of help than German tanks and *Panzergrenadiers* attacked in force, quickly knocking out Miller's only heavy weapons, a light tank and four half-tracks mounting

quad-50s. When Miller ordered everybody out, most made it, in the process evacuating all remaining ammunition but leaving behind 15,000 rations and 25,000 gallons of gasoline. As the evacuation was in progress,
two armored cars and six Shermans from Task Force Orr appeared, but
the German tanks quickly knocked out all six Shermans. Picking up survivors among the tank crews, the armored cars fell back on Dochamps.

Although the fight at Samrée further delayed the 116th Panzer Division, it paid off with the acquisition of rations and precious gasoline. That
was only the second occasion (the first was at Büllingen) when the Germans captured appreciable amounts of fuel. Aware that an undetermined
number of Americans were in La Roche, General Krüger saw no need to
fight for that town when little seemed to stand in the way of continuing to
the Ourthe at Hotton. Once he had a crossing of the river there, he could
proceed southwest to Marche, gaining excellent roads emanating from
that town toward the Meuse, and any Americans left in La Roche would
be cut off. He told General von Waldenburg to send a task force composed of four Panthers and a company of *Panzergrenadiers* marching
through the night to grab the bridge at Hotton.

At Hotton, the valley of the Ourthe is wide. The village was on generally flat ground with most of the buildings on the south bank, but a few
houses, the schoolhouse, and the little Hôtel de la Paix stood on the
north bank. Most of the 120 or so support troops of the 3d Armored
Division that were there—clerks, signalmen, mechanics, medics—were
billeted in the schoolhouse. At a sturdy two-way bridge erected by U.S.
Army Engineers to replace a permanent span demolished by retreating
Germans in September, a platoon of the 51st Engineer Combat Battalion
was on guard. There were two tanks in the village, a light and a medium,
both stragglers awaiting minor repairs.

At 7:30 A.M. on December 21, the men were eating breakfast when
mortar shells began falling in the schoolyard. Minutes later, two Panthers
appeared on a trail leading from a finger of wooded high ground overlooking the village and rolled toward the bridge over the Ourthe. Moving
out to meet them, the lone Sherman got in the first shot but in vain, and
return fire from the leading Panther knocked it out.

A rocket from a bazooka fired by Sgt. Vern Sergent and Pvt. Hugh
Lander hit the Panther near its gasoline tank and ignited spilled gasoline.
Thinking the tank doomed, the crew jumped out and ran, but the fire
quickly dissipated. Although the second Panther knocked out the light
tank, a rocket from another bazooka manned by Cpl. Phillip Popp and
Pfc. Carl Nelson hit the turret, and again the crew bailed out and ran.

The loss of the two tanks discouraged further German attack for the
moment, but the *Panzergrenadiers* began digging in on the high ground,
which commanded not only the village but also the highway leading from
Soy, the location of General Rose's small reserve. That highway followed

the forward slopes of a narrow ridgeline, the last before the ground dropped away to the wide valley of the Ourthe and beyond it, the broad plateau of the Condroz. To German tankers so long confined amid the woods and gorges of the eastern Ardennes, the view of the open ground—tank country—was tantalizing.

After radioing division headquarters for help, the senior officer in Hotton, Maj. Jack W. Fickessen, organized a defense. At Rose's order, the commander of the 36th Armored Infantry Regiment, Col. Robert L. Howze, Jr., doubling in brass as commander of the reserve, tried to send tanks and infantry down the road from Soy, but the Germans commanded the road. Only after nightfall was Howze able to send two platoons of tanks and a company of armored infantry along back roads to Hotton.

The Germans before Hotton were awaiting reinforcements, which General von Waldenburg was doing his best to send; yet instead of the weak opposition General Krüger had anticipated, the Germans had to contend with Task Force Orr at Dochamps. That interfered with the movement of German reinforcements, and not until near nightfall was the German armor, with the help of a battalion of the 560th Volksgrenadier Division, able to force Colonel Orr to abandon Dochamps and pull back to the hamlet of Amonines, only three miles short of Colonel Howze's reserve position in Soy.

Samuel Mason Hogan was a small-town Texan who grew up hunting, fishing, and riding horses. After two years at a local junior college, he obtained an appointment to West Point and finished with the class of 1938. Whatever vehicle Hogan rode in flew the Lone Star flag of Texas.

Daylight was beginning to break on December 21 when Sam Hogan downed a quick cup of coffee and with his driver and orderly set out, as ordered the night before, to check in at his division's headquarters. Hogan's operations officer, Maj. Travis M. Brown, and the leader of his reconnaissance platoon, 1st Lt. Clark V. Worrell, were to come along in another jeep and lead the way.

After traveling four miles, Travis and Worrell spotted a group of soldiers in the road ahead, gathered around a jeep and two half-tracks and eating K-rations. Two of the soldiers were wearing American overcoats, but as the officers drew closer, they made out in the growing light that the others were unquestionably Germans. The driver brought the jeep to a halt little more than ten yards from them. As Hogan and his jeep closed up, Worrell whispered as loud as he dared: "They're Germans, Colonel!"

Jumping from their jeeps, Hogan and the others began to run, which sent the Germans scurrying for their weapons. Hogan was sure he would be hit, for he was wearing fleece-lined British flying boots and they were made neither for walking nor running. He nevertheless reached a clump of bushes moments after the others—only the driver of Brown and Worrell's jeep was missing—and after catching their breath, they continued running. They escaped, Hogan believed, because the booty in the jeeps diverted the Germans: cigarettes, K-rations, and two good old Texas fruitcakes Hogan had received for Christmas.

On the theory that they were closer to Hotton than to their starting point in La Roche, Hogan headed for Hotton, but at every turn they ran into more Germans. In escaping from one group, Brown and Worrell became separated from Hogan, his driver, and his orderly.

After all three spent the night huddled in the woods under Hogan's trench coat, Hogan decided he might make better progress returning to La Roche. In a hamlet, civilians told him there was an American force in the next village of Marcouray. It was Task Force Hogan.

In Marcouray, Hogan learned from his executive officer, Maj. W. Stewart Walker, that a medical sergeant going back for supplies had come upon the driver of Brown and Worrell's jeep, and from him Walker learned something of what had happened to Hogan. When he radioed that information to division headquarters, he received orders to bring the task force out. Walker had gotten as far as Marcouray, on the upper reaches of a slope overlooking the Ourthe, when at dusk a *Panzerfaust* knocked out the lead tank. Walker had holed up in the village for the night.

Although the orders were still to break out, patrols soon determined that a sizable German force blocked the way. Since Marcouray had some forty solidly built stone houses and good fields of fire in all directions, Hogan decided to hold in the hope that somebody could break through to him.

Afforded a battalion from the 517th Parachute Infantry—a separate regiment that had been resting in northern France when the German offensive opened—Colonel Howze early on December 22 again tried to break through from Soy to Hotton. Yet again the attempt got nowhere, for the Germans still held the high ground overlooking the highway. The defense of Hotton would be left to the little band of original defenders and the tanks and armored infantrymen that had gained the village during the night.

It was late afternoon of the 22d before the Germans attacked once more at Hotton, to meet, as a German commander noted, "a hailstorm of fire." *Panzergrenadiers* got into some of the houses, splitting the defenders, but fire from the two platoons of Shermans and the threat of bazookas kept the German tanks at a distance. Night had fallen and a crisis was approaching when the German firing inexplicably died down, and with incredulity the Americans became aware that their foe was falling back. They could only wonder why.

As the result of the resistance at Hotton, an apparently strong American presence in Soy, armor at Amonines, and armor again (albeit surrounded) at Marcouray, General Krüger had come to the conclusion that he faced a powerful American force and would be unable to get across the Ourthe at Hotton without a hard fight and a long delay. Krüger had learned that the Americans had abandoned La Roche and also that the 2d Panzer Division of the 47th Panzer Corps had gained a crossing of the west branch of the Ourthe, and there was something to be said for advancing close alongside another panzer division.

Once again Krüger, master of the countermarch, ordered General von Waldenburg to backtrack. While the 560th Volksgrenadier Division continued to seek a crossing of the river at Hotton, the panzer division was to cross at La Roche and continue the thrust to the Meuse.

Although General Rose had far less strength than his adversary imagined, he did enjoy a brief hope of sizable reinforcement when the army commander, General Hodges, released CCA from its back-up position near Eupen. By daylight of the 22d, most of the combat command had arrived, but orders soon followed to send the bulk of CCA to form a screen along the west branch of the Ourthe to protect the assembly of the 84th Infantry Division at Marche, a part of the counterattacking force to operate under General Collins's VII Corps. All that was left as reinforcement for General Rose was a company of armored infantry and a battalion of medium tanks.

With the departure of the 116th Panzer Division, Rose's position improved. Nevertheless, as he and his men soon found out, the 560th Volksgrenadiers still had a lot of fight in them. So, too, the sharply compartmented, hilly, heavily wooded countryside with few roads better than farm tracks favored infantry far more than it did armor, and Rose was particularly short of infantry. There was also a real possibility that the Germans might break through along Rose's north flank, for there, at the crossroads known as Baraque de Fraiture, a crisis was developing.

To the men involved, it seemed light-years ago. In reality it had been only a few days since the executive officer of the 598th Field Artillery Battalion, Maj. Arthur C. Parker III, had brought three of his battalion's 105mm. howitzers out of their positions beyond the Our River in the shadow of the Schnee Eifel and through Schoenberg and St. Vith. Two days later, on December 19, the commander of the 7th Armored Division, General Hasbrouck, had arranged with the commander of the 106th Division's artillery to send Parker and his howitzers back along the supply route leading to La Roche to help keep that route open at Baraque de Fraiture.

An X-shaped crossroads, Baraque de Fraiture stands on high, windswept ground where the snow was soon to be deep. At an elevation of just over 2,200 feet, it is the second highest point in the Ardennes, and much of the countryside nearby is wooded and marshy, much like that on the Hautes Fagnes. There was no village, only three farmhouses with their outbuildings; the village from which the crossroads took its name was a thousand yards to the northeast. The roads crossing at Baraque de Fraiture were the generally east-west Salmchâteau–La Roche highway and the major north-south route—Highway N-15—linking Bastogne, Houffalize, and Liège. Although the ground close about the crossroads was cleared, thick fir forests closed in on all sides.

To the American commanders, who still saw Liège as a primary German objective, Baraque de Fraiture and Highway N-15 were obviously of critical importance. Although the crossroads was the objective assigned by General Rose to his Task Force Orr, the task force had failed to get past Samrée.

Highway N-15—and Baraque de Fraiture—was roughly in the center of what turned out to be the sector of the XVIII Airborne Corps, which extended for some thirty miles from Trois Ponts to Hotton. To the east of the highway, the 82d Airborne Division had to defend the line of the Salm River, a long stretch of the Salmchâteau–La Roche highway, and, so long as *Kampfgruppe Peiper* remained a threat, much of the south bank of the Amblève River as well. Thus General Gavin had nothing left with which to block Highway N-15. Once the small available portion of the 3d Armored Division got involved between the Ourthe and the little Aisne River, neither did General Rose, even though according to the interdivisional boundary the highway was Rose's responsibility. Thus, at first, Major Parker's three artillery pieces and their crews, plus a few men of the 589th Field Artillery Battalion's Service Battery, who had also escaped from the shadow of the Schnee Eifel, were all that stood in the way of German advance past Baraque de Fraiture. A total of 110 men.

The next morning, December 20, a detachment from an antiaircraft battalion with three half-tracks mounting quad-50s and a self-propelled 37mm. gun joined Parker. When at noon an order arrived from the 106th Division for the three artillery pieces to be moved well to the rear where the 598th Field Artillery Battalion was to be reconstituted, Major Parker recognized that if he left, the little band of antiaircraft troops would have no hope of holding the vital crossroads. He ignored the order.

As an indirect result of the Sixth Panzer Army's failure to get across the Elsenborn Ridge, a threat to the crossroads was soon building. In keeping with Field Marshal Model's order of December 20, the Sixth Panzer Army's uncommitted 2d SS Panzer Corps under General der Waffen-SS Willi Bittrich began to move forward in pursuit of the new mission of protecting the north flank of the Fifth Panzer Army, which at that point was making the main effort.

One of the two divisions under Bittrich's command, the 9th SS Panzer Division, began the difficult task of negotiating the jammed roads through the Losheim Gap and crossing the Salm River, while the other, the 2d SS Panzer Division, circled behind St. Vith and entered the gap through which General Krüger's 58th Panzer Corps had begun to pass early on December 19. (The 2d SS Panzer Division and its commander, Generalleutnant Heinz Lammerding, were infamous for one of the war's worst atrocities. In June, the troops had destroyed the French village of Oradour-sur-Glâne and murdered 642 of the inhabitants, including women and children.)

When the 2d SS Panzer Division reached the gap southwest of St. Vith, it was out of gasoline. Only during the night of December 21 did enough fuel arrive to enable Major Krag's reconnaissance battalion to try to open the Salmchâteau–La Roche highway for the division's advance; but Krag had achieved nothing and had eventually turned on Salmchâteau. Not until the morning of the 22d did enough gasoline arrive to move a *Panzergrenadier* regiment, some tanks, and an artillery battalion, and even then, to stretch available fuel, each vehicle towed at least one other and in most cases two. Because outposts of the 82d Airborne Division still denied the Salmchâteau–La Roche highway, those troops had to trudge through the day's heavy snowfall over back roads to reach Highway N-15 at Houffalize and there turn north to Baraque de Fraiture.

By that time, the night of December 22, the little American force at the crossroads had received some reinforcement. Sent to guard the 7th Armored Division's supply route at Samrée, a troop of the 87th Armored Reconnaissance Squadron had found the enemy there and joined Parker's force, and the 3d Armored Division's Task Force Kane sent two self-propelled 105mm. assault guns.

Parker himself was no longer around. Late on December 21, a fragment from a mortar shell wounded him seriously; he refused evacuation, but when he lost consciousness, that was no longer his to say. Another officer of the 589th Field Artillery Battalion, Maj. Elliott Goldstein, took over. To Goldstein it was fairly obvious that the crossroads was soon to come under attack by the 2d SS Panzer Division, for the men repulsed a reconnaissance patrol from that division and captured the leader of the patrol.

The commander of the 82d Airborne Division, General Gavin, was in the meantime growing increasingly concerned about Highway N-15. If the Germans drove up the highway, they might either trap the airborne division in the angle formed by the Amblève and Salm Rivers or at least force the division's withdrawal, in either case preventing Gavin from accomplishing his mission of covering the exodus of American troops from the St. Vith salient. During the afternoon of December 21, in company with the commander of the regiment closest to the highway, Col. Charles Billingslea of the 325th Glider Infantry, Gavin went to see the 3d Armored Division's General Rose. He found him on the second floor of a house at the crossroads behind Baraque de Fraiture at Manhay.

Since the highway was Rose's responsibility, Gavin asked what Rose had available for blocking it. Not much, responded Rose. He had had to send Task Force Kane, which had earlier been at Manhay, to help Task Force Orr near Dochamps; his CCB was still fighting Peiper; and although CCA was at last on the way, he had the impression he was going to have to send the bulk of that combat command to the other side of the Ourthe River to screen the assembly of the 84th Division. He would nevertheless try to hold part of CCA at Manhay.

Little encouraged by that visit, Colonel Billingslea moved a platoon into the hamlet of Regné, astride the Salmchâteau–La Roche highway, which extended his line to within two miles of Baraque de Fraiture. Yet he was still unhappy and asked Gavin to release his 2d Battalion, which Gavin had withheld as a division reserve. When Gavin agreed, Billingslea sent a company to Baraque de Fraiture and the rest of the battalion to high ground overlooking the crossroads at the village of Fraiture itself. Both forces moved into position during the heavy snowfall of December 22.

That night, men and tanks of the 2d SS Panzer Division moved into attack positions in front of both the crossroads and the village. Just before daylight on the 23d, seventy-five *SS-Panzergrenadiers* hit the 2d Battalion, 325th Glider Infantry, at the village, coming close to carrying the position when they caught most of the glider infantrymen out of their foxholes eating breakfast in the houses. A counterattack led by the battalion commander, Maj. Richard M. Gibson, restored the situation.

All morning the Germans kept up a drumbeat of mortar and artillery fire against Baraque de Fraiture. In quest of help, Major Goldstein, taking with him a captured German captain and sergeant as proof that he faced attack by the SS, went by jeep to the crossroads at Manhay. There he found a newly arrived task force of the 3d Armored Division's CCA under Lt. Col. Walter B. Richardson, the only part of CCA remaining for General Rose's use. Richardson agreed to send a platoon each of armored infantry and medium tanks to help and added a company of paratroopers from a separate parachute infantry battalion, the 509th, the U.S. Army's oldest, whose men had fought in one place or another since North Africa, and, like the 517th Parachute Infantry, had been moved forward from a rest area in northern France.

Shortly after midday, as the tanks and infantry started down the highway toward Baraque de Fraiture, they ran into a roadblock the Germans had established behind the crossroads. While the platoon of armored infantrymen and company of paratroopers dismounted to take out the roadblock, the commanders of the five tanks buttoned their hatches and kept going. They reached Baraque de Fraiture around 1 P.M.

Dusk was approaching when at four o'clock German mortars and artillery began a heavy shelling. For twenty minutes the guns pounded, then as the fire lifted onto the highway behind the crossroads, eight Mark IVs accompanied by what looked to the defenders to be hordes of *SS-Panzergrenadiers* attacked up the road from the south, while other *SS-Panzergrenadiers* accompanied by half-tracks attacked along the road from the west, the direction of Samrée.

Except for one tank, which found cover behind a masonry wall, the Shermans were in the open on flat ground, fully exposed to enemy fire. Pausing at the woodsline, the Mark IVs quickly knocked out two of them; but the Shermans also got two Mark IVs and one of the 598th Field Artillery Battalion's howitzers accounted for two more.

Because the Mark IVs had yet to close in, the defenders were holding their own against the *SS-Panzergrenadiers* when two Panthers appeared along the road from the east, the direction of Salmchâteau. Fire from the Panthers quickly knocked out two more of the Shermans. The one taking cover behind the wall would drive into the open, fire a shot at the Panthers, then return to its cover. Yet for all the effect the rounds had on the heavy frontal armor, it was "like throwing peas at a plate glass window." Once again the Sherman emerged from its hiding place to get in another shot, but that was one time too many. A round from one of the Panthers blew it apart.

It was fully dark and *SS-Panzergrenadiers* were swarming over the crossroads when the commander of Company F, 325th Glider Infantry, Capt. Junior R. Woodruff, radioed his battalion commander, Major Gibson, that the defense of the crossroads was falling to pieces and asked permission to withdraw. When the request reached Colonel Billingslea, he refused in the hope of getting other reinforcements from the 3d Armored Division. Moments later, Woodruff radioed again: German tanks were grinding down the foxholes. That time Billingslea said, OK, get out.

As the Germans engulfed the crossroads, small bands of men tried to make stands in barns and farmhouses. In one farmhouse, Major Goldstein's operations officer, Capt. George Huxel, although wounded, tried to hold with a few men; but when the attached barn collapsed, Huxel saw no choice but to run for it. As three cows dashed bellowing from the barn, Huxel and those with him took advantage of the confusion to escape.

Men in another house holed up in the cellar until the building caught fire and forced them out, hands overhead. German shells and small-arms fire cut down others as they tried to gain the woods.

All three of the 589th Field Artillery Battalion's howitzers were lost, as were the two assault guns of Task Force Kane, the antiaircraft half-tracks, and all the vehicles of the troop of the 87th Armored Cavalry Squadron. The total of men who died or were captured would never be known, but of the 116 glider infantrymen of Captain Woodruff's company F, only 45 got away. In tribute to the officer who first established a defense at Baraque de Fraiture, the men who survived the fight renamed it Parker's Crossroads.

With news of the collapse at Baraque de Fraiture, General Gavin risked pulling out one of the battalions of the 504th Parachute Infantry that was watching *Kampfgruppe Peiper* and sent it to regain the crossroads. Yet on second thought Gavin decided that a counterattack by a single battalion would be an exercise in futility. (Said Major Gibson: "I wouldn't attack that damned place with a regiment, not to mention a battalion.") It would be wiser, Gavin decided, to use the parachute infantry to help Major Gibson protect the division's ruptured flank.

Gavin had nothing left with which to try to block the critical highway behind Baraque de Fraiture, and General Rose had little more. Rose did order Colonel Richardson at Manhay to send a platoon each of armored infantry and medium tanks under Richardson's executive officer, Maj. Olin F. Brewster, to join the armored infantry and company of paratroopers that had earlier tried to get through. That force dug in astride the highway inside the forest, roughly midway between Manhay and Baraque de Fraiture, at a spot that on the maps had a name, Belle Haie.

Although General Ridgway had been pressing General Hodges for release of the 3d Armored Division's CCB from the fight against *Kampfgruppe Peiper*, he had yet to succeed. That meant that the only uncommitted troops left to him were those that had begun withdrawing early that morning from the salient near St. Vith. Those men were disorganized, scattered about in various villages, and obviously in need of rest. Although reluctant to call on them, Ridgway considered that he had no choice.

General Hoge's CCB of the 9th Armored Division had been the first unit to get out of the salient as an integral force. Early in the afternoon of December 23, even before the Germans hit Baraque de Fraiture, Ridgway ordered Hoge to back up the 82d Airborne Division's western flank. To cover the assembly of the combat command, Hoge sent a company of tanks to Manhay and the 27th Armored Infantry Battalion to Malempré, a village two miles southeast of Manhay, which was off Highway N-15 but on ground that looked down onto the highway.

Ridgway and the other American commanders fully expected the 2d SS Panzer Division to exploit its success at Baraque de Fraiture by continuing without pause up Highway N-15 to Liège. That city was indeed the formal objective of Bittrich's 2d SS Panzer Corps, for under the changed mission whereby the Sixth Panzer Army was to protect the Fifth Panzer Army's northern flank, that might be best accomplished by pushing the Americans back across the Meuse at and around Liège. In fact Field Marshal Model saw that as beyond the capabilities of the Sixth Panzer Army at the moment. He indicated instead that he would be happy establishing a line along the Amblève River and on high ground north of Manhay, thereby uncovering the Trois Ponts–Hotton highway. Then the 2d SS Panzer Division was to veer northwest to get across the Ourthe River and onto the Condroz plateau, there to provide the Fifth Panzer Army with flank protection for the continuing drive to the Meuse.

Yet even to gain that line was for the moment beyond the means of the Sixth Panzer Army, for only on December 23 with the American withdrawal from the St. Vith salient had the road network there become available. It would take time to reposition divisions to assist the 2d SS Panzer Division. Indeed, not until the next day, December 24, was Hitler to agree to end the futile battering against the Elsenborn Ridge; and shortages of gasoline, aggravated by the break in the weather that turned loose Allied fighter-bombers, complicated the task of shifting units.

Kampfgruppe Peiper by that time was reduced to a shell, its commander intent only on getting his men out of their trap on foot; and the rest of the 1st SS Panzer Division had been so punished that the division was capable for the moment of nothing more than holding a defensive sector facing Stavelot and Trois Ponts. The other armor of the 1st SS Panzer Corps—the 12th SS Panzer Division—had also lost heavily and would need several days to re-form into any kind of an effective fighting force. Freed by the American withdrawal from the St. Vith salient, the two *Volksgrenadier* divisions of General Lucht's 66th Corps were to defend along the lower reaches of the Salm River, between Vielsalm and Trois Ponts, thereby enabling the 9th SS Panzer Division, which had made no headway in crossing the river, to shift upstream and cross in the vicinity of Vielsalm and Salmchâteau.

The 2d SS Panzer Division thus might anticipate help soon from that division operating on its right flank; more immediate help was meanwhile to come at Field Marshal Model's order from Colonel Remer's *Führer Begleit Brigade*. Remer was to follow the trace of the 2d SS Panzer Division and attack close along the division's right flank near Baraque de Fraiture.

Even had the division commander, General Lammerding, not wanted to await that brigade's arrival, he had other reasons for delaying an attack up Highway N-15 beyond Baraque de Fraiture, not the least of which were the mounting swarms of P-38 Lightnings and P-51 Mustangs that seemingly pounced upon anything moving in the open by daylight. (General Dietrich complained that the pilots showed no respect for general officers.) Because of the dense forest on both sides of N-15, an attack directly up the highway would be restricted, as far as tanks were concerned, to twenty-two feet of macadam, and Lammerding wanted no part of that. He intended instead to move through villages off either side of the highway, then converge on Manhay at a point close to the crossroads where the woods ran out.

To prepare the way for his maneuver, *SS-Panzergrenadiers* during the night of the 23d infiltrated through the woods and attacked the village of

Odeigne, just west of the highway and roughly parallel with Major Brewster's position at Belle Haie. In the darkness, the Germans quickly routed a platoon of light tanks protected by only a squad of riflemen. Yet Lammerding would be unable to exploit that gain until his engineers could improve a dirt track leading to the village to enable his tanks to get forward. Not until near nightfall on Christmas Eve—December 24—were the engineers to complete that task.

For the American command, it became increasingly unfortunate that Highway N-15 represented the approximate boundary between the 82d Airborne and 3d Armored Divisions. Although General Ridgway had tried to ease the problem by assigning responsibility for the highway to one division, the 3d Armored, his superior, General Hodges, in late afternoon of the 23d, introduced a complication. Because the bulk of the 3d Armored Division was screening the assembly of General Collins's VII Corps and was eventually supposed to form a part of Collins's counterattacking force, Hodges transferred the division to Collins's command. Highway N-15 lay close at that point not only to an interdivisional but to an inter-corps boundary; but responsibility for the highway remained with Ridgway's XVIII Airborne Corps, which meant that it was no longer a responsibility of the 3d Armored Division, which was no longer a part of that corps. Since the highway was also the approximate boundary between two German corps—Bittrich's 2d SS Panzer and Krüger's 58th Panzer—Field Marshal Model solved the problem by placing the 2d SS Panzer Division under Krüger's command. As events were soon to demonstrate, Hodges would have been well advised to adopt a similar solution.

Even though Major Brewster's little task force at Belle Haie belonged to the 3d Armored Division, nobody moved immediately to order Brewster to withdraw. Indeed, a second company of the 509th Parachute Infantry Battalion reinforced Brewster, but the task of finding a force capable of prolonged defense in front of Manhay remained Ridgway's. Ridgway turned to the commander of the 7th Armored Division, General Hasbrouck, just back from the St. Vith salient. Hasbrouck in turn called on Colonel Rosebaum and CCA, which had emerged from the salient in considerably better shape than had General Clarke's CCB.

As a defensive position, the village of Manhay suffered from the fact that it was dominated by high ground to the south in the direction of Baraque de Fraiture. Thus Colonel Rosebaum prepared to push his defenses out beyond the crossroads to block the road linking Odeigne to Highway N-15, to cut the main highway itself, and to relieve armored infantry of Hoge's CCB, 9th Armored Division, at Malempré. That done, Hoge's CCB was to become General Ridgway's reserve, and Major Brewster's task force at Belle Haie was to withdraw.

Late on the morning of December 24, as Rosebaum's troops moved to their positions, a contingent of tanks and infantry from the *Führer Begleit Brigade* attacked Regné, the hamlet on the Salmchâteau–La Roche highway only two miles from Baraque de Fraiture. The lone platoon of glider infantrymen in the hamlet was no match for the German tanks. General Gavin was considerably concerned about losing the village, for from it led a road into the valley of the little Lienne Creek to both Gavin's and Ridgway's command posts. Afforded a company of medium tanks from Hoge's CCB, Gavin in early afternoon used parachute infantry riding on the tanks to retake Regné.

Much to the delight of the commander of the *Führer Begleit Brigade*, Colonel Remer, who still nursed the ambition of garnering glory by driving to the Meuse, Field Marshal Model ordered his brigade to disengage. He needed it more, Model had decided, to help the Fifth Panzer Army reach the river.

Not long after that, the 82d Airborne Division also relinquished Regné. Gavin's division was getting ready to withdraw.

Hardly had the 82d Airborne Division moved up to the Salm River and the Salmchâteau–La Roche highway than the officer known for his dislike of withdrawals, General Ridgway, told Gavin to reconnoiter for a defensive line to his rear that might be occupied once the troops had pulled back from the St. Vith salient. Like Ridgway, Gavin also disliked withdrawals and protested. Ridgway nevertheless insisted, pointing out that the Germans might threaten the 82d Airborne Division's western flank (which was in fact what had happened). The line Gavin chose ran generally along the highway linking Trois Ponts and Manhay.

Early on December 24, Ridgway issued a warning order to Gavin to prepare for possible withdrawal to that line. Despite Gavin's concern for his western flank, the possibility of withdrawing still disturbed him. He prided himself on the fact that his division had never relinquished any ground it had gained. More important, the spectacle of tired and in some cases dispirited troops from the St. Vith salient passing through the airborne division's positions was fresh in Gavin's mind. To withdraw so soon after his men had gone through that experience, and while belief was widespread that the Germans were using American vehicles and men in American uniforms, might lead to panic.

As it turned out, Gavin would be unable even to argue his case, for in mid-morning of December 24, General Ridgway had a visitor at his farmhouse headquarters in Werbomont who insisted on withdrawal: Field Marshal Montgomery. Arriving in an open car without escort, Montgomery jauntily acknowledged the salutes of the guards and went inside. It was essential, he told Ridgway, that the First Army build a solid northern flank by shortening the line in preparation for counterattack by General Collins's VII Corps. The new line was to be a southwestward extension of the solid positions already established on the Elsenborn Ridge and at Malmédy and Stavelot.

As worked out with Ridgway, the line was to extend from Trois Ponts along the road leading to Manhay, the line that General Gavin had previously reconnoitered; but at Manhay, Colonel Rosebaum's CCA, 7th Armored Division, was to leave only an outpost at the crossroads and occupy high ground behind it. To the west of Manhay, the 3d Armored Division was to continue to defend generally along the Trois Ponts–Manhay–Hotton highway.

The choice of the night of December 24 for the withdrawal and reshuffling of the line—the same night that *Kampfgruppe Peiper* was withdrawing from La Gleize—proved to be unfortunate, for it coincided with a renewed attack by the 2d SS Panzer Division. Task Force Brewster and the 7th Armored Division's CCA were destined to pay the consequences.

Not until well after dark, around 6 P.M., did Colonel Rosebaum receive the order to withdraw. His men were still making their preparations when at 9 P.M., in bright moonlight glistening on a frozen snow cover, *SS-Panzergrenadiers* supported by tanks began moving from Odeigne toward Highway N-15 and Manhay.

The Americans standing in the way astride the little road from Odeigne consisted of under-strength companies of the 48th Armored Infantry Battalion and the 40th Tank Battalion, the latter with only seven medium tanks. Tankers and infantrymen were both on the alert, but as a column of tanks approached, quite clearly the first was a Sherman. It had the silhouette, the characteristic engine noise, and an unmistakable blue exhaust.

They all knew that contingents of the 3d Armored Division were in the vicinity, and nobody wanted to be guilty of firing on a friendly column. A call to the rear failed to clarify anything, for in the confusion resulting from the shifts in boundaries and from the fact that the units that had withdrawn from the St. Vith salient had yet to establish viable communications, there was no communication between the two American armored divisions.

Before anybody could discern that it was no friendly column but Mark IVs and Panthers that were approaching, *SS-Panzergrenadiers* opened fire with *Panzerfausts*. They knocked out four tanks with the first rockets and crippled two more. After six days in the embattled salient near St. Vith, the American crews had had all they could take. The crippled tanks and the one that had escaped damage took off. They fled toward Manhay, leaving the armored infantrymen to plead for authority to fall back. Denied that, they broke in disorder.

In the attacking force, SS-Sgt. Ernst Barkmann of the 4th Panzer Company commanded a Panther, Panzer 401. In the confusion, Barkmann and his tank became separated from the others and soon emerged alone on Highway N-15. Thinking the rest had gone ahead of him, Barkmann continued along the highway until he reached a small clearing. Fifty paces ahead he saw a tank, its commander's upper body visible in the turret. That was his platoon leader SS-Sgt. Maj. Franz Frauscher, thought Barkmann, but as Barkmann's tank drew abreast and Barkmann started to speak, the man in the turret disappeared and slammed the hatch shut. For the first time Barkmann noticed that the tank had not the green panel lights of a panzer but dark red lights. It was a Sherman.

Over the intercom, Barkmann shouted for the gunner to fire, but as the turret swung in the direction of the American tank, the barrel of the cannon slammed against the Sherman's turret. Discerning immediately what was wrong, Barkmann's driver needed no orders to back up. That freed the panzer's traverse and at a distance of precisely one yard, Barkmann's gunner slammed a round into the rear of the Sherman.

Still convinced that SS-Sergeant Major Frauscher and the other tanks were ahead, Barkmann continued along the highway. Rounding a sharp curve, he came again to a clearing. Then he gasped. Ahead of him he counted nine American tanks partially dug in. To stop or to turn back would be suicide. "Keep driving," Barkmann ordered the driver. "Full speed." As they passed the American position, nine turrets turned as if in unison, but nobody fired.

Once past those tanks, Barkmann halted and tried to raise his company on the radio but without success. Quite obviously, he was ahead of Frauscher and the rest of his platoon; but if he tried to withdraw, he would have to pass the dug-in American tanks again. *Wenn schon, denn schon!* (What the hell!) Barkmann decided to keep going.

As the forest again enveloped each side of the highway, he saw American infantrymen falling back along both sides of the road. Swearing as only foot soldiers can swear at men who ride, they made way for the tank, obviously unaware in the darkness that it was German.

Then came a broad clearing and Panzer 401 was inside Manhay. American tanks and other vehicles were parked alongside the buildings. At a café, such was the activity that Barkmann was convinced it was a command post, but nobody paid his tank any heed other than to get out of the way.

Reaching the crossroads in the center of the village, Barkmann wanted to turn left, toward the west, which he knew to be the direction the attack was to take from Manhay, but down that road three Shermans were approaching. Barely pausing, he told his driver to continue straight up the highway in the direction of Liège.

Moments later, Panzer 401 was passing one American tank after another, all pulled over to one side of the road, their crews standing outside, talking and smoking. Again there was no choice but to keep moving. And again American soldiers leaped aside to allow the tank to pass, but that time some of them recognized it for what it was. Jumping into their own tanks, the crews swung their turrets; but being in column, one tank masked the fire of another, and Barkmann dropped a smoke grenade onto the highway to cloud their vision further.

Up ahead a jeep approached, somebody standing in it and shouting over and over to halt. When the driver at last realized he was approaching a German tank, he screeched to a halt and tried to back up. "Roll over it!" ordered Barkmann.

The impact of crushing the jeep threw Barkmann's tank against a Sherman parked alongside the road, and the treads of the two behemoths interlocked. Panzer 401's motor choked and stopped. Small-arms fire erupted, forcing Barkmann to close his hatch. Unless the driver could restart the motor quickly, some American gun was sure to do the tank in. Again and again the driver tried, and Barkmann was beginning to despair when at last the motor caught.

Back up! Barkmann commanded. With little difficulty, the Panzer broke free and again headed up the highway.

However brief the delay, it provided time for the Shermans to organize a pursuit. Although Barkmann dropped another smoke grenade onto the road, the pursuing Shermans came on. Swinging the turret all the way around to the rear, the gunner fired, hitting the first American tank and setting it on fire, which blocked the highway.

A few hundred yards down the road, Barkmann saw a trail and ordered the driver to pull onto it. There the crew found a sheltered position affording a view of the highway, and Barkmann permitted his men to dismount for a breath of air.

Back at the sharp curve in the highway overlooking Manhay where Barkmann and his Panther had passed dug-in American tanks, an experience similar to that at Odeigne occurred. There the American commanders and men of another under-strength rifle company supported by ten tanks also hesitated to fire on what looked to be an American column, for again a Sherman was in the lead with its characteristic silhouette and blue exhaust. The delay proved fatal. As on the Prümerberg outside St. Vith, the German tanks fired high-velocity flares, blinding the American crews. They knocked out most of the tanks. All the crews fled, and when *SS-Panzergrenadiers* closed in, so did the armored infantrymen.

Beyond the highway, in the village of Malempré, men of another task force of armored infantrymen and tanks could see the fight along the highway taking place. Their orders were to withdraw to the new positions behind Manhay at 11 P.M. and to do so even should communications fail. Since it was almost that hour, the infantry and tank commanders, unable to reach their battalion commanders by radio, moved the timetable up by fifteen minutes. Close behind them, a column of *SS-Panzergrenadiers* occupied Malempré.

In Manhay, there was no real contest. An American platoon leader got two tanks into position for a brief stand at the crossroads, knocking out two German tanks, but in what became a general hegira, they failed to stand for long.

Every commander who has ever executed a planned withdrawal has worried lest his enemy should strike while the withdrawal was in process. That was what happened at Manhay, and it happened along a unit boundary where responsibilities were ill-defined, to exhausted, battle-weary men who had yet to get a good night's sleep after six days in the line in the St. Vith salient. Predictably, a rout ensued, possibly abetted by the knowledge of many men that at least one German tank had already penetrated the village.

From their hiding place north of Manhay, SS-Sergeant Barkmann and his crew could discern that German tanks were firing inside Manhay. It was "like music to their ears." As the noise of battle at last faded in the darkness, Panzer 401 inched back onto the highway and returned past burning American vehicles to the village.

The debacle at Manhay left a small American force standing alone astride Highway N-15 at Belle Haie: Major Brewster's task force, composed of seven tanks and a platoon of armored infantry of the 3d Armored Division and two companies of the 509th Parachute Infantry Battalion. The German advance on Manhay had cut off the force from the rear, and *SS-Panzergrenadiers* were thick and close in the woods.

Early in the evening when Brewster's superior, Colonel Richardson, had learned that the 7th Armored Division was to withdraw to a new line behind Manhay, he himself had received no orders to pull back. Thus he radioed Major Brewster to stand fast. Even when Brewster reported that German tanks had cut the road behind him, Richardson still ordered him to hold. "Don't give an inch unless I approve it," said Richardson.

In less than an hour Manhay was a scene of confusion and panic, and Richardson realized that it was pointless for Brewster to continue to hold at Belle Haie. By radio he told him to get out fast. If it was necessary, to save his men, he was to destroy his remaining vehicles, including the tanks.

Although Brewster tried to move down the highway to gain a secondary road leading to Malempré, German tanks knocked out a tank at each end of his column, making it impossible for the remaining vehicles to move either backward or forward off the constricted road. Brewster ordered all vehicles to be damaged and left behind: a half-track, a 6 × 6 truck, a jeep, and five Shermans. Moving on foot through the woods, Brewster and his men reached positions of the 82d Airborne Division beyond Malempré not long before daylight.

When Brewster later in the day reported to his division commander, General Rose, he was startled to find Rose antagonistic. "Why did you destroy government equipment?" demanded Rose. Brewster replied that he had authority from his commander, Colonel Richardson, and that he had thought it better to save his men rather than lose everybody trying to salvage a few vehicles. "Major," said Rose, "I call that misbehavior."

A strict disciplinarian, Rose ordered court-martial charges prepared against Brewster for cowardice before the enemy. Neither Colonel Richardson nor the commander of CCA, Brig. Gen. Doyle A. Hickey, would endorse them, and nothing had come of the charges when three months later, beyond the Rhine River, General Rose died in battle.

That Christmas Eve yet another surrounded American force was seeking a way out: the 3d Armored Division's Task Force Hogan, which since December 21 had been trapped near the Ourthe River in the village of Marcouray. The rest of the 3d Armored Division had been too hard-pressed to attempt a rescue, and an attempt at firing medical supplies in artillery shells had gone awry.

Close to noon on Christmas Eve, a German jeep approached under a white flag with a lieutenant who, when ushered before Colonel Hogan, demanded that he surrender. The American troops were surrounded by three panzer divisions, their situation hopeless. He was authorized, said the lieutenant, to take an officer on a tour of the German positions to verify the Americans' plight. Hogan responded that he had orders to fight to the death, and as a soldier, he would obey his orders.

That afternoon seven C-47 aircraft attempted to drop supplies, but German flak shot down all but one. Some of the airmen tried to parachute, but so low were the planes that Hogan and his men feared none would survive. Two pilots, nevertheless, entered Hogan's perimeter that night, their falls having been checked by the treetops.

Reconnaissance that same night revealed that there was no way out of Marcouray for vehicles other than the main road, and that was thick with German troops and vehicles. Hogan radioed the news to the rear. The next day, he and his men had just finished a Christmas dinner of K-rations when a message arrived from General Rose directing Hogan to destroy his heavy weapons and vehicles and get out on foot.

Through the afternoon, the men drained the oil from the tanks and other vehicles, put sugar in the gasoline, then ran the motors a few at a time until they froze. Just before leaving, the crews of the tanks and artillery pieces were to drop their breech blocks into a well. The surgeon, Capt. Louis Spigelmann, and several of his medics volunteered to stay with the wounded and the next day were to attempt (unsuccessfully, as it turned out) to pass through German lines under a white flag. Some of the less seriously wounded were to guard German prisoners until the Germans arrived. A detail buried the only one of Hogan's men killed at Marcouray and a German prisoner whom an impetuous lieutenant had shot in the back of the head before anybody could knock his weapon away.

After nightfall, faces blackened with burnt cork, steel helmets left behind to cut down on noise, a force that the American press had by that time come to call "Hogan's 400" started out. A reconnaissance platoon led the way, followed by the rest of the men in groups of twenty with an interval of thirty seconds between each.

Much to Colonel Hogan's regret, he was still wearing those fleece-lined British flying boots. Struggling uphill in the dark over rough terrain, it seemed to Hogan that he slid two steps backward for every step forward, and going downhill was like "a modified ski slide." His orderly and his driver helped, but so slow was Hogan's progress that in time the three ended up at the tail of the column. Daylight was about to break when Hogan felt he had no choice but to rest. Once again the three huddled together under Hogan's trench coat.

It was well after daylight when they resumed their march, eventually coming upon a company of infantry from a newly arrived unit of the 75th Infantry Division. By jeep they traveled to the 3d Armored Division's command post and there found that everybody else had arrived safely except for one man killed by a nervous sentry.

When General Rose saw Hogan, he wanted to know why he was the last man out. Hogan thought of several heroic answers he might give but decided finally to stick with the truth, even though for a stalwart, outdoors Texan, it was a difficult admission.

Said Hogan: "My feet hurt."

For the German drivers of the 2d SS Panzer Division's 2d SS Medical Company and their wounded, traveling in a convoy of sixteen ambulances, Christmas Eve was a nightmare. In fourteen regular and two high-capacity ambulances, with SS-Capt. Hans Winkler riding in the last vehicle, the convoy started off at 1 P.M. from the division's main field-dressing station near Houffalize. Because American fighter-bombers sometimes attacked individual ambulances, the medical company had grouped its ambulances in convoy on the theory that that would minimize the chance of pilots failing to spot the Red Cross markings. Their goal was a hospital a few miles inside Germany at Neuerburg.

The convoy had gone only a few miles when at the edge of the village of Sommerain one of the ambulances had a flat tire. As all the vehicles halted briefly, the walking wounded took advantage of the pause to stretch their legs and grab a smoke.

At that moment a P-38 Lightning flew over, buzzing the column at such a low level that Winkler could make out the pilot's features. As that plane soared away, another approached. For a moment Winkler thought the pilots were playing a game of nerves, but it was more than that. The second plane opened fire with all its machine guns, strafing the column. Five more Lightnings followed closely, and all came back for a second run.

The two high-capacity ambulances immediately burst into flames. Ignoring continued strafing, the drivers, assistant drivers, and walking wounded braved the flames to enter the vehicles, cut the straps holding the patients to their litters, and throw the wounded outside, where other men seized blankets and overcoats to try to smother their fiery uniforms. "Despairing, pain-filled cries for help" filled the air. Despite every effort, many of the wounded burned to death, "black and ashened."

As the Lightnings flew away, everybody able to help redistributed the wounded among those vehicles that could still operate. The less seriously wounded, including two American prisoners whose faces appeared to be white from fear that the Germans might take revenge on them, sat on fenders or held onto the tops of the ambulances. At a nearby headquarters, Captain Winkler left the two Americans and his less seriously wounded to be taken to the nearest field-dressing station.

It was near midnight when the convoy reached the hospital at Neuerburg, but the hospital was already overtaxed with patients. At the direction of the officer in charge, Winkler continued another fourteen miles to Bitburg. Once again there was no room. It was the same at the next hospital in Bad Bertrich.

By that time it was daylight, and the wounded had been on the road for almost seventeen hours in unheated ambulances with little to eat or drink. When a lieutenant said there was no room, Winkler seethed with anger. As he left the building, he noted that the rooms did, indeed, appear to be full; but there were no patients in the corridors, and the corridors were far warmer than the ambulances. Once the patients were there, thought Winkler, the doctors and nurses could hardly ignore them.

Winkler and his drivers had deposited most of the wounded in the corridors when a senior officer ordered Winkler to either remove the patients or face arrest. "Neither I nor one of my comrades," said Winkler defiantly, "is going to be arrested here, and we will depart only when our wounded are cared for."

The confrontation attracted a crowd of surgeons, nurses, and visiting civilians, and the senior officer departed. People began to mutter, and nurses hurried to find hot drinks and cookies for the wounded. My God, thought Winkler, Christmas cookies! What a Christmas!

Accompanied by two guards, the officer in charge came back, but again Winkler refused to return the wounded to the ambulances. He did agree to bring in no more but to take those who remained to a Luftwaffe hospital in the nearby town of Andernach. With that, the officer let him go. Although Winkler heard later that his division headquarters intended charging him with "refusing orders and unsoldierly conduct," nothing ever came of it.

For long Captain Winkler pondered which had been more traumatic: the enemy's attack upon the convoy or "the refusal to admit our wounded in the homeland."

*   *   *

At headquarters of the First Army in a Belgian Army barracks at Tongres, the situation on the night of December 24 looked "if anything, worse than before." There were reports of armored columns of the Fifth Panzer Army nearing the Meuse, and the G-2, Colonel Dickson, was convinced that the Germans at Manhay were intent on taking Liège.

Yet despite the debacle that occurred later that night at Manhay, the situation was in fact brighter than General Hodges and his staff realized. The 82d Airborne Division had withdrawn to new positions with little interference from the enemy, and the 7th Armored Division had begun to form a new line north of Manhay astride N-15 leading to Liège. A battalion of the 106th Division's 424th Infantry, which had been in the St. Vith salient, was sufficiently reorganized to become a part of that line. Other battalions of that regiment, plus those of the 28th Division's 112th Infantry, also might be called on in an emergency; and as part of the readjustment of the line, General Hoge's CCB, 9th Armored Division, had retired to afford the XVIII Airborne Corps a reserve.

Along that part of the Trois Ponts–Hotton highway between Manhay and Hotton, the 3d Armored Division was soon to receive reinforcements. Seriously short of infantry from the start, General Rose had already received help from the separate 509th Parachute Infantry Battalion and from two battalions of the separate 517th Parachute Infantry (a third had joined the 30th Division for the mop-up of *Kampfgruppe Peiper*). On the morning of December 24, the 290th Infantry of the 75th Infantry Division—the untried division only recently arrived on the Continent—had begun to attack to help drive the Germans back from the highway between Soy and Hotton. That night a second regiment, the 289th Infantry, arrived and was able to help the armor on the other flank near Manhay. On Christmas Day, Rose was also to get help from his own CCB, released at last from the fight against *Kampfgruppe Peiper*.

On Christmas morning, one message after another reached General Ridgway from the First Army's headquarters insisting that the crossroads at Manhay be retaken. They reflected the continuing concern of Hodges and his staff that Liège might fall and imperil all American positions south of the Meuse, but they failed to take into consideration the fact that Field Marshal Montgomery had ordered the new line behind Manhay.

Contingents of the 2d SS Panzer Division did make a stab up Highway N-15 from Manhay early on Christmas morning, but after meeting heavy fire, the Germans turned back. General Lammerding's goal was not Liège but a turn to the northwest, to get across the Ourthe River and onto the Condroz plateau where he could protect the flank of the Fifth Panzer Army. For Lammerding, Manhay was but a pivot for that turn.

Goaded by the messages from Hodges's headquarters and unaware of Lammerding's intentions, General Ridgway ordered the 7th Armored Division to retake the village, but General Hasbrouck had precious little with which to do the job. Furthermore, retreating tankers the night before had felled trees across the highway to block a German advance, and they just as effectively blocked American tanks trying to go the other way. Not until two nights later with the help of a battalion of the 517th Parachute Infantry was Manhay retaken and then primarily because the village had ceased to be important to the 2d SS Panzer Division.

General Lammerding's first objective after making the turn at Manhay was to move down the highway toward Hotton to take two villages—Grandmenil and Erezée—from which roads led northwest to a crossing of the Ourthe River at Durbruy, six miles downstream from Hotton. No sooner were the Germans in control of the crossroads at Manhay than Lammerding sent an under-strength company of Panthers moving on Grandmenil, just a mile away, with *SS-Panzergrenadiers* following closely. Only a platoon of self-propelled tank destroyers of the 3d Armored Division's Task Force Kane, without infantry support, stood in the way at Grandmenil; and when the *SS-Panzergrenadiers* closed in under darkness, the tank destroyers retired along the highway toward Erezée.

Meanwhile, the 75th Division's 289th Infantry, commanded by Col. Douglas B. Smith, which had arrived the night before, was in an assembly area near Grandmenil. The commander of the 3d Armored Division's CCA, General Hickey, whom General Rose had put in charge of the division's eastern flank, ordered Smith to block both the main highway between Grandmenil and Erezée and a secondary road leading northwest toward the Ourthe.

Although a roadblock was soon in place on the highway, the inexperienced U.S. infantrymen manning it succumbed to the same ploy that earlier had tricked the veterans of the 7th Armored Division's CCA: An American tank appeared first. Followed closely by eight Panthers, the Sherman continued past the roadblock. Even as the German tanks shot up the main body of the battalion, somebody got off a round from a bazooka, which knocked out one of the tanks at a spot where the road ran along the side of a cliff. Unable to get past, the remaining German tanks fell back on Grandmenil.

For General Hickey, it was too much to ask the green infantrymen to retake Grandmenil without armored support. That came in early afternoon with the arrival of a first contingent of the 3d Armored Division's CCB, Task Force McGeorge, which had a company each of armored infantry and medium tanks.

Task Force McGeorge was getting ready to attack when eleven P-38 Lightnings of the 430th Squadron, flying a mission for the 7th Armored Division, mistook the formation for Germans and bombed and strafed the assembly area. Although the American tanks were displaying orange identification panels, they were just outside the no-bomb line designated by the air control officer with the 7th Armored Division, and the airmen took the panels for a ruse. Task Force McGeorge lost thirty-nine officers and men killed. It was near nightfall the next day, December 26, when the task force, assisted by a battalion of the 289th Infantry, finally retook Grandmenil.

As that happened, it was becoming clear on the German side that General Lammerding's 2d SS Panzer Division had gone about as far as it could go. The *SS-Panzergrenadiers*, in particular, had lost heavily in the opening attack at Baraque de Fraiture, and by Christmas Day there were eighteen American field artillery battalions (more than two hundred guns) in position to crush any movement along the roads in the vicinity of Manhay and Grandmenil. Because of the seemingly omnipresent fighter-bombers, little of Lammerding's artillery had come forward.

Nor was Lammerding getting the promised help from the 9th SS Panzer Division, which was to have attacked up the valley of the Lienne Creek along the 2d SS Panzer Division's eastern flank. Beset by air attacks and short of gasoline, only a few of that division's tanks had arrived. In the end, only one of the division's *SS-Panzergrenadier* regiments, composed mainly of ethnic Germans from the Black Sea region of Russia, posed any real problem for the 82d Airborne Division.

The fighting along the northern shoulder of the German penetration was to continue for several more days, but by nightfall of December 26 the worst was over. The next morning, the commander of the Sixth Panzer Army, General Dietrich, ordered Lammerding to turn over the sector around Baraque de Fraiture to the 9th SS Panzer Division, then join what was left of the 560th Volksgrenadier Division and of the 12th SS Panzer Division (at last brought forward from the vicinity of the Elsenborn Ridge) in a new attack to break through Hotton and Soy onto the Condroz plateau. That too was to turn out to be futile, an exercise accomplishing nothing but to prolong the agony for both sides.

All four of the once-proud SS panzer divisions had been reduced to little more than shells and were to have little impact on the continuing battle. At least as important for the Americans at the moment, none of the German divisions had succeeded in crossing the Ourthe River, which meant that the troops of the Fifth Panzer Army struggling for the Meuse had no protection on their northern flank.

CHAPTER TWENTY-SEVEN

Crisis Before the Meuse

One of the principal waterways of western Europe, the Meuse River rises in northeastern France, meanders past Sédan, where the Germans in 1940 made their principal crossing to drive triumphantly to the sea, and enters Belgium near the French town of Givet. Along much of the course downstream from Givet, the banks are steep, sometimes cliffs up to 300 feet high; but there are level stretches, as at a point near Dinant where in 1940 the first Germans to cross the river used a weir. Within Belgium, the river in most places is about 120 yards wide, the current swift. At Namur, where it absorbs the waters of the Sambre River, it becomes wider still for the northeastward flow past Liège and the turn north into the Netherlands, where it is known as the Maas. So critical is the trench of the Meuse to the defense of Belgium that in the years between the two world wars, the Belgian government limited the number of bridges spanning the river. There were a number of crossing sites, nevertheless, mainly at the towns of Dinant, Namur, and Huy, and at Liège.

On the second day of the German offensive, General Eisenhower charged the commander of the Communications Zone (the Services of Supply), Lt. Gen. John C. H. Lee, with defending the bridges over the Meuse. Although they were to be prepared for demolition, none was to be blown except on specific order.

To do the job, General Lee called for the most part on general service engineer regiments. Within France, he used six French light infantry battalions, only recently organized and equipped with a diverse collection of small arms and makeshift uniforms. For the bridges considered to be most critical, Lee had a separate regiment, the 29th Infantry, which had long provided the demonstration troops for The Infantry School at Fort Benning, Georgia. At the time, the 29th Infantry was guarding railroads in France and searching for what constituted a small corps of AWOL American soldiers engaged in a lucrative black market business in rations, cigarettes, and gasoline.

During the first days of the offensive, some American commanders—particularly General Middleton of the VIII Corps—were concerned that the Germans might turn south along the valley of the Meuse toward Sédan and Paris. The route was wide open, for the western flank of the VIII Corps between Neufchâteau and the Meuse (a distance of thirty miles) hung in the air. Although there was hope of filling the gap with the 11th Armored and 17th Airborne Divisions, which General Eisenhower on December 18 ordered to move from England to the Continent, those divisions would not be available for several days.

Thus General Lee ordered the 29th Infantry to cover not only the bridges in Belgium but those in France as far south as Verdun. Starting on December 18, the regiment sent small contingents to all the bridges and a platoon to the radio repeater station at Jemelle, near Marche, with orders to defend the station against paratroopers and patrols. If threatened by a large attack, the equipment was to be sabotaged before falling back.

Even before assuming command in the north, Field Marshal Montgomery had hurried a scratch force of three hundred men to the bridges from Huy to Givet with an assignment to delay the Germans as long as possible, for the thinking at that point was that the Germans would get across the Meuse, whereupon the 30th Corps—assembled under Lt. Gen. Brian G. Horrocks as a reserve behind the Meuse northwest of Liège—was to counterattack. By the 20th, when Eisenhower gave Montgomery command in the north, the staunch American stand at various points—particularly in front of the Elsenborn Ridge—led General Horrocks to conclude that "the enemy's hopes of bouncing the Meuse crossing have almost vanished." The line of the Meuse was to be held.

Montgomery ordered the 29th Armoured Brigade, consisting of three regiments (the equivalent of American battalions), to defend the principal crossing sites from Huy to Givet; and by nightfall on December 21, the 23d Hussars was in position at Givet, the 3d Royal Tank Regiment at Dinant, and the 2d Fife and Forfar Yeomanry at Namur. Patrols from yet another British unit, the 2d Household Cavalry, crossed the river and probed as far east as the road center of Marche. Those deployments freed the bulk of the 29th Infantry to move to Liège, there to guard the bridges and defend supply installations.

With those dispositions, the chance of the Germans getting a bridge across the Meuse by a *coup de main* was remote. There remained, nevertheless, a real possibility that German armor might reach the river and force a crossing.

Despite the despair over the prospects for the offensive that senior German field commanders had begun to voice as early as December 18, Field Marshal von Rundstedt's staff on December 22 prepared an optimistic estimate of the situation. Not until January 1, the staff predicted, would American reserves be able to mount major attacks from north and south, and not until near the end of December would the Americans be capable of defending the Meuse in strength. There was apparently still time for the armor of von Manteuffel's Fifth Panzer Army to get across the Meuse. That was in Hitler's mind the next day, the 23d, when he released the 9th Panzer and 15th Panzergrenadier Divisions to the Fifth Panzer Army.

The German estimate came on the very day that General Patton launched his attack from the south, and an American force to attack in the north was already assembling. Under General Collins and the headquarters of the VII Corps, that force was scheduled to consist of the 4th Cavalry Group, the 75th and 84th Infantry Divisions, the 2d Armored Division, and at least a part of the 3d Armored Division.

On the other hand, whether those units, as Field Marshal Montgomery had ordered, could stay out of the defensive battle to get ready to attack was problematical. When the vanguard of the 3d Armored Division arrived early on the 20th, the troops were fighting before the day was out. So, too, the leading regiment of the 84th Division had been in Marche only a few hours when the likelihood developed that not only that regiment but the entire division soon might be engaged.

Early on December 21, the commander of the 84th Division, Brig. Gen. Alexander R. Bolling, having established his headquarters in Marche, learned of the German attack against the bridge over the Ourthe River nearby at Hotton. Aware from talking with the commander of the 51st Engineer Combat Battalion, Lt. Col. Harvey R. Fraser, that only Fraser's men guarding bridges and manning roadblocks stood between the enemy and Marche, Bolling felt compelled to position his leading regiment in a semicircular defense of the town.

That same morning, December 21, General Collins arrived at Hodges's command post in the Hôtel des Bains in Chaudfontaine, where he learned his mission and the divisions that were to make up his corps. The big question before the two commanders was whether in assembling as far forward as Marche, they risked getting Collins's troops drawn into the fight prematurely. They were still conferring when at 11 A.M. General Bolling telephoned. It looked, said Bolling, as if he might be involved in a fight for Marche. Should he pull back and await the rest of his division or should he hold the town?

"Yes," replied Hodges, "hold." With that decision, whatever Field Marshal Montgomery's orders, another portion of the troops earmarked for the VII Corps was bound to be caught up in the defensive fight.

When a second regiment arrived just before nightfall on the 21st, General Bolling adjusted the defense of Marche to put two regiments in the line, leaving his third as a reserve behind the town. The 334th Infantry dug in forward of the highway connecting Marche and Hotton, while the 335th Infantry defended in front of the town and bent its line back to protect the division's open southern flank.

The next morning, December 22, as motorized patrols of the 84th Division probed in search of the enemy, General Collins again visited General Hodges, concerned lest the Germans penetrate the undefended sector south of Marche and get behind the town, thereby threatening the assembly of the rest of the VII Corps on the Condroz plateau. In reaction to that concern, Hodges told Bolling to push out a screen well to the south and southwest of Marche.

That deployment increased the chances of the 84th Division becoming involved in the defensive battle. Yet when Montgomery visited Hodges early in the afternoon, the mission of the VII Corps remained unchanged: Avoid battle and prepare to attack. To allow time for the last of the 2d Armored Division and corps artillery to arrive, the attack was to be delayed for two days. The 2d Armored Division was to form the right—or southern—wing, the 84th Division the center, and the 3d Armored Division the left—or northern—wing, while the untested 75th Division was to constitute a reserve.

As General Bolling readily deduced, the Germans needed Marche, for the town was as much a road center as was Bastogne. The most important routes were a highway leading north to Liège and the Bastogne–Marche–Namur highway, N-4, from which lesser roads ran west to the Meuse at Dinant. It was Highway N-4 that General von Manteuffel was after. Not only did it afford access to the tank country of the Condroz plateau but also to the Meuse at the bend in the river at Namur, the most direct route to Brussels and Antwerp. To a commander who from the first had seen Antwerp as beyond reach, it would hardly go unnoticed that gaining the Meuse at Namur would position his army if not for implementing the Small Solution, then at least for trapping those Americans still holding south of the Meuse and Liège.

Failure to gain Marche and its roads would force von Manteuffel onto a much less desirable route to the Meuse in the vicinity of Dinant, a route running along the southern rim of the Condroz through what geologists call the Famenne Depression. That is an extension of the rugged country of the main body of the Ardennes, with steep-sided ridges and deep-cut, meandering streams, including that of the Lesse River, which joins the Meuse near Dinant.

Even as Colonel von Lauchert's 2d Panzer Division engaged Major Desobry's force at Noville just north of Bastogne during the night of December 19, patrols from the division's reconnaissance battalion were exploring the roads leading west. Just before dawn on the 20th, some of the reconnaissance troops, supported by a few light tanks, approached the bridge over the west branch of the Ourthe at Ourtheuville. It was a

BEFORE THE MEUSE
DEC 24-26

U.S. POSITIONS, MORNING OF DEC 24

GERMAN CONCENTRATIONS, DEC 24

U.S. ATTACKS, DEC 24-25

GERMAN ATTACKS, DEC 24-26

Scale:
0 1 2 3 4 5
MILES

sturdy Bailey Bridge, the bridge that General Krüger of the 58th Panzer Corps had assumed the Americans would demolish before troops of the 116th Panzer Division could seize it.

There a platoon of the 299th Engineer Combat Battalion and a company of the 158th Engineer Combat Battalion, hurried to the bridge after having screened in front of Bastogne until the airborne troops arrived, had prepared the span for demolition. They had support from the eight tank destroyers of the 705th Tank Destroyer Battalion, which their commander, Colonel Templeton, had dropped off to cover the move of the rest of his battalion to Bastogne.

As the Germans reached the bridge, the engineers pushed down on the detonator to set off the explosives, but nothing happened. Although a light tank started across the bridge, one of the tank destroyers knocked it out. With that, the Germans fell back, and the rest of the day passed quietly. Some motor traffic going to and from Bastogne resumed, and several groups of civilian refugees crossed the bridge, among them the Abbé Musty and his fifty boys from the Bastogne Seminary.

That night the Germans came back. After mortars and artillery shelled the defenders intermittently for two hours, *Panzergrenadiers* at midnight waded the shallow river. Again the demolition charges on the bridge failed to go off.

With Germans ensconced in houses around the bridge, the commander of the 1128th Engineer Combat Group, to which the engineer defenders were attached, authorized withdrawal. To the surprise of a handful of men of the 51st Engineer Combat Battalion, who were manning a roadblock just three miles from the bridge at a crossroads known as Barrière de Champlon, the Germans made no immediate effort to exploit their success. The engineers had no way of knowing it, but the 2d Panzer Division had run out of gasoline.

It was that delay—all through the 21st and 22d—that afforded time for the 84th Division to reach Marche, whereupon, once the engineers at Barrière de Champlon had further blocked the highway by felling trees and blowing a big crater in the road, their battalion commander, Colonel Fraser, ordered them to retire. The delay also afforded time for General Bolling to send a rifle company seven miles southwest of Marche to the town of Rochefort, a first step in implementing General Hodges's order to push out a screen beyond Marche. It also provided time for a task force of the 3d Armored Division's CCA to come forward to bolster the defensive screen in front of Marche.

By nightfall of December 22, enough gasoline had at last arrived to enable the 2d Panzer Division's reconnaissance battalion to resume its advance. Bypassing the felled trees and crater in the highway behind Barrière de Champlon by using trails in the woods, the light tanks and armored cars then returned to Highway N-4 and soon swung west to avoid Marche to the south. At the highway connecting Marche and

Rochefort, the column hit a screening force of the 3d Armored Division's CCA and lost five vehicles, but it bounced off along a side road to reach the highway at the village of Hargimont.

General Bolling in the meantime reinforced the screen south of Marche by sending two motorized infantry battalions, one to augment the company already sent to Rochefort, the other to continue six miles to the west to block a crossing of the Lesse River. Both columns ran into German fire at Hargimont but backtracked, swung well around to the west, and reached their objectives without further difficulty.

The next day, December 23, the main body of the 2d Panzer Division had hardly begun to advance when the leading *Kampfgruppe* came to a halt. The commander reported a roadblock, heavily defended. Doubting the report, the corps commander, General von Lüttwitz, went forward himself and found only a light barricade, no defenders in sight. He relieved the commander on the spot, and at last, in mid-afternoon, the advance began, only to come to a halt again at the crater in the highway behind the Barrière de Champlon. It took four hours to construct a route around it capable of handling the medium tanks.

Based on the progress of the reconnaissance battalion south of Marche, von Lüttwitz decided for the moment merely to block in the direction of Marche with a *Panzergrenadier* battalion while turning the rest of the division westward in the wake of the reconnaissance troops. Before halting for the night, the head of the column got as far as Buissonville, five miles beyond the Marche-Rochefort highway; but the rest of the long column was still toiling forward.

As the 2d Panzer Division began its advance in earnest, the bulk of the American 2d Armored Division had reached the division's assembly area on the Condroz plateau. During the morning of December 23, the commander, Maj. Gen. Ernest N. Harmon, a man noted for his gravel voice and his swearing, who had commanded the division long ago in North Africa and then rejoined it in Normandy, called on his corps commander, General Collins, at the corps command post in the Château de Bessines ten miles north of Marche. The 84th Division, said Collins, was fast being drawn into the battle, but he still hoped to keep the arrival of Harmon's division secret long enough to mount a surprise attack.

Returning to the armored division's headquarters in a small château a few miles away at Havelange, Harmon had lunch with his staff and senior commanders. All were relaxing over coffee when a lieutenant, Everett C. Jones, arrived, a bloody bandage on his head.

At a village ten miles to the south near the town of Ciney, he explained, his patrol from the 82d Armored Reconnaissance Battalion had received fire from several German armored vehicles, including what Jones saw as two Mark IV tanks. Although his armored car had been hit and burned, he and his crew had escaped.

It would be determined later that Jones's patrol had tangled not with Germans but with a British patrol probing east from Dinant. Yet it appeared to Harmon at the time that the engagement had compromised the attempt to keep the 2d Armored Division's arrival secret and that the German spearhead, avoiding a fight at Marche, was headed for the Meuse, only nine miles beyond Ciney.

Running across a field to a grove of trees where a tank battalion had bivouacked, Harmon asked a company commander, Capt. Charles B. Kelley, how long it would take him to get on the road. If he could break radio silence, said Kelley, five minutes. So be it, replied Harmon. "You get down that road to a town called Ciney . . . block the entrances and exits and start fighting. The whole damn division is coming right behind you."

With all of CCA soon following Kelley's tank company, Harmon reported to General Collins what he had done. Having already received reports of German armor bypassing Marche and of another column heading for Rochefort (it was the *Panzer Lehr Division*), Collins not only approved but ordered Harmon to attack immediately to take Buissonville, thereby securing the 84th Division's open flank, and to continue forward to help the battalion of the 84th Division that had occupied Rochefort. Quite clearly, Collins believed, his VII Corps would be unable to "remain aloof from the defensive battle."

Under orders from Harmon, the commander of CCA, Brig. Gen. John H. ("Pee Wee") Collier, left half his command to block the roads around Ciney until CCB could arrive and sent a task force under the commander of the 66th Armored Regiment's 2d Battalion, Lt. Col. Hugh O'Farrell, southeast toward Buissonville. A skirmish delayed the column at the first village of Leignon, so that it was close to midnight before the column got going again. Made cautious by the skirmish, O'Farrell put Company F of the 41st Armored Infantry Regiment in the lead on foot. The armored infantrymen marched in single file on either side of the road; the night was bright, with light from a full moon reflecting off a thin cover of snow.

The men were nearing a farm close to the village of Haid, where Lieutenant Jones had encountered fire that afternoon, when the company commander, Capt. George E. Bonney, who was moving up and down the column in a jeep, heard vehicles approaching. Riding slowly back along the column, he told his men to pull off the road into the shadows of big trees lining either side. They were to fire only after the first vehicle of what was apparently a German column reached the rear of the company.

Germans in two American jeeps led the column, followed by three-quarter-ton American trucks, an American ambulance, and German scout cars, motorcycles, and two half-tracks towing 88mm. guns—twelve vehicles in all. Who started the firing remained unclear, but "all hell broke loose." As the riflemen fired, so did the .50-caliber machine guns on their half-tracks at the rear of their column. Wounded Germans "screamed in agony." Some Germans tried to break away across the fields, but the machine guns on the half-tracks cut them down. Others raised their hands above their heads and tried frantically to surrender.

Only minutes had passed when Captain Bonney shouted as loud as he could to cease fire. It took some time for the firing to die away, and even then, as the infantrymen began to march some thirty prisoners toward the rear (another thirty Germans were dead), somebody opened fire with a machine gun on a half-track. Two .50-caliber bullets almost severed Captain Bonney's right leg.

It was not until December 22 that the main body of the *Panzer Lehr Division*, which had left behind a *Panzergrenadier* regiment at Bastogne, began moving in the direction of the Meuse. Following an encounter with an American artillery unit near the village of Tillet, the head of the column entered the road center of St. Hubert after nightfall without further delay or fighting. Not until noon on the 23d was there sufficient gasoline to continue the march along two roads leading in the direction of Rochefort.

Soon after nightfall on the 23d, a *Kampfgruppe* under Lt. Col. Joachim Ritter von Porschinger approached the town and paused to send out patrols. The patrols returned with word that the town was undefended.

The word was wrong. The 335th Infantry's 3d Battalion, commanded by Maj. Gordon A. Bahe, was in Rochefort, albeit short two of its companies. One had been left behind on the Marche-Rochefort highway to face the Germans at Hargimont, and the other had left Rochefort to scout villages farther south. Yet Major Bahe also had two platoons of 57mm. antitank guns; a platoon of the 51st Engineer Combat Battalion, sent to Rochefort to repair a bridge damaged earlier; and a platoon of the 29th Infantry that had been defending the radio repeater station at Jemelle but had conformed with orders to sabotage the equipment and withdraw. Once fighting began, Bahe was to recall the company that was reconnoitering to the south.

Just before the road from St. Hubert entered Rochefort, it passed between two commanding hills. Going forward to supervise the attack personally, the *Panzer Lehr*'s commander, General Bayerlein, recognized the danger of passing through such a defile without first securing the hills; but in view of the reports from the patrols, he decided to make a dash into the town. "OK," he shouted, "let's go! Shut your eyes and go in!"

As if on cue, heavy fire from small arms and antitank guns rained down on the road. Several vehicles caught fire. Quickly ordering withdrawal, Bayerlein sent a platoon of tanks circling the town to cut the highway beyond it while he prepared for a deliberate assault to begin at midnight.

Since Rochefort was a sizable town, Major Bahe had no hope of defending all the buildings, so that in the darkness the Germans had little trouble gaining entry. Fighting proceeded from house to house until by daylight the American infantrymen were confined to buildings on one side of the town square with a strongpoint in the Grand Hôtel de l'Etoile.

Early in the morning, word arrived from the commander of the 335th Infantry, Col. Hugh C. Parker, to withdraw, for Bahe's mission was delay, not last-ditch defense. Yet most of the men were so closely engaged that only the battalion headquarters and the weapons company managed to reach trucks waiting beyond the damaged bridge. Endangered by German fire, the trucks had left when the rest of the men threw smoke grenades into the square and made a break for it on foot. All but a few were eventually to make their way back to Marche by roundabout routes, many of them going as far south as Givet, then traveling back along the west bank of the Meuse.

At that point the *Panzer Lehr Division* would have been free to continue toward the Meuse, its route blocked only by another of the 84th Division's battalions sent to delay in the valley of the Lesse River (and that battalion withdrew under orders during the night), but General Bayerlein, conscious of the utter fatigue of his troops, nevertheless decided to delay in Rochefort. Although he sent reconnaissance patrols up the valley of the Lesse, he wanted his men to enjoy "the success of the day" and "special rations" that had arrived for Christmas.

On the night of December 23, Generals von Manteuffel and von Lüttwitz conferred. Quite obviously, noted von Manteuffel, the Americans held Marche in strength, thereby barring access to Highway N-4 onto the Condroz plateau and to the Meuse at Namur. On the other hand, the 2d Panzer Division had already bypassed Marche to the south, and the *Panzer Lehr Division* should soon have access to the valley of the Lesse River beyond Rochefort. While not the most desirable route to the Meuse, because it cut across the grain of the Famenne Depression, it was the shortest: from Rochefort to the Meuse at Dinant was only fourteen miles.

Continuing the thrust in that direction was not without peril, for the two panzer divisions—as von Manteuffel put it—constituted nothing more than "a pointed wedge" with both flanks open. Both divisions would have to drop off troops, as indeed they had already begun to do, to guard the flanks. Still there was some hope that the 9th Panzer Division would arrive if not the next day, the 24th, as promised, then soon afterward, and that division could protect the 2d Panzer Division's north flank at Marche, probably taking the town. There was also hope that the 15th

Panzergrenadier Division would soon arrive, and even though von Manteuffel had already designated a sizable portion of that division for Bastogne, the presence of the rest of the division would alleviate a chronic shortage of infantry in the panzer divisions.

Furthermore, von Manteuffel intended to go personally to visit the commander of the 116th Panzer Division, General von Waldenburg, to prod him into getting on with cutting the Marche-Hotton highway and Highway N-4 beyond it. That would prevent the Americans from pouring reinforcements into Marche to hit the army's north flank. That done, and entry gained to the Condroz plateau, von Waldenburg was to drive westward to Ciney, thereby extending the flank protection.

Neither von Manteuffel nor von Lüttwitz saw the plan as ideal, particularly in view of the fatigue of German troops, who had been fighting almost without respite for eight days. Yet to both it appeared to be the only way any German force was going to reach the Meuse River. They would have considered it even less ideal had they been aware of the presence of General Harmon's 2d Armored Division, part of which had already gone into action against the foremost troops of the 2d Panzer Division.

On the day before, December 22, General von Waldenburg had begun conforming to the order from his corps commander, General Krüger, to pull the 116th Panzer Division back to La Roche and there cross the Ourthe River and proceed to cut the Marche-Hotton highway. Von Waldenburg noted, not without a touch of bitterness, that that would put the division almost exactly where it would have been had Krüger allowed him to try for the bridge over the west branch of the Ourthe at Ourtheuville. He had a point and more, for had his troops crossed the west branch on the night of December 19, they could have beaten the Americans to Marche. As it was, they had lost "three important days."

While the bulk of the 116th Panzer Division was toiling through the narrow streets of La Roche and over a single bridge which men of the 7th Armored Division's Trains had damaged as they left, reconnaissance troops pushed ahead. Soon they reported a thin American line on high ground just forward of the Marche-Hotton highway. As along the Hotton-Soy portion of the highway, which von Waldenburg's troops had so recently left, that high ground commanded the highway behind it and represented the last major obstacle before German tanks might debouch onto the more open ground—tank country—of the Condroz.

When the approach of darkness brought relief from Allied fighter-bombers, two companies of *Panzergrenadiers* pushed ahead of the main column in half-tracks and captured American trucks. During the night, while German artillery shelled a line of hamlets on the ridge, those two companies—120 men—infiltrated on foot through a thin line of foxholes outside the hamlet of Verdenne and holed up in a fir forest between the hamlet and the Marche-Hotton highway.

Just before daylight on December 24, Pfc. Frank A. Carroll of Company I, 334th Infantry, awakened to find his foxhole mate, Pvt. Eddie Korecki, on full alert. "A bunch of people," said Korecki, had come through the line during the night; he assumed they were men of mine-laying details that had been at work in front of the line, but he thought it might be a good idea to check with their platoon leader.

The two Americans found the foxholes of both their platoon leader and their platoon sergeant empty. Although there were no signs of blood or a struggle, footprints in the snow revealed that a large body of men had been there during the night. Going to the company command post, Carroll gave the alarm, and a patrol following the trace of the footsteps into the forest came under heavy small-arms fire.

When the commander of the 334th Infantry, Col. Charles E. Hoy, learned of the presence of the German force, he ordered an immediate attack to clear the Germans out. In mid-afternoon of December 24, the 3d Battalion's reserve company, supported by two platoons of Shermans of the attached 771st Tank Battalion, moved toward the woodsline. There they found the Germans in skirmish formation, ready to plunge from the woods toward the houses of Verdenne in support of a frontal attack against the hamlet. Fire from the infantrymen and tanks prompted most of the Germans to surrender (there were almost a hundred of them) while the others either were killed or fled back into the forest.

The attacking force those men were to have helped was nearly an hour late in reaching its line of departure. With the support of five Panthers, two half-tracks, and an armored car, a company of *Panzergrenadiers* broke into Verdenne and continued as far as an imposing edifice, the Château de Verdenne, three hundred yards beyond near the edge of the forest.

The commander of the 84th Division, General Bolling, called on his reserve regiment, the 333d Infantry, to send a battalion to retake Verdenne. One of that battalion's rifle companies was away on another mission, and the other two were considerably under strength; for like the rest of the infantry companies of the 84th Division, they had recently undergone a severe and costly baptism of fire in an attack near Aachen. Company K, for example, had four officers and little more than a hundred men.

The two companies rendezvoused late in the evening at the village of Bourdon, behind Verdenne astride the Marche-Hotton highway. As they left Bourdon to gain a line of departure at an escarpment along the edge of the woods overlooking Verdenne, a guide sent from the company that had relinquished the hamlet put them on the wrong route. Instead of taking a trail leading directly through the woods, Company K in the lead began to move up a circuitous woods road.

Inside the woods, the night was black. Plodding up the steep road, the men came upon a stationary column of tanks. Those, thought the company commander, 1st Lt. Harold P ("Bud") Leinbaugh, were Shermans from the 771st Tank Battalion that were to support the attack on Verdenne. Leinbaugh told his communications sergeant, Donald Phelps, to tell the tankers to hitch onto the tail of Company K.

Feeling in the darkness along the side of one of the tanks, Phelps pounded on the turret with his rifle. "Hey, you guys, open up!" He pounded again. The hatch opened slowly, and the head and shoulders of a man appeared. "*Was ist los*?" a voice demanded. "*Was ist los*?"

As machine guns on the tanks blazed, Leinbaugh and his men plunged into ditches alongside the road. They had stumbled upon a column of Panthers, some thirty to forty, operating under their battalion commander, Maj. Gerhard Tebbe. Earlier in the evening, Tebbe and his tanks had pushed through a burning Verdenne and entered the woods. Although under orders to cut the Marche-Hotton highway and continue to the west, Tebbe had halted to allow *Panzergrenadiers* and artillery to catch up and to await reports from patrols sent to investigate the terrain just beyond the Marche-Hotton highway, which from Tebbe's map appeared to be marshy. Since his men were exhausted, Tebbe had told them to button up and get some rest. It was, after all, Christmas Eve, and over a radio in Tebbe's tank he could hear the bells of the cathedral in Cologne tolling the approach of the Yuletide.

Although the drivers of the Panthers started their motors, they made no effort to move, and the gunners, unable to depress their 75s low enough to hit the Americans in the ditches, fired into the surrounding woods. Recovering from his surprise, Sergeant Phelps grabbed a bazooka and got in a shot at one of the tanks, but before he could fire again, shell fragments mangled his left hand.

Over the company's SCR-300, Leinbaugh reported to his battalion commander that he had run into German tanks. "Get that stuff out of your way and get moving," came the reply. Snapping off the radio, Leinbaugh said to the men around him: "Let's get the hell out of here." Company K fell back and once out of sight of the tanks, dug in to block the road to Bourdon and the Marche-Hotton highway.

The mishap that befell Leinbaugh's Company K delayed the attack to retake Verdenne for an hour; but at 1 A.M. on Christmas morning, the company of the 333d Infantry that had been following Leinbaugh teamed with a company of the 334th Infantry and behind heavy artillery fire, got into the hamlet. Clearing it was another matter. All through Christmas Day the men fought, dodging under covering fire from house to house, digging Germans out of cellars only to see others take their places.

The Château de Verdenne—where the owner, a Belgian nobleman of Polish origin, Baron Charles de Radzitsky d'Ostrowick, his daughter,

Elizabeth, and fifteen other civilians took refuge in the cellar—changed hands several times. The baron and his companions learned to tell who controlled the floors above them by the sound of the footsteps: soft thuds meant Americans in rubber overshoes; loud clicking, Germans in hob-nailed boots.

On one occasion, when the baron ventured upstairs to get water for a wounded German tanker who had taken refuge in the cellar, he found that only the dead controlled the upper floors. The once beautiful grand salon was a shambles, ancestral coats-of-arms along the staircase riddled with bullet holes, tapestries and draperies sagging and shredded, and a billiard table (one leg missing) matted with blood. Moonlight streamed through holes cut by artillery fire in the roof, and dead men littered the floor.

Even with Verdenne reduced to rubble at last in American hands, the German threat to break across the Marche-Hotton highway and onto the Condroz remained. All through Christmas Day and the day after, the 116th Panzer Division's tanks and *Panzergrenadiers* tried to retake Verdenne and seize adjacent hamlets, while Colonel Remer's *Führer Begleit Brigade* entered the fight close along the Ourthe River to try to get past the hamlet of Hampteau and at last seize the bridge across the Ourthe at Hotton. So, too, Major Tebbe's Panthers in the woods behind Verdenne might at any moment break out to cut the highway.

That the infantrymen gave no ground was attributable in large measure to their valor and determination, but almost to a man they paid tribute to the fire support behind them. As on the Elsenborn Ridge and in the vicinity of Manhay, the array of artillery pieces was overwhelming. All the 84th Division's 48 pieces were able to fire into the sector, plus the 334th Infantry's Cannon Company, 18 pieces of armored artillery of the 3d Armored Division's CCA, and 72 pieces of VII Corps artillery, which included a battalion of 8-inch howitzers, a total of 150 pieces.

It was the artillery that eventually crushed Major Tebbe's Panthers. From the positions of Company K, 333d Infantry, near the German tanks, Lieutenant Leinbaugh adjusted the fire of one of the battalions, which set a Panther to burning. Once that firing data had been passed to other battalions, all of them fired in one tremendous Time-on-Target, a cascade of deadly shells such as Leinbaugh and his men had never witnessed before. "Whole trees were blown into the air, tanks and trucks exploded, and as the rain of shells slackened, the screams of dying Germans carried clearly to the watching men of Company K."

Those Germans who survived, including Major Tebbe, had no intention of staying in the woods to await more of that kind of punishment. Although patrols had determined that Americans held the nearby hamlet of Marenne, Tebbe hoped that in the darkness he might be able to sneak through. American vehicles, including tanks, lined the road through the little village, houses so close on either side that the German tankers would have been unable to rotate their turrets to open fire; but all was quiet.

At a house just beyond Marenne, a few men of the 333d Infantry had been detailed, upon the approach of German tanks, to pull a daisy chain of seven antitank mines across the road. Although the men were alert, the approach of tanks from their rear disconcerted them, and they made no effort to pull the mines into the road. One of the Panthers nevertheless blundered onto the pile of mines and blew up in a tremendous explosion.

The carcass partially blocked the road, forcing the remaining tanks and other vehicles into a field which turned out to be laced with antitank mines. As one vehicle after another hit mines, American artillery fire, some of it shells fitted with the POZIT fuse, descended on the field. Noting a bright moon in the sky to the east, Major Tebbe over his radio ordered all the drivers to "head for the moon." Many of the tanks and other vehicles made it, but seventeen stayed behind in the field.

Although General von Waldenburg continued for several days to try to gain the Condroz plateau, the final outcome of the engagement had been determined by the end of the day after Christmas. There was to be no protection on the Condroz for the north flank of the 2d Panzer Division.

Late on December 20, the Abbé Musty and his fifty students from the seminary in Bastogne reached the village of Bande on Highway N-4 between the Ourthe River and Marche. Exhausted from the long hike, the Abbé accepted invitations from the villagers to pass the night. The next day he decided to discontinue his flight and take his chances with the people of Bande.

By Christmas Eve, Germans were all over Bande, mainly support troops of the 2d Panzer Division, but there was also a group wearing the black and white shoulder patch of the *Sicherheitsdienst*, the SD, the security service of the SS. Those soldiers camped out in the ruins of the buildings along Highway N-4, the Grand' Rue, which the Germans had put to the torch back in September in retaliation for the attack by the *Armée Secrète* on German troops in the nearby St. Hubert Forest.

During the morning of December 24, which was a Sunday, the Abbé Musty celebrated mass in the stone church among the farmhouses on the hill above the Grand' Rue. As he emerged after the service, he learned that the SD had been going from house to house arresting all men of the village age seventeen and over, and they quickly seized those who had attended the mass. Among them were four of Abbé Musty's students. To the Abbé and disturbed relatives, the Germans insisted that they were merely conducting a check of identity cards. Everybody would be home for Christmas dinner.

Other SD soldiers were doing the same in the neighboring hamlet of

Grune. They brought all the men together at a sawmill alongside the Grand' Rue and through most of the afternoon questioned them, some alone, some in groups. They were looking for information about the *Armée Secrète*.

Worried that the men were to be deported to Germany, Mme. René Tournay headed for the sawmill with two overcoats, one her husband's and the other belonging to her landlord's son. An officer stopped her, promising to deliver the coats and demanding that Madame Tournay bring him some cognac. When she returned with three bottles, she begged the officer to release her husband. "Don't bargain with me," snapped the officer. "I'm not a Jew!"

Inside the sawmill, an interrogator learned that Albert Schmitz ran a soft-drink bottling plant and sent him to bring back a hundred bottles of lemonade. (Schmitz seized the opportunity to escape.) Another learned that Armand Toussaint was a farmer and sent him to bring back twenty bottles of wine, promising that when he brought them, he would free Toussaint and his son. To Toussaint's amazement, the German held to his promise.

As the afternoon wore on and people gathered outside the sawmill with coats and food, the Germans finally allowed them to deliver their gifts and speak briefly with the men. In that way, Mlle. Marthe Picard had a short talk with her fiancé, twenty-one-year-old Léon Praile.

Dusk was approaching and a few flakes of snow were falling when the interrogators divided their captives into two groups, those who were over thirty-two in the first, those under that age in the second. They ordered the younger men outside, thirty-three of them, including the four seminary students from Bastogne, lined them up in three rows, and stripped them of such personal belongings as pocketbooks, money, rings, watches, rosaries.

There were six guards armed with rifles and burp guns and three officers, everybody wearing the shoulder patch of the SD. Ordering the Belgians to put their hands over their heads, they marched them down the highway. At the ruins of a house beside the Café de la Poste, which had also been burned but had been replaced by a one-story wooden building, they halted them and still in three rows, made them turn their backs to the house.

One of the guards put a hand on the shoulder of the last man in the front row and led him to the door of the damaged house. A shot rang out. The man tumbled through the door into the cellar. Another guard executed the last man in the next row, then another the last man in the third row. Then the next man in row after row. When the Germans fired, some of the victims cried out, but a second round silenced them.

As the executions proceeded, Léon Praile, tall, solidly built, broad shoulders, whispered to those near him. They stood no chance unless they fought back, said Praile. If they all turned on the guards, surely some of them would escape. Several nodded agreement, and Praile was about to act when he felt a heavy hand on his shoulder.

As the guard—a sergeant—led Praile toward the door, Praile perceived that the man was weeping. Praile made up his mind: There was no way he was going to submit docilely to execution. They were three paces from the door when Praile wrenched free and with every ounce of his strength jammed a fist into the sergeant's face. The German fell.

In the gathering darkness, Praile dashed across the road, jumped a hedge, plunged into a little stream, and ran into a field beyond it. Although the Germans fired, none of the bullets found him. Beyond the field he penetrated deep inside a forest before at last daring to pause for breath. Despite his wet clothes, he spent the night in the forest and the next day tried to gain American lines; but there were too many Germans. That night he crept back to the edge of Bande and hid himself in the hayloft of his uncle's house.

Praile's flight did nothing to stay the other executions. When they were over, the bodies of thirty-two young men lay in the cellar, crudely concealed by planks torn from burned houses nearby. The next day the Germans released the older men at the sawmill to return to their homes.

When the massacre at Bande became known, many of the villagers recalled the departure of the Germans in September as American troops approached. The Germans had brandished their fists and shouted: "We'll be back!"

During the night of December 23, as Colonel O'Farrell's task force of the 2d Armored Division's CCA was moving toward Buissonville under orders to continue to Rochefort, the reconnaissance battalion and a leading *Kampfgruppe* of the 2d Panzer Division passed through the village on their way to the Meuse. Composed of forty Mark IV and Panther tanks, twenty-five self-propelled guns, and *Panzergrenadiers* in half-tracks, both the reconnaissance troops and the *Kampfgruppe* had gone before O'Farrell's task force, having paused for the night after ambushing the German vehicles, resumed its advance. That was shortly before daylight on December 24, and since CCB had begun to arrive at Ciney to hold that town, the rest of General Collier's CCA joined the advance on roads paralleling that taken by O'Farrell's tanks and armored infantry.

After an occasional brush with antitank guns and a few tanks left behind to guard the 2d Panzer Division's flank, both task forces of CCA in the early afternoon approached Buissonville. As O'Farrell's tanks and armored infantry entered the village, the other task force reached the crest of a ridge looking down over it and much of the surrounding countryside.

Below them the men could see a long German column approaching Buissonville. Tanks and self-propelled pieces of the 14th Armored Field Artillery Battalion opened a devastating fire. Those Germans who survived the first salvo tried to flee, leaving behind four antitank guns, six artillery pieces, and thirty-six vehicles, most of which were destroyed. A few Germans escaped; many were killed and a hundred captured.

With Buissonville in hand and Rochefort by that time abandoned by the troops of the 335th Infantry, CCA holed up around Buissonville while patrols scouted in the vicinity. Nearby, the commander of the 4th Cavalry Group, Col. John C. MacDonald, moved his 24th Cavalry Reconnaissance Squadron into the village of Humain, between Buissonville and the 335th Infantry's open flank. The presence of American forces in the two villages effectively blocked the route the 2d Panzer Division had been using to toil toward the Meuse. Unless the Germans swung far to the south, the only road left to them was the highway from Rochefort up the valley of the Lesse River.

Before daylight that morning, as the 2d Panzer Division's reconnaissance battalion reached the village of Celles, the commander paused at the main crossroads for a look at his map. As he was studying it, his leading Panther hit a mine in a daisy chain that a squad of American engineers had placed across the road.

The explosion awakened a Belgian woman, Mme. Marthe Monrique, who was the proprietress of an inn, the Pavillon Ardennais, just across the road from where the German commander was standing. Although Madame Monrique's neighbors had fled to the woods, she had stayed behind to try to prevent the Germans from destroying her inn, hopeful that the fact that she spoke German would help. With the noise of the explosion, she turned on a light and pulled back the blackout curtain to see what was happening.

Seeing the light, two Germans knocked at the inn. "How many kilometers to Dinant?" one of them asked. Aware that there was a signpost just across the road, Madame Monrique saw no point in trying to deceive them. "Ten kilometers," she said in German. "How's the road?" the German came back. At that point, a lie seemed credible. "The Americans mined the whole road," said Madame Monrique; "they've been working night and day burying mines in the road—for miles."

The loss of the leading Panther to a mine gave credence to what the Belgian woman said, but her stratagem failed to delay the Germans for long. Because the *Kampfgruppe* bringing up the rear had had to halt two miles back at the village of Conjoux, almost out of gasoline, the commander of the reconnaissance battalion was under considerable compulsion to push ahead, for his was the only force that might quickly gain the Meuse. It was still dark when the battalion resumed its march.

Although the Germans encountered no more mines, trouble lay ahead in the form of five British-operated Shermans. Part of the 3d Royal Tank Regiment, commanded by Col. A. W. Brown, which was defending the west bank of the Meuse at Dinant, each tank covered a road leading to

BATTLE OF THE BULGE
DEC 16 - 26

— LIMIT OF GERMAN
PENETRATION

Scale:
0   10   20   30
MILES

N

the highway bridge at the town. The tanks were to delay long enough for the bridge to be blown, then form a roadblock for a last-ditch defense. The thinking was that nobody would come back.

Along the road that the main body of the German reconnaissance battalion was taking, everybody in a Sherman covering the road—including the commander, Sgt. F. ("Geordie") Probert—had fallen asleep. They awoke with a start to "the sound of straining engines and the clank of tank tracks." In gathering light, Probert saw a long column of German vehicles along a twisting road below him.

In the excitement, Probert's gunner failed to lower the range on his sight. When he fired, he hit not the leading vehicle for which he aimed but another far down the column, a truck apparently loaded with ammunition, for it exploded and burst into flame. A second truck behind it, loaded with gasoline, also caught fire. When a Panther pushed past the burning vehicles and headed toward the British tank, Probert ordered the driver to pull back behind the ridge.

Discouraged by the unexpected resistance and almost out of gas, the German commander ordered his vehicles to cover among the houses of a nearby village, Foy–Notre Dame. There they holed up, precisely three miles from the Meuse. Although an order eventually filtered down from Field Marshal Model to continue to the Meuse on foot, nobody paid any heed. By that point—Christmas Day—it had become a matter not of the Meuse but of survival.

Early in the afternoon of December 24, Field Marshal Montgomery, seriously perturbed about what the Germans still might accomplish, visited the First Army's headquarters at Tongres. As Montgomery had notified General Eisenhower two days earlier, he had little confidence that General Patton's attack into the southern flank of the German penetration would be strong enough to deter the advance of the Fifth Panzer Army, in which case he would be left to deal "unaided" with both the Fifth and Sixth Panzer Armies. It was Montgomery's broad concern about the enemy's next move that had prompted him that morning to direct General Ridgway to pull back the 82d Airborne Division from its salient along the Salm. Montgomery was so worried that he attached the British 51st Highland Division to the First Army to assemble as a reserve south of the Meuse near Liège.

As to the threat to Collins's VII Corps, Montgomery told Hodges that he was releasing Collins from his mission to attack. Instead, "if forced," Collins was authorized to pull back the 2d Armored and 84th Divisions all the way to a line extending from Hotton northwest to the Meuse at the town of Andenne, twelve miles downstream from the bend in the river at Namur.

As Hodges noted with concern, that would allow the Germans to occupy almost all of the Condroz plateau and a great stretch of the eastern and southern banks of the Meuse, thereby driving a deep wedge into the First Army's western flank. He was not advocating such a withdrawal, Montgomery assured him, merely authorizing it if the Germans forced it, and that line from Hotton to Andenne was to be a final defensive position. Whether to fall back was to be up to Collins.

Hardly had Montgomery left Hodges's headquarters when in mid-afternoon General Harmon telephoned headquarters of the VII Corps. He wanted permission to attack immediately against panzer formations in the vicinity of Celles. He knew they were there because Belgian telephone operators and police in the towns through which the Germans had passed were reporting to the Belgian police in Harmon's headquarters town of Harvelange.

Since General Collins was away from the headquarters, his artillery commander, Brig. Gen. Williston B. Palmer, a curmudgeon and a perennial bachelor (he had no time, Palmer told friends, for both the army and a wife), took the call. Aware of the effort to keep troops of the VII Corps out of the defensive battle, Palmer told Harmon to wait, that he expected Collins to return soon. "Furious," Harmon unleashed a few of the expletives for which he was noted.

To Palmer, it seemed that he had hardly put down the telephone before Harmon called again. As aggressive a commander as Harmon himself, Palmer considered for a moment giving Harmon the permission he sought, but he thought better of it. Wait, he said again, for Joe Collins to return.

A few minutes later Palmer was again called to the telephone. That time it was the First Army's chief of staff, General Kean. Montgomery had visited Hodges, said Kean, with new instructions for Collins. To make sure Collins understood them, he was sending an assistant G-3, Col. R. F. ("Red") Akers, Jr., to Collins's headquarters. In the meantime, he wanted to make sure that Collins understood that he had "unrestricted use of all of his troops" and, if necessary, authority to alter his defensive positions.

Unwilling to talk openly on the telephone, Kean asked Palmer if he could find on his map a town beginning with the letter A and another with the letter H. Studying the map, Palmer picked out the towns of Achêne and Le Houisse, both southwest of Ciney in the direction of Celles—the direction in which Ernie Harmon wanted to attack. Yes, said Palmer, he saw the two towns. Collins was authorized, said Kean, to change his defensive positions to a line between those two towns.

Palmer was jubilant. That meant Harmon could attack.

Having learned that General Collins had arrived at Harmon's command post, Palmer sent his aide with a written message (Harmon's telephone was out) passing on what Kean had told him, including the word about the two towns, Achêne and Le Houisse.

The lieutenant had been gone only a few minutes when General Kean telephoned again to say that, on reflection, he doubted whether Palmer had understood him correctly. Colonel Akers was on the way, he reiterated, with a full explanation. In the meantime: "Now get this. I'm only going to say it once. Roll with the punch."

Viewed in the context of rolling with the punch, Palmer realized that his identification of the towns A and H southwest of Ciney, forward of the 2d Armored Division's positions at Ciney, made no sense. Looking again at the map, Palmer spotted Andenne and Huy, both on the Meuse well over thirty miles to the rear. On a carbon of the original message to Collins, he explained that he had misconstrued the double-talk about the towns A and H. Calling a liaison officer to take the message to Collins, Palmer quickly added a note: "I think you had better come home."

When General Collins received the second message, it was too late in the day in any case for General Harmon to attack. Telling Harmon to prepare for attack early the next morning, Collins returned to the Château de Bessines.

While awaiting the arrival of Red Akers, Collins discussed the situation with his staff. To a man they agreed with Collins: They should attack. When Akers did arrive—"his lips blue with cold and his face almost frozen"—Collins gave him a drink of rum, then listened "a bit aghast" as Akers told of a possible withdrawal to the line Andenne-Hotton. On the other hand, noted Collins, he was only authorized to withdraw to that line, not obligated to. He also had unrestricted use of all his divisions, no longer having to withhold them for a counterattack, and the decision to withdraw was his alone.

Having lectured as an instructor at The Infantry School on events of World War I, Collins was well aware of the incident in which an emissary of von Moltke's, Lt. Col. Richard Hentsch, acting on oral orders, directed premature withdrawal of the German First Army, which contributed to a French victory. Wanting no part of the kind of recriminations that later befell Hentsch, Collins directed Akers to put his instructions, as derived from Montgomery by way of Hodges, in writing.

With that piece of paper in hand, Collins told Ernie Harmon to attack.

A survey on December 24 of the German order of battle in or near the eastern end of the bulge that the Germans had driven into the American line would lend some credence to Field Marshal Montgomery's immense concern. Five panzer divisions were already in action and a sixth on the way: the *Panzer Lehr* and the 2d Panzer pushing past Marche for the Meuse; the 116th Panzer trying to get across the Marche-Hotton highway onto the Condroz plateau to assist that push; the 2d SS Panzer and the 9th SS Panzer on the other side of the Ourthe River also trying to get onto the plateau; and the 9th Panzer on the way to help at Marche. There was also the *Führer Begleit Brigade* and such as was left of the 12th SS Panzer after its futile efforts to get past the Elsenborn Ridge. It was that formidable array that convinced Montgomery the Germans were getting ready for a powerful, concentrated effort—perhaps the most powerful blow since the start of the offensive.

The array was actually more formidable on a G-2 map than in reality, for except for the 9th Panzer Division, all the panzer formations had already incurred heavy losses. Allied aircraft sharply curtailed their maneuvers by day; and the men still fighting were close to exhaustion, their supplies (including gasoline) sharply diminished. The goal of the Meuse River was nevertheless close at hand.

In quest of that goal, the commander of the 47th Panzer Corps, General von Lüttwitz, early on Christmas Day sent contingents of the *Panzer Lehr Division* from Rochefort to retake Humain and Buissonville, hoping thereby to reopen the shortest route westward and secure the north flank at the base of what von Manteuffel called the "pointed wedge." At Humain, the light tanks and armored cars of the 24th Cavalry Reconnaissance Squadron were no match for the German tanks and relinquished the village; but the loss made little difference, for General Collier's CCA maintained a firm hold on Buissonville. With Collier's powerful force on the north flank, neither von Lüttwitz nor von Manteuffel was willing to send anybody else marching for the Meuse until at least a portion of the 9th Panzer Division arrived to hold that flank.

In the countryside close to the Meuse River near Dinant, Christmas Day dawned with a light cloud cover, but that cleared early and both American and British fighter-bombers were soon overhead. There were at first few targets, for the tanks and other vehicles of the two advanced forces of the 2d Panzer Division—one in and around Foy–Notre Dame, the other in woods between Conjoux and Celles, both with gasoline tanks almost dry—kept under cover. It remained for the 3d Armored Division's CCB under Brig. Gen. I. D. White to flush them.

CCB began to advance shortly after daylight on Christmas morning with two task forces marching down roughly parallel roads from assembly areas outside Ciney with plans to link at Celles. Neither task force had any great difficulty. One moving from Achêne on Celles dug a few Germans from a forest alongside the road and beyond the forest came under fire from tanks concealed among the buildings of a farm, but American fighter-bombers drove the tanks out (four Panthers), and the American tanks and tank destroyers quickly destroyed them. The other task force had a brief engagement near Conjoux, then pushed on in the face of fire from an occasional tank or antitank gun.

In mid-afternoon, the two tasks forces linked on high ground overlooking Celles and continued down into the village without resistance. Near the Pavillon Ardennais, the men saw a Panther that had been disabled by a mine, but that was the only sign of the enemy.

Covering the western flank of the advance, the 82d Armored Reconnaissance Battalion approached Foy–Notre Dame. Seeing German vehicles in the village, the commander of Company A, Capt. James Hartford, sent a platoon to reconnoiter. When the Germans fired on the platoon, Hartford committed the rest of his company, then called on another company to help. Once the men knocked out an antitank gun near the center of the village, the rest was mop-up. Just under 150 Germans surrendered.

In the attack, the reconnaissance troops were helped by the five Shermans of the 3d Royal Tank Regiment, whose crews were relieved that the arrival of the American armor eliminated the requirement for them to make a last-ditch stand in front of the highway bridge at Dinant. Unfortunately, in the first meeting, the crew of an American tank mistook one of the British-operated Shermans for a German tank and knocked it out.

As night fell on Christmas Day and General White made plans for mopping up the German pockets the next day, the only hope for the trapped Germans lay in relief forces breaking through. When a *Kampfgruppe* of the 9th Panzer Division arrived at last near Marche, General von Lüttwitz could send help, but not much. Through the night a *Kampfgruppe* of the 2d Panzer Division—all that was left—and another of the *Panzer Lehr Division* toiled up the valley of the Lesse River toward Celles. Each force had not quite a company of tanks (about fifteen), a few *Panzergrenadiers* and engineers, a light artillery battalion, and part of an antiaircraft battalion.

The *Kampfgruppe* of the 2d Panzer Division was the first to arrive. As the column came within two miles of Celles, it seemed to the Germans that the ridge ahead of them was "crawling with tanks." Before they could disperse into an attack formation, fire from American tanks and from artillery directed from spotter aircraft began to riddle their ranks. By way of the British tanks at Foy–Notre Dame, General White called in a squadron of British Typhoons, but since the Americans had no radio contact with the planes, the little artillery observation aircraft had to dive dangerously low to point out the German column, whereupon the British pilots went to work with deadly rockets.

When the *Kampfgruppe* of the *Panzer Lehr Division* arrived, it received much the same reception. Learning of the disasters, General von Lüttwitz ordered both columns to fall back on Rochefort, leaving the trapped men of the 2d Panzer Division's spearhead to fend for themselves. That night General von Manteuffel authorized them to break out on foot.

Around six hundred Germans eventually escaped. They had to leave behind all the vehicles and equipment of an entire *Panzergrenadier* regiment, a battalion of tanks, three artillery battalions, and the bulk of an antiaircraft battalion. In the whole engagement, including the fighting at Buissonville, the 2d Armored Division knocked out or captured 82 tanks, 83 antitank and artillery pieces, and 500 other vehicles of various types; the division captured 1,213 Germans and killed at least another 900. The American division lost 28 medium tanks (26 of which were soon back in action), 201 men wounded, and 43 killed.

The day after Christmas marked if not the absolute end, then at least the beginning of a precipitous end to the German offensive as Adolf Hitler had originally planned it. On that day, December 26, the American defenders on the Elsenborn Ridge were still holding firm; the big attack on Christmas Day at Bastogne had failed; General Patton's attack against the southern flank was still under way and a relief column entered Bastogne; the attempt by the 2d SS and the 9th SS Panzer Divisions to break past Manhay failed; so, too, did the 116th Panzer Division's attempt to push beyond the Marche-Hotton highway.

Many long, bitter days of combat were to pass before Hitler would finally admit that his grand offensive had failed. Indeed, that same day he was to announce new, grandiose plans to salvage something from it. Yet saner heads recognized that the Führer's desperate ambition, like a lone panther in the garden of the curé of Foy–Notre Dame three miles short of the Meuse River, lay broken in the snow.

BOOK
VI

THE
ROAD
BACK

CHAPTER TWENTY-EIGHT

Crises in Command

In the underground concrete chambers of the *Adlerhorst* near Ziegenberg Castle, Alfred Jodl, chief of *OKW*'s operations staff, received a telephone call on the night of December 24 from General von Manteuffel. On the eve of the all-out attack to take Bastogne—to be launched just a few hours later on Christmas Day—von Manteuffel said it was impossible for him to continue driving for the Meuse River and still hope to take Bastogne. The time had come, he said, for a completely new plan. Upon nearing the Meuse, he would wheel north and drive between the Ourthe and the Meuse. That would bring him in on the flank and rear of the American forces fighting south of Liège, at Malmédy, and on the Elsenborn Ridge. Such a plan clearly inferred abandoning Antwerp as an objective, and that, Jodl responded emphatically, the Führer would never countenance. He nevertheless promised to pass along von Manteuffel's recommendation.

On Christmas Day, when Hitler finally arose, he appeared to be cheerful. Late in the day he joined his staff around a candlelit Christmas tree and to everyone's surprise drank a glass of wine and seemed to enjoy it. Yet his physical appearance continued to disturb everybody: "his face was haggard and his voice quavered. . . . His handclasp was weak and soft; all his movements were those of a senile man."

Late that night his military advisers, along with Field Marshal von Rundstedt, joined him for a review of the military situation. There was immense concern about Russian advances in Hungary and speculation as to why the Russians had failed to open a new offensive in Poland.

When the discussion turned to the Ardennes, there was a late report from Field Marshal Model. His chief of staff, General Krebs, had drafted it while Model was visiting the front. Yet for all the gloom Model had encountered there, he made no effort to alter the optimistic tone of Krebs's draft. Even though Model often still spoke frankly to the Führer, he saw little point in inviting Hitler's wrath.

Although the Fifth Panzer Army would soon reach the Meuse, noted Model, the Sixth Panzer Army had been unable to get across the Ourthe so that von Manteuffel's north flank was exposed. Meanwhile, the Seventh Army was under heavy attack from the south. The Fifth Panzer Army might be able to seize some "unoccupied crossings" of the Meuse (he failed to elaborate on what he meant by that), but Model considered it essential for von Manteuffel to turn his main force northward and in conjunction with the Sixth Panzer Army eliminate the Americans fighting south of the Meuse and Liège. And Bastogne would have to be taken. Once all those goals were achieved, Model concluded—but merely as a sop to the Führer's ambition, not through any personal conviction—the drive for Antwerp might be resumed.

After reviewing Model's report, General Jodl, who was another of the few still able to speak candidly to the Führer, paused for a moment. "*Mein Führer*," he continued, "we must face the facts squarely and openly. We cannot force the Meuse River."

Hitler refused to accept that. "We have had unexpected setbacks," he said, "because my plan was not followed to the letter." On the other hand, "all is not yet lost."

As Hitler continued, it became clear that he had accepted von Manteuffel's and Model's recommendation to concentrate on eliminating the Americans south of the Meuse in the vicinity of Liège; but as a prerequisite, to remove the threat to the rear of the two panzer armies, he insisted on capturing Bastogne. Rejecting a proposal to seize Luxembourg City so as to bolster the morale of the troops, he also turned down a proposal from von Rundstedt to return to the earlier plan for the Fifteenth Army to drive down the valley of the Meuse behind Aachen and link with the forces in the Ardennes. That, he said—no doubt thinking of his field commanders' espousal of the Small Solution—would be too costly and would take away resources from the final objective, which he still intended to pursue: Cross the Meuse and capture Antwerp.

Three days later, on December 28, Hitler admitted that the situation in the Ardennes was serious, even desperate, but then added: "As much as I may be tormented by worries and even physically shaken by them, nothing will make the slightest change in my decision to fight on until at last the scales tip to our side." By attacking in the Ardennes, he said, he had forced the Americans to withdraw 50 percent of their strength from other parts of the front, which left those sectors "extraordinarily thin."

Jabbing a finger at a large map on the wall, he indicated the province of Alsace in the northeastern corner of France. There, on New Year's Eve, he announced, he was launching a new offensive (it had been in preparation since December 22) to be known as Operation *NORDWIND*. It would force the Americans to pull back the divisions that were threatening the southern flank in the Ardennes, and with the collapse of that threat, the main offensive in the Ardennes would "*then be resumed* [he stressed the words] with a fresh promise of success."

Field Marshal Model, said Hitler, was "to consolidate his holdings and reorganize for a new attempt on the Meuse." He was also to "make another powerful assault on Bastogne. Above all, we must have Bastogne!"

At Field Marshal Montgomery's invitation, General Bradley flew on Christmas Day (by a roundabout route avoiding the bulge in the American line) to confer with Montgomery. When Bradley landed at St. Trond, northwest of Liège, nobody from Montgomery's staff was there to meet him, which Bradley took to be "a calculated insult." He was tempted to turn around and go home; but when General Hodges's aide-de-camp, Maj. William C. Sylvan, arrived in a staff car, he decided to proceed.

Montgomery's headquarters was in a modest house in Zonhoven, a few miles north of Hasselt. Montgomery offered neither food nor drink (Bradley had had only an apple for lunch) but began immediately to lecture his guest. "I was absolutely frank with him," Montgomery reported later to Field Marshal Brooke. "I said the Germans had given us a real 'bloody nose'; it was a proper defeat, and we had much better admit it." It was, said Montgomery, "entirely our own fault" for trying to advance in two columns rather than putting everything behind the thrust north of the Ardennes. "The enemy saw his chance and took it. Now we were in a proper muddle."

Montgomery told Brooke he felt sorry for Bradley; he "looked thin, and worn and ill at ease." According to Montgomery, Bradley agreed entirely with everything he said. "Poor chap; he is such a decent fellow and the whole thing is a bitter pill for him. But he is man enough to admit it and he did."

Bradley saw it quite differently. He found Montgomery "more arrogant and egotistical" than ever, lecturing and scolding him "like a schoolboy." Bradley was "so enraged and so utterly exasperated" that it was all he could do, while "seething inside," to keep silent.

Most disturbing of all to Bradley was Montgomery's view on attacking to erase the German bulge. Convinced that the Germans were still capable of another major blow, Montgomery said he had no intention of attacking until "he was certain the enemy had exhausted himself." The First Army was too weak to go on the offensive, and the Third Army's attack would accomplish little. The proper course was for everybody to go on the defensive and in the south to withdraw to a shorter defensive line (possibly as far back as the Vosges Mountains) in order to free divisions to strengthen Hodges's First Army. As Bradley understood him—although Montgomery subsequently denied it—he believed it would be three months before Hodges would be capable of a major offensive.

The meeting lasted only half an hour, and Bradley flew back to his headquarters in a mood to match the gathering blackness of the night. Late that evening he had a talk with George Patton, who found Montgomery's ideas "disgusting." If ordered to fall back, Patton thought he would "ask to be relieved." Montgomery was just "a tired little fart."

The next morning, Bradley telephoned Eisenhower's headquarters, talked with the chief of staff, Bedell Smith, and "let him have it with both barrels." Montgomery, he said, was throwing away "an opportunity to inflict a devastating defeat on the enemy." He wanted the First and Ninth Armies returned to his command immediately, whereupon he would move his headquarters to Namur to assure proper coordination and "get some action in the north."

Still seething, Bradley took "the extraordinary step" of writing to one not then under his command, Courtney Hodges. While making it clear that his letter should in no way be considered a directive, he said he failed to view the German situation "in as grave a light" as did Montgomery. Although conscious that the First Army had absorbed a heavy blow, he believed the Germans had lost much more heavily and were so weak that an attack by the First Army would force them "to get out in a hurry." He urged Hodges to look for an opportunity to attack "as soon as the situation seems to warrant."

That night, December 26, aware of the death blow that Ernie Harmon's 2d Armored Division was administering to the spearhead of the German offensive near Celles, Bradley again telephoned Bedell Smith. "Damn it, Bedell," he said, "can't you people get Monty going in the north? As near as we can tell, the other fellow's reached the highwater mark today."

Before daylight on Christmas Eve, two small converted cargo ships—one British, the SS *Cheshire*, the other Belgian, the *Léopoldville*—set sail from Southampton across the rough waters of the English Channel, bound for the French port of Cherbourg. Each carried 2,200 American soldiers of the 262d and 264th Infantry Regiments, the vanguard of the 66th Infantry Division, scheduled to relieve the 94th Infantry Division that was containing Germans holding out in ports in Brittany and so release that division for commitment in the Ardennes. Three British destroyers and a French frigate served as escort.

A German submarine, *U-486*—one of a new class equipped with a snorkel—lay on the Channel floor five miles outside the breakwater at Cherbourg. As part of the German Navy's support of the offensive in the Ardennes, *U-486* and a number of other submarines had received orders early in December to begin operations in the Channel. Under the command of 1st Lt. Gerhard Meyer, *U-486* had assumed its station the night before, December 23.

As the Allied convoy reached open waters, the sea was running heavy. It was bitterly cold. All through the day most of the soldiers aboard the two troopships were seasick. In the crowded compartments below decks on the *Léopoldville*, the air was fetid.

By 5 P.M. it was dark enough for Lieutenant Meyer to chance bringing his craft to the surface. Some thirty minutes later, a lookout picked up the approaching convoy. Slightly before six o'clock, Meyer gave the order to fire a torpedo, which headed unerringly for the *Léopoldville*.

The torpedo struck the vessel starboard side aft and exploded in number four hold. At least three hundred soldiers died from the explosion or drowned in the water that swiftly flooded two of the troop compartments.

All lights went out, and the ship's engines stopped. Among the troops, there was no panic; they took their places on deck as they had learned to do earlier in the day in a lifeboat drill. While some helped carry injured to the ship's infirmary, word passed among the men that tugs were coming to tow the ship into the harbor at Cherbourg. That seemed logical, for the lights of the port were clearly visible—to shore-trained eyes, only a short distance away.

There were indeed plenty of tugs at Cherbourg and many another vessel that might be used for rescue, but for a long time nobody notified American Army and Navy headquarters in the port about the disaster. The senior British commander, Lt. Comdr. John Pringle, captain of HMS *Brilliant*, had no radio communications with Cherbourg, and even though he notified authorities in Southampton, they failed to pass the word along. Not until 6:25 P.M., almost half an hour after the torpedo hit, did anybody notify Cherbourg, and then it was a blinker message from HMS *Brilliant* stating only that the *Léopoldville* had been hit and needed assistance.

That message mystified officials at the port. What kind of assistance? Every request by blinker message for additional information went unanswered. That contributed to the delay in sending help. Even greater delay stemmed from the fact that it was Christmas Eve and every man who could be spared was on leave. It was close to 7 o'clock, a full hour after the torpedoing, before the first rescue craft left the harbor.

Meanwhile, HMS *Brilliant*, along with the other British destroyers and the French frigate, was looking for the German submarine and dropping depth charges. All the while, *U-486* lay on the bottom of the Channel, its motors silent. Neither Lieutenant Meyer nor any of his forty-eight-man crew felt any elation. They knew they had scored a hit but thought they had only grazed their target.

The big problem aboard the *Léopoldville* was that nobody knew how extensive was the damage. The skipper, Capt. Charles Limbor, made no attempt to check it, and somebody (nobody would ever determine who it was) kept announcing over the public address system that there was no danger of sinking. Several times the word went out that tugs were coming to tow the *Léopoldville* into port. At other times, that all passengers were to be transferred to other ships. Yet always, no danger of sinking.

To the soldiers, that made the behavior of the Belgian crew—mostly men from the Belgian Congo—incomprehensible. The entire crew except for the four senior officers early made for the lifeboats, climbed aboard, and launched them. A few U.S. soldiers joined them, and others filled one of the boats until an officer ordered them out. There was no danger of sinking.

As the powerless *Léopoldville* began to drift, Commander Pringle aboard the *Brilliant* ordered Captain Limbor by blinker signals to drop anchors. Learning finally that there were many wounded aboard the troopship, Pringle stopped his search for the U-boat and came alongside the *Léopoldville*. Although he intended only to remove the wounded, the British sailors encouraged other soldiers to come aboard.

In the rough seas, getting anybody across from the *Léopoldville* to the *Brilliant* was more than perilous, it was death-defying. With virtually no crew left aboard the troopship, hardly anybody knew how to moor the two vessels. It took considerable time before British sailors manning the *Léopoldville*'s antiaircraft guns and American soldiers accomplished the task. Even then the lines broke constantly, and others had to be secured to keep the two vessels close together.

They were never exactly parallel. Over and over again, both vessels rose and fell in the heaving seas, came together with a grinding, crushing noise, pulled apart, then came together once more. Many men nevertheless heeded the cries of the British sailors: "Jump, Yank!" Some mistimed their jumps and fell between the two ships, there to be crushed when next the two vessels surged together. That discouraged many others from jumping, and even though the *Léopoldville* had developed a strong list, there was still no word from anybody in authority that it was sinking. Was it safer to stay with the ship or jump?

As 2d Lt. Harry Peiper saw it: "It was like trying to jump on a big, bobbing cork on a rough pond. . . . At one second, [*Brilliant*] was crashing the side of our ship some fifteen feet below me, then it was at my level but fifteen feet out. There was no telling where it was going to be at the next second." A former football player at the University of California, Peiper finally jumped and just managed to grab a handhold on the lifelines of the destroyer's deck. Seconds before the two ships crashed together again, he swung his feet over the railing.

They tried at first to transfer the wounded by means of lines and pulleys, but there was no way to keep the stretchers flat, and even though strapped down, men slipped off into the sea between the two vessels. One soldier with both arms in splints began slipping while halfway across, slowly, headfirst, "desperately but futilely clutching the sides of the litter with his feet."

The better way seemed to be to throw the wounded across, either on their stretchers or in wicker basket sea litters, sometimes in a sheet or a blanket. Aboard the *Brilliant*, British sailors and American soldiers who had made the jump tried to catch them, to cushion their fall, but some hit the deck hard.

There was still no word to abandon ship. Although Captain Limbor ordered the few of his crew who were still aboard to leave, nobody told the soldiers what to do. Again, why make that perilous jump when there was no danger of the *Léopoldville* going down? Nor did anybody tell Commander Pringle that the *Léopoldville* was mortally wounded.

For the better part of an hour, the *Brilliant* remained alongside; but as boats from Cherbourg began to arrive, Captain Pringle pulled away. He had already taken on a heavy load, he needed to get the wounded to Cherbourg for medical attention, and he presumed that the arriving craft would be able to take the other troops off, should that prove necessary. Had he realized that the *Léopoldville* was sinking, he might have considered towing the vessel; but that would have been difficult because the *Léopoldville*, at his order, had dropped anchors, and no crewmen remained to hoist them.

Not long after the *Brilliant* departed, word began to pass among the soldiers that the *Léopoldville* was doomed. The ship's list was becoming "more pronounced every minute."

When two small tugs came alongside, some soldiers got aboard. Others turned to nine remaining lifeboats, which they managed with great difficulty to launch, but none carried its full capacity. (In lifeboats with a total capacity of 590 men, 300 got away.) There were still many men who made no effort to leave the ship, for as a battalion commander, Lt. Col. J. Ralph Martindale, later noted: "Until one minute prior to sinking, all indications and all information indicated that the ship would stay afloat."

At close to 8:30 P.M., the ship gave a sudden lurch. Then came "a rumbling, like the beating of drums in a serious symphony . . . the drums getting louder and louder." Hatch covers blew off. The ship began to upend, going down by the stern while at the same time rolling to one side. Life rafts broke loose, crashing among the soldiers. Steel helmets careened about the decks. Some men fell overboard; others threw themselves into the water. Almost to a man they still wore their heavy woolen overcoats beneath their little life jackets. When waterlogged, those pulled many a man to his death. Some still refused to enter the icy water, but as the ship assumed the vertical, they had no choice. Others were still trying to climb the rapidly rising decks when the ship plunged beneath the water.

Once in the water, panic at last engulfed many of the men. They grabbed at other people, dragging them under. They fought for positions on the small life rafts, to be first to be pulled aboard lifeboats, tugs, PT boats, destroyers. Many a man hefted aboard one of the craft was already dead from hypothermia or drowning; the crews threw their bodies overboard to make room for the living.

When the ghastly ordeal was finally over, five hundred more men from the *Léopoldville*—plus Captain Limbor, who went down with his ship—were dead. Counting the three hundred who died at the start, that made a total of eight hundred or more, the worst disaster to befall a troopship carrying American soldiers during the course of the war.

Between the time the torpedo struck and the *Léopoldville* went under, two and a half hours elapsed. At least five hundred men went to their deaths in the cold waters of the English Channel who should have lived; yet in view of the delay in communications with Cherbourg, the bungling and indecision, the early departure of the Belgian crew, and the lack of information or direction from the bridge, it was incredible that the toll was no higher.

Like General Bradley, General Eisenhower was anxious for Field Marshal Montgomery to attack; but in one respect he was thinking like Montgomery. Because of the slowness of General Patton's advance on Bastogne, Eisenhower saw a pressing need for more divisions. The 17th Airborne Division had yet to arrive from England, and the tragedy at sea meant that the 94th Infantry Division would have to continue the task of containing Germans in the ports of Brittany. That left him with only two divisions not yet committed: the 11th Armored Division, just arrived from England, and the 87th Infantry Division, which the Seventh Army had pulled from the line by extending the sectors of other divisions. Yet so long as the Germans continued to attack, Eisenhower was reluctant to commit those two divisions. At his daily staff conference on December 26, he ruled that the commander of the 6th Army Group, General Devers, would have to withdraw from the Saar and Rhine Rivers back to the Vosges, thereby shortening the line and freeing two or three divisions.

That decision taken (although yet to be implemented), Eisenhower prepared to meet Montgomery in Brussels. Even though telephone communications were functioning satisfactorily, Eisenhower found the telephone no substitute for face-to-face conversation. Because of his staff's continuing concern for his safety, he agreed to go by special train, planning to depart that night, the 26th; but before anybody boarded the train, the Luftwaffe bombed it, and it was noon the next day when Eisenhower finally got under way. At a staff conference before leaving, he learned that Montgomery was at last contemplating attack, to which Eisenhower responded: "Praise God from Whom all blessings flow!"

Partly because of security precautions, which annoyed Eisenhower, the journey was slow, and the roads were so icy that he headed not for Brussels but for Hasselt, which was considerably closer to Montgomery's forward headquarters. It was near midday on December 28 before the train reached Hasselt and Montgomery came aboard.

Eisenhower found Montgomery still convinced that the Germans had one more full-blooded attack left in them. He apparently based that belief on the estimates of his G-2, Brigadier Williams, who like most Allied intelligence officers was at that point living by the adage, once burned, twice cautious. An aerial reconnaissance report of a concentration of five hundred German vehicles led Williams's staff to speculate that the Germans might be moving up one, perhaps two more SS panzer divisions to assemble a corps behind the SS panzer divisions on the northern flank, "to deliver next breakout." The British Joint Intelligence Committee was also being cautious, noting that the Germans had failed to reach either their intermediate or long-range objective and thus "might well release additional reserves for a final lunge."

That kind of caution failed to meld with the intercepts that ULTRA was producing. Most intercepts pointed to the Germans' being in serious straits, with heavy tanks losses, and suffering from an acute shortage of gasoline. Although there were indications that they were shifting some formations already committed toward Bastogne, there was none indicating a buildup in the north.

Montgomery told Eisenhower that while he awaited the expected blow, he was beginning to replace General Collins's troops at the tip of the bulge from Rochefort to Hotton with British troops, thereby enabling Collins finally to assemble for an attack. When Eisenhower raised the possibility that the Germans might not in fact mount another major thrust, Montgomery promised that if it failed to develop, he would start General Collins's attack six days later, on January 3. With that assurance, Eisenhower telephoned his headquarters to direct release of the 11th Armored and 87th Divisions to General Patton.

Before Eisenhower departed, Montgomery raised the issue that had so long complicated Allied command relationships: When the Allied armies renewed the drive into Germany, Montgomery insisted that he be designated overall ground commander and in particular that he have command over Bradley's 12th Army Group. As Eisenhower left, Montgomery thought he had won his point. So he reported to Field Marshal Brooke; but Brooke thought otherwise. "It looks to me," Brooke confided in his diary, "as if Monty, with his usual lack of tact, has been rubbing into Ike the results of not having listened to Monty's advice!"

Nevertheless emboldened, Montgomery the next day wrote Eisenhower a letter that if not insubordinate, was at least insolent and arrogant. Because of Eisenhower's failure to designate an overall commander for a principal Allied thrust north of the Ardennes, he inferred, they had already had "one very definite failure," so that the time had come for Eisenhower "to be very firm on the subject . . . no loosely worded statement" would do. He proceeded even to write Eisenhower's directive for him: "From now onwards full operational direction, control and co-ordination . . . is vested in the C.-in-C. 21 Army Group, subject to such instructions as may be issued by the Supreme Commander from time to time." He considered it essential that "*all* available offensive power" be assigned to a northern thrust and that "one man" should direct and control that thrust, without which, he concluded, "I am certain that . . . we shall fail again."

In view of all the earlier disagreements over ground command and a single thrust into Germany, that letter in itself would have been enough to submit the Supreme Commander's patience to rigorous testing. As it happened, it came at a time when the voice of the British press had become strident, maintaining that Montgomery "had saved the Americans from the consequence of their follies and that he would rightly go on to lead all the Allies to victory."

Once General Marshall in Washington learned that the British press was predicting that Eisenhower was to name Montgomery as overall ground commander, he cabled Eisenhower that in his opinion, there should "under no circumstances" be "any concessions of any kind whatsoever," for that would create "a terrific resentment" in the United States. (At that point there were forty-two American divisions on the Continent as against nineteen from Britain and the Commonwealth countries, and the margin was bound to increase.) "You are doing a fine job," Marshall concluded, "and go on and give them hell."

As for Eisenhower and many senior members of his staff, Montgomery's letter generated deep resentment. They saw it as an ultimatum. Almost everybody, including Eisenhower's British deputy supreme commander, Air Marshal Tedder, considered that the time had come for a showdown. Either Eisenhower or Montgomery had to go; and given the preponderance of forces that the United States was contributing to the alliance, quite clearly it would not be Eisenhower.

Through a PHANTOM liaison officer at Bradley's headquarters in Luxembourg City, Montgomery's chief of staff, General de Guingand, learned of the deep resentment the reports and editorials in the British press had generated. That prompted him to telephone Walter Bedell Smith at Versailles, from whom he learned that Montgomery's message had upset everybody. An "extremely dangerous situation" had developed.

Despite de Guingand's position on Montgomery's staff, the Americans trusted him, and he knew it. If he could get from Brussels to Versailles in time, thought de Guingand, perhaps he could head off a showdown. Yet throughout the morning of December 30, abominable flying weather appeared to forestall that. Not until early afternoon did the weather clear sufficiently to risk takeoff; even then it was a hair-raising ride, and several times the pilot contemplated turning back, until at last he got a glimpse of the Seine and followed it at treetop level to Orly Airfield outside Paris.

At the Trianon Palace Hotel, de Guingand learned from Bedell Smith that he might be too late. Together, the two went to a small house in a nearby forest where Eisenhower's security officers had insisted that Eisenhower stay until the apparent threat to his life passed. "In a somberly lighted room, full of smoke from [Air Marshal] Tedder's pipe but made somewhat more cheerful by a healthy blaze in the fireplace," Eisenhower explained the intolerable position in which the British press reports and Montgomery's insistence on overall command placed General Bradley.

Eisenhower said he was "tired of the whole business" and had concluded that it had become a matter to be decided by the Combined Chiefs of Staff. He had already drafted a message to be sent through General Marshall to the Combined Chiefs, stating explicitly that they would have to choose between him and Montgomery. Should the Combined Chiefs decide in favor of Eisenhower, the British commander in Italy, Field Marshal Sir Harold Alexander, would be an acceptable substitute for Montgomery.

Well aware that it would be Montgomery who would have to go, but wanting no showdown in any case, de Guingand insisted that his chief had no inkling of the resentment his letter had fostered. He was convinced that once Montgomery understood, he would back down and cooperate. Withhold the message to Marshall for twenty-four hours, implored de Guingand, to afford him an opportunity to talk with Montgomery.

To both Eisenhower and Tedder it seemed that the damage had already been done, and neither was inclined to agree. Only when Bedell Smith took de Guingand's side did Eisenhower relent. He would sit on the message for a day.

Back in General Smith's office, de Guingand sent a message to Montgomery, saying that he planned to fly back the next day and come to Zonhoven to discuss an important matter; but because of continued bad weather, it was 4:30 P.M. before he reached Montgomery's headquarters. Since Montgomery was just sitting down to tea, de Guingand joined him. Neither man interrupted the ritual to discuss business. Rising, Montgomery said: "I'm going upstairs to my office, Freddie. Please come up when you have finished your tea."

When de Guingand came upstairs, he put the matter bluntly. "I've just come from SHAEF and seen Ike," he said, "and it's in the cards that you might have to go." Explaining the hard feelings at Eisenhower's headquarters in some detail, de Guingand told of the message Eisenhower was planning to send to Marshall. He "believed the situation could be put right," de Guingand concluded, but "it required immediate action."

To de Guingand, Montgomery seemed "genuinely and completely taken by surprise" and "found it difficult to grasp" what he was saying. He "looked completely non-plussed—I don't think I had ever seen him

so deflated. It was as if a cloak of loneliness had descended upon him."
Asked Montgomery: "What shall I do, Freddie?"

De Guingand pulled out a message he had already drafted, and with a
few changes, Montgomery approved it. He had "seen Freddie," the message began, and understood from him that Eisenhower was "greatly worried by many considerations." He had given Eisenhower his "frank
views" because that was what he believed Eisenhower wanted, but he was
"sure there are many factors which have a bearing quite beyond anything
I realize." The message concluded:

> Whatever your decision may be you can rely on me one hundred
> per cent to make it work and I know Brad will do the same. Very
> distressed that my letter may have upset you and I would ask you to
> tear it up. Your very devoted subordinate Monty.

Over icy roads, de Guingand drove to the 21st Army Group's rear
headquarters in Brussels, where he spoke candidly to four prominent
British news correspondents. Montgomery's command of American
forces, he explained, had been a temporary expedient, and in view of the
overwhelming number of American troops in Europe, pressure for an
overall British ground commander was not only self-defeating but dangerous. With the newsmen promising to consult their editors, de
Guingand telephoned Versailles. Bedell Smith told him that Eisenhower
had received Montgomery's message, had been "most touched," and the
signal to Washington "now reposed in the waste-paper basket."

The next day, Eisenhower forwarded to all three army group commanders an outline plan for future operations, which he had just finished
drafting when the crisis with Montgomery arose. In it, he proposed to
reduce the bulge in the Ardennes "by immediate attacks from north and
south" with Montgomery continuing to command in the north until the
First and Third Armies linked, whereupon Bradley was to resume command of the First Army. As he explained to Montgomery in a covering
letter, also written before he received Montgomery's apology, he was
leaving the Ninth Army under Montgomery for reasons of "military necessity," a decision, he said, that "most assuredly reflects my confidence
in you personally. Yet in the matter of command, he could "go no further."

That crisis between Eisenhower and Montgomery was as close as Adolf Hitler came to precipitating a break in the Western alliance, and it
was nowhere near a break. However heated and serious, it remained
merely another difference of opinion between field commanders, a controversy in large measure generated by a mercurial press always ready to
champion dissension and preach disaster. (Not just the British press; for
the American press was complaining vehemently that Montgomery had
committed no British troops to help in the Ardennes.) The insensitive
Montgomery was destined to provoke controversy again a few days later,

and the Chief of the Imperial General Staff, Field Marshal Brooke, who constantly lamented the inexperience of senior American commanders in "handling large masses in battle," would for long persist in raising the issue of "a more effective overall control of the ground forces"; but it remained an intramural issue among military men that in the end had no appreciable effect on conduct of the war by the Anglo-American alliance.

The bulge in the American line was forty miles wide at its base, sixty miles deep at the apex. The problem was how to eliminate it.

To George Patton, who had disliked the assignment of relieving Bastogne because it diverted him from the obvious solution, the answer was simple—the same as that taught between wars at the Command and General Staff College—cut it off at the base. ("If you get a monkey in the jungle hanging by his tail," said Patton, "it is easier to get him by cutting his tail than kicking him in the face.") He wanted to assume the defensive at Bastogne and with a reinforced XII Corps under Manton Eddy in the lead attack northeastward across the Sûre and Our Rivers into Germany to Bitburg and Prüm, there to link with a drive by the First Army southeastward from the Elsenborn Ridge. Those drives would penetrate deep into the enemy's rear and trap all the forces that had plunged into the Ardennes.

The First Army's Courtney Hodges agreed, but only "in principle." Hodges saw the roadnet leading southeast from the Elsenborn Ridge to Prüm as too limited to support a major advance, a view that the German commanders who had had such a task toiling through the Losheim Gap would certainly have seconded.

The man whom Montgomery had designated to spearhead the attack from the north, Joe Collins, had a proposal that would eliminate that problem and still cut the base of the German salient: Move his corps behind Malmédy and drive southeast on St. Vith while Patton drove north up the Skyline Drive.

When Montgomery visited Collins in the Château de Bessines on several occasions after the stopping of the 2d Panzer Division near Celles, Collins pressed that plan while at the same time urging Montgomery to get on with the attack before the Germans could consolidate their gains. Yet every time, Montgomery reiterated his concern for still another major German blow, which might well pierce the First Army's lines. Nobody, replied Collins, was going to break through "such top-flight divisions" as the 1st, 2d, 9th, and 30th, the 3d Armored, and the 82d Airborne. When Montgomery insisted it would be impossible to supply a corps over "a single road" (that from Malmédy to St. Vith), Collins responded: "Well, Monty, maybe you British can't but we can."

On December 27, Collins presented his plan to drive from Malmédy to St. Vith to General Hodges, but in view of Montgomery's objection, he proposed two other possibilities, both aimed at Houffalize for link-up with troops of the Third Army advancing north from Bastogne. Hodges chose to endorse one of those.

On the same day, before Eisenhower left by train for his meeting with Montgomery, Bradley visited him with his own proposal for eliminating the bulge. Patton, said Bradley, should attack with Middleton's VIII Corps from Bastogne on Houffalize and with Millikin's III Corps northeastward on St. Vith. (To ensure that Patton did not shift instead to the drive he wanted on Bitburg and Prüm, Bradley specified that the two new divisions afforded Patton, the 11th Armored and the 87th, had to be employed with the VIII Corps in the vicinity of Bastogne.) Hodges was to drive with Collins's VII Corps on Houffalize and with Ridgway's XVIII Airborne Corps push southeast on St. Vith. Again Bradley urged Eisenhower to return the First and Ninth Armies to his command and again he said that he would shift his headquarters to Namur.

While disapproving any immediate change in command, Eisenhower approved Bradley's plan of attack. When Montgomery subsequently agreed—at last persuaded by Joe Collins not to strike at the tip of the German salient, not to kick the monkey in the face—it became the Allied plan. It was no drive to cut the enemy's feet from under him and trap him in the Ardennes; it was instead a conservative push against his waist, combined with drives not unlike two windshield wipers sweeping the enemy back like raindrops toward St. Vith. When von Rundstedt learned the nature of his enemy's riposte, he called it, not without a touch of irony, the "Small Solution."

In ordering a diversionary attack against the 6th Army Group to force the Americans to pull some of their divisions from the Ardennes, Adolf Hitler displayed considerable prescience; for in taking over much of the Third Army's front to allow Patton to attack and in releasing the 87th Division, General Devers's command had become gravely overextended. Devers's Seventh U.S. Army and First French Army held a line 240 miles long, which included a big reentrant known as the Colmar Pocket that afforded the Germans a sally port west of the Rhine. General Eisenhower constantly worried about that extended line and told Devers on several occasions that he had to be prepared to give ground rather than endanger the integrity of his forces.

By Christmas Eve, it was already apparent that the Germans were planning an attack of some kind in the south. "Excellent agent sources [for which read ULTRA]," noted Devers's G-2, Brig. Gen. Eugene L. Harrison, "report enemy units building up in the Black Forest area [just east of the Rhine] for offensive."

That was one consideration behind General Eisenhower's decision two days later, on December 26, for Devers to pull back to the Vosges Mountains; but Devers interpreted that not as a directive but as another warning of what he might be called upon to do. On New Year's Eve the

6th Army Group was still in place along the German frontier and the Rhine in the sharp angle that is the extreme northeastern corner of France and around the periphery of the Colmar Pocket.

By that time indications of a German buildup and probable attack were clearer still. As before the attack in the Ardennes, ULTRA was telling nothing specific but was providing considerable information on the assembly of German troops. Several reports provided fairly accurate indications of the enemy order of battle. Another noted that replacements for the 17th SS Panzergrenadier Division were being rushed forward, and yet another revealed that the 21st Panzer Division was moving south. Those intercepted messages, when combined with prisoner interrogations and aerial reconnaissance, made it clear that an attack was coming, either on New Year's Eve or at the latest on New Year's Day.

In response to Eisenhower's warnings about possible withdrawal, General Devers—the only senior American commander whom Eisenhower had had no hand in selecting and thus one in whom he was never fully confident—had designated three fall-back positions, the last being the line of the Vosges; but he had ordered no withdrawal. One reason was Devers's concern for French sensibilities, for any large-scale withdrawal involved relinquishing the city of Strasbourg.

The French, Devers knew, saw Strasbourg symbolically as the capital of Alsace and Lorraine, the two provinces lost to the Germans from 1870 to 1918 and again from 1940 to late 1944. No Frenchman could forget that it was in Strasbourg in 1792 that Rouget de Lisle had composed what became the revered national anthem, *La Marseillaise.* Nor was there a French schoolchild who had not been moved to tears reading *"La Dernière Leçon"* ("The Last Lesson"), a touching short story by Alphonse Daudet about a schoolmaster's last class in the French language before German authorities in 1871 took charge. To abandon Strasbourg meant exposing thousands of Frenchmen to cruel German reprisal. More than that, to abandon Strasbourg was to serve up a part of the very soul of France.

When the German First Army attacked an hour before midnight on New Year's Eve with five divisions and with two panzer divisions in reserve, the importance of Strasbourg to the French either escaped General Eisenhower or else he deemed military considerations to be overriding. At the first word of the attack, Eisenhower told Bedell Smith to "call up Devers and tell him he is not doing what he was told." He wanted Devers to leave light screening forces on the plain between the Rhine and the Vosges and fall back on the mountains. That was as much as to say: Abandon Strasbourg.

As soon as the head of the French provisional government, Charles de Gaulle, learned of Eisenhower's directive, he promptly sent the chief of staff of the French Ministry of Defense, General Pierre Juin, to Versailles to protest. In a fury, Juin told Bedell Smith that France would never relinquish Strasbourg. Already de Gaulle had ordered the commander of the First French Army, General Jean de Lattre de Tassigny, to take responsibility for defending the city.

General Smith's well-known temper flared, for de Gaulle's action not only represented defiance of Eisenhower as Supreme Commander but unilateral alteration of an interarmy boundary. You go through with it, said Bedell Smith, and not one more bullet, not one more gallon of gasoline would the French Army receive.

In that case, responded Juin, the French government might deny American use of French railroads. If Eisenhower persisted, de Gaulle was prepared to withdraw the First French Army from his command.

It sounded like an argument in a school yard. It was in fact a clever ploy. Juin departed knowing that he had left General Smith visibly shaken and that Smith would tell his chief everything. That would afford Eisenhower time to reconsider before he met with de Gaulle at de Gaulle's request the next afternoon. Lest the stratagem miscarry, de Gaulle that night cabled President Roosevelt and Prime Minister Churchill for help. Roosevelt declined to intervene in what he considered to be a military matter. Scheduled to fly to Paris on January 3 to lunch with Eisenhower, Churchill withheld his judgment.

When the prime minister, delayed by bumpy flying weather over the Channel, reached Versailles around 2 P.M., General de Gaulle had already arrived, and at Eisenhower's invitation, Churchill sat in on the conference. Explaining the vital symbolic importance of Strasbourg to the French people, de Gaulle said that unless Eisenhower defended the city, he himself as head of state would be compelled to act independently. Of such importance was Strasbourg that he was prepared to risk losing the entire First French Army rather that relinquish the city without a fight.

Losing his temper, Eisenhower repeated Bedell Smith's threat to deprive the French Army of supplies; but in reality, even before opening the conference, he had begun to reconsider. The crisis in the Ardennes was past, and although Operation NORDWIND was a heavy blow, troops of the Seventh Army by nightfall of the second day had almost brought the main effort to a halt. Besides, there must be no threat by the French to the U.S. Army's lines of communication across France.

He would instruct General Devers, said Eisenhower, to withdraw only from the tip of the salient in the extreme northeastern corner of France back some twenty miles to the little Moder River. He would adjust the interarmy boundary to give responsibility for defending Strasbourg to the French. As de Gaulle departed, immensely relieved, Prime Minister Churchill, who had said not a word during the deliberations, remarked quietly to Eisenhower: "I think you've done the wise and proper thing."

So did the commander of the 6th Army Group, General Devers, and the commander of the Seventh Army, General Patch, for both saw Eisenhower's order to withdraw as premature. Fighting in bitter cold and heavy snow continued until January 25. One column advancing out of the Colmar Pocket got within thirteen miles of Strasbourg while another north of the city got within nine miles; but Operation *NORDWIND* ended with the Germans gaining nothing more than twenty miles of flat landscape of no tactical or strategic importance.

The offensive cost the Germans 25,000 casualties; the Americans, 15,600. Contrary to Adolf Hitler's goal, it produced no diminution of the American effort in the Ardennes. Lest the German operation should expand to the north, Eisenhower and Bradley on January 10 ordered Patton, over his strenuous objections, to send a division to back up his overextended XX Corps in defensive positions facing the Saar; Patton chose the 4th Armored Division, which was down to forty-two medium tanks and badly needed a rest in any case. That was all.

CHAPTER TWENTY-NINE

Erasing the Bulge

Once burned, twice cautious. Having perceived no intruders at all before December 16, Allied commanders and their intelligence officers in the days that followed saw a burglar under every bed. Their alarm persisted even after the Germans in front of the Meuse on Christmas Day and the next day suffered "one of the most serious things that can possibly happen to one in battle"—as Tweedledee explained it to Alice—getting one's head cut off.

At the height of the battle on December 22, General Eisenhower had issued an order of the day in which he noted that "By rushing out from his fixed defenses the enemy may give us the chance to turn his great gamble into his worst defeat." Everybody was to hold before him "a single thought—to destroy the enemy on the ground, in the air, everywhere—destroy him!" Yet when it came down to how to do that, the specter of all those burglars dictated caution. Not as much caution as Field Marshal Montgomery had urged, but caution nevertheless. As von Rundstedt put it: the Small Solution.

Concern for burglars was also evident in other actions of the Supreme Commander. Near the end of December Eisenhower suggested raising Belgian, Polish, and more French divisions, and plans were soon under way for equipping eight French divisions and close to 500,000 men— mostly Frenchmen—to guard lines of communication. In Washington, at Eisenhower's request, the Joint Chiefs of Staff stepped up the sailing dates of an airborne, three infantry, and three armored divisions to Europe. They also allocated to Eisenhower three more infantry divisions not previously scheduled for his command. General Marshall began to comb out support units in the United States, Alaska, and Panama to provide infantry replacements.

What about transferring divisions from Italy? asked Eisenhower. Perhaps 100,000 U.S. Marines? He set his staff to work on a plan for obtaining volunteers from segregated Negro support units to join the infantry.

On the theory that Hitler might be shifting divisions from the Eastern Front to the Ardennes, Eisenhower asked Marshall to obtain from the Russians "at the earliest possible moment some indication of their strategical and tactical intentions." The Red Army had been lying low since late summer; when would the Russians begin their long-awaited winter offensive?

On December 26, General Marshall notified Eisenhower that the Russian dictator, Joseph Stalin, would be pleased to confer with any senior officer whom Eisenhower might send to Moscow. Eisenhower promptly sent his British deputy, Air Marshal Tedder, but because of delays caused by bad weather in both Naples and Cairo, Tedder reached Moscow only in the middle of January. Said Eisenhower: "His trip is of the utmost importance," but by the time Tedder saw Stalin, events had overtaken his mission.

Even before visiting Versailles on January 3, Prime Minister Churchill had directed his service chiefs to find another quarter of a million men from somewhere, a perplexing requirement in view of the heavy levies already imposed on limited British manpower over six long years of war, and he wrote President Roosevelt urging more American troops. On January 6, Churchill, with Eisenhower's approval, wrote personally to Stalin: "The battle in the West is very heavy. . . . I shall be grateful if you can tell me whether we can count on a major Russian offensive during January. I regard the matter as urgent."

Stalin answered promptly, to explain that bad weather had held up the Red Army's offensive, but "taking into account the position of our Allies on the Western Front," the Russian high command had decided "to accelerate the completion of our preparations" and regardless of the weather, "open an offensive along the entire Central Front no later than the second half of January."

Whether Stalin would speed up his offensive remained problematical. In terms of his long-range goal of dominating as much of Europe as possible, he had no need to help his Western Allies, but he did have a need to get the Red Army moving westward to occupy as much territory as possible before the armies of America and Britain got there. Whatever Stalin's motivation, fourteen infantry divisions and two tank corps attacked across the Upper Vistula River on January 12, the start of what was to become a mammoth offensive.

The offensive did nothing to ease the situation for American forces in the Ardennes; for by that time the issue was no longer in doubt, and in any case, the Germans had shifted only one unit from the Eastern Front, a *Volksgrenadier* division that had been in reserve in Hungary. Born out of an unjustified concern (not far from panic), the call for help from Stalin was ill-considered and unnecessary. It was to help put Stalin in a strong bargaining position a few weeks later at Yalta, where, in response to an invitation long sought by Churchill and Roosevelt but issued only three days after Churchill's plea for help, the Allied heads of state came to discuss the postwar face of Europe. The Red Army's drive, proclaimed Stalin in an order of the day in February, "resulted in breaking the German attack in the West." At Yalta, he would play that for all it was worth when, in reality, Hitler's ill-starred adventure in the Ardennes actually eased the task of the Red Army.

Although Hitler insisted that the drive to gain the Meuse was to continue even as General von Manteuffel reduced Bastogne, the commander of the Fifth Panzer Army, with Field Marshal Model's tacit approval but without notifying the *Adlerhorst,* went on the defensive at Rochefort and Marche and directed full attention to Bastogne. It was essential to attack quickly, before the Americans could broaden their thin corridor into the town. Yet von Manteuffel could not be ready until December 30, and on the 27th, the 9th Armored Division's CCA, shifted hurriedly from Luxembourg, retook Sibret to open the Neufchâteau highway into Bastogne.

Von Manteuffel put much of his hope for severing the corridor in Colonel Remer's *Führer Begleit Brigade*, shifted from its brief commitment near Hotton, for the brigade had incurred nothing like the heavy losses in men and machines incurred by the panzer and SS panzer divisions. The brigade was to attack the corridor from the west to seize Sibret and cut the Neufchâteau highway, while another force struck simultaneously from the east across the Arlon highway.

That second force consisted of the *Führer Grenadier Brigade*; the 3d Panzergrenadier Division, its numbers sharply reduced after battering futilely against the Elsenborn Ridge; and the 1st SS Panzer Division, Joachim Peiper's outfit, which had enough repaired and replacement tanks to form a *Kampfgruppe* with the strength of a separate American tank battalion, perhaps forty to fifty tanks. The second force also had a powerful fresh unit, the 167th Volksgrenadier Division, hurried from a reserve position in Hungary.

Aware from radio intercepts that it would be several days before the American First Army attacked from the north, von Manteuffel assumed that General Patton would delay a renewed attack until the First Army was ready. In fact, Patton was already widening the corridor into Bastogne and was preparing for a major attack on December 30, the same day as von Manteuffel, in the direction of Houffalize.

Close along the Arlon highway an experienced 35th Infantry Division had entered the line between the 4th Armored and 26th Infantry Divisions, and an experienced 6th Armored Division was on the way. With the 9th Armored Division's CCA and the two divisions that Eisenhower released on the 28th (the 11th Armored and 87th Infantry Divisions), General Middleton's VIII Corps was to pass west of Bastogne and head for Houffalize.

On both sides of the corridor, the opposing attacks ran head-on into each other just as a foggy day was dawning, and predictable confusion ensued. Predictably, too, the inexperienced 11th Armored and 87th Infantry Divisions lost heavily, particularly in junior officers, but so did the Germans. Fighting with far greater determination than had been exhibited in a first commitment in Luxembourg, the 9th Armored Division's CCA brought the *Führer Begleit Brigade* to a halt well short of Sibret and the Neufchâteau highway. As the fighting resumed the next day, the Americans began to gain ground—however laboriously—toward the highway leading west out of Bastogne to St. Hubert.

On the night of December 30, the Luftwaffe returned to Bastogne with a raid far heavier than that of Christmas Eve. Since there was by then a way out of the town, many of the civilians grabbed a few personal belongings and took it.

Southeast of Bastogne, the veteran 35th Infantry Division stood full in the path of the German attack. A bloody melee ensued, and before the day was done the Germans had trapped and wiped out three American rifle companies. Although the 35th Division had arrived without its customary supporting tank battalion, communications were good to the adjacent 4th Armored Division, and General Gaffey's tanks lent a hand. The heaviest fighting was for the village of Lutrebois, only two and a half miles from the little road through Assenois over which supplies were moving into Bastogne. By early afternoon the weather had cleared sufficiently to bring American fighter-bombers to the scene, and the 35th Division's artillery made liberal use of the POZIT fuse. Even so, as night came, the *Volksgrenadiers* held Lutrebois.

There the German attack stalled. Although the day's gain extended what was already a salient in the American line to a depth of three miles and a width of four, a firm line sealed it on all three sides. The 26th Division attacking in the direction of Wiltz threatened one flank of the German salient, while the 6th Armored Division passed through Bastogne and on New Year's morning attacked northeast, threatening the other flank. The fresh armored troops quickly took three places that had figured prominently in the early fighting for Bastogne: Bizory, Neffe, and Mageret.

The failure to sever the corridor into Bastogne convinced General von Manteuffel that he stood no chance of taking the town and that the time had come to abandon all thought of continuing the offensive in the Ardennes. Lest the troops in the tip of the salient be trapped, he appealed to Field Marshal Model on the night of January 2 for permission to fall back to a line anchored on Houffalize. Von Lüttwitz, who still had troops in the tip of the bulge, lent his voice to the appeal. He was convinced the British were soon going to hit the tip, a possibility lent credence by the identification near Rochefort of a British division.

Although Model agreed professionally, he had no authority to sanction withdrawal or even to desist in trying to take Bastogne. For his troubles in asking, von Manteuffel received merely another order to attack. What was left of the 12th SS Panzer Division was on the way, along with a *Volksgrenadier* division transferred from the vicinity of Aachen. With these reinforcements, von Manteuffel was to try once again to capture Bastogne on January 4.

On January 3, Hitler at last admitted that his original plan to cross the Meuse and capture Antwerp had failed. Yet he was convinced—or so he said—that the bulge forged in the Ardennes could be turned to German advantage. In launching the offensive, Hitler reasoned, he had forced General Eisenhower to employ almost all his resources; was not the use of elite airborne divisions to do the brutal defensive work of infantry proof of that? By holding the bulge, he might keep the Allies spread thin elsewhere while he assembled divisions for spoiling attacks, such as Operation *NORDWIND*. That way he could prevent Eisenhower from concentrating for a renewed offensive to gain the Ruhr. Yet if the bulge was to be held, he had to have Bastogne, both to anchor the southern flank and to deny the town's roads to his enemy.

Hitler by that time had already demonstrated how much he wanted Bastogne—enough to risk what remained of the Luftwaffe to prevent Allied fighter-bombers from intervening in von Manteuffel's efforts to take the town. At his order, the Luftwaffe mustered every available plane to strike British and American airfields in the Netherlands, Belgium, and northeastern France. In the hope that Allied pilots and antiaircraft gunners would be less than alert in the wake of New Year's Eve, the Luftwaffe struck early on New Year's Day.

Over the Netherlands that morning, the pilot of an artillery observation plane yelled unbelievingly into his radio: "At least two hundred Messerschmitts flying low on course 320 degrees!" What he saw was the vanguard of three groups of planes, a total of 1,035 Focke-Wulf 190s and Messerschmitt 109s coming in on the deck to hit twenty-seven Allied airfields where row after row of fighter-bombers stood in close formation.

No source of intelligence, including ULTRA, had provided any warning. In what Allied airmen would later call the "Hangover Raid," the Germans destroyed 156 planes, 36 of them American, most of them hit on the ground or while trying to take off. The losses included Field Marshal Montgomery's personal C-47.

They were heavy losses, but they could be quickly replaced (Eisenhower sent Montgomery his own C-47). The Germans paid with over three hundred planes and as many irreplaceable pilots, their heaviest losses in a single day during the entire war. As a senior German air commander noted, it was the Luftwaffe's "death blow."

The snow was deeper than ever in the Ardennes, the temperatures lower, the fog thicker, the chill winds more penetrating when early on

BATTLE OF THE BULGE
DEC 26 - JAN 28

- GERMAN FRONT, DATE INDICATED

- AXIS OF ALLIED ATTACKS

Scale:
0   10   20   30
MILES

January 3, Joe Collins sent the 2d and 3d Armored Divisions driving southeast from the Hotton-Soy-Manhay highway toward Houffalize. Three old adversaries—the 12th and 560th Volksgrenadier and the 2d SS Panzer Divisions—stood in the way. The *Volksgrenadier* divisions had only three thousand men each, the SS panzer division six thousand; yet that was sufficient, when added to the cruel terrain and weather, to impose a crablike advance.

So murky was the atmosphere that not a single fighter-bomber could support the attack, and sorties by artillery planes were possible for no longer than an hour. It was a pattern that underwent little change for a fortnight. On only three days were fighter-bombers able to take to the air at all. Much of the time the men advanced through snow flurries, followed on the fourth day by a heavy snowfall that piled drifts in places to a depth of several feet.

Tanks stalled on icy hillsides. Trucks towing antitank guns or artillery pieces skidded, jackknifed, collided, and blocked vital roads for hours. Two trucks towing 105mm. howitzers plunged off a cliff. Bridges everywhere were out, the sites defended. The Germans occasionally counterattacked—a brace or so of tanks, a company or a battalion of infantry. Under those conditions, two miles a day was a major achievement.

For men of the Third Army, it was even rougher, for the foe around Bastogne was himself trying to attack and represented the best the Germans still had to offer. Bitterly cold, stung by biting winds and driven snow, nostrils frozen and lungs seared by the cold, Patton's troops saw little change in a pattern long familiar. Such well-known names as *Panzer Lehr*, the *Führer Begleit* and *Grenadier Brigades*, the 5th Parachute Division, the 26th Volksgrenadier Division, the 1st, 9th, and 12th SS Panzer Divisions. Not the elite formations that had plunged out of the mists and snow on December 16, but worthy adversaries nevertheless. Familiar, too, were many of the place names, the same villages where small clumps of paratroopers, armored infantrymen, and a few tanks a fortnight before had thwarted the Germans in the race for Bastogne; Senonchamps, Champs, Mageret, Longvilly, Noville.

Having had no success against the corridor south of Bastogne, von Manteuffel struck from the north astride the Houffalize highway. Under the command of General Priess and the 1st SS Panzer Corps, there were four divisions: the 26th and 340th Volksgrenadier, the latter recently arrived from the vicinity of Aachen, and the 9th and 12th SS Panzer Divisions. The two SS panzer divisions between them had only fifty-five tanks.

Von Manteuffel anticipated that the attack would get nowhere, and he was right. Before the day of January 4 was out, Field Marshal Model ordered him to release the 9th SS Panzer Division to move north to help the Sixth Panzer Army, and the next day von Manteuffel took it upon himself to pull what was left of the 12th SS Panzer Division to form a reserve. A threat to Bastogne no longer existed.

Three days later, on January 8, Hitler finally agreed to a limited withdrawal from the tip of the bulge. It was not to go all the way back to Houffalize, as his field commanders wanted, but to a line anchored on the point where the two branches of the Ourthe join five miles west of the town. That was Adolf Hitler's first grudging admission that the offensive in the Ardennes had failed utterly.

*   *   *

Freddie de Guingand's appeal to four senior British newsmen in Brussels failed to stop the British newspapers from praising Montgomery and criticizing Eisenhower for not giving him overall command of the Allied ground forces. In an effort to quell it, SHAEF's public relations office on January 5 made the first public announcement of the shift of command in the Ardennes, noting that it had come about "by instant agreement of all concerned" and only because the German thrust had severed communications between Bradley's headquarters and the First and Ninth Armies. Yet far from quieting the British press, the announcement fueled the outcry.

At Luxembourg City, General Bradley was furious that SHAEF's announcement made no mention that the shift in command was temporary, and he and his staff saw the furor in the British press as "a cataclysmic Roman Holiday." So much of the comment involved either direct or implied criticism of Eisenhower that Prime Minister Churchill felt impelled to write President Roosevelt that "His Majesty's Government have complete confidence in General Eisenhower and feel acutely any attacks made on him."

According to Montgomery, he too was "perturbed. . . about the sniping at Eisenhower which was going on in the British press." He informed Churchill that he intended holding a press conference to explain "how the whole Allied team rallied to the call" in the Ardennes and "put in a strong plea for Allied solidarity." Churchill approved.

Most of what Montgomery had to say to newspapermen at his headquarters on January 7 reflected that purpose. He paid high tribute to the American soldier, who was "basically responsible for Rundstedt not doing what he wanted to do." He would "never want to fight alongside better soldiers" and singled out three particularly heroic stands: the Elsenborn Ridge, St. Vith, and Bastogne.

So, too, he praised Eisenhower. He was "absolutely devoted" to him, and it grieved him when he saw "uncomplimentary remarks about him in the British press." Eisenhower bore "a great burden," needed "our fullest support," and had "a right to expect it." "Let us all rally round the captain of the team."

Had that been all Montgomery said, no repercussions would have occurred; but some of his other remarks were imperious, after the manner of "St. George come to slay the dragon." Von Rundstedt, he said, had driven "a deep wedge into the center of the United States First Army and the split might have become awkward"; but "As soon as I saw what was happening I took certain steps myself to ensure that if the Germans got to the Meuse they would certainly not get over that river." He took "precautions," he was "thinking ahead." Nevertheless, "the situation began to deteriorate." Yet "the whole Allied team rallied to meet the danger; national considerations were thrown overboard; General Eisenhower placed me in command of the whole Northern front." (No mention of why.)

Then: "I employed the whole available power of the British Group of Armies," bringing it "into play very gradually" so as not to interfere with American lines of communication. "Finally, it was put into battle with a bang and today British divisions are fighting hard on the right flank of the United States First Army." Thus British troops were fighting alongside "American forces who have suffered a hard blow. This is a fine Allied picture."

Much of that was patently untrue. For a legitimate reason—so low were British manpower reserves that Montgomery had to husband the 30th Corps for the renewal of the drive into Germany—Montgomery had moved British troops only into reserve positions, sparing them the heavy casualties they were bound to incur if he sent them east of the Meuse. As he talked, "British divisions" were not "fighting hard on the right flank of the United States First Army," only the 29th Armoured Brigade, two battalions of the 6th Airborne Division, and the 53d Welsh Division, under orders to push the Germans back from the tip of the bulge, but cautiously, in order to avoid undue losses. Hardly "the whole available power of the British Group of Armies." Was that commitment "with a bang"?

The battle, Montgomery continued, had been "most interesting . . . possibly one of the most interesting and tricky" he had ever "handled." The first step, he said, was to "'head off' the enemy from the tender spots and vital places," then "rope him in and make quite certain that he could not get to the places he wanted, *and also* that he was slowly but surely removed away from those places."

Yet how much of that had Montgomery actually done?

- He wanted to pull back from the Elsenborn Ridge even as the battle there was almost won, but bowed to Hodges's objection.
- He wanted to pull back immediately from St. Vith, which would have afforded the Germans early use of a vital road network but again bowed to Hodges's objection; and by the time he specifically ordered withdrawal, Hodges had already specified that the decision on withdrawal was to be up to the man on the ground: Hasbrouck.
- He ordered the 82d Airborne Division to withdraw from the Salm River to the Trois Ponts–Manhay line, but Ridgway had already directed Gavin to prepare for such a withdrawal.
- He ordered relinquishing the Manhay crossroads, but in recognition that that opened to the Germans another route to the Ourthe River, Hodges ordered the crossroads retaken.
- He ordered Joe Collins to assemble for an attack, but when most of Collins's force became involved in the defensive battle, authorized with-

drawal. Collins attacked instead and stopped the Germans short of the Meuse.

- When it came to reducing the bulge, Montgomery moved so slowly— however "surely"—that the Germans were able to regroup undisturbed by the First Army for new assaults on Bastogne.

What, then, had Montgomery accomplished? His presence assured what conceivably might not have been possible with Bradley remaining in Luxembourg City: one hand at the helm. Yet Hodges and Simpson of the Ninth Army were old friends from the days of the Great War, and every division that moved to the Ardennes from the Ninth Army, with the exception of the 2d Armored Division, was on the way when Montgomery assumed command. Even without Montgomery's request for the 2d Armored Division, which was the Ninth Army's reserve, there was hardly any likelihood that Simpson would have withheld it; and even before Montgomery asked for Collins and the headquarters of the VII Corps, Hodges had already alerted Collins to move to the Ardennes and prepare to attack.

Montgomery's contribution rested in those "certain steps," the "precautions," the "thinking ahead," essential to positioning the divisions of the 30th Corps as a reserve behind the Meuse, which made it possible for Simpson to release divisions without undue concern that the Germans might take advantage of a thinned front. Yet as a loyal member of the Allied team, as Montgomery professed to be and was, he had already made that move even before Eisenhower put him in command.

There was no question but that Montgomery was highly complimentary on the achievements of American troops (wrote *The New York Times:* "No handsomer tribute was ever paid to the American soldier"), and the appeal for solidarity behind Eisenhower rang of sincerity. Yet the other remarks left the impression, as de Guingand noted, that Montgomery was saying: "What a good boy am I!" That as Montgomery himself later noted, he "appeared, to the sensitive, to be triumphant—not over the Germans but over the Americans."

For one as sensitive as Omar Bradley over the transfer of the Ninth Army and, most especially, his beloved First Army, probably anything Montgomery said would have rankled. ("Not only should I not have held the conference," wrote Montgomery later, "but I should have been even more careful than I was trying to be.") Bradley learned of Montgomery's remarks by what he took to be a broadcast by the BBC. In fact an Australian newsman, Chester Wilmot, believed what Bradley heard was his own dispatch to the BBC which the Germans had intercepted, altered, and rebroadcast over a propaganda station in the Netherlands. Whatever the case—and Bradley was as livid in later years, when he had had time to read accounts of the press conference, as he had been at the time—Bradley was "all-out right-down-to-his-toes mad."

He quickly telephoned Eisenhower, protesting both Montgomery's remarks and SHAEF's failure to note in its announcement that the transfer of command was temporary. Although fairly certain that Eisenhower would never make Montgomery overall ground commander, Bradley wanted to make his position unmistakably clear. "After what has happened," he said, "I cannot serve under Montgomery." If Eisenhower put Montgomery in overall command, he "must send me home." He added that Patton too had told him he would refuse to serve under Montgomery.

Without consulting Eisenhower (nor had Montgomery), Bradley called his own press conference, in which he defended his decision to hold the Ardennes lightly. Describing the circumstances of Montgomery's assuming command, he used the word "temporary" three times. He also said that as soon as the forces of the First and Third Armies joined hands, he was to reassume command of both the First and Ninth Armies. Although he knew that Eisenhower had already decided to leave the Ninth Army with Montgomery, he hoped his misstatement might prompt Eisenhower to reconsider.

A fortnight later Winston Churchill entered the arena to set matters right. Before the House of Commons on January 18, he noted that the battle in the Ardennes was primarily an American battle. "The Americans have engaged 30 or 40 men for every one we have engaged and they have lost 60 to 80 men for every one of us." It was, Churchill continued, "the greatest American battle of the war and will, I believe, be regarded as an ever famous American victory."

With that, the tempest was over. Adolf Hitler may well have learned of it and taken some comfort from it, but it was again no more than an intramural issue among proud military commanders and posed no threat to the Anglo-American alliance. Indeed, when Bradley told Eisenhower that if he had to serve under Montgomery, he would forfeit "the confidence of my command," he was overrating the importance of the issue. They read British newspapers and listened to the BBC at Versailles and Luxembourg City, but down in the foxholes, nobody read newspapers other than the *Stars & Stripes* (usually a day or so late) and nobody had radios.

Did it really matter to the American soldier, fighting for his life in the harsh cold and snow of the Ardennes, who commanded him at the top? Who was this Montgomery? Who was Bradley? Who, even, was Hodges or Gerow, Collins, or Ridgway? (Patton was another matter.) A front-line soldier was immensely well informed if he knew the name of his company commander, who had just arrived the day before to replace that other one who had lasted only a week.

As British units—the 29th Armoured and 34th Tank Brigades, the 6th

Airborne, 51st Highland, and 53d Welsh Divisions—left the tip of the bulge to regroup for a renewed drive to the Rhine, troops of the First and Third Armies plowed slowly but inexorably toward Houffalize. As juncture neared, a division in each army set out to achieve the honor of making the link-up.

In the First Army, that was the 84th Infantry Division, which formed a thirty-three-man patrol representing all battalions of the 334th Infantry. Shortly before noon on January 15, the patrol crossed the Ourthe near the confluence of the two branches of the river and settled down in a village to await arrival of troops of the 11th Armored Division. Word came late that night that the patrol was to move closer to Houffalize. At two thirty in the morning, cold and exhausted, the men holed up in a Belgian farmhouse, where the owner and his family welcomed them with bread, butter, and coffee.

At nine thirty the next morning, January 16, the second-in-command of the patrol, Pfc. Rodney Himes, spotted a soldier outside the farmhouse. Since all the men were under orders to stay inside, Himes beckoned the man in order to chew him out. He wasn't from the 84th Division, said the soldier; he was from the 41st Armored Cavalry Reconnaissance Squadron, 11th Armored Division.

That man had apparently strayed from his unit, which on orders from the commander of the 11th Armored Division, Brig. Gen. Charles S. Kilburn, acting on word from General Patton, had started out on January 15 to establish contact with the First Army. Because the squadron commander, Lt. Col. Miles Foy, was at the moment away, his executive officer, Maj. Michael J. L. Greene, led the advance.

Early on the 16th, Greene and his men reached high ground overlooking the east branch of the Ourthe and the rubble of a town nestled in the valley, which a sign along the road indicated was Houffalize. Some of Greene's men spotted soldiers moving along a crest on the far side of the river—they could be Americans, they could be Germans—and Greene sent a six-man patrol to investigate. When the squadron commander, Colonel Foy, arrived in his jeep, he set off in the wake of the patrol.

On the north bank, a motion picture cameraman, Staff Sgt. Douglas Wood, arrived in mid-morning at positions of a task force of the 2d Armored Division's CCA commanded by Colonel O'Farrell. Wood said he thought juncture between the American armies was imminent and he wanted to be on hand to film it. Having paid little attention to the possibility of a link-up and expecting relief momentarily by another unit, O'Farrell discouraged him. Wood was on the point of giving up when the commander of Company F, 41st Armored Infantry Regiment, asked Wood to film his men.

As Wood began filming the infantrymen in their foxholes, a figure emerged from a nearby wood. The men waved him forward, but the soldier paused briefly to beckon others behind him. They were from the 41st

Armored Cavalry Reconnaissance Squadron, 11th Armored Division, said the men, and having waded the river, they were goddamned wet and cold.

Close behind the patrol came Colonel Foy with his driver and radio operator, their jeep left down at the river. When Foy said he wanted to make contact with a senior officer, Sergeant Wood took him to find Colonel O'Farrell.

As they approached O'Farrell's tank, Wood called out: "There's a colonel here from the 11th Armored to see you, sir."

O'Farrell's head and shoulders emerged from the turret. "Well, Jesus Christ," blurted Foy, "if it isn't O'Farrell . . . Haven't seen you since Fort Knox."

That night the 2d Armored Division moved into Houffalize, and the next day, January 17, the First Army went back to the open arms of Omar Bradley.

On January 12, Hitler ordered the four SS panzer divisions pulled from the line to reserve positions near St. Vith, ostensibly to guard against an American attack along the base of the bulge, but in reality a first step in extricating the Sixth Panzer Army and leaving responsibility for what remained of the bulge to the Fifth Panzer Army. To von Rundstedt, that indicated that Hitler was at last facing reality in the Ardennes. Upon arriving at the *Adlerhorst* two days later and receiving no long lecture, he was sure of it. He seized the opportunity to ask not only for an immediate withdrawal behind Houffalize but for authority to withdraw by stages all the way to the Rhine, whose broad moat provided the only hope of stopping the Allied armies.

Even though Hitler had, indeed, accepted the inevitability of losing the ground gained in his offensive, von Rundstedt was asking too much. Approving withdrawal behind Houffalize, Hitler also authorized further withdrawal, when forced by American pressure, to the frontier and the West Wall. There the German armies were to stand. Soon after that he left the *Adlerhorst* for Berlin, and a week later, on January 22, he ordered the SS panzer divisions with the two SS corps headquarters shifted to the Eastern Front.

Although the soldiers of the German Army in the Ardennes deeply resented the withdrawal of the SS divisions, thinking they were to get a rest, they continued to resist with a tenacity that to American soldiers and their commanders defied explanation. For the most part, their resistance centered on occasional key high ground, at road junctions, and in villages. The villages were of importance to both sides, for only there was to be found protection from the cold. In most cases, it took direct fire from tanks and tank destroyers to blast the Germans out.

As the days passed, von Manteuffel and his corps and division commanders began to exceed the authority granted them by Hitler and sometimes authorized withdrawal even without American pressure, for it was vital to begin getting men and such vehicles as had gasoline back across the few tactical bridges spanning the Our River. When that happened, American units might advance for an hour or even half a day without a shot fired at them. Then, suddenly, at a stream bank, a farmhouse, the edge of a wood or a village, a flurry of fire from automatic weapons or shelling from mortars and artillery would erupt. Again a slow, costly fight to dig the Germans out, and then they almost always counterattacked with a company or a battalion.

Most of the American divisions that fought in the defensive phase joined the drive back. As a part of the First Army were the 1st, 30th, 75th, and 84th Infantry Divisions; the 82d Airborne Division; the 2d Division's 23d Infantry; the surviving regiment of the 106th Division; the 4th Cavalry Group; the separate 517th Parachute Infantry; and the 2d, 3d, and 7th Armored Divisions. As a part of the Third Army, the 4th, 5th, 26th, 35th, 80th, and 87th Infantry Divisions; the 101st Airborne Division; and the 6th and 11th Armored Divisions. Joining them were four units new to the Ardennes: with the First Army, the 83d Infantry Division; with the Third Army, the 6th Cavalry Group and the 17th Airborne and 90th Infantry Divisions.

Back to places with bitter memories: Baugnez, where the 30th Division found grisly snow-covered evidence of murder; Vielsalm, Salmchâteau, St. Vith, where a new commander of the V Corps, General Huebner, afforded the honor of entering the demolished town to the 7th Armored Division and General Hasbrouck in turn afforded it to Bruce Clarke's CCB; the Café Schumann crossroads; Wiltz, Clervaux, Consthum, Marnach, Diekirch, Fouhren.

On January 18, General Patton at last got a drive going—as he had always wanted—along the base of the bulge, an attack by General Eddy's XII Corps across the Sûre River and up the Skyline Drive. It was too late at that point to hope to trap large German forces, but the thrust speeded up an already frantic German scramble for the tactical bridges across the Our. On the 22d, as leaden skies finally cleared, pilots were early in the air, jubilant to find German vehicles stalled bumper to bumper waiting their turn to cross ice-encrusted bridges. Astride the Skyline Drive, infantrymen cheered to see the carnage that air and artillery wrought. By January 26, 1945, only a few small German delaying detachments remained, and they were all eliminated by the 28th, the official date set by the U.S. Army for the end of the Ardennes campaign.

Adolf Hitler in his desperate gamble had failed not only to reach Antwerp, which his generals never expected to gain, but he also fell short of his interim objective, the Meuse River, which his generals saw as a reasonably realistic goal. However it might be argued that Hitler had no alternative to ultimate defeat except, as von Clausewitz put it, "to regard the greatest daring as the greatest wisdom," to concentrate his forces in "one desperate blow . . . employing the assistance of subtle stratagem," all he accomplished was to assure swift success for the Red Army's renewed drive in the East and, possibly, to delay the Allied advance by a few weeks. In the end, he probably speeded his country's ultimate collapse.

Among 600,000 Americans eventually involved in the fighting—including 29 divisions, 6 mechanized cavalry groups, and the equivalent of 3 separate regiments—casualties totaled 81,000, of which 15,000 were captured and 19,000 killed. Among 55,000 British—2 divisions and 3 brigades—casualties totaled 1,400, of which just over 200 were killed. The Germans, employing close to 500,000 men—including 28 divisions and 3 brigades—lost at least 100,000 killed, wounded, and captured.

Both sides lost heavily in weapons and equipment, probably as many as 800 tanks on each side, and the Germans a thousand planes. Yet the Americans could replace their losses in little more than a few weeks, while the Germans could no longer make theirs good. Only foul weather, German ingenuity, and American recourse to the Small Solution prevented the Germans from losing even more men and machines.

The German soldier in the Ardennes amazed his adversary. Short of transport, short of gasoline, short of artillery because of the lack of transport and gasoline, his nation on the brink of defeat, he nevertheless fought with such courage and determination that the American saw him as fanatic. What motivated him to such ends? Was it the tradition of discipline dating from Frederick the Great? Unit loyalty? Personal honor? Fear of what defeat held in store for his country? Harsh discipline? Threats to his family? A pistol at his back? Whatever his motivation, he performed with heroism and sacrifice, marred only by the excesses of a few, primarily by the SS.

The victory in the Ardennes belonged to the American soldier, for he provided time to enable his commanders—for all their intelligence failure—to bring their mobility and their airpower into play. At that point the American soldier stopped everything the German Army threw at him.

A belief would long persist that when the Germans first struck, some American troops fled in disarray. In a book published as late as the fortieth anniversary of the battle, one historian noted that "during the early stages . . . hundreds of American troops fled to the safety of the rear in sheer panic."

That was patently false. Some individuals deserted, often getting as far back as Liège or Dinant before being apprehended. Yet with the possible exception of the conglomerate group of infantrymen hurriedly thrown together from men in a rest center to hold Honsfeld against Peiper's tanks, no front-line American unit fled without a fight. After hard fighting—out of ammunition, overwhelmed by tanks—some fell back in disorder, and there was indeed brief panic within the 9th Armored Division's CCR at Longvilly; but anybody with any knowledge of what it is like to confront the enemy would recognize that exigent circumstances were involved.

There were many cases where retreating troops, halted and thrown back into the line with some other unit, quickly melted away. Yet that is not an uncommon occurrence on the battlefield, for the individual lacks unit loyalty, his own noncommissioned and junior officers are no longer there either to inspire or to discipline him, and he has nobody to let down but strangers. On the other hand, those same men, again afforded unit identity, almost always rallied. A case in point was Team SNAFU in Bastogne.

What many did see—including Major Boyer on the road behind St. Vith—were supporting units hastily falling back. Yet in most cases those units had authority to withdraw. Why expose corps artillery pieces, big antiaircraft guns, ordnance and quartermaster depots, hospitals, replacement depots, whatever, to devastation or capture? Was anything gained by delaying withdrawal of the platoon of the 47th Field Hospital from Waimes so long that 2d Lt. Mabel Jessop and nine other nurses almost became victims of the massacre at Baugnez? Only when the withdrawing units clogged the roads did any form of panic develop. Anybody who has difficulty differentiating between hurried (even harried) withdrawal and panic should read Ernest Hemingway's *A Farewell to Arms*.

Except for a few individuals, the front-line American soldier stood his ground. Surprised, stunned, unbelieving, incredulous, not understanding what was hitting him, he nevertheless held fast until his commanders ordered withdrawal or until he was overwhelmed. If nobody ever achieved sufficient superiority on the battlefield to overwhelm his enemy and compel him to surrender or flee, nobody would ever win. It happens to one side or another in every battle, else there is stalemate, and it is folly to think that in every case the American soldier will be the one who wins.

Hitler saw the American soldier as the weak component (the "Italians") of the Western alliance, the product of a society too heterogeneous to field a capable fighting force. Bouck, Crawford, Tsakanikas, Umanoff, Moore, Reid, Descheneaux, O'Brien, Jones, Erlenbusch, Goldstein, McKinley, Mandichak, Spigelman, Garcia, Russamano, Wieszcyk, Nawrocki, Campbell, Barcellona, Leinbaugh. Black men, too, although their color was hardly to be reflected in their names. The heterogeneity was indeed there, but at many a place—at Krinkelt-Rocherath, at Dom. Bütgenbach, in the Losheim Gap, behind the Schnee Eifel, at St. Vith, atop the Skyline Drive, at the Parc Hôtel, Echternach, Malmédy, Stavelot, Stoumont, Bastogne, Verdenne, Baraque de Fraiture, Hotton, Noville—the American soldier put the lie to Hitler's theory. His was a story to be told to the sound of trumpets.

Epilogue

Well before the final victory in Europe, the U.S. Army began canvassing prisoner-of-war compounds in search of German soldiers who might have been involved in war crimes against soldiers and civilians in the American sectors, with particular attention to a search for the perpetrators of the Malmédy Massacre. Not until several months after the war ended was the search completed and five hundred former members of *Kampfgruppe Peiper*, along with their superiors, assembled for interrogation.

Among them was the commander of the Sixth Panzer Army, Dietrich; his chief of staff, Kraemer; the commander of the 1st SS Panzer Corps, Priess; and Peiper himself. All four were charged with an illegal order in regard to treatment of prisoners or with transmitting on illegal order and Peiper, in addition, with failing to give instructions on the disposition of prisoners of war.

Along with sixty-nine other suspects winnowed from the five hundred, the officers were transferred in the spring of 1946 to a detention barracks at the site of one of the most notorious Nazi concentration camps at Dachau. The trial began at Dachau on May 16, officially designated as *U.S.* v. *Valentin Bersin, et al.* (after a tank commander whose name came first alphabetically among the defendants). The prosecution charged that the defendants as a group

> did willfully, deliberately, and wrongfully permit, encourage, aid, abet and participate in the killing, shooting, ill treatment, abuse and torture of members of the Armed Forces of the United States of America, and of unarmed allied civilians.

There was a separate bill of particulars for each of twenty-four officers and forty-nine noncommissioned officers or enlisted men.

Among survivors of the massacre who testified for the prosecution either in pre-trial depositions or at the trial were Lieutenant Lary and Sergeant Zach; and among the Belgian civilians, André Schroeder on the

620

killings at Honsfeld and Madame Grégoire on the killings of civilians at Stavelot. Major McCown testified in defense of Peiper, basically to the effect that there were no killings of American prisoners at La Gleize and that Peiper and his men exhibited high military competence and treated their prisoners humanely.

During the course of the trial, the prosecution freely admitted gaining confessions through the use of hoods (as if the man was to be executed), false witnesses, and mock trials. All seventy-three defendants were nevertheless convicted. On July 11, 1946, they were sentenced:

> to death: 43, including Peiper.
> to life imprisonment: 22, including Dietrich.
> to prison for 10, 15, or 20 years: 18, including Priess (20 years) and Kraemer (10 years).

The prisoners were transferred to Landsberg fortress, where Adolf Hitler served time following his abortive *putsch* in Munich in 1923. An exhaustive review process then began. Each of two review boards recommended reductions in some of the sentences, citing irregularities in pretrial investigations and the trial itself, including a number of questionable procedural rulings by the bench. As finally recommended by the Theater Judge Advocate for War Crimes to the commander of the American Zone of Occupation, General Lucius Clay, Dietrich's sentence of life imprisonment should be confirmed, but thirteen convictions should be disallowed, and only thirteen of the forty-three death sentences (including Peiper's) should be carried out.

Those recommendations came only in the spring of 1948, by which time a Cold War had begun, and many Americans had come to look more kindly on their erstwhile enemy. Returned to civilian life, the chief defender, Col. Willis M. Everett, Jr., began a fervent campaign in behalf of the defendants. Like the review boards, Everett deplored both the methods used in the pre-trial investigation (two of the principal interrogators were German Jews who had emigrated to the United States upon the rise of Hitler) and the trial itself. Although Everett had never been in combat, he was convinced that the SS troops had acted without premeditation in the heat of battle and maintained that many an American soldier had killed prisoners under similar circumstances. Everett appealed to the Judge Advocate General in Washington, to the Supreme Court (which declined to hear the case), to the newspapers, and to a friend in Congress, who succeeded in getting the allegations before Secretary of the Army Kenneth Royall.

Royall created a three-man commission to review Everett's allegations (the commission upheld the thirteen death sentences) and called on General Clay in Germany for yet another review. Religious leaders and others in Germany began to appeal to the American Congress and to air their distress in the German press. More stories—not always substantiated—of ill-treatment of the prisoners emerged: broken teeth, blows to the genitals. Some American newspapers were soon expressing doubt about the findings of all war crimes trials and deploring the depths to which American military justice had sunk. A strange alliance of pacifists and right-wing, anti-Semitic groups joined the din; on the other side were the veterans' organizations.

In March, 1949, the Senate Armed Services Committee appointed a subcommittee to investigate the trial and Colonel Everett's allegations and invited the participation of a member of the Senate Investigations Subcommittee, who had tried unsuccessfully to obtain the investigation for his subcommittee. He was a junior senator, eager to distract attention from his own indictment for unethical conduct as an attorney and judge in his home state and equally eager for exposure to establish himself on the national scene. Since some of his constituents were wealthy, right-wing, and pro-German, the case was tailormade for him: Joseph McCarthy of Wisconsin.

McCarthy made a circus of the hearings. To demonstrate that he knew what was meant by the heat of battle, he paraded his own dubious war record as a pilot in the Pacific. It was pitiful, he shouted, that "16- or-17-year-old boys" should be "kicked in the testicles, crippled for life." So often did McCarthy raise the subject of genitals that "It sometimes seemed that [he] believed the quality of postwar American military justice to hinge on the condition of the sexual organs of German prisoners." He viciously attacked one of the pre-trial interrogators, a German-Jewish immigrant, and bluntly accused him time after time of perjury. He wondered if the officer would submit to a lie detector test; there would be, he said snidely, "no kicking in the groin or anything like that."

On May 20, 1949, McCarthy issued a press release, then took the floor before the subcommittee to accuse the U.S. Army of "Gestapo and OGPU tactics" and the subcommittee of attempts to "whitewash" the army's conduct in the Malmédy case. Declaring the hearings a "shameful farce," he stalked out of the room, soon to find another *cause célèbre* through which to project himself into the national limelight.

The final report of the Senate subcommittee proved or disproved nothing, but the widely publicized hearings put additional pressure on General Clay in Europe. Even as the hearings were under way, he commuted six of the thirteen remaining death sentences to life imprisonment. All the while furor was mounting in the German press, which, with the end of military government, had markedly increased. (Poor Peiper—his wife, his three blond children.) Yet another review board conducted a continuing examination of all cases of war crimes, and before long, the seven remaining death sentences for the Malmédy Massacre, including Peiper's, were commuted to life imprisonment.

As the Federal Republic of Germany neared full sovereignty and acceptance into the European family of nations, custody of the remaining prisoners passed to the Germans, and a board composed of three Germans and a representative each of the United States, Great Britain, and France was empowered to make recommendations for clemency and parole. In 1954, the board reduced Peiper's sentence to thirty-five years. In 1955, Dietrich was paroled; and shortly before Christmas, 1956, the last prisoner still in the Landsberg fortress, Joachim Peiper, having served (including pre-trial determent) eleven years, departed a free man.

Despite the campaign in Germany for the release of the Malmédy prisoners, Peiper found the environment hostile. He soon moved to Alsace to the village of Traves, where he supported himself and his family by translating books. All seemed to be well until in the summer of 1976 a sensational article on the notorious resident of Traves appeared in the French Communist newspaper *L'Humanité*. Two weeks later, fire bombs destroyed Peiper's house and killed the sixty-year-old former commander of *Kampfgruppe Peiper*.

Author's Note

At twenty-two years of age, I fought in the Battle of the Bulge as a rifle company commander and subsequently wrote an account of my wartime experiences, *Company Commander,* which led me to a career as a civilian historian with the United States Army.

During the forty years since the battle, there have been four histories by American authors, including a superb official military history by my friend and former mentor, Hugh M. Cole, which is the essential starting point for any research on the battle. Although I admire the three general works, I eventually became convinced that only someone who knew the fighting firsthand could capture the special aura of the battle, one who knew what it was like to live in a frozen foxhole under German shelling, to see German soldiers in greatcoats charging toward you like—it seemed to us—men possessed, to experience the numbing horror of mammoth tanks clanking toward you, their long cannon preceding them like something obscene.

I was further convinced that whoever that person was should also be able to bring to the story knowledge of military factors at the command level, what it meant to senior commanders to face the greatest crisis to hit the Western Front during the course of the war. At the same time, he should provide an interpretive account of the military campaign sufficiently interesting and understandable to attract the general reader.

With the encouragement of my friend John Toland, who wrote one of the early books on the battle, I concluded upon my retirement in early 1979 that I should attempt the assignment. I approached the work with a kind of messianic zeal, for I wanted to tell the story to my own satisfaction (the battle had shaped my life, and I have always felt that I left a little something of me in the Ardennes). I also wanted to tell it for the veteran of the battle, who in many cases knew little of what went on beyond hand grenade range of his foxhole, the veteran whose attention would surely be refocused on the battle upon its fortieth anniversary in

1984. And I wanted to tell it in terms understandable to the generations who have come after us, to demonstrate that we were no cardboard figures of history but young men with human frailties like everybody else, suddenly involved in a terrible struggle with which we somehow coped, almost always with fear, sometimes with cowardice, sometimes with courage that we never knew we had.

During my five years of research and writing, I returned to the Ardennes four times for months at a time. I traveled what seemed to me every way and by-way of what is today a beautiful region, found old foxholes (including my own) in fir forests, dug from them spent cartridges and corroded fragments of shells. I talked with many civilians who shared our ordeal, and I became closely acquainted with local historians and in particular with a group of men and women in Luxembourg who are dedicated to studying the battle and unearthing previously undisclosed information, the *Cercle d'Etudes sur la Bataille des Ardennes*.

Although considerable material exists on the actions and decisions of senior German commanders, I wanted to find out from soldiers of lesser ranks what it was like to fight us. Thus I arranged to interview many German veterans, corresponded with others, and obtained more than a thousand pages of published and unpublished materials, both personal accounts and unit histories.

In pursuit of fresh material from American veterans, I placed notices in veterans' publications and received a heart-warming response. I was particularly touched by the responses of two men who survived the dreadful Malmédy Massacre, who told me that they had never before talked publicly of their experience but were persuaded to do so in the belief that the man who wrote *Company Commander* would understand.

I can only trust that I have fulfilled their faith and my assumed responsibility to other veterans, as well as to readers from later generations.

Acknowledgments

Many people helped make this book possible. Credit to some is provided in the documentation by chapters, but there are others—Americans, Belgians, British, Germans, and Luxembourgers—to whom I owe special tribute.

United States: In the U.S. Army Center of Military History, Carol Anderson, Jefferson Powell, Mary Sawyer, John Wilson, and Hannah Zeidlick; in the National Security Agency, Wallace Winkler (now retired); in the Modern Military Records Branch, National Archives, John P. Taylor; in the Cartographic Branch, William Cunliffe, and Robert Richardson; in the Washington Federal Records Center, Victoria Washington and Fred Pernell; in the Office of Air Force History, William Heindahl; and in the Navy History Center, Dr. Dean Allard.

For diligent help in unraveling events on the northern shoulder, Ralph G. Hill, Jr., Wyomissing, Pa.; for assistance with events of their former divisions: Haynes W. Dugan, Shreveport, La., 3d Armored Division; Brig. Gen. Hal C. Pattison, Fairfax, Va., 4th Armored Division; Walter Berry, Falls Church, Va., 4th Division; Ken Danielson, East Point, Ga., and Generals Robert W. Hasbrouck, Washington, D.C., and Bruce Clarke, Arlington, Va., 7th Armored Division; Raymond L. Lewis, San Diego, Calif., CCB, 9th Armored Division; Robert H. Phillips, Springfield, Va., 28th Division; John Campbell, Rockville, Md., and Harold Leinbaugh, Fairfax Station, Va., 84th Division; Dr. Lyle J. Bouck, Jr., St. Louis, Mo., and Joseph C. Doherty, Alexandria, Va., 99th Division; and Francis H. Aspinwall, Ponchatoula, La., 106th Division.

For an order of battle and for commenting on the entire manuscript, a knowledgeable student of the battle, Danny S. Parker, Helena, Mont,.; for German translation, Greg Kitsock, Ashland, Pa.; for the loan of unit histories, Fleming Fraker, Arlington, Va., and David Ruby, Pitcairn, Pa.; for permission to use Colonel Dickson's papers, Mrs. Benjamin Abbot Dickson, Paoli, Pa.; for the use of General Sibert's papers, Mrs.

626

Edwin Sibert, Martha's Vineyard, Mass.; for loan of research materials gathered for earlier books, my friends John Eisenhower and John Toland; and for maps, of which I am proud, my longtime friend Billy C. Mossman, and Robert Love and Harry Bruenhoefer of Blair, Inc., Falls Church, Va.

Belgium: For access to his voluminous files on events around St. Vith and for commenting on the entire manuscript, my friend Dr. Maurice Delaval, Vielsalm; for a conducted terrain study of the site of the gasoline depot near Stavelot, Lt. Col. Roger Hardy, Blankenberge; for help with interviews, Joseph Scholzen, Büllingen; for guiding me through the forests around Krinkelt-Rocherath, Paul Droesch, Büllingen; for unsurpassed Belgian hospitality and help with interviews, Sanny and Nicolas Schugens, Lanzerath; for help on events near Celles, Comte Jacques de Villenfagne de Sorinne; for the tragic story of Renée Lemaire, her sisters, Mmes. Gisèle Lemaire and Jacques Bourlet (Maggy Lemaire), Brussels; in the Syndicat d'Initiative, Bastogne, Simonne Schmitz; in the Bibliothèque de Stavelot, Maria DuBois and Marie-Louise Lejeune; in the Syndicat d'Initiative, Rochefort, Maria De Leeuw; at the Château de Froid-Cour, M. and Mme. Charles-Albert de Harenne; at Spa, George R. de Lame and members of the *gendarmerie;* at La Gleize, Gerard Grégoire; and as a host, guide, research assistant, and long-suffering consultant, a British subject currently living in Hedomont, my friend William C. C. Cavanagh.

Great Britain: In the Cabinet Office Historical Section, London, Eve Streatfeild and Mrs. H. E. Forbes; for help with ULTRA, Peter Calvocoressi, London, and Ralph Bennett, President, Magdalene College, Cambridge; for help on events at the tip of the bulge, historian and former Troop Sergeant, 3d Tank Regiment, Peter Elstob, London; and for incidental assistance, Roger Bell, Goodmayes, Essex, and Patrick Hargreaves, Keighley, Yorkshire.

Germany: For finding materials in German veterans' publications and locating veterans, Günter von der Weiden, Stolberg, and for a mammoth task of translation, Heino Brandt, Stolberg; and to both, my appreciation for traipsing about their country with me to help with interviews and to find Ziegenberg Castle and the site of the *Adlerhorst;* appreciation also to Dr. Adolf Hohenstein, Höfen, and Prof. Dr. Jürgen Rohwer, Bibliothek für Zeitgeschichte, Stuttgart; and to those who granted interviews which I was unable to use, particularly Fritz Schmäschke, München-Gladbach.

Luxembourg: For serving as a guide and reviewer of chapters, Pierre Eicher, Marnach; for interview and research assistance, Jean Milmeister, Tuntange; for locating headquarters sites, Jean Welter, Luxembourg City; and for hospitality and general assistance, President Camille Kohn and members of the *Cercle d'Etudes sur la Bataille des Ardennes (CEBA),* Clervaux.

Special thanks to my agent, Carl D. Brandt, and my editor, Bruce Lee, both of whom displayed faith in this book long before they probably should have, and to one who should receive a campaign star, my superb copy editor, Ann Adelman. Special appreciation also to my editor with Weidenfeld & Nicolson in England, John Curtis.

U.S. INFANTRY REGIMENT
Strength: 3,257

Headquarters and Headquarters Company

- Cannon Company — 6 105mm. hows.
- Antitank Company — 9 57mm. AT Guns
- 1st Battalion A,B,C,D
  - 2nd Battalion E,F,G,H
  - 3rd Battalion I,K,L,M
- Service Company

U.S. INFANTRY BATTALION
Strength: 836

Headquarters and Headquarters Company

- Antitank Platoon — 3 57mm. AT Guns
- Mine Platoon
- I & R Platoon
- Ammunition and Pioneer Platoon
- Rifle Company
  - Rifle Company
  - Rifle Company — Strength: 193 *
- Heavy Weapons Company — Strength: 166 **

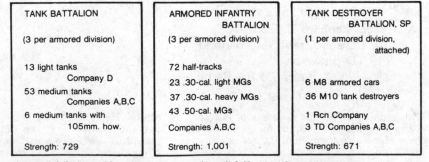

TANK BATTALION	ARMORED INFANTRY BATTALION	TANK DESTROYER BATTALION, SP
(3 per armored division)	(3 per armored division)	(1 per armored division, attached)
13 light tanks — Company D	72 half-tracks	6 M8 armored cars
53 medium tanks — Companies A,B,C	23 .30-cal. light MGs	36 M10 tank destroyers
6 medium tanks with 105mm. how.	37 .30-cal. heavy MGs	1 Rcn Company
	43 .50-cal. MGs	3 TD Companies A,B,C
	Companies A,B,C	
Strength: 729	Strength: 1,001	Strength: 671

* (each with 3 rifle platoons of 3 squads each and weapons platoon with 2 .30-cal. light MGs and 3 .60mm. mortars)

** (8 .30-cal. heavy MGs and 6 81mm. mortars)

Order of Battle

BY DANNY S. PARKER*

Supreme Headquarters Allied Expeditionary Forces (SHAEF)

General of the Army Dwight D. Eisenhower

UNITED STATES ARMY
(organization as of January 1, 1945)

12th U.S. Army Group

Lt. Gen. Omar N. Bradley

First U.S. Army

Lt. Gen. Courtney H. Hodges
5 Belgian Fusilier Battalion
143 and 413 AA Gun Battalions

V Corps

Maj. Gen. Leonard T. Gerow
102 Cavalry Group, Mechanized
613 TD Battalion
186, 196, 200, and 955 FA Battalions

*With appreciation for the assistance of Michael Cox, Winston Hamilton, Victor Madej, William F. Murphy, Jr., Bruno Sinigaglio, Shelby Stanton, and Charles V. P. von Luttichau. Material is drawn from the author's war game, *The Last Gamble* (Tokyo: Hobby Japan, 1984).

254 Engineer C (Combat) Battalion
187 FA Group
    751 and 997 FA Battalions
190 FA Group
    62, 190, 272, and 268 FA Battalions
406 FA Group
    76, 941, 953, and 987 FA Battalions
1111 Engineer C Group
    51, 202, 291, and 296 Engineer C Battalions
134, 387, 445, 460, 461, 531, 602, 639, and 863 AAA AW Battalions

1st Infantry Division ("Big Red One")*

Brig. Gen. Clift Andrus
    16, 18, and 26 Inf Regiments
    5, 7, 32, and 33 FA Battalions
    1 Engineer C Battalion
    745 Tank Battalion†
    634 and 703 TD Battalions
    103 AAA AW Battalion

The division fought in North Africa, Sicily, Normandy, Aachen, and the Hürtgen Forest.

2d Infantry Division ("Indianhead")

Maj. Gen. Walter M. Robertson
    9, 23, and 38 Inf Regiments
    12, 15, 37, and 38 FA Battalions
    2 Engineer C Battalion
    741 Tank Battalion
    462 AAA AW Battalion
    612 and 644 TD Battalions

9th Infantry Division ("Octofoil")

Maj. Gen. Louis A. Craig
    39, 47, and 60 Inf Regiments
    26, 34, 60, and 84 FA Battalions
    15 Engineer C Battalion
    38 Cav Rcn Squadron (attached)

---

*In most cases, nicknames came from shoulder patches; some units had no nickname.
†Tank, TD, and AAA AW (Automatic Weapons) Battalions in infantry divisions were attached.

746 Tank Battalion
376 and 413 AAA AW Battalions

The division fought in North Africa, Sicily, Normandy, and the Hürtgen Forest.

78th Infantry Division ("Lightning")

Maj. Gen. Edwin P. Parker, Jr.
    309, 310, and 311 Inf Regiments
    307, 308, 309, and 903 FA Battalions
    303 Engineer C Battalion
    709 Tank Battalion
    628 and 833 TD Battalions
    552 AAA AW Battalion
    CCR, 5th Armored Division (attached)
    2 Ranger Battalion (attached)

The attack in support of the 2d Division's attack on the Roer River dams was the division's first action.

99th Infantry Division ("Checkerboard")

Maj. Gen. Walter E. Lauer
    393, 394, and 395 Inf Regiments
    370, 371, 372, and 924 FA Battalions
    324 Engineer C Battalion
    801 TD Battalion
    535 AAA AW Battalion

The division had held a long defensive front in the Ardennes since mid-November, its only action.

VII Corps

Maj. Gen. Joseph Lawton Collins
    4 Cavalry Group, Mechanized
    29 Inf Regiment
    French Light Inf Brigade
    509 Parachute Inf Battalion
    298 Engineer C Battalion
    740 Tank Battalion
    18, 83, 87, 183, 193, 957, and 991 FA Battalions
    18 FA Group
        188, 666, and 981 FA Battalions
    142 FA Group
        195 and 266 FA Battalions

188 FA Group
 172, 951, and 980 FA Battalions
 342, 366, 392, 1308, and 1313 Engineer Gen Service Regiments

2d Armored Division ("Hell on Wheels")

Maj. Gen. Ernest N. Harmon
 41 Armored Inf Regiment
 66 and 67 Armored Regiments
 14, 78, and 92 Armored FA Battalions
 17 Armored Engineer Battalion
 18 Ren Battalion
 702 TD Battalion
 195 AAA AW Battalion

The division fought in North Africa, Sicily, Normandy, and in the vicinity of Aachen.

3d Armored Division ("Spearhead")

Maj. Gen. Maurice Rose
 36 Armored Inf Regiment
 32 and 33 Armored Regiments
 54, 67, and 391 Armored FA Battalions
 23 Armored Engineer Battalion
 83 Rcn Squadron
 643 TD Battalion
 486 AAA AW Battalion

The division fought in Normandy, the pursuit across France, and costly fall battles in the vicinity of Aachen.

83d Infantry Division ("Thunderbolt")

Maj. Gen. Robert C. Macon
 329, 330, and 331 Inf Regiments
 322, 323, 324, and 908 FA Battalions
 308 Engineer C Battalion
 772 TD Battalion
 453 AAA AW Battalion

The division fought in Normandy and at Brest, then after having rested briefly in the Ardennes, moved to the Hürtgen Forest.

84th Infantry Division ("Railsplitters")

Brig. Gen. Alexander R. Bolling
 333, 334, and 335 Inf Regiments

325, 326, 327, and 909 FA Battalions
309 Engineer C Battalion
771 Tank Battalion
638 TD Battalion
557 AAA AW Battalion

The division underwent its baptism of fire in November in the vicinity of Aachen.

XVIII Airborne Corps

Maj. Gen. Matthew B. Ridgway
    14 Cavalry Group, Mechanized
    254, 275, 400, and 460 FA Battalions
    79 FA Group
        153, 551, and 552 FA Battalions
    179 FA Group
        259 and 965 FA Battalions
    211 FA Group
        240 and 264 FA Battalions
    401 FA Group
        187 and 809 FA Battalions

7th Armored Division ("Lucky Seventh")

Brig. Gen. Robert W. Hasbrouck
    CCA, CCB, and CCR
    23, 38, and 48 Armored Inf Battalions
    17, 31, and 40 Tank Battalions
    434, 440, and 489 Armored FA Battalions
    33 Armored Engineer Battalion
    87 Rcn Squadron
    814 TD Battalion
    203 AAA AW Battalion

The division arrived in time to participate in the pursuit across France, encountered heavy fighting near Metz in September, and had another costly encounter in October in Holland.

30th Infantry Division ("Old Hickory")

Maj. Gen. Leland S. Hobbs
    117, 119, and 120 Inf Regiments
    113, 118, 197, and 230 FA Battalions
    105 Engineer C Battalion
    743 Tank Battalion
    823 TD Battalion

99 Inf Battalion (attached)
517 Parachute Inf Regiment (attached)
526 Armored Inf Battalion (attached)
110 and 431 AAA AW Battalions

The division began fighting in Normandy in June, figured prominently in repelling a German attack at Mortain, and fought in November near Aachen.

75th Infantry Division

Maj. Gen. Fay B. Prickett
    289, 290, and 291 Inf Regiments
    730, 897, 898, and 899 FA Battalions
    275 Engineer C Battalion
    750 Tank Battalion
    629 and 772 TD Battalions
    440 AAA AW Battalion

The division's first action was alongside the 3d Armored Division in front of the Ourthe River.

82d Airborne Division ("All American")

Maj. Gen. James M. Gavin
    504, 505, and 508 Parachute Inf Regiments
    325 Glider Inf Regiment
    551 Parachute Inf Battalion (attached)
    376 and 456 Parachute FA Battalions
    307 Airborne Engineer Battalion
    80 AAA AW Battalion

The division made combat jumps in Sicily, Normandy, and Holland.

106th Infantry Division ("Golden Lions")

Maj. Gen. Alan W. Jones
    422, 423, and 424 Inf Regiments
    589, 590, 591, and 592 FA Battalions
    81 Engineer C Battalion
    820 TD Battalion
    634 and 563 AAA AW Battalions

The division's first action was in the Ardennes.

Third U.S. Army

Lt. Gen. George S. Patton, Jr.

109, 115, 217, and 777 AA Gun Battalions
456, 465, 550, and 565 AAA AW Battalions

III Corps

Maj. Gen. John Millikin
6 Cavalry Group, Mechanized
179, 274, 776, and 777 FA Battalions
193 FA Group
177, 253, 696, 776, and 949 FA Battalions
203 FA Group
278, 742, and 762 FA Battalions
183 and 243 Engineer C Battalions
1137 Engineer C Group
145, 188, and 249 Engineer C Battalions
467 and 468 AAA AW Battalions

4th Armored Division

Maj. Gen. Hugh J. Gaffey
CCA, CCB, CCR
10, 51, and 53 Armored Inf Battalions
8, 35, and 37 Tank Battalions
22, 66, and 94 Armored FA Battalions
24 Armored Engineer Battalion
704 TD Battalion
25 Cav Squadron
489 AAA AW Battalion

The division first saw action in Normandy in July and during the fall experienced heavy fighting in Lorraine and with the Third Army's drive to the Saar River.

6th Armored Division ("Super Sixth")

Maj. Gen. Robert W. Grow
CCA, CCB, CCR
9, 40, and 50 Armored Inf Battalions
15, 68, and 69 Tank Battalions
128, 212, and 231 Armored FA Battalions
25 Armored Engineer Battalion
86 Cav Squadron
777 AAA AW Battalion

The division entered combat in Normandy and exploited the breakout into Brittany, then fought through the fall in Lorraine.

26th Infantry Division ("Yankee")

Maj. Gen. Willard S. Paul

101, 104, and 328 Inf Regiments
101, 102, 180, and 263 FA Battalions
101 Engineer C Battalion
735 Tank Battalion
818 TD Battalion
390 AAA AW Battalion

The division experienced heavy combat near Verdun in September and had only recently been pulled from the line to absorb replacements when sent to the Ardennes.

35th Infantry Division ("Santa Fe")

Maj. Gen. Paul W. Baade
134, 137, and 320 Inf Regiments
127, 161, 216, and 219 FA Battalions
60 Engineer C Battalion
654 TD Battalion
448 AAA AW Battalion

The division entered the line in Normandy in July and figured prominently in stopping the enemy attack near Mortain, then fought through the fall in Lorraine.

90th Infantry Division ("Tough Hombres")

Maj. Gen. James A. Van Fleet
357, 358, and 359 Inf Regiments
343, 344, 345, and 915 FA Battalions
315 Engineer C Battalion
773 TD Battalion
537 AAA AW Battalion

The division took heavy losses in its first engagements in Normandy in June and through the fall fought in the vicinity of Metz and in the drive to the Saar River.

VIII Corps

Maj. Gen. Troy H. Middleton
687 FA Battalion
174 FA Group
965, 969, and 700 FA Battalions
333 FA Group
333 and 771 FA Battalions
402 FA Group
559, 561, and 740 FA Battalions

    422 FA Group
        81 and 174 FA Battalions
    178 and 249 Engineer C Battalions
    1102 Engineer Group
        341 Engineer Gen Service Regiment
    1107 Engineer C Group
        159, 168, and 202 Engineer C Battalions
    1128 Engineer C Group
        35, 44, and 158 Engineer C Battalions
    French Light Infantry (six Metz Light Inf Battalions)
    467, 635, and 778 AAA AW Battalions

9th Armored Division

Maj. Gen. John W. Leonard
    CCA, CCB, CCR
    27, 52, and 60 Armored Inf Battalions
    2, 14, and 19 Tank Battalions
    3, 16, and 73 Armored FA Battalions
    9 Armored Engineer Battalion
    89 Cav Squadron
    811 TD Battalion
    482 AAA AW Battalion

The Battle of the Bulge was the division's first action.

11th Armored Division ("Thunderbolt")

Brig. Gen. Charles S. Kilburn
    CCA, CCB, CCR
    21, 55, and 63 Armored Inf Battalions
    22, 41, and 42 Tank Battalions
    490, 491, and 492 Armored FA Battalions
    56 Armored Engineer Battalion
    602 TD Battalion
    41 Cav Squadron
    575 AAA AW Battalion

The division's first action was west of Bastogne.

17th Airborne Division ("Golden Talon")

Maj. Gen. William M. Miley
    507 and 513 Parachute Inf Regiments
    193 and 194 Glider Inf Regiments
    680 and 681 Glider FA Battalions
    466 Parachute FA Battalion

139 Airborne Engineer Battalion
155 Airborne AAA AW Battalion

The division entered the line for the first time in late December west of Bastogne.

28th Infantry Division ("Keystone")

Maj. Gen. Norman D. Cota
109, 110, and 112 Inf Regiments
107, 108, 109, and 229 FA Battalions
103 Engineer C Battalion
707 Tank Battalion
630 TD Battalion
447 AAA AW Battalion

The division's first action was in Normandy in late July, followed by an attack into the Siegfried Line near St. Vith and heavy combat in the Hürtgen Forest.

87th Infantry Division ("Golden Acorn")

Brig. Gen. Frank L. Culin, Jr.
345, 346, and 347 Inf Regiments
334, 335, 336, and 912 FA Battalions
312 Engineer C Battalion
761 Tank Battalion
549 AAA AW Battalion

Although committed briefly in the Saar region, the division's first major action was west of Bastogne.

101st Airborne Division ("Screaming Eagles")

Brig. Gen. Anthony C. McAuliffe
(Maj. Gen. Maxwell D. Taylor)
501, 502, and 506 Parachute Inf Regiments
327 Glider Inf Regiment
1 Battalion, 401 Glider Infantry
321 and 907 Glider FA Battalions
377 Parachute FA Battalion
326 Parachute Engineer Battalion
705 TD Battalion
377 Airborne AAA AW Battalion

The division jumped on D-Day in Normandy and later in Holland.

XII Corps

Maj. Gen. Manton S. Eddy

2 Cavalry Group, Mechanized
161, 244, 277, 334, 336, and 736 FA Battalions
177 FA Group
    215, 255, and 775 FA Battalions
182 FA Group
    802, 945, and 974 FA Battalions
183 FA Group
    695 and 776 FA Battalions
404 FA Group
    273, 512, and 752 FA Battalions
1303 Engineer Gen Service Regiment
452 and 457 AAA AW Battalions

4th Infantry Division ("Ivy"—for IV)

Maj. Gen. Raymond O. Barton
    8, 12, and 22 Inf Regiments
    20, 29, 42, and 44 FA Battalions
    4 Engineer C Battalion
    70 Tank Battalion
    802 and 803 TD Battalions
    377 AAA AW Battalion

The division landed on UTAH Beach on D-Day, fought in Normandy, helped liberate Paris, penetrated the Siegfried Line on the Schnee Eifel, and fought in the Hürtgen Forest.

5th Infantry Division ("Red Diamond")

Maj. Gen. S. Leroy Irwin
    2, 10, and 11 Inf Regiments
    19, 21, 46, and 50 FA Battalions
    7 Engineer C Battalion
    737 Tank Battalion
    818 TD Battalion
    449 AAA AW Battalion

The division entered combat in Normandy in July and took heavy casualties in the fall fighting for Metz.

10th Armored Division ("Tiger")

Maj. Gen. William H. H. Morris, Jr.
    CCA, CCB, CCR
    20, 54, and 61 Armored Inf Battalions
    3, 11, and 21 Tank Battalions
    419, 420, and 423 Armored FA Battalions

609 TD Battalion
55 Armored Engineer Battalion
90 Rcn Squadron
796 AAA AW Battalion

The division entered the line in Lorraine in late September and participated in the encirclement of Metz and the drive to the Saar River.

80th Infantry Division ("Blue Ridge")

Maj. Gen. Horace L. McBride
317, 318, and 319 Inf Regiments
313, 314, 315, and 905 FA Battalions
305 Engineer C Battalion
702 Tank Battalion
610 TD Battalion
633 AAA AW Battalion

The division began fighting in Normandy in August, had a hard fight for a crossing of the Moselle River in September, and in November participated in the drive to the Saar River.

U.S. ARMY AIR FORCES

U.S. Strategic Air Forces in Europe

General Carl Spaatz

Eighth Air Force (strategic)

Lt. Gen. James H. Doolittle

Ninth Air Force

Lt. Gen. Hoyt S. Vandenberg

IX Bombardment Division

Maj. Gen. Samuel E. Anderson

IX Troop Carrier Command

Maj. Gen. Paul L. Williams

IX Tactical Air Command (supporting First Army)

Maj. Gen. Elwood R. ("Pete") Quesada

XIX Tactical Air Command (supporting Third Army)

Brig. Gen. Otto P. Weyland

XXIX Tactical Air Command (supporting Ninth Army)

Maj. Gen. Richard E. Nugent

BRITISH ARMY

21 Army Group

Field Marshal Sir Bernard L. Montgomery

30 Corps

Lt. Gen. Brian G. Horrocks
    2 Household Cavalry Regiment
    11 Hussars and Cavalry Regiment
    73 Antitank Regiment
    4 and 5 Royal Horse Artillery Regiments
    7, 64, and 84 Royal Artillery Regiments
    27 Light AA Regiment

6th Airborne Division

Maj. Gen. Eric L. Bols
    3 and 5 Parachute Brigades
    6 Airlanding Brigade
    53 Light Royal Artillery Regiment
    3 and 4 Airlanding AT Battalions
    6 Royal Armoured Car Regiment

The division jumped on D-Day in Normandy.

51st Infantry Division (Highland)

Maj. Gen. T. G. Rennie
    152, 153, and 154 Inf Brigades
    126, 127, and 128 Royal Artillery Regiments
    2 Derby Yeomanry
    61 Antitank Regiment
    40 Light AA Regiment

A veteran division that had been fighting since Normandy.

53d Infantry Division (Welsh)

Maj. Gen. R. K. Ross

71, 158, and 160 Inf Brigades
81, 83, and 133 Royal Artillery Regiments
53 Rcn Regiment
71 Antitank Regiment
25 Light AA Regiment

Another veteran division that had seen heavy fighting in Holland.

29th Armoured Brigade

Brig. Gen. C. B. C. Harvey
23 Hussars Regiment
3 Royal Tank Regiment
8 Rifle Brigade
2 Fife and Forfar Yeomanry

A veteran brigade that had been scheduled to draw new tanks and equipment when ordered to the Ardennes.

33d Armoured Brigade

Brig. Gen. H. B. Scott
144 Royal Armoured Car Regiment
1 Northamptonshire Yeomanry
1 East Riding Yeomanry

A veteran brigade that had seen hard fighting in Normandy.

34th Army Tank Brigade

Brig. Gen. W. S. Clarke
9 Royal Tank Regiment
107 and 147 Royal Armoured Car Regiments

Having no infantry, the brigade fought closely with the 6th Airborne Division.

(In reserve, 43d and 50th Infantry Divisions and Guards Armoured Division.)

ROYAL AIR FORCE

Bomber Command

Air Chief Marshal Sir Arthur T. Harris

Fighter Command

Air Marshal Sir Roderic M. Hill

Second Tactical Air Force

Air Marshal Sir Arthur Coningham

GERMAN ARMY
(organization as of December 28, 1944)

OB WEST

Field Marshal Gerd von Rundstedt

Army Group B

Field Marshal Walter Model

Fifth Panzer Army

General der Panzertruppen Hasso von Manteuffel
    19 Flak Brigade
    207 and 600 Engineer Battalions
    653 Heavy Antitank Battalion
    669 Ost (East) Battalion
    638, 1094, and 1095 Heavy Artillery Batteries
    25/975 Fortress Artillery Battery
    1099, 1119, and 1121 Heavy Mortar Batteries
    3 Todt Brigade (paramilitary engineers)

47th Panzer Corps

General der Panzertruppen Heinrich von Lüttwitz
    15 Volkswerfer Brigade
    182 Flak Regiment
    766 Volksartillerie Corps

2d Panzer Division

Col. Meinrad von Lauchert
    3 Panzer Regiment
    2 and 304 Pzgr Regiments
    74 Artillery Regiment
    2 Rcn Battalion
    38 Antitank Battalion

38 Engineer Battalion
273 Flak Battalion

Reorganized after heavy losses in Normandy, the division had more than a hundred tanks and assault guns and many veterans still in its ranks.

9th Panzer Division

Genmaj. Harald von Elverfeldt
33 Panzer Regiment
10 and 11 Pzgr Regiments
102 Artillery Regiment
9 Rcn Battalion
50 Antitank Battalion
86 Engineer Battalion
287 Flak Battalion
301 Heavy Panzer Battalion (attached)

A veteran division recovering from losses incurred in Normandy when ordered from Holland to the Ardennes; with attached Tigers, the division had just over a hundred tanks.

Panzer Lehr Division

Genlt. Fritz Bayerlein
130 Panzer Regiment
901 and 902 Pzgr Regiments
130 Rcn Battalion
130 Antitank Battalion
130 Engineer Battalion
311 Flak Battalion
559 Antitank Battalion (attached)
243 Assault Gun Brigade (attached)

Virtually destroyed in Normandy, the division had been rebuilding when hastily committed to counterattack the Third Army in the Saar region. With no time to replace men and tanks before commitment in the Ardennes, the division was beefed up with attachments.

26th Volksgrenadier Division

Col. Heinz Kokott
39th Fusilier and 77 and 78 VG Regiments
26 Artillery Regiment
26 Rcn Battalion
26 Antitank Battalion
26 Engineer Battalion

Often destroyed on the Eastern Front, the division was rebuilt for the Ardennes offensive under the old organization of three infantry battalions per regiment and had a strength of over 17,000 men.

Führer Begleit Brigade

Col. Otto Remer
  102 Panzer Battalion
  100 Pzgr Regiment
  120 Artillery Regiment
  120 Rcn Battalion
  120 Antitank Battalion
  120 Engineer Battalion
  828 Grenadier Battalion
  673 Flak Regiment

Built around a cadre of troops from Hitler's headquarters guard, the brigade included a tank battalion from the *Gross Deutschland Panzer Division* (still on the Eastern Front) and some infantry fillers from that division. It was strongly reinforced with assault guns and 88mm. and 105mm. pieces.

66th Corps

General der Artillerie Walter Lucht
  16 Volkswerfer Brigade
    86 and 87 Werfer Regiments
  244 Assault Gun Brigade
  460 Heavy Artillery Battalion

18th Volksgrenadier Division

Col. Hoffman-Schonborn
  293, 294, and 295 VG Regiments
  1818 Artillery Regiment
  1818 Antitank Battalion
  1818 Engineer Battalion

Formed in September in Denmark around a cadre from a Luftwaffe field division with many fillers from the Luftwaffe and the Navy; at full strength and with two months of experience on the defensive in the Eifel.

62d Volksgrenadier Division

Col. Frederich Kittel
  164, 193, and 190 VG Regiments
  162 Artillery Regiment

162 Antitank Battalion
162 Engineer Battalion

Rebuilt almost from scratch from a division destroyed on the Eastern Front with many Czech and Polish conscripts who spoke no German.

58th Panzer Corps

General der Panzertruppen Walter Krüger
    7th Volkswerfer Brigade
        84 and 85 Werfer Regiments
    401 Volksartillerie Corps
    1 Flak Regiment

116th Panzer Division ("Greyhounds")

Genmaj. Siegfried von Waldenburg
    16 Panzer Regiment
    60 and 156 Pzgr Regiments
    146 Artillery Regiment
    146 Rcn Battalion
    226 Antitank Battalion
    675 Engineer Battalion
    281 Flak Battalion

The division had strong unit pride. Although losses were heavy in Normandy and the Hürtgen Forest, replacements of fairly good caliber filled the ranks, and the division had over a hundred tanks and antitank and assault guns.

560th Volksgrenadier Division

Col. Rudolf Langhauser
    1128, 1129, and 1130 VG Regiments
    1560 Artillery Regiment
    1560 Antitank Battalion
    1560 Engineer Battalion

Formed from occupation troops in Norway in late summer of 1944, the division was poorly trained and was at first missing the 1129th Regiment; but the troops quickly gained battle experience and fought effectively in front of the Ourthe River.

29th Panzer Corps

Genlt. Karl Decker
(Brought forward at the end of December to control some of the troops at Bastogne: 1st SS Panzer Division; 901st Pzgr Regiment, *Panzer Lehr Division;* and the 167th Volksgrenadier Division.)

167th Volksgrenadier Division

> Genlt. Hans-Kurt Höcker
> > 331, 339, and 387 VG Regiments
> > 167 Artillery Regiment
> > 167 Antitank Battalion
> > 167 Engineer Battalion

Virtually destroyed on the Eastern Front, the division was reformed in Hungary with replacements mainly from a Luftwaffe field division.

Sixth Panzer Army

> Oberstgruppenführer der Waffen-SS Josef ("Sepp") Dietrich
> > Von der Heydte Battalion
> > 506 Heavy Panzer Battalion
> > 683 Heavy Antitank Battalion
> > 217 Assault Panzer Battalion
> > 394, 667, and 902 Assault Gun Battalions
> > 741 Antitank Battalion
> > 1098, 1110, and 1120 Heavy Howitzer Batteries
> > 428 Heavy Mortar Battery
> > 1123 K-3 Battery
> > 2 Flak Division
> > > 41 and 43 Regiments
> > 4 Todt Brigade

1st SS Panzer Corps

> SS-Gruppenführer Hermann Priess
> > 4th Volkswerfer Brigade
> > > 51 and 53 Werfer Regiments
> > 9th Volkswerfer Brigade
> > > 14 and 54 Werfer Regiments
> > 388 Volksartillerie Corps
> > 402 Volksartillerie Corps
> > 501 SS-Artillery Battalion

1st SS Panzer Division ("Liebstandärte Adolf Hitler")

> SS-Oberführer Wilhelm Mohnke
> > 1 SS-Panzer Regiment
> > 1 and 2 SS-Pzgr Regiments
> > 1 SS Artillery Regiment
> > 1 SS Rcn Battalion
> > 1 SS Antitank Battalion
> > 1 SS Engineer Battalion
> > 1 SS Flak Battalion

501 SS Heavy Panzer Battalion (attached)

The division had a reputation for daring and ruthlessness; with 22,000 men, it was one of the more powerful German divisions.

3d Parachute Division

Genmaj. Wadehn
5, 8, and 9 Parachute Inf Regiments
3 Artillery Regiment
3 Rcn Battalion
3 Antitank Battalion
3 Engineer Battalion

Practically destroyed in Normandy, the division had been rebuilt in Holland, mainly from rear echelon Luftwaffe ground troops. Both troops and commanders were inexperienced.

12th SS Panzer Division ("Hitler Jugend")

SS-Standartenführer Hugo Kraas
12 SS-Panzer Regiment
25 and 26 SS-Pzgr Regiments
12 SS Artillery Regiment
12 SS Rcn Battalion
12 SS Antitank Battalion
12 SS Engineer Battalion
12 SS Flak Battalion
560 Heavy Antitank Battalion (attached)

The division had been rebuilt following heavy losses in Normandy and had approximately 22,000 men but was short of experienced junior officers.

12th Volksgrenadier Division

Genmaj. Gerhard Engel
27 Fusilier and 48 and 89 VG Regiments
12 Artillery Regiment
12 Antitank Battalion
12 Fusilier Battalion
12 Engineer Battalion

After heavy losses in the summer of 1944 in Russia, the division was hastily rebuilt and hurried to halt American attacks around Aachen, where it earned the honorific *"Volksgrenadier."*

277th Volksgrenadier Division

Col. Wilhelm Viebig

289, 990, and 991 VG Regiments
277 Artillery Regiment
277 Antitank Battalion
277 Engineer Battalion

The division had only about a thousand veterans, many of the others being ethnic Germans from conquered border regions. A weak division.

150th Panzer Brigade

Obersturmbannführer der Waffen-SS Otto Skorzeny
    Two panzer cos., two Pzgr cos., and two antitank cos.
    A heavy mortar battalion (two batteries)
    600 Parachute Battalion
    Kampfgruppe 200 (Luftwaffe ground unit)
    An anti-partisan company

A makeshift formation hurriedly assembled to meet the special requirements that Hitler imposed on Skorzeny.

2d SS Panzer Corps

SS-Obergruppenführer Willi Bittrich
    410 Volksartillerie Corps
    502 SS Heavy Artillery Battalion

2d SS Panzer Division ("Das Reich")

SS-Brigadeführer Heinz Lammerding
    2 SS-Panzer Regiment
    3 and 4 SS-Pzgr Regiments
    2 SS Artillery Regiment
    2 SS Rcn Battalion
    2 SS Engineer Battalion
    2 SS Flak Battalion

A division with a reputation for brutality, it had experienced heavy fighting in Russia and then in Normandy. Rebuilt during the fall with replacements considered better than average.

9th SS Panzer Division ("Hohenstaufen")

SS-Oberführer Sylvester Stadler
    9 SS-Panzer Regiment
    19 and 20 SS-Pzgr Regiments
    9 SS Artillery Regiment
    9 SS Rcn Battalion
    9 SS Antitank Battalion

9 SS Engineer Battalion
9 SS Flak Battalion
519 Heavy Antitank Battalion (attached)

Rebuilt after heavy losses in Normandy and Holland, the division had many ethnic Germans from border regions and few veterans, but ethnic Germans from the Black Sea region of Russia were excellent soldiers. The division was badly short of transport.

67th Corps

Genlt. Otto Hitzfeld
17 Volkswerfer Brigade
88 and 89 Werfer Regiments
405 Volksartillerie Corps
1001 Heavy Assault Gun Company

3d Panzergrenadier Division

Genmaj. Walter Denkert
8 and 29 Pzgr Regiments
103 Panzer Battalion
3 Artillery Regiment
103 Rcn Battalion
3 Antitank Battalion
3 Engineer Battalion
312 Flak Battalion

Transferred from Italy in the summer of 1944, the division lost heavily in fighting around Metz and later around Aachen. Refitted hurriedly for the Ardennes, the division lacked 20 percent of its strength in troops and 40 percent in equipment.

246th Volksgrenadier Division

Col. Peter Koerte
352, 404, and 689 VG Regiments
246 Artillery Regiment
246 Antitank Battalion
246 Engineer Battalion

Virtually destroyed on the Eastern Front, the division also lost heavily in the fall fighting around Aachen. Scheduled to attack at Monschau, the division arrived late.

272d Volksgrenadier Division

Col. Georg Kosmalla

>980, 981, and 982 VG Regiments
>272 Artillery Regiment
>272 Antitank Battalion
>272 Engineer Battalion

Virtually destroyed in Normandy, the division had been hastily rebuilt and committed in the vicinity of Monschau, where it was scheduled to attack but instead fought defensively against the American 78th Division.

326th Volksgrenadier Division

>Col. Erwin Kaschner
>751, 752, and 753 VG Regiments
>326 Artillery Regiment
>326 Antitank Battalion
>326 Engineer Battalion

Rebuilt following the withdrawal from France with generally inexperienced and poorly trained troops.

Seventh Army

>General der Panzertruppen Erich Brandenberger
>657 and 668 Heavy Antitank Battalions
>501 Fortress Antitank Battalion
>47 Engineer Battalion
>1092, 1093, 1124, and 1125 Heavy Howitzer Batteries
>660 Heavy Artillery Battery
>1029, 1039, and 1122 Heavy Mortar Batteries
>999 Penal Battalion
>44 Machine Gun Battalion
>15 Flak Regiment
>1 Todt Brigade

53d Corps

>General der Kavallerie Edwin von Rothkirch
>(Brought forward on December 22 to command the 5th Parachute—see 85th Corps—and 15th Panzergrenadier Divisions and the *Führer Grenadier Brigade* at Bastogne.)

9th Volksgrenadier Division

>Col. Werner Kolb
>36, 57, and 116th VG Regiments
>9 Artillery Regiment
>9 Antitank Battalion

9 Engineer Battalion

After heavy losses in Romania in the fall of 1944, refitted and moved to Denmark for training. First committed in the Ardennes on December 28.

15th Panzergrenadier Division

Col. Hans-Joachim Deckert
104 and 115 Pzgr Regiments
115 Panzer Battalion
115 Artillery Regiment
115 Rcn Battalion
33 Antitank Battalion
33 Engineer Battalion
315 Flak Battalion

Transferred from Italy in late summer of 1944, the division during the fall served as a kind of fire brigade, fighting both around Aachen and in the Vosges. Not fully refitted for the Ardennes.

Führer Grenadier Brigade

Col. Hans-Joachim Kahler
99 Pzgr Regiment
101 Panzer Battalion
911 Assault Gun Brigade
124 Antitank Battalion
124 Rcn Battalion
124 Engineer Battalion
124 Flak Battalion
124 Artillery Regiment

Formed from a nucleus of troops who provided the outer rim of defense for Hitler's headquarters, the brigade had a brief and costly commitment on the Eastern Front before arriving piecemeal in the Ardennes.

80th Corps

General der Infanterie Franz Beyer
408 Volksartillerie Corps
8 Volkswerfer Brigade
2 and *Lehr* Werfer Regiments

212th Volksgrenadier Division

Genmaj. Franz Sensfuss
316, 320, and 423 VG Regiments
212 Artillery Regiment
212 Antitank Battalion

212 Engineer Battalion

Despite heavy losses on the Eastern Front, the division retained a large cadre of experienced officers and noncommissioned officers, and its replacements, largely from Bavaria, were above average. It was the best division in the Seventh Army.

276th Volksgrenadier Division

Gen. Kurt Möhring (later Col. Hugo Dempwolff)
986, 987, and 988 VG Regiments
276 Artillery Regiment
276 Antitank Battalion
276 Engineer Battalion

Formed from the shell of another division destroyed in Normandy, the division had a number of hospital returnees but not enough to make up for other poorly trained replacements and inexperienced leaders.

340th Volksgrenadier Division

Col. Theodor Tolsdorff
(committed in late December at Bastogne under the 1st SS Panzer Corps)
694, 695, and 696 VG Regiments
340 Artillery Regiment
340 Antitank Battalion
340 Engineer Battalion

Having absorbed the remnants of another division, the division had more veterans than most, but since it had only recently come from the line near Aachen, it was considerably under strength.

85th Corps

General der Infanterie Baptist Kniess
406 Volksartillerie Corps
18 Volkswerfer Brigade
21 and 22 Werfer Regiments

5th Parachute Division

Col. Ludwig Heilmann
13, 14, and 15 Parachute Inf Regiments
5 Artillery Regiment
5 Rcn Battalion
5 Engineer Battalion
5 Flak Battalion

11 Assault Gun Brigade

Virtually destroyed in Normandy, the division had been refitted over the fall and had close to 16,000 men. Both the division commander and the regimental commanders were inexperienced in combat.

352d Volksgrenadier Division

Col. Erich Schmidt
914, 915, and 916 VG Regiments
352 Artillery Regiment
352 Antitank Battalion
352 Engineer Battalion

Reconstructed almost from scratch with a great influx of Luftwaffe and Navy replacements to a strength of 13,000, the division was poorly trained and lacked experienced officers.

79th Volksgrenadier Division

Col. Alois Weber
208, 212, and 226 VG Regiments
179 Artillery Regiment
179 Antitank Battalion
179 Engineer Battalion

Totally destroyed in the summer of 1944 on the Eastern Front (one man survived), the division had men culled mainly from rear area headquarters.

LUFTWAFFE

II Fighter Corps

Genmaj. Dietrich Peltz

III Flak Corps

Genlt. Wolfgang Pickert

Notes

PROLOGUE

For events at Bande: Commission des Crimes de Guerre, Ministère de la Justice, Royaume de Belgique, *Les Crimes de Guerre—Bande* (Liège: Georges Thone, 1950).

"I have made a momentous decision" (p. 11), Cole, *The Ardennes*, p. 2.

For the story of Elise Delé-Dunkel, author's interview (assisted by Jean Milmeister) with Mme Delé, Bivels, Luxembourg, 24 Aug 81; corrections of an early draft by Mme Delé, 30 Aug 82; and G-2 journals as noted.

CHAPTER I: THE DECISION, THE SETTING, AND THE PLAN

For "knocked from Britannia's hand" (p. 17), MS # C-065i, *Ministerialrat im OKW* Dr. Helmut Greiner, "Operation *BARBAROSSA*."

"Probing the Soviet attitude" (p. 19), Irving, *Hitler's War*, p. 773.

"Ultra-capitalist states on one side" (p. 20), Stenographic Account of Staff Conferences of Adolf Hitler and German High Command, Fragment No. 39, S. L. A. Marshall Military History Collection, University of Texas, El Paso.

Von Rundstedt at the *Wolfschanze* (p. 21), Warlimont, *Inside Hitler's Headquarters*, p. 477.

Marshall Foch and "If you go into that death-trap" (p. 23), Charles B. MacDonald, "The Neglected Ardennes," *Military Review*, Apr 63.

Oshima's conference with Hitler (p. 25), War Dept—ACofS G-2—No. 897, 8 Sep 44, RG (Record Group) 457 (Records of the National Security Agency), Box 10, "MAGIC" Diplomatic Summary, 1944, NA (National Archives).

"One of the most important tasks in this offensive" and following quotations (p. 32), Otto Skorzeny, *Special Mission* (London: Futura Publications, no date but c. 1958), p. 145.

For "excessively modest, too reserved" (p. 33) and following quotations, MS # B-344, Gen der Inf Günther Blumentritt, "Three Marshals, National Character, and the 20 July Complex."

"His manner was rough" and "My dear Bayerlein" (p. 33), Brett-Smith, *Hitler's Generals*, p. 200, citing von Manteuffel to B. H. Liddell-Hart.

"A field marshal does not become a prisoner" (p. 34), MS # B-593, Genmaj Carl Wagener, "*Army Group B* (22 Mar–17 Apr 45)."

For "to change the guards" (p. 34), Elstob, *Hitler's Last Offensive,* p. 36n, citing von Rundstedt to B. H. Liddell-Hart.

For "correct but not cordial" (p. 34), Cole, *The Ardennes,* pp. 23–24.

For "a stroke of genius" and "all, absolutely all" (p. 35), Rundstedt Testimony, *Trial of the Major War Criminals Before the International Military Tribunal,* Vol. XXXI, p. 29.

"This plan hasn't got a damned leg to stand on" (p. 35), Charles V. P. von Luttichau, Report on the Interview (14–19 May 52) with Thuisko von Metzsch (one of Model's staff officers) on Operations of *Army Group B* and Its Role in the German Ardennes Offensive 1944, CMH (Center of Military History).

For "unalterable" and "In our present situation" (p. 36), ltr, Jodl to Westphal, 1 Nov 44, *OB WEST, KTB Anlage 50,* Vol. I. pp. 30–31, as cited in Cole, p. 28.

"I think under your plan" (p. 36), Eisenhower interv with von Manteuffel.

"Preparations for an improvisation" (p. 37), msg, Jodl to von Rundstedt, 22 Nov 44, *OB WEST, KTB Anlage 50,* Vol. II, p. 12, as cited in Cole, p. 31.

"All Hitler wants me to do" (p. 37), Elstob, p. 56.

For "continue this battle" (p. 38), Gilbert, ed., *Hitler Directs His War,* p. 106.

CHAPTER II: THE DECEPTION AND THE INTELLIGENCE APPARATUS

For "there can be no doubt" (p. 40), *OB WEST KTB,* 6 Nov 44, as cited in MacDonald, *The Siegfried Line Campaign,* p. 394.

"Miracle of the West" (p. 43), MacDonald, p. 392.

For "a broken man" (p. 47), MS # B-151a, von Manteuffel, "The *5 Pz Army* and the Offensive in the Ardennes."

"Our thoughts wandered" (p. 48), ltr, Stiegeler to Günter von der Weiden, 18 Jan 82.

For Oshima's report on conference with von Ribbentrop (p. 49), War Dept—ACofS G-2—No. 970, 20 Nov 44, RG 457, Box 10, "MAGIC" Diplomatic Summary, 1944, NA, and additional msg No. 79712, 22 Nov 44.

"Monty's suggestion is simple" (p. 50), Kay Summersby, *Eisenhower Was My Boss* (New York: Prentice-Hall, 1948), p. 170.

"Two and a half months of bitter fighting" (p. 51), SHAEF Weekly Intelligence Summary 22, 27 Aug 44.

"The defeat . . . is complete" (p. 51), Diary, Office of the Commander-in-Chief, 5 Sep 44, SHAEF files.

For political upheaval within Germany (p. 51), FUSA (First U.S. Army) G-2 Estimate 24, 3 Sep 44.

For "deliver the original in thirty days" (p. 51), Bradley, *A Soldier's Story,* p. 426.

For Colonel Koch's G-2 estimate (p. 52), TUSA G-2 Estimate 9, 28 Aug 44.

"The dwindling fire brigade" (p. 53), SHAEF G-2 Weekly Intelligence Summary 30, 15 Oct 44.

For large-scale surrenders (p. 53), FUSA G-2 Estimate 36, 20 Nov 44.

"It is now certain" (p. 53), 12th AGp (Army Group) G-2 Summary 18, 12 Dec 44.

"I wonder what is wrong with him" (p. 54), Pogue interv with Sibert, 11 May 51. (All Dr. Pogue's interviews conducted for his volume *The Supreme Command* are in the U.S. Army Military History Research Collection, Carlisle Barracks, Pa.)

For personality conflict between Dickson and Kean (p. 55), Pogue interv with Adolph G. Rosengarten, Jr., ULTRA officer in G-2 Sect, FUSA, 22 Dec 47, and author's intervs with various members of the FUSA staff.

For "hated Sibert and the latter reciprocated" (p. 55), *ibid.*

For Dickson visits to Williams (p. 55), Pogue intervs with Williams, 30–31 May 45, and with Sibert, *op. cit.*

"Monk's shrubbery" and a man who sometimes had to be sat on (p. 55), Pogue intervs with Williams. See also Pogue interv with Rosengarten and ltr to the author from Rosengarten, 4 Jun 82.

"I don't want a man from OSS" (p. 56), Pogue interv with Sibert and Col. William H. Jackson, Sibert's deputy, 11 May 51.

"He fools some of the people" (p. 56), Baldwin, *Battles Lost and Won*, p. 363.

For not a single OSS agent (p. 56), CIA, memo to Sibert by Luman B. Kirkpatrick, subj: Operations of OSS with 12th Army Group, no date, Sibert papers.

For "absolutely no indication" (p. 57), Histories of Radio Intelligence Units European Theater September 1944 to March 1945, Vol. I, NA.

"No confirmation" (p. 57), 106th Div G-2 Periodic Rpt, 12 Dec 44.

"A sonnet written by a machine" (pp. 57–58), Lewin, *Ultra Goes to War*, p. 20.

For "the unpredictable waywardness of genius" (p. 58), Lewis, p. 40.

For "long hair . . . dirty clothes" (p. 58), Garlinski, *The Enigma War*, p. 69.

For "a large copper-coloured cupboard" (p. 58), Garlinski, p. 68.

CHAPTER III: WHAT DID THE ALLIES KNOW?

All direct quotes from German messages are either from Bennett, *Ultra in the West*, or from the messages themselves as found in the Cabinet Office Historical Section. For uses of ULTRA in American headquarters, see: American Embassy, London, Memorandum for Colonel Taylor, subj: Report of Lt. Col. Munane and Lt. Col. Orr on Use of Ultra at 12th Army Group, and subj: Report on Ultra Intelligence at First U.S. Army, Lt. Col. Adolph G. Rosengarten, Jr., both in NA; and Lt. Col. M. C. Helfers, unpublished MS, "My Personal Experience with High Level Intelligence," Nov 74, courtesy of the author.

Strong's G-2 Rpt of 1 Oct (p. 62), SHAEF Weekly Intelligence Summary 28, 1 Oct 44.

Strong's G-2 Rpt on *Fifth Panzer Army* (p. 63), SHAEF Weekly Intelligence Summary 33, 5 Nov 44.

Sibert's report (p. 63), 12th AGp Weekly Intelligence Summary 9, 7 Oct 44.

For "a truly colossal effort" and "final showdown" (p. 64), SHAEF Weekly Intelligence Summary 34, 12 Nov 44.

Summary of Allied intelligence view (pp. 64–65), Lt. Col. Harry L. Dull, Jr., Classified Annex to Addendum to U.S. Army War College Military Research Program Paper, "The Ultra Study," 25 May 77, NA.

For "a calculated risk" (p. 68), Bradley and Blair, *A General's Life*, p. 373.

For "the First Army is making a terrible mistake" (p. 68), Blumenson, *The Patton Papers*, p. 582.

For "to launch a spoiling . . . offensive" and "We'll be in a position" (pp. 68–69), Brig. Gen. Oscar W. Koch with Robert G. Hays, *G-2: Intelligence for Patton* (Philadelphia: Whitmore Publishing Co., 1971), p. 86.

For "to mount a spoiling offensive" (p. 69), TUSA G-2 Periodic Rpts 186 and 188, 13 and 14 Dec 44.

Skorzeny's order (p. 69) is reproduced in a preliminary draft of an unpublished MS by Dickson in Toland files, LofC (Library of Congress). See also Eisenhower, *The Bitter Woods*, pp. 165–166.

For "desperate men" (p. 69), Pogue interv with Rosengarten.

For Mendenhall's study (p. 69), see Col. B. A. Dickson and Ivan H. Peterman, unpublished MS, "We Wouldn't Be Warned in the Bulge," Toland files, LofC.

For "deft, sure hand" (p. 70), Dickson, unpublished MS known as Monk Dickson's Journal and entitled "Algiers to the Elbe," Dickson papers.

For "when anyone attacks" (p. 71), Bradley, *A Soldier's Story*, p. 454.

For "we could chew them up" (p. 71), Sibert, unpublished MS, "Military Intelligence Aspects of the Period Prior to the Ardennes Counteroffensive," Sibert papers.

For "get Dickson straightened out" (p. 72) and "stressed the optimistic picture" (p. 73), Pogue interv with Sibert and Jackson, *op. cit.*

"We cannot really feel satisfied" (p. 73), SHAEF Weekly Intelligence Summary 38, 10 Dec 44.

For "at least a fortnight" (p. 73), Pogue, *The Supreme Command*, p. 365n, citing ltr from Strong, 31 Aug 45.

For "a nasty little Kasserine" (p. 73), Pogue, p. 361.

For "aware of the danger" (p. 73), Pogue citing ltr from Strong, p. 365n. See also Pogue interv with Sibert and Jackson, *op. cit.*

For "to make a fighting withdrawal" (p. 74), Bradley and Blair, p. 354.

"The enemy's present practice" (p. 74), Eisenhower, *The Bitter Woods*, pp. 174–175. Judge Malcolm R. Wilkey, Washington, D.C., formerly a member of the G-2 Sect, VIII Corps, provided the author with an unpublished MS prepared over the period January–March 1945, "Summary of G-2 Estimates re Battle of the Bulge, 15 November 1944–9 March 1945."

"Whereas previously the Germans" (p. 75), Hanson W. Baldwin, "The Battle of the Bulge as a Case History in Battlefield Intelligence," *Combat Forces Journal*, citing ltr from Simpson, 29 May 46.

For "the relief is now complete" (p. 75), 2d Div G-2 Periodic Rpt, 10 Dec 44.

"Go back to sleep, Robbie," (p. 75), author's interv with Maj. Gen. Ralph W. Zwicker, CofS, 2d Inf Div, 4 Mar 82.

For "in towns close to the front" (p. 75), V Corps G-2 Periodic Rpt, 15 Dec 44.

For "a major counterattack" and "probable" (p. 75), 2d Div G-2 Periodic Rpts, 11 and 12 Dec 44.

For "many PWs" and "between the 17th and 25th of December" (p. 76), FUSA G-2 Periodic Rpt 189, 15 Dec 44, which reflected information available to Dickson on the 14th.

"It's the Ardennes!" (p. 76), Dickson draft MS, Toland files, *op. cit.*

For the "black propaganda" incident (p. 76), Bradley, *A Soldier Reports*, pp. 426–427; Dickson's involvement provided by Rosengarten.

"A very interesting report" (p. 77), FUSA G-2 Periodic Rpt 189.

For Tasker's prediction (p. 77), see Lt. Gen. Lewis H. Brereton, *The Brereton Diaries* (New York: William Morrow, 1946), p. 387.

For "visiting galaxy" (p. 77), unpublished diary kept by Hodges's aide, Maj. William C. Sylvan, CMH.

Allied air commanders' conference (p. 78) and for "the enemy could still do something" and "had looked in a mirror" (p. 79), Cole.

CHAPTER IV: THE LAST FEW HOURS

For "had more forces hidden" (p. 85), Eisenhower interv with Von Manteuffel, 12 Oct 66.

For "strong enemy forces" (p. 85), MS # B-151a, von Manteuffel.

"There will be no deviation" (p. 86), Eisenhower, *The Bitter Woods*, p. 161.

On the wearing of enemy uniforms (p. 87), Skorzeny, *Special Mission*, p. 149. For a more studied analysis of the subject, see Eisenhower, p. 124n.

For "deceive very young American troops" (pp. 87–88) and "Well, go and think it all over" (pp. 88), Skorzeny, pp. 155 and 158–159.

For "more fit for bicycles" (p. 89), ETHINT (European Theater Historical Interview) 10, Peiper.

For "not necessarily a great victory" (p. 90), author's interv with Wortmann, 16 Oct 82.

For "perhaps in the process" (p. 90), author's interv with Osterhold, 16 Oct 82.

"There is a general feeling of elation" (p. 90), Merriam, *Dark December*, p. 37.

"I write during one of the great hours" (p. 90), Annex 3 to 1st Div G-2 After Action Rpt, Dec 44, "Captured Letter" ('We March')." See observations on morale in MS # B-151a, Von Manteuffel.

For "a temper when tested" (p. 91), ltr, Col. Ralph V. Steele, Exec O, 9th Inf, to Joseph C. Doherty, 8 Apr 82.

For "in a large-scale offensive" (p. 94), Royce L. Thompson, "American Intelligence on the German Counteroffensive," prepared in support of Cole, *The Ardennes*, CMH.

For "sound of vehicles . . . barking dogs" (p. 94), 106th Div G-2 Periodic Rpt, 15 Dec 44.

For "much saluting" (p. 94), Thompson, *op. cit.*

For "large enemy formations in Bitburg" (p. 94), author's interv with Barton, 10 Jun 54, CMH.

"Don't worry" (p. 94), author's interv with Col. Léon Kimmes, Luxembourg Army, 21 Aug. 81.

For "a more active participant" (p. 95), ltrs to the author from Allard, 17 May and 9 Jun 82. Allard's twin brother survived as a prisoner of war.

"Tomorrow the heavies'll start firing again" (p. 95), Charles Whiting, *Death of a Division* (New York: Stein and Day, 1980), p. 4. Whiting has some new material from interviews with Belgian civilians but depends almost entirely for the tactical story on Cole. His analyses and criticisms of the 106th Division are ill-considered.

For "didn't have the chance of a snowflake" (p. 96), Combat Interv with men of Troop C, 18th Cav Rcn Sqdn.

"Soldiers of the West Front!!" and "Tomorrow brings the beginning" (p. 97), Thompson, *op. cit.*

CHAPTER V: IN FRONT OF ST. VITH

Combat Interviews for the 14th Cav Gp are many and detailed but understandably less so for the 106th Div, although the division has an excellent unit history by the distinguished military historian Col. R. Ernest Dupuy, *St. Vith: Lion in the Way* (Washington, D.C.: Infantry Journal Press, 1949).

For "in the true Prussian tradition" (p. 101), Brownlow, *Panzer Baron*, p. 62.

"You remember our conversation" (p. 102) and "How do you know" (p. 102), Eisenhower interv with Von Manteuffel.

"Surrender, Americans" and "Take a ten-minute break" (p. 106), Combat Intervs with 14th Cav. Gp.

The story of Sanny Schür (pp. 106–107), author's interv with Mme Susanne Schür Schugens, Lanzerath, 5 Aug 81.

"If they can't sign off" (pp. 107–108), Eisenhower, *The Bitter Woods*, p. 185.

For "seventy-five yards from CP" (p. 109), Combat Intervs with 14th Cav Gp.

For "a volcano about to erupt" (p. 110), author's interv with Col. Pierce Timberlake, who knew Devine well, 21 Oct 83.

"I'll stay" (p. 111), Combat Interv with Co A, 81st Engr Bn.

For "a major offensive in this sector" (p. 115), 2d Div Ltr of Instructions, 132400A Nov 44, in 2d Div G-3 Jnl file, 13–14 Nov 44. Cole, *The Ardennes*, says that in the event of enemy attack, the 2d Division intended withdrawing the two regiments from the Schnee Eifel to the Auw-Bleialf road and using one to counterattack into the Losheim Gap. The author finds no evidence of such a plan. Robertson in a letter to Dr. Delaval, Vielsalm, confirmed the possibility of withdrawal but mentioned no counterattack plan, and neither the former division CofS, General Zwicker, nor the G-3, Maj. Gen. John H. Chiles, nor the artillery commander, Maj. Gen. John H. Hinds, recalls such a plan.

"If you can't hold" (p. 118), Combat Interv with Troop B, 18th Cav Rcn Sqdn.

"Subject: Undertaking *GREIF*" (p. 119). The order is reproduced in Dupuy, *Lion in the Way*, p. 235. Differing from Dupuy's account of the findings of the order, the author's account is based on ltr to *The Cub* (106th Div. Ass. newsletter), 24 Jan 47, from Lt. Col. Charles F. Girand (copy in Robert C. Ringer, unpublished MS, "The End Is Not Yet.")

"*Marschiert schnell!*" (p. 120) and "Somebody's got to stay here" (p. 121), Combat Interv with Cannon Co., 424th Inf.

For "might go half-way to Paris" (p. 123), Combat Interv with Middleton in ETO Historian's file, NA.

For "not to get heavily engaged" (p. 123), Combat Interv with Puett.

"*Bonn hier*" (p. 128), ltr, Hill to Joseph C. Doherty, 15 Oct 80 and author's intervs with Hill, Jul 82.

For "two keys . . . two big friends" (p. 128), Hill, unpublished MS, "The Battle of the Bulge."

"You know how things are" (p. 128), Toland, *Battle*, p. 32.

For "but I agree" (p. 129), Hill MS, *op. cit.*

"Well, that's it" and "I just talked to Jones" (p. 129), Toland, p. 33. See also Combat Interv with Middleton and accompanying ltr, Middleton to Theater Historian ETO, 30 Jul 45.

Additional sources: ltr, Col. Joseph F. Puett to author, 7 Apr 83; extensive correspondence between the author and Ralph G. Hill and Francis H. Aspinwall; ltr, Col. Joseph C. Matthews, Exec O, 422d Inf, to Hill, 7 Jul 82; tp intervs by the author with Maj. Gen. John H. Hinds (CG, 2d Div Arty), Aug 82; author's interv with Zwicker, *op. cit.;* and ltr, Maj. Gen. John H. Chiles (G-3, 2d Div) to author, 18 Dec 82.

CHAPTER VI: THE SKYLINE DRIVE

Combat interviews are detailed for the 109th and 112th Inf Regts but probably because so many men were lost, few for the 110th Inf. Robert H. Phillips, *To Save Bastogne* (New York: Stein and Day, 1983), filled the lacuna with interviews he himself conducted.

"Get them when they cross" (p. 133), Combat Interv with Cannon Co., 112th Inf.

"Nobody able to sleep" (p. 134), Cole, *The Ardennes*, pp. 198–199.

"What do you make of it?" (p. 138), Maj. Gen. Daniel B. Strickler, unpublished MS, "The Battle of the Bulge," Toland files, LofC.

For "in friendly fashion" (p. 139), Cole, p. 184n.

Additional sources: author's interv with prof. Dr. Joseph Maertz, Clervaux, 22 Aug 81; Maj. Georg Loos, "The Operations of *Army Engineer Battalion 600* during the Battle of the Bulge."

CHAPTER VII: THE SOUTHERN SHOULDER

Combat interviews with all units are extensive, and there is an excellent regimental history: Col. Garden F. Johnson, *History of the Twelfth Infantry Regiment in World War II* (privately printed, 1947).

For "a good-looking blonde" (p. 149), and action (pp. 150–151), James V. Christy, unpublished and untitled MS written for the author.

For "fanatically hopped up" and following quotations (p. 151), Maj. Harry M. Kemp, "The Operations of the 3d Battalion, 109th Infantry, in the Vicinity of

Diekirch, Luxembourg," monograph prepared for Advanced Infantry Officers' Course, Ft. Benning, Ga., 1949–50.

For "very bloody fighting" (p. 151), MS # A-876, Brandenberger, *"Seventh Army* in the Ardennes Offensive," vol. II.

For "no cause for alarm" and following quotations (p. 152), Combat Interv with Rudder.

For quotations and action at the Parc Hôtel (pp. 156–158), Combat Intervs with Leake, *et al.* and "Notes on Parc Hôtel," Toland files, LofC.

For "no retrograde movement" (p. 159), 12th Inf AAR, Dec 44.

For "a matter of making the breakthrough" (p. 159), MS # A-876, Brandenberger.

CHAPTER VIII: THE NORTHERN SHOULDER

Combat Interviews are detailed and comprehensive for all units of the 2d and 99th Divisions. Unit histories: *Combat History of the Second Infantry Division in World War II* (Baton Rouge, La.: Army & Navy Publishing Co., 1946); Maj. Gen. Walter E. Lauer, *Battle Babies: The Story of the 99th Infantry Division* (Baton Rouge, La.: Military Press of Louisiana, 1951); and *741 Tank Battalion D-Day to V-E Day* (privately printed, 1982).

For "attached to him perpetually" (p. 160), Cole, *The Ardennes*, p. 76.

For "decent, but stupid" (p. 160), Merriam, *Dark December*, p. 18.

For shooting of Russians (p. 160), Brett-Smith, *Hitler's Generals*, p. 157.

For "an earth-shaking inferno" (p. 163), Frühbeiser, "The *9th Parachute Regiment* in the Offensive Against the Americans," *Der Deutsche Fallschirmjäger*, No. 12, 1964.

For "all hell broke loose" (p. 163), Nawrocki, unpublished MS, "Battle of the Bulge, 99th Infantry Division, December 1944, Co B, 393."

For "thunderous" (p. 163), Combat Interv with Kempton.

For "a terrifying experience" (p. 163), Ronningen, unpublished MS, "The Battle of the Bulge," courtesy of William C. C. Cavanagh.

For "the earth seemed to break open" (p. 163), Holz, *"Panzerjäger 12* in the Battle of the Bulge," Part II, *Der Alte Kameraden*, No. 12, 1972.

For "could see them against the skyline" (p. 164), ltr, Macay to Cavanagh (no date).

For "in swarms" (p. 164), Maj. Keith P. Fabianich, "The Defense of Höfen, Germany," *Infantry School Quarterly*, Jul 48.

The definitive work on the proximity fuse (p. 165) is Ralph B. Baldwin, *The Deadly Fuze: Secret Weapon of World War II* (San Rafael, Cal.: Presidio Press, 1980).

For "headlong retreat" (p. 166), 38th Cav Rcn Sqdn AAR, Dec 44.

For "every weapon" and "practically swept" (p. 166), Fabianich, *op. cit.*

For "just as startled" and "didn't know and didn't care" (pp. 172–173), ltr, Newbrough to Cavanagh, 7 Oct 79.

All material on Adolf Schür (pp. 176–178), author's interv with Schür, 10 Aug 81.

"What shall we do then?," "Hold," "No, I have orders to hold" and "hanging limply" (p. 178), Eisenhower, *The Bitter Woods*, pp. 188, 190, 191. Dr. Bouck confirmed the story as written by Eisenhower.

"Can't we go to your CP" (p. 179), ltr, Hinds to Cavanagh, 2 Feb 82, and author's tp intervs with Hinds, 20 and 22 Nov 82.

"Go slow and watch your step" (p. 180), Robertson, "Operations 2nd Infantry Division—6-20 December 1944," attachment to 2d Div AAR, Dec 44.

For "entire front was practically reestablished" (p. 181), Lauer, *Battle Babies*, p. 25n.

For "could be decisive" (p. 182), Skorzeny, *Special Mission*, p. 166.

For "gone to bed" (p. 182), ltr, Peiper to Lyle Bouck, 9 Dec 66, courtesy of Bouck.

Additional source: Hubert Meyer, *Kriegegeschichte der 12 SS-Panzerdivision (Hitlerjugend)*, Vol. II (Osnabrück: Munin Verlag, Gmb H., 1982).

CHAPTER IX: REACTION AT THE TOP

For "might be the answer" (p. 185), 12th AGp Briefings, 16 Dec 44, 12th AGp files.

"Well, Brad" and "A counterattack, yes" (p. 186), Bradley, *A Soldier's Story*, p. 450.

For "send Middleton some help" (p. 186), ibid., p. 451.

"Tell him" (p. 186), Eisenhower, *The Bitter Woods*, p. 215.

"I hate like hell to do it" (p. 186), Bradley, p. 475.

For "cracked a bottle of champagne" (p. 186), unpublished diary kept by Bradley's aide, Lt. Col. Chet Hansen, entry of 17 Dec 44 (copy in U.S. Army Military History Research Collection).

Signal to *Jadgkorps II* (p. 186), Ultra files.

For "do whatever they wish" and "I wish everybody could see them" (p. 187), Sylvan Diary.

"God gave him a face" (p. 188), MacDonald, *The Mighty Endeavor*, pp. 406–407, citing author's interv with Eisenhower.

For "implicit faith" (p. 188), MacDonald in Parrish, ed., *The Encyclopedia of World War II*, p. 282.

For "the heaviest artillery fire" (p. 188), First Light Rpts, 160645 Dec 44, FUSA G-2 Jnl file.

For "in large patrol strength" (p. 188), Sylvan Diary, entry of 16 Dec 44.

"This call to arms" (p. 189), tp msg from V Corps, 161244 Dec 44, FUSA G-2 Jnl file.

For "the situation for the division" (p. 189), msg, 161415 Dec 44, VIII Corps G-3 Jnl file.

For "neither optimistic nor pessimistic" (p. 189), Sylvan Diary, *ibid*.

"These documents indicate" (p. 190), Annex 3, VIII Corps G-2 Periodic Rpt, 162400 Dec 44.

For "by 1130 hours" (p. 190), msg from 99th Div, 161300 Dec 44, V Corps G-2 Jnl file.

"The sudden attacks" and "Until the magnitude" (p. 190), 12th AGp G-2 Periodic Rpt, 162300 Dec 44.

For "did not come up to expectations" (p. 191), MS # B-151a, Von Manteuffel.

"Hold on as long as possible" (p. 191), Nobécourt, *Hitler's Last Gamble*, p. 186.

On the German parachute drop (pp. 191–192*ff.*), see Willy Volberg, unpublished MS, "Operation STÖSSER," a personal experience account prepared for the author (translation by Maj. Dieter Kopac, Würselen).

For "crush everything" (p. 192), Nobécourt, p. 152.

"Balck! Balck!" (p. 193), Toland, *Battle*, p. 39.

For "the Italian" (p. 194), Irving, *Hitler's War*, p. 741.

CHAPTER X: *Kampfgruppe Peiper*

An essential source is Giles, *The Damned Engineers*. Immensely helpful also were the correspondence and interviews with Col. David E. Pergrin and Ralph Hill, Jr.

For "well bred . . . resourceful" (p. 197), Weingartner, *Crossroads of Death*, pp. 21, 88.

For "the decisive role in the offensive" (p. 197), ETHINT 10, Peiper.

For "the decisive hour," "wave of terror," and without "humane inhibitions" (p. 197), sworn statement by Dietrich, 22 Mar 46, in Royce L. Thompson, "The ETO Ardennes Campaign: Operations of the Combat Group Peiper, 16–26 December 1944," prepared in support of Cole, *The Ardennes*, CMH.

For quotations from Peiper (pp. 197–198), sworn statement by Peiper, 21 Mar 46, in *ibid.*

For "fight in the old SS spirit" and following quotations (p. 198), prosecution exhibits in Case No. 6-24, *U.S. vs. Valentin Bersin, et al.*, NA.

For "biggest damn tank" (p. 201), Toland, *Battle*, p. 47.

For "in wild scramble," (p. 201), Combat Interv with 14th Cav gp.

Material on Karl Wortmann (pp. 202*ff.*) from author's interv with Wortmann, 16 Oct 82.

"Those don't sound like ours" and following quotations (pp. 202–203), Toland, pp. 46–47.

For war crimes at Honsfeld (pp. 203–204), see affidavits in SHAEF War Crimes files.

For the story of Erna Collas (p. 204), author's interv with André Schroeder, 14 Aug 81, and ltr, Schroeder to author, 10 Sep 81.

"The Germans are coming!" (p. 206) and the actions oJ Meads, Yager, Rapp, Paul J. Rutka, and Charles W. Smith, ltrs to Ralph Hill and the author, 3 Jun, 2 Jul, 15 Aug, 1 Sep, and 11 Dec 82.

"My God! They shot Pappel" (p. 207), ltr, Yager to Ralph Hill, 2 Jul 82. See also Case 6-107, SHAEF War Crimes files.

"The enemy had the key to success" (p. 209), Cole, p. 91.

For "a last ditch defense of the CP" (p. 210), personal diary provided the author by Matt F. C. Konop.

For "the usual cold, tasteless mixture" (p. 211) and expected "to be blown up" (p. 212), Mabel Jessop, "The Teams of Majors Hurwitz and Higgenbotham," in Dr. Clifford L. Graves, ed., *Front Line Surgeons* (San Diego: Frye and Smith, 1950).

"Hey, why don't you ride with me" (p. 213) and Bechtel's story, Bechtel, unpublished MS, "Untold Story of Battery B," and ltr, Bechtel to the author, 7 Jun 82.

"We're going to blow" (p. 215), Giles, p. 92.

"There's a big Kraut column" and "That little FAOB outfit" (p. 215), Giles, pp. 93–94.

For "those beautiful trucks" (p. 217), Peiper testimony in Thompson, *op. cit.*

For "almost like a lowing" (p. 219), James P. Mattera (with C. M. Stephan, Jr.), "Murder at Malmédy," *Army* magazine, Dec 81.

For "for a few minutes" and following quotations (p. 219), prosecution exhibits in *U.S. vs. Valentin Bersin, et al.*

Lieutenant Lary's account (p. 220), 1st Lt. Virgil P. Lary, Jr., "The Massacre at Malmédy," *Field Artillery Journal*, Feb 46.

"Let's go!" (p. 220) and "Forget the password" (p. 222), Mattera, *op. cit.*

For Lieutenant Lary's story (p. 220) see Hugh Mulligan, article based on interviews with Mesdames Martin, *Ohio State Journal*, 16 Dec 69, copy with Ringer MS, *op. cit;* also interview with Mesdames Martin by William C.C. Cavanagh, 9 Mar 84.

"There is absolutely no question" (p. 222), Sylvan Diary, entry of 17 Dec 44.

Additional sources: Richard Gallagher, *Malmédy Massacre* (New York: Paperback Library, 1964); Charles Whiting, *Massacre at Malmédy* (London: Leo Cooper, 1971); Gerard Grégoire, *Les Panzers de Peiper Face à l'U.S. Army* (privately printed, n.d.); Charles A. Hammer, ed., *History of the 285th Field Artillery Observation Battalion* (privately printed, n.d.); 81st Cong., 1st Sess., Report of the Subcommittee on Armed Services, United States Senate, Malmédy Massacre Investigation (13 Oct 49); Steven P. Kane, *The 1st SS Panzer Division in the Battle of the Bulge* (Bennington, Vt.: International Graphics Corporation, 1982); Kenneth C. Parker, "More on the Massacre at Malmédy," *Field Artillery Journal*, May 46; Marshall Andrews, "10 Years After, Malmédy Massacre," *Washington Post*, 16 Dec 54; Sgt. Ed Cunningham, "Massacre at Malmédy," *YANK* magazine, Jan 44; Maj James B. Kemp, "Operations of the 612th Tank Destroyer Battalion, Second Infantry Division, in the Battle of the Bulge, Vicinity of Elsenborn Corner," Advanced Infantry Officers' Course, Ft. Benning, Ga. 1949–50; author's interv with Haley Marshall, 394th Inf, 17 Jul 82; unidentified CO, Co B, 2d Engr Bn, "Diary of a Prisoner of War," in *The Checkerboard* (newsletter of the 99th Div Assn), Dec 82; author's interv with Samuel M. Barrett, Btry B, 285th FA Obsn Bn, 10 Aug 81; ltrs to the author from Albert M. Valenzi, 20 Jan 83, William H. Merriken, 24 Jan 83, and Michael Sciranko, 8 Feb 83; Statement of Pfc Homer D. Ford in ETO Historians' file; and ltr to the author from Ralph A. Logan, date missing but late 1983.

CHAPTER XI: "THE DAMNED ENGINEERS"

Many of the sources for Chapter X also apply for this chapter, particularly Giles, Grégoire, and Pergrin.

"They're Krauts!" (p. 225). Giles, *The Damned Engineers*, p. 293.

"German tanks," (p. 227), "If anything happens" (p. 228), and "Murderer!" (p. 229), Toland, *Battle*, p. 58.

"The people of the village" (p. 231), Giles, p. 53, and with the exception of the next entry, all following quotations.

"Go to the devil" (p. 234), author's interv with Schugens, 8 Aug 81.

Additional sources: Charles Foley, *Commando Extraordinary* (London: Longmans Green, 1954); Howard R. Bergen, *History of the 99th Infantry Battalion* (Oslo: Emil Moestueas, n.d.); Cecil E. Roberts, *A Soldier from Texas* (Fort Worth, Tex.: Branch-Smith, 1978); Raymond L. Lewis (CCB, 9th Armd Div), unpublished MS, "Eight Days at St. Vith"; Ken C. Rust, *The 9th Air Force in World War II* (Fallbrook, Cal.: Aero Publishers, 1967); testimony of Marie Lochem in SHAEF War Crimes files; and Roger Hardy, *Le 5e Bataillon de Fusiliers Belges Durant L'Hiver 1944–1945* (privately printed, 1983). A photograph of a German officer at the Kaiserbaracke, a crossroads between Ligneuville and St. Vith, was for long mistakenly identified as Peiper, which led a number of writers (including Giles) to conclude that Peiper split his column. That was not the case. The editors of the British periodical *After the Battle* have conclusively proven that the photograph is not of Peiper. See No. 4, Nov 74.

CHAPTER XII: THE RACE FOR BASTOGNE: THE FIRST PHASE

A basic source is Phillips, *To Save Bastogne*. Unit histories are: *History of the 110th Infantry Regiment, United States Army, World War II*, and *The 28th Infantry Division* (both Atlanta: Albert Love Enterprises, 1945 and 1946).

"I don't know any details" (p. 262), Hewitt, *Workhorse of the Western Front*, p. 173 (full citation under Chapter XXI).

"I'll put it up to Ike" (p. 262), Eisenhower, *The Bitter Woods*, p. 226.

"Pardon my French" and "I will never move backwards" (p. 262), Hansen Diary, entry of 17 Dec 44.

For "considered the situation . . . critical" and "prepared for any eventuality" (p. 263), Gavin, *On to Berlin*, pp. 204–205.

"Get all your boys together" (p. 267) and "From now on" (p. 268), extract from a ltr from Col. Gustin M. Nelson to his father, written in May 45, Toland files, LofC.

For "the sharpshooter of Munshausen," "swinging a souvenir American bayonet," and "measures would be taken" (pp. 272–273), Toland, *Battle*, p. 79, and ltr to the author from Pierre Eicher, 22 Aug 83. Eicher corrects Toland's identification of the village as Marnach.

"We've blown up everything" (p. 274), Combat Interv with Company K, 110th Infantry.

For "no more time to talk" (p. 277), Col. Hurley Fuller, unpublished MS, "Report of Operations of the 110th Infantry Combat Team, December 16–18, 1944," Toland files, LofC.

"This switchboard is now closed" (p. 278), author's interv with Malcom R. Wilkey, G-2 Sect, VIII Corps, 20 Jan 83.

Additional sources: Prof. Dr. Joseph Maertz, *Luxemburg im Der Ardennenoffen-*

sive 1944/45 (Luxembourg City: Sankt-Paulus-Druckerei, 1969); Richard V. Grulich, Hq Co, 110th Inf, unpublished MS, "Three Days Plus 102"; John B. Allard, unpublished MS, "A Replacement in the 'Bloody Bucket,'" prepared for the author, and ltrs to the author, 17 May and 9 Jun 82; ltr to the author from John E. Peiper, Co I, 112th Inf, 18 Apr 82; and author's interv with Jean Servais, 22 Aug 81.

CHAPTER XIII: THE RACE FOR BASTOGNE: THE SECOND PHASE

Phillips, *To Save Bastogne*, was again highly useful, and some other sources cited for Chapter XII also apply.

For "already imperiled" and "could seriously endanger" (p. 280), MS # B-151a, Von Manteuffel.

For "flowing to the west" (p. 281), MS # B-040, Genmaj. Heinz Kokott, *"26th Volksgrenadier Division* in the Ardennes Offensive."

For "go find your regiment" (p. 284), ltr, Seely to Marshall S. Reid, no date, but published in the newsletter of the Southwest Chapter, 3d Armd Div Assn, Mar 82, courtesy of Haynes W. Dugan.

"My God, this is the sort of thing" (p. 285), Charles T. Johnson, unpublished and untitled MS prepared for the author and ltr, 10 Sep 82.

"There's a tank coming" (p. 287), Seely ltr, *op. cit.*

For "a fantastic aspect" (p. 289), MS # A-942, Genlt. Fritz Bayerlein, *"Panzer Lehr Division* (15–22 Dec 1944)."

"How many teams?", "Three," and "Sir, I want authority" (p. 290), Combat Interv with Roberts.

For "cut the column in the middle" (p. 294), CCR, 9th Armd Div AAR, Dec 44.

For "young, blonde, and beautiful" and following quotations (p. 295), B. H. Liddell-Hart, *History of the Second World War* (New York: G. P. Putnam's Sons, 1971), p. 651n, and Marshall, *Bastogne: The First Eight Days* (full citation under Chapter XXIV), p. 185. Both historians received their information from Bayerlein himself.

For "mischance and confusion" (p. 297), Cole, *The Ardennes*, p. 303.

Additional sources: History of the 58th Armored Field Artillery Battalion (privately printed, n.d.), provided by Raymond T. Summers; Lt. Gen. William F. Train, unpublished MS, "My Memories of the Battle of the Bulge," prepared for the author, Dec 82; and Lester M. Nichols, *Impact: The Battle Story of the Tenth Armored Division* (New York: Bradbury, Sayles, O'Neill Co., 1967).

CHAPTER XIV: THE DEFENSE OF WILTZ

See again Phillips, *To Save Bastogne*, and for the Americans hiding in Wiltz, Toland, *Battle*.

For "like autumn leaves" (p. 303), Phillips, p. 240.

For "mud, fields, streams" (p. 306), Col. Daniel B. Strickler, "Action Report of the German Ardennes Breakthrough as I Saw It from 16 December 1944–2 January 1945," in *History of the 110th Infantry Regiment*.

Additional sources: G. Martin, "Fighting Around the 'Schumann Café,'" *Der Deutsche Fallschirmjäger*, No. 2, 1976; and "The Second Platoon of the 42d Field Hospital at Wiltz" in Graves, ed., *Front Line Surgeons*.

CHAPTER XV: DEVELOPING CRISIS AT ST. VITH

Combat Interviews for the 7th Armored Division are extensive. Unit histories are Dupuy, *op. cit.; The Lucky Seventh: History of the Seventh Armored Division and the Seventh Armored Divison Association* (privately printed, 1982); and *The Valiant 275th Armored Field Artillery Battalion* (privately printed, 1978). Correspondence conducted with veterans by Francis H. Aspinwall was most helpful.

For "the canvas on the truck" (p. 315), ltr, Brown to Aspinwall, 24 Aug 81.

For "men in greenish uniforms" (pp. 316–317), Aspinwall, unpublished MS, "Memorandum of Personal Experience, 589th FA Bn."

For "very big and powerful" and following quotation (p. 319), Dupuy, *Lion in the Way*, p. 153, citing affidavits from civilians in Meyerode obtained by General Wood.

"Withdraw from present positions" (p. 320), Cole, *The Ardennes*, p. 165.

"Find out what you can" (p. 322) and "break that ring" (p. 323), Eisenhower, *The Bitter Woods*, pp. 227, 229.

For "a final delaying position" (p. 324), Cole, p. 163.

For "mad as hell" and "anytime and any place" (p. 325), *The Valiant 275th Armored Field Artillery Battalion*, p. 13.

Quotations from Boyer (pp. 325–326), Eisenhower, *The Bitter Woods*, pp. 231–232.

"And how is your situation, Baron" and following quotations (p. 327), Toland, *Battle*, p. 66, and confirmed in Eisenhower interv with Von Manteuffel, 12 Oct 66.

"We'll be in good shape" (p. 327) and following quotations, Eisenhower, *The Bitter Woods*, pp. 229–230. See also Toland, pp. 54, 62.

"I want to shoot" (p. 330), Eisenhower, p. 233.

For "take over," "left the room," and "the commander of the 14th Cavalry Group" (p. 331), 14th Cav Gp AAR, Dec 44.

Additional sources: The Armored School, *The Defense of St. Vith, Belgium, 17–23 December 1944*; Lewis, "Eight Days at St. Vith," *op. cit.*; William Donohue Ellis and Col. Thomas J. Cunningham, Jr., *Clarke of St. Vith: The Sergeant's General* (Cleveland: Dillon/Liederbach, 1974); ltr, Col. Charles C. Cavender to Toland, 13 Mar 59, and day-by-day account by Cavender, Toland files, LofC; ltrs to the author from Cavender, 20 Jun and 3, 14, and 16 Jul 83; interv with Col. George Descheneaux, Toland files, LofC; Maj. Gerald K. Johnson, "The Black Soldier in the Ardennes," *Soldiers* magazine, Feb 81; Capt. Alan W. Jones, Jr., "The Operations of the 423d Infantry (106th Infantry Division) in the Vicinity of Schoenberg during the Battle of the Ardennes," Maj. Lewis M. Keyes, "Operations of the 106th Infantry Division in the Battle of the Bulge," and Maj. John C.

Hollinger, "The Operations of the 422d Infantry Regiment in the Vicinity of Schlausenbach, Germany," Advanced Infantry Officers' Course, Ft. Benning, 1949–50; *The Lion's Tale—Short Stories of the 106th Infantry Division* (limited edition by Seventh Annual 106th Division Convention Committee, 1953); Thomas J. Riggs, "An Engineer's Seven Day War," (published article but journal not identified) in Ringer, unpublished MS, *op. cit.*; ltr to author from Lawrence J. Smith, 14th Cav Gp S-3, 22 Oct 83; and ltr to the author from Lt. Col. Levin L. Lee, 14th Cav Gp, 7 Sep 83.

CHAPTER XVI: SHAPING THE DEFENSE OF ST. VITH

Most sources for Chapter XV also apply to this chapter.
"Can't, Lieutenant" (p. 334), Combat Interv with 14th Cav Gp.
For "all hell break loose" and following quotations (p. 335), Combat Intervs with Whiteman and 1st Sgts. Frederick J. Mabb and Andrew J. Ellmer.
For "drove like mad" (p. 336), Lewis, "Eight Days at St. Vith."
"My poor men" (p. 339), Dupuy, *Lion in the Way*, p. 121, citing ltr, Tech. Sgt. T. Wayne Black, 422d Inf.
For "to destroy by fire" (p. 339), *ibid.*, p. 104, and Cole, *The Ardennes*, p. 167.
"Attack Schoenberg" (p. 340), "It is now exactly," and "It sounded like" (p. 341), Dupuy, pp. 128, 137.
"We're sitting like fish in a pond" (p. 343) and following quotations, Toland interv with Descheneaux, Toland files, LofC.
"OK, Colonel, I'll go" (p. 344), Eisenhower, *The Bitter Woods*, p. 293.
"I know it's no use" and following quotations (p. 345), Toland, *Battle*, p. 122.
"Supplies have not been dropped" (p. 347), Dupuy, p. 134.
"Who do I work for?" (p. 348), Eisenhower, p. 285.

CHAPTER XVII: IN FRONT OF LUXEMBOURG CITY

Combat Interviews are extensive and have valuable covering narratives.
"Use your own judgment" (p. 355), Combat Interv with Rudder.
For the evacuation of Diekirch (p. 356), Lt. E. T. Melchers, "Rapport sur l'Activité de la Gendarmerie Grand-Ducale du Bombardment et de l'Evacuation de la Ville de Diekirch," courtesy Lt. Col. Melchers.
For "drive the enemy into the river" (p. 357), FO 3, CCA, 9th Armd Div, in CCA AAR, Dec 44.
For "it was a desperate fight" (p. 364), Combat Interv with Leake, *et al.*
"Really it was swell" (p. 365), Daniel B. Stresow, unpublished MS, "E Company's Last Stand," Toland files, LofC.
Barton's sending a message (p. 366), author's interv with Barton.
For "for God's sake get out the tanks" (p. 367), Combat Interv with Cook.
For "heard groaning" and following quotations (p. 368), Stresow MS.

Additional information on the stand in Echternach obtained in author's tp interv with Paul H. Dupuis, 15 Aug 83.

CHAPTER XVIII: IN DEFENSE OF THE TWIN VILLAGES

Most sources cited for Chapter VIII apply.

"I want to talk with your commander" (p. 374), author's interv with Osterhold, *op. cit.*

Lieutenant Goffigon's story (pp. 375–376 and 378–379), author's interv with Goffigon, 11 Mar 82, and Charles B. MacDonald, *Company Commander* (Washington, D.C.: Infantry Journal Press, 1947; current edition Bantam Books).

"We're doing all we can!" (p. 379), Walter E. Eisler, Jr., CO, Co L, 23d Inf, unpublished MS, "The Breakthrough, 16–19 Dec 1944, L Co, 23d Inf, 2d Inf Div," prepared for the author, Sep 81.

For "the Germans had broken through" (p. 380), Combat Interv with Robertson.

For "until ordered otherwise" (p. 380), Combat Interv with McKinley, *et al.*, 1st Bn, 9th Inf.

For "absolutely black" and following quotation (p. 381), Combat Interv with Maj. William F. Hancock, Exec O, 1st Bn, 9th Inf.

For "splashing Billy and me" (p. 382), Herbert P. Hunt, unpublished MS, "A Rifle Company That Would Not Budge: The Sequence of Events," prepared for the author, fall 81.

"If you don't get it out right now" and two following quotations (p. 383), Combat Interv with Hancock.

For "a scene of wild confusion" (p. 384), Combat Interv with McKinley, *et al.*

For "the night was ablaze" (p. 384), MacDonald, *Company Commander*, p. 139.

The story of Private Fisher (pp. 385–386), is from SHAEF War Crimes files and ltr, Fisher to author, 10 Sep 81. Fisher's testimony was corroborated by that of Staff Sgt. Charles Hunt.

The actions of Colonel Zeiner's tanks (pp. 386–387), Meyer, *Kriegegeschichte der 12 SS-Panzerdivision*, *op. cit.*

"Action quieting" (p. 387), historian's narrative of 38th Inf action in Combat Interv files.

For "a quivering hulk" (p. 387), Maj. Ben W. Legare, "The Operations of the 2d Batallion, 394th Infantry, in the German Counteroffensive, Vicinity of Losheimergraben, Germany," Advanced Infantry Officers' Course, Ft. Benning, Ga., 1949–50.

"Pull back to new positions" and "Withdraw immediately" (p. 388), Combat Interv with Capt. Frank W. Luchowski, S-3, 1st Bn, 23d Inf.

For "a state of shock" (p. 389), ltr, Sutherland to Joseph G. Doherty, 18 Oct 81. See also taped remarks, Col. Oscar A. Axelson, CO, 406th FA Gp, for William C. C. Cavanagh, no date, but in 1981.

"We fight and die here" (p. 390), Maj. Thomas J. Gendron, "The Operations of the 2d Battalion, 26th Infantry at Dom. Bütgenbach, Belgium," Advanced Infantry Officers' Course, Ft. Benning, Ga., 1949–50.

Additional sources: Royce L. Thompson, "Tank Fight of Rocherath-Krinkelt, 17–19 December 1944," prepared in support of Cole, *The Ardennes*, CMH; "The *12th Division* in the Battle of the Bulge 1944," *Der Alte Kameraden*, No. 11, 1975, and Nos. 2, 6, and 11, 1976; ltr, John W. Reid, 3d Bn, 393d Inf, to Toland,

18 Jan 58, Toland files, LofC; ltr, Lee Smith, CO, Co K, 23d Inf, to author, 26 Mar 82; ltrs, Daniel W. Franklin, Co K, 38th Inf, to author, 21 May and 2 and 17 Aug 82; and ltr, F. G. Prutzman, Hq, 2d Div Arty, to John H. Hinds, 2 Jul 47.

CHAPTER XIX: TO GAIN THE ELSENBORN RIDGE

See sources previously cited for Chapters VIII and XVIII.

For "a withering hail" (p. 392), historian's narrative in Combat Interv file.

"Hell, yes!," "unbelievable control," and "You have saved my regiment" (p. 397), *ibid.*

For "like a crippled goose" (p. 398), Cole, *The Ardennes*, p. 125.

For "tank grave" and "a cruel sight" and following quotations (p. 399), *"Die dritte Kompanie"* (unit history, *Co C, 12th SS-Pz Regt, 12th SS-Pz Div*, 1978).

"You got him" and following quotations (p. 400), ltr to author from Hugh Berger, Co I, 23d Inf, 28 Dec 81.

For "to move to new positions" (p. 402), historian's narrative.

"Your hospital is under arrest" (p. 403), Jessop, "The Teams of Majors Hurwitz and Higgenbotham," *op. cit.*

For "exceedingly heavy artillery" and following quotations (p. 405), Captured Combat Report, *3d Bn, 12th SS-Tank Regt*, in 1st Div, Annex 4 to Monthly Intell Activities Rpt, Dec 44.

For "a ring of steel" (p. 406), Gendron, *op. cit.*

For "as common as grass" (p. 407), Combat Interv with Daniel, *et. al.*

"I don't know where they got the ammo" and "knocked a part of Hitler's personal operations plan" (p. 408), Cole, pp. 132, 135.

For "a pretty good day's work" (pp. 409–410), Combat Interv with Robertson.

"What the 2d Division has done" (p. 410), historian's narrative of 1st Bn, 9th Inf, in Combat Interv files.

Additional sources: Maj. Gen. Derrill M. Daniel, unpublished MS, "The Operations of the 2d Battalion, 26th Infantry, at Dom. Bütgenbach, Belgium," Toland files, LofC; ltr, Daniel to Joseph C. Doherty, no date but in 1982; ltrs, Daniel to author, 23 Jun and 2 Jul 83; ltr, William Boehme, G-2 Sect, 1st Div, to Joseph C. Doherty, 16 Jan 82; Capt. Donald E. Rivette, "The Hot Corner at Dom. Bütgenbach," *Infantry Journal*, Oct 45); Diary, Col. Robert E. Snetzer, CO, 2d Engr C Bn, 12 Dec 44–20 Jan 45, courtesy of Tom C. Morris; ltr, Robert L. Dudley, plat ldr, 741st Tk Bn, to Joseph C. Doherty, no date but in 1982; and author's intervs with Joseph Scholzen and Albert Kohnenmergen, 14 Aug 81.

CHAPTER XX: COMMAND DECISIONS

For a heaven-sent opportunity (pp. 415–416), Sir Francis de Guingand, *Generals at War* (London: Hodder and Stoughton, 1964), p. 106.

For "great confusion" and following quotations (p. 416), Bryant, *Triumph in the West*, pp. 270–273.

For "worse than it was at noon" (p. 418) and "Well, I knew my staff would get here" (p. 420), Hansen Diary, entries of 18 and 19 Dec 44.

"The present situation" and "Hell, let's have the guts" (p. 420), Eisenhower, *Crusade in Europe*, p. 350.

"When can you start?" and following quotations (p. 420), Eisenhower, *The Bitter Woods*, pp. 256–257.

"Remember how a tarpon" (p. 421), Blumenson, *The Patton Papers*, p. 603.

For "a completely Allied outlook" (p. 421) and "General Eisenhower says" (p. 422), Eisenhower, *The Bitter Woods*, p. 368.

For "completely dumbfounded" (p. 422), Bradley and Blair, *A General's Life*, p. 363.

For "the logical thing to do" and "There's no doubt" (p. 423), Bradley, *A Soldier's Story*, p. 276.

For "one of my biggest mistakes" (p. 423), Bradley and Blair, p. 363.

For "British troops will always" (p. 423), Eisenhower, *The Bitter Woods*, p. 270.

For "through the machinations of the Prime Minister" and following quotation (p. 423), Blumenson, p. 601.

For "would be a most opportune time" (p. 423), Chandler, ed., Vol IV, *The War Years*, p. 2367.

For "created undercurrents of unhappiness" and "cocky mannerisms" (p. 424), Monk Dickson journal.

For "like Christ come to cleanse the temple" (p. 424), Wilmot, *The Struggle for Europe*, p. 592.

For "the quiet reticent type" (p. 426), Chandler, ed., Vol IV, p. 2369.

Material on public reaction (pp. 427–428) provided by J. Vanwelkenhuyzen, director, *Centre de Recherches et d'Etudes Historiques de la Seconde Guerre Mondiale*, Brussels, and Mme. Gracie Delépine, *Bibliothèque de Documentation Internationale Contemporaine*, Nanterre.

For "sheer hysteria" and "What could have been an unholy mess" (p. 428), Phillip Knightley, *The First Casualty—From the Crimea to Vietnam: The War Correspondent as Hero, Propagandist, and Myth Maker* (New York: Harcourt Brace Jovanovich, 1975), p. 324.

For the "angry session" (p. 428), *New York Times*, 20 Dec 44.

For "tinged by sorrow" (p. 429), *Washington Post*, 25 Dec 44.

For "the situation should not be viewed with panic" (p. 429), *New York Times*, 21 Dec 44.

CHAPTER XXI: THE WAR AGAINST *KAMPFGRUPPE PEIPER*

Most sources for Chapters X and XI are applicable. The 30th Division has an excellent unit history, Robert L. Hewitt, *Workhorse of the Western Front* (Washington, D.C.: Infantry Journal Press, 1946), and each of the regiments has a published history. See also *Spearhead in the West: The Third Armored Division* (compiled by the division staff in Germany, 1945), and Lt. Col. George Kenneth Rubel, *Daredevil Tankers, The Story of the 740th Tank Battalion* (privately printed, no date). Although there were detailed interviews for the 30th Division, they were combined into a general narrative, Capt. Franklin Ferriss, "The German Offensive of 16 November: The Defeat of the *1st SS Panzer Division Adolf Hitler*." Interviews with CCB, 3d Armored Division, and the 82d Airborne Division are extensive.

"I'm Jim Gavin" and following quotations (p. 433), Edward C. Arn, CO, Co F, 119th Inf, unpublished MS, "The Saga of a Civilian Soldier," and ltrs to the author, 17 Sep 82 and 30 Jan 83.

"They've killed a good few" and following quotations (p. 436), Whiting, *Massacre at Malmédy*, pp. 96–97 and 137–138.

For "such a crime" (p. 436), Skorzeny, *Special Mission*, p. 177.

All quotation reference to the killing of civilians (pp. 437–438), Commission des Crimes de Guerre, *Les Crimes de Guerre—Stavelot*, p. 16.

For "to take care of a tank," "Biggest Goddamned noise," and following quotation (p. 439), "AAA Units in Ardennes Battle," ETO Historian's file.

For "every commander to shoot him down" (p. 440), Peiper testimony, Thompson MS, *op. cit.*

"They're bastard tanks" (p. 441), Ferriss MS.

"I'll bet you guys" (p. 444), Giles, *The Damned Engineers*, p. 279.

"You have nothing to fear" (p. 445) and subsequent quotations from L'Abbé Hanlet from "La Tragédie de la Maison St-Edouard," courtesy William C. C. Cavanagh.

For "opened its muzzle up like a rose" (p. 446), Ferriss MS.

"Let's get the sons of bitches!" (p. 448), Combat Interv with officers of 1st Bn, 504th Prcht Inf.

CHAPTER XXII: THE LAST DAYS OF *KAMPFGRUPPE PEIPER*

Most sources for Chapters X, XI, and XXI are applicable.

For "a motley crew" (p. 451) and "*Kamerad!*" (p. 452), Cole, *The Ardennes*, p. 361.

"Surrender or die!" (p. 452), Giles, *The Damned Engineers*, p. 312.

"That place is very strong" and following quotation (p. 456), 30th Div Tp jnl 21 Dec 44.

"We're eliminating the Communist menace" and "We will keep what is best" and "I give you my word" (p. 459), Toland, *Battle*, p. 178. For McCown's story, see also ltrs to the author from McCown, 15 and 27 Jul 83, and Annex 3 to XVIII Corps (AB), G-2 Per Rpt No. 11, Observations of an American Field Officer Who Escaped from the *1st SS Panzer Division "Adolf Hitler."*

"If *Kampfgruppe Peiper* does not punctually report" (p. 460) and "May we break out?" (p. 461), Toland, p. 211.

"Colonel, that proposal is a farce" (p. 460), Eisenhower, *The Bitter Woods*, p. 278.

For "by all means bring back," "Merry Christmas," and "immediate escape" (p. 461) and "fierce, wild shooting" (p. 462), Karl Wortmann, "Password: 'Merry Christmas,'" *Der Freiwillige*, No. 12, 1978 (translation by Hans Holtkamp).

"Halt, Goddamn it!" (p. 462), Toland, p. 243, and ltrs to the author from McCown.

For the bombings of Malmédy (pp. 464–465), Royce L. Thompson, "Malmédy, Belgium, Mistaken Bombing, 23 and 25 December 1944," prepared in support of Cole, *The Ardennes*, CMH; 120th Inf AAR, Dec 44, and 30th Div G-3 Jnls, 23–25 Dec 44.

CHAPTER XXIII: THE DEFENSE OF ST. VITH

See previous citations for Chapters XV and XVI.

"This terrain is not worth a nickel" (p. 466), ltr, Clarke to author, 6 Apr 83.

For "in bad shape" (p. 468), Hasbrouck msg as cited in Cole, *The Ardennes*, pp. 394–395.

"Come on out!" and "Fuck you" (p. 473), Combat Interv with Britton, *et al.*

For "to plan alternative positions" (p. 473), Riggs, "An Engineer's Seven Day War."

"What are our orders?" and "Go west!" (p. 474), Combat Interv with 1st Lt. Roger W. Cresswell, Exec O, Co A, 23d Armd Inf Bn.

For "a kind of scavenger hunt" (p. 475), Cole, p. 411.

Hasbrouck msg (p. 477) and unless otherwise noted, messages exchanged between Hasbrouck and the First Army and the XVIII Airborne Corps are in 7th Armd Div Combat Interv file.

For "not expected to sacrifice his command" (p. 478), tp conv, Ridgway and Kean, 212350 Dec 44, Ridgway papers.

"Did you read this?" and "Yes, sir" (p. 480), author's interv with Hasbrouck, 20 Aug 83.

For "calm, courageous, imperturbable" and following quotations (p. 480), Ridgway, *Soldier*, pp. 119–120.

"The mud makes it pretty difficult" (p. 481) and "That cold snap" (p. 482), Eisenhower, *The Bitter Woods*, p. 302.

For "the opportunity will be over" and quotations following (p. 482), Cole, p. 415.

For "like subway trains" (p. 484), Train MS.

"The earth shook" (p. 487), Lewis MS.

"They can come back with all honor" (p. 487), Cole, p. 413.

"*A bas les Boches!*" (p. 487), MacDonald, *The Mighty Endeavor*, p. 386.

CHAPTER XXIV: THE DEFENSE OF BASTOGNE

The historian for the European Theater, Col. S. L. A. Marshall, assisted by Capt. John G. Westover and 1st Lt. A. Joseph Webber, conducted detailed interviews with the 101st Airborne Division, CCR, 9th Armored Division, and CCB, 10th Armored Division, whereupon Marshall wrote a narrative summary, which is in the Combat Interv files. The author has been unable to find the original interviews with the 101st, although it is evident from the interviews with the armored units that Marshall adhered scrupulously to the interview material. His narrative was subsequently published semi-officially as *Bastogne: The First Eight Days* (Washington, D.C.: Infantry Journal Press, 1946). In an appendix, "The Enemy Story," Marshall provides valuable material obtained through postwar interviews with von Lüttwitz, Bayerlein, Kokott, and von Lauchert. Any direct quotation without a citation is attributable to Marshall.

One of the better unit histories is Leonard Rapport and Arthur Northwood, Jr., *Rendezvous with Destiny: A History of the 101st Airborne Division* (101st Airborne Division Association, 1948). For the first days at Bastogne, the authors reprinted Marshall's account, but where they developed additional material, inserted it and marked it with an asterisk.

For "as if it were a [theater] curtain" (p. 490), Combat Interv with officers and men of Team Desobry. Maj. Gen. William R. Desobry provided detailed corrections to an early draft accompanying ltr to the author, 24 Aug 83.

For "it looked as if" (p. 491), Eisenhower, *The Bitter Woods*, p. 311.

"Don't be afraid" and "The Germans are coming" (p. 493), Toland, *Battle*, p. 129.

For "the son of a bitch" (p. 500), Combat Interv with Desobry.

For "to aid CCB" (p. 504), Cole, *The Ardennes*, p. 514.

For civilians in Bastogne (pp. 505–507), see Joss Heintz, *In the Perimeter of Bastogne* (Kiwanis Club, Bastogne, 1975), and Nobécourt, *Hitler's Last Gamble*.

For the story of Renée LeMaire (p. 507*ff.*), the author is deeply indebted to her two sisters, as noted in the acknowledgments. See also Dr. John T. Prior, "The Night Before Christmas—Bastogne, 1944," *The Bulletin*, Dec 72.

For "the hole in the doughnut" (p. 510), Fred MacKenzie, *The Men of Bastogne* (New York: David McKay, 1968), p. 151.

Most published accounts of the demand for surrender (pp. 511–513) are similar, and Rapport and Northwood (pp. 510–511), reproduce the German and English versions of the demand. New material is from Mme Simonne Schmitz of the Syndicat d'Initiative, Bastogne, and an account by one of the parliamentaries, Lt. Hellmuth Henke, provided by CEBA (with special thanks to Jean Milmeister). Although there has been speculation that instead of "Nuts!" General McAuliffe used a vulgarity, he assured the author in an interview in 1949 that he did indeed say "Nuts!"

Additional sources: Robert J. Houston, *D-Day to Bastogne: A Paratrooper Recalls World War II* (Smithtown, N.Y.: Exposition Press, 1980); and Rudolf Siebert, *2d Pz Div Rcn Bn*, "Die Schlacht in den Ardennes," *The Bulge* (CEBA), No. 2-81.

CHAPTER XXV: TO RELIEVE BASTOGNE

Sources listed for Chapter XXIV are applicable, particularly Marshall; and again no quotations from that source are cited. There are good Combat Intervs for the 4th Armored Division.

For "wrote knowingly" (p. 514), Martin Blumenson, *The Patton Papers 1895–1940* (Boston: Houghton Mifflin, 1972), p. 15.

"Troy, of all the goddamned crazy things" (p. 515), Eisenhower, *The Bitter Woods*, p. 333.

"All right, Troy" and "to cut off the Krauts" (p. 515), Price, *Troy H. Middleton*, p. 262.

"The general impression" (p. 515), Combat Interv with Lt. Col. Hal C. Pattison, Exec O, CCA, 4th Armd Div.

For "to drive like hell" (p. 519), "Sorry I did not get to shake hands," and "like shoals of silver minnows" (p. 521), Cole, *The Ardennes*, pp. 515, 531, and 468.

For "resupply coming from the sky" and following quotations (p. 522), ltr to the author from Mme. Jacques Boulet (Maggy LeMaire).

For "not to feel a sentimental pride" and following quotations (p. 522), Laurence Critchell, *Four Stars of Hell* (New York: The Declan X. McMullen Co., 1947), p. 267.

For "close enough for government work" (p. 522), Mackenzie, p. 189.

For McAuliffe at the police station (p. 525), Heintz, *In the Perimeter of Bastogne*, p. 67

"Xmas Eve present coming up" (p. 525), Cole, p. 475.

For "an all but imperceptible movement" (p. 526), MacKenzie, p. 212.

For "wore that ghastly air" (p. 527), Critchell, p. 274.

For "desperate effort" (p. 529), and "three tanks believed friendly" (p. 532), Cole, p. 480.

"This is it" (p. 531) and two following quotations, Combat Interv with Abrams, *et al*.

"Come here!" (p. 532), Toland, *Battle*, p. 264.

"How are you" and "Gee" (p. 532), Eisenhower, p. 345.

Additional sources: Capt. William A. Dwight, "Events Preceding Entry into Bastogne," in 4th Armd Div Combat Interv file; ltr, Maj. Gen. Joseph H. Harper to William C. C. Cavanagh, 3 Aug 69; and Lt. Col. Joseph A. Wyant, historian, Ninth Air Force, "Battle of the Ardennes," Office of Air Force History.

CHAPTER XXVI: IN FRONT OF THE OURTHE RIVER

"They're Germans, Colonel!" (p. 539), Samuel M. Hogan, unpublished and untitled MS, courtesy of Dr. Maurice Delaval; also ltr to the author from Hogan, 13 Nov 83.

For "a hailstorm of fire" (p. 540), Cole, *The Ardennes*, p. 379.

For "like throwing peas at a plate glass window" (p. 545), ltr to the author from Frank Evans, Trp D, 87th Cav Rcn Sqdn, 7th Armd Div, 22 Oct 83.

For "I wouldn't attack" (p. 546), Combat Interv with Billingslea.

SS-Sgt. Ernst Barkmann's story (pp. 550–552) is from Otto Weidinger, *Division Das Reich (The Path of the 2d SS Panzer Division 'Das Reich'—The History of the Backbone Division of the Waffen-SS)* (Osnabrück Verlag, 1982), Vol. V, Chapter V (translation by M. Trevor Shanklin).

"Don't give an inch" and "Why did you destroy" (p. 553), Toland, *Battle*, pp. 230, 251.

For the story of SS-Capt. Hans Winkler (pp. 555–556), Weidinger, *op. cit*.

For "if anything, worse than before" (p. 557), Sylvan Diary, entry of 24 Dec 44.

Additional sources: "Action at Samrée, Belgium: The Role of the Division Quartermaster in Defense of Samrée," *The Lucky Seventh, op. cit.*; William R. Breuer, *Bloody Clash at Sadzot: Hitler's Final Strike for Antwerp* (St. Louis: Zeus Publishers, 1981); Gert Schmager, *"Regiment 'Der Führer'—*22d until 27th December 1944," *Der Freiwillige*, Vol. 12, 1964; Committee 3, Officers Advanced Course, The Armored School, 1948–1949, Armor Under Adverse Conditions (2d and 3d Armored Divisions in the Ardennes Campaign, 16 Dec 44–16 Jan 45); and XVIII Abn Corps, Rpt of Investigation, CCA, 7th Armd Div, Manhay (Dec. 24–25, 1944).

CHAPTER XXVII: CRISIS BEFORE THE MEUSE

Combat Interviews are good for both the 2d Armored and 84th Divisions. Both have excellent unit histories: Donald E. Houston, *Hell on Wheels: The 2d Armored Division* (San Rafael, Cal.: Presidio Press, 1977), and Theodore Draper, *The 84th Infantry Division in the Battle of Germany, November 1944— May 1945* (New York: The Viking Press, 1946). See also Perry S. Wolff, *Fortune Favored the Brave: A History of the 334th Infantry, 84th Division* (printed in Germany, 1945). For British operations, see in addition to the official history, Operations of 30 (Br) Corps During German Attack in the Ardennes, December 1944–January 1945, in ETO Historian's file.

"Yes, hold" (p. 562), Sylvan Diary, entry of 21 Dec 44.

"You get down that road" (p. 567), Maj. Gen. E. N. Harmon (with Milton MacKaye and William Ross MacKaye), *Combat Commander: Autobiography of a Soldier* (Englewood Cliffs, N.J.: Prentice-Hall, 1970).

For "remain aloof" (p. 567), Collins, *Lightning Joe*, p. 285.

For "all hell broke loose" and "screamed in agony" (pp. 567–568), "The Battle of Eastern Belgium" in 2d Armd Div Combat Interv file.

"Ok, let's go!" (p. 568), Cole, *The Ardennes*, p. 437.

For "the success of the day" and "special rations" (p. 569), Helmut Ritgen, "The Battle of the Ardennes" in *Die Geschichte der Panzer-Lehr-Division im Westen, 1944–1945* (Stuttgart: Motorbuch Verlag, 1979) (translation by Maj. Dieter Kopac).

For "a pointed wedge" (p. 569), MS # B-151a, Von Manteuffel.

For "three important days" (p. 570), MS # A-873, Genmaj. Siegfried von Waldenburg, "Commitment of the *116th Panzer Division* in the Ardennes (16–26 Dec 1944)."

Story of Carroll and Korecki (p. 571), Eisenhower, *The Bitter Woods*, p. 363.

"Hey, you guys, open up!" and "Let's get the hell out of here" (p. 572), and "Whole trees were blown" (p. 573), Harold P. Leinbaugh and John D. Campbell, "Christmas in Verdenne," *The Washington Post Magazine*, 23 Dec 79, p. 7. Also intervs with Leinbaugh and Campbell; Videotape interv, Leinbaugh and Campbell with Gerhard Tebbe; and F. Memminger, "As the Law Demanded—In Remembrance of the Breakthrough of the Combat Group Bayer North of Verdenne and of 1st Lt. Hans Joachim Weissflog," Journal of the *116th Panzer Division*, No. 1, 1958 (translation by Hans Holtkamp).

"Don't bargain with me" (p. 575) and the crime at Bande, Commission des Crimes de Guerre, *Bande, op. cit.*

The story of Madame Monrique (p. 577) is from Toland, *Battle*, pp. 217–218. See also Nobécourt, *Hitler's Last Gamble*, pp. 237–238.

The story of the British tanks (pp. 577–579) is from Elstob, *Hitler's Last Offensive*, p. 393, and ltr to the author from Elstob, 20 Dec 83.

For "unaided" (p. 579), Montgomery to Eisenhower, M-389, 22 Dec 44, Eisenhower personal file, as cited in Pogue, *The Supreme Command*, p. 382.

For "if forced" (p. 579), Baldwin, *Battles Lost and Won*, p. 347. See also Baldwin, "Great Decisions," *The Infantry Journal*, May 47.

"Furious" (p. 580), Houston, *Hell on Wheels*, p. 341.

For "unrestricted use," "Now get this" and "I think you had better come home" (pp. 580–581), Brig. Gen. Williston B. Palmer, "Narrative from Memory of Actions and Orders at CP VII Corps on 24 December 1944," 7 May 47, in 2d Armd Div Combat Interv file.

For "his lips blue" and "a bit aghast" (p. 581), Collins, p. 289.

For "crawling with tanks" (p. 583), Cole, 562.

CHAPTER XVIII: CRISES IN COMMAND

For "his face was haggard" (p. 587), Irving, *Hitler's War*, p. 821.

For "unoccupied crossings" (p. 588), Von Luttichau and Bauer, "Key Dates During Ardennes Offensive," Pt I, p. 39.

"*Mein Führer*" (p. 588), Merriam, *Dark December*, p. 151.

"We have had unexpected setbacks" (p. 588), "As much as I may be tormented," *then he resumed*," and "to consolidate his holdings" (p. 589), Toland, *Adolf Hitler*, pp. 837–839.

For "a calculated insult" and "more arrogant and egotistical" and following quotations, (p. 589), Bradley and Blair, *A General's Life*, pp. 369–370.

"I was absolutely frank with him," "entirely our own fault," "looked thin" and "Poor chap" (p. 589), Bryant, *Triumph in the West*, p. 278.

For "he was certain" (p. 589), Bradley, *A Soldier's Story*, p. 481.

Montgomery's denial (p. 589), John Eisenhower interv with Montgomery, 1 Oct 66.

For "a tired little fart" (p. 590), and preceding quotations, Blumenson, *The Patton Papers*, pp. 606, 608.

For "let him have it" and following quotations, "the extraordinary step" and "Damn it, Bedell" (p. 590), Bradley and Blair, pp. 370–371.

For the story of the troopship *Léopoldville* (pp. 590–594), Jacquin Sanders, *A Night Before Christmas: The Sinking of the Troopship Léopoldville* (New York: G. P. Putnam's Sons, 1963). Additional German material provided by Prof. Dr. Jürgen Rohwer, Bibliothek für Zeitgeschichte, 16 Apr 82. There are detailed interviews with survivors in 66th Div Combat Interv file.

"Praise God" (p. 594), Cole, p. 612.

For "to deliver next breakout" and "might well release" (p. 595), Weigley, *Eisenhower's Lieutenants*, pp. 541–542.

"It looks to me" (p. 595), quoted in Bryant, p. 279.

For Montgomery's letter to Eisenhower (pp. 595–596), Montgomery, *Memoirs*, pp. 284–285.

For "had saved the Americans" (p. 596), Weigley, p. 543.

For "under no circumstances" and three following quotations (p. 596), Marshall to Eisenhower, W-84337, 30 Dec 44, Eisenhower personal file, as cited in Pogue, *The Supreme Command*, p. 386.

For "extremely dangerous situation" (p. 596) and following quotations, unless otherwise noted, de Guingand, *Generals at War*, pp. 106–115.

"In a somberly lighted room" and "tired of the whole buisness" (p. 597), Eisenhower, *The Bitter Woods*, p. 383.

"Whatever your decision" (p. 598), Montgomery, p. 286.

For "handling large masses" (p. 599), Bryant, p. 287.

"If you get a monkey" (p. 599), Weigley, p. 566, citing Patton news conference, 1 Jan 45.

For "in principle" (p. 599), Cole, p. 611.

For "such top-flight divisions" and "Well, Monty" (p. 599), Collins, *Lightning Joe*, p. 292.

For "the Small Solution" (p. 600), Cole, p. 605, citing *OB WEST* War Diary.

"Excellent agent sources" (p. 600), John Frayn Turner and Robert Jackson, *Destination Berchtesgaden: The Story of the United States Seventh Army in World War II* (New York: Charles Scribner's Sons, 1975), p. 106.

For "call up Devers" (p. 601), Ambrose, *The Supreme Commander*, p. 577.

"I think you've done" (p. 602), Eisenhower, *Crusade in Europe*, p. 363. Nobécourt, *Hitler's Last Gamble*, has more detail on the encounter, particularly from the French viewpoint.

CHAPTER XXIX: ERASING THE BULGE

A detailed account of the fighting around Bastogne is in Cole, *The Ardennes*, and more detail on erasing the bulge in MacDonald, *The Last Offensive*.

For the allusion to Tweedledee and Alice (p. 604), the author is indebted to Strowson, *The Battle for the Ardennes*, p. 115. Eisenhower's order of the day is in Pogue, *The Supreme Command*, p. 547.

For "at the earliest possible moment" and "His trip" (p. 605), Irving, *The War Between the Generals*, p. 362.

"The battle in the West" and "taking into account" (p. 605), Elstob, *Hitler's Last Offensive*, pp. 445–446.

For "resulted in breaking" (p. 606), Cole, *The Ardennes*, p. 676.

For "death blow" (p. 608), the head of the German fighter forces, Lt. Gen. Adolf Galland.

For "by instant agreement" (p. 611), Bradley and Blair, *A General's Life*, pp. 380–381.

For "a catacylsmic Roman Holiday" (p. 611), Hansen Diary, entry of 7 Jan 45.

"His Majesty's Government" (p. 611), Eisenhower, *The Bitter Woods*, p. 386.

For "perturbed . . . about the sniping" (p. 611), the press conference, and "appeared to be sensitive" (p. 613), Montgomery, *Memoirs*, pp. 278–282.

For Chester Wilmot (p. 613), Wilmot, *The Struggle for Europe*, p. 611n.

For "all-out . . . mad" (p. 614), Bradley and Blair, p. 383, citing Ralph Ingersoll.

"After what has happened" (p. 614) and "The Americans have engaged" (p. 614), Pogue, p. 389.

"There's a colonel here" and following quotations (p. 616), historian's narrative with 2d Armd Div Combat Intervs.

For "during the early stages" (p. 618), Carlo D'Este, *Decision in Normandy* (New York: E. P. Dutton, 1983).

EPILOGUE

All quotations from Weingartner, *Crossroads of Death*. Professor Weingartner is kinder to the defendants than one who lay on the ground that dreadful day would be, but his is a careful, detailed, scholarly account, focusing primarily on the trial and subsequent events.

Bibliography

PUBLISHED WORKS

Articles and books, including unit histories, applicable to only one or two chapters are listed with the appropriate chapter documentation.

Stephen E. Ambrose, *The Surpreme Commander: The War Years of General Dwight D. Eisenhower* (Garden City, N.Y.: Doubleday, 1970).

Hanson W. Baldwin, *Battles Lost and Won: Great Campaigns of World War II* (New York: Harper & Row, 1966).

Ralph Bennett, *Ultra in the West: The Normandy Campaign of 1944–45* (New York: Charles Scribner's Sons, 1980).

Martin Blumenson, *The Patton Papers 1940–45* (Boston: Houghton Mifflin, 1974).

Omar N. Bradley, *A Soldier's Story* (New York: Henry Holt and Co., 1951).

—— and Clay Blair, *A General's Life* (New York: Simon and Schuster, 1983).

Richard Brett-Smith, *Hitler's Generals* (San Rafael, Cal.: Presidio Press, 1977).

Donald Grey Brownlow, *Panzer Baron: The Military Exploits of General Hasso von Manteuffel* (North Quincy, Mass.: The Christopher Publishing House, 1975).

Arthur Bryant, *Triumph in the West: A History of the War Years Based on the Diaries of Field-Marshal Lord Alanbrooke, Chief of the Imperial General Staff* (Garden City, N.Y.: Doubleday, 1959).

Peter Calvocoressi, *Top Secret Ultra* (London: Cassell, 1980).

Alfred D. Chandler, Jr., ed., *The Papers of Dwight David Eisenhower*, Vol. IV, *The War Years* (Baltimore: Johns Hopkins Press, 1970).

Hugh M. Cole, *The Ardennes: Battle of the Bulge,* US ARMY IN WORLD WAR II (Washington, D.C.: Government Printing Office, 1965).

J. Lawton Collins, *Lightning Joe, An Autobiography* (Baton Rouge, La.: Louisiana State University Press, 1979).

Wesley Frank Craven and James Lea Cate, eds., *Europe—ARGUMENT to V-E*

Day, Vol. III, *The Army Air Forces in World War II* (Chicago: University of Chicago Press, 1951).

David Downing, *The Devil's Virtuosos: German Generals at War 1940–5* (New York: St. Martin's Press, 1977).

Dwight D. Eisenhower, *Crusade in Europe* (Garden City, N.Y.: Doubleday, 1948).

John Eisenhower, *The Bitter Woods* (New York: G. P. Putnam's Sons, 1969).

Maj. L. F. Ellis, with Lt. Col. A. E. Warhurst, *Victory in the West,* Vol. II, *The Defeat of Germany* (London: Her Majesty's Stationery Office, 1968).

Peter Elstob, *Hitler's Last Offensive* (London: Secker & Warburg, 1971).

Jósef Garlinski, *The Enigma War* (New York: Charles Scribner's Sons, 1980).

James M. Gavin, *On to Berlin: Battles of an Airborne Commander 1943–1946* (New York: The Viking Press, 1978).

Felix Gilbert, ed., *Hitler Directs His War* (New York: Oxford University Press, 1950).

Janice Holt Giles, *The Damned Engineers* (Boston: Houghton Mifflin, 1970).

David Irving, *Hitler's War* (New York: The Viking Press, 1977).

————, *The War Between the Generals: Inside the Allied High Command* (New York: Congdom & Lattés, 1981).

John Keegan, *Waffen-SS: The Asphalt Soldiers* (New York: Ballantine Books, 1970).

Ronald Lewin, *Ultra Goes to War* (New York: McGraw-Hill, 1978).

Charles B. MacDonald, *The Mighty Endeavor: American Armed Forces in The European Theater in World War II* (New York: Oxford University Press, 1969).

————, *The Siegfried Line Campaign,* US ARMY IN WORLD WAR II (Washington, D.C.: Government Printing Office, 1963).

————, *The Last Offensive,* US ARMY IN WORLD WAR II (Washington, D.C.: Government Printing Office, 1973).

Robert E. Merriam, *Dark December* (Chicago: Ziff-Davis, 1947; current edition: *The Battle of the Bulge,* Bantam Books).

Bernard L. Montgomery, *The Memoirs of Field-Marshal the Viscount Montgomery of Alamein, K.G.* (Cleveland: World, 1958).

————, *Normandy to the Baltic* (Boston: Houghton Mifflin, 1946).

Jacques Nobécourt, *Hitler's Last Gamble: The Battle of the Bulge* (New York: Schocken Books, 1967).

Thomas Parrish, ed., *The Simon and Schuster Encyclopedia of World War II* (New York: Simon and Schuster, 1978).

Forrest C. Pogue, *The Supreme Command,* US ARMY IN WORLD WAR II (Washington, D.C.: Government Printing Office, 1954).

Frank James Price, *Troy H. Middleton: A Biography* (Baton Rouge, La.: Louisiana State University Press, 1974).

Matthew B. Ridgway and Harold H. Martin, *Soldier: The Memoirs of Matthew B. Ridgway* (New York: Harper & Bros., 1956).

John Strowson, *The Battle for the Ardennes* (London: B. T. Batsford, 1972).

John Toland, *Battle: The Story of the Bulge* (New York: Random House, 1959).

————, *Adolph Hitler* (Garden City, N.Y.: Doubleday, 1976).

Walter Warlimont, *Inside Hitler's Headquarters 1943–1945* (New York: Praeger, 1964).

Russel F. Weigley, *Eisenhower's Lieutenants: The Campaign of France and Germany 1944–1945* (Bloomington, Ind.: Indiana University Press, 1981).

James J. Weingartner, *Crossroads of Death: The Story of the Malmédy Massacre and Trial* (Berkeley: University of California Press, 1979).

Chester Wilmot, *The Struggle for Europe* (New York: Harper & Bros., 1952).

OFFICIAL RECORDS

During periods of combat, each headquarters from army down through regiment and separate battalion submitted a monthly narrative after action report, along with such supporting documents as G-2 and G-3 daily journals, daily periodic reports, G-2 estimates, messages, and overlays. Although use of the after action reports is essential, commands often put the best possible light on their activities; for that reason, the G-2 and G-3 journals are vital, for in the manner of a ship's log, no entry in the journals was to be erased or altered. It would take a score of years to study every unit's journals in detail, but I have used them where something was unclear, where something appeared to have been covered up, and for such critical periods as the days immediately preceding the German attack.

After action reports of the V Corps, First and Third Armies, and the 12th Army Group were published officially. Copies may be found with the World War II unit records in the National Archives. The raw files of the First Army and the 12th Army Group are nevertheless important, particularly for G-2 estimates and periodic reports.

COMBAT INTERVIEWS

Soon after an important action, teams of historians in uniform working under the European Theater Historical Section descended upon the units involved, interviewed commanders and men at various levels, and sometimes provided an overall covering narrative based on the interviews and the historians' own observations. The materials are in rough typescript with the World War II records in the National Archives, filed by division or corps. They provide much more human interest material than do the official records, and, like the G-2 and G-3 journals, can sometimes be used as a corrective for after action reports.

AUTHOR'S INTERVIEWS AND
UNPUBLISHED MANUSCRIPTS

In response to notices in veterans' publications, more than a hundred veterans of the battle provided information on their experiences and some provided unpublished manuscripts. I corresponded at length with some of the veterans and interviewed others. Where I have used the material, identification is provided in the chapter documentation; to all who responded, I am grateful.

Through the kindness of John Toland, I used interviews he conducted for his earlier work on the battle, located in the Library of Congress, and through the kindness of John Eisenhower, his interviews with Field Marshals Montgomery and von Manteuffel, located in the Dwight D. Eisenhower Library.

Credit for interviews with civilians in Belgium and Luxembourg is included in the chapter documentation.

SPECIAL MATERIALS

MAGIC files in the National Archives and ULTRA files, September 1944–January 1945, normally in the Public Records Office, London, but temporarily withdrawn for the use of official historians in the Cabinet Office Historical Section, London, where I was premitted to use them.

Other special materials are noted in the chapter documentation.

GERMAN MATERIALS

Under the auspices of the European Theater Historical Section, German generals in captivity immediately after the war prepared narrative accounts of their experiences. Every German general who was involved in the Ardennes at division level and above (with the exception of General Dietrich) wrote an account. They vary in quality but are essential to telling the German story; they are stored in the National Archives. Although I have used all the manuscripts for the Ardennes, citations are provided only for direct quotations.

In support of the official histories, historians in the U.S. Army Center of Military History prepared detailed studies based on the German manuscripts and official German records. Identified by the letter R and a number, the studies are also in the National Archives. Of particular value for my work were three studies by Charles V. P. von Luttichau—R-12, "Ardennes Offensive—Preliminary Planning"; R-13, "Framework of *Wacht am Rhein*"; and R-14, "The Strategic Concentration"—plus another by von Luttichau in collaboration with Magna E. Bauer, R-15, "Key Dates in the Ardennes Offensive."

With the help of Günter von der Weiden and Heino Brandt, I traveled the length and breadth of West Germany interviewing German veterans who served at regimental level or below. Again with their help, I obtained well over a thousand pages of published German material, including unofficial unit histories and personal accounts. Since my work is focused on the American view, I was able to use only portions of that material where it dovetailed with the story from the American side; the use is reflected in the chapter documentation. I am nevertheless grateful to all who consented to interviews.

Index

687